# WORD
# BIBLICAL
# COMMENTARY

# WORD
# BIBLICAL
# COMMENTARY

## Volume 33B

## Matthew 14–28

# DONALD A. HAGNER

# WORD BOOKS, PUBLISHER · DALLAS, TEXAS

Word Biblical Commentary
Matthew 14–28
Copyright © 1995 by Word, Incorporated

**Library of Congress Cataloging-in-Publication Data**
Main entry under title:

Word biblical commentary.

    Includes bibliographies.
    1. Bible—Commentaries—Collected works.
BS491.2.W67    220.7'7    81–71768
ISBN 0–8499–1096–X (v. 33B) AACR2

Printed in the United States of America

The author's own translation of the Scripture text appears in italic type under the heading *Translation*.

5 6 7 9  AGF  9 8 7 6 5 4 3 2 1

*To Beverly*

# Contents

# Editorial Preface

The launching of the *Word Biblical Commentary* brings to fulfillment an enterprise of several years' planning. The publishers and the members of the editorial board met in 1977 to explore the possibility of a new commentary on the books of the Bible that would incorporate several distinctive features. Prospective readers of these volumes are entitled to know what such features were intended to be; whether the aims of the commentary have been fully achieved time alone will tell.

First, we have tried to cast a wide net to include as contributors a number of scholars from around the world who not only share our aims but are in the main engaged in the ministry of teaching in university, college, and seminary. They represent a rich diversity of denominational allegiance. The broad stance of our contributors can rightly be called evangelical, and this term is to be understood in its positive, historic sense of a commitment to Scripture as divine revelation and to the truth and power of the Christian gospel.

Then, the commentaries in our series are all commissioned and written for the purpose of inclusion in the *Word Biblical Commentary*. Unlike several of our distinguished counterparts in the field of commentary writing, there are no translated works, originally written in a non-English language. Also, our commentators were asked to prepare their own rendering of the original biblical text and to use those languages as the basis of their own comments and exegesis. What may be claimed as distinctive with this series is that it is based on the biblical languages, yet it seeks to make the technical and scholarly approach to the theological understanding of Scripture understandable by—and useful to—the fledgling student, the working minister, and colleagues in the guild of professional scholars and teachers as well.

Finally, a word must be said about the format of the series. The layout, in clearly defined sections, has been consciously devised to assist readers at different levels. Those wishing to learn about the textual witnesses on which the translation is offered are invited to consult the section headed *Notes*. If the readers' concern is with the state of modern scholarship on any given portion of Scripture, they should turn to the sections on *Bibliography* and *Form/Structure/Setting*. For a clear exposition of the passage's meaning and its relevance to the ongoing biblical revelation, the *Comment* and concluding *Explanation* are designed expressly to meet that need. There is therefore something for everyone who may pick up and use these volumes.

If these aims come anywhere near realization, the intention of the editors will have been met, and the labor of our team of contributors rewarded.

General Editors: *David A. Hubbard*
*Glenn W. Barker†*
Old Testament: *John D. W. Watts*
New Testament: *Ralph P. Martin*

# Author's Preface

Since the publication of this second volume occurs nearly two full years after the first volume, a few fresh prefatory remarks are in order.

In the preparation of this volume I have severely missed the two major, multivolume Matthew commentaries that were my constant companions and dialogue partners in the final stages of the preparation of the first volume, namely that of Ulrich Luz (chaps. 1–7 were available in English; chaps. 8–17 were available in German) and that of Davies and Allison (chaps. 1–18 were available in two volumes). On the other hand, for the passion narrative I have been grateful to have available the new, masterly two-volume commentary by R. E. Brown, *The Death of the Messiah*. These volumes have enriched my study of Matthew in much the same way that Brown's comparable commentary on *The Birth of the Messiah* was an aid in the writing of the early chapters of the first volume.

Many of the persons who were thanked in the preface to the first volume deserve thanks again here. Two new names, however, deserve special mention in connection with the second volume: my doctoral student, Steve Wilkinson, for superbly compiling the indexes that appear at the end of this volume, and also doctoral student Max Lee, for research help in the passion and resurrection narratives.

Thanks must also be given again specifically to Professor Ralph P. Martin, Dr. Lynn Losie, and Ms. Melanie McQuere for their editorial work. And again I express my admiration and thanks to the staff of the word-processing office at Fuller Seminary, Michael Kennedy, Anne White, and especially Susan Carlson Wood, who patiently and expertly put most of the present volume into its present shape.

Finally, again warm thanks are due to my wife, Beverly, to whom this commentary is dedicated. I am deeply grateful for her unfailing love and support, not only during the completion of this project but in all circumstances and at all times.

Well, yes, I should also like to offer half-hearted thanks to my colleagues and friends at Fuller Seminary, who in celebration of the completion of the commentary prepared a mock Festschrift for me entitled *Did You Not Believe That I Would Complete It?* in which essays explored, among other imponderables, the problem of "delay and imminence" in the appearance of the second volume. To them and all other friendly skeptics I now say: "O ye of little faith!"

Donald A. Hagner

*July 1995*
*Fuller Theological Seminary*
*Pasadena, California*

# Abbreviations

## A. General Abbreviations

| | |
|---|---|
| A | Codex Alexandrinus |
| *ad* | comment on |
| Akkad. | Akkadian |
| א | Codex Sinaiticus |
| Ap. Lit. | Apocalyptic Literature |
| Apoc. | Apocrypha |
| Aq. | Aquila's Greek Translation of the OT |
| Arab. | Arabic |
| Aram. | Aramaic |
| B | Codex Vaticanus |
| C | Codex Ephraemi Syri |
| c. | *circa,* about |
| cent. | century |
| cf. | *confer,* compare |
| chap(s). | chapter(s) |
| cod., codd. | codex, codices |
| contra | in contrast to |
| D | Codex Bezae |
| dat. | dative |
| DSS | Dead Sea Scrolls |
| ed. | edited by, editor(s) |
| e. g. | *exempli gratia,* for example |
| et al. | *et alii,* and others |
| ET | English translation |
| EV | English Versions of the Bible |
| fem. | feminine |
| frag. | fragments |
| FS | *Festschrift,* volume written in honor of |
| ft. | foot, feet |
| gen. | genitive |
| Gr. | Greek |
| *hap. leg.* | *hapax legomenon,* sole occurrence |
| Heb. | Hebrew |
| Hitt. | Hittite |
| ibid. | *ibidem,* in the same place |
| id. | *idem,* the same |
| i. e. | *id est,* that is |
| impf. | imperfect |
| infra | below |
| Jos. | Josephus |
| lat | Latin |
| lit. | literally |
| LXX | Septuagint |
| masc. | masculine |
| mg. | margin |
| MS(S) | manuscript(s) |
| MT | Masoretic text (of the Old Testament) |
| n. | note |
| N.B. | *nota bene,* note well |
| n. d. | no date |
| Nestle | Nestle (ed.), *Novum Testamentum Graece* [26], rev. K. and B. Aland |
| no. | number |
| n.s. | new series |
| NT | New Testament |
| obs. | obsolete |
| o.s. | old series |
| OT | Old Testament |
| p., pp. | page, pages |
| *pace* | with due respect to, but differing from |
| //, par(s). | parallel(s) |
| par. | paragraph |
| *passim* | elsewhere |
| pl. | plural |
| Pseudep. | Pseudepigrapha |
| Q | Quelle ("Sayings" source for the Gospels) |
| q.v. | *quod vide,* which see |
| rev. | revised by, reviser, revision |
| Rom. | Roman |
| RVmg | Revised Version margin |
| Sam. | Samaritan recension |
| sc. | *scilicet,* that is to say |
| Sem. | Semitic |

| sing. | singular | Ugar. | Ugaritic |
|-------|----------|-------|----------|
| Sumer. | Sumerian | UP | University Press |
| s.v. | *sub verbo,* under the word | u.s. | *ut supra,* as above |
| sy | Syriac | v, vv | verse, verses |
| Symm. | Symmachus | vg | Vulgate |
| Tg. | Targum | viz. | *videlicet,* namely |
| Theod. | Theodotion | v.l. | *varia lectio,* alternative |
| TR | Textus Receptus | | reading |
| tr. | translator, translated by | vol. | volume |
| | | x | times (2x = two times, etc.) |

For abbreviations of Greek MSS used in *Notes,* see Nestle[26].

## B. Abbreviations for Translations and Paraphrases

| AmT | Smith and Goodspeed, *The Complete Bible, An American Translation* | Moffatt | J. Moffatt, *A New Translation of the Bible* (NT 1913) |
|-----|------|---------|------|
| | | NAB | The New American Bible |
| ASV | American Standard Version, American Revised Version (1901) | NEB | The New English Bible |
| | | NIV | The New International Version (1978) |
| AV | Authorized Version = KJV | NJB | New Jerusalem Bible (1985) |
| GNB | Good News Bible = Today's English Version | NRSV | New Revised Standard Version (1989) |
| JB | Jerusalem Bible | Phillips | J. B. Phillips, *The New Testament in Modern English* |
| JPS | Jewish Publication Society, *The Holy Scriptures* | | |
| | | REB | Revised English Bible |
| KJV | King James Version (1611) = AV | RSV | Revised Standard Version (NT 1946, OT 1952, Apoc. 1957) |
| Knox | R. A. Knox, *The Holy Bible: A Translation from the Latin Vulgate in the Light of the Hebrew and Greek Original* | RV | Revised Version, 1881–85 |
| | | Wey | R. F. Weymouth, *The New Testament in Modern Speech* |
| | | Wms | C. B. Williams, *The New Testament: A Translation in the Language of the People* |

## C. Abbreviations of Commonly Used Periodicals, Reference Works, and Serials

| AARSR | American Academy of Religion Studies in Religion | *AcOr* | *Acta orientalia* |
|-------|------|--------|------|
| | | ACW | Ancient Christian Writers |
| | | ADAJ | Annual of the Department of Antiquities of Jordan |
| *AAS* | *Acta apostolicae sedis* | | |
| AASOR | Annual of the American Schools of Oriental Research | *AER* | *American Ecclesiastical Review* |
| | | *AfO* | *Archiv für Orientforschung* |
| | | AGJU | Arbeiten zur Geschichte des antiken Judentums und des Urchristentums |
| AB | Anchor Bible | | |
| *AbrN* | *Abr-Nahrain* | | |
| ACNT | Augsburg Commentary on the New Testament | | |

| | | | |
|---|---|---|---|
| AGSU | Arbeiten zur Geschichte des Spätjudentums und Urchristentums | ANTZ | Arbeiten zur Neutestamentlichen Theologie und Zeitgeschichte |
| AH | F. Rosenthal, *An Aramaic Handbook* | AOAT | Alter Orient und Altes Testament |
| AHW | W. von Soden, *Akkadisches Handwörterbuch* | AOS | American Oriental Series |
| AJA | *American Journal of Archaeology* | AP | J. Marouzeau (ed.), *L'Année philologique* |
| AJAS | *American Journal of Arabic Studies* | APOT | R. H. Charles (ed.), *Apocrypha and Pseudepigrapha of the Old Testament* |
| AJBA | *Australian Journal of Biblical Archaeology* | ARG | *Archiv für Reformationsgeschichte* |
| AJBI | Annual of the Japanese Biblical Institute | ARM | Archives royales de Mari |
| AJP | *American Journal of Philology* | ArOr | *Archiv orientální* |
| AJSL | *American Journal of Semitic Languages and Literature* | ARW | *Archiv für Religionswissenschaft* |
| AJT | *American Journal of Theology* | ASB | *Austin Seminary Bulletin* |
| ALBO | Analecta lovaniensia biblica et orientalia | ASNU | Acta seminarii neotestamentici upsaliensis |
| ALGHJ | Arbeiten zur Literatur und Geschichte des hellenistischen Judentums | ASS | *Acta sanctae sedis* |
| | | AsSeign | *Assemblées du Seigneur* |
| | | ASSR | *Archives des sciences sociales des religions* |
| ALUOS | Annual of Leeds University Oriental Society | ASTI | *Annual of the Swedish Theological Institute* |
| AnBib | Analecta biblica | ATAbh | Alttestamentliche Abhandlungen |
| AnBoll | Analecta Bollandiana | | |
| ANEP | J. B. Pritchard (ed.), *Ancient Near East in Pictures* | ATANT | Abhandlungen zur Theologie des Alten und Neuen Testaments |
| ANESTP | J. B. Pritchard (ed.), *Ancient Near East Supplementary Texts and Pictures* | ATD | Das Alte Testament Deutsch |
| | | ATDan | Acta theologica danica |
| ANET | J. B. Pritchard (ed.), *Ancient Near Eastern Texts* | ATR | *Anglican Theological Review* |
| | | AusBR | *Australian Biblical Review* |
| ANF | The Ante-Nicene Fathers | AUSS | *Andrews University Seminary Studies* |
| Ang | *Angelicum* | | |
| AnnThéol | *L'Année théologique* | | |
| AnOr | Analecta orientalia | BA | *Biblical Archaeologist* |
| ANQ | *Andover Newton Quarterly* | BAC | Biblioteca de autores cristianos |
| ANRW | *Aufstieg und Niedergang der römischen Welt* | BAGD | W. Bauer, *A Greek-English Lexicon of the New Testament and Other Early Christian Literature*, ET, ed. W. F. Arndt and F. W. Gingrich; 2d ed. rev. F. W. Gingrich and F. W. |
| ANTF | Arbeiten zur Neutestamentlichen Textforschung | | |
| ANTJ | Arbeiten zum Neuen Testament und zum Judentum | | |
| Anton | *Antonianum* | | |

|  |  |  |  |
|---|---|---|---|
| | Danker (University of | | (Neukirchen, 1951–) |
| | Chicago, 1979) | *BIES* | *Bulletin of the Israel Explora-* |
| *BARev* | *Biblical Archaeology Review* | | *tion Society (= Yediot)* |
| *BASOR* | *Bulletin of the American Schools* | *BIFAO* | *Bulletin de l'institut français* |
| | *of Oriental Research* | | *d'archéologie orientale* |
| *BASP* | *Bulletin of the American Society* | *BiTod* | *The Bible Today* |
| | *of Papyrologists* | *BJRL* | *Bulletin of the John Rylands* |
| BBB | Bonner biblische Beiträge | | *University Library of* |
| BBET | Beiträge zur biblischen | | *Manchester* |
| | Exegese und Theologie | BJS | Brown Judaic Studies |
| *BCSR* | *Bulletin of the Council on the* | BK | *Bibel und Kirche* |
| | *Study of Religion* | BKAT | Biblischer Kommentar: Altes |
| BDB | F. Brown, S. R. Driver, and C. | | Testament |
| | A. Briggs, *Hebrew and* | *BLE* | *Bulletin de littérature* |
| | *English Lexicon of the Old* | | *ecclésiastique* |
| | *Testament* | *BLit* | *Bibel und Liturgie* |
| BDF | F. Blass, A. Debrunner, and R. W. | BNTC | Black's New Testament |
| | Funk, *A Greek Grammar of* | | Commentaries |
| | *the NT* | *BO* | *Bibliotheca orientalis* |
| BDR | F. Blass, A. Debrunner, and | *BR* | *Biblical Research* |
| | F. Rehkopf, *Grammatik des* | *BSac* | *Bibliotheca Sacra* |
| | *neutestamentlichen* | *BSO(A)S* | *Bulletin of the School of* |
| | *Griechisch* | | *Oriental (and African)* |
| *BeO* | *Bibbia e oriente* | | *Studies* |
| BETL | Bibliotheca ephemeridum | BSR | Bibliothèque de sciences |
| | theologicarum | | religieuses |
| | lovaniensium | *BT* | *The Bible Translator* |
| BEvT | Beiträge zur evangelischen | *BTB* | *Biblical Theology Bulletin* |
| | Theologie | *BTS* | *Bible et terre saint* |
| BFCT | Beiträge zur Förderung | *BTZ* | *Berliner theologische Zeitschrift* |
| | christlicher Theologie | BU | Biblische Untersuchungen |
| BGBE | Beiträge zur Geschichte der | *BVC* | *Bible et vie chrétienne* |
| | biblischen Exegese | *BW* | *Biblical World* |
| *BHH* | *Biblisch-Historisches* | BWANT | Beiträge zur Wissenschaft |
| | *Handwörterbuch* | | vom Alten und Neuen |
| *BHK* | R. Kittel, *Biblia hebraica* | | Testament |
| *BHS* | *Biblia hebraica stuttgartensia* | *BZ* | *Biblische Zeitschrift* |
| BHT | Beiträge zur historischen | BZAW | Beihefte zur *ZAW* |
| | Theologie | BZNW | Beihefte zur *ZNW* |
| *Bib* | *Biblica* | BZRGG | Beihefte zur *ZRGG* |
| BibB | Biblische Beiträge | | |
| *BibLeb* | *Bibel und Leben* | *CAD* | *The Assyrian Dictionary of the* |
| *BibNot* | *Biblische Notizen* | | *Oriental Institute of the* |
| BibOr | Biblica et orientalia | | *University of Chicago* |
| *BibRev* | *Bible Review* | *CAH* | *Cambridge Ancient History* |
| BibS(F) | Biblische Studien (Freiburg, | CAT | Commentaire de l'Ancien |
| | 1895–) | | Testament |
| BibS(N) | Biblische Studien | *CB* | *Cultura bíblica* |

| | | | |
|---|---|---|---|
| *CBQ* | *Catholic Biblical Quarterly* | *CTR* | *Criswell Theological Review* |
| CBQMS | CBQ Monograph Series | *CurTM* | *Currents in Theology and* |
| CCath | Corpus Catholicorum | | *Mission* |
| CChr | Corpus Christianorum | | |
| *CE* | *Cahiers Évangiles* | *DACL* | *Dictionnaire d'archéologie* |
| CGTC | Cambridge Greek Testament | | *chrétienne et de liturgie* |
| | Commentary | *DBSup* | *Dictionnaire de la Bible,* |
| CGTSC | Cambridge Greek Testa- | | *Supplément* |
| | ment for Schools and | *Diak* | *Diakonia* |
| | Colleges | *DISO* | C.-F. Jean and J. |
| *CH* | *Church History* | | Hoftijzer, |
| *CHR* | *Catholic Historical Review* | | *Dictionnaire des inscriptions* |
| *ChrTod* | *Christianity Today* | | *sémitiques de l'ouest* |
| *CIG* | *Corpus inscriptionum* | DJD | Discoveries in the Judean |
| | *graecarum* | | Desert |
| *CII* | *Corpus inscriptionum* | *DJG* | J. B. Green and S. McKnight |
| | *iudaicarum* | | (eds.), *Dictionary of Jesus* |
| *CIL* | *Corpus inscriptionum* | | *and the Gospels* |
| | *latinarum* | *DL* | *Doctrine and Life* |
| *CIS* | *Corpus inscriptionum* | *DOTT* | D. W. Thomas (ed.), |
| | *semiticarum* | | *Documents from Old* |
| *CJT* | *Canadian Journal of Theology* | | *Testament Times* |
| CNT | Commentaire du Nouveau | *DR* | *Downside Review* |
| | Testament | DS | Denzinger-Schönmetzer, |
| ConB | Coniectanea biblica | | *Enchiridion symbolorum* |
| ConBNT | Coniectanea biblica, New | *DTC* | *Dictionnaire de théologie* |
| | Testament | | *catholique* |
| *Concil* | *Concilium* | *DTT* | *Dansk teologisk tidsskrift* |
| *ConNT* | *Coniectanea neotestamentica* | *DunRev* | *Dunwoodie Review* |
| *CQ* | *Church Quarterly* | | |
| *CQR* | *Church Quarterly Review* | *EAJT* | *East Asia Journal of Theology* |
| *CRAIBL* | *Comptes rendus de l'Académie* | EBib | Etudes bibliques |
| | *des inscriptions et belles-* | *EBT* | *Encyclopedia of Biblical* |
| | *lettres* | | *Theology* |
| *CRev* | *Classical Review* | *EcR* | *Ecclesiastical Review* |
| *CrQ* | *Crozier Quarterly* | *EDNT* | H. Balz and G. Schneider |
| CSCO | Corpus scriptorum christian- | | (eds.), *Exegetical Dictionary* |
| | orum orientalium | | *of the New Testament* |
| CSEL | Corpus scriptorum ecclesias- | *EF* | *Études franciscaines* |
| | ticorum latinorum | EHAT | Exegetisches Handbuch zum |
| *CTA* | A. Herdner, *Corpus des* | | Alten Testament |
| | *tablettes en cunéiformes* | EKKNT | Evangelisch-katholischer |
| | *alphabétiques* | | Kommentar zum Neuen |
| *CTJ* | *Calvin Theological Journal* | | Testament |
| *CTM* | *Concordia Theological* | *EKL* | *Evangelisches Kirchenlexikon* |
| | *Monthly* | *EnchBib* | *Enchiridion biblicum* |
| *CTQ* | *Concordia Theological* | *EncJud* | *Encyclopedia judaica* (1971) |
| | *Quarterly* | *EpR* | *Epworth Review* |
| | | *ER* | *Ecumenical Review* |

| | | | |
|---|---|---|---|
| *ErJb* | *Eranos Jahrbuch* | *GRBS* | *Greek, Roman, and Byzantine* |
| *EstBib* | *Estudios bíblicos* | | *Studies* |
| ETL | *Ephemerides theologicae* | *Greg* | *Gregorianum* |
| | *lovanienses* | GTA | Göttinger Theologische |
| *ETR* | *Etudes théologiques et* | | Arbeiten |
| | *religieuses* | *GTJ* | *Grace Theological Journal* |
| ETS | Erfurter Theologische | | |
| | Studien | *HALAT* | W. Baumgartner et al., |
| *EV* | *Esprit et Vie* | | *Hebräisches und* |
| *EvJ* | *Evangelical Journal* | | *aramäisches Lexikon zum* |
| EvK | Evangelische Kommentar | | *Alten Testament* |
| *EvQ* | *Evangelical Quarterly* | HAT | Handbuch zum Alten |
| *EvT* | *Evangelische Theologie* | | Testament |
| *EWNT* | H. Balz and G. Schneider | *HBT* | *Horizons in Biblical* |
| | (eds.), *Exegetisches* | | *Theology* |
| | *Wörterbuch zum Neuen* | HDR | Harvard Dissertations in |
| | *Testament* | | Religion |
| *Exp* | *Expositor* | *HeyJ* | *Heythrop Journal* |
| *ExpTim* | *The Expository Times* | *HibJ* | *Hibbert Journal* |
| | | HKAT | Handkommentar zum Alten |
| FB | Forschung zur Bibel | | Testament |
| FBBS | Facet Books, Biblical Series | HKNT | Handkommentar zum |
| FC | Fathers of the Church | | Neuen Testament |
| FRLANT | Forschungen zur Religion | *HL* | *Heiliges Land* |
| | und Literatur des | HNT | Handbuch zum Neuen |
| | Alten und Neuen | | Testament |
| | Testaments | HNTC | Harper's NT Commentaries |
| FTS | Frankfurter theologische | *HR* | *History of Religions* |
| | Studien | HSM | Harvard Semitic Mono- |
| *FV* | *Foi et Vie* | | graphs |
| | | HTKNT | Herders theologischer |
| *GAG* | W. von Soden, *Grundriss der* | | Kommentar zum Neuen |
| | *akkadischen Grammatik* | | Testament |
| GCS | Griechische christliche | *HTR* | *Harvard Theological Review* |
| | Schriftsteller | HTS | Harvard Theological Studies |
| GKB | Gesenius-Kautzsch- | *HTS* | *Hervormde Teologiese Studies* |
| | Bergsträsser, *Hebräische* | *HUCA* | *Hebrew Union College Annual* |
| | *Grammatik* | HUT | Hermeneutische |
| GKC | *Gesenius' Hebrew Grammar,* ed. | | Untersuchungen zur |
| | E. Kautzsch, tr. A. E. | | Theologie |
| | Cowley | | |
| *GL* | *Geist und Leben* | *IB* | *Interpreter's Bible* |
| GNT | Grundrisse zum Neuen | *IBS* | *Irish Biblical Studies* |
| | Testament | ICC | International Critical |
| *GOTR* | *Greek Orthodox Theological* | | Commentary |
| | *Review* | *IDB* | G. A. Buttrick (ed.), |
| *GPM* | *Göttinger Predigtmeditation* | | *Interpreter's Dictionary of the* |
| *GR* | *Greece and Rome* | | *Bible* |

| | | | |
|---|---|---|---|
| IDBSup | Supplementary volume to IDB | JRelS | Journal of Religious Studies |
| IEJ | Israel Exploration Journal | JRH | Journal of Religious History |
| Int | Interpretation | JRS | Journal of Roman Studies |
| ISBE | G. W. Bromiley (ed.), International Standard Bible Encyclopedia, rev. ed. | JRT | Journal of Religious Thought |
| | | JSJ | Journal for the Study of Judaism |
| | | JSNT | Journal for the Study of the New Testament |
| ITQ | Irish Theological Quarterly | JSNTSup | JSNT Supplement Series |
| | | JSOT | Journal for the Study of the Old Testament |
| JA | Journal asiatique | | |
| JAAR | Journal of the American Academy of Religion | JSOTSup | JSOT Supplement Series |
| | | JSS | Journal of Semitic Studies |
| JAC | Jahrbuch für Antike und Christentum | JSSR | Journal for the Scientific Study of Religion |
| JANESCU | Journal of the Ancient Near Eastern Society of Columbia University | JTC | Journal for Theology and the Church |
| JAOS | Journal of the American Oriental Society | JThSB | Jahrbuch der theologischen Schule Bethel |
| JAS | Journal of Asian Studies | JTS | Journal of Theological Studies |
| JBC | R. E. Brown et al. (eds.), The Jerome Biblical Commentary | Judaica | Judaica: Beiträge zum Verständnis . . . |
| JBL | Journal of Biblical Literature | | |
| JBR | Journal of Bible and Religion | KAI | H. Donner and W. Röllig, Kanaanäische und aramäische Inschriften |
| JCS | Journal of Cuneiform Studies | | |
| JDS | Judean Desert Studies | | |
| JEA | Journal of Egyptian Archaeology | KAT | Kommentar zum Alten Testament |
| JEH | Journal of Ecclesiastical History | | |
| JES | Journal of Ecumenical Studies | KB | L. Koehler and W. Baumgartner, Lexicon in Veteris Testamenti libros |
| JETS | Journal of the Evangelical Theological Society | | |
| JHS | Journal of Hellenic Studies | KD | Kerygma und Dogma |
| JIBS | Journal of Indian and Buddhist Studies | KlT | Kleine Texte |
| | | KNT | Kommentar till Nya Testament |
| JIPh | Journal of Indian Philosophy | | |
| JJS | Journal of Jewish Studies | | |
| JMES | Journal of Middle Eastern Studies | LCC | Library of Christian Classics |
| | | LCL | Loeb Classical Library |
| JMS | Journal of Mithraic Studies | LD | Lectio divina |
| JNES | Journal of Near Eastern Studies | Leš | Lešonénu |
| JPOS | Journal of the Palestine Oriental Society | LexTQ | Lexington Theological Quarterly |
| | | LingBib | Linguistica Biblica |
| JQR | Jewish Quarterly Review | LLAVT | E. Vogt, Lexicon linguae aramaicae Veteris Testamenti |
| JQRMS | Jewish Quarterly Review Monograph Series | LPGL | G. W. H. Lampe, Patristic Greek Lexicon |
| JR | Journal of Religion | | |
| JRAS | Journal of the Royal Asiatic Society | LQ | Lutheran Quarterly |
| | | LQHR | London Quarterly and Holborn Review |
| JRE | Journal of Religious Ethics | | |

| | | | |
|---|---|---|---|
| *LR* | *Lutherische Rundschau* | NCB | New Century Bible (new ed.) |
| *LS* | *Louvain Studies* | | |
| LSJ | Liddell-Scott-Jones, *Greek-English Lexicon* | NCCHS | R. C. Fuller et al. (eds.), *New Catholic Commentary on Holy Scripture* |
| *LTK* | *Lexikon für Theologie und Kirche* | NCE | M. R. P. McGuire et al. (eds.), *New Catholic Encyclopedia* |
| *LTP* | *Laval théologique et philosophique* | | |
| LUÅ | Lunds universitets årsskrift | *NedTTs* | *Nederlands theologisch tijdschrift* |
| *LumVie* | *Lumière et Vie* | | |
| LumVieSup | Supplement to LumVie | *Neot* | *Neotestamentica* |
| *LVit* | *Lumen Vitae* | *NewDocs* | *New Documents Illustrating Early Christianity, A Review of Greek Inscriptions, etc.*, ed. G. H. R. Horsley, North Ryde, NSW, Australia |
| *LW* | *Lutheran World* | | |
| *McCQ* | *McCormick Quarterly* | | |
| MDOG | Mitteilungen der deutschen Orient-Gesellschaft | NFT | New Frontiers in Theology |
| MeyerK | H. A. W. Meyer, *Kritisch-exegetischer Kommentar über das Neue Testament* | NHS | Nag Hammadi Studies |
| | | *NIDNTT* | *New International Dictionary of New Testament Theology* |
| *MGWJ* | *Monatschrift für Geschichte und Wissenschaft des Judentums* | NICNT | New International Commentary on the New Testament |
| MHT | J. H. Moulton, W. F. Howard, and N. Turner, *A Grammar of New Testament Greek* | NIBC | New International Biblical Commentary |
| | | NIGTC | New International Greek Testament Commentary |
| MM | J. H. Moulton and G. Milligan, *The Vocabulary of the Greek Testament* | *NKZ* | *Neue kirchliche Zeitschrift* |
| | | *NorTT* | *Norsk Teologisk Tijdsskrift* |
| | | *NovT* | *Novum Testamentum* |
| MNTC | Moffatt NT Commentary | NovTSup | Supplement to *NovT* |
| *MPAIBL* | *Mémoires présentés a l'Académie des inscriptions et belles-lettres* | NPNF | Nicene and Post-Nicene Fathers |
| | | *NRF* | *Nouvelle revue française* |
| *MScRel* | *Mélanges de science religieuse* | *NRT* | *La nouvelle revue théologique* |
| MTS | Marburger theologische Studien | *NTA* | *New Testament Abstracts* |
| | | NTAbh | Neutestamentliche Abhandlungen |
| *MTZ* | *Münchener theologische Zeitschrift* | NTD | Das Neue Testament Deutsch |
| *MUSJ* | *Mélanges de l'université Saint-Joseph* | NTF | Neutestamentliche Forschungen |
| MVAG | Mitteilungen der vorder-asiatisch-ägyptischen Gesellschaft | NTL | New Testament Library |
| | | *NTR* | *New Theology Review* |
| | | *NTS* | *New Testament Studies* |
| NABPR | National Association of Baptist Professors of Religion | NTTS | New Testament Tools and Studies |
| *NB* | *New Blackfriars* | *Numen* | *Numen: International Review for the History of Religions* |

| | | | |
|---|---|---|---|
| NZSTR | Neue Zeitschrift für systematische Theologie und Religionsphilosophie | PTMS | Pittsburgh (Princeton) Theological Monograph Series |
| | | PTR | Princeton Theological Review |
| OBO | Orbis biblicus et orientalis | PVTG | Pseudepigrapha Veteris Testamenti graece |
| ÖBS | Österreichische biblische studien | PW | Pauly-Wissowa, Real-Encyklopädie der classischen |
| OCD | Oxford Classical Dictionary | | |
| OCP | Orientalia christiana periodica | | Altertumswissenschaft |
| OGI | W. Dittenberger (ed.), Orientis graeci inscriptiones selectae (1903–5) | PWSup | Supplement to PW |
| | | QD | Quaestiones disputatae |
| OIP | Oriental Institute Publications | QDAP | Quarterly of the Department of Antiquities in Palestine |
| OLP | Orientalia lovaniensia periodica | QLP | Questions liturgiques et paroissiales (Leuven) |
| OLZ | Orientalische Literaturzeitung | | |
| Or | Orientalia (Rome) | RA | Revue d'assyriologie et d'archéologie orientale |
| OrAnt | Oriens antiquus | | |
| OrChr | Oriens christianus | RAC | Reallexikon für Antike und Christentum |
| OrSyr | L'orient syrien | | |
| OTM | Oxford Theological Mono-graphs | RB | Revue biblique |
| | | RBén | Revue bénédictine |
| OTS | Oudtestamentische Studiën | RCB | Revista de cultura biblica |
| | | RE | Realencyklopädie für protestantische Theologie und Kirche |
| PAAJR | Proceedings of the American Academy of Jewish Research | | |
| PCB | M. Black and H. H. Rowley (eds.), Peake's Commentary on the Bible | REA | Revue des études anciennes (Bordeaux) |
| | | RechBib | Recherches bibliques |
| PEFQS | Palestine Exploration Fund, Quarterly Statement | RefRev | Reformed Review |
| | | REg | Revue d'égyptologie |
| PEQ | Palestine Exploration Quarterly | REG | Revue des études grecques |
| | | REJ | Revue des études juives |
| PG | J. P. Migne, Patrologia graeca | RelS | Religious Studies |
| PGM | K. Preisendanz (ed.), Papyri graecae magicae | RelSoc | Religion and Society |
| | | RelSRev | Religious Studies Review |
| PhEW | Philosophy East and West | RES | Répertoire d'épigraphie sémitique |
| PhRev | Philosophical Review | | |
| PJ | Palästina-Jahrbuch | ResQ | Restoration Quarterly |
| PLL | Papers on Language and Literature | RevExp | Review and Expositor |
| | | RevistB | Revista bíblica |
| PO | Patrologia orientalis | RevQ | Revue de Qumrân |
| POxy | Oxyrhynchus Papyri | RevScRel | Revue des sciences religieuses |
| PRS | Perspectives in Religious Studies | RevSém | Revue sémitique |
| PRU | Le Palais royal d'Ugarit | RevSR | Revue des sciences religieuses (Strasbourg) |
| PSTJ | Perkins (School of Theology) Journal | | |
| | | RevThom | Revue thomiste |

| | | | |
|---|---|---|---|
| RGG | Religion in Geschichte und | ScEs | Science et esprit |
| | Gegenwart | SCR | Studies in Comparative |
| RHE | Revue d'histoire ecclésiastique | | Religion |
| RHPR | Revue d'histoire et de | Scr | Scripture |
| | philosophie religieuses | SD | Studies and Documents |
| RHR | Revue de l'histoire des religions | SE | Studia Evangelica 1, 2, 3, 4, 5, |
| RivB | Rivista biblica | | 6 (= TU 73 [1959], 87 |
| RNT | Regensburger Neues | | [1964], 88 [1964], 102 |
| | Testament | | [1968], 103 [1968], 112 |
| RR | Review of Religion | | [1973]) |
| RRéf | Revue Réformée | SEÅ | Svensk exegetisk årsbok |
| RSO | Rivista degli studi orientali | Sef | Sefarad |
| RSPT | Revue des sciences philoso- | SeinSend | Sein und Sendung |
| | phiques et théologiques | Sem | Semitica |
| RSR | Recherches de science religieuse | SHT | Studies in Historical |
| RTL | Revue théologique de Louvain | | Theology |
| RTP | Revue de théologie et de | SJLA | Studies in Judaism in Late |
| | philosophie | | Antiquity |
| RTR | Reformed Theological Review | SJT | Scottish Journal of Theology |
| | | SKK | Stuttgarter kleiner |
| SacPag | Sacra Pagina | | Kommentar |
| Sal | Salmanticensis | SMSR | Studi e materiali di storia delle |
| SANT | Studien zum Alten und | | religioni |
| | Neuen Testament | SNT | Studien zum Neuen |
| SAQ | Sammlung ausgewählter | | Testament |
| | kirchen- und | SNTSMS | Society for New Testament |
| | dogmengeschichtlicher | | Studies Monograph |
| | Quellenschriften | | Series |
| SB | Sources bibliques | SNTU | Studien zum Neuen Testament |
| SBF | Studii biblici franciscani | | und seiner Umwelt |
| SBJ | La sainte bible de Jérusalem | SNTUMS | SNTU Monograph Series |
| SBLASP | Society of Biblical Literature | SO | Symbolae osloenses |
| | Abstracts and Seminar | SOTSMS | Society for Old Testament |
| | Papers | | Study Monograph Series |
| SBLDS | SBL Dissertation Series | SPap | Studia papyrologica |
| SBLMasS | SBL Masoretic Studies | SPAW | Sitzungsberichte der |
| SBLMS | SBL Monograph Series | | preussischen Akademie |
| SBLSBS | SBL Sources for Biblical | | der Wissenschaften |
| | Study | SPB | Studia postbiblica |
| SBLSCS | SBL Septuagint and Cognate | SR | Studies in Religion/Sciences |
| | Studies | | religieuses |
| SBLTT | SBL Texts and Translations | SSS | Semitic Study Series |
| SBM | Stuttgarter biblische | ST | Studia theologica |
| | Monographien | STÅ | Svensk teologisk årsskrift |
| SBS | Stuttgarter Bibelstudien | STDJ | Studies on the Texts of the |
| SBT | Studies in Biblical Theology | | Desert of Judah |
| SC | Sources chrétiennes | StimmZeit | Stimmen der Zeit (Munich) |
| ScEccl | Sciences ecclésiastiques | STK | Svensk teologisk kvartalskrift |

| | | | |
|---|---|---|---|
| Str-B | [H. Strack and] P. Billerbeck, *Kommentar zum Neuen Testament* | TQ | *Theologische Quartalschrift* |
| | | TRE | *Theologische Realenzyklopädie* |
| StudBib | Studia Biblica | TRev | *Theologische Revue* |
| StudNeot | Studia neotestamentica | TRu | *Theologische Rundschau* |
| STZ | *Schweizerische theologische Zeitschrift* | TS | *Theological Studies* |
| | | TSK | *Theologische Studien und Kritiken* |
| SUNT | Studien zur Umwelt des Neuen Testaments | TT | *Teologisk Tidsskrift* |
| | | TTh | *Tijdschrift voor theologie* |
| SVTP | Studia in Veteris Testamenti pseudepigrapha | TToday | *Theology Today* |
| | | TTZ | *Trierer theologische Zeitschrift* |
| SWJT | *Southwestern Journal of Theology* | TU | Texte und Untersuchungen |
| | | TWAT | G. J. Botterweck and H. Ringgren (eds.), *Theologisches Wörterbuch zum Alten Testament* |
| SymBU | Symbolae biblicae upsalienses | | |
| TantY | *Tantur Yearbook* | TWNT | G. Kittel and G. Friedrich (eds.), *Theologisches Wörterbuch zum Neuen Testament* |
| TAPA | *Transactions of the American Philological Association* | | |
| TBei | *Theologische Beiträge* | | |
| TBl | *Theologische Blätter* | TynB | *Tyndale Bulletin* |
| TBü | Theologische Bücherei | TZ | *Theologische Zeitschrift* |
| TC | Theological Collection (SPCK) | UBSGNT | United Bible Societies *Greek New Testament* |
| TCGNT | B. M. Metzger, *A Textual Commentary on the Greek New Testament* | UF | *Ugaritische Forschungen* |
| | | UNT | Untersuchungen zum Neuen Testament |
| TD | *Theology Digest* | USQR | *Union Seminary Quarterly Review* |
| TDNT | G. Kittel and G. Friedrich (eds.), *Theological Dictionary of the New Testament* | | |
| | | UT | C. H. Gordon, *Ugaritic Textbook* |
| TextsS | Texts and Studies | UUÅ | Uppsala universitetsårsskrift |
| TF | *Theologische Forschung* | | |
| TGeg | *Theologie der Gegenwart* | VC | *Vigilae christianae* |
| TGl | *Theologie und Glaube* | VCaro | *Verbum caro* |
| Th | *Theology* | VChr | *Vigiliae Christianae* |
| THKNT | Theologischer Handkommentar zum Neuen Testament | VD | *Verbum domini* |
| | | VF | *Verkündigung und Forschung* |
| | | VKGNT | K. Aland (ed.), *Vollständige Konkordanz zum griechischen Neuen Testament* |
| ThViat | *Theologia Viatorum* | | |
| TJT | *Toronto Journal of Theology* | | |
| TLZ | *Theologische Literaturzeitung* | VS | Verbum salutis |
| TNTC | Tyndale New Testament Commentaries | VSpir | *Vie spirituelle* |
| | | VT | *Vetus Testamentum* |
| TP | *Theologie und Philosophie* | VTSup | Vetus Testamentum, Supplements |
| TPQ | *Theologisch-praktische Quartalschrift* | | |

| | | |
|---|---|---|
| WA | M. Luther, Kritische Gesamtausgabe (="Weimar" edition) | |
| WBC | Word Biblical Commentary | |
| WD | *Wort und Dienst* | |
| WDB | *Westminster Dictionary of the Bible* | |
| WHAB | *Westminster Historical Atlas of the Bible* | |
| WMANT | Wissenschaftliche Monographien zum Alten und Neuen Testament | |
| WO | *Die Welt des Orients* | |
| WortWahr | *Wort und Wahrheit* | |
| WTJ | *Westminster Theological Journal* | |
| WUNT | Wissenschaftliche Untersuchungen zum Neuen Testament | |
| WW | *Word and World* | |
| WZKM | *Wiener Zeitschrift für die Kunde des Morgenlandes* | |
| WZKSO | *Wiener Zeitschrift für die Kunde Süd- und Ostasiens* | |
| ZA | *Zeitschrift für Assyriologie* | |
| ZAW | *Zeitschrift für die alttestamentliche Wissenschaft* | |

| | |
|---|---|
| ZDMG | *Zeitschrift der deutschen morgenländischen Gesellschaft* |
| ZDPV | *Zeitschrift des deutschen Palästina-Vereins* |
| ZEE | *Zeitschrift für evangelische Ethik* |
| ZHT | *Zeitschrift für historische Theologie* |
| ZKG | *Zeitschrift für Kirchengeschichte* |
| ZKT | *Zeitschrift für katholische Theologie* |
| ZMR | *Zeitschrift für Missionskunde und Religionswissenschaft* |
| ZNW | *Zeitschrift für die neutestamentliche Wissenschaft* |
| ZRGG | *Zeitschrift für Religions- und Geistesgeschichte* |
| ZSSR | *Zeitschrift der Savigny-Stiftung für Rechtsgeschichte* |
| ZST | *Zeitschrift für systematische Theologie* |
| ZTK | *Zeitschrift für Theologie und Kirche* |
| ZWT | *Zeitschrift für wissenschaftliche Theologie* |
| ZZ | *Zwischen den Zeiten* |

**D. Abbreviations for Books of the Bible, the Apocrypha, and the Pseudepigrapha**

### NEW TESTAMENT

| | | |
|---|---|---|
| Gen | 2 Chr | Dan |
| Exod | Ezra | Hos |
| Lev | Neh | Joel |
| Num | Esth | Amos |
| Deut | Job | Obad |
| Josh | Ps(s) | Jonah |
| Judg | Prov | Mic |
| Ruth | Eccl | Nah |
| 1 Sam | Cant | Hab |
| 2 Sam | Isa | Zeph |
| 1 Kgs | Jer | Hag |
| 2 Kgs | Lam | Zech |
| 1 Chr | Ezek | Mal |

### OLD TESTAMENT

| | |
|---|---|
| Matt | 1 Tim |
| Mark | 2 Tim |
| Luke | Titus |
| John | Philem |
| Acts | Heb |
| Rom | Jas |
| 1 Cor | 1 Peter |
| 2 Cor | 2 Peter |
| Gal | 1 John |
| Eph | 2 John |
| Phil | 3 John |
| Col | Jude |
| 1 Thess | Rev |
| 2 Thess | |

## APOCRYPHA

| | | | |
|---|---|---|---|
| 1 Kgdms | 1 Kingdoms | Ep Jer | Epistle of Jeremiah |
| 2 Kgdms | 2 Kingdoms | S Th Ch | Song of the Three Children (or |
| 3 Kgdms | 3 Kingdoms | | Young Men) |
| 4 Kgdms | 4 Kingdoms | Sus | Susanna |
| 1 Esdr | 1 Esdras | Bel | Bel and the Dragon |
| 2 Esdr | 2 Esdras | Pr Azar | Prayer of Azar |
| 4 Ezra | 4 Ezra | Pr Man | Prayer of Manasseh |
| Jdt | Judith | 1 Macc | 1 Maccabees |
| Add Esth | Additions to Esther | 2 Macc | 2 Maccabees |
| Wis | Wisdom of Solomon | 3 Macc | 3 Maccabees |
| Sir | Ecclesiasticus (Wisdom of | 4 Macc | 4 Maccabees |
| | Jesus the son of Sirach) | Tob | Tobit |
| Bar | Baruch | | |

## E. Abbreviations of the Names of Pseudepigraphical and Early Patristic Books

| | | | |
|---|---|---|---|
| Adam and Eve | Life of Adam and Eve | 1–2 Clem. | 1–2 Clement |
| Apoc. Abr. | Apocalypse of Abraham (1st | Did. | Didache |
| | to 2nd cent. A.D.) | Diogn. | Diognetus |
| 2–3 Apoc. Bar. | Syriac, Greek Apocalypse of | Herm. Man. | Hermas, Mandates |
| | Baruch | Sim. | Similitudes |
| Apoc. Mos. | Apocalypse of Moses | Vis. | Visions |
| As. Mos. | (See T. Mos.) | Ign. Eph. | Ignatius, Letter to the |
| 1–2–3 Enoch | Ethiopic, Slavonic, | | Ephesians |
| | Hebrew Enoch | Magn. | Ignatius, Letter to the |
| Ep. Arist. | Epistle of Aristeas | | Magnesians |
| Jub. | Jubilees | Phil. | Ignatius, Letter to the |
| Mart. Isa. | Martyrdom of Isaiah | | Philadelphians |
| Odes Sol. | Odes of Solomon | Pol. | Ignatius, Letter to Polycarp |
| Pss. Sol. | Psalms of Solomon | Rom. | Ignatius, Letter to the |
| Sib. Or. | Sibylline Oracles | | Romans |
| T. 12 Patr. | Testaments of the Twelve | Smyrn. | Ignatius, Letter to the |
| | Patriarchs | | Smyrnaeans |
| T. Abr. | Testament of Abraham | Trall. | Ignatius, Letter to the |
| T. Judah | Testament of Judah | | Trallians |
| T. Levi | Testament of Levi, etc. | Mart. Pol. | Martyrdom of Polycarp |
| T. Sol. | Testament of Solomon | Pol. Phil. | Polycarp, Letter to the |
| | | | Philippians |
| Gos. Eb. | Gospel of the Ebionites | Irenaeus, Adv. | Irenaeus, Against All |
| Gos. Heb. | Gospel of the Hebrews | Haer. | Heresies |
| Gos. Naass. | Gospel of the Naassenes | Tertullian, De | Tertullian, On the |
| Gos. Pet. | Gospel of Peter | Praesc. Haer. | Proscribing of Heretics |
| Barn. | Barnabas | | |

## F. Abbreviations of Names of Dead Sea Scrolls and Related Texts

| | | | |
|---|---|---|---|
| CD | Cairo (Genizah text of the) Damascus (Document) | 1QM | *Milḥāmāh* (War Scroll) |
| | | 1QS | *Serek hayyaḥad (Rule of the Community, Manual of Discipline)* |
| Ḥev | Naḥal Ḥever texts | | |
| Mas | Masada texts | 1QSa | Appendix A *(Rule of the Congregation)* to 1QS |
| Mird | Khirbet Mird texts | | |
| Mur | Wadi Murabbaʿat texts | 1QSb | Appendix B *(Blessings)* to 1QS |
| P | Pesher (commentary) | | |
| Q | Qumran | 3Q*15* | Copper Scroll from Qumran Cave 3 |
| 1Q, 2Q | | | |
| 3Q, etc. | Numbered caves of Qumran, yielding written material; followed by abbreviation of biblical or apocryphal book | 4QFlor | *Florilegium* (or *Eschatological Midrashim)* from Qumran Cave 4 |
| | | 4QMess ar | Aramaic "Messianic" text from Qumran Cave 4 |
| QL | Qumran literature | 4QPrNab | Prayer of Nabonidus from Qumran Cave 4 |
| 1QapGen | *Genesis Apocryphon* of Qumran Cave 1 | 4QTestim | *Testimonia* text from Qumran Cave 4 |
| 1QH | *Hôdāyôt (Thanksgiving Hymns)* from Qumran Cave 1 | 4QTLevi | *Testament of Levi* from Qumran Cave 4 |
| 1QIsaᵃ,ᵇ | First or second copy of Isaiah from Qumran Cave 1 | 4QPhyl | Phylacteries from Qumran Cave 4 |
| | | 11QMelch | *Melchizedek* text from Qumran Cave 11 |
| 1QpHab | *Pesher on Habakkuk* from Qumran Cave 1 | 11QtgJob | *Targum of Job* from Qumran Cave 11 |

## G. Abbreviations of Targumic Material

| | | | |
|---|---|---|---|
| *Tg. Onq.* | *Targum Onqelos* | *Tg. Ps. -J.* | *Targum Pseudo-Jonathan* |
| *Tg. Neb.* | *Targum of the Prophets* | *Tg. Yer. I* | *Targum Yerušalmi I** |
| *Tg. Ket.* | *Targum of the Writings* | *Tg. Yer. II* | *Targum Yerušalmi II** |
| *Frg. Tg.* | *Fragmentary Targum* | *Yem. Tg.* | *Yemenite Targum* |
| *Sam. Tg.* | *Samaritan Targum* | *Tg. Esth I,* | *First or Second Targum of* |
| *Tg. Isa.* | *Targum of Isaiah* | *II* | *Esther* |
| *Pal. Tgs.* | *Palestinian Targums* | | |
| *Tg. Neof.* | *Targum Neofiti I* | *optional title | |

## H. Abbreviations of Other Rabbinic Works

| | | | |
|---|---|---|---|
| ʾAbot R. Nat. | *ʾAbot de Rabbi Nathan* | Der. Er. Zuṭ. | *Derek Ereṣ Zuṭa* |
| ʾAg. Ber. | *ʾAggadat Berešit* | Gem. | *Gemara* |
| Bab. | *Babylonian* | Kalla | *Kalla* |
| Bar. | *Baraita* | Mek. | *Mekilta* |
| Der. Er. Rab. | *Derek Ereṣ Rabba* | Midr. | *Midraš;* cited with usual |

|  | abbreviation for biblical book; but *Midr. Qoh.* = *Midraš Qohelet* |  | periods] = *Genesis Rabbah*) |
|---|---|---|---|
|  |  | *Sem.* | *Semahot* |
| *Pal.* | *Palestinian* | *Sipra* | *Sipra* |
| *Pesiq. R.* | *Pesiqta Rabbati* | *Sipre* | *Sipre* |
| *Pesiq. Rab Kah.* | *Pesiqta de Rab Kahana* | *Sop.* | *Soperim* |
| *Pirqe R. El.* | *Pirqe Rabbi Eliezer* | *S. ʿOlam Rab.* | *Seder ʿOlam Rabbah* |
| *Rab.* | *Rabbah* (following abbreviation for biblical book: Gen. Rab. [with | *Talm.* | *Talmud* |
|  |  | *Yal.* | *Yalqut* |

## I. Abbreviations of Orders and Tractates in Mishnaic and Related Literature

(Italicized *m.*, *t.*, *b.*, or *y.* used before name to distinguish among tractates in Mishnah, Tosepta, Babylonian Talmud, and Jerusalem Talmud.)

| | | | |
|---|---|---|---|
| *ʾAbot* | *ʾAbot* | *Maʿaś. Š.* | *Maʿaśer Šeni* |
| *ʿArak.* | *ʿArakin* | *Našim* | *Našim* |
| *ʿAbod. Zar.* | *ʿAboda Zara* | *Nazir* | *Nazir* |
| *B. Bat.* | *Baba Batra* | *Ned.* | *Nedarim* |
| *Bek.* | *Bekorot* | *Neg.* | *Negaʿim* |
| *Ber.* | *Berakot* | *Nez.* | *Neziqin* |
| *Besa* | *Besa* (= *Yom Tob*) | *Nid.* | *Niddah* |
| *Bik.* | *Bikkurim* | *Ohol.* | *Oholot* |
| *B. Meṣ.* | *Baba Meṣiʿa* | *ʿOr.* | *ʿOrla* |
| *B. Qam.* | *Baba Qamma* | *Para* | *Para* |
| *Dem.* | *Demai* | *Peʾa* | *Peʾa* |
| *ʿEd.* | *ʿEduyyot* | *Pesah.* | *Pesahim* |
| *ʿErub.* | *ʿErubin* | *Qinnim* | *Qinnim* |
| *Giṭ.* | *Gittin* | *Qidd.* | *Qiddušin* |
| *Hag.* | *Hagiga* | *Qod.* | *Qodašin* |
| *Hal.* | *Halla* | *Roš. Haš.* | *Roš Haššana* |
| *Hor.* | *Horayot* | *Sanh.* | *Sanhedrin* |
| *Hul.* | *Hullin* | *Šabb.* | *Šabbat* |
| *Kelim* | *Kelim* | *Šeb.* | *Šebiʿit* |
| *Ker.* | *Keritot* | *Šebu.* | *Šebuʿot* |
| *Ketub.* | *Ketubot* | *Šeqal.* | *Šeqalim* |
| *Kil.* | *Kilʾayim* | *Soṭa* | *Soṭa* |
| *Maʿaś.* | *Maʿaśerot* | *Sukk.* | *Sukka* |
| *Mak.* | *Makkot* | *Taʿan.* | *Taʿanit* |
| *Makš.* | *Makširin* (=*Mašqin*) | *Tamid* | *Tamid* |
| *Meg.* | *Megilla* | *Tem.* | *Temura* |
| *Meʿil.* | *Meʿila* | *Ter.* | *Terumot* |
| *Menah.* | *Menahot* | *Tohar.* | *Toharot* |
| *Mid.* | *Middot* | *T. Yom* | *Tebul Yom* |
| *Miqw.* | *Miqwaʾot* | *ʿUq.* | *ʿUqṣin* |
| *Moʿed* | *Moʿed* | *Yad.* | *Yadayim* |
| *Moʿed Qaṭ.* | *Moʿed Qaṭan* | *Yebam.* | *Yebamot* |

| | | | |
|---|---|---|---|
| *Yoma* | *Yoma (= Kippurim)* | *Zebaḥ.* | *Zebaḥim* |
| *Zabim* | *Zabim* | *Zer.* | *Zeraᶜim* |

## J. Abbreviations of Nag Hammadi Tractates

| | | | |
|---|---|---|---|
| *Acts Pet. 12* | *Acts of Peter and the Twelve* | *Marsanes* | *Marsanes* |
| *Apost.* | *Apostles* | *Melch.* | *Melchizedek* |
| *Allogenes* | *Allogenes* | *Norea* | *Thought of Norea* |
| *Ap. Jas.* | *Apocryphon of James* | *On Bap. A* | *On Baptism A* |
| *Ap. John* | *Apocryphon of John* | *On Bap. B* | *On Baptism B* |
| *Apoc. Adam* | *Apocalypse of Adam* | *On Bap. C* | *On Baptism C* |
| *1 Apoc. Jas.* | *First Apocalypse of James* | *On Euch. A* | *On the Eucharist A* |
| *2 Apoc. Jas.* | *Second Apocalypse of James* | *On Euch. B* | *On the Eucharist B* |
| *Apoc. Paul* | *Apocalypse of Paul* | *Orig. World* | *On the Origin of the World* |
| *Apoc. Pet.* | *Apocalypse of Peter* | *Paraph. Shem* | *Paraphrase of Shem* |
| *Asclepius* | *Asclepius 21–29* | *Pr. Paul* | *Prayer of the Apostle Paul* |
| *Auth. Teach.* | *Authoritative Teaching* | *Pr. Thanks.* | *Prayer of Thanksgiving* |
| *Dial. Sav.* | *Dialogue of the Savior* | *Prot. Jas.* | *Protevangelium of James* |
| *Disc. 8–9* | *Discourse on the Eighth and Ninth* | *Sent. Sextus* | *Sentences of Sextus* |
| | | *Soph. Jes. Chr.* | *Sophia of Jesus Christ* |
| *Ep. Pet. Phil.* | *Letter of Peter to Philip* | *Steles Seth* | *Three Steles of Seth* |
| *Eugnostos* | *Eugnostos the Blessed* | *Teach. Silv.* | *Teachings of Silvanus* |
| *Exeg. Soul* | *Exegesis on the Soul* | *Testim. Truth* | *Testimony of Truth* |
| *Gos. Eg.* | *Gospel of the Egyptians* | *Thom. Cont.* | *Book of Thomas the Contender* |
| *Gos. Phil.* | *Gospel of Philip* | *Thund.* | *Thunder, Perfect Mind* |
| *Gos. Thom.* | *Gospel of Thomas* | *Treat. Res.* | *Treatise on Resurrection* |
| *Gos. Truth* | *Gospel of Truth* | *Treat. Seth* | *Second Treatise of the Great Seth* |
| *Great Pow.* | *Concept of our Great Power* | *Tri. Trac.* | *Tripartite Tractate* |
| *Hyp. Arch.* | *Hypostasis of the Archons* | *Trim. Prot.* | *Trimorphic Protennoia* |
| *Hypsiph.* | *Hypsiphrone* | *Val. Exp.* | *A Valentinian Exposition* |
| *Interp. Know.* | *Interpretation of Knowledge* | *Zost.* | *Zostrianos* |

**Note:** The textual notes and numbers used to indicate individual manuscripts are those found in the apparatus criticus of *Novum Testamentum Graece*, ed. E. Nestle and K. Aland et al. (Stuttgart: Deutsche Bibelgesellschaft, 1979[26]). This edition of the Greek New Testament is the basis for the *Translation* sections.

# Commentary Bibliography

**Albright, W. F.,** and **Mann, C. S.** *Matthew.* AB. Garden City, NY: Doubleday, 1971. **Allen, W. C.** *A Critical and Exegetical Commentary on the Gospel according to St. Matthew.* 3rd ed. ICC. Edinburgh: T. & T. Clark, 1912. **Argyle, A. W.** *The Gospel according to Matthew.* CBC. Cambridge: Cambridge University Press, 1963. **Barclay, W.** *The Gospel of Matthew.* Rev. ed. 2 vols. The Daily Study Bible. Philadelphia: Westminster, 1975. **Beare, F. W.** *The Gospel according to Matthew: A Commentary.* Oxford: Blackwell, 1981. **Bengel, J. A.** *Gnomon of the New Testament.* 7th ed. Edinburgh: T. & T. Clark, 1857. 1:71–490. **Benoit, P.** *L'Évangile selon saint Matthieu.* 3rd ed. La Sainte Bible. Paris: Letouzey et Ané, 1961. **Blomberg, C. L.** *Matthew.* New American Commentary. Nashville: Broadman, 1992. **Bonnard, P.** *L'Évangile selon saint Matthieu.* 2nd ed. CNT. Neuchâtel: Delachaux & Niestlé, 1970. **Bruner, F. D.** *The Christbook: A Historical/Theological Commentary: Matthew 1–12.* Waco, TX: Word, 1987. ———. *The Churchbook: A Historical/Theological Commentary: Matthew 13–28.* Dallas, TX: Word, 1990. **Calvin, J.** *Commentary on a Harmony of the Gospels.* 3 vols. Reprint. Grand Rapids: Eerdmans, 1956–57. **Carson, D. A.** "Matthew." In *The Expositor's Bible Commentary,* ed. F. E. Gaebelein. Grand Rapids: Zondervan, 1985. 8:1–599. **Dahl, N. A.** *Matteus Evangeliet.* 2 vols. 2nd ed. Oslo: Universitetsforlaget, 1973. **Davies, M.** *Matthew: Readings, a New Biblical Commentary.* Sheffield: JSOT, 1992. **Davies, W. D.,** and **Allison, D. C., Jr.** *A Critical and Exegetical Commentary on the Gospel according to Saint Matthew.* 2 vols. (1–7; 8–18). ICC. Edinburgh: T. & T. Clark, 1988, 1991. **Fenton, J. C.** *Saint Matthew.* Pelican Commentaries. Baltimore: Penguin, 1964. **Filson, F. V.** *A Commentary on the Gospel according to St. Matthew.* BNTC. London: A. & C. Black, 1960. **Fornberg, T.** *Matteusevangeliet 1:1–13:52.* KNT 1A. Uppsala: EFS, 1989. **France, R. T.** *The Gospel according to Matthew.* TNTC 1. Grand Rapids: Eerdmans, 1985. **Gaechter, P.** *Das Matthäus-Evangelium.* Innsbruck: Tyrolia, 1963. **Garland, D. E.** *Reading Matthew: A Literary and Theological Commentary on the First Gospel.* New York: Crossroad, 1993. **Gerhardsson, B.** "Ur Matteusevangeliet" (chaps. 1–2; 5–7; 26–28). In *Ur Nya Testamentet: Kommentar till valda texter,* ed. L. Hartman. Lund: Gleerup, 1970. **Gnilka, J.** *Das Matthäusevangelium.* 2 vols. HTKNT. Freiburg: Herder, 1986, 1988. **Green, H. B.** *The Gospel according to Matthew.* New Clarendon Bible. Oxford: Clarendon, 1975. **Grundmann, W.** *Das Evangelium nach Matthäus.* THKNT. Berlin: Evangelische Verlagsanstalt, 1968. **Gundry, R. H.** *Matthew: A Commentary on His Literary and Theological Art.* Grand Rapids: Eerdmans, 1982. ———. *Matthew: A Commentary on His Handbook for a Mixed Church under Persecution.* 2nd ed. Grand Rapids: Eerdmans, 1994. **Hagner, D. A.** *Matthew 1–13.* WBC 33a. Dallas: Word, 1993. **Harrington, D. J.** *The Gospel of Matthew.* SacPag. Collegeville, MN: Liturgical, 1991. **Hendricksen, W.** *The Gospel of Matthew.* Edinburgh: Banner of Truth, 1974. **Hill, D.** *The Gospel of Matthew.* NCB. London: Marshall, Morgan, and Scott, 1972. **Klostermann, E.** *Das Matthäusevangelium.* 2nd ed. HNT. Tübingen: Mohr, 1927. **Kvalbein, H.** *Matteus-Evangeliet.* 2 vols. Oslo: Nye Luther, 1989, 1990. **Lachs, S. T.** *A Rabbinic Commentary on the New Testament: The Gospels of Matthew, Mark and Luke.* Hoboken, NJ: Ktav, 1987. **Lagrange, M.-J.** *Évangile selon Saint Matthieu.* EBib. Paris: Gabalda, 1923. **Lenski, R. C. H.** *The Interpretation of St. Matthew's Gospel.* Columbus, OH: Wartburg, 1943. **Limbeck, M.** *Matthäus-Evangelium.* SKK NT 1. Stuttgart: Katholisches Bibelwerk, 1986. **Lohmeyer, E.** *Das Evangelium des Matthäus.* 4th ed. Ed. W. Schmauch. MeyerK. Göttingen: Vandenhoeck & Ruprecht, 1967. **Luz, U.** *Matthew 1–7: A Commentary.* Trans. W. C. Linss. Continental Commentaries. Minneapolis: Augsburg, 1989. ———. *Das Evangelium nach Matthäus.* Vol. 2, Matt 8–17. EKK. Neukirchen-Vluyn: Benzinger & Neukirchener, 1990. **Maier, G.** *Matthäus-Evangelium.* 2 vols. Bibel-Kommentar. Neuhausen-Stuttgart: Hänssler, 1979. **McNeile, A. H.** *The Gospel according to St. Matthew.* London: Macmillan, 1915. **Meier, J. P.** *Matthew.* NT

Message 3. Wilmington, DE: Glazier, 1981. **Montefiore, C. G.** *The Synoptic Gospels.* Vol 2. 2nd ed. London: Macmillan, 1927. **Morris, L.** *The Gospel according to Matthew.* Pillar Commentary. Grand Rapids: Eerdmans, 1992. **Mounce, R. H.** *Matthew.* NIBC. Peabody, MA: Hendrickson, 1991. **Patte, D.** *The Gospel according to Matthew: A Structural Commentary on Matthew's Faith.* Philadelphia: Fortress, 1987. **Plummer, A.** *An Exegetical Commentary on the Gospel according to St. Matthew.* London: Stock, 1909. **Robinson, T. H.** *The Gospel of Matthew.* MNTC. Garden City, NY: Doubleday, 1928. **Sabourin, L.** *The Gospel according to St Matthew.* 2 vols. Bombay: St Paul, 1982. **Sand, A.** *Das Evangelium nach Matthäus.* RNT. Regensburg: Pustet, 1986. **Schlatter, A.** *Der Evangelist Matthäus.* 2nd ed. Stuttgart: Calwer, 1933. **Schmid, J.** *Das Evangelium nach Matthäus.* RNT. Regensburg: Pustet, 1965. **Schnackenburg, R.** *Matthäusevangelium.* 2 vols. Die neue echter Bibel. Würzburg: Echter, 1985, 1987. **Schniewind, J.** *Das Evangelium nach Matthäus.* 8th ed. NTD. Göttingen: Vandenhoeck & Ruprecht, 1956. **Schweizer, E.** *The Good News according to Matthew.* Atlanta: John Knox, 1975. **Smith, R. H.** *Matthew.* ACNT. Minneapolis: Augsburg, 1989. **Stendahl, K.** "Matthew." In *Peake's Commentary on the Bible,* ed. M. Black and H. H. Rowley. Rev. ed. New York: Nelson, 1962. 769–98. **Strack, H. L.,** and **Billerbeck, P.** *Kommentar zum Neuen Testament aus Talmud und Midrasch.* 4 vols. 3rd ed. Munich: Beck, 1951–56. **Tasker, R. V. G.** *The Gospel according to St. Matthew.* TNTC. London: Tyndale, 1961. **Trilling, W.** *The Gospel according to St. Matthew.* New York: Herder & Herder, 1969. **Viviano, B. T.** "The Gospel according to Matthew." In *The Jerome Biblical Commentary,* ed. R. E. Brown, J. A. Fitzmyer, and R. E. Murphy. Englewood Cliffs, NJ: Prentice Hall, 1990. 630–74. **Weiss, B.** *Das Matthäus-Evangelium.* 9th ed. Göttingen: Vandenhoeck & Ruprecht, 1898. **Zahn, T.** *Das Evangelium des Matthäus.* 2nd ed. Leipzig: Deichert, 1903.

# General Bibliography

**Abrahams, I.** *Studies in Pharisaism and the Gospels.* 2 vols. Cambridge: Cambridge University, 1917, 1924. **Albertz, M.** *Die synoptischen Streitgespräche.* Berlin: Trowitzsch, 1921. **Allison, D. C., Jr.** *The End of the Ages Has Come: An Early Interpretation of the Passion and Resurrection of Jesus.* Philadelphia: Fortress, 1985. **Alsup, J. E.** *The Post-Resurrection Appearance Stories of the Gospel Tradition.* Stuttgart: Calwer, 1975. **Arens, E.** *The HΛΘON-Sayings in the Synoptic Tradition: A Historico-Critical Investigation.* OBO 10. Göttingen: Vandenhoeck & Ruprecht, 1976. **Aune, D. E.** *Prophecy in Early Christianity and the Ancient Mediterranean World.* Grand Rapids: Eerdmans, 1983. **Baarlink, H.** *Die Eschatologie der synoptischen Evangelien.* BWANT 120. Stuttgart: Kohlhammer, 1986. **Bacon, B. W.** *Studies in Matthew.* New York: Holt, 1930. **Balch, D. L.**, ed. *Social History of the Matthean Community: Cross-Disciplinary Approaches.* Minneapolis: Fortress, 1991. **Baltensweiler, H.** *Die Verklärung Jesu.* ATANT 33. Zürich: Zwingli, 1959. **Banks, R.** *Jesus and the Law in the Synoptic Tradition.* SNTSMS 28. Cambridge: Cambridge University, 1975. **Barrett, C. K.** *The Holy Spirit and the Gospel Tradition.* London: SPCK, 1966. ———. *Jesus and the Gospel Tradition.* Philadelphia: Fortress, 1968. **Barth, G.** "Matthew's Understanding of the Law." In *Tradition and Interpretation in Matthew,* ed. G. Bornkamm et al. Philadelphia: Westminster, 1963. 58–164. **Bauer, D. R.** *The Structure of Matthew's Gospel: A Study in Literary Design.* JSNTSup 31. Sheffield: JSOT, 1988. **Bayer, H. F.** *Jesus' Predictions of Vindication and Resurrection.* WUNT 2.20. Tübingen: Mohr, 1986. **Beasley-Murray, G. R.** *Jesus and the Kingdom of God.* Grand Rapids: Eerdmans, 1986. ———. *Jesus and the Last Days: The Interpretation of the Olivet Discourse.* Peabody, MA: Hendrickson, 1993. **Benoit, P.** *The Passion and Resurrection of Jesus Christ.* New York: Herder & Herder, 1969. **Berger, K.** *Die Amen-Worte Jesu: Eine Untersuchung zum Problem der Legitimation in apokalyptischer Rede.* BZNW 39. Berlin: de Gruyter, 1970. ———. *Die Gesetzesauslegung Jesu: Ihr historischer Hintergrund im Judentum und im Alten Testament: Teil I. Markus und Parallelen.* WMANT 40. Neukirchen-Vluyn: Neukirchener, 1972. **Betz, O.** *Jesus: Der Messias Israels.* WUNT 42. Tübingen: Mohr, 1987. ——— and **Grimm, W.** *Wesen und Wirklichkeit der Wunder Jesu.* Frankfurt: Lang, 1977. **Black, M.** *An Aramaic Approach to the Gospels and Acts.* 3rd ed. Oxford: Clarendon, 1967. **Blass, F., Debrunner, A.,** and **Funk, R. W.** *A Greek Grammar of the New Testament.* Chicago: University of Chicago Press, 1961. **Blair, E. P.** *Jesus in the Gospel of Matthew.* Nashville: Abingdon, 1960. **Blomberg, C. L.** *Interpreting the Parables.* Downers Grove, IL: InterVarsity, 1990. **Böcher, O.** *Christus Exorcista.* BWANT 90. Stuttgart: Kohlhammer, 1972. **Borgen, P.** *Paul Preaches Circumcision and Pleases Men and Other Essays on Christian Origins.* Trondheim: Tapir, University of Trondheim, 1983. **Boring, M. E.** *Sayings of the Risen Jesus: Christian Prophecy in the Synoptic Tradition.* SNTSMS 46. Cambridge: Cambridge University, 1982. **Bornkamm, G.** "The Authority to 'Bind' and 'Loose' in the Church in Matthew's Gospel." In *The Interpretation of Matthew,* ed. G. Stanton. Philadelphia/London: SPCK/Fortress, 1983. 85–97. ———. "End-Expectation and Church in Matthew." In *Tradition and Interpretation in Matthew,* ed. G. Bornkamm et al. Philadelphia: Westminster, 1963. 15–51. **Bornkamm, G., Barth, G.,** and **Held, H. J.** *Tradition and Interpretation in Matthew.* Philadelphia: Westminster, 1963. **Brandenburger, E.** *Das Recht des Weltrichters: Untersuchung zu Matthäus 25, 31–46.* SBS 99. Stuttgart: Katholisches Bibelwerk, 1980. **Bratcher, R. G.** *A Translator's Guide to the Gospel of Matthew.* New York: United Bible Societies, 1981. **Braun, H.** *Qumran und das Neue Testament.* 2 vols. Tübingen: Mohr, 1966. **Broer, I.** *Freiheit vom Gesetz und Radikalisierung des Gesetzes: Ein Beitrag zur Theologie des Evangelisten Matthäus.* SBS 98. Stuttgart: Katholisches Bibelwerk, 1980. **Brooks, S. H.** *Matthew's Community: The Evidence of His Special Sayings Material.* JSNTSup 16. Sheffield: JSOT, 1987. **Brown, R. E.** *The Birth of the Messiah.* Garden City, NY: Doubleday, 1977. ———. *The Gospel according to John.* 2 vols. AB.

Garden City, NY: Doubleday, 1966, 1970. ———. *New Testament Essays.* Milwaukee: Bruce, 1965. ———. *The Virginal Conception and Bodily Resurrection of Jesus.* New York: Paulist, 1973. ———, **K. P. Donfried, J. A. Fitzmyer, and J. Reumann,** eds. *Mary in the New Testament.* Philadelphia: Fortress, 1978. ———, **K. P. Donfried, and J. Reumann,** eds. *Peter in the New Testament.* Minneapolis: Augsburg, 1973. **Bultmann, R.** *History of the Synoptic Tradition.* 2nd ed. Oxford: Blackwell, 1968. **Burger, C.** *Jesus als Davidssohn.* FRLANT 98. Göttingen: Vandenhoeck & Ruprecht, 1970. **Burnett, F. E.** *The Testament of Jesus-Sophia: A Redaction-Critical Study of the Eschatological Discourse in Matthew.* Washington, DC: University Press of America, 1979. **Butler, B. C.** *The Originality of St. Matthew: A Critique of the Two Document Hypothesis.* Cambridge: Cambridge University, 1951. **Caird, G. B.** *The Language and Imagery of the Bible.* Philadelphia: Westminster, 1980. **Caragounis, C. C.** *Peter and the Rock.* BZNW 58. Berlin: de Gruyter, 1989. **Carlston, C. E.** *The Parables of the Triple Tradition.* Philadelphia: Fortress, 1975. **Chilton, B. D.** *God in Strength: Jesus' Announcement of the Kingdom.* SNTUMS B.1. Freistadt: Plöchl, 1979. **Cope, O. L.** *Matthew: A Scribe Trained for the Kingdom of Heaven.* CBQMS 5. Washington, DC: Catholic Biblical Association, 1976. **Crossan, J. D.** *In Fragments: The Aphorisms of Jesus.* San Francisco: Harper & Row, 1983. ———. *In Parables: The Challenge of the Historical Jesus.* New York: Harper & Row, 1973. **Cullmann, O.** *Peter: Disciple, Apostle, Martyr.* 2nd ed. Philadelphia: Westminster, 1962. **Dahl, N. A.** *Jesus the Christ: The Historical Origins of Christological Doctrine.* Ed. D. H. Juel. Minneapolis: Fortress, 1991. **Dalman, G.** *Jesus-Jeshua: Studies in the Gospels.* 1929. New York: Ktav, 1971. ———. *The Words of Jesus.* Edinburgh: T. & T. Clark, 1909. **Danby, H.** *The Mishnah.* Oxford: Oxford University, 1933. **Daube, D.** *The New Testament and Rabbinic Judaism.* London: Athlone, 1956. **Davies, W. D.** *The Setting of the Sermon on the Mount.* Cambridge: Cambridge University, 1966. **Davison, J. E.** "*Anomia* and the Question of an Antinomian Polemic in Matthew." *JBL* 104 (1985) 617–35. **Deutsch, C.** *Hidden Wisdom and the Easy Yoke: Wisdom, Torah and Discipleship in Matthew 11.25–30.* JSNTSup 18. Sheffield: JSOT, 1987. **Dibelius, M.** *From Tradition to Gospel.* New York: Scribner, 1965. **Didier, M.,** ed. *L'Évangile selon Matthieu: Rédaction et théologie.* BETL 29. Gembloux: Duculot, 1972. **Dobschütz, E. von.** "Matthew as Rabbi and Catechist." In *The Interpretation of Matthew,* ed. G. Stanton. Philadelphia/London: Fortress/SPCK, 1983. 85–97. **Dodd, C. H.** *The Parables of the Kingdom.* London: Nisbet, 1935/New York: Scribners, 1936. **Donaldson, T. L.** *Jesus on the Mountain: A Study in Matthean Theology.* JSNTSup 8. Sheffield: JSOT, 1985. **Dupont, J.** *Les Béatitudes: I. Le problème littéraire; II. La bonne nouvelle; III. Les Évangelistes.* Paris: Gabalda, 1958, 1969, 1973. **Edwards, J. R.** "The Use of ΠΡΟΣΕΡΧΕΣΘΑΙ in the Gospel of Matthew." *JBL* 106 (1987) 65–74. **Edwards, R. A.** *Matthew's Story of Jesus.* Philadelphia: Fortress, 1985. **Ellis, P. F.** *Matthew: His Mind and His Message.* Collegeville, MN: Liturgical, 1974. **Feldmeier, R.** *Die Krisis des Gottessohnes.* WUNT 2.21. Tübingen: Mohr, 1987. **Fiedler, M. J.** "Gerechtigkeit im Matthäus-Evangelium." *Theologische Versuche* 8 (1977) 63–75. **Fitzmyer, J. A.** *Essays on the Semitic Background of the New Testament.* SBLSBS 5. Missoula, MT: Scholars, 1974. ———. *A Wandering Aramean.* SBLMS 25. Missoula, MT: Scholars, 1981. **Ford, D.** *The Abomination of Desolation in Biblical Eschatology.* Washington, DC: University Press of America, 1979. **France, R. T.** *Jesus and the Old Testament.* London: Tyndale, 1971. ———. *Matthew: Evangelist and Teacher.* Grand Rapids: Zondervan, 1989. **Frankemölle, H.** "Amtskritik im Matthäus-Evangelium?" *Bib* 54 (1973) 247–62. ———. *Jahwebund und Kirche Christi.* NTAbh n.s. 10. Münster: Aschendorff, 1974. **Freyne, S.** *Galilee, Jesus and the Gospels: Literary Approaches and Historical Investigations.* Philadelphia: Fortress, 1988. **Fuller, R. H.** *Interpreting the Miracles.* Philadelphia: Westminster, 1963. ———. *The Mission and Achievement of Jesus.* SBT 1.12. London: SCM, 1967. **Gaechter, P.** *Die literarische Kunst im Matthäusevangelium.* SBS 7. Stuttgart: Katholisches Bibelwerk, 1965. **Gerhardsson, B.** *The Gospel Tradition.* ConBNT 15. Malmö: Gleerup, 1986. ———. "Gottes Sohn als Diener Gottes: Agape und Himmelsherrschaft nach dem Matthäusevangelium." *ST* 27 (1973) 25–50. ———. "'An ihren Früchten sollt ihr sie erkennen': Die Legitimitätsfrage in der matthäischen Christologie." *EvT* 42 (1982) 113–26. ———. *Memory and Manuscript.* Tr. E.

J. Sharpe. ASNU 22. Lund: Gleerup, 1961. ————. *The Mighty Acts of Jesus according to the Gospel of Matthew.* Lund: Gleerup, 1979. ————. *Tradition and Transmission in Early Christianity.* ConBNT 20. Lund: Gleerup, 1964. **Giesen, H.** *Christliches Handeln: Eine redaktionskritische Untersuchung zum δικαιοσύνη-Begriff im Matthäus-Evangelium.* Frankfurt am Main: Lang, 1982. **Goulder, M. D.** *Midrash and Lection in Matthew.* London: SPCK, 1974. **Grässer, E.** *Das Problem der Parusieverzögerung in den synoptischen Evangelien und in der Apostelgeschichte.* 2nd ed. BZNW 22. Berlin: Töpelmann, 1966. **Gray, S. W.** *The Least of My Brothers: Matthew 25:31–46: A History of Interpretation.* SBLDS 114. Atlanta: Scholars, 1989. **Green, J. B.** *The Death of Jesus.* WUNT 2.33. Tübingen: Mohr, 1988. **Gundry, R. H.** *The Use of the Old Testament in St. Matthew's Gospel.* NovTSup 18. Leiden: Brill, 1967. **Hagner, D. A.** "Apocalyptic Motifs in the Gospel of Matthew: Continuity and Discontinuity." *HBT* 7 (1985) 53–82. ————. "Matthew, Gospel according to." In *The International Standard Bible Encyclopedia,* ed. G. W. Bromiley et al. Grand Rapids: Eerdmans, 1986. 3:280–88. ————. "Righteousness in Matthew's Theology." In *Worship, Theology and Ministry in the Early Church.* FS R. P. Martin, ed. M. J. Wilkins and T. Paige. Sheffield: JSOT, 1992. 101–20. ————. "The *Sitz im Leben* of the Gospel of Matthew." In *SBL 1985 Seminar Papers.* Atlanta: Scholars Press, 1985. 243–69. ————. *The Use of the Old and New Testaments in Clement of Rome.* NovTSup 34. Leiden: Brill, 1973. **Hahn, F.** *The Titles of Jesus in Christology.* New York: World, 1969. **Hare, D. R. A.** *The Theme of Jewish Persecution of Christians in the Gospel according to St. Matthew.* SNTSMS 6. Cambridge: Cambridge University, 1967. **Harrington, D. J.** "Matthean Studies Since Joachim Rohde." *HeyJ* 16 (1975) 375–88. **Hartman, L.** *Prophecy Interpreted.* ConBNT 1. Lund: Gleerup, 1966. **Harvey, A. E.** *Jesus and the Constraints of History.* Philadelphia: Westminster, 1982. **Hasler, V.** *Amen.* Zürich: Gotthelf, 1969. **Heil, J. P.** *The Death and Resurrection of Jesus: A Narrative-Critical Reading of Matthew 26–28.* Minneapolis: Fortress, 1991. **Held, H. J.** "Matthew as Interpreter of the Miracle Stories." In *Tradition and Interpretation in Matthew,* ed. G. Bornkamm et al. Philadelphia: Westminster, 1963. 165–299. **Hengel, M.** *The Atonement.* Philadelphia: Fortress, 1981. ————. *The Charismatic Leader and His Followers.* New York: Crossroad, 1981. ————. *Crucifixion in the Ancient World and the Folly of the Message of the Cross.* Philadelphia: Fortress, 1977. ————. *Judaism and Hellenism.* 2 vols. Philadelphia: Fortress, 1981. ————. *Property and Riches in the Ancient Church.* Philadelphia: Fortress, 1974. ————. *The Son of God.* Philadelphia: Fortress, 1976. **Hill, D.** *New Testament Prophecy.* Atlanta: John Knox, 1979. ————. "Some Recent Trends in Matthean Studies." *IBS* 1 (1979) 139–49. ————. "Son and Servant: An Essay on Matthean Christology." *JSNT* 6 (1980) 2–16. **Hoehner, H.** *Herod Antipas.* SNTSMS 17. Cambridge: Cambridge University, 1972. **Hoffmann, P.** *Studien zur Theologie der Logienquelle.* Münster: Aschendorf, 1972. ————, ed. *Orientierung an Jesus: Zur Theologie der Synoptiker.* Freiburg: Herder, 1973. **Houlden, J. L.** *Backward into Light: The Passion and Resurrection of Jesus according to Matthew and Mark.* London: SCM, 1987. **Hubbard, B. J.** *The Matthean Redaction of a Primitive Apostolic Commissioning: An Exegesis of Matthew 28:16–20.* SBLDS 19. Missoula, MT: Scholars, 1974. **Hübner, H.** *Das Gesetz in der synoptischen Tradition.* Witten: Luther-Verlag, 1973. **Hummel, R.** *Die Auseinandersetzung zwischen Kirche und Judentum im Matthäusevangelium.* 2nd ed. BEvT 33. Munich: Kaiser, 1966. **Humphrey, H. M.** *The Relationship of Structure and Christology in the Gospel of Matthew.* New York: Fordham, 1977. **Iersel, B. M. F. van.** *"Der Sohn" in den synoptischen Jesusworten.* 2nd ed. NovTSup 3. Leiden: Brill, 1964. **Jeremias, J.** *Abba.* Göttingen: Vandenhoeck & Ruprecht, 1966. ————. *The Eucharistic Words of Jesus.* London: SCM, 1990. ————. *Jerusalem in the Time of Jesus.* 3rd ed. London: SCM, 1969. ————. *Jesus' Promise to the Nations.* 2nd ed. SBT 1.24. London: SCM, 1967. ————. *New Testament Theology: The Proclamation of Jesus.* New York: Macmillan, 1971. ————. *The Parables of Jesus.* New York: Scribner, 1972. ————. *The Prayers of Jesus.* Philadelphia: Fortress, 1978. **Johnson, M. D.** "Reflections on a Wisdom Approach to Matthew's Christology." *CBQ* 36 (1974) 44–64. **Juel, D.** *Messiah and Temple.* SBLDS 31. Missoula, MT: Scholars, 1977. ————. *Messianic Exegesis.* Philadelphia: Fortress, 1987. **Jülicher, A.** *Die Gleichnisreden Jesu.* 2 vols. 2nd ed. Tübingen: Mohr, 1911. **Käsemann, E.** *New Testament Questions of Today.*

Philadelphia: Fortress, 1969. **Kertelge, K.,** ed. *Der Tod Jesu.* QD 74. Freiburg: Herder, 1976. **Kilpatrick, G. D.** *The Origins of the Gospel according to St. Matthew.* Oxford: Clarendon, 1959. **Kingsbury, J. D.** *Jesus Christ in Matthew, Mark, and Luke.* Philadelphia: Fortress, 1981. ———. *Matthew.* Proclamation Commentaries. Philadelphia: Fortress, 1977. ———. *Matthew as Story.* Philadelphia: Fortress, 1986. ———. *Matthew: Structure, Christology, Kingdom.* Philadelphia: Fortress, 1975. ———. *The Parables of Jesus in Matthew 13.* Richmond: John Knox, 1969. ———. "The Title 'Kyrios' in Matthew's Gospel." *JBL* 94 (1975) 246–55. ———. "The Title 'Son of God' in Matthew's Gospel." *BTB* 5 (1975) 3–31. ———. "The Title 'Son of David' in Matthew's Gospel." *JBL* 95 (1976) 591–602. **Klauck, H.-J.** *Allegorie und Allegorese in synoptischen Gleichnistexten.* Münster: Aschendorff, 1978. **Kratz, R.** *Auferweckung als Befreiung: Eine Studie zur Passions- und Auferstehungstheologie des Matthäus.* SBS 65. Stuttgart: Katholisches Bibelwerk, 1973. **Kretzer, A.** *Die Herrschaft der Himmel und die Söhne des Reiches.* SBM 10. Stuttgart: Katholisches Bibelwerk, 1971. **Kruijf, T. de.** *Der Sohn des lebendigen Gottes.* AnBib 14. Rome: Biblical Institute, 1962. **Kümmel, W. G.** *Promise and Fulfilment.* SBT 23. London: SCM, 1961. **Künzel, G.** *Studien zum Gemeindeverständnis des Matthäus-Evangeliums.* Stuttgart: Calwer, 1978. **Kunzi, M.** *Das Naherwartungslogion Markus 9, 1 par.* BGBE 21. Tübingen: Mohr, 1977. **Kynes, W. L.** *A Christology of Solidarity: Jesus as the Representative of His People in Matthew.* Lanham, MD: University Press of America, 1991. **Ladd, G. E.** *The Presence of the Future.* Grand Rapids: Eerdmans, 1974. **Lange, J.** *Das Erscheinen des Auferstandenen im Evangelium nach Matthäus.* Würzburg: Echter, 1973. ———, ed. *Das Matthäus-Evangelium.* Wege der Forschung 525. Darmstadt: Wissenschaftliche Buchgesellschaft, 1980. **Lee, M. Y.-H.** *Jesus und die jüdische Autorität.* FB 56. Würzburg: Echter, 1986. **Lentzen-Deis, F.** *Die Taufe Jesu nach den Synoptikern.* FTS 4. Frankfurt: Knecht, 1970. **Léon-Dufour, X.** *Études d'Évangile.* Paris: Editions du Seuil, 1965. **Levine, A. J.** *The Social and Ethnic Dimensions of Matthean Salvation History: "Go nowhere among the Gentiles . . ." (Matt 10:5b).* Lewiston, NY: Mellen, 1988. **Lindars, B.** *New Testament Apologetic.* London: SCM, 1961. **Linnemann, E.** *Studien zur Passionsgeschichte.* FRLANT 102. Göttingen: Vandenhoeck & Ruprecht, 1970. **Ljungman, H.** *Das Gesetz erfüllen.* Lund: Gleerup, 1954. **Lohse, E.** *History of the Suffering and Death of Jesus Christ.* Philadelphia: Fortress, 1967. **Loos, H. van der.** *The Miracles of Jesus.* NovTSup 8. Leiden: Brill, 1965. **Lührmann, D.** *Die Redaktion der Logienquelle.* WMANT 33. Neukirchen-Vluyn: Neukirchener, 1969. **Luz, U.** "The Disciples in the Gospel according to Matthew." In *The Interpretation of Matthew,* ed. G. Stanton. Philadelphia/London: Fortress/SPCK, 1983. 98–128. ———. "Die Erfüllung des Gesetzes bei Matthäus (Mt 5.17–20)." *ZTK* 75 (1978) 398–435. ———. "Die Wundergeschichten von Mt 8–9." In *Tradition and Interpretation in the New Testament.* FS E. E. Ellis, ed. G. F. Hawthorne and O. Betz. Grand Rapids/Tübingen: Eerdmans/Mohr, 1987. 149–65. **Malina, B. J.,** and **Neyrey, J. H.** *Calling Jesus Names: The Social Value of Labels in Matthew.* Sonoma, CA: Polebridge, 1988. **Manson, T. W.** *The Sayings of Jesus.* 2nd ed. London: SCM, 1949. ———. *The Servant-Messiah.* Cambridge: Cambridge University, 1953. ———. *The Teaching of Jesus.* 2nd ed. Cambridge: Cambridge University, 1935. **Marcus, J.** *The Mystery of the Kingdom of God.* SBLDS 90. Atlanta: Scholars, 1986. **Marguerat, D.** *Le Jugement dans l'Évangile de Matthieu.* Geneva: Éditions Labor et Fides, 1981. **Martin, R. P.** "St. Matthew's Gospel in Recent Study." *ExpTim* 80 (1968–69) 132–36. **Massaux, E.** *The Influence of the Gospel of Saint Matthew in the Christian Literature before Saint Irenaeus.* Tr. N. J. Belval and S. Hecht. Ed. A. J. Bellinzoni. 2 vols. New Gospel Studies 5.1–2. Leuven/Macon, GA: Peters/Mercer, 1990, 1992. **Matera, F. J.** *Passion Narratives and Gospel Theologies.* New York: Paulist, 1986. **McConnell, R. S.** *Law and Prophecy in Matthew's Gospel.* Basel: Reinhardt, 1969. **McGuckin, J.** *The Transfiguration of Christ in Scripture and Tradition.* Lewiston, NY: Mellen, 1986. **Meier, J. P.** *Law and History in Matthew's Gospel.* AnBib 71. Rome: Biblical Institute, 1976. ———. *The Vision of Matthew: Christ, Church and Morality in the First Gospel.* New York: Paulist, 1979. **Merklein, H.** *Jesu Botschaft von der Gottesherrschaft.* SBS 11. Stuttgart: Katholisches Bibelwerk, 1983. **Metzger, B. M.** *A Textual Commentary on the Greek New Testament.* New York: United Bible Societies, 1971. **Meyer, B. F.** *The Aims of Jesus.* London: SCM, 1979.

**Minear, P. S.** *Commands of Christ.* Edinburgh: St. Andrew, 1972. ———. *Matthew: The Teacher's Gospel.* New York: Pilgrim, 1982. **Moffatt, J.** *An Introduction to the Literature of the New Testament.* 3rd ed. New York: Scribner's, 1922. **Mohrlang, R.** *Matthew and Paul: A Comparison of Ethical Perspectives.* SNTSMS 48. Cambridge: Cambridge University, 1984. **Montefiore, C. G.** *Rabbinic Literature and Gospel Teachings.* London: Macmillan, 1930. **Moo, D. J.** *The Old Testament in the Gospel Passion Narratives.* Sheffield: Almond, 1983. **Moore, A. L.** *The Parousia in the New Testament.* NovTSup 13. Leiden: Brill, 1966. **Moore, G. F.** *Judaism in the First Centuries of the Christian Era.* 3 vols. Cambridge, MA: Harvard University, 1955–58. **Moore, S. D.** *Literary Criticism and the Gospels: The Theoretical Challenge.* New Haven: Yale, 1989. **Moule, C. F. D.** *Essays in New Testament Interpretation.* Cambridge: Cambridge University, 1982. ———. *The Phenomenon of the New Testament.* SBT 2.1. London: SCM, 1967. **Neirynck, F.** *The Minor Agreements of Matthew and Luke against Mark.* BETL 37. Louvain: Louvain University, 1974. **Nepper-Christensen, P.** *Das Matthäusevangelium: Ein judenchristliches Evangelium?* Aarhus: Universitetsforlaget, 1954. **Newman, B. M.,** and **Stine, P. C.** *A Translator's Handbook on the Gospel of Matthew.* New York: United Bible Societies, 1988. **Nissen, A.** *Gott und der Nächste im antiken Judentum.* WUNT 15. Tübingen: Mohr, 1974. **Nolan, B.** *The Royal Son of God: The Christology of Mt 1–2.* OBO 23. Göttingen: Vandenhoeck & Ruprecht, 1979. **Ogawa, A.** *L'histoire de Jésus chez Matthieu: La signification de l'histoire pour la théologie matthéenne.* Frankfurt am Main: Lang, 1979. **Orton, D. E.** *The Understanding Scribe and the Apocalyptic Ideal.* JSNTSup 25. Sheffield: JSOT, 1989. **Overman, J. A.** *The Gospel of Matthew and Formative Judaism: A Study of the Social World of the Matthean Community.* Minneapolis: Fortress, 1990. **Percy, R.** *Die Botschaft Jesu.* Lund: Gleerup, 1953. **Pesch, R.** *Jesu ureigene Taten?* QD 52. Freiburg: Herder, 1970. ———. *Naherwartungen: Tradition und Redaktion in Mk 13.* Düsseldorf: Patmos, 1968. **Piper, J.** *"Love Your Enemies."* SNTSMS 38. Cambridge: Cambridge University, 1979. **Piper, R. A.** *Wisdom in the Q-Tradition: The Aphoristic Teaching of Jesus.* SNTSMS 61. Cambridge: Cambridge University, 1989. **Polag, A.** *Die Christologie der Logienquelle.* WMANT 45. Neukirchen-Vluyn: Neukirchener, 1979. ———. *Fragmenta Q.* Neukirchen-Vluyn: Neukirchener, 1979. **Przybylski, B.** *Righteousness in Matthew and His World of Thought.* SNTSMS 41. Cambridge: Cambridge University, 1980. **Reumann, J.** *Righteousness in the New Testament.* Philadelphia: Fortress, 1982. ———. *The Supper of the Lord.* Philadelphia: Fortress, 1985. **Riches, J.** *Jesus and the Transformation of Judaism.* New York: Seabury, 1980. **Ridderbos, H.** *Matthew's Witness to Jesus Christ.* New York: Association Press, 1958. **Riesenfeld, H.** *The Gospel Tradition and Its Beginnings.* London: Mowbray, 1961. **Riesner, R.** *Jesus als Lehrer.* WUNT 2.7. Tübingen: Mohr, 1981. **Rigaux, B.** *The Testimony of St. Matthew.* Chicago: Franciscan Herald, 1968. **Riley, H.** *The First Gospel.* Macon, GA: Mercer, 1992. **Robertson, A. T.** *A Grammar of the Greek New Testament in Light of Historical Research.* 4th ed. New York: Hodder & Stoughton, 1923. **Roloff, J.** *Das Kerygma und der irdische Jesus.* Göttingen: Vandenhoeck & Ruprecht, 1970. **Rothfuchs, W.** *Die Erfüllungszitate des Matthäus-Evangeliums.* BWANT 88. Stuttgart: Kohlhammer, 1969. **Sand, A.** *Das Gesetz und die Propheten: Untersuchungen zur Theologie des Evangeliums nach Matthäus.* Biblische Untersuchungen 11. Regensburg: Pustet, 1974. ———. *Das Matthäus-Evangelium.* Erträge der Forschung 275. Darmstadt: Wissenschaftliche Buchgesellschaft, 1991. ———. "Propheten, Weise, und Schriftkundige in der Gemeinde des Matthäusevangeliums." In *Die Kirche im Werden,* ed. J. Hainz. Munich: Schöningh, 1976. 167–85. **Schaberg, J.** *The Father, the Son and the Holy Spirit: The Triadic Phrase in Matthew 28:19b.* SBLDS 19. Chico, CA: Scholars, 1982. **Schenk, W.** *Die Sprache des Matthäus.* Göttingen: Vandenhoeck & Ruprecht, 1987. **Schenke, L.,** ed. *Studien zum Matthäusevangelium.* Stuttgart: Katholisches Bibelwerk, 1988. **Schlatter, A.** *Die Kirche des Matthäus.* Gütersloh: Bertelsmann, 1929. **Schmidt, T. E.** *Hostility to Wealth in the Synoptic Tradition.* JSNTSup 15. Sheffield: JSOT, 1987. **Schnackenburg, R.** "Petrus im Matthäusevangelium." In *À cause de l'Évangile: Études sur les Synoptiques et les Actes.* FS J. Dupont, ed. F. Refoulé. LD 123. Paris: Cerf, 1985. 107–25. ———. *Schriften zum Neuen Testament.* Munich: Kösel, 1971. ——— et al., eds. *Die Kirche des Anfangs.* FS H. Schürmann. Freiburg: Herder, 1978. **Schottroff, L.** "Das geschundene Volk und die

Arbeit in der Ernte: Gottes Volk nach dem Matthäusevangelium." In *Mitarbeiter der Schöpfung: Bibel und Arbeitswelt,* ed. L. and W. Schottroff. Munich: Kaiser, 1983. **Schulz, S.** *Q: Die Spruchquelle der Evangelisten.* Zürich: Theologischer, 1972. ———. *Die Stunde der Botschaft.* Hamburg: Furche, 1967. **Schürer, E.** *The History of the Jewish People in the Age of Jesus Christ.* Rev. ed. Ed. G. Vermes et al. 3 vols. Edinburgh: T. & T. Clark, 1973–87. **Schürmann, H.** *Jesu ureigener Tod.* Freiburg: Herder, 1975. ———. *Traditionsgeschichtliche Untersuchungen zu den synoptischen Evangelien.* Düsseldorf: Patmos, 1968. **Schweizer, E.** "Gesetz und Enthusiasmus bei Matthäus." In *Beiträge zur Theologie des Neuen Testaments,* ed. E. Schweizer. Zürich: Zwingli, 1970. 49–70. ———. *Matthäus und seine Gemeinde.* SBS 71. Stuttgart: Katholisches Bibelwerk, 1974. ———. "Matthew's Church." In *The Interpretation of Matthew,* ed. G. Stanton. Philadelphia/London: Fortress/SPCK, 1983. 129–55. **Senior, D.** *Invitation to Matthew.* Garden City: Doubleday, 1977. ———. *The Passion of Jesus in the Gospel of Matthew.* Wilmington, DE: Glazier, 1985. ———. *What are they saying about Matthew?* New York: Paulist, 1983. **Shuler, P. L.** *A Genre for the Gospels: The Biographical Character of Matthew.* Philadelphia: Fortress, 1982. **Sigal, P.** *The Halakah of Jesus of Nazareth according to the Gospel of Matthew.* Lanham, MD: University Press of America, 1986. **Soares-Prabhu, G. M.** *The Formula Quotations in the Infancy Narrative of Matthew.* AnBib 63. Rome: Biblical Institute, 1976. **Solages, M. de.** *La composition des Évangiles de Luc et de Matthieu et leurs sources.* Leiden: Brill, 1973. **Stanton, G. N.** *A Gospel for a New People: Studies in Matthew.* Edinburgh: T. & T. Clark, 1992. ———. "The Origin and Purpose of Matthew's Gospel: Matthean Scholarship from 1945 to 1980." In *ANRW* 2.25.3 (1983) 1889–1951. ———, ed. *The Interpretation of Matthew.* Philadelphia/London: Fortress/SPCK, 1983. **Stendahl, K.** *The School of St. Matthew.* 2nd ed. Philadelphia: Fortress, 1968. **Stonehouse, N. B.** *The Witness of Matthew and Mark to Christ.* 2nd ed. Grand Rapids: Eerdmans, 1958. **Strauss, D. F.** *The Life of Jesus Critically Examined.* 1892. Philadelphia: Fortress, 1972. **Strecker, G.** "The Concept of History in Matthew." In *The Interpretation of Matthew,* ed. G. Stanton. Philadelphia/London: Fortress/SPCK, 1983. 67–84. ———. *Der Weg der Gerechtigkeit: Untersuchung zur Theologie des Matthäus.* FRLANT 82. Göttingen: Vandenhoeck & Ruprecht, 1962. **Stuhlmacher, P.** *Jesus von Nazareth—Christus des Glaubens.* Stuttgart: Calwer, 1988. ———, ed. *The Gospel and the Gospels.* Grand Rapids: Eerdmans, 1991. **Suggs, M. J.** *Wisdom, Christology and Law in Matthew's Gospel.* Cambridge, MA: Harvard University, 1970. **Suhl, A.** "Der Davidssohn im Matthäus-Evangelium." *ZNW* 59 (1968) 36–72. **Taylor, V.** *The Historical Evidence for the Virgin Birth.* Oxford: Clarendon, 1920. **Telford, W. R.** *The Barren Temple and the Withered Tree.* JSNTSup 1. Sheffield: JSOT, 1980. **Theissen, G.** *The Miracle Stories of the Early Christian Tradition.* Philadelphia: Fortress, 1983. **Thompson, W. G.** *Matthew's Advice to a Divided Community: Mt. 17,22–18,35.* AnBib 44. Rome: Biblical Institute, 1970. **Tilborg, S. van.** *The Jewish Leaders in Matthew.* Leiden: Brill, 1972. **Trilling, W.** "Amt und Amtsverständnis bei Matthäus." In *Mélanges bibliques.* FS B. Rigaux, ed. A. Descamps. Gembloux: Duculot, 1969. 29–44. ———. *Studien zur Jesusüberlieferung.* Stuttgarter biblische Aufsatzbände 1. Stuttgart: Katholisches Bibelwerk, 1988. ———. *Das wahre Israel: Studien zur Theologie des Matthäusevangeliums.* 3rd ed. Leipzig: St. Benno, 1975. **Turner, N.** *A Grammar of New Testament Greek: Vol. 3. Syntax.* Edinburgh: T. & T. Clark, 1963. **Verseput, D.** *The Rejection of the Humble Messianic King: A Study of the Composition of Matthew 11–12.* Frankfurt am Main: Lang, 1986. **Vögtle, A.** *Das Evangelium und die Evangelien.* Düsseldorf: Patmos, 1971. **Walker, R.** *Die Heilsgeschichte im ersten Evangelium.* FRLANT 91. Göttingen: Vandenhoeck & Ruprecht, 1967. **Walter, N.** "Zum Kirchenverständnis des Matthäus." *Theologische Versuche* 12 (1981) 25–46. **Weder, H.** *Die Gleichnisse Jesu als Metaphern.* FRLANT 120. Göttingen: Vandenhoeck & Ruprecht, 1984. **Weiser, A.** *Die Knechtsgleichnisse der synoptischen Evangelien.* SANT 10. Munich: Kösel, 1971. **Westcott, B. W.** *An Introduction to the Study of the Gospels.* London: Macmillan, 1875. **Westerholm, S.** *Jesus and Scribal Authority.* ConBNT 10. Lund: Gleerup, 1978. **White, R. E. O.** *The Mind of Matthew.* Philadelphia: Westminster, 1979. **Wilkins, M. J.** *The Concept of Disciple in Matthew's Gospel.* NovTSup 59. Leiden: Brill, 1988. **Wink, W.** *John the Baptist in the Gospel Tradition.* SNTSMS 7. Cambridge: Cambridge University, 1968. **Wrede, W.** *The Messianic Secret.* Cambridge, MA: Clarke, 1971. **Zeller, D.** *Die weisheitlichen Mahnsprüche bei den Synoptikern.* Würzburg: Echter, 1977. **Zumstein, J.** *La condition du croyant dans l'Évangile selon Matthieu.* OBO 16. Göttingen: Vandenhoeck & Ruprecht, 1977.

# Matthew 14:1–28:20

# Further Ministry and Confrontation
# with the Religious Authorities   (14:1–16:20)

## The Fate of John the Baptist   (14:1–12)

### Bibliography

**Aus, R.** *Water into Wine and the Beheading of John the Baptist: Early Jewish-Christian Interpretation of Esther 1 in John 2:1–11 and Mark 6:17–29.* BJS 150. Atlanta: Scholars, 1988. **Cope, O. L.** "The Death of John the Baptist in the Gospel of Matthew." *CBQ* 38 (1976) 515–19. **Derrett, J. D. M.** "Herod's Oath and the Baptist's Head." *BZ* 9 (1965) 49–59, 233–46. **Gnilka, J.** "Das Martyrium Johannes des Täufers." In *Orientierung an Jesus.* FS J. Schmid, ed. P. Hoffmann. Freiburg: Herder, 1973. 78–92. **Hoehner, H. W.** *Herod Antipas.* SNTSMS 17. Cambridge: Cambridge UP, 1972. 112–22, 149–65. **Meier, J. P.** "John the Baptist in Matthew's Gospel." *JBL* 99 (1980) 383–405. **Potterie, I. de la.** "Mors Johannis Baptistae." *VD* 44 (1966) 142–51. **Riesner, R.** "Johannes der Täufer auf Machärus." *BK* 39 (1984) 176. **Schenk, W.** "Gefangenschaft und Tod des Täufers." *NTS* 29 (1983) 453–83. **Schütz, R.** *Johannes der Täufer.* ATANT 50. Zürich: Zwingli, 1967. **Trilling, W.** "Die Täufertradition bei Matthäus." *BZ* 3 (1959) 271–89.

### Translation

[1]*At that time Herod the tetrarch heard of the fame of Jesus,* [2]*and he said to his servants: "This one is* [a] *John the Baptist.* [b] *He has been raised from the dead, and because of this these powers are working in him."*

[3]*For Herod* [c] *had seized John, bound* [*him*],[d] *and put him in prison because of Herodias the wife of Philip,* [e] *his brother.* [4]*For John kept saying to him, "It is not lawful for you to have her."* [5]*And although he wanted to have him killed, he was afraid of the crowd because they regarded him as a prophet.*

[6]*When the birthday of Herod arrived,* [f] *the daughter of Herodias danced among the guests,* [g] *and she pleased Herod,* [7]*for which reason he swore with an oath to give to her whatever she asked.* [8]*And she, put forward by her mother, said: "Give me here upon a platter* [h] *the head of John the Baptist."* [9]*And the king, having become distressed* [i] *because of the oaths he had sworn and those reclining at the meal with him, commanded it to be given to her.* [10]*And he sent and beheaded John in the prison.* [11]*And John's* [j] *head was brought upon a platter, and it was given to the girl, and she brought it to her mother.* [12]*And when his disciples came, they took the body,* [k] *and they buried it,* [l] *and they went and reported everything* [m] *to Jesus.*

### Notes

[a] D vg[mss] and a few other witnesses begin the sentence with μήτι, thus forming a question: "Is not this John the Baptist?" (But μήτι expects a negative answer, which is strange in light of the following verse.)

ᵇ D ff¹ vgᵐˢˢ add ὃν ἐγὼ ἀπεκεφάλισα, "whom I beheaded" (from Mark 6:16), anticipating the narrative that follows.

ᶜ B Θ f¹³ sa mae insert τότε, "then." Despite Matthew's favoring of τότε, the shorter text is supported by a diversity of text types; the τότε was probably added to alert the reader that vv 3–12 are a flashback. See *TCGNT*, 34–35.

ᵈ The critical text has αὐτόν, "him," in brackets because it is omitted by the important MSS ℵ* and B, as well as other witnesses. The pronoun is in any event required in English (unlike Gr.).

ᵉ D and lat omit φιλίππου, "of Philip" (cf. shorter text of Luke 3:19), perhaps to harmonize with the evidence reflected in Jos., *Ant.* 18.5.4 §§136–37. Cf. *TCGNT*, 35.

ᶠ A variant reading, "when the birthday was celebrated," is found in some MSS: γενεσίοις δὲ ἀγομένοις (f¹); γενεσιῶν δὲ ἀγομένων (W f¹³ TR); and γενεσιῶν δὲ γενομένων (C K N Θ).

ᵍ Lit. "in the middle/midst."

ʰ D omits ἐπὶ πίνακι, "upon a platter."

ⁱ A number of MSS (ℵ C [L] W Zᵛⁱᵈ TR lat sy co) read ἐλυπήθη ὁ βασιλεύς. διὰ δέ: "the king was distressed. But on account of . . . ," thereby relieving the ambiguity of the syntax as it stands in the critical text, where διὰ τοὺς ὅρκους καὶ τοὺς συνανακειμένους, "on account of his oaths and the dinner guests," could be linked with λυπηθείς, "being grieved," rather than with ἐκέλευσεν, "he commanded." See *TCGNT*, 35–36.

ʲ Lit. "his."

ᵏ πτῶμα, "body" (in agreement with Mark 6:24). Some witnesses (W TR lat syʰ sa boᵐˢˢ) have the more common synonym σῶμα. The former is to be preferred on the basis of superior textual evidence. See *TCGNT*, 36.

ˡ The critical Gr. text reads αὐτό[ν], "it," reflecting the divided witnesses. The neuter, although strongly attested, is expected because of πτῶμα and thus might be a correction of scribes; αὐτόν, on the other hand, is found in ℵ* B ff¹ boᵐˢˢ. See *TCGNT*, 36.

ᵐ "Everything" is the implied object of the verb, although it does not appear in the Gr. text.

### *Form/Structure/Setting*

A. Matthew is now content to follow the order of Mark, as he will do for the most part in the remainder of the Gospel. Omitting the sending out of the twelve (Mark 6:7–13), which was presented earlier (10:5–23), Matthew follows the rejection of Jesus at Nazareth with the fearful and incorrect estimate of Jesus from Herod. This in turn leads, as in Mark, to the retrospective account of the death of John the Baptist, thus rounding out the story of John.

B. Matthew depends upon Mark (Mark 6:14–24; cf. Luke 9:7–9; 3:19–20, but Luke lacks the narrative concerning John's death). For Matthew's first two verses, the following differences from Mark should be noted. First, Matthew's opening words, ἐν ἐκείνῳ τῷ καιρῷ, "at that time," are his own transition to the present pericope. Matthew (with Luke) substitutes τετράρχης, "tetrarch," for Mark's βασιλεύς, "king" (but cf. v 9 where Matthew uses βασιλεύς), perhaps to distinguish him clearly from Herod the Great, who figured so largely in chap. 2, and Herod Agrippa I (cf. Acts 12). Matthew alone has Herod speak τοῖς παισὶν αὐτοῦ, "to his servants," the declarative sentence οὗτός ἐστιν Ἰωάννης ὁ βαπτιστής, "This one is John the Baptist." Other changes in vv 1–2 are only minor rephrasing of Mark. Matthew omits entirely, however, the material that follows in Mark 6:15–16, with its alternative evaluation of John as Elijah or one of the prophets (cf. 16:14; Mark 8:28) and Herod's reassertion that it was John, risen from the dead. In the remainder of the pericope (vv 3–12), Matthew follows Mark closely but abridges the narrative quite frequently (by more than one third). Beyond this common practice of Matthew, the following can be noted: whereas according to Mark it was Herodias who wanted to kill John (Mark 6:19), Matthew's rewriting makes Herod the one who wanted to do so (this conflicts with Mark 6:20); whereas Mark writes that Herod "was afraid of John, knowing he was a righteous and holy man" (ἐφοβεῖτο τὸν Ἰωάννην, εἰδὼς αὐτὸν ἄνδρα δίκαιον καὶ ἅγιον), Matthew writes that ἐφοβήθη τὸν ὄχλον ὅτι ὡς προφήτην αὐτὸν εἶχον, "he was afraid of the crowd because they regarded him as a prophet" (v 5). The result of these changes is a much more negative view of Herod than in the Markan account (cf. too the omission of Mark 6:20b) as well as an emphasis on the motif of the suffering of the prophets (cf. 13:57; 23:30–31, 34, 37). Among further omissions for the sake of brevity, Matthew lacks the note that the daughter of Herod pleased Herod's guests too (καὶ τοῖς συνανακεμένοις; Mark 6:22) and the offer of Herod to give the girl ἕως ἡμίσους τῆς βασιλείας μου, "up to as much as half my kingdom" (Mark 6:23). Finally to be noted is Matthew's substitution of καὶ ἔθαψαν αὐτό[ν], "and they buried him (it)," for Mark's καὶ ἔθηκαν αὐτὸ ἐν μνημείῳ, "and they placed it in a tomb" (Mark 6:29), and the concluding words, unique to Matthew, that bridge also to the opening of the next pericope: καὶ ἐλθόντες ἀπήγγειλαν τῷ Ἰησοῦ, "and they went and reported everything to Jesus" (v 12; cf. Mark 6:30, which, however, is hardly here "misunderstood" by Matthew [contra Fenton]).

C. The pericope as defined here has two main parts, which, because they are closely associated, are treated together as one pericope. The first concerns Herod's reaction to the reports concerning Jesus; the second is a flashback describing the murder of John the Baptist. The pericope may be outlined as follows: (1) Herod hears (v 1) and reacts to (v 2) the report concerning Jesus; (2) the fate of John the Baptist: (a) his arrest, provocation, and imprisonment (vv 3–5), (b) the dance of Herodias' daughter and the promise of Herod (vv 6–7), (c) the request of Herodias (v 8), (d) the fulfillment of the request (vv 9–11), and (e) the action of John's disciples (v 12). There is very little syntactic parallelism in the pericope, which consists of a straightforward, economical narrative prose style.

## Comment

**1–2** ἐν ἐκείνῳ τῷ καιρῷ, "at that time," is Matthew's own transitional phrase here and has no chronological significance. This pericope is the only place in Matthew where Herod Antipas, son of Herod the Great and tetrarch (τετραάρχης, ruler of part [originally, a fourth] of a territory) of Galilee (cf. Luke 3:1), is mentioned. When Herod heard of the ἀκοήν, "fame" (the same word is used in the same sense in 4:24), of Jesus, his uneasy conscience made him fearful that John the Baptist had come back from the dead: οὗτός ἐστιν Ἰωάννης ὁ βαπτιστής, "this one is John the Baptist." Such a conclusion points both to the awe in which John was held by him and also to the commonness of the belief that holy servants of God, such as prophets (cf. v 5), could return to the earth after their death and would do so in connection with the approach of the end of the age. That others entertained the same ideas concerning John the Baptist is indicated by 16:14. Thus αἱ δυνάμεις ἐνεργοῦσιν ἐν αὐτῷ, "these powers are working in him," points not only to the invasion of the present age by the world beyond but has eschatological intimations as well. (For αἱ δυνάμεις, "the powers," see 13:54; for the idea of powers working in persons, cf. Gal 3:5.) In answering the question of the source of Jesus' power (cf. 13:54, 56), Herod thus gives his own explanation, one caused very much by his own guilty conscience.

**3–4**  We are now given the background to Herod's fears about John the Baptist in a narrative that, returning to an earlier time, provides an account of John's death by the hand of Herod. Earlier in his Gospel, Matthew had been content merely to mention John's arrest (4:12). Herod had seized John, bound him, and put him in prison (the fortress of Machaerus, according to Jos., *Ant.* 18.5.1 §§109–15) for his apparently public opposition to Herod's marriage to Herodias, Herod's niece but more importantly his brother Philip's wife. There is some uncertainty about this Philip, since the Philip we know as Herod's brother from the Gospels (i.e., the tetrarch of Luke 3:1) was apparently married not to Herodias but to Salome her daughter (cf. Jos., *Ant.* 18.5.4 §136). The Philip mentioned in our pericope was probably a half brother of Antipas and is referred to as Herod by Josephus; the mother of this Herod-Philip was Mariamne II. However this problem is to be solved, John opposed Herod's marriage to his brother's wife, not simply on the grounds of the impropriety of divorce and remarriage (cf. 19:9) but on the basis of the OT prohibition reflected in Lev 18:16 and 20:21 (in the case of a childless widow, such a "levirate" marriage was obligatory; see Deut 25:5; cf. Matt 22:24). This lies behind John's strong statement: οὐκ ἔξεστίν σοι ἔχειν αὐτήν, "it is not lawful for you to have her." The imperfect tense of ἔλεγεν implies repetition: "he kept saying." Herod would not tolerate John's condemnation and so had him arrested. (Josephus, on the other hand, states that John was arrested for sedition [*Ant.* 18.5.2 §§118–19]. Any form of opposition from an apocalyptic preacher could easily have been regarded as seditious.)

**5**  According to Matthew, Herod wanted to silence John permanently by killing him (θέλων is a concessive participle, thus "although wanting to") but was afraid of τὸν ὄχλον, "the crowd," because they held John to be a προφήτην, "prophet" (for Markan differences, see above *Form/Structure/Setting* §B; cf. exactly the same fear concerning Jesus, but pertaining to his arrest, in 21:46). In 21:21 Matthew again notes that John was widely held to be a prophet (cf. 11:9). John had made a great impact on the populace as a prophet or "spokesman" for God (cf. 3:5–6), and although he had been arrested, he had apparently not been forgotten; and this Herod knew.

**6–7**  At a great banquet celebrating Herod's birthday, the daughter of Herodias (Salome, though not named here or in the Markan parallel; cf. Jos., *Ant.* 18.5.4 §136) danced and so delighted Herod that before everyone he rather boastfully and recklessly promised to give the girl whatever she requested. Though perhaps unusual, it is not improbable that a girl probably not much older than twelve (note the diminutive form of κοράσιον in v 11, lit. "little girl"; cf. Mark 5:42) would dance before guests on a special occasion, though she was a princess. The Semitism μεθ᾽ ὅρκου ὡμολόγησεν, "he swore with an oath," indicates the strength and seriousness of the promise and thus Herod's sense of obligation. The opening construction of the verse, γενεσίοις δὲ γενομένοις, "when the birthday celebration arrived," is very unusual. Matthew apparently borrowed γενεσίοις from Mark and then added the concordant participle of γίνεσθαι on the model of Matthew's favorite, the genitive absolute (giving "the appearance of a Lat. ablative absolute" [Wellhausen, cited by McNeile]).

**8**  The girl followed her mother's prompting (προβιβασθεῖσα, "put forward," the only occurrence of the word in the NT) in making the astonishing request for John's head on a platter. That the request could be made and granted at a banquet underlines the degradation of the royal court. Herodias is described in the Markan account as wanting the death of John (Mark 6:19).

**9–11** The "king" (the title was probably used for Herod as ruler but was not strictly true) regretted having made the foolish promise: λυπηθείς, "having become distressed." The following accusative phrase governed by διά, "because of," can be taken either with the preceding participle, thus giving the grounds for Herod's grief, or with the following verb, ἐκέλευσεν, "he commanded," giving the grounds for the command. The difference is slight. It was because he had made "the oaths" (τοὺς ὅρκους, plural, is perhaps to be understood as one oath; cf. BDF §142; cf. the singular in v 7) before "those reclining at the meal with him" (τοὺς συνανακειμένους) that he felt obligated, almost against his will (cf. v 4 with Mark 6:20), to carry out the request. He "sent" (πέμψας) soldiers to do his dirty work; the singular verb ἀπεκεφάλισεν [τὸν] Ἰωάννην ἐν τῇ φυλακῇ, "he beheaded John in the prison," places the responsibility upon his shoulders. When the head was brought to the girl, ἤνεγκεν τῇ μητρὶ αὐτῆς, "she brought it to her mother," Herodias, the real instigator of John's murder.

**12** The disciples of John (αὐτοῦ, "his") took the body and buried it (cf. 27:57–61, for Jesus; Acts 8:2, for Stephen). Having fulfilled this duty to their master, they reported his death to Jesus (ἀπήγγειλαν τῷ Ἰησοῦ). This last piece of information, found only in Matthew, again points to the close ties between Jesus and John (cf. 3:11–16; 11:7–19; 17:12; 21:32). John's disciples know that because of their association Jesus must immediately hear about John's death (for previous contact between John's disciples and Jesus, see 9:14; 11:2; we have no way of knowing what John's response was to the report of 11:4–6).

### Explanation

Although John the Baptist came in the eschatological role of Elijah, "they did to him whatever they pleased" (17:12). As John was regarded as a prophet, he suffered the fate of the prophets (cf. this important theme in 23:31–35). Described by Jesus as greater than any other "born of woman" (11:11), he was murdered through a bizarre sequence of events, part of the "entertainment" of the evening, by the whim and caprice of the wicked. A horrendous crime of this kind is self-indicting. Yet God no more prevents this outrageous deed than he will the death of Jesus, or later of Stephen and the thousands of martyrs who have followed in his footsteps. John's murder is a foreshadowing of the murder of Jesus, and Matthew's narrative is designed to indicate a number of parallels. "So also the Son of Man will suffer at their hands" (17:12). Death, the temporary end of physical life, is not the worst enemy of humanity. Alienation from God is. And thus those who murdered John are far more pitiable than is John himself. In this instance, to be "dead" is more blessed than to be "alive"; for the one murdered truly lives, while those who murdered him are in reality the dead. As Jesus was soon to follow in John's path, so are his disciples also to be prepared for death (cf. 10:21–22, 39; 24:9).

# The Feeding of the Five Thousand    (14:13-21)

### Bibliography

**Bammel, E.** "The Feeding of the Multitude." In *Jesus and the Politics of His Day*, ed. E. Bammel and C. F. D. Moule. Cambridge: Cambridge UP, 1984. 211–40. **Buse, I.** "The Gospel Accounts of the Feeding of the Multitudes." *ExpTim* 74 (1963) 167–70. **Cangh, J. M. van.** *La multiplication des pains et l'eucharistie.* LD 86. Paris: Cerf, 1975. **Cerfaux, L.** "La section des pains." In *Recueil Lucien Cerfaux.* Gembloux: Duculot, 1954. 1:471–86. **Clavier, H.** "La multiplication des pains dans le ministère de Jésus." *SE* 1 [= TU 73] (1959) 441–57. **Cousins, P. E.** "The Feeding of the Five Thousand." *EvQ* 39 (1967) 152–54. **Farrer, A. M.** "Loaves and Thousands." *JTS* 4 (1953) 1–14. **Fowler, R. M.** *Loaves and Fishes: The Function of the Feeding Stories in the Gospel of Mark.* SBLDS 54. Chico, CA: Scholars, 1981. **Grant, R. M.** *The Problem of Miraculous Feedings in the Greco-Roman World.* Berkeley: University of California, 1982. **Hebert, A. G.** "History in the Feeding of the Five Thousand." *SE* 2 [= TU 87] (1964) 65–72. **Heising, A.** *Die Botschaft der Brotvermehrung.* SBS 15. Stuttgart: Katholisches Bibelwerk, 1966. ———. "Exegesis und Theologie der alt- und neutestamentlichen Speisewunder." *ZTK* 86 (1964) 80–96. **Iersel, B. van.** "Die wunderbare Speisung und das Abendmahl in der synoptischen Tradition." *NovT* 7 (1964–65) 167–94. **Knackstedt, J.** "Die beiden Brotvermehrungen im Evangelien." *NTS* 10 (1964) 309–35. **Körtner, H. J.** "Das Fischmotiv im Speisungswunder." *ZNW* 75 (1984) 24–35. **Masuda, S.** "The Good News of the Miracle of the Bread." *NTS* 28 (1982) 191–219. **Neugebauer, F.** "Die wunderbare Speisung (Mark 6.30–44 parr.) und Jesu Identität." *KD* 32 (1986) 254–77. **Patsch, H.** "Abendmahlsterminologie ausserhalb der Einsetzungsberichte." *ZNW* 62 (1971) 210–31. **Potterie, I. de la.** "Le sens primitif de la multiplication des pains." In *Jésus aux origines de la christologie*, ed. J. Dupont. BETL 40. Gembloux: Duculot, 1975. 303–29. **Repo, E.** "Fünf Brote und zwei Fische." In *Probleme der Forschung*, ed. A. Fuchs. SNTU A3. Vienna: Herold, 1978. 99–113. **Richardson, A.** "The Feeding of the Five Thousand." *Int* 9 (1955) 144–49. **Schenke, L.** *Die wunderbare Brotvermehrung.* Würzburg: Echter, 1983.

### Translation

[13]*And when Jesus heard this, he went away from there in a boat[a] privately to a deserted place. And when the crowds heard this, they followed him from the cities by foot.* [14]*And when he disembarked,[b] he saw a huge crowd, and he was moved with compassion for them, and he healed their sick.*

[15]*But when it was evening, his disciples came to him and said: "This is a deserted place, and the day[c] is already gone. Send the crowds away[d] so that they may return to their villages[e] and buy food for themselves." *[16]*But Jesus[f] said to them: "There is no need for them to go away. You give them something to eat." *[17]*But they said to him: "We have nothing here except five loaves and two fish." *[18]*And he said: "Bring them here to me." *[19]*And having commanded[g] the crowds to recline on the grass, he took the five loaves and the two fish, looked up into the sky and blessed God, and when he had broken the loaves into pieces, he gave them to the disciples, and the disciples gave it to the crowds.* [20]*And everyone ate and was full, and they took up twelve baskets full of leftover fragments.* [21]*And those who ate numbered about[h] five thousand, not counting the women and children.*

### Notes

ᵃ Γ sy$^{s,c}$ and a few other witnesses omit ἐν πλοίῳ, "in a boat."

ᵇ A few witnesses (a b ff² sy$^{s,c}$) omit ἐξελθών, "having disembarked" or "having come out."

ᶜ ἡ ὥρα, lit. "the hour." See BAGD, s.v.

ᵈ ℵ C Z f¹ sy$^{hmg}$ sa$^{mss}$ bo add οὖν, "therefore."

ᵉ Some MSS (C* Θ sy$^{hmg}$ sa$^{mss}$) read κύκλῳ, "surrounding (area)," for κώμας, "villages," through the influence of the parallel in Mark 6:36.

ᶠ A number of MSS (ℵ* D Z$^{vid}$ e k sy$^{s,c,p}$ sa bo) omit Ἰησοῦς, "Jesus," with the result that the definite article functions as a pronoun. On the other hand, many MSS include Ἰησοῦς (ℵ¹ B C L W Θ f$^{1,13}$ TR lat sy$^h$ sa$^{ms}$ mae) so that the critical text places the name in the text but encloses it in brackets.

ᵍ B* reads κελεύσατε, "[you] command (them)."

ʰ A few witnesses (W lat sy$^{s,c,p}$ bo) omit ὡσεί, "about."

### Form/Structure/Setting

A. The narrative now turns to the recounting of two dramatic "nature" miracles, the multiplying of the loaves and fish and Jesus' walking on the water. These have the effect of sharpening further the question concerning the power and identity of Jesus. The feeding of the five thousand, furthermore, has unmistakable messianic implications.

B. In this pericope, which is the only miracle of Jesus found in all four Gospels (cf. John 6:1–15), Matthew is dependent on Mark (Mark 6:32–44; cf. Luke 9:10b–17). Again Matthew's clear tendency is to abbreviate Mark's account but not by quite as much as elsewhere. Matthew's opening words, ἀκούσας δὲ ὁ Ἰησοῦς, "and when Jesus heard this," are his own transition from the preceding pericope (on the problem thereby caused, see *Comment*). Matthew (so too Luke) omits Mark's καὶ εἶδον αὐτοὺς ὑπάγοντας, "and they saw them departing" (Mark 6:33), and Mark's note, καὶ προῆλθον αὐτούς, "they arrived before them" (Mark 6:33), since Matthew reports only the movement of Jesus. Matthew omits Mark's hyperbolic πασῶν, "all," before "the cities" (v 13; Mark 6:33). Matthew (so too Luke) does not include Mark's "because they were like sheep not having a shepherd" (Mark 6:34), which he has used already in another context (9:36). He also omits the immediately following words, "and he began to teach them many things" (Mark 6:34), adding instead the reference to healing: καὶ ἐθεράπευσεν τοὺς ἀρρώστους αὐτῶν, "and he healed their sick" (v 14; cf. Luke 9:11). There follow some very slight changes, from which we note only the omission of τοὺς κύκλῳ ἀγρούς, lit. "the surrounding fields (hamlets)," of Mark 6:36 and the substitution of βρώματα, "food," for τί φάγωσιν, "something they might eat" (v 15; Mark 6:36). In v 16 Matthew inserts οὐ χρείαν ἔχουσιν ἀπελθεῖν, "there is no need for them to go away." Matthew (so too Luke) further omits Mark's reference to the disciples' extraordinary question whether they should buy 200 denarii (a denarius was a day's wages) worth of bread (Mark 6:37) as well as Jesus' response, "How many loaves do you have? Go see" (Mark 6:37), thus necessitating the addition of οὐκ ἔχομεν ὧδε εἰ μή, "we have nothing here except" (v 17; cf. Luke 9:13). Matthew further adds ὁ δὲ εἶπεν· φέρετέ μοι ὧδε αὐτούς, "and he said, 'Bring them here to me'" (v 18), thus underlining the sovereign authority of Jesus. Matthew (so too Luke) omits the detailed information concerning the crowd sitting in "companies," "groups" of "hundreds" and "fifties," as well as the note that the grass was "green" (Mark 6:39–40).

By contrast, however, Matthew and Luke follow Mark very closely in the description of Jesus' actions at this point, omitting only Mark's τοὺς ἄρτους, "the loaves" (Mark 6:41). Matthew and Luke also appear uninterested in the fish, omitting Mark's reference to Jesus' dividing of the fish for everyone (Mark 6:41), as well as the notice that the leftover fragments included the fish (Mark 6:43). The focus on the bread, and omission of reference to the fish, may be related to a eucharistic understanding of the passage wherein the latter had no place (see *Comment* on vv 18–19). Finally, Matthew adds τὸ περισσεῦον, "the abundance left over" (v 20; cf. Luke 9:14), and the concluding notice that the number five thousand was χωρὶς γυναικῶν καὶ παιδίων, "without women and children" (v 21). The numerous minor agreements between Matthew and Luke against Mark in this pericope are remarkable. They are very probably to be explained through the influence of oral tradition (thus rightly Luz) and do not constitute an insuperable obstacle to the two-source hypothesis and Markan priority, as sometimes claimed. Note especially, for example, the nearly verbatim agreement in the description of the actions of Jesus (v 19b; Mark 6:41; Luke 9:16), probably influenced by the eucharistic tradition.

C. As a "gift miracle" narrative (thus Theissen, *Miracle Stories*, 104), the form of the story is a little unusual. In particular, there is surprisingly neither a comment on the reaction of the people nor a christological conclusion drawn by the evangelist. The remarkable story is thus left to make its own statement. The following outline of the pericope may be suggested: (1) the setting, consisting of (a) Jesus' withdrawal (v 13a) and (b) the following of the crowd (v 13b); (2) compassionate healings (v 14); (3) the problem (v 15); (4) Jesus' incredible suggestion (v 16); (5) the scanty resources (v 17); and (6) the solution, consisting of (a) the miracle itself (vv 18–19), (b) the abundance (v 20), and (c) the number fed (v 21). There is only a small amount of parallel structure in the pericope: e.g., v 13a and 13b (participles of ἀκούειν, "hear"; main verbs; the datives ἐν πλοίῳ, "in a boat," πεζῇ, "on foot"; and the statements about ὁ τόπος, "the place," and ἡ ὥρα, "the hour" [v 15]). V 19 is noteworthy in this respect for the two main verbs εὐλόγησεν, "he blessed," and ἔδωκεν, "he gave," together with the aorist participles subordinated to them.

D. This pericope finds a close parallel and possible doublet in the feeding of the four thousand in 15:32–39 (cf. Mark 8:1–10). See the discussion of the problem there (*Form/Structure/Setting* §D). Both feeding pericopes are alluded to in 16:5–12 (cf. Mark 8:14–21).

E. The question of the historicity of this miracle has proved problematic for many modern scholars. The healing miracles of Jesus constitute far less of a problem because of the well-known phenomenon of psychosomatic healings. Those such as the present one and the walking on the water in the next pericope (vv 22–33), however, involve direct contravention of natural law. If the world view of the interpreter does not allow this possibility, implausible naturalistic explanations will be sought: e.g., Jesus was able to get those who had food in the crowd to share it with their neighbors, or Jesus walked the beach or on stones just below the surface of the water. Such explanations are far from the intention of the evangelists and out of line with the Gospel narratives.

But are such nature miracles to be automatically excluded as impossibilities? If, as the Bible claims, God works in history and uniquely and supremely in Jesus Christ, may not such events have actually happened? If we do not allow the transcendent within history, the Bible suddenly becomes a very different collection of writings, a book of parables concerning human existence rather than the account of salvation worked out in the historical process.

The historicity of miracles that transcend the laws of nature cannot be established here. It is an assumption of the present commentary that the miracles recorded by Matthew were historical events. With the evangelist, we are driven to the question of who this Jesus is (cf. 8:27; 16:13–15), for this issue is at the bottom a christological one.

## Comment

**13** Matthew's ἀκούσας, "when he heard," ties this passage to the end of the preceding one about the death of John the Baptist. (In Mark the preceding passage [Mark 6:30–31] records not the death of John but the return of the apostles from their missionary journey; thus Jesus' going off privately in a boat is not a response to the news of John's death, as it is in Matthew.) That is, in Matthew when Jesus heard of the death of John, he went off by himself for a while. The effect of this, however, is to ignore the fact that the story of John's death was a flashback and so to throw the entire sequence of narratives that follow back to that earlier time. Perhaps Matthew regarded John's death as having occurred only a few days earlier (thus McNeile). The suggestion that, given the parenthetical nature of vv 3–12, the object of ἀκούσας, "having heard," is Herod's evaluation of John in v 2 (Carson, Morris, Blomberg) ignores the placement of ἀκούσας immediately following the reference to the report of John's death to Jesus (v 22). This verse is a counterpart to 4:12, which refers to Jesus' response to John's imprisonment using the same participle, ἀκούσας, "having heard," and main verb, ἀνεχώρησεν, "he went away." Presumably Jesus had gone εἰς ἔρημον τόπον κατ' ἰδίαν, "privately to a deserted place," in order to pray, the death of John perhaps turning his mind to his own approaching passion (cf. v 23). There is no indication at all that Jesus is attempting to flee from Herod Antipas (or, indeed, that Jesus was now newly threatened by the latter), despite the assumption of many commentators (cf. too on 14:22). The crowds (οἱ ὄχλοι), however, followed him as always (cf. 4:25; 8:1; 19:2; 20:29). They came ἀπὸ τῶν πόλεων, "from the cities," probably Capernaum and others along the lake, πεζῇ, "by foot," following the shoreline with their eyes on Jesus' boat.

**14** When Jesus got out of the boat at a deserted place along the shore, he was confronted with πολὺν ὄχλον, "a large crowd," and he was "moved with compassion" (ἐσπλαγχνίσθη; used in the same sense in 9:36; 15:32). In a summary way, Matthew notes (cf. Luke 9:11) that ἐθεράπευσεν τοὺς ἀρρώστους αὐτῶν, "he healed their sick" (ἄρρωστος is used in Matthew only here; for θεραπεύειν in miracle summaries, see 4:23–24; 8:16; 9:35; 12:15; 15:30; 19:2; 21:14).

**15** The disciples (οἱ μαθηταί), who have not yet been mentioned in the pericope but who, like the crowds, must have walked to the spot, articulate the problem posed by the large crowd and the end of the day. ἡ ὥρα, which usually means "the hour," here is to be understood as "the day" (see BAGD, 896a). ἡ ὥρα ἤδη παρῆλθεν, "the day is already gone," is thus the equivalent of ὀψίας δὲ γενομένης, "when it was evening," the words with which this verse begins. The disciples propose that Jesus dismiss the crowds so that they can go to τὰς κώμας, "the villages," i.e., probably nearby communities, in order to acquire food (βρώματα; the only occurrence of the word in Matthew) for themselves. Under the circumstances this clearly seemed the best thing to do.

**16–17** Jesus' response to this suggestion must have seemed incomprehensible to the disciples. The crowd didn't need to go away, because the disciples could give them something to eat: δότε αὐτοῖς ὑμεῖς φαγεῖν, "You give them (food) to eat" (emphasis from the unnecessary pronoun). In Matthew's account they express their incredulity in the simple words "we have nothing here except five loaves and two fish." At this point the story bears some intentional similarity to the comment of Elisha in the miraculous provision of food from twenty loaves of barley and the response of the man from Baal-shalishah (2 Kgs 4:42–44; cf. John 6:9, "but what are those among so many?").

**18–19** The miracle of the multiplication of the loaves and fish is not described—indeed, it is not even mentioned as such but only first discovered by the reader through its results, mentioned in v 20. Confronted with the problem, Jesus first asks for the five loaves and two fish to be brought to him and commands the crowds to sit down (ἀνακλιθῆναι, "to recline," as at a meal—indeed, as at a banquet) on the grass. He then takes the bread, looks up to heaven, and in rabbinic fashion blesses God for the gift of food. (The traditional prayer was: "Blessed art thou, O Lord our God, King of the universe, who bringest forth bread from the earth"; cf. *m. Ber.* 8:7; *b. Ber.* 35a; 46a.) Then he breaks the bread (and fish) and gives it to his disciples, who in turn give it to the crowds. The sequence of verbs or participles, i.e., λαμβάνειν, "take," εὐλογεῖν, "bless," κλᾶν, "break," διδόναι, "give," is the same as in the account of the Last Supper (26:26–27), suggesting an inevitable association of the two stories (but cf. the similarity with the description of the ordinary meal in Acts 27:35). ἀναβλέψας εἰς τὸν οὐρανόν, "having looked up into the sky," lacking in 26:26, reflects a common practice in connection with prayer (cf. Mark 7:34; John 11:41; 17:1; for OT background, Ps 123:1).

**20** The statement of the miracle is really found in this verse in the observation that ἔφαγον πάντες καὶ ἐχορτάσθησαν, "everyone ate and was full." The last verb, χορτάζειν, has the nuance of being "completely satisfied"; it has already been used with clearly eschatological associations in 5:6. The miracle in this sense anticipates the messianic age in which the hungry are to be fed (cf. Luke 1:53; 6:21). Messianic blessing also appears to be intended in the overabundance of food. Thus the leftover fragments filled δώδεκα κοφίνους, "twelve baskets." This word for "basket," κόφινος, "considered typical for the Jews" (BAGD, 447), is used in the NT only in reference to the leftovers collected in the feeding of the five thousand (16:9; Mark 6:43; 8:19; Luke 9:17; John 6:13). A different word for "basket," σπυρίς, a term used also among the Greeks, is used in reference to the collection of the fragments left over from the feeding of the four thousand (15:37; 16:10; Mark 8:8, 20). The fact that "twelve" baskets are referred to in this pericope probably symbolizes the twelve tribes of Israel (contra Luz), i.e., a portrayal of messianic fulfillment brought to the Jews. The number of baskets in the two feedings is made important by 16:9–10. This alone encourages the intepreter to think of the significance of the numbers; it does not suggest, however, that every number in the passage (e.g., five loaves, two fishes, five thousand men) has symbolic significance. This miracle recalls God's miraculous, abundant provision of manna, "bread," ἄρτος in the LXX, in the wilderness (cf. Exod 16:13–35; Num

11:7–9, 31–32). The eschatological connotation of the manna miracle is evident in *2 Apoc. Bar.* 29:8 (cf. Rev 2:17).

**21** The number of those who were miraculously fed is reckoned as "about [ὡσεί] five thousand." Matthew alone among the four evangelists notes that this was a count of the men and did not include the women and children who were fed. No attempt is made, however, to give a total count of those who were fed.

### Explanation

The miracle of the feeding of the five thousand is much more than just the supernatural provision for the physical hunger of a large crowd on a specific occasion. There is no need to deny the historicity of the miracle simply because we have never witnessed a miraculous multiplication of food. At the same time, however, the literal, historical miracle of Jesus on this occasion is full of ongoing and important significance for Matthew's community and for us. Indeed, the miracle is a deed filled with symbolism at more than one level, which is why Matthew (following Mark) takes the trouble to tell the very similar story of the feeding of the four thousand (see *Comment* on 15:32–39). The primary symbolism is that of messianic provision, which both points to the reality of present fulfillment and foreshadows the blessings of the eschaton (the Fourth Gospel develops this idea, relating the feeding miracle also to the eucharist; John 6). This provision takes place in the wilderness, just as manna was provided in the wilderness. It is a kind of messianic banquet in which the people recline at table (cf. 8:11). Jesus is the messianic provider, the Christ—a point left implicit by Matthew in this passage. The hungry are filled now as they will also be filled in the future. The miracle typifies the full and complete blessing of humanity in the meeting of human need and the experience of ultimate well-being, universal shalom. The feeding of the multitude is thus the harbinger of good news for Matthew's church and for Christians of every era. At another level and in specific contrast to the feeding of the four thousand (which, as will be seen, points to the Gentiles), the symbolism of the twelve baskets suggests the special significance of this miracle for Israel. Messianic fulfillment means (and especially for Matthew!) that Jesus will provide for Israel before considering the Gentiles. And the feeding of the five thousand is an indication to the Jews that the Messiah is in their midst, offering to them—as in the miracle of manna in the wilderness—the reality of salvation, the fulfillment of the promises.

# *Walking on the Water* (14:22–33)

### Bibliography

**Achtemeier, P.** "Person and Deed: Jesus and the Storm-Tossed Sea." *Int* 16 (1962) 169–76. **Berg, W.** *Die Rezeption alttestamentlicher Motive im Neuen Testament dargestellt an den Seewandelerzählungen.* Freiburg: Hochschule, 1979. **Braumann, G.** "Der sinkende Petrus." *TZ* 22 (1966) 403–14. **Carlisle, C. R.** "Jesus' Walking on the Water: A Note on Matthew 14:22–

33." *NTS* 31 (1985) 151–55. **Denis, A. M.** "La marche de Jésus sur les eaux." In *De Jésus aux Évangiles*, ed. I. de la Potterie. BETL 35. Gembloux: Duculot, 1967. 233–47. **Derrett, J. D. M.** "Why and How Jesus Walked on the Sea." *NovT* 23 (1981) 330–48. **Heil, J. P.** *Jesus Walking on the Sea.* AnBib 87. Rome: Biblical Institute, 1981. **Hill, D. F.** "The Walking on the Water." *ExpTim* 99 (1988) 267–69. **Kratz, R.** "Der Seewandel des Petrus." *BibLeb* 15 (1974) 86–101. **Lövestam, E.** "Wunder und Symbolhandlung: Eine Studie über Matthäus 14.28–31." *KD* 8 (1962) 124–35. **Ritt, H.** "Der 'Seewandel Jesu' (Mark 6.45–52 par.)." *BZ* 23 (1979) 71–84. **Smit-Sibinga, J.** "Matthew 14,22–33: Text and Composition." In *New Testament Textual Criticism.* FS B. M. Metzger, ed. J. E. Epp and G. D. Fee. Oxford: Clarendon, 1981. 15–33.

## Translation

[22] *And immediately*[a] *he instructed the disciples*[b] *to get into the*[c] *boat and to go before him*[d] *to the other side while he dismissed the crowds.* [23]*And after he had dismissed the crowds, he went up to the mountain privately in order to pray. And when evening came, he was there alone.* [24]*But the boat was already*[e] *a long distance*[f] *from the land, being tossed about by the waves, for the wind was contrary.* [25]*And in the fourth watch of the night, he came to them, walking across the lake.* [26]*But when his disciples saw him walking on the sea, they were terrified, saying: "It is a ghost." And they cried out in fear.* [27]*But immediately [Jesus]*[g] *spoke to them, saying: "Be of good courage. It is I! Do not be afraid."* [28]*And Peter answered him and said: "Lord, if it is you, command me to come to you on the water."* [29]*And he said: "Come." And Peter got out of the boat and walked on the water, and he came*[h] *to Jesus.* [30]*But seeing the [strong]*[i] *wind, he was afraid, and when he began to sink, he cried out, saying: "Lord, save me."* [31]*And Jesus immediately stretched out his hand and took hold of him, and he said to him: "You of little faith, why did you doubt?"* [32]*And when they got into the boat, the wind stopped.* [33]*And those who were in the boat worshiped him, saying: "Truly you are the Son of God."*

## Notes

[a] εὐθέως, "immediately," is omitted in ℵ* C* (ff¹) sy^{s.c}, an "accidental omission" according to the committee. See *TCGNT*, 36.

[b] Some MSS (B K P Θ ƒ¹³ it vg^{mss} sy) read αὐτοῦ, "his," after "disciples," probably from the influence of the parallel in Mark 6:45. See *TCGNT*, 36.

[c] A few MSS (B Σ ƒ¹ 33 bo^{ms} mae) omit the definite article τό, "the," thus producing "a boat."

[d] D it omit αὐτόν, "him."

[e] D lat sy^{c.p} co omit ἤδη, "already."

[f] σταδίους πολλούς, lit. "many stadia." Θ has, in addition to a different word order, σταδίους ἱκανούς, with approximately the same meaning; many MSS (ℵ C D L W 084 0106 ƒ¹ sy^h TR) refer to μέσον τῆς θαλάσσης, "the middle of the lake" (cf. Mark 6:47). Since harmonization with Mark (and not John 6:19) is probable, the committee concludes that the text of B ƒ¹³ best accounts for the other readings. See *TCGNT*, 37.

[g] ℵ* D 084 sy^c sa bo omit ὁ Ἰησοῦς, "Jesus." Other witnesses (C L W Θ 0106 ƒ¹.¹³ TR) place αὐτοῖς, "to them," before ὁ Ἰησοῦς. Although the shorter reading may be original, it is also possible that the name dropped out through homoioteleuton (*OIC* ὁ Ἰησοῦς] with *AYTOIC*). The committee thus places the name in brackets. See *TCGNT*, 37.

[h] Some witnesses (ℵ¹ C² D L W Θ 073 0119 ƒ¹.¹³ TR) omit καί, "and," and have ἐλθεῖν, "to come," a scribal softening of the completed action implied by ἦλθεν, "he came." ℵ has both ἐλθεῖν and ἦλθεν.

[i] Some important witnesses (ℵ B* 073 33 sa bo) omit ἰσχυρόν, "strong," which may have been added to heighten the cause of Peter's fear (cf. the addition of σφόδρα in W). A majority of the committee, however, regarded the word as necessary to explain Peter's increased fear. Thus the word is enclosed in brackets. See *TCGNT*, 38.

## Form/Structure/Setting

A. As in both Mark and John, this miracle occurs immediately after the feeding of the five thousand. The effect of these successive narratives is powerful. The question of the identity of this Jesus, which has been before the readers previously (cf. 7:28–29; 11:3; 13:54–56; 14:2), especially in 8:27, and which was left implicit in the preceding narrative, again cries out for an answer that is now unequivocally given in v 33. This conclusion can be said to serve also as a fitting one to the miracle of the feeding (cf. the association of the passages in Mark 6:52). Green (141) appropriately describes the pericope as "an epiphany of Jesus to the disciples, in the same category as the Transfiguration" (17:1–8).

B. In vv 22–27 and 32–33, Matthew is dependent on Mark 6:45–52 (cf. John 6:16–21). Beginning with this passage down through 16:12 there are no Lukan parallels. Vv 28–31, on the other hand, are unique to Matthew and are drawn from his own special source. Matthew again abridges Mark, but not to the same extent as usual. The changes to be noted are the following: in v 22 Matthew omits Mark's problematic πρὸς βηθσαϊδάν, "to Bethsaida" (Mark 6:45; cf. John 6:17: "to Capernaum"), and Mark's (Mark 6:45) αὐτός, "he (himself)," before the verb "dismissed"; in v 23 he adds a favorite phrase, κατ᾽ ἰδίαν, "privately," in describing Jesus going up the mountain; in v 24 he replaces Mark's ἐν μέσῳ τῆς θαλάσσης, "in the middle of the lake" (Mark 6:47), with ἤδη σταδίους πολλοὺς ἀπὸ τῆς γῆς, "already many stadia from the land" (cf. John 6:19: "twenty five or thirty stadia"), and omits Mark's καὶ ἰδὼν αὐτούς, "and seeing them," i.e., presumably from the land (Mark 6:48); in v 25 he omits Mark's enigmatic καὶ ἤθελεν παρελθεῖν αὐτούς, "and he was ready to pass them by" (Mark 6:48), which does not fit his portrayal of Jesus. In v 26 he adds the word μαθηταί, "disciples," as well as ἀπὸ τοῦ φόβου, "out of fear," to stress the mental state of the disciples. At the very end of the pericope (v 33), he substitutes the remarkable προσεκύνησαν αὐτῷ λέγοντες· ἀληθῶς θεοῦ υἱὸς εἶ, "they worshiped him, saying: 'Truly you are the Son of God,'" for Mark's much weaker "they were exceedingly astonished" (Mark 6:51). Matthew furthermore omits Mark's closing sentence, "For they did not understand concerning the loaves, but their heart was hardened" (Mark 6:52). By contrast the disciples in Matthew know the identity of Jesus and without hesitation confess him to be the Son of God. In this passage Matthew has thus more often altered Mark deliberately rather than merely for the sake of abridgement. The earlier pericope describing Jesus' stilling of the storm at sea (8:23–27) is parallel in many respects to the present pericope (see *Form/Structure/Setting* §D on that pericope).

C. Although the narrative of the events themselves constitutes the primary matter in this pericope, the words spoken by Jesus (vv 27, 31), Peter (v 30), and the disciples (v 33) assume a special importance. The passage can be outlined in the following way: (1) the departure of the disciples and the dismissal of the crowd (vv 22–23a); (2) Jesus prays alone on the mountain (v 23); (3) the strong wind on the sea (v 24); (4) the appearance of Jesus and the fear of the disciples (vv 25–26); (5) the self-revelation of Jesus and announcement of comfort (v 27); (6) Peter's request and his walking on the water (vv 28–29); (7) Peter's wavering and his cry for help (v 30); (8) the saving and rebuke of Peter (v 31); (9) the end of the wind (v 32); and (10) the disciples' confession of faith (v 33). (5) occurs exactly at the center of the "double story" (Gerhardsson, *Mighty Acts*, 57). It is clear from the structure of the pericope (as well as from comparison with Mark) that vv 28–31 are a curious parenthetical intrusion into the main story. In form, the narrative is thus similar to the miracles of healing: i.e., the expression of the need of the disciples (and Peter), (Peter's request for help), the miracle of the calm sea, and the response of the disciples. It is at the same time, however, an epiphany story. Although there are some correspondences in the structure of the text (e.g., "It is a ghost"—"It is I"—"if it is you" [vv 26–28]; "Lord, save me"— "You of little faith, why did you doubt" [vv 30–31]), there is practically no syntactic parallelism to be noted.

D. On the problem of the historicity of this pericope, see *Form/Structure/Setting* §E for the preceding pericope (vv 13–21). For (unpersuasive) Hellenistic parallels as well as the Buddhist story (*Jâtaka* 190) of a disciple who walked on water or sank depending on whether he focused on the Buddha, see Luz.

### Comment

**22**  εὐθέως, "immediately," joins this passage closely with the preceding one, as also in Mark. Jesus apparently orders the disciples to return by boat without him (εἰς τὸ πέραν, "to the other side," presumably to Capernaum on the west shore of the lake [cf. v 13] but left vague in Matthew), not simply in order to dismiss the crowds properly but that he might linger in prayer according to his original intention (cf. v 13). It is at least possible that the disciples were sent away in order to keep them from possible involvement in designs for a messianic revolt (cf. John 6:15). Perhaps Matthew's omission of "he was ready to pass them by" (Mark 6:48) indicates the assumption of Jesus' deliberate plan to teach the disciples through his mastery of the sea. (Matthew seems oblivious to Mark's apparently theophanic language [cf. Exod. 33:22].) Since there is no evidence of imminent danger from Herod, a return to the western shore of the lake is not at all impossible (cf. John 6:17). The boat with disciples in it suggests the church, as also in 8:23.

**23**  Jesus went up εἰς τὸ ὄρος, "into the mountain" (cf. 5:1; 15:29; 17:1), one of the hills along the northeast or east shore of the sea of Galilee. κατ' ἰδίαν, "privately," picks up again the same phrase used in v 13 (cf. 17:1), and the point is further strengthened by μόνος ἦν ἐκεῖ, "he was there alone." Moses typology hardly seems to be intended here (contra Davies-Allison), the reference to the mountain being merely borrowed from Mark. The solitude of Jesus is the important motif for Matthew at this point. The other references to Jesus praying (προσεύχεσθαι) in Matthew are in 26:36, 39, 42, 44 (cf. Luke 9:28), all in connection with his own imminent suffering and death. In the present instance, the same thoughts may be presumed to be in Jesus' mind, prompted perhaps by the report of John the Baptist's death (cf. the initial departure of Jesus into the wilderness privately in v 13 following the report referred to in v 12). The time reference ὀψίας δὲ γενομένης, "when it was evening," given the εὐθέως, "immediately," of v 22, may mean simply a time somewhat later in the evening than that referred to by the same phrase in v 15 (cf. too the reference to "the fourth watch of the night" in v 25). But the phrase may simply be a relic of the separate transmission of the story in oral tradition.

**24** The boat, which had left some time earlier, was "already many stadia" (σταδίους, the only occurrence of the word in Matthew) from the land. A stadion was an ancient measure of distance equal to 185 meters (see BAGD, 764); hence, the boat was perhaps a mile or two from shore. The disciples had to fight a contrary (ἐναντίος; the only occurrence of the word in Matthew) wind, and the boat was "harassed" (βασανιζόμενον) by the waves (cf. 8:24), so that it is not strange that they had been able to row only a relatively short distance.

**25–26** The Romans divided the night (between 6 P.M. and 6 A.M.) into four watches. The fourth "watch" (φυλακῇ; cf. the same use of the word in 24:43) was accordingly between 3 A.M. and 6 A.M., and thus the disciples had been fighting the storm for a large part of the night. Although the disciples were undoubtedly exhausted, cold, and wet, Matthew's narrative focuses on one supreme element, their fear. They were already afraid for their lives, but the specter of someone "walking on the water" among the waves in the darkness must have been absolutely terrifying (the words περιπατεῖν and ἐπί occur in both v 25 and v 26, once with the accusative, i.e., "across," and once with the genitive, "upon"; cf. v 28). It is thus perfectly understandable that the disciples ἐταράχθησαν, "were terrified" (the word is used again in Matthew only in 2:3, but in a different sense), concluded they were seeing some kind of "ghost" (φάντασμα; in the NT only here and in the parallel in Mark 6:49), and ἀπὸ τοῦ φόβου ἔκραξαν, "cried out in fear" (as Matthew alone notes). Given the popular belief that the sea was the home of evil spirits (cf. Rev 13:1), they undoubtedly thought the "ghost" meant to do them ill. In Luke 24:37, the risen Jesus appears to the disciples, who are filled with fear and conclude they are seeing "a spirit" (πνεῦμα; but D: φάντασμα; as in our text; for a similar word, see Wis 18:17). OT symbolism concerning the mastery of God over the sea and specifically his walking upon it (e.g., Ps 77:16, 19; Job 9:8; 38:16; cf. wisdom in Sir 24:5), while significant in retrospect, could hardly have occurred to the disciples at the time, although for the evangelist and his readers it must have been suggestive.

**27** Jesus immediately (εὐθύς) acts to calm the great fear of the disciples by identifying himself: "Be of good courage [θαρσεῖτε, used elsewhere in Matthew only in 9:2, 22]. It is I! Do not be afraid" (for φοβεῖσθαι used similarly in exceptional situations, see 17:7; 28:5, 10). ἐγώ εἰμι, "It is I," probably had a deeper meaning to Matthew and his readers than the simple self-identification of Jesus that it is to the disciples. In a theophany-like context such as this, the words allude to the definition of the name Yahweh (ἐγώ εἰμι = I AM) given in the LXX of Exod 3:14 (cf. Matt 22:32; John 8:58; Mark 14:62) and Isa 43:10; 51:12. God is present uniquely in Jesus.

**28–29** The section now inserted by Matthew (vv 28–31) focuses on Peter, who is of exceptional importance to the evangelist (cf. esp. 16:16–19; 17:24–27 in this section of the Gospel). The passage is marked by Matthean vocabulary, and thus Matthew may have composed the passage, or at least has left his impress on the material if it derives from oral tradition (thus Schweizer, Davies-Allison). Similarities reflecting possible dependence on the story of the stilling of the storm may also be kept in mind. Peter is here paradoxically a model both of faith and of lack of faith. The story is also a demonstration of the saving power of the Lord. If we take the narrative as historical, it is difficult to know what lay behind Peter's request. It may be that Peter wanted to participate with Jesus in this miracle as he had in the preceding one. Perhaps it was no more than impulsiveness or the desire to do something excitingly dangerous—to have a once-in-a-lifetime experience—which appealed to him. The impossible would be possible through the power of Jesus. Thus Peter's request is based upon faith in Jesus and not upon an uncertainty about whether the apparition really was Jesus (this reality is assumed in the protasis of the condition). He did get out of the boat and did walk toward Jesus: περιεπάτησεν ἐπὶ τὰ ὕδατα, "he walked on the water" (cf. vv 25, 26; the substitution of ὕδατα [the plural here, as in 8:32] is probably a Semitism; "water," for θάλασσα, "sea," may reflect simply the short distance he walked). For OT and Jewish background, see Lövestam.

**30** Peter's lack of faith is caused by a failure of concentration: he is distracted by the fierce wind. His mind became more affected by the circumstances than by faith in the power of Jesus, and once again he became filled with fear (cf. a similar sad turn in his life in 26:69–75). He began then to sink (καταποντίζεσθαι) and cried out in desperation: κύριε, σῶσόν με, "Lord, save me." Almost exactly the same cry is made by the disciples in the storm-tossed boat in 8:25. There is undeniably a paradigmatic character to this cry for salvation. In the moment of most dire human need, there is but one cry, just as there is but one source of salvation.

**31** Jesus responds to this desperate cry "immediately" (εὐθέως), stretching out his hand (as in 8:3) to save Peter. Jesus then addresses Peter as ὀλιγόπιστε, "you of little faith" (see *Comment* on 6:30 for this word in Matthew), just as he did the disciples in the boat according to 8:26, and asks εἰς τί ἐδίστασας, "Why did you doubt?" (the only other use of διστάζειν in the NT is in 28:17; it means "to be of a divided mind"). Here the object of the doubt is whether it was possible indeed to walk on the water and hence indirectly expresses a doubt concerning the power of Jesus. Peter was nevertheless saved. The underlying message here is as much for the disciples and for Matthew's church as it is for Peter himself.

**32** A sometimes unnoticed aspect of the story is the miraculous cessation of the powerful wind. This makes the story quite similar to that of the stilling of the storm in 8:23–27. ἐκόπασεν ὁ ἄνεμος, "the wind stopped," not apparently in response to a command of Jesus (as in 8:26) but simply in response to his presence in the boat.

**33** Matthew's own ending to the pericope makes a most remarkable contrast to the ending of the similar story in 8:23–27. There the men "marvel" and ask the question, "What sort of person is this that the winds and the sea obey him?" Here the disciples "worshiped him" (for προσκυνεῖν, "worship," applied to Jesus, see 2:2, 8, 11; 8:2; 9:18; 15:25; 28:9, 17) and conclude with the confession ἀληθῶς θεοῦ υἱὸς εἶ, "Truly you are the Son of God." (Modified by θεοῦ [emphatic in position], υἱός is definite despite the lack of the definite article: in the context the translation "a" Son of God is absurd.) For "Son of God," see *Comment* on 4:3. As the one who walks upon the water and calms the storm, Jesus embodies the very presence of God (see *Comment* on v 26). Here "Son of God" is probably understood by the disciples as the unique messenger of God, God's messianic agent, and not, as the later church will make explicit, the actual incarnation of God. This conclusion has an inevitability about it, given the preceding two narratives. It strangely anticipates the answer given to the direct question of Jesus in 16:16, which gives the impression of being the first time the question has received this answer. Yet Matthew's Christology builds throughout the narrative of the words and deeds of Jesus that begins in chap. 5. The present passage and verse are a climactic point in the narrative thus far (cf. Mark 15:39; Matt 27:54). 16:16 is yet a higher climax and a turning point of the whole Gospel.

### Explanation

Jesus has power over the sea: he walks upon the deep as God alone does, and the sea respects his wishes. If the Israelites regarded the sea as the domain of evil powers (see *Comment* on 8:23–27), then the terrifying experience of a storm at sea in the dead of night becomes even more symbolic of the human experience of evil (cf. Ps 69:15–16). The fear of the disciples is like the fear of all who are threatened by insecurity in the face of the unknown. But when Jesus appears to those in extreme need, it is as one who has sovereign power, not only over the forces of nature but over evil itself. Thus his words, "Be of good courage. It is I! Do not be afraid," are not empty or meaningless. Fear is unwarranted where Jesus is present. If in circumstances of personal need one responds in faith and, like Peter, steps out into the unknown but begins to submerge again through doubt under the all-too-real presence of evil, then at the cry, "Lord, save me," Jesus is immediately there to deliver the believer (cf. Ps 18:16–17). Then will come the gentle rebuke: "You of little faith, why did you doubt?" In the experience of the Christian, Jesus is "God with us" (1:23), the ever-present source of deliverance (cf. 28:20). (For a similar meditation upon God's deliverance employing the symbol of the water and storm, see Pss 69:1–3, 13–15; 107:23–32.) In some such way as this, the miracle of this pericope was meant to be understood by and find practical application in Matthew's church. The Jesus who multiplied the loaves and fish and who appeared to the disciples walking on the water and who saved Peter from sinking, this same Jesus is the Lord of the church who has brought salvation and who stands similarly prepared to save his people, even when they may doubt, from the evils that beset them. This Jesus who rules over nature and even the realm of evil is rightly worshiped as "truly the Son of God."

# Healing of the Sick: A Summary Passage    (14:34–36)

### Translation

³⁴*And when they had crossed over, they came to the shore at Gennesaret.*ᵃ ³⁵*And the people of that place recognized him and sent word into the whole of that region. And they brought to him all who were not well,* ³⁶*and they were pleading with him that they might only touch the hem of his garment. And as many as touched it were made whole.*

### Notes

ᵃ According to D* lat syˢ·ᶜ·ᵖ, Γεννησάρ, "Gennesar" (Dᶜ: Γεννησαράτ, "Gennesarat"); according to (L) Θ *f*¹³ TR, Γεννησαρέθ, "Gennesareth"; the spelling Γεννησαρέτ, "Gennesaret," however, is found in ℵ B C (N) W Γ 0119 *f*¹.

*Form/Structure/Setting*

A. As in Mark and John, the two preceding miracle narratives are followed in Matthew by a summary of healings done by Jesus. These two narratives are similarly preceded by a summary of Jesus' healings (vv 13–14). These formulaic summaries are of particular importance in Matthew (cf. 4:24–25; 8:16–17; 9:35; see Gerhardsson, *Mighty Acts,* 20–37), reminding the readers continually of the reality of the good news of Jesus' proclamation. Jesus heals again, although this is not his primary calling or his supreme work.

B. Matthew is closely dependent on Mark (Mark 6:53–56; cf. John 6:22–25) but as usual abbreviates his source. In v 34 Matthew omits Mark's note καὶ προσωρμίσθησαν, "and they came into the harbor" (Mark 6:53), and in v 35, Mark's succeeding words, "and when they got out of the boat, immediately" (Mark 6:54). On the other hand, in v 35 Matthew adds the words οἱ ἄνδρες τοῦ τόπου ἐκείνου, "the people of that place," to identify the subject of the verbs and alone refers to the people of the region bringing πάντας, "all," their sick folk. Matthew also smooths Mark's rough syntax (Mark 6:55b). He further omits Mark 6:56a, "and wherever he came into villages or cities or into the fields, they laid their sick in the marketplaces," thus restricting the summary of healings to Gennesaret.

C. The straightforward narrative form of the pericope is dictated by the close dependence on Mark. The content can be outlined as follows: (1) arrival in Gennesaret (v 34); (2) the recognition of Jesus and the bringing of the sick (v 35); and (3) healings even by the touching of Jesus' garment (v 36). Little structural parallelism is evident.

*Comment*

**34** The verb διαπερᾶν, "cross over," is used elsewhere in Matthew only in 9:1, where it also refers to crossing the lake from the east shore to the west. In Luke 5:1 (the only other occurrence of "Gennesaret" in the NT besides the Markan parallel to the present passage [Mark 6:53]), the sea itself is called "the lake [λίμνην] of Gennesaret." Gennesaret, or Gennesar, is either a village or a region (or both) that lies on the shore just a couple of miles southwest of Capernaum. No threat to the life of Jesus is implied.

**35** Given Gennesaret's proximity to Capernaum, it was to be expected that people there would recognize Jesus (and his disciples). They sent word (ἀπέστειλαν, "sent," i.e., sent the message) of Jesus' presence there to the whole of the surrounding region (a general rather than specific reference) in order that others too might be helped, but perhaps too because it was good for business. Hearing the report, people brought all (πάντας) their needy. For the expression κακῶς ἔχοντας, "being sick," see too the summaries of 4:24; 8:16 as well as 9:12.

**36** Although no mention is made of the size of the crowds who came, this verse suggests the numbers were very large. Jesus probably healed in his normal way, i.e., directly. But there were apparently so many people in need of healing that they pressed around him and begged (παρεκάλουν; for the same use of the verb, cf. 8:5) to touch the hem of his garment (for this, see *Comment* on 9:20). Such is the power of Jesus that all who touched him on this occasion were instantly cured of their maladies. The word for "made whole," διεσώθησαν, occurs in Matthew only here (where it carries no further meaning than the similar meaning of σῴζειν; cf. 9:21–22); in itself, however, it hints at the "salvation" ultimately to be accomplished by the Savior (cf. 1:21). The christological significance of the pericope is left implicit in Matthew (as in Mark).

### Explanation

Jesus again engages in a healing ministry as part of his proclamation of the dawning of the kingdom of God. The healings and their inclusiveness ("all") point to and foreshadow the blessings of the eschatological order in its final realization in the future. Jesus is central to the experience of, and even the possibility of, these healings. His power is so overwhelming that simply to touch his garment is to experience immediate healing. The same presence and power of Jesus are available to the church in ways that transcend temporary, ad hoc healings of this kind. The salvation experienced by the church goes beyond what was experienced at Gennesaret; the healings at Gennesaret are at best only anticipations of the eschatological wholeness of the church to be experienced by every believer.

# *Jesus' Criticism of the Pharisees* (15:1–11)

### Bibliography

**Baumgarten, A. I.** "*Korban* and the Pharisaic Paradosis." *JANESCU* 16 (1984) 5–17. **Berger, K.** *Gesetzesauslegung Jesu.* 1:272–77, 461–507. **Booth, R. P.** *Jesus and the Laws of Purity.* JSNTSup 13. Sheffield: JSOT, 1986. **Broer, I.** *Freiheit vom Gesetz und Radikalisierung des Gesetzes.* SBS 99. Stuttgart: Katholisches Bibelwerk, 1980. **Carlston, C. E.** "The Things That Defile (Mark 7,14) and the Law in Matthew and Mark." *NTS* 15 (1968–69) 75–96. **Daube, D.** "Responsibilities of Master and Disciples in the Gospels." *NTS* 19 (1972–73) 1–15. **Derrett, J. D. M.** "*KOPBAN, O ΕΣΤΙΝ ΔΩPON.*" *NTS* 16 (1970) 364–68. **Fitzmyer, J.** "The Aramaic Qorban Inscription from Jebel Hallet et-Turi and Mk 7:11/Mt 15:5." *JBL* 78 (1959) 60–65. **Hübner, H.** *Gesetz.* 176–82. **Käsemann, E.** "Matthäus 15,1–14." In *Exegetische Versuche und Besinnungen.* Göttingen: Vandenhoeck & Ruprecht, 1960. 1:237–42. **Krämer, H.** "Eine Anmerkung zum Verständnis von Mt 15,6a." *WD* 16 (1981) 67–70. **Kümmel, W. G.** "Äussere und innere Reinheit des Menschen bei Jesus." In *Das Wort und die Wörter.* FS G. Friedrich, ed. H. Balz and S. Schulz. Stuttgart: Kohlhammer, 1973. 35–46. **Lambrecht, J.** "Jesus and the Law: An Investigation of Mark 7:1–23." *ETL* 53 (1977) 24–82. **Lührmann, D.** ". . . womit er alle Speisen für rein erklärte (Mk 7.19)." *WD* 16 (1981) 71–92. **Merkel, H.** "Markus 7.15: Das Jesuswort über die innere Verunreinigung." *ZRGG* 20 (1968) 340–63. **Paschen, W.** *Rein und Unrein.* SANT 24. Munich: Kösel, 1970. **Räisänen, H.** "Jesus and the Food Laws: Reflections on Mark 7.15." *JSNT* 16 (1982) 79–100. **Schoeps, H. J.** "Jésus et la loi juive." *RHPR* 33 (1953) 1–20.

### Translation

[1] *Then Pharisees* [a] *and scribes* [b] *from Jerusalem came to Jesus, saying:* [2] *"Why do your disciples transgress the tradition of the elders? For they do not wash their hands whenever*

*they eat bread."* ³*And he answered and said to them: "And why do you yourselves transgress the commandment of God because of your tradition?* ⁴*For God said:* ᶜ *'Honor your* ᵈ *father and your* ᵉ *mother,' and, 'Let the one who speaks evil of father or mother most certainly be put to death.'* ⁵*But you say: 'Whenever one says to one's father or mother: "Whatever you would have benefited from me is* ᶠ *now* ᵍ *'a gift,'"* ⁶*one need not at all support one's parents.'* ʰ *And you cancel out the word* ⁱ *of God because of your tradition.* ⁷*Hypocrites, Isaiah prophesied rightly concerning you, saying:*

⁸*This people* ʲ *honors me with their lips,*
*but their heart is distant from me.*
⁹*And vainly they worship me*
*teaching doctrines which are human commandments."*

¹⁰*And when he had called the crowd together, he said to them: "Hear and understand.* ¹¹*It is not* ᵏ *what goes into the mouth that defiles a person, but it is what comes out of the mouth—this is what defiles a person."*

### Notes

ᵃ C L W 0119 TR add οἱ, "the," the definite article going with "Pharisees," probably through influence of the Markan parallel (Mark 7:1).

ᵇ Many witnesses (C L W 0119 TR lat syᵃ·ᶜ·ʰ mae boᵐˢˢ) have the order "scribes and Pharisees," probably because of its frequency in Matthew.

ᶜ Some witnesses (א*·² C L W 0106 TR *f* syʰ) read ἐνετείλατο λέγων, "commanded, saying," probably a scribal expansion (cf. ἐντολήν, "commandment," in v 3). See *TCGNT*, 38.

ᵈ Translating τόν, lit. "the," as "your." Some MSS (C² K L N W Θ *f* ¹³ lat sy) add σοῦ, "your," to produce exact correspondence with the LXX text of Exod 20:12 and Deut 5:16. Cf. too the parallel in Mark 7:10. See also next *Note.*

ᵉ Translating τήν, lit. "the," as "your." Some MSS (N W it syᵃ·ᶜ·ᵖ) add σοῦ, "your," thus conforming the text exactly to that of the LXX (Deut 5:16). Cf. the parallel in Mark 7:10.

ᶠ א* adds οὐδέν ἐστιν, "is nothing," at the end of the verse, resulting in the meaning "the gift you would have gained from me is nothing."

ᵍ "Now" is added to the translation for clarity.

ʰ The critical text reads τὸν πατέρα αὐτοῦ, "his father." Some MSS (C L W Θ 0106 *f*¹ TR vgᶜˡ syᵖ·ʰ) add ἢ τὴν μητέρα αὐτοῦ, "or his mother," and others slight variants thereof. The phrase could have been added to bring about agreement with vv 4–5 and the parallel in Mark 7:12, or it could have accidentally dropped because of the similar ending αὐτοῦ, "his" (or deliberately omitted for stylistic reasons). The committee omits the phrase based on the weight of א B D. See *TCGNT*, 38. "Parents" is used in the translation to reflect the inclusiveness of vv 4–5.

ⁱ א*·² C 084 *f*¹³ read τὸν νόμον, "the law"; L W 0106 *f*¹ TR lat syʰ read τὴν ἐντολήν, "the commandment." The latter appears to be a harmonization with v 3. While τὸν λόγον, "the word," could be caused by Mark 7:13, the committee preferred the weight of א¹ B D. See *TCGNT*, 38.

ʲ A number of MSS (C W 0106 [*f*¹] TR syʰ) harmonize the citation with the LXX of Isa 29:13 by adding ἐγγίζει μοι ὁ λαὸς οὗτος τῷ στόματι αὐτῶν καί, "the people is near to me with their mouth and."

ᵏ D adds πᾶν, "everything," thus softening the reading to "not everything."

### Form/Structure/Setting

A. Matthew follows Mark in alternating passages revealing the power and identity of Jesus with confrontations with those who refuse Jesus and his message. In the present instance, religious authorities come to Galilee from Jerusalem and initiate contact with Jesus. This passage and the closely related following one (cf. v 20) are of key importance in Matthew because the Pharisees represent established Judaism for his readers. Although Matthew, as will be seen, softens the radical teaching of Jesus found in Mark, he does not do away with it altogether.

B. For this pericope Matthew depends again on Mark (Mark 7:1–15; cf. Luke 11:37–41 for a partial parallel). Two major changes should be noted to begin with: (1) Matthew omits Mark 7:2–4, with its detailed description of the ritual cleansings of the Pharisees—this background being unnecessary for his Jewish-Christian readers—and (2) Matthew displaces Mark's quotation of Isa 29:13 by putting it after Jesus' illustration of the way in which the Pharisees violate the commandment of God (vv 3–6) rather than having Jesus begin with the quotation, as in Mark 7:6. Most interesting from a theological point of view is Matthew's conservative rewriting of Mark's statement, changing "there is nothing [οὐδέν] outside of a person which entering is able to [ὃ δύναται] defile that person" (Mark 7:15) to "it is not what goes into the mouth which defiles a person" (v 11). Matthew's avoidance of "nothing" and "is able to" (cf. the same omission in v 17) makes the passage more acceptable to Jewish Christians who no doubt continued to observe the dietary laws (cf. too especially the omission in v 17 of the editorial comment in Mark 7:19b that "thus he declared all foods clean").

Among smaller changes, the following are to be noted: Matthew's own opening words τότε προσέρχονται τῷ Ἰησοῦ, "then they came to Jesus"; his omission of τινές, "some," before scribes (v 1; cf. Mark 7:1); his substitution of the stronger παραβαίνουσιν, "transgress" (v 2; cf. same verb in v 3), replacing ἀφέντες, "forsaking," in Mark 7:8), for οὐ περιπατοῦσιν . . . κατά, "not walk . . . according to" (Mark 7:5); his substitution of διὰ τὴν παράδοσιν ὑμῶν, "because of your tradition" (v 3), for κρατεῖτε τὴν παράδοσιν τῶν ἀνθρώπων, "you hold the tradition of human beings" (Mark 7:8); the omission of Mark 7:9: "and he said to them: 'You are good at [καλῶς, lit. "well"] rejecting the commandment of God, in order that you might establish your tradition," perhaps because it is repetitive (cf. v 3) but also perhaps because it (esp. καλῶς) is susceptible to misunderstanding; the substitution of θεός, "God" (v 4), for Μωϋσῆς, "Moses" (Mark 7:10), to emphasize the gravity of the commandment in contrast to human tradition; the omission (v 5) of the technical term κορβᾶν ("Corban") in Mark 7:11, probably simply because it is an unnecessary encumbrance of the text; the heightening of Mark's οὐκέτι ἀφίετε αὐτόν, "no longer permit him" (Mark 7:12), to an emphatic countercommand οὐ μὴ τιμήσει, "one need not support" (v 6); the omission of "which you hand on; and you do many similar things" (Mark 7:13b) in v 6, of ὡς γέγραπται, "as it is written," in v 7 (cf. Mark 7:6b), of πάλιν, "again," in reference to calling the crowd together in v 10 (cf. Mark 7:14), and of πάντες, "all," in the same verse; finally, εἰς τὸ στόμα, "into the mouth," and ἐκ τοῦ στόματος, "out of the mouth," replace εἰς αὐτόν, "into him," and ἐκ τοῦ ἀνθρώπου, "out of the person" (v 11; Mark 7:15). Many of the changes noted here and other less significant ones not noted are mainly abbreviations, but a few are stylistic, and several appear to be theologically motivated.

C. This controversy pericope, which contains two OT citations, is carefully structured by Matthew. The passage can be outlined as follows: (1) the coming of the Pharisees and scribes (v 1), further subdivided into (a) the question and implied charge (v 2a) and (b) the grounds of the charge (2b); (2) Jesus' counter question and implied charge, on the model of rabbinic controversies (v 3), further subdivided into (a) the teaching of scripture (v 4) and (b) the practice of the Pharisees (vv 5–6); (3) the prophecy of Isaiah (vv 7–9); and (4) a revolutionary general principle (vv 10–11). In typical controversy narrative form, the question of the Pharisees is answered in turn by a parallel question of Jesus, and each question is backed up with supporting argumentation. The following structural features are notable. The structure of v 2, containing an implied charge of the Pharisees in the form of a question followed by the grounds of the former introduced by γάρ, "for," is paralleled exactly in vv 3–6 in the response of Jesus (where, however, the grounds take considerably more space [vv 4–6]). A further structural observation is that v 6b forms an inclusio with v 3, both making the same point in the same way, though with v 6b using somewhat different vocabulary: cf. παραβαίνετε, "transgress" (v 3), with ἠκυρώσατε, "cancel out" (v 6b), and τὴν ἐντολὴν τοῦ θεοῦ, "the commandment of God" (v 3), with τὸν λόγον τοῦ θεοῦ, "the word of God" (v 6b). Matthew's placement of the quotation from Isa 29:13 after the argument of Jesus has the effect of reinforcing the point. Finally we may note the nearly exact parallelism in the two main clauses of v 11, broken only by the τοῦτο, "this," in the second clause, producing a rhetorical emphasis on "what comes out of a person."

D. V 11 finds a parallel in *Gos. Thom.* 14, which is probably dependent on Matt 15:11 (cf. "mouth" rather than "person" as in Mark).

## Comment

**1–2**  Matthew's abbreviation of Mark has the effect of making it the purpose of the Pharisees and scribes to come to Jesus, who had acquired a reputation as an interpreter of the law, in order to test him on the issue of obedience to the law (i.e., as understood by the Pharisees). This was possibly a formal or semiformal delegation of leading Pharisaic authorities and scripture scholars sent from Jerusalem in order to gain more information about Jesus' views on the subject (cf. Mark 3:22; John 1:19; crowds from Jerusalem had followed Jesus from the beginning [4:25]). Of the seven times in which scribes and Pharisees are linked in Matthew, this is the only occurrence of the order "Pharisees and scribes" (for γραμματεῖς, "scribes," see *Comment* on 2:4), probably because of dependence on Mark (7:1), as well as a desire to emphasize that the view represented here is that of the Pharisees. τὴν παράδοσιν τῶν πρεσβυτέρων, "the tradition of the elders," is a technical term that refers to the oral tradition of the Pharisees (Jos., *Ant.* 13.10.6 §297; *m. ʾAbot* 1:1; cf. Gal. 1:14), which was an interpretation of the written laws of the Torah, meant at the same time to be a hedge around them. For the Pharisees *the* measure of righteousness and thus of loyalty to the Torah was obedience to this sacred tradition (cf. *b. Sukk.* 20a). The particular instance of violation the Pharisees focus upon is that of eating with unwashed hands (cf. Luke 11:38). The reference to eating "bread" (ἄρτον), which was the staple of the everyday meal, is a synecdoche for eating food. In view here is not physical cleanliness but ritual purity. There is no OT commandment concerning the ceremonial washing of hands before the eating of ordinary meals. The Pharisees, however, had as their main project the reapplication of the ritual purity required of priests in connection with their temple duties to the table conduct of the ordinary family at home. The Pharisees in this instance had taken the commandment to priests concerning the washing of hands (and feet) before performing their temple duties (cf. Exod 30:17–21; for handwashing as a protection against ritual impurity, cf. Lev 15:11) and had applied it to all Jews in the blessing preceding the eating of meals (see *m. Ber.* 8:2–4; *y. Šabb.* 1.3d; cf. Mark 7:3–4). This reapplied rule of ritual purity had perhaps already been

widely adopted by the general populace (contra Booth; see Mark 7:3). The accusation against Jesus' disciples is also of necessity an accusation against the master of
the disciples, i.e., Jesus himself (cf. 12:2; Daube).

**3** Rather than defending the conduct of his disciples by answering the Pharisees (an answer, however, *is* given in v 20b), Jesus turns to the offensive by asking
the Pharisees a similar question but one that refers to a much more serious in-
fringement: "Why do *you* [ὑμεῖς is emphatic] transgress the commandment of
God [τὴν ἐντολὴν τοῦ θεοῦ] because of your tradition [παράδοσιν]?" The very
heart of Pharisaism, the tradition of the elders (= "your tradition"; contra Luz)
that was supposed to protect against the violation of the Torah, had in fact become responsible for (διά, "because of") the grievous transgression of God's
command. This accusation proves to be more devastating than that of the Pharisees against Jesus' disciples (v 2).

**4** That the charge contained in the preceding rhetorical question was not an
empty one is now shown through the evidence (γάρ, "for") provided in vv 4–6.
The direct citation of the Torah is set forth as the standard of righteousness. Matthew portrays the fifth commandment as being spoken by God himself: ὁ γὰρ
θεὸς εἶπεν, "For God said." Not merely human tradition is at stake here (cf. vv 3,
6, 9b). The commandment is cited in verbatim agreement with the LXX of Exod
20:12 and Deut 5:16, except for the omission of the pronoun σοῦ, "your" (one
occurs after πατέρα, "father," in the former passage; two occur in the latter). τίμα,
"honor," means to look after and hence to support one's parents financially and
not simply to revere them (cf. 1 Tim 5:3). The commandment is quoted again in
Matt 19:19 (cf. Eph 6:2). To the commandment itself is added the further, related commandment regarding "speaking evil" (κακαλογῶν) against one's parents.
In effect, denial of support to one's parents was the same as speaking evil against
them. The LXX of Exod 21:17 (cf. Lev 20:9; Ezek 22:7a) is cited nearly verbatim.
θανάτῳ τελευτάτω, lit. "with death let that one die," is a Semitism (reflecting the
Hebrew infinitive absolute) that brings special emphasis to the supreme penalty.
The teaching of the written Torah is unmistakable and emphatic: parents are to
be cared for and, indeed, with proper respect.

**5–6** By contrast with what God says, however, the Pharisees (ὑμεῖς δέ, "but
*you*," is emphatic) promoted a practice (λέγετε, "you say") that violated the spirit
and letter of the fifth commandment. If one designated by a formal vow one's
material wealth as a "gift" (δῶρον, used here in a technical sense; cf. the transliterated Hebrew κορβᾶν [קָרְבָּן, *qorbān*], "(temple)-gift" or "offering," in Mark 7:11,
translated δῶρον in both Matthew and the LXX), i.e., for the support of the temple
ritual, one was discharged from responsibility to one's parents, indeed—as Matthew makes explicit with the double negative οὐ μή, "not at all" or "in no wise"
(cf. Mark's οὐκέτι ἀφίετε, "you do not permit")—the money was no longer available for the support of parents. The tradition of v 6a is the exact opposite of the
biblical commandment (cf. v 4). This vow to give one's wealth to the temple was
regarded as sacred and one that once made could not be altered (cf. Deut 23:21–
23; Num. 30:3–5). For the sacredness of a vow taking precedence over even a
biblical precept, see *t. Ned.* 1.6.4. At an apparently later time the rabbis did allow
for the reversal of a Corban vow in order to uphold the commandment to honor
one's parents (see *m. Ned.* 9:1). Thus ὃ ἐὰν ἐξ ἐμοῦ ὠφεληθῇς, "whatever you would
have benefited from me," the parents' right to expect provision from a son, was

invalidated or nullified; in this way the parents were robbed of their rightful privilege (cf. Prov 28:24). The clear commandment of Torah was transgressed. And so Jesus concludes ἠκυρώσατε τὸν λόγον τοῦ θεοῦ διὰ τὴν παράδοσιν ὑμῶν, "you cancel out the word of God because of your tradition" (cf. v 3). See Fitzmyer for nonbiblical parallels to the Corban vow.

**7–9** Matthew adjoins the OT citation (Isa 29:13) at this point, following the preceding argument, in order to seal the case against the Pharisees. At bottom, the issue is one of hypocrisy, i.e., the pretense of obeying the will of God while in fact transgressing it. Hypocrisy, the art of seeming to be what one is not, is a particularly important subject in Matthew (see *Comment* on 6:2; cf. esp. chap. 23 *passim*, where ὑποκριταί, "hypocrites," is also applied repeatedly to the scribes and Pharisees). Isaiah had already talked about such hypocrisy in words that fit the pattern of the present situation so well that they amount to a prophecy, i.e., in the sense of typological correspondence between Isaiah's day and the time of Jesus. (This perspective accords well with Matthew's understanding of the fulfillment of the OT in the events concerning and surrounding Jesus.) The citation of Isa 29:13 is almost verbatim from the LXX, with only very minor changes in the first and last lines (i.e., vv 8a and 9b). The contrast between the lips or mouth and the heart in v 8 is found also in Ps 78:36–37. It is the last line in particular, however, that is so amazingly appropriate to the Pharisees: διδάσκοντες διδασκαλίας ἐντάλματα ἀνθρώπων, lit. "teaching doctrines, the commandments of human beings." Jesus' accusation is precisely that the Pharisees have supplanted the commandment of God with human commandments (cf. the allusion to "human commandments" drawn from Isa 29:13 in a similar connection in Col 2:22; Titus 1:14). Matthew elsewhere provides other examples of their practice (cf. chap. 23).

**10–11** Jesus calls the crowd together in order to make an important—indeed revolutionary—pronouncement that goes far beyond the issue of washed or unwashed hands by addressing the whole issue of ritual purity. The importance of the principle is emphasized through the opening exhortation ἀκούετε καὶ συνίετε, "hear and understand" (a formula used in Matthew only here; the combination of the two verbs, however, is found also in 13:23; cf. 13:13–15). Although Matthew has downplayed the radicality of the Markan account in the first half of the statement of v 11, especially in his omission of Mark 7:19b (see above *Form/ Structure/Setting* §B), the latter half of the statement in Matthew still contains the core of a revolutionary understanding of the law (see the interpretation in vv 18–20). The statement "what goes into the mouth does not defile a person" taken on its own terms can even here be understood to challenge the dietary restrictions of Lev 11 (cf. v 17), although that is far from Matthew's purpose (cf. v 20b). Matthew's use of στόματος, "mouth" (where Mark has ἀνθρώπου, "person," or the personal pronoun αὐτόν, "him"), is more in keeping with the explanation given in v 17 but may also have been prompted by its use in 12:34. The stress of v 11, at least as it stands in Matthew, however, is not on the first half but on the second half (cf. the emphatic τοῦτο, "this") of the statement (cf. v 19). The Pharisees, who might have been wary of the way in which the first half of the statement is expressed, even according to Matthew, would not have disagreed with the point of the second half (as explained in v 19). Defilement here refers to being made ritually unclean or impure (the verb κοινοῖ, "defiles," occurs in Matthew only here and in vv 18, 20; cf. Acts 10:15; 11:8, which refer exactly to becoming unclean through what goes into one's mouth; see too Acts 21:28; cf. 1 Macc 1:47, 62). On the importance of what comes out of the mouth, i.e., one's speech, see Eph 4:29; Jas 3:6. Matthew here is thus hardly to be understood as overthrowing the law, not even the ritual law (rightly Luz, Davies-Allison; contra Meier).

### Explanation

The error of the Pharisees and their scribes as revealed here can only be called a tragic irony. Those who were in principle the most deeply committed to the practice of the righteousness of the Torah, whose very tradition was invented to realize that righteousness, are shown here to oppose and invalidate a commandment of God through that tradition. In chap. 23 Jesus will return to criticism of the Pharisees. It would be a sad mistake, however, to let these passages dominate our assessment of the Pharisees and of Judaism generally. (See further *Comment* in chap. 23 on this subject.) Although the criticism of the Pharisees in Matthew goes back to the Jesus of history, it is beyond question that the degree of the harshness against them is to some extent heightened by the evangelist who, in addition to writing a historical narrative, is also addressing his Jewish-Christian community in their own debate with the synagogue, the contemporary manifestation of Pharisaic Judaism. Matthew, as we have seen, probably minimizes the implicit revolutionary significance of v 11a because he is writing to Jewish Christians (Mark, on the other hand, writing to gentile Christians, maximizes the point and makes it quite explicit with the editorial comment: "Thus he declared all foods clean" [Mark 7:19]). Even so, Matthew has not totally suppressed the radical truth that Jesus' words open the door to a new evaluation of the dietary restrictions, i.e., to the commands of the written Torah itself. For Matthew, Jesus alone is the true interpreter and upholder of the ultimate meaning of the Torah. It should be no surprise that it took some time for the implicit teaching of Jesus to be fully understood and implemented in the early church, especially by Jewish Christians. Thus we see Peter struggling with the issue in Acts 10:10. Yet even Jewish Christians such as Peter (Acts 10:28) and Paul, himself a former Pharisee, learn eventually that the distinctions of ritual purity have been done away with in Christ (Rom 14:14, 20). Matthew's conservative Jewish-Christian church may well have continued to observe the dietary laws as a matter of custom and to support their claim vis-à-vis the synagogue that they were the fulfillment of Judaism, but they would surely have been aware that their Christian counterparts in gentile communities and perhaps even other Jewish-Christian congregations had done away with such observances.

# Explanation of the Criticism of the Pharisees (15:12–20)

### Bibliography

See *Bibliography* for 15:1–11.

## Translation

¹²*Then the* ª *disciples came and said to him: "Do you know that when the Pharisees heard the statement, they were scandalized?"* ¹³*And he answered and said: "Every plant which my heavenly Father has not planted will be pulled up.* ¹⁴*Let them* ᵇ *be: they are blind guides [of the blind];* ᶜ *but if a blind person leads a blind person,* ᵈ *both will fall into a pit."*
¹⁵*Peter answered and said to him: "Explain [this]* ᵉ *analogy to us."* ¹⁶*But he* ᶠ *said: "Are you yourselves even yet also without understanding?* ¹⁷*Are you not* ᵍ *aware that everything that goes into the mouth goes into the stomach and passes into the latrine?* ¹⁸*But the things that come out of the mouth come from the heart, and they are the things that defile the person.* ¹⁹*For from the heart* ʰ *come evil deliberations, murders, adulteries, acts of fornication, robberies, lies, blasphemies.* ²⁰*These are the things that defile the person, but eating with unwashed hands does not defile the person."*

## Notes

ª Many witnesses (C L W 0106 *f*¹ TR lat sy) add αὐτοῦ, "his."

ᵇ D has τοὺς τυφλούς, "the blind."

ᶜ B D 0237 omit τυφλῶν, "of the blind," and the word is thus placed in brackets in the critical text. The shorter reading is not simply preferred over the others, despite the weight of B and D, since the longer reading more easily explains the various variant readings. See *TCGNT*, 39.

ᵈ Θ *f*¹³ mae have ὁδηγῶν σφαλήσεται καί, for ἐὰν ὁδηγῇ, "if he leads," resulting in the reading "If a blind person causes a blind one of the leaders to slip, also both will have fallen into the pit."

ᵉ ℵ B *f*¹ sa bo omit ταύτην, "this." Yet the word could have been deliberately omitted by scribes since the intended "parable" or "analogy" is not that which immediately precedes. Thus the word is placed in the text, but in brackets. See *TCGNT*, 39.

ᶠ C L W Θ 0119 *f*¹,¹³ TR syʰ insert Ἰησοῦς, "Jesus."

ᵍ ℵ C L W 0119 *f*¹ TR syʰ bo read οὔπω, "not yet," for οὐ, "not."

ʰ ℵ* W boᵐˢ omit ἐξέρχεται, κἀκεῖνα κοινοῖ τὸν ἄνθρωπον. ἐκ γὰρ τῆς καρδίας, "they come out, and they are the things that defile the person. For from the heart . . ." This is a clear example of omission due to homoioteleuton (καρδίας—καρδίας).

## Form/Structure/Setting

A. This passage extends the preceding pericope through further criticism of the Pharisees but most importantly through an explanation of the path-breaking statement of v 11. Teaching rather than controversy is the focus of the passage. The viewpoint of the Pharisees does not reflect the will of the Father but reflects instead an unfortunate blindness. Here again the full and harsh criticism of chap. 23 is anticipated.

B. Just as in the preceding passage, Matthew follows Mark (7:17–23; Luke has only the parable of the blind leading the blind [6:39]). The significant alterations to be noted are the following. Matthew inserts vv 12–14, the analogies of the plant and the blind leaders, the former probably from his own source, the latter probably from Q (cf. Luke 6:39). Matthew omits, just as previously in v 11, Mark's phraseology "Nothing [πᾶν] outside entering into a person is able [δύναται] to defile" (Mark 7:18), probably again because it is too radical for his Jewish-Christian readers. Matthew preserves Mark's πᾶν, "everything," but applies it to the fact that all food is digested and passes out of the body. Similarly, Matthew will have nothing of Mark's editorializing for his gentile readers, καθαρίζων πάντα τὰ βρώματα, "declaring all foods clean" (Mark 7:19), which he omits. Then at the very end of the pericope Matthew adds the words τὸ δὲ ἀνίπτοις χερσὶν φαγεῖν οὐ κοινοῖ τὸν ἄνθρωπον, "but eating with unwashed hands does not defile the person" (v 20), to conclude formally the controversy with the Pharisees in good rabbinic fashion. Attention is thus taken away from the issue of unclean food and directed to the original question (v 2) of eating with unwashed hands.

Among the less significant changes, the following may also be noted. Matthew adds ἀκμήν, "even yet," in v 16, thus sharpening the criticism of the disciples. In vv 17, 18 Matthew again (cf. v 11) substitutes στόμα, "mouth," for Mark's ἄνθρωπος, "person" (Mark 7:18, 20). In v 18 Matthew adds ἐκ τῆς καρδίας ἐξέρχεται, "come from the heart" (cf. v 19; 12:34; Mark 7:20–21). Matthew, in v 19, abbreviates Mark's list of vices (Mark 7:21–22) from thirteen to seven (the number reflecting representative completeness). In this list Matthew substitutes the adjective πονηροί ("evil") for Mark's κακοί ("evil"), modifying διαλογισμοί, "deliberations," and includes, as the sixth item, one item not found in Mark, ψευδομαρτυρίαι, "lies" (the word occurs again in the NT only in Matt 26:59; cf. *Did.* 5.1). Matthew omits six items from Mark's list simply to abbreviate, as is the case too with the omission (in v 20) of πάντα, "all" (Mark 7:23), and τὰ πονηρὰ ἔσωθεν ἐκπορεύεται, "the evil things proceed from within." Matthew thus abbreviates, as usual, but also changes his Markan source for theological reasons.

C. As in 13:36, the disciples, represented by Peter, seek and are given an explanation of the enigmatic saying of v 11, called here, in the broadest sense, a "parable" (v 15). Before that, the Pharisees are characterized through two different analogies. The passage may be outlined as follows: (1) the disciples' question concerning the Pharisees (v 12); (2) Jesus' answer through the analogies of (a) the plant not planted by the Father (v 13) and (b) the blind leading the blind (v 14); (3) the request for an explanation (v 15); and (4) the explanation of the earlier statement (v 11) by means of a description of (a) what goes in the mouth of a person (v 17) and of (b) what comes out of a person (vv 18–19) and (c) a concluding statement (v 20). An interesting syntactical parallelism is evident in the clause of v 17 beginning with τὸ εἰσπορευόμενον, "what goes into," and the initial clause of v 18, beginning τὰ δὲ ἐκπορευόμενα, "but the things that come out," each having two parallel prepositional phrases. A further structural feature is the function of v 20 as the inclusio of v 18b, so that the list of seven vices occurs between the two statements that those are the things that defile a person. Finally v 20b is itself a kind of inclusio with v 2, thus rounding out the pericope by bringing it back to its starting point.

D. *Gos. Thom.* 40 contains the same logion as in v 13 but probably is dependent on Matthew (cf. too Ign. *Trall.* 11.1 and Pol. *Phil.* 3.1). *Did.* 5.1 appears to quote part of the vice list of v 19 (cf. Mark 7:21–22) in the Matthean order and hence is probably dependent on Matthew.

## Comment

**12** Matthew's familiar τότε, "then," introduces the passage and the question of the disciples. That the disciples were disturbed that the Pharisees ἐσκανδαλίσθησαν, "were scandalized" (see *Comment* on 11:6), by the preceding exchange (vv 1–11) indicates that they too held the Pharisees in high regard. If the popularly recognized authorities on the righteousness of the law found Jesus' teaching objectionable, was not this something to be pondered? τὸν λόγον, lit. "the word," is here to be understood more broadly as "the matter" or "the statement," i.e., presumably that of v 11. Did Jesus know that he had offended the Pharisees, and if so, did it not matter to him?

**13**   Jesus' two-part answer was undoubtedly a surprise to the disciples because of its strong, unreserved rejection of the Pharisees. First Jesus implies that the Pharisees are not ἐφύτευσεν, "planted," by God, and thus God will pull them out of the ground (ἐκριζωθήσεται, lit. "will be uprooted," a divine passive), a veiled metaphor for destruction (cf. 13:29, the only other occurrence of the verb in Matthew). φυτεία, "plant," occurs only here in the NT; for the verb φυτεύειν, "plant," see 21:33, where the householder who plants a vineyard is God (cf. Isa 60:21; *Pss. Sol.* 14:3–4). The expression ὁ πατήρ . . . ὁ οὐράνιος, "heavenly Father," is a favorite of Matthew's (see *Comment* on 5:48). Only here and in 18:35 is this specific phrase modified not by ὑμῶν, "your," but by μου, "my" (but cf. 7:21; 10:32–33; 11:27; 12:50; 16:17; 18:10, 19, 35; 20:23; 25:34, 26:29, 39, 42, 53). This points to the special relationship between Jesus and God that enables Jesus to speak with incomparable authority and thus to exclude the viewpoint of the Pharisees so absolutely.

**14**   ἄφετε αὐτούς, "let them be," is apparently Jesus' response to the concern of the disciples reflected in their initial question. That the Pharisees were offended by Jesus' comment should not worry the disciples. For the Pharisees are but τυφλοί . . . ὁδηγοὶ τυφλῶν, "blind guides of the blind" (the same description, "blind guides," is used of the Pharisees in 23:16, 24; for the Jew as a "guide to the blind," see Rom 2:19). Those who follow the lead of the Pharisees are themselves described as "the blind." The absurdity of the situation of the Pharisees and their disciples is set forth in the proverbial image of a blind person leading another blind person, both of them falling into a pit (cf. Luke 6:39). It would be hard to find a more vivid image of lostness, hopelessness, and futility.

**15–16**   Peter, doubtless as the spokesmen of the other disciples, asks for an explanation of τὴν παραβολὴν [ταύτην], lit. "[this] parable," i.e., what so upset the Pharisees. The textually uncertain ταύτην, "this," would seem to refer to the analogy just given in v 14, or possibly v 13. But the explanation shows clearly that v 11 is in mind (with Davies-Allison, contra Schweizer). In Mark the request for interpretation of the "parable" comes immediately after the saying about what does and what does not defile (Mark 7:17). παραβολή (*māšāl*; see *Comment* on 13:3) is used here in the broad sense of proverb, riddle, or wisdom saying, suitable to the content of v 11. φράσον, "explain," is used only here in the NT (cf. the different word in 13:36). The response of Jesus involves a mild rebuke of the disciples (unusual in Matthew) contained in καὶ ὑμεῖς, "you yourselves also," and in ἀκμήν, "even now" (the only NT occurrence of the word). The disciples had already been initiated into the secrets of the kingdom (13:11) expressed through parables and had affirmed that they had understood "all these things" (13:51). Yet despite the fundamental importance of understanding (cf. 13:23), they were unable to understand what Jesus was saying (cf. the same failure in connection with the teaching of the Pharisees in 16:9–12).

**17**   What is ingested by humans (τὸ εἰσπορευόμενον εἰς τὸ στόμα, "what goes into the mouth") passes through "the dietary tract" (τὴν κοιλίαν) and into the "latrine" (ἀφεδρῶνα). Food is accordingly of little consequence to the spiritual state of a person. It would be possible from this verse to conclude that such defilement as may occur in eating certain foods is only temporary, except for the clear statement in v 11 that what is eaten "does not defile a person."

**18–19** By direct contrast, "the things that come out of the mouth" (τὰ δὲ ἐκπορευόμενα ἐκ τοῦ στόματος), i.e., the words one speaks, do defile a person (cf. v 11; cf. Jas 3:1–11). The words come ἐκ τῆς καρδίας, "from the heart," and thus have to do with the very nature of a person (see 12:34–35). And "from the heart" comes a veritable stream of wickedness. Matthew provides only a representative list of seven items (cf. Mark's thirteen), with one item, ψευδομαρτυρίαι, "lies," not from Mark's list, probably thought by Matthew to be particularly appropriate to things from the heart uttered by the mouth. It also brings to four the number of the second table of the ten commandments that are represented (in addition to murder, adultery, and stealing, which Matthew reorders to agree with the OT order, both in the MT and in the LXX). But if this was a concern of Matthew's, why did he omit Mark's "covetousness," i.e., the tenth commandment?

**20** The thought of v 18b is now repeated for emphasis. ταῦτα, "those things," are what truly make a person unclean (cf. τοῦτο, "this" [v 11]). Matthew's added final words in v 20b recall in a somewhat anticlimactic manner the initial accusation of the Pharisees and scribes in v 2, and at the same time divert the reader's attention from the possible implications of Jesus' words for the dietary law itself. Thus in Matthew's portrayal (in striking contrast to Mark's), Jesus criticizes only the tradition of the Pharisees and makes no radical reformation of the written Torah itself. What does not defile is eating with unwashed hands. For Matthew, Jesus and Jesus alone is the true interpreter of the law.

### Explanation

Above all others the Pharisees were respected and admired for their serious pursuit of righteousness (cf. 23:2–3). Perhaps this is exactly why Jesus criticized them so harshly. The source of their perspective was not God; they were themselves but blind guides of blind disciples. As had been pointed out in the preceding passage, they sadly allowed human teachings to cancel out the very commandments of God. They so valued the items of minor significance and a ritualistic formalism that they neglected emphasizing what truly makes a person unclean (cf. 23:23). The passage thus stands as a warning to all those who concern themselves with the intensive pursuit of righteousness and who in so doing elevate human tradition and formalism to a level equal with or even higher than scripture itself. The true problem of sin is not to be found in a failure to perform correctly some external minutiae of human making; sin is an interior matter that concerns the evil thought, words, and deeds that come from the heart. Moral righteousness is thus far more important than ritual purity. The fundamental problem of humanity is more basic than the Pharisees dreamed. The Pharisees simply failed to address sin as a radical human problem. The overcoming of sin, however, was essential to the purpose and work of Jesus (cf. 1:21; 26:28).

# The Faith of the Canaanite Woman     (15:21–28)

## Bibliography

**Burkill, T. A.** "The Historical Development of the Story of the Syrophoenician Woman." *NovT* 9 (1967) 161–77. **Dermience, A.** "La pericope de la Cananéenne (Mt 15,21–28)." *ETL* 58 (1982) 25–49. **Harrisville, R. A.** "The Woman of Canaan: A Chapter in the History of Exegesis." *Int* 20 (1960) 274–87. **Légasse, S.** "L'épisode de la Cananéenne d'après Mt 15,21–28." *BLE* 73 (1972) 21–40. **Neyrey, J. H.** "Decision Making in the Early Church: The Case of the Canaanite Woman." *ScEs* 33 (1981) 373–78. **Ringe, S. H.** "A Gentile Woman's Story." In *Feminist Interpretation of the Bible,* ed. L. M. Russell. Philadelphia: Westminster, 1985. 65–72. **Russell, E. A.** "The Canaanite Woman and the Gospels (Mt 15,21–28; cf. Mark 7,24–30)." In *Studia Biblica 1978,* ed. E. A. Livingstone. Sheffield: JSOT, 1979. 2:263–300. **Schwarz, G.** "ΣΥΡΟΦΟΙΝΙΚΙΣΣΑ—ΧΑΝΑΝΑΙΑ (Markus 7.26/Matthäus 15.22)." *NTS* 30 (1984) 626–28. **Theissen, G.** "Lokal- und Sozialkolorit in der Geschichte von der syrophönikischen Frau (Mk 7,24–30)." *ZNW* 75 (1984) 202–25 [ET in *The Gospels in Context.* Minneapolis: Fortress, 1991. 61–80]. **Woschitz, K. M.** "Erzählter Glaube: Die Geschichte vom starken Glauben als Geschichte Gottes mit Juden und Heiden (Mt 15,21–28 par)." *ZKT* 107 (1985) 319–32.

## Translation

[21]*And Jesus came away from there and went into the regions of Tyre and Sidon.* [22]*And look, a Canaanite woman from those regions came and was crying out,*[a] *saying: "Have mercy on me, Lord, Son of David. My daughter suffers severely from being possessed by a demon."* [23]*But he did not answer her with so much as*[b] *a word. And his disciples came to him and were asking him as follows:*[c] *"Send her away because she keeps hounding*[d] *us."* [24]*And he answered and said: "I was sent to no one except to the*[e] *lost sheep of the house of Israel."* [25]*But she came and began to worship*[f] *him, saying: "Lord, help me."* [26]*But he answered and said: "It is not right*[g] *to take the bread of the children and to throw it to the dogs."* [27]*But she said: "True, Lord, but*[h] *even the dogs do eat the crumbs that fall from the table of their masters."* [28]*Then Jesus*[i] *answered and said to her: "O woman, your faith is indeed*[j] *great. Be it to you as you want." And her daughter was healed from that very hour.*

## Notes

[a] א\* Z *f*[13] have the aorist ἔκραξεν, "cried out," instead of the impf. tense of the same verb; other witnesses (C L W 0119 TR) have the synonym ἐκραύγασεν, "cried out." Some MSS (K L W Γ Δ 0119 TR lat sy[h]) add αὐτῷ, "to him," while D has ὀπίσω αὐτοῦ, "after him," modeled on ὄπισθεν ἡμῶν, "after us," in v 23.

[b] Lit. "did not answer a word."

[c] λέγοντες, lit. "saying."

[d] κράζει ὄπισθεν ἡμῶν, lit. "she keeps crying out after us."

[e] D adds ταῦτα, "these."

[f] προσεκύνει, taken as an inceptive impf., "began to worship." Some witnesses (א² C L W 0119 TR mae bo), however, have the aorist προσεκύνησεν, "worshiped."

[g] D it sy[a,c] have the stronger οὐκ ἔξεστιν, "it is not permitted." See *TCGNT,* 40.

ʰ γάρ, lit. "for." B syˢˑᵖ sa boᵐˢ omit γάρ, probably by influence from the Markan parallel (Mark 7:28).

ⁱ A few witnesses (D Γ saᵐˢˢ) omit ὁ Ἰησοῦς, perhaps through influence of the preceding narrative (i.e., vv 23, 24, 26).

ʲ "Indeed" is added to the translation to bring out the emphasis on μεγάλη, "great," apparent from the Gr. word order.

## Form/Structure/Setting

A. The narrative returns to the miraculous deeds of Jesus, in this instance to a healing from a distance. Yet the focus here is not on the healing but on the gentile woman who makes the request. This raises the whole question of the relation between the ministry of Jesus and the Gentiles, a question that has already been raised in the Gospel (cf. 8:10–12, and especially 10:5–6 in the sending out of the twelve to extend Jesus' message and ministry). The remarkable persistence of the woman in this pericope, despite her open admission of the priority of Israel in the saving purposes of God, wins out in the end, and her faith is praised by Jesus.

B. Although Matthew is dependent on Mark for the story (Mark 7:24–30; the narrative is lacking in Luke), he has reworked it and has added important new material. The insertion of vv 23–24 gives Matthew's pericope its special character. There, after his initial silence to the woman's request and after her perseverance, which annoys the disciples to the extent that they ask Jesus to send the woman away, Jesus announces in a very strong statement that his mission is directed only to the house of Israel (cf. 10:6, in nearly verbatim agreement). But the remarkable woman is not discouraged by this implicit rejection and effectively presses her case. The other major change Matthew makes of his Markan source is in introducing direct discourse almost at the beginning (i.e., from v 22), whereas Mark begins direct discourse only in v 27. Thus Matthew recasts the earlier Markan material (Mark 7:25–26).

Among other changes Matthew makes, the following are the most interesting and significant. Matthew's transitional words are, as usual, his own (cf. his favorite vocabulary, e.g., ἐξελθών, ἀνεχώρησεν). Matthew adds καὶ Σιδῶνος, "and Sidon," to Mark's simple Τύρου, "Tyre" (the two names occur in Matthew only together; cf. 11:21–22). Matthew omits Mark 7:24b, 25a, which refers to Jesus going into a house, his desire for anonymity, the impossibility of keeping his presence a secret, and the woman hearing about him. Matthew goes directly to the woman's request for help in the words ἐλέησόν με, κύριε υἱὸς Δαυίδ, "Have mercy on me, Lord, Son of David" (v 22). Matthew then alters Mark's third-person statement that the woman's daughter had a πνεῦμα ἀκάθαρτον, "unclean spirit" (Mark 7:25), to the direct statement ἡ θυγάτηρ μου κακῶς διαμονίζεται, "my daughter suffers severely from being possessed by a demon" (v 22). Matthew furthermore describes the woman as Χαναναία ἀπὸ τῶν ὁρίων ἐκείνων, "a Canaanite from those regions" (v 22), in contrast to Mark's Ἑλληνίς, Συροφοινίκισσα τῷ γένει, "a Greek, Syrophoenician by race" (Mark 7:26). Matthew replaces Mark's προσέπεσεν πρὸς τοὺς πόδας αὐτοῦ, "fell at his feet" (Mark 7:25), with the stronger προσεκύνει αὐτῷ, "began to worship him" (v 25). Mark's third-person request that the demon might be cast out of the woman's daughter (Mark 7:26) is replaced in Matthew with the direct κύριε, βοήθει μοι, "Lord, help me" (v 25). Matthew omits Mark's ἄφες πρῶτον χορτασθῆναι τὰ τέκνα, "allow the children to be fed first" (Mark 7:21). Although theologically this fits Matthew's perspective, it takes the edge off the story of the woman's amazing faith. Matthew replaces Mark's παιδίων, "children," with the more appropriate κυρίων, "masters" (v 27). Matthew's climactic ὦ γύναι μεγάλη σου ἡ πίστις· γενηθήτω σοι ὡς θέλεις, "O woman, your faith is indeed great. Be it to you as you desire" (v 28), replaces Mark's "on account of this word, go; the demon has departed from your daughter" (Mark 7:29). Finally Matthew abbreviates Mark's closing sentence considerably by avoiding the mention of the woman returning home and finding her daughter well (Mark 7:30), instead simply noting that in that hour the girl was healed, without specific reference to the exorcism of the demon (v 28; this last verse is very much patterned after 8:13). Matthew thus again abbreviates Mark in this pericope but more importantly reformulates the story so as to put great emphasis on the exclusivity of Jesus' mission to the Jews and yet at the same time to recognize the reality of the faith of a Gentile.

C. Matthew's narrative consists of dialogue from almost the very beginning. In the exchanges, which are quite brief, the woman speaks three times (vv 22, 25, 27), Jesus three times (vv 24, 26, 28), and the disciples once (v 23). This gives the narrative a sense of motion leading to the final statements in v 28. Thus the healing miracle becomes primarily a framework and vehicle for the teaching with its climactic apothegm preceding the short notice that the girl was healed, as the following outline indicates: (1) transition to present pericope (v 21); (2) the woman's request (v 22); (3) Jesus' initial silence (v 23a); (4) the disciples' plea (v 23b); (5) the statement concerning Jesus' mission (v 24); (6) the woman's persistence (v 25); (7) the objection of Jesus (v 26); (8) the woman's retort (v 27); (9) acclamation of the woman's faith (v 28a); and (10) granting of the woman's request (v 28b). The most notable structural features are in the alternating definite articles (ὁ δέ/ἡ δέ) functioning as pronouns in the description of the dialogue (cf. vv 23–27) and the fourfold use of ἀποκρίνεσθαι in Jesus' response (vv 23, 24, 26, 28). Within this structure, the plea of the apostles (v 23b) is parenthetical. In the content of the dialogue, the two appeals of the woman are parallel (ἐλέησόν με, "have mercy on me" [v 22], and βοήθει μοι, "help me" [v 25]), and it is worth noting that each of the three times the woman speaks she addresses Jesus as κύριε, "Lord" (vv 22, 25, 27). Matthew's literary artistry is again at work in the construction of this pericope.

D. The similarity between this story and that of the centurion's request (8:5–13) deserves special notice. In both cases a Gentile asks for the healing of a valued child—respectively, a servant (if this is a son, the similarity is even more striking) and a daughter, both of whom lie in beds of torment. In both cases the strangeness of a Gentile's coming to Jesus is apparent. And especially if 8:7 is taken as a question, both demonstrate a striking perseverance. Both are ultimately praised highly for their faith (8:10; 15:28). Finally and most remarkable of all are the nearly verbatim parallel final notices about the granting of the respective healings.

## Comment

**21** Matthew's transition has Jesus leaving "there" (with Mark, deliberately vague). Gennesaret was the last place mentioned (14:34), but there is no necessity to hold that the events of 15:1–20 also occurred there. He went away, or possibly "withdrew" (ἀνεχώρησεν, a favorite Matthean word; cf. *Comment* on 2:12), into an area where he may have been less known, namely Tyre and Sidon. This could refer to the actual gentile towns along the Syrophoenecian coast (cf. 11:21–22; but also Mark 3:8) or to the larger territories known by those names extending far to the east of the towns, in which case the population could still have been largely Jewish. It is possible, but by no means necessary, to conclude from the Greek text (ἀνεχώρησεν εἰς, taken as "to come up to the borders of") that Jesus did not enter these territories and that the woman came onto Jewish soil to make her request (ἀπὸ τῶν ὁρίων ἐκείνων ἐξελθοῦσα, "she, coming out of those boundaries," in v 22). Cf. Mark 7:31.

**22** Matthew's ἰδού, "look," calls attention to the remarkable occurrence of a gentile woman approaching Jesus with a request. Matthew describes her simply as a Χαναναία, "Canaanite" (the only occurrence of the word in the NT), "from those regions." The term "Canaanite" has inevitable OT associations with the pagan inhabitants of Palestine displaced by the Jews and thus contrasts the woman all the more with the people of God (the term is also used for non-Jews in the rabbinic literature; cf. *m. Qidd.* 1:3; *b. Sota* 35a). As Mark's description of her as a Ἑλληνίς, "Greek," suggests, she was Hellenized to some extent, and almost certainly the conversation between her and Jesus would have been held in Greek. Yet, as emerges from the terminology used in her initial request as well as from her perspective in v 27, she was apparently acquainted with Judaism to some extent. Thus her opening words are properly Jewish: ἐλέησόν με, κύριε υἱὸς Δαυίδ, "have mercy on me, Lord, Son of David" (cf. the same cry of the blind men in 9:27; 20:30–31). The title "Son of David" (see *Comment* on 9:27) is a Jewish title for the Messiah (cf. 1:1; 12:23; 21:9; 22:42). For κύριε, "Lord," which the woman uses three times in succession in appeals for healing (cf. vv 25, 27), see *Comment* on 8:2 (cf. 8:6; 17:15; 20:30–31, 33). The verb ἐλέησον is commonly used with these appellations (see the same references). The verb ἔκραζεν in the imperfect tense, "was crying out," suggests the woman had to work hard to get the attention of Jesus, who was probably protected by his disciples (cf. v 23b). Although her cry is for mercy on herself (με, "me"), her request actually concerns her daughter who suffered severely (κακῶς, a word used often by Matthew for those who suffer; e.g., 4:24; 17:15) because she was "demon possessed" (δαιμονίζεται; see 4:24; 9:32; 12:22). See *Comment* on 4:24 regarding demon possession.

**23** Jesus at first ignores the woman's request altogether, speaking not a word (λόγον) to her. The justification for this surprising lack of response will be given in the following verse. The silence of Jesus, however, did not dissuade her, and she apparently continued crying out, much to the annoyance of the disciples (ὅτι κράζει ὄπισθεν ἡμῶν, "because she keeps crying out after us"). They repeatedly asked Jesus (ἠρώτων, imperfect tense, "were asking") to "send her away" (ἀπόλυσον αὐτήν), perhaps implying that Jesus should heal her (cf. 8:13; the verb ἀπόλυσον could be taken to mean "set free" [thus Légasse]). But Jesus does not heed their request.

**24** Indeed he announces again the purpose of his mission. These words appear to be spoken to the disciples, who may have expected Jesus to grant her request. They provide a justification for sending the woman away without healing her daughter. They confirm the limits he set upon their mission in 10:5–6. οὐκ ἀπεστάλην, "I was not sent," refers to being sent by God. As God did not send him to the Gentiles but to the Jews, so also he had restricted the disciples' mission to the Jews. The expression τὰ πρόβατα τὰ ἀπολωλότα οἴκου Ἰσραήλ, "the lost sheep of the house of Israel," is found verbatim in 10:6 (see *Comment* there; cf.

9:36; 18:12 and Jer 50:6). Jesus' mission to Israel is a matter of God's faithfulness to Israel (cf. Rom. 15:8), a point that must have been extremely important to Matthew and his readers in their argument against the synagogue. The apparent absoluteness of Jesus' statement here is conditioned immediately in this very pericope by his healing of the Canaanite's daughter and will be further altered as the Gospel proceeds (cf. 21:43; 24:14; 28:19). But if Jesus was perhaps about to send the woman away without answering her request, her renewed approach, recorded in the next verse, persuaded him otherwise.

**25** The remarkable persistence of the woman continues even after the rebuff contained in the exclusivism of the preceding statement. She is convinced that he is the Jewish Messiah and that he can heal her daughter. She thus "began to worship" (προσεκύνει, imperfect tense) him, a verb used with reference to Jesus in 8:2; 9:18 (see especially for parallels to the present story); 14:33; 20:20 (cf. 28:9, 17). Driven by a mother's love for her child, she again made her plea: κύριε, βοήθει [the only occurrence of this verb in Matthew] μοι, "Lord, help me," a re-expression of the request in v 22 but in more idiomatic Greek (cf. Ps 109:26).

**26–27** In the remarkable exchange that follows, the Jewish view of the salvation-historical primacy of Israel is assumed by Jesus and accepted without challenge by the woman. τὸν ἄρτον τῶν τέκνων, "the bread of the children," here is a symbol of the messianic fulfillment (cf. Luke 14:15; see *Comments* on 4:3 and 6:11) promised to and now in some way being made actual to Israel (cf. the symbolism of the feeding of the five thousand in 14:15–21). The "children" here are those who belong to the household and thus those whose right it is to receive bread (the children are equal to those who belong to the kingdom, οἱ υἱοὶ τῆς βασιλείας, lit. "the sons of the kingdom"; cf. 8:12). It is wrong (οὐκ ἔστιν καλόν, lit. "it is not good") to throw to dogs what belongs to the children. The Jews universally assumed that eschatological fulfillment belonged to Israel in an exclusive sense. Many also expected that the overflow of the abundant eschatological blessing of God would be made available to "righteous" Gentiles (i.e., by keeping the Noachic laws [Gen 9:1–17]). The woman seems to know of this widespread idea and thus that as a Gentile, though she had no right to the eschatological banquet itself, she might well be allowed to enjoy something of the overflow, here described in the image of "the crumbs" (τῶν ψιχίων, a word occurring in the NT only here and in the Markan parallel) that fall from the table (cf. Luke 16:21) to the "house dogs" (κυναρίοις, again in the NT only in these verses and in the Markan parallel). This word, used first by Jesus and then by the woman, recalls that Gentiles were sometimes likened to the unclean dogs that roamed the streets (cf. 7:6). κυρίων, "masters," suggests the superiority of Israel as the people of God over the Gentiles. The disarming response of the woman, ναί, κύριε, "true, Lord," reflects an acceptance of her position, but also a constancy of faith that impresses Jesus.

**28** The words of Jesus, μεγάλη σου ἡ πίστις, lit. "great is your faith," spoken here to a gentile woman, recall the compliment paid to the gentile centurion in the parallel story in chap. 8 (cf. 8:10, where a deliberate contrast with Israel is made). They also recall, by contrast, Jesus' rebuke of Peter's little faith in 14:31 (cf. 16:8), not to mention the unbelief of the Jews (e.g., 13:58). The address, ὦ γύναι, "O woman," reveals the degree to which Jesus was moved by this gentile woman's faith. The reward of faith with the granting of a request for healing is an important theme in Matthew (cf. 8:13; 9:22, 29; see *Comment* on 21:22). Jesus thus finally responds to the woman's faith with the good news γενηθήτω σοι ώς θέλεις, "be it to you as you want" (cf. a similar formula in 8:13). The short notice at the end of the pericope that her daughter "was healed" (ἰάθη) from that hour is exactly paralleled in the conclusion to the story of the healing of the centurion's son (cf. 8:13, with the only differences being ὁ παῖς αὐτοῦ, "his son," and the use of ἐν with the dative rather than ἀπό with the genitive, "in that hour" for "from that hour"; cf. 9:22 and 17:18, both with ἀπό and the genitive). The exorcism itself is not described. Matthew, like Mark, lets the conclusion of the story have its own impact and records neither the joy of the woman nor any christological conclusion that might well be drawn from the story.

### Explanation

The eventual answering of the request of the Canaanite woman, as with the healing of the centurion's son (8:5–13), are exceptions in the ministry of Jesus that are at the same time anticipations of the ultimate goal of the mission of the Christ, which is to bring blessing to humankind universally. The gentile mission will become increasingly clear later in Matthew (e.g., 24:14; 28:19), but it is especially important for the evangelist to stress the faithfulness of God initially to Israel, which is her salvation-historical right (cf. Rom 1:16). Jesus strictly limited his own mission, as he did that of his disciples, to Israel; but the time of the blessing of the Gentiles was indicated by Jesus explicitly and is foreshadowed here and there in the narratives. What becomes clear again from the present passage is a basic principle: that it is ultimately receptive faith and not physical Jewishness that determines the blessing of God. Paul maximized this truth as the apostle to the Gentiles. The latter can receive the privilege of the Jews through faith (cf. esp. Rom 4; Gal 3). Accordingly, the privilege of the Jews is no longer unique but is to be enjoyed by all who respond in faith (cf. 21:43).

# Healings on the Mountain    (15:29–31)

### Bibliography

**Gerhardsson, B.** *Mighty Acts.* 28. **Ryan, T. J.** "Matthew 15.29–31: An Overlooked Summary." *Horizons* 5 (1978) 31–42.

### Translation

²⁹*And passing on from there, Jesus came beside the Sea of Galilee, and having gone up on the mountain, he sat down there.* ³⁰*And large* ᵃ *crowds came to him, having with them those who were lame, blind, deformed, mute,* ᵇ *and many others. And they laid them at his* ᶜ *feet, and he healed them,* ᵈ ³¹*with the result that the crowd* ᵉ *marveled, seeing the*

*mute speaking,[f] the deformed whole,[g] and the lame walking and the blind seeing. And they glorified the God of Israel.*

### Notes

[a] πολλοί, lit. "many."

[b] The order of the preceding four groups varies considerably in the textual evidence. See apparatus in Nestle-Aland. The last word, κωφούς, can mean either "deaf" or "mute," or perhaps both.

[c] Many witnesses (C K P W Γ Δ f¹ TR sy^{p.h}) have τοῦ Ἰησοῦ, hence, the feet "of Jesus."

[d] D it sa^{mss} bo^{ms} add πάντας, "all."

[e] Many witnesses (B L W TR lat sy^{c.p.h} mae) have the pl. τοὺς ὄχλους, "the crowds," in keeping with v 30.

[f] B Φ and a few other witnesses have ἀκούοντας, "hearing"; others (N O Σ have ἀκούοντας καὶ λαλοῦντας, "hearing and speaking." These alterations are caused by the ambiguity of κωφούς. See above, *Note* b.

[g] A few witnesses (א f¹ lat sy^{s.c} bo) omit κυλλοὺς ὑγιεῖς, "the deformed whole," perhaps because it was thought to be redundant in light of the next clause concerning the lame walking, or because there are no other references to the healing of the deformed in the Gospels. On the other hand, more probably the phrase was added to make the list of those cured more nearly parallel with the four categories of need mentioned in v 30. The broad character of witnesses containing the words favors their retention in the text. See *TCGNT*, 40.

### Form/Structure/Setting

A. As in the similar sequence in 14:13–14, Jesus heals large numbers of people of a variety of maladies prior to the miraculous feeding of the multitude. This miracle summary is the last of a series (cf. 4:23–25; 8:16–17; 9:35–36; 14:13–14, 34–36), except for the brief note in 19:2, presented in this section of Matthew and represents a climax in Jesus' Galilean ministry (note especially the concluding reference in v 31 to the people glorifying the God of Israel). With the multitude in place, the narrative setting for the miracle of the feeding of the four thousand (vv 32–39) is established.

B. Matthew's miracle summary passage stands here in place of the story of a specific healing of a deaf mute in Mark 7:31–37 (lacking in Luke). Some similarities suggest that Matthew's summary is to some extent based on, or at least prompted by, the Markan story. Thus, although Matthew avoids the difficulties of Mark's geographical notice, both evangelists at the beginning make reference to τὴν θάλασσαν τῆς Γαλιλαίας, "the Sea of Galilee" (v 29; Mark 7:31); both refer to the bringing of the needy to Jesus, and Matthew's reference to κωφούς, "deaf" (or "mute") corresponds to Mark's κωφόν (v 30; Mark 7:32); both refer to healing (v 30; Mark 7:33–37); both refer to the amazement of the people (v 31; Mark 7:37); and, finally, both conclude with a statement of response from the crowd (ἐδόξασαν τὸν θεὸν Ἰσραήλ, "they glorified the God of Israel" [v 31]; "he has done all things well" [Mark 7:37]). Yet among all these similarities the actual wording of Matthew is totally different from that of Mark. Beyond these agreements, furthermore, are a number of important differences in addition to the basic point that Mark describes a specific incident while Matthew generalizes concerning Jesus' healings, referring to four basic types of malady. Matthew's healings occur on a "mountain" beside the Sea of Galilee, Mark's apparently in the region of the Decapolis. While in Matthew the sick are placed at the feet of the seated Jesus (v 30), in Mark those who bring the deaf mute beseech Jesus to lay his hand on him (Mark 7:32). Furthermore, while Mark goes into considerable detail concerning the technique used by Jesus on this particular occasion, Matthew simply records that "he healed them" (ἐθεράπευσεν αὐτούς), i.e., the sick. Furthermore, Matthew lacks the messianic secret motif of Mark 7:36. Thus this pericope is really Matthew's own formulation, suggested by Mark's narrative more than drawn from it or even based upon it. In Matthew, more than in Mark, this pericope serves as a transition between the preaching narrative and the feeding of the multitude (thus on the pattern of 14:13–14).

C. The pericope may be simply outlined as follows: (1) Jesus goes up on the mountain (v 29); (2) the sick are brought to him (v 30a–b); (3) he heals them (v 30c); (4) they are visibly restored to health (v 31a); and (5) the people respond (v 31b). Structurally, the most interesting feature is the list of four maladies in v 30 and the corresponding list of those healed in v 31. The latter is partly in chiastic relation with the former, except for the last two items, which occur in the wrong order (the χωλούς, "lame," should be last, and the τυφλούς, "blind," next to last for a perfect chiasm). It is a wonder that among the several textual variants pertaining to this material, none appears to be concerned to produce the exact chiasm. Two other items hinder perfect parallelism: the lack of a corresponding element in v 31 to match καὶ ἑτέρους πολλούς, "and many others" (v 30), and the use of the adjective ὑγιεῖς, "whole," to modify κυλλούς, the "deformed," instead of a participle as in the other three cases (v 31). V 29 reveals parallelism in the use of participles (μεταβάς; ἀναβάς) with the respective finite verbs.

## Comment

**29** According to Matthew, Jesus moves from the Syrophoenician coast (ἐκεῖθεν, "from there") to the Sea of Galilee and a "mountain" (τὸ ὄρος), i.e., a hillside along the shore of the lake (παρά, "alongside"), although which shore is not specified (cf. Mark 7:31, where the reference to the Decapolis necessitates the eastern shore). Matthew gives no indication that the crowds were composed of Gentiles. Jesus went up on the mountain and "sat there" (ἐκάθητο ἐκεῖ), very much as though he intended to teach (cf. 5:1) rather than to heal (teaching indeed may generally have preceded healing, and the fact that the crowd was with Jesus for three days suggests the same). This setting serves in turn the narrative of the feeding of the four thousand (vv 32–38; cf. John 6:3). For the significance of ὄρος, "mountain," in Matthew, see *Comment* on 5:1. Donaldson (followed by Davies-Allison; denied by Luz) has argued that the complex of ideas in 15:29–39, e.g., eschatological gathering of the people, healing, and the messianic banquet, point to the mountain as symbolic of Mount Zion and Zion eschatology (*Jesus on the Mountain*, 130–31). These ideas *are* in close conjunction here and make Donaldson's conclusion possible, though not quite necessary.

**30** As usual, the crowds flock to Jesus for healing. Here they bring those in need of healing, and they put them at the feet of Jesus in a gesture of obeisance and expectation. Of the four specific categories of need mentioned, only the κυλλούς, "the deformed," are not mentioned again in Matthew in healing contexts (nowhere else in the Gospels is there mention of the healing of the κολλούς, although the healing of the withered hand [12:10–14] could be included in this category; the only other occurrence of the word in Matthew is in 18:8). The three remaining words all occur in 11:5, and there are specific stories of the healing of the "mute" (κωφός) in 9:32–33 and of the healing of the "blind" (τυφλοί) in 9:27–31; 20:29–34. Both of these last two words occur in 12:22 (a man who was blind and deaf), while in the summary of 21:14 the blind and the lame are mentioned together. The representative character of the list is made clear by the words καὶ ἑτέρους πολλούς, "and many others." The healings are described only in the brief, direct statement at the end of the verse: καὶ ἐθεράπευσεν αὐτούς, "and he healed them" (cf. similar brevity and directness in other summaries: 4:24; 8:16; 12:15; 14:14; 19:2; 21:14).

**31** ὥστε, "so that," introduces the result: the crowd marveled (for θαυμάζειν, "marvel," cf. 8:27; 9:33). What they saw is described using the same four specific categories mentioned in the preceding verse, though not in the same order (note the similarity with 11:5). κωφούς, which can mean either deaf or mute, occurs here with the participle λαλοῦντας, "speaking," and thus is understood in the latter sense (cf. Mark 7:37). Seeing the evidence for these healings before their very eyes, the people responded by praising the God of Israel. This expression underlines God's faithfulness to his people and thus inevitably implies the fulfillment of prophecy (cf. the correspondence with Isa 35:5–6, where three of the four maladies are specifically mentioned; cf. too Isa 29:18–19), though this is not mentioned. It is particularly appropriate for Jews to glorify God in this way (for δοξάζειν, "glorify," in this sense in Matthew, see too 5:16 and esp. 9:8). The familiar OT phrase τὸν θεὸν Ἰσραήλ, "the God of Israel" (cf. Pss 41:13; 72:18; 106:48; 1 Kgs 1:48), occurs again in the NT only in Luke 1:68 and Acts 13:17. Contrary to many commentators (e.g., Gundry, Carson, France) it cannot be insisted that this language must come from Gentiles (cf. Isa 29:19, 23; Pss 41:13; 72:18; 106:48). The idea that the healings of this pericope were performed for Gentiles makes 15:24 and the narrative of the Canaanite woman absurd. Had the evangelist intended Gentiles, he would have made that clear. There can be no doubt that praising the God of Israel is appropriate in the mouths of Jews (cf. 5:16; 6:9). The implicit Christology involved whereby Jesus is the channel of such blessing to God's people, however, is also inescapably clear to the readers of the narrative in the larger context of the Gospel.

*Explanation*

Jesus' healing ministry continues, although as but part of the larger purpose of his ministry. The miracles point to the reality of Jesus' proclamation of the kingdom and of his identity as messianic king (note the resemblance to 11:5 in response to John the Baptist's question). It is the God of Israel who is at work in the miracles of Jesus. Matthew's emphasis on fulfillment elsewhere is exactly in keeping with this assessment. That this was particularly meaningful to Matthew's Jewish-Christian church in its defense against the counterarguments of the synagogue is obvious. If it is the God of Israel who is at work in the ministry of Jesus, then God's faithfulness to his people is confirmed in the same way that the limitation of Jesus' mission to Israel confirms it. Matthew's Jewish-Christian church never ceased giving thanks to the God of Israel, who was the God of Jesus and of the church.

# The Feeding of the Four Thousand    (15:32–38)

## Bibliography

**Donaldson, T. L.** *Jesus on the Mountain.* 122–35.

See also *Bibliography* for 14:13–21.

## Translation

[32]*And Jesus, when he had called his* [a] *disciples together, said: "I feel compassion for the crowd, because it is already* [b] *three days that they have remained with me and they do not have anything to eat. And I do not want to dismiss them when they are hungry, lest they should give out on the road."* [c] [33]*And the* [d] *disciples said to him: "Where in this wilderness will we get an adequate supply of loaves so that such a crowd can be filled?"* [34]*And Jesus said to them: "How many loaves do you have?" And they said: "Seven and a few small fish."* [35]*And after he had ordered* [e] *the crowd to recline upon the ground,* [36]*he took* [f] *the seven loaves and the fish, and* [g] *having given thanks, he broke the bread and was giving* [h] *it to the* [i] *disciples, and the disciples were giving it to the crowds.* [j] [37]*And all ate and were filled, and of the abundance of fragments they took up seven baskets full.* [38]*And the number of those who ate was four thousand* [k] *men, not counting women and children.* [l]

## Notes

[a] A few MSS (א W Θ) omit αὐτοῦ, "his."

[b] B omits ἤδη, "already."

[c] D* omits μήποτε ἐκλυθῶσιν ἐν τῇ ὁδῷ, "lest they should give out on the road," probably through homoioteleuton (θέλω—ὁδῷ).

[d] Many witnesses (C D L W Θ *f*[1] TR sy) add αὐτοῦ, "his."

[e] A number of MSS (C L W TR sy[h]) have the synonym ἐκέλευσε, "commanded," for παραγγείλας, thus conforming the text more to the narrative of the feeding of the five thousand (cf. 14:19).

[f] The witnesses in the preceding note have the participle λαβών, "taking," conforming the word exactly to the parallel in 14:19 (but cf. too the parallel in Mark 8:6).

[g] Many MSS (C[2] L* W TR sy[h]) omit καί, "and," probably by influence of the parallel in Mark 8:6.

[h] Many MSS (C L W *f*[1] TR) have the aorist ἔδωκεν, "he gave," instead of the impf. ἐδίδου, "he was giving" (cf. 14:19).

[i] C L W TR lat add αὐτοῦ, "his," in agreement with the parallel in Mark 8:6.

[j] C D W Θ TR lat sy[h] sa[mss] mae have the sing. τῷ ὄχλῳ, "the crowd," again as in the parallel in Mark 8:6.

[k] B Θ *f*[13] (א, ὡσεί) add ὡς, "about," through the influence of the parallel in Mark 8:9.

[l] The important witnesses א D lat sy[c] sa bo reverse the order, thus reading παιδίων καὶ γυναικῶν, "children and women." Although this is the harder reading (i.e., unlike the usual order and thus

perhaps original), the textual evidence in favor of the accepted reading is of a wider variety. See *TCGNT*, 40–41.

### Form/Structure/Setting

A. The healing ministry of Jesus is here followed again, as in 14:14–21, by the miraculous feeding of a multitude. This is the last narrative concerning Jesus' miraculous deeds before the decisive confession by Peter that Jesus is the Christ and the radically new turn taken by Jesus in the announcement of his suffering and death (16:13–21). Quite probably the pericope, although for Matthew it is a feeding of Jews, also contains symbolism that anticipates the ultimate blessing of the Gentiles—something also in view in the reality of the cross. The passage is thus a climax to the first main part of the Gospel as well as a preparation for the final and climactic part of the story of Jesus.

B. Matthew is again dependent on Mark for this pericope (Mark 8:1–10; it is lacking in Luke). Matthew follows the wording of Mark rather closely. Beyond small changes and rewriting, the following more significant differences are to be noted. To begin with, Matthew omits Mark's opening words, which seem to suggest a new setting, one later than the preceding narrative: "In those days again there was a great crowd, and they did not have anything to eat" (Mark 8:1). Matthew appends the present narrative directly to the preceding healings narrative, which provides the setting. Matthew alters the indirect statement of Mark 8:3 (ἐάν, "if . . .") concerning the dismissal of the crowd to the direct statement οὐ θέλω, μήποτε, "I do not want to . . . , lest" (v 32). Matthew omits Mark's note "and some of them had come from afar" (Mark 8:3; cf. v 32) in characteristic abbreviation of his source. Similarly, Matthew omits Mark's separate notice about the fish (i.e., all of Mark 8:7) and places the reference to fish earlier in the disciples' response to Jesus' question, on the model of the feeding of the five thousand (Mark 8:5; v 34; cf. 14:17), as well as in Jesus' blessing of the bread (v 36; cf. Mark 8:6). As in the narrative of the feeding of the five thousand (14:19), Matthew abbreviates Mark by omitting the verb παρατιθέναι, "distribute," which occurs here twice (Mark 8:6). In v 37 Matthew adds two words to heighten the impact of the narrative: πάντες, "all," ate (cf. 14:20; Mark 6:42) and the seven baskets of fragments were πλήρεις, "full" (cf. 14:20). This emphasis continues in the last verse of Matthew's narrative, where οἱ δὲ ἐσθίοντες, "those who ate," is added as well as ἄνδρες χωρὶς γυναικῶν καὶ παιδίων, "men, without women and children," after the reference to the number "four thousand" (cf. the same wording in 14:21). Matthew thus has abbreviated Mark, though not as much as usual because Mark's narrative is already terse; Matthew has also intensified the report of the miracle by slight modifications.

C. The structure of this pericope, especially after the opening verse, is very similar to that of the narrative of the feeding of the five thousand (see *Form/Structure/Setting* for 14:13–21). Here again there is no concluding reference to the crowd's reaction, nor is a christological point drawn. The story stands by itself. The pericope may be outlined as follows: (1) Jesus' compassion upon the hungry people (v 32); (2) the problem (v 33); (3) the scanty resources (v 34); and (4) the solution, consisting of (a) the miracle (vv 35–37a), (b) the abundance (v 37b), and (c) the number fed (v 38). No striking syntactic parallelism is evident in the pericope, which consists of straightforward narrative.

D. Why do Mark and Matthew have two such remarkably similar stories of the miraculous feedings of multitudes (with the present pericope and its Markan parallel, cf. 14:13–21 and Mark 6:32–44), and what is the relationship between the two stories? It is clear that both Mark and Matthew regard the accounts as describing separate events. Both evangelists indeed deliberately compare and contrast the two feedings at a later point (16:5–12; cf. Mark 8:14–21), and there, as in the respective narratives themselves, the specific details of the two stories are kept carefully distinct.

Thus in particular we may note in the feeding of the five thousand the consistent reference to: the lateness of the hour; five loaves and two fish ($i\chi\theta\dot{\nu}\alpha\varsigma$); the crowd lying on the grass ($\chi\dot{o}\rho\tau\sigma\varsigma$), and twelve baskets ($\kappa o\phi\dot{\iota}\nu\sigma\nu\varsigma$) of remainders. By contrast, in the feeding of the four thousand note the consistent reference to: the third day; seven loaves and a few fish ($i\chi\theta\dot{\nu}\delta\iota\alpha$, diminutive, "little fish" [but also $i\chi\theta\dot{\nu}\alpha\varsigma$ in v 36]); the crowd lying on the ground ($\gamma\tilde{\eta}\nu$); and seven baskets ($\sigma\pi\nu\rho\dot{\iota}\delta\alpha\varsigma$) of remainders. A few of these are deliberately emphasized in 16:9–10 (cf. Mark 8:19–20). There are further differences to be noted as well, especially toward the beginning of the pericopes. In the narrative of the feeding of the five thousand, it is the disciples who take the initiative and approach Jesus concerning the need of the people, suggesting that Jesus dismiss the crowds so they can obtain food. Then Jesus says "you give them something to eat" (14:15; cf. Mark 6:37). In the narrative of the feeding of the four thousand, it is Jesus who takes the initiative (so too in the question of Jesus in John 6:5), noting that the crowds have nothing to eat and that he does not want to send them on the road with such hunger.

The differences between the two narratives noted thus far are important. They underline the fact that both Mark and Matthew believed the stories described two separate events (so especially 16:9–10; Mark 8:19–20). On the other hand, the remarkable similarities between the stories point to the possibility, or perhaps probability, that the narratives describe what was originally one miraculous feeding.

The similarities to be noted are the following. First, the larger framework of the two narratives is quite parallel: each occurs after an extensive healing ministry (14:14 [cf. Luke 9:11]; 15:29–31 [Mark 7:31–37]); each is followed by a boat trip (14:22–33 [Mark 6:45–51]; 15:39 [Mark 8:10]). Within the narratives themselves are the following similarities: both occur in a deserted area ($\check{e}\rho\eta\mu\sigma\varsigma$: 14:15 [Mark 6:35]; $\dot{e}\rho\eta\mu\dot{\iota}\alpha$: 15:33 [Mark 8:4]); both employ $\check{\eta}\delta\eta$, "already," though the first relates to the hour, the second to the third day; both take up the question of the dismissal of the crowd; in both Jesus asks concerning the resources (Mark 6:38, repeated verbatim in the second narrative, Matt 15:34); in both the disciples report what is available. What follows in both narratives is the particularly striking common succession, in nearly verbatim language, of the command to recline, taking the food, giving thanks for it, breaking it, giving it to the disciples and thereby then to the crowd, the reference to all eating and being filled, the taking up of the leftover fragments, and finally the report of the number who had eaten.

It can hardly be denied that even if the feedings of the four and five thousand were actually different events, the second narrative is patterned after the first and there has been crossover or reciprocal influence in the language used to describe them. But these similarities may equally well point to the conclusion that we have here variant versions describing what was originally but one event. What inclines one to this conclusion more than anything else is the extreme improbability that after experiencing the feeding of the five thousand and now being confronted with an almost identical situation with seven loaves of bread and a few small fish in their baskets, the disciples should ask, "Where are we to get bread enough in the desert to feed so great a crowd?" (v 33 [Mark 8:4]; RSV).

But if these two narratives were originally variant versions of the same miraculous feeding of a multitude, why does Mark, and Matthew following Mark (but note that Luke and John include only the story of the feeding of the five thousand), include both and deliberately insist on their independence (i.e., in 16:9–10; Mark 8:19–20)? Mark had available to him two very similar stories that were different, however, in important specific details—some of which had probably already assumed symbolic importance (see below). Rather than choosing only one account and omitting the other, Mark included both, thereby preserving the important symbolic meaning in each, the one feeding representing the provision for the Jews, the other for the nations. If, as Mark may imply (but cf. Mark 8:1, which makes somewhat of a break with the preceding narrative), the feeding of the four thousand took place in the region of the Decapolis (Mark 7:31), this may also suggest gentile associations, even though there is little hint from Mark (even less from Matthew) that the four thousand were anything other than Jews. Note too how the Gentiles are considered earlier in the chapter, explicitly in vv 21–28 and perhaps implicitly in vv 11, 17–20, with their critique of the ceremonial law that divides Jew and Gentile. It may furthermore have been thought desirable to preserve the accounts of the two feeding miracles to match the two of Moses (Exod 16; Num 11) and Elijah (2 Kgs 4:1–7, 38–44), who are soon to be mentioned in 17:1–8, although they are eclipsed in importance by Jesus.

Although it is of course not impossible that there were two similar, miraculous feedings, the data surveyed above seem more consistent with the hypothesis of one original event that came to be transmitted in two different versions, each with its own symbolism.

## Comment

**32** The presence of the crowd with Jesus for "already three days" (ἤδη ἡμέραι τρεῖς; "a parenthetical nominative," see BDF §144) presupposes the setting of the previous pericope (cf. vv 29–30). Jesus "calls together" his disciples (προσκαλεσάμενος; cf. 10:1; 15:10; 20:25) and announces σπλαγχνίζομαι ἐπὶ τὸν ὄχλον, "I feel compassion for the crowd" (similarly, 9:36; 14:14; cf. 20:34), because they had nothing to eat. In keeping with this compassion, Matthew has Jesus assert ἀπολῦσαι αὐτοὺς νήστεις οὐ θέλω, "I do not want to dismiss them when they are hungry [the adjective νῆστις, "hungry," occurs in the NT only here and in the Markan parallel (Mark 8:3)], "lest they should give out" (ἐκλυθῶσιν, in the Gospels only here and Mark 8:3). Thus in this pericope the suggestion of the disciples in 14:15 seems to be anticipated and answered before it is made. Furthermore, here Jesus is the one who initially feels concern for the people and thus will not send them away. The fear that the people might faint on the road is unique to this pericope.

**33** Matthew's abbreviation of Mark in the narrative of the feeding of the five thousand results in the omission of the question or the equivalent of the question that is asked here (cf. Mark 6:37, which, however, is implied in the disciples' remark in 14:17). The disciples' question virtually precludes any knowledge of a previous miraculous feeding, such as that of the five thousand in chap. 14. They apparently know of no way that this multitude (ὄχλον τοσοῦτον, "such a crowd") could be fed short of dismissing them to make their way home. χορτάσαι, "to feed" or "to be filled," is the same verb found in 14:20 and in v 37 in the report that all were filled.

**34** The opening words, λέγει αὐτοῖς ... πόσους ἄρτους ἔχετε, "said to them: 'How many loaves do you have?'" agree verbatim with Mark 6:38 in the narrative concerning the five thousand (cf. Mark 8:5). The answer of the disciples, according to Matthew, is at once similar and dissimilar to the answer of the disciples in the feeding of the five thousand. By the addition of ὀλίγα ἰχθύδια, "a few small fish" (lacking in Mark at this point [8:6] but drawn from 8:7), the answer becomes similar to that in 14:17. At the same time, the difference is also clear. Here it is ἑπτὰ καὶ ὀλίγα ἰχθύδια, "seven (loaves) and a few small fish," whereas in the feeding of the five thousand it is πέντε ἄρτους καὶ δύο ἰχθύας, "five loaves and two fish" (14:17). On the number "seven" in the "seven loaves," see *Comment* on v 37. The difference in the number of loaves is specifically noted in 16:9–10, where, however, the number of fish is not mentioned. The use of the diminutive ἰχθύδια, "small fish," used only here and in the Markan parallel, would be more important except that the ordinary word ἰχθύας, "fish," is used in v 36.

**35–36** The statement of v 35 agrees with that of 14:19a, although the vocabulary differs: παραγγείλας is used for κελεύσας (both meaning "having commanded"); ἀναπεσεῖν is used for ἀνακλιθῆναι (both meaning "to recline"); and γῆν, "ground," is used for χόρτου, "grass." After this, however, the vocabulary agrees closely, reflecting as it does the church's liturgical language used in celebrating the eucharist. Thus the four verbal forms, ἔλαβεν, "he took" (cf. λαβών, "having taken" [14:19]), the seven loaves and the fish, εὐχαριστήσας, "having given thanks" (cf. εὐλόγησεν, "he blessed" [14:19]), ἔκλασεν, "he broke (them)" (cf. κλάσας, "having broken [them]" [14:19]), and ἐδίδου, "he began to give" (ἔδωκεν, "he gave" [14:19]), it to the disciples, all correspond closely to the same verbs used in the institution of the Lord's Supper in 26:26. If there are gentile associations in the symbolism of seven loaves and the seven baskets of fragments left over (see *Comment* on v 37; cf. 16:9–10), the allusions to the eucharist, with its universal implications, take on special meaning. Only one element of 14:19 not found here, namely the "looking up into the sky," is also not found in 26:26. The close correspondence among v 36, 14:19, and 26:26 is striking. Matthew's ἰχθύας, "fish," is lacking in the Markan account at this point and fails to preserve the distinction between the "fish" of the narrative of the feeding of the five thousand and the "little fish" (ἰχθύδια) of the present narrative (v 34; Mark 8:7).

**37** This verse repeats 14:20 verbatim except for a very slight change in word order in the middle of the verse and the key words at the end of the verse, ἑπτὰ σπυρίδας, "seven baskets" (cf. δώδεκα κοφίνους, "twelve baskets," in 14:20). The importance of this difference is clear from the notice taken of it in 16:9–10. The type of basket referred to here was a more flexible basket than the baskets (probably wicker) referred to in the narrative of the feeding of the five thousand (cf. 14:20). That there were seven loaves and seven baskets full of remaining fragments in this feeding of the multitude cannot be accidental. The number seven points to fullness and perfection, or, somewhat less plausibly, to the "seventy" gentile nations. Much less likely is Lohmeyer's suggestion that the number refers to the seven deacons of Acts 6:1–6, who after all were Hellenistic Jews and not Gentiles. If it is taken in conjunction with the twelve baskets full of remainders in the feeding of the five thousand, which almost certainly points to the twelve tribes of Israel (or the twelve disciples), i.e., the Jews, then the sevens—even though those who actually had been fed were Jews—may well symbolize the meeting of the needs of the Gentiles, i.e., the fullness of messianic provision for the entire world. "All" ($\pi\acute{a}\nu\tau\epsilon\varsigma$) ate and "were satisfied" ($\acute{\epsilon}\chi o\rho\tau\acute{a}\sigma\theta\eta\sigma a\nu$), together with the abundance ($\tau\grave{o}$ $\pi\epsilon\rho\iota\sigma\sigma\epsilon\hat{v}o\nu$) reflected in the seven baskets of remainders, has here as in 14:20 eschatological overtones (see *Comment* there) that are consistent with this interpretation.

**38** This statement is merely a verbatim repetition of 14:21, the only changes being obviously the number itself, the omission here of $\acute{\omega}\sigma\epsilon\acute{\iota}$, "about," the transposition of $\acute{a}\nu\delta\rho\epsilon\varsigma$, "men," and the number $\tau\epsilon\tau\rho a\kappa\iota\sigma\chi\acute{\iota}\lambda\iota o\iota$, "four thousand." The number is regarded as approximate, despite the omission of $\acute{\omega}\sigma\epsilon\acute{\iota}$, "about." If we are correct in thinking that the feeding of the five thousand is associated with the Jews (twelve baskets of fragments) and that the present feeding suggests provision for the Gentiles (seven loaves and seven baskets of fragments), then the smaller number of four thousand in reference to the Gentiles may subtly point to Israel's priority in the reception of the abundance of eschatological blessing.

### Explanation

At first glance this miracle involving the feeding of the four thousand seems to be merely a less impressive repetition of the miracle of the feeding of the five thousand. Both stories are clearly stories of messianic provision foreshadowing the blessings of the eschaton, and this one, especially in retrospect, intimates the extension of messianic blessing even to the Gentiles. The fulfillment brought by Jesus is finally to involve the feeding of the hungry of the nations. The universalism implicit here is important to the evangelist's understanding of the meaning and significance of Jesus' messianic mission. Theologically, this feeding, like that of the five thousand, is closely related to the feeding symbolized in the eucharist, which also points in its own way to the experience of eschatological blessing. The feeding of the four thousand points to the blessing of the Gentiles, who, together with Israel, will also be the recipients of eschatological blessing through the provision of Jesus.

# The Seeking of a Sign    (15:39–16:4)

### Bibliography

**Edwards, R. A.** *The Sign of Jonah.* SBT 2.18. London: SCM, 1971. **Hirunima, T.** "Matthew 16,2b–3." In *New Testament Textual Criticism.* FS B. M. Metzger, ed. E. J. Epp and G. D. Fee. Oxford: Clarendon, 1981. 35–45. **März, C.-P.** "Lk 12,54b–56 par Mt 16,2b.3 und die Akoluthie der Redequelle." *SNTU* 11 (1986) 83–96.

## Translation

³⁹*And when he had dismissed the crowd, he got into the boat, and he came to the region of Magadan.*[a]

¹⁶:¹*And the Pharisees and Sadducees came to him, and to test*[b] *him they asked him to show them a sign from heaven.* ²*But he, answering, said to them: "[When evening has come, you say: 'It will be fair weather, for the sky is red.'* ³*And early in the morning: 'It will be stormy today, for the sky*[c] *is dark and red.' How, on the one hand, do you know how to discern the face of the sky, but, on the other, you are not able to discern*[d] *the signs of the times?]*[e] ⁴*An evil and adulterous*[f] *generation seeks a sign, and no sign will be given to it except the sign of Jonah."*[g] *And he left them and went away.*

## Notes

[a] Many MSS have Μαγδαλά, "Magdala" (L Θ f¹,¹³ TR syʰ), or Μαγδαλάν, "Magdalan" (C N W 33 mae bo), both of which mean in Aram. and Heb. "Tower," rather than Μαγαδάν, "Magadan" (thus ℵ* B D). The variants may have in mind the town of Migdal on the west coast of the Sea (cf. Luke 8:2, "Magdalene," i.e., from Migdal). Magadan is a name not known elsewhere (the same is true of Δαλμανουθά, "Dalmanutha," from the parallel in Mark 8:10). It is the "harder" reading and contained in the best MSS.

[b] The translation "to test" takes the participle πειράζοντες, lit. "testing," as indicating purpose.

[c] In place of οὐρανός "sky," D reads ἀήρ, "air."

[d] "To discern" is added in the translation. A few MSS add δοκιμάζειν (G N) or δοκιμάσαι (W), "to test," or γνῶναι (1012 lat), "to know," or for δύνασθε, "able," substitute συνίετε (S 700), "understand," or δοκιμάζετε (L), "test," by influence of the Lukan parallel (Luke 12:56).

[e] The long passage in brackets (vv 2–3) is omitted by important witnesses (ℵ B X Γ f¹³ sy ˢ·ᶜ sa mae boᵖᵗ). It may have been inserted from Luke 12:54–56 (although the wording is very different) or from some other source; contrariwise, if original, it may have been deliberately omitted by copyists in regions where a red morning sky does not indicate a storm, as, for example, in Egypt. It might, on the other hand, have been omitted because it is not found in the Markan parallel or in the otherwise identical pericope in 12:38–39. The passage is accordingly retained by the *UBSGNT* committee, but in brackets to indicate the uncertainty of the text. See *TCGNT*, 41.

[f] D it omit καὶ μοιχαλίς, "and adulterous."

[g] Many MSS (C W Θ f¹,¹³ TR it vgᶜˡ sy mae bo) add τοῦ προφήτου, "the prophet," through the influence of the earlier parallel in 12:39.

## Form/Structure/Setting

A. There is a certain irony in the sequence of the narrative, which has this request for a sign follow the healings and the feeding of the four thousand in 15:30–39. The "signs of the times" fill Jesus' messianic ministry, yet the religious leadership of Israel, represented in the Pharisees and Sadducees, is unwilling to accept available evidence. It is doubtful, however, that they would have found any sign convincing since Jesus did not fit their preconceptions and furthermore criticized their teaching (cf. the following pericope, vv 5–12).

B. Apart from the textually questionable material in vv 2b–3 (bracketed in the translation), this pericope is found in almost identical form in 12:38–39, where, however, it is the scribes and Pharisees who ask to see a sign. Indeed, vv 2a and 4 (except the last four words) agree verbatim with 12:39, which, however, adds τοῦ προφήτου, "the prophet," after Jonah.

The present pericope, like the former one, is drawn from Mark 8:11–13. Lukan parallel material is found in three different places (with v 1, cf. Luke 11:16; with vv 2–3, cf. Luke 12:54–56, where the thought is the same but the examples and language differ; with v 4, cf. Luke 11:29).

The differences between this pericope and its Markan source are minimal (if we disregard vv 2b–3). Matthew adds καὶ Σαδδουκαῖοι, "and Sadducees" (cf. the addition of τινὲς τῶν γραμματέων, "some of the scribes," in 12:38), in v 1, as well as rewriting Mark's slightly awkward sentence. The preposition ἐκ, "from" (with Luke 11:16, against Mark), replaces ἀπό, "from" (Mark 8:11), in the phrase "a sign from heaven." In v 2 Matthew omits Mark's note concerning the human emotions of Jesus, καὶ ἀναστενάξας τῷ πνεύματι αὐτοῦ, "and sighing deeply in his spirit" (Mark 8:12). In v 4 he adds καὶ μοιχαλίς, "and adulterous" (as also in 12:39), in describing γενεά, "generation." He again (cf. 12:39) omits Mark's ἀμὴν λέγω ὑμῖν, "truly I say to you" (Mark 8:12), and rephrases the content of the following saying, adding the reference to the one sign that will be given, τὸ σημεῖον Ἰωνᾶ, "the sign of Jonah" (the same addition is made in Luke 11:29; cf. "the sign of Jonah the prophet" [τοῦ προφήτου] in 12:39). Matthew's final note, καὶ καταλιπὼν αὐτοὺς ἀπῆλθεν, "and he left them and went away," is close to the content of Mark 8:13, where, however, there is also reference to getting a boat and crossing to "the other side," omitted by Matthew (but cf. v 5).

As for the bracketed material in vv 2b–3, it appears that we have a version of something that may have been in Q or different versions of Q (cf. Luke 12:54–56). The Lukan parallel is quite the same in concept, with the cloud in the west and the wind from the south being meteorological observations corresponding to the red and red-gloomy sky in Matthew. In the sentence of the application (v 3b; Luke 12:56), Luke begins with the addition ὑποκριταί, "hypocrites," refers to discerning the face τῆς γῆς, "of the earth," as well as that of the sky, has οἴδατε δοκιμάζειν, "you know how to test," for Matthew's γινώσκετε διακρίνειν, "you know how to discern," and finally has τὸν καιρὸν δὲ τοῦτον, "but this age," for Matthew's τὰ δὲ σημεῖα τῶν καιρῶν, "but the signs of the times." *Gos. Thom.* 91 contains a close parallel to the statement of v 3b. The version of the logion of Jesus given in v 4 is quoted by Justin Martyr in *Dialogue* 107.1, but in dependence on Matthew.

C. This controversy pericope continues an exchange between Jesus and his enemies, consisting basically of a request and a response, including a rebuke. It may be outlined as follows (1) transition (15:39); (2) the request of the Jewish leaders (v 1); (3) the response of Jesus, consisting of (a) an acknowledgement of their ability to "read" the sky concerning future weather (vv 2–3a) and (b) a faulting of them for their inability to read signs of a more important kind (v 3b); (4) rebuke and refusal (v 4a–b); and (5) transition (v 4c). The little parallelism in the passage is found in the response of Jesus in vv 2–3. In vv 2–3a each weather prediction is followed by a supporting clause πυρράζει γὰρ ὁ οὐρανός, "the sky is red," though in the second instance, the participle στυγνάζων, "being dark," precedes ὁ οὐρανός, "the sky." In v 3b, furthermore, the μὲν—δέ, "on the one hand—but on the other," clauses are syntactically parallel, although the infinitive διακρίνειν, "to discern," or its counterpart is lacking. The object of the first, τὸ μὲν πρόσωπον τοῦ οὐρανοῦ, "the face of the sky," corresponds to the object of the second, τὰ δὲ σημεῖα τῶν καιρῶν, "the signs of the times."

### Comment

**39** The dismissing of the crowd (cf. 14:15, 22, 23), which perhaps occurred with a formal blessing, is followed by a boat trip (cf. the boat trip following the feeding of the five thousand [14:22, 32]), which brings Jesus (but apparently not his disciples according to 16:5; contrast Mark 8:10) εἰς τὰ ὅρια Μαγαδάν, "to the region of Magadan." The name Magadan is unknown in ancient literature outside this occurrence, as is its location (cf. the textual variants mentioned in the *Notes*). Mark's Δαλμανουθά, "Dalmanutha," in the parallel (Mark 8:10) is similarly unknown. From Matthew alone it is unclear whether the healings of 15:29–31 and the feeding of the four thousand occurred on the western or the eastern shore of the Sea of Galilee. In Mark, on the other hand, the healings occur on the eastern shore in the region of the Decapolis (Mark 7:31), although the setting for the feeding of the four thousand is different in time and perhaps place too. Matthew's substitution of Magadan for Mark's Dalmanutha may have helped his readers, but it does not help us. If it was on the west side of the lake, then "the other side" of 16:5 would again be the east side of the lake.

**16:1** Matthew's grouping together of the Pharisees and Sadducees (the single definite article οἱ, "the," links them together) happens again in Matthew only in 3:7. It is particularly problematic when the two very different groups are linked in connection with their teaching (as in vv 6, 11, 12). The Sadducees have not been referred to by Matthew since 3:7. Although members of both groups sat together on the Sanhedrin, serving as the leadership for Israel, they were opposed to each other, differing quite extensively, especially in their doctrine (see discussion in next pericope). It is not unusual, however, for traditional enemies to unite against what is perceived to be potentially threatening to the status and welfare of each group. In this instance, Jesus' teaching overturned that of the Pharisees, and the clear messianic intimations of his ministry could well have suggested the danger of a popular revolt to the Sadducees. That their request for a sign was not an innocent one, i.e., in order to have the ministry of Jesus validated for them, is made clear by the participle πειράζοντες, "testing (him)." Their minds were already made up concerning Jesus, and now they merely tried to entrap him by finding something that could be used against him (cf. πειράζειν again in 19:3; 22:18, 35). The request for a σημεῖον ἐκ τοῦ οὐρανοῦ, "a sign from heaven," is for a display of power for its own sake and one that would present proof that was irrefutable (Luz: "a cosmic sign"). "Heaven" here is a circumlocution for God; hence, the request is for a sign from God. But when Jesus has been performing a host of signs of the kingdom and the response is unbelief, this is exactly the kind of request he will deny. Had he produced some extraordinary sign, his enemies would doubtless have accused him of sorcery. For further comment pertinent to this verse, see *Comment* on 12:39.

**2–3** The response of Jesus to this request begins with a criticism of these leaders for their inability to interpret the signs he has been doing. He alludes perhaps to a popular weather proverb concerning signs in the sky that could be interpreted to predict the weather that would follow (see *Notes* on the textual problem of vv 2b–3). The words εὐδία, "fair weather," and πυρράζει, "is red," occur in the NT only here. Although, on the one hand, the Pharisees and Sadducees could thus τὸ μὲν πρόσωπον τοῦ οὐρανοῦ . . . διακρίνειν, "discern the face of the sky" (perhaps here is a deliberate play on the word "heaven/sky" as it occurs in the request, v 1), from the signs that were available, they were, on the other hand, unable (οὐ δύνασθε, "you are not able") similarly to discern τὰ δὲ σημεῖα τῶν καιρῶν, "the signs of the times," i.e., the signs in the ministry of Jesus marking the dawning of the messianic age (the expression is used in the NT only here; for a similar use of the plural καιροί, "times," cf. Acts 3:20; for the singular in an eschatological sense, cf. 8:29; 13:30; 21:34; 24:34). How could such a situation be?

**4** For this verse, see the *Comment* on the nearly verbatim 12:39. Here the words τοῦ προφήτου, "the prophet," are lacking after the name Jonah, as is the further explanation given in 12:40. The sign of Jonah needs no explanation here, since it has been defined in 12:40. Here, as there, it is the sign of Jesus' resurrection from the dead (see further *Comment* on 12:40). That is the one spectacular and overwhelming sign to be given to that generation. The final four words of the pericope, καὶ καταλιπὼν αὐτοὺς ἀπῆλθεν, "and he left them and went away," serve as an abrupt ending of the conversation and a transition, together with the opening words of v 5, to the next pericope (cf. Mark 8:13, where the reference to going to "the other side" is included).

### Explanation

See the *Explanation* for 12:38–42. Given the new material of vv 2b–3, the following may be added. It is surprising that in a wide variety of different fields of knowledge human beings can be so knowledgeable and perceptive, yet in the realm of the knowledge of God exist in such darkness. The explanation of the latter sad state is not to be found in a lack of intellectual ability—no more for the Pharisees and Sadducees than for today. The evidence is there, examinable and understandable for those who are open to it and who welcome it. The issue in the knowledge of God is not intellect but receptivity. The "signs of the times," i.e., as narrated in the gospel of the ministry of Jesus, are there to be received and affirmed by faith. That is the key point. Again the further request for a sign under these circumstances only reveals an adamant refusal to receive the truth. To those in this unfortunate frame of mind the truth is that no sign will suffice.

# The Leaven of the Pharisees and Sadducees (16:5–12)

### Bibliography

**Mitton, C. L.** "Leaven." *ExpTim* 84 (1973) 339–43. **Negoitta, A.,** and **Daniel, C.** "L'Énigme du levain." *NovT* 9 (1967) 306–14.

### Translation

⁵*And when the disciples* ᵃ *came to the other side of the lake,*ᵇ *they had forgotten to bring bread.* ⁶*And Jesus said to them: "Be on your watch* ᶜ *and beware of the leaven of the Pharisees and Sadducees."* ⁷*But* ᵈ *they were considering this* ᵉ *among themselves, saying: "We did not bring bread."* ⁸*Jesus knew their thoughts* ᶠ *and said: "O you of little faith, why are you thinking among yourselves that you have* ᵍ *no bread?* ⁹*Do you not yet comprehend? Do you not remember the five loaves of the five thousand and how many baskets you took up?* ¹⁰*Or the seven loaves of the four thousand and how many baskets*

*you took up?* [11] *How is it that you do not understand that I did not speak to you concerning bread? But beware* [h] *of the leaven of the Pharisees and Sadducees.*" [12] *Then they understood that he did not say to beware of the leaven in bread* [i] *but of the teaching of the Pharisees and Sadducees.*

## Notes

[a] Some MSS (L W *f*[1] TR lat sy) add αὐτοῦ, "his" disciples, a natural but unnecessary addition.

[b] "Of the lake," is added to the translation for clarity.

[c] ὁρᾶτε, lit. "look."

[d] D it sy[s] have τότε, "then."

[e] "This" is added to the translation for clarity.

[f] "Their thoughts" is added to the translation for clarity.

[g] Many MSS (C L W *f*[1] TR sy sa) have ἐλάβετε, "took," a reading that can be explained by the οὐκ ἐλάβομεν, "we did not take," in v 7. It is less likely that ἐλάβετε, "took," would have been altered to ἔχετε, "have," despite its occurrence in the Markan parallel (Mark 8:17). Moreover, the MS evidence in favor of ἔχετε is much superior. See *TCGNT*, 42.

[h] Many MSS (D[c] W TR sy[h]) put the infinitive προσέχειν, "to beware," immediately after εἶπον ὑμῖν, "I said to you," thus making the last clause of the verse a part of the question rather than a new command (cf. KJV: "concerning bread that ye should beware of the leaven of the Pharisees and of the Sadducees?"). In favor of the critical text as it stands are א B C* L Θ *f*[1] sy[p] co.

[i] A few MSS (א* [33] ff[1] sy[c]) have τῶν Φαρισαίων καὶ Σαδδουκαίων, "of the Pharisees and Sadducees," in place of τῶν ἄρτων, lit. "of the loaves," probably through the influence of the phrase "the leaven of the Pharisees and Sadducees" in vv 6 and 11. Some other witnesses (D Θ *f*[13] sy[s]) have no modifier whatsoever, resulting in "not to beware of leaven, but of the teaching of the Pharisees and Sadducees." The modifier "in bread" could be an expansion; on the other hand, if original, it may well have been deleted as superfluous. The *UBSGNT* committee favors inclusion of the modifier τῶν ἄρτων, lit. "of the loaves," based on the important witnesses א[2] B (*f*[1]) lat co; Origen. See *TCGNT*, 42.

## Form/Structure/Setting

A. This pericope is placed here undoubtedly because of the reference to the Pharisees and Sadducees in the preceding passage. They had there requested that Jesus produce a sign from heaven, apparently not in sincere quest of the truth but in order to entrap Jesus. The negative view of the Jewish leadership, representing "an evil and adulterous generation," prompts a comment concerning the danger of their teaching. So much is clear in the present passage. At the same time, however, much in this pericope, which has been called "the most enigmatic" in the whole of Matthew (Green, 148), remains clouded and difficult, even mysterious. This passage, combined with the one that precedes, serves as a kind of final indictment of the Pharisees (and Sadducees) in the first main part of the Gospel.

B. Matthew continues here to be dependent on Mark (Mark 8:14–21; only a partial parallel is found in Luke 12:1). Matthew departs from his source in making certain changes, and as usual he also abridges Mark. The important differences are as follows. Matthew's opening reference to the disciples having come to the other side finds its parallel in the last verse of the preceding pericope in Mark (Mark 8:13). After these opening words and the note that the disciples had forgotten to bring bread, Matthew omits Mark's reference to the one loaf that was in the boat (Mark 8:14). In v 6 Matthew softens Mark by substituting εἶπεν, "he said," for Mark's διεστέλλετο, "he ordered" (Mark 8:15). In the same verse Matthew further substitutes the synonym προσέχετε, "beware," for Mark's βλέπετε. For Mark's difficult καὶ τῆς ζύμης Ἡρῴδου, "and the leaven of Herod," Matthew substitutes the more general καὶ Σαδδουκαίων, "and Sadducees," in keeping with the representation of the Jewish leadership in v 1. Among the few minor changes in v 7, we need mention only Matthew's ἐλάβομεν, "we brought," for Mark's ἔχομεν, "we have." In v 8 Matthew adds ὁ Ἰησοῦς, "Jesus," ἐν αὑτοῖς, "among yourselves," and his favorite ὀλιγόπιστοι, lit. "little faiths," and he deletes Mark's redundant οὐδὲ συνίετε, "nor understood" (Mark 8:17). Matthew omits the rest of Mark 8:17 and most of 8:18, which contain a harsh rebuke of the disciples for being hard hearted and for having eyes that do not see and ears that do not hear (in Matthew, the latter criticism is reserved for those unreceptive of the kingdom; cf. 13:15–16). Matthew abridges the remainder of Mark (Mark 8:18b–21), primarily by omitting the repeated reference to the baskets being "filled with fragments" as well as the answer of the disciples in each case, where they respond concerning the number of baskets, i.e., twelve and seven. Matthew apparently assumes these are well known from the earlier narratives and need not be repeated at this point. He also twice substitutes the synonymous verb ἐλάβετε, "take up," for Mark's ἦρατε. Finally, Matthew adds vv 11 and 12 to the Markan account, apparently to clarify Jesus' point in the pericope. The result is a return to the beginning of the pericope by the repetition of the warning concerning the leaven of the Pharisees and Sadducees together with the provision of the interpretation that the leaven is τῆς διδαχῆς, "the teaching," of these groups (v 12). We can thus see Matthew's special interests at work in some of his alterations of and additions to the Markan text as well as some of the customary tendency to abbreviate when possible. Above all, it is clear how Matthew has brought light to the meaning of Mark 8:15 by his addition in vv 11–12.

C. The passage consists basically of a warning given by Jesus that is misunderstood by the disciples because of their own exasperation at having forgotten to bring bread with them to their apparently isolated destination. The following outline may be suggested: (1) the problem of the disciples (v 5); (2) Jesus' warning (v 6); (3) the confusion of the disciples (v 7); (4) Jesus' rebuke, consisting of (a) the disciples' lack of faith (v 8), (b) the reference to the feedings (vv 9–10), and (c) the misunderstanding (v 11a); (5) the repetition of the warning (v 11b); and (6) the disciples' comprehension (v 12). The warning of v 6 is repeated verbatim (minus the initial ὁρᾶτε, "look") in v 11b, which serves therefore as an inclusio (cf. also v 12), lacking in Mark. Further exact parallelism is to be seen especially in vv 9 and 10 in the double question pertaining to the two miraculous feedings, although it is to be noted that the different Greek words for "baskets" are carefully maintained for the respective feedings, as, of course, are the respective numbers. Other formal connections can be seen in the repeated use of the verb διαλογίζεσθαι, "reason, consider," in vv 7 and 8, as well as the repeated νοεῖτε, "understand," in vv 9 and 11. The parallel prepositional phrases in v 11 present the distinctive Matthean interpretation of the Markan pericope, equating the leaven with the teaching of the Pharisees (and Sadducees). The leaven of the Pharisees in Luke, on the other hand, is identified as ὑπόκρισις, "hypocrisy" (Luke 12:1; cf. Matt 23).

*Comment*

**5** According to Matthew, the disciples apparently join Jesus, who has already come εἰς τὸ πέραν, "to the other side," of the lake. According to Mark, the discussion recorded here seems to have taken place "in the boat" (Mark 8:14). If Magadan (15:39) was on the west side of the lake, this appears to be the more deserted east side of the lake, perhaps with Jesus and the disciples on their way northward toward Caesarea Philippi (cf. v 13). The disciples embarrassingly had forgotten (the only occurrence of the verb ἐπιλανθάνεσθαι in Matthew) to bring food (basically "bread") with them and were accordingly upset.

**6** At this point Jesus delivers a strong warning to them (note the combination of ὁρᾶτε, "be on your watch," lit. "see," and προσέχετε, "beware," which is emphatic) concerning τῆς ζύμης τῶν Φαρισαίων καὶ Σαδδουκαίων, "the leaven of the Pharisees and the Sadducees." The disciples, with only bread on their minds (cf. v 7), apparently misunderstood the import of Jesus' statement. What Jesus meant by this rather cryptic statement will dawn upon the disciples only in v 12. It can only be guessed whether Jesus' choice of metaphor was itself occasioned by the disciples' concern over the bread. The warning is repeated verbatim in v 11, and its interpretation is given in v 12. The dynamic potential of leaven, but in a good sense, has already been used by Matthew in describing the kingdom of God (13:33, the only occurrence in Matthew of ζύμη, "leaven," outside the present passage). Here again the metaphor points to the spreading and permeating effect of leaven, but in a corrupting sense (the more normal use of the metaphor; cf. Str-B 1:728–29; 4:469, 474) and therefore as something to be wary of (cf. 1 Cor 5:6–8). The linking together of the Pharisees and the Sadducees with one definite article is again surprising (see *Comment* on v 1), especially when the leaven is defined as τῆς διδαχῆς, "the teaching," of these groups. See further *Comment* on v 12.

**7–8** These verses show the preoccupation of the disciples with bread, which causes them to miss the point being made by Jesus. The reference to ζύμη, "leaven," has apparently only the effect of exacerbating their anxiety concerning the lack of bread (cf. v 11a); to all else the disciples were oblivious. Notable in this connection is the repeated use of the verb διαλογίζεσθαι, "discuss" (a word with a negative connotation in Matthew; cf. 21:25 and the cognate noun in 15:19), with ἐν ἑαυτοῖς, "among themselves/yourselves." Jesus rebukes them for being so caught up with this problem, addressing them with the word ὀλιγόπιστοι, "people of little faith." In every instance of the use of this word in Matthew, it is addressed to disciples in a context where the question concerns their ultimate welfare and the reality of God's provision for them (cf. 6:30; 8:26; 14:31). The implication here seems to be that the disciples can trust God's provision for their physical need and that they ought not to be so distracted by the lack of bread that they miss altogether the point of an important spiritual warning Jesus gives them. The participle γνούς, "knowing," suggests an unusual or miraculous ability of Jesus to know what has not been told to him (note ἐν ἑαυτοῖς, "among themselves/yourselves"; cf. the similar use of the same participle in 12:15; 22:18; 26:10; cf. 9:4).

**9–10** The reference now to the two miraculous feedings is designed to remind the disciples of how faithful God is in meeting human need, even particularly in the matter of bread. The questions, οὔπω νοεῖτε, οὐδὲ μνημονεύετε, "Do you not yet comprehend? Do you not remember?" have the effect of sharpening the rebuke. Matthew emphasizes the abundance of God's provision in the specific mention of the five loaves and the five thousand and the seven loaves and the four thousand. His deletion of the answer to the question of how many baskets were taken up in each instance (cf. Mark 8:19–20) is an interesting touch. As in Mark, the question of the number of baskets (using the different vocabulary, κοφίνους and σπυρίδας) is raised, but the answer is left to be supplied by the reader on the basis of the accounts that have been presented in the immediately preceding chapters (14:15–21; 15:32–38). This test of the memory has the effect of drawing a heightened attention to the numbers involved in each case—the very numbers that are the key to the underlying symbolism of the two feedings, twelve and seven respectively, pointing, as we argued above, to the provision for Israel and the nations. Thus even in this passing mention of the two miraculous feedings, where the focus is on the divine provision for human need (cf. Mark 6:52), the numbers and their symbolism remain significant. Jesus makes the point that the disciples should not have become so concerned about their mundane needs, for which they could trust God, that they lost sight of things that really mattered (cf. 6:33).

**11** Jesus again expresses his disappointment (cf. v 8) over the disciples' failure to understand (νοεῖτε, as in v 9) his point by mistaking it for some comment about literal bread. He then turns to the truly important issue, repeating verbatim (except for the opening word ὁρᾶτε, "be on your watch") the original warning given in v 6 concerning the danger of "the leaven of the Pharisees and Sadducees."

**12** The disciples finally understand their mistake (contrast the disciples in Mark 8:21) in not realizing that Jesus had not been talking about leaven in bread but about the leaven that was τῆς διδαχῆς τῶν Φαρισαίων καὶ Σαδδουκαίων, "the teaching of the Pharisees and Sadducees." Here we have not only the strangeness of the linking of two such antithetical groups but the further and more difficult problem of the reference to their teaching (διδαχή) as though this were something they held in common. The teaching of the Pharisees, however, consisted essentially of the oral tradition constructed around the written Torah so as to insure obedience to it—the "tradition of the elders" (15:2). The Lukan version of this logion (Luke 12:1) appears to have this in mind to some extent in the description of the leaven of the Pharisees (there is no mention of the Sadducees) as being "hypocrisy" (cf. 23:13–36). The teaching of the Sadducees, if one may indeed refer to their views as any kind of coherent teaching, consisted of a denial of the authority of the Pharisaic tradition and of any accretions, such as even the prophetic writings, to the five books of Moses, which were alone regarded by them as canonical. Most notorious in the NT is their disagreement with the Pharisees over the question of the resurrection of the dead (noted by Matthew in 22:23–33; cf. Acts 23:6–10). In terms of their essential religious perspectives, it thus makes no sense to speak of "the teaching of the Pharisees and the Sadducees" (moreover, if the Pharisaic tradition is in view, the command stands in some tension with 23:2–3). But if instead we look for a particular "teaching" held in common by the Pharisees and Sadducees, keeping in mind the immediately preceding passage (vv 1–4) and the unified front of the two groups against Jesus (cf. 22:34; Acts 5:17), it could be found in a preconception of the nature of the Messiah and messianic fulfillment—a fulfillment that of necessity would include a national-political dimension (cf. their inability to read the "signs of the times" [v 3]). The "teaching" would thus be that of the united front of Jewish leadership, which was also widely held by the masses (and even the disciples, hence the appropriateness of the warning here). It disqualified Jesus from any claim to being the agent of messianic fulfillment. This "teaching" was indeed like leaven in that it affected all else and would indeed ultimately bring Jesus to his death.

### Explanation

The disciples had not yet learned that they could trust in God's provision for their needs. They therefore fell into that very common error of letting relatively unimportant and mundane concerns block out the teaching of their Lord. The point was not that they should expect another miraculous provision of food but rather that they should not have allowed themselves to become so distraught over something so relatively minor that it controlled their very thinking (and hearing). If God is the faithful provider, as the miraculous feedings demonstrate, then no disciple should be threatened by insecurity and thus become sidetracked from the truly important or fall prey to false teaching. Once the kingdom is one's priority, mundane matters should no longer cause undue anxiety (cf. 6:25–33). It was more important to be vigilant against untruthful opponents.

# Peter's Confession and Commissioning (16:13–20)

### Bibliography

**Anderson, B. W.** "The Messiah as the 'Son of God' in the Old Testament." In *Christological Perspectives.* FS H. K. McArthur, ed. R. F. Berkey and S. A. Edwards. New York: Pilgrim, 1982. 157–69. **Basser, H. W.** "Derrett's 'Binding' Reopened." *JBL* 104 (1985) 297–300. **Betz, O.** "Felsenmann und Felsengemeinde." *ZNW* 48 (1957) 49–77. **Bornkamm, G.** "The Authority to 'Bind' and 'Loose' in the Church in Matthew's Gospel: The Problem of Sources in Matthew's Gospel." *Perspective* 11 (1970) 37–50. ———. *Jesus of Nazareth.* New York: Harper & Row, 1960. **Bousset, W.** *Kyrios Christos.* Nashville: Abingdon, 1970. **Brown, C.** "The Gates of Hell and the Church." In *Church, Word and Spirit.* FS G. W. Bromiley, ed. J. Bradley and R. Muller. Grand Rapids: Eerdmans, 1987. 15–43. **Brown, R. E., Donfried, K. P., and Reumann, J.** *Peter in the New Testament.* Minneapolis: Augsburg, 1973. **Büchsel, F.** "δέω (λύω)." *TDNT* 2:60–61. **Bultmann, R.** "Die Frage nach dem messianischen Bewusstsein Jesu und das Petrus-Bekenntnis." In *Exegetica.*, ed. E. Dinkler. Tübingen: Mohr, 1967. 1–9. ———. "Die Frage nach der Echtheit von Mt 16,17–19." In *Exegetica,* ed. E. Dinkler. Tübingen: Mohr, 1967. 255–77. **Cadbury, H. J.** "The Meaning of John 20.23, Matthew 16.19, and Matthew 18.18." *JBL* 58 (1939) 251–54. **Caragounis, C. C.** *Peter and the Rock.* BZNW 58. Berlin: de Gruyter, 1989. **Carroll, K. L.** "Thou Art Peter." *NovT* 6 (1963) 268–76. **Claudel, G.** *La confession de Pierre: Trajectoire d'une péricope évangélique.* EBib n.s. 10. Paris: Gabalda, 1988. **Cullmann, O.** *Peter: Disciple, Apostle, Martyr.* Cleveland: Meridian, 1958. ———. "Πέτρος, Κηφᾶς." *TDNT* 6:100–112. **Derrett, J. D. M.** "Binding and Loosing (Matthew 16:19; 18:18; and John 20:23)." *JBL* 102 (1983) 112–17. ———. "'Thou Art the Stone, and upon This Stone . . . .'" *DR* 106 (1988) 276–85. **Duling, D. C.** "Binding and Loosing: Matthew 16:19; Matthew 18:18; John 20:23." *Forum* 3/4 (1987) 3–31. **Emerton, J. A.** "Binding and Loosing—Forgiving and Retaining." *JTS* 13 (1962) 325–31. **Falk, Z. W.** "Binding and Loosing." *JJS* 25 (1974) 92–100. **Fitzmyer, J. A.** "Aramaic *Kepha'* and Peter's Name in the New Testament." In *To Advance the Gospel.* New York: Crossroad, 1981. 112–24. **Fornberg, T.** "Peter—The High Priest of the New Covenant?" *EAJT* 4 (1986) 113–21. **Gero, S.** "The Gates or the Bars of Hades? A Note on Matthew 16.19." *NTS* 27 (1981) 411–14. **Grelot, P.** "'Sur cette pierre je bâtirai mon Église' (Mt 16.18b)." *NRT* 109 (1987) 641–59.

Gundry, R. H. "The Narrative Framework of Matthew 16.17–19." *NovT* 7 (1964) 1–9. **Hahn, F.** "Die Petrusverheissung Mt 16,18f." In *Das kirchliche Amt im Neuen Testament,* ed. K. Kertelge. Freiburg: Herder, 1977. 543–63. **Harnack, A. von.** "Der Spruch über Petrus als den Felsen der Kirche." *Sitzungsberichte der Preussischen (Deutschen) Akademie der Wissenschaften zu Berlin (Philosophisch-historische Klasse)* 1 (1918) 637–54. **Hiers, R. H.** "'Binding and Loosing': The Matthean Authorizations." *JBL* 104 (1985) 233–50. **Hoffmann, P.** "Die Bedeutung des Petrus für die Kirche des Matthäus." In *Dienst an der Einheit,* ed. J. Ratzinger. Düsseldorf: Patmos, 1978. 9–26. ———. "Der Petrus-Primat im Matthäusevangelium." In *Neues Testament und Kirche.* FS R. Schnackenburg, ed. J. Gnilka. Freiburg: Herder, 1974. 94–114. **Hommel, H.** "Die Tore des Hades." *ZNW* 80 (1989) 124–25. **Howard, G.** "The Meaning of Petros-Petra." *ResQ* 10 (1967) 217–21. **Immisch, O.** "Matthäus 16.18." *ZNW* 17 (1916) 18–26. **Jeremias, J.** "κλείς." *TDNT* 3:744–53. **Kähler, C.** "Zur Form- und Traditionsgeschichte von Mt 16,17–19." *NTS* 23 (1976–77) 36–58. **Kahmann, J.** "Die Verheissung an Petrus." In *L'Évangile selon Matthieu,* ed. M. Didier. 261–80. **Kingsbury, J. D.** "The Figure of Peter in Matthew as a Theological Problem." *JBL* 98 (1979) 67–83. **Klein, H.** "Das Bekenntniss des Petrus und die Anfänge des Christusglaubens im Urchristentum." *EvT* 47 (1987) 176–92. **Knight, G. A. F.** "Thou Art Peter." *Today* 17 (1960) 168–80. **Korting, G.** "Binden oder lösen: Zu Verstockungs- und Befreiungstheologie in Mt 16,19; 18,18.21–35 und Joh 15,1–17; 20,23." *SNTU* 14 (1989) 39–91. **Lambrecht, J.** "'Du bist Petrus.'" *SNTU* 11 (1986) 5–32. **Lampe, P.** "Das Spiel mit dem Petrus-Namen—Mt 16,18." *NTS* 25 (1978–79) 227–45. **Luz, U.** "Das Primatwort Matthäus 16.17–19 aus wirkungsgeschichtlicher Sicht." *NTS* 37 (1991) 415–33 = "The Primacy Text (Mt. 16:18)." *Princeton Seminary Bulletin* 12 (1991) 41–55. **Mantey, J. R.** "Distorted Translations in John 20:23; Matthew 16:18–19 and 18:18." *RevExp* 78 (1981) 409–16. **Marcus, J.** "The Gates of Hades and the Keys of the Kingdom." *CBQ* 50 (1988) 443–55. **Menken, M.** "The References to Jeremiah in the Gospel according to Matthew." *ETL* 60 (1984) 5–25. **Moule, C. F. D.** "Some Reflections on the 'Stone' Testimonia in Relation to the Name Peter." *NTS* 2 (1955) 56–58. **Porter, S. E.** "Vague Verbs, Periphrastics, and Matt. 16.19." *Filologia Neotestamentaria* 2 (1988) 155–73. **Robinson, B. P.** "Peter and His Successors: Tradition and Redaction in Matthew 16:17–19." *JSNT* 21 (1984) 85–104. **Schenk, W.** "Das 'Matthäusevangelium' als Petrusevangelium." *BZ* n.s. 27 (1983) 58–80. **Schmid, J.** "Petrus der 'Fels' und die Petrusgestalt der Urgemeinde." In *Evangelienforschung,* ed. J. B. Bauer. Graz: Styria, 1968. 159–75. **Schnackenburg, R.** "Das Vollmachtswort vom Binden und Lösen, traditionsgeschichtlich gesehen." In *Kontinuität und Einheit,* ed. P.-G. Müller and W. Stenger. Freiburg: Herder, 1981. 141–57. **Stauffer, E.** "Zur Vor- und Frühgeschichte des Primatus Petri." *ZKG* 62 (1943–44) 3–34. **Vögtle, A.** "Das Problem der Herkunft von 'Matthew 16,17–19.'" In *Offenbarungsgeschehen und Wirkungsgeschichte.* Freiburg: Herder, 1985. 109–40. **Wall, R. W.** "Peter, 'Son' of Jonah: The Conversion of Cornelius in the Context of Canon." *JSNT* 29 (1987) 79–90. **Wilcox, M.** "Peter and the Rock: A Fresh Look at Matthew 16:17–19." *NTS* 22 (1975) 73–88.

*Translation*

[13] *When Jesus came into the region of Caesarea Philippi, he began asking his disciples:* [a] *"Who do people say* [b] *the Son of Man is?"* [14] *They said: "Some,* [c] *on the one hand, say John the Baptist, but others Elijah, and still others Jeremiah or one of the prophets."* [15] *He said to them: "But you yourselves, who do you say I am?"* [16] *Simon Peter answered and said:* [d] *"You are the Christ, the Son of the living* [e] *God!"* [17] *Jesus responded and said to him: "You are blessed, Simon bar-Jonah,* [f] *because flesh and blood are not the source of this revelation* [g] *but my Father who is in heaven.* [18] *And I say to you that you are Peter, and upon this rock I will build my church and the gates of Hades will not overpower it.* [19] *I will give you the keys of the kingdom of heaven and whatever* [h] *you bind on earth*

*shall have been bound in heaven; and whatever* [i] *you set loose upon the earth shall have been set loose in heaven.*" [20] *Then he ordered* [j] *the* [k] *disciples to tell no one that he* [l] *was* [m] *the* [n] *Christ.*

## Notes

[a] The translation omits the redundant λέγων, "saying."

[b] Many witnesses (D L Θ *f* [1,13] TR it vg[mss] sy[(s,c),p,h]) add με, lit. "me," which gives the resultant translation "I, the Son of man, am," thus making it quite clear that Jesus asks about himself and not another. This addition, however, almost certainly results from its inclusion in the parallels (Mark 8:27; Luke 9:18). Cf. too v 15. See *TCGNT*, 42.

[c] D W it omit οἱ μέν, "some, on the one hand."

[d] D bo[ms] add αὐτῷ, "to him."

[e] D* reads σῴζοντος, "saving."

[f] A few MSS (L Γ *f* [1,13]) separate the two parts of the name, thus βὰρ Ἰωνᾶ, "bar Jonah."

[g] οὐκ ἀπεκάλυψέν σοι, lit. "have not revealed to you."

[h] Some witnesses (Θ *f* [1] it Or Cyp Eus Cyr) have the pl. ὅσα ἄν, "whatever," in place of the sing., with the corresponding participle δεδεμένα, "bound," also in the pl.

[i] Same variant as preceding *Note*, with corresponding pl. participle λελυμένα, "set free."

[j] B* D sy[c] have ἐπετίμησεν, "warned sternly," for διεστείλατο, "ordered," through influence of the Markan parallel (Mark 8:30).

[k] L W Θ *f* [1,13] TR lat sy co insert αὐτοῦ, "his."

[l] D Θ q read οὗτος, "this one," in place of αὐτός, "he."

[m] ἐστίν, lit. "is." Cf. preceding *Note* (i.e., "this one is the Christ").

[n] Many later MSS (ℵ[2] C D W TR lat sy[h] mae bo) add Ἰησοῦς, "Jesus," i.e., "Jesus the Christ" (but D, "Jesus Christ"), clearly an expansion.

## Form/Structure/Setting

A. As it is in Mark and Luke, this passage in Matthew is clearly the climax of the first main part of the Gospel, devoted to the description of the Galilean ministry of Jesus (i.e., 4:17–16:20). It presents in a paradigmatic form an unequivocal and definitive confession of Jesus as the promised Messiah. This is the only adequate conclusion to the preceding, lengthy description of the deeds and words of Jesus. And without question, much in the preceding accounts has been anticipating this powerful confession. Thus we have repeatedly heard the question asked concerning the identity of the one who could speak and act in this unique way (cf. 8:27, "What sort of man is this?"; 11:2, "Are you he who is to come, or shall we look for another?"; 12:23, "Can this be the Son of David?"). There have been intimations of his identity throughout, such as his authority (7:29; 9:8), his power to heal (cf. 15:31), and his uniqueness (9:33, "Never was anything like this seen in Israel"). The demons know his identity as the "Son of God" (8:29). And even the disciples in the excitement of the moment have already exclaimed "Truly you are the Son of God" (14:33). But now in a private, peaceful, meditative setting, Jesus for the first time elicits from the disciples, represented by Peter, the reasoned and careful conclusion that he is indeed the Christ, the Messiah of promise.

B. Matthew, who has been following Mark's order closely since the beginning of chap. 14 (Mark 6:14), omits the preceding Markan pericope concerning the healing of the blind man at Bethsaida (Mark 8:22–26). Matthew was probably not impressed with the Markan story since it suggests the use of means to heal (cf. his omission of the similar healing in Mark 7:32–35) and that more than one attempt was needed to do the job right. It does not fit well with the Christology Matthew has been developing, with immediate healings by a spoken word, and is thus omitted, especially just before Peter's confession. So far as source criticism of the present pericope is concerned, it can be divided into two parts. The first, vv 13–16, 20, is drawn from Mark 8:27–30 (paralleled in Luke 9:18–21, with a Johannine counterpart in John 6:67–69). The second part is vv 17–19, which are unique to Matthew (for v 19, cf. John 20:23).

In the first part, the following alterations of Mark are to be noted. In the introductory verse (v 13), Matthew omits Mark's καὶ ἐν τῇ ὁδῷ, "and on the road" (Mark 8:27), perhaps regarding such an important passage as deserving a setting of its own. He also omits Mark's "and his disciples," it being obvious from the following clause that the disciples are with Jesus, and he changes τὰς κώμας, "the villages" (Mark 8:27), to τὰ μέρη, "the region." In the question asked of the disciples about what others were saying, Matthew replaces Mark's με, "I," with the common title Jesus used of himself, τὸν υἱὸν τοῦ ἀνθρώπου, "the Son of Man" (v 13; Mark 8:27). In v 14 Matthew alters Mark's second ἄλλοι, "others," to ἕτεροι, "others," for stylistic reasons and inserts immediately after it Ἰερεμίαν ἤ, "Jeremiah or," perhaps to give an example (cf. Mark 8:28). In v 15 he substitutes λέγει αὐτοῖς, lit. "he says to them," for Mark's καὶ αὐτὸς ἐπηρώτα αὐτούς, "and he asked them" (Mark 8:29), again for reasons of style. In v 16 Matthew adds the name Σίμων, "Simon," before the name "Peter," and then in the confession itself adds to Mark's simple ὁ Χριστός, "the Christ" (Mark 8:29), the words ὁ υἱὸς τοῦ θεοῦ τοῦ ζῶντος, "the Son of the living God" (cf. Luke's τὸν Χριστὸν τοῦ θεοῦ, "the Christ of God" [Luke 9:20], and John's ὁ ἅγιος τοῦ θεοῦ, "the Holy One of God" [John 6:69]). In v 20 Matthew inserts a characteristic τότε, "then," and substitutes διεστείλατο τοῖς μαθηταῖς, "ordered his disciples," for Mark's stronger ἐπετίμησεν αὐτοῖς, "he sternly charged them." Finally, he replaces Mark's simple περὶ αὐτοῦ, "concerning him" (Mark 8:30; cf. Luke's τοῦτο, "this" [Luke 9:21]), with ὅτι αὐτός ἐστιν ὁ Χριστός, "that he was the Christ"—thus adding emphasis to the point.

In his alterations of Mark, we again see Matthew making stylistic changes, but little of the usual abridgment is to be seen. Instead Matthew makes several interesting theological expansions of Mark, the most important, of course, being in the high point of the passage, the words of the confession itself (v 16). To the material borrowed from Mark, Matthew has added new material from his own special sources (vv 17–19). On this material, see below, §D.

C. This important pericope is very carefully constructed. A simple outline is as follows: (1) the setting and the question concerning the public's estimate of Jesus (v 13); (2) the answer to the first question (v 14); (3) the question asked of the disciples (v 15); (4) Peter's answer to the second question (v 16); (5) Jesus' affirmation of the answer (v 17); (6) the commissioning of Peter, consisting of (a) the saying concerning the church (v 18) and (b) the authority of the keys (v 19); and (7) the command to silence (v 20). A fair amount of structural parallelism is to be found in the passage. Thus, the structure of the two questions is exactly parallel in form (vv 14, 16), despite the substitution of τὸν υἱὸν τοῦ ἀνθρώπου, "the Son of Man," for με, "I," in the first one. The answer to the first question presents the various options in parallel syntax. Each of the three verses 17–19 consists of three elements: a main statement followed by a couplet (see Jeremias, TDNT 3:7). Peter's confession σὺ εἶ ὁ Χριστός, "You are the Christ" (v 16), finds a syntactic parallel in the response of Jesus, σὺ εἶ Πέτρος, "You are Peter" (v 18). Antithetic parallelism can be seen in the contrast between "flesh and blood" and "my heavenly Father" in v 17. A striking instance of symmetrical parallelism is found in v 19b and c. Finally, Matthew's restatement of the Markan ending, i.e., αὐτός ἐστιν ὁ Χριστός, "he is the Christ," has the emphatic effect of an inclusio with v 16. The confession is thereby in a sense repeated. Matthew's artistry is thus again to be seen in this pericope, both by means of certain alterations of his Markan source and through his presentation of his special material.

D. Although relatively few scholars deny the historicity of Peter's confession itself, the historicity of the special Matthean material that follows (vv 17–19) is widely regarded as dubious. Not only is the latter material lacking in the other Gospels (but cf. Luke 22:31–32; John 21:15–23 for passages consonant with the present one), but it also seems to be full of anachronisms, including the reference to the ἐκκλησία, "church," the security of the church, as well as the authority of office and power granted to Peter. It is certainly the case that the language of the passage as it stands reflects to a considerable extent the conceptions and self-consciousness of the later church. But this is a long way from necessarily concluding that Jesus could not have said something along these lines or that Matthew has simply invented the material out of thin air.

Davies-Allison correctly resist the conclusion that vv 17–19 are the result of Matthean composition. They also deny that the verses represent a displaced resurrection story (Stauffer; Strecker, *Weg*, 206–7; C. Kähler) or reflect an incident originally in the context of the Last Supper (Cullmann, *Peter*). Instead, they tentatively propose that the entire narrative is an early account (reflected in scattered Johannine parallels), earlier than the Markan and Lukan parallels, that may well reflect a historical event. Not all the evidence they provide (e.g., evidence of Peter's authority in Paul's letters, Semitisms, parallel ideas at Qumran, criteria of consistency and dissimilarity) is equally strong, as they admit, but they have at least shown that the common negative assessment of historicity is hardly justifiable.

Certain frequent objections to the historicity of these verses can be met (vv 18–19 are the bigger problem; see Wilcox). Can Jesus have referred to building "my church"? Luz regards this as the "most important" argument against the authenticity of the words. The word ἐκκλησία, "church," however, should not be thought to be a problem since Jesus would have been speaking in Aramaic and not Greek. Thus he would not have used the word ἐκκλησία but probably an Aramaic equivalent meaning "community" (see *Comment* on v 18 for possibilities). But can Jesus have referred to building "*my*" community? Luz says we should expect "the community of God" since Jesus assembled God's people and not a holy remnant. The point, however, is that the calling of God's people demanded a decision for the kingdom of God as announced by and embodied in Jesus himself. It was a decision to be related to Jesus. In this perspective, to become a member of the community of God was to become a member of the community of Jesus (cf. the fate of "the children of the kingdom" in 8:12). A division was inevitable. It should therefore by no means be regarded unthinkable that Jesus could have talked of *his* community.

Can Jesus have been interested at all in building a *future* community? Although this is often assumed to be impossible because of the apparent imminence of Jesus' eschatological expectation, certain facts indicate otherwise. The very choice of twelve disciples, the trouble taken to teach them, and the commission given to them point to Jesus' preparation for the future. That Jesus would himself be active in the future building of the church is not an impossibility if he was able to speak of his own resurrection (cf. v 21) and promise his future presence with the disciples (28:20; cf. 18:20). Davies-

Allison seem unnecessarily to deny the post-resurrection aspect of the promise of Jesus building his community by taking it as fulfillable in the life of Jesus, translating "from this point on" (2:614).

Despite the claims of some who deny the authenticity of the passage, the authority of Peter here is not out of keeping with the picture of him in the rest of the NT (thus, e.g., Beare). Although Peter's authority as witnessed in Acts or Galatians is not absolute (nor is that part of the promise here), his central position in the early chapters of Acts is quite consonant with the importance granted him here as the rock upon which the church is to be built.

Worth indicating are the Semitisms in the passage, which, though they do not prove the point, are consistent with the claim that the material is early. Thus Peter is designated as μακάριος, "blessed" or "happy" (אֶשֶׁר [ʾešer]), and referred to as bar-Jonah, "Son of Jonah." Further Semitisms are the word play on the Aramaic כֵּיפָא (kêpāʾ), "rock," the reference to humans as "flesh and blood," the expression "the gates of Hades," and finally and especially the figurative language of "binding and loosing."

Finally we note that much of the language in this passage has its parallels in earlier portions of the Gospel. V 17 contains the language concerning revelation to Peter from "my Father who is in heaven," and v 19 cites "the kingdom of heaven." Jesus elsewhere in the Gospel pronounces others "blessed" (5:3–11) and employs the image of building on rock (7:24–25).

If Jesus affirmed Peter's confession of him as the Christ, then he was conscious of his messianic identity and accordingly would have thought in terms of constituting the messianic community. This conclusion is by no means canceled out even if Jesus had expected the parousia to occur within that generation (cf. v 28), a point that is in any event debatable. In support of the historicity of the passage, see further Cullmann, Jeremias. For an overview of the study of the passage up to the 1950s, see Cullmann, *Peter,* 163–70.

In short, although the authenticity of the passage cannot be demonstrated, there is no convincing reason to doubt that Jesus the Messiah could have contemplated and founded a messianic community (a "church"), spoken of its security, and given Peter the role of leadership in that community. To be sure, this passage gains increasing significance for the increasingly self-conscious church as it moves to the end of the first century and later, but that surplus of meaning must not be read into the passage or put into the mouth of Jesus.

### Comment

**13** When Jesus takes his disciples north of the Sea of Galilee (about twenty-five miles) to the region of Caesarea Philippi (so named because it was rebuilt by the tetrarch Herod Philip in honor of the emperor Tiberius; modern "Baniyas," formerly "Paneas"), a beautiful area in the foothills of Mount Hermon, it is ostensibly in order to retreat from the press of the crowds. But there is also another special reason, for what transpires here is both a climax and a dramatic turning point in the Gospel (as it is also in Mark and Luke). It is unlikely that Jesus chooses Caesarea Philippi because of its pagan associations, including the shrine to Pan, in order to assert his own authority over the world's religions (contra Bruner, following Barclay). He takes the disciples there merely as a place of retreat where he can be alone with them. The location of Caesarea Philippi may, however, have prompted some of the imagery used (e.g., "rock," "building" of church, "gates of

Hades"; see Immisch). Jesus takes the initiative by directly asking the question that has been in the minds of the disciples (and the readers of the Gospel) from the beginning of his ministry. What were people saying about him? How did they classify him, having seen him heal and heard him teach? Matthew's use of τὸν υἱὸν τοῦ ἀνθρώπου, "the Son of Man," in the question is probably meant as a circumlocution for the first-person pronoun, "I," used regularly by Jesus (contra Davies-Allison). Thus the question means here, as in Mark 8:27, "Who do people say I am?" See the repetition of the question using "I" in v 15. Jesus is hardly asking here for the identification of one who fits the title "the Son of Man" (contra Gundry), which was at best of ambiguous meaning. At the same time, however, the answer given by Peter in v 16 is consonant with the meaning of the "Son of Man" in its titular sense (for which, see *Comment* on 8:20), and the readers can hardly have failed to think of this (cf. 10:23, 13:41). There is thus at least an anticipation of the answer in the question as posed in Matthew.

**14** The disciples report that the people hold a variety of opinions about Jesus. Common to the three names and the more general "one of the prophets" is the idea of one who appears in connection with the coming of the end times, but as a precursor or attendant figure rather than the promised one himself. John the Baptist seemed clearly to be such a figure, who indeed portrayed his ministry as one of preparation for an imminent end and just for this reason caused such a sensation. Some apparently were of the opinion that Jesus was the martyred John resurrected to life (see especially 14:2 for the articulation of this view by Herod). Others thought of Jesus as Elijah, a prophet who in the OT was assigned the preparatory role of forerunner to the Messiah (cf. Mal 3:1; 4:5–6) and who for just this reason became identified with the work of John the Baptist (by Jesus already in 11:9–10, 14; cf. 17:12–13). Matthew's addition of the name Jeremiah (which in the NT occurs only in Matthew; cf. also 2:17; 27:9) suggests that Jeremiah was thought by some to be a key OT figure who would play a role in the coming of the eschaton (on Jeremiah in the intertestamental period, see 2 Macc 15:13–16 and esp. 2 Esdr 2:18, which refers to an eschatological appearance of Jeremiah with Isaiah [but the date of this reference is debatable]). There are, furthermore, a number of obvious parallels between Jesus and Jeremiah, such as the preaching of judgment against the people and the temple, and especially in suffering and martyrdom (see Menken). The general phrase ἢ ἕνα τῶν προφητῶν, "or one of the prophets," points to the widespread view that the greatest figures of the OT would return in a preparatory role just before the end of this age (cf. the importance of Enoch in the intertestamental literature and Melchizedek at Qumran). We have no evidence of Jeremiah being named explicitly in such a connection, and it may be that Jeremiah is named as representative of the prophetic corpus (Jeremiah appears first in a rabbinic list of prophets; cf. the *baraita* in *b. B. Bat.* 14b). Special OT men who had not died, e.g., Enoch and Elijah, were ideal candidates for returning in the time just prior to the eschatological era. There is no record of the death of Jeremiah in the Bible. On the other hand, others, such as the prophets, could well be raised from the dead in order to participate in the events of the end (cf. Luke 9:19). The crowds also identify Jesus as a "prophet" in 21:11. Exalted as these evaluations of Jesus are, placing him as an important figure connected with the coming of the eschatological age, they are inadequate, although partially true.

**15** Jesus repeats the question (this time in verbatim agreement with Mark), now directing it to the disciples (note the emphatic ὑμεῖς, "you yourselves"). The first-person pronoun με stands in place of "Son of Man" in v 13. The question is asked not so much for information but to elicit from the disciples an explicit confession of his messianic identity.

**16** Simon Peter (for the double name, see 4:18; 10:2; cf. v 17) answers for himself as well as for the other apostles (see esp. 15:15; cf. 19:27 for Peter as spokesman for the others). This was something they had undoubtedly discussed again and again, and they had already come to their conclusion. While it must be granted that it *is* Peter who responds and upon whom the singular pronouns and verbs of vv 17–19 focus (thus rightly Davies-Allison), Peter is never regarded as isolated from the twelve. To be sure, he is their leader and spokesman (*primus inter pares*), but he is also *their* representative, indeed the representative of the entire church (rightly Luz). Cf. too the plural verbs in the similar logion in 18:18, which in principle involve the same authority, even if at a local level (cf. Kingsbury, *JBL* 98 [1979] 67–83). Peter thus boldly declares: σὺ εἶ ὁ Χριστὸς ὁ υἱὸς τοῦ θεοῦ τοῦ ζῶντος, "You are the Christ, the Son of the living God." This answer differs categorically from those offered by the people. That is, here Jesus is not identified as one of the figures involved in the coming of the end times, but as *the* coming one, the determinative person who brings with him the messianic age and the transformation of the present order. Χριστός, "Christ," is the Greek word for "anointed one" (Hebrew: מָשִׁיחַ [*māšîaḥ*]). For the title, see *Comment* on 1:1, 16. This is the first occurrence of the title in direct speech. For the closely related title "Son of David," see 9:27; 12:23; 15:22.

In 1 Sam 7:4–16, the passage that gives rise to the expectation of the Son of David, it is said that "the LORD will make you a house" and that that house "shall be made sure forever before me" and that throne "shall be established forever" (2 Sam 7:16). Davies-Allison stress this passage as the background for the present pericope, which serves as its fulfillment: "Mt 16.13–20 records the eschatatological realization of the promises made to David" (Davies-Allison, 2:603; see too Anderson for Davidic and Zionist links with Peter's confession). Matthew's interpretive expansion, ὁ υἱὸς τοῦ θεοῦ, "the Son of God," defines the Messiah as more than a human figure, as someone who is uniquely a manifestation of God, the very agent of God who somehow participates in God's being (see Gundry, Davies-Allison; on the title, see *Comment* on 3:17; and 4:3; 8:29; 11:27). The disciples had earlier already confessed Jesus as the Son of God (14:33). There it was under pressure of extraordinary circumstances; here it is the result of calm reflection as well as the product of divine revelation. And to this second confession the revelation of Jesus' call to suffer and die is appended. The high priest later asks Jesus whether he is "the Christ, the Son of God" (26:63), thereby again bringing together the two titles (for the same juxtaposition of titles, see also John 11:27; 20:31). For the background of the conception of the Messiah as God's Son, cf. 2 Sam 7:14; Ps 2:6–8, 12; 4QFlor 10–14. See also 27:40, 43, 54 for the "Son of God" title. The title is, of course, extremely important in the Fourth Gospel (besides references above, see 1:34, 49; 19:7; cf. 6:69). The expression τοῦ θεοῦ τοῦ ζῶντος, "the living God," is an OT expression (cf. Deut 5:26; Pss 42:2; 84:2), found elsewhere in Matthew in 26:63 (cf. 22:32) and frequently in the NT (see 1 Tim 3:15; 4:10 [where it furthermore modifies the noun ἐκκλησία, "church"]; Acts 14:15; Rom 9:26; 2 Cor 3:3, 6:16; 1 Thess 1:9; Heb 3:12; 9:14; 10:31; 12:22; 1 Peter 1:23; Rev 7:2; 15:7; cf. John 6:57; Rev

1:18; 4:9). It describes the true God, as opposed to the gods of the world who were not alive, such as the deities of the region of Caesarea Philippi (cf. its use by Jews in pagan contexts, e.g., 2 Macc 7:33; 15:4; 3 Macc 6:28). Implied in the phrase (but only implied) is the fact that God is uniquely the source of all life (see Meier, Davies-Allison).

**17** In his response, Jesus proclaims Peter to be μακάριος, "blessed," i.e., one in the state of being deeply happy through the proleptic experience of the eschatological blessing of God. For, in fact, Peter's confession is the truth. Jesus affirms it not merely as the result of human effort and reasoning (σὰρξ καὶ αἷμα, "flesh and blood," is a Semitic expression for human agency; cf. Gal 1:16), although these were clearly at work in the process, but as a revelation from God, i.e., divinely certified truth. In distinctively Matthean language, ὁ πατήρ μου ὁ ἐν τοῖς οὐρανοῖς, "my Father who is in heaven," has revealed to Peter the identity of his Son, Jesus (cf. 11:27, "No one knows the Son except the Father"). Paul can use similar language in describing God's revelation of the Son to him (cf. Gal. 1:15–16). The verb ἀπεκάλυψεν, "revealed," with God as the acting subject has connotations of the imparting of eschatological knowledge (see also *Comments* on 11:25, 27). Davies-Allison link this with the notion of the unveiling of a hidden Messiah (cf. John 7:27; Justin, *Dial.* 8.4; 100.1). In short, divine revelation has been at work in bringing Peter and his disciples to this conclusion about Jesus. And that divine authority serves as a guarantee of the correctness of their assessment. Peter is addressed here by his proper name, Simon (Σίμων, from Hebrew שִׁמְעוֹן [ Šim⁽ôn]; cf. Συμεών, "Simeon" [2 Peter 1:1]), by which he is first introduced in 4:18 (cf. 10:2).

The name Βαριωνά, "bar-Jonah," i.e., the transliterated Aramaic for "son of Jonah," is quite problematic, since in the best MSS of John 1:42 and 21:15, Simon Peter is called the son of Ἰωάννου, "John." If we are not faced here with a textual corruption (oddly no textual witnesses have harmonized the present passage to agree more closely with the Johannine references), then we may have simply an Aramaic alternate to the Greek name John. Although the Aramaic *bar-Yôḥānān* is quite different, the Lucianic text of the LXX can use Ἰωνάν (*Yōnan*) for "John" (*Yôḥānān*); see, e.g., Neh 6:18; 2 Kgs 25:23; 1 Chr 3:24. See Jeremias, *TDNT* 3:407; cf. Luz, 461, n. 59. On the other hand, it may be that the ascription is a deliberate Matthean redaction (cf. B. P. Robinson), and it is possible that some special meaning is in view through the association of Peter with the prophet Jonah. A number of suggestions have been made. A particularly interesting one is the parallel between the two figures in their common reluctance to preach repentance to the Gentiles (see R. W. Wall). Some have seen the connection in the sign of Jonah. Thus Gundry argues that in the name "bar-Jonah" is "a warning of death by martyrdom and a promise of resurrection." This seems to read rather too much into the name, however. C. Brown (37) goes even further, nevertheless, in the actual identification of Jesus with Jonah so that "bar-Jonah" means that Peter was spiritually the son of Jesus, who is the new Jonah. Also possible, but unlikely, is the claim that "bar-Jonah" is derived from the word for "terrorist" or "revolutionary" and that Peter was once a Zealot (thus Cullmann; cf. M. Hengel, *The Zealots* [Edinburgh: T. & T. Clark, 1989] 55). Davies-Allison regard as more probable the simple solution that "John" was changed to "Jonah" by Matthew to elevate Peter to the status of a prophet; perhaps, on the other hand, "Jonah" was inadvertently changed in the Fourth Gospel to the more popular "John."

**18** This verse has rightly been described as "among the most controversial in all of Scripture" (Davies-Allison, 2:623). As Peter had made a declaration concerning Jesus, now Jesus makes an important declaration concerning Peter: σὺ εἶ

Πέτρος, "you are Peter," and that name is now to take on special significance because Peter is also the "rock" upon which Jesus the Messiah will build his community. It is more probable that new significance is given to a name by which Simon was already known (with Gundry, contra Davies-Allison) than that Jesus first at this point gives him the name "Peter" (by which he has repeatedly been referred to in the preceding narratives). Davies-Allison, however, speak of the gaining of a new name in connection with the founding of a new people, noting (with Cullmann) the parallel with Abraham and the reference in Isa 51:1–2, which refers to the "rock from which you were hewn." The suggestion is intriguing but based more on speculation than evidence and furthermore must face the very different metaphors of being hewn from rock and being built upon rock. The word play is clear in the Greek (Πέτρος [*Petros*], "Peter [lit. 'stone']"—πέτρα [*petra*], "rock") despite the shift required by the feminine form of the noun for "rock." It is even more obvious in the Aramaic, where the name כֵּיפָא, *Kêpā*ʾ, is exactly the same for the word "rock." Since *kêpā*ʾ usually means "stone," not something one builds upon, Luz argues for the derivation of the word play from the Greek words. But word play does not demand the usual meaning of words, especially in metaphorical applications such as the present one. The Aramaic word play on the same word remains the most convincing explanation. Fortunately, the play also worked in Greek. For evidence that *kêpā*ʾ was a name in current use, contrary to the claim of many scholars, see Fitzmyer. (For Κηφᾶς [*Kēphas*], "Cephas," the Greek form of the name, see John 1:42; 1 Cor 1:12; Gal 1:18).

The natural reading of the passage, despite the necessary shift from *Petros* to *petra* required by the word play in the Greek (but not the Aramaic, where the same word *kêpā*ʾ occurs in both places), is that it is Peter who is the rock upon which the church is to be built (thus rightly Morris, France, Carson, Blomberg, Cullmann [*Peter*, 207], Davies-Allison; so too the interconfessional volume by Brown, Donfried, and Reumann [*Peter in the NT*, 92]). The frequent attempts that have been made, largely in the past, to deny this in favor of the view that the confession itself is the rock (e.g., most recently Caragounis) seem to be largely motivated by Protestant prejudice against a passage that is used by the Roman Catholics to justify the papacy. Not infrequently these attempts reveal the improper influence of passages such as 1 Cor 3:11 and Eph 2:20. But to allow this passage its natural meaning, that Peter is the rock upon which the church is built, is by no means either to affirm the papacy or to deny that the church, like the apostles, rests upon Jesus as the bedrock of its existence. Jesus is after all the builder, and all that the apostles do they do through him. For a similar point, buttressed with OT allusions, see Knight, who refers finally to the rock as "none other than God-in-Christ" (179; cf. Moule). As has often been pointed out, it is none other than the confessing Peter who is in view here as the rock, and it is as the representative of Christ that the authority to be mentioned in the next verse is given to him in his custody of the gospel of Christ.

Luz follows the argument of P. Lampe that *kêpā*ʾ meant a round stone rather than rock and would not have been thought of as suitable to build upon. (For this reason Luz regards vv 18–19 as deriving from a Greek-speaking context.) As Davies-Allison (following Fitzmyer) note, however, *kêpā*ʾ can mean rock (as, e.g., at Qumran and in the Targumim). Even if one were to think only of a stone, Davies-Allison point out that the Greek equivalent, λίθος, "stone," is the word used for the foundation stone for the temple (cf. Isa 28:16). For a possible link with the stone passage of Ps 118:22, see Wilcox (cf. Moule). Cullmann sees a connection with the block of stone in Dan 2:34–35, 44–45, which Judaism associated with the Messiah (*Peter*, 191–92).

The rock imagery implies both stability and endurance (cf. 7:24–25), even before the gates of Hades (see below). For Jewish background concerning a community built upon a "rock," see Str-B 1:732–33. "Rock" of course refers here not to Peter's character, as will become clear later in the narrative, but to his office and function (see too France) as leader of the apostles.

As argued above, underlying the Greek word ἐκκλησία, "church," is an Aramaic word spoken by Jesus meaning "community" (קָהָל [qāhāl]; עֵדָה, [ʿēḏâ] = συναγωγή, "synagogue," in LXX; or possibly כְּנִישְׁתָּא [kĕnîštāʾ]). The word ἐκκλησία appears often in the LXX, usually as the translation of קָהָל (qāhāl). Israel can be called קְהַל יהוה (qĕhāl YHWH), ἐκκλησία τοῦ κυρίου, "community of the LORD." The word for community in Jesus' day was עֵדָה (ʿēḏâ), usually translated συναγωγή. If Jesus is the Christ, then it is natural to expect that the community Jesus refers to is the messianic community or the eschatological people of God. Jesus says "my community," where the μοῦ, "my," is emphatic by its position. It is the messianic community of the Messiah, and the statement is thus an implicit messianic claim (Carson; cf. Brown, 33). Naturally Matthew and his readers understood by ἐκκλησία the church, and they did so justifiably. (The word ἐκκλησία occurs only here and in 18:17 in the four Gospels.) The point of the assertion is that Jesus, i.e., the risen Jesus, will build his new community in the first instance through the labor of the apostles (cf. Eph 2:20), and Peter has been designated as the leader of the apostles (cf. the early chapters of the book of Acts). The metaphorical use of "build" (οἰκοδομήσω) is appropriate to a community conceived of as a spiritual "house" or "temple" (cf. "house of Israel" and note the description of the church as "God's building" in 1 Cor 3:9; cf. Eph 2:19–21).

Jesus further assures Peter and the other disciples that πύλαι ᾅδου οὐ κατισχύσουσιν αὐτῆς, "the gates of Hades will not overpower it." The metaphor "gates of Hades" is found in the OT and intertestamental writings (where in Hebrew it is the "gates of Sheol" [שַׁעֲרֵי שְׁאוֹל, šaʿărê šĕʾôl]), e.g., in Isa 38:10; Wis 16:13; 3 Macc 5:51; Pss. Sol. 16:2 (in all of which cases the Greek agrees exactly with Matthew's phrase). It is essentially synonymous with "gates of death" (as in Job 38:17; Pss 9:13; 107:18; see too 1QH 6:24–26), Hades/Sheol being understood to be the realm of the dead.

The word πύλαι, "gates," in this stereotyped phrase has become symbolic of "the power of" or, as is more likely, it is a case of pars pro toto (thus Jeremias), where Hades itself is in view. Marcus (47) regards the gates of Hades as an antitype of the implied gates of heaven (cf. metaphor of Peter's keys) with the background being one of apocalyptic conflict.

The meaning of this statement has been much debated (summaries are available in C. Brown and Davies-Allison). Almost all the explanations that have been offered focus on or start with the idea of the overcoming of death. Some hypotheses stress the positive side by referring to resurrection, whether general resurrection (Schlatter), the resurrection of Jesus (McNeile), or the immortality of Peter or his office (Harnack and B. P. Robinson, taking πέτρᾳ, "rock," rather than ἐκκλησίαν, "church," as the antecedent of αὐτῆς, "it"). Such an understanding also underlies the quite speculative suggestion that the statement refers to Christ's descent into Hades to bring the righteous dead to life (Bousset, Kyrios, 65). Other hypotheses are content to speak merely of the triumph over death (Schweizer, Hill, Schnackenburg, Gundry [more specifically over martyrdom through persecution]; note RSV: "the powers of death"; but now NRSV returns to the literal: "the gates of Hades"). A key exegetical question is whether one should extend the metaphor of "the gates of Hades" to include more than merely death, in other words as having distinctly eschatological overtones. Many do so: the powers of evil (Allen); rulers of Hades, by metonymy (Marcus); the powers of the underworld (Bornkamm, *Jesus of Nazareth*, 187; Jeremias, *TDNT* 6:924–28; Davies-Allison); or the power of Satan (Hiers). There is risk in some of these more adventuresome proposals, yet since the ultimate survival of the church is in view, certainly the ultimate defeat of all evil is at least implied.

With the help of his association of Jesus with Jonah in this passage, C. Brown finds in the phrase a passion prediction. That is, for Jesus the gates of Jerusalem and the temple (cf. Ps 118:19–26) will become the gates of Sheol. Jesus will be put to death by the hostile Jewish authorities, but neither Jesus nor his community will ultimately be overcome. If this is a passion prediction, however, it is at very best only implicit, for Matthew has reserved the passion predictions until after v 21 with its formulaic "from that time." The general point is true enough, however: nothing—not even the death of the Messiah—can prevent the community from arriving victoriously at its eschatological goal.

Given the usual understanding of the phrase, it is probably best taken as meaning "the power of death" or perhaps simply "death"; it is this that shall not overpower (κατισχύσουσιν) the church. αὐτῆς, "it," has as its antecedent not πέτρα, "rock," but more naturally the nearer antecedent ἐκκλησίαν, "church" (contra B. P. Robinson). That is, the church as God's eschatological community will never die or come to end—this despite the eventual martyrdom of the apostles and even, more imminently, the death of its founder (soon to be announced; cf. v 21). Since death is one of the weapons of Satan and his horde, the "extended meaning" of the passage wherein the church survives the attack upon it from the realm of the evil one is not far from the mark, though it goes beyond what the text actually says. If the church escapes destruction despite the death of its leadership, so too will it escape anything that the enemy might bring upon it. Implied too is that those who die as a part of that church cannot be defeated by death but will be raised at the end time. The church—conceived of as the community of saints at any particular time, or as the saints of every age who cumulatively make up the church *in toto*—can never be destroyed.

**19** Peter, as the leader of the twelve, is the "rock" upon which the new community will be built. With this commissioning of Peter comes the authority symbolized by his possession of τὰς κλεῖδας τῆς βασιλείας τῶν οὐρανῶν, "the keys of the kingdom of heaven." For "kingdom of heaven," see *Comment* on 3:2. "Keys" are above all a symbol of authority and, hence, a symbol of power over something. This may be possessed by means of knowledge (as in Luke 11:52; cf. Matt 23:13; *b. Šabb.* 31a–b) or, in the case of Jesus, by divine right. In the context of our passage, note especially Rev 1:18: "I died, and behold I am alive for evermore, and I have the keys of Death and Hades" (cf. Rev 3:7 [cf. Isa 22:22]; 9:1; 20:1). See Emerton for the links between v 19 and Isa 22:22. Peter's possession of the keys of the kingdom grants him the right to admit or deny admittance into the kingdom, i.e., into the experience of the beginning blessings of eschatological salvation, as the following words confirm. This authority is expressed through the distinctive rabbinic idiom of "binding and loosing" (see Str-B 1:741–47 for numerous references).

Again, the question of the meaning of "binding and loosing" has given rise to much discussion. Among the options that have been offered, the following may be mentioned (see the review in Davies-Allison). "Binding and loosing" can be regarded as the language of demon exorcism (cf. Hiers), but this interpretation cannot be made to fit the context. Equally unlikely is the suggestion that the phrase refers to the placing and removing of magical curses (F. C. Conybeare, "Christian Demonology," *JQR* 9 [1897] 444–70). More reasonable, but still unconvincing, is the application of the words to a ban, i.e., of excommunication (Büchsel, *TDNT* 2:60–61). Most likely the words refer in the first instance to some kind of conduct that one is bound to or released from. One possibility is that they might concern vows (Falk), although this again does not fit the context. The words are better taken in the wider sense of wrong and right conduct, on the rabbinic model of specific, practical interpretation of the Torah, the determination of what was permitted and what was forbidden (so too B. H. Streeter, *The Primitive Church* [New York: Macmillan, 1929] 63; Derrett; Zahn; Davies-Allison; Luz), or somewhat more generally "teaching authority" (Bornkamm, *Perspective* 11 [1970] 37–50). This interpretation may by extension be construed to include the forgiveness or nonforgiveness of sins (Schlatter; Basser) and thus the determination of salvation or damnation (A. Schweitzer, *The Quest of the Historical Jesus* [New York: Macmillan, 1910] 371; Falk). That is, admission or nonadmission to the kingdom is now to be determined by the disciples' proclamation of what may be called the Jesus tradition—his proclamation and his teaching (see Korting). Cf. the commission of 28:16–20.

In its primary meaning, the phrase "binding and loosing" refers to the allowing and disallowing of certain conduct, based on an interpretation of the commandments of the Torah, and thus it concerns the issue of whether or not one is in proper relationship to the will of God (contrast the reference to the Pharisees' misuse of their authority [note implied keys!] in 23:13). In Matthew, Jesus is the true interpreter of Torah. His disciples will pass on that interpretation and extend it. Thus Matthew may have in mind the teaching office of Peter and the apostles (for whom the power of binding and loosing is also assumed in the plural verbs of 18:18 in the discourse on "church discipline"). Peter is in this sense *the* scribe trained for the kingdom of heaven (13:52). This would be a more Matthean description (cf. 23:8) than the reference to Peter as "chief rabbi" by B. P. Robinson (98) and Davies-Allison (2:639). He is the primary custodian and guarantor of the tradition of the teaching of Jesus (thus rightly Bornkamm, *Perspective* 11 [1970] 37–50). This means the words of Jesus and would, of course, include the ethical teaching of Jesus—his authoritative exposition of the law. But it also includes the kerygmatic utterances of Jesus concerning the coming of the kingdom of God as well as those that point to his own unique position in the mediation of salvation (e.g., 10:32–33, 39; 11:27). Thus, despite the rabbinic idiom, more is in view than halachic renderings (although Matthew and his community would have relished this aspect). In construing the meaning here more widely so as to include gospel with law, we may appeal to the closely related saying in John 20:23 (indeed, probably a variant of the present logion [thus Emerton on the basis of underlying Aramaic]): "If you [plural] forgive the sins of any, they are forgiven; if you [plural] retain the sins of any, they are retained." The Matthean logion has an extended meaning quite like this, which refers to the declaration of the forgiveness of sins, i.e., of salvation itself (cf. 18:18; Fornberg thus likens Peter to the high priest of the new covenant). The authority spoken of, then, is in effect that of being able to declare whether a person becomes fully a part of the community of salvation or not, no longer simply on the basis of obedience to Torah but on the basis of response or lack of response to the good news of the kingdom (cf. the practice of the disciples in 10:13–15). It is the conveying of "the word of grace and judgment" (Jeremias, *TDNT* 3:752). Thus it is not wrong to say, as Knight does, that ultimately the power of the keys is given to the people of God as a whole (178). Marcus (453) regards this as an apocalyptic change that alters the cosmos (including the law), involving the transfer of authority from the scribes and Pharisees to Peter.

To indicate the final authority of this "binding and loosing," the unusual Greek construction of the future tense and the perfect participle is employed (ἔσται δεδεμένον ἐν τοῖς οὐρανοῖς, "shall have been bound in heaven"; ἔσται λελυμένον ἐν τοῖς οὐρανοῖς, "shall have been loosed in heaven"). The meaning of these tenses is not altogether clear (see Porter's discussion). Many take them as referring to decisions already taken in heaven, thus giving a predestinarian sense to the statement (e.g., Gundry, Carson, Mantey, Marcus). That Matthew has a doctrine of election is clear from 11:25–27, as we have seen, and thus this interpretation of the tenses must be taken seriously. At the same time, the thrust of the present passage (like that of 18:18) has more to do with the establishment of the authority of Peter (the apostles and the church) in his mission to the world. The judgment of Peter, and by implication that of the church, reflects what is in accord with what is settled in heaven as the fully determined will of God (see Mantey, Porter). Whether this is already decreed in the will of God or subsequently ratified as the will of God is not the issue here. Peter's authority, in short, is such that he speaks on behalf of heaven (i.e., God).

**20** Jesus "then" (τότε) "ordered" (διεστείλατο, the only occurrence of the verb in Matthew) the disciples to keep quiet about his messianic identity, i.e., ὅτι αὐτός ἐστιν ὁ Χριστός, lit. "that he is the Christ," a repetition of the confession of v 16 for emphasis. This logion is perhaps the key one in establishing the motive of the "messianic secret" (see further *Comment* on 8:4). Here the reason for the secrecy is about to become particularly clear. Jesus is not the kind of Messiah that the masses have in mind. Far from overpowering the evil powers of the world there and then and establishing a national-political kingdom, Jesus is now to talk of another, dramatically different path upon which his messianic calling will take him.

*Explanation*

The climax of the first main part of the Gospel is found in this resounding confession of Jesus as "the Christ, the Son of the living God." It is this to which all (beginning especially with 4:17) has led. It is this that must be established with all possible fixity before the narrative takes that startling turn that will dominate the second half of the Gospel and that seems almost to contradict the point just established. With this supremely important confession of Jesus as Messiah, confirmed by Jesus' declaration of the divinely certified truth of the confession (v 17), it is not surprising that several other important ideas emerge, i.e., the church, the authority of Peter (and the other apostles), and inclusion or exclusion from the kingdom. For all of these—as indeed Christianity itself—are dependent on the identity of Jesus. It is because Jesus is who he is that Peter and the disciples can fulfill their calling and the church can be "built." The extended meaning of the logion spoken to Peter (vv 18–19) coincides with what took place in the early history of the church according to the book of Acts. Peter and the apostles were the proclaimers of the gospel, the perpetuators of the tradition, and they were vitally a part of each new stage of advancement in the overcoming of traditional barriers. And although Paul would ultimately become the "apostle to the Gentiles," it was through Peter's preaching that the gospel first came to Gentiles (Acts 10). It is especially here, in a major turning point for the history of the church, that Peter makes the most exemplary use of the "keys" and of his authority to "loose." (Had Paul been the initiator of gentile evangelization, it perhaps would have been forever suspect.) Matthew's Jewish-Christian readers would have taken pride in the knowledge that Christianity was Jewish before the influx of the Gentiles and that the church as a whole depended upon its Jewish roots in Peter and the apostles.

# The Turning Point:
# The Announcement of the Cross  (16:21–17:27)

## The First Announcement of the Suffering and
## Death of the Messiah  (16:21–23)

### Bibliography

**Bastin, M.** "L'annonce de la passion et les critères de l'historicité." *RevScRel* 50 (1976) 289–329; 51 (1977) 187–213. **Black, M.** "The 'Son of Man' Passion Sayings in the Gospel Tradition." *ZNW* 60 (1969) 1–8. **Feuillet, A.** "Les trois grandes prophéties de la passion et de la résurrection des évangiles synoptiques." *RevThom* 67 (1967) 533–60; 68 (1968) 41–74. **Neirynck, F.** "Ἀπὸ τότε ἤρξατο and the Structure of Matthew." *ETL* 64 (1988) 21–59. **Schaberg, J.** "Daniel 7,12 and the New Testament Passion-Resurrection Predictions." *NTS* 31 (1985) 208–22. **Vögtle, A.** "Todesankündigungen und Todesverständnis Jesu." In *Der Tod Jesu,* ed. K. Kertelge. QD 74. Freiburg: Herder, 1976. 51–113. **Willaert, B.** "La connexion littéraire entre la première prédiction de la passion et la confession de Pierre chez les synoptiques." *ETL* 32 (1956) 24–45.

### Translation

[21]*From that time Jesus* [a] *began to show his disciples that it was necessary for him to go to Jerusalem, and to suffer many things at the hands of* [b] *the elders and chief priests and scribes,* [c] *and to be put to death and to be raised to life on the third day.* [d] [22]*And Peter took him aside and began to reprove him, saying: "Far be this from you, Lord; this will in no wise happen to you!"* [23]*But he turned and said to Peter: "Get behind me, Satan. You are a cause of stumbling to me, because you are setting your mind not on the things of God but on the things of human beings."*

### Notes

[a]The important witnesses א* and B* (as well as sa^mss mae bo) add Χριστός, "Christ." The addition is clearly caused by the preceding verse (and pericope). Because of its rarity elsewhere (e.g., in Matthew only in 1:1, 18), the *UBSGNT* committee regards the addition as made by a scribe rather than the evangelist, although the latter is far from impossible. In favor of the simple Ἰησοῦς, "Jesus," see א² C L W Θ *f*^1,13 TR latt sy sa^ms bo^mss. A few MSS (א¹ 892) omit both names, probably through accidental omission of both abbreviated names (X̅C̅ and I̅C̅ ) in an attempt to correct the reading. See *TCGNT*, 42–43.

[b]"At the hands of" translates ἀπό, lit. "from."

[c]A few witnesses (Θ *f*^1,13 mae) add τοῦ λαοῦ, "of the people" (cf. 2:4).

[d]D (it) bo have μετὰ τρεῖς ἡμέρας ἀναστῆναι, "after three days to rise again," through the influence of Mark 8:31.

## Form/Structure/Setting

A. The second main part of the Gospel begins at this point, signaled by the opening ἀπὸ τότε, "from that time," placing Jesus on the road to Jerusalem and the cross. Not that Jesus' ministry of healings or his teaching has come to an end. Both indeed continue, but no longer as the main focus of attention. From now on the focus is upon what is to befall Jesus in Jerusalem. Although Jesus' death has been alluded to earlier in the Gospel (cf. 9:15; 12:40), in the present pericope it is first announced openly as the explicit intention of Jesus. This passage is thus no less of key importance in the Gospel than the preceding one. It can be no accident that the announcement of Jesus' imminent death is delayed until after Peter's bold confession at Caesarea Philippi in the immediately preceding pericope. It was important for Jesus' identity as Messiah to be firmly fixed in the minds of the disciples before they could be told of Jesus' death since the death could well seem to rule out such a conclusion. Peter's reaction in the present passage—which stands in such bold contrast to his praiseworthy confession in the preceding pericope—shows how incongruous he regarded the ideas. This passage and even more so the closely related following passage seem to contradict everything that raced through the disciples' minds when they thought of the presence of the Messiah and the dawning of the messianic age. The turn the Gospel now takes will necessitate the radical redefining of categories for the disciples. The narrative now inexorably moves toward the heart of the story of Jesus the Christ. Thus Martin Kähler was theologically correct when he described the Gospels as "passion narratives with extended introductions" (*The So-Called Historical Jesus and the Historic Biblical Christ* [Philadelphia: Fortress, 1964] 80, n. 11).

B. Matthew here is dependent on Mark 8:31–33 (cf. Luke 9:22). The changes Matthew makes at the beginning have the effect of establishing the pericope as one of particular importance. Matthew's own initial ἀπὸ τότε, "from that time," informs the reader that a major turning point in the narrative has been reached (cf. 4:17). Among further changes in v 21 (Mark 8:31), the following should be noted. Matthew adds ὁ Ἰησοῦς, "Jesus," and τοῖς μαθηταῖς αὐτοῦ, "to his disciples," to emphasize the significance of the passage. Matthew's δεικνύειν, "to show," for Mark's διδάσκειν, "to teach," is more appropriate to the nature of the material about to be revealed. Matthew substitutes the simple αὐτόν, "him," for Matthew's τὸν υἱὸν τοῦ ἀνθρώπου, "the Son of Man," probably because the title, or even the circumlocution, seems weak and anticlimactic after the confession of v 16. Matthew adds the phrase εἰς Ἰεροσόλυμα ἀπελθεῖν, "to go to Jerusalem" (cf. 20:18), and deletes Mark's καὶ ἀποδοκιμασθῆναι, "and be rejected," probably because it seemed redundant in the context. Matthew is content with one definite article, τῶν, "the," for the three groups, "elders, chief priests, and scribes," thus linking them together (as does Luke 9:22). Finally, in v 21 Matthew substitutes τῇ τρίτῃ ἡμέρᾳ ἐγερθῆναι, "on the third day to be raised to life" (Luke 9:22 agrees with this change, against Mark), for Mark's less accurate μετὰ τρεῖς ἡμέρας ἀναστῆναι, "after three days to rise again," probably reflecting the more precise language used in the kerygma and liturgy of the church (cf. 1 Cor 15:4, including the passive use of the verb). Matthew omits the opening words of Mark 8:32, καὶ παρρησίᾳ τὸν λόγον ἐλάλει, "and with boldness he was speaking the word," probably because the boldness seemed self-evident. Matthew, expanding Mark's mere reference to Peter's reproof of Jesus, supplies the content of the reproof with the added direct discourse: λέγων· ἵλεώς σοι, κύριε· οὐ μὴ ἔσται σοι τοῦτο, "God be gracious to you, Lord; this will in no wise happen to you" (v 22). In v 23 Matthew omits Mark's curious note καὶ ἰδὼν τοὺς μαθητὰς αὐτοῦ, "and looking at his disciples" (Mark 8:33), with the result that the focus remains on Peter. Matthew further softens Mark's ἐπιτίμησεν, "he rebuked" (Peter), to εἶπεν, "he said." Finally to be noted is Matthew's addition of the clause σκάνδαλον εἶ ἐμοῦ, "you are a cause of stumbling to me," which sharpens the already sharp rebuke of Peter. Thus in this passage Matthew again follows Mark quite closely, with only a couple of omissions of Markan material and with a number of significant additions designed to highlight the passage and to help the reader with further information at important points.

C. The structure of this brief pericope can be seen in this simple outline: (1) announcement of the divinely willed necessity of Jesus' suffering and death (v 21); (2) Peter's reproof of Jesus (v 22); and (3) Jesus' rebuke of Peter (v 23). The most interesting syntactic feature is without question that of v 21, where αὐτόν, "he," is the subject of four parallel infinitives, ἀπελθεῖν, "go," παθεῖν, "suffer," ἀποκτανθῆναι, "be put to death," and ἐγερθῆναι, "be raised to life"—all of which together serve as the subject controlled by the single verb δεῖ, "it is necessary," thus pointing to divine necessity. Three of the infinitives have modifiers (only ἀποκτανθῆναι, "to be put to death," does not), and παθεῖν is modified by the threefold πρεσβυτέρων καὶ ἀρχιερέων καὶ γραμματέων ("elders and chief priests and scribes"). Other syntactic parallelisms to be noted are: the parallel clauses in Peter's reproof (the first positive, ἵλεώς σοι, "God be gracious to you"; the second strongly negative, οὐ μὴ ἔσται σοι τοῦτο, "this will in no wise happen to you" [v 22]) and the parallelism in Jesus' rebuke: τὰ τοῦ θεοῦ, "the things of God," and τὰ τῶν ἀνθρώπων, "the things of human beings" (v 23). The contrast between the two vocatives, κύριε, "Lord" (v 22), and σατανᾶ, "Satan" (v 23), is striking.

D. This is the first of three predictions (all of which are found also in Mark and Luke) of the suffering and death of Jesus (cf. 17:22–23; 20:17–19; cf. 26:2). Matthew depends on Mark for all three. Of these, the second is the shortest while the third is the most detailed. Common to all three are the essential elements of being killed (in the third, crucified explicitly) and being raised on the third day. Thus, in the passion predictions of Jesus, we have the two elements that are of key importance in the kerygma of the early church (as witnessed in 1 Cor 15:3–8; cf. the sermons in the book of Acts). This does not necessarily mean that the historical Jesus could not have predicted his own suffering and death, and even his resurrection (see the discussion in Davies-Allison, 2:657–61). Of the three passion predictions, the one that most bears the detailed marks of being written with the events already in mind (vaticinia ex eventu) is the third. That Jesus' predictions in these passages line up with the kerygma of the church is not sufficient reason to reject the possibility of their authenticity, or at least of an authentic core. A variety of scripture passages were available to Jesus in understanding what lay ahead (e.g., Pss 22; 118:17–18, 22; Isa 53; Dan 7; 12; Wis 3).

*Comment*

**21**   The opening words, ἀπὸ τότε ἤρξατο ὁ Ἰησοῦς, "from that time Jesus began," repeat verbatim the formula of 4:17, thus bringing the readers to the second main stage of the entire Gospel narrative, which, as this verse announces, will focus on the death of Jesus. Immediately following the triumphant announcement of Peter that Jesus is the Messiah, Jesus begins "to show" (δεικνύειν; the verb occurs elsewhere in Matthew only in 4:8 and 8:4), i.e., to make vividly clear, to his disciples something that at this point is mysterious and completely out of their purview. But as unthinkable as it would seem, what Jesus now says will happen to him is a matter of divine necessity (to be distinguished from the blind fate of the Greek world). The verb δεῖ, "it is necessary," points to nothing less than the will of God (cf. the use of δεῖ in connection with the passion and the fulfilling of scripture in 26:54; cf. Luke 24:26–27). It is thus the compulsion of God's will that lies behind the following four infinitives, which are together syntactically governed by δεῖ. The first of these is εἰς Ἱεροσόλυμα ἀπελθεῖν, "to go to Jerusalem." This element is also part of the third passion prediction (20:18). The narrative concerning the ministry of Jesus is to find its climax in the Holy City itself in a final and fateful confrontation with the Jewish leadership (on the association of Jerusalem with the death of prophets, see 23:37 and Luke 13:33).

The second infinitive clause, πολλὰ παθεῖν, "to suffer many things," refers generally (cf. too 17:12) to what will befall Jesus in Jerusalem, something described more fully in the third passion prediction (in 20:19). The three groups mentioned as responsible for what Jesus will suffer, τῶν πρεσβυτέρων καὶ ἀρχιερέων καὶ γραμματέων, "the elders and chief priests and scribes," apparently represent the leadership of Israel (which may account for the single article for the three). The elders were those whose age, experience, and piety accorded to them the responsibilities of leadership. The chief priests were the intermediate hierarchy between the single high priest, the presiding officer of the Sanhedrin (see 26:62–68), and the priesthood generally (for the chief priests and the Sanhedrin, see 26:59). The scribes were the professional Torah scholars (cf. 2:4 and see *Comment* on 13:52). The three are mentioned together again only in 27:41 (though in a different order, i.e., 2, 3, 1), which records the partial fulfillment of the present prediction (cf. 26:57, where the scribes and elders are mentioned together with the high priest, Caiaphas). Most commonly linked in the passion narrative itself are the high priests and elders (cf. 26:3, 47; 27:1, 3, 12, 20; 28:11–12; outside the passion narrative, cf. 21:23). The chief priests and scribes are linked only in 2:4; in the third passion prediction, 20:18; and in 21:15.

The third infinitive stands unmodified, ἀποκτανθῆναι, "to be put to death," posing at once the supreme mystery of this Messiah and an apparent contradiction of what the disciples had finally confessed openly in the preceding pericope. The same verb is used in the second passion prediction (17:23; cf. its use in 14:5; 21:38–39; 26:4), while the more specific σταυροῦν, "crucify," is used in the third prediction (20:19; cf. its use in 26:2; 27:22–44).

The fourth infinitive governed by δεῖ is used in the clause τῇ τρίτῃ ἡμέρᾳ ἐγερθῆναι, "to be raised to life on the third day." The same verb (also passive in form, reflecting divine agency) in the same phrase is found in the second and third passion predictions (17:23; 20:19; cf. 27:63; 26:32). These predictions find their fulfillment in 28:1, 6, and this affirmation in turn becomes the central element of the kerygma of the early church (cf. 1 Cor 15:4; Acts 2:23–24; 3:15; 4:10, etc.). The related reference "three days" is found in 12:40 (together with "three nights") in connection with the sign of Jonah and in 26:61 and 27:40 in connection with the metaphor of destroying the temple and rebuilding it in three days (cf. John 2:19–

22). A further possible background to the prediction "on the third day" is in Hos 6:2. "On the third day" requires inclusive reckoning (Friday–Sunday). Thus at this major turning point in the Gospel, Jesus through his prediction provides what amounts to a programmatic prospect of what lies ahead, determined already in the will of God.

**22** Jesus' statement was fully incomprehensible to Peter. In no way did the messianic identity of Jesus fit the program now laid out by Jesus. To Peter and the other disciples what Jesus now began to say to them seemed flatly contradictory of their confession of him as Messiah (cf. 1 Cor 1:23) and his unqualified acceptance of that confession. Peter accordingly took Jesus aside to reprove him. This was quite a remarkable act in itself, given Peter's confession of Jesus as Messiah and that he addresses Jesus as κύριε, "Lord," but it is also indirect evidence that for Peter the deity of Jesus was hardly yet clear despite his confession. Peter's statement falls into two parts. The first ἵλεώς σοι, is an abbreviated form of εἴη ὁ θεὸς ἵλεώς σοι, "May God be gracious to you," which in the context means something like "May God mercifully spare you this" (BAGD, 376a). But cf. BDF §128(5), which more convincingly takes the clause as "a Septuagintism" meaning more directly "far be it from," thus making it synonymous with the second clause (for this use of ἵλεως in the LXX, see 2 Kgdms 20:20; 23:17 [= 1 Chr 11:19]; 2 Macc 2:21). This is followed by a very strong negation (the double negative, οὐ μή) of the possibility of the things just mentioned by Jesus: οὐ μὴ ἔσται σοι τοῦτο, "this will in no wise happen to you." Peter's confidence in this response depends upon his faulty concept of the nature of the Messiah and his work. He has yet to understand that God has willed another path for the Messiah.

**23** Although none of the evangelists tells us of Peter's reaction to this harsh response of Jesus, it is obvious that he would have been bewildered and crushed. In opposing the death of Jesus, Peter was going *against* the will of God and had unwittingly taken a position identical with that of Satan, who early on in Matthew's narrative had attempted to sidetrack Jesus from his Father's will (see 4:1–11). For this reason, Jesus speaks to Peter addressing him as "Satan"; it is as though Peter's response were inspired by Satan. Jesus' rebuke, ὕπαγε ὀπίσω μου, σατανᾶ, "get behind me, Satan," is thus almost exactly the same as that of 4:10 (where only the ὀπίσω μου, "behind me," is missing). Peter, "the rock" (v 17), had become in effect a stone of offense or a "rock of stumbling" (Isa 8:14) to Jesus (as Jesus himself would become to others [cf. Rom 9:33; 1 Peter 2:6–8]), a σκάνδαλον, a "stumbling block" (cf. the cognate verb in 11:6), in the path to the accomplishment of God's will (for parallel testings of Jesus along this line, see 26:36–46, but especially 27:40–44). The command to get "behind me" (ὀπίσω μου) refers to the clearing of Jesus' path by the removal of an obstacle (and perhaps hints at the proper place for a disciple following Jesus; cf. esp. v 24; and 4:19; 10:38). The essence of Peter's mistake was setting his mind upon τὰ τῶν ἀνθρώπων, "the things of human beings," rather than upon τὰ τοῦ θεοῦ, "the things of God" (a very similar point is made in the imperative, using the same verb, φρονεῖν, in Col 3:2). Peter's focus, like that of the other disciples (cf. 20:21), was on the triumphant aspects of the Messiah and the messianic kingdom. But if Peter would set his mind on the will of God, he needed to make room for the necessity of the suffering and death of Jesus. And as they next will be told, the disciples must face that reality in their own lives.

*Explanation*

If the Messiah was present among his people and the messianic kingdom was already beginning with the promise that its full realization lay in the near future, then the line between promise and fulfillment seemed simple and direct. Given such a scheme, dominated by Israel's national-political hope, it is no surprise that the disciples were baffled by Jesus' somber announcement, which seemed not so much a serious detour as a blatant contradiction of their hopes (cf. Luke 24:21). Lacking in the disciples' perspective was a sense of the gravity of sin and thus of the necessity of the cross as the instrumental means to the very possibility of the experience of the kingdom. Jesus' purpose was far greater than the blessing of Israel with the establishment of political independence and the experience of material blessing. His purpose was to counteract the effects of sin universally (cf. Gal 3:13) and thus to deliver humanity from a far greater enemy than the Roman oppressors. It is this purpose that makes the work of Jesus the turning point of the ages and that controls Jesus in the accomplishment of God's will. It is this that drives him to the cross (20:28).

# The Path of Discipleship    (16:24–28)

*Bibliography*

**Chilton, B. D.** "'Not to Taste Death': A Jewish, Christian and Gnostic Usage." In *Studia Biblica 1978*, ed. E. A. Livingstone. Sheffield: JSOT, 1980. 2:29–36. **Dautzenberg, G.** *Sein Leben bewahren.* SANT 14. Munich: Kösel, 1966. 68–82. **Fletcher, D. R.** "Condemned to Die: The Logion on Cross-Bearing: What Does it Mean?" *Int* 18 (1964) 156–64. **Künzi, M.** *Das Naherwartungslogion Markus 9,1 par.: Geschichte seiner Auslegung.* BGBE 21. Tübingen: Mohr, 1977. **Riesenfeld, H.** "The Meaning of the Verb ἀρνεῖσθαι." *ConNT* 11 (1947) 207–19. **Satake, A.** "Das Leiden der Jünger 'um meinetwillen.'" *ZNW* 67 (1976) 4–19.

*Translation*

²⁴*Then Jesus said to his disciples: "If any* ᵃ *desire to come after me, they must practice self-denial* ᵇ *and take their cross and keep following me.* ²⁵*For those who want to preserve their lives* ᶜ *will lose them; but those who lose their lives on my account will find them.* ²⁶*For what will* ᵈ *any profit if they should gain the whole world but lose their lives? Or what will people give in exchange for their lives?* ²⁷*For the Son of Man is about to come in the glory of his Father with his angels, and then he will render to all according to what they have done.* ᵉ ²⁸*Truly I tell you: There are some standing here who will by no means die* ᶠ *before they see the Son of Man coming in his kingdom."*

*Notes*

ᵃVv 24–27, originally in the sing. (e.g., "anyone . . . his [her]"; "whoever . . . his [her]"), have been recast in the pl. to avoid the masc. pronouns.

ᵇ ἀπαρνησάσθω ἑαυτόν, lit. "let him deny himself [herself]."

ᶜ ψυχή, lit. "soul," but here in the Hebraic sense of life animating the body.

ᵈ Some witnesses (C D W TR lat) have the present tense ὠφελεῖται, "does (profit)."

ᵉ τὴν πρᾶξιν αὐτοῦ, lit. "his [her] deed." Some MSS (ℵ* f¹ it vg⁽ᶜ⁾ syᶜ·ᵖ·ʰ co) have τὰ ἔργα αὐτοῦ, "his [her] works," thus harmonizing with Ps 61:13(LXX).

ᶠ γεύσωνται θανάτου, lit. "taste of death."

### Form/Structure/Setting

A. Jesus now confronts his disciples with what must have been yet a further unsettling revelation. True discipleship must entail a readiness to accept a path of self-denial and even martyrdom. This is a motif that has been broached earlier in the Gospel (cf. 10:17–28), and indeed 10:38–39 corresponds closely to vv 24–25. Yet with the present passage preceded by the jarring announcement of the necessity of Jesus' imminent suffering and death, the sayings here lose their theoretical character and sound proportionately more ominous. If the slave is not above the master and may thus expect similar treatment (10:24–25), the disciples are here confronted vividly with the cost of discipleship.

B. In this triple tradition passage Matthew depends as usual on Mark (Mark 8:34–9:1; cf. Luke 9:23–27). Matthew deletes Mark's opening words "and calling the crowd together," thereby restricting the passage to the hearing of the disciples. Matthew begins instead with the opening τότε ὁ Ἰησοῦς, "then Jesus." The dominical logion that follows (i.e., vv 24–25) is in verbatim agreement with Mark except for the following changes.

Matthew's ἐλθεῖν, "come," takes the place of Mark's ἀκολουθεῖν, "follow" (Mark 8:34; cf. ἔρχεσθαι, "come," in Luke 9:23); the more proper subjunctive, ἀπολέσῃ, "lose" (so too Luke 9:24), is used for Mark's ἀπολέσει, "lose" (Mark 8:35); Matthew (so too Luke 9:24) omits Mark's καὶ τοῦ εὐαγγελίου, "and the gospel's" (Mark 8:35), thereby focusing more on Jesus; and he substitutes εὑρήσει, "will find" (thus breaking the symmetrical parallelism; cf. 10:39), for Mark's σώσει, "will save" (Mark 8:35). Matthew revises the syntax of the next logion (v 26), making use of the future rather than the present tense, but still closely follows the Markan vocabulary. The following logion, Mark 8:38a–b ("whoever is ashamed of me and my words in this adulterous and sinful generation, the Son of Man will also be ashamed of") is omitted by Matthew, probably because it is seen as a digression (a similar logion has already been given in 10:33). Matthew takes the final part of the same logion (the subordinate clause "when he comes in the glory of his Father with the holy angels") and makes an independent statement of it (using μέλλει, "about to," and omitting the modifier τῶν ἁγίων, "holy," with ἀγγέλων, "angels"), adding an OT quotation concerning judgment (v 27; Ps 62:12). V 28 omits Mark's opening "and he said to them" (Mark 9:1), thereby attaching this final logion more closely to the preceding passage.

Otherwise, Matthew in this logion follows Mark very closely except in the final object clause following ἴδωσιν, "they see," where for Mark's τὴν βασιλείαν τοῦ θεοῦ ἐληλυθυῖαν ἐν δυνάμει, "the kingdom of God having come in power" (Mark 9:1), he has the more specific τὸν υἱὸν τοῦ ἀνθρώπου ἐρχόμενον ἐν τῇ βασιλείᾳ αὐτοῦ, "the Son of Man coming in his kingdom" (cf. in Luke 9:27, the simple τὴν βασιλείαν τοῦ θεοῦ, "the kingdom of God"). In this pericope, Matthew has thus followed Mark very closely but at the same time has put his own stamp upon the material.

C. The passage consists of an initial main saying (v 24), followed by three supporting logia reminiscent of wisdom sayings (vv 25, 26, 27, each with an initial post-positive γάρ, "for"). V 28 functions as a stress on the imminence of the coming of the Son of Man referred to in v 27. The following outline may be suggested: (1) the main condition of discipleship (v 24); (2) a paradoxical principle (v 25); (3) the supreme value of life (v 26); (4) the reality of the parousia and future judgment (v 27); and (5) the imminence of the parousia (v 28). Some parallelism is found in each of the first three logia. Thus v 24 has three parallel third-person imperatives; v 25 consists of two structurally parallel sentences (the εὑρήσει, "will find," in the second main clause breaks the exact verbal parallelism of Mark's σώσει, "will save" (perhaps through the influence of the similar saying in 10:39); and in v 26 there is syntactic parallelism in the two main parts (introduced by τί, "what") as well as in the contrast in the subordinate clause between τὸν κόσμον ὅλον κερδήσῃ, "gain the whole world," and τὴν δὲ ψυχὴν αὐτοῦ ζημιωθῇ, "but lose his life." Finally to be noted are the parallel references to the coming of the Son of Man in vv 27 and 28. The Markan pericope contains most of the parallelism (which is a part of the Jesus tradition itself in its oral form), which is then taken over and improved by Matthew.

D. The exact relationship between the similar sayings in 10:38–39, also addressed to the disciples, and vv 24–25 is difficult to establish (cf. too Luke 17:33). We may well have here variants of the same saying, the former coming to Matthew via Q and utilized in the free composition of the discourse in chap. 10 (thereby also accounting for their anachronistic character there), the latter via Mark. On the other hand, it is not at all impossible that very similar sayings about the essence of discipleship may have been uttered by Jesus on different occasions. John 12:25 provides a saying similar to v 25, but it is obviously given with a clearly Johannine imprint. Matthew's unique citation of the OT in v 27b is probably alluded to in *2 Clem.* 11:6. Justin Martyr probably alludes to v 26 in *Apol.* 1.15.12 (in the context of a montage of Matthean allusions).

## Comment

**24** The initial, typically Matthean, τότε, "then," in this case links this pericope closely with the preceding one. Jesus now proceeds to instruct his disciples and through them the church (note: "if any") in a discipleship patterned on his own self-denial and suffering. The disciple must be modeled on the example of the master (cf. 10:24–25). Discipleship involves a deliberate decision to follow Jesus by denying self and putting one's life on the line, taking up one's cross (cf. the Lukan addition καθ᾿ ἡμέραν, "daily" [Luke 9:23]). ἐλθεῖν, "to come," is used referring to discipleship only here in Matthew (but cf. 4:19, δεῦτε, "come"). Here the self-denial (ἀπαρνησάσθω, in Matthew only here) is a preliminary to the central imperative to "take up one's cross" (ἀράτω τὸν σταυρὸν αὐτοῦ; cf. 10:38, where however the verb is λαμβάνει, "take"). The latter metaphor does not mean bearing up under some difficulty or malady in life but a deliberate dying to oneself (a point confirmed by the following verses). To deny oneself—indeed to die to oneself—this is what it means to "follow" Jesus (ἀκολουθείτω; see *Comment* on 4:20 for the importance of this word for Matthew). In contrast to the preceding aorist imperatives, this verb is in the present tense, suggesting the ongoing practice of following. Thus the revelation of Jesus' own imminent suffering and death in the preceding pericope is now seen to be full of significance for the disciples themselves.

**25** The first reason (γάρ, "for") for this death to self is presented in the articulation of the paradoxical principle that the attempt to preserve one's life (σῶσαι, lit. "save," is to be understood in this sense) results in the loss of it (ἀπολέσει, "will lose," with overtones of eschatological judgment; cf. 10:39), while the deliberate giving up of one's life for the sake of Jesus results in the "finding" of it (εὑρήσει; cf. 10:39). ἕνεκεν ἐμοῦ, "on my account" (cf. 5:11; 10:18, 39; 19:29; see Satake), not only establishes this service as discipleship to Jesus (note the christological implications) but sets this material apart from other general, secular sentiments concerning a similar principle of self-giving and self-discovery (for a rabbinic parallel, cf. *b. Tamid* 32a). While ψυχή is clearly to be translated "life" here, rather than "soul," the "life" intended is not merely physical life but life in the deeper and more fundamental sense of one's true being, and thus life that transcends death (see *Comments* on 10:28, 39). Although it is difficult to articulate, the concept of "finding one's life" is not very different from experiencing the ultimate well-being meant by the word "salvation" (cf. *shalom*). The dying to self may or may not involve a literal martyr's death, but the person who dies to self in discipleship to Jesus (cf. 5:11; 10:18, 39; 19:29) will discover life in this fundamental sense. In sharp contrast, those persons who try selfishly to guard their existence will not know the full commitment of discipleship and will tragically end up losing the very thing they tried to protect (cf. Luke 12:33; John 12:25; Rev 12:11).

**26** A second reason (again γάρ, "for") for heeding the instruction of Jesus concerning discipleship builds upon the first one. If it is a matter of nothing less than gaining or losing one's "life," what could be of more importance to an individual? Thus if a person were to "gain the whole world" (τὸν κόσμον ὅλον κερδήσῃ) but "suffer the loss of life" in some fundamental sense (τὴν δὲ ψυχὴν αὐτοῦ ζημιωθῇ; the only occurrence of this verb in Matthew)—ψυχή, "life," here again understood as more than physical life—what would be the good of that (cf. esp. Luke 12:20; Jas 4:13–14)? Here ὠφεληθήσεται means "profit" or "benefit" (the word is used elsewhere in Matthew only in 15:5 and 27:24). The reference to the possibility of gaining "the whole world," i.e., its wealth, is reminiscent of 4:8, where Satan offers Jesus "all the kingdoms of the world and their glory" if he will only worship him—i.e., if Jesus would look out for himself and avoid the path of obedience (suffering and death) God had marked out for him. It is hard to imagine a more powerful polemic against wealth that squeezes out discipleship (cf. 6:19–21). The second question asks rhetorically whether there is any conceivable ἀντάλλαγμα ("thing given in exchange"; the only occurrence in the NT is here and in the Markan parallel) with which a person could again acquire possession of his or her ψυχή, "life," itself (cf. *2 Apoc. Bar.* 51:15). The answer is self-evident. Given the supreme value of life, the person's very being, nothing can be imagined that could warrant an exchange. Any conceivable answer would be fundamentally self-contradictory, such is the *sine qua non* of one's being (cf. Ps 49:8–9). The only sensible course for the disciple is the way of Jesus, i.e., the way of self-denial and the cross.

**27** As a third reason for the commitment of full discipleship (again, γάρ, "for"), building on the preceding material, Matthew has placed special emphasis on the reality of the coming of the Son of Man and human accountability at that time. This emphasis is fully in keeping with the common use of eschatology in the NT as a motivation for ethics. Given the preceding announcement of the imminent suffering and death of Jesus, the reference here to the Son of Man coming ἐν τῇ δόξῃ τοῦ πατρὸς αὐτοῦ μετὰ τῶν ἀγγέλων αὐτοῦ, "in the glory of his Father with his angels," must refer to what will follow those announced events. The μέλλει, "is about to," is indeterminate but suggests something in the not distant future (cf. the use of the same verb in the second passion prediction; 17:22; cf. 17:12; 20:22). The time reference is, however, made more specific in the verse that follows. The Son of Man who must suffer and die (v 21) is also destined to return ἐν τῇ δόξῃ τοῦ πατρὸς αὐτοῦ, "in the glory of his Father" (cf. Rom 6:4). The glorious coming of the Son of Man is referred to again in 24:30 (μετὰ δυνάμεως καὶ δόξης πολλῆς, "with power and great glory"; cf. the reference to the Son of Man's "throne of glory" in 19:28) and in 25:31 (ἐν τῇ δόξῃ αὐτοῦ, "in his glory"). The latter passage also includes a reference to πάντες οἱ ἄγγελοι μετ᾽ αὐτοῦ, "all his angels with him." The αὐτοῦ, "him," in the present reference to angels probably refers to the Son of Man (e.g., 13:41; 24:31, 2 Thess 1:7; so too perhaps 25:31; for OT background, cf. Zech 14:5). At this point Matthew inserts the further apocalyptic motif of the coming judgment by the use of explicit OT language: καὶ τότε ἀποδώσει ἑκάστῳ κατὰ τὴν πρᾶξιν αὐτοῦ, "and then he will render to each person according to what he or she has done." These words, which are cited elsewhere in the NT (Rom 2:6; cf. allusions in 2 Cor 11:15; 2 Tim 4:14; 1 Peter 1:17; Rev 2:23, 18:6; 20:12–13; 22:12), are in nearly verbatim agreement with Ps 61:13 (LXX), where only the number of the verb (second person) differs and the final phrase is κατὰ τὰ ἔργα αὐτοῦ, "according to his [her] works." The identical words, however, are also found in Prov 24:12 (but where the verb is in the present tense, ἀποδίδωσιν, "renders"; cf. too Sir 35:22 [LXX], where the last phrase is found nearly verbatim, κατὰ τὰς πράξεις [plural] αὐτοῦ, "according to his [her] deeds," but where the first part is somewhat differently put). The concept is a common one in the OT (cf. Jer 17:10) and had by the NT era (as the above references show) become nearly proverbial in character. Matthew's singular τὴν πρᾶξιν, lit. "the deed," is a summarizing noun. His point is clear. After his death and resurrection, Jesus will return in glorious manner as the apocalyptic Judge of humanity (cf. 7:22–23; 13:41–42; cf. 25:31–46). In light of this, one's decisions about one's ψυχή, "very being," become not only crucially important but also urgent.

**28** In a saying that is given grave importance by the introductory ἀμήν, "truly," Jesus assures his disciples (although Mark's inclusion of the crowd [Mark 8:34] makes more sense here) that some of those hearing his words at that time, τινες τῶν ὧδε ἑστώτων, "some standing here," would still be alive to see τὸν υἱὸν τοῦ ἀνθρώπου ἐρχόμενον ἐν τῇ βασιλείᾳ αὐτοῦ, "the Son of Man coming in his kingdom." This is the meaning of οὐ μὴ γεύσωνται θανάτου, lit. "by no means taste death," i.e., not die (for the same expression, see John 8:52; Heb 2:9; 2 Esdr 6:26; rabbinic references: *Gen. Rab.* 9.2; *b. Yoma* 78b). For a look at the problem raised by a similar verse, see the discussion of 10:23. By far the most natural understanding of this verse, given especially the context of the preceding verse to which Matthew has closely attached it, is that the consummation of the present age and the coming of the eschaton proper with its concomitant blessing and judgment would be experienced within not many decades through the triumphant return of the Son of Man. (Understanding the verse as referring to the parousia proper are Grundmann, Gundry, Luz, Gnilka, Sabourin.) Thus the length of the interim period between the death of the Son of Man and his glorious return would be limited, so that the latter would occur within the lifetime of some standing there at that moment. (The ἕως, "before" or "until," does not require the conclusion that these persons will die *after* seeing the coming of the Son of Man in power and that therefore the parousia cannot be meant since it will usher in the final age.) As we have noted in the discussion of 10:23, such a conclusion, which from our later perspective must be judged as chronologically incorrect, is not out of keeping with the theological unity of eschatology (i.e., wherein the first and second coming of Jesus are part of one eschatological process, with the former anticipating and guaranteeing the reality of the latter) as well as with Jesus' own self-confessed ignorance of the actual time of his return (24:36). Of key importance in deciding the interpretation of this verse is the necessity of giving full heed to the statement that some would still be alive to see the coming of the Son of Man in power. The idea that ἑστώτων, "standing," could be taken in the sense of faithfulness in the midst of persecution (thus "very tentatively" Davies-Allison; cf. Strecker, *Weg*, 43) is hardly convincing without more evidence from the immediate context.

Some have tried to ease the problem by understanding "death" as referring to some kind of "second death" or eschatological punishment, but this explanation goes against the natural meaning of to "taste death" and creates as many of its own problems as it solves. There is, alternatively, as we have also seen above (on 10:23), the possibility of a range of meanings for the expression "the coming of the Son of Man in his kingdom." Some encouragement to ponder these comes from the parallel expressions in Mark and Luke, namely, "the kingdom of God come in power" and simply "the kingdom of God," respectively. It is obvious that whereas Matthew has made Mark's clause more specific (perhaps over-specific), Luke has made it more general. If we look for an event within the lifetime of at least some who were present, which could correspond to the powerful coming of the kingdom, and perhaps even of Matthew's coming of the Son of Man, the following options are conceivable. (1) Since in all three Synoptics this statement is followed by the transfiguration of Jesus (a revelation of his glorious identity), it has been argued that this is what is intended. This view was held already by the early Fathers (cf. Harrington [tentatively]; Blomberg). But an event that was to occur in a mere six days is hardly compatible with the strange statement that some would live to see it. (2) Another candidate is the resurrection of Jesus (cf. Rom 1:4) and/or the subsequent ascension of Jesus and the experience of the Holy Spirit at Pentecost fifty days later (thus among others, Luther, Calvin, McNeile, Albright-Mann, Tasker, and Meier, who speaks of the resurrection as "an anticipated parousia"). Although an easier interpretation than the transfiguration, the time interval (probably less than a year) again seems too short for the language used. (3) A further possibility sometimes considered is the gentile mission and the rapid expansion of the church, or simply Christ's role in the church (thus Hill, Green, France). Without doubt, these involve a realization of the kingdom in power. They fit Mark and Luke better, however, than Matthew's reference to the coming Son of Man who comes in powerful judgment (cf. v 27). It is of course possible to opt for a combination of these. Thus Carson opts for a combination of (2) and (3). Davies-Allison opt for a combination of the resurrection and the second coming, regarding the one as a foreshadowing of the other. Bruner sees truth in each of the options (cf. too Morris). (4) A fourth possibility and one that fits particularly well with the time interval (with the lapse of about forty years) is the destruction of Jerusalem (already J. J. Wettstein ['Η Καινὴ Διαθήκη, 2 vols. (Amsterdam, 1751–52)] in 1752; among other authors: H. Alford [*The Greek New Testament*, 2 vols. (Chicago: Moody, 1968)]; Morison [*Gospel according to St.*

*Matthew* (London: Hodder and Stoughton, 1895)]; so too Lagrange, Benoit, Gaechter). Because the coming of the kingdom by definition means not only blessing but judgment and because the destruction of Jerusalem can be conceived of as the judgment of God upon national Israel for her unbelief, this event can be thought of itself as a form of the coming of the kingdom of the Son of Man in power. Matt 24, as we will see, associates the destruction of Jerusalem with the eschatological judgment of the end time (Luke's version of the eschatological discourse of Jesus also gives special place to the destruction of Jerusalem [cf. Luke 21:20–24]). See further the *Comment* on 24:34. The interpretation of this logion as anticipating the destruction of Jerusalem fits Matthew's language concerning the returning of the Son of Man as Judge. In this way, the judgment upon Jerusalem can be seen as paradigmatic of the final, eschatological judgment itself (rightly Alford: "a *type* and *earnest* of the final coming of Christ" [1:177]).

This typology is apparent in chap. 24, but there in the examination of 24:29–30 we will see that it is nevertheless the case, if the eschatological discourse intends any chronology, that Matthew conceives of the Son of Man as gloriously returning in connection with, i.e., immediately after, the destruction of Jerusalem. As we will argue there, probably Jesus predicted the destruction of Jerusalem within that generation—an event the disciples could not imagine without the end of the age and the parousia of the Son of Man. Then what may easily have happened was that the imminence became associated with the coming of the Son of Man in power. Although Matthew in the present instance regarded the glorious parousia of the Son of Man as occurring within the lifetime of some who were standing there, what Jesus may have referred to was the destruction of Jerusalem and the temple. From our perspective, because of the typological interconnection, the latter may be regarded as an anticipation of the final judgment. Given the unity of eschatology, the theological point remains justifiable; i.e., to see the destruction of Jerusalem was in a sense to see the coming of the Son of Man in his kingdom. What Jesus had already brought and accomplished pointed dramatically to the coming eschaton.

### Explanation

The path of discipleship is the path of the cross for everyone who would follow Jesus. Paradoxically, it is the one who gives up his or her life in discipleship to Jesus who will truly find life, both in the present and in the future, while the one who seeks to have life on his or her own terms will in effect lose it. This self-denial means a new set of priorities that will look foolish to the world. This dying to self makes possible the radical love and service that are the essence of discipleship. The stakes are exceedingly high, for what could be more important to an individual than life itself? Furthermore, when Jesus comes—and because of the theological unity of eschatology, the time could even now be chronologically imminent—he will hold all people accountable for what they have done with their lives. Taking up the cross, death to self, the reality of suffering even in the new era inaugurated by Jesus—these were hardly what the bewildered disciples anticipated for themselves in their association with Jesus (cf. 19:27–30; 20:20–28). Thus as Jesus startled them with a redefinition of the work of the Messiah, so too he startled them with his concept of discipleship for them. Triumph and glory would indeed come for the disciples—as it would for Jesus—but not until after the present era was brought fully to its end.

# The Transfiguration of Jesus    (17:1–8)

### Bibliography

**Bacon, B. W.** "After Six Days." *HTR* 8 (1915) 94–121. ———."The Transfiguration Story." *AJT* 6 (1902) 236–65. **Baltensweiler, H.** *Die Verklärung Jesu.* ATANT 33. Zürich: Zwingli, 1959. **Baly, D.** "The Transfiguration Story." *ExpTim* 82 (1971) 70. **Bernadin, J. B.** "The Transfiguration." *JBL* 52 (1933) 181–89. **Best, T. F.** "The Transfiguration: A Select Bibliography." *JETS* 24 (1981) 157–61. **Blinzler, J.** *Die neutestamentlichen Berichte über die Verklärung Jesu.* NTAbh 17.4. Münster: Aschendorff, 1937. **Caird, G. B.** "The Transfiguration." *ExpTim* 67 (1956) 291–94. **Carlston, C. E.** "Transfiguration and Resurrection." *JBL* 80 (1961) 233–40. **Chilton, B. D.** "The Transfiguration: Dominical Assurance and Apostolic Vision." *NTS* 27 (1980) 115-24. **Dabrowski, E.** *La transfiguration de Jésus.* Rome: Biblical Institute, 1939. **Danker, F. W.** "God with Us: Hellenistic Christological Perspectives in Matthew." *CurTM* 19 (1992) 433–39. **Dodd, C. H.** "The Appearances of the Risen Christ: An Essay in Form-Criticism of the Gospels." In *Studies in the Gospels,* ed. D. E. Nineham. Oxford: Blackwell, 1955. 9–35. **Feuillet, A.** "Les perspectives propres à chaque évangéliste dans le récits de la transfiguration." *Bib* 39 (1958) 281–301. **Frieling, R.** *Die Verklärung auf dem Berge.* Stuttgart: Katholisches Bibelwerk, 1969. **Kee, H. C.** "The Transfiguration in Mark: Epiphany or Apocalyptic Vision?" In *Understanding the Sacred Text,* ed. J. Reumann. Valley Forge, PA: Judson, 1972. 135–52. **Léon-Dufour, X.** "La transfiguration de Jésus." In *Études.* 83–122. **Liefeld, W. L.** "Theological Motifs in the Transfiguration Narrative." In *New Dimensions in New Testament Study,* ed. R. N. Longenecker and M. C. Tenney. Grand Rapids: Zondervan, 1974. 162–79. **Lohmeyer, E.** "Die Verklärung Jesu nach dem Markus-Evangelium." *ZNW* 21 (1922) 185–215. **McGuckin, J. A.** "Jesus Transfigured: A Question of Christology." *Clergy Review* 69 (1984) 271–79. ———. *The Transfiguration of Christ in Scripture and Tradition.* Lewiston, NY: Mellen, 1986. **Müller, H.-P.** "Die Verklärung Jesu." *ZNW* 51 (1960) 56–64. **Murphy-O'Connor, J.** "What Really Happened at the Transfiguration?" *BibRev* 3 (1987) 8–21. **Neirynck, F.** "Minor Agreements: Matthew-Luke in the Transfiguration Story." In *Orientierung an Jesus.* FS J. Schmid, ed. P. Hoffman et al. Freiburg: Herder, 1973. 253–66. **Niemand, C.** *Studien zu den Minor Agreements der synoptischen Verklärungsperikopen.* Frankfurt am Main: Lang, 1989. **Pamment, M.** "Moses and Elijah in the Story of the Transfiguration." *ExpTim* 92 (1981) 338–39. **Pedersen, S.** "Die Proklamation Jesu als des eschatologischen Offenbarungsträgers (Mt. xvii.1-13)." *NovT* 17 (1975) 241–64. **Ramsey, A. M.** *The Glory of God and the Transfiguration of Christ.* London: Longmans, Green, 1949. **Refoulé, F.** "Jésus, nouveau Moïse, ou Pierre, nouveau grand prêtre?" *RTL* 24 (1993) 145–62. **Riesenfeld, H.** *Jésus transfiguré.* ASNU 16. Copenhagen: Munksgaard, 1947. **Roehrs, W. R.** "God's Tabernacles among Men: A Study of the Transfiguration." *CTM* 35 (1964) 18–25. **Sabbe, M.** "La rédaction du récit de la transfiguration." In *La venue du Messie,* ed. E. Massaux. RechBib 6. Bruges: Desclée de Brouwer, 1962. 65–100. **Smith, M.** "The Origin and History of the Transfiguration Story." *USQR* 36 (1980) 39–44. **Stein, R. H.** "Is the Transfiguration (Mark 9:2-8) a Misplaced Resurrection-Account?" *JBL* 95 (1976) 79–96. **Trites, A. A.** "The Transfiguration of Jesus: The Gospel in Microcosm." *EvQ* 51 (1979) 67–79. **Williams, W. H.** "The Transfiguration—A New Approach?" *SE* 6 [= TU 112] (1973) 635–50.

## Translation

[1] And [a] *after six days Jesus took Peter and James and his brother John, and he brought them up to a high mountain alone.* [b] [2] *And he was transfigured* [c] *before them, and his face shone like the sun, and his garments became as white as light.* [d] [3] *And behold Moses and Elijah, who were talking with him, appeared to them.* [4] *And Peter responded and said to Jesus: "Lord, it is good for us to be here. If you would like,* [e] *I* [f] *will put up three shrines here, one for you, one for Moses, and one for Elijah."* [5] *While he was still speaking, look, a bright cloud came down over them, and, look, a voice from the cloud said: "This is my beloved Son, in whom I am well pleased. Hear him."* [g] [6] *And when the disciples heard the voice, they fell on their faces, and they were terrified.* [h] [7] *And Jesus came to them, touched them, and said: "Rise and do not be afraid."* [8] *And when they lifted their eyes, they saw no one except him,* [i] *Jesus, alone.*

## Notes

[a] D Θ it add ἐγένετο, "it came to pass" (cf. Luke 9:28).

[b] D reads λίαν, "very (high mountain)," for κατ᾽ ἰδίαν, "alone."

[c] D e (sy^p) read μεταμορφωθείς ὁ Ἰησοῦς, "having been transfigured, Jesus," and they accordingly omit the καί, "and," after ἔμπροσθεν αὐτῶν, "before them."

[d] For τὸ φῶς, "light," D lat sy^c bo^mss read χιών, "snow"(cf. 28:3).

[e] W Θ f¹ sa^mss bo omit εἰ, "if," thereby turning Peter's statement into a question: "Do you want . . . ?"

[f] D W Θ it sy^{c.p} sa bo TR have ποιήσωμεν, "let us make," a harmonization with the Markan and Lukan parallels.

[g] Many MSS (C L W Θ f¹³ TR lat sy mae) reverse the order of ἀκούετε αὐτοῦ, "hear him," thereby bringing greater stress to the αὐτοῦ, "him"(cf. Luke 9:35).

[h] ἐφοβήθησαν σφόδρα, lit. "they were exceedingly afraid."

[i] Many MSS (B² C [D] L f^{1,13} TR) have τόν, the definite article, before Ἰησοῦν, "Jesus," instead of αὐτόν, "him"; W omits αὐτόν, "him," putting nothing in its place; in support of the text (i.e., αὐτόν) are ℵ (but after Ἰησοῦν ) B* Θ 700.

## Form/Structure/Setting

A. All three synoptic Gospels preserve the sequence of (1) the confession at Caesarea Philippi, (2) the announcement of Jesus' suffering and death (together with the subsequent saying about true discipleship), and (3) the transfiguration. Matthew and Mark include immediately after the present pericope (4) a repetition of the prophecy about the passion of the Son of Man. The logic of this sequence is clear. Jesus elicits the confession concerning his messiahship but then proceeds to instruct the disciples in the unexpected way of this strange Messiah and those who would follow him. It is for the purpose of confirming the truth of Jesus' identity as the Messiah, the Son of God—despite the shocking and apparently contradictory revelation of his imminent suffering and death—that the inner circle of disciples is allowed a glimpse of the true glory of Jesus in his transfiguration before their eyes. Thus Schweizer appropriately names the pericope "God's answer to the announcement of the passion." The real context of our passage is thus to be found not in the logion of 16:28 (contra Chilton) but in the passion announcement of 16:21–23. No other narrative between those of the birth and those of the resurrection is quite like this one. For whereas Jesus' ministry regularly has a veiled character to it, here is the only time that veil is briefly taken away, and something of Jesus' transcendent glory is directly seen by the disciples. Despite his coming death, Jesus is the Messiah, the glorious personage, confessed by Peter in the preceding pericope.

B. Matthew follows his Markan source quite closely in this pericope (Mark 9:2–8; cf. Luke 9:28–36). The major changes are the additions of καὶ ἔλαμψεν τὸ πρόσωπον αὐτοῦ ὡς ὁ ἥλιος, "and his face shone like the sun" (v 2; cf. Mark 9:2; Luke also refers to the image [εἶδος] of his face becoming "other" [ἕτερον], Luke 9:29), and vv 6–7 in their entirety, concerning the fear of the disciples (which is placed after the experience of the cloud and the divine voice) and Jesus' comforting touch and words. In the first instance, we probably have a tradition other than Mark—one reflected also in Luke; in the second, we have perhaps Matthean elaboration of the reference to fear in Mark 9:6 (omitted by Matthew from what would have been its place following v 4). The larger omissions of Markan material in Matthew's narrative are the subordinate clause of Mark 9:3, "as no fuller on earth could bleach them" (which becomes pointless given Matthew's likening of the garments to light itself), and all of Mark 9:6, about the fear of the disciples (but perhaps reflected in v 6).

Among the smaller alterations of Mark, the following should be noted. In v 1 Matthew omits the definite articles before the names Ἰάκωβον, "James," and Ἰωάννην, "John" (so too Luke 9:28, which for stylistic reasons omits the article in all three instances); in the same verse Matthew adds τὸν ἀδελφὸν αὐτοῦ, "his brother," after John (cf. 4:21; 10:2) and deletes Mark's redundant μόνους, "alone" (Mark 9:2), after κατ' ἰδίαν, "privately." In v 2 Matthew changes Mark's στίλβοντα λευκὰ λίαν, "very gleaming white" (Mark 9:3), to λευκὰ ὡς τὸ φῶς, "white as light" (cf. Luke 9:29: ἐξαστράπτων, "flashing like lightning"). In v 3 Matthew adds ἰδού, "behold" (so too Luke 9:30), reverses (as does Luke 9:30) the order of names to "Moses and Elijah" (Mark has Ἠλίας σὺν Μωϋσεῖ, "Elijah with Moses" [Mark 9:4], perhaps with Mark 9:11–13 in mind; but the order "Moses and Elijah" appears in Peter's proposal in Mark 9:5), and changes Mark's τῷ Ἰησοῦ, "to Jesus" (Mark 9:4), to the smoother μετ' αὐτοῦ, "with him." In v 4 Mark's ῥαββί, "Rabbi" (Mark 9:5), in Peter's address to Jesus becomes the more christologically suitable (especially after Caesarea Philippi) κύριε, "Lord" (cf. Luke 9:33: ἐπιστάτα, "Master"); Matthew further indicates Peter's deference to Jesus by adding εἰ θέλεις, "if you want," to the idea of building three shrines there (Mark 9:5). In v 5 Matthew inserts an initial genitive absolute, ἔτι αὐτοῦ λαλοῦντος, "while he was yet speaking" (cf. a similar genitive absolute in Luke 9:34), followed by ἰδού, "behold" (cf. Mark 9:7); there Matthew also adds the adjective φωτεινή, "bright," to describe the cloud that comes over the disciples (cf. Mark 9:7), as well as a further ἰδού, "behold," before the reference to the voice from the cloud. Matthew (and Luke 9:35) employs the participle λέγουσα, "saying," before the spoken words (cf. 3:17), while into the latter Matthew inserts ἐν ᾧ εὐδόκησα, "in whom I am well pleased" (on the model of 3:17). Finally, in v 8 Matthew rephrases Mark, writing ἐπάραντες δὲ τοὺς ὀφθαλμοὺς αὐτῶν, "and when they lifted their eyes," and omitting Mark's final redundant μεθ' ἑαυτῶν, "with themselves" (Mark 9:8). Apart from these changes Matthew is content to follow Mark nearly verbatim.

C. The narrative, in the form of an epiphany story, centers on the revelation of Jesus' glory and the voice from heaven. Peter's proposal is a parenthetical misunderstanding. The following outline may be suggested: (1) the setting (v 1); (2) the revelation of Jesus' glory, consisting of (a) his physical alteration (v 2) and (b) the appearance of key OT figures (v 3); (3) Peter's proposal (v 4); (4) the divine confirmation of Jesus' uniqueness (v 5); (5) the fear of the disciples (v 6) and the comfort of Jesus (v 7); and (6) the return to the ordinary (v 8). Arguably v 9, with its injunction of temporary silence about the event, could be considered the closing verse of this pericope (thus K. Aland's *Synopsis Quattuor Evangeliorum* [Stuttgart: Deutsche Bibelgesellschaft, 1985] 236–39). On the other hand, taking it as the introduction to the next pericope has the effect of linking the two pericopes closely together and serving as the reminder that prompts the disciples' question in v 10. Since the pericope is basically narrative, it contains little structural parallelism. Only to be mentioned are the exactly parallel clauses in v 2b and c, the parallelism in Peter's "one for . . ." (v 4c), and the parallelism in Jesus' words in v 7. V 8, furthermore, in its reference to "Jesus alone," comes close to forming an inclusio with the κατ᾽ ἰδίαν, "alone," in v 1. A possible chiastic analysis places the divine voice of v 5 at the center of the pericope (see Davies-Allison).

D. The words of v 5b, beginning with καὶ ἰδού, "and look," are in verbatim agreement with those of 3:17 at the baptism of Jesus, except for ἐκ τῆς νεφέλης, "from the cloud," for ἐκ τῶν οὐρανῶν, "from heaven," and the final two words, ἀκούετε αὐτοῦ, "hear him," which are lacking in 3:17. Thus exactly the same words are spoken concerning Jesus at the crucial point of the beginning of his public ministry and at the major turning point of the initial open announcement of his death. The same words (though not quite verbatim) are found in 2 Peter 1:6–17, where in a quite explicit allusion to the present passage (cf. "with him on the holy mountain") the author says "we were eyewitnesses of his majesty" (μεγαλειότητος), thus drawing out the christological import of the passage. The voice itself is described as that of "the Majestic Glory" (μεγαλοπρεποῦς δόξης). Here we have dependence either on our Matthew or on the tradition that underlay it.

E. Because the transfiguration story by its nature is closely linked theologically to the resurrection narratives, where the glory of Jesus is again unmistakably revealed, a number of scholars (esp. R. Bultmann [*Theology of the New Testament* (New York: Scribner's, 1951) 1:26] and his followers; see too Carlston, Murphy-O'Connor) have regarded the present pericope as a "displaced resurrection story," brought forward into the account of Jesus' ministry to aid the reader in assessing the real significance of Jesus. No evidence exists, however, to confirm this hypothesis, which is based solely on the unique character of the narrative in its setting in the ministry of Jesus. The argument of Carlston and Murphy-O'Connor, that if the event had actually happened before the resurrection, these disciples would never again have experienced doubt or fear, seems psychologically naive. Furthermore, the narrative differs from the resurrection narratives in many particulars (see esp. Dodd; Stein; Baltensweiler).

The unusual nature of the story is not to be denied, nor its similarity to the resurrection stories, which in a sense it foreshadows. But although this narration is so difficult "as to almost defy historical investigation" (I. H. Marshall, *The Gospel of Luke* [Grand Rapids: Eerdmans, 1978] 381), there is no necessity to dismiss the historicity of the event out of hand. (Chilton tries to sidestep the question of historicity altogether by a strictly literary approach.) Murphy-O'Connor's attempt to reconstruct an original historical kernel involving Jesus' realization, aided by two "explaining angels" (which in the first century were "understood by all to have a literary function" [17]), of the role of his death in God's purposes is inventive but highly speculative. Matthew will record that Jesus referred to the event as a ὅραμα, "vision" (v 9). This points unquestionably to the unusual character of what happened. But it should also be clearly noted that this word indicates something really seen (according to Kee, it was an "apocalyptic vision") and not something merely imagined (see BAGD, 577a). We may add that an *a priori* bias against the possibility of an event such as this does not put one in an advantageous position with respect to much of the Gospel.

Literary and more general parallels, both Jewish and Hellenistic, have led some scholars to conclude that the story of the transfiguration was originally the creation of the early church. Thus the similarities that can be seen between the transfiguration and the Exod 34 story of the glowing face of Moses on Mount Sinai (see below) are taken by D. F. Strauss (*The Life of Jesus Critically Examined* [reprint, Philadelphia: Fortress Press, 1972] 544) as an indication that the one story is modeled on the other. More popular, on the other hand, is the explanation based on the similarity with epiphany motifs in Hellenistic literature, as for example held by E. Lohmeyer, W. G. Kümmel (*The Theology of the New Testament* [Nashville: John Knox, 1975] 123), and F. Hahn (*The Titles of Jesus in Christology*, 340–41). The similar motifs that may be pointed to, however, can hardly be made to substantiate the claim that the transfiguration story is a concocted version of a Hellenistic epiphany narrative.

## Comment

**1** Matthew's exceptionally precise time indication μεθ᾽ ἡμέρας ἕξ, "after six days," follows Mark (cf. Luke 9:28, "about the eighth day") and may allude to Exod 24:12–18, where Moses sees the glory of Yahweh on the mountain and on the seventh day hears the voice of God. Jesus took with him the inner circle of disciples, Peter, James, and John (cf. Exod 24:1, 9, where Moses takes three close co-workers with him, Aaron, Nadab, and Abihu). These three are again privileged to accompany Jesus into the deeper recesses of the Garden of Gethsemane (26:37; see too Mark 5:37[par. Luke 8:51] and 13:3, where they are joined by Andrew). The fact that Jesus restricts this experience to the inner core of the disciples points to its particularly special character and the necessity to keep it secret (cf. v 9). These three disciples witness the glory of Jesus κατ᾽ ἰδίαν, "alone," just as the twelve themselves in 16:21 had been given the privileged knowledge that Jesus was to suffer and die. Jesus took them εἰς ὄρος ὑψηλόν, "to a high mountain," corresponding in a sense to Mount Sinai (not the traditional site, Mount Tabor, where there was a Roman post at the time [cf. Jos., *J.W.* 2.20.6 §573; 4.1.8 §§54–55], but some other, now unknown, high place; Mount Meron, between Caesarea Philippi and Capernaum, is a good guess [so Liefeld]). For the importance of mountains as places of special revelation in Matthew, see *Comment* on 4:8, and Donaldson, *Jesus on the Mountain.*

**2** The central event is described simply, in the words μετεμορφώθη ἔμπροσθεν αὐτῶν, "he was transfigured before them"; i.e., his physical appearance was transformed or dramatically altered. μεταμορφοῦν occurs in the physical sense only here and in the Markan parallel; in a spiritual sense it occurs in Rom 12:2 and 2 Cor 3:18 (in a passage that is a midrash on Exod 34), the latter possibly in a deliberate allusion to the transfiguration story. What happened is spelled out further, though only partially, in the following statements that ἔλαμψεν τὸ πρόσωπον αὐτοῦ ὡς ὁ ἥλιος, "his face shone like the sun" (the same expression is used figuratively of the righteous in the kingdom following the judgment [cf. 13:43]; cf. Moses' face in

Exod 34:29–35 and for further OT background, Dan 12:3; cf. 2 Esdr 7:97; *2 Apoc. Bar.* 51.3), and that his garments became λευκὰ ὡς τὸ φῶς, "as white as light" (cf. the whiteness of the angel's raiment in 28:3, ὡς χιών, "as snow"). The disciples see Jesus as they had never seen him before. What they saw must surely have reminded them of what they had often read in the narratives concerning Moses on Mount Sinai (cf. Exod 24), and this may to some extent influence the form of the present passage. It is clear that in this manifestation of Jesus they were somehow suddenly in direct contact with the glory of the divine presence (cf. Liefeld).

3 But now a further remarkable event witnessing to the glory of Jesus occurs, announced by Matthew's flag-words καὶ ἰδού, "and look." Two of the most important OT figures, Moses and Elijah, appear to the disciples (ὤφθη αὐτοῖς, "appeared to them"), and they converse with Jesus. This suggests at once the unity of the work of Jesus with the meaning of the OT, Moses and Elijah perhaps representing both the law and the prophets, as well as the imminence of the end of the age (cf. v 10), in connection with which key OT individuals were expected to reappear (cf. on 16:14). Both Moses and Elijah were associated with Mount Sinai, the mountain of revelation (for Elijah, "Horeb, the mount of God" [1 Kgs 19:8]). Elijah furthermore was taken directly to heaven without dying (2 Kgs 2:11–12), and rabbinic tradition (based on Deut 34:6) held too that Moses had been taken directly to heaven (cf. *b. Soṭa* 13b and the book known as *The Assumption of Moses* [= *Testament of Moses?*]). Possibly Elijah and Moses are further linked in Rev 11:1–13 (see esp. vv 5–6). Clearly, to be associated with Moses and Elijah, indeed on such a personal basis (which is what the conversation indicates), also indicated something about the greatness of Jesus. But it is apparently just this line of thinking that leads Peter to his well-meant but mistaken proposal in v 4, which in turn receives its correction in v 5.

4 Although Matthew downplays Peter's bewildered and fearful state of mind (by omitting Mark 9:6), it is obvious here too that Peter's suggestion involved a serious mistake. Apparently feeling that some response from him was called for, Peter began lamely with the statement "Lord, it is good [καλός, BAGD, 400b: "pleasant, desirable, advantageous"] for us to be here." He proposes to put up τρεῖς σκηνάς, lit. "three tents," probably little huts made of branches, not for providing the hospitality of overnight lodging or to prolong the experience (which after all was terrifying) but possibly as a kind of honorary gesture, a commemoration of this remarkable event, i.e., three shrines or holy places, similar to the OT tent shrine itself, which would symbolize the remarkable communion between heaven and earth represented by these three figures. (Cf. the "tent of meeting," where Yahweh spoke to Moses [Exod 33:7–11; Num 12:5–9].) God in this instance, however, would speak to the disciples without a tent of meeting. Riesenfeld and others make the alternative, but less convincing, suggestion that the proposal refers to the huts or "booths" that were put up during the autumn harvest festival in commemoration of God's deliverance in the wilderness wandering and at the same time as a sign of the coming eschatological deliverance (cf. Lev 23:39–44). No indication of the time of the year is given, and further, as Carson rightly notes, it is difficult to suppose that Jesus traveled with his disciples to the mountain during the Feast of Tabernacles. It would be hard, however, to deny the eschatological allusions intrinsic to this passage, and they perhaps hold the key to understanding Peter's unusual suggestion. Did he think the eschaton was beginning and that some sort of permanent dwelling should be provided for

these key eschatological figures? The basic mistake of Peter, as the following verse shows, is the relativizing of Jesus so that he becomes one of three, even if the first named. Rather the focus was upon Jesus, who was seen in divine splendor and who was announced by the Shekinah glory as the unique Son.

**5** While Peter was still speaking, another remarkable event occurred (cf. ἰδού, "look"): a "bright cloud" (νεφέλη φωτεινή) came upon the disciples. This cloud symbolizes the Shekinah glory, the very presence of God (cf. Exod 40:35; *Odes Sol.* 35:1, where the same noun and verb ἐπισκιάζειν, "come upon, overshadow" [cf. Exod 19:19], are used to describe the presence of Yahweh in the tent-shrine). The future coming of the Son of Man will also be accompanied by clouds (cf. 16:27; 24:30; 26:64; for the expectation of a return of the cloud of the Shekinah glory in the eschatological era, see 2 Macc 2:8; cf. Isa 4:5). Directly from this cloud of the divine presence comes another startling occurrence (Matthew uses ἰδού, "look," for the second time in the verse): the voice (φωνή) of God is heard from the cloud (cf. the equivalent ἐκ τῶν οὐρανῶν, "from heaven," in 3:17). The words spoken are exactly the same as in 3:17 but now with the added ἀκούετε αὐτοῦ, "hear him," calling further attention to the unique authority of Jesus, and are probably an intentional allusion to Deut 18:15, where Moses speaks of the prophet "like me," whom God would raise up for his people (cf. the NT use of this passage in Acts 3:22–23). Matthew particularly, with his catechetical interests, focuses on the authority of Jesus' teachings (see esp. Pedersen), specifically his exposition of the Torah, but the passion predictions need not therefore be ruled out of consideration. For the exegesis of the oracle "This is my beloved [Luke: ἐκλελεγμένος, "chosen"] Son, in whom I am well pleased," see *Comment* on 3:17. If the second clause contains an allusion to the suffering Servant of Isaiah (as argued there), this now takes on enormously heightened significance, given the preceding announcement by Jesus of his suffering and death. Jesus is the Messiah in whom God delights (Isa 42:1) but also the suffering Servant upon whom "the Lord has laid the iniquity of us all" (Isa 53:6). The divine voice thus identifies Jesus as the unique Son of God who possesses unique authority. Moses and Elijah are but his attendants. The focus is upon Jesus who is about to accomplish God's saving purposes in the redemption of the world (this point emerges more clearly in the parallel passage in Luke, where Moses and Elijah are described as speaking to Jesus concerning "his death [ἔξοδος] which he was about to accomplish in Jerusalem" [Luke 9:31]). Thus in the very midst of Jesus' supreme exaltation the divine voice alludes to his fate as the suffering Servant who must die. The idea of erecting three shrines reflected a misunderstanding of the uniqueness of Jesus and of his centrality to the whole sweep of salvation history.

**6–7** The disciples were terrified by the phenomena they were witnessing (in 3:17 the voice was probably heard only by Jesus). Fear at hearing the voice of God is a common experience in the OT (cf. Deut 4:33; Hab 3:2[LXX]; for fear as a reaction to a "vision," see Dan 8:17). When the disciples heard the voice of God, they fell on their faces, probably partly in fear (ἐφοβήθησαν σφόδρα, "they were terrified"; cf. the same words in 27:54) and partly in worship (for the connection between falling down before Jesus and worship of him, see 2:11; 4:9; 18:26). As he had done on a previous occasion when the disciples were filled with terror, Jesus comes to them, he touches them (ἁψάμενος αὐτῶν; the verb is usually used in conjunction with healings: cf. 8:3, 15; 9:29; 20:34), and he tells them to rise and not to be afraid (cf. 14:27). The recording of the touch of Jesus here may well have the purpose of showing that it was the real Jesus they had seen transfigured and talking to Moses and Elijah and that they therefore had not simply experienced an illusion. The Jesus of transcendent glory remains the compassionate Master who led them into discipleship. (The three elements of falling down, being touched, and being told not to fear are found in Rev 1:17.)

**8** This final verse serves not only to bring the account of the experience to an end but to emphasize the exclusive focus upon Jesus. The repetition involved in the syntax effectively makes this point: when they looked up "they saw no one [οὐδένα] except" αὐτόν 'Ιησοῦν μόνον, "him [emphatic], Jesus alone." Moses and Elijah were no longer to be seen. As they had played their respective roles in the history of salvation leading to this point in time, so now too they, returning to normal experience, must yield to Jesus, who alone remains on center stage, who alone is to be heard, and who alone can bring salvation history to its goal. It is that human Jesus, whose glory now recedes again until the resurrection, who alone can accomplish the will of God through the cross.

### Explanation

Whereas in our day most Christians need to have a revelation concerning the full humanity of Jesus, who has been abstracted into the doctrine of the Trinity, it was not so with the disciples. They, having a few days earlier heard Jesus speak in a most unexpected and disconcerting way about his death, needed at this point some assurance of the true identity of Jesus as Messiah, Son of God. This was especially important if they were to be able later to hold on to the continuity between the Jesus they had followed and the glory of the risen Christ they were also to experience. It may well be, however, that even in our day a sense of the transcendent glory of Jesus, such as is afforded by this pericope, is also very important. With the unveiling of Jesus' glory comes the divine exhortation: "Hear him!" For Matthew and his community, this exhortation undoubtedly emphasized the authority of Jesus' teaching (cf. 7:29). This prompted G. B. Caird (294) to write: "The whole history of Christian ethics could be written as a commentary on the Transfiguration." The present-day church needs once again to discover the absolute authority of the teaching of Jesus. Jesus, as our passage shows, stands in continuity with the revelation of the OT, symbolized by Moses and Elijah, but because of who he is and what he brings (i.e., the kingdom of God, the climax of salvation history), his utterances have a final and incomparable authority. The transfiguration dramatically underlines that fact.

# The Coming of Elijah (17:9–13)

### Bibliography

**Allison, D. C.** "'Elijah must come first.'" *JBL* 103 (1984) 256–58. **Blomberg, C. L.** "Elijah, Election, and the Use of Malachi in the New Testament." *CTR* 2 (1987) 100–108. **Faierstein,**

M. M. "Why do the Scribes say that Elijah must come first?" *JBL* 100 (1981) 75–86. **Fitzmyer, J. A.** "More about Elijah Coming First." *JBL* 104 (1985) 295–96. **Holzmeister, U.** "Einzeluntersuchungen über das Geheimnis der Verklärung Christi." *Bib* 21 (1940) 200–210. **Martyn, J. L.** "We have found Elijah." In *Jews, Greeks, and Christians,* ed. R. G. Hamerton-Kelly and R. Scroggs. SJLA 21. Leiden: Brill, 1976. 181–219. **Robinson, J. A. T.** "Elijah, John, and Jesus." *NTS* 4 (1958) 263–81. **Taylor, J.** "The Coming of Elijah, Mt 17,10–13 and Mk 9,11–13: The Development of the Texts." *RB* 98 (1991) 107–19.

## Translation

⁹*And when they were coming down from the mountain, Jesus commanded them, saying: "Tell no one of the vision until the Son of Man is risen* ᵃ *from the dead."* ¹⁰*And the* ᵇ *disciples asked him: "Why therefore do the scribes say that Elijah must come first?"* ¹¹*And he* ᶜ *answered and said: "As the scriptures say:* ᵈ *'Elijah is coming,* ᵉ *and he will restore* ᶠ *everything.'* ¹²*But I say to you that Elijah has already come, and they did not recognize him but did to* ᵍ *him whatever they wanted to do. Thus too the Son of Man is about to suffer at their hands."* ʰ ¹³*Then the disciples understood that he spoke to them concerning John the Baptist.*

## Notes

ᵃ ἐγερθῇ, "is raised"; many MSS (ℵ C L W Z Θ *f* ¹,¹³ TR) have the synonym ἀναστῇ, influenced by the parallel in Mark 9:9.

ᵇ B C D *f* ¹³ TR sy mae bo^pt add αὐτοῦ, "his." This is more likely a secondary addition (commonly occurring with οἱ μαθηταί, "the disciples") than an intentional omission resulting from the preceding αὐτόν, "him." See *TCGNT*, 43.

ᶜ Some witnesses (C Θ *f* ¹³ TR sy^p,h) add Ἰησοῦς, "Jesus."

ᵈ "As the scriptures say" is added to the translation to point out that Jesus here quotes the OT (see *Comment*).

ᵉ C L Z *f* ¹³ TR sy^p,h add πρῶτον, "first," probably influenced by the parallel in Mark 9:12. Favoring the critical text, however, are ℵ B D W Θ *f* ¹ lat sy^c co.

ᶠ D it have the infinitive ἀποκαταστῆσαι, "to restore"; thus "Elijah is coming to restore everything"; bo has ἀπαγγέλει, "will proclaim," in place of ἀποκαταστήσει, "will restore."

ᵍ ἐν, lit. "in"; since it is an unnecessary preposition, it is omitted by ℵ D W *f* ¹³ sy^h bo.

ʰ Lit. "by them."

## Form/Structure/Setting

A. It is obvious that this passage is closely related to what immediately precedes, even if one were to take v 9 as the end of that pericope rather than as the beginning of the present one. Having seen Jesus talking with Elijah, who was very clearly prophesied to return in connection with the end of the age (cf. Mal 3:1; 4:5), the disciples understandably wonder about his promised coming. They had apparently not yet understood what Jesus had said explicitly earlier in the narrative about John the Baptist functioning in the role of Elijah (11:10, 14). The disciples should not be thought of as stupid. They were being bombarded with one new and surprising thing after another, as was inevitable at this decisive juncture in the history of salvation. This question is a natural one, given their circumstances.

B. Matthew continues to be dependent on Mark (Mark 9:9–13; lacking in Luke). The major departures are Matthew's omission of Mark 9:10, where the disciples are reported to have "kept the matter to themselves, questioning what the rising of the dead meant" (probably Matthew regarded this as a diversion or as too negative a portrayal of the disciples); Matthew's altering of Jesus' question in the rather difficult Mark 9:12b ("And how it is written of the Son of Man that he should suffer many things and be treated with contempt?" with unmistakable verbal allusions to Isa 53) to the clear statement of v 12, οὕτως καὶ ὁ υἱὸς τοῦ ἀνθρώπου μέλλει πάσχειν ὑπ' αὐτῶν, "thus too the Son of Man is about to suffer at their hands"; and Matthew's addition of the following and final verse: "Then the disciples understood that he spoke to them concerning John the Baptist" (v 13). Other changes to be noted are: in v 9 (cf. Mark 9:9) Matthew's insertion of ὁ Ἰησοῦς λέγων, "Jesus saying," the substitution of ὅραμα (lit. "vision," though not in any technical sense) as an equivalent to Mark's ἃ εἶδον, "the things they saw," and the substitution of ἐγερθῇ, "is raised" (in keeping with 16:21 and the language of the church; cf. 1 Cor 15:4) for Mark's ἀναστῇ, "rises." In v 10 (cf. Mark 9:11), Matthew inserts οἱ μαθηταί, "the disciples," for clarity, and in v 11 (cf. Mark 9:12) he deletes Mark's πρῶτον, "first," regarding it as self-evident (it has been used in the preceding verse). In v 12 (cf. Mark 9:13) Matthew alters Mark's ἐλήλυθεν, "has come," to the more decisive ἤδη ἦλθεν, "has already come;" he adds the clarifying words καὶ οὐκ ἐπέγνωσαν αὐτόν, "and they did not recognize him"; and finally he deletes Mark's καθὼς γέγραπται ἐπ' αὐτόν, "just as it is written concerning him" (after the references to the people treating "him" [Elijah; i.e., John] however they wanted), perhaps regarding this as confusing (there is no prophecy of Elijah suffering) and as detracting from attention to Jesus as the fulfiller of scripture in his passion. Beyond these changes, Matthew as usual follows the wording of Mark's narrative very closely. There is a small degree of abbreviation, but Matthew's main purpose in the changes appears to be to make the Markan narrative as clear as possible by removing what is awkward, confusing, or potentially difficult for his readers.

C. At the heart of the pericope are the quotations of the prophet Malachi concerning Elijah and Jesus' revolutionary understanding of this material. The central issue is a hermeneutical one, and to the extent that Jesus must counter the interpretation of the "authorities," the scribes (cf. v 10), the passage has the shape of a controversy pericope, with the offering of thesis (Elijah must come) and counterthesis (Elijah has come). It can be outlined as follows: (1) the command to silence concerning the transfiguration (v 9); (2) the disciples' question concerning Elijah (v 10); (3) Jesus' answer, further divided into (a) the coming of Elijah (v 11), (b) John the Baptist (v 12a–b), and (c) the suffering of the Son of Man (v 12c); and (4) the disciples' comprehension (v 13). Consisting of dialogue with relatively brief exchanges, the pericope contains very little structural parallelism. We mention only the contrasting assertions of vv 11 and 12 (μέν . . . δέ) and the parallel verbs of v 12b.

D. The pericope is closely related to the earlier assertion of Jesus in 11:14, "And if you are willing to receive it, he is Elijah, 'the one about to come.'" The function of John the Baptist as Elijah is important for the evangelist's portrayal of Jesus as the Messiah who brings eschatological fulfillment. The present pericope is employed effectively by Justin Martyr in his *Dialogue with Trypho the Jew* in response to the same problem raised by the scribes in v 10 (*Dial.* 49.1–5).

*Comment*

**9** On the way down from the mountain, Jesus commanded the disciples to "tell no one" (μηδενὶ εἴπητε) what they had just seen. Matthew uses ὅραμα, regarding it as suitable for a theophany. The word here means a supernatural "vision," not in the sense of something imagined but in the sense of something seen. It replaces Mark's ἃ εἶδον, "what you have seen," as a kind of technical term, but not to take away from the reality of the event. (Only Matthew among the Gospels uses this word. The frequent use of it in Acts [e.g., 9:10; 10:3; 11:5; 16:9] is usually connected with divine revelations or "visions" in the proper sense of the word.) The command to secrecy is a variant of the messianic secret motif (see *Comment* on 8:4). If Jesus regularly exhorted silence concerning his messianic identity lest the people misunderstand his messianic calling, how much more would he do so in the present case where his divine glory was briefly seen. The secret was to be kept until his resurrection (ὁ υἱὸς τοῦ ἀνθρώπου, "the Son of Man," is here a circumlocution for "I"; cf. *Comment* on 8:20), that is, until Jesus had finished his work on the cross and again assumed his glorious status, now as the Risen One. In this sense the transfiguration was a foreshadowing of Jesus' glorious resurrection (cf. the appearance on the mountain in 28:16–20). When the resurrection became the center of the early church's proclamation, then too the story of the transfiguration could be made known. But the disciples surely would have been hard pressed to comprehend at this point Jesus' intent (despite Matthew's omission of Mark 9:10).

**10** With the sight of Elijah and Moses talking to Jesus fresh in their minds, the disciples are prompted to ask about the coming of Elijah. They knew well the scribes' (γραμματεῖς, the professional scripture scholars; see further *Comment* on 2:4) insistence (perhaps even in response to Jesus' and their proclamation of the kingdom) that the coming of the eschatological age had the precondition of the return of Elijah. The οὖν, "therefore," probably is linked not with the reference to the resurrection but to the transfiguration narrative as a whole and in particular to the appearance of Elijah. According to the prophet Malachi, 'Ηλίαν δεῖ ἐλθεῖν πρῶτον, "Elijah must come first." On the nuance of δεῖ, "it is necessary," as the divine will, cf. *Comment* on 16:21. This is essentially a distillation of Mal 4:5: "Behold I will send you Elijah the prophet before the great and terrible day of the LORD comes" (cf. LXX [Mal 3:22]). For the rabbinic expectation of Elijah, see *m. ʿEd.* 8:7; *m. B. Meṣ.* 3:5. Thus the disciples shared the question of the scribes concerning whether the Elijah they had just seen was going to return yet again before the end of the age. With their uncertainty and lack of understanding of the resurrection saying (cf. Mark 9:10), however, it is unlikely that their question was specifically how Elijah could return before the imminent death and resurrection of Jesus (contra Fenton, Gundry, Patte). Their question concerns, rather, the meaning of the Malachi passage.

It has been pointed out by M. M. Faierstein (so too J. A. T. Robinson and J. L. Martyn) that it is far from clear that the Malachi passage or Jewish tradition brought the prior coming of Elijah specifically into relation with the coming of the Messiah. The response of D. C. Allison, however, shows that the association is not to be regarded as a Christian invention. Fitzmyer calls attention to the difficulty of establishing a general Jewish expectation that the Messiah was to come on the "day of the Lord." The question about Elijah in the present verse concerns only the meaning of the Malachi prophecy that Elijah must come before the end of the age. Undoubtedly, the disciples also wondered how this expectation was to be related to the eschatological realities being announced by Jesus, whom they had just confessed to be the Messiah (16:16).

**11** Jesus responds to their question by alluding to the same passage with the words Ἡλίας μὲν ἔρχεται, "Elijah is coming" (ἔρχεται being reminiscent of the LXX's ἐλθεῖν), going a step further by adding καὶ ἀποκαταστήσει πάντα, "and he will restore everything." The verb ἀποκαταστήσει, "will restore," is drawn verbatim from the LXX of Mal 3:23, where, however, the object clause is "the heart of the father to the son and the heart of a man to his neighbor" (the Hebrew of Mal 4:6 is only slightly different). The future tense, therefore, does not suggest that Jesus expects a future return of John the Baptist (contra Gundry). The restoration of "everything" (πάντα) must here refer not to the eschatological renewal of the present order itself (which would make Elijah the Messiah himself, rather than the forerunner of the Messiah), as, for example, apparently in Acts 1:6 (and cf. especially the cognate noun ἀποκατάστασις, "restoration" or "establishing," in Acts 3:21 in an allusion to the return of Jesus), but to a preparatory work of repentance and renewal (as in the Malachi passage; see especially Luke 1:17 and cf. Sir 48:10). Only an interpretation of this kind can make possible Jesus' identification of John the Baptist with Elijah in the verse that follows. In short, Jesus responds initially by fully agreeing with the scribes in their understanding of Malachi's prophecy that Elijah is to come and accomplish his preparatory work. It is only in the astonishing conclusion now to be drawn that Jesus parts company with the scribes.

**12** λέγω δὲ ὑμῖν, "but I say to you," carries a degree of emphasis to the following statement. The scribes were right in thinking that Elijah had to come before the commencement of the eschatological age, but now Jesus flatly asserts that Ἠλίας ἤδη ἦλθεν, "Elijah has already come" (cf. the explicit statement in 11:14). The allusion here is to John's ministry of repentance and renewal. The forerunner had in fact come, but "they did not recognize him" (οὐκ ἐπέγνωσαν αὐτόν) and furthermore did to him whatever they pleased (cf. 14:6–12; cf. for the historical Elijah, 1 Kgs 19:2, 10). There is an unmistakable typological correspondence between the fate of John the Baptist and that of Jesus (cf. 11:16–19). Jesus too, coming as the promised Messiah to his people, was largely unrecognized (cf. 16:13–14; John 1:10), although this is implied rather than stated here (both John and Jesus were regarded as prophets; cf. 21:26, 46). The second point, however, is made very explicit: "thus too [οὕτως καὶ] the Son of Man is about to suffer [πάσχειν] at their hands" (cf. the first passion prediction in 16:21 and the second, which will occur in vv 22–23). ὁ υἱὸς τοῦ ἀνθρώπου, "the Son of Man," as in v 9, is here a circumlocution for "I." If the scribes and the Jewish leaders had not recognized John as Elijah, their culpability in not recognizing Jesus was, if anything, even greater, given the public ministry of Jesus.

**13** The reference to an Elijah who had come, and to whom they did as they pleased, apparently jogged the memory of the disciples (cf. 11:14; 14:12), and "then they understood" (τότε συνῆκαν) that Jesus spoke of John the Baptist. The startling conclusion is left implicit. If John was Elijah, then Jesus is the one whose way was prepared by John (3:3), the Messiah and the one who brings with him the eschatological kingdom. The proper identification of John leads to the appropriate Christology.

### Explanation

At the heart of this pericope lies the hermeneutical question of the meaning of Malachi's prophecy. The scribes had done their job well in concluding "Elijah must come first." Their insistence on this point, however, was determined to a large extent by their *a priori* convictions about how the eschatological fulfillment had to occur, and it was probably motivated by their unwillingness to accept Jesus or his message. As they saw nothing in John's fate in Herod's prison that corresponded with their expectations of Elijah, so also they saw nothing in Jesus' claims or in his humility that corresponded with their conception of the Messiah. And when he was crucified, that served only to confirm that he could not have been the Messiah. Thus their rigid, preconceived notions tragically caused them to be blind to the very heart of God's mission in his Messiah. What was required of them was to revise their categories and to understand, with Paul among other Jews, that "Christ crucified" (1 Cor 1:23), rather than being a self-contained and intolerable contradiction, is the glorious high point of God's promises to Israel— and through Israel to the nations of the world.

## *The Healing of the Epileptic Boy by Jesus after the Disciples' Failure   (17:14–20[21])*

### Bibliography

**Aichinger, H.** "Zur Traditionsgeschichte der Epileptiker-Perikope Mk 9,14–29 par Mt 17,14–21 par Lk 9,37–43a." In *Probleme der Forschung*, ed. A. Fuchs. SNTU A3. Vienna: Herold, 1978. 114–43. **Barth, G.** "Glaube und Zweifel in den synoptischen Evangelien." *ZTK* 72 (1975) 269–92. **Bornkamm, G.** "πνεῦμα ἄλαλον: Eine Studie zum Markusevangelium." In *Geschichte und Glaube*. Gesammelte Aufsätze II. BEvT 53. Munich: Kaiser, 1971. 21–36. **Derrett, J. D. M.** "Moving Mountains and Uprooting Trees (Mk 11:22; Mt 17:20, 21:21; Lk 17:6)." *BO* 30 (1988) 231–44. **Duplacy, J.** "La foi qui déplace les montagnes (Mt 17,20; 21,21 et par)." In *A la rencontre de Dieu*. FS A. Gelin, ed. M. Jourjon et al. Bibliothèque de la faculté de théologie de Lyon 8. Le Puy: Mappus, 1961. 272–87. **Hahn, F.** "Jesu Wort vom bergeversetzenden Glauben." *ZNW* 76 (1985) 149–69. **Klein, H.** "Das Glaubensverständnis im Matthäusevangelium." In *Glaube im Neuen Testament*. FS H. Binder, ed. F. Hahn and H. Klein. Biblisch-theologische Studien 7. Neukirchen: Neukirchener, 1982. 29–42. **Léon-Dufour, X.** "L'episode de l'enfant épileptique." In *La formation des évangiles*. RechBib 2. Bruges: Desclée de Brouwer, 1957. 85–115. **Schmithals, W.** "Die Heilung des Epileptischen." *ThViat* 13 (1976) 211–34. **Wilkinson, J.** "The Case of the Epileptic Boy." *ExpTim* 79 (1967) 39–42. **Zmijewski, J.** "Der Glaube und seine Macht." In *Begegnung mit dem Wort*. FS H. Zimmermann, ed. J. Zmijewski and E. Nellessen. BBB 53. Bonn: Hanstein, 1980. 81–103.

## Translation

[14] *And when they had come* [a] *to the crowd, a man came to him, knelt before him,* [15] *and said: "Lord, have mercy on my son, because he is epileptic and suffers* [b] *terribly. For often he falls into the fire, and often* [c] *into the water.* [16] *And I brought him to your disciples, but they were not able to heal him."* [17] *And* [d] *Jesus, answering, said: "O unfaithful* [e] *and depraved generation, how long will I be with you? How long will I put up with you? Bring him here to me."* [18] *And Jesus rebuked the demon,* [f] *and it* [g] *came out of him, and the child was healed from that hour.*

[19] *Then coming to Jesus privately, the disciples said: "Why were we unable to cast it out?"* [20] *And he* [h] *said to them: "Because of your little* [i] *faith. For truly I tell you, if you have faith only as small as* [j] *a mustard seed, you will say to this mountain, 'Move from here to there,' and it will be moved. And nothing will be impossible for you."* [k]

## Notes

[a] Complementing the single ἐλθόντων of the text to produce a proper genitive absolute, C L W Θ TR add αὐτῶν, thus producing "when they had come down." D lat (sy$^{s,c}$) bo$^{pt}$, on the other hand, change the pl. ἐλθόντων into the sing. nominative adverbial participle ἐλθών, "when he came down." Clearly the difficult ἐλθόντων is to be preferred.

[b] The important witnesses ℵ B L Z$^{vid}$ Θ have ἔχει, "has." Nevertheless, πάσχει, "suffers" (C D W f$^{1,13}$ TR lat sy$^{c,h}$), is preferred by the committee since κακῶς πάσχει, "suffers terribly," is the more difficult reading, being pleonastic as well as being less idiomatic Gr. than κακῶς ἔχει, lit. "he has (is) poorly" (cf. 4:24; 8:16; 9:12; 14:35).

[c] D Θ f$^1$ it mae have ἐνίοτε, "sometimes," for the repeated πολλάκις, "often" (omitted by W).

[d] ℵ$^1$ Z and a few other witnesses have τότε, "then."

[e] Z Φ and a few other witnesses have πονηρά, "evil," for ἄπιστος, "unfaithful."

[f] αὐτῷ, "him" or "it," is changed in the translation to "the demon" for clarity. See *Comment* for the ambiguity of the pronoun.

[g] τὸ δαιμόνιον, "the demon." See preceding *Note*.

[h] C L W f$^1$ TR lat sy$^{p,h}$ add Ἰησοῦς, "Jesus."

[i] C D L W TR sy$^{s,p,h}$ have the more common word ἀπιστίαν, "lack of faith." The word ὀλιγοπιστία (*hap. leg.* in NT) in its adjectival form (ὀλιγόπιστος, "of little faith") is furthermore a Matthean favorite. See *TCGNT*, 43. Another probable reason for the change to ἀπιστία, "lack of faith," is that in the same verse the point is made that only a little faith (as of a mustard seed) is sufficient to move mountains.

[j] ὡς, lit. "faith *as* a mustard seed."

[k] Many MSS (ℵ$^2$ C D L W f$^{1,13}$ TR lat (sy$^{p,h}$) (mae) bo$^{pt}$ add another sentence (v 21): τοῦτο δὲ τὸ γένος οὐκ ἐκπορεύεται εἰ μὴ ἐν προσευχῇ καὶ νηστείᾳ, "But this kind does not come out except by fasting and prayer." But the verse is lacking in ℵ* B Θ 33 sy$^{s,c}$ sa bo$^{pt}$, and there is no apparent reason that it would have been omitted other than that Matthew chooses to make another point. Thus it has almost certainly been inserted from the parallel passage (Mark 9:29). See *TCGNT*, 43.

## Form/Structure/Setting

A. There is no obvious reason why the narrative of the healing of the possessed boy is placed here in the Markan sequence, which Matthew continues to follow. It does not have any particular connection with what precedes or follows and strikes one as parenthetical or incidental to the new direction the narrative has taken from 16:21 (Mark 8:31). Healing miracles in the second main part of Matthew are very few (specific miracles after the present pericope only in 20:29–34, the healing of two blind men; general or summarizing references only in 19:1

and 21:14 in the temple). The story may be placed here for no other reason than that this is chronologically about when it occurred (cf. Luke's specific reference to the time [Luke 9:37]). Although the miracle does have an obvious christological aspect, this is left implicit by the evangelists (only Luke notes any concluding observation at all [9:43]). The focus is the importance of faith—a theme that does have special relevance at this stage of the overall narrative.

B. Matthew depends on Mark again (Mark 9:14–29) but abbreviates to the point of omitting nearly two thirds of the Markan account in the first part of the passage (Matt 17:14–18 has 10.3 lines of the Nestle-Aland Greek NT compared to Mark's 28.3 lines; the Lukan parallel [9:37–43a] also abbreviates this material to a considerable extent [15.5 lines]). The extensive agreements between Matthew and Luke against Mark prompt Luz to argue for the influence of oral tradition or a different version of the Markan text. Matthew gives only the basics of the story, omitting the following: Mark's setting with its reference to the dispute with the scribes (Mark 9:14–16), the description of the symptoms of the boy's possession (Mark 9:18a), the lengthy section prior to the actual healing, including Jesus' question about the length of the possession (Mark 9:20–24; v 15b picks up a little of Mark 9:22; and the striking discussion concerning faith and unbelief in Mark 9:23–24 finds its counterpart in the emphasis on faith, Matthean style, in v 20, which is lacking in Mark [and in the Lukan parallel, but cf. Luke 17:6]), and finally the details of the exorcism itself (Mark 9:25–28).

Matthew's skeletal story draws upon Mark's wording. The following changes can be noted. At the beginning of v 14, Matthew has the disciples and Jesus come πρὸς τὸν ὄχλον, "to the crowd," rather than as in Mark πρὸς τοὺς μαθητάς, "to the disciples" (i.e., the other nine; Mark 9:14). Matthew adds that the father was "kneeling before him" (γονυπετῶν αὐτόν) and that (v 15) he addressed Jesus as κύριε, "Lord" (Mark 9:17 has the address διδάσκαλε, "teacher"; so too Luke 9:38), with the direct appeal ἐλέησόν μου τὸν υἱόν, "have mercy on my son" (in Mark the appeal, in the words "help us," does not occur until 9:22). Matthew employs the technical term σεληνιάζεται, "is epileptic," and simply writes κακῶς πάσχει, "he suffers terribly," in place of Mark's detailed description (Mark 9:18). In v 17 Matthew adds καὶ διεστραμμένη, "and depraved" (with Luke 9:41), in the description of that "faithless generation" (Mark 9:19). At the end of v 18 Matthew indicates the healing in the words καὶ ἐθεραπεύθη ὁ παῖς ἀπὸ τῆς ὥρας ἐκείνης, "and the child was healed from that hour" (for this Matthean language, cf. 9:22; 15:28). In the second part of the passage, vv 19–20, Matthew begins with an added, characteristic τότε, "then," and then replaces the Markan answer of Jesus, "This kind is able to be cast out by no one except by prayer" (cf. the textually dubious v 21 in Matthew), with v 20 and its reference to little faith—faith as small as a mustard seed (probably a Q saying; cf. Luke 17:6 where, however, it is a sycamin tree that is rooted up and planted in the sea [cf. Matt 21:21 for a mountain being moved into the sea, a mixing of the two traditions])—and the possibility of all through faith. Clearly, in much of this Matthew's abbreviation is to conserve space. But the omission of Mark 9:22b–24 probably results from Matthew's dissatisfaction with the man saying "if you can" and admitting his ἀπιστία, "unbelief." In Matthew, by contrast, the man addresses Jesus as "Lord" and exhibits no uncertainty in his appeal, "have mercy on my son" (v 15). Similarly, the answer of Jesus in Mark 9:29 could be seen as limiting Jesus' power (esp. in the rendering of v 21, "by prayer and fasting"). Matthew's message, on the contrary, is that nothing is impossible for one who has faith even as small as a mustard seed (v 20).

C. This pericope is one of mixed genre, consisting of a healing narrative (but minus the reaction of the crowd or any christological conclusion) mixed with teaching in a final apothegm about faith growing out of the disciples' inability to heal the possessed boy. The story is told more for the accompanying teaching than for its own sake (Davies-Allison describe it as "on its way to becoming a pronouncement story" [2:720]). As an outline, the following may be suggested. Part 1 (the healing): (a) a man entreats Jesus for his son, subdivided into (i) the request (v 14–15a), and (ii) the symptoms (v 15b-c); (b) the previous failure of the disciples (v 16); (c) Jesus' response of lament (v 17); (d) the healing (v 18). Part 2 (the subsequent discussion): (a) the disciples' question (v 19); and (b) Jesus' answer, including a further statement concerning faith (v 20). The pericope consists mainly of direct discourse and contains little structural parallelism or symmetry. To be noted in this connection are the parallel clauses in v 15c (where πίπτει, "he falls," is understood in the second clause), the parallel interrogatory clauses in Jesus' lament (v 17), the three parallel clauses, each with an independent subject, in v 18, and finally the parallelism in v 20 in the instruction concerning faith. These parallelisms are the result of Matthew's redaction of the passage (except for that of v 17, which is borrowed from Mark).

D. A related, but probably independent, version of the logion in v 20 is found in 21:21 (in the context of the withering of the fig tree, parallel to Mark 11:23). There the power of faith is illustrated by the figure of casting a mountain into the sea (cf. the Lukan parallel to the present passage, where a tree is rooted up and cast into the sea [Luke 17:6]). It is not unlikely that Jesus used various, related metaphors on different occasions to make the same point about faith. Cf. the general reference simply to moving mountains in *Gos. Thom.* 48 (where, however, the teaching is about peace rather than faith).

## Comment

**14–15** When Jesus and the three disciples had come down from the mountain to join the other disciples (cf. Mark 9:14), they encountered a crowd. The disciples had attempted an exorcism only to fail, and now the same man approached Jesus himself for the healing of his boy. Matthew presents the man as worshiping Jesus, using not only προσῆλθεν, "came to" (on which, see *Comments* on 5:1; 8:2) but γονυπετῶν, "kneeling down" (used again in Matthew only in 27:29, mockingly), as well as the address κύριε, "Lord." In his direct appeal, furthermore, he is a man of faith: ἐλέησόν μου τὸν υἱόν, "have mercy on my son" (cf. also, with possibly a liturgical echo, the similar request using the same verb in 9:27; 15:22; 20:30; contrast Mark 9:22b, 24b). Matthew uses the term σεληνιάζεται, lit. "moonstruck" (cf. "lunacy," probably a case of epilepsy; in the NT the word is used only by Matthew here and in 4:24, where it occurs in a list of those healed by Jesus and follows the word δαιμονιζομένους, "demon possessed"), to indicate the boy's condition, adding κακῶς πάσχει, "suffers terribly," to indicate its severity. Matthew's statement that "he falls" (πίπτει) frequently into the fire and into the water points to a serious lack of motor control that repeatedly put the boy's life in danger. (This is attributed in Mark to the attempt of the demon to kill the boy;

Mark 9:22: ἔβαλεν, "it has cast.") The fact that the curing of the boy in v 18b is by means of an exorcism indicates that Matthew also understood the disease of the boy to be caused by a demon (for a similar connection between disease and demon possession, see *Comments* on 9:32; 12:22).

**16** The man relates that he had already brought his son to the disciples, i.e., the nine who had not accompanied Jesus up the mountain but found they were "not able" (οὐκ ἠδυνήθησαν) "to heal" (θεραπεῦσαι; cf. *Comment* on 4:23; and v 18) his son. The inability of the disciples to perform this exorcism could call in question Jesus' own power (cf. Mark 9:22b), since it was he who had bestowed the power upon them to perform such miracles (10:1, 8). But Jesus has not the slightest problem with the exorcism (v 18). In this instance, which may have alarmed as well as frustrated the disciples, they were to learn an important lesson about faith. (For a parallel instance, cf. 2 Kgs 4:31.)

**17** Jesus' lament here is addressed not so much to the man, who after all seemed to believe in Jesus' power (but not that of the disciples?), or to the disciples, as it is to the unbelieving crowd that had become involved (note the repeated plural ὑμῶν, "you," and the plural verb φέρετε, "you bring," and the "privately" of v 19). That "generation" (γενεά) is addressed as being ἄπιστος καὶ διεστραμμένη, "unfaithful and depraved" (both words in Matthew only here; cf. Deut 32:5, 20 and the identical address in Luke 9:41; cf. too the other Matthean description of that generation as πονηρὰ καὶ μοιχαλίς, "evil and adulterous," in 12:39, 45 [only "evil"], and 16:4; cf. Mark 8:38; Phil 2:15). The repeated rhetorical question in the style of prophetic lament beginning with "How long?" (ἕως πότε) has an added edge for the disciples (and the readers) now after the prediction of his suffering and death. There is an undeniable frustration in Jesus' questions—a frustration over the breakdown of the dawning kingdom in his absence, reflected in the powerlessness of the disciples. They appear themselves to have been affected by the unbelief of the crowd, and they will receive their rebuke in v 20. But here the hardheartedness of the crowd is primarily in view, and Jesus asks how long he will have to be with them (cf. John 14:9) and "put up" with them (ἀνέχεσθαι occurs in Matthew only here). The whole episode seems to have reminded Jesus of Israel's unbelief. There was no doubt some impatience in Jesus when he ordered φέρετέ μοι αὐτὸν ὧδε, "bring him to me here" (cf. the command of 14:18).

**18** The object of Jesus' rebuke indicated by αὐτῷ (masculine or neuter), "him" or "it," is ambiguous: it could be the boy (cf. RSV; and NEB: "Jesus then spoke sternly to the boy") or the demon, which is about to be mentioned. Since Matthew is following Mark and the latter is explicit (the object of the verb in Mark 9:25 is τῷ πνεύματι τῷ ἀκαθάρτῳ, "the unclean spirit"; cf. Mark 1:25), it is likely that Matthew's αὐτῷ refers to the demon, thus anticipating rather than following the noun to which it refers. At the rebuke of Jesus, the demon immediately came out of the boy, and it is recorded that the boy "was healed" (ἐθεραπεύθη) ἀπὸ τῆς ὥρας ἐκείνης, "from that hour" (cf. the similar ending formulae in 8:13 and 9:22, both referring to "that hour"). This verse is remarkable for its directness and the conciseness of its three main clauses, each with a different subject: ὁ Ἰησοῦς, "Jesus," τὸ δαιμόνιον, "the demon," and ὁ παῖς, "the child."

**19–20a** The disciples came to Jesus κατ' ἰδίαν, "privately," reflecting their embarrassment over the episode, to inquire why in this instance they were unable to cast out the demon. The ἡμεῖς, "we," is emphatic. They were surprised at their failure because they knew that Jesus had given them authority and the power to exorcise demons (10:1, 8) and they undoubtedly had already themselves performed numerous exorcisms (cf. Luke 10:17). Was it perhaps a matter of technique? Probably the disciples were dismayed by Jesus' crisp answer: διὰ τὴν ὀλιγοπιστίαν ὑμῶν, "because of your little faith." Perhaps in this instance they had become uneasy over the extreme symptoms displayed by the boy (described much more fully by Mark). Perhaps surrounded by a doubting crowd, and without Jesus or Peter, James, and John, their confidence was shaken and their power thereby dwindled so that they were unable to drive the demon out. The noun ὀλιγοπιστία, "little faith," occurs in the NT only here (for the cognate adjective, see 6:30; 8:26; 14:31; 16:8). It suggests not total lack of faith (as does ἀπιστία) but a weak faith that nevertheless produces the same effect as no faith (cf. Jas 1:6–7). In light of the statement that follows, this "little faith" apparently does not qualify to be called genuine faith at all, even of a minimal amount. No distinction is made in this passage between "saving faith" and a "special faith" adequate for healing (contra Davies-Allison, Luz).

**20b** Matthew introduces this accompanying logion with the formula ἀμὴν γὰρ λέγω ὑμῖν, "truly I say to you," thus heightening its authority (see *Comment* on 5:18). πίστιν ὡς κόκκον σινάπεως, "faith as a mustard seed" (cf. the same phrase in Luke 17:6), refers to the smallest possible amount (as the mustard seed is "the smallest of all seeds" [13:31–32]). Just that small amount of faith has unlimited potential and through God's power makes everything possible. (On the importance of πίστις, "faith," in Matthew, see *Comment* on 8:10.) This point is driven home with the proverbial and hyperbolic analogy of moving mountains (cf. 21:21, also in reference to faith; the analogy is picked up by Paul in 1 Cor 13:2; for rabbinic background see *b. Sanh.* 4a; *b. Soṭa* 9b; *b. B. Bat.* 3b) and the concluding affirmation that οὐδὲν ἀδυνατήσει ὑμῖν, "nothing will be impossible for you." While the full range of possibility here is not to be missed, at the same time the limitations imposed by the immediate context, as well as that of the Gospel as a whole, must not be ignored. Consideration of the context leads to the conclusion that the clause "nothing will be impossible" refers to the signs of the kingdom, which the disciples in their office were commissioned to perform in chap. 10. There is furthermore the conditioning factor of the faith of the intended recipients of these signs (cf. 13:58), as well as—and most basic of all—the will of God itself.

### Explanation

The relation between faith and healing, in this case exorcism, is the central concern of the pericope. But here, unlike other places in the Gospel where the issue is addressed, the focus is not on the faith of the recipient (cf. 9:28–29) but on the faith of those who would be the means of that healing. In Matthew the question concerns faith, even as small as a mustard seed, as opposed to no faith (cf. Mark, where the man reveals a mixture of faith and unbelief [Mark 9:22–24]). With the smallest conceivable amount of faith, the possibilities are limitless, and to emphasize this, only hyperbole will serve. The emphasis is rightly on what a small amount of faith can do. Yet the conditions, which can become limitations, are also repeatedly presumed in the Gospel: the passage pertains to the signs of the kingdom, not miracles of any kind; it applies also to the uniqueness of the apostles' commission, though the pericope is not without its application to Matthew's church (and the church of our day), where healing too may be expected; the receptivity of those in need is an obvious factor; and finally the will of God always constitutes the final determinant. Healings require faith, yet faith, even genuine faith, whether of the healer or the would-be-healed, cannot demand healing. Disciples, moreover, cannot depend on a mechanistic approach to the works of the kingdom. With faith all things are possible—but only within the sovereign and sometimes mysterious will of God. In this instance, as we come to know, it was God's will for the healing of the man's son, but that healing was at first hindered by the uncertainty of the disciples. Nothing is impossible for the disciple of Jesus who with faith works within the established will of God. It is therefore the case that not every failure in the performance or reception of healing is the result solely of insufficient faith.

# The Second Passion Prediction    (17:22–23)

### Bibliography

Brodie, T. "Fish, Temple, Tithe, and Remission: The God-based Generosity of Deuteronomy 14–15 as One Component of Matt 17:22–18:35." *RB* 99 (1992) 697–718. **Thompson, W. G.** *Matthew's Advice to a Divided Community: Mt 17,22–18,35.* AnBib 44. Rome: Biblical Institute, 1970. 16–49.

See also *Bibliography* for 16:21–23.

### Translation

²²*And as they were gathering around him* ᵃ *in Galilee, Jesus said to them: "The Son of Man is about to be betrayed into human hands,*ᵇ ²³*and they will kill him, and on the third day* ᶜ *he will be raised."*ᵈ *And they became very sorrowful.*ᵉ

### Notes

ᵃ Many witnesses (C D L W Θ *f*¹³ TR saᵐˢˢ mae bo) have ἀναστρεφομένων, "living," in place of the rare and more difficult συστρεφομένων, "gathering around (him)" (ℵ B *f*¹), which is to be preferred. Cf. *TCGNT*, 44. The pronoun "him" is implied.

ᵇ Lit. "the hands of men."

ᶜD it syˢ bo have μετὰ τρεῖς ἡμέρας, "after three days," by influence of the parallel in Mark 9:31.

ᵈ ἐγερθήσεται. B 047 *f*¹³ have ἀναστήσεται, "he will rise," by influence of the parallel in Mark 9:31.

ᵉ K and a few other witnesses omit this sentence, probably for theological reasons.

### Form/Structure/Setting

A. This second announcement of Jesus' suffering and death sustains the tension created by the first announcement (16:21–23) and further orients the second half of the Gospel (cf. 20:17–19) to the central events in the ministry of Jesus that were to take place in Jerusalem. This is the shortest of the three predictions (discounting v 12c, which is an incidental reference to the death of Jesus). In Mark 9:30–32 this pericope leads directly into the teaching that true greatness is to be found in service, of which naturally the great model is the passion of Jesus.

B. Matthew depends on Mark 9:30–32 for this pericope (cf. Luke 9:43b–45). The biggest changes are at the beginning and end. Thus Matthew begins with his own genitive absolute, συστρεφομένων δὲ αὐτῶν, "and as they were gathering around (him)," in (ἐν) Galilee (cf. Mark's "passing through [διά] Galilee") and then omits Mark's following two clauses about Jesus not wanting anyone to know and that he "was teaching his disciples" (Mark 9:30b and 31a). Matthew reserves the verb "teach" (διδάσκειν) for matters other than the passion predictions. At the end of the pericope, Matthew omits Mark 9:32, "They were ignorant of the matter and were afraid to ask him." Matthew here probably wants to minimize the ignorance of the disciples. As for the central logion itself (v 22b–23; cf. Mark 9:31b to end of verse), Matthew has μέλλει ("is about to") with the infinitive παραδίδοσθαι, "be betrayed" (both also in Luke 9:44, probably through the influence of oral tradition). Matthew omits Mark's redundant participle ἀποκτανθείς, "having been killed," replaces Mark's μετὰ τρεῖς ἡμέρας, "after three days," with the more accurate τῇ τρίτῃ ἡμέρᾳ, "on the third day," and replaces the verb ἀνιστάναι, "rise," with ἐγείρειν in the passive, "be raised" (the latter two changes occur in all three passion predictions, probably through the influence of the kerygma of the early church; cf. 1 Cor 15:4). Finally Matthew adds καὶ ἐλυπήθησαν σφόδρα, "and they became very sorrowful," suggesting comprehension at least at one level of what Jesus meant (contra Mark 9:32). In contrast to the other passion predictions, there is no reference to going to Jerusalem (16:21; 20:18), suffering many things (16:21), the chief priests and scribes (20:18; 16:21 adds elders), or the other details mentioned in 20:18–19 (i.e., being condemned to death and deliverance to the Gentiles for mocking, scourging, and crucifixion).

C. This short pericope has three parts: (1) announcement of the betrayal into hands of men (v 22); (2) announcement of the death and resurrection of Jesus (v 23a–b); and (3) the response of the disciples (v 23c). Apart from the slight parallelism of the second and third clauses of the prediction itself (v 23c–b), the passage reveals no noteworthy structural features.

## Comment

**22** Matthew's opening genitive absolute, συστρεφομένων ... αὐτῶν, "as they were gathering around (him)," suggests another, a second, private (cf. Mark 9:30) and explicit announcement "in Galilee" (ἐν τῇ Γαλιλαίᾳ) of what was to befall Jesus in Jerusalem in the not distant future (μέλλει, "is about to"). ὁ υἱὸς τοῦ ἀνθρώπου, "the Son of Man," is here, as earlier (see *Comment* on 8:20), a circumlocution for "I," i.e., for Jesus himself. Now for the first time the important word παραδίδοσθαι, "to hand over, be betrayed," is used in referring to Jesus' death (cf. 20:18–19; and especially chaps. 26–27, where it occurs no less than fifteen times, underlining the fulfillment of the predictions; Acts 3:13; Rom 4:25; 1 Cor 11:23; cf. Rom 8:32, where God is said to hand over his own Son). Possibly there is also an intended allusion to the verb in the LXX of Isa 53:6, 12. A divine handing over of Jesus is reminiscent of the δεῖ, "it is necessary," in 16:21. The verb reminds the reader that the disciples have been warned of a day when they will be "handed over" (cf. 10:17–22; 24:9–10). εἰς χεῖρας ἀνθρώπων, lit. "into the hands of men," is a general reference to the Jewish authorities and the Romans (cf. 26:45: εἰς χεῖρας ἁμαρτωλῶν, "into the hands of sinners") as opposed to the specific references to the chief priests and scribes (20:18) and elders (added in 16:21). Behind it may lie the Aramaic "the sons of men," in which case there would be a wordplay with "the Son of Man" (see Thompson).

**23** The verb ἀποκτενοῦσιν, "will kill," is also used in the first passion prediction (16:21; only in the third prediction is σταυροῦν, "crucify," used; for ἀποκτείνειν, cf. 21:38–39; 26:4). It too recalls and anticipates instances where the same verb is used referring to the persecution the disciples are to expect (cf. 10:28; 23:34; 24:9). Jesus will be killed, but τῇ τρίτῃ ἡμέρᾳ ἐγερθήσεται, "on the third day he will be raised." This last clause is found again verbatim in the third prediction (20:19) and very nearly verbatim in the first (16:21). It finds its fulfillment in 28:6. See further *Comment* on 16:21. The final words ἐλυπήθησαν σφόδρα, "they became very sorrowful," are again juxtaposed in 26:22 (cf. too 18:31), where Jesus announces that one of the twelve will betray him; the verb is used of Jesus himself in the Garden of Gethsemane with the passion in full view (26:37). Matthew thus records the emotion of the disciples. Though quite beyond their understanding at this time, because the resurrection is beyond their mental horizon, these words fill them with trouble.

### Explanation

The performance of another healing miracle in Galilee is not to be understood as a return to the business of the kingdom as before the turning point (cf. 16:21) of the first passion prediction. Jesus does not return to Capernaum to settle down or reestablish a base for future missions. No, Jesus' purpose is to accomplish the will of the Father through his own suffering and death. The cross is now the orientation point of the Gospel narrative. And Jesus' words remind the disciples, and readers, that they must be prepared to follow in Jesus' footsteps in faithfulness to his calling (cf. 16:24–26).

# Paying the Temple Tax    (17:24–27)

### Bibliography

**Aarde, A. G. van.** "Resonance and Reception: Interpreting Mt 17:24–27 in Context." *Scr* 29 (1989) 1–12. **Banks, R.** "Jesus and Custom." *ExpTim* 84 (1973) 265–69. **Bauckham, R.** "The Coin in the Fish's Mouth." In *Gospel Perspectives 6,* ed. D. Wenham and C. L. Blomberg. Sheffield: JSOT, 1986. 219–52. **Cassidy, R. J.** "Matthew 17:24–27—A Word on Civil Taxes." *CBQ* 41 (1979) 571–80. **Daube, D.** "The Temple Tax." In *Appeasement or Resistance? and Other Essays on New Testament Judaism.* Berkeley, CA.: University of California, 1987. 39–58.

**Dautzenberg, G.** "Jesus und der Tempel: Beobachtungen zur Exegese der Perikope von der Tempelsteuer (Mt 17, 24–27)." In *Salz der Erde—Licht der Welt: Exegetische Studien zum Matthäusevangelium*. FS A. Vögtle, ed. L. Oberlinner and P. Fiedler. Stuttgart: Katholisches Bibelwerk, 1991. 223–38. **Derrett, J. D. M.** "Peter's Penny: Fresh Light on Matthew xvii. 24–27." In *Law in the New Testament*. London: Darton, Longman & Todd, 1970. 1:247–65. **Flusser, D.** "Matthew 17.24–7 and the Dead Sea Sect." *Tarbiz* 31 (1961–62) 150–56. **Garland, D.** "Matthew's Understanding of the Temple Tax (Matt 17:24–27)." *SBL Seminar Papers.* Atlanta: Scholars, 1987. (1987) 190–209. **Homeau, H. A.** "On Fishing for Staters: Matthew 17.27." *ExpTim* 85 (1974) 340–42. **Horbury, W.** "The Temple Tax." In *Jesus and the Politics of His Day*, ed. E. Bammel and C. F. D. Moule. Cambridge: Cambridge UP, 1984. 265–86. **Légasse, S.** "Jésus et l'impôt du Temple (Mt 17, 24–27)." *ScEs* 24 (1972) 361–77. **Liver, J.** "The Half-Shekel Offering in Biblical and Post-Biblical Literature." *HTR* 56 (1963) 173–98. **Mandell, S.** "Who Paid the Temple Tax When the Jews Were under Roman Rule?" *HTR* 77 (1984) 223–42. **McEleney, N.** "Matthew 17:24–27—Who Paid the Temple Tax?" *CBQ* 38 (1976) 178–92. **Montefiore, H.** "Jesus and the Temple Tax." *NTS* 10 (1963–64) 60–71. **Schwarz, G.** "ἀνοίξας τὸ στόμα αὐτοῦ? (Matthäus 17.27)." *NTS* 38 (1992) 138–41.

### Translation

[24]*And when they had come into Capernaum, those who collect the temple tax* [a] *came to Peter and said: "Your teacher pays the temple tax,* [b] *doesn't he?"* [25] *He said: "Yes." And when Peter* [c] *had come into the house, Jesus came to him and said: "How does it seem to you, Simon? From whom do the kings of the earth receive revenues or taxes? From their children* [d] *or from others?"* [26] *And when he answered,* [e] *"From others," Jesus said to him: "As a result, then, the children are free.* [f] [27] *But lest we offend them, go to the lake, cast out a fishhook, take the first fish that comes up, and when you have opened its mouth, you will find* [g] *a coin.* [h] *Take it and give it to them for me and for you."*

### Notes

[a] τὰ δίδραχμα, lit. "the didrachmas" (two-drachma pieces), here used in the special sense of the temple tax.

[b] See preceding *Note.* Here the definite article τά appears in brackets, since ℵ* D mae bo omit it. W sa have the sing. article τό, since Jesus would have paid only one didrachma for the tax. The pl. article is witnessed to by ℵ² B C L Θ *f* [1,13] TR and sy[h].

[c] "Peter" added for clarity, reflecting the accusative case of ἐλθόντα, lit. "having come." Several other readings seem to have been caused by the unusual ἐλθόντα . . . αὐτόν. Thus C and a few other witnesses have ὅτε ἦλθον, "when they came"; L W (adding ὁ Ἰησοῦς) and TR have ὅτε εἰσῆλθεν, "when he came in"; other MSS (ℵ*² [D]) add the prefix εἰς- to ἐλθόντα, while still others have the pl. εἰσελθόντων.

[d] τῶν υἱῶν, lit. "sons," as also in v 26.

[e] εἰπόντος δέ, a partial genitive absolute construction without the corresponding noun, is judged by the *UBSGNT* committee to have given rise to a number of other readings: ℵ has ὁ δὲ ἔφη, "but he said," changing the following ἔφη to εἶπεν δέ, "and he said"; C L W *f* [13] TR sy[c.p.h] (mae) have λέγει αὐτῷ ὁ Πέτρος, "Peter said to him"; D sy[s] have λέγει αὐτῷ, "he said to him." In favor of the text are B Θ *f* [1] sa bo[pt]. See *TCGNT*, 44.

[f] A twelfth-century minuscule (713; cf. Arabic form of Tatian's *Diatessaron* 25.6 and Ephraim's commentary on the latter [14.17]) adds ἔφη Σίμων· ναί. λέγει ὁ Ἰησοῦς· δὸς οὖν καὶ σὺ ὡς ἀλλότριος αὐτῶν, "Simon said: 'Yes.' Jesus says: 'You therefore also give as their alien.'" See *TCGNT*, 44.

[g] D it sy[s.c] add ἐκεῖ, "there."

[h] στατῆρα, lit. "stater." See *Comment.*

*Form/Structure/Setting*

A. It is difficult to know why Matthew has inserted this pericope just at this point after following Mark closely since 14:1 (with only two exceptions, both omissions [Mark 6:30–31; 8:22–26]). The often-encountered suggestion that the avoidance of offending the tax collectors (v 27) is associated with the avoidance of offending in 18:6–7 fails to see the very great differences between the offending there and that of the present passage. Possibly the reason for Matthew's placing of the passage here is chronological, since the tax was collected in the month of Adar (approximately March) shortly before the season of Passover (cf. Jos., *Ant.* 3.8.2 §§193–96; *m. Šeqal.* 1:1), and Jesus and his disciples in the narrative are now on their way to Jerusalem for just that festival. It is in a sense an encounter with the Jewish authorities, but in this case (unlike the others) Jesus surprisingly agrees to go along with their request, lest unnecessary offense be caused. The uncertainty of the tax collectors about Jesus' compliance with the tax suggests they may have thought of him as an eschatological prophet in some sense in conflict with the temple (cf. the Qumran community's opposition to the temple cult; others seem to have avoided the tax too). Obviously, Matthew has special interest in the story since it presents Jesus as a loyal Jew who pays the temple tax. Although Jesus pays the tax, it is clear from 24:1–2 that he does not regard the temple as permanent or ultimate in its significance (cf. too 12:6).

B. The pericope is unique to Matthew and was probably drawn from his special fund of oral tradition (so too Davies-Allison). Among the evangelists, if the material was known to them, Matthew alone has interest in preserving the narrative, with his Jewish-Christian church in mind. The story is also found in the *Epistula Apostolorum* 5 (second century), which is probably dependent on the Gospel of Matthew.

C. Although the pericope contains the account of an unusual miracle (v 27), this is only an accessory to its main purpose, which is its teaching concerning the temple and the avoidance of offense. A simple outline may be offered: (1) the question about the temple tax and Peter's answer (vv 24–25a); (2) Jesus' question and Peter's answer (v 25b–26a); (3) the articulation of the basic principle (v 26b); and (4) the divine provision of the tax (v 27). The teaching in the passage occurs through the short exchanges of the dialogue. The only noteworthy structural feature is the parallelism in the instructions of v 27, where each of the four main clauses has a subordinate participle and where all four are modified by the negative purpose clause, beginning with ἵνα δὲ μή ("lest").

D. The evangelist presents the narrative as something that occurred toward the end of the ministry of Jesus when the temple was still standing. It is of course unnecessary to suppose that this story would have been of no interest or of no use to Matthew's church after the destruction of the temple in A.D. 70, or to suppose with Montefiore that Matthew's Jewish-Christian community applied the teaching to the *fiscus iudaicus*, i.e., the perpetuation of the temple tax by the Romans after A.D. 70 for the support of the Roman temple of Jupiter Capitolinus (cf. Jos. *J.W.* 7.9.6 §218; Dio Cassius, *Epitome* 66.7.2). If this were the case, payment of the tax, not nonpayment, would have been an offense to the Jews. The pericope contains important theological teaching as well as a practical principle that transcends the setting in which it was originally articulated. It is, furthermore, of importance to Matthew to continue to press his argument about the loyalty of the Jesus of history to fundamental Jewish realities such as the law and the temple. Matthew's Jewish-Christian readers needed just such information in maintaining their Christian viewpoint in opposition to the counterclaims of the synagogue. Although the present pericope hardly requires an early date for the Gospel, a pre-70 date makes especially good sense of it. For various rabbinic and other parallels to the story of the coin in the fish's mouth, see Bauckham, 237–44.

> Some scholars (see esp. Cassidy) have argued that this pericope concerns not the temple tax but Roman taxation. They have, on the one hand, pointed out problems with the traditional interpretation, such as uncertainty about whether the temple tax was compulsory (and if so, for whom) and, assuming a late date for the Gospel, the apparent irrelevance of the matter for Matthew's readers. On the other hand, they point to the similarities between the taxation of this pericope and the practice of Roman taxation (even to a similar amount, the equivalent of two drachmae). Davies-Allison answer the various arguments in detail, pointing out with Bauckham that the decisive point in favor of a Jewish taxation is that the tax under discussion is one levied in effect by God (whose children are free from it).

## Comment

**24–25a** Having returned to Capernaum, the center of Jesus' Galilean ministry (cf. *Comment* on 4:13; most recently 9:1) but also the official residence (for taxation purposes) of both Peter and Jesus, Peter, as the leading disciple of Jesus, was approached by the temple tax collectors and asked whether his master paid the tax. τὰ δίδραχμα, "the two-drachma piece," was approximately equal in value to the half-shekel collected annually from every Jew to support the temple (i.e., from males over twenty years of age; cf. Exod 30:13–16; cf. 38:26; Neh 10:32–33.; *m. Šeqal.* 3–4; Jos., *Ant.* 18.9.1 §312). The Roman authorities allowed this significant exception to their policy of not allowing subject nations to levy taxes on their populations. There was some debate regarding whether the Torah required the annual tax, with the Pharisees supporting it and the Essenes opposing it (see Horbury, who finds this issue to be the original concern of the passage). The form of the question, using οὐ, "not" (rather than μή), hints that the tax collectors expected a positive answer. The tax collectors refer to Jesus, as non-disciples commonly do in Matthew, as διδάσκαλος, "teacher" (cf. 9:11; 12:38; 19:16; 22:16, 24, 36). In the related passage, 22:15–22, where Jesus is asked about the propriety of paying taxes to the Romans, the Pharisees and the Herodians also address Jesus as διδάσκαλε, "teacher." Peter's response, ναί, "yes," may well have been based more on assumption than actual knowledge.

**25b–26a** The telescoped narrative need not imply supernatural knowledge on Jesus' part (despite 12:15, 25) of Peter's conversation with the tax collectors. Jesus asks Peter for his opinion on the subject apparently as a teaching device, leading to the key statement of v 26b. In this private discussion in the house, Jesus addresses Peter by his Aramaic name, Σίμων, "Simon" (cf. 4:18; 10:2; 16:16–17). The question τί σοι δοκεῖ, "what do you think?" will occur often in the succeeding chapters (but cf. esp. 22:17). οἱ βασιλεῖς τῆς γῆς, "the kings of the earth," refers generally to pagan kings who exercise rule over others (cf. 10:18; 11:8; OT background: Ps 2:2; cf. the same expression in Rev 6:15; 17:2, 18; 18:3, 9; 19:19; 21:24). This reference is only an analogy concerning the nature of taxation and should not mislead one into taking the passage as a whole as referring to Roman taxation. The distinction between τέλη, "(indirect) tax, customs, duties" (thus BAGD, 812a; cf. Rom 13:7b) and κῆνσον, "tax, poll tax" (thus BAGD, 430b; cf. 22:17–22), is not great, but the former may be more general taxation and the latter the head-tax connected with the census. Peter, of course, knows that rulers do not exact taxes ἀπὸ τῶν υἱῶν αὐτῶν, "from their children" (lit. "sons"), but ἀπὸ τῶν ἀλλοτρίων, "from others," or from "aliens," as the word may also be translated (cf. Acts 7:6). Kings tax the peoples over whom they have authority, not their own families.

**26b** The central teaching of the pericope is now presented by Jesus. The opening ἄρα γε, "as a result," indicates the dependence of this statement on the preceding conclusion. The basic principle is ἐλεύθεροί εἰσιν οἱ υἱοί, "the children [lit. 'sons'] are free" (ἐλεύθεροι, "free," is in the emphatic initial position; this is the only occurrence of the word in the Gospels, except for John 8:33, 36; cf. 1 Cor 9:1). The children of the king are accordingly free from the necessity of paying taxes. In this instance the king is God and the "sons" are his children (cf. 5:9, 45), not the Jews but the children of the kingdom (cf. 13:38). The argument of Horbury, Bauckham, and Luz that "the sons" should be understood as the Israelites is not impossible, but the most natural understanding, given their association with Jesus, is that they are the Christians, the children of God by adoption. Quite probably, then, the ἀλλότριοι, the "others" of vv 25–26, are the unbelieving Jews (thus Garland, 208). The disciples of Jesus are thus not obligated to pay taxes to their Father (cf., e.g., 5:16, 48; 6:1; 23:9). The implied conclusion is that they are free from the burden of the temple tax. Here again the surprising authority of Jesus over the commandment of Torah (Exod 30:13–14) is evident.

**27** Although there is no necessity for the children of their heavenly Father to pay this tax, yet Jesus is willing to pay it in order to avoid unnecessary offense, ἵνα δὲ μὴ σκανδαλίσωμεν αὐτούς, "lest we offend them." Since Jesus can make his point through this teaching, confirmed by the miracle that now follows, there is no need to offend the Jewish authorities (as, for example, had to be the case in 15:12; cf. 13:57). The avoiding of unnecessary offense is the central point of the pericope (see esp. Garland, 204–5). This same principle of freedom, yet with voluntary sacrifice of that freedom in practice, is advocated later by Paul (cf. Rom 14:13–23; 1 Cor 8:13–9:1, 12). The instructions Jesus now gives to Peter involve not simply mysterious foreknowledge (as in 21:2 or Mark 14:13) but a miracle of divine provision. This miracle is, however, unique in the NT in that Jesus performs it for his and Peter's own convenience (in this sense it is more like the *ad hoc* miracle stories of the NT apocrypha). But like the miracle of the withering of the fig tree (21:19), its primary function is to provide a "sign" to underline a theological truth: that God provides the fish (not a symbol of Christ, *pace* McEleney) with the coin in its mouth (which the fish had apparently seen shining in the water and taken for food). This serves to underline the truth of Jesus' point that the children of the king do not themselves have to pay the tax. Peter is to fish in the Sea of Galilee using an ἄγκιστρον, "fishhook" (the only occurrence of the word in the NT), and in the mouth of the first fish he takes he will find a στατῆρα, "stater," a silver coin worth four drachmas, or the equivalent of a shekel, just enough to pay the temple tax for two (cf. a parallel story of a pearl in a fish in *b. Šabb.* 119a–b). Peter is then to take it to the tax collectors for himself and for Jesus (ἀντὶ ἐμοῦ καὶ σοῦ, "for me and for you"). Jesus thus would pay the temple tax once more before he accomplished in his death on the cross the unique sacrifice that would make the temple superfluous. The fulfillment of Jesus' directions and their truthfulness are not recorded but left assumed. Thus the miraculous provision is itself de-emphasized in favor of the underlying lessons.

## Explanation

The issue of the pericope concerns not the paying of taxes to the state, i.e., the secular authorities (this issue comes up specifically in 22:15–22), but a specifically religious tax for the maintenance of the temple and its ritual, wherein atonement for sins was made possible. Given the present situation of the dawning of the kingdom of God in the ministry and person of Jesus, the paying of the temple tax was or would be, strictly speaking, no longer a necessity (cf. 12:6). That nearness is an inescapable aspect of this pericope, given the larger context of the Gospel. Those who participate in this new reality are the children of the king and thus need not pay the tax to support what will after all soon belong to the old order (cf. the prophecy of the destruction of the temple [24:1–2]). Yet for Jesus more important things are at hand, and there is no point to make an issue out of this, thereby offending the Jewish authorities. And so Jesus chooses *not* to exercise his and Peter's rightful freedom as the children of God not to pay the tax, thereby anticipating what would become a basic principle of Pauline practice and the practice of all knowledgeable and "stronger" Christians: the avoidance of unnecessary offense of the "weaker." At bottom here is love and concern for others rather than the use of one's rightful freedom. The two aspects of the pericope—loyalty to the temple together with freedom from the law of the temple tax—would have been particularly appropriate for those grappling with issues of continuity and discontinuity and, of course, would have had important ramifications for relationships with the Jewish community.

# The Fourth Discourse:
# Life in the Community of the Kingdom
# (18:1–35)

## Bibliography

**Barth, G.** "Auseinandersetzungen um die Kirchenzucht im Umkreis des Matthäusevangeliums." *ZNW* 69 (1978) 158–77. **Butler, B. C.** "M. Vaganay and the 'Community Discourse.'" *NTS* 1 (1954–55) 283–90. **Pesch, W.** "Die sogenannte Gemeindeordnung Mt 18." *BZ* 7 (1963) 220–35. **Schweizer, E.** "Die matthäische Sicht der Gemeinde in Kapitel 18." In *Matthäus und seine Gemeinde*. 106–15. **Trilling, W.** "Die 'Gemeindeordnung' Kapitel 18." In *Das wahre Israel*. 106–23. **Vaganay, L.** "Le schématisme du discours communautaire à la lumière de la critique des sources." *RB* 60 (1953) 203–44. **Zimmermann, H.** "Die innere Struktur der Kirche und das Petrusamt nach Matthew 18." *Catholica* 30 (1976) 168–83.

## Introduction

Matthew's fourth discourse is widely known as a discourse devoted to church order or church discipline. This designation comes primarily from the content of the central pericope of vv 15–20, where specific instructions are provided for dealing with a member of the community who has offended another member. In fact, however, the subject of the discourse is rather wider than this. The evangelist appears again to have brought together diverse materials into the form of a single discourse. In general it may be said that the discourse concerns relations between members of the community, dealing in turn with such particular matters as humility, the avoidance of causing others to stumble, and the importance of forgiveness.

Contrary to the opinion of a number of commentators (e.g., Davies-Allison), vv 1–14 do not concern children. A child is presented in v 2 only as an example of humility, not because children are the subject of the verses that follow. The use of the little child (the Greek word is a diminutive form) as a model prompts the subsequent references to disciples, i.e., members of the community, as "little ones" (vv 6, 10, 14). The "little ones" are specifically designated as those "who believe in me" (v 6). Already in v 5 the word "little child" is applied, as argued below, to the disciple.

It seems clear that Matthew meant this discourse, like the other discourses, to be a practical guide to the Christian community. Yet the discourse falls well short of being an actual handbook of church order. It is very unlikely too that the evangelist has used such a handbook for his source, even for vv 15–20. Davies-Allison have rightly observed that the disciplinary section of vv 15–20 is surrounded in the discourse with material that, by its emphasis on matters such as humility, concern for others, and forgiveness, conditions its severity.

There is no unanimity concerning the structure of the discourse. Its various segments are for the most part loosely related, often with the help of catchwords brought from one paragraph to another. Many interpreters regard the discourse as having two main parts, vv 1–14 and 15–35, each ending with a parable (thus Gnilka, Davies-Allison). On the other hand, the only significant break in the discourse occurs at the beginning of v 21. We offer for structural analysis only the following tabulation of discrete passages:

I. Greatness in the Kingdom (vv 1–4)
II. Warning against Causing Others or Allowing Oneself to Stumble (vv 5–9)
III. The Father's Concern that No Disciple Perish (vv 10–14) (with supporting parable, vv 12–14)
IV. Handling Matters of Church Discipline (vv 15–20)
V. The Necessity of Forgiveness (vv 21–35) (with supporting parable, vv 23–35)

# Greatness in the Kingdom of Heaven (18:1– 4)

### Bibliography

**Brown, R. N.** "Jesus and the Child as Model of Spirituality." *IBS* 4 (1982) 178–92. **Crossan, J. D.** "Kingdom and Children: A Study in the Aphoristic Tradition." *Semeia* 29 (1983) 75–95. **Dupont, J.** "Matthieu 18.3." In *Neotestamentica et Semitica.* FS M. Black, ed. E. E. Ellis and M. Wilcox. Edinburgh: T. & T. Clark, 1969. 50–60. **Maisch, I.** "Christsein in Gemeinschaft." In *Salz der Erde—Licht der Welt.* FS Anton Vögtle, ed. L. Oberlinner and P. Fiedler. Stuttgart: Katholisches Bibelwerk, 1991. 223–38. **Martinez, E. R.** "The Interpretation of *hoi mathetai* in Matthew 18." *CBQ* 23 (1961) 281–92. **Patte, D.** "Jesus' Pronouncement about Entering the Kingdom like a Child: A Structural Exegesis." *Semeia* 29 (1983) 3–42. **Robbins, V. K.** "Pronouncement Stories and Jesus' Blessing of the Children: A Rhetorical Approach." *Semeia* 29 (1983) 43–74. **Schilling, F. A.** "What Means the Saying about Receiving the Kingdom of God as a Little Child?" *ExpTim* 77 (1965) 56–58. **Schnackenburg, R.** "Grosssein im Gottesreich." In *Studien zum Matthäusevangelium.* FS W. Pesch, ed. L. Schenke. Stuttgart: Katholisches Bibelwerk, 1988. 269–82. **Wenham, D.** "A Note on Mark 9.33–42/Matt 18.1–6/Luke 9.46–50." *JSNT* 14 (1982) 113–18.

### Translation

[1]*Then* [a] *the disciples came to Jesus, saying: "Who indeed is the greatest in the kingdom of heaven?"* [2]*And calling* [b] *to him a* [c] *little child, whom he placed in their midst,* [3]*he said: "Truly I say to you: Unless you revise your ways and become like little children, you absolutely will not enter into the kingdom of heaven.* [4]*Therefore whoever will humble himself or herself* [d] *as this little child is humble, this person is the greatest in the kingdom of heaven."*

### Notes

[a] ἐν ἐκείνῃ τῇ ὥρᾳ, lit. "in that hour." Some witnesses (Θ *f*¹ 33 it syˢ·ᶜ) read ἡμέρᾳ, "day," in place of ὥρᾳ, "hour."

[b] Many MSS (D W Θ *f*¹³ TR latt sy sa mae) add ὁ Ἰησοῦς, "Jesus," as the subject of the participle and the verbs that follow. The text without the addition is attested by ℵ B L Z *f*¹ bo.

[c] D e syˢ·ᶜ add ἕν, "one."

<sup>d</sup> "Or herself" added to translation.

*Form/Structure/Setting*

A. Matthew's fourth discourse, treating a variety of aspects of life in the church, is occasioned by the question concerning who is the greatest in the kingdom of heaven (v 1). Thus the first main theme discussed is the especially important one of humility, a theme that is central to the ministry of Jesus himself. Jesus uses a child as the model of the simple humility that makes for greatness in the kingdom (vv 1–4), and the analogy of children or "little ones" dominates the first part of the discourse (through v 14).

B. In vv 1–2 Matthew has quite freely rewritten his Markan source (Mark 9:34–35; cf. Luke 9:46–47). He has omitted Mark 9:33 (cf. 17:24 for the return to Capernaum) and alters Mark 9:24 so that the disciples ask Jesus directly the question about the greatest in the kingdom of heaven, rather than having Jesus inquire about their conversation "on the road." Thus too the setting in Mark 9:35a can be done away with. The result is that Matthew has made the disciples appear less guilty than they do in Mark. Matthew begins with ἐν ἐκείνῃ τῇ ὥρᾳ, "in that hour" (v 1), and broadens the question from Mark's simple "who is the greatest?" (i.e., of the disciples, Mark 9:34; cf. Luke 9:46, αὐτῶν, "of them") to "who is the greatest" ἐν τῇ βασιλείᾳ τῶν οὐρανῶν, "in the kingdom of heaven?" The logion of Mark 9:35b, "If anyone would be first, that person must be last of all and servant of all," is omitted at this point (its counterpart is found in 20:26–27; cf. 23:11–12). Matthew also inserts two new logia (vv 3–4) after the reference to Jesus setting the child in their midst (v 2). The first of these is almost exactly the same as Mark 10:15 and is omitted in the parallel pericope (cf. 19:13–15). In v 2 Matthew employs the participle προσκαλεσάμενος, "having called to him," for Mark's λαβών, "having taken," and Matthew, who commonly avoids human emotions in Jesus, omits (as does Luke 9:47) Mark's ἐναγκαλισάμενος αὐτό, "having taken it in his arms" (Mark 9:36). The first half of the logion that follows in Mark (Mark 9:37) is found in v 5, which, it will be argued below, belongs to the next pericope rather than to the present one. Thus, as we have also seen in the other major teaching discourses, Matthew takes much more liberty with his source than is generally the case in his narrative. Matthew here, as throughout the discourse, makes use of different sources, piecing them together in a fresh and stimulating manner, mainly with an eye to the catechetical value of the whole.

C. This initial pericope consists of the question of the disciples and the answer of Jesus, with the last words of the answer, οὗτός ἐστιν ὁ μείζων ἐν τῇ βασιλείᾳ τῶν οὐρανῶν (v 4), "this one is the greatest in the kingdom of heaven," forming an inclusio with the question of the disciples (v 1). The brief passage may be outlined as follows: (1) the question about greatness (v 1); (2) Jesus' answer, subdivided into (a) the need to become childlike (vv 2–3) and (b) the definition of greatness as humility (v 4). The little structural parallelism in the pericope begins in v 3, with the parallel verbs in the subordinate clause (στραφῆτε, lit. "turn," and γένησθε, "become") as well as the parallel phrases of vv 3 and 4, ὡς τὰ παιδία, "like the little children," and ὡς τὸ παιδίον τοῦτο, "like this little child."

## Comment

**1** The opening ἐν ἐκείνῃ τῇ ὥρᾳ, "in that hour," is here general, amounting to "then" (cf. the same use of the phrase in 26:55). If, on the other hand, this pericope originally followed the second passion prediction (17:22–23), as it does in Mark, the more specific phrase would have had an added poignancy. But even as the sequence stands, however, the irony of the disciples' prepossession with greatness, so recently after Jesus spoke of his own suffering and death, is apparent. Jesus' answer in vv 3–4 shows that the disciples thought of greatness exclusively in terms of power, position, and glory rather than, say, in terms of righteousness, as greatness in the kingdom had earlier been defined (5:19). The disciples are apparently not so much interested in the reasons for greatness as in the state itself of being "greatest" (μείζων, comparative adjective used as superlative). It is clear what Matthew has in mind from the added ἐν τῇ βασιλείᾳ τῶν οὐρανῶν, "in the kingdom of heaven," namely the people of the kingdom, i.e., the church (cf. Luke's μείζων αὐτῶν, "greatest of them," the disciples [Luke 9:46]). It is unlikely that a future greatness in the eschatological kingdom is meant here, although this possibility cannot be excluded (the verb ἐστίν could be a futuristic present, but the future tense was available if the evangelist desired unmistakable clarity on the point). The question thus does not concern a theoretical debate concerning the greatness of Moses, Elijah (cf. 11:11b), or Jesus, who as Lord is automatically to be excluded from the question. Instead, Matthew extends it to "the kingdom of heaven," in the sense of the church, to bring the question home to his readers. This phrase furthermore could stand as a rubric over the entire discourse, which concerns the church (cf. v 17), and specifically life in the church. That the question was more than theoretical among the disciples becomes evident later from the painful episode of 20:20–28 (note 20:24; cf. esp. Luke 22:24).

**2–3** When Jesus called a "little child" (παιδίον) over to him and put the child in their midst, he gave substance to what he was about to teach. The social insignificance, if not the innocent unself-consciousness of the little child, was the very antithesis of the disciples' interest in power and greatness. The logion of v 3 is introduced with the formula ἀμὴν λέγω ὑμῖν, "truly I say to you," to stress its importance (see *Comment* on 5:18). The disciples, Jesus insists, must στραφῆτε, lit. "turn" (from the Heb. שׁוּב, šûb, "turn," in the sense of "return" or "repent"; the same word underlies μετανοεῖν, "repent," in 3:2; 4:17), i.e., they must change their ways. The content of the required reversal is indicated in the following exhortation, καὶ γένησθε ὡς τὰ παιδία, "and become like little children" (cf. 19:14). Unless the disciples exhibit a childlike indifference to greatness by the world's standards, they "cannot" (the double negative of the Greek emphasizes this) expect to "enter the kingdom of heaven" (οὐ μὴ εἰσέλθητε εἰς τὴν βασιλείαν τῶν οὐρανῶν; the same expression occurs verbatim in 5:20, which formally is also very similar; cf. too 7:21; 19:23–24; 23:13). Intended here specifically is an eschatological entry into, or experience of, the kingdom of God. At the same time, as throughout the Gospel, the words can refer also to a present entering of the kingdom. Disciples enter in the present what they shall more fully enter in the future. A parallel idiom in Matthew is "to enter into life" (see vv 8–9; 19:17; cf. 25:21, 23: "enter into the joy of your Lord"; for the remainder of the NT, Acts 14:22; 1 Cor 15:50; Gal 5:21; Eph 5:5; 1 Thess 2:12; 2 Tim 4:18; 2 Peter 1:11). In a passage related in content to the present logion, the Gospel of John uses the idiom "to see the kingdom of God," which is paralleled by "to enter into the kingdom of God" (John 3:3, 5)—this in a passage that speaks of being born "again" or "from above" and "of water and spirit."

**4** To become like a little child means to humble oneself. Thus this verse builds directly on the preceding statements (note the οὖν, "therefore") as well as supplying the direct answer to the question asked in v 1. τὸ παιδίον τοῦτο, "this little child," points to the concrete example before their eyes (cf. v 2). Jesus here reverses the perspective of the world by his statement of a fundamental paradox: greatness in the kingdom is a matter of humility, not power or position. The child's humility is its lack of status, not its actions or feelings of humbleness. This paradox is articulated dramatically in 23:11–12, the only other place in Matthew where the verb ταπεινοῦν, "humble," is used (cf. 5:5 and Jas 4:10; 1 Peter 5:6; and for the example of Jesus, Phil 2:8–9; the adjective ταπεινός is applied to Jesus in 11:29; for rabbinic background, cf. *b. B. Mes.* 85b). To become humble, i.e., to be without status and in this sense unself-conscious like a little child (cf. the description of the disciples as "infants" in 11:25 and as "little ones" in 10:42), is to be great by the standards of the kingdom of God. Any further stipulation of the symbolism of a child's humility leads to unwarranted allegorizing (cf. the review of options in Davies-Allison and even their own suggestion that the point of comparison lies in the need to see one's life "as being in need of a new beginning" [2:758]).

*Explanation*

The disciples must have been shocked when in response to their question about who was the greatest in the kingdom of heaven, Jesus turned on them and asserted that unless their perspective changed they would not enjoy the blessings of the eschatological kingdom in the present or the future. From Jesus' point of view, the disciples were so fundamentally on the wrong track in their admiration of, and quest of, what *they* considered to be greatness that it was questionable whether they really understood the kingdom he proclaimed and, in particular, that its basis lay in God's free grace (cf. Mark 10:15). The status of the disciples before God was like that of dependent little children, and their corresponding attitude was to be a childlike humility, not pride of position or power (cf. 1 John 2:16–17). Clearly, a primary virtue of those who would be disciples, hence for those in the church, is a humility that marks them off radically from a world obsessed with the quest for greatness construed only as power and status. The disciple is called to be like his or her Master, whose demeanor even as the Christ was one of humility (cf. 12:18–21; 21:5).

# Warning against Causing Others or Allowing Oneself to Stumble (18:5–9)

## Bibliography

**Basser, H. W.** "The Meaning of 'Shtuth': Gen. R. 11 in Reference to Mt 5.29–30 and 18.8–9." *NTS* 31 (1985) 148–51. **Derrett, J. D. M.** "Cutting off the Hand that Causes Offense." In *Jesus's Audience: The Social and Psychological Environment in which He Worked.* London: Darton, Longman & Todd, 1973. 201–4. ———. "μύλος ὀνικός (Mk 9.42 par.)." *ZNW* 76 (1985) 284–85. **Humbert, A.** "Essai d'une théologie du scandale dans les synoptiques." *Bib* 35 (1954) 1–28. **Kossen, H. B.** "Quelques remarques sur l'ordre des paraboles dans Luc XV et sur la structure de Matthieu XVIII 8–14." *NovT* 1 (1956) 75–80.

## Translation

⁵ *"And whoever receives one such little child in my name receives me.* ⁶ *But whoever it may be that causes one of these little ones who believe in me to stumble, it would be better for them* [a] *that a large* [b] *millstone were hung around their necks and they were drowned in the depths* [c] *of the sea.* ⁷ *Woe to the world for the stumbling blocks it brings.* [d] *For although it is necessary for such causes of stumbling to come, woe to the* [e] *one through whom the stumbling block comes.* ⁸ *But if your hand or your foot causes you to stumble, cut it* [f] *off and cast it from you. For it is better to enter into life crippled or lame than having two hands or two feet to be cast into eternal fire.* ⁹ *And* [g] *if your eye causes you to stumble, pluck it out and cast it from you. For it is better to enter into life with but one eye than having two eyes to be cast into the Gehenna of fire."*

## Notes

[a] αὐτῷ, "him," changed to pl. together with other pronouns and nouns in the sentence in order to avoid masc. language.

[b] ὀνικός, lit. "pertaining to a donkey," i.e., the large revolving millstone pulled by a donkey, rather than any smaller millstone.

[c] πελάγει can also mean "high" or "open" sea.

[d] "It brings" added in translation for clarity.

[e] Many MSS (B W Θ *f*¹³ TR it vg^cl sa^mss) add ἐκείνῳ, "that." Against the addition are ℵ D L *f*¹ and many ancient translations. The *UBSGNT* committee argues that the word was added because the context "seems to call for such a demonstrative." *TCGNT*, 44. Possibly too the influence of 26:24b encouraged the addition.

[f] αὐτῷ. W TR sy^h bo have αὐτά, "them"; U 28 aur have the feminine αὐτήν, "it," thus agreeing with the gender of the first noun, χείρ, "hand."

[g] D reads τὸ αὐτὸ εἰ καί, "the same thing (is true), if also. . . ."

## Form/Structure/Setting

A. Because v 5 refers to ἓν παιδίον τοιοῦτο, "one such little child," it is possible to take this verse as the end of the preceding pericope. Yet v 5 moves away altogether from the issue of "the greatest in the kingdom of heaven," the inclusio with which v 4 ends. The opening construction of v 6, ὃς δ' ἄν, "whoever," corresponds to the opening of v 5, καὶ ὃς ἐάν, "and whoever," which, on the other hand, stands in contrast to the structure of v 4, which begins with ὅστις, "whoever." The shift in terminology that produces τῶν μικρῶν τούτων, "these little ones," in v 6, is a deliberate one, intended to show that now, indeed beginning in v 5 where the transition takes place (contra Davies-Allison), those in view are not little children but disciples, i.e., Christians in the church, who are being likened to little children. Pursuing the theme of the discourse, which can be characterized as life in the kingdom of heaven on earth (or here we may say "the church"), Matthew turns to the importance of not causing others or oneself to stumble, i.e., to fall away from faith in, and commitment to, the gospel. "These little ones" or disciples of Jesus will continue to be the subject of attention through v 14 (where the phrase occurs yet again; see too v 10), after which Matthew moves to cases of church discipline.

The issue of "causing one to stumble" is seen by many to link up with the "giving of offense" in 17:27 because of the use of words of the same root for both (σκανδαλίζειν in 17:27). Thereby it is thought that this discourse, or its first third, can be related to 17:24–27 (cf. too ἐν ἐκείνῃ τῇ ὥρᾳ, "in that hour," of v 1). Against this view, however, is the fact that vv 2–5 relate only indirectly to the theme represented by σκανδαλίζειν but, more importantly, that the evidence of offense in 17:27 has to do with Jewish tax collectors—a mere expedience—whereas the causing to stumble in the present chapter has to do with disciples or church members being caused to lose their faith (cf. v 14)—a matter of dire importance and something quite different from that referred to in 17:27.

B. In this pericope Matthew continues to depend on Mark (Mark 9:42–50; cf. Luke 17:1–2). Having embarked on one of his major discourses, however, Matthew omits Mark 9:38–41, the discussion of one not of the circle of Jesus' disciples who was casting out demons (although Mark's last verse is represented in 10:42). The more significant changes made by Matthew in the remainder are the insertion of v 7 (reflected, however, in Luke 17:1, and therefore probably originally a Q saying), the coalescing of the reference to hand and foot in one verse (v 8), thereby enabling the omission of Mark 9:45 with its repetition, and the omission of Mark 9:48 (a quotation of Isa 66:24). The obscure Mark 9:49–50 is also omitted. Among smaller changes, the following may be noted: in v 6 Matthew's substitution of συμφέρει, "be better for," for Mark's more awkward καλὸν . . . μᾶλλον, "good . . . rather" (Mark 9:42), κρεμασθῇ, "hang," for περίκειται, "hang around" (Mark 9:42), and καταποντισθῇ, "drown," for Mark's βέβληται, "cast" (Mark 9:42; cf. ἔρριπται, "cast" [Luke 17:2]). In v 6 Matthew adds the words ἐν τῷ πελάγει, "in the depths," thereby heightening the judgment (cf. Mark 9:42). In v 8, the coalescing of hand and foot made necessary other slight changes in the syntax; Matthew substitutes βληθῆναι, "to be cast," for ἀπελθεῖν, "to depart," omits Mark's εἰς τὴν γέενναν, "into Gehenna" (a phrase that *is* picked up from Mark in v 9; cf. Mark 9:43), and substitutes αἰώνιον, "eternal," for ἄσβεστον, "unquenchable." In v 9 only one important change need be noted: Matthew's substitution of εἰς τὴν ζωήν, "into life" (a phrase Matthew likes; it occurs again in v 8 [where, however, it is borrowed from Mark 9:43] and in 19:17), for Mark's εἰς τὴν βασιλείαν τὸν θεόν, "into the kingdom of God" (Mark 9:47; but in the parallel

statement in 9:43 Mark too has ζωή, "life"). We see again Matthew's careful following of Mark and yet his practice of abridging, of smoothing out awkward
constructions, and of inserting new material from Q and perhaps his special
source, as happens especially in the discourses.

C. The pericope is mainly concerned with the avoidance of offense, here in
the sense of causing one to stumble. The opening saying (v 5) concerns the
proper treatment of disciples, who are to be welcomed, not offended. As an outline, the following can be suggested: (1) the importance of receiving disciples
(v 5); (2) the importance of not causing disciples to stumble, subdivided into (a)
the severe judgment of one who does (v 6) and (b) the necessity of stumbling
blocks, yet the culpability of those who cause them (v 7); and (3) the importance
of not causing oneself to stumble, subdivided into (a) the offensive hand or foot
(v 8) and (b) the offensive eye (v 9). The impressive structural parallelism in
Matthew is largely taken over from Mark and probably reflects the prewritten
form of the transmission of the sayings of Jesus. The first part of the pericope
contains little such parallelism (cf. the parallel clauses governed by ἵνα, "in order
that" [v 6]). The complicated syntactical structure of v 9, on the other hand, is
structurally the mirror of v 8. What is said about the eye is said in almost verbatim
agreement with what was said about hand or foot (Mark's separate treatment of
the latter produces a threefold parallelism in structure [Mark 9:43–47]). Only
slight changes keep the correspondence from being verbatim (e.g., ἔξελε, "tear
out," for ἔκκοψον, "cut out" ; εἰς τὴν γέενναν τοῦ πυρός, "into the Gehenna of
fire," for εἰς τὸ πῦρ τὸ αἰώνιον, "into the eternal fire"). Remarkably, these same
logia with only slight changes are found, in reverse order, in 5:29–30, where the
offending members are the right eye and the right hand. Except for συμφέρει σοι
in 5:29 (for καλόν σοί ἐστιν, both meaning "it is better for you") and the following repeated "that one of your members perish and not the whole body be cast
into Gehenna," the two passages are nearly identical syntactically. Almost certainly
in these two passages we have variants of the same original logia.

D. The content of vv 6–7 is reflected in *1 Clem.* 46.8 where, however, dependence seems rather to be on the oral tradition that underlies Matthew. The
occurrence of similar material in Justin Martyr, *Apol.* 1.15.2, on the other hand, is
clearly dependent on Matthew (v 9, but influenced by the language of v 8). Dependence on Matthew (v 7) is also apparent in *Pseudo-Clementine Homilies* 12.29.1.

*Comment*

5   The first main part of chap. 18 (vv 1–14) is about disciples, not children.
Even the reference to the παιδίον, "little child," in vv 1–4 is only for the purpose
of encouraging childlikeness in the disciples. Thus v 5 too is not about receiving
children (*pace* Gundry, Davies-Allison), as is the case in 19:13–15, but about welcoming the disciple of Jesus, who for the moment in this transitional verse is
referred to as ἓν παιδίον τοιοῦτο, "one such child" (thus correctly Thompson,
*Matthew's Advice*, 105), the disciple who has become childlike. The later equivalent of the phrase understood in this sense is ἕνα τῶν μικρῶν τούτων, "one of
these little ones" (vv 6, 10, 14). Thus the real parallel to the present verse is in
10:40 (where just a few lines later the disciple is also referred to as "one of these

little ones" [10:42]). Receiving a disciple here, as there (where the same verb, δέχεται, "receive," is used), apparently means showing hospitality and consideration to disciples in pursuit of their calling, and hence especially in missionary work. This reception of the disciple is to be ἐπὶ τῷ ὀνόματί μου, "in my name," says Jesus (a fundamental characteristic of discipleship in Matthew is acting in the name of Jesus; cf. v 20; 28:19). To give hospitable reception to a childlike disciple is furthermore to receive Jesus himself (cf. 10:40; exactly along the same line is 25:40, 45).

**6** Jesus next presents a contrasting treatment of disciples in this reference to causing them "to stumble." The verb σκανδαλίζειν, which occurs here and in vv 8 and 9 (cf. the cognate noun σκάνδαλον in v 7), obviously is to be understood in the serious sense of causing someone to stumble or fall into sin, or perhaps even to lose their faith in Jesus and the gospel. It is thus to hinder in some fundamental sense and not simply in the giving of mere personal offense as in 17:27. ἕνα τῶν μικρῶν τούτων, "one of these little ones," refers to disciples (see *Comment* on the preceding verse), as the added modifier τῶν πιστευόντων εἰς ἐμέ, "who believe in me," makes clear (the only place where this common Johannine idiom appears explicitly in the synoptic tradition [the Mark 9:42 parallel is textually uncertain]). Matthew especially likes this expression, describing disciples as "little ones" (cf. vv 10, 14; 10:42; cf. the same idea, but different terminology, in 11:25), which is apparently meant to portray not merely their humble demeanor (v 3) but also their utter dependence on their heavenly Father (7:11). It would "be better" (συμφέρει; cf. similar use in 5:29–30) for one who causes another to fall to suffer an abrupt end of life than to become the means for the destruction of others. The μύλος ὀνικός, "large millstone," was the revolving upper millstone drawn by a donkey (hence ὀνικός, "pertaining to a donkey"). The throwing of a millstone into the sea, as a convincing image of sinking, may have been a common idiom (cf. Rev 18:21; the proverbial metaphor of a millstone around one's neck is found in *b. Qidd.* 29a; see Jos., *Ant.* 14.15.10 §450). The verb καταποντίζειν, "sink, drown," is used earlier in Matthew in describing Peter as he begins to sink in the water (14:30; these are the only occurrences of the word in the NT). Here it means "to drown." ἐν τῷ πελάγει, "in the depth" or "open (sea)," is added by Matthew for effect (it occurs in the NT only here and in Acts 27:5).

**7** The gravity of causing others to fall is emphasized further by the pronouncing of woe (for οὐαί, see *Comment* on 11:21) upon the world generally as well as upon the individual through whom these offenses come. Misery will come upon the world because it is the source of much stumbling (ἀπὸ τῶν σκανδάλων, "because of stumbling blocks," i.e., enticements to sin and apostasy [BAGD, 753a]). Jesus realistically affirms that such enticements are ἀνάγκη, "necessary" (only here in Matthew), presumably because of the nature of a fallen world, but perhaps too as affording the testing of the disciple (cf. 1 Cor 11:19). On the other hand, ἐλθεῖν, "to come," may point to their presence prior to the end of the age (24:6, 10). But this is in no way to lessen the culpability of those who cause such offenses against disciples (cf. 13:41). A similar tension is found in the divine necessity of the death of Jesus (δεῖ, "must" [16:21; 26:54]) and the culpability of the one who betrays him (26:24). This last-mentioned verse is similar to the present verse in that it is said that the Son of Man goes "as it is written concerning him"; but then woe is pronounced upon "that man" (οὐαὶ δὲ τῷ ἀνθρώπῳ ἐκείνῳ, "woe to that man") through whom the betrayal takes place, about whom it is furthermore said that it would "have been better for him" (καλὸν ἦν αὐτῷ) had he not been born. For the pronouncing of οὐαί, "woe," upon culpable persons, see *Comment* on 11:21 (cf. chap. 23 *passim*; 24:19; 26:24).

**8–9** The gravity of sinning and falling away is now further stressed, but along a somewhat different line (although what causes oneself to fall can also become the cause of others' falling), which focuses upon specific offending members of the human body, the hand or the foot (v 8) and the eye (v 9). The practically identical logia of 5:29–30, which concern specifically right eye and right hand, are given in the context of the enticement of sexual lust (see *Comment* there). Here the context is broader. Again, however, the point is the desirability of drastic action (though the exhortations are hyperbolic and not to be taken literally) to overcome the instrument of stumbling. The new element in these verses, altogether lacking in 5:29–30, is the positive reference in the repeated words (in slightly different order) εἰσελθεῖν εἰς τὴν ζωήν, "to enter into life." These words, which stand in direct contrast to βληθῆναι εἰς τὸ πῦρ τὸ αἰώνιον, "to be cast into the eternal fire" (second instance: εἰς τὴν γέενναν τοῦ πυρός, "into the Gehenna of fire"), refer to entrance into the eschatological kingdom at the time of the last judgment (note Mark's third instance, referring to the eye, where the clause becomes εἰσελθεῖν εἰς τὴν βασιλείαν τοῦ θεοῦ, "to enter into the kingdom of God").

Thompson (*Matthew's Advice*, 116–20) argues that the repeated verb σκανδαλίζειν, "to offend, cause to stumble," should be understood as causative (the stem -ιζ is often causative, cf. BDF §108[3]), in which case it refers to causing *others* rather than oneself to stumble. This attractive proposal has the advantage of bringing vv 8–9 more into accord with the other pericopes of the discourse in chap. 18, and especially with the immediate context, by turning the focus away from concern for oneself to concern for others. Thompson's conclusion, though it remains a possible one, is nevertheless not compelling. In both occurrences the verb is followed by the singular σε, "you," which functions as the direct object of the verb (as in the parallel of 5:29–30). Had the evangelist intended the causing of *others* to fall, he could have made this quite unmistakable by substituting or adding the word ἄλλους, "others," or some equivalent. The function of vv 8–9 is to underline the gravity of stumbling.

The use of ζωή, "life," as a synonym for the future life of the kingdom can also be seen in 7:14; 19:16–17, 29; 25:46. On the subject of the πῦρ, "fire," of eschatological judgment, see *Comment* on 3:10. The phrase εἰς τὸ πῦρ τὸ αἰώνιον, "into the eternal fire" (v 8), occurs also in 25:41 (cf. 3:12). The phrase εἰς τὴν γέενναν τοῦ πυρός, "into the Gehenna of fire" (v 9), occurs also in 5:22. So high are the stakes—eschatological blessing or judgment—that it is far better to suffer some degree of self-imposed limitation in this life, and thus to enter the life of the eschaton, than to take no such self-limiting action and thereby to be caused to fall, and so to enter eschatological judgment.

*Explanation*

It is a fundamentally important matter how one treats disciples of Jesus—that is, how one treats fellow members of the church. So important are fellow believers that to receive them is to receive Jesus himself. On the other hand, it is of very great importance to avoid anything that will cause them to fall, and indeed it is also important for members of the church themselves to avoid all that may be adverse to their own faith and life in the kingdom. The practiced application of this principle is easily seen in the Pauline letters. Paul, building on the tradition of the teaching of Jesus, insists on the importance of not causing one's brother or sister to stumble (Rom 14:13, 21; 1 Cor 8:9, 13); and he knows that action must be taken so that one does not stumble oneself. Thus he exhorts the Christian to put to death the members of his or her old nature (cf. Rom 6:12–13; Col 3:5). Matthew's community receives, through the evangelist's transmission of the teaching of Jesus, instruction that is all important for the survival of the church. If the attacks against the faith of Christians from outside are real, there can be no tolerance of stumbling blocks originating from within the community, from brothers or sisters, or from oneself.

# The Father's Concern That No Disciple Perish (18:10–14)

### Bibliography

**Arai, S.** "Das Gleichnis vom verloren Schaf: Eine traditionsgeschichtliche Untersuchung." AJBI 2 (1976) 111–37. **Bishop, E. F. F.** "The Parable of the Lost or Wandering Sheep." ATR 44 (1962) 44–57. **Derrett, J. D. M.** "Fresh Light on the Lost Sheep and the Lost Coin." NTS 26 (1979) 36–60. **Dupont, J.** "Les implications christologiques de la parabole de la brebis perdue." In Jésus aux origenes de la christologie. 2nd ed. BETL 40. Leuven: Leuven UP, 1989. 331–50. ———. "La parabole de la brebis perdue." Greg 49 (1968) 265–87. **Héring, J.** "Un texte oublié: Mt 18.10: A propos des controverses recentes sur le pedobaptisme." In Aux sources de la tradition chrétienne. FS M. Goguel, ed. P. Benoit et al. Neuchâtel/Paris: Delachaux et Niestlé, 1950. 95–102. **Petersen, W. L.** "The Parable of the Lost Sheep in the Gospel of Thomas and the Synoptics." NovT 23 (1981) 128–47. **Roloff, J.** "Das Kirchenverständnis des Matthäus im Spiegel seiner Gleichnisse." NTS 38 (1992) 337–56. **Schnider, F.** "Das Gleichnis vom verloren Schaf und seine Redaktoren." Kairos 19 (1977) 146–54. **Trau, J. M.** "The Lost Sheep: A Living Metaphor." BiTod 28 (1990) 277–83.

### Translation

[10]"*See that you do not treat one of these little ones* [a] *with contempt. For I tell you that their angels in heaven* [b] *always behold my Father's face who is in heaven.* [c]

[12]"*What do you think? If someone has a hundred sheep and one of them goes astray, will not that person leave the ninety-nine* [d] *on the hills* [e] *and go and seek the straying sheep?* [f] [13]*And if that person finds it, truly I say to you, that person will rejoice over it more than over the ninety-nine who have not strayed.* [14]*Thus it is not the will of* [g] *your* [h] *Father who is in heaven that one* [i] *of these little ones should perish.*"

## Notes

a D it vg[mss] sy[c] sa[mss] add *τῶν πιστευόντων εἰς ἐμέ*, "who believe in me," probably by the influence of 18:6.

b *ἐν οὐρανοῖς*, "in heaven" (cf. the same phrase at the end of the verse); B (33) sa[mss] alter this to the equivalent *ἐν τῷ οὐρανῷ*, "in heaven," while N *f*[1] aur sy[s] sa[mss] omit the phrase altogether.

c Many MSS (D L[c] W TR lat sy[c.p.h] bo[pt]) have inserted (as v 11) *ἦλθεν γὰρ ὁ υἱὸς τοῦ ἀνθρώπου* [(L[mg]) 892[c] 1010 c sy[h] bo[pt] insert *ζητῆσαι καί*] *σῶσαι τὸ ἀπολωλός*, "For the Son of Man came (to seek and) to save the lost." Lacking the sentence are א B L* Θ *f*[1.13] 33 sy[s] mae bo[pt]. The addition is borrowed from Luke 19:10 and was probably designed to link v 10 more closely with vv 12–14. See *TCGNT*, 44–45.

d B Θ *f*[13] sa[mss] mae add *πρόβατα*, "sheep."

e א* omits *ἐπὶ τὰ ὄρη*, "on the hills."

f "Sheep" added to translation.

g *ἔμπροσθεν*, lit. "before." This awkward preposition is omitted by א *f*[13] (sy[s.c]) bo. See *Comment*.

h Some MSS (B N Γ Θ *f*[13] sy[s.h] co) read *μου*, "my," in place of *ὑμῶν*, "your" (so א D [*ἡμῶν*, "our"] K L W Δ *f*[1] latt sy[c.p.hmg]), probably through the influence of v 10 (cf. v 35). The occurrences of "my Father" and "your Father" in Matthew are nearly equal in number (19x, 18x [*σου* or *ὑμῶν*], respectively). *TCGNT*, 45.

i *ἕν*, "one," neuter and appropriate to *πρόβατα*. Many MSS (W Θ *f*[1.13] TR lat) change it to *εἷς*, masc. as more appropriate to "the little ones," who are disciples. For text as is, א B D L N.

## *Form/Structure/Setting*

A. The importance of every disciple, every "little one," is now stressed by a glimpse of their importance to the Father. This is accomplished by reference to their angels and especially by the parable of the one lost sheep, the point of which Jesus emphasizes in the statement of v 14. The function of this pericope in the larger discourse is to provide a foundation for right conduct in the church. That is, because every little one is so important to the Father, the way one acts toward any of them is extremely important in God's sight. The passage thus provides a theological rationale for the preceding passage concerning not causing others to stumble, as well as for the admonitions concerning proper conduct toward disciples in the remainder of the chapter.

B. From this pericope to the end of the discourse (i.e., the end of chap. 18), Matthew no longer depends on Mark but instead depends partly upon Q and partly upon his own source. In the present instance, apart from v 10, which is unique to Matthew, Matthew apparently depends on Q (cf. Luke 15:3–7), although there is practically no word-for-word agreement between Matthew and Luke. There is, to be sure, a common story line, wherein "a certain person" (Matthew: *τινὶ ἀνθρώπῳ*; Luke: *τίς ἄνθρωπος*) has a hundred sheep, one of which becomes lost, and the owner seeks the lost one, leaving the ninety-nine (Matthew: *ἐπὶ τὰ ὄρη*, "on the hills"; Luke: *ἐν τῇ ἐρήμῳ*, "in the desert area"), finds it, and rejoices over that fact. But the differences are extensive. Whereas Luke introduces the pericope explicitly as a parable (Luke 15:3), Matthew begins with the question *τί ὑμῖν δοκεῖ*, "What do you think?" (cf. 17:25; 21:28, etc.). Matthew's *πλανηθῇ ἓν ἐξ αὐτῶν*, "one of them strayed" (v 12), puts the responsibility more on the sheep rather than on the shepherd as in Luke's *ἀπολέσας ἐξ αὐτῶν ἕν*, "having lost one of them" (Luke 15:4); in line with this, Luke's *τὸ ἀπολωλός*, "the lost one" (Luke 15:4; cf. Luke 15:6), becomes in Matthew *τὸ πλανώμενον*, "the one having strayed" (v 12). But it is toward the end of the pericope that the differences are the most marked. According to Luke, the shepherd, rejoicing, places the sheep on his shoulder, goes home, and gathers his friends and neighbors to announce the good news, whereupon is presented the concluding logion: "I say to you that there will be more joy in heaven over one sinner who repents than over the ninety-nine righteous people who have no need of repentance" (Luke 15:7). Matthew ends the pericope more abruptly with the logia of vv 13 and 14, where there is reference to rejoicing more over the one than over the ninety-nine who did not stray, finally stating that it is not the will of "your Father" that one of these "little ones" should perish. Matthew has probably abbreviated his Q source and has clearly adapted the parable freely to accomplish his own purpose in the discourse so that in its new application it refers now not, as in Luke, to the lost sinner but to the one who strays and is brought back to the fold (see Jeremias, *Parables*). *Gos. Thom.* 107 has an allusion to the parable (which, however, turns it on its head) that is probably dependent on the synoptic tradition (cf. too v 14 with 2 Peter 3:9).

C. The pericope consists of a parable prefaced and followed by separate logia, as the following outline indicates: (1) the importance of the "little ones," subdivided into (a) the command not to look down on them (v 10a) and (b) the evidence of their importance (v 10b); (2) the parable of the lost sheep, subdivided into (a) the straying of the one sheep (v 12) and (b) the joy at the restoration of the one (v 13); and (3) the importance of each little one to the Father (v 14). The surprisingly little symmetry or parallelism in the pericope is found only in the parable, since the opening and concluding logia are so brief. In the parable itself, vv 12 and 13 each begin with ἐάν, "if," clauses and have or imply double main clauses, while the main clauses of each verse are parallel, dealing with the ninety-nine and the one (and vice versa). The reference to ἓν τῶν μικρῶν τούτων, "one of these little ones," at the end of the final logion forms an inclusio with the same phrase in v 10a.

### Comment

**10**   Disciples, i.e., members of the Christian community, are to "see to it" (ὁρᾶν, in the sense of stern warning; see 8:4; 9:30; 16:6; 24:6) that they do not "act contemptuously" (καταφρονήσητε) toward another disciple, ἑνὸς τῶν μικρῶν τούτων, lit. "one of these little ones" (cf. v 6, and *Comment* there). καταφρονεῖν means "to despise" or "to treat with contempt" (cf. BAGD, 420a; the verb is used elsewhere in Matthew only in 6:24; cf. 1 Tim 4:12). All disciples, all members of the community, are of inestimable worth and significance. To make this remarkable point more evident, reference is made to the angels of each of these "little ones," οἱ ἄγγελοι αὐτῶν ἐν οὐρανοῖς, "their angels in heaven," who themselves "always behold" (διὰ παντὸς βλέπουσι) the face of the Father in heaven. (Carson's interpretation, following B. B. Warfield, of the "angels" as the spirits of the little ones after death, while not impossible, is not convincing. If this view were correct, a different vocabulary might have been expected, as well as a future tense, "will behold.") These supernatural creatures are thus able to do what no human being can do and live (Exod 33:20). Since in Jewish tradition only some angels are able to see the face of God (cf. Isa 6:2; *1 Enoch* 14:21; contrast "angels of the Presence" in *Jub.* 2:2, 18; cf. *1 Enoch* 40), these angels are therefore to be regarded as especially significant. The idea of key angels who have access to the very presence of God is reflected also in Luke 1:19 (Gabriel), Tob 12:15 (Raphael), and Rev 8:2; more generally the author of Hebrews can describe angels as "ministering spirits sent forth to serve for the sake of those who are to obtain salvation" (Heb 1:14; for OT background, cf. Gen 48:16 and esp. Ps 91:11; see too 1QH 5:20–22; *3 Apoc. Bar.* 12:3; Str-B 1:781–83; 3:437–40 for rabbinic references). So important are the disciples of Jesus, these "little ones," that they have "their" (αὐτῶν) angels, who presumably look after their welfare primarily through intercession, but perhaps also in other ways. This passage falls short of describing "guardian" angels (despite the "guardian angels" of NEB; corrected in REB to "angels") assigned to each individual Christian, who attempt to keep her or him out of danger. A more general idea is in view, namely, that angels represent the "little ones" before the throne of God. The point here is not to speculate on the *ad hoc* role of angels in aiding disciples of Jesus but rather simply to emphasize the importance of the latter to God. If the very angels of God's presence are concerned with the "little ones," how much more then should also fellow Christians be for one another! They are to be received and esteemed; special care must furthermore be taken not to cause them to stumble.

**12** The opening question, τί ὑμῖν δοκεῖ, "What do you think?" is an invitation to consider a matter seriously, and here a rhetorical device to strengthen the assumed affirmative answer (cf. too οὐχί, which anticipates a positive answer) to the question that follows (Matthew uses this introductory question several times; cf. 17:25; 21:28; 22:17, 42; 26:66). The imagery of the people of God as a flock of sheep, and of straying sheep, is found at several places in the OT. Ezek 34 in particular presents interesting contacts with details of the parable (cf. Ezek 34:6 [with reference to ὄρει, "hill"], 12 [ζητεῖ, "seeks"], 16 [with specifically τὸ πλανώμενον, "the straying one"; so too Ezek 34:4]). Similar imagery is also found elsewhere in the OT (cf. Ps 119:176; Jer 23:1–4; 50:6; Isa 53:6) as well as in the NT (1 Peter 2:25; John 10:11–18). The imagery of the one straying sheep out of the ninety-nine, however, finds no real parallel elsewhere. Here the parable concerns members of the community ("little ones" [v 14]) who go astray, i.e., lapse, and are brought back (unlike the use of the imagery in 9:36; 10:6; 15:24, where the scattered, "lost [τὰ ἀπολωλότα]" sheep are Israelites who have not received the gospel). The verb πλανᾶν, "stray," assumes importance again in the apocalyptic discourse (24:4, 5, 11, 24). Such is the value of each individual sheep that the shepherd "will leave" (ἀφήσει) the ninety-nine "on the hills" (ἐπὶ τὰ ὄρη, perhaps an allusion to Ezek 34:6) to seek the one who has strayed (again probably a deliberate change of Q [cf. Luke 15:6], perhaps with Ezek 34 or other OT passages in mind). The security of the remaining ninety-nine while the shepherd is absent is not a matter of concern in the parable. Matthew does not specify the cause of the straying of such a disciple, but from the context it must be the conduct of other disciples. The perfect applicability of Luke 19:10, "For the Son of Man came to seek and to save the lost," makes it no surprise that in later manuscripts scribes inserted the verse (i.e., v 11) just prior to the parable. Very probably Matthew and his original readers think of Jesus as the shepherd who goes in search of the stray (see 26:31; cf. 9:36; 15:24; elsewhere in the NT, John 10:11–30).

**13**  The finding (and rescuing) of the lost sheep is the cause of great joy, a point emphasized by the ἀμὴν λέγω ὑμῖν, "truly I say to you" (cf. on 5:18). This joy is even greater than that for the ninety-nine who did not stray but remained safe in the fold. The joy at the restoration of one who had strayed points to the importance of each sheep in the shepherd's eye.

**14**  The application of the short parable (cf. οὕτως, "thus"), and thus its place in the discourse, is made quite explicit in this concluding logion. It is against the will of "your Father who is in heaven" (τοῦ πατρὸς ὑμῶν τοῦ ἐν οὐρανοῖς; for this expression, see *Comment* on 5:16; it occurs verbatim in 5:45) that "one of these little ones" (ἐν τῶν μικρῶν τούτων, cf. vv 6, 10; 10:42) should perish. The improper preposition ἔμπροσθεν, lit. "before," is a reverential way of speaking about God's activity (cf. 11:26; Isa 45:1 LXX) or will (θέλημα), as here. The reference to "your" Father is in keeping with the address of the discourse to the members of the community. ἀπόληται, "perish," is a particularly strong word to describe the fate of one who stumbles or falls away (cf. 10:28). This ultimate ruin or destruction is itself a further sobering reason for care in one's conduct with others. This then is the reason that disciples, members of the community, are to be received and welcomed by their brothers and sisters in the faith and why one is to be careful not to cause them to stumble: each of "these little ones" is precious in the sight of God, whose very angels seek their welfare and whose will it is that not one perish.

*Explanation*

This pericope substantiates the importance of proper conduct between Christians, using paradoxical categories to do so. In this passage, disciples are described, on the one hand, as "these little ones," who have humbled themselves by assuming a childlike lack of status, and as sheep in danger of straying but, on the other hand, as those who have even their angels in heaven and who are so important that if one should stray, the shepherd will spare no energy to save it. The shepherd/sheep imagery is especially rich in its ability to call attention to the value placed upon the sheep. As the shepherd would not lose one sheep, so it is the will of the Father that not one of these little ones perish. If this is so, then the demeanor of disciple to disciple in the community is a matter of grave importance. Human beings must not be allowed to overturn the saving purpose of God. And thus a disciple must esteem every other disciple in the same way that God esteems them all.

# Handling Matters of Church Discipline    (18:15–20)

*Bibliography*

**Barth, G.** "Auseinandersetzung um die Kirchenzucht im Umkreis des Matthäusevangelium." *ZNW* 69 (1978) 158–77. **Catchpole, D. R.** "Reproof and Reconciliation in the Q Community: A Study of the Tradition-History of Matthew 18.15–17, 21–2/Lk 17.3–4." *SNTU* 8 (1983) 79–90. **Christian, P.** "Was heisst für Matthäus 'In meinen Namen versammelt'

(Mt 18, 20)." In *Dienst und Vermittlung*, ed. W. Ernst. Leipzig: St. Benno, 1977. 97–105. **Derrett, J. D. M.** "'Where two or three are convened in my name . . .': A sad misunderstanding." *ExpTim* 91 (1979) 83–86. **Duling, D. C.** "Binding and Loosing: Matthew 16:19; Matthew 18:18; John 20:23." *Forum* 3 (1987) 3–31. **Forkman, G.** *The Limits of the Religious Community.* ConBNT 5. Lund: Gleerup, 1972. 124–32. **Hickling, C. J. A.** "Conflicting Motives in the Redaction of Matthew: Some Considerations on the Sermon on the Mount and Matthew 18.15–20." *SE* 7 [= TU 126] (1982) 247–60. **Korting, G.** "Binden oder lösen: Zu Verstockungs- und Befreiungstheologie in Mt 16,19; 18,18. 21–35 und Joh 15,1–17; 20,23." *SNTU* 14 (1989) 39–91. **Matthew, P. K.** "Authority and Discipline: Matt. 16:17–19 and 18:15–18 and the Exercise of Authority and Discipline in the Matthean Community." *Communio Viatorum* 28 (1985) 119–25. **Pesch, R.** "'Wo zwei oder drei versammelt sind auf meinen Namen hin . . .' (Mt 18,20)." In *Studien zum Matthäusevangelium.* FS W. Pesch, ed. L. Schenke. Stuttgart: Katholisches Bibelwerk, 1988. 227–43. **Pfitzner, V. C.** "Purified Community—Purified Sinner: Expulsion from the Community according to Matthew 18.15–18 and 1 Corinthians 5.1–5." *AusBR* 30 (1982) 34–55. **Sievers, J.** "'Where Two or Three . . .': The Rabbinic Concept of Shekinah and Matthew 18:20." In *Standing before God.* FS J. M. Oesterreicher, ed. A. Finkel and L. Frizzell. New York: Ktav, 1981. 171–82. **Zimmermann, H.** "Die innere Struktur der Kirche und das Petrusamt nach Mt 18,15–35." In *Petrus und Papst*, ed. A. Brandenburg and H. J. Urban. Münster: Aschendorff, 1977. 4–19.

*Translation*

[15] *"And if your brother or sister* [a] *sins [against you],* [b] *go and rebuke him or her just between the two of you. If she or he listens, you have gained your sister or brother.* [16] *But if he or she does not listen, take with you one or two others, in order that 'Every matter may be established by the mouth of two or three witnesses.'* [c] [17] *But if he or she does not listen to them, tell it to the church. And if he or she does not listen to the church, let that person be to you as a Gentile and a* [d] *tax collector.* [18] *Truly I say to you: Whatever you bind on earth shall have been bound in heaven,* [e] *and whatever you loose on earth* [f] *shall have been loosed in heaven.* [g] [19] *Again, [truly]* [h] *I say to you that if two of you agree concerning any matter about which you ask, it will be done for them by my Father who is in heaven.* [20] *For where two or three are* [i] *gathered together in my name, there am* [j] *I in their midst."*

*Notes*

[a] "Brother or sister" and "he or she" represent inclusive-language translations of masc. nouns and pronouns in the Gr.

[b] The important MSS ℵ B *f* [1] sa bo[pt] omit εἰς σέ, "against you"; including these words are D L W Θ *f* [13] TR latt sy mae bo[pt]. Possibly the words were inserted on the pattern of εἰς ἐμέ, "against me," in v 21. On the other hand, they could have been deliberately omitted for theological reasons so that the verse could apply to sin generally. The *UBSGNT* committee accordingly includes the words but places them within brackets. *TCGNT*, 45.

[c] The order of the last four words varies in the MSS. Thus ℵ Θ 700 have δύο ἢ τριῶν μαρτύρων; L has μαρτύρων δύο ἢ τριῶν; and D has just δύο ἢ τριῶν, "two or three."

[d] D adds ὡς, "as."

[e] ἐν οὐρανῷ, "in heaven"; some MSS (ℵ L 33), perhaps influenced by 16:19, change οὐρανός to the pl. and add the definite article, ἐν τοῖς οὐρανοῖς; many MSS (W *f* [1] TR) have the sing. τῷ οὐρανῷ. For the text, B Θ *f* [13].

[f] D* n omit the words following the first occurrence of τῆς γῆς, "the earth," up to and including the second occurrence of τῆς γῆς, a clear example of omission through homoioteleuton. The resultant reading makes no sense: "Whatever you bind on earth shall have been loosed in heaven."

<sup>g</sup> ἐν οὐρανῷ, "in heaven"; as in *Note* e, some MSS (D L 33) have ἐν τοῖς οὐρανοῖς; others (W *f*¹ TR) ἐν τῷ οὐρανῷ. For the text, א B Θ *f*¹³.

<sup>h</sup> Some MSS (א D L Γ *f*¹ lat sy<sup>p</sup> bo) omit ἀμήν, "truly"; others (N W Δ sy<sup>h</sup>) have δέ, "but," instead. In favor of ἀμήν are B (Θ) *f*¹³ TR it sy<sup>s,c</sup> sa mae bo<sup>ms</sup>. Because of the divided testimony, the word is put in brackets in the Gr. text.

<sup>i-j</sup> A few MSS (D [g¹] sy<sup>s</sup>) have οὐκ εἰσὶν γάρ, "For where are not (two or three)," together with a second negative παρ' οἷς οὐκ, "with them (I am) not."

## Form/Structure/Setting

A. The conduct of disciple toward disciple has thus far been dealt with in general terms. Now the problem of specific offenses against members of the community by other members of that community is addressed. Again the grave importance of such offenses is evident, as is the consequent need of a proper disciplinary procedure. This is as close as we come in Matthew to an actual handbook of rules for the community. Of course, in a broader sense the catechetical nature of the Gospel is meant to be a guide to Christian righteousness. In this pericope we see church discipline pragmatically at work, its basis in OT precedent, the authority once again of those in positions of leadership, and the promise of the continued presence of Jesus in his gathered community.

B. Apart from some similarity between v 15 and Luke 17:3, thus possibly reflecting a Q saying, the pericope is from Matthew's own source. V 18 is a nearly verbatim repetition of 16:19b–c (cf. John 20:23 for a related saying). The only differences are the plurals ὅσα (for ὅ), δεδεμένα (for δεδεμένον), λελυμένα (for λελυμένον), the singular ἐν οὐρανῷ (twice, for ἐν τοῖς οὐρανοῖς), and finally and most important, the plural endings of the verbs δήσητε (for δήσῃς) and λύσητε (for λύσῃς). V 15 differs from Luke 17:3 by lacking the opening words προσέχετε ἑαυτοῖς, "give heed to yourselves," the insertion of ὕπαγε, "go," the verb ἔλεγξον for ἐπιτίμησον, both meaning "rebuke" (Matthew perhaps influenced by the LXX of Lev 19:17), the inclusion of the words μεταξὺ σοῦ καὶ αὐτοῦ μόνου, lit. "between you and him alone," and in the final clause Matthew's ἐάν σου ἀκούσῃ ἐκέρδησας τὸν ἀδελφόν σου, "if he listens, you have gained your brother," for Luke's καὶ ἐὰν μετανοήσῃ ἄφες αὐτῷ, "and if he repents, forgive him." Although the changes are thus considerable, it is possible that the different sayings reflect an earlier common, original logion, which Matthew has adapted to his purposes in this pericope. *Did.* 15.3 betrays probable knowledge of the Matthean pericope. Vv 19–20 are probably reflected in Ign. *Eph.* 5.2 (cf. *Gos. Thom.* 30; cf. 48).

C. This pericope is in the form of specific community regulations in instances where one member has sinned against another. It includes in extreme cases the command to ostracize the offending member. Furthermore, an authoritative basis is provided for the entire process, together with the promises of answered prayer and the presence of Jesus. The following outline can be suggested: (1) procedure in cases of specific offense (v 15a), further divided into (a) a private meeting (v 15b–d), (b) a meeting with two or three others, with OT basis (v 16), and (c) public exposure and ostracizing (v 17); (2) statement of the authority behind such discipline (v 18); (3) the answer to prayer in such matters (v 19); and (4) the presence of Jesus in such circumstances (v 20). The most striking structural parallelism is found in the repeated ἐάν, "if," clauses at the beginning of vv 15, 16, 17, 17b, and 19. Each of these clauses, except for the last, introduces a potential situation and is followed in the apodosis by what is deemed the appropriate action. The appended logion of v 18 consists of two exactly symmetrical halves (cf. 16:19b–c). The form of the material is eminently suitable for memorization and may reflect its transmission in oral tradition.

D. There is without question a certain anachronism about this pericope, which views the church as a distinct entity and, indeed, one with considerable organization. The present form of the discourse speaks obviously to the church of Matthew's day. If, however, Jesus was able to conceive of and plan for a community to carry on the work of the kingdom after his death (see *Comment* on 16:18), then he could also have made provision for the future existence of that community through the type of teaching found in this pericope. Matthew has probably taken sayings from the tradition and molded them into this pericope (as he has for the discourse as a whole) and thus given them somewhat more immediate relevance for his church.

## Comment

**15** The reference to ὁ ἀδελφός σου, "your brother," indicates that conduct within the community of disciples continues to remain in view. The content of ἁμαρτήσῃ [εἰς σέ], "should sin [against you]," is probably left deliberately imprecise so that a broad variety of offenses can be included. Presumably, however, given the procedure that follows, the type of sin being considered is of a substantial rather than trivial or merely personal nature (the verb ἁμαρτάνειν, "sin," occurs in Matthew only here, in v 21, and in 27:4). When a member of the community has been sinned against, that person is to go (ὕπαγε) to the other person and "rebuke" (ἔλεγξον; the verb occurs in Matthew only here) him or her. The meaning here is not to scold someone or to abuse them verbally for their conduct but rather to bring the offensive matter to their attention in the hope that they will repent of their actions and be restored to the community. The same verb occurs in the LXX of Lev 19:17 (cf. 1QS 5:25–6:1, CD 9:2–8, also with three stages in the process; for rabbinic background, see *b. Tamid* 62a; *b. Šabb.* 119b). It is also to be seen in passages reflecting the practice of the church (e.g., 1 Tim 5:20; 2 Tim 4:2; Titus 2:15; cf. too Gal 6:1; Titus 3:10). This first stage is to be done strictly in private, μεταξὺ σοῦ καὶ αὐτοῦ μόνου, lit. "between you and him alone," so as to avoid spreading unnecessarily the knowledge of the person's sin (cf. Prov 25:9). If the person "listens" (ἀκούσῃ), i.e., responds appropriately, probably assuming repentance and a request for forgiveness, then restoration takes place: ἐκέρδησας τὸν ἀδελφόν σου, "you have gained your brother." This last clause may have the nuance of restoring the lapsed person to full membership in the community (i.e., the opposite of the excommunication of v 17b). The person who has been sinned against is thus to bring the matter to the perpetrator (contrast the otherwise similar *y. Yoma* 45c), as much for the latter's own good as to ease the pain of the offense. The offender is thus like the stray sheep of the preceding passage, who must be brought back to the fold. Only in such a way can the community remain intact (cf. Jas 5:19–20).

**16** Once the first stage has proven fruitless, a second stage is to come into effect. The procedure is repeated but now in the presence of one or two other members of the community. This procedure is explicitly on the pattern of the

OT stipulation in Deut 19:15 (cf. Deut 17:6; for rabbinic background, *m. Soṭa* 1:1), which Matthew proceeds to quote at this point: ἵνα ἐπὶ στόματος δύο μαρτύρων ἢ τριῶν σταθῇ πᾶν ῥῆμα, "in order that every matter may be established by the mouth of two or three witnesses." The parallel is not exact, however, since in the OT the witnesses are witnesses of the deed itself, whereas here they serve as witnesses of the reproof and appeal for repentance or, if the person refuses to respond, of his or her recalcitrance. Matthew abbreviates the LXX by replacing the repeated καὶ ἐπὶ στόματος τριῶν μαρτύρων, "and by the mouth of three witnesses," with ἢ τριῶν, "or three," and alters the verb σταθήσεται, "shall stand," to the subjunctive σταθῇ, "may stand," agreeing with the ἵνα, "in order that." Beyond these slight changes, the quotation is verbatim. The appeal to two or three witnesses, with the same OT background in view, is found also in 26:60; John 8:17 (cf. Heb 6:18; Rev 11:3). This small group of disciples is to proceed along the same lines laid out in v 15. The hope is for repentance and restoration. But in this intermediate stage at the same time the matter acquires the status of legality (cf. 2 Cor 13:1; 1 Tim 5:19), which can serve to bring the process to the third stage, including excommunication, if necessary.

**17** When the offending person does not listen to the group of two or three (παρακούσῃ, twice in this verse, means to "disregard"), the matter is to be brought to the attention of "the community" as a whole (τῇ ἐκκλησίᾳ, "the [local] church"). Only in this verse and in 16:18 is this word used in the four Gospels (see *Comment* on 16:18). The community itself then apparently makes its plea, indeed the final plea, to the offender to repent. At this point it is felt that enough opportunity for repentance has been given, and that if the person has failed to respond appropriately, the only course of action that remains is ostracism from the community. This is the force of the stipulation ἔστω σοι ὥσπερ ὁ ἐθνικὸς καὶ ὁ τελώνης, "let him be to you as a Gentile and a tax collector." The derogatory use of ἐθνικός, "Gentile," reflects Matthew's Jewish-Christian community and is to be understood in the sense of "heathen," i.e., pagan (cf. its use in 5:47 and 6:7; the only other occurrence of the word in the NT is in 3 John 7). The "tax collector" (ὁ τελώνης) was also despised by the Jews (see esp. *Comment* on 5:46–47 and 10:3; the reference here stands in no tension with a passage such as 21:31–32, contra McNeile). Thus the unrepentant offender is not simply put out of the community but categorized as among the worst sort of persons. (The Pauline admonitions of 1 Cor 5:9–13 and 2 Thess 3:14–15 are similar in effect; cf. Titus 3:10.)

**18** See *Comment* on the nearly verbatim statement in 16:19. Several important differences are to be noted. In 16:19 Peter is addressed; here, by contrast, the verbs are plural, and thus other disciples and leaders of the community are also given the authority to "bind and loose." Here the binding and loosing have to do directly with matters of church discipline, whereas in 16:19 they concern matters of conduct more generally. However, in both instances the ultimate issue concerns membership in the community. In the present instance, which addresses the case of one who has "sinned" (v 15), the connection with John 20:23 ("If you forgive [ἀφῆτε] the sins of any, they are forgiven; if you retain [κρατῆτε] the sins of any, they are retained") becomes more apparent. Loosing is the equivalent of forgiving, binding of retaining. The leadership thus has the ability to make decisions concerning unrepentant sinners in the community—decisions that carry authority such that they are said to be likewise fixed in heaven. At stake is nothing less than the ultimate welfare of the offending individual.

**19** An emphatic (ἀμήν, "truly," "amen") promise is introduced here to encourage the church in its administration of church discipline. That Jesus continues to address this issue is indicated both by the initial πάλιν, "again," as well as by the use of παντὸς πράγματος, "every matter" (the only occurrence of this word in Matthew; see 1 Cor 6:1; cf. πᾶν ῥῆμα, "every matter" [v 16]). In instances of discipline, the community leaders will "ask" (αἰτήσωνται) for guidance; where two (δύο; cf. v 16) are agreed (συμφωνήσωσιν; the verb occurs again in Matthew only in 20:2, 13), they can be assured of God's guidance in their decisions. Quite possibly in view is the agreement of two members of a three-member court representing the community (cf. *m. Sanh.* 1:1; cf. too *b. Sanh.* 7a; *b. Ber.* 6a, where the Shekinah abides with the court that judges justly). It seems very unlikely, on the other hand, that the "two" refers to the offender and the one offended against (*pace* Derrett). The contrast between ἐπὶ τῆς γῆς, "on the earth," and being granted their request παρὰ τοῦ πατρός μου τοῦ ἐν οὐρανοῖς, "from my Father who is in heaven" (for this Matthean phrase, see *Comment* on 7:21), reflects the same polarity as that of v 18 (ἐπὶ τῆς γῆς, "upon the earth"—ἐν οὐρανῷ, in heaven") and indicates that a similar point is being made. What the disciples agree to on earth in disciplinary matters of the church may be taken as also the will of heaven. This promise is by its context thus more restricted in character than those of 7:7 and 21:22. The fact that the Father is referred to as "my" (μου) rather than "your" hints at the involvement of Jesus in the concerns of his community and anticipates the verse that follows.

**20** This verse adds a promise to the preceding statements. In the conduct of its business, and again by context especially in the handling of church discipline (cf. 1 Cor 6:1–6), where two or three (cf. v 16) are gathered together "in my name" (εἰς τὸ ἐμὸν ὄνομα; cf. v 5; see *Comment* on 7:22), there Jesus will be in their midst. "In my name" is another way of saying "under my rule." This presence of Jesus should not be understood as a metaphor (as in the case of Paul's statement in 1 Cor 5:4) but is the literal presence of the resurrected Christ, in keeping with the promise to be articulated in 28:20 (cf. 1:23b). The community founded by Jesus (16:18) is assured that he will be present in that community until the close of the age. The saying is closely paralleled by the rabbinic saying that where two gather together to study Torah, the Shekinah glory is present with them (in *m. ʾAbot* 3:2; 3:6; *b. Sanh.* 39a; *b. Ber.* 5b). The differences, gathering in the name of Jesus (for study of Torah) and the presence of Jesus (for the Shekinah glory), point to the enormous christological implications of this final logion. It is not far from this sense of the divine presence (cf. Joel 2:27; Zech 2:10–11) to the Christology of Paul or of the author of Hebrews.

### Explanation

A premise basic to this pericope is the importance of personal relationships between members of the community. Just as it is important not to cause any of "these little ones" to stumble, so it is important that one not impudently sin against another. Accordingly, Jesus outlines a procedure for cases where one sins in this way and displays a hard-heartedness about it. It would be a mistake to think that in similar circumstances this procedure can be applied today, primarily because excommunication or ostracism today has nowhere near the same effect as it did in the first century. That is, in Matthew's day to be cast out left one with no other options for Christian community. Today a person may simply walk down the street to the next church or next denomination. This is not to say that the church must give up on the possibility of church discipline but simply to say that the process will take on its own character appropriate to the present-day situation. It is also worth pointing out that the notion of an "isolated, individual Christian" (e.g., a "TV" Christian) was not then considered a possibility. The Christian is always to be accountable to a community. And the importance of the community receives indirect confirmation in the divinely granted authority of its leaders, in the promise of answered prayer in the administration of the church, and in the promise of the continuing presence of the risen Christ in the midst of those gathered in his name. The supreme mark of Christ's community is Christ's presence.

# The Necessity of Forgiveness: The Parable of the Unforgiving Servant    (18:21–35)

### Bibliography

**Breukelmann, F. H.** "Eine Erklärung des Gleichnisses vom Schalksknecht (Matth. 18,23–35)." In *Parrhesia.* FS K. Barth, ed. E. Busch et al. Zürich: EVZ, 1966. **Broer, I.** "Die Parabel vom Verzicht auf das Prinzip von Leistung und Gegenleistung." In *À cause de l'Evangile.* FS J. Dupont. LD 123. Paris: Cerf, 1985. 145–64. **Buckley, T. W.** *Seventy Times Seven: Sin, Judgment, and Forgiveness in Matthew.* Collegeville, MN: Liturgical Press, 1991. **De Boer, M. C.** "Ten Thousand Talents? Matthew's Interpretation and Redaction of the Parable of the Unforgiving Servant (Matt. 18:23–35)." *CBQ* 50 (1988) 214–32. **Deidun, T.** "The Parable of the Unmerciful Servant (Mt 18:23–35)." *BTB* 6 (1976) 203–24. **Dietzfelbinger, C.** "Das Gleichnis von der erlassenen Schuld." *EvT* 32 (1972) 437–51. **Fuchs, E.** "The Parable of the Unmerciful Servant." *SE* 1 [= TU 73] (1959) 487–94. **Merklein, H.** "Der Prozess der Barmherzigkeit." In *Studien zum Matthäusevangelium.* FS W. Pesch, ed. L. Schenke. Stuttgart: Katholisches Bibelwerk, 1988. 201–7. **Patte, D.** "Bringing Out of the Gospel-Treasure What Is New and What Is Old: Two Parables in Matthew 18–23." *Quarterly Review* 10 (1990) 79–108. **Scott, B. B.** "The King's Accounting: Matthew 18:23–34." *JBL* 104 (1985) 429–42.

### Translation

[21] *Then Peter came and said to him:*[a] *"Lord, How many times will my brother or sister*[b] *sin against me, and I must forgive that person? As many as seven?"* [22]*Jesus said to him: "I tell you not as many as seven, but as many as seventy times seven.*[c]

[23]*"Because of this, the kingdom of heaven is like the situation of*[d] *a king, who desired to settle accounts with his servants.* [24]*As he began to do this,*[e] *a man was brought to him who owed him ten thousand*[f] *talents.* [25]*But when he was unable to pay it back, the*

*sovereign* [g,h] *commanded him to be sold, together with his wife and children and every-thing he had, in order that the debt might be paid.* [26] *The* [i] *servant, therefore, falling down, prostrated himself before him, saying:* [j] *'Be patient toward me, and I will repay everything to you.'* [k] [27] *And the sovereign of that servant* [l] *was moved with compassion, released him, and canceled the debt.* [28] *But that* [m] *servant came out and found one of his fellow servants, who owed him a hundred denarii, seized him, and began to* [n] *choke him, saying: 'Pay me what you owe.'* [29] *His fellow servant, therefore, fell down* [o] *and pleaded with him, saying: 'Be patient toward me, and I will repay you.'* [30] *And he would not listen,* [p] *but departed and had him thrown* [q] *into prison until he paid what was owed.* [31] *When his fellow servants, therefore, saw the things that had happened, they were greatly distressed, and they went and related to their sovereign everything that had happened.* [32] *Then his sovereign called him and said to him: 'Evil servant, I canceled all that debt for you when you pleaded with me.* [33] *Ought not you also* [r] *to have been merciful to your fellow servant as I was merciful to you?'* [34] *And his sovereign was angry and handed him over to the torturers until he should render to him all* [s] *that was owed.* [t] [35] *Thus also my heavenly Father will do to you, unless each one of you forgives your brother or sister* [u] *from your heart.'*

## Notes

[a] Many MSS ($\aleph^2$ L W Θ $f^{1,13}$ TR aur sy[p,h]) move αὐτῷ, "to him," to after the earlier participle, προσελθών, lit. "having come." A few MSS omit αὐτῷ altogether ($\aleph^*$ sy[s]), perhaps by accident. If the αὐτῷ was originally in the earlier position, it is difficult to understand why it was moved to the later position. Thus the *UBSGNT* committee accepts the later position as original (*TCGNT*, 45).

[b] "Or sister" added to translation, and the object of the second verb is changed accordingly.

[c] ἑβδομηκοντάκις ἑπτά can also mean "seventy-seven" (cf. JB; NIV). The larger number is opted for here as more effectively pointing to the implication of an unlimited number of times.

[d] "The situation of" added in translation for clarity.

[e] συναίρειν, lit. "to reckon," the same verb used in the preceding verse.

[f] For μυρίων, "ten thousand," a few MSS ($\aleph^*$ co) have πολλῶν, "many," and one (c) has ἑκατόν, "a hundred." These changes are obvious attempts to soften the hyperbole.

[g] Many MSS (W Θ $f^{13}$ TR it vg[cl] sy[p,h]) add αὐτοῦ, "his"; some others ($f^1$ 700 g[1] sy[s,c]) omit the words ὁ κύριος, lit. "the lord," altogether.

[h] In keeping with the reference to a "king" in v 23, ὁ κύριος, lit. "the lord," is translated as "sovereign" throughout the parable.

[i] A number of MSS ($\aleph^2$ D L Δ Θ lat sy mae bo) add ἐκεῖνος, "that" (cf. v 28).

[j] Many MSS ($\aleph$ L W $f^{1,13}$ TR it sy [p,h] co) add the vocative κύριε, "lord" or "master." If the word were original, it could have been omitted to conform this verse more closely to v 29. The *UBSGNT* committee, however, notes that the addition may have been made "to adapt the expression to a spiritual interpretation" and cites the variety of witnesses that support the shorter reading (B D Θ vg sy[s,c] arm geo). *TCGNT*, 46.

[k] Θ omits the words καὶ πάντα ἀποδώσω σοι, "and I will repay everything to you," through an obvious case of homoioteleuton (cf. ἐμοί—σοι).

[l] B Θ $f^1$ sa[mss] omit ἐκεῖνον, "that"; sy[c] has ὁ κύριος αὐτοῦ, "his master"; and sy[s] omits altogether the words ὁ κύριος τοῦ δούλου ἐκείνου, "the master of that servant," perhaps as unnecessary in the context.

[m] ἐκεῖνος, "that," is omitted by B.

[n] "Began to" interprets the verb as an inceptive impf.

[o] πεσών, lit. "falling." Many MSS ( C[2] W $f^{13}$ TR sy[p,h] mae) accordingly add εἰς τοὺς πόδας αὐτοῦ, "at his feet" (rather than this phrase being omitted through homoioteleuton); cf. *TCGNT*, 46. One MS (28) adds προσεκύνει αὐτόν, "kneeled before him," in imitation of v 26.

[p] "Listen" added to translation as a complement to οὐκ ἤθελεν, "he would not."

[q] ἔβαλεν, lit. "he cast (him)." The translation reflects the departure of the master and the action of others in fulfillment of his command in casting the man into prison.

ʳ 𝔓²⁵ sy replace καὶ σέ, "you also," with οὖν, "therefore"; D Θ saᵐˢˢ have οὖν καὶ σέ, "therefore you also."

ˢ D syˢ omit πᾶν, "all."

ᵗ Many MSS (ℵ*·² C L W f¹ TR syᵖ·ʰ) add αὐτῷ, "to him." The *UBSGNT* committee prefers the shorter reading, which has wide textual representation (ℵ¹ B D Θ f¹³ latt syˢ·ᶜ).

ᵘ Many MSS (C W f¹³ TR syⁱᵖⁱ·ʰ) add τὰ παραπτώματα αὐτῶν, "their transgressions," at the very end of the verse. The *UBSGNT* committee regards the words as "a natural expansion," perhaps on the model of 6:14. *TCGNT*, 46. "Or sister" is added to the translation (cf. *Note* b above).

### Form/Structure/Setting

A. Continuing the theme of the discourse, relationships between members of the community, Matthew now turns to the important subject of forgiveness (cf. the earlier attention given to it in 6:12, 14–15). Forgiveness will be a necessity whenever human beings exist together as disciples. Forgiveness among members of the community is to know no limit. It is clear from the parable of the unforgiving servant that one who has been forgiven must in turn forgive others. And it is not allegorizing to interpret this parable as portraying God's forgiveness of the members of the community as the model for their forgiveness of one another. Disciples are the forgiven who forgive. And as God's forgiveness is inexhaustible, so too must disciples cultivate their ability to renew their forgiveness of others again and again.

B. The parable of the unforgiving servant is found only in Matthew, being drawn from his own fund of tradition. Vv 21–22, on the other hand, find a partial parallel in Luke 17:4 (which, along with 17:1–3, follows the order of the material in Matthew) and thus may be based on an original Q saying. Luke's logion is joined to those that precede and is not given as an answer to a question asked by Peter. In Matthew Peter asks whether he (and by implication the other disciples) is to forgive someone who sins against him as many as "seven" (ἑπτάκις) times. The Lukan logion runs: "If anyone should sin against you seven times in a day, and seven times should turn to you, saying, 'I repent,' forgive him" (Luke 17:4). The differences from Matthew are notably the reference to "in the day" (τῆς ἡμέρας), probably a Lukan addition, and the reference to repentance, which Matthew probably assumes. Matthew's "seventy times seven" may well be his own expansion, if it is not a variant stemming from the tradition.

C. Vv 21–22 are independent from the parable that follows. The subject is similar, however, and Matthew has brought his discourse to an effective conclusion with the juxtaposition of this material. The dialogue of vv 21–22 consists simply of (1) question (v 21) and (2) answer (v 22). The parable of the unforgiving servant may be outlined as follows:

I. The King and His Subjects (vv 23–27)
   A. The King's Decision to Settle Accounts with His Subjects (v 23)
   B. The Servant with the Impossible Debt (v 24)
   C. The Decision to Force Payment (v 25)
   D. The Plea for Mercy (v 26)
   E. The Canceling of the Debt (v 27)
II. The Servant and His Fellow Servant (vv 28–31)
   A. The Servant Forcing His Fellow Servant to Pay a Small Debt (v 28)

I and II are strikingly parallel in several respects, especially in the demand of payment (the debts are contrasted dramatically) and the plea for mercy (the language of vv 26 and 29 is very nearly identical). Also there is some similarity between the treatment of the fellow servant (final clause of v 30) and the treatment eventually accorded the unforgiving servant himself in III (final clause of v 34). Although the parable concerns financial indebtedness, it is clear that the underlying principle is to be understood more broadly. Thus v 33 speaks of showing mercy, while v 35 speaks of forgiving (which is the language used also to refer to the cancellation of debt; cf. vv 27, 32); vv 21–22 are also concerned explicitly with forgiveness.

## Comment

**21–22** For the second time in the discourse, the teaching of Jesus is prompted by a question (cf. v 1). There is a sense too in which the parable that follows may be understood to grow out of the question (cf. διὰ τοῦτο, "therefore" [v 23]). Peter, again the spokesman for the disciples (cf. 15:15; 16:16; 17:4, etc.), knows already that Jesus taught the necessity of forgiving others (cf. 6:12, 14–15). Now in the context of a discussion of practical matters in the life of the community, Peter wants to determine what the limit is for the number of times forgiveness is to be extended to another. Thinking of the high standards of righteousness in Jesus' teaching, Peter probably regarded "seven times" (ἑπτάκις), the traditional number of fullness, as a quite generous proposal. The rabbis had considered three times sufficient for the forgiveness of the same sin (*b. Yoma* 86b–87a; but see *m. Yoma* 8:9 for a harsher view). Here, as earlier in the discourse (v 15), the verb ἁμαρτάνειν, "sin," is left general, presumably in order to include as wide a variety of phenomena as possible. εἰς ἐμέ, "against me," echoes the εἰς σέ, "against you," of v 15. The difference between vv 15–20 and the present passage is that in the former the repentance of the sinning one is lacking, whereas here it is assumed (cf. Luke 17:4). The subject here, therefore, is one who sins and repents (asks for forgiveness). In the answer of Jesus, ἑβδομηκοντάκις ἑπτά, whether it is to be taken as "seventy-seven" (cf. Gen 4:24, where in the LXX exactly the same Greek words are used) or "seventy times seven," points not to a limit of literally seventy-seven or even of 490 times but indicates forgiving an unlimited number of times (cf. too Luke 17:4: "seven times in a day"). Unlimited frequency of forgiveness goes with the unlimited scope of what is to be forgiven. This emphasis on the extravagant character of forgiveness is taken up in the parable that follows, which places the disciple's forgiveness of others squarely upon the foundation of God's forgiveness of the disciple (vv 33, 35).

**23** The διὰ τοῦτο, "on account of this," or "therefore," links the parable closely with the preceding verses. The parable, like those of chap. 13, explicitly concerns ἡ βασιλεία τῶν οὐρανῶν, "the kingdom of heaven" (for this phrase, see *Comment* on 3:2), and thus the discourse returns to a theme with which it began (cf. vv 1, 3–4). The kingdom, and thus the life of the members of the community of the kingdom, "is like" (ὡμοιώθη; see *Comment* on 13:24) the situation revealed in the story now to be told. These opening words, ὡμοιώθη ἡ βασιλεία τῶν οὐρανῶν ἀνθρώπῳ βασιλεῖ, lit. "the kingdom of heaven is like a man, a king," are found again verbatim in the introduction to the parable of the marriage feast in 22:2. The reference to a "king," a word that, being replaced by ὁ κύριος, "the lord," does not occur again in the parable and is not vital to it, was probably inserted to facilitate the analogy with God in v 35 (i.e., "my heavenly Father"). The repeated use of the title ὁ κύριος, "the lord," is consonant with this understanding (cf. vv 25, 27, 31, 32, 34). The expression συνᾶραι λόγον, "to settle accounts" (by ὁ κύριος, "the master," with his δοῦλοι, "servants"), is found again in the parable of the talents in 25:19 (this and the two occurrences of συναίρειν in our passage are the only NT occurrences of the word). Inevitably the idea of settling accounts has eschatological overtones (cf. v 35; 25:30), as does the use of ὁ κύριος, "the lord," although they are left implicit at this point.

**24–25** As the settling of the accounts with the servants began, the special case of a servant with an astronomically high debt was brought before the sovereign. The servant (possibly a "governor" or other high official) owed his master "ten thousand talents" (μυρίων ταλάντων). The use of μύριοι, "myriad" or "ten thousand," which itself could mean "beyond number," is a deliberate hyperbole pointing to a debt that was so high it was practically incalculable. Although the value of the talent, the largest monetary designation, varied, it was "always comparatively high" (BAGD, 803b). According to Josephus (*Ant.* 17.11.4 §§317–20) 600 talents in taxes were collected from all of Judea, Idumea, and Samaria in 4 B.C. The debt of the man, in short, ran into billions of dollars. It was clearly outside the ability of the servant to pay, and thus the sovereign ordered that he and his family members be sold, i.e., into slavery (for OT background: 2 Kgs 4:1; Neh 5:3–5; Amos 2:6; 8:6; Isa 50:1) and his property be liquidated. (Even with this, the payment could never have come close to meeting the amount of the debt; yet this was the customary and rightful punishment.) Some have worried about the unrealistic sum owed by the servant and have accordingly suggested that originally the parable referred to a smaller amount (De Boer: ten thousand denarii; T. W. Manson [*Sayings of Jesus*, 213]: ten talents, which Matthew then heightened [so too, Davies-Allison]). Parables, however, by their nature often employ hyperbole for effect, and there is no reason to require that every point correspond to historical reality.

**26** The slave fell before his sovereign and "prostrated himself" (προσεκύνει, which usually means or implies worship, should be understood here in a lesser sense of obeisance before a monarch; see other possible instances of this use of the word in 8:2; 9:18; 15:25; 20:20, though in these instances worship may be implied). He then appealed to his master to "be patient" (μακροθύμησον; the verb is used in Matthew only here and in v 29) and promises—unrealistically, given the size of the debt—καὶ πάντα ἀποδώσω σοι, "and I will pay you everything" (πάντα, "everything," is furthermore in an emphatic position). The servant's petition in this verse agrees exactly with that of his fellow servant in v 29, where, however, the πάντα ("everything") is lacking.

**27** The phrase ὁ κύριος τοῦ δούλου ἐκείνου, "the lord of that servant," occurs again in 24:50 in a context of eschatological judgment. Here ἐκείνου, "that," anticipates the ἐκεῖνος, "that," of the next verse, where it effectively distinguishes the first servant from the fellow servant. The sovereign was "moved with compassion" (σπλαγχνισθείς; in all the other instances of this word in Matthew, it refers to Jesus: 9:36; 14:14; 15:32; 20:34), "released [ἀπέλυσεν] him," and canceled the debt. The verb here for "cancel" (ἀφιέναι) is the verb used regularly to refer to "forgiveness" pertaining to sins (cf. 6:12 [where the word for sins, ὀφειλήματα, is literally "debts"], 14–15; 9:2, 5–6; 12:31–32). τὸ δάνειον, "the debt," technically a "loan," occurs in the NT only here. The metaphor of forgiven debt for the forgiveness of sins is found in Luke 7:40–43 (where the greater the debt, the greater the love of the debtor for the creditor). In response to the plea of the servant for clemency in the form of the time to repay the enormous debt, the sovereign responds with nearly unimaginable grace in the full dismissal of all indebtedness. It is not difficult to hear the echo of the gospel of the forgiveness of sins in this verse.

**28** The forgiven servant (ὁ δοῦλος ἐκεῖνος, "that servant"; cf. v 27), however, proceeds to pressure a fellow servant to pay a relatively small debt of a "hundred denarii" (ἑκατὸν δηνάρια), especially small in comparison with the debt from which he himself had been released (a denarius was the average daily wage of a workman [BAGD, 179a]; there were six thousand denarii to a single talent, and thus the servant had himself been forgiven a debt 600,000 times greater, if we ignore the obvious hyperbole). He even resorts to physical violence in his demand for payment (ἔπνιγεν, "he began to choke him"; cf. the wicked servant beating a fellow servant in 24:49).

**29** The plea of the fellow servant for mercy is deliberately patterned after the plea of the first servant. Thus this verse is nearly an exact repetition of v 26. The fellow servant is in the same hopeless plight his creditor himself had recently been in, despite the relatively small debt, and he accordingly makes the same plea (παρεκάλει, "pleaded," is more appropriate in reference to a fellow servant than the προσεκύνει, "prostrated," of v 26, used in reference to the master): "Be patient with me and I will repay you" (the deliberate omission of πάντα, "everything" [cf. v 26], is perhaps related to the smaller sum involved, or it may underline the extravagance of the unrealistic claim of the first servant in v 26).

**30** The response of the creditor in this instance stands in sharp contrast to the response of the creditor in v 27. The servant refused to listen to his fellow servant (οὐκ ἤθελεν, lit. "he would not"), a point that is reinforced by the participle ἀπελθών, "having gone away." He had his fellow servant thrown into prison, ἕως ἀποδῷ τὸ ὀφειλόμενον, "until he paid what was owed"(for casting into prison and payment of the last penny, cf. 5:25–26). This payment could occur only through money given by family and friends on his behalf.

**31** The other servants were distraught (ἐλυπήθησαν σφόδρα, "were greatly distressed"; the phrase occurs also in 17:23) over the fate of their fellow servant and went to their master to inform him of the matter (διασαφεῖν, "inform, explain," occurs in the NT only here and in 13:36). The reader is probably to assume that they knew of the cancellation of the first servant's huge debt.

**32–33** Having summoned the servant, and addressing him as δοῦλε πονηρέ, "evil servant"(the expression is used in Matthew also in 25:26, with the two words reversed), "his master" (ὁ κύριος αὐτοῦ) reminds him of πᾶσαν τὴν ὀφειλὴν ἐκείνην, "all that debt" (cf. v 24), which had been canceled when he had pled for mercy (v 26). But v 33 is the very heart of the parable: "Should not you also have shown mercy [ἐλεῆσαι] to your fellow servant, as I have shown you mercy [ἠλέησα]?" We encounter here a central principle in the teaching of Jesus, which is expressed in a variety of ways. God's forgiveness of a person must be reflected in that person's forgiveness of others (6:12, 14–15). It is the merciful (ἐλεήμονες) that are pronounced blessed and who will themselves obtain mercy (ἐλεηθήσονται, 5:7). As the disciple judges others, so will God judge the disciple; and by the measure in which the disciple gives to others, by the same measure will God give to the disciple (7:2). Disciples, in short, are to act toward others as God has acted toward them—in mercy (cf. Luke 6:36), in forgiveness, and in love (cf. especially 1 John 4:11; Jas 2:13, which closely resembles the present passage).

**34** The servant's master was filled with anger (ὀργισθείς) and revoked his earlier cancellation of the servant's great debt. He handed the man over to "the torturers" (τοῖς βασανισταῖς, i.e., the jailers in charge of the prison; the word occurs in the NT only here; for the cognate verb see 8:29) until the debt was fully paid (πᾶν τὸ ὀφειλόμενον, "everything owed"; cf. 5:26). Torturers, though disallowed by the Jews, were common in Roman prisons; in the case of unpaid debt, friends and relations would have accordingly been more urgent in raising money. Given the enormity of the debt, the imprisonment would have been permanent. This together with the reference to the torturers may hint (cf. v 35) at eschatological punishment. This verse is the close counterpart of v 30, which describes in similar language the servant's imprisonment of his fellow servant until his debt was paid. It demonstrates concretely the teaching that as one treats others so also will one be treated, a point made explicit in the application of the parable in the following verse.

**35** From the application in this verse, it becomes clear that in the parable the "king" (v 23) and "master" or "lord" (κύριος [vv 25, etc.]) stands for God and that the "servants" symbolize disciples. The enormity of the debt forgiven the first servant points to God's forgiveness of sin, in comparison with which disciples' sins against other disciples are to be regarded as petty. As the master of the slave revoked the earlier cancellation of his servant's debt, so too (οὕτως, "thus") God will revoke his forgiveness of a disciple's sins if that disciple, like the servant in the parable, refuses to forgive the sins of another disciple. For ὁ πατήρ μου ὁ οὐράνιος, "my heavenly Father," see *Comment* on 15:13. The reference to forgiving here indicates the real concern of the imagery of debts, canceled or not canceled, in the parable and at the same time recalls earlier material in the discourse and hence serves as an inclusio to the question of forgiveness in vv 21–22. ἀπὸ τῶν καρδιῶν ὑμῶν, "from your hearts," means in all sincerity, not just in word or appearance (cf. Rom 6:17; 1 Peter 3:4; cf. *Jub.* 35:13).

### Explanation

Conduct in the community of disciples called "the church" is to be patterned after the mercy and grace of God's free forgiveness of sins—which is an important basis for the very existence of the community. As God freely forgives those who have sinned against him, so are disciples to freely forgive those who sin against them. In both instances the repentance of the sinner is assumed. The failure to forgive one who is repentant casts doubt on the genuineness of a person's discipleship. The refusal to forgive others will be reflected upon the disciple in God's refusal to forgive him or her. Thus, in keeping with the thrust of the larger discourse, we see again the high importance of a person's conduct toward other members of the community. The community must treat its members as God treats them. Failure in this respect creates an intolerable inconsistency at the very point where the kingdom is to manifest itself: in the community of the redeemed, living in a fallen world.

# On the Way to Jerusalem: Increasing Confrontation (19:1–20:34)

## Beginning the Journey (19:1–2)

### Bibliography

**Slingerland, H. D.** "The Transjordanian Origin of St. Matthew's Gospel." *JSNT* 3 (1979) 18–28.
**Van Den Branden, A.** "Mt. 19,1–12 dans une perspective historique." *BO* 34 (1992) 65–82.

### Translation

[1] *And it came to pass that when Jesus finished* [a] *these words, he went away from Galilee, and he came to the districts of Judea across the Jordan.* [2] *And large crowds followed him, and he healed them there.* [b]

### Notes

[a] D it bo$^{ms}$ have ἐλάλησεν, "spoke."
[b] ἐκεῖ, "there," is lacking in P$^{25}$ sy$^s$.

### Form/Structure/Setting

A. With the end of the fourth teaching discourse, Matthew turns in the following two chapters (19–20) to the journey to Jerusalem. The new section begins with two verses of transition, which include reference to Jesus' journey and to the performance of healings on the way.

B. Although the opening words, which serve as the concluding formula to the preceding discourse, and μετῆρεν ἀπὸ τῆς Γαλιλαίας, "he went away from Galilee," are from Matthew himself, the material that follows is drawn from Mark (Mark 10:1; cf. Luke 9:51). In v 2 Matthew makes several changes: he substitutes ἠκολούθησαν, "followed" (suggesting discipleship), for Mark's συμπορεύονται, "were going with," and adds πολλοί, "many" or "large," after ὄχλοι "crowds"; he omits Mark's twofold πάλιν, "again," as well as Mark's ὡς εἰώθει, "as was his custom"; and finally he changes Mark's ἐδίδασκεν αὐτούς, "he was teaching them," to ἐθεράπευσεν αὐτοὺς ἐκεῖ, "he healed them there" (thus alternating a reference to teaching with one to healing and avoiding a reference to further teaching just after the long preceding discourse).

C. V 1a consists of the formula Matthew uses, with only slight variations, to close each of the five discourses (cf. 7:28; 11:1; 13:53; 26:1). Following this formula, these transition verses (1–2) consist of two clauses each (with all four verbs being in the aorist tense), giving each verse a balanced structure.

## Comment

**1** On the formula used to conclude the discourse, see *Introduction,* in Hagner, *Matthew 1–13,* li. In one other instance (13:53–54), the formula is coupled, as here, with a geographical notice employing μετῆρεν, "he went away," and a form of the verb ἔρχεσθαι in a reference to Jesus "coming" or "going" into a different region. In the present instance Jesus leaves Galilee, thus concluding the major component of his teaching and healing ministry, which was centered there, and moves on now in the direction of Jerusalem (cf. the announcements in 16:21; 20:17; cf. Luke 9:51). Considerable difficulty has been caused by the reference to τὰ ὅρια τῆς Ἰουδαίας πέραν τοῦ Ἰορδάνου, "the districts of Judea beyond the Jordan." This refers not to the *author's* Transjordanian location (*pace* Slingerland) but probably indicates that Jesus, like most Galilean pilgrims on their way to Jerusalem, crossed the Jordan River on his way south, thus avoiding Samaria (cf. the reference to the departure from Jericho in 20:29, suggesting a crossing of the river there on the way to Jerusalem). He thus entered an area east of the Jordan that, perhaps because of the number of Jews residing there, was regarded as belonging to Judea (see Strabo, *Geo.* 16.2.21; Tacitus, *Hist.* 5.6; cf. Mark 10:1). Alternatively, allowing for a gap in the narrative, the crossing of the Jordan from the Transjordan into Judea near Jericho could be in view (thus Blomberg).

**2** This verse, referring to the crowds that seemed always to follow Jesus and his ministry of healing among them, is typical of transitional passages. Exactly the same generalizing elements are found at earlier transitional points in 12:15 (virtually identical with the present verse) and 15:29–30. Matthew does not refer here to any specific deeds of healing, but the general reference nevertheless continues the alternating pattern of words and deeds.

### Explanation

Although Jesus' Galilean ministry is formally at an end and Jesus now pursues another—indeed, his main—goal, that of the cross, he does not turn away the crowds or refuse to heal the sick. He cannot be other than he is: the Messiah of Israel, who brings healing to his people (see too 20:29–34).

# The Question of Divorce   (19:3–12)

### Bibliography

**Allison, D. C.** "Divorce, Celibacy and Joseph (Matthew 1.18–25 and 19.1–12)." *JSNT* 49 (1993) 3–10. **Baltensweiler, H.** "Matthäusevangelium (Kap. 19, 1–12; 5, 27–32)." In *Die Ehe im Neuen Testament.* Zürich: Zwingli, 1967. 82–119. **Bauer, J. B.** "Ehescheidung wegen Ehebruch?" *BLit* 24 (1956–57) 118–21. ———. "Die matthäische Ehescheidungsklausel." *BLit* 38 (1964–65) 101–6. **Blinzler, J.** "Εἰσὶν εὐνοῦχοι." *ZNW* 48 (1957) 254–70. **Blomberg, C. L.** "Marriage, Divorce, Remarriage, and Celibacy: An Exegesis of Matthew 19:3–12."

*Trinity Journal* 11 (1990) 161–96. **Bockmuehl, M.** "Matthew 5.32; 19.9 in Light of Pre-Rabbinic Halakhah." *NTS* 35 (1989) 291–95. **Catchpole, D. R.** "The Synoptic Divorce Material as a Traditio-Historical Problem." *BJRL* 57 (1975) 92–127. **Côté, P.-R.** "Les eunuques pour le royaume (Mt 19,12)." *Église et Théologie* 17 (1986) 321–34. **Daniel, C.** "Esséniens et eunuques (Matthieu 19, 10–12)." *RevQ* 6 (1968) 353–90. **Derrett, J. D. M.** "The Teaching of Jesus on Marriage and Divorce." In *Law in the New Testament*. London: Longman and Todd, 1970. 363–88. **Descamps, A.-L.** "Les textes évangéliques sur le mariage." *RTL* 9 (1978) 259–86; 11 (1980) 5–50. **Dinter, P. E.** "Disabled for the Kingdom: Celibacy, Scripture and Tradition." *Commonweal* [New York] 117 (1990) 571–77. **Dupont, J.** *Mariage et divorce dans l'Évangile: Matthew 19, 3–12 et parallèles.* Bruges: Addaye de Saint-André & Desclée de Brouwer, 1959. **Fahy, T.** "St. Matthew 19:9—Divorce or Separation?" *ITQ* 24 (1957) 173–74. **Fitzmyer, J. A.** "The Matthean Divorce Texts and Some New Palestinian Evidence." *TS* 37 (1976) 197–226. **Fleming, T. W.** "Christ and Divorce." *TS* 24 (1963) 106–20. **Harrington, W.** "Jesus' Attitude towards Divorce." *ITQ* 37 (1970) 199–209. **Heth, W. A.** "The Meaning of Divorce in Matthew 19:3–9." *Churchman* 98 (1984) 136–52. ————. "Unmarried 'for the Sake of the Kingdom' (Matthew 19:12) in the Early Church." *GTJ* 8 (1987) 55–88. ———— and **Wenham, G. J.** *Jesus and Divorce.* Nashville: Nelson, 1985. **Holmes, M. W.** "The Text of the Matthean Divorce Passages: A Comment on the Appeal to Harmonization in Textual Decisions." *JBL* 109 (1990) 651–64. **Isaksson, A.** *Marriage and Ministry in the New Temple: A Study with Special Reference to Mt. 19.12–13 and 1 Cor. 11.3–16.* Lund: Gleerup/Copenhagen: Munksgaard, 1965. **Kaye, B.** "'One Flesh' and Marriage." *Colloquium* 22 (1990) 46–57. **Keener, C. S.** *. . . And Marries Another: Divorce and Remarriage in the Teaching of the New Testament.* Peabody, MA: Hendrickson, 1991. **Kilgallen, J. J.** "To What Are the Matthean Exception-Texts (5,32 and 19,9) an Exception?" *Bib* 61 (1980) 102–5. **Kodel, J.** "The Celibacy Logion in Matthew 19:12." *BTB* 8 (1978) 19–23. **LaMarche, P.** "L'indissolubilité selon Matthieu 19,9." *CHR* 30 (1983) 475–82. **Leeming, B., and Dyson, R. A.** "Except It Be for Fornication?" *SCR* 8 (1956) 75–82. **Lövestam, E.** "Die funktionale Bedeutung der synoptischen Jesusworte über Ehescheidung und Wiederheirat." In *Theologie aus dem Norden,* ed. A. Fuchs. SNTU A2. Freistadt: F. Plöchl, 1977. 409–30. **Mahoney, A.** "A New Look at the Divorce Clauses in Mt 5.32 and 19.9." *CBQ* 30 (1968) 29–38. **Moingt, J.** "Le divorce (pour motif d'impudieité) (Mt 5.32, 19.9)." *RSR* 56 (1968) 337–84. **Molldrem, M. J.** "A Hermeneutic of Pastoral Care and the Law/Gospel Paradigm Applied to the Divorce Texts of Scripture." *Int* 45 (1991) 43–54. **Moloney, F. J.** "Matthew 19,3–12 and Celibacy: A Redactional and Form Critical Study." *JSNT* 2 (1979) 42–60. **Osburn, C. D.** "The Present Indicative of Matthew 19:9." *ResQ* 24 (1981) 193–203. **Porter, S. E., and Buchanan, P.** "On the Logical Structure of Matt 19:9." *JETS* 34 (1991) 335–39. **Quesnell, Q.** "Made Themselves Eunuchs of the Kingdom of Heaven (Mt 19,12)." *CBQ* 30 (1968) 335–58. **Sand, A.** *Reich Gottes und Eheverzicht im Evangelium nach Matthäus.* SBS 109. Stuttgart: Katholisches Bibelwerk, 1983. ————. "Die Unzuchtsklausel in Mt 5,31.32 und 19,3–9." *MTZ* 20 (1969) 118–29. **Schneider, G.** "Jesu Wort über die Ehescheidung in der Überlieferung des Neuen Testaments." *TTZ* 80 (1971) 65–87. **Stein, R. H.** "Is It Lawful for a Man to Divorce His Wife?" *JETS* 22 (1979) 115–22. **Stenger, W.** "Zur Rekonstruktion eines Jesusworts anhand der synoptischen Ehescheidungslogien (Mt 5,32; Lk 19,11; Mk 10,11f)." *Kairos* 26 (1984) 194–205. **Tannehill, R. C.** "Matthew 19:12: Eunuchs for the Kingdom." In *The Sword of His Mouth.* Philadelphia: Fortress, 1975. 134–40. **Trautman, D. W.** *The Eunuch Logion of Matthew 19,12: Historical and Exegetical Dimensions as Related to Celibacy.* Rome: Catholic Book Agency, 1966. **Vawter, B.** "The Divorce Clauses in Mt. 5,32 and 19,9." *CBQ* 16 (1954) 155–67. ————. "Divorce and the New Testament." *CBQ* 39 (1977) 528–42. **Wenham, G. J.** "Matthew and Divorce: An Old Crux Revisited." *JSNT* 22 (1984) 95–107. ————. "The Restoration of Marriage Reconsidered." *JJS* 30 (1979) 36–40. ————. "The Syntax of Matthew 19.9." *JSNT* 28 (1986) 17–23. **Wiebe, P. H.** "Jesus' Divorce Exception." *JETS* 32 (1989) 327–33. **Witherington, B.** "Matthew 5.32 and 19.9—Exceptional Situation?" *NTS* 31 (1985) 571–76. **Yamauchi, E. M.** "Cultural Aspects of Marriage in the Ancient World." *BSac* 135 (1978) 241–52.

See also *Bibliography* for 5:31–32.

## *Translation*

*3And Pharisees[a] came to him, testing him and saying:[b] "Is it lawful for a man[c] to divorce his wife for any reason whatever?" 4He answered and said:[d] "Have you not read that the One who created[e] made them from the beginning male and female? 5And he said: 'Because of this a man will leave his father and mother and will be joined[f] to his wife, and the two will become one flesh.'[g] 6So that no longer are they two, but they are one flesh. What therefore God has yoked together,[h] let no one separate." 7They said to him: "Why therefore did Moses command a husband[i] to give a certificate of divorce and thus to divorce his wife?"[j] 8He[k] said to them, "Moses permitted you to divorce your wives because of your hard-heartedness, but it was not so from the beginning. 9I tell you that[l] whoever divorces his wife except for sexual immorality and marries another commits adultery."[m,n]*

*10[His][o] disciples said to him:[p] "If the relationship between a man and his wife is like this, it is better not to marry." 11And he said to them: "Not everyone accepts [this][q] matter; only those to whom it has been granted. 12For there are eunuchs who have been born thus from their mother's womb, and there are eunuchs who have been made eunuchs by others, and there are eunuchs who have made themselves eunuchs for the sake of the kingdom of heaven. Let the one who is able to accept this accept it."*

## *Notes*

[a] Many MSS (א D TR sa[mss]) have the definite article *οἱ*, "the," before Pharisees. But the article is missing in MSS of good quality and diversity (P[25] B C L W Δ Θ $f^{1,13}$ sa[ms] mae bo), and it would be natural for copyists to insert the definite article. Cf. *TCGNT*, 47.

[b] D W Δ sy[h] mae add *αὐτῷ*, "to him."

[c] A few important MSS (א* B L Γ) omit *ἀνθρώπῳ*, "for a man"; a few (e.g., 1424[c]) substitute *ἀνδρί*, "for a man," through the influence of Mark 10:2. The *UBSGNT* committee judges it more probable that *ἀνθρώπῳ* is original, rather than being added later, and that the Alexandrian witnesses deleted the word in the interest of conciseness of literary style. *TCGNT*, 47.

[d] C W Θ $f^{1,13}$ TR lat sy mae all add *αὐτοῖς*, "to them."

[e] *κτίσας*, "created" (B Θ $f^1$ co). Many MSS (א C D [L] W Z $f^{13}$ TR lat sy) have *ποιήσας*, "made," probably to harmonize the text with the LXX of Gen 1:27 (quoted immediately following). *TCGNT*, 47.

[f] *κολληθήσεται* (so B D W Θ $f^{13}$). Other MSS (א C K L Z Γ Δ $f^1$) read *προσκολληθήσεται* in conformity with the LXX text of Gen 2:24.

[g] Possibly the question mark is to be moved from the end of v 5 and placed here, so that both vv 4 and 5 are understood as the question.

[h] D it add *εἰς ἕν*, "into one."

[i] "A husband" added in translation.

[j] *αὐτήν*, "her." The *UBSGNT* committee puts the pronoun in brackets because of the divided textual evidence: for inclusion, B C W $f^{13}$ TR sy[p,h]; for omission, א D L Z Θ $f^1$ lat. The word can have been added to complete the sense or deleted through the influence of Mark 10:4. *TCGNT*, 47. "His wife" is added to the translation to complete the sense.

[k] A few MSS (א Φ mae) add *ὁ Ἰησοῦς*, "Jesus."

[l] *ὅτι*, "that," is omitted by B D Z it, probably through the influence of Mark 10:11.

[m] Several different readings exist for the ending of the verse. In place of the final *μοιχᾶται*, "commits adultery," C* N (the latter also omits *καὶ γαμήσῃ ἄλλην*, "and marries another") B $f^1$ bo have *ποιεῖ αὐτὴν μοιχευθῆναι*, "makes her commit adultery," almost certainly from 5:32. For *μὴ ἐπὶ πορνείᾳ*, "except for sexual immorality," a number of MSS (B D $f^{1,13}$ it [sy[c]] sa mae bo) read *παρεκτὸς λόγου πορνείας*, "except on the ground of sexual immorality," again by assimilation to the text of 5:32. In favor of the adopted reading are א C[3] L (W) Z Θ TR vg sy[s,p,h]. *TCGNT*, 47–48.

[n] Many MSS (B C* W Θ $f^{1,13}$ TR lat sy[p,h] bo) add to the verse *καὶ ὁ ἀπολελυμένην* [*γαμῶν γαμήσας*, B TR] *μοιχᾶται*, "and the one who marries a divorced woman commits adultery," again almost certainly an assimilation to 5:32. *TCGNT*, 48.

ᵒ P⁷¹ᵛⁱᵈ ℵ B Θ saᵐˢ mae omit αὐτοῦ, "his," perhaps because of the preceding αὐτῷ, "to him." For its inclusion are P²⁵ C D L W Z f¹,¹³ TR lat sy saᵐˢˢ bo. The committee reflects the difficulty by placing the word in brackets. *TCGNT*, 48.

ᵖ P²⁵ ℵ* omit αὐτῷ, "to him."

�q Some MSS (B f¹ boᵐˢ) omit τοῦτον, "this." In favor of its inclusion are ℵ C D L W Z f¹³ TR lat sy co. The ambiguity of the pronoun may have caused its deletion. The committee retains the word, but in brackets. *TCGNT*, 48–49.

### Form/Structure/Setting

A. This pericope, with its reference to the Pharisees coming to "test" Jesus, sustains the tension, encountered earlier, between Jesus and the religious authorities (cf. 12:14; 15:12), and anticipates the opposition Jesus will encounter in Jerusalem. The latter point becomes even more significant in light of the unacceptable answer of Jesus, which seems yet again to challenge the authority of Moses. Jesus, however, appeals to Moses in making his response (vv 4–5) and speaks to the question of divorce in terms of the ethics of the kingdom of God (cf. chaps. 5–7).

B. Except for vv 10–12, which are unique to Matthew, Matthew here continues to depend on Mark (Mark 10:2–12). The basic alteration made by Matthew is that of moving forward the quotation of the OT (vv 4–5; cf. Mark 10:6–7) to the beginning of Jesus' response to the Pharisees' question (cf. the similar transposition of an OT quotation to an earlier position in 15:4). Matthew avoids the question of Jesus in Mark, "What did Moses command you?" (Mark 10:3); instead Jesus quotes the OT material asking οὐκ ἀνέγνωτε, "Have you not read?" (v 4). The response of the Pharisees to Jesus' question in Mark 10:4 becomes in turn a question of the Pharisees concerning why Moses commanded what he did (v 7; the contrast between "permit" [Mark's ἐπέτρεψεν, Mark 10:4] and the intensifying "command" [Matthew's ἐνετείλετο] is noteworthy). Mark's ἀπὸ δὲ ἀρχῆς, "from the beginning," which occurs at the beginning of Mark 10:6 (in connection with the Genesis quotation), becomes ἀπ' ἀρχῆς δὲ οὐ γέγονεν οὕτως, "from the beginning it was not so" (v 8b). Matthew omits Mark 10:10, which refers to the disciples asking Jesus privately about the teaching, with the result that v 9 seems to be addressed to the Pharisees (λέγω δὲ ὑμῖν, "But I say to you"). In the logion that follows (v 9), Matthew adds the exception clause, μὴ ἐπὶ πορνεία, "except for sexual immorality" (see *Comment*; cf. 5:32), and omits Mark's last two words ἐπ' αὐτήν, "against her" (Mark 10:11), as well as Mark's final sentence, "and if she divorces her husband and marries another man, she commits adultery" (Mark 10:12), an assertion that made sense to Mark's gentile readers but not in Matthew's Jewish ethos where divorce was exclusively the husband's option. Finally to be noted is Matthew's addition in v 3 (cf. Mark 10:2) of the words κατὰ πᾶσαν αἰτίαν, "for any cause," words that reflect the Pharisaic debate on the subject (see *Comment*). Matthew is thus clearly dependent on Mark, with verbatim agreement at many points, but at the same time the evangelist in characteristic fashion has reshaped the passage with his own concerns and readers in view.

A close parallel to the present passage is found in the Sermon on the Mount, 5:31–32, where Jesus also disallows divorce, "except on the grounds of sexual immorality" (παρεκτὸς λόγου πορνείας). The only other significant difference between 5:32 and v 9 is the former's ποιεῖ αὐτὴν μοιχευθῆναι, "he makes her commit adultery," which is lacking in the present pericope. Quite probably the two verses represent variant versions of one original logion. Paul may well allude to this material in its oral form in 1 Cor 6:16; 7:10–12 (cf. especially "not I, but the Lord"). The Matthean pericope, or possibly the tradition underlying it, is cited or alluded to specifically in Justin, *Apol.* 1.15.4 (cf. vv 10–12) and in Ptolemaeus, *Epist. ad Floram* 2.4 (as found in Epiphanius, *Pan. haer.* 33.4.4).

C. The character of the pericope as a controversy or argumentative dialogue is obvious not only from the explicit reference to "testing" in v 3 but also from the structure and content of the pericope. The Pharisees initiate the dialogue with their question (v 3), to which Jesus responds (vv 4–6); the Pharisees then pose a counterquestion (v 7), which Jesus also answers (vv 8–9). The final section consists of a comment from the disciples (v 10) and a response from Jesus (vv 11–12). The following outline may be suggested: (1) the test question (v 3); (2) the answer, subdivided into (a) the teaching of Moses in Genesis (vv 4–6a) and (b) the application (v 6b); (3) the Pharisees' objection, based on Moses' teaching (v 7); (4) Jesus' explanation (v 8); (5) conclusion (v 9); (6) the disciples' comment (v 10); and (7) Jesus' response, further divided into (a) the hardness of the saying (v 11), (b) the saying concerning eunuchs for the kingdom of God (v 12a–c), and (c) the exhortation to hear (v 12d). As usual, there is little to note concerning structural parallelism in that portion of the passage characterized mainly by dialogue (i.e., vv 3–10). Vv 10–12, on the other hand, which are apparently added from Matthew's special source and were originally independent from the preceding verses, reveal a remarkably symmetrical structure in the threefold εἰσὶν εὐνοῦχοι, "there are eunuchs," each of which is modified by an οἵτινες, "who," clause with a main verb modified by a prepositional phrase. On either side of this threefold structure stands χωρεῖν, "receive," the final exhortation serving thus as an inclusio with v 11. The form of the logia in these verses almost certainly results from their transmission in oral tradition.

## Comment

**3** The Pharisees come to test Jesus (they do so elsewhere in 16:1; 22:18, 35; in each case πειράζειν, "test," is used as here) on a question they had frequently debated among themselves. The issue was not divorce itself, the right to which they took for granted, but rather the justifiable grounds for divorce. Would Jesus side with the school of Shammai, which allowed divorce only on the grounds of sexual immorality, or would he side with the school of Hillel, which sanctioned divorce on the most trivial grounds? (Cf. *m. Giṭ.* 9:10; *b. Giṭ.* 90a; Jos., *Ant.* 4.8.23 §§244–59, *Vita* 76; Philo, *Spec. Leg.* 5.) Matthew's added words κατὰ πᾶσαν αἰτίαν, "for any cause," however, can be taken in two ways, i.e., "for every reason whatever" (i.e., Hillel's position) or "for any reason (at all)." If the grammar is ambiguous, the context favors the former alternative. Underlying the question of the lawful grounds for divorce (ἔξεστιν, "is it lawful," occurs in the same sense in 12:2, 10, 12, concerning the sabbath; cf. 14:4; 22:17) was the question of the exegesis of the word "indecency" in Deut 24:1 (Heb. עֶרְוַת דָּבָר, ʿerwat dābār, lit. "nakedness of a thing," i.e., "a matter of uncleanness"; LXX: ἄσχημον πρᾶγμα, lit. "unseemly thing [or deed]"), which the Shammaites interpreted narrowly and the Hillelites broadly. The subject of divorce has already been discussed early in Matthew in the Sermon on the Mount (see *Comment* on 5:31–32; cf. v 9 below).

**4–5**   In Matthew Jesus begins his answer by quoting several lines from Genesis, which provide the basis of the viewpoint he will argue in vv 6, 9. The Pharisees should remember how "the creator" (ὁ κτίσας; lit. "the one having created"; only here in Matthew) designed things ἀπ᾽ ἀρχῆς, "from the beginning." The words of the first citation, ἄρσεν καὶ θῆλυ ἐποίησεν αὐτούς, "male and female he made them," are found verbatim in Gen 1:27; 5:2 (this material is cited in CD 4:21 in an argument against polygamy). In the brief introductory formula at the beginning of v 5, καὶ εἶπεν, "and he said," the subject of the verb is probably to be understood not as Jesus (as at the beginning of v 4) but as the Creator, who is regarded as speaking through Moses. The citation in v 5 agrees almost exactly with the LXX (the Hebrew text differs slightly) of Gen 2:24 (a passage cited again in the NT in Eph 5:31). The slight differences are the omission of αὐτοῦ, "his," after πατέρα, "father," and μητέρα, "mother" (it is clearly implied), the dropping of the prepositional prefix προσ- in the verb κολληθήσεται, "will be joined to," and finally the substitution of τῇ γυναικί for the equivalent πρὸς τὴν γυναῖκα, "to his wife." The Genesis account describes the will of God (cf. Mal 2:16), indeed, the original will of God as established in the account of creation itself. When a man and a woman become husband and wife, they become united in one flesh.

**6**   ὥστε, "so that," introduces a result clause that emphasizes the final point of the preceding citation as well as providing the basis for the conclusion drawn in the second half of the verse. According to God's plan, the union of husband and wife means that the two have become σὰρξ μία, "one flesh." God has "yoked [them] together" (συνέζευξεν; in the NT only here and in the parallel in Mark 10:9) in a mysterious union, described as "one flesh" (Paul seems to interpret this as sexual intercourse in 1 Cor 6:16). The unity, as instituted by God himself in the creation of humankind, is *not* to be broken apart by human beings (μὴ χωριζέτω, "let one not divide," the only occurrence of the word in Matthew; cf. 1 Cor 7:10–11). Divorce, therefore, is not in accord with God's design and is to be prohibited since it breaks what is a unique and holy union.

**7**   With Jesus' prohibition of divorce, the Pharisees must have felt they had Jesus trapped since after all it was clear that Moses had in fact allowed and regulated divorce, according to Deut 24:1–4. The authority of Moses for the Pharisees (cf. 23:2) is evident in the use of ἐνετείλατο, "commanded." The βιβλίον ἀποστασίου, "certificate of divorce" (cf. Deut 24:1–3; cf. Jer 3:8), was a legal document that recorded the separation and the reason for the separation, which enabled the divorced woman to enter into a new marriage. (The only stipulation in Deut 24:4 is that the divorced woman was not allowed again to become the wife of her former husband.)

**8**   Jesus responds by admitting that Moses "permitted" (ἐπέτρεψεν, elsewhere in Matthew only in 8:21; contrast ἐνετείλατο, "commanded," in the preceding verse) divorce but at the same time declaring that, rather than the ideal will of God, this was a concession to "your [i.e., the people's] hard-heartedness" (σκληροκαρδίαν ὑμῶν; the only occurrence of the word in Matthew). The Mosaic legislation in Deut 24:1–4 was thus not normative but only secondary and temporary, an allowance dependent on the sinfulness of the people. In that context it served as a control against abuse and excess (for a similar kind of argument, cf. Gal 3:15–19). "From the beginning" (ἀπ᾽ ἀρχῆς, a deliberate recalling of the phrase in v 4), argues Jesus, this was not the situation, as the cited OT material made clear. Jesus thus pits Moses against Moses. The implication is that the new era of the present kingdom of God involves a return to the idealism of the pre-fall Genesis narrative. The call of the kingdom is a call to the ethics of the perfect will of God (cf. the Sermon on the Mount), one that makes no provision for, or concession to, the weakness of the flesh.

**9** For this verse, see also the *Comment* on 5:32, which is almost its exact equivalent. λέγω ὑμῖν, "I say to you," is emphatic (see *Comment* on 5:20). The prohibition of divorce is here again qualified by Matthew's added exception clause, which makes allowance for his Jewish-Christian readers, μὴ ἐπὶ πορνείᾳ, "except for sexual immorality" (this is the equivalent of the phrase in 5:32: παρεκτὸς λόγου πορνείας, "except on the ground of sexual immorality"; cf. Dupont, 102–6).

> It is unlikely that the phrase is to be understood as *not* involving an exception, but in the sense of "not even in the case of," thereby making the prohibition absolute (Vawter, who once held this view, accepted later [1977] that the phrases are exceptive). If this argument were correct, we should expect μηδέ, "not even," rather than the simple μή. The evangelist adds the exception clauses for the sake of the moral sensitivities of his Jewish-Christian readers. Rabbinic Judaism required a husband to divorce an unfaithful wife (cf. *m. Soṭa* 5:1; *m. Yebam.* 2:8; at Qumran, 1QapGen 20:15; see Bockmuehl). For discussion of the possibility that πορνεία means illicit marriage, i.e., within the forbidden degrees of relationship (thus LaMarche; Witherington), see *Comment* on 5:32.

Apart from the allowed exception, any one who divorces his wife and marries another μοιχᾶται, "commits adultery" (cf. Luke 16:18; Matt 5:32, the only other place in the Gospel where this verb occurs, is not exactly parallel since it refers to marrying a divorced woman). Thus divorce is not allowed, except in special cases, and remarriage after divorce is similarly ruled out (see Dupont, Heth, Quesnell, Wenham [*JSNT* 28 (1986) 17–23]). For a contrasting view, see Carson and Wiebe, who take the exception clause as governing the protasis in its entirety, thereby allowing remarriage in the case of divorce for reasons of sexual infidelity. Exegetically, Wenham (see too Heth and Wenham) is more convincing on this passage. The Matthean addition of the exception clause (cf. the absolute statements of Mark 10:11 and Luke 16:18) has the effect of making Jesus side with the Shammaites, i.e., that divorce was allowable in cases of sexual misconduct. The addition not only softens the ethics of the kingdom, but it also stands in tension with the absolutism of v 6, weakens the argument of vv 7–8, and makes the disciples' comment in v 10 and Jesus' statements in v 11–12 less appropriate than they would be in the case of an absolute prohibition of divorce.

**10** The disciples are not slow to catch the radical character of Jesus' teaching, which to judge from their comment seemed more narrow than they had themselves viewed the subject. This comment was probably made in private (cf. Mark 10:10) after the Pharisees had departed (a common pattern of conduct among rabbinic disciples in controversy passages). The strict view of Jesus concerning the permanence of the "relationship" (αἰτία; for this definition see BAGD, 26b) between husband and wife led to the conclusion that οὐ συμφέρει γαμῆσαι, lit. "it is not advantageous to marry." The risks of becoming inseparably linked with an unsatisfactory wife, in whatever way, were too great in their estimate.

**11** Jesus does not challenge the disciples' assessment of the difficulty of abiding by his high standards, i.e., the standards of the kingdom. He admits that the alternative of non-marriage is one that not all will be able to "accept" (χωροῦσιν; for χωρεῖν in this sense, see BAGD, 890a.) "This word" refers most probably to the immediately preceding statement, "It is better not to marry" (cf. v 12 [esp. the final sentence] concerning the renunciation of marriage), which in turn, however, is prompted by the teaching of v 9 (see Quesnell). If by the world's standards and the standards even of the Pharisees, the prohibition of divorce is unacceptable, so perhaps more so is the alternative of no marriage. Those "to whom it has been granted" (οἷς δέδοται; cf. 13:11) refers to those disciples who are willing and able to make this sacrifice (cf. the same point in 1 Cor 7:7, 17).

**12** Three groups of "eunuchs" (εὐνοῦχοι; the word occurs only here and in Acts 8 in the NT) are mentioned here, two literal and one metaphorical. Among literal eunuchs are those born thus (the impotent) and those made thus by others (those castrated for certain high positions in a royal court; cf. the Ethiopian eunuch of Acts 8:27). Such literal eunuchs were not allowed in the assembly of the people according to Deut 23:1 (cf. *m. Yebam.* 8:4–6 and 6:6). A third group of "eunuchs" are those who figuratively are said to have "made themselves eunuchs" (εὐνούχισαν ἑαυτούς; the verb occurs only in this verse in the NT) "for the sake of the kingdom of heaven" (διὰ τὴν βασιλείαν τῶν οὐρανῶν; for this expression see *Comment* on 3:21). The latter phrase is to be understood in the sense of those who have renounced marriage (such as John the Baptist and Jesus himself) to give priority to the work of the kingdom (cf. 1 Cor 7:32–34) and not to the requirement of sexual continence on the part of those who have been divorced (as claimed by Dupont, Moloney; cf. Gundry) or who have renounced their wives (thus Côté). The kingdom thus can take priority over the interpretation of Gen 1:28 as the obligation to marry and to have children. If Jesus, like John the Baptist and Paul (cf. 1 Cor 7:29, 31), expected the imminent end of the age, the idea of celibacy would take on a less objectionable aspect. ὁ δυνάμενος χωρεῖν, "the one who is able to accept (it)," is the one to whom God grants (v 11) the ability to accept non-marriage. Two alternatives thus lie open to the disciples of Jesus: marriage without the option of divorce (cf. v 6, stated absolutely; v 9, with the added exception clause; cf. 1 Cor 7:39) or celibacy for the cause of the kingdom (on this, see Blinzler, Kodel, Moloney). For celibacy at Qumran, see 1QSa 1.25; 2.11.

### Explanation

Again in this pericope we encounter the absoluteness of the kingdom of God and its ethics. In his answer to the question about divorce, Jesus appeals to the creation narrative of Genesis. The kingdom of God brought by Jesus is ultimately to involve the restoration of the perfection of the pre-fall creation, and the ethics of the kingdom as taught by Jesus reflect this fact. As God intended no divorce for the garden of Eden, so divorce is not to be allowed in the new era of the kingdom of God. The call of some to celibacy also reflects the priority of the kingdom in the present time frame. But if provision was made through Moses for the "hard-heartedness" of Israel by the allowing and regulating of divorce, it may well be asked, ought not some similar provision be made for those who still exist "between the times," i.e., who participate in the kingdom of God but also remain at the same time fallen creatures in a fallen world that remains short of the eschaton? Although realistically a positive answer must be given to this question (as indeed the introduction of the exception clause already indicates), it is not possible for the ethics of the kingdom to be articulated in anything less than ideal terms. The righteousness of the kingdom is ever before the disciples as a call and a challenge, yet in the present interim era it must not be thought surprising that the disciples will continue to fall short of the goal—a goal whose full realization awaits the parousia and eschaton. Only an unjustifiable biblicism will force the idealism of NT ethics in a cruel and heartless manner by an adamant insistence upon the teaching of this passage as merely a collection of detailed laws (see Stein for a sensible approach). The goal of no divorce remains an ideal we continue to strive toward.

# Jesus and the Little Children   (19:13–15)

## Bibliography

**Brown, R.** "Jesus and the Child as a Model of Spirituality." *IBS* 4 (1982) 178–92. **Clavier, H.** "Jésus et l'enfant." *ETR* 8 (1933) 243–55. **Crossan, J. D.** "Kingdom and Children: A Study in the Aphoristic Tradition." *Semeia* 29 (1983) 75–95. **Derrett, J. D. M.** "Why Jesus Blessed the Children (Mk. 10:13–16)." *NovT* 25 (1983) 1–18. **Légasse, S.** "Jésus accueille les enfants: Marc x, 13–16 et parallèles." In *Jésus et l'enfant.* Paris: J. Gabalda, 1969. 36–43. **Patte, D.** "Jesus' Pronouncement about Entering the Kingdom like a Child: A Structural Exegesis." *Semeia* 29 (1983) 3–42. **Ringshausen, G.** "Die Kinder der Weisheit: Zur Auslegung von Mk 10:13–16 par." *ZNW* 77 (1986) 34–63. **Robbins, V. K.** "Pronouncement Stories and Jesus' Blessing of the Children: A Rhetorical Approach." *Semeia* 29 (1983) 43–74.

## Translation

[13]*Then little children were brought to him in order that he might lay his hands on them and pray. But the disciples rebuked them.* [14]*But Jesus said:*[a] *"Let the little children come to me and do not forbid them, for of such is the kingdom of heaven."* [15]*And having laid his hands on them, he went away from there.*

## Notes

[a] Some MSS (א C D L W *f*[13] lat sy sa[ms] mae bo) add αὐτοῖς, "to them." Supporting the text as is are B Θ *f*[1] TR it sa[mss].

## Form/Structure/Setting

A. That Jesus does not regard marriage unfavorably in the preceding pericope is made clear in the present passage by his affirming attitude toward children. Here we have what might be considered an extension of the discussion of familial matters. Although the passage reminds the reader of the importance of childlikeness for those who belong to the kingdom (cf. v 14b), this pericope regards literal children.

B. Matthew here continues to depend on Mark (Mark 10:13–16; cf. Luke 18:15–17). Matthew's only major departure from Mark is in the omission of Mark 10:15, "Truly I say to you, whoever does not receive the kingdom of God as a child shall in no wise enter it." The equivalent to this logion, however, has already been given in 18:3. Matthew makes the following significant changes of Mark: After an inserted introductory τότε, "then" (v 13), typical of Matthew, Mark's αὐτῶν ἅψηται, "he might touch them" (Mark 10:13), is altered to τὰς χεῖρας ἐπιθῇ αὐτοῖς καὶ προσεύξηται, "he might lay his hands upon them and pray" (v 13; cf. Mark 10:16). As he does frequently, Matthew omits the emotional language of Mark in ἠγανάκτησεν, "he was indignant" (Mark 10:14), together with the unnecessary participle ἰδών, "seeing" (Mark 10:14). He further omits Mark's ἐναγκαλισάμενος αὐτὰ κατευλόγει, "taking them up in his arms, he blessed them" (Mark 10:16), probably to abbreviate (blessing is assumed in the laying on of hands) or because of a varying practice in the laying on of hands. Finally Matthew adds ἐπορεύθη ἐκεῖθεν, "he departed from them" (cf. the beginning of the next pericope, Mark 10:17). Matthew has also characteristically changed Mark's ἡ βασιλεία τοῦ θεοῦ, "the kingdom of God," to ἡ βασιλεία τῶν οὐρανῶν, "the kingdom of heaven" (v 14; cf. Mark 10:14). Further changes involve minor syntactical differences. Matthew follows Mark closely, but again with a degree of freedom.

C. The focus of this short pericope is on the teaching logion of v 14, for which the remainder provides the context and an illustration. The simple structure of the passage may be outlined in the following manner: (1) the presentation of little children for blessing (v 13a); (2) the disciples' objection (v 13b); (3) Jesus' affirmation of the children, consisting of (a) the invitation (v 14a) and (b) the grounds for the invitation (v 14b); and (4) the blessing and Jesus' departure (v 15). Only two structural features of the passage need be noted: the positive (ἄφετε, "permit") and negative (μὴ κωλύετε, "do not forbid") form of the invitation, providing emphasis (v 14a), and the correspondence between the action of Jesus in the laying on of hands (v 15) and the opening request (v 13). The passage is brief and direct, with no diversion from the main point.

*Comment*

**13** Matthew's initial τότε, "then," is a general word of transition rather than a chronological notice (cf. 9:14; 12:38; 15:1; 18:21; etc.). The verb προσηνέχθησαν, "they were brought," is commonly used in bringing the sick for healing (cf. 4:24; 8:16; 9:2, 32; 12:22; 14:35; 17:16). Parents brought their children (Luke specifies βρέφη, "babies") to be "blessed" by Jesus (cf. Mark 10:16 for the verb). This is the point of the laying on of hands and the prayer. (The laying on of hands was also done for healing [cf. 9:18; Mark 6:5; 7:32; 8:23, 25; Luke 4:40; Acts 9:12, 17; 28:8], for reception of the Holy Spirit [Acts 8:17–19; 19:6], and for ordination [Acts 6:6; 13:3; 1 Tim 4:14; 5:22; 2 Tim 1:6]; OT background exists only for ordination [Num 27:18, 23; cf. Deut 34:9] and for the blessing of the father [Gen 48:14], a parallel overstressed by Derrett.) The objection of the disciples, directed against those who brought the children and not the children themselves, was presumably based on their belief that Jesus had more important things ahead of him to do than to spend his time and energy blessing little children. Although children were not considered very important, precedent for elders blessing little children can be found in *Soṗ.* 18:5 (on the evening of the Day of Atonement). (A similar occurrence of ἐπιτιμᾶν, "rebuke," is found in 20:31, where the crowd rebukes the blind men who cry out to Jesus to be healed.)

**14** Jesus' response must have surprised the disciples, for he emphatically invites the little children to come to him: ἄφετε, "permit (them)" (for ἀφιέναι in this sense, cf. 8:22; 13:30; 23:13), and μὴ κωλύετε, "do not forbid them" (κωλύειν occurs in Matthew only here; cf. Mark 9:38; Acts 10:47). It is unlikely that the latter phrase constitutes a technical term referring to baptism and hence an allusion to infant baptism (an argument based on the use of the same verb in Acts 8:36; 10:47; cf. Matt 3:14; see O. Cullmann, *Baptism in the New Testament*, SBT 1 [London: SCM, 1950] 71–80). Little children in their dependence and receptivity belong to the kingdom by their very nature. τῶν γὰρ τοιούτων ἐστὶν ἡ βασιλεία τῶν οὐρανῶν, "for of such is the kingdom of heaven," at the same time recalls the teaching of 18:2–5, where the disciples were told that they had themselves to become like "little children" (παιδία, the same word as here) if they hoped to enter the kingdom of heaven (see *Comment* on that passage). If little children are a model for disciples, then they obviously have their proper place in the presence of Jesus. They illustrate in a vivid way what the kingdom is about and how it is received. Jesus does not miss the opportunity to point this out.

**15** Thus Jesus is happy to lay his hands on the little children to bless them. It is recorded that he did so and then proceeded on his way, the way to Jerusalem.

### Explanation

For all the seriousness of the issues relating to the dawning of the kingdom in and through the work of Jesus, the nature of the kingdom is such that even little children find their place in it. Little children indeed intrinsically have an affinity for the kingdom. They too in their way are members of the community of faith. Even more remarkable, little children can serve as a paradigm for the conduct of disciples. Jesus is not too busy even on the way to the cross to bless the little ones who can by example teach the "little ones" who are the adult members of the community of disciples. He blesses alike the little children and the childlike.

# The Rich Young Man   (19:16–22)

### Bibliography

**Berger, K.** *Die Gesetzesauslegung Jesu: Ihr historischer Hintergrund im Judentum und im Alten Testament.* WMANT 40. Neukirchen: Neukirchener, 1972. 396–460. **Brunner, A.** "Einer nur ist der Gute (Mt. 19,17)." *GL* 38 (1965) 411–16. **Cope, O. L.** "'The Good is One'—Mt

19:16–22 and Prov 3:35–4:4." In *Matthew: A Scribe Trained for the Kingdom of Heaven.* Washington: Catholic Biblical Assn. of America, 1976. 111–19. **Coulot, C.** "La structuration de la péricope de l'homme riche et ses différentes lectures (Mc 10,17–31; Mt 19,16–30; Lc 18,18–30)." *RevSR* 56 (1982) 240–52. **Grimme, H.** "Drei Evangelienberichte in neuer Auffassung." *TGl* 34 (1942) 83–90. **Klijn, A. F. J.** "The Question of the Rich Young Man in a Jewish-Christian Gospel." *NovT* 8 (1966) 149–55. **Légasse, S.** "Le 'jeune homme' riche." In *L'appel du riche.* EBib. Paris: Beauchesne, 1966. 184–214. **Luck, U.** "Die Frage nach dem Guten: Zu Mt 19,16–30 und Par." In *Studien zum Text und zur Ethik des Neuen Testaments.* FS H. Greeven, ed. W. Schrage. Berlin: de Gruyter, 1986. 282–97. **Murray, G.** "The Rich Young Man." *DR* 103 (1985) 144–46. **Neuhäusler, E.** "Allem Besitz entsagen." In *Anspruch und Antwort Gottes: Zur Lehre von den Weisungen innerhalb der synoptischen Jesusverkündigung.* Düsseldorf: Patmos, 1962. 170–85. **Thomas, R. L.** "The Rich Young Man in Matthew." *GTJ* 3 (1982) 235–60. **Tillard, J. M. R.** "Le propos de pauvreté et l'exigence évangélique." *NRT* 100 (1978) 207–32, 359–72. **Trilling, W.** *Christusverkündigung in den synoptischen Evangelien: Beispiele gattungsgemässer Auslegung.* Munich: Kösel, 1969. 128–45. **Wenham, J. W.** "Why Do You Ask about the Good? A Study of the Relation between Text and Source Criticism." *NTS* 28 (1982) 116–25. **Yarnold, E.** "*Teleios* in St. Matthew's Gospel." *SE* 4 [= TU 102] (1968) 269–73. **Zimmerli, W.** "Die Frage des Reichen nach dem ewigen Leben." *EvT* 19 (1959) 90–97.

## Translation

[16]*And look, one came to him* [a] *and said: "Teacher,* [b] *what good thing must I do in order to gain* [c] *eternal life?"* [17]*And he said to him: "Why are you asking me about what is good? There is One who is good.* [d,e] *But if you want to enter into life, keep the commandments."* [18]*He said to him: "Which commandments?"* [f] *And Jesus said: "These: 'You shall not murder; you shall not commit adultery; you shall not steal; you shall not bear false witness;* [19]*honor your father and mother'; and 'you shall love your neighbor as yourself.'"* [20]*The young man said to him: "All these things I have kept.* [g] *What do I still lack?"* [21]*Jesus said to him: "If you want to be perfect, go, sell your possessions and give the money* [h] *to [the]* [i] *poor, and you will have a treasure in heaven, and come, follow me."* [22]*But when the young man heard the statement,* [j] *he went away in sorrow, for he had many possessions.*

## Notes

[a] Many MSS (C [D] L W f[1] TR sy) have αὐτῷ, "to him," after the verb εἶπεν, "said."

[b] Many MSS (C W Θ f[13] TR lat sy sa mae bo[pt]) add ἀγαθέ, i.e., "good," probably because of the parallel text in Mark 10:17; Luke 18:18. Supporting the shorter reading are א B D L f[1] bo[pt].

[c] σχῶ, lit. "might have." א L (sy[s,c,hmg]) have ποιήσας ζωὴν αἰώνιον κληρονομήσω, "do that I might inherit eternal life," probably through the influence of the parallel in Luke 18:18.

[d] Many MSS (C [W] f[13] TR sy[p,h] sa bo[ms]) have τί με λέγεις ἀγαθόν; οὐδεὶς ἀγαθὸς εἰ μὴ εἷς ὁ θεός, "Why do you call me 'good'? No one is good except one: God." This is almost certainly the result of assimilation to the parallels in Mark 10:18; Luke 18:19. Supporting the text as is: א B (* minus εἷς) (D) L Θ (f[1]) (lat, sy[s,c,hmg]) mae bo. See *TCGNT*, 49.

[e] Lat sy[c] mae bo add ὁ θεός, "God."

[f] "Commandments" added to translation.

[g] Many MSS (א[2] C D [except for μου, "my"] W f[13] TR it vg[cl] sy co) add ἐκ νεότητός μου, "from my youth," through the influence of the parallel in Mark 10:20 (cf. Luke 18:21). In favor of the shorter text are: א* B L Θ f[1] lat.

[h] "The money" added to translation.

[i] τοῖς, "the," is lacking in א C L W Z f[1,13] TR; it is found, however, in B D Θ co. The *UBSGNT* committee thus puts the word in brackets.

ʲ B it syˢ·ᶜ·ᵖ mae boᵐˢˢ have τὸν λόγον τοῦτον, "this word"; א L Z, on the other hand, omit τὸν λόγον, "the word," altogether. In favor of the accepted text are C D W Θ *f* ¹·¹³ TR lat syʰ sa bo. The *UBSGNT* committee accepts τὸν λόγον, "the word," as the reading that most readily explains the others. See *TCGNT*, 49.

### Form/Structure/Setting

A. The narrative now turns to the story of a young man whose great riches kept him from the full and unreserved commitment required of one who would become a disciple. This in turn leads to a brief discussion of the difficulty of the rich entering the kingdom (vv 23–26) and the rewards of sacrificial discipleship (vv 27–30). The absolute value of the kingdom provides the underlying unity of these passages. If the kingdom demands one's all, the rewards more than compensate for the sacrifices.

B. Matthew, following the Markan sequence, depends again on Mark (Mark 10:17–22; cf. Luke 18:18–23). The following changes should be noted. In v 16 (= Mark 10:17) Matthew omits Mark's ἐκπορευομένου αὐτοῦ εἰς ὁδόν, "as he was setting out on the road" (cf. the reference to Jesus' departure of the end of v 15), beginning instead with his own distinctive ἰδού, "look." Matthew further omits the dramatic touches of Mark, προσδραμών, "running" (which becomes προσελθών, "coming to [him]"), and καὶ γονυπετήσας αὐτόν, "falling on his knees," regarding them as unnecessary to the story. Mark's κληρονομήσω, "might inherit," becomes σχῶ, "might have" (cf. ἔχων, "having," in v 22). In v 17 Matthew omits Mark's Ἰησοῦς, "Jesus" (Mark 10:18), reserving it for the articulation of the commandments in v 18. Matthew makes a significant change in the question asked by the young man: Mark's διδάσκαλε ἀγαθέ, τί ποιήσω, "Good teacher, what shall I do . . . ?" becomes διδάσκαλε, τί ἀγαθὸν ποιήσω, "Teacher, what good thing shall I do . . . ?" In keeping with this alteration in v 17, Matthew changes Mark's τί με λέγεις ἀγαθόν, "Why do you call me good?" (Mark 10:18), to τί με ἐρωτᾷς περὶ τοῦ ἀγαθοῦ, "Why are you asking me about the good?" as well as modifying the sentence that follows in Mark, οὐδεὶς ἀγαθὸς εἰ μὴ εἷς ὁ θεός, "no one is good except God alone," to εἷς ἐστιν ὁ ἀγαθός, "there is One who is good." Thus Matthew, with obvious christological interests, avoids the conclusion that Jesus is not to be considered "good." In Matthew the question is solely the defining of what is "good" ethically. V 17c, εἰ δὲ θέλεις εἰς τὴν ζωὴν εἰσελθεῖν, τήρησον τὰς ἐντολάς, "but if you want to enter into life, keep the commandments," is Matthew's own addition, as is v 18a, λέγει αὐτῷ ποίας, "He said to him, 'Which ones?'" a question replacing Mark's τὰς ἐντολὰς οἶδας, "you know the commandments" (Mark 10:19). Matthew introduces the commandments with ὁ δὲ Ἰησοῦς εἶπεν, "and Jesus said"(v 18b; cf. Mark 10:19), thus emphasizing Jesus as the teacher of Torah. In citing the commandments, Matthew follows the LXX in using οὐ with the future indicative rather than Mark's μή with the subjunctive (so too Luke). In v 18 Matthew omits Mark's μὴ ἀποστερήσῃς, "do not defraud" (Mark 10:19; omitted also in Luke 18:20), a commandment not found among the ten, although it can be taken to approximate the tenth. On the other hand, in v 19 Matthew adds the commandment from Lev 19:18, καὶ ἀγαπήσεις τὸν πλησίον σου ὡς σεαυτόν, "and 'you shall love your neighbor as yourself.'" Matthew alone identifies the man as ὁ νεανίσκος (v 20; just as Luke alone identifies him as an ἄρχων, "ruler" [Luke

18:18]) and accordingly omits Mark's ἐκ νεότητός μου, "from my youth" (Mark 10:20). In the same verse Matthew omits Mark's διδάσκαλε, "teacher" (so too Luke 18:21), adds the question τί ἔτι ὑστερῶ, "what yet do I lack?" (but cf. Mark 10:21b, ἔν σε ὑστερεῖ, "one thing you lack"), and omits the poignant Markan statement ὁ δὲ Ἰησοῦς ἐμβλέψας αὐτῷ ἠγάπησεν αὐτόν, "and Jesus looked at him and loved him" (Mark 10:21, also omitted in Luke 18:22). In v 21 Matthew substitutes εἰ θέλεις τέλειος εἶναι, "if you want to be perfect," for Mark's ἔν σε ὑστερεῖ, "one thing you lack" (Mark 10:21b; cf. Matt v 20). In the same verse Matthew substitutes σου τὰ ὑπάρχοντα, "your possessions," for Mark's ὅσα ἔχεις, "whatever you have." Matthew adds ὁ νεανίσκος once again in v 22, as well as substituting ἀκούσας, "when he heard" (see too Luke 18:23), for στυγνάσας, "having become gloomy" (Mark 10:22). Thus Matthew has extensively reworked the passage, more so than is usually the case and with a number of his own special interests in mind. Close agreement with Mark is found only in the quotation of the commandments and at the end of the pericope (vv 21b–22). The reference to "treasure in heaven," found in all three Synoptics, also occurs earlier in 6:20. The citation of Lev 19:18 is found again in 22:38.

Origen (*Comm. on Matt.* 15.14) records a similar story from the *Gospel of the Hebrews*, where Jesus draws the conclusion that the young man could not have fulfilled the commandment to "love one's neighbor as oneself" since many of the man's Jewish brethren were poor and hungry. In the *Gospel of the Nazaraeans* (E. Hennecke, *New Testament Apocrypha*, ed. W. Schneemelcher [Philadelphia: Westminster, 1963] 1:148–49), Jesus presents his own interpretation of the commandments, showing that the man had in fact not kept the commandments.

C. The pericope consists of dialogue between Jesus and a young man seeking eternal life. There is no controversy here; the young man comes as a sincere inquirer, receives instruction from Jesus through the asking of questions, and makes his decision. The following outline may be suggested: (1) the inquirer's question (v 16); (2) Jesus' response, pointing to the commandments (v 17); (3) the young man's request for specificity (v 18a); (4) Jesus' citation of the commandments (v 18b–19); (5) the young man's assertion of compliance with the commandments and further question (v 20); (6) the remaining obstacle and invitation to discipleship (v 21); and (7) the sorrowful departure of the rich man (v 22). The alternation of question and answer produces an overlapping of terms or concepts: e.g., "good" in vv 16–17; "life eternal/life" in vv 16–17; "commandments" in vv 17–20; "lack"/ "be perfect" in vv 20–21; and "your possessions"/"treasure in heaven"/"many possessions" in vv 21–22. Structural features include the parallelism in the citing of the commandments, in particular the first four, which are negative (the final two are positive, and each has an expressed direct object). Also striking are the five parallel imperative verbs of v 21: "go," "sell," "give," "come," and "follow."

*Comment*

**16** Matthew's ἰδού, "look," calls attention as usual to a particularly remarkable happening, in this case the recorded exchange between Jesus and a young seeker of eternal life. The address διδάσκαλε, "teacher" (i.e., in the sense of rabbi), is one of respect but not of commitment (see *Comment* on 8:19). Sensing a lack in his life, he asks Jesus what (further) "good" (ἀγαθόν; cf. 12:35), i.e. what righteous deed, he must yet perform in order that σχῶ ζωὴν αἰώνιον, "I may have eternal life." The latter is mentioned in 25:46, referring to the future inheritance of eschatological blessing (cf. entering "the kingdom of God" in 19:23–24). Elsewhere in Matthew, the shorter "enter into life" is used in the same sense (cf. v 17; 7:14; 18:8–9).

**17**  Jesus responds to the young (cf. v 20) man with a question, saying according to Matthew, "Why are you asking me about the good [περὶ τοῦ ἀγαθοῦ]?" This is followed by the statement that εἷς ἐστιν ὁ ἀγαθός, "There is One who is good," perhaps an allusion to the Shema of Deut 6:4. God, who is alone the ultimate measure of good, has already defined what is good in his commandments. "The good" is to be understood as a reference to Torah (thus, rightly, Murray). (Torah is defined as "good" in *m. ʾAbot* 6:2; *b. Ber.* 28b.) By his extensive editing of Mark's stronger statements (see above *Form/Structure/Setting* §B), Matthew has avoided any implication that Jesus is not to be thought of as good, which could be inferred from the Markan parallel. The issue in Matthew, however, concerns the definition of the good. God has given the commandments precisely to define righteousness, and Jesus, loyal to the law, stands behind them. While Jesus interprets the meaning of those commandments, they themselves are the beginning point for the definition of righteousness. One who seeks eternal life should accordingly look to the commandments (cf. Lev 18:5): τήρησον τὰς ἐντολάς, "keep the commandments" (the only such direct exhortation in Matthew; cf. 5:19; 28:20). εἰς τὴν ζωὴν εἰσελθεῖν, "to enter into life," is the equivalent of σχῶ ζωὴν αἰώνιον, "have eternal life," in the preceding verse (see above; cf. Luke 10:28).

**18–19**  The response ποίας, "which ones?" is a request for Jesus to indicate the type of commandments he has in view rather than to assign an order of importance to the commands, as in 22:35–40. Thus Jesus here neither lists all the commandments, nor does he put them in order of importance. He points instead to some of the commandments as representative of the whole (cf. the τό, "the" [which amounts to "such as"], before the listing of the commandments and the similar citation of representative commandments for the whole in Rom 13:9). The commandments cited are mainly from the second table of the ten, the exceptions being the fifth commandment concerning the honoring of one's parents and the addition of the commandment of Lev 19:18 concerning loving one's neighbor as oneself, which itself summarizes the second table of the law (cf. the important Matthean emphasis in 22:39–40; the commandment is alluded to also in 5:43; cf. *Did.* 1.2). Matthew cites the sixth through the ninth commandments in the order of the MT (of both Exod 20:12–16 and Deut 5:16–20) rather than in the order of the LXX (in either of the two passages). These are followed by the fifth commandment and finally that of Lev 19:18. The text of the commandments, on the other hand, agrees exactly with the LXX wording (of both Exodus and Deuteronomy) except for the insignificant omission of the pronoun σου, "your," after "father and mother" (occurring only after "father" in Exod 20:12).

**20**  These commandments were well known, and the young man heard nothing thus far that surprised him. For the first time in the narrative the interrogator is described as ὁ νεανίσκος, "the young man" (in Matthew the word occurs only here and in v 22; only the parallel in Luke 18:18 describes the man as an ἄρχων, "ruler"). The young man asserts with no lack of self-confidence πάντα ταῦτα ἐφύλαξα, "all these things I have kept." By this statement he meant not just the six commandments mentioned by Jesus but the totality they represented (note πάντα, "all," which is emphatic by position). Although at one level the claim may well have been legitimate (cf. the claim of the young Saul of Tarsus, "as to righteousness under the law blameless" [Phil 3:6; cf. Sir 15:15]), he could hardly have been successful in obeying the commandments as interpreted by Jesus in the Sermon on the Mount. Nevertheless, Jesus does not fault the young man for his claim but instead goes directly to what he perceived as the heart of the man's problem in response to the sincere question τί ἔτι ὑστερῶ; "What yet do I lack?" (cf. b. Soṭa 22b for a similar question).

**21** Jesus now elevates the discussion to a new level: to the standards of discipleship in the kingdom. The demands of that discipleship involve more than obedience to discrete commandments; they are absolute. They involve the desire to be τέλειος, "perfect" (cf. the same word in 5:48), and result in gaining "treasure" (θησαυρόν) in heaven (cf. 6:20) and in following Jesus (δεῦρο, ἀκολούθει μοι, "come, follow me"; cf. 4:22; 8:22; 9:9). The discipleship of the kingdom is not simply a matter of obeying commandments; it requires an absolute commitment (cf. 8:22; 10:38–39; 16:24–26). And this perfection is not simply a challenge offered to a special class of people in the kingdom (pace Harrington; cf. Viviano); it is the call given to all who would enter the kingdom (cf. vv 23–26). In the case of this particular young man, it was his wealth (which paradoxically was considered God's blessing) that kept him from total, uninhibited commitment, and it is just this fact that is pointed out in Jesus' command ὕπαγε, πώλησόν σου τὰ ὑπάρχοντα καὶ δὸς [τοῖς] πτωχοῖς, "go, sell your possessions and give the money to [the] poor." The young man, who had almost certainly given some of his wealth to the poor, as a righteous man would have done, was undoubtedly shocked to hear the command to give away all his wealth to the poor (this went against rabbinic teaching; cf. b. Ketub. 50a). Only by this radical action, however, can the young man hope to enter into the life of the eschatological order. In this case the treasures of this world must be given up for the greater θησαυρὸν ἐν οὐρανοῖς, "treasure in heaven" (6:19–21; cf. 13:44–46; Luke 12:33). Participation in the kingdom (cf. 6:33), whence alone comes eternal life, is offered to the young man in the accompanying invitation to follow Jesus.

**22** τὸν λόγον, "the statement," that made the young man depart sorrowfully is that of the preceding verse. He was not prepared to accept Jesus' commandment and invitation, ἦν γὰρ ἔχων κτήματα πολλά, "for he had many possessions." The periphrastic construction ἦν ἔχων, with its emphasis on continuing action, suggests a preoccupation with his wealth. The noun κτήματα, "possessions" (the only occurrence of the word in Matthew; cf. Acts 2:45; 5:1), means not only fields and houses but other kinds of property (see BAGD, 455a). The young man's rejection of Jesus' invitation proved Jesus' own logion that "wherever your treasure is, there too will be your heart" (6:21 and b. Ber. 61b). It is in fact impossible to serve both God and money (see 6:24).

### Explanation

The pericope (esp. v 17c) should not be taken as teaching that salvation can be gained by simple obedience to the commandments. This is already evident in that although the young man was able to answer that he had kept the commandments, he was nevertheless conscious of falling short of entering, or being able to enter, eternal life. Jesus' conversation with the young man is designed from the start to bring him to the understanding that participation in the kingdom, through becoming Jesus' disciple, is the only way to the eschatological blessing of eternal life. Genuine obedience to the commandments—i.e., as interpreted by Jesus!— is possible only through participation in the kingdom. But the earlier teaching in the Gospel concerning the discipleship of the kingdom has shown repeatedly the absolute claim of the kingdom upon the disciple's life. It is just at this point, as Jesus knows, that this young man was most vulnerable. So attached was he to his great wealth that he was unwilling to part with it. Such is the insidiousness of riches that, as Bengel notes, "If the Lord had said, Thou art rich, and art too fond of thy riches, the young man would have denied it." He had to be confronted with all the force of a radical alternative. The seeming inevitability of the young man's decision raises the question whether *any* rich people can participate in the kingdom—a question that is addressed in the pericope that follows.

# Can the Rich Enter the Kingdom of Heaven?
## (19:23–26)

### Bibliography

**Aicher, G.** *Kamel und Nadelöhr: Eine kritisch-exegetische Studie über Mt 19,24 und Parallelen.* Münster: Aschendorff, 1908. **Best, E.** "The Camel and the Needle's Eye (Mk 10:25)." *ExpTim* 82 (1970–71) 83–89. **Derrett, J. D. M.** "A Camel through the Eye of a Needle." *NTS* 32 (1986) 465–70. **Herklotz, F.** "Miszelle zu Mt 19,24 und Parallelen." *BZ* 2 (1904) 176–77. **Lehmann, R.** "Zum Gleichnis vom Kamel und Nadelöhr und Verwandtes." *TBl* 11 (1932) 336–38. **Minear, P. S.** "The Needle's Eye: A Study in Form Criticism." *JBL* 61 (1942) 157–69.

### Translation

[23]*And Jesus said to his disciples, "Truly I say to you, a rich person will enter into the kingdom of heaven with difficulty.* [24]*And again I say to you, it is easier for a camel* [a] *to go through* [b] *the eye* [c] *of a needle than for a rich person to enter the kingdom of God."* [d] [25]*But when the* [e] *disciples heard this, they were quite astonished* [f] *and said: "Who then is able to be saved?"* [26]*But Jesus looked at them and said, "With human beings this is impossible, but with God all things are possible."*

### Notes

[a] Some relatively unimportant witnesses (59 l[188] arm geo) have κάμιλον (in pronunciation the same as κάμηλον, "camel"), "a rope" or "ship's hawser," thus avoiding the incongruity of the metaphor. (See Luke 18:25; *TCGNT*, 169.)

[b] διελθεῖν, "pass through" (thus B D Γ Θ latt sy[c] sa[mss] mae), as in Mark 10:25. Other MSS (א C K L [W] Z Δ f[1,13] sy[s,p,h] sa[mss] bo) have εἰσελθεῖν, "enter into" (cf. the following εἰσελθεῖν [which, however, is omitted by א L], v 23; Luke 18:25).

<sup>c</sup> τρυπήματος, "eye" (so אℵ² D L W Z Γ Δ *f*<sup>1,13</sup>); אℵ* B have the synonym τρήματος, perhaps by harmonization with the parallel in Luke 18:25; C K Θ, on the other hand, have yet another synonym, τρυμαλιᾶς, in accord with the parallel in Mark 10:25.

<sup>d</sup> A few MSS (Z *f*<sup>1</sup> sy<sup>s,c</sup> bo<sup>ms</sup>) have τῶν οὐρανῶν, "of heaven," by influence of v 23.

<sup>e</sup> Many MSS (C³ W *f*<sup>1</sup> TR sy<sup>c</sup> mae) add αὐτοῦ, "his"; cf. v 23. *TCGNT*, 50.

<sup>f</sup> D it vg<sup>mss</sup> sy<sup>c</sup> add καὶ ἐφοβήθησαν, "and they were afraid."

### Form/Structure/Setting

A. After the immediately preceding episode of the encounter between the rich young man and Jesus, this brief, general discussion of wealth and participation in the kingdom is presented. The fact that the young man was unwilling to respond to Jesus' invitation to discipleship raises the question of the salvation of the wealthy. Granted the perspective of Jesus in the preceding pericopes, is it possible for the rich to be saved, and if so, how?

B. Matthew depends on Mark 10:23–27 for this pericope (cf. Luke 18:24–27). For the most part Matthew's changes consist of the usual omission of redundancy and the abridgment of Mark's text. Thus Matthew omits the whole of Mark 10:24 (as does Luke), which refers to the amazement of the disciples (found again in Mark 10:26; cf. Matt 19:25) and repeats the statement about the difficulty of entering the kingdom (cf. Mark 10:23; Matt 19:23), although without reference to the rich in this instance. In v 23 Matthew omits Mark's περιβλεψάμενος, "having looked around" (Mark 10:23; cf. ἐμβλέψας, "looking at," in v 26 [cf. Mark 10:27]). In the same verse Matthew inserts the formula ἀμὴν λέγω ὑμῖν, "truly I say to you," for emphasis (cf. too the abbreviated formula inserted at the beginning of v 24). Immediately following, Matthew inserts an unnecessary ὅτι, "that," and then substitutes πλούσιος, "rich person," for Mark's longer οἱ τὰ χρήματα ἔχοντες, "those who have riches," and his preferred βασιλείαν τῶν οὐρανῶν, "kingdom of heaven" (but cf. "kingdom of God" in v 24) for Mark's βασιλείαν τοῦ θεοῦ, "kingdom of God" (Mark 10:23). V 24 essentially follows Mark 10:25. In v 25 Matthew adds a beginning ἀκούσαντες δέ, "but when they heard," adds μαθηταί, "disciples," substitutes σφόδρα, "exceedingly," for Mark's less common synonym περισσῶς, and omits Mark's πρὸς ἑαυτούς, "to themselves" (Mark 10:26), thus continuing the open dialogue. In v 26 Matthew moves Mark's αὐτοῖς, "at (to) them," from after ἐμβλέψας, "looked at," to after εἶπεν, "said," inserts an emphatic τοῦτο, "this," and omits Mark's repetitive ἀλλ' οὐ παρὰ θεῷ, "but not with God" (Mark 10:27).

C. Further teaching about the wealthy is presented by means of the dialogue between Jesus and the disciples, consisting of the simple form of basic statement, question, and clarifying comment. The following outline brings out this structure: (1) the difficulty of the rich entering the kingdom, further divided into (a) the basic assertion (v 23) and (b) an analogy (v 24); (2) the disciples' question (v 25); and (3) Jesus' response: with God everything is possible (v 26). Although the simple dialogue does not lend itself to much structural parallelism, v 24 contains syntactic parallelism in the infinitive clauses. There is further parallelism in the contrasting predicate nominatives and accompanying prepositional phrases in v 26. The repeated motif of "entering the kingdom of God" (vv 23–24) finds its counterpart in σωθῆναι, "be saved," of v 25. Also to be noted are the formulas ἀμὴν λέγω ὑμῖν, "truly I say to you," and πάλιν λέγω ὑμῖν, "again I say to you," in vv

23–24. The vivid, aphoristic sayings of Jesus in vv 23–24, 26 lend themselves by their form to easy memorization.

*Comment*

**23–24** ἀμὴν λέγω ὑμῖν, "truly I say to you," is one of Matthew's favorite devices for emphasizing the words of Jesus (see *Comment* on 5:18). The word πλούσιος, "rich person," occurs in Matthew only in 27:57 besides this pericope. No doubt with the preceding episode in mind, Jesus asserts with considerable force that the rich will enter the kingdom of heaven only with great difficulty (δυσκόλως, "with difficulty," is found in the NT only here in all three Synoptics). For βασιλεία τοῦ οὐρανῶν, "kingdom of heaven," see *Comment* on 3:2; for the expression "enter [εἰσέρχεσθαι] the kingdom of heaven," see *Comment* on 5:20. In v 24 the unusual τὴν βασιλείαν τοῦ θεοῦ, "the kingdom of God" (elsewhere in Matthew only in 12:28; 21:31, 43), stands in exact parallelism with τὴν βασιλείαν τῶν οὐρανῶν, "the kingdom of heaven," confirming that for Matthew the difference is merely terminological. The difficulty of the rich entering the kingdom is now portrayed in terms of the proverbial analogy of a camel, the largest animal of the region, going through the eye of a needle. (The analogy is not known elsewhere in ancient literature, although similar analogies occur, such as that of the impossibility of an elephant going through a needle's eye [*b. Ber.* 55b; *b. B. Meṣ.* 38b; cf. Matt 23:24].) The attempts to make the analogy more "reasonable" by reading κάμιλον, "hawser," for κάμηλον, "camel" (pronounced the same because of itacism), or by understanding the "eye of the needle" as a narrow doorway miss the very point of the imagery. The analogy is deliberately ludicrous and hyperbolic. Nor is it to be taken as pointing to the literal impossibility of the rich entering the kingdom (despite even εὐκοπώτερον, "easier") but as a way of underlining the exceptional difficulty of this occurring (note δυσκόλως, "with difficulty" [not "impossible"], in v 23; cf. v 26).

**25** The disciples were very surprised at Jesus' statement (ἐξεπλήσσοντο σφόδρα, "exceedingly amazed"; elsewhere in Matthew the verb is used only in reference to Jesus' teaching; cf. 7:28; 13:54). They shared the common view of the time that riches were a sign of God's blessing (together with the righteousness of the blessed; cf. Deut 28:1–14) and provided the possibility of both deeds of charity (almsgiving) and leisure for the study of Torah and the pursuit of righteousness. If the rich, such as the sincere and righteous inquirer of the preceding pericope, with those exceptional advantages could only be saved with great difficulty, then the disciples understandably inquire τίς ἄρα δύναται σωθῆναι, "who then is able to be saved?" The verb σῴζειν, "save," is used here in the sense of eschatological salvation (cf. the use of the same verb in 1:21; 10:22; 16:25; 18:11) and functions as the equivalent of "to have eternal life" and "to enter the kingdom of heaven." In the teaching of Jesus, this salvation is both present and future (cf. vv 16–17).

**26** The initial ἐμβλέψας, "having looked at (them)," has the effect of bringing extra intensity to the logion that follows (the verb occurs elsewhere in Matthew only in 6:26). The τοῦτο, "this," that is impossible for human beings can mean either the salvation of the rich or, more probably, the broader possibility of human salvation at all. That is, humanly speaking, it is impossible that anyone should be "saved" (cf. *Comment* on preceding verse for this word). All human salvation depends exclusively upon God; παρὰ ἀνθπώποις, "with human beings," this is ἀδύνατον, "impossible" (the only occurrence of this adjective in Matthew). In the second, contrasting clause, πάντα, "everything," replaces τοῦτο, "this." If παρὰ δὲ θεῷ, "with God," everything is δυνατά, "possible," that includes not only the salvation of human beings in general but even the salvation of the rich. The latter would include not only those who, like the rich young man in the preceding pericope, must give up their wealth to enter the kingdom but other rare individuals who are able to live with their wealth as if it were nothing. For OT background for God's ability to do everything, see esp. Job 10:13 (LXX: πάντα δύνασαι, ἀδυνατεῖ δέ σοι οὐθέν, "you are able to do everything, and nothing is impossible for you"); cf. Job 42:2; Zech 8:6 (LXX); Luke 1:37. For a possible allusion in this verse to the LXX of Gen 18:14, see Gundry.

*Explanation*

Preoccupation with their wealth is a notorious fault of the rich. The wealthy are generally held captive by their wealth. Exactly for this reason Jesus warned that "wherever your treasure is, there too will be your heart" (6:21). And it was also for this reason that the young rich man of vv 16–22 was required to part with his fortune. Discipleship is a matter of total, undistracted, and unqualified commitment. When Jesus said "you cannot serve God and money" (6:24), he also indirectly indicated the difficulty of the rich entering the kingdom. On the other hand, it seems clear that Jesus had a few relatively wealthy followers (e.g., Joseph of Arimathea, Lazarus, Zacchaeus, and perhaps Matthew) and was happy to take advantage of their hospitality (cf. Luke 8:3). If it is not theoretically impossible that the rich can be saved (i.e., without giving up their wealth), it is practically the case that only a relative few are able by the grace of God to live with their riches in a way that does not compromise their full, undivided commitment to Jesus in discipleship. But to live with wealth in this way is tantamount to giving it all away. It remains generally true that wealth "is a stumbling block to those who are avid for it, and every fool will be taken captive by it" (Sir 31:7). We should recognize that by the standards of first-century Palestine, most upper-middle-class Westerners and those on the Pacific rim would be considered wealthy. For all such persons the questions of wealth, discipleship, and the poor cannot be sidestepped if following Christ and his teaching means anything at all.

# The Rewards of the Disciples   (19:27–30)

*Bibliography*

**Baumgarten, J. M.** "The Duodecimal Courts of Qumran, Revelation, and the Sanhedrin." *JBL* 95 (1976) 59–78. **Broer, I.** "Das Ringen der Gemeinde um Israel: Exegetischer Versuch über Mt 19,28." In *Jesus und der Menschensohn.* FS A. Vögtle, ed. R. Pesch and R.

Schnackenburg. Freiburg: Herder, 1975. 148–65. **Burnett, F. W.** *"Palingenesia* in Matt. 19:28: A Window on the Matthean Community?" *JSNT* 17 (1983) 60–72. **Derrett, J. D. M.** *"Palingenesia* (Matthew 19.28)." *JSNT* 20 (1984) 51–58. **Dupont, J.** "Le logion des douze trônes (Mt 19,28; Lc 22,28–30)." *Bib* 45 (1964) 335–92. **May, D. M.** "Leaving and Receiving: A Social-Scientific Exegesis of Mark 10:29–31." *PRS* 17 (1990) 141–54. **Schmidt, T. E.** "Mark 10:29–30; Matthew 19:29: 'Leaves Houses . . . and Region'?" *NTS* 38 (1992) 617–20. **Sim, D. C.** "The Meaning of παλιγγενεσία in Matthew 19.28." *JSNT* 50 (1993) 3–12. **Theissen, G.** "Wir haben alles verlassen." *NovT* 19 (1977) 161–96.

### Translation

[27] *Then Peter responded and said to him: "Look, we ourselves have left everything and have followed you. What then will we have?"* [28] *And Jesus said to them: "Truly I tell you that you who have followed me, in the age of the renewing of the world when the Son of Man sits upon his glorious throne, you* [a] *also will sit upon twelve thrones, judging the twelve tribes of Israel.* [29] *And every person who has left houses, or brothers or sisters, or father or mother,* [b] *or children, or fields for the sake of my name will receive them a hundred times over* [c] *and will inherit eternal life.* [30] *But the many who would be first will be last, and the last will be first."*

### Notes

[a] Some MSS (‫ א‬D L Z *f*[1]) read αὐτοί, "yourselves," in place of ὑμεῖς, "you" (thus B C W Θ *f*[15] TR latt), probably a change designed to avoid the repeated ὑμεῖς.

[b] A large number of MSS (‫ א‬C* C[3] L W Θ *f*[13] TR lat sy[(c).p.h] sa mae bo) add ἤ γυναῖκα, "or wife," after ἤ μητέρα, "or mother," probably through the influence of the parallel in Luke 18:29. Some other MSS (*f*[1]) substitute ἤ γονεῖς, "or parents," for ἤ πατέρα ἤ μητέρα, "or father or mother," perhaps also through the influence of Luke 18:29.

[c] Some MSS (B L sa mae) substitute πολλαπλασίονα, "many times over," for ἑκατονταπλασίονα, "a hundred times over," again perhaps an assimilation to the parallel in Luke 18:30 (cf. the Western text of Luke, however, with the further reduction to ἑπταπλασίονα, "seven times over," a reading that apparently also found its way into a few MSS of Matthew [thus Ephraem]). *TCGNT*, 50.

### Form/Structure/Setting

A. This pericope is obviously related closely to the preceding material, both to the general discussion of the possibility of the rich being saved as well as, and even more closely, to the story of the rich young man who was not willing to give away his wealth. With such a great sacrifice and unqualified commitment required of those who would participate in the kingdom, the disciples find themselves particularly interested in the compensatory rewards that will be theirs in the future.

B. Matthew here continues to depend on Mark (Mark 10:28–31; cf. Luke 18:28–30; 22:28–30). Matthew begins v 27 with a characteristic τότε, "then," as well as the following ἀποκριθείς, "answered," not found in Mark, while omitting Mark's initial ἤρξατο λέγειν, "began to say" (Mark 10:28). At the end of v 27 Matthew inserts the question that is only implied in Mark: τί ἄρα ἔσται ἡμῖν, "what then will we have?" The inserted logion in v 28, not found in Mark, is perhaps partly from Matthew's own source and partly from Q (the second half of the logion, about sitting on thrones and judging the twelve tribes of Israel, is found also in

Luke 22:30b, which is not, however, in sequence with the present pericope). Matthew recasts the logion of v 29 from Mark's negative form into a positive statement (e.g., substituting πᾶς ὅστις, "everyone whoever," for Mark's οὐδείς, "no one," and omitting Mark's ἐὰν μή, "except"). In the same verse Matthew abbreviates Mark's ἕνεκεν ἐμοῦ καὶ ἕνεκεν τοῦ εὐαγγελίου, "for my sake and for the sake of the gospel," with the simple ἕνεκεν τοῦ ὀνόματός μου, "for the sake of my name." Matthew omits Mark's νῦν ἐν τῷ καιρῷ τούτῳ, "now in the present time," together with the list that follows (Mark 10:30), as well as the contrasting ἐν τῷ αἰῶνι τῷ ἐρχομένῳ, "in the coming age," with the resultant effect being that the "hundredfold" compensation becomes exclusively future, standing alongside the future inheritance of eternal life (κληρονομήσει, "will inherit," is Matthew's addition). Matthew thereby avoids the confusion of present and future blessings in the Markan text. Matthew, in his familiar practice, thus takes up much of Mark verbatim but also freely shapes the passage, making alterations and adaptations to suit his own perspective.

C. Further teaching is now given through the vehicle of question and answer, together with an appended, apparently independent logion (v 30). The following is a suggested outline: (1) the disciples' question concerning rewards (v 27); (2) Jesus' answer, further divided into (a) sitting on thrones (v 28) and (b) future rewards and eternal life (v 29); and (3) a concluding logion about reversal (v 30). Structural features to be noted are: especially the sevenfold list of v 29, with each of the last six preceded by ἤ, "or"; the repeated and emphatic ὑμεῖς, "you," of v 28 (which corresponds to the ἡμεῖς, "we," of v 27) together with the appositive οἱ ἀκολουθήσαντές μοι, "the ones following me," which corresponds to the ἠκολουθήσαμέν σοι, "we have followed you"; the correspondence between Jesus sitting upon a throne and the disciples sitting on twelve thrones; the ἀφῆκεν, "has left," of v 29, which corresponds with ἀφήκαμεν, "we have left," in v 27; and the parallel main clauses of v 29 (λήμψεται, "will receive"; κληρονομήσει, "will inherit"). In v 28–29, "following" and "leaving all" are in chiastic relationship with the order of v 27. There is also striking syntactic parallelism in the logion of v 30. Again the form of the logia of Jesus looks like it bears the stamp of oral transmission. The logion of v 30 will be repeated, but in reverse order, in 20:16.

### Comment

**27** Peter, as spokesman for the others (cf. 15:15; 16:16; 17:4), raises the question of what rewards the disciples may expect for having left all in order to follow Jesus (cf. 4:20; Luke 5:28). The question may well have been prompted by the earlier refusal of the young rich man to sell his possessions and give the money to the poor (vv 16–22; the verb ἠκολουθήσαμεν recalls esp. the invitation of v 21; cf. v 28). To that man Jesus held out the prospect of "treasures in heaven." The disciples were interested in what compensation they were to receive for their obedience (cf. the very specific request in 20:20–28). They, after all, had left everything in order to follow Jesus (see esp. Theissen). The emphatic ἰδοὺ ἡμεῖς, "look, we," betrays a certain self-satisfaction, for example, in comparison to the rich young man, to which v 30 (and 20:16) as well as the parable of the workers in the vineyard may be directed.

**28** The first part of Jesus' response is given with a similar emphasis, ἀμὴν λέγω ὑμῖν, "truly I say to you" (see *Comment* on 5:18). The ὑμεῖς, "you," and καὶ ὑμεῖς, "even you" (which is partly resumptive), lend great emphasis to the reply and correspond to the emphatic pronouns of v 27. In a similar way οἱ ἀκολουθήσαντές μοι, "those who have followed me," corresponds to the ἠκολουθήσαμέν σοι, "we have followed you," of v 27. The temporal dative phrase ἐν τῇ παλιγγενεσίᾳ, "in the renewing of the world," probably modifies what follows rather than what precedes; i.e., it is at that time, when the Son of Man assumes his throne, that the disciples will also sit on thrones. παλιγγενεσία, which literally means "rebirth" or "regeneration" (the only other NT occurrence of the word, in Titus 3:5, is used in a personal sense; cf. John 3:3; 1 Peter 1:3; 2 Cor 5:17), refers here to the eschatological renewal of the world at the end of the present age (cf. ἀποκατάστασις, "restoration," in Acts 3:21; cf. Rom 8:21–23; Rev 21:1–4; 2 Peter 3:13; given the extensive background for this understanding of the word, Derrett's suggestion that the word should be translated "resurrection" is unconvincing; see Sim, who relates the word to the reference to the passing away of this world in 5:18; 24:35). Although the word was familiar in Greco-Roman (esp. Stoic) circles as referring to the cyclical renewal of the world (see BAGD, s.v.), it is the Jewish background that is more important here. Josephus (*Ant.* 11.3.9 §66) uses the word to refer to the rebirth of the Jewish nation following the exile; Philo (*Mos.* 2.65) of the new earth following the flood (cf. *1 Clem.* 9.4). For OT background see such passages as Isa 65:17; 66:22; and for intertestamental literature see *1 Enoch* 45:3–5; 72:1; *2 Apoc. Bar.* 32:1–4; 44:12; 57:2 (cf. at Qumran, 1QS 4:25; 1QH 13:11–12). If the phrase is taken as modifying the preceding, it would mean "those who follow me in personal regeneration" and thus be a phrase more reminiscent of the Johannine or Pauline writings rather than typically Matthean apocalyptic. The reference to the time when καθίσῃ ὁ υἱὸς τοῦ ἀνθρώπου ἐπὶ θρόνου δόξης αὐτοῦ, "the Son of Man will sit upon his glorious throne," alludes to Dan 7:9 (cf. the dependence on Dan 7:13 in the references to a glorious coming of the Son of Man in 16:27, 24:30; 25:31). The number of the twelve disciples (cf. 10:1–2, 5; 11:1; 20:17; 26:20) is now seen to correspond to the twelve tribes of Israel. The eschatological rule of disciples with their Lord is also found in Rev 3:21; 20:6 (cf. the parable in Luke 22:30; 1 Cor 6:2–3; with regard to "judgment" given to the people of God, cf. Dan 7:22, 27; cf. Wis 3:8 for κρίνειν in the sense of "ruling over"). The rule of the twelve over τὰς δώδεκα φυλὰς τοῦ Ἰσραήλ, "the twelve tribes of Israel," however, has special symbolic significance referring to an eschatological Israel with the reconstituted twelve tribes (nine and a half of which were "lost" by the day of Jesus). The idea of an eschatological "judging" (κρίνοντες) of the φυλὰς λαοῦ, "tribes of the people," is found in *Pss. Sol.* 17:26 (cf. *Pss. Sol.* 17:29). (Cf. Philo, *Quest. in Ex.* 2.114; *T. Judah* 25 for the rule of the twelve patriarchs in heaven.) The twelve disciples, representing the true Israel, will thus be vindicated before unbelieving Israel by assuming authority over them—an authority to judge or rule over them delegated to the twelve by the Son of Man himself (cf. Rev 21:12, 14; see Baumgarten). The disciples, who have given up everything now and appear insignificant, can expect in the future to become powerful figures of rule and authority.

**29** The πᾶς ὅστις, lit. "everyone whoever," broadens the answer of Jesus beyond the twelve to include all disciples of Jesus. Those who have suffered the loss of family and possessions ἕνεκεν τοῦ ὀνόματός μου, "for the sake of my name" (i.e., for the sake of Jesus himself), ἑκατονταπλασίονα λήμψεται, "will receive them a hundred times over." This is typically poetic language that employs hyperbole in the description of the bounteousness of eschatological blessing, the point being that the latter will exceed beyond calculation the losses incurred in the first place. The representative list of seven items (the number of fullness) itself stands symbolically for all such losses. The first and last items, οἰκίας, "houses," and ἀγρούς, "fields," point to material possessions, although the former can imply "households" and thus suggest the personal relationships that follow. The absolute commitment required by the discipleship of the kingdom may well involve the sacrifice of such relationships (cf. 4:22; 8:21–22; and esp. 10:37; cf. Luke 14:26). All losses of this kind will be wonderfully compensated for in the eschatological blessing to be enjoyed by disciples of Jesus. But the greatest blessing of all will be the inheritance of eternal life (κληρονομεῖν is used in 5:5 to refer to the eschatological inheritance of the earth and in 25:34 to refer to "the kingdom prepared for you from the foundation of the world"). This reference to ζωὴν αἰώνιον, "eternal life," recalls the question of the rich young man in v 16 (cf. 25:46). What he was unable to acquire because of his riches will be freely given to the disciples together with their "treasure in heaven" (cf. v 21), the incalculable blessings of the eschaton.

**30**   This probably originally independent logion (but it is already appended in Mark 10:31 to the preceding discussion) seems to function at the end of the present pericope as a reminder that the blessing and glory just referred to remain something yet future. The disciples must not presume upon their special status in the present. Those πολλοί, "many," who push themselves to the top in the present to be πρῶτοι, "first," e.g., the rich, will in the end find themselves at the bottom as the ἔσχατοι, "last," i.e., the impoverished. Those, on the other hand (not many), who are willing to be "last" by the standards of this world will paradoxically be exalted to the first rank with the coming of the eschaton (for a similar rabbinic saying, cf. *b. B. Bat.* 10a). Those who deny themselves in the present in following the teaching of Jesus may be sure of a dramatic reversal when the eschatological era comes in all its fullness (the saying receives a slightly different application at the end of the parable that follows, v 16; cf. Luke 13:30).

### Explanation

Although the demands of discipleship are great, the eventual rewards will be far greater. It is always the case that our thinking and language are so conditioned by the realities of the present time frame that the blessings of the age to come can only be described in suggestive, poetical images. But it is a fundamental component of the teaching of Jesus that a glorious future awaits those who have followed him. Not only will the twelve have their position of privilege and authority, but all disciples of Jesus will enjoy the bountiful blessings that will accompany eternal life. It is this expectation that is to motivate disciples in the present time of self-sacrifice and denial. They who are now last in the eyes of the world will be first when the Son of Man returns in power.

# *The Parable of the Vineyard Workers* (20:1–16)

*Bibliography*

Barré, M. L. "The Workers in the Vineyard." *BiTod* 24 (1986) 173–80. Bauer, J. B. "Gnaden oder Tagelohn (Mt 20,8-16)?" *Bib* 42 (1961) 224–28. Blinzler, J. "Gottes schenkende Güte: Mt 20,1–16." *BLit* 37 (1963–64) 229–39. Cadbury, H. J. "The Single Eye." *HTR* 47 (1954) 69–74. Culbertson, P. "Reclaiming the Matthean Vineyard Parables." *Encounter* 49 (1988) 257–83. De Chalendar, X. "L'argent: Matthieu 19,30–20,16." *CHR* 28 (1981) 450–56. Derrett, J. D. M. "Workers in the Vineyard: A Parable of Jesus." *JJS* 25 (1974) 64–91. Dietzfelbinger, C. "Das Gleichnis von den Arbeiten im Weinberg als Jesuswort." *EvT* 43 (1983) 126–37. Duplacy, J. "Le maître généreux et les ouvriers égoïstes." *BVC* 44 (1962) 16–30. Dupont, J. "Les ouvriers de la onzième heure (Mt 20)." *AsSeign* 56 (1974) 16–27. ———. "Les ouvriers de la vigne (Mt 20,1–16)." *AsSeign* 22 (1965) 28–51. ———. "La parabole des ouvriers de la vigne (Matthieu, XX, 1–16)." *NRT* 79 (1957) 785–97. Eichholz, G. "Von den Arbeitern im Weinberg (Matth. 20, 1–6a)." In *Gleichnisse der Evangelien*. Neukirchen: Neukirchener, 1971. 85–108. Elliott, J. H. "Matthew 20:1–15: A Parable of Invidious Comparison and Evil Eye Accusation." *BTB* 22 (1992) 52–65. Feuillet, A. "Les ouvriers envoyés à la vigne (Mt XX, 1–16)." *RevThom* 79 (1979) 5–24. Fortna, R. T. "'You have made them equal to us!' (Mt 20:1–16)." *Journal of Theology for Southern Africa* 72 (1990) 66–72. Glover, F. C. "Workers for the Vineyard, Mt. 20,4." *ExpTim* 86 (1975) 310–11. Gryglewicz, F. "The Gospel of the Overworked Workers." *CBQ* 19 (1957) 190–98. Harnisch, W. "The Metaphorical Process in Matthew 20:1–15." *SBL 1977 Seminar Papers* (1977) 231–50. Hatch, W. H. P. "A Note on Matthew 20:15." *ATR* 26 (1944) 250–53. Haubeck, W. "Zum Verständnis der Parabel von den Arbeitern im Weinberg (Mt 20,1–15)." In *Wort in der Zeit*. FS K. H. Rengstorf, ed. W. Haubeck and M. Bachmann. Leiden: Brill, 1980. 95–107. Heinemann, H. "The Conception of Reward in Matt 20.1–16." *JJS* 1 (1948–49) 85–89. Hezser, C. *Lohnmetaphorik und Arbeitswelt in Mt 20,1–16*. Göttingen: Vandenhoeck & Ruprecht, 1990. Hoppe, R. "Gleichnis und Situation: Zu den Gleichnissen vom guten Vater (Lk 15,11–32) und gütigen Hausherrn (Mt 20,1–15)." *BZ* 29 (1984) 1–21. Manns, F. "L'arrière-plan socio-économique de la parabole des ouvriers de la onzième heure et ses limites." *Anton* 55 (1980) 259–68. Meurer, S. "Zur Beziehung der Gerechtigkeit Gottes zum Recht: Dazu Auslegung von Mt 20,1–16." In *Das Recht in Dienst der Versöhnung und des Friedens*. ATANT 63. Zürich: Theologischer, 1972. 29–44. Mitton, C. L. "Expounding the Parables—The Workers in the Vineyard." *ExpTim* 77 (1965–66) 307–11. Nelson, D. A. "Matthew 20:1–16." *Int* 29 (1975) 288–92. Patte, D. "Bringing out of the Gospel-Treasure What Is New and What Is Old: Two Parables in Matthew 18–23." *Quarterly Review* [Nashville, TN] 10 (1990) 79–108. Rodríguez, J. D. "The Parable of the Affirmative Action Employer." *CurTM* 15 (1988) 418–24. Roloff, J. "Das Kirchenverständnis des Matthäus im Spiegel seiner Gleichnisse." *NTS* 38 (1992) 337–56. Schenke, L. "Die Interpretation der Parabel von den 'Arbeitern im Weinberg' (Mt 20, 1–15) durch Matthäus." In *Studien zum Matthäusevangelium*. FS W. Pesch, ed. L. Schenke. Stuttgart: Katholisches Bibelwerk, 1988. 245–68. Schnider, F. "Von der Gerechtigkeit Gottes: Beobachtungen zum Gleichnis von den Arbeitern) im Weinberg (Mt 20,1–16)." *Kairos* 23 (1981) 88–95. Sutcliffe, E. F. "Many Are Called but Few Are Chosen." *ITQ* 28 (1961) 126–31. Tevel, J. M. "The Labourers in the Vineyard: The Exegesis of Matthew 20,1–7 in the Early Church." *VC* 46 (1992) 356–80. Williams, W. T. "The Parable of the Labourers in the Vineyard (Mt 20,1–16)." *ExpTim* 50 (1938–39) 526. Zimmermann, H. "Die Gottesoffenbarung der Gleichnisse Jesu: Das Gleichnis von den Arbeitern im Weinberg: Mt 20,1–16." *BibLeb* 2 (1961) 100–104.

## Translation

[1]*"For the kingdom of heaven is like the story of*[a] *a man who was master of a household, who once went out early to hire workers for his vineyard.* [2]*And when he had agreed with the workers on the rate of*[b] *a denarius a day, he sent them into his vineyard.* [3]*And when he went out about the third hour, he saw*[c] *others standing idle in the marketplace.* [4]*And he said to them: 'You go into the*[d] *vineyard too, and I will pay*[e] *you whatever is just.'*[5]*And they went to the vineyard.*[f] *[But]*[g] *when he went out again about the sixth and ninth hours, he did the same.* [6]*And at about the eleventh hour*[h] *when he went out, he found still others standing there,*[i] *and he said to them: 'Why have you stood here idle the whole day?'* [7]*They said to him: 'Because no one has hired us.' He said to them: 'You too go into the*[j] *vineyard.'*[k] [8]*And when evening came, the lord of the vineyard said to his foreman: 'Call the workers and give them*[l] *their pay, beginning with those who came last*[m] *to those who came first.'*[n] [9]*And the ones who came about the eleventh hour each received a denarius.* [10]*And those who came first thought they would receive more. But they themselves received [the]*[o] *one denarius each.* [11]*And when they had received their pay,*[p] *they began to murmur against the master of the household,* [12]*saying: 'Those who came*[q] *last worked one hour, yet you have made them equal to us who have borne the burden of the day and its heat.'*[13]*But he answered and said to one of them: 'My friend, I have done you no injustice. Did you not agree with me*[r] *to one denarius?* [14]*Take what is yours and go. But I*[s] *want to give to this one who came last just what I gave to you.* [15]*[Or]*[t] *is it not proper for me to do what I want among what is mine. Or is your eye jealous because I am good to others?'*[u] [16]*Thus the last will be first, and the first will be last."*[v]

## Notes

[a] "The story of" added to translation.

[b] "The rate of" added to translation.

[c] D it have εὗρεν, "he found," probably by the influence of v 6.

[d] ℵ C Θ $f^{13}$ it vg$^{cl}$ sa mae add μου, "my."

[e] δώσω, lit. "I will give."

[f] "To the vineyard" added to translation.

[g] Many MSS (B W Θ $f^{1,13}$ TR it mae bo) omit δέ, "but." Yet in favor of its inclusion are ℵ C D L lat sy$^{h**}$ sa. The *UBSGNT* committee, reflecting the divided evidence, retains the word, but in brackets.

[h] "Hour" added in translation. The word ὥραν, "hour," is added to the text by C W $f^{1,13}$ TR it to avoid the awkwardness.

[i] C$^{*,3}$ W $f^{1,13}$ TR sy$^{p,h}$ add ἀργούς, "idle" (cf. v 3). "There" is added to the translation.

[j] C$^3$ D Z it vg$^{cl}$ sy$^s$ sa mae add μου, "my" (cf. *Note* d above).

[k] Many MSS (C$^*$ W $f^{13}$ TR sy$^{(c),p,h}$ [bo$^{mss}$]) add καὶ ὃ ἐὰν ᾖ δίκαιον λή(μ)ψεσθε, "and you will receive whatever is just" (cf. v 4).

[l] αὐτοῖς, "to them," is omitted by ℵ C L Z.

[m] τῶν ἐσχάτων, lit. "the last" (pl.).

[n] τῶν πρώτων, lit. "the first" (pl.).

[o] B D W $f^{1,13}$ TR omit τό, "the," and, except for B, have καὶ αὐτοί, "even they," before, rather than after, ἀνὰ δηνάριον, "each a denarius." ℵ L Z Θ 33 support the text. The divided evidence results in the *UBSGNT* committee's decision to place the word in brackets.

[p] "Their pay" added in translation.

[q] "Who came" is added in translation (cf. *Notes* m and n above).

[r] L Z sy$^s$ sa$^{mss}$ bo have συνεφώνησά σοι, "Did not I agree with you."

[s] B adds an emphatic ἐγώ, "I."

[t] B D L Z Θ sy$^{s,c}$ omit ἤ, "or." Favoring its inclusion are ℵ C W $f^{1,13}$ TR lat sy$^{p,h}$ co. The word could have been accidentally dropped because of the similar sounding σοι just ahead of it (itacism). Be-

cause of the divided textual evidence, the word is put in brackets. See *TCGNT*, 50–51.

<sup>u</sup> "To others" is added to translation.

<sup>v</sup> Many MSS (C D W Θ *f*<sup>1,13</sup> TR latt sy mae bo<sup>pt</sup>) add πολλοὶ γάρ εἰσιν κλητοί, ὀλίγοι δὲ ἐκλεκτοί, "for many are called, but few are chosen," words found verbatim in 22:14. The words, which are lacking in ℵ B L Z sa bo<sup>pt</sup>, could accidentally have dropped out through homoioteleuton (ἔσχατοι—ἐκλεκτοί), but in the opinion of the *UBSGNT* committee were more probably added later. See *TCGNT*, 51.

## Form/Structure/Setting

A. The theme of rewards is continued in the present parable (cf. the opening γάρ, "for") where, however, the new elements of length of service and grace shown to the unworthy enter into the picture. There is a sense in which the parable is directed to the attitude reflected in Peter's question in 19:27. The parable serves as a vivid illustration of the maxim about the first and last in 19:30, which is cited again in reverse order at the end of the parable. Although the interpretation here is given a new dimension, this maxim is almost certainly the reason Matthew inserts the parable at this point in his narrative.

B. The parable is unique to Matthew and constitutes the first major departure from the Markan material and its sequence since 18:23–35. V 16 finds a parallel in Mark 10:31 but is dependent on the similar logion underlying 19:30 as the reversed order of "first" and "last" shows. The parallel in 13:30 agrees in the order, but the wording is rather different. The logion probably circulated independently in slightly different forms in the oral tradition (cf. *Barn.* 6.13). Matthew's parable, including the final logion, derives from his own special fund of material.

C. This lengthy parable begins with the formulaic introduction ὁμοία γάρ ἐστιν ἡ βασιλεία τῶν οὐρανῶν, "for the kingdom of heaven is like." As in the preceding material, Jesus remains the speaker, and thus the parable begins somewhat abruptly. Although the concluding logion (v 16) may have been originally separate, it functions particularly well as the emphatic concluding statement of the parable (cf. οὕτως, "thus"). The parable can be outlined as follows: (1) the master sends workers into the vineyard, subdivided into (a) early in the morning (vv 1–2), (b) about the third hour (vv 3–5a), (c) about the sixth and ninth hours (v 5b), and (d) about the eleventh hour (vv 6–7); (2) the payment of the workers, divided into (a) instructions to the foreman (v 8), (b) the payment of those who came last (v 9), and (c) the payment of those who came first (v 10); (3) the complaint of those who worked all day (vv 11–12); (4) the response of the master, subdivided into (a) the fairness of the payment (vv 13–14a), (b) the will of the master (v 14b), and (c) two penetrating questions (v 15); and (5) a concluding logion (v 16). The first part of the parable, where five groups are sent out into the vineyard (vv 1–7), has interesting structural parallelism. The pattern is found most clearly in the sending out of the first, second, and fifth groups. In v 5, however, the sending out of the third and fourth groups (the sixth and ninth hours) is abbreviated and summarized with the simple ἐποίησεν ὡσαύτως, "he did the same," thus breaking with the parallelism before and after. A further major departure from the parallelism is found in the sending out of the last group with the addition of a question and answer (v 6b–7a) not found in the other sendings. Apart from these exceptions, the following pattern can be seen: (1) the reference to the master going out (ἐξῆλθεν, "he went out," in v 1; ἐξελθών, "having gone out," in vv 3, 5, 6); (2) reference to the hour (περὶ . . . ὥραν, "about . . . hour," in vv 3, 5, 6); (3) reference to those "standing" (ἐστῶτας, vv 3, 6); (4) mention of the wages (vv 2, 4); and (5) the invitation to work (ὑπάγετε . . . εἰς τὸν ἀμπελῶνα, "go . . . into the vineyard" (vv 4, 7; cf. v 2). Other parallelism exists in the second half of this parable between v 8b, the reference to "the last" and "the first," and v 16 (cf. too the reference to "the last" in vv 12 and 14), in the reference to the payment received by the last and the first (vv 9–10) and the references to the original agreement to a wage of one denarius (vv 2, 13).

## Comment

**1–2** The formulaic opening ὁμοία ἐστιν ἡ βασιλεία τῶν οὐρανῶν, "the kingdom of heaven is like . . ." occurs often in Matt 13 (see 13:31, 33, 44, 45, 47). The comparison to ἀνθρώπῳ οἰκοδεσπότῃ, "a man, the master of a household," is also found in 13:52 and 21:33, the latter instance also concerning a vineyard. The kingdom of heaven is here (as in 13:24, 45) not like the man but like the story that is narrated. Although not vital to the point being made, the analogy between the οἰκοδεσπότης, "the master of the household," and Jesus (cf. 10:25; and perhaps 13:27), on the one hand, and those called to work in the "vineyard" (ἀμπελῶνα; cf. 21:28, 33, 41) and disciples of Jesus called to work in the kingdom, on the other, is clearly implied. (The vineyard of God is a frequent OT symbol for Israel; cf. Isa 5:1–7; Jer 12:10.) The agreement at the beginning with those first sent out concerning the wage of "a denarius for the day" (ἐκ δηναρίου τὴν ἡμέραν) becomes very important at the end of the parable (v 13). A "denarius" (δηνάριον; cf. 18:28) was the average daily wage for such laborers (cf. the approximately equal drachma in Tob 5:15[LXX]). Everything in the story is thus far straightforward and without surprise: a master of a household early in the morning, i.e., at dawn, hires workers to work in his vineyard for the day at an agreed upon and average pay for such work.

**3–5a** Here too everything is quite ordinary. At περὶ τρίτην ὥραν, "about the third hour," i.e., on the Roman reckoning of time, 9:00 A.M., the master "saw others standing idle [ἀργούς] in the marketplace." The "marketplace" (ἀγορά) was where workers seeking work could be found and hired (presumably the first group, too, had been hired there, although the word is not mentioned). These workers are hired with the agreement καὶ ὃ ἐὰν ᾖ δίκαιον δώσω ὑμῖν, "and I will give you whatever is just," implying that they would receive pay proportionate to the amount of time they worked. There is no hint of the surprise that lay ahead. And so they joined the other workers (*pace* Glover, who argues that the middle groups of vv 3–5 did *not* go to work in the vineyard).

**5b** At about the sixth and ninth hours (i.e., noon and 3:00 in the afternoon), the master ἐποίησεν ὡσαύτως, "did the same," hiring further groups of workers, presumably with the same stipulation that they would be compensated justly. Again there is nothing unusual in this, although one might conclude that the work of the vineyard had some urgency about it that made the master interested in hiring as late as 3:00 in the afternoon, or indeed as late as 5:00, in the invitation to the final group. Was it perhaps harvest time, and if so, does that urgency point to the urgency of the work of the kingdom (cf. 9:37; 13:39)? This would tie in with the implied idea of the last judgment.

**6–7** Those invited to work at "the eleventh" hour (i.e., 5:00 in the afternoon) are first asked why they have stood "idle" (ἀργοί) the whole day. Their answer is that no one had hired them. There is an important reason for this conversation and especially this answer of those hired last, which is hardly to be considered a lame excuse for laziness (the same answer could well have been made by others). Why is this statement made? The purpose of this insertion, which breaks the pattern of the previous hirings, is apparently to underline the fact that these are the ones rejected by other employers as unworthy. These "last" ones assume particular importance in the second half of the parable (cf. vv 8–9, 12, 14, 16). They are analogous to the tax collectors and the harlots invited into the kingdom by Jesus (see esp. 21:31). To these workers, regarded as undesirable by others, the master gives the invitation "even you [καὶ ὑμεῖς] go into the vineyard"—the same invitation given to the earlier groups.

**8–10** It was customary to pay day workers in the evening (in compliance with Lev 19:13; Deut 24:15). ὁ κύριος τοῦ ἀμπελῶνος, "the lord of the vineyard" (the expression occurs again in 21:40; cf. 9:38; 18:27), is probably the same as ὁ οἰκοδεσπότης, "the master of the household" (vv 1, 11). The word for "foreman" (ἐπίτροπος) occurs in Matthew only here. The master orders the wages to be paid ἀρξάμενος ἀπὸ τῶν ἐσχάτων ἕως τῶν πρώτων, "beginning with the last to the first" (cf. v 16). But not only are the last paid first (see Williams), they are paid—and here is the jolting element of the parable as it departs from the real, work-a-day world—the same as the first, i.e., a denarius each. When "the first," those who had worked the whole day, saw this, they understandably expected that they would receive proportionately "more" (πλεῖον) than the latecomers. But καὶ αὐτοί, "even they themselves," received each a denarius and no more.

**11–12** The complaint (ἐγόγγυζον, "they were murmuring," the only occurrence of the verb in Matthew) of those who had come first was that the master had made those who had come last ἴσους ἡμῖν, "equal to us" (ἴσος occurs in Matthew only here). That is, no difference was made between those who had worked one hour in the cool evening and those who had "borne the burden [τὸ βάρος, in Matthew only here] and heat [τὸν καύσωνα, in Matthew only here] of the day." From one point of view, and it was this point of view that dominated their thinking, a great injustice was being done to them. Should not they who had worked so long and hard have been paid more than the latecomers (who in any case, not having been hired by others, were not as worthy)? The parable resembles that of the prodigal son and the reaction of the elder brother (see Hoppe).

**13–14** The master responds to the complaint by speaking to one of those who had worked all day, addressing him gently as ἑταῖρε, "my friend" (the word is also used in 22:12; 26:50, but nowhere else in the NT). The answer consists of two arguments: (1) because the master kept to the terms of the initial agreement (cf. v 2), no real injustice had been done to the worker (therefore, he should take his pay and be satisfied), and (2) it was the specific wish of the lord of the vineyard to treat τούτῳ τῷ ἐσχάτῳ, "this last one," i.e., an individual representing the group who began work at the eleventh hour, as he treated the representative of the group who began work in the early morning. There is a distinct note of grace (θέλω . . . δοῦναι, "I wish . . . to give") in this second statement. The "last ones" in fact did not deserve what they were given. Their pay, equal to that of others, depended purely on the will of the lord of the vineyard. Contrast a rabbinic version of the parable (*y. Ber.* 2.5c, 15), which could have been inspired by Matthew (see Grundmann; Str-B 4:484–500), in which those who worked a shorter period of time accomplished as much as those who worked longer and thus in fact earned their pay! This is not to deny that the rabbis could also speak of grace (rightly, Derrett, Heinemann, Hezser).

**15**    The two questions asked here presuppose the premise of grace to the unworthy. In the first instance, it is the prerogative of the owner of the vineyard and the employer of the workers, including those of the eleventh hour, to do as he pleases with what is his (the θέλω, "I want," here corresponds with the same verb in the preceding verse). If he wills to give to the unworthy what they do not deserve, that is his perfect right (the initial οὐκ expects a positive answer). The second question is based on the master's having been good to the unworthy (ἐγὼ ἀγαθός εἰμι, "I am good," an emphatic statement). The parable is thus about the goodness (cf. 19:17), *sc.* the mercy, of God (cf. Jeremias, *Parables of Jesus*, 38, 139). Consequently, Fortna suggests titling it "The Good (or Generous) Employer" (72). ὁ ὀφθαλμός. . . πονηρός, "the evil eye," refers here, as elsewhere in the Gospel (cf. 6:23; Mark 7:22; Sir 14:8–10), to an envious eye (see esp. Elliott). The spirit of envy, like the insistence on "justice" reflected in the complaint of the workers who were hired first, stands in sharp contradiction to the reality of grace.

**16**    This appended logion brings the parable to an end (note οὕτως, "thus") by focusing attention on the reversal wherein the last are made first and the first last. It thus repeats the logion of 19:30 but alters the order so that here the last are appropriately referred to before the first. The point does not concern the time when the disciples, who are certainly to identify themselves with those who have worked the whole day (*contra* Mitton, who sees these as the Pharisees, and Barré, who identifies the disciples with the last workers hired), will receive their reward, i.e., after those who came later, but rather the fact that those who come last, the "unworthy" (cf. v 6b–7a), will receive a reward equal to that given the disciples. (Cf. the rabbinic parallel: "Some obtain and enter the kingdom in an hour, while others reach it only after a lifetime" [*b. ʿAbod. Zar.* 17a; cf. *Sem.* [= *Ebel Rabbati*] 3.) The last are thus not the last in time but the last in rank, i.e., in terms of worthiness. Thus the parable and also its concluding logion have the effect of underlining the impropriety of the disciples' question in 19:27. The fundamental assertion of the parable is that God's grace is granted also to those who come last. Those who come to work in the vineyard after the twelve, even those who come in the eleventh hour, the unwanted and the unworthy, will receive before the disciples the same reward to be given the disciples. In this sense the last will be first and the first last. The surprise of this reversal is similar to that referred to in 19:30, where there is more emphasis on the "first."

### Explanation

The teaching of the parable focuses on the grace shown to those enlisted in the eleventh hour, those regarded by others as not worth hiring. Only in the realm of grace is the equal treatment of all the workers possible. And it is precisely the latest comer, the least worthy, who is the most conspicuous example of the grace of the kingdom of God. The parable is thus a variation of the important theme of the Gospel articulated by Jesus in the words "For I did not come to call the righteous but sinners" (9:13) and illustrated in his table fellowship with "tax collectors and sinners" (cf. 9:11; 11:19; 21:31; cf. Luke 15:11–32). In the realm of grace upon which the kingdom proclaimed by Jesus is based, it is wrong to set one's mind on the rewards that will set one on a higher level than others. Indeed, even where such differences in future reward may be real (cf. 5:19; 10:41–42; 19:28), in comparison with the common reward that will be shared by all in the kingdom, they amount to nothing. The parable focuses on those who come last, not those who came first (see Rodríguez for an intriguing modern application). In the kingdom where grace reigns supreme, the equality of saints is significantly conditioned only by the priority of the last. The sovereignty of grace relegates the doctrine of rewards to a position of lesser importance. Although nothing in the context suggests this (rightly, Hezser), Matthew's church possibly identified those who worked the whole day with Israel and those who came last with the Gentiles, thus understanding the parable to signify the equality of gentile Christians with Jewish Christians.

# The Third Prediction of Jesus' Suffering and Death    (20:17–19)

## Bibliography

**Feuillet, A.** "Les trios propéties de las passion et de la résurrection des évangiles synoptiques." *RevThom* 67 (1967) 533–61; 68 (1968) 41–78.

See also *Bibliography* for 16:21–23 and for 17:22–23.

## Translation

[17]*And as Jesus was going up* [a] *to Jerusalem, he took aside the twelve [disciples]* [b] *privately and on the road* [c] *said to them:* [18] *"Behold, we are going up to Jerusalem, and the Son of Man will be handed over to the chief priests and scribes, and they will condemn him to death,* [19] *and they will hand him over to the Gentiles for mocking, and scourging and crucifixion, and on the third day he will be raised."* [d]

## Notes

[a] A few MSS (B [*f*[1]] sy[p] sa bo) have μέλλων δὲ ἀναβαίνειν Ἰησοῦς, "and Jesus being about to go up," which is probably a correction since the departure from Jericho on the road up to Jerusalem is referred to only in v 29. See *TCGNT*, 51.

[b] Some MSS (א D L Θ *f*[1,13] sy[s,c] bo) omit μαθητάς, "disciples," perhaps through assimilation to the synoptic parallels (Mark 10:32; Luke 18:31). On the other hand, μαθηταί is often added by scribes to the simple οἱ δώδεκα, "the twelve." The text with μαθηταί is witnessed to by B C W TR lat sy[h] sa[mss] mae. Accordingly, the word is included, but in brackets. See *TCGNT*, 51–52.

<sup>c</sup> Many MSS (C D W TR sy) have the word order ἐν τῇ ὁδῷ καί, "on the road and," which probably represents a smoothing of the text. Cf. *TCGNT*, 52.

<sup>d</sup> Many MSS (B C² D W Θ *f*<sup>1,13</sup> TR) have ἀναστήσεται, "he will rise," probably through assimilation to the synoptic parallels (Mark 10:34; Luke 18:33).

### Form/Structure/Setting

A. The narrative returns again to the goal of Jerusalem and what will befall Jesus there. For the third (cf. 16:21; 17:22–23) and last time before his arrival in the holy city (21:10), Jesus predicts his suffering and death (a fourth, brief prediction just prior to the events themselves is found in 26:2). This prediction makes a particularly sharp contrast with both the preceding sections, where the disciples seem preoccupied with rewards (19:27–30), and the following pericope describing the overt ambition of the sons of Zebedee (vv 20–23). Jesus again affirms the cross as his goal and thus serves as the model according to which the disciples must learn to pattern their own lives. But while he is "last," his disciples compete for being "first." This prediction serves the function of building up the tension prior to the momentous events that will happen in Jerusalem, where the earthly work of Jesus will find its climax.

B. Matthew depends on Mark (Mark 10:32–34; cf. Luke 18:31–34) and, as customary, abbreviates his source by the omission of what is regarded as unnecessary. Thus in v 17 Matthew omits Mark's note that "Jesus was going before them, and they were wondering, and as they followed they were afraid" (Mark 10:32). This omission is in keeping with Matthew's tendency to portray the disciples more positively than does Mark. Matthew's only insertion in the passage, besides the probable addition of μαθητάς, "disciples," occurs in this verse in the words κατ' ἰδίαν, "privately" (something assumed in the parallels but regarded as important by Matthew). Matthew further omits at the end of this verse Mark's ἤρξατο, "he began (to say)," and the redundant object clause "the things being about to happen to him" (Mark 10:32). Vv 18–19, on the other hand, follow Mark very closely. Vv 18–19a follow Mark verbatim, and in the remainder of v 19 Matthew employs εἰς and infinitives for Mark's future indicative verbs, thus focusing on the purpose of the handing over of Jesus. No equivalent, however, is found for Mark's ἐμπτύσουσιν αὐτῷ, "they will spit upon him," and Matthew substitutes the more specific καὶ σταυρῶσαι, "and to crucify," for Mark's καὶ ἀποκτενοῦσιν, "and they will kill (him)" (Mark 10:34). Finally, as in the first two predictions, ἐγερθήσεται, "will be raised," is substituted for ἀναστήσεται, "will rise" (cf. Mark 10:34; Luke 18:33), and τῇ τρίτῃ ἡμέρᾳ, "on the third day" (cf. Luke 18:33), replaces Mark's μετὰ τρεῖς ἡμέρας, "after three days," in keeping with the language of the early church (cf. 1 Cor 15:4). The language of the prediction itself and especially the specific details are thus governed to a considerable extent by the kerygma of the post-resurrection Christian communities, which has left its impress on the tradition.

This third prediction is the most specific of the three (cf. 16:21; 17:22–23). Although it lacks the reference to the πρεσβύτεροι, "elders," and the general reference πολλὰ παθεῖν, "to suffer many things" (both in 16:21), it alone refers to the condemnation to death, the handing over to the Gentiles, the mocking, the scourging, and specifically the crucifixion (the latter is referred to only in this synoptic passion prediction; but cf. Luke 24:7).

C. This brief passion prediction may be outlined as follows: (1) Jesus on the road to Jerusalem (v 17) and (2) the third prediction of Jesus' fate in Jerusalem, divided further into (a) the handing over to the Jewish authorities in Jerusalem (v 18a–b), (b) the condemnation to death (v 18c), (c) the handing over to the Gentiles, suffering, and death (v 19a–b), and (d) the resurrection (v 19c). The prediction itself (vv 18–19) has very simple syntax and striking parallelism. After the initial main verb (describing the setting and not part of the actual prediction) of v 18 (ἀναβαίνομεν, "we are going up"), the prediction begins with a future passive verb, παραδοθήσεται, "will be handed over" (the passive probably reflecting the divine will), matched by the final ἐγερθήσεται, "will be raised" (i.e., by God). In between are two future indicative verbs, κατακρινοῦσιν, "they will condemn," and παραδώσουσιν, "they will hand over," describing the action of the Jewish authorities. Further parallelism is found in the three infinitives ἐμπαῖξαι ("to mock"), μαστιγῶσαι ("to scourge"), and σταυρῶσαι ("to crucify"), all governed by εἰς, "to," and describing the deeds of the Gentiles. In each instance the verb παραδιδόναι, "to hand over," is further described by the parallel dative nouns for the Jewish authorities and the Gentiles. The form of the material may be dependent to a considerable extent on the transmission of this important material in the early post-resurrection church.

## Comment

**17** The third formal prediction of Jesus' suffering and death takes on a special dramatic note because it is given as Jesus is actually on the way to Jerusalem, ἀναβαίνων . . . εἰς Ἱεροσόλυμα, "going up to Jerusalem" (cf. the same verb in v 18), and, even more pointedly, ἐν τῇ ὁδῷ, "on the road" (cf. Luke's use of this motif in 9:51–53; 19:28). The use of παρέλαβεν, "took aside," is paralleled in the special taking aside of the inner circle of disciples for the experience of the transfiguration (17:1, where κατ' ἰδίαν, "privately," is also used in a parallel way) and Jesus' agony in Gethsemene (26:37). Here it is all "the twelve" (τοῖς δώδεκα) who are privileged to be the recipients of the revelation.

**18** The opening words ἰδοὺ ἀναβαίνομεν εἰς Ἱεροσόλυμα, "behold, we are going up to Jerusalem," amount to an announcement of the imminence of the climactic events now to occur. Jesus' reference to himself as ὁ υἱὸς τοῦ ἀνθρώπου, "the Son of Man," occurs also in the second passion prediction (17:22) but not in the first (16:21), although it is in the Markan statement of the first prediction (Mark 8:31). See above the *Comment* on 8:20 for the title "the Son of Man." The Son of Man will be "handed over" (παραδοθήσεται; cf. 17:22) to the Jewish authorities (cf. the same verb in John 18:36), the "chief priests and scribes" (ἀρχιερεῦσιν καὶ γραμματεῦσιν; cf. 16:21, where πρεσβυτέρων, "elders," are included). Behind the passive verb is probably the divine will (cf. δεῖ, "it is necessary," in 16:21; 26:24) and not only the betrayal of Jesus by Judas (cf. 10:4; 26:24). The Jewish authorities "will condemn him to death" (κατακρινοῦσιν, "will condemn," is a legal term that implies some form of legal process). While the Jewish authorities could judge Jesus as deserving death (θανάτῳ; cf. 26:66), Roman law did not permit them to carry out the sentence (cf. John 18:31), and thus he had to be turned over to the Romans. Matthew stresses the culpability of the Jewish leaders throughout (so too in chap. 27).

**19**  The handing over of Jesus specifically τοῖς ἔθνεσιν, "to the Gentiles," is mentioned here for the first time in the predictions (the second prediction refers to being handed over "into the hands of men" [17:22]). The handing over of Jesus by the Jewish authorities to the Romans, i.e., Pilate, is explicitly stated in John 18:30, 35 (cf. Acts 21:11, for Paul being handed over to the Gentiles). Matthew's account of the passion refers also to the "mocking" (ἐμπαίζειν occurs in 27:29, 31; cf. 27:41) and to the "scourging," but with the synonym φραγελλοῦν (27:26). (Surprisingly, despite the use of the word in the third prediction as found in all three synoptic Gospels, only the Johannine account of the passion uses the verb μαστιγοῦν [John 19:1]). The verb σταυροῦν, found only here in the three synoptic passion predictions (which otherwise consistently use the more general verb ἀποκτείνειν, "kill") but also in 26:2 (cf. Luke 24:7), is the most important verb in all the passion narratives (cf. 27:22–31). Crucifixion was a Roman form of capital punishment, exercised only upon non-Romans, and not a Jewish form of execution (cf. *m. Sanh.* 7:1). It could be interpreted as the cursing of Jesus by God (Deut 21:23; cf. Gal 3:13). Crucifixion is also prophesied to be literally the lot of the followers of Jesus in 23:34, and figuratively the taking up of one's cross is required of all disciples (cf. 10:38; 16:24). As the final infinitive in Matthew's series of three, σταυρῶσαι, "crucify," indicates the final climactic goal to be realized by Jesus in his earthly life. The prophecy καὶ τῇ τρίτῃ ἡμέρᾳ ἐγερθήσεται, "and on the third day he will be raised," is found verbatim in the second prediction (17:22) and nearly so in the first (16:21; cf. too 12:40). It finds its fulfillment in 28:6 (cf. 27:63) and becomes the very core of the early church's kerygma (cf. 1 Cor 15:4; Acts 10:40).

### Explanation

For the third time Jesus predicts his imminent suffering and death in Jerusalem. This time the prediction includes very specific details meant to convey the sovereign direction of God in these events. Jesus' fate in Jerusalem will be no tragic accident of history but the outworking of God's saving purposes for humanity. This is the preeminent work of Jesus—not his powerful deeds and words, nor his ministry among the Jews of Galilee and Judea, but his death on the cross. Although the meaning of that death has not yet been addressed in the Gospel (it has been hinted at more than once, however: e.g., 1:22; 3:17), the next pericope will culminate in a statement that can leave no doubt concerning it (v 28). Jesus goes the way of the cross for the sake of others.

# A Request for Positions of Honor    (20:20–28)

### Bibliography

**Barrett, C. K.** "The Background of Mark 10.45." In *New Testament Essays*. FS T. W. Manson, ed. A. J. B. Higgins. Manchester: Manchester UP, 1959. 1–18. ———. "Mark 10.45: A Ransom for Many." In *New Testament Essays*. London: SPCK, 1972. 20–26. **Clark, K. W.** "The Meaning of [κατα]κυριεύειν." In *Studies in New Testament Language and Text*, ed. J. K. Elliott. NovTSup 44. Leiden: Brill, 1976. 100–105. **Davies, R. E.** "Christ in Our Place—The Contribution of the Prepositions." *TynB* 21 (1970) 71–91. **Feuillet, A.** "Le logion sur la rançon." *RSPT* 51 (1967) 365–402. **France, R. T.** "The Servant of the Lord in the Teaching of Jesus." *TynB* 19 (1966) 26–52. **Goguel, M.** "Duex notes d'exégèse." *RSR* 123 (1941) 27–56. **Hengel, M.** *The Atonement*. Philadelphia: Fortress, 1981. **Hooker, M. D.** *Jesus and the Servant*. London: SPCK, 1959. ———. *The Son of Man in Mark*. Montreal: McGill UP, 1967. 140–47. **Légasse, S.** "Approche de l'épisode préévangélique des fils de Zébédée [Mark x.35–40 par.]." *NTS* 20 (1974) 161–77. **O'Callaghan, J.** "Fluctuación textual en Mt 20,21.26.27." *Bib* 71 (1990) 552–58. **Page, S. H. T.** "The Authenticity of the Ransom Logion (Mark 10:45b)." In *Gospel Perspectives*, ed. R. T. France and D. Wenham. Sheffield: JSOT, 1980. 1:137–61. **Stuhlmacher, P.** "Vicariously Giving His Life for Many: Mark 10:45 (Matt. 20:28)." In *Reconciliation, Law, and Righteousness: Essays in Biblical Theology*. Tr. E. Kalin. Philadelphia: Fortress, 1986. 16–29.

### Translation

[20] *Then the mother of the sons of Zebedee came with her sons to him, falling down before him and asking something from him.* [21] *And he said to her: "What do you want?" She said: "Say that these two sons of mine might sit at your side, one on your* [a] *right and one on your* [b] *left, in your kingdom."* [22] *But he answered and said: "You don't know what you are asking. Are you able to drink the cup which I am about to drink?"* [c] *They said to him: "We are able."* [23] *He said to them: "You will drink my cup,* [d] *but sitting at my right and* [e] *left,* [f] *[this]* [g] *is not mine to give, but it will be given* [h] *to those for whom it is prepared by my Father."*

[24] *And when the ten heard of this, they were angry at the two brothers.* [25] *But Jesus called them together and said: "You know that the rulers of the Gentiles rule over them like lords and the great leaders exercise authority over them.* [26] *It is not to be* [i] *so among you. But whoever desires to become great among you, let that person be* [j] *your servant.* [27] *And whoever desires to be first among you, let that person be* [k] *your slave.* [28] *In the same way,* [l] *the Son of Man did not come to be served, but to serve, that is, to give his life as a ransom for many."* [m]

### Notes

[a] ℵ B omit σου, "your." See next *Note*.

[b] D Θ f[1] lat mae omit σου, "your." Copyists apparently omitted this σου (or the preceding one) in order to avoid the unnecessary duplication. Cf. μου, "my," in v 23 and *Note* f below.

[c] Many MSS (C W TR sy[p,h] bo[pt]) add ἢ τὸ βάπτισμα ὃ ἐγὼ βαπτίζομαι βαπτισθῆναι, "or to be baptized with the baptism with which I am baptized," through the influence of the parallel in Mark 10:38. See next *Note*.

[d] Many MSS (C W TR sy[p,h] bo[pt]) add καὶ τὸ βάπτισμα ὃ ἐγὼ βαπτίζομαι βαπτισθήσεσθε, "and you will be baptized with the baptism with which I am baptized," again through the influence of the parallel in Mark 10:39. The shorter text is here, as in the preceding *Note*, supported by Alexandrian, Western, and Caesarean witnesses. See *TCGNT*, 52.

[e] B L Θ f[1] it vg[cl] sa mae bo[pt] have ἤ, "or," instead of καί, "and," apparently a further assimilation to the Markan text (Mark 10:40).

[f] W Γ Δ sy add μου, "my." See *Note* b.

[g] Many MSS (ℵ B L Z Θ f[1,13] TR lat sy[p] co) omit τοῦτο, "this," probably, though not certainly, through assimilation to the parallel in Mark 10:40. It is included in C D W Δ sy[(s,c),h] and retained by the *UBSGNT* committee, but in brackets.

ʰ "It will be given" (= δοθήσεται) supplies the ellipsis in the Gr. text.

ⁱ ἔσται, lit. "will (not) be." A few MSS (B Δ Z saᵐˢˢ) substitute ἐστίν, "is (not)." The textual witnesses for the future tense are more impressive. See *TCGNT*, 52–53.

ʲ ἔσται, lit. "will be." A few witnesses (ℵ² L S lat mae bo) have ἔστω, "let him be." See next *Note*.

ᵏ ἔσται, lit. "will be." A few witnesses (B Γ mae bo) have ἔστω, "let him be."

ˡ ὥσπερ, lit. "just as."

ᵐ D (Φ it syᶜ) add here "a piece of floating tradition, an expanded but inferior version of Luke 14:8–10" (*TCGNT*, 53). Metzger translates the lengthy insertion: "But seek to increase from that which is small, and from the greater to become less. When you enter into a house and are invited to dine, do not recline in the prominent places, lest perchance one more honorable than you comes in, and the host come and say to you, 'Go farther down'; and you will be put to shame. But if you recline in the lower place and one inferior to you comes in, the host will say to you, 'Go farther up'; and this will be advantageous to you."

### Form/Structure/Setting

A. After the immediately preceding announcement of the suffering and death that await Jesus, the two disciples' quest for power and status in the present pericope seems all the more shocking and objectionable (note Matthew's τότε, "then" [v 20]). It provides the occasion for yet further teaching from Jesus concerning the nature of greatness and priority in the kingdom. The sons of Zebedee are thus shown to be completely wrong in their concept of greatness. They demonstrate that they have not understood Jesus' teaching in the preceding material about the first being last and the last being first (19:30; 20:16). True greatness, the greatness of the kingdom, is reached only through service and self-sacrifice. Jesus is himself the supreme model of that kind of greatness.

B. In this pericope Matthew continues to depend on Mark (Mark 10:32–45), more closely in the second half, vv 24–28 (for this half of the pericope, cf. Luke 22:24–27, which, however, does not follow Mark closely), than in the first half, vv 20–23. Matthew softens the objectionable character of the request by making the ambitious mother of the two disciples, who is not mentioned in Mark, mainly responsible. Although she is accompanied by her two sons (μετὰ τῶν υἱῶν αὐτῆς, "with her two sons"), it is she in v 20 who comes προσκυνοῦσα, "falling down before [Jesus]," and making the request (αἰτοῦσα, "asking") for οὗτοι οἱ δύο υἱοί μου, "these my two sons" (v 21). Further, Matthew refuses to name the two disciples (although their identity is not in doubt since they are specified, with Mark, as the "sons of Zebedee"). Thus Mark's Ἰάκωβος καὶ Ἰωάννης, "James and John," is omitted in v 20 and becomes τῶν δύο ἀδελφῶν, "the two brothers," in v 24 (cf. Mark 10:41). The request of the mother is left much the same as that of the brothers in Mark, except that Matthew substitutes the more Jewish expression ἐν τῇ βασιλείᾳ σου, "in your kingdom" (v 21), for the Markan ἐν τῇ δόξῃ σου, "in your glory" (Mark 10:37). Matthew's rewriting of Mark 10:35b–36 in vv 20–21 avoids the considerable awkwardness of the Markan syntax. Beginning first in v 22 Jesus' response is made, as in Mark throughout, using second-person plural verbs, thus addressing the sons themselves and confirming the impression that in the preceding verses Matthew is responsible for adding the reference to their mother. Matthew omits Mark's second metaphor to describe Jesus' death, the reference to being baptized with a baptism, both in Jesus' question (v 22; cf. Mark 10:38) and in his prediction of the fate of the disciples (v 23; cf. Mark 10:39). Matthew adds to Mark's ἡτοίμασται, "is prepared" (Mark 10:40), the phrase ὑπὸ τοῦ πατρός μου, "by my Father" (v 23).

Among the minor changes made in the second half of the pericope, the following may be noted: in v 24 Matthew omits Mark's ἤρξαντο, "began" (Mark 10:41); in v 25 Matthew omits δοκοῦντες, "supposing," and αὐτῶν, "their," after οἱ μεγάλοι, "great ones" (Mark 10:42); in v 26 Matthew substitutes ἔσται, "will be," for Mark's ἐστίν, "is" (Mark 10:43); in v 27 ὑμῶν δοῦλος, "your servant," for πάντων δοῦλος, "servant of all" (Mark 10:44); and finally in v 28 ὥσπερ, "just as" (focusing on Jesus as example), for Mark's γάρ, "for" (Mark 10:45). The agreement in the wording of vv 24–28 with Mark 10:41–45 is very close; in the final logion (v 28; Mark 10:45) it is verbatim except for Matthew's opening ὥσπερ, "just as." The logion about service in Luke 22:27 reflects a tradition independent from the present pericopes. Vv 26–27 find a close parallel in the short logion of 23:11, "the one who is the greatest of you will be your servant [διάκονος]."

C. The passage consists of two main sections, one of dialogue (vv 20–23), which in turn serves as the basis for what follows, and one of teaching (vv 24–28). As a suggested outline the following may be offered: (1) the request of the mother and sons (vv 20–21); (2) Jesus' response, subdivided into (a) the ignorance reflected in the question (v 22a), (b) the necessity of "the cup" (v 22b–23a), and (c) the Father's prerogative (v 23b–c); (3) the indignation of the ten (v 24); and (4) Jesus' teaching, further divided into (a) greatness among the Gentiles (v 25), (b) greatness in the kingdom (vv 26–27), and (c) the example of the Son of Man (v 28). The parallelism of the first part involves a chiasm with similar syntax in the respective parallels: (*a*) the request of mother and sons (v 21) is followed by (*b*) the question about drinking the cup (v 22); (*b'*) Jesus in turn says they will drink the cup (v 23a) and then says (*a'*) he cannot grant their request (v 23b). In the second half of the pericope the following parallelism is to be noted: the parallel sentences of v 25b and c; the exactly parallel sentence of vv 26b and 27, with the corresponding μέγας, "great," and πρῶτος, "first," as well as διάκονος, "servant," and δοῦλος, "slave"; and finally the parallel infinitives of v 28, διακονηθῆναι, "to be served," and διακονῆσαι, "to serve," the latter being expanded by δοῦναι, "to give." The parallelism in the second half of the pericope may well result from the prior oral transmission of the material.

D. A word is necessary about the authenticity of v 28b as a logion of Jesus. It is unfortunate that much of contemporary NT scholarship regards it as improbable that Jesus was able to interpret his own imminent death in terms of a sacrifice for sin. The interpretive clause at the end of v 28 is widely regarded as the retrojection of the post-resurrection church's understanding of the death of Jesus as an atoning death. It is pointed out that the ransom logion does not fit the service logion, that the aorist ἦλθεν, "came," reflects a later perspective, and that Jesus nowhere else uses λύτρον, "ransom," imagery. Yet several things should be noted. None of the objections is compelling. There is no reason that a summarizing aorist, ἦλθεν (as, e.g., in 9:13c; 10:34; 11:19), cannot reflect the perspective of Jesus toward his work. The λύτρον image, furthermore, is not very different from the language of the Lord's Supper (see esp. 26:28). On the positive side, we may note the following. First, the reference occurs only in an incidental and fully natural manner in a parenetic context, whereas if it is church theology, one might expect it to assume a more central or important position. Second, the language, although it is clearly the language of redemption, is not nearly as specific or detailed as that encountered in the passages of the NT that do interpret the death of Jesus from a later perspective. The language here is more restrained and suggestive. Third, several Semitisms are apparent in the logion (cf. *Comment*), which would fit the strong probability that Jesus spoke Aramaic (cf. J. Jeremias, *Eucharistic Words*, 179–82). Fourth, there is the ready background of Isa 53 or, less probably, 2 Macc 7:37–38; 4 Macc 6:28–29 (see *Comment*) to account for Jesus' understanding of his death in the categories of a sacrifice for sin. If Jesus knew of, indeed purposely went to, his death (note the threefold announcement), it is unimaginable that he would not have meditated upon the meaning of his death. If he spoke to his disciples of service and spoke of his own ministry as service, it is natural that he would have thought of the servant songs of Isaiah, and thought of his own calling in light of them. One cannot remove a key element from Jesus' consciousness, such as in v 28b, without the negative effect of putting a great amount of his deeds and words beyond understanding. Jesus goes to the cross in the knowledge that he is to fulfill the saving purposes of his Father. For a recent and cogent defense of the authenticity of Mark 10:45, see R. H. Gundry, *Mark: A Commentary on His Apology for the Cross* (Grand Rapids: Eerdmans, 1993) 587–90; see too Page and Stuhlmacher.

### Comment

**20–21** According to Matthew, the mother and her sons come to Jesus together, but it is the mother who implores Jesus for the special privilege of her sons. Her name may have been Salome (cf. Mark 15:40; Matt 27:56), and perhaps she was Jesus' aunt, the sister of Jesus' mother (cf. John 19:25), which may have been thought to add a certain leverage to the request. In the context, προσκυνοῦσα probably means "falling down before" Jesus to make her request. The phrase αἰτοῦσά τι ἀπ᾽ αὐτοῦ, "asking something from him," by its anticipation of what follows, calls special attention, as does Jesus' question τί θέλεις, "what do you want?" to the unusual character of the request. Although he avoids their names in the entire pericope, Matthew has earlier identified "the sons of Zebedee" as James and John (4:21; 10:2). The request is even more disappointing when it is realized that James and John were members, together with Peter, of the specially privileged inner circle of disciples (cf. 17:1; 26:37). It is possible that Matthew puts the request in the mouth of the mother in order to avoid the implication that James and John challenged the position of priority granted to Peter in 16:18. The faithfulness of the mother to Jesus becomes evident when she, together with the other women, is seen at the foot of the cross (27:56). The request is not merely that the sons might rule with Jesus (a promise already granted in 19:28) but that in that glorious manifestation of the reign of Jesus, they might enjoy the most exalted positions of importance, first and second in the kingdom, on his right and left hands, respectively (in keeping with the custom of ancient monarchs; cf. Jos., *Ant.* 6.11.9 §235). ἐν τῇ βασιλείᾳ σου, "in your kingdom," means the overt and thus eschatological manifestation of that kingdom (cf. "your glory" in Mark 10:37), which the disciples apparently associated with Jesus' arrival in Jerusalem. The kingdom is referred to as Jesus' kingdom also in 13:41; 16:28 (both referring to the Son of Man; cf. Luke 22:29; 23:42).

**22** Jesus responds that the brothers (who are now addressed directly, as they are in Mark) did not know what they were asking. To be identified with Jesus' future glory means first to be identified with his suffering and death. Jesus refers to the latter under the metaphor of "drinking the cup": τὸ ποτήριον ὃ ἐγὼ μέλλω πίνειν, "the cup which I am about to drink" (cf. τὸ ποτήριον τοῦτο, "this cup," in 26:39; John 18:11; for the OT background of the metaphor, see Pss 11:6; 75:8; Isa 51:17, 22). It is questionable, however, whether the brothers understood at this point that drinking Jesus' cup meant their own martyrdom. Their easy answer, δυνάμεθα, "we are able," comes too quickly to conclude that. When they heard the metaphor, they probably thought only of a limited suffering prior to glory (cf. 26:56c).

**23** Jesus responds with what amounts to a prophecy that the brothers will suffer and/or be martyred for their association with him: they will drink his cup. (The martyrdom of James is recorded in Acts 12:2; for the suffering of John, who was apparently not a martyr; cf. John 21:20–23.) The sons of Zebedee would indeed drink the cup that Jesus was about to drink. They would accordingly share in Jesus' glory, but the request to sit at the favored positions on Jesus' right and left hands could not be granted by Jesus. That prerogative was not his but his Father's (cf. 24:36). Thus Jesus here, as always in Matthew, yields in subordination to the will of his Father. The seats of extraordinary honor in the eschaton belong to those for whom ἡτοίμασται ὑπὸ τοῦ πατρός μου, "it has been prepared by my Father" (cf. similar language with reference to the kingdom in 25:34). The request was therefore not only improper in itself, but it was completely inconsistent with the pattern of the obedience of Jesus to the will of his Father.

**24–25** The other ten disciples were understandably "indignant" (ἠγανάκτησαν; the verb is used elsewhere in Matthew of the disciples in 26:8 and of the chief priests and scribes in 21:15) when they heard about James and John's request. Probably what bothered them was not so much the impropriety of the request but rather that the two had made an attempt to gain for themselves alone the highest places in the eschatological kingdom. Thus Jesus calls together not just the two but all the disciples to give them further teaching on this subject. The values of the two brothers, and probably of the other ten disciples, reflected the values of the world and not those of the kingdom. In the world it is οἱ ἄρχοντες, "the rulers," and μεγάλοι, "great ones," of the pagan Gentiles who quest for power and who relish it. κατακυριεύειν, "rule over like lords," occurs in Matthew only here (cf. 1 Peter 5:3, where the RSV translates "domineering"; Ps 9:26, 31 [LXX]). κατεξουσιάζειν, "exercise authority over," occurs in the NT only here and in the Markan parallel (Mark 10:42). The expression ἄρχοντες τῶν ἐθνῶν, "rulers of the Gentiles," occurs in the NT only here (cf. John 12:31; 14:30; 16:11; 1 Cor 2:6, 8; Rev 1:5). Cf. the important parallel in Luke 22:25–27. Greatness, honor, and prestige in the kingdom of God are reckoned by a completely different standard in the community of Jesus' disciples (cf. the disciples' question and Jesus' teaching in 18:1–4).

**26–27** Therefore, says Jesus, "It is not to be so among you." Matthew's future ἔσται, "will (not) be," really amounts to an imperative as in its next two occurrences in these verses. The words μέγας, "great," and πρῶτος, "first," obviously correspond to the initial request of the two brothers ("right hand" and "left hand" would be the first and second positions). The person who would be such in the community of the kingdom must not strive for positions of honor but become "your" (i.e., the community's) διάκονος, "servant" (for nearly the same saying, see 23:11; cf. Mark 9:35), and δοῦλος, "slave." "First" and "slave" are nearly polar opposites. The greatness of the kingdom is thus of a paradoxical nature, as the disciples should by now have understood (cf. 10:39; 16:25; 19:30). The disciples are called to follow in the footsteps of their Lord and to follow his example of humility (cf. 5:5), service, and self-sacrifice.

**28** The very center of the Son of Man's work, indeed, is in the service of others: he came οὐκ . . . διακονηθῆναι, "not to be served," ἀλλὰ διακονῆσαι, "but to serve." The "Son of Man" (for ὁ υἱὸς τοῦ ἀνθρώπου, see *Comment* on 8:20), who as such will come in apocalyptic glory (cf. 16:27; 19:28) and who then will indeed be served (cf. Dan 7:14), has come first in the humble service of others (cf. Phil 2:7). In this sense Jesus is a model (cf. ὥσπερ, lit. "just as") for the disciples, who are also called to serve (23:11). But although following Jesus' example may entail drinking the cup that he must drink (v 22), the specific way the Son of Man is to serve, as spelled out in the final clause (the καί, lit. "and," is thus epexegetical and should be translated "that is"), is unique: καὶ δοῦναι τὴν ψυχὴν αὐτοῦ λύτρον ἀντὶ πολλῶν, "that is, to give his life as a ransom for many." "Ransom," although drawn from the background of purchasing the freedom of a slave or captive (i.e., to free by payment), is here used in a metaphorical sense for a setting free from sin and its penalty at the cost of the sacrifice of Jesus. This is the service performed by the suffering servant of Isa 53 (see esp. Isa 53:10–12, where the servant [v 11] gives himself up to death as an offering for sin and bears the sin of "many" [v 12]). Jesus has already been identified with that servant by the quotation of Isa 53:4 in 8:17 and Isa 42:1–4 in 12:18–21.

Dependence here on Isa 53 has been challenged by C. K. Barrett and M. D. Hooker, among others, who point out that the verb used here, διακονεῖν, "serve," or its cognates, is *not* used in the LXX servant songs of Isaiah (where παῖς rather than διάκονος is used). Further, the word in Isaiah for offering is אָשָׁם, 'āšām, which the LXX never translates using λύτρον (or cognates). These objections are not insurmountable. The lack of actual linguistic parallels at these points (they *are* present in the case of ψυχή and πολλοί) cannot obscure the significant conceptual parallels. It is simply too easy to insist on the difference of the words and to attribute different nuances to them, while at the same time ignoring their similarities. In both passages one who has been designated as rendering service gives his life for the salvation of the people. The אָשָׁם, 'āšām, "guilt offering," can without difficulty connote payment to release from penalty of sin (the meaning of λύτρον). The allusion to Isaiah is easier to see in Matthew than in Mark because of the earlier association of Jesus with Isaiah's servant (e.g., 8:17; 12:17–21). Agreeing with this understanding of the background are France, Carson, Blomberg, Harrington, Morris (tentatively), and Gundry (but see a reversal of his opinion concerning the nearly verbatim logion of Mark 10:45 in *Mark* [Grand Rapids: Eerdmans, 1993] 591–92).

λύτρον, "ransom," occurs only here and in the Markan parallel in the NT, although the cognate noun ἀντίλυτρον, "ransom," occurs in 1 Tim 2:6 and the related λύτρωσις, "redemption," occurs in Luke 1:68; 2:38; Heb 9:12. But apart from these technical terms, the reference to the giving of the Son as a sacrifice for sin is common in the

NT (e.g., 2 Cor 5:15; Gal 1:4; 2:20; Eph 5:2, 25; the cognate verb λυτροῦσθαι, "redeem" [i.e., freely ransom], occurs in Titus 2:14 and 1 Peter 1:18; for OT background see Ps 48:8–9[LXX]). The use of τὴν ψυχήν for "life" (cf. נַפְשׁוֹ, *napšô*, "his soul," in Isa 53:11–12) and the final πολλοί, lit. "many" (perhaps "all" in the sense of the community of the elect; cf. Isa 53:12 [רַבִּים, *rabbîm*]; Matt 26:28; see too 1QS 6:1–23), are Semitisms. The preposition ἀντί, "for," has the idea of substitution; hence what is meant here is "a ransom in the place of many" (see R. E. Davies; M. J. Harris, "Prepositions and Theology in the Greek New Testament," *NIDNTT* 3:1179–80). A further possible, but less likely, background to this logion (cf. Barrett) may be found in 2 Macc 7:37–38; 4 Macc 6:28–29; 17:21–22 (ἀντίψυχον); cf. 1:11; this background involves the sacrificial suffering and death of martyrs but lacks explicit mention of service or servanthood. Thus for the first time in the Gospel the meaning of his death is articulated by Jesus himself. Although Jesus has predicted his death in three formal prophecies (16:21; 17:22–23; 20:17–19; cf. 17:12), only now and almost incidentally does he mention the purpose of what will befall him in Jerusalem (aside from allusions [e.g., 1:21; 3:17], the only other direct interpretation of Jesus' death is found in the Last Supper narrative [26:28]). On the question of the authenticity of this final logion, see above *Form/Structure/Setting* §D.

### Explanation

The sons of Zebedee make a request that from one point of view seems natural and acceptable. That point of view, however, reflects the distorted perspective of human fallenness, wherein the greatest good appears to be that which serves the self, i.e., honor, position, glory, and prestige. It is the perspective that dominates the pagan world and its powerful rulers. The kingdom brought by Jesus defines greatness in an entirely opposite way (cf. 18:1–4) in terms of servanthood. This way is foreign to the world and to human nature. Yet it is the way of Jesus, and it is thus to be the way of his disciples. There will be eschatological rewards for the disciples, of course, but these are not for the present, nor are the disciples to have them uppermost in their minds. Instead the disciples are to be marked by the humility, servanthood, and obedience to death that characterized Jesus, in the knowledge that to suffer with him may mean to drink the cup that he drank before ultimately reigning with him (cf. Rom 8:17). As McNeile (290) rightly notes, "'*Servire est regnare*' [to serve is to reign] is the essence of Christian ethics (cf. 1 Cor 9:19; 2 Cor 4:5; Gal 5:13; Rom 12:10; Phil 2:3)."

# Two Blind Men Receive Their Sight   (20:29–34)

### Bibliography

**Berger, K.** "Die königliche Messiastraditionen des Neuen Testaments." *NTS* 20 (1973–74) 1–44. **Burger, C.** "Der Davidssohn bei Matthäus." In *Jesus als Davidssohn.* FRLANT 98.

Göttingen: Vandenhoeck & Ruprecht, 1970. 72–106. **Chilton, B. D.** "Jesus *ben David*: Reflections on the *Davidssohnfrage*." *JSNT* 14 (1982) 88–112. **Duling, D. C.** "Matthew's Plurisignificant 'Son of David' in Social Science Perspective: Kinship, Kingship, Magic, and Miracle." *BTB* 22 (1992) 99–116. ———. "Solomon, Exorcism, and the Son of David." *HTR* 68 (1975) 235–52. ———. "The Therapeutic Son of David: An Element in Matthew's Christological Apologetic." *NTS* 24 (1978) 392–410. **Fisher, L. R.** "Can This Be the Son of David?" In *Jesus and the Historian*. FS E. C. Colwell, ed. F. T. Trotter. Philadelphia: Westminster, 1968. 82–97. **Gibbs, J. M.** "Purpose and Pattern in Matthew's Use of the Title 'Son of David.'" *NTS* 10 (1963–64) 446–64. **Ketter, P.** "Zur Localisierung der Blindenheilung bei Jericho." *Bib* 15 (1934) 411–18. **Kingsbury, J. D.** "The Title 'Son of David' in Matthew's Gospel." *JBL* 95 (1976) 591–602. **Loader, W. R. G.** "Son of David, Blindness, Possession, and Duality in Matthew." *CBQ* 44 (1982) 570–85. **Lövestam, E.** "Davids-son-kristologin hos synoptikerna." *SEÅ* 37–38 (1972–73) 196–210. **Mullins, T. Y.** "Jesus, the 'Son of David.'" *AUSS* 29 (1991) 117–26. **Steinhauser, M. G.** "The Form of the Bartimaeus Narrative (Mark 10:46–52)." *NTS* 32 (1986) 583–95.

## *Translation*

[29]*And as they were coming out of Jericho, a great crowd* [a] *followed him.* [30]*And look, two blind men who were sitting beside the road heard that Jesus was passing by, and they cried out, saying: "Have mercy on us, [Lord,]* [b] *Son* [c] *of David."* [31]*But the crowd rebuked them in order to silence them. But they cried out all the more, saying: "Have mercy on us, Lord,* [d] *Son of David."* [32]*And Jesus stopped and called to them and said: "What do you want me to do for you?"* [33]*They said to him: "Lord, that our eyes may be opened."* [e] [34]*And Jesus, moved with compassion, touched their eyes, and immediately they received their sight,* [f] *and they followed him.*

## *Notes*

[a] $P^{45}$ (Γ) it vg[mss] sy[h] bo[mss] read ὄχλοι πολλοί, lit. "many crowds."

[b] א D Θ $f^1$ it sy[c] mae omit κύριε, "Lord," perhaps through the influence of the parallel in 9:27. On the other hand, the word could be an insertion to bring about exact accord with v 31. Since the position of κύριε in the word order also varies (see too below, *Note* d), the *UBSGNT* committee puts the word in brackets. Supporting the text are $P^{45vid}$ C W $f^1$ TR sy[p.h] sa[ms]. See *TCGNT*, 53–54.

[c] Some witnesses (א L Θ $f^{13}$ sa[mss] mae bo) insert Ἰησοῦ, "Jesus," before υἱέ, "Son," the latter being changed from the nominative to the vocative case (as happens also in some other MSS).

[d] א B D L Z Θ $f^{13}$ lat sy[p] sa[mss] bo have the word order κύριε ἐλέησον ἡμᾶς, "Lord, have mercy on us" (so too in v 30, B L Z lat sa[mss] bo). Despite the strong textual attestation for this order, the committee regards it as an assimilation to the common liturgical order of the words. See *TCGNT*, 54.

[e] sy[c] adds καὶ βλέπωμεν σε, "and we may see you."

[f] ἀνέβλεψαν, lit. "they saw"; many MSS (C K N W Γ Δ TR sy[p.h] sa[ms]) add after the verb the words αὐτῶν οἱ ὀφθαλμοί, i.e., "their eyes (saw)."

## *Form/Structure/Setting*

A. Just before arriving in Jerusalem, Jesus performs a striking miracle in the healing of two blind men, who appeal to him using the title Son of David. This is the same title with which Jesus will be greeted on his entry into Jerusalem (21:9). In the temple Jesus will again heal the blind and the lame too (21:14). The present passage thus at once rounds out the preceding main section of the Gospel and serves as a transition to the arrival of Jesus in Jerusalem and the events to occur there. The present miracle has the effect of confirming the messianic identity of Jesus as the Son of David. With sovereign power he brings sight to the blind, and they respond by following him in discipleship—all this in strong contrast to the way he will be received by the Jerusalem authorities.

B. Matthew continues to depend on Mark (Mark 10:46–52; cf. Luke 18:35–43), despite the basic difference that Matthew refers to two blind men (v 30) rather than Mark's single blind man, who is given the name Bartimaeus (Mark 10:46). Matthew's story, furthermore, parallels an earlier one in the Gospel (9:27–31), which also concerns two blind men, and which may be a doublet of the present story (see below for an analysis of the differences). The significant Matthean departures from Mark are the following. Matthew omits Mark's opening sentence καὶ ἔρχονται εἰς Ἰεριχώ, "and they came into Jericho," which serves no real purpose and stands in tension with the reference in the following sentence to coming out of Jericho. Matthew omits Mark's specific reference καὶ τῶν μαθητῶν αὐτοῦ, "and his disciples," including them instead in the plural genitive absolute, with which Matthew begins. Matthew refers to ὄχλος πολύς, "a great crowd," instead of Mark's ὄχλου ἱκανοῦ, "a considerable crowd," and unlike Mark has the crowd follow Jesus (ἠκολούθησεν αὐτῷ, "they followed him"). Matthew omits the reference to "Bartimaeus the Son of Timaeus," as well as the word "a beggar" (it is clearly implied that his two blind men, sitting beside the road, are also begging), and prefaces his reference to the two blind men with his favorite flag-word, ἰδού, "look" (v 30). Matthew omits Mark's ὁ Ναζαρηνός, "the Nazarene" (Mark 10:47), after Ἰησοῦς, "Jesus" (v 30). Mark's υἱὲ Δαυὶδ Ἰησοῦ, ἐλέησόν με, "Son of David, Jesus, have mercy on me" (Mark 10:47), becomes ἐλέησον ἡμᾶς, [κύριε,] υἱὸς Δαυίδ, "have mercy on us, [Lord,] Son of David" (v 30; cf. 9:27); the same is true of the repeated cry in the following verse in each Gospel, except for Mark's omission of Ἰησοῦ, "Jesus." In v 31 Matthew has also substituted ὄχλος, "crowd," for Mark's πολλοί, "many," and μεῖζον, "greater," for Mark's πολλῷ μᾶλλον, "much more" (Mark 10:48). Matthew omits the reference to the crowd telling the blind man the good news that Jesus was calling him and the blind man throwing off his mantle and jumping up (Mark 10:49b–50); Matthew comes directly to the exchange between Jesus and the blind men. He alters the blind man's address of Jesus as ῥαββουνί, "Rabbi," to the more appropriate κύριε, "Lord," and the request in Mark, ἵνα ἀναβλέψω, "that I may see," is expanded to ἵνα ἀνοιγῶσιν οἱ ὀφθαλμοὶ ἡμῶν, "that our eyes may be opened" (v 33; Mark 10:51). In v 34 Matthew inserts σπλαγχνισθεὶς δὲ ὁ Ἰησοῦς ἥψατο τῶν ὀμμάτων αὐτῶν, "moved with compassion, Jesus touched their eyes" (an unusual type of insertion for Matthew), while omitting Mark's ὕπαγε, ἡ πίστις σου σέσωκέν σε, "go, your faith has healed you" (Mark 10:52), a point with which Matthew does not want here to distract his readers (but cf. 9:29). Finally, Matthew omits ἐν τῇ ὁδῷ, "on the road," after the concluding note that the men who had been healed followed Jesus (v 34; Mark 10:52), thus pointing to true discipleship rather than the mere accompanying of Jesus to Jerusalem.

Clearly our passage is much closer to Mark 10:41–52 than is the earlier narrative of the healing of two blind men in 9:27–31. It seems probable that the latter is a doublet of the present passage. The common elements between the two Matthean pericopes are particularly striking: (1) both concern two blind men (δύο τυφλοί), who (2) cry out with nearly the same cry, ἐλέησον ἡμᾶς [κύριε not in 9:27], υἱὸς Δαυίδ, "have mercy on us, [Lord,] Son of David," (3) to Jesus as he passes by, and (4) whom Jesus heals by touching their eyes (ἥψατο τῶν ὀφθαλμῶν/ ὀμμάτων αὐτῶν, "he touched their eyes"). These common elements between the two passages are more impressive than the differences, such as that in 9:27 the blind men follow Jesus (rather than sitting beside the road) and go into a house for their healing, that in the earlier narrative faith is stressed (as it is not here), and that the earlier passage closes with the messianic secret motif (whereas secrecy is here no longer a factor; cf. the imminence of the entry into Jerusalem). Thus what was probably originally a single story serves two different purposes in Matthew's narrative. If these two passages represent what were originally separate stories, the least that must be concluded is that the language of the one has exercised considerable influence upon the other. It is worth reminding ourselves that we have only a select handful of specific cases of healing in the Gospels and that many more individual stories could have been told. On Matthew's special interest in the evidence of "two" who are healed, see *Form/Structure/Setting* §C on 8:28-34.

C. The most striking structural feature of this healing pericope is the repeated cry of the blind men (vv 30-31), which is obviously important for the evangelist. The pericope can be outlined as follows: (1) the departure from Jericho and the cry of the blind men (vv 29-30); (2) the rebuke and the repeated cry (v 31); (3) the response of Jesus and the specific request of the blind men (vv 32-33); and (4) the healing (v 34). This form is similar to that of other healing pericopes, yet it is conspicuous that no reaction of the crowd is noted. Furthermore, no direct christological conclusion is drawn at the end of the passage, although the healing implies the truth of the blind men's designation of Jesus as "Lord, Son of David." The final note, furthermore, that the blind men "followed" (ἠκολούθησαν) Jesus also serves indirectly as a pointer to Christology. This reference to following Jesus stands as an inclusio in relation to the note about the crowds following Jesus at the beginning of the pericope. The only other parallelism in the pericope is related to the two cries of the blind men, which are identical (the κύριε, "Lord," of the second being more textually secure than of the first) and which are introduced with the identical ἔκραξαν λέγοντες, "they cried out, saying" (this combination is a favorite of Matthew's: cf. 8:29; 9:27; 14:30; 15:22; 21:9, 15; 27:23). The result is particular emphasis on the words with which the blind men appeal to Jesus.

### Comment

**29** Jesus and his disciples (thus the plural αὐτῶν, "they"; cf. v 24), on the last leg of their journey to Jerusalem, depart from Jericho (just a few miles west of the Jordan River, about fifteen miles northeast of Jerusalem), accompanied by a large crowd (for ἀκολουθεῖν, "follow," used with large crowds, see 4:25; 8:1; 12:15; 14:13; 19:2). The crowd of this passage anticipates the excitement and jubilation of 21:8-11. It is not difficult to imagine the eager anticipation of the crowd concerning Jesus' arrival in Jerusalem and the confrontation between Jesus and the Romans that was sure to take place there.

**30** Matthew's ἰδού, "look," focuses the readers' attention on the emerging story that now unfolds. "Two" (δύο; cf. 8:28; 9:27; 18:16; 26:60) blind men sat παρὰ τὴν ὁδόν, "beside the road," probably near the western entrance to the city (i.e., the road from Jerusalem) where there would be the most traffic, in order to beg for alms. The blind men, who would have heard the noise of the crowd, were informed that Jesus was passing by. Either the blind men were told something about Jesus then and there, or, more probably, they had already heard of him and his ability to perform miracles. If he had healed others, he might be able to heal them too. And thus they cried out: ἐλέησον ἡμᾶς [κύριε] υἱὸς Δαυίδ, "Have mercy on us, [Lord,] Son of David" (exactly the same cry, except for the singular pronoun, is found on the lips of the Canaanite woman in 15:22, and, except for κύριε, "Lord," in the appeal of the two blind men in 9:27; cf. 17:15 for ἐλέησον, "have mercy"). κύριε, in conjunction with Son of David as it is here, must be translated "Lord" (on the title, see *Comment* on 7:21; for the vocative, as here, cf. 8:2, 6, 8, 21, 25; 14:30; 15:22, 25; 17:15). For the messianic implications of the title υἱὸς Δαυίδ, "Son of David," see *Comment* on 1:1 (cf. 9:27; 12:23; 15:22). Here the use of the title anticipates the cry of the crowds in Jerusalem (21:9, 15) as well as Jesus' discussion of the title in 22:42–45. The blind men believe in the power of the Son of David, who was to bring the fulfillment of the messianic age, to heal them of their blindness (Isa 29:18; 35:5; cf. Matt 11:5).

Some (e.g., Burger, Duling, Chilton, Fisher, Lövestam) have argued that "Son of David" here has for its background the Hellenistic Jewish development of Solomon as exorcist and healer (based on the mastery mentioned in 1 Kgs 4:29–34; cf. Jos., *Ant.* 8.2.5 §§45–49; *T. Sol.* 20.1). There are problems with this explanation, however (see R. H. Gundry, *Mark* [Grand Rapids: Eerdmans, 1993] 600), and it is far more likely that "Son of David" is to be understood specifically in terms of Jesus' messiahship (cf. 1:1; 21:9, 15; 22:41–45). Despite the lack of texts that speak of the Messiah as healer, it is not difficult to imagine that the one by whose appearance the new age was to dawn would also be thought of as one who could heal.

**31** The rebuke of the blind men by the crowd apparently finds its motivation in the conviction that Jesus had something more important on his mind at the moment, namely, the arrival and subsequent events in Jerusalem. Perhaps the disciples were behind this rebuke (cf. their similar rebuke of others in 19:13; the verb σιωπᾶν, "to be silent," is used elsewhere in Matthew only in 26:63). The rebuke, however, had no effect on the blind men, except to increase the fervency of their cry (μεῖζον, "more greatly"). They knew that at that moment a unique opportunity presented itself to them, and they would not be silenced. The cry is repeated verbatim, according to Matthew, but undoubtedly a few decibels louder (see *Comment* on preceding verse).

**32–33** When Jesus stops and calls (the only such use of φωνεῖν in Matthew) the men to come to him, he shows that even on the way to the climactic point of his ministry, the cross, he will not let the cry of the needy go unheard. The question he asks, τί θέλετε ποιήσω ὑμῖν, "What do you want me to do for you?" is not for information but to provide an opportunity for the blind men to express their faith through their request. Thus although this pericope does not stress faith as does the similar story in 9:28 (or the parallel in Mark 10:52), it is clearly implied in the request ἵνα ἀνοιγῶσιν οἱ ὀφθαλμοὶ ἡμῶν, "that our eyes may be opened" (for the verb, cf. 9:30). The address κύριε, "Lord," reinforces the implied faith of the blind men.

**34** Jesus was moved with compassion for the blind men (σπλαγχνίζειν is used three other times in Matthew to describe Jesus' compassion, all in reference, however, to crowds [9:36; 14:14; 15:32]). ἥψατο τῶν ὀμμάτων αὐτῶν, "he touched their eyes" (for Jesus touching as he heals, cf. 8:3, 15; 9:29). The more literary ὀμμάτων, "eyes," used here instead of the synonym ὀφθαλμῶν (cf. 9:29), occurs elsewhere in the NT only in Mark 8:23. This deliberate and noticeable difference in vocabulary serves to keep the pericope separate from its doublet in 9:27–31 (cf. the similar phenomenon in the two miraculous feeding narratives). The healing is direct and immediate (cf. εὐθέως, "immediately," used also in the healing of 8:3; cf. 14:31). The blind men, liberated from their darkness, followed Jesus as new disciples, the only such note that someone healed by Jesus followed him directly. The men with their new sight were fully confident that they had encountered and had been healed by the Messiah, the Son of David. It need hardly be said that they followed him in great anticipation of what he would do in Jerusalem.

### Explanation

Jesus on the way to his death in Jerusalem does not cease being the Messiah who meets the needs of individuals. The giving of sight to the blind is a dramatic miracle that points to the dawning of the era of messianic fulfillment. The Son of David is present among his people. And as he compassionately delivers them from their literal darkness, so he continues on his way to Jerusalem, where in his sacrificial death he will deliver all of humanity from an even greater darkness—that of the bondage to sin and death. Thus the cry of the blind men, "Lord, have mercy on us," becomes in the Kyrie Eleison of the church's liturgy the cry for deliverance from sin and its judgment. This healing pericope thus may be seen as the gospel in a microcosm.

# The Last Days in Jerusalem    (21:1–22:46)

## Bibliography

**Doeve, J. W.** "Purification du temple de desséchement du figuier: Sur la structure du 21ème chapitre de Matthieu et parallèles (Marc xi.1–xii.12; Luc xix.28–xx.19)." *NTS* 1 (1954–55) 297–303. **Kretzer, A.** "Das mt Basileiaverständnis im Rückblick auf Israel nach der Parabeltrilogie Mt 21, 28–22, 14." In *Der Herrschaft der Himmel und die Söhne des Reiches.* Würzburg: Echter, 1971. 150–86. **Luz, U.** "Matthew's Anti-Judaism: Its Origin and Contemporary Significance." *CurTM* 19 (1992) 405–15. **Petersen, S.** "Zum Problem der vaticinia ex eventu." *ST* 19 (1965) 167–88. **Schweizer, E.** "Matthäus 21–25." In *Orientierung an Jesus.* FS J. Schmid, ed. P. Hoffmann. Freiburg: Herder, 1973. 364–71.

# The Dramatic Entry into Jerusalem    (21:1–11)

## Bibliography

**Barnicki, R.** "Das Zitat von Zach 9:9–10 und die Tiere im Bericht von Matthäus über dem Einzug Jesu in Jerusalem (Mt 21:1–11)." *NovT* 18 (1976) 161–66. **Bauer, W.** "The 'Colt' of Palm Sunday (Der Palmesel)." *JBL* 72 (1953) 220–29. **Bergen, P. van.** "L'Entrée messianique de Jésus à Jérusalem." *QLP* 38 (1957) 9–24. **Bishop, E. F. F.** "Hosanna: The Word of the Joyful Jerusalem Crowds." *ExpTim* 53-54 (1941–43) 212–14. **Blenkinsopp, J.** "The Hidden Messiah and His Entry into Jerusalem." *Scr* 13 (1961) 51–56, 81–88. ———. "The Oracle of Judah and the Messianic Entry." *JBL* 80 (1961) 55-64. **Brandscheidt, R.** "Messias und Tempel: Die alttestamentlichen Zitate in Mt 21,1–17." *TTZ* 99 (1990) 36–48. **Burger, C.** *Jesus als Davidssohn.* FRLANT 98. Göttingen: Vandenhoeck & Ruprecht, 1970. 81–87. **Catchpole, D. R.** "The 'Triumphal' Entry." In *Jesus and the Politics of His Day,* ed. E. Bammel and C. F. D. Moule. Cambridge: Cambridge UP, 1982. 319–34. **Derrett, J. D. M.** "Law in the New Testament: The Palm Sunday Colt." *NovT* 13 (1971) 241–58. **Du Buit, M.** "La dernière semaine." *CE* 76 (1969) 4–59. **Dupont, J.** "L'entrée de Jésus à Jérusalem dans le récit de saint Matthieu (XXI, 1–17)." *LumVie* 48 (1960) 1–8. ———. "L'entrée messianique de Jésus à Jérusalem (Mt 21, 1–17)." *AsSeign* 37 (1965) 46–62. **Fahy, T.** "The Triumphal Entry into Jerusalem." In *New Testament Problems.* London: Burns and Oates, 1963. 126–39. **Fitzmyer, J. A.** "Aramaic Evidence Affecting the Interpretation of Hosanna in the New Testament." In *Tradition and Interpretation in the New Testament.* FS E. E. Ellis, ed. G. F. Hawthorne and O. Betz. Grand Rapids/Tübingen: Eerdmans/Mohr, 1987. 110–18. **Frenz, A.** "Mt XXI 5.7." *NovT* 13 (1971) 259–60. **Haeusler, B.** "Zu Mt 21:3b und Parallelen." *BZ* 14 (1917) 153–58. **Harvey, A. E.** "Jesus the Christ: The Options in a Name." In *Jesus and the Constraints of History.* London: Duckworth, 1982. 120–51. **Jacob, R.** *Les péricopes de l'entrée à Jérusalem et de la préparation de la cène: Contribution à l'étude du problème synoptique.* Paris: Gabalda, 1973. **Johnson, S. L.** "The Triumphal Entry of Christ." *BSac* 124 (1967) 218–29. **Kennard, J. S.** "'Hosanna' and the Purpose of Jesus." *JBL* 67 (1948) 171–76. **Lohfink, N.** "Der Messiaskönig und seine Armen kommen zum Zion: Beobachtungen zu Mt 21,1–17." In *Studien zum Matthäusevangelium.* FS W. Pesch, ed. L. Schenke. Stuttgart: Katholisches

Bibelwerk, 1988. 179–200. **Lohse, E.** "Hosianna." *NovT* 6 (1963) 113–19. **Mackay, W. M.** "The Contrasts of Palm Sunday." *ExpTim* 44 (1932–33) 275–77. **März, C.-P.** *"Siehe, dein König kommt zu dir . . .": Eine traditionsgeschichtliche Untersuchung zur Einzugsperikope.* ETS 43. Leipzig: St. Benno, 1980. **Mariadasan, V.** *Le triomphe messianique de Jésus et son entrée à Jérusalem.* Tindivanam, India: Catechetical Centre, 1978. **Mastin, B. A.** "The Date of the Triumphal Entry." *NTS* 16 (1969–70) 76–82. **Meyer, P. W.** "Matthew 21:1–11." *Int* 40 (1986) 180–85. **Michel, O.** "Eine philologische Frage zur Einzugsgeschichte." *NTS* 6 (1959–60) 81–82. **Patsch, H.** "Der Einzug in Jerusalem." *ZKT* 68 (1971) 1–26. **Paul, A.** "L'entrée de Jésus à Jérusalem (Mc 11; Mt 21; Lc 19; Jn 12)." *AsSeign* 19 (1971) 4–26. **Pesch, R.,** and **Kratz, R.** "Jesus zieht ein in Jerusalem." In *So liest man synoptische.* Frankfurt am Main: Knecht, 1979. 6:64–72. **Pope, M. H.** "Hosanna—What It Really Means." *BibRev* 4 (1988) 16–25. **Richardson, C. C.** "Blessed Is He That Cometh in the Name of the Lord." *ATR* 29 (1947) 96–98. **Rodd, C. S.** "The Way of the Cross." *ExpTim* 91 (1980) 178–79. **Schweizer, E.** "Matthäus 21–25." In *Orientierung an Jesus.* FS J. Schmid, ed. P. Hoffmann. Freiburg: Herder, 1973. 364–71. **Scott, W.** "Hosanna." *ExpTim* 53–54 (1941–43) 167. **Spitta, F.** "Der Volksruf beim Einzug Jesu in Jerusalem." *ZWT* 52 (1910) 307–20. **Stanley, D. M.** "Études matthéennes: l'entrée messianique à Jérusalem." *ScEccl* 6 (1954) 93–106. **Trilling, W.** "Der Einzug in Jerusalem." In *Neutestamentlichen Aufsätze.* FS J. Schmid, ed. J. Blinzler et al. Regensburg: Pustet, 1963. 303–9. **Visser 't Hooft, W. A.** "Triumphalism in the Gospels." *SJT* 38 (1985) 491–504. **Werner, E.** "'Hosanna' in the Gospels." *JBL* 65 (1946) 97–122. **Winterbothom, R.** "The Ass and the Ass's Colt: St. Matthew xxi. 1–7." *ExpTim* 28 (1916–17) 380–81. **Wood, C. T.** "The Word ὡσαννά in Matthew xxi. 9." *ExpTim* 52 (1940–41) 357.

*Translation*

[1]*And when they* [a] *drew near to Jerusalem and they* [b] *came to Bethphage on* [c] *the Mount of Olives, then Jesus sent two disciples,* [2]*saying to them: "Go into the village which lies before you, and immediately* [d] *you will find an ass tied and a colt with her. Untie the animals* [e] *and bring them* [f] *to me.* [3]*And if anyone says anything to you, say that 'the Lord has need of them.'* [g] *And immediately he will* [h] *send them."* [4]*And this* [i] *took place in order that the word spoken through the prophet* [j] *might be fulfilled, which says:*
    [5]*Say to the daughter of Zion:*
        *Behold, your king is coming to you,*
        *meek and mounted upon an ass,*
        *and upon* [k] *a colt, a foal* [l] *of a beast of burden.*
    [6]*And the disciples went and did just as Jesus had commanded them, and* [7]*brought the ass and the colt, and they put upon them* [m] *garments,* [n] *and he sat upon them.* [8]*A very large crowd spread out their own garments on the road, but others were cutting down branches from the trees and spreading* [o] *them on the road.* [9]*And the crowds who were going before him,* [p] *as well as those who followed, were crying out, saying:*
        *Hosanna to the Son of David;*
        *Blessed is the one who comes in the name of the Lord;*
        *Hosanna in the highest.* [q]
    [10]*And when he came into Jerusalem, the whole city was shaken, saying: "Who is this?"* [11]*And the crowds were saying: "This is the prophet Jesus,* [r] *the one from Nazareth of Galilee."*

*Notes*

[a] A few MSS (C³ vg^mss sy^c.p bo^mss) have ἤγγισεν, "he drew near." Cf. next *Note.*

[b] A few MSS (א* C³ syᶜ·ᵖ saᵐˢ mae) have ἦλθεν, "he came."

[c] εἰς, lit. "to." Many MSS (א D L W Θ *f*¹·¹³ TR) have πρός, "to," through assimilation to the parallel in Mark 11:1; Luke 19:29.

[d] A few MSS (it [syᶜ] bo) omit εὐθέως, "immediately."

[e] The direct object, "the animals," is added to the translation.

[f] The direct object, "them," is added to the translation.

[g] א Θ have αὐτοῦ, "him" or "it."

[h] Many MSS (C L W Z Θ *f*¹·¹³ TR) have the present tense ἀποστέλλει (but with future meaning) probably through assimilation to the parallel in Mark 11:3. The subject of the verb is somewhat ambiguous. It could be "the Lord" of the preceding clause, in which case the sentence would mean that the Lord would send them (back) immediately (after having used them). Cf. the Markan parallel and see *Comment.*

[i] Many MSS (B C³ W *f*¹·¹³ TR vgᶜˡ syʰ sa mae boᵐˢ) add ὅλον, "whole (thing)."

[j] A few MSS (Mᵐᵍ itᵃ·ᶜ·ʰ boᵐˢ) add Ζαχαρίου, "Zechariah"; others (vg⁴ᵐˢˢ boᵐˢ eth) add Ἠσαΐου, "Isaiah."

[k] Many MSS (C D W Θ *f*¹³ TR latt mae bo) omit ἐπί, "upon."

[l] A few MSS (א¹ L Z) omit υἱόν, "foal."

[m] Θ *f*¹³ 33 have the sing. αὐτῷ, "it"; D Φ have αὐτόν, "it." These changes may be motivated by the desire to avoid the implication that Jesus sat upon both animals.

[n] Many MSS (א¹ C L W *f*¹·¹³ TR lat syʰ) insert αὐτῶν, "their," after ἱμάτια, "garments."

[o] א* D bo have the aorist ἔστρωσαν, "they spread."

[p] Many MSS (K N W Γ Δ Θ TR lat) omit αὐτόν, "him," probably through the influence of the parallel in Mark 11:9.

[q] (Φ) syᶜ add "and many came out to meet him rejoicing and glorifying God for everything they saw." This is probably a combination of Luke 19:37 and John 12:13.

[r] A few MSS (*f*¹³ aur) omit Ἰησοῦς, "Jesus." Others (C L W *f*¹ TR lat sy mae boᵐˢ) put Ἰησοῦς, "Jesus," in the emphatic position before ὁ προφήτης, "the prophet."

## *Form/Structure/Setting*

A. Jesus' arrival in Jerusalem is an important dividing point in the Gospel. The Galilean ministry has come to an end, and the journey to Jerusalem has been completed. Now all that remains are the events, the deeds and teaching in Jerusalem, that are preliminary to the goal and climax of the entire Gospel narrative. We now meet in chaps. 21–23 the final encounter between Jesus and Israel, consisting of a trio of parables (21:28–22:14), conflict stories (22:15–46), and the diatribe against the Pharisees in chap. 23 (cf. Schweizer, "Matthäus 21–25," who includes the Olivet discourse). This pericope describing the actual arrival in the holy city presents a poignant mixture of truth and irony. Jesus is welcomed for what he in truth is, the Son of David, the Messiah of Israel, yet it is precisely as such that he will be rejected by the people. For the moment, however, Jesus will receive the acclaim of the people, and Matthew will record the impact of his arrival in Jerusalem. But when Jesus shows that he is a different kind of Messiah than that of the popular expectation, the people will no longer support him. Paradoxically they will send the one they now receive with such jubilation to his death on the cross. Thus the triumphal entry is a prelude to the passion.

B. Matthew is here dependent on Mark 11:1–10 (cf. Luke 19:28–40; John 12:12–19), except for vv 10–11. Matthew does his usual abridging and makes one important addition: the fulfillment quotation (a combination of Isa 62:11 and Zech 9:9) in vv 4–5. The more significant changes made by Matthew are the following: in v 1 (Mark 11:1) the omission of καὶ βηθανίαν, "and Bethany," and the additions of καὶ ἦλθον, "and they came," before the reference to Bethphage and τότε Ἰησοῦς, "then Jesus," before the verb "sent"; in v 2 (Mark 11:2) the omission of the redundant εἰσπορευόμενοι εἰς αὐτήν, "going into it," and Mark's "upon which no one has yet sat" (apparently regarded by Matthew as unimportant), the substitution of ὄνον δεδεμένην καὶ πῶλον μετ' αὐτῆς, "an ass tethered and a colt with her," for Mark's simple πῶλον δεδεμένον, "an ass tethered" (with the coming OT citation in view), the consequent omission of Mark's αὐτόν, "it," and the insertion of μοι, "to me"; in v 3 (Mark 11:3) the omission of the unnecessary ποιεῖτε τοῦτο, "do this," the insertion of ὅτι, "that," and the further necessary alterations from the singular to the plural of the pronouns referring to the animals. Matthew also alters the tense of ἀποστέλλει, "sends," to the future ἀποστελεῖ, "will send," while omitting Mark's πάλιν ὧδε, "again here," with the result that the subject of the verb is understood as the man in the village rather than Jesus (i.e., returning the animals). After the inserted OT citation, Matthew condenses Mark 11:4–6 into the simpler summary statement of v 6. In v 7 (cf. Mark 11:7) Matthew again introduces τὴν ὄνον, "the ass," and changes the final pronoun from singular to the necessary plural (αὐτῶν); in v 8 (Mark 11:8) ὁ δὲ πλεῖστος ὄχλος, "a very large crowd," replaces Mark's simple πολλοί, "many," and κλάδους ἀπὸ τῶν δένδρων, "branches from the trees," takes the place of στιβάδας ... ἐκ τῶν ἀγρῶν, "leaves from the fields"; Matthew adds ἐστρώννυον ἐν τῇ ὁδῷ, "spreading (them) on the road," for parallelism and emphasis. Similarly, in v 9 (cf. Mark 11:9–10) Matthew inserts οἱ δὲ ὄχλοι, "and the crowds," and adds λέγοντες, "saying," after ἔκραζον, "cried out." In the actual words of acclaim, Matthew adds τῷ υἱῷ Δαυίδ, "to the Son of David," after the initial ὡσαννά, "Hosanna," while omitting altogether Mark's third line (Mark 11:10a), εὐλογημένη ἡ ἐρχομένη βασιλεία τοῦ πατρὸς ἡμῶν Δαυίδ, "Blessed is the coming kingdom of our father David." Matthew's version of the crowds' slogan, by focusing on the agent of the coming kingdom, permits a more ready christological interpretation. Vv 10–11 are Matthew's own addition, perhaps from his special source. Because of the similarity between v 10a and Mark 11:11a, where Jesus enters the temple, vv 10–11 are sometimes included with the following pericope (as in K. Aland, *Synopsis Quattuor Evangeliorum* [Stuttgart: Deutsche Bibelgesellschaft, 1985] 370–71). But as they stand in Matthew, these verses serve as the conclusion to the triumphal entry into Jerusalem rather than the introduction to his entering the temple (vv 12–17). Again in Matthew's use of Mark, we see close dependence but considerable abridgment together with free alteration for his own purposes, especially in the specific adaptations of Markan material with the OT citation in mind.

C. The narrative of this pericope, which tells of Jesus' entry into Jerusalem, centers on the two high points of the fulfillment of scripture (vv 4–5) and the jubilant cry of the crowds in v 9. The following outline may be suggested: (1) the arrival in Bethphage (v 1); (2) the instructions to the two disciples (vv 2–3); (3) the fulfillment of scripture (vv 4–5); (4) the return of the two disciples (vv 6–7b); (5) the entry into Jerusalem, subdivided into (a) Jesus' ride into Jerusalem (v 7c) and (b) the crowds' preparation of his way (v 8); (6) the cry of the crowds (v 9); and (7) the impact on Jerusalem and the question of Jesus' identity (vv 10–11). As usual in narrative of this kind, there is not much structural parallelism in the pericope. The reference to the two animals in the quotation (v 5) is responsible for the reference to the ὄνος, "ass," and πῶλος, "colt," both before and after the quotation (vv 2, 7). Matthew creates parallelism (not in Mark) by the addition of a clause referring explicitly to the spreading of branches on the road (parallel to the spreading of garments). Further parallelism may be seen in the reference to those going before and those following Jesus (οἱ προάγοντες; οἱ ἀκολουθοῦντες) and in the question and answer of vv 10b–11a. Finally to be noted is the parallel ὡσαννά, "Hosanna," at the beginning and end of the crowds' public acclamation of Jesus. The first line of this acclaim, ὡσαννὰ τῷ υἱῷ Δαυίδ, "Hosanna to the Son of David," will occur again in v 15, while the second, εὐλογημένος ὁ ἐρχόμενος ἐν ὀνόματι κυρίου, "Blessed is the one who comes in the name of the Lord," will be quoted by Jesus against unbelieving Jerusalem in 23:39.

## Comment

**1** βηθφαγή (בֵּית פַּגֵּא, *bêṭ paggēʾ*, "house of unripe figs"), mentioned only here and in the synoptic parallels, is unknown, but it was apparently on τὸ ὄρος τῶν ἐλαιῶν, "the Mount of Olives," just overlooking Jerusalem and close to Bethany, with which it is linked in Mark 11:1; Luke 19:28. The village to which the two disciples were sent (v 2) was probably this Bethany. Zech 14:4 (a passage with messianic associations) speaks of Yahweh standing on the Mount of Olives in the time of eschatological fulfillment, and perhaps for this reason it is from the Mount of Olives that Jesus ascends to heaven and to that site that he will return when the eschaton is fully and finally to dawn (cf. Luke 24:50–51; Acts 1:11–12; Jos., *Ant.* 20.8.6 §169; *J.W.* 2.13.5 §§261–62).

**2–3** The instructions to the disciples assume the divine ordering of all that is now to happen (cf. 26:18). This conclusion is strengthened by εὐθέως, "immediately," as well as Matthew's future tense ἀποστελεῖ, "he will send." That is, the disciples will immediately find the two animals, and when they are challenged in taking them, their explanation will be accepted and their owner will send them εὐθύς, "immediately" (there is no difference in the meaning of the two words). This alteration of Mark so that Jesus is the subject of the verb strengthens the notion of divine control in the whole affair (contrast Mark 11:3). It may be that we are to infer that Jesus had earlier made arrangement for this loan of the animals (cf. Morris, who describes the words "the Lord has need of them" as a "prearranged password"), but in the narrative all is thus predetermined solely by ὁ κύριος αὐτῶν χρείαν ἔχει, "the Lord has need of them." As Matthew will point out in v 4, Jesus' instructions to the two disciples and the divine superintendence are designed to fulfill OT prophecy. Indeed, with the latter in view, Matthew refers in v 2 to two animals, ὄνον . . . καὶ πῶλον μετ᾽ αὐτῆς, "an ass and a colt with her," rather than Mark's single "colt" (see further *Comment* on v 7).

**4–5** The entry of Jesus into Jerusalem at this crucial juncture of his ministry is thus deliberately staged by Jesus so as to agree with and fulfill OT prophecy (for rabbinic background referring to the Messiah riding an ass and colt, cf. *Gen. Rab.* 98.9; *b. Sanh.* 98a–99a, *Koh. Rab.* 1.9; on Matthew's fulfillment formula quotations generally, see *Introduction*, in Hagner, *Matthew 1–13*, liii–lvii). τὸ ῥηθὲν διὰ τοῦ προφήτου, "what was spoken through the prophet," in this case points to Zech 9:9 (with the slight influence of Isa 62:11 on the form of the first line, either through conflation in memory or liturgical usage). The address τῇ θυγατρὶ Σιών, "to the daughter of Zion" (which in Zech 9:9 is parallel with θύγατερ Ἰερουσαλήμ, "daughter of Jerusalem"), means the inhabitants of the city of Jerusalem. εἴπατε τῇ θυγατρὶ Σιών is found verbatim in Isa 62:11, where the coming of ὁ σωτήρ, "the Savior," is announced in a passage similar to Zech 9:9. The remainder of the quotation is drawn verbatim from Zech 9:9, except for the omission of the LXX's words δίκαιος καὶ σῴζων αὐτός, lit. "just and saving is he" (although appropriate, the words are omitted perhaps to focus on the humility of Jesus), which follow the line "behold, your king comes to you," and the departure from the LXX's simpler ἐπὶ ὑποζύγιον καὶ πῶλον νέον, "upon an ass [i.e., a beast of burden; see W. Bauer; Michel's response shows that πῶλον was used for "ass"] and a new colt," for which Matthew has ἐπὶ ὄνον καὶ ἐπὶ πῶλον υἱὸν ὑποζυγίου, "upon an ass and upon a colt, the foal of an ass [a beast of burden]," which is closer in form to the Hebrew of Zech 9:9 (which unlike the LXX refers specifically to an "ass") than are our LXX manuscripts. It is clear that the prophecy of the arrival of the messianic king was that he would arrive in meekness (πραΰς, "meek"; cf. Jesus' application of this word to himself in 11:29), riding not the white stallion of a conqueror but in servant fashion riding the lowly and ordinary beast of burden, the ass, and thus bringing peace (cf. Zech 9:10) rather than war.

But was it one or two animals? It is commonly argued that Matthew, who alone among the evangelists speaks explicitly of two animals, has misunderstood the device of synonymous parallelism (e.g., McNeile, Grundmann, Gnilka, Meier, Beare), so common in the Hebrew Bible: the second phrase is the restatement, and perhaps refinement, of the first phrase, to be translated (if at all) with a preceding "even" (thus Zech 9:9 points to a single animal). It is very difficult, however, to believe that with the full Jewishness of Matthew's perspective he would have been ignorant of something as obvious as synonymous parallelism (so too K. Stendahl, *School of St. Matthew*, 119, 200). And it is almost impossible to argue that Matthew believed two animals were necessary, rather than the single animal of Mark, for the prophecy of Zechariah to be regarded as fulfilled. Although it is less natural to do so, it is possible to read both the Hebrew of Zech 9:9 and the Greek version of it given by Matthew as referring to two animals. That Matthew opts to understand Zechariah this way and goes out of his way to stress that there were two animals indicates that Matthew was particularly excited about a correspondence that presented itself. Clearly the key to the problem lies in the fact that an unbroken colt (note Mark 11:2, "upon which no one had sat," which is known to Matthew although omitted by him) was usually introduced into service while accompanied by its parent (on the inseparability of the two, see *m. B. Bat.* 5:3; on the importance of the Judah oracle [Gen 49:11] for the coming of the Messiah, see Blenkinsopp). And the tumult with which Jesus would enter Jerusalem would make such accompaniment all the more necessary (see Winterbotham). There is thus an *ipso facto* probability that historically two animals were involved in the entry of Jesus into Jerusalem. Matthew, either deducing this fact from general probability or possibly knowing from an eyewitness tradition that there were two animals (Gundry, *Matthew* [409], speaks of "a historical reminiscence"), maximizes the correspondence with a somewhat unnatural interpretation of Zechariah that finds reference to two animals. This is precisely the detailed kind of agreement, however, that would impress and delight the rabbinical taste and inclinations of both Matthew and his readers. Although Matthew is the only evangelist to quote Zech 9:9, it is clear that for all the Gospel writers there is special messianic significance in the manner in which Jesus chooses to enter Jerusalem. Zech. 9:9 is the deliberate frame of reference Jesus chooses to create by riding into the city on the foal of an ass. He comes as ὁ βασιλεύς, "the king," i.e., the messianic Son of David, yet as one who is πραΰς, "meek" (cf. 11:29–30), as a king indeed who will hang on a cross for his people (cf. 27:29, 37). Thus the entry is triumphant only in a paradoxical sense (cf. Visser 't Hooft).

**6–7** The report that the disciples went and did "just as" (καθώς) Jesus commanded them, returning with the two animals, enhances the fulfillment motif (v 4) and points to the divine sovereignty over the events of this last stage of Jesus' work. The animals, τὴν ὄνον καὶ τὸν πῶλον, "the ass and the colt," correspond exactly to the immediately preceding quotation of Zech 9:9, understood in Matthew's literal way (see *Comment* on preceding verses). The two animals of Matthew's account require the two plural pronouns αὐτῶν, "them," in v 7. The first clearly refers to the two animals—that is, the disciples put their outer garments over the backs of both the ass and its colt. In the second instance the αὐτῶν is ambiguous, although it probably refers again to the two animals (thus Grundmann, Gnilka) rather than to the garments upon which Jesus sat (in any case, the garments were put on both animals). If this is true, it hardly means that the evangelist alleges that Jesus actually sat upon both animals at once (!) or even in succession. Instead it means that here the two animals, which were kept so closely together, are conceptually regarded as a single, inseparable unit (which is probably also how Matthew understood the Zechariah quotation with its literally understood coming "upon" two animals; see Frenz), despite the plural language, which, as argued above, is kept by Matthew for the detailed coincidence with the OT quotation. Thus when Jesus sat upon "them," we are probably to understand simply that Jesus sat upon the colt with the ass just beside it. Clearly Matthew is pleased to note the detailed accord with the OT prophecy. (For an OT reference to Solomon, the new king, riding on a mule, cf. 1 Kgs 1:33.) For the significance of Zech 9:9 for the ministry of Jesus, see France, *Jesus and the Old Testament*, 105–6.

**8** The crowd, an exceptionally large one (the superlative πλεῖστος is used; cf. Mark 4:1), understanding something of the festivity of this royal entry into Jerusalem, joins in by carpeting Jesus' path, some with their clothes (for this practice at the recognition of a king, cf. 2 Kgs 9:13; for rabbinic background, *Yal. Exod.* 168; *b. Ketub.* 66b), others with cut branches (palm branches according to John 12:13; cf. 1 Macc 13:51; 2 Macc 10:7). Thus although the king rides into the city humbly upon the lowly colt of an ass, the crowds bring him into the city with a public demonstration befitting a king.

**9** The pilgrims preceding him and those following him (οἱ προάγοντες αὐτὸν καὶ οἱ ἀκολοθοῦντες) constitute a kind of royal procession, and their repeated cry (ἔκραζον, imperfect tense) proclaims Jesus as the messianic king. The repeated word "Hosanna" (ὡσαννά) represents a Greek transliteration of the Aramaic הֹושַׁע נָא (hôšaʿ nāʾ), which means literally "O save" (cf. the LXX, which rather than transliterating the word, translates it σῶσον δή, "save now"; see LXX Ps 117:25; cf. 2 Kgdms 14:4). The word became in common liturgical usage a cry of jubilation, and in the present passage it amounts to "God save" (on this connotation, see Pope) or more probably "praise be" to the messianic king (see Fitzmyer; cf. Luke's translation, δόξα, "glory," in Luke 19:38). To the first "Hosanna" is added the dative phrase τῷ υἱῷ Δαυίδ, resulting in the meaning "praise/glory be to the Son of David" (cf. 20:30–31), i.e., the Davidic king (cf. 2 Sam 7:12–16; on the title in Matthew, see *Comment* on 9:27). Children continue this cry in the temple area according to v 15. To the second "Hosanna" is added the phrase ἐν τοῖς ὑψίστοις, "in the highest," thus "praise/glory in the highest" (cf. Luke 2:14, 19:38). The word "Hosanna" is drawn from the Hebrew text of Ps 118:25, since the middle line εὐλογημένος ὁ ἐρχόμενος ἐν ὀνόματι κυρίου, "Blessed is the one who comes in the name of the Lord," is drawn verbatim from the LXX text of that same verse (i.e., Ps 117:25 LXX). In this Psalm, as in the crowds' acclamation here, there is a note of triumph and of eschatological salvation. This made the psalm, which was in the pilgrims' minds with the approaching Feast of Passover, appropriate for an application such as the present one. With the entry of the king into Jerusalem, eschatological salvation (conceived of in national-political terms) was about to be experienced (cf. *b. Pesaḥ.* 119a; *Midr. Ps.* 118.24 [242a]). Here the one "who comes in the name of the Lord" is not simply a pilgrim approaching the temple during a festival (as the language was normally used) but none other than that promised descendant of David who would bring the promised blessing of that kingdom. The same line is quoted verbatim again in 23:39 where, however, it refers to the proper eschatological coming of Jesus (for ὁ ἐρχόμενος, "the coming one," cf. 3:11; 11:3; John 1:15; 11:27; Acts 19:4). The enthusiastic shouting of the crowds would have been consistent with the nationalistic fervor of pilgrims having come to Jerusalem for a great festival.

**10–11** The impact of the arrival of Jesus in Jerusalem was great: according to Matthew "the whole city was shaken" (ἐσείσθη πᾶσα ἡ πόλις; the verb σείειν, "shake," is used figuratively again only in 28:4; cf. the whole of Jerusalem being "troubled" at the report of the birth of the messianic king in 2:3). The question τίς ἐστιν οὗτος, "who is this?" asks for an explanation of who it is that enters the city so audaciously, receiving and accepting the accompanying crowds' affirmation of him as the messianic king of the line of David. The crowds, probably to be distinguished from the crowds of the procession itself, supply that information in the repeated (ἔλεγον, imperfect, "were saying") "this is the prophet Jesus, the one from Nazareth of Galilee." Probably many in the crowds of pilgrims in Jerusalem for the festival of Passover had heard reports about this Jesus and his work in Galilee. The title "the prophet" (ὁ προφήτης) is probably only a title of great respect here (cf. v 46) rather than an evaluation of Jesus as *the* prophet in the absolute sense, i.e., the eschatological prophet of Deut 18:15 (cf. John 6:14; 7:40). Hence it is not simply "the prophet," or "the prophet to come," but rather "Jesus the prophet from Nazareth of Galilee." From Matthew's perspective this statement is informational rather than confessional. The crowds of the city thus do not appear ready to accept the hasty identification of Jesus as the messianic king, and their assessment of Jesus falls short of the full truth (cf. 16:14).

### Explanation

Jesus enters Jerusalem humbly, seated upon a lowly beast of burden, while being acclaimed the messianic king of the line of David and accepting this acclaim. The arrangements for the entry are made under divine superintendence and in fulfillment of prophecy. Yet in spite of this the crowds hardly understood the significance of this humble entry of Jesus into the capital. Their thoughts concerning the messianic king, the Son of David, were dominated by ideas of power, glory, the overthrow of the Roman authorities, and the establishment of a national-political kingdom. It was precisely for this reason that earlier Jesus tried to keep his messianic identity a secret (which was now no longer necessary). If the crowds' identification of Jesus as the Davidic king was correct, they missed the paradoxical character of that kingship. The irony was that the king, who really was the promised Messiah, came to Jerusalem not as a warrior upon a stallion but humbly as a servant—indeed, as the servant who had come to die. The goal was a more fundamental salvation and a kingdom that was universal in scope, one that far transcended the limited horizon of the crowds.

# *The Son of David in the Temple*   *(21:12–17)*

## *Bibliography*

**Barrett, C. K.** "The House of Prayer and the Den of Thieves." In *Jesus und Paulus*. FS W. G. Kümmel, ed. E. E. Ellis and E. Grässer. Göttingen: Vandenhoeck & Ruprecht, 1975. 13–20. **Bauckham, R. J.** "Jesus' Demonstration in the Temple." In *Law and Religion: Essays on the Place of the Law in Israel and Early Christianity*, ed. B. Lindars. Cambridge: Clarke, 1988. 72–89, 171–76. **Braun, F.-M.** "L'expulsion des vendeurs du Temple." *RB* 38 (1929) 178–200. **Buchanan, G. W.** "Symbolic Money-Changers in the Temple?" *NTS* 37 (1991) 280–90. **Burkitt, F. C.** "The Cleansing of the Temple: Mt 21.12–17." *JTS* 25 (1923) 386–90. **Buse, I.** "The Cleansing of the Temple in the Synoptics and in John." *ExpTim* 70 (1958–59) 22–24. **Caldecott, A.** "The Significance of the Cleansing of the Temple." *JTS* 24 (1923) 382–86. **Carmichael, J.** "Jésus-Christ et le Temple." *NRF* 12 (1964) 276–95. **Cooke, F. A.** "The Cleansing of the Temple." *ExpTim* 63 (1951–52) 321–22. **Derrett, J. D. M.** "The Zeal of the House and the Cleansing of the Temple." *DR* 95 (1977) 79–94. **Doeve, J. W.** "Purification du temple et desséchement du figuier: Sur la structure du 21ème chapitre de Matthieu et parallèles (Marc xi.1–xii.12, Luc xix.28–xx.19)." *NTS* 1 (1954–55) 297–308. **Dupont, J.** "L'entrée messianique de Jésus à Jérusalem (Mt 21, 1–17)." *AsSeign* 37 (1965) 46–62. **Eppstein, V.** "The Historicity of the Gospel Account of the Cleansing of the Temple." *ZNW* 55 (1964) 42–58. **Evans, C. A.** "Jesus' Action in the Temple: Cleansing or Portent of Destruction?" *CBQ* 51 (1989) 237–70. **Hamilton, N. Q.** "Temple Cleansing and Temple Bank." *JBL* 83 (1964) 365–72. **Harvey, A. E.** "Jesus the Christ: The Options in a Name." In *Jesus and the Constraints of History*. London: Duckworth, 1982. 120–51. **Hiers, R. H.** "Purification of the Temple: Preparation for the Kingdom of God." *JBL* 90 (1971) 82–90. **Hooker, M. D.** "Traditions about the Temple in the Sayings of Jesus." *BJRL* 70 (1988) 7–19. **Jeremias, J.** "Zwei Miszellen: 1. Antik-jüdische Münzdeutung; 2. Zur Geschichtlichkeit der Tempelreinigung." *NTS* 23 (1976–77) 177–80. **Kallemeyn, H.** "Un Jésus intolérant? (Matthieu 21:12–17)." *RRéf* 43 (1992) 85–91. **Lohmeyer, E.** "Die Reinigung des Tempels." *TBl* 20 (1941) 257–64. **Losie, L. A.** "The Cleansing of the Temple: A History of a Gospel Tradition in Light of Its Background in the Old Testament and in Early Judaism." Diss., Fuller Theological Seminary, 1984. **Manson, T. W.** "The Cleansing of the Temple." *BJRL* 33 (1950–51) 271–82. **Mendner, S.** "Die Tempelreinigung." *ZNW* 47 (1956) 93–112.

**Neusner, J.** "Money-Changers in the Temple: The Mishnah's Explanation." *NTS* 35 (1989) 287–90. **Richardson, P.** "Why Turn the Tables? Jesus' Protest in the Temple Precincts." In *SBL 1992 Seminar Papers*, ed. E. H. Lovering, Jr. Atlanta: Scholars, 1992. 507–23. **Roth, C.** "The Cleansing of the Temple and Zechariah xiv. 21." *NovT* 4 (1960) 174–81. **Schnider, F.,** and **Stenger, W.** "Die Tempelreinigung." In *Johannes und die Synoptiker*. Münster: Kösel, 1971. 26–53. **Schweizer, E.** "Matthäus 21, 14–17." In *Matthäus und seine Gemeinde*. Stuttgart: Katholisches Bibelwerk, 1974. 132–37. **Söding, T.** "Die Tempelaktion Jesu: Redaktionskritik— Überlieferungseschichte—historische Rückfrage (Mk 11,15–19; Mt 21,12–17; Lk 19,45–48; Joh 2,13–22)." *TTZ* 101 (1992) 36–64. **Spiegel, E.** "War Jesus gewalttätig? Bemerkungen zur Tempelreinigung." *TGl* 75 (1985) 239–47. **Trautmann, M.** *Zeichenhafte Handlungen Jesu: Ein Beitrag zur Frage nach dem geschichtlichen Jesus*. FB 37. Würzburg: Echter, 1980. 96–103. **Trilling, W.** "Der Einzug in Jerusalem." In *Neutestamentliche Aufsätze*. FS J. Schmid, ed. J. Blinzler et al. Regensburg: Pustet, 1963. 303–9. **Trocmé, É.** "L'expulsion des marchands du Temple." *NTS* 15 (1968–69) 1–22. **Wagner, G.** "The Cleansing of the Temple." In *Survey Bulletin*. Rüschlikon: Baptist Theological Seminary, 1967. 30–42. **Watty, W. W.** "Jesus and the Temple— Cleansing or Cursing?" *ExpTim* 93 (1982) 235–39.

## Translation

[12]*And Jesus came into the temple,*[a] *and he threw out all those who were selling and buying in the temple, and he overturned the tables of the money changers and the chairs of those selling pigeons,* [13]*and he said to them: "It is written:*

*My house shall be called a house of prayer,*
*But you are making*[b] *it a den of thieves."*

[14]*And the blind and the lame came to him in the temple, and he healed them.* [15]*But when the chief priests and the scribes saw the wonders he performed and heard*[c] *the children who were crying out in the temple and saying: "Hosanna to the Son of David," they were indignant* [16]*and said to him: "Do you hear what these children*[d] *are saying?" And Jesus said to them: "Yes. Have you never read that:*[e]

*'From the mouth of babes and those who suckle I will bring forth praise'?"*

[17]*And when he left them he went outside of the city to Bethany, and he spent the night there.*

## Notes

[a] Many MSS (C D W *f*[1] TR lat sy) add τοῦ θεοῦ, "of God," an insertion that emphasizes the sanctity of the temple and thus the appropriateness of Jesus' response to the pecuniary activities there. Cf. Metzger in *TCGNT*, 54–55, who calls it "a natural expansion."

[b] Many MSS (C D W *f*[13] TR) have ἐποιήσατε, "you made," and others (*f*[1]) have πεποιήκατε, "you have made," through the influence of the parallels Luke 19:46 and Mark 11:17, respectively.

[c] "Heard" is added to the translation.

[d] "Children" is added to the translation.

[e] ὅτι, "that," is omitted by ℵ D it.

## Form/Structure/Setting

A. The first thing Jesus does in Jerusalem is to go to the temple, not as a pilgrim to worship but as the messianic king to purge it of practices that mocked its divinely intended purpose. Jesus also heals in the temple, and he again accepts the designation "Son of David." This pericope points inescapably to the authority of Jesus (cf. the raising of this issue in v 23) and to the eschatological significance of his mission with its consequences for the temple itself (cf. 24:2).

B. For the first half of this pericope, the cleansing of the temple, Matthew depends on Mark 11:15–17 (cf. Luke 19:45–46; the Johannine counterpart, John 2:13–16, while it contains similarities to the synoptic narratives, is also distinctive). Matthew moves this narrative forward chronologically, putting it before the cursing of the fig tree (vv 18–19) rather than sandwiching it between the cursing of the fig tree and its withering as in Mark. And whereas Mark explicitly puts the cleansing on the day after the entry (Mark 11:11, 12, 15), Matthew implies that it took place immediately after the entry. The second half of the pericope (vv 14–17) is unique to Matthew (but with v 17, cf. Mark 11:11b). In the material dependent upon Mark, Matthew makes two significant omissions: he omits Mark 11:16, "and he would not allow anyone to carry anything through the temple" (a typical Matthean abridgment of what is regarded as unnecessary to the pericope), and in the citation of Isa 56:7 he omits (with Luke 19:46) the words πᾶσιν τοῖς ἔθνεσιν, "for all the Gentiles" (see *Comment* on v 13). Other changes to be noted are: Matthew's addition of πάντας, "all," before τοὺς πωλοῦντας, "those selling" (v 12; cf. Mark 11:15), and the omission of οὐ, "not," before γέγραπται, "it is written," thus altering Mark's question into a more forceful statement (v 13; cf. Mark 11:17) and allowing for the question in v 16. Apart from a few additional minor changes, Matthew follows Mark closely, often verbatim, in these verses.

C. The pericope blends several types of material together under the common theme of things that take place "in the temple." Thus the pericope begins with prophetic or sign-bearing deeds performed by Jesus (vv 12–13), refers to healings of the blind and lame (v 14), continues with a controversy between the Jewish authorities and Jesus (vv 15–16), and concludes with a narrative note (v 17). As an outline of the passage, the following may be recommended: (1) casting out the merchants from the temple (v 12); (2) their violation of the purpose of the temple (v 13); (3) Jesus' healing of the blind and lame in the temple (v 14); (4) the indignation of the Jewish authorities, further divided into (a) the claim concerning the Son of David (v 15), (b) the offense caused by the cry of the children (v 16a), and (c) Jesus' appeal to scripture (16b–c); and (5) the return to Bethany (v 17). Following the introductory phrase εἰς τὸ ἱερόν, "into the temple" (v 12), the passage is unified by the threefold occurrence of the phrase ἐν τῷ ἱερῷ, "in the temple" (vv 12, 14, 15). The passage is further marked structurally by syntactical pairs: πωλοῦντας, "sellers," and ἀγοράζοντας, "buyers"; τραπέζας, "tables," and καθέδρας, "chairs"; τῶν κολλυβιστῶν, "of the money changers," and τῶν πωλούντων, "of the sellers"; τυφλοί, "blind," and χωλοί, "lame"; and ἀρχιερεῖς, "chief priests," and γραμματεῖς, "scribes." A notable contrast between οἶκος προσευχῆς, "house of prayer," and σπήλαιον λῃστῶν, "den of thieves," occurs in v 13. The ἐξῆλθεν, "he went out," of v 17 matches the εἰσῆλθεν, "he came in," of v 12. Matthew's literary artistry is again evident in his presentation of this pericope.

D. It is possible that Matthew's unique reference in vv 15–16 to the crying out of the children is related to the mention of the stones crying out in the parallel in Luke 19:39–40. The underlying similarity of the Aramaic (אבניא, ʾabnayyāʾ, "stones," and בניא, bĕnayyāʾ, "sons," respectively) may point to a common original, which was then read in two different ways. Yet, in fact, the stones do not cry out in Luke as do the children in Matthew. For an actual play on the two words, see 3:9 (cf. the quotation of Ps 118:22–23 in 21:42 and the appendix on the wordplay in K. Snodgrass, *The Parable of the Wicked Tenants*, 113–18).

E. The positioning of the cleansing of the temple at the beginning of the ministry of Jesus according to the Gospel of John (John 2:13–17) almost certainly results from that evangelist's concern to emphasize Jesus' break with Judaism from the outset of the Gospel. The differences between the Johannine and synoptic accounts hardly need point to two separate occurrences. It is highly unlikely that such a dramatic event occurred twice. And given the obvious freedom of the evangelists to order their materials and shape them in keeping with their purposes, it is also unnecessary to conclude that there were two separate cleansings of the temple.

*Comment*

**12** Matthew's juxtaposition of this pericope with the triumphal entry of Jesus into the city has the effect of emphasizing the identity of the one who now enters the temple: it is the messianic king, the Son of David (cf. v 15, which repeats the cry of the crowds in v 9). He enters the temple in a confrontational mood, and his initial actions must have been perceived as the beginning of the literal revolution he was expected to bring (cf. *Pss. Sol.* 17:30 for the expectation that the coming Son of David would, in connection with the setting up of his kingdom, "cleanse Jerusalem"; cf. Mal 3:1–5; see Hiers). In the temple precincts, and especially during the major festivals, provision was made for pilgrims to purchase animals and birds (cf. Luke 2:24) for sacrifice. Money changers exchanged Roman currency for Tyrian coins (the tetradrachma equaled the shekel), which alone could actually be used in making offerings or paying the temple tax (cf. 17:24–27). Jesus was not against these practices in principle, which were necessary for the functioning of the sacred cultus, but only the stationing of them in the temple area, probably in the court of the Gentiles (there is evidence that animals for the sacrifices were also available for purchase at special facilities on the Mount of Olives). No comment is made on the fairness of prices or rates of exchange, which are again not Jesus' concern (but v 13b suggests that profit was certainly a motivating factor for the merchants; for evidence of inflated prices charged for birds, see *m. Ker.* 1.7; cf. *b. Pesaḥ.* 57a; *y. Ḥag.* 2.3). The issue simply concerns the turning of the temple precincts into a place of business. Thus ἀγοράζοντας, "buyers," as well as πωλοῦντας, "sellers," are thrown out of the temple. Jesus turns over the "tables" (τραπέζας) of the "money changers" (κολλυβιστῶν, in Matthew only here and in the NT only in the gospel parallels) and the "chairs" (καθέδρας) of those selling birds, yet we are not here to think of Jesus as violent (see Spiegel). Jesus meant the action as an eschatological sign rather than a practical reform of the objectionable practices (cf. references given above and in a clearly eschatological context Zech 14:21: "And there shall no longer be a trader in the house of the Lord of hosts on that day"; cf. Roth). An era has come wherein the temple has necessarily lost importance (cf. 12:6; see too Schnider and Stenger; Caldecott), yet the messianic king cannot countenance proceedings within the temple precincts that violate its divinely intended purpose.

**13** Jesus bases his concrete opposition to the mercantile activities in the temple upon the definition of the essential meaning of the temple given by the prophet

Isaiah: ὁ οἶκός μου οἶκος προσευχῆς κληθήσεται, "my house shall be called a house of prayer." For Jesus' use of the introductory formula γέγραπται, "it is written," see *Comment* on 4:4. This quotation, which otherwise agrees verbatim with the LXX of Isa 56:7, omits the final three words πᾶσιν τοῖς ἔθνεσιν, "for all the Gentiles" (cf. Mark 11:17). Matthew deletes these words from his Markan source probably because he sees no continuing or eschatological significance of the temple for the Gentiles. The temple, after all, is soon to come to an end (cf. 24:2), and the hope of the Gentiles is centered on the kingdom brought by Jesus (cf. v 43; 24:14; 28:19). Moreover, this gentile hope is not to be realized until after the resurrection. The temple was meant to be a place of prayer, of communion with God, but instead it had become a place where people were distracted with the transaction of business. "You" (ὑμεῖς, emphatic), argues Jesus, "are making" (ποιεῖτε) it by contrast a σπήλαιον λῃστῶν, "den of thieves," a phrase drawn verbatim from the LXX of Jer 7:11 (where it is also applied to God's house, the temple, and in a context of judgment upon the temple). The point does not concern the impropriety of the sacrifices (defended by Isa 56:7, just prior to the quoted words) or profiteering by the temple businessmen, despite the fact that they probably *were* profiteers, or the corruption of the priesthood but the failure to understand the fundamental significance of the temple. (For the temple as God's "house," cf. Isa 60:7.) Jesus' critique resembles that given by the prophets: i.e., the mechanics of the temple ritual were allowed to obscure the point of authentic communion with God (e.g., Jer 7:21–23; Amos 5:21–24; Mic 6:6–8). Consequently, the temple cleansing is followed by the cursing of the fig tree, which dramatically symbolizes judgment upon Israel for her failure (vv 18–19). Thus the Son of David's clearing of the temple symbolizes a broader failure of Israel to realize God's purposes and will. It is not in itself a portent of the temple's destruction (*pace* Hooker; Watty; rightly Evans). Since λῃστής can also mean "insurrectionist" (as it does in 26:55, and possibly in 27:38, 44), it may be that Jesus' criticism focuses on the making of the temple into a "nationalist stronghold" (see Barrett; for political associations, cf. Hamilton).

**14** Matthew's record of Jesus' healings in the temple (the only such mention of Jesus' healings in Jerusalem in the Synoptics) underlines his identity as the Son of David (cf. 20:30–31, where the blind men appeal to Jesus with just this title; 11:5, where the healing of "blind" and "lame" points to Jesus' messianic identity; 15:31). The τυφλοὶ καὶ χωλοί, "blind and lame," whose access to the temple was severely restricted, probably to the court of the Gentiles (cf. Lev 21:18–19; 2 Sam 5:8; and for other Jewish background, 1 QSa 2:5–22, CD 15:15–17, and *m. Hag.* 1:1), having apparently heard of Jesus' presence in the temple, seek him out (προσῆλθον, "came to"; see *Comment* on 5:1), and ἐθεράπευσεν αὐτούς, "he healed them." The Messiah thus manifests the blessings of the kingdom precisely in the precincts of the temple (see Trautmann), which is thereby transformed from a commercial center to a place of healing (one cannot but think of Matthew's earlier citation of Hos 6:6 [Matt 9:13; 12:7]).

**15** Matthew now records the reaction of the Jewish authorities, specifically οἱ ἀρχιερεῖς καὶ οἱ γραμματεῖς, "the chief priests and the scribes" (the same groups are mentioned together in 2:4). They had seen the θαυμάσια, "wonders" (the only occurrence of the word in the NT) performed by Jesus. Despite these remarkable healings, however, they were unwilling to draw the appropriate conclusion concerning Jesus' messianic identity. In this connection Matthew mentions a new element. Children had apparently gathered near Jesus and were, apparently in all good fun, mimicking the chant they had earlier heard (they may already have known the words from the Hallel, which was taught to children; *t. Soṭa* 6.2–3) their elders direct to Jesus (see *Comment* on v 9): ὡσαννὰ τῷ υἱῷ Δαυίδ, "Hosanna to the Son of David." The chief priests and the scribes seemed particularly bothered by this: ἠγανάκτησαν, "they were indignant" (the word occurs elsewhere in Matthew in 20:24 and 26:8).

**16** Their question to Jesus already implies that Jesus too should have been upset at this cry of the children and that he should have stopped them or at least have somehow dissociated himself from the designation. The presumption of the Jewish authorities throughout is that any claim of Jesus to the title could have no truth. They were undoubtedly shocked and further offended when Jesus acknowledged hearing the children with his ναί, "yes," and was prepared to accept the very designation they chanted. Although the children had little, if any, understanding of the meaning of their chant, they were saying the truth. Thus Jesus asks (the words οὐδέποτε ἀνέγνωτε, "have you never read?" are found verbatim in Mark 2:25) whether the chief priests and scribes had not read the scripture that says "From the mouth of babes and those who suckle I will bring forth praise." Matthew's Greek agrees exactly with that of the LXX of Ps 8:3. The LXX continues with ἕνεκα τῶν ἐχθρῶν σου, "for the sake of your enemies," which words, if in Jesus' mind, would have made the text all the more relevant to the situation. In place of "praise," the Hebrew text has עֹז, *ʿoz*, "strength," so that the argument appears to depend on the LXX and go back to Matthew rather than to Jesus. But as France (*Jesus and the Old Testament*, 251–52) has shown, the Hebrew text of Ps 8:3 could be understood as an ascription of praise ("strength to the Lord"; cf. Pss 29:1; 59:16[MT 59:17]; 68:35[MT 68:34]; 96:7), and thus the LXX may represent a valid interpretation of the Hebrew original. Unknowingly, the children utter the truth of God (cf. the revelation of divine truth to νήπιοι, "babes," in 11:25, where, however, the subject is the childlikeness of the disciples of Jesus). As the infants referred to in Ps 8:3 spontaneously utter the praise of God's creation, so these children give appropriate praise to the Son of David.

**17** Matthew records at this point a seemingly abrupt departure (perhaps itself implying a note of condemnation) from the Jewish authorities and from the city itself. It was not yet time for the more escalated confrontation concerning what authority Jesus claimed, as in vv 23–27 (cf. vv 45–46) or narratives to follow (cf. 22:15–46; 26:3–5). For the moment Jesus returns to Bethany (modern El Aziriyeh, a mile and a half away, on the Mount of Olives) where, Matthew reports, he "spent the night" (ηὐλίσθη; cf. the only other occurrence of the word in the parallel of Luke 21:37). The crowds of the festival necessitated that, like Jesus, many pilgrims find lodging outside the city.

*Explanation*

When the Son of David, the messianic king, comes to Jerusalem, he goes directly to the temple, the physical center of the Jewish faith. There he performs a symbolic act in clearing the temple of mercantile activity by which he points to his own authority and identity as well as to a symptom of the failure of Judaism. In the temple, furthermore, he heals the blind and the lame, thereby pointing to the real presence of the messianic kingdom in and through his ministry, the rule of God wherein the unhindered communion between God and humanity—the very thing the temple had symbolized—alone is realized. He finally allows himself to be proclaimed Son of David and accepts the affirmation as he had in the entry into the city. One "greater than the temple" is here (12:6). The Messiah is thus among his people in judgment and in healing. The truth of Jesus' identity can be made public; the claim will not be widely received but instead will bring Jesus to the cross.

# *The Cursing of the Fig Tree* (21:18–22)

## Bibliography

**Bartsch, H.-W.** "Die 'Verfluchung' des Feigenbaums." *ZNW* 53 (1962) 256–60. **Duplacy, J.** "La foi qui déplace les montagnes." In *À la recontre de Dieu.* FS A. Gelin. Le Puy: X. Mappus, 1961. 273–81. **Ellul, D.** "Dérives autour d'un figuier: Matthieu 21,18–22." *FV* 91 (1992) 69–76. **Giesen, H.** "Der verdorrte Feigenbaum—Eine symbolische Aussage? Zu Mk 11.12– 14.20f." *BZ* 20 (1976) 95–114. **Hahn, F.** "Jesu Wort vom bergeversetzenden Glauben." *ZNW* 76 (1985) 149–69. **Kahn, J. G.** "La parabole du figuier stérile et les arbres récalcitrants de la Genèse." *NovT* 13 (1971) 38–45. **Münderlein, G.** "Die Verfluchung des Feigenbaumes." *NTS* 10 (1963) 89–104. **Schwarz, G.** "Jesus und der Feigenbaum am Wege (Mk 11,12–14, 20–25/Mt 21,18–22)." *BibNot* 61 (1992) 36–37. **Telford, W. R.** *The Barren Temple and the Withered Fig Tree.* JSNTSup 1. Sheffield: JSOT, 1980.

## Translation

[18]*Early in the morning as he was returning to the city, he became hungry.* [19]*And seeing one fig tree beside the road, he came up to it and found nothing on it except only leaves, and he said to it: "May no fruit ever come* [a] *from you again." And the fig tree withered immediately.*

[20]*And when the disciples saw this,* [b] *they marveled, saying: "How did the fig tree suddenly wither?"* [21]*And Jesus said to them: "Truly I tell you, if you have faith and do not doubt, you will do not only this marvel of the withered fig tree,* [c] *but also if you say to this mountain, 'Be raised up and cast into the sea,' it will happen.* [22]*And everything, whatever you ask in prayer, believing, you will receive."*

## Notes

[a] B L begin the sentence with the negative *oú*, "not" or "no," thus emphasizing the negation.
[b] "This" added in translation.
[c] The translation expands *τὸ τῆς συκῆς*, lit. "the of the fig tree."

## Form/Structure/Setting

A. In its context immediately following the cleansing of the temple, the withering of the fig tree serves as an enacted parable of judgment upon unfruitful

Israel. Only when understood as an anticipation of the destruction of the temple (24:2, 15) and the end of national Israel (cf. 23:38) does the miracle make sense. The second part of the pericope (vv 20–22), on the other hand, stands out in the narrative as a parenthetical diversion, as it also does in Mark, but here presents a theme already handled earlier in the Gospel (e.g., 7:7–11; 17:20).

B. Matthew depends on Mark (Mark 11:12–14, 20–24) for this pericope, but by having extracted the account of the clearing of the temple (Mark 11:15–17; Matthew omits Mark 11:18–19; 11:25 altogether) and placing it just prior to this pericope, he is able to put the cursing of the fig tree together with its withering and the discussion that follows. Although the dependence on Mark is clear, Matthew takes considerable freedom with Mark's wording. The more important changes are: in v 18 Matthew adds πρωΐ, "early" (but cf. Mark 11:20), and ἐπανάγων εἰς τὴν πόλιν, "returning to the city" (cf. Mark 11:12); in v 19 (cf. Mark 11:13) Matthew refers to "one" (μίαν) fig tree ἐπὶ τῆς ὁδοῦ, "beside the road," in place of Mark's ἀπὸ μακρόθεν, "(seeing) from a distance," and omits Mark's description of the tree as "having leaves," the clause "if perhaps he might find something on it" (both omissions being probably simply abbreviation), and the sentence "for it was not the season of figs" (omitted perhaps as not only misleading but as an unnecessary complication, irrelevant to Jesus' prophetic action); Matthew adds μόνον, "only," after "leaves" to stress the point of unfruitfulness; further in v 19 (cf. Mark 11:14), Matthew omits Mark's redundant ἀποκριθείς, "answering," restates the curse of the fig tree (and sharpens it by replacing Mark's optative φάγοι, "may [not] eat," expressing a wish, with the strong prohibitive subjunctive γένηται, "[not] be"), and omits Mark's reference to the disciples hearing Jesus (which is no longer needed, given the immediate withering of the tree in Matthew). Also in v 19, Matthew's καὶ ἐξηράνθη παραχρῆμα ἡ συκῆ, "and suddenly the tree withered," is, of course, unique to Matthew (cf. Mark 11:20). In v 20 Matthew can accordingly have οἱ μαθηταὶ ἐθαύμασαν, "the disciples marveled," in place of Mark's "and Peter remembered" (Mark 11:21). Matthew omits Mark's ῥαββί, "Rabbi," with which Peter addresses Jesus, as well as changing the comment "Look, the tree which you cursed has withered" (Mark 11:21) to the question πῶς παραχρῆμα ἐξηράνθη ἡ συκῆ, "How did the fig tree suddenly wither?" V 21 involves free rewriting of Mark 11:23, with the same emphasis on faith without doubt. Most notably, Matthew omits Mark's ἔχετε πίστιν θεοῦ, "Have faith in God" (Mark 11:22). Matthew's οὐ μόνον τὸ τῆς συκῆς ποιήσετε, "not only will you do the [cursing] of the fig tree," is an addition to the Markan material. Finally, in v 22 Matthew makes minor changes of Mark 11:24: the omission of διὰ τοῦτο λέγω ὑμῖν, "on account of this I say to you," the omission of the object of πιστεύοντες, "believing," i.e., ὅτι ἐλάβετε, "that you will receive," and the alteration of Mark's ἔσται ὑμῖν, "it will be to you," to Matthew's favorite λήμψεσθε, "you will receive." Mark 11:25 (and 26) is omitted since this material has already been used in the Sermon on the Mount (6:14–15; cf. 5:23–24).

In the second part of Matthew's pericope, v 22 finds Johannine parallels in John 14:13–14; 15:7; 16:23. The reference to the moving of mountains finds a parallel earlier in Matthew, i.e., 17:20. This is the only material that finds a parallel in Luke (Luke 17:6), although the parable of the unfruitful fig tree, Luke 13:6–9, bears a striking similarity to the present pericope.

C. The pericope consists of two main parts: the prophetic sign of the cursing and withering of the fig tree and the discussion about the power of faith that follows. The material of the first part bears no relation to the second part except in providing the occasion for the disciples' question and the subsequent teaching about faith. The disciples are not interested in the meaning of what Jesus has done but in the mechanics of how he did it (cf. the question of v 20). The result is that the prophetic sign receives no comment (except indirectly from the preceding context; in Mark, where the withering is separated from the cursing by the clearing of the temple narrative, the problem is reduced considerably). The pericope may be outlined as follows: (1) Jesus' hunger (v 18), (2) the curse and withering of the fig tree (v 19), (3) the disciples' question (v 20), (4) the lesson concerning faith (v 21), and (5) the general promise to the prayer of faith (v 22). Such parallelism as there is in the pericope is limited to v 21, where one may mention ἄρθητι, "be raised up," and βλήθητι, "be cast," and the parallel subjunctives governed by ἐάν, "if": ἔχητε πίστιν, "have faith," and μὴ διακριθῆτε, "do not doubt."

## Comment

**18** After spending the night in Bethany (cf. v 17), Jesus "returns" (ἐπανάγων; the only occurrence in Matthew) to Jerusalem early in the morning of the next day (cf. Mark 11:20 for πρωΐ, "early"; Mark's chronology, however, differs from that of Matthew). The reference to Jesus becoming hungry provides the occasion for Jesus' approach to the fig tree (πεινᾶν, "hunger," is used in reference to Jesus elsewhere in Matthew only in 4:2; cf. too 25:34–46).

**19** Jesus came up to the fig tree along the side of the road in the hope of finding figs to eat. But he found no fruit on the tree despite the presence of leaves, which ordinarily come after the fruit and thus should have indicated the presence of fruit (at least in an early, yet still edible form; i.e., the fruit-bud known to modern Palestinian Arabs as *taqsh*). Jesus found φύλλα [the word occurs again in 24:32] μόνον, "only leaves." The surprising curse (note esp. εἰς τὸν αἰῶνα, "forever," with the connotation of final judgment), its harshness, and the immediate withering of the tree disclose that what occurs here is a prophetic sign that points beyond itself to a far more grievous kind of barrenness. In an earlier situation where Jesus was hungry (4:2–4), he refused to make use of his power to perform miracles; so too the present miracle has nothing to do with Jesus' hunger and frustration. The tree in effect is judged for its barrenness, with the result that it "immediately" (παραχρῆμα occurs in Matthew only here and in the following verse) shrivels up and dies. For the seriousness of the lack of καρπός, "fruit," see 3:10; 7:19; and the parables of eschatological judgment that follow later in this and the next chapter, which provide the key to understanding the application of this prophetic act to Israel (see esp. v 43; 22:3; and the whole of chap. 23). Matthew's redaction of Mark thus does not avoid the judgment symbolism in favor of lessons on prayer and faith (*pace* Telford). The prophetic sign in effect curses Israel (*pace* Carson, who finds only hypocrisy cursed), which despite outward indications (cf. the leaves of the fig tree) was nevertheless without fruit. The withering of the fig tree is thus an apocalyptic word of judgment (Bartsch) that will find its analogue in the future destruction of Jerusalem and its temple (rightly, Hill, Münderlein, Gnilka, Blomberg; cf. 24:2–28). Luke's parable of the fig tree (Luke 13:6–9) makes, in its way, the same point as the present enacted parable. For the unfruitful fig tree as a symbol for Israel, see esp. Jer 8:13; Mic 7:1 (cf. Isa 5:1–7; Hos 9:10, 16).

**20** The disciples are so "amazed" (ἐθαύμασαν; see *Comment* on 8:27) at the immediate withering of the fig tree that they apparently ignore the meaning of what Jesus has done. Their somewhat irrelevant question concerning how Jesus had made the tree wither so suddenly is nevertheless honored by Jesus and the evangelist. And thus we move from the barrenness of Israel to the faith with which the disciples will be kept from being powerless and hence themselves also barren. There is no need to relate these verses directly to the subject of the preceding verses so that the prayer of faith must concern the judgment of Israel (as H. van der Loos wrongly argues [*The Miracles of Jesus*, 695]).

**21** Jesus responds to the disciples' question with a short discourse on the importance of faith. In a statement made emphatic by the introductory ἀμὴν λέγω ὑμῖν, "Truly I say to you," and by the double statement ἐὰν ἔχητε πίστιν καὶ μὴ διακριθῆτε, "if you have faith and do not doubt" (the same combination, using the same words, is found in Rom 4:20 and Jas 1:6), Jesus indicates that the disciples can do what is otherwise impossible. The allusion to casting "this mountain" (a stereotyped expression, not the Mount of Olives) into the sea, as in the earlier use of the metaphor in 17:20 (cf. Paul's use of it in 1 Cor 13:2; *Gos. Thom.* 48 may be a related logion), points to the hyperbolic character of what is being said, including the reference to repeating the miracle of causing the tree to wither. For a mixing of the two metaphors, i.e., the uprooting and the planting of a sycamine tree in the sea, cf. Luke 17:6. (Telford's suggestion that in the parallel passage in Mark the mountain is symbolic of the temple and its imminent doom is unconvincing.)

**22** This statement at once generalizes and limits the point being made. The πάντα ὅσα, lit. "everything whatever," is limited by the words that follow: ἂν αἰτήσητε ἐν τῇ προσευχῇ, "you ask in prayer" (the last word may serve as a link to v 13 and the narrative of the clearing of the temple). The effect of this is to limit the granting of requests to the will of God (cf. the limitations of ἐν τῷ ὀνόματί μου, "in my name" [John 14:13–14; 16:23], and of mutual indwelling [John 15:7] in the Johannine parallels). Jesus does not offer his disciples magical power to do whatever they please or to perform extraordinary feats for their own sake, such as the withering of a fig tree. All must be related to the purpose of God that is in the process of being realized. The present participle πιστεύοντες, "believing," reaffirms the stress on faith (see Hahn) in the preceding verse. This verse repeats and reaffirms the similar teaching in 6:8; 7:7–11; 18:19, where limitations are also built into the passages. It is unlikely that the limitation here regards requests that have to do with the replacement of the temple cult (as Blomberg contends).

*Explanation*

The two apparently unrelated main points of this pericope, the acted-out parable of judgment against unfruitful Israel and the power of prayer to those who believe, may have been kept together in the tradition because the latter was understood in terms of the possibility of fruitfulness for the disciples (in contrast to

Israel). Whether or not this is true, it is clear that vv 21–22, any more than their earlier Matthean parallels, do not offer the disciples or the Christians of Matthew's church (or of the modern church) the promise that if only they will believe they will be able to do anything they want, perform any miracle, or astound the world with wonders or even miracles that make good sense (in terms of human need). The wonderful promise of vv 21–22 points instead to the miraculous power available to the disciples to fulfill their calling, that is, in the living of the Christian life in fruitful discipleship. In short, where the apparently unlimited character of the promise is stressed, where the language is taken in all seriousness, it is especially important to condition the promise in terms of what God will universally provide to those who ask. The miraculous character of *such* provision and answered prayer, however, should not be underestimated. The promise thus concerns the experience of eschatological life in anticipation and foretaste of the eschaton proper.

# *The Question about Jesus' Authority (21:23–27)*

### Bibliography

**Kim, S.** "Die Vollmacht Jesu und der Tempel (Markus 11/12): Der Sinn der 'Tempelreinigung' und der geschichtliche und theologische Zusammenhang des Prozesses Jesu." *ANRW* 2.26.1. Forthcoming. **Kremer, J.** "Jesu Antwort auf die Frage nach seiner Vollmacht: Eine Auslegung von Mk 11, 27–33." *BibLeb* 9 (1968) 128–36. **Shae, G. S.** "The Question on the Authority of Jesus." *NovT* 16 (1974) 1–29.

### Translation

[23]*And when he had come into the temple, the chief priests and the elders of the people came to him while he was teaching and said: "By what authority are you doing these things? And who gave this authority to you?"* [24]*Jesus answered and said to them: "I will also ask you concerning one matter, which if you tell me, I too will tell you by what authority I do these things.* [25]*From whence came the baptism practiced by John? From heaven or from human beings?" And they began reasoning among themselves, saying: "If we say 'from heaven,' he will say to us, 'Why therefore did you not believe him?'* [26]*But if we say 'from human beings,' we must*[a] *fear the crowd, for everyone regards John as a prophet."* [27]*And they answered Jesus and said: "We do not know." He*[b] *himself*[c] *said to them: "Neither do I say to you by what authority I do these things."*

### Notes

[a] φοβούμεθα, lit. "we fear."
[b] καὶ αὐτός, lit. "even he."
[c] A few MSS (א it sy[c, p]) have ὁ Ἰησοῦς, "Jesus," in place of καὶ αὐτός; a few others (700 l sa) omit both, having simply ἔφη αὐτοῖς, "he said to them."

*Form/Structure/Setting*

A. The question of the authority of Jesus has been raised sharply by the events recorded with the beginning of chap. 21, i.e., the triumphal entry and Jesus' actions in the temple, all pointing to Jesus' identity as the Son of David. The question that was surely in the minds of the Jewish authorities from that first day and that one expected to hear from them in vv 15–17 is now asked with all possible bluntness. But because they are inflexibly unreceptive to the truth, Jesus does not answer them directly. But in his indirect way, and by their evasive response (which confirms their immovable unbelief), the implicit answer is nonetheless clear. Their unbelief, representative of Israel's unbelief, prompts the three parables that follow (i.e., 21:28–22:14).

B. Matthew, continuing to follow the order of Mark, draws this material from Mark 11:27–33 (cf. Luke 20:1–8). The agreement is very close, and only minor changes are made, among which the following may be noted. Matthew omits Mark's opening notice that "they came again to Jerusalem" (cf. 21:18). In v 23 (cf. Mark 11:27) Matthew substitutes ἐλθόντος, "came," for Mark's περιπατοῦντος, "walking about"; adds διδάσκοντι, while he was "teaching" (perhaps to prepare for the question about authority); omits καὶ οἱ γραμματεῖς, "and the scribes" (perhaps for no other reason than brevity or because the question does not involve the law); adds τοῦ λαοῦ, "of the people," after οἱ πρεσβύτεροι, "the elders" (cf. the same addition in 26:47; 27:1); and omits the redundant clause ἵνα ταῦτα ποιῇς, "in order that you might do these things" (Mark 11:28; the same omission is made in Luke 20:2). In v 24 (cf. Mark 11:29) Matthew inserts ἀποκριθείς, "he answered" (so too Luke 20:3), and substitutes εἴπητε, "tell," for ἀποκρίθητε, "answer" (cf. Luke 20:3). In v 25 (cf. Mark 11:30) Matthew turns Mark's single question into two questions (producing more emphasis) by adding πόθεν ἦν, "from whence was it?" Matthew (so too Luke 20:4) further omits Mark's ἀποκρίθητέ μοι, "answer me."

The remaining changes are relatively insignificant, and only two need be noted. In v 26 Matthew clears up somewhat the break in the syntax of Mark 11:32 by substituting φοβούμεθα, "we fear," for Mark's ἐφοβοῦντο, "they were afraid" (but only Luke 20:6 really succeeds in smoothing out Mark's awkwardness). In keeping with this change to direct discourse, Matthew alters Mark's following verb εἶχον, all "held" that John was a prophet, to ἔχουσιν, all "hold" that John was a prophet, thereby preserving the direct discourse. Finally, in v 27 Matthew replaces ὁ Ἰησοῦς, "Jesus" (Mark 11:33), with καὶ αὐτός, "even he himself," thereby avoiding the repetition of the name that occurs in the first half of the verse.

C. This exchange between Jesus and his opponents contains no fewer than five questions. The controversy centers on the authority of Jesus, who responds by raising the associated issue of John the Baptist's authority. The passage may be outlined as follows: (1) the question about Jesus' authority (v 23); (2) Jesus' counter question (vv 24–25b); (3) the dilemma of the Jewish leaders (vv 25c–26); (4) their answer (v 27a); and (5) Jesus' refusal to answer the initial question directly (v 27b). As for structural features, it should be noted that Matthew balances the two questions of the Jewish authorities (v 23) with a double question from Jesus (v 25). Syntactic parallelism can be seen in the two ἐάν, "if," clauses of vv

25–26 (cf. the ἐάν clause of v 24b) with the corresponding opposites ἐξ οὐρανοῦ, "from heaven," and ἐξ ἀνθρώπων, "from human beings" (reflecting the opposition uttered by Jesus in v 25b). Finally, the concluding statement of Jesus in v 27b functions as an inclusio to the initial question of v 23. An answer, albeit an indirect one, is paradoxically provided through the rationale underlying the negative answer given by the Jewish leaders in v 27a.

## Comment

**23** According to Matthew's chronology, on the day following the clearing of the temple Jesus returned and was "teaching" (διδάσκοντι) there. No reference is given to the content of the teaching of Jesus at this point, but it would be a fair assumption that he was again proclaiming the dawn of the kingdom of God (cf. εὐαγγελιζομένου, "proclaiming good news," in Luke 20:1). Jesus' public teaching affords the Jewish authorities the opportunity to interrogate him regarding the authority he presumed to underlie the things he was doing. The representatives of the Sanhedrin, i.e., οἱ ἀρχιερεῖς καὶ οἱ πρεσβύτεροι τοῦ λαοῦ, "the chief priests and the elders of the people," are mentioned together again in 26:3, 47; 27:1, 3, 12, 20, where they take the leading role in the death of Jesus (cf. 16:21; 26:57; 27:41, where they are mentioned with the γραμματεῖς, "scribes"). It is clear that Jesus acted and spoke in a way that assumed a certain ἐξουσία, "authority" (cf. 7:29; 9:6; and finally, 28:18). The questions of the Jewish leaders, for whom much was at stake, were the obvious and expected ones. First, ἐν ποίᾳ ἐξουσίᾳ, "with what authority," was Jesus doing ταῦτα, "these things" (i.e., the actions of the preceding day, the clearing of the temple and the healings [vv 12–15] as well as probably the present teaching [thus Gnilka])? And second, what was the source of that authority (τίς σοι ἔδωκεν τὴν ἐξουσίαν ταύτην, "who gave to you this authority," is repeated for emphasis)? (Cf. a similar question put to Peter and John in Acts 4:7.) The questions are hardly asked for the sake of information. They represent instead an attempt to gain more ammunition to be used against Jesus when the time was right.

**24–25b** For this reason Jesus does not give a direct answer to their questions. He counters instead with a question of his own in good rabbinic fashion (cf. for example *b. Taʿan.*7a; *b. Sanh.* 65b), which, if answered, would at once reveal the source of Jesus' authority, which stands in continuity with that of John the Baptist, and expose the guilt of the Jewish authorities. Jesus' counter question is anything but a clever ploy designed to sidestep their questions. The λόγον ἕνα, "one matter," concerning which Jesus asks the chief priests and elders, as they themselves perceive, cannot be answered without revealing the unreceptive hearts of his questioners: What was the authority that underlay the baptizing work of John? Was that baptizing ἐξ οὐρανοῦ ἤ ἐξ ἀνθρώπου, "from heaven or from human beings"? These are the only, and mutually exclusive, alternatives (cf. Acts 5:38–39) for explaining the work of the Baptist and that of Jesus. ἐξ οὐρανοῦ, "from heaven," is a Jewish circumlocution for "from God" (cf. "kingdom of heaven" in Matthew). If these Jewish leaders are willing to answer this question, which Jesus knows they are not, then he will answer theirs, ἐρῶ ἐν ποίᾳ ἐξουσίᾳ ταῦτα ποιῶ, "I will tell you by what authority I am doing these things" (words that exactly repeat the initial question).

**25c–26** Jesus' question puts the Pharisees on the defensive, and as "they began reasoning" (διελογίζοντο as an inceptive imperfect tense), the dilemma it posed became evident. On the one hand, if they admitted that John's baptism came from God (Jesus' view; see 11:7–15; cf. John 1:25, 33), they knew they could be faulted for not believing him (as in fact they are in v 32) and in turn for not believing that Jesus too had been sent by God, for John had prepared the way for Jesus. On the other hand, if they said that his baptism depended merely on human authority (which was in fact their view), they feared the reaction of the crowd. In a public setting such as this, they did not want to be perceived as denying outright that John had been a prophet sent by God. In turning Mark's editorial comment ἐφοβοῦντο τὸν ὄχλον, "they were afraid of the crowd," into direct discourse, Matthew produces the rather awkward φοβούμεθα τὸν ὄχλον, lit. "we are afraid of the crowd," which is then better taken in the sense of "we must fear the crowd." The fact that the crowd, i.e., the people generally, held John the Baptist to be a προφήτην, "prophet,"—i.e., one sent by and speaking for God—has been mentioned earlier in 14:5 (cf. too 11:9), where the opinion was responsible for Herod's fear of killing John. A similar fear, according to v 46, prevents the Jewish authorities from seizing Jesus (the crowds "held him to be a prophet" [προφήτην]) in order to kill him (cf. v 11; 26:5 and the parallel in Luke 22:2; cf. Acts 5:26).

**27** The chief priests and elders did not want to antagonize the crowds, thus further weakening their leadership or, worse, bringing physical violence upon themselves. Their answer was an evasive, noncommittal οὐκ οἴδαμεν, "we do not know," that indirectly reveals their incompetence as religious leaders of the people. Jesus in turn refuses to answer the initial question concerning his authority and its source. ἐν ποίᾳ ἐξουσίᾳ ταῦτα ποιῶ, "by what authority I am doing these things," repeats the same words in v 24 (verbatim) and v 23. The words καὶ αὐτός, "even he himself," appear to be emphatic, making the point that in the face of hardened unbelief Jesus refused to disclose himself to the Jewish authorities. The result is that the final logion takes on the character of a judgment oracle. The answer to the question was certainly not in doubt. If Jesus regarded the work of John as ἐξ οὐρανοῦ, "from heaven," it is clear that the same answer was implied with regard to his own ministry (cf. Bengel). That was implied already in the message that through his ministry the kingdom of God was being made manifest (cf.12:28; 13:16–17).

### Explanation

The real issue in the passage concerns not information about the authority of Jesus but the unbelief and unreceptivity of the Jewish leadership. The latter knew well enough that Jesus would have claimed divine authority for his doings in the temple area. Their question thus reflects not an inquisitive openness but an already established rejection of Jesus and the attempt to gain evidence that could later be used against him. As they had responded negatively to John the Baptist, so they responded negatively to Jesus and his claims. The result was the unfortunate exchange recorded in this pericope. Jesus confronts the chief priests and elders with their unbelief; they respond evasively; and Jesus refuses to play their game, asserting that no answer will be given to their question. Their rejection of Jesus brings their condemnation. Not infrequently the request of information can hide, as here, a lack of receptivity and commitment.

# The Parable of Two Sons    (21:28–32)

## Bibliography

**Bratcher, R. G.** "Righteousness in Matthew." *BT* 40 (1989) 228–35. **Derrett, J. D. M.** "The Parable of the Two Sons." *ST* 25 (1971) 109–16. **Dupont, J.** "Les deux fils dissemblables (Mt. 21)." *AsSeign* 57 (1971) 20–32. **Gibson, J.** "*Hoi telonai kai hai pornai.*" *JTS* 32 (1981) 429–33. **Guy, H. A.** "The Parable of the Two Sons." *ExpTim* 51 (1939–40) 204. **Hagner, D. A.** "Righteousness in Matthew's Theology." In *Worship, Theology and Ministry in the Early Church.* FS R. P. Martin, ed. M. J. Wilkins and T. Paige. Sheffield: JSOT, 1992. 101–20. **Kleist, J. A.** "Greek or Semitic Idiom: A Note on Mt. 21, 32." *CBQ* 8 (1946) 192–96. **Kretzer, A.** "Das mt Basileiaverständnis im Rückblick auf Israel nach der Parabeltrilogie Mt 21, 28–22, 14." In *Der Herrschaft der Himmel und die Söhne des Reiches.* Würzburg: Echter, 1971. 150–86. **Légasse, S.** "Jésus et les prostituées." *RTL* 7 (1976) 137–54. **Macgregor, W. M.** "The Parable of the Two Sons." *ExpTim* 38 (1926–27) 498. **Merkel, H.** "Das Gleichnis von den 'ungleichen Söhnen' (Matth. xxi. 28–32)." *NTS* 20 (1974) 254–61. **Michaels, J. R.** "The Parable of the Regretful Son." *HTR* 61 (1968) 15–26. **Ogawa, A.** "Paraboles de l'Israël véritable? Reconsidération critique de Mt. xxi 28–xxii 14." *NovT* 21 (1979) 121–49. **Popkes, W.** "Die Gerechtigkeitstradition im Matthäus-Evangelium." *ZNW* 80 (1989) 1–23. **Przybylski, B.** "Matthew 21:32." In *Righteousness in Matthew and His World of Thought.* SNTSMS 41. Cambridge: Cambridge UP, 1980. 94–96. **Read, D. H. C.** "When What You Believe Is What You Do." *ExpTim* 90 (1979) 367–68. **Richards, W. L.** "Another Look at the Parable of the Two Sons." *BR* 23 (1978) 5–14. **Schmid, J.** "Das textgeschichtliche Problem der Parabel von den zwei Söhnen." In *Vom Wort des Lebens.* FS M. Meinertz. Münster: Aschendorff, 1951. 68–84. **Weder, H.** "Die Parabel von den ungleichen Söhnen (Mt 21,28–32)." In *Die Gleichnisse Jesu als Metaphern.* FRLANT 120. Göttingen: Vandenhoeck & Ruprecht, 1978. 230–38. **Wulf, F.** "Die ungleichen Söhne." *GL* 44 (1971) 75–77.

## Translation

[28] *"What does it seem to you? A[a] man had two sons. And[b] he went to the first and said, 'Son, go today and work in the[c] vineyard.' [29]But he answered and said, 'I will not,' although[d] afterwards he changed his mind and went.[e,f] [30]And the man[g] went and said the same to the other[h] son. And he answered and said, 'I will go,[i] sir,'[j] but he did not go. [31]Which of the two did the will of his father?" They said,[k] "The first."[l] Jesus said to them, "Truly I say to you that the tax collectors and the harlots go into the kingdom of God before you. [32]For John came to you in the way of righteousness, and you did not believe him. But the tax collectors and the harlots believed him. But you yourselves, although having seen, did not[m] change your mind afterwards and believe him."*

## Notes

[a] A number of MSS (C Δ Θ *f*[1,13] it vg[cl] sy) add τις, "certain." Cf. Luke 15:11.

[b] A few MSS (ℵ* L Z [sy[s,c]] co) omit καί, "and."

[c] Some MSS (B C² W Z lat sa mae bo[pt]) add μου, "my."

[d] δέ, lit. "but," omitted by ℵ* (B) it sa[mss].

[e] A few MSS (B Θ *f*[13] sa[mss] bo) reverse the order of the two sons, putting second the one who said he would not go but afterwards went (cf. NEB; NASB). This also involves for these MSS changing ὁ

πρῶτος, "the first," in the answer of the Jewish leaders in v 31 to ὁ ἔσχατος, "the last," or ὁ ὕστρος, lit. "the afterwards one" (B). Cf. *Note* l. The change in order may have been motivated by the order of salvation history, wherein the Jews first refuse the kingdom while the Gentiles later receive it (cf. too the parable of the prodigal son, where the prodigal is the younger son). The other order, where the first son refuses to go, better explains the request then given to the second son. See the full discussion in *TCGNT*, 55–56.

f D it sy[s.(c)] add εἰς τὸν ἀμπελῶνα, "into the vineyard."

g "The man" added to translation for clarity.

h A number of MSS (ℵ[2] B C[2] L Z f[1] mae bo) substitute δευτέρῳ, "second."

i The Gr. text has merely ἐγώ, lit. "I," with the verb "will go" understood. A few MSS (Θ f[13]) substitute ὑπάγω, "I go."

j κύριε can also be translated "Lord." Θ omits κύριε, probably in light of the disobedience of this son.

k Many MSS (C W f[1] TR it vg[cl] sy sa mae bo[ms]) add αὐτῷ, "to him."

l B sa[mss] bo have ὁ ὕστερος, lit. "the afterwards one," meaning apparently not the second son but the first son, who "afterwards" changed his mind and went into the vineyard. These variants are linked with the order of the sons in vv 28–30. See *Note* e above. D it sy[s.(c)] have ὁ ἔσχατος, "the last." Because the latter is the more difficult reading, it is preferred by many (cf. J. R. Michaels, *HTR* 61 [1968] 15–26). The *UBSGNT* committee regards this reading as either a "transcriptional blunder" or perhaps the result of wanting to have the Pharisees affirm the hypocrisy of which Jesus later accuses them (cf. 23:3). See again the full discussion in *TCGNT*, 55–56.

m οὐδέ, lit. "neither"; ℵ C L W TR have οὐ, "not." D sy[s] omit the negative altogether. The *UBSGNT* committee regards the omission as "accidental." See *TCGNT*, 57.

## *Form/Structure/Setting*

A. The parable now offered by Jesus, the first of a series of three related parables, has as its purpose the depiction of the unfaithfulness of the Jewish leaders. For this reason Jesus begins by asking the Jewish leaders for their opinion concerning which of the two sons was the faithful one. Their correct answer becomes in turn, through typically parabolic procedure, a self-indictment (cf. v 45). In this instance, as also in the following parable, the application is made absolutely unmistakable by Jesus' subsequent comment (vv 31b–32). Those who had just questioned Jesus about his authority are thus shown themselves to be rejecting the kingdom of God. Viviano accordingly refers to this pericope as a midrash on the preceding pericope (21:23–27).

B. This parable is unique to Matthew and may be regarded as being drawn from his own special source. The closest synoptic parallel, pertinent only to the application of the parable in vv 31–32, is found in Luke 7:29–30, which is not at all close to the actual wording of the Matthean pericope.

C. The pericope consists of two clearly distinct parts, the parable and its application. The opening question and corresponding answer (v 31) have the effect of sharpening the application to the listeners. The pericope may be outlined as follows: (1) the parable of the two sons, divided into (a) the invitation to, and response of, the first (vv 28–29) and (b) the invitation to, and response of, the second (v 30); and (2) the application of the parable, divided into (a) the faithful response of the first son (v 31a–b), (b) the faithful response of tax collectors and harlots (v 31c), (c) the contrast between the unbelief of the Jewish leaders and the faith of the tax collectors and harlots with respect to John the Baptist (v 32a–b), and (d) a repeated indictment of the Jewish leaders for their hardheartedness (v 32c). The pericope exhibits numerous parallelisms. In the parable itself the parallelism occurs mainly in the structure supporting the dialogue. Thus προσελθὼν τῷ πρώτῳ εἶπεν, "he came to the first and said" (v 28), is paralleled by προσελθὼν δὲ τῷ ἑτέρῳ εἶπεν, "and he came to the other and said" (v 30); the response of each of the sons is introduced with the words ὁ δὲ ἀποκριθεὶς εἶπεν, "and he answered and said" (vv 29 and 30); and there is the narrative opposition ἀπῆλθεν, "he went" (v 29), and οὐκ ἀπῆλθεν, "he did not go" (vv 29, 30). In the application of the parable, the repeated οἱ τελῶναι καὶ αἱ πόρναι, "the tax collectors and the harlots," bears mention. The phrase occurs chiastically with "you" in vv 31–32. The opposition of οὐκ ἐπιστεύσατε αὐτῷ, "you did not believe him," and ἐπίστευσαν αὐτῷ, "they believed him," in v 32 is striking. Further to be noted is the direct application of the language of v 29 in the final indictment of v 32, οὐδὲ μετεμελήθητε ὕστερον, "you did not change your mind afterward." The parable and application thus reveal considerable artistry as well as subtlety (see below).

## Comment

**28–29** The preliminary question τί δὲ ὑμῖν δοκεῖ, "What do you think?" involves the listeners (cf. Matthew's use of the same device in 17:25; 18:12), namely, the Jewish leaders of the preceding pericope, in active engagement with a parable that will be applied to them. The very different parable of Luke 15:11–32 begins almost exactly as the present parable: "A certain man had two sons" (but υἱούς, rather than τέκνα as here). The father approaches the πρώτῳ, "first," son, presumably the eldest, and asks him to go σήμερον, "today," and ἐργάζου ἐν τῷ ἀμπελῶνι, "work in the vineyard" (cf. the same language in 20:1–16). Again the reference to the vineyard associates the parable with Israel (cf. 20:1–16). The negative response of the first son, οὐ θέλω, "I will not," indicates outright rejection of and rebellion against the father's authority; culturally this was unacceptable since obedience would have been the only proper response of a son (see Sir 3:3–11). Yet this son, having ὕστερον, "afterwards" (cf. the use of the word again in v 32), μεταμεληθείς, "changed his mind" (which can also connote "regret" and "repentance"; cf. its other use in Matthew in 27:3), ἀπῆλθεν, "went," and obeyed his father's original request. Thus the initial refusal was followed by eventual obedience.

**30** The father then approached the ἑτέρῳ, "other," son with the same request (εἶπεν ὡσαύτως, "he spoke in the same way"). This son responded in a manner exactly opposite to the response of the first son. That is, he agreed to go (ἐγώ, lit. "I," is short for ἰδοὺ ἐγώ, i.e., "Here am I" [Heb. הִנֵּנִי, hinnēnî], a Septuagintal formula of consent), addressing his father as κύριε, "sir" or perhaps "lord" (thereby strengthening the apparent agreement to obey); yet in fact οὐκ ἀπῆλθεν, "he did not go," to work in the vineyard. Thus initial agreement was followed by eventual disobedience.

**31** When Jesus asked his listeners which son had done "the will of the father" (τὸ θέλημα τοῦ πατρός, language very reminiscent of passages such as 7:21 and 12:50, where Jesus refers to the will of "my" Father), the chief priests and elders responded with the obvious answer, ὁ πρῶτος, "the first" (cf. v 28). This much was perfectly clear. But the Jewish leaders must have been shocked and offended by the application that Jesus proceeded to draw from the parable. For he links *them* with the son who was so ready with words implying obedience but disobeyed and did not go into the vineyard to work. They had received the law and they gave assent to it, yet they had not obeyed it, nor did they obey the messengers God had now sent them. On the other hand, the sinful outcasts of society, "the tax collectors and the harlots" (οἱ τελῶναι καὶ αἱ πόρναι; Matthew refers to the latter only here and in v 32; for the former, cf. 9:10–11; 11:19, where they are linked with ἁμαρτωλοί, "sinners"), are identified with the son who first refused to obey his father but afterwards changed his mind and did so. It is thus they rather than the Jewish authorities who were entering the kingdom. Going εἰς τὴν βασιλείαν τοῦ θεοῦ, "into the kingdom of God" (cf. 6:20; 7:21; for "kingdom of God," see *Comments* on 6:33; 12:28), becomes the analogue of going into the vineyard. It is difficult to conclude anything about a possible subsequent repentance of the Jewish leaders on the basis of the temporal element in going into the kingdom "before you" (προ[άγουσιν]). See *Comment* on 5:18 for the use of the formula ἀμὴν λέγω ὑμῖν, "truly I say to you."

**32** Jesus now provides the logic underlying his explanation of the parable. God had provided an invitation to the Jewish leaders in the preaching of John the Baptist (in mind from the preceding pericope), which they had rejected. John had come ἐν ὁδῷ δικαιοσύνης, "in the way of righteousness." Probably this is to be understood as a reference to the process of the accomplishment of salvation in history through God's sending of John as the forerunner of Jesus (see *Comment* on 3:15; the phrase occurs also in Prov 8:20; 12:28; 21:21[LXX]; 2 Peter 2:21, but in these instances the emphasis is clearly on ethical righteousness). John came preaching the imminence of the kingdom of God (cf. 3:2; 11:11–12). Yet the Jewish leaders "did not believe him" (οὐκ ἐπιστεύσατε αὐτῷ; cf. v 25). The tax collectors and harlots, on the other hand, responded to John's message (for the response of the former, cf. Luke 3:12; 7:29). Jesus further contrasts the Jewish leadership with the first, initially disobedient son by noting that unlike him they did not "change their mind afterwards" (οὐδὲ μετεμελήθητε ὕστερον; cf. the same language in v 29) and respond appropriately by believing him. The words τοῦ πιστεῦσαι αὐτῷ, "and believe him," ordinarily expressing purpose, here are epexegetical, providing the content of the preceding verb (see MHT 1.216–17). Their culpability is stressed by the participle ἰδόντες, which may be taken as concessive, hence "although seeing." The object of the participle remains unexpressed, although presumably intended is the witnessing of the response of the unrighteous to the ministry of the Baptist. The Jewish authorities thus have no excuse. The contrast noted here between the receptivity of sinners and the hardheadedness of the Jewish religious leadership in relation to the message of Jesus is a common motif in the Gospel tradition (cf. 9:10–13; Luke 7:29–30, 35–50; 18:9–14; John 7:48). The connection between John the Baptist and Jesus is such that those who reject John also reject Jesus.

### Explanation

Doing the will of the Father, for Jesus, is more than simply a matter of words; it is always a matter of deeds (cf. esp. 7:21–27; 25:31–46). It is one thing to say one does or will do the will of the Father; it is another thing actually to do it. Words alone mean nothing. A certain claim of serving God and being faithful to Torah went with being the religious leadership of the Jewish people. Yet in fact these leaders were not obedient to God. They had not heeded the message of John the

Baptist, just as they now opposed the message of Jesus himself. But the paradox lay in the fact that the despised sinners, the tax collectors and harlots—those with no claim to righteousness whatsoever—believed both John and Jesus. Thus they, rather than the "righteous" establishment (cf. 9:13), were entering the kingdom of God. They who knew themselves to be desperately needy of grace were the ones open to it and thus the ones who received it.

# The Parable of the Rented Vineyard   (21:33–46)

### Bibliography

**Bayer, H. F.** *Jesus' Predictions of Vindication and Resurrection: The Provenance, Meaning, and Correlation of the Synoptic Predictions.* WUNT 2.20. Tübingen: Mohr, 1986. **Black, M.** "The Christological Use of the Old Testament in the New Testament." *NTS* 18 (1971–72) 1–14. ———. "The Parable as Allegory." *BJRL* 42 (1959–60) 273–87. **Brown, R. E.** "Parable and Allegory Reconsidered." *NovT* 5 (1962) 36–45. **Bruce, F. F.** "New Wine in Old Wineskins: III. The Corner Stone." *ExpTim* 84 (1972–73) 231–35. **Crossan, J. D.** "The Parable of the Wicked Husbandmen." *JBL* 90 (1971) 451–65. **Derrett, J. D. M.** "Allegory and the Wicked Vinedressers." *JTS* 25 (1974) 426. ———. "Fresh Light on the Parable of the Wicked Vinedressers." In *Law in the New Testament.* London: Longman and Todd, 1970. 286–312. ———. "The Stone That the Builders Rejected." In *SE* 6 [= TU 102] (1968) 180–86. **Dillon, R. I.** "Towards a Tradition-History of the Parables of the True Israel (Mt 21,33–22,14)." *Bib* 47 (1966) 1–42. **Dombois, H.** "Juristische Bemerkungen zum Gleichnis von den bösen Weingärtnern." *NZSTR* 8 (1966) 361–73. **Feldmeier, R.** "Heil im Unheil: Das Bild Gottes nach der Parabel von den bösen Winzern (Mk. 12, 1–12 par)." *TBei* 25 (1994) 5–22. **Gray, A.** "The Parable of the Wicked Husbandmen (Matthew xxi. 33–41; Mark xii. 1–9; Luke xx. 9–16)" *HibJ* 19 (1920–21) 42–52. **Harnisch, W.** "Der bezwingende Vorsprung des Guten: Zur Parabel von den bösen Winzern (Markus 12, 1ff. und Parallelen)." In *Die Sprache der Bilder: Gleichnis und Metapher in Literatur und Theologie,* ed. H. Weder. Gütersloh: Mohn, 1989. 22–38. **Hengel, M.** "Das Gleichnis von den Weingärtnern: Mc 12, 1–12 im Lichte der Zenonpapyri und der rabbinischen Gleichnisse." *ZNW* 59 (1968) 1–39. **Hester, J. D.** "Socio-Rhetorical Criticism and the Parable of the Tenants." *JSNT* 45 (1992) 27–57. **Hubaut, M.** "La parabole des vignerons homicides: Authenticité et visée première." *RTL* 6 (1975) 51–61. ———. *La parabole des vignerons homicides.* Cahiers de la Revue Biblique 16. Paris: Gabalda, 1976. **Iersel, B. M. F. van.** "Das Gleichnis von den bösen Winzern." In *"Der Sohn" in den synoptischen Jesusworten.* NovTSup 3. Leiden: Brill, 1964. 124–45. **Jeremias, J.** "Κεφαλὴ γωνίας—Ἀκρογωνιαῖος." *ZNW* 29 (1930) 264–80. **Kim, S.** "Jesus—The Son of God, the Stone, the Son of Man, and the Servant: The Role of Zechariah in the Self-Identification of Jesus." In *Tradition and Interpretation in the New Testament.* FS E. E. Ellis, ed. G. F. Hawthorne and O. Betz. Grand Rapids: Eerdmans, 1987. 134–48. **Kingsbury, J. D.** "The Parable of the Wicked Husbandmen and the Secret of Jesus' Divine Sonship in Matthew: Some Literary-Critical Observations." *JBL* 195 (1986) 643–55. **Klauck, H.-J.** "Das Gleichnis vom Mord im Weinberg (Mk 12, 1–12; Mt 21, 33–46; Lk 20, 9–19)." *BibLeb* 11 (1970) 118–45. **Kümmel, W. G.** "Das Gleichnis von den bösen Weingärtnern." In *Heilsgeschehen und Geschichte.* MTS 3. Marburg: Elwert, 1965. 207–17. **Kuhn, K. H.** "*Kakiē kakōs* in the Sahidic Version of Matthew 21:41." *JTS* 36 (1985) 390–93. **Lebreton, J.** "Les vignerons." In *La vie* *et l'enseignement de Jésus Christ notre seigneur.* Paris: Beauchesne, 1931. 178–83. **Léon-Dufour, X.** "The Murderous Vineyard-Workers." *TD* 15 (1967) 30–36. ———. "La parabole des vignerons homicides." *ScEccl* 17 (1965) 365–96. **Lohmeyer, E.** "Das Gleichnis von den bösen Weingärtnern." *ZST* 18 (1941) 242–59. **Lowe, M.** "From the Parable of the Vineyard to a Pre-Synoptic Source." *NTS* 28 (1982) 257–63. **Morice, W. G.** "The Parable of the Tenants and the Gospel of Thomas." *ExpTim* 8 (1987) 104–7. **Mussner, F.** "Die bösen Winzer nach Mt 21.33–46." In *Antijudaismus im Neuen Testament? Exegetische und systematische Beiträge,* ed. P. Eckert et al. Munich: Kaiser, 1967. 129–34. **Newell, J. E.,** and **Newell, R. R.** "The Parable of the Wicked Tenants." *NovT* 14 (1972) 226–37. **O'Neill, J. C.** "The Source of the Parables of the Bridegroom and the Wicked Husbandmen." *JTS* 39 (1988) 485–89. **Pedersen, S.** "Zum Problem der vaticinia ex eventu: Eine Analyse von Mt. 21, 33–46 par.; 22, 1–10 par." *ST* 19 (1965) 167–88. **Robinson, J. A. T.** "The Parable of the Wicked Husbandmen: A Test of Synoptic Relationships." *NTS* 21 (1975) 443–61. **Snodgrass, K. R.** "The Parable of the Wicked Husbandmen: Is the Gospel of Thomas Version the Original?" *NTS* 21 (1974–75) 142–44. ———. *The Parable of the Wicked Tenants.* WUNT 27. Tübingen: Mohr, 1983. **Swaeles, R.** "L'Arrière-fond scripturaire de Matt. xxi. 43 et son lien avec Matt xxi. 44." *NTS* 6 (1959–60) 310–13. ———. "La parabole des vignerons homicides (Mt 21,33–46)." *AsSeign* 29 (1966) 36–51. **Trilling, W.** "Gericht über das falsche Israel (Mt 21,33–46)." In *Christusverkündigung in den synoptischen Evangelien.* Munich: Kösel, 1969. 165–90. ———. "Les vignerons homicides (Mt 21, 33–46)." *AsSeign* 58 (1974) 55–65. ———. "Das Winzergleichnis: 21,33–45." In *Das wahre Israel.* Munich: Kösel, 1964. 55–65.

## Translation

[33] *"Hear another parable: A man, the master of a house, planted a vineyard. And he put a fence around it, and he dug a wine press in it, and he built a watchtower. Then[a] he leased it to tenant farmers and went off on a journey.* [34] *But when the time of the harvest[b] drew near, he sent his servants to the tenants to receive his fruit.* [35] *And the tenants took his servants, beat one, killed another, and stoned a third.* [36] *Again[c] he sent other servants, more than the first time, and they did the same to them.* [37] *Finally he sent his own son to them, saying: 'They will have regard for my son.'* [38] *But when the tenant farmers saw the son, they said among themselves: 'This one is the heir. Come, let us kill him, and we will have[d] his inheritance.'* [39] *And they took him, cast him out of the vineyard, and killed him.[e]* [40] *When therefore the lord of the vineyard comes, what will he do to those tenants?"* [41] *They said to him: "He will mercilessly destroy those evil persons, and he will lease the vineyard to other tenant farmers, who will give over to him its fruits in their seasons."*

[42] *Jesus said to them: "Have you never read in the scriptures:*
*The stone which the the builders rejected,*
*This one has become the corner stone.*
*This is from the Lord,*
*and it is marvelous in our[f] eyes?*

[43] *Therefore I tell you that[g] the kingdom of God will be taken from you, and it will be given to a people producing its fruit. [[44]And the one who falls upon this stone will be dashed to pieces; but it will crush whomever it falls upon.][h]*

[45] *And when the chief priests and the Pharisees heard his parables, they knew that he was speaking about them.* [46] *And although they wanted to seize him, they were afraid of the crowds, since they held him to be a prophet.*

*Notes*

ᵃ "Then" added to translation; the text has καί, "and."

ᵇ τῶν καρπῶν, lit. "the fruits."

ᶜ ℵ* syᵖ have καὶ πάλιν, "and again"; D has πάλιν οὖν, "again therefore"; d has πάλιν δέ, "but again."

ᵈ For σχῶμεν many MSS (C W *f*¹³ TR syᵖ· ʰ) have κατάσχωμεν, "possess."

ᵉ A few MSS representing the Western text (D Θ it) reverse the order of the casting out of the vineyard and the killing of the son, with the result that the son is first killed and then cast out of the vineyard. This is probably due to the harmonization of the sequence with the Markan parallel (Mark 12:8). See *TCGNT*, 57, and *Comment* below.

ᶠ D* *f*¹·¹³ sa mae have ὑμῶν, "your."

ᵍ ὅτι, "that," is omitted by ℵ B* Θ.

ʰ The entire verse is omitted by D 33 it syˢ; Eusebius. The *UBSGNT* committee regards the verse as "an accretion" to Matthew's text (perhaps from Luke 20:18), yet it is retained in brackets "because of the antiquity of the reading and its importance." See *TCGNT*, 58. Snodgrass (*The Parable of the Wicked Tenants*, 66–68), on the other hand, argues for the authenticity of the verse.

## *Form/Structure/Setting*

A. The second parable in the series of three directed against the Jewish leaders is particularly interesting, not only because of its specifically prophetic character, pointing to the death of the son, but also because of the motif of judgment against Israel and the concept of the "transference" of the kingdom to a different people. The leaders thus function as representatives of Israel. Their rejection of Jesus and his message mean in turn the removal of Israel's privilege as the people of God. God's saving purposes are now directed to his new people, the church, consisting of both Jews and Gentiles.

B. Matthew depends here on Mark 12:1–12 (cf. Luke 20:9–19), although he does not feel obligated to follow the Markan text very closely, especially toward the end of the parable where a fair amount of new material is inserted. Noting first the more important insertions, we may call attention to the following: in v 41b Matthew adds not only γεωργοῖς, "tenants," but also the following clause, οἵτινες ἀποδώσουσιν αὐτῷ τοὺς καρποὺς ἐν τοῖς καιροῖς αὐτῶν, "who will give to him the fruits in their seasons" (in keeping with Matthew's emphasis on "fruit" in vv 34, 43); Matthew adds from his own source the entirety of v 43 concerning the transference of the kingdom from the Jews to the Gentiles and perhaps also the Q saying of v 44 (cf. Luke 20:18), which however is textually uncertain (see *Note* h above). A further insertion is the clause of v 40a ὅταν οὖν ἔλθῃ ὁ κύριος τὸν ἀμπελῶνος, "when therefore the lord of the vineyard comes" (probably an allusion to the parousia of Jesus; cf. Mark's ἐλεύσεται, "he will come," in Mark 12:9). Most of the remaining differences involve Matthew's usual abbreviation and smoothing of the Markan text.

To be noted are the following: In v 33 Matthew's introductory ἄλλην παραβολὴν ἀκούσατε, "hear another parable," is distinctive, as is his description of the man as an οἰκοδεσπότης, "house master" (a favorite Matthean word, which is found seven times in Matthew compared to Mark's single use); in v 34 Matthew expands Mark's simple τῷ καιρῷ (lit. "in the season"; Mark 12:2) to ὅτε δὲ ἤγγισεν ὁ καιρὸς τῶν καρπῶν, "and when the season of the harvest drew near" (reflecting Matthew's interest in the imminence of eschatology); Matthew furthermore writes the plural τοὺς δούλους αὐτοῦ, "his servants," for Mark's singular δοῦλον, "a servant" (Mark 12:2); Matthew's alteration of

Mark's τοῦ ἀμπελῶνος, "of the vineyard" (Mark 12:2), to αὐτοῦ, "his" (although it is possible to translate αὐτοῦ as "its," i.e., of the vineyard; cf. KJV), emphasizes the master's ownership of, and thus right to, the vineyard's fruit. Whereas Mark first refers to three individual servants (Mark 12:3–5; cf. Luke's enumeration τρίτον, "a third" [Luke 20:12]), only the third of whom is killed (though none is killed in the Lukan account), Matthew begins with the plural τοὺς δούλους, "the servants" (resumed from the preceding verse), and then differentiates individual servants, the first of whom is beaten, while the second two are killed (in the third instance Matthew alone employs the word ἐλιθοβόλησαν, "they stoned"). Matthew also omits the reference to the first servant being sent away empty-handed as well as Mark's verbs ἐκεφαλαίωσαν, "they struck on the head" (probably an allusion to stoning), and ἠτίμασαν, "they dishonored" (Mark 12:4). In v 36 Matthew's second group is described with the words ἄλλους δούλους πλείονας τῶν πρώτων, "other servants, more than the first," which replace Mark's simple καὶ πολλοὺς ἄλλους, "and many others" (Mark 12:4). Furthermore, whereas Mark refers again specifically to the beating and killing of these other servants, Matthew abbreviates with the words καὶ ἐποίησαν αὐτοῖς ὡσαύτως, "and they did the same to them" (v 36). In v 37 Matthew omits Mark's ἔτι ἕνα εἶχεν, "he had yet one," beginning instead with the word ὕστερον, "afterwards." Surprisingly, Matthew omits Mark's adjective ἀγαπητόν, "beloved" (Mark 12:6), in describing the son (cf. Matthew's application of the adjective to Jesus in 3:17; 12:18; 17:5). No less surprising is the fact that scribes have not inserted the adjective in later manuscripts. (Snodgrass [*Parable*, 59] concludes that Matthew's form of the parable is more original.) In v 38 (cf. Mark 12:7) Matthew inserts ἰδόντες τὸν υἱόν, "seeing the son" (which may indirectly intensify the guilt of the tenants' rejection of the son), and adds αὐτοῦ, "his," to "inheritance" (stressing the relation between the inheritance and the son). In v 39 Matthew reverses Mark's order of the killing of the son and the casting of him out of the vineyard (Mark 12:8), thereby producing accord with the historical fact that Jesus was executed outside the city of Jerusalem. In v 40 Matthew's insertion of τοῖς γεωργοῖς ἐκείνοις, "to those tenants," also has the effect of intensifying their guilt. At the beginning of v 41, Matthew's addition of λέγουσιν αὐτῷ, "they said to him," puts the answer to the preceding question in the mouth of the guilty tenants. Matthew's addition of κακοὺς κακῶς, "evil ones terribly," intensifies the severity of the deserved judgment. The formula at the beginning of v 42, λέγει αὐτοῖς ὁ Ἰησοῦς, "Jesus said to them," is required by the change of speakers made at the beginning of v 41. The OT quotation of v 42 is in verbatim agreement with Mark 12:10–11. In v 45 Matthew specifies οἱ ἀρχιερεῖς, "the chief priests" (cf. vv 15, 23), and οἱ Φαρισαῖοι, "the Pharisees," as those who knew the parable was directed against them and who thus plot against Jesus. Finally to be noted are Matthew's addition of the reason for their fear of arresting Jesus, ἐπεὶ εἰς προφήτην αὐτὸν εἶχον, "since [the crowds] held him to be a prophet" (v 46), and the omission of Mark's καὶ ἀφέντες αὐτὸν ἀπῆλθον, "and leaving him, they departed" (because Matthew has yet a third parable addressed to them).

Again, together with the clear dependence on Mark, Matthew shows a considerable freedom in adapting the parable with his own concerns in mind.

C. The pericope consists basically of two main parts: the parable and its application. It may be outlined as follows: (1) the parable of the evil tenant farmers, subdivided into (a) the setting up of the vineyard (v 33), (b) the sending of servants to receive the harvest and their rejection, further divided into (i) the first group (vv 34–35) and (ii) the second group (v 36), (c) the sending of the son (v 37), and (d) the killing of the son (vv 38–39); (2) the application of the parable, subdivided into (a) punishment and the transference of the vineyard to new tenants (vv 40–41), (b) the logion concerning the rejected stone (v 42), (c) the transference of the kingdom (v 43), and (d) the decisive significance of the stone (v 44); and (3) the negative response of the Jewish leaders (vv 45–46). To be noted among structural features of the parable are the following: In v 33 six parallel aorist verbs, each linked by καί, provide the predicate of the relative pronoun ὅστις, "who." In vv 34, 36, and 37, the verb ἀπέστειλεν, "he sent," occurs three times, the second time being modified by πάλιν, "again," the third by ὕστερον, "finally." In the third instance the object τὸν υἱὸν αὐτοῦ, "his son," stands parallel to τοὺς δούλους αὐτοῦ, "his servants" (and in the second instance to ἄλλους δούλους, "other servants"). V 35 contains three parallel aorist verbs, each with the distributive pronoun ὅν. The second of these, ἀπέκτειναν, "they killed," finds its parallel in v 39 in reference to the killing of the son (cf. too the parallel participle λαβόντες, "having taken," in each instance). In the remainder of the pericope, structural parallelism is hardly to be found. This half of the pericope is somewhat disjointed because of the insertion of the OT quotation in v 42 and the enigmatic logion of v 44, if authentic. The only notable parallelism is to be found in the verbs ἀρθήσεται, "it will be taken away," and δοθήσεται, "it will be given" (v 43). Each has a further modifying phrase—the first, ἀφ᾽ ὑμῶν, "from you," the second, ἔθνει, "to a people"—but this parallelism is broken by the addition to the latter of the words ποιοῦντι τοὺς καρποὺς αὐτῆς, "producing its fruits," which corresponds to the reference to τοὺς καρπούς, "the fruits," in v 41. The pericope as a whole is thus formed of the parable, its controversial application (including OT citation), and the reference to the hostile response of the Jewish leaders who wanted to apprehend Jesus in order to do away with him.

D. Much discussion has been given to the question of whether this parable can be said to derive from Jesus or to be a composition of the early church. A number of factors seem to argue in favor of the latter: (1) the obviously allegorical character of the parable; (2) the detailed knowledge of the future reflected at several points; (3) the clear salvation-history perspective; (4) dependence upon the LXX in the form of the OT quotations; and (5) the existence of a simpler version of the parable in *Gos. Thom.* 65–66. At the same time, however, it is by no means certain that the parable cannot have been spoken by Jesus essentially as we have it in the Synoptics. There is no reason why Jesus could not have spoken an allegorical parable (there are obvious allegorical elements in the other parables attributed to Jesus). On this point, see Black, Brown, and Snodgrass (*Parable*, 12–26). Nor is there any compelling reason why Jesus could not have thought of himself as "the son" (cf. van Iersel), anticipated his own death (cf. the passion predictions of 16:21; 17:22–23; 20:18–19), prophesied the fall of Jerusalem (cf. 24:2; see Pedersen), and perceived his own role in bringing the kingdom as the climax of God's salvific program for Israel and the world. It would be natural for the post-resurrection church to draw out the significance of these allegorical aspects more confidently with the passing of time. It is clear that the evangelist, like his Markan source, has left his impress on the material as it came to him (e.g., in putting the death of the son outside the vineyard). The conformity of the OT allusions and quotations to the text of the LXX is the work of the Hellenistic Jewish redactor of the Gospel, if it had not already occurred earlier in the oral form of the material when it was translated into Greek. As for the relationship between Matthew's parable and that of the *Gospel of Thomas*, the latter, rather than being original, is almost certainly dependent on the synoptic tradition (see K. R. Snodgrass, *NTS* 21 [1974–75] 142–44). It is therefore unnecessary to reject the essential authenticity of the parable as we have it in the synoptic Gospels.

### Comment

**33** The Jewish leaders to whom the first parable was addressed (cf. vv 23, 28) are now directed to ἀκούσατε, "hear" (cf. 13:18), ἄλλην παραβολήν, "another parable" (cf. 13:24, 31, 33). The parable of 20:1–16, based on the same imagery of vineyard, householder, and tenant farmers, also begins with reference to ἄνθρωπος ... οἰκοδεσπότης, "a man, a master of a house" (the same juxtaposition is found in 13:52; for the latter word see too 13:27; 20:11; 24:43). The detailed description of the setting up of the vineyard, although realistic in itself, is based on the LXX text of Isa 5:2, where each of Matthew's first four clauses, beginning with ἐφύτευσεν ἀμπελῶνα, "he planted a vineyard," and including reference to the hedge, wine press, and tower, is found in almost exactly the same language (although the order of the clauses in the LXX is 2, 1, 4, 3). The image of the vineyard, which is otherwise irrelevant to the parable itself, points to "the house of Israel" as in Isa 5:7—or more precisely "the kingdom of God" (cf. vv 41, 43)— and thus prepares the way for the indictment of the Jewish leaders for not producing fruit—in this case for not giving the yield of the vineyard to its lord. Not found in Isa 5 is the reference to letting the vineyard out to tenant farmers and the going away of the absentee landlord on a journey (ἀπεδήμησεν; cf. a similar use of this verb in 25:14–15). These two items reinforce the responsibility of Israel and its leadership in particular for the care of the vineyard. The latter may allude to the transcendence of God, necessitating the use of servants as intermediaries.

**34** Behind the reference to the drawing near (ἤγγισεν, "draw near," is the same verb used in reference to the dawning of the kingdom in 3:2; 4:17; 10:7) of ὁ καιρὸς τῶν καρπῶν, lit. "the season of the fruits," is probably also an allusion to the eschatological harvest (cf. 13:30). At the approach of this crucial time, the master ἀπέστειλεν τοὺς δούλους αὐτοῦ, "sent his servants" (words that occur again verbatim in the third parable [22:3]; here probably an allusion to the OT prophets; cf. *Comment* on the next verse), to collect τοὺς καρποὺς αὐτοῦ, "his fruit," i.e., now not the portion that was due to him as the owner of the vineyard but what was due to him as the lord of the vineyard and the entire harvest.

**35–36** The servants sent by the master of the vineyard were not only resisted, as were the OT prophets sent by God (cf. 2 Chr 24:19; Jer 7:25–26; 25:4 [called specifically δοῦλοι, "servants," in the LXX of both passages; cf. too Wisdom's sending of her servants in Prov 9:3 LXX]), but were severely treated and even put to death (the persecution of the prophets is a familiar theme in the OT; cf. Jeremiah, who was beaten, according to Jer 20:2, and Uriah the prophet, killed in Jer 26:21–23; Zechariah is stoned in 2 Chr 24:21; cf. the general reference to the killing of the prophets in Neh 9:26). In the following, third parable, Matthew alludes again to this treatment of the prophets in his reference to the king's servants who are treated shamefully and killed (22:6; cf. 5:12; 23:31, 34; esp. 23:37 with its reference to the killing and "stoning" [λιθοβολεῖν, as here] of the prophets). The words πάλιν ἀπέστειλεν ἄλλους δούλους, "again he sent other servants," alluding to the long-suffering compassion of God in sending generation after generation (cf. πλείονας τῶν πρώτων, "more than the first") of prophets to Israel (perhaps in this case the latter prophets in contrast to the former prophets), are repeated verbatim (except that πάλιν, "again," occurs after ἀπέστειλεν, "he sent") in 22:4. Repeatedly the lord of the vineyard sent servants and repeatedly they were beaten or killed (ἐποίησαν αὐτοῖς ὡσαύτως, "they treated them similarly").

**37** "Finally" (for ὕστερον in this sense, see BAGD, 849b) the master decides to send τὸν υἱὸν αὐτόν, "his son" (cf. Heb 1:1–2). The allusion here to the Father's sending of his Son, Jesus (cf. 10:40; 15:24 for the sending; 3:17; 11:27; 17:5 for the sonship), is unmistakable despite Matthew's omission of Mark's ἀγαπητόν, "beloved" (Mark 12:6; so too, Luke 20:13). ἐντρέπειν means to "have regard" or "respect" for someone. The master of the vineyard thus sends the one closest to him, his son—his own flesh and blood—in the confidence that such an emissary will not receive the same treatment but will be received as the master himself would be. Then the final τὸν υἱόν, "my son," where a simple αὐτόν, "him," would have sufficed, takes on a special emphasis. The secondary meaning is clear: at the end of a long history of revelation to Israel through the prophets, God sends his own Son to his people Israel (cf. 15:24). For Jesus' self-consciousness of his identity as God's unique Son, see, among others, such passages as 3:17; 11:27. This is his first public assertion of his divine sonship (see Kingsbury). For Jewish background for the designation of the Messiah as the "Son of God," cf. 4QFlor 10–14.

**38–39** The tenant farmers recognize the son as ὁ κληρονόμος, "the heir," and decide to kill him and thus σχῶμεν τὴν κληρονομίαν αὐτοῦ, "have his inheritance" (the words κληρονόμος, "heir," and κληρονομία, "inheritance," occur in Matthew only here). Here the parallel with Jesus and the Jews who plot to kill him breaks down. They did not recognize him as the son or the heir, nor did they anticipate receiving anything by doing away with him; instead they moved against him as a dangerous charlatan whose false claims had to be stopped. But a parable need not, indeed seldom does, correspond to its symbolized referent at every point. In the framework of the parabolic story, the tenant farmers clearly failed to reckon with the possibility of the return of the lord of the vineyard himself and the punishment they might in turn receive (cf. v 41). In v 39 Matthew, altering the Markan order, has the son first cast out of the vineyard and then killed (so too Luke 20:15). This reversal shows beyond doubt that Matthew has the death of Jesus in mind since Jesus was in fact killed outside the city walls (the same point is emphasized in Heb 13:12; cf. John 19:20). McNeile notes that if the parable had been created by the early church, some allusion to the resurrection of Jesus would almost certainly have been included.

**40–41** The coming of the master of the vineyard to punish the tenants of the vineyard suggests a judgment that is eschatological in tone—something that appears to be reinforced in the reference to the οἰκοδεσπότης, "master of a house," now as ὁ κύριος τοῦ ἀμπελῶνος, "the lord of the vineyard." The question concerning what he will do with the evil tenant farmers becomes more than rhetorical in Matthew since the self-condemning answer is put into the mouth of the Jewish leaders in the verse that follows. If the Jewish leaders did answer the question, it is unlikely that they responded with the entirety of v 41 since that answer corresponds too exactly with the purpose of Jesus and the evangelist in the pericope (cf. the anticipation of v 43). Matthew intensifies the guilt of the Jewish leaders in the unusual syntax and assonance caused by the addition of the adjective κακούς, "evil" (modifying αὐτούς, "them"), and the adverb κακῶς, "evilly" or "severely," modifying the verb ἀπολέσει, "will destroy"; cf. NEB: "He will bring those wretches to a wretched end"). These words may well constitute an allusion to the destruction of Jerusalem (cf. 24:3, 21). It is unlikely that the Jewish leaders would naturally have thought of the idea that the vineyard would be let out to ἄλλοις γεωργοῖς, "other tenant farmers," and of course certainly not in terms of another ἔθνει, "nation," as these words are interpreted in v 43. It is clear, nevertheless, that the parable, even in its supposed earliest form, is not basically about issues of land ownership (*pace* Newell and Newell; Hester). The last clause of v 41, added by Matthew alone, οἵτινες ἀποδώσουσιν αὐτῷ τοὺς καρποὺς ἐν τοῖς καιροῖς αὐτῶν, "who will render to him the fruits in their seasons" (cf. Ps 1:3), is particularly consonant with Matthew's interests in the fruit of righteousness throughout the Gospel (cf. v 43; cf. 3:8, 10; 7:16–20; 12:33). The new "nation" of v 43, unlike Israel, *will* produce the fruit of the kingdom.

**42**   For the formula favored by Matthew, οὐδέποτε ἀνέγνωτε ἐν ταῖς γραφαῖς, "have you never read in the scriptures," cf. 12:3, 5; 19:4; 21:16; 22:31. The citation, which follows the LXX text of Ps 118(117 LXX):22–23 verbatim, focuses on one element of the preceding parable, namely the rejection of the son, now clearly the rejection of Jesus. This OT passage, which was probably first used independently of the parable, is one of several "stone" passages (v 44 alludes to another of these; see below) that became important in the apologetic of the early church (see esp. 1 Peter 2:4–8, where some of these "stone" passages [i.e., besides Ps 118:22; Isa 8:14; Isa 28:16] are quoted together; Ps 118:22 is also alluded to in Acts 4:11; see Kim for an argument that passages from Zechariah lie behind this pericope). The citation may initially have been related to the parable through the wordplay and association of בֵּן, *ben*, "son," and אֶבֶן, *ʾeben*, "stone." The λίθον, "stone," that ἀπεδοκίμασαν, "they rejected" (cf. the use of this verb in the passion predictions of Mark 8:31; Luke 9:22; 17:25), has been made the most important of all, the κεφαλὴν γωνίας, lit. "the head of the corner," i.e., the most important foundational stone (cf. Isa 28:16) or, more probably, the keystone or capstone at the top of the arch of a doorway (thus Jeremias; see BAGD, 430b). The unusual feminine pronoun αὕτη, "this," at the end of the third line of the quotation probably reflects the corresponding Hebrew pronoun זֹאת, *zoʾt*, "this," which is feminine either because of the feminine אֶבֶן, *ʾeben*, "stone," or more probably because it sums up the whole of the preceding clause (the feminine serves as the pronoun for the general statement; cf. BDF §138[2]). Following its use by Jesus, the early Christian found in this cryptic proverb concerning the rejected stone that was made the most important one a perfect analogy to the rejection and exaltation of Christ (on the vindication theme, see Bayer, 90–109). This odd turn of events was indeed παρὰ κυρίου, "from the Lord," and something θαυμαστή, "marvelous," to behold. It was in this strange way that God brought salvation to his people (see Feldmeier). The context of this material in Ps 118 is one of salvation (Ps 118:25–26 is quoted by Matthew, following Mark, in connection with the entry into Jerusalem in v 9). It is possible, though far from certain, that the OT citation was a part of the original parable uttered by Jesus (in favor of this conclusion, see Snodgrass, *Parable;* Kim; against it, see Feldmeier).

**43** The διὰ τοῦτο, "on account of this," refers back not to the immediately preceding quotation but to the parable itself. That is, because of their rejection of the Son sent by the Father, just as the vineyard was let out to other tenants who would hand over the fruit of the vineyard, so will ἡ βασιλεία τοῦ θεοῦ, "the kingdom of God" (see *Comment* on 12:28 for this expression in Matthew), be taken away from the Jewish leaders and given ἔθνει ποιοῦντι τοὺς καρποὺς αὐτῆς, "to a people producing the fruit of it [i.e., the kingdom]." The verbs here are "divine passives," reflecting God as the acting subject. This setting aside of the privilege of Israel as the unique people of God in favor of another people, namely, the church (*pace* Snodgrass, *Parable*), is of course nothing short of revolutionary. The singular ἔθνος, which means "people" or "nation," inevitably alludes to the eventual mission to the Gentiles, the ἔθνοι, plural of the same word (cf. 12:21; 24:14; 28:19). The word in the singular here need not be thought of as excluding Jews, however, since the new nation, the church (cf. 16:18), consists of both Jews and Gentiles (and Jews are included in 28:19). Matthew's church, after all, consists mainly, if not exclusively, of Jewish Christians. To be sure, as several have pointed out (e.g., Harrington), it is not *necessary* to interpret the ἔθνος as meaning the church. But given the total context of the Gospel, this is the most natural interpretation of the passage (see Grundmann). The singular form of the word is applied to the church in 1 Peter 2:9 (also in the context of the "stone" passages). The emphasis on this new group producing the appropriate fruit (cf. v 41) is thoroughly consonant with Matthew's frequent stress on the righteousness of the kingdom (e.g., 5:20; 6:33) that Jesus embodies and brings. The new people of God have a similar responsibility to live in the righteousness of the law (as interpreted by Jesus).

**[44]** This obscure proverb-like logion, if authentic here (see *Note* h above), returns to the "stone" motif of v 42. As it stands in the present context, it appears to function as warning of the judgment (something not mentioned in v 43) that will come upon Israel for her rejection of the Son. Snodgrass appropriately suggests that the parable should be named "The Parable of the Rejected Son" (*Parable*, 109). The first part of the saying (πεσὼν ἐπὶ τὸν λίθον, "falling on the stone") probably alludes to the "stone of the stumbling" of Isa 8:14–15, whereas the second half, where the stone falls upon and crushes a person, may be based on Dan 2:34–35, 44–45. Here it is the rejected stone—now the cornerstone (Ps 118:22 in v 42)—who becomes to those who have rejected him either the stone of stumbling or the stone that crushes, in both cases bringing ruin to them. This sober judgment oracle may thus be thought of not as out of place but as supplementing v 43, which spoke only of the kingdom being taken away, and as corresponding to the judgment referred to in v 41.

**45–46** Matthew records the response of "the chief priests and the Pharisees" (οἱ ἀρχιερεῖς καὶ οἱ φαρισαῖοι; the only other linking of these two groups in Matthew is in 27:62), who heard the parables (i.e., from v 28 to v 44) and realized that they had been directed against them (περὶ αὐτῶν, "concerning them"). The last mention of addressees was in vv 23–24, where the chief priests were linked with "the elders of the people." The reference to the Pharisees (only in Matthew) seems to have been added to intensify their culpability as the religious leaders of the Jewish people. The self-recognition shows the effectiveness of the parables as a means of disclosure. The desire of these Jewish leaders to seize Jesus is thwarted only by their fear of the crowds because they held Jesus εἰς προφήτην, "to be a prophet." This deliberately parallels the statement of v 26, where they similarly feared the crowd because they held John the Baptist to be a prophet (cf. 14:5). Although the crowds were wrong in their evaluation of Jesus (cf. v 11; 16:14; and of John too, cf. 11:9–10), their conviction was enough to deter the authorities, at least for the moment, in their evil designs (the reason becomes clear in 26:5). The events related in this chapter, and here at the end of it, provide the background for the escalation of the confrontation in the following chapters.

*Explanation*

As in the parables on either side of this one, the emphasis here again falls on the unreceptivity of the Jews and in particular upon the Jewish religious establishment. This is heightened by the motif of the rejection and murder of the servants and finally the son. Here the correspondence between the story of the parable and the historical rejection of the prophets and the Son of God is nothing less than remarkable. The reference to the killing of the son (v 39) and the rejection of the stone (v 42) become in effect further prophecies of what is to befall the Son (cf. 16:21; 17:22–23; 20:18–19). What is most astonishing, however, is the salvation-historical perspective contained in the reference to the transferring of the vineyard from the original tenants to new ones—spelled out specifically as the transference of the kingdom of God to a new people (v 43). For Matthew's Christian-Jewish readers, this served to explain both the present futility of the contemporary Judaism of the synagogue and the emergence of the new entity, largely but not exclusively Gentile in composition, the church. Finally determinative for this sequence of events was the response given to the Son sent by the Father. Those who reject the Son, who has become the cornerstone of the new reality of the church, which becomes in effect the new Israel, forfeit their favored position and bring themselves into judgment (v 44), while those who receive the Son receive with him the blessed reality of the now-dawning kingdom of God (for the decisive importance of relation to the Son, cf. 10:32–33). Then, as now, relationship to Jesus is finally what matters.

# The Parable of the Wedding Banquet   (22:1–14)

*Bibliography*

**Ballard, P.** "Reasons for Refusing the Great Supper." *JTS* 23 (1972) 341–50. **Beare, F. W.** "The Parable of the Guests at the Banquet: A Sketch of the History of Its Interpretation." In *The Joy of Study: Papers on the New Testament and Related Subjects.* FS F. C. Grant, ed. S. E. Johnson. New York: Macmillan, 1951. 1–7. **Bergen, P. van.** "La parabole des invités qui se derobent." *LumVie* 49 (1960) 1–9. **Boissard, E.** "Many Are Called, Few Are Chosen." *TD* 3 (1955) 46–50. **Cripps, K. R. J.** "A Note on Matthew xxii.12." *ExpTim* 69 (1957–58) 30.

**Dawson, W. S.** "The Gate Crasher." *ExpTim* 85 (1974) 304–6. **Derrett, J. D. M.** "The Parable of the Great Supper." In *Law in the New Testament*. London: Darton, Longman and Todd, 1970. 126–55. **Dschulnigg, P.** "Positionen des Gleichnisverständnisse im 20. Jahrhundert: Kurze Darstellung von fünf wichtigen Positionen der Gleichnistheorie (Jülicher, Jeremias, Weder, Arens, Harnisch)." *TZ* 45 (1989) 335–51. **Eichholz, G.** "Vom grossen Abendmahl (Luk. 14, 16–24) und von der königlichen Hochzeit (Matth. 22, 1–14)." In *Gleichnisse der Evangelien*. Neukirchen: Neukirchener, 1971. 126–47. **Grimme, H.** "Drei Evangelienberichte in neuer Auffassung: I. Mt 22,11ff; II. Jo 2,3; III. Mt 19,16ff." *TGl* 34 (1942) 83–90. **Haacker, K.** "Das hochzeitliche Kleid von Mt 22,11–13 und ein palästinisches Märchen." *ZDPV* 87 (1971) 895–97. **Haenchen, E.** "Das Gleichnis vom grossen Mahl." In *Die Bibel und wir: Gesammelte Aufsätze*. Tübingen: Mohr, 1968. 2:135–55. **Hahn, F.** "Das Gleichnis von der Einladung zum Festmahl." In *Verborum Veritas*. FS G. Stahlin, ed. O. Böcher and K. Haacker. Wuppertal: Brockhaus, 1970. 51–82. **Hasler, V.** "Die königliche Hochzeit, Matth. 22, 1–14." *TZ* 18 (1962) 25–35. **Lemcio, E. E.** "The Parables of the Great Supper and the Wedding Feast: History, Redaction and Canon." *HBT* 8 (1986) 1–26. **Lewis, A. S.** "Matthew xxii. 4." *ExpTim* 24 (1912–13) 427. **Linnemann, E.** "Überlegungen zur Parabel vom grossen Abendmahl, Lc 14,15–24 Mt, 22 1–14." *ZNW* 51 (1960) 246–55. **Manns, F.** "Une tradition rabbinique réinterprétée dans l'évangile de Mt 22,1–10 et en Rm 11,30–32." *Anton* 63 (1988) 416–26. **Matura, T.** "Les invités à la noce royale (Mt 22, 1–14)." *AsSeign* 59 (1974) 16–27. **Merriman, E. H.** "Matthew xxii. 1–14." *ExpTim* 66 (1954–55) 61. **Meyer, B. F.** "Many (=All) Are Called, but Few (=Not All) Are Chosen." *NTS* 36 (1990) 89–97. **Musurillo, H.** "Many Are Called, but Few Are Chosen." *TS* 7 (1946) 583–89. **Navone, J.** "The Parable of the Banquet." *BiTod* 1 (1964) 923–29. **Pedersen, S.** "Zum Problem der vaticinia ex eventu: Eine Analyse von Mt. 21, 33–46 par.; 22, 1–10 par." *ST* 19 (1965) 117–88. **Pesch, R.,** and **Kratz, R.** "Gleichnis vom grossen Gastmahl." In *So liest man synoptisch*. Frankfurt am Main: Knecht, 1978. 39–60. **Pesch, W.** "Berufene und Auserwählte: Homilie zu Matthäus 22,14." *BK* 20 (1965) 16–18. **Radl, W.** "Zur Struktur der eschatologischen Gleichnisse Jesu." *TTZ* 92 (1983) 122–33. **Reicke, B.** "Synoptic Prophecies on the Destruction of Jerusalem." In *Studies in New Testament and Early Christian Literature*, ed. D. E. Aune. NovTSup 33. Leiden: Brill, 1972. 121–34. **Rengstorf, K. H.** "Die Stadt der Mörder (Mt 22,7)." In *Judentum, Urchristentum, Kirche*. FS J. Jeremias, ed. W. Eltester. Berlin: Töpelmann, 1960. 106–29. **Sanders, J. A.** "The Ethic of Election in Luke's Great Banquet Parable." In *Essays in Old Testament Ethics*. FS J. P. Hyatt, ed. J. C. Crenshaw and J. T. Willis. New York: Ktav, 1974. 245–71. **Schlier, H.** "The Call of God." In *The Relevance of the New Testament*. New York: Herder and Herder, 1968. 249–58. **Schottroff, L.** "Das Gleichnis vom grossen Gastmahl in der Logienquelle." *EvT* 47 (1987) 192–211. **Selbie, W. B.** "The Parable of the Marriage Feast (Matthew xxii. 1–4)." *ExpTim* 37 (1925–26) 266–69. **Sim, D. C.** "The Man without the Wedding Garment (Matthew 22:11–13)." *HeyJ* 31 (1990) 165–78. ———. "Matthew 22.13a and 1 Enoch 10.4a: A Case of Literary Dependence?" *JSNT* 47 (1992) 3–19. **Suttcliffe, E. F.** "Many Are Called but Few Are Chosen." *ITQ* 28 (1961) 126–31. **Swaeles, R.** "L'orientation ecclésiastique de la parabole du festin nuptial en Mt., XXII, 1–14." *ETL* 36 (1960) 655–84. ———. "La parabole du festin nuptial (Mt 22,1–14)." *AsSeign* 74 (1963) 33–49. **Trilling, W.** "Zur Überlieferungsgeschichte des Gleichnisse vom Hochzeitsmahl Mt 22, 1–14." *BZ* 4 (1960) 251–65. **Vaccari, A.** "La parabole du festin des noces (*Mt.*, 22,1–14): Notes d'exégèse." In *Mélanges Jules Lebreton*. RSR 39 (1951) 138–45. **Via, D. O.** "The Relationship of Form to Content in the Parable: The Wedding Feast." *Int* 25 (1971) 171–84. **Vögtle, A.** "Die Einladung zum grossen Gastmahl und zum königlichen Hochzeitsmahl: Ein Paradigma für den Wandel des geschichtlichen Verständnishorizonts." In *Das Evangelium und die Evangelien*. Düsseldorf: Patmos, 1971. 171–218. **Wainwright, E.** "God Wills to Invite All to the Banquet, Matthew 22:1–10." *International Review of Mission* 77 (1988) 185–93. **Wainwright, G.** "Mt. XXII.11–13: Une controverse primitive sur l'admission à la Sainte Cène."

*SE* 6 [= TU 102] (1973) 595–98. **Weder, H.** "Die Parabel vom grossen Mahl (Mt 22,1–10; Lk 14,15–24; ThEv 64)." In *Die Gleichnisse Jesu als Metaphern.* FRLANT 120. Göttingen: Vandenhoeck & Ruprecht, 1978. 177–93. **Wrembek, C.** "Das Gleichnis vom königlichen Hochzeitsmahl und vom Mann ohne hochzeitliches Gewand: Eine geistliche-theologische Erwägung zu Mt 22,1–14." *GL* 64 (1991) 17–40.

## Translation

¹*Jesus answered and again spoke to them in parables, saying:* ² *"The kingdom of heaven is like the situation of a man, a king, who held a wedding banquet for his son.* ³*And he sent his servants to call those who had been invited to the banquet, but they did not want to come.* ⁴*Again he sent other servants, saying: 'Say to those who have been invited: "Look, I have prepared my food, my bulls and fatted cattle have been slaughtered and everything is ready. Come to the wedding banquet." '*⁵*But they paid no attention and went away, this one to his own field, and that one to his business.* ⁶*The others, however, seized his servants, treated them shamefully, and killed them.* ⁷*But the king*ᵃ *became angry, and he sent his troops,*ᵇ *and he destroyed those murderers and burned their city.* ⁸*Then he said to his servants: 'The wedding banquet is ready, but those who had been invited were not worthy.* ⁹*Go therefore to where the highways exit from the city and invite as many as you encounter to the wedding banquet.'* ¹⁰*And those servants went out onto the highways and gathered together all whom*ᶜ *they found, both bad and good. And the wedding banquet*ᵈ *was filled with guests.*

¹¹*"But when the king entered to survey those who were reclining at the tables, he saw there a man who was not clothed in a garment appropriate to a wedding banquet.*ᵉ ¹²*And he said to him: 'Friend, how did you enter here without a wedding garment?' But he was silent.* ¹³*Then the king said to the servants: 'Bind*ᶠ *him hand and foot and cast*ᵍ *him into the outer darkness. There will be weeping and grinding of teeth there.'* ¹⁴*For all are called,*ʰ *but not all are chosen."*ʰ

## Notes

ᵃ Some MSS (Θ *f*¹³ lat syᵖ mae boᵖᵗ) insert ἀκούσας, "having heard"; many other MSS (C [D] W TR syʰ) read καὶ ἀκούσας ὁ βασιλεὺς ἐκεῖνος, "and when that king heard."

ᵇ D *f*¹ it syᶜ boᵖᵗ have the sing. τὸ στράτευμα αὐτοῦ, "his army."

ᶜ οὕς, "whom." Many MSS (B² C L W Θ *f*¹ TR it syʰ) have ὅσους, "as many as," probably through the influence of the preceding verse.

ᵈ γάμος, "wedding banquet." ℵ B* L have νυμφών, in the sense of "wedding hall," described by Metzger as "an Alexandrian correction" to avoid the awkwardness of referring to a banquet as "filled." *TCGNT*, 58.

ᵉ ἔνδυμα γάμου, lit. "a wedding garment."

ᶠ D it (syᵃ·ᶜ) have ἄρατε αὐτὸν ποδῶν καὶ χειρῶν καὶ βάλετε, "take him by the feet and hands and cast (him)."

ᵍ Many MSS (C W TR [syʰ]) insert ἄρατε αὐτὸν καί, "take him and."

ʰ L *f*¹ sa add the definite article οἱ before each of the nouns for "called" and "chosen." Lit., the verse reads "Many are called, but few are chosen." For a justification of the translation above, see *Comment.*

## Form/Structure/Setting

A. The final parable in this closely interrelated sequence of three parables (beginning in 21:28) speaks again concerning the lack of response among the Jews to Jesus and his message. As in the preceding and parallel parable of the wicked tenant farmers, again there is reference to the killing of servants and the loss on the part of those who ignore the invitation to the banquet, including the loss of their favored status. The invitation to the messianic banquet is opened up to all, "both bad and good" (cf. 21:31). And thus the failure of the Jews to respond to the invitation of the king becomes the opportunity of all others. Yet the final semi-independent verses (vv 11–14) indicate that this does not mean that the issue of righteousness becomes unimportant.

B. Except for vv 11–14, which are drawn from Matthew's special source, the parable is probably derived from Q (cf. Luke 14:15–24). Although Matthew and Luke agree substantially enough to posit a common source, the actual agreement in wording is small, and there are also a number of important differences between them. Thus whereas in Luke the story concerns "the master of a house" (οἰκοδεσπότης; Luke 14:21) who is holding a "great dinner" (δεῖπνον μέγα; Luke 14:16), in Matthew (v 2) it concerns a "king" (βασιλεύς) who held a "wedding banquet" (γάμος/γάμοι) "for his son" (τῷ υἱῷ αὐτοῦ). Probably Luke follows Q more closely, and Matthew's form of the story is influenced by the reference to the "son" in the preceding parables ("wedding banquet" is also consonant with Matthew's eschatological perspective in these parables). In contrast to Luke's single servant who is sent (Luke 14:17), Matthew uses the plural τοὺς δούλους αὐτοῦ, "his servants" (v 3), and then refers to the sending of ἄλλους δούλους, "other servants" (v 4), changes that again conform the story more closely to that of the preceding parable (cf. 21:36). The same is true of Matthew's addition of the shameful treatment and killing of these servants (v 6; cf. 21:35–36). Matthew's statement, "Look, I have prepared my food [τὸ ἄριστόν μου], my bulls and fattened cattle have been slaughtered" (v 4c), was either omitted by Luke (who refers explicitly to an evening meal [δεῖπνον]) or is an unusual addition to Q by Matthew. In v 5 Matthew's "this one went to his field, that one to his business," in comparison with Luke's longer description (Luke 14:18–20) together with Matthew's omission of Luke's third instance (the man who had just taken a wife), appears to be characteristic Matthean abbreviation. Totally missing in Luke, and probably Matthean additions to Q, are the sending of the soldiers, the destruction of those who had killed the king's servants, and the burning of their city (22:7). Luke's note of judgment is found only at the end: "For I tell you that none of these people who were called will taste of my banquet" (12:24, omitted by Matthew). Probably another Matthean addition is found in the statement of v 8, οἱ δὲ κεκλημένοι οὐκ ἦσαν ἄξιοι, "but those who had been invited were not worthy." In v 9 Matthew's ὅσους, "as many as," is apparently an abbreviation of the material reflected in Luke ("the poor, the crippled, blind and lame"). Matthew's emphasis in the pericope is not here but in the added words πονηρούς τε καὶ ἀγαθούς, "both bad and good" (v 10). Finally, Matthew also omits the reference to the return of the servant with the report that after he had done as ordered, there was yet space, and the second sending out of the servant with instructions to "compel them to enter" (Luke 14:22–23). This material, probably in Q, was not pertinent to his purposes. Considerable freedom is thus seen in Matthew's adaptation of the Q material for his own emphasis.

Vv 11–14 find no parallels in Mark or Luke and are appended by Matthew from some source other than Mark or Q. The judgment oracle of v 13 finds a close parallel with that of 8:12 in reference to "the sons of the kingdom," agreeing verbatim with that passage in the words about casting εἰς τὸ σκότος τὸ ἐξώτερον· ἐκεῖ ἔσται ὁ κλαυθμὸς καὶ ὁ βρυγμὸς τῶν ὀδόντων, "into the outermost darkness; there there will be weeping and the grinding of teeth." The concluding logion of v 14 is found nearly verbatim in *Barn.* 4.14, but without the conjunction and the verb γάρ εἰσιν, "for they are."

C. The parable of the wedding banquet probably concluded originally with v 10, with its reference to the filling up of the hall with guests. Matthew has appended a further brief parable to this (vv 11–13), which, despite the skill with which it is joined to the preceding parable, makes a different point altogether. This is in turn followed by an originally separate logion (v 14). The following outline may be suggested: (1) the parable of the wedding banquet, divided further into (a) (i) the first call to the banquet (vv 1–3a) and (ii) the first refusal (v 3b); (b) (i) the second call to the banquet (v 4) and (ii) the second refusal (v 5); (c) the killing of the servants (v 6); (d) the wrathful response of the king (v 7); (e) the extension of the call to all (vv 8–9); and (f) the in-gathering of bad and good (v 10); (2) the parable of the required wedding garment, divided into (a) the king's question (vv 11–12) and (b) the judgment of the one without a wedding garment (v 13); and (3) a final logion (v 14). The syntactical structure of the pericope provides only a few parallelisms. The two sendings of servants employ the same verb, ἀπέστειλεν, "he sent," and direct object, δούλους, "servants" (vv 3, 4). The three clauses in the Matthean material beginning with ἰδού, "look," in v 4c, end similarly, in euphonic if not syntactic parallelism: ἡτοίμακα . . . τεθυμένα . . . ἕτοιμα. Matthew has constructed the clauses of v 5b and c (beginning ὃς μέν . . . ὃς δέ . . . ) in parallelism. The parallel aorist verbs in v 7, ἀπώλεσεν, "he destroyed," and ἐνέπρησεν, "he burned," may also be noted. The logion of v 8 also displays syntactic parallelism. The parallel epexegetical πονηρούς τε καὶ ἀγαθούς, "both evil and good" (v 10), should be noted. And finally the parallelism of the concluding logion (v 14) is striking. Matthew's hand is responsible for many of these structural features, though some may have come to him already in his special source.

D. A cluster of related questions emerges in the interpretation of the reference in 22:7 to the angry king who "sent his soldiers, destroyed those murderers, and burned their city." Two main issues are raised by these words: (1) Do they refer to the destruction of Jerusalem, and (2) if so, what does this entail for the date of the Gospel? With regard to the first of these, it must be admitted from the start that the details, especially of the sending of the soldiers and the burning of the city (not hitherto mentioned in the parable), seem somewhat strange in the context of the parable. On the other hand, it may be that these details are innocent elements of the parable—simply a part of the story—and no more; i.e., they may allude to nothing beyond themselves. Rengstorf, for example, has shown that the language used here is typical of that used in the ancient world in referring to punitive expeditions. If this is stock phraseology, there is no need to see a reference to the destruction of Jerusalem here (indeed, according to Josephus, only the temple, and not the city, was destroyed by fire). Reicke also shows that the language in question does not necessarily point to the destruction of Jerusalem, as is so often concluded. Even if one nevertheless feels compelled to understand the words as an allusion to the destruction of Jerusalem, this hardly demonstrates a post-70 date for the Gospel. Jesus is shortly to prophesy the fall of the city (24:2–26), and thus the present passage could itself be an anticipation of the future rather than *post eventum.* Gundry hence concludes that the prophecy of chap. 24 "may have triggered Matthew's present insertion [v 6]" (437). For further discussion of the date of the Gospel, see *Introduction,* in Hagner, *Matthew 1–13,* lxxiii–lxxv.

E. As with the preceding parable, the question of the authenticity of this parable is often raised. Again we have the obvious allegorical character of the parable, a perspective that seems to be after the fact, especially in the possible allusion to the fall of Jerusalem, and again a parallel in *Gos. Thom.* 64. The same comments made in connection with the authenticity of 21:33–44 are applicable here (see on that pericope, *Form/Structure/Setting* §D). On allegory in the parables of Jesus, see "The Interpretation of Parables," in Hagner, *Matthew 1–13,* 364–65.

## Comment

**1–2** The introductory καὶ ἀποκριθείς, "and he answered," is apparently formulaic rather than actually referring to a response or answer to those being addressed. The plural ἐν παραβολαῖς, "in parables" (cf. 13:3, 13, 34–35), may also be formulaic, unless it points to the original separateness of vv 11–13 as a second parable. Like those of chap. 13, this parable deals again with ἡ βασιλεία τῶν οὐρανῶν, "the kingdom of heaven" (for the formula beginning with ὡμοιώθη, "is similar," cf. 13:24 [including ἀνθρώπῳ, "to a man"]; 18:33 [verbatim agreement with v 2 through ἀνθρώπῳ βασιλεῖ, "a man, a king"]; 25:1). The "kingdom of heaven," the eschatological reality dawning in and through the ministry of Jesus, is paralleled by the analogy of a γάμος, "wedding banquet" (used alternately in the plural and singular [vv 8, 10, 11–12] with no difference in meaning). The analogy of eschatological fulfillment and a wedding banquet has already been encountered in Matthew (see 9:15) and is based on the expectation of the so-called messianic banquet (see *Comment* on 9:15; cf. Rev 19:7, 8–9). As in the preceding parable, a "son" (υἱός), now of a king, figures in the story (cf. the reference to the "bridegroom" in 9:15; 25:1; for bridegroom as "Messiah," see John 3:29). Again, as in the preceding parable, the son represents Jesus.

**3** The king ἀπέστειλεν τοὺς δούλους αὐτοῦ, "sent his servants" (the words are found verbatim in 21:34, and here, as there, are probably an allusion to the prophets), to call to the banquet τοὺς κεκλημένους, "those who had been invited," i.e., the "sons of the kingdom," the Jewish people. καὶ οὐκ ἤθελον ἐλθεῖν, "and they were not willing to come" (the imperfect tense emphasizing repeated unwillingness), alludes to the unresponsiveness of Israel to God's repeated invitation (cf. καὶ οὐκ ἠθελήσατε, "and you were not willing," in 23:37; cf. John 5:40).

**4–5** These verses repeat and expand on the preceding verse. As in the preceding parable, a second group of servants is sent with the call (πάλιν ἀπέστειλεν ἄλλους δούλους, "again he sent other servants," agrees verbatim with the beginning of 21:36). Now the emphasis is strongly on eschatological fulfillment: the animals (ταῦροι, "bulls," occurs in the Gospels only here, and σιτιστά, "fattened cattle," occurs in the NT only here) have been slaughtered, the feast (ἄριστον, "meal," occurs in Matthew only here) is prepared (cf. similar imagery in Wisdom's invitation to her banquet in Prov 9:2, 5), καὶ πάντα ἕτοιμα, "and everything is ready." Thus this second group probably consists in Matthew's mind not of the latter prophets, as in the preceding parable, but of John the Baptist, Jesus, and his disciples, i.e., those who bring the message of eschatological readiness. The call is issued with all force and clarity: δεῦτε εἰς τοὺς γάμους, "come to the wedding banquet." Yet the people of Israel were largely unresponsive. They "paid no attention" (ἀμελήσαντες, the only occurrence of the word in the Gospels; cf. Heb 2:3), they returned to their ordinary pursuits, to the field and to the shop (ἐμπορίαν, "business," occurs only here in the NT), as though no such invitation had been given or received. They denied the reality of what was announced and being celebrated.

**6** Worse than that, οἱ λοιποί, "the others," probably because they regarded the servant-messengers as deceivers, seized them, ὕβρισαν καὶ ἀπέκτειναν, "treated them shamefully and killed (them)." The applicability of the language to the fate of John the Baptist, Jesus (the verb ὑβρίζειν, "treat shamefully," occurring in Matthew only here, is used in the passion prediction of Luke 18:32; cf. its application to Paul in 1 Thess 2:2), and eventually the disciples is obvious (they thus share the same end as the prophets; cf. 21:35; 23:37).

**7** The response of the king to the ungrateful and unresponsive people who refused his invitation is not left to be supplied by the listeners, as in the preceding parable (cf. 21:40–41) but here is given as a part of the parable itself. The wrathful reaction of the king (in 18:34 ὀργίζεσθαι, "be wrathful," is also used in reference to a "king" [18:23], to whom Jesus likens his "heavenly Father") results in the sending of soldiers, the destruction of the guilty and treasonous people (τοὺς φονεῖς ἐκείνους, "those murderers," intensifies that guilt; cf. 21:41), and the burning of "their city" (τὴν πόλιν αὐτῶν). These details, on the one hand, seem rather far-fetched for the story of the parable itself and, on the other hand, correspond remarkably to the destruction of Jerusalem in A.D. 70 so that it is easy (though hardly necessary) to see a reference to that event here. However that may be, it is virtually impossible for post-70 readers of the Gospel not to see the destruction of Jerusalem alluded to in these words. See Gundry (436–37) for an argument that the language of this verse depends upon Isa 5:24–25. (For further discussion of this verse and its meaning for the date of Matthew, see above *Form/Structure/Setting* §D.)

**8–9** The king reiterates to his (remaining) servants that the wedding banquet is ἕτοιμος, "ready" (cf. v 4), a hint of realized eschatology, οἱ δὲ κεκλημένοι οὐκ ἦσαν ἄξιοι, "but those who had been invited were not worthy" (cf. the use of ἄξιος, "worthy," in Acts 13:46). The servants were therefore to go out to places on the highways where many were sure to pass (ἐπὶ τὰς διεξόδους τῶν ὁδῶν probably means not "street crossings" but "outlets," i.e., "the places where a street cuts *through* the city boundary and goes *out* into the open country"; so BAGD, 194A) and to call to the banquet ὅσους, "as many as," they found. This open invitation serves in this parable as the counterpart to the letting out of the vineyard to other tenants in the preceding parable (21:41, 43). The result in both cases is the loss of Israel's privileged position, here as those who had initially been invited.

**10** This verse records the fulfillment of the command contained in the preceding verse. The servants gathered all they found, πονηρούς τε καὶ ἀγαθούς, "both bad and good" (the emphasis thus falls on "the bad"; the same two words occur in the same order in 5:45). This mixture coincides with the parable of the dragnet, where the kingdom is likened to a net that gathered fish of every kind

(13:47–48) prior to the separation of good and bad. The stress thus is not, as one might have expected, on the gathering of Gentiles and Jews indiscriminately (although this too is probably implied) but on an earlier theme, the inclusion of the "unrighteous" with the "righteous" (cf. 21:31 with its reference to "tax collectors and harlots"; cf. 9:13). The result of the gathering of "all whom they found" was that the banquet ἐπλήσθη, "was filled," with guests (ἀνακειμένων, lit. "those reclining at table"). The messianic banquet thus finds its eschatological fullness in the inclusion of such unlikely people as Gentiles (cf. Rom 11:25) and those widely regarded as "the unrighteous."

**11–12** The material added by Matthew at this point (vv 11–14) apparently has as its purpose to emphasize the very great importance of righteousness for those who would enter the kingdom (cf. 5:20) and thus to balance the point made in v 10 concerning "both bad and good." This added material corresponds to the emphasis in the preceding parable on the giving of fruit in its season by the new tenant farmers (21:41, 43). Although these verses are carefully joined with what precedes (note: king, those reclining at table, wedding garment), it is difficult not to notice the awkwardness in the surprising requirement that one person called in off the street should be clothed in a "wedding garment." It is little wonder that the person was left "speechless" (RSV) under the circumstances. If, however, Matthew here adjoins a parable, or part of a parable, originally independent of this context, the problem is somewhat alleviated. The king observes at the messianic banquet someone (note Sim's conclusion [*HeyJ* 31 (1990) 165–78] that the man could also represent the Jewish leadership who decline the invitation in the first section of the pericope [vv 3–6]) who is not properly clothed, i.e., does not have an ἔνδυμα γάμου, "wedding garment." For such a garment as a metaphor for righteousness, cf. Rev 19:8, where at the marriage of the Lamb the Bride is granted to wear "fine linen, bright and pure," whereupon follows the statement: "for the fine linen is the righteous deeds [τὰ δικαιώματα] of the saints." To the king's inquiry (for the address ἑταῖρε, "friend," cf. 20:13; 26:58) as to how he had come to be there without the proper garment, no answer is given, for the person was without excuse. Although it has been suggested by some (e.g., Haacker, Gundry, Blomberg), the idea that the host provided the proper garment for the wedding feast is both difficult to substantiate and moreover irrelevant to Matthew's point (rightly Carson). There is, furthermore, no fundamental incompatibility between an invitation to all and the subsequent requirement of righteousness (*pace* Radl, who concludes that the latter emphasis must derive from the early church rather than from Jesus).

**13** Except for the reference to the binding of hands and feet, the king's severe pronouncement of judgment employs formulae used several times in the Gospel. Thus ἐκβάλετε αὐτὸν εἰς τὸ σκότος τὸ ἐξώτερον, "cast him into the outer darkness," is found also in 8:12, in reference to "the sons of the kingdom" who exhibit no faith, and verbatim in 25:30, where it is spoken to the "worthless servant" who is described as "wicked and slothful" in 25:26. (For the possible dependence of v 13a on *1 Enoch* 10:4a, see Sim.) The sentence of judgment in both of these passages (8:12; 25:30) also contains the second formula from Matthew's stock of apocalyptic imagery, ἐκεῖ ἔσται ὁ κλαυθμὸς καὶ ὁ βρυγμὸς τῶν ὀδόντων, "there then will be weeping and grinding of teeth," which is found verbatim also in 13:42, 50; 24:51, where it is applied to the unrighteous or wicked. The severity of the judgment pronounced upon the person without the wedding garment is similarly related to the person's failure in righteousness. The future judgment of the church is also to be considered (cf. Weder, 191–92).

**14** This final logion ties in well with the preceding and especially the parable of vv 1–10. In πολλοὶ γάρ εἰσιν κλητοί, "for many are called," the πολλοί is probably to be taken as a universalizing Semitism, which can be translated "everyone" (cf. the same word in the same sense in 20:28; see J. Jeremias, *TDNT* 6:541–42). Thus in keeping with the opening of the invitation to all, "as many as you find" (v 9), the point is that "everyone is invited." Counterbalancing this, however, is the second half of the logion, ὀλίγοι δὲ ἐκλεκτοί, "but few are chosen." The word ὀλίγοι, "few," is here very probably also to be understood as a Semitism meaning "fewer than" in the sense of "not all." The term does not indicate the smallness of the actual number of the chosen but merely that in contrast to the scope of the call not all are chosen (see esp. B. F. Meyer). The notion of election here works together with, rather than against, the reality of human responsibility constantly before the reader of Matthew. The mystery of election has already been presented in 11:27. The word οἱ ἐκλεκτοί, "the elect," becomes in 24:22, 24, 31 shorthand for the disciples of Christ. The statement here that only some are the "elect" describes from the divine perspective something very well known to Matthew's readers: that not all are receptive to Jesus and his message and not all bring forth the righteousness of the kingdom (cf. 7:13–14). Tragically, the people who had long been known by the adjective "chosen" lose their privilege through their unresponsiveness to the invitation. Their chosenness was in the final analysis a calling—a calling to which finally they were not true. A similar distinction between the saved and the lost is found in 2 Esdr 8:3, 41.

### Explanation

This final parable of the series of three focuses on the general unresponsiveness of the people of Israel generally and not merely the leadership of Israel. Ironically, the "chosen people" show in their refusal of the invitation that they are *not* all among the "elect" but only among the "called." Those initially invited are accordingly designated as "not worthy," and the invitation is broadened to include all, the "bad" as well as the "good," and by implication, finally, Gentiles as well as Jews. Those who would come must nevertheless respond appropriately, i.e., in a discipleship that produces the righteousness of the kingdom. In the end, although all are invited, not all will show themselves to be truly among the "elect." The pericope thus contains not only the good news of an open, rather than a restricted, invitation but also the sobering reminder of the seriousness of discipleship for those who respond. Matthew never tires of the theme of the righteousness of this discipleship—that of the kingdom of God. It constitutes a dividing point for all humanity and is the sole demonstrating criterion for membership among the elect.

# *Tribute to Caesar?*  *(22:15–22)*

## Bibliography

**Abel, E. L.** "Jesus and the Cause of Jewish National Independence." *REJ* 128 (1969) 247–52. **Abrahams, I.** "Give unto Caesar." In *Studies in Pharisaism and the Gospels.* Reprint. New York: Ktav, 1967. 1:62–65. **Barrett, C. K.** "The New Testament Doctrine of Church and State." In *New Testament Essays.* London: SPCK, 1972. 1–19. **Bruce, F. F.** "Render to Caesar." In *Jesus and the Politics of His Day,* ed. E. Bammel and C. F. D. Moule. Cambridge: Cambridge UP, 1984, 249–63. **Cuvillier, E.** "Marc, Justin, Thomas et les autres: Variations autour de la péricope de denier à César." *ETR* 67 (1992) 329–44. **Daube, D.** "Four Types of Questions: Mt 22.15–46." *JTS* n.s. 2 (1951) 45–48 (= *The New Testament and Rabbinic Judaism.* London: Athlone, 1956. 158–63). **Derrett, J. D. M.** "'Render to Caesar . . . .'" In *Law in the New Testament.* London: Darton, Longman and Todd, 1970. 313–38. **De Surgy, P.** "Rendez à César ce qui est à César, et à Dieu ce qui est à Dieu (Mt 22)." *AsSeign* 60 (1975) 16–25. **Giblin, C. H.** "'The Things of God' in the Question concerning Tribute to Caesar." *CBQ* 33 (1971) 510–27. **Goppelt, L.** "The Freedom to Pay the Imperial Tax (Mk 12, 17)." *SE* 2 [= TU 87] (1964) 185–94. **Hart, H. St. J.** "The Coin of 'Render unto Caesar . . .' (A Note on Some Aspects of Mark 12:13–17; Matt. 22:15–22; Luke 20:20–26)." In *Jesus and the Politics of His Day,* ed. E. Bammel and C. F. D. Moule. Cambridge: Cambridge UP, 1984. 241–48. **Kennard, J. S.** *Render to God: A Study of the Tribute Passage.* New York: Oxford UP, 1950. **Klemm, H. G.** "De censu Caesaris: Beobachtungen zu J. Duncan M. Derretts Interpretation der Perikope Mk. 12:13–17 par." *NovT* 24 (1982) 234–54. **Loewe, H. M. J.** *"Render unto Caesar": Religious and Political Loyalty in Palestine.* Cambridge: Cambridge UP, 1940. **Oster, R. E.** "'Show me a denarius': Symbolism of Roman Coinage and Christian Beliefs." *ResQ* 28 (1985–86) 107–15. **Stock, A.** "Render to Caesar." *BiTod* 62 (1972) 929–34.

## Translation

[15] *Then the Pharisees went and plotted concerning how they might trap him on some matter.*[a] [16] *And they sent their disciples together with the Herodians to him, saying:*[b] *"Teacher, we know that you are true, and that you teach the way of God in truth, and that no one matters specially to you, for you do not regard the status* [c] *of persons.* [17] *Tell us, therefore,*[d] *what you think: Is it right to pay tax to Caesar, or not?"* [18] *Jesus, knowing their evil intent,*[e] *said: "Why do you test me, hypocrites?* [19] *Show me the coin used for paying the tax."* *And they brought him a denarius.* [20] *And he*[f] *said to them: "Whose image and inscription are these?"* [21] *They said to him:*[g] *"Caesar's."* *Then he said to them: "Give the things that are Caesar's to Caesar and the things that are God's to God."* [22] *And when they heard this, they marveled, and leaving him, they departed.*

## Notes

[a] ἐν λόγῳ, lit. "in word," may also be translated "in something."

[b] λέγοντες, "saying" (thus C D W Θ *f*[1,13] and TR), a nominative, has as its subject the Pharisees, who thus speak through their disciples. A few important MSS (א B L) have the accusative λέγοντας, which would be translated "who said," i.e., the disciples who had been sent. This, however, is a construction found nowhere else in Matthew.

[c] Lit. "face." See *Comment.*

ᵈ D it syˢ omit εἰπὲ οὖν ἡμῖν, "Tell us, therefore."
ᵉ "Intent" added to translation for clarity.
ᶠ D L Z Θ *f*¹³ lat syˢ·ᶜ·ᵖ mae bo add ὁ Ἰησοῦς, "Jesus."
ᵍ ℵ B syᵖ omit αὐτῷ, "to him."

### Form/Structure/Setting

A.  Following the preceding three parables directed largely at Israel's religious leadership, a succession of controversies is initiated alternatively by the Pharisees (vv 15–21), Sadducees (vv 27–31), and again the Pharisees (vv 34–40). In all three instances Jesus passes the difficult tests that are set for him. The first concerns the sticky question of paying the head tax to Caesar. By catching Jesus on the horns of a dilemma, the Pharisees hope not only to discredit him as a teacher but to gain some information that might prove useful against him on some future occasion.

The final passage of the chapter (vv 41–46) involves a fourth question, in this instance initiated by Jesus. Daube has found in the four questions a grouping similar to that found in rabbinic tradition, consisting of questions of the following four types: (1) *hokmāh*, "wisdom" (halakhic interpretation of legal texts); (2) *bôrût*, "vulgarity" (questions ridiculing a belief); (3) *derek* ʾ*ereṣ*, "the way of the land" (questions of moral conduct); and (4) *haggādāh*, "legend" (interpretation of biblical texts with apparent contradictions). The correspondence of these four types with the nature of the four questions discussed in the remaining four pericopes of the chapter is remarkable.

B. Matthew here resumes his dependence on Mark (Mark 12:13–17; cf. Luke 20:20–26). There are no major differences between Matthew and Mark, and Matthew's wording follows Mark very closely. The few differences amount mainly to slight dislocations of Markan material, as, e.g., the transposition of the clause "you teach the way of God in truth" (v 16) to before the reference to Jesus not respecting persons rather than after it (cf. Mark 12:14). Apart from these few differences in word order and slight variations in vocabulary, only the following differences are worth noting. The opening verse (v 15) provides a transition not found in Mark, except for the reference to the attempt to "entrap" Jesus (Matthew uses παγιδεύσωσιν for Mark's ἀγρεύσωσιν), which is pulled ahead of the reference to the sending of the Pharisees' delegation (cf. Mark 12:13). In v 17 Matthew adds the words εἰπὲ οὖν ἡμῖν τί σοι δοκεῖ, "Tell us, therefore, what do you think?" and deletes Mark's redundant second question, "Shall we pay or shall we not pay?" (Mark 12:14). In v 18 Matthew supplants Mark's ὑπόκρισιν, "hypocrisy," with πονηρίαν, "evil," but then uses that word in the vocative ὑποκριταί, "hypocrites" (cf. Mark 12:15). In v 19 Matthew's τὸ νόμισμα τοῦ κήνσου, lit. "the coin of the tax," replaces Mark's δηνάριον, "denarius," though this word is used in the next clause (cf. Mark 12:15–16). Matthew's added final transition clause καὶ ἀφέντες αὐτὸν ἀπῆλθαν, "and leaving him, they departed," is apparently picked up verbatim from the end of the parable of the evil tenant farmers according to Mark (cf. Mark 12:12b), where it was originally omitted by Matthew.

C.  In keeping with its nature as a controversy or more particularly a "testing" pericope, this passage consists mainly of dialogue between the Pharisees and Jesus. The following may be suggested as an outline: (1) the Pharisees' attempt to entrap Jesus, divided into (a) the plotting (v 15), (b) the hypocritical preface (v

16), and (c) the question (v 17); (2) Jesus' response, divided into (a) the question of motive (v 18), (b) the image on the coin (vv 19–21a), and (c) the determining principle (v 21b); and (3) the amazement and departure of the delegation (v 22). The relatively brief exchanges between Jesus and his opponents provide little opportunity for structural parallelism. Some parallelism may be detected in the preface to the Pharisees' question (v 16), where four clauses employing present verbs occur, two referring to truth and two with negatives referring to the non-respect for persons. The articulation of Jesus' answer in v 21 is parallel in structure, although the verb ἀπόδοτε, "render," is assumed rather than stated in the second clause. The pericope is notable for its conciseness, except ironically for the redundancies of the preface to the Pharisees' question (v 16).

## Comment

**15** The Pharisees were last referred to in 21:45, where it was noted that they knew Jesus' parable of the evil tenant farmers was directed against them. Already in 12:14 the Pharisees "took counsel" (as here, συμβούλιον ἔλαβον) against Jesus concerning "how they might destroy him" (further parallel syntax except for the verb, which is here παγιδεύσωσιν, "might entrap," to which is added ἐν λόγῳ, lit. "in a word" or "in some matter"). On at least two previous occasions the Pharisees have come to Jesus "testing" him (πειράζοντες; 16:1; 19:3; cf. in the present chapter vv 18, 35). The purpose of the Pharisees here, as on those occasions, is clear: to "entrap" Jesus by getting him to say something that might be used against him in their attempt to get rid of him.

**16** The "disciples" (μαθητάς) of the Pharisees are mentioned only here in the NT. This delegation is apparently sent to carry out the purposes of the Pharisaic leadership. The "Herodians," who are linked with the Pharisees again in the Gospel tradition only in Mark 3:6 where they plot to destroy Jesus, were apparently royalists who supported the family of Herod and had a vested interest in the maintenance of peace and the status quo in Palestine. These Herodians and disciples of the Pharisees approach Jesus with complimentary words, not as a *captatio benevolentiae* so much as a deliberate attempt to incline Jesus from the start to an answer that might incriminate him. διδάσκαλε, "teacher," is a title of respect, not unlike "rabbi" (cf. 23:8), but is used regularly in Matthew when non-disciples address Jesus (cf. 9:11; 12:38; 17:24; 19:16; 22:24, 36). The assertions ἀληθὴς εἶ, "you are true," and τὴν ὁδὸν τοῦ θεοῦ ἐν ἀληθείᾳ διδάσκεις, "you teach the way of God in truth," seem designed to flatter Jesus into speaking as boldly as possible. The questioners hardly believed what they said at this point or they would have taken Jesus and his message more seriously than they did. For οἴδαμεν ὅτι, "we know that," used similarly, cf. John 3:2. τὴν ὁδὸν τοῦ θεοῦ, "the way of God," probably alludes to the teaching of Jesus concerning righteousness (cf. Gen 18:19; Ps 25:9; Matt 3:3; 7:14). The following two clauses, "no one matters to you specially, for you do not look on the face of the people" (for the last clause, cf. 1 Sam 16:7), seem to be designed to invite Jesus to give an incriminating answer to the question that follows. If Jesus was no respecter of the wealth, position, or power of a person, he might well speak critically of the emperor's taxation of the Jews.

**17**   The question itself was a brilliant one because either of the alternative answers could be used against Jesus. If he were to answer that it is right to give tribute to Caesar, he would be discredited among the people as compromising on a basic principle and as thus not being worthy of the name "prophet." If, on the other hand, he were to disallow the paying of the tax to Caesar, that could be used against him in any later presentation of Jesus to the Roman authorities as a dangerous revolutionary. The question τί δοκεῖ, lit. "what does it seem," is generally in the mouth of Jesus (17:25; 18:12; 21:28; 22:42) rather than in that of his opponents as here. κῆνσον, "tax," was an annual head tax (cf. *census*) paid by all adults. It was a painful reminder of the Roman occupation.

**18**   Jesus saw through their pretense (for γνούς, "knowing," in the sense of Jesus' special knowledge, cf. 12:15; 16:8; 26:10), referred to here as their "evil" (τὴν πονηρίαν αὐτῶν; this is the only use of the noun in Matthew, but the cognate adjective πονηρός is applied to the Pharisees in 12:34, 39; 16:4). Jesus refers to the Pharisees as ὑποκριταί, "hypocrites," in 15:7 and of course repeatedly in chap. 23. For the verb πειράζειν, "test," which is applied only to Jesus in Matthew, cf. 4:1, 3; 16:1; 19:3; 22:35 (in five of the seven instances, the subject of the verb is the Pharisees).

**19–20**   Jesus asks to see the coin used to pay the tax (a Roman coin was required in this case) in order to provide a visual aid that will serve to strengthen his answer. When the denarius is brought to him, he asks his questioner to identify the picture and name on the coin (εἰκών, "image," and ἐπιγραφή, "inscription," both occur in Matthew only here). The reason for this question becomes clear in the following verse.

**21**   The Pharisees and Herodians quickly respond that it is the picture and name "of Caesar" (Καίσαρος). The simplicity and yet stunning appropriateness of Jesus' next statement, which nicely resolves the problem, is striking to say the least. Since the coin has the emperor's picture and name on it (for details, see Hart), it may be regarded as belonging to him, and thus it is right and proper to give it to him. Indeed, because of the offensiveness of a human image on a coin, it would be most appropriate for Jews to be rid of such a coin (see Bruce). If Jesus was willing to pay the temple tax (17:4), he was equally willing to pay the tax to the Romans. But this concession is balanced by the complementary command to give God the things that are his (τὰ τοῦ θεοῦ, "the things of God"). This way of expressing God's claim on his children makes it practically all inclusive (Giblin suggests an implied reference to the "image" and "inscription" of God in relation to his creatures). We must render to God our very selves in obedience and service, which will in time touch all we have and own. Caesar can have his paltry tax if only one gives to God his due (cf. Bruce, 261). Later NT emphasis on paying taxes and rendering honor to secular rulers (Rom 13:7; 1 Peter 2:17) depends to no small extent on this logion. (See Goppelt for insightful discussion.) Derrett's notion that by obeying Caesar one obeys the commandments of God does not seem to be the point here.

**22**   The insincere questioners could not themselves help admiring this answer (ἀκούσαντες ἐθαύμασαν, "when they heard, they marveled"; in the other occurrences of the word in Matthew, it describes the response to what Jesus did, rather than what he said; cf. 8:27; 9:33; 15:31; 21:20). Jesus has indeed shown himself to be one who teaches "the way of God in truth" (v 16). They departed without accomplishing their purpose (the identical words καὶ ἀφέντες αὐτὸν ἀπῆλθαν, "and leaving him, they departed," borrowed here by Matthew, occur in Mark 12:12 where they describe a similar departure of Jesus' opponents in frustration).

### Explanation

The design of the Pharisees to entrap Jesus failed because he was able to transcend the dilemma they forced on him. And in so doing, Jesus was at the same time able to articulate a fundamental principle by which the disciples could chart their existence as the people of God's kingdom living in a yet imperfect world governed by secular authorities. This logion served as the beginning point of what was to be elaborated centuries later in the Lutheran two-kingdom theory. The later NT writers regard the ruling powers as instituted by God and as worthy of honor, faithfulness, support, and intercession (e.g., Rom 13:1–17; 1 Peter 2:13–17). It is right to render to Caesar what is Caesar's. Jesus was no Zealot or revolutionary who advocated the overthrow of the Roman government. But neither did he put priority upon loyalty to secular government. If one rendered to the state its restricted due, all the more was one to render to God his unrestricted due—the totality of one's being and substance, one's existence, was to be rendered to God and nothing less. Loyalty to Caesar must always be set in the larger context and thus be relativized by the full submission of the self to God. The bottom line for the disciple of Jesus is to "render to God the things that are his."

# Whose Wife Will She Be in the Resurrection? (22:23–33)

### Bibliography

**Baumbach, G.** "Der sadduzäische Konservativismus." In *Literatur und Religion des Frühjudentums,* ed. J. Maier and J. Schreiner. Würzburg: Echter, 1973. 201–13. **Blakeney, E. H.** "A Note on St. Matthew xxii. 29." *ExpTim* 4 (1892–93) 382. **Carton, G.** "Comme des anges dans le ciel." *BVC* 28 (1959) 46–52. **Cohn-Sherbok, D. M.** "Jesus' Defence of the Resurrection of the Dead." *JSNT* 11 (1981) 64–73. **Downing, F. G.** "The Resurrection of the Dead: Jesus and Philo." *JSNT* 15 (1982) 42–50. **Dreyfus, F.** "L'argument scripturaire de Jésus en faveur de la résurrection des morts." *RB* 66 (1959) 213–24. **Ellis, E. E.** "Jesus, the Sadducees and Qumran." *NTS* 10 (1963–64) 274–79. **Janzen, J. G.** "Resurrection and Hermeneutics: On Exodus 3.6 in Mark 12.26." *JSNT* 23 (1985) 43–58. **Kilgallen, J. J.** "The Sadducees and Resurrection from the Dead: Luke 20, 27–40." *Bib* 67 (1986) 478–95. **Manns, F.** "La technique du 'Al Tiqra' dans les évangiles." *RevScRel* 64 (1990) 1–7. **Müller, K.** "Jesus und die Sadduzäer." In *Biblische Randbemerkungen.* FS R. Schnackenberg, ed. H. Merklein and J. Lange. Würzburg: Echter, 1974. 3–79. **Reicke, B.** "The God of Abraham, Isaac, and Jacob in New Testament Theology." In *Unity and Diversity in New Testament Theology.* FS G. E. Ladd, ed. R. A. Guelich. Grand Rapids: Eerdmans, 1978. 186–94. **Rigaux, B.** *Dieu l'a ressuscité: Exégèse et théologie biblique.* Gembloux: Duculot, 1973. **Schubert, K.** "Die Entwicklung der Auferstehungslehre von der nachexilischen bis zur frührabbinischen

Zeit." *BZ* 6 (1962) 177–214. **Schwankl, O.** *Die Sadduzäerfrage (Mk. 12, 18–27 par.): Eine exegetisch-theologische Studie zur Auferstehungserwartung.* BBB 66. Frankfurt am Main: Athenäum, 1987.

## Translation

²³*On that day Sadducees came to him, asserting*ᵃ *that there is no resurrection, and asked him a question,*ᵇ ²⁴*saying: "Teacher, Moses said: 'If anyone dies not having had children, his brother shall marry his wife*ᶜ *and shall raise up children*ᵈ *for his brother.'* ²⁵*Now there were seven brothers among us. And the first, after he had married, died, and, not having offspring,*ᵈ *he left his wife to his brother.* ²⁶*The same thing happened with*ᵉ *the second and third brothers,*ᶠ *even to the seventh.* ²⁷*And last of all the wife died.*ᵍ ²⁸*In the resurrection, therefore, whose wife of the seven will she be? For they all had her as a wife."*ʰ ²⁹*Jesus answered and said to them: "You are misled because you know*ⁱ *neither the scriptures nor the power of God.* ³⁰*For in the resurrection they will*ʲ *not marry nor will they give a daughter*ᵏ *to be married, but they will be as the angels*ˡ *in heaven are.*ᵐ ³¹*But as to the issue of the resurrection of the dead, have you not read the word spoken by God to you, saying:* ³²*'I am the God of Abraham and the*ⁿ *God of Isaac and the*ⁿ *God of Jacob'? He*ᵒ *is not [the]*ᵖ *God of the dead but of the living."* ³³*And when the crowds heard this, they were amazed at his teaching.*

## Notes

ᵃ λέγοντες, lit. "saying." The reading οἱ λέγοντες, "who say," is in fact found in ℵ² K L Θ *f*¹³, but the insertion of the article is probably caused by scribal assimilation to the parallels (Mark 12:18; Luke 20:27). The article could have been omitted through homoioteleuton (cf. the last syllable of Σαδδουκαῖοι), but if it were originally present, "this would be the only place where Matthew has provided an explanation of this sort concerning Jewish affairs" (*TCGNT*, 58).

ᵇ "A question" added to translation.

ᶜ D omits τὴν γυναῖκα αὐτοῦ, "his wife," probably through homoioteleuton (cf. αὐτοῦ following ὁ ἀδελφός).

ᵈ σπέρμα, lit. "seed."

ᵉ "The same thing happened with" translates ὁμοίως καί, lit. "similarly also."

ᶠ "Brothers" added to translation for clarity.

ᵍ Many MSS (D Θ *f*¹³ TR lat syᵖ·ʰ saᵐˢˢ mae bo) insert καί, "also," probably through assimilation to the parallels (Mark 12:22; Luke 20:32).

ʰ "As a wife" added to translation.

ⁱ Lit. "not knowing." See *Comment.*

ʲ All the verbs in this verse are in the present tense. They are translated here with future tenses because the resurrection is a future event.

ᵏ "A daughter" added to translation for clarity.

ˡ A large number of MSS (ℵ L W *f*¹³ TR) add θεοῦ or τοῦ θεοῦ, "of God," which may well be a "natural expansion." If, on the other hand, the words were original, it is difficult to know why they would have been omitted from B and D (see *TCGNT*, 58–59).

ᵐ "Are" is added to translation.

ⁿ The definite article ὁ, "the," is omitted twice by ℵ, perhaps to conform the text more closely to the LXX of Exod 3:6.

ᵒ Many MSS ([Θ *f*¹³] TR syʰ) have ὁ θεὸς θεός, "God is (not) a God . . . ." See too the following Note.

ᵖ ὁ, "the," found in B L Γ Δ *f*¹, is omitted by ℵ D W. The *UBSGNT* committee found it difficult to decide whether ὁ was omitted to conform the text to the parallel in Mark 12:27 or was added to conform to the immediately preceding occurrences of ὁ θεός. Thus the word is retained in brackets. See *TCGNT*, 59.

## Form/Structure/Setting

A. The Pharisees, having left the scene in frustration (although they will again be on the offensive in vv 34–40), are followed next by the Sadducees in the rapid-fire attempt to challenge and overthrow the authority of Jesus as a teacher. The clever question they bring to Jesus grows directly out of their denial of the resurrection. Although they think they have trapped Jesus by their unusual case study, as well as established their point of view in opposition to the Pharisees (who with Jesus believed in the resurrection), they instead receive a rather sharp rebuke from Jesus for being ignorant of both the scripture and the power of God (v 29). Jesus' handling of the question confirms his authority as a most exceptional teacher.

B. As in the preceding pericope, Matthew depends on Mark (Mark 12:18–27; cf. Luke 20:27–40), whose wording is followed rather closely. Among differences, the following should be noted: Matthew's opening phrase ἐν ἐκείνη τῇ ἡμέρᾳ, "on that day," and concluding verse, "And when they heard, the crowds were amazed at his teaching," are his own additions to the Markan pericope. In v 23 Matthew omits Mark's οἵτινες, "who" (Mark 12:18), thus transforming the participial clause into a statement of the Sadducees. In v 24 Matthew shortens Mark's formula ἔγραψεν ἡμῖν ὅτι, "wrote to us that" (Mark 12:19), to the simple εἶπεν, "said." In the words drawn from the OT in v 24 (cf. Mark 12:19), Matthew makes a few minor changes that have the effect of aligning the wording a little more closely with the OT texts in question. Thus after the abbreviation of Mark's τινος ἀδελφός, "a brother of someone," to the simple τις, "someone," Matthew omits Mark's καὶ καταλίπῃ γυναῖκα, "and leaves a wife," and ἵνα, "that" (which are not in the OT texts alluded to), substitutes ἐπιγαμβρεύσει, "will marry" (cf. γάμβρευσαι in Gen 38:8) for Mark's λάβῃ, "take," and substitutes ἀναστήσει (cf. Gen 38:8) for ἐξαναστήσῃ, both meaning "will raise up." In v 25 Matthew adds παρ' ἡμῖν, "among us" (bringing a degree of realism to the story), and the explanatory clause ἀφῆκεν τὴν γυναῖκα αὐτοῦ τῷ ἀδελφῷ αὐτοῦ, "he left his wife to his brother" (pointing clearly to the law of levirate marriage). V 26 abbreviates Mark 12:21–22a by the simple use of ὁμοίως, "similarly." In v 28 Matthew omits Mark's redundant ὅταν ἀναστῶσιν, "when they rise" (if it was originally in Mark's text). In v 29 Matthew recasts Mark's question into a more forceful statement, omitting οὐ διὰ τοῦτο, "is it not on account of this?" (Mark 12:24). In v 31 Matthew omits Mark's ἐν τῇ βίβλῳ Μωϋσέως ἐπὶ τοῦ βάτου, "in the book of Moses, concerning the thorn bush" (Mark 12:26), perhaps regarding it as unnecessary for his readers. Mark follows this with πῶς εἶπεν αὐτῷ ὁ θεός, "how God said to him [Moses]," which in Matthew becomes τὸ ῥηθὲν ὑμῖν ὑπὸ τοῦ θεοῦ, "what was spoken to you by God" (again the adaptation may have in mind Matthew's Jewish readers). Matthew's addition of the verb εἰμί, "am," in the citation itself (v 32; cf. Mark 12:26) conforms it more closely to the LXX of Exod 3:6. Finally, Matthew omits Mark's anticlimactic πολὺ πλανᾶσθε, "you err seriously" (Mark 12:27), thereby ending the response of Jesus with reference to the OT citation. Other Matthean changes of Mark not noted here are minor and mainly of a stylistic nature.

C. This second "testing" pericope is very similar in form to the preceding pericope. Again the dialogue between Jesus and his opponents holds center stage. The following outline may be suggested: (1) the question of the Sadducees, divided further into (a) the initial denial of the resurrection (v 23), (b) the Mosaic command of levirate marriage (v 24), and (c) the specific case of a woman who had had seven brothers as her husbands (vv 25–28); (2) the response of Jesus, divided further into (a) the ignorance of the Sadducees (v 29), (b) the nature of resurrection life (v 30), and (c) God as the God of the living (vv 31–32); and (3) the reaction of the crowds (v 33). The dialogical character of the passage and the citation of the OT do not present much opportunity for structural symmetry or parallelism. What is to be found interestingly occurs in the words of Jesus, where we may note the parallel direct objects γραφάς, "scriptures," and δύναμιν, "power" (v 29), the parallel verbs γαμοῦσιν, "marry," and γαμίζονται, "give in marriage" (v 30), and the truncated parallelism in v 32 between νεκρῶν, "of the dead," and ζώντων, "of the living." The threefold formula "the God of Abraham, the God of Isaac, and the God of Jacob" (v 31), although drawn from Exod 3:6, also bears noting.

D. The story of the woman married (necessarily) to seven brothers bears a striking similarity to that of Sarah in the book of Tobit, who married seven husbands only to see each of them die without bringing to her the benefit of children (Tob 3:7–8). Although it is not mentioned in Tobit, it may be assumed that, following the law of levirate marriage, some of her seven husbands were brothers. The main difference between the two stories is that none of Sarah's marriages was consummated since each husband died on the wedding night, being slain by the demon Asmodeus "before he had been with her as his wife" (Tob 3:8), whereas in the Sadducees' story all of the seven brothers had her as wife, yet without success in producing children. The Sadducees' story seems to have a legendary character (despite Matthew's παρ' ἡμῖν, "among us"), and if based in reality rather than being simply an elaboration of the Tobit story, it seems at least to have been influenced by Tobit (e.g., perhaps in the number "seven").

### Comment

**23**   Matthew's bridge from the preceding passage, ἐν ἐκείνῃ τῇ ἡμέρᾳ, "on that day" (cf. 13:1), to the present passage may be a way of linking similar passages rather than a strictly chronological note. Although no indication is given by Matthew, it is clear that the Sadducees, like the Pharisees, have come to "test" Jesus as a teacher. In the present instance, if Jesus could be made to side with the Sadducees against the Pharisees on the question of the resurrection, Jesus would lose face, they would be vindicated, and their position with the people might be strengthened. The Sadducees come insisting on their position from the start, λέγοντες μὴ εἶναι ἀνάστασιν, "saying there is no resurrection." The Sadducees held only the five books of Moses as inspired and found no evidence there for believing in the resurrection (the disbelief in the resurrection referred to in 1 Cor 15:12 stems from quite different causes). Their disagreement with the Pharisees on the question was notorious (cf. Acts 23:8). Since the resurrection of Jesus and hence of all the dead was to become so critically important in the church (cf. Acts 4:2), much is at stake in the present exchange.

**24**   The Sadducees, like the Pharisees in the preceding pericope, address Jesus as διδάσκαλε, "teacher" (see *Comment* on v 16; cf. v 36). Their question is prefaced by the quotation of the words of Moses, establishing the practice of levirate marriage. The words are a rather free quotation drawn from two passages, Deut 25:5

and Gen 38:8. In the ἐάν, "if," clause only the words ἐάν, "if," and ἀποθάνῃ, "dies," agree exactly with the LXX of Deut 25:5; τις, "anyone," and μὴ ἔχων τέκνα, "not having children," are paraphrases of the LXX text. The remainder of the quoted words, beginning with the verb ἐπιγαμβρεύσει, "shall marry" (LXX: γάμβρευσαι), closely resemble the LXX of Gen 38:8, especially the last clause καὶ ἀναστήσει [LXX: ἀνάστησον] σπέρμα τῷ ἀδελφῷ αὐτοῦ [LXX: σου], "and he shall raise up seed for his brother," which agrees nearly verbatim. This presentation of the Mosaic legislation serves as the premise explaining the unusual story that follows.

**25–28** Matthew's addition of παρ᾽ ἡμῖν, "among us," makes the case more than simply a hypothetical one. Something of the kind must not have been that unusual given the levirate practices (even if "seven" brothers represents an extreme example; cf. above *Form/Structure/Setting* §D). The problem raised by the Sadducees exists even where two brothers may have been concerned. In the Sadducees' story, none of the six brothers was able to fulfill the raising up of children to the first brother. For ὕστερον, lit. "afterwards" (v 27), in the sense of "last," see BAGD, 849b, and cf. 21:37; 26:60. With the death of the wife, the problem is fully set: whose wife will she be ἐν τῇ ἀναστάσει, "in the resurrection"? The final clause, following the question, πάντες γὰρ ἔσχον αὐτήν, "for all had her," makes clear that each had truly been her husband in the sense of having consummated the marriage sexually (unlike the parallel in Tob 3:7–8).

**29** The error of the Sadducees was their denial of the resurrection. Jesus attributes this error to their ignorance (μὴ εἰδότες may be translated as a causal participle, i.e., "because you do not know") of the scriptures and the power of God. τὰς γραφάς, "the scriptures," would normally refer to approximately our OT canon, but here the implication may be that the Sadducees did not even know their own canonical scriptures, i.e., the five books of Moses, as the citation of Exod 3:6 in v 32 seems to confirm. τὴν δύναμιν τοῦ θεοῦ, "the power of God," obviously refers to the ability of God to raise the dead in a final, eschatological resurrection (cf. 1 Cor 6:14). The scriptural argument is pursued further in vv 31–32, but the argument concerning God's power is left at this point.

**30** The problem raised by the Sadducees' story is in fact an imagined one, based on an incorrect extrapolation from life in the present age to that of the future. The life of the resurrection order, while presumably in many respects in continuity with present experience, is at least different from the present in that there will be no marriage. οὔτε γαμοῦσιν οὔτε γαμίζονται, "neither marry nor give in marriage," are mutually reinforcing but make the same point: there will be no marriage in the resurrection order. Jesus' answer must here depend on supernatural knowledge. The concluding clause ἀλλ᾽ ὡς ἄγγελοι ἐν τῷ οὐρανῷ εἰσιν, "but they will be like the angels in heaven," must not be generalized to mean altogether or in every respect. The only point made here is that so far as marriage (and sex?) is concerned, human beings will be like the angels, i.e., not marrying.

**31–32** Having thus solved the Sadducees' problem case with an authoritative pronouncement on the subject, Jesus returns to the basic issue of the reality of the resurrection itself. περὶ δὲ τῆς ἀναστάσεως τῶν νεκρῶν, lit. "but concerning the resurrection of the dead," means in effect "to return to the initial problem." These words are not to be applied to the OT citation of v 32, from which only an inference is drawn concerning the reality of the resurrection. The formulaic question οὐκ ἀνέγνωτε, "have you not read?" is used often by Jesus in Matthew in responding to his opponents (cf. 12:3, 5; 19:4; 21:16, 42). In all of Matthew's introductory formulae to his OT quotations, only here do we find ὑμῖν, "to you" (to the Jewish people, including the Sadducees), and τὸ ῥηθὲν . . . ὑπὸ τοῦ θεοῦ, "what was spoken by God" (cf. ὑπὸ κυρίου, "by the Lord," in 1:22; 2:15). The latter is probably occasioned by the fact that God speaks in the cited material.

The passage cited in v 32, drawn from material accepted as canonical by the Sadducees, agrees verbatim with the LXX of Exod 3:6 except for the omission of τοῦ πατρός σου θεός, "your father, God," and the insertion of the definite articles before θεός, "God," in its second and third occurrences (cf. the same formula "the God of Abraham, and the God of Isaac, and the God of Jacob" in Exod 3:15, 16). Long after the death of Abraham, Isaac, and Jacob, God revealed himself to Moses as the God of the patriarchs. This implies that they are still alive since it would mean little to say that God "is" (εἰμί, present tense) the God of dead men. The concluding explanatory words following the quotation make just this point: οὐκ ἔστιν [ὁ] θεὸς νεκρῶν ἀλλὰ ζώντων, "he is not the God of the dead but of the living." The point that Abraham, Isaac, and Jacob, although having died, "are alive in God" (ζῶσιν τῷ θεῷ) is also made in 4 Macc 7:19; 16:25. If God is the God of the patriarchs, they are by implication alive after their death (whether in Sheol [thus Ellis] or otherwise is of no consequence to the argument), and thus the ground is prepared for the reality of the future resurrection. For this reason, in 8:11 Matthew can earlier refer to the coming time when "many from east and west will come and recline at table with Abraham and Isaac and Jacob in the kingdom of heaven." Jesus' argument is distinctive and does not follow the commonly used rules of rabbinic argument from scripture (see Cohn-Sherbok; for a parallel with Philo's argument from the same Exodus passage, see Downing).

**33** οἱ ὄχλοι, "the crowds," having overheard the exchange between the Sadducees and Jesus, ἐξεπλήσσοντο ἐπὶ τῇ διδαχῇ αὐτοῦ, "were amazed at his teaching," as is said verbatim (except for word order) in 7:28, after Matthew's presentation of the Sermon on the Mount (cf. too the amazement recorded in 13:54; 19:25). The wisdom of Jesus the teacher is thus vindicated a second time under the fire of his opponents (cf. v 22 and especially v 46).

### Explanation

The Sadducees denied the resurrection because they did not find it explicitly taught in the five books of Moses. Limiting himself to their abbreviated canon, Jesus shows that the reality of the future resurrection is clearly implied in the simple affirmation of Exod 3:6. The specific problem they raised, moreover, was based on the failure to realize the newness that the resurrection age will bring.

Modern disbelief in the future resurrection of the dead is the result of an entirely different set of circumstances, especially the naturalism of modern science. Such a viewpoint, however, is not dissimilar to that of the Sadducees, especially in the underestimating of the power of God and the misunderstanding of the NT view of the resurrection and the world to come. If God is truly God, then the raising of the dead can be no problem for him. The power to revivify cannot be denied to the One who created life in the first place. Furthermore, resurrection bodies and the world of the eschaton are neither to be misunderstood as "spiritual" or immaterial, intangible realities completely discontinuous with life as we know it nor, on the other hand, as flesh and blood, material realities completely continuous with the world we know. Although we know little concerning the nature of the world to come and our own existence in it, that future reality will be both continuous in some ways and discontinuous in other ways with what we have known. For one thing, we will have bodies, and thus we will not be disembodied spirits, yet those bodies will not be of flesh and blood but bodies of a new kind that we have yet to experience (*the* NT discussion of this subject is, of course, 1 Cor 15:35–50). Then the creation will have become the new creation of God.

# Which Is the Great Commandment of the Law? (22:34–40)

## Bibliography

**Berger, K.** "Die Schriftauslegung in Mt 22, 34–40." In *Die Gesetzesauslegung Jesu.* 202–8. **Bockmuehl, K.** "The Great Commandment." *Crux* 23.3 (1987) 10–20. **Bornkamm, G.** "Das Doppelgebot der Liebe." In *Neutestamentliche Studien.* FS R. Bultmann, ed. W. Eltester. BZNW 21. Berlin: Alfred Töpelmann, 1954. 85–93 (reprinted in *Geschichte und Glaube. Gesammelte Aufsätze III.* BEvT 48. Munich: Kaiser, 1968. 37–45). **Burchard, C.** "Das doppelte Liebesgebot in der frühen christlichen Überlieferung." In *Der Ruf Jesu und die Antwort der Gemeinde.* FS J. Jeremias, ed. E. Lohse and B. Schaller. Göttingen: Vandenhoeck & Ruprecht, 1970. 39–62. **Derrett, J. D. M.** "'Love Thy Neighbor as a Man Like Thyself'?" *ExpTim* 83 (1971) 55–56. **Diezinger, W.** "Zum Liebesgebot Mk xii, 28–34 und Parr." *NovT* 20 (1978) 81–83. **Donaldson, T. L.** "The Law That 'Hangs' (Mt 22:40): Rabbinic Formulation and Matthean Social World." In *Society of Biblical Literature 1990 Seminar Papers*, ed. D. J. Lull. Atlanta: Scholars, 1990. 14–33. **Ernst, J.** "Die Einheit von Gottes—und Nächstenliebe in der Verkündigung Jesu." *TGl* 60 (1970) 3–14. **Fuchs, E.** "Was heisst: 'Du sollst deinen Nächsten lieben wie dich selbst'?" *TBl* 11 (1932) 129–40 (reprinted in *Zur Frage nach dem historischen Jesus.* Tübingen: Mohr, 1960. 1–20). **Fuller, R. H.,** ed. *Essays on the Love Commandment.* Philadelphia: Fortress, 1978. **Furnish, V. P.** *The Love Command in the New Testament.* Nashville: Abingdon, 1972. **Gerhardsson, B.** "The Hermeneutic Program in Matthew 22:37–40." In *Jews, Greeks and Christians.* FS W. D. Davies, ed. R. Hamerton-Kelly and R. Scroggs. Leiden: Brill, 1976. 129–50. **Grundmann, W.** "Das Doppelgebot der Liebe." *ZZ* 11 (1957) 449–55. **Hultgren, A. J.** "The Double Commandment of Love in Mt 22:34–40." *CBQ* 36 (1974) 373–78. **Iersel, B. van.** "Les lignes fondamentales de notre vie chrétienne (Mt. 22,34–36)." *AsSeign* 71 (1963) 27–44. **Kiilunen, J.** *Der Doppelgebot der Liebe in synoptischer Sicht: Ein redaktionskritischer Versuch über Mk 12, 28–34 und die Parallelen.* Helsinki: Suomalainen Tiedeakademia, 1989. **Lohfink, N.** "Das Hauptgebot." In *Das Siegeslied am Schilfmeer: Christliche Auseinandersetzungen mit dem Alten Testament.* Frankfurt am Main: Knecht, 1965. 19–50. **Michel, O.** "Das Gebot der Nächstenliebe in der Verkündigung Jesu." In *Zur sozialen Entscheidung: Vier Vorträge*, ed. N. Koch. Tübingen: Mohr, 1947. 53–101. **Miller, J. S.** "The Neighbor." *ExpTim* 96 (1984–85) 337–39. **Montefiore, H.** "Thou Shalt Love Thy Neighbor as Thyself." *NovT* 5 (1962) 157–70. **Nissen, A.** *Gott und der Nächste* *im antiken Judentum.* WUNT 15. Tübingen: Mohr, 1974. **Osborn, E.** "The Love Command in 2nd-Century Christian Writing: Mt 22.36–79." *Second Century* 1 (1981) 223–43. **Perkins, P.** *Love Commands in the New Testament.* New York: Paulist, 1982. **Schneider, G.** "Die Neuheit der christlichen Nächstenliebe." *TTZ* 82 (1973) 257–75. **Stern, J. B.** "Jesus' Citation of Dt 6,5 and Lv 19,18 in Light of Jewish Tradition." *CBQ* 28 (1966) 312–16. **Strecker, G.** "Gottes- und Menschenliebe in Neuen Testament." In *Tradition and Interpretation in the New Testament.* FS E. E. Ellis, ed. G. F. Hawthorne and O. Betz. Grand Rapids/Tübingen: Eerdmans/Mohr, 1987. 53–67. **Wolpert, W.** "Die Liebe zum Nächsten, zum Feind und zum Sünder." *TGl* 74 (1984) 262–82.

### Translation

³⁴*Now the Pharisees, when they heard that he had silenced the Sadducees, gathered together in one place,*[a] ³⁵*and one of them [—an expert in the law—],*[b] *testing him,*[c] *asked:* ³⁶*"Teacher, which is the great commandment in the law?"* ³⁷*And he* [d] *said to him: "You shall love the Lord your God with the whole of your heart and with the whole of your life and with the whole of your mind.'* [e] ³⁸*This is the great and first commandment.* ³⁹*And* [f] *the second is similar to it.*[g] *'You shall love your neighbor as yourself.'* ⁴⁰*On these two commandments hang the whole* [h] *law and the prophets."*

### Notes

[a] A few witnesses (D it sy^{s,c} mae?) have ἐπ' αὐτόν, "against him," for ἐπὶ τὸ αὐτό, "in one place."

[b] νομικός, lit. "lawyer," is omitted by f¹ sy^s. This together with its omission also in "widely scattered versional and patristic witnesses" suggests the possibility that the word (not used elsewhere by Matthew) was introduced early through the influence of the parallel in Luke 10:25. However, because of the weight of all the remaining textual evidence, the word is retained, but in brackets. Cf. *TCGNT*, 50. F G H have νομικός τις, "a certain lawyer."

[c] Many MSS (D W Θ f^{1,13} TR it sy^{(s,c)h} sa^{mss} mae) insert καὶ λέγων, "and saying."

[d] Many MSS (D W Θ f^{1,13} TR lat sy^{p,h} mae) insert ὁ Ἰησοῦς, "Jesus."

[e] A few witnesses (c sy^{s,c} Clement of Alexandria) substitute ἰσχύι, "strength," perhaps thereby bringing a degree of conformity to the LXX text of Deut 6:5 (which has δυνάμεως), while rather more (Θ f^{13} [sy^p] bo^{mss}) substitute ἰσχύι σου καὶ ἐν ὅλῃ τῇ διανοίᾳ σου, "with your strength and with the whole of your mind," probably through the influence of the parallels (Luke 10:27; cf. Mark 12:30).

[f] δέ, lit. "but," is omitted by ℵ* B sa^{ms} bo^{mss}.

[g] K Γ f^{13} sa mae have αὕτη, "this," while D Z*^{vid} bo have ταύτῃ, "this." B has the simple ὁμοίως, "similarly."

[h] ὅλος, "whole," is omitted by ℵ* sy^{s,c,p} sa bo^{pt}.

### Form/Structure/Setting

A. The third and last of this series of confrontations of Jesus by his opponents brings another test question from the Pharisees. The question is one of fundamental importance, for the answer to it will establish whether Jesus belongs to some radical fringe group or within the piety of mainstream Judaism. Matthew's abrupt ending suggests that the Pharisees had no particular problem with his answer (cf. Mark 12:32–34).

B. Matthew continues to depend on Mark (Mark 12:28–34; cf. the secondary parallel in Luke 10:25–28), but less closely than in the preceding pericope. Matthew makes several substantial omissions, the longest of these being the omission of the entirety of Mark 12:32–34. The reason for this omission seems obvious: the friendly discourse between the scribe and Jesus, ending with the remark of Jesus, "You are not far from the kingdom of God," does not fit well with the pattern of increasing hostility that Matthew has been building up in his narrative (cf. the climactic denunciation of the Pharisees in chap. 23). Matthew has turned Mark's didactic story (*Schulgespräch*) into a conflict story (*Streitgespräch*). Cf. Bornkamm, "Das Doppelgebot." The last statement of Mark 12:34, "and no one dared to question him any more," is delayed until the end of the following pericope (v 46), the last in this section of the Gospel. A second, and perhaps surprising, omission is that of the opening words of the Shema in v 37: "Hear, Israel, the Lord our God is one Lord" (Mark 12:29). It is unlikely that this omission has anything to do with tensions between Matthew's church and the synagogue. More likely Matthew omits it because it is not essential to the argument and because he can assume the readers' association of the good commandment with the Shema, which his community probably continued to say twice a day. The final omission to be noted is of Mark's fourth phrase, modifying the love commandment (v 37), "and with the whole of your strength" (Mark 12:30). It is surprising that Matthew omits this phrase, which is found in the Hebrew Bible, rather than $\kappa a\grave{\iota}$ $\dot{\epsilon}\xi$ $\ddot{o}\lambda\eta\varsigma$ $\tau\hat{\eta}\varsigma$ $\delta\iota a\nu o\acute{\iota}a\varsigma$ $\sigma o\upsilon$, "and with the whole of your mind," which is an addition of the LXX to the Hebrew text. Still, by merely reducing the number of qualifying phrases to three, Matthew brings about more resemblance to the Hebrew formula of Deut 6:5, which also contains three phrases. It should also be noted that Matthew (v 37) has altered Mark's Greek (Mark 12:30) in these phrases, changing $\dot{\epsilon}\xi$, "from," and the genitive (as also in LXX) to the better Greek of $\dot{\epsilon}\nu$, "with," and the dative (cf. the mixed constructions in Luke 10:27). Matthew also makes some additions to his Markan source. The entirety of v 34 is added, in which Matthew focuses on the alternate attempts of Sadducees and Pharisees to find fault with his teaching. Matthew's "one of them," i.e., of the Pharisees, takes the place of Mark's "one of the scribes." Matthew's $\nu o\mu\iota\kappa\acute{o}\varsigma$, "lawyer" (v 35), if original, is also an addition. Matthew substitutes $\pi\epsilon\iota\rho\acute{a}\zeta\omega\nu$ $a\grave{\upsilon}\tau\acute{o}\nu$, "testing him" (v 35), for the appreciative attitude reflected in Mark's "seeing that he answered them well" (Luke 10:25 agrees with Matthew against Mark in his $\dot{\epsilon}\kappa\pi\epsilon\iota\rho\acute{a}\zeta\omega\nu$, "testing"). Matthew inserts at the beginning of v 36 the address $\delta\iota\delta\acute{a}\sigma\kappa a\lambda\epsilon$, "teacher" (so too Luke 10:25). In the same verse Matthew substitutes $\mu\epsilon\gamma\acute{a}\lambda\eta$, "great," for $\pi\rho\acute{\omega}\tau\eta$, "first," and adds $\dot{\epsilon}\nu$ $\tau\hat{\omega}$ $\nu\acute{o}\mu\omega$, "in the law." Matthew also adds v 38: $a\ddot{\upsilon}\tau\eta$ $\dot{\epsilon}\sigma\tau\grave{\iota}\nu$ $\dot{\eta}$ $\mu\epsilon\gamma\acute{a}\lambda\eta$ $\kappa a\grave{\iota}$ $\pi\rho\acute{\omega}\tau\eta$ $\dot{\epsilon}\nu\tau o\lambda\acute{\eta}$, "this is the great and first commandment," giving emphasis to the point (cf. Mark 12:31b). In v 39 Matthew adds $\acute{o}\mu o\acute{\iota}a$ $a\grave{\upsilon}\tau\hat{\eta}$, "similar to it." Finally, Matthew adds a distinctive concluding statement to Mark's account: "On these two commandments hang the whole of the law and the prophets" (v 40). The agreements between Matthew and Luke against Mark ($\nu o\mu\iota\kappa\acute{o}\varsigma$, [$\dot{\epsilon}\kappa$] $\pi\epsilon\iota\rho\acute{a}\zeta\omega\nu$, $\delta\iota\delta\acute{a}\sigma\kappa a\lambda\epsilon$) are thought by some scholars (e.g., Berger, Hultgren) to point to the existence of a form of the pericope parallel to the Markan form that was used by Matthew and Luke.

C. The third confrontation story is similar in form to the two preceding narratives, although it lacks any reference to a response either of the Pharisees or of the crowds. The passage may be outlined as follows: (1) another question from the Pharisees, divided into (a) the gathering of the Pharisees (v 34) and (b) the law expert's presentation of the question (vv 35–36); and (2) Jesus' definitive answer, divided into (a) the first commandment (vv 37–38), (b) the second commandment (v 39), and (c) the commandments as the heart of the law and the prophets (v 40). Again the dialogue dominates the actual structure of the passage. The only noticeable structural feature, beyond the three parallel phrases of v 37 drawn from Mark (and in turn the LXX), is the syntactic parallel in the presentation of the two commandments (vv 37 and 39), both with the verb ἀγαπήσεις, "you shall love," accompanied by a direct object and a verbal modifier. A chiasm occurs in vv 37–39, where after the citation of the first commandment the notice "this is the first and great commandment" is given and then the notice "the second is similar to it" is followed by the citation of the second commandment. The lack of any word concerning the response of those who heard Jesus' answer is undoubtedly caused by Matthew's close joining of this passage to that which follows. The result is that the response of v 46 is also relevant to the present passage.

### Comment

**34** While the Pharisees may inwardly have rejoiced in the report concerning Jesus' refutation of the Sadducees (in particular their denial of the resurrection), they must also have been frustrated in yet another triumph of Jesus the teacher. συνήχθησαν ἐπὶ τὸ αὐτό, "were gathered together in the same place" (the identical phrase occurs in the LXX of Ps 2:2 in a context of opposition against the Lord's "anointed" [τοῦ χριστοῦ]), suggests the concerted action of a group of Pharisees for whom the spokesman of the following verse acts as a representative (cf. the sending of disciples of the Pharisees in v 16). This gathering of the Pharisees serves also as the context for the following pericope (cf. v 41).

**35–36** The νομικός, "law expert" (used in Matthew only here, although the text is questionable; see *Note* b above), cannot be distinguished from the γραμματεύς, "scribe," of the parallel in Mark 12:28. In this case the law expert was clearly of the party of the Pharisees. Again the question in Matthew is not a sincere one but is asked with the motive of πειράζων, "testing" (cf. v 18 where this attitude receives a rebuke; cf. 16:1; 19:3), in the hope of catching him in some fundamental error. For the third time in these successive pericopes, Jesus' opponents address him as διδάσκαλε, "teacher" (cf. vv 16, 24; see *Comment* on 9:11). There is evidence that the question concerning the most important commandment (μεγάλη, "great," is a Semitism for "greatest") was of considerable interest in rabbinic discussions (cf. for OT background esp. Mic 6:8; Hillel summarized the law in the negative form of the Golden Rule [*b. Šabb.* 31a]; R. Simlai [*b. Mak.* 24a; *Midr. Tanhuma B* on Judg §10 (16b)] refers to the reduction of the 613 commandments of Moses to 11 by David [Ps 15], 6 by Isaiah [Isa 33:15–16], 3 by Micah [Mic 6:8], 2 by Isaiah again [Isa 56:1], 1 by Amos [Amos 5:4], and 1 again by Habakkuk [Hab 2:4]; for specific reference to Lev 19:18 used similarly to the present passage, cf. *Sifra Lev.* 19:18 [Rabbi Akiba]; *Gen. Rab.* 24 [16b]; cf. too *m. ʾAbot* 1:2). Nevertheless, the wrong answer—i.e., other than that given by Jesus, which could be construed as including within it all the other commandments—could have proved useful to the Pharisees in their attempt to get rid of Jesus.

**37–38** Jesus draws his answer from the Shema, which was recited twice daily by the Jews. After the opening words, "Hear, Israel, the Lord our God is one Lord," which are included in Mark 12:29, comes the commandment quoted by Jesus. The wording of the citation itself agrees nearly verbatim with the LXX of Deut 6:5, except for Matthew's use of ἐν and the dative for ἐκ and the genitive (no doubt reflecting the Hebrew preposition בְּ, *bĕ*, "with," of the Hebrew text of Deut 6:5) and the alteration of the third noun from δυνάμεως, "strength," to διανοίᾳ, "mind" (the latter, however, occurs in a cognate passage in the LXX of Josh 22:5). διανοία is derived from Matthew's source, Mark 12:30 (which, however, has four modifying nouns; cf. above *Form/Structure/Setting* §B). The first and great commandment is to love God with all one's being: with heart, soul, mind, and whatever else one might care to add. This commandment from Deut 6:5 can easily be recognized as a kind of elaboration on the first commandment of the Decalogue: "I am the Lord your God . . . you shall have no other gods besides me." In its fundamental character, this is clearly ἡ μεγάλη [cf. v 36] καὶ πρώτη ἐντολή, "the great and first commandment." Included within it is the duty of obedience to the other commandments given by God, and thus the answer would have been a good one in the eyes of the Pharisees.

**39** Jesus adds a second, companion (ὁμοία αὐτῇ, "similar to it") commandment to his answer, linked with the first by the common word ἀγαπήσεις, "you shall love" (reflecting the rabbinic practice known as *gĕzĕrâ šāwâ*, "equal category," namely the association of scripture passages on the basis of a common word), as a way of presenting a comprehensive picture of one's duty to God and to brothers and sisters of the human family (cf. *T. Iss.* 5:2; *T. Dan.* 5:3). ἀγαπήσεις τὸν πλησίον σου ὡς σεαυτόν, "you shall love your neighbor as yourself," agrees verbatim with the LXX of Lev 19:18 (cf. too Lev 19:34). Matthew has already cited the commandment in 5:43 (partially) and 19:19, both citations being unique to Matthew. It is quoted by Paul in Rom 13:9 as the summing up of "the commandments," in Gal 5:14 as the fulfillment of the "whole law," and it is cited in Jas 2:8 as "the royal law according to scripture." Its high significance in all these instances traces back to Jesus' teaching in the present passage. It is also clearly the fundamental ground upon which the ethical teaching of the NT church is built. (Strecker relates this passage to the statement in 1 John 4:8 that "God is love.") The Pharisees would clearly accept the importance of this additional commandment, even if they may not have given it quite the same degree of prominence. See *Comment* on 19:19 for further exegesis of the commandment itself.

**40** So important are these two commandments, indeed, that Jesus can conclude that on these two commandments ὅλος ὁ νόμος κρέμαται καὶ οἱ προφῆται, "hang the whole law and the prophets." This is a way of saying that the commandments of the law and the teaching of the prophets cannot be fulfilled apart from the twofold love commandment. This is put conversely in 7:12, where the Golden Rule is said "to be," i.e. "to fulfill," the law and the prophets: "For this is the law and the prophets" (cf. Rom 13:10: "Love is the fulfilling of the law"). G. Bertram rightly concludes: "κρέμαται, ἀνακεφαλαιοῦται [Rom 13:9] and πεπλήρωται [Gal 5:14] are exact material parallels which have the same fact in view" (*TDNT* 3:920–21). Jesus, in Matthew's view, does not cancel the commandments of the law through his teaching concerning the critical importance of love but instead regards the latter as the true fulfillment of the heart of the former (cf. too, 9:13; 12:7; esp. 23:23). The twofold commandment as set forth in this passage may appropriately be thought of as nothing less than a "hermeneutic program" for the understanding and application of the law and the prophets (thus Gerhardsson).

## Explanation

The two love commandments belong together, covering the vertical (relationship with God) and the horizontal (relationship with others) dimensions. The first entails the second; the second presupposes and depends on the first. It is obvious, however, that the use of the verb ἀγαπήσεις, "you shall love," does not mean the same thing in both places. In neither case is love construed as an emotion. Love for one's neighbor means acting toward others with their good, their well-being, their fulfillment, as the primary motivation and goal of our deeds. Such love is constant and takes no regard of the perceived merit or worth of the other person. Love of God, on the other hand, is to be understood as a matter of reverence, commitment, and obedience. It is at once an acknowledgment of his identity as Creator and Redeemer and a reflection of that reality in the ordering of our lives. With this orientation toward God and others, the law and the prophets have reached their ultimate goal. Further concern with commandments, further elaboration of ethical stipulations—these all depend upon the real manifestation of the love commandments for their legitimacy.

# David's Greater Son    (22:41–46)

## Bibliography

**Burger, C.** *Jesus als Davidssohn.* **Chilton, B. D.** "Jesus *ben David*: Reflections on the *Davidssohnfrage.*" *JSNT* 14 (1982) 88–112. **Daube, D.** *The New Testament and Rabbinic Judaism.* 158–69. **Fitzmyer, J. A.** "The Son of David Tradition and Mt 22:41–46 and Parallels." In *Essays on the Semitic Background of the New Testament.* 113–26. **Friedrich, G.** "Messianische Hohepriestererwartung in den Synoptikern." *ZTK* 53 (1956) 265–311. **Gagg, R. P.** "Jesus und die Davidssohnfrage." *TZ* (1951) 18–30. **Gibbs, J. M.** "Purpose and Pattern in Matthew's Use of the Title 'Son of David.'" *NTS* 10 (1963–64) 446–64. **Gourgues, M.** "Marc 12:36 et parallèles (Mt 22:44; Lc 20:42)." In *À la droite de Dieu.* EBib. Paris: J. Gabalda, 1978. 127–43. **Hay, D. M.** *Glory at the Right Hand: Psalm 110 in Early Christian Literature.* SBLMS 18. Nashville: Abingdon, 1973. **Hays, D.,** and **Suhl, A.** "Der Davidssohn in Matthäus-Evangelium." *ZNW* 59 (1968) 57–81. **Iersel, B. M. F. van.** *"Der Sohn" in den synoptischen Jesusworten.* **Johnson, S. E.** "The Davidic-Royal Motif in the Gospels." *JBL* 87 (1968) 136–50. **Lövestam, E.** "Die Davidssohnfrage." *SEÅ* 27 (1962) 77–82. **Lohse, E.** "Der König aus Davids Geschlecht: Bemerkungen zur messianischen Erwartung der Synagoge." In *Abraham unser Vater.* FS O. Michel, ed. O. Betz et al. AGSU 5. Leiden: Brill, 1963. 337–45. **Michaelis, W.** "Die Davidssohnschaft Jesu als historisches und kerygmatisches Problem." In *Der* *historische Jesus und der kerygmatische Christus,* ed. H. Ristow and K. Matthiae. Berlin: Evangelische Verlagsanstalt, 1962. 317–30. **Neugebauer, F.** "Die Davidssohnfrage (Mark xii. 35–7 parr.) und der Menschensohn." *NTS* 21 (1974–75) 81–108. **Schneider, G.** "Die Davidssohnfrage (Mk 12, 35–37)." *Bib* 53 (1972) 65–90. ———. "Zum Vorgeschichte des christologischen Prädikats 'Sohn Davids.'" *TTZ* 80 (1971) 247–53. **Wrede, W.** "Jesus als Davidssohn." In *Vorträge und Studien.* Tübingen: Mohr, 1907. 147–77.

## Translation

[41] *While the Pharisees were gathered, Jesus asked them a question,*[a] [42]*saying: "What do you think concerning the Messiah? Whose son is he?" They said to him: "David's!"* [43]*He*[b] *said to them: "How therefore does David by the Spirit call him lord,*[c] *saying:*

[44]*The*[d] *Lord said to my lord:*
*Sit at my right hand*
*Until I put your enemies*
*Below*[e] *your feet?*

[45]*If therefore David*[f] *calls him lord, how is he his son?"* [46]*And no one was able to answer him with even a word, nor did anyone dare from that day*[g] *to question him any longer.*

## Notes

[a] "A question" added to translation.

[b] L Z *f*[1] vg[mss] mae bo add ὁ Ἰησοῦς, "Jesus."

[c] In B*, αὐτοῦ, "his," follows κύριον, i.e., "his lord."

[d] Although ℵ B D Z lack the definite article before κύριος, "Lord," it must nevertheless be translated as definite. The LXX includes the article, and thus scribes were inclined to insert it here.

[e] Many MSS (W *f*[1] TR lat mae) read ὑποπόδιον, "a footstool," a conforming of the citation to the LXX of Ps 110:1.

[f] D K Δ Θ *f*[13] it vg[mss] sy[h**] mae bo[pt] add ἐν πνεύματι, "by the Spirit," through the influence of v 43.

[g] D W *f*[1] sy[s,c] bo[ms] read ὥρας, "hour."

## Form/Structure/Setting

A. This pericope comes as the climax to the preceding series of testings of Jesus by his opponents, each one of which Jesus has brilliantly passed, demonstrating further his authority as a teacher. Now, however, *he* takes the initiative against his opponents, here again the Pharisees, by putting a difficult question before them. This question is not one designed for its cleverness but one that has to do with Jesus' own identity and calling. The Pharisees are unable to draw the required conclusion, just as they have been earlier unable to accept Jesus, his message, or his personal claims. Whereas he has passed the tests they put to him, they fail in the test he puts to them.

B. Matthew continues to depend on Mark for this pericope (Mark 12:35–37a; cf. Luke 20:41–44), but he connects it much more closely with the preceding narrative. Mark makes a break with what precedes by referring to a new teaching context: διδάσκων ἐν τῷ ἱερῷ, "teaching in the temple" (Mark 12:35), words omitted by Matthew. Furthermore, Matthew has Jesus address the question to the "gathered" Pharisees directly, rather than rhetorically to the crowd as in Mark.

The resultant direct discourse between Jesus and his opponents in vv 42–43 is thus missing in Mark. The other major difference from his Markan source is Matthew's addition of v 46, which is, however, partly borrowed from Mark's ending to the preceding pericope (Mark 12:34b). Matthew omits Mark 12:37b, "and the large crowd heard him gladly," since it does not fit well with his purpose, i.e., showing the failure of Jesus' opponents. This prepares the way for the sharp criticism of the Pharisees in chap. 23. The quotation of Ps 110:1 in v 44 agrees exactly with its form in Mark 12:36 (note especially ὑποκάτω, "below," for the LXX's ὑποπόδιον, "footstool"). A further slight change to note is Matthew's εἰ οὖν, "if therefore" (v 45; cf. Mark 12:37), which adds a little more sharpness to the question that follows, and the substitution of the more usual πῶς for πόθεν, "how" (cf. Luke 20:44). Finally, Matthew's omission of τῷ ἁγίῳ, "the Holy" (Mark 12:36), as a modifier of τῷ πνεύματι, "the Spirit," is probably simply an abbreviation.

C. The beginning of the pericope is characterized by the simple syntax of direct discourse. As in the two preceding passages, the citation of the OT plays a central role. The second question of Jesus, however, is left unanswered. Matthew's readers are left to supply the answer themselves, depending on the Christology of the early church. As an outline, the following is suggested: (1) Jesus' question (vv 41–42b); (2) the Pharisees' answer (v 42c); (3) Jesus' second question (vv 43–45); and (4) the final silence of his opponents (v 46). The only structural feature that bears noting is the repetition of the clause Δαυὶδ καλεῖ αὐτὸν κύριον, "David calls him lord," in v 45a, just after the citation of Ps 110:1 (the identical clause with ἐν πνεύματι, "by the Spirit," occurs in v 43 immediately before the quotation).

D. Ps 110:1, which is cited in v 44, became a particularly important OT text in the early church (see Hay). It generally is used in referring to the resurrection/ ascension and heavenly rule of Christ (cf. 26:64; Acts 2:34–35; 1 Cor 15:25; Eph 1:20; Col 3:1; Heb 1:3, 13; 8:1; 10:12–13). Only in the present instance is the focus on the introductory "the Lord said to my lord." The use of this pericope by *Barn.* 12.10–11 misunderstands the sonship question altogether (as does much modern critical scholarship) by understanding it as denying that Jesus is the Son of David.

*Comment*

**41–42**  By connecting this pericope so closely with the preceding through the use of the genitive absolute, συνηγμένων δὲ τῶν φαρισαίων, "while the Pharisees were gathered together," Matthew has Jesus' question directed at the Pharisees, his questioners also in vv 15–22 and 34–40. The question asked by Jesus must have seemed very easy to the Pharisees. It was common knowledge that the promised Messiah (ὁ Χριστός, "the Christ," i.e., "the anointed One") was to be of the lineage of David (cf. John 7:42; for OT background, see 2 Sam 7:12–13; Ps 89:4; Jer 23:5; cf. *Ps. Sol.* 17:21). Conversely, throughout the Gospel the references to Jesus as the Son of David (e.g., 1:1, 20; 9:27; 12:23; 15:22; 20:30–31; 21:9) amount to assertions of his messianic identity.

**43–44**  Jesus now points the Pharisees to Ps 110:1 (LXX 109:1), where David ἐν πνεύματι, "by the Spirit," that is, by divine inspiration (cf. 2 Sam 23:2), refers to the coming messianic ruler, and hence his son, as κύριον, "lord." The citation agrees verbatim with the LXX except for the omission of the article before the first occurrence of κύριος, "Lord," and the substitution of the adverb ὑποκάτω, "beneath," for the noun ὑποπόδιον, " footstool." Underlying the two uses of κύριος are two different Hebrew words: the first is the tetragrammaton יהוה (the personal name "Yahweh," which was not spoken by the Jews, who substituted the word ʾ*ăḏonay*, i.e., a word virtually identical to the second word); the second is אֲדֹנִי (ʾ*ăḏonî*, "my lord"). David calls his son not Yahweh but ʾ*ăḏonî*, "my lord": "Yahweh [the Lord] said to my lord." But it is astonishing that David should call his son "my lord"; by Jewish standards of familial respect, it is rather the son who might refer to his father as "my lord."

**45** The question is repeated for emphasis. How can it be that David calls his son κύριος, "lord"? This question, which goes unanswered either by the Pharisees or by Jesus, must not be taken as an implicit denial that the Messiah is in fact the Son of David (*pace* Chilton), an ascription that the evangelist repeatedly uses in referring to Jesus and that Jesus himself willingly accepts (see *Comment* on vv 41–42). The point of the question addressed to the Pharisees is apparently to elevate the concept of Messiah from that of a special human being to one who uniquely manifests the presence of God—and thus one whom David has also to address as his lord. This pericope serves thus in one sense as a kind of justification for the extravagant claims made by Jesus, or concerning him, earlier in the Gospel (e.g., 10:32–33, 40; 11:27; 14:33; 16:16). As in Peter's confession, so here, the Christ, the Son of David, is to be recognized as uniquely "the Son of the living God" (cf. Gibbs, 460–64). He is the living Lord of the church (Burger, 88–89) who sits at God's right hand. The Pharisees accordingly reject Jesus at their very great peril. They have rejected not merely a human messianic claimant but the unique emissary of God, whom even David had called "my lord." κύριος, "lord," in reference to Jesus here, as Fitzmyer points out, suggested to the evangelist and his community that Jesus "was somehow on a par with Yahweh of the Old Testament" (125). On the usefulness of seeing the present pericope in relation to such passages as Acts 2:29–35; 13:23–39; Heb 1:5–13, see Lövestam.

**46** Matthew rounds out this major section of his narrative by making the point that Jesus' opponents had to give up trying to outsmart Jesus or to trap him in his words. The wisdom of Jesus the teacher has been vindicated. His opponents cannot so much as answer a λόγον, "word," and none dared to engage him in such debates again. Too easily their attempts had been turned against them. The process against Jesus, which comes to its culmination in chaps. 26–28, must therefore find some other basis before it can proceed.

## *Explanation*

The Pharisees assumed they had sufficient knowledge concerning the promised Messiah. They saw no problem in the question Jesus put to them. The Messiah was to be a descendant of David. Yet they could not explain why David referred to his son as "my lord." They had not confronted the mystery of a human being who was also the divine agent of God, the unique Son of God. It was because God uniquely manifested himself in his Messiah for the gracious fulfillment of his promises to Israel that David referred to his descendant as "my lord." So too today repeated attempts are being made to explain Jesus in strictly human categories. Yet if we limit our understanding of Jesus to analogies that from the beginning rule out the supernatural and the divine, we will never arrive at an adequate view of Jesus. This is the very point the Gospel desires to press home to its readers. Jesus' question to the Pharisees—How then does David call him "my lord"?—must also be asked of those modern scholars who allow Jesus to be no more than a human teacher. The burning question "Who do you say I am?" (16:15) has only one adequate answer.

# Castigation of the Scribes and Pharisees (23:1–39)

## Bibliography

**Baumbach, G.** "Jesus und die Pharisäer." *BLit* 41 (1968) 112–31. **Farbstein, D.** "Waren die Pharisäer und die Schriftgelehrten Heuchler?" *Judaica* 8 (1952) 193–207. **Flusser, D.** "Two Anti-Jewish Montages in Matthew." *Immanuel* 5 (1975) 37–45. **Frankemölle, H.** "'Pharisäismus' in Judentum und Kirche." In *Gottesverächter und Menschenfeinde?* ed. H. Goldstein. Düsseldorf: Patmos, 1979. 123–89. **Garland, D. E.** *The Intention of Matthew 23.* NovTSup 52. Leiden: Brill, 1979. **Glasson, T. F.** "Anti-Pharisaism in St. Matthew." *JQR* 51 (1960–61) 316–20. **Haenchen, E.** "Matthäus 23." *ZTK* 48 (1951) 38–63. **Hagner, D. A.** "Pharisees." In *Zondervan Pictorial Encyclopedia of the Bible,* ed. M. C. Tenney. Grand Rapids: Zondervan, 1975. 4:745–52. **Johnson, L. T.** "The New Testament's Anti-Jewish Slander and Conventions of Ancient Rhetoric." *JBL* 108 (1989) 419–41. **Légasse, S.** "'L'antijudäisme' dans l'Évangile selon Matthieu." In *L'Évangile selon Matthieu,* ed. M. Didier. BETL 29. Gembloux: Duculot, 1972. 417–28. ———. "Scribes et disciples de Jésus." *RB* 68 (1961) 321–45. **McKnight, S.** "A Loyal Critic: Matthew's Polemic with Judaism in Theological Perspective." In *Anti-Semitism and Early Christianity: Issues of Polemic and Faith,* ed. C. A. Evans and D. A. Hagner. Minneapolis: Fortress, 1993. 55–79. **Michel, O.** "Polemik und Scheidung." *Judaica* 15 (1959) 193–212. **Minear, P. S.** "False Prophecy and Hypocrisy in the Gospel of Matthew." In *Neues Testament und Kirche.* FS R. Schnackenburg, ed. J. Gnilka. Freiburg: Herder, 1974. 76–93. **Newport, K. G. C.** "The Pharisees in Judaism Prior to A.D. 70." *AUSS* 29 (1991) 127–37. **Niedner, F. A.** "Rereading Matthew on Jerusalem and Judaism." *BTB* 19 (1989) 43–47. **Pesch, W.** "Drohweissagungen." In *Der Lohngedanke in der Lehre Jesu.* Munich: Zink, 1955. 40–50. ———. "Theologische Aussagen der Redaktion von Matthäus 23." In *Orientierung an Jesus.* FS J. Schmid, ed. P. Hoffmann et al. Freiburg: Herder, 1973. 286–99. **Russell, E. A.** "'Antisemitism' in the Gospel of Matthew." *IBS* 8 (1986) 183–96. ———. "The Image of the Jew in Matthew's Gospel." *Proceedings of the Irish Biblical Association* 12 (1989) 37–57. **Schürmann, H.** "Die Redekomposition wider 'dieses Geschlecht' und seine Führung in der Redenquelle (vgl. Mt 23,1–39 par Lk 11,37–54): Bestand—Akoluthie—Kompositionsformen." *SNTU* 11 (1986) 33–81. **Szabó, A.** "Anfänge einer judenchristliche Theologie bei Matthäus." *Judaica* 16 (1960) 193–206. **Tilborg, S. van.** *The Jewish Leaders in Matthew.* Leiden: Brill, 1972. **Viviano, B. T.** "The Pharisees in Matthew 23." *BiTod* 27 (1989) 338–44. **Westerholm, S.** *Jesus and Scribal Authority.* ConBNT 10. Lund: Gleerup, 1978. **Wild, R. A.** "The Encounter between Pharisaic and Christian Judaism: Some Early Gospel Evidence." *NovT* 27 (1985) 105–24.

## Introduction

Chap. 23 forms a distinct discourse within the Gospel, one that has become notorious for its vitriolic condemnation of the scribes and Pharisees. It is not itself, however, exactly comparable to the five major discourses of Matthew (see *Introduction,* in Hagner, *Matthew 1–13,* li). Unlike the other discourses, its content is largely negative and condemnatory, being aimed at the criticism of a specific group. In keeping with these distinctions, it does not have an ending like the formulaic ending of the five discourses. But, like them, it is a composition of the evangelist using a variety of traditional materials.

Some (e.g., Bacon, *Studies in Matthew;* Gundry; Blomberg) have argued, however, that this chapter should be considered as a part of the fifth and final discourse of the Gospel, found in the two chapters that follow. The strength of this suggestion is that it recognizes the close relation between the material of chap. 23 and that of chaps. 24–25. Chap. 23 can thus be seen as the formal indictment for the judgment that is described in chaps. 24–25. Yet this function of chap. 23 and its natural relatedness to chaps. 24–25 can be affirmed without the insistence that structurally the three chapters should be thought of as forming a single discourse (rightly Gnilka, Carson). In both content and form chap. 23 is distinct from chaps. 24–25. There is, furthermore, a very clear break between the two discourses: Jesus was in the process of departing from the scene of his previous remarks (24:1: ἐπορεύετο, "he departed") when the disciples, by posing their question, initiated a new and independent discourse. This break, when combined with the new subject matter of chaps. 24–25, is a far more significant break than that of 13:36 (sometimes referred to in defense of the unity of chaps. 23 and 24–25), where the same discussion is in fact continued but now in the requisite privacy, with the disciples alone.

The discourse of chap. 23 is somewhat puzzling because of its mixed form and the change of addressees beginning in v 13. In order, the discourse consists of (1) an exhortation (vv 2–12); (2) seven woes pronounced upon the Pharisees (vv 13–33; for structural analysis of these, see *Form/Structure/Setting* §C for that pericope); (3) a prophecy (vv 34–36); and (4) a lament (vv 37–39). The woes are undoubtedly the centerpiece of the chapter, and the material that follows them coheres much more readily with them than does the material that precedes. This agrees with the understanding that ostensibly the addressees are the scribes and the Pharisees, beginning with v 13 (note the plural pronoun ὑμῖν, "you") through to the end of the discourse. The first part of the discourse, on the other hand, is addressed specifically "to the crowds and to his disciples" (v 1). This has led some (e.g., Frankemölle) to conclude that the entire discourse is addressed to the church and that the hypocrisy being criticized in the woes is that of the church and not that of the Pharisees. Such a conclusion allows one to sidestep the difficult anti-Judaism of the woes.

It is true that the church must guard against the danger of hypocrisy and that it can read the woes and find material relevant to itself. But that is at best a secondary application of the passage. Historically there can be little question that the evangelist means to present a polemic against the scribes and Pharisees. Furthermore, we must face the fact that Jesus is portrayed as castigating the religious leadership of Israel in the harshest language. We must first account for this and then raise an appeal against the anti-Semitic use of this passage.

When Jesus refers to the Pharisees positively in 23:2–3a, he indicates that in principle Pharisaism's quest for righteousness is worthy and admirable. We can, therefore, with the best recent scholarship affirm Pharisaism as something to be held in high esteem (see Farbstein). The problem Jesus focuses on is not Pharisaism but those Pharisees whose practice contradicted their professed quest for righteousness. The Pharisees themselves were sensitive to the danger of hypocrisy. A well-known passage (*b. Soṭa* 22b) denounces six types of hypocritical Pharisees, focusing on some of the same elements of hypocrisy denounced by Jesus (cf. too *y. Ber.* 9:5). Presumably many Pharisees would have agreed with Jesus' criticism of hypocrisy, and therefore his criticism is not to be construed as falling upon all Pharisees. How tragic, therefore, that in common parlance "Pharisee" is often regarded as synonymous with "hypocrite." Two further points need to be made. First, the language of the woes, so harsh to modern ears, reflects the conventions of ancient polemic (see esp. Johnson). Thus the severe language is not as exceptional as it may seem to us. Second, the debate between Jesus and the Pharisees is to be understood as in some respects an intramural one (see McKnight). Certainly for Matthew the issue concerns who is the more reliable interpreter of Torah: the Pharisees or Jesus? Beneath that question, however, lies the matter of Christology. Jesus is sovereign in the matter of the interpretation of righteousness because of who he is. It is this matter that underlies the growing hostility between the synagogue and church that has undoubtedly left its impact upon the material presented here.

Finally, in light of what has been said above, it is unthinkable that chap. 23 be used to portray the Pharisees or Judaism negatively. This passage has a very specific historical context (see Glasson), and therefore it is totally improper to attempt to apply it to Jews or Judaism today. Even in its historical setting, as we have seen, the bitter rhetoric of chap. 23 must yield to an adequate and fair understanding of Pharisaic Judaism. Thus this chapter provides *no* basis whatsoever for anti-Semitic attitudes or actions (see Michel). And the same must be said of all the "anti-Judaistic" passages in the Gospel (see further *Introduction*, in Hagner, *Matthew 1–13*, lxxi–lxxiii).

# The Pharisees' Pride and the Disciples' Humility (23:1–12)

## Bibliography

**Barbour, R. S.** "Uncomfortable Words: VIII. Status and Titles." *ExpTim* 82 (1970–71) 137–42. **Becker, H.-J.** *Auf der Kathedra des Mose: Rabbinisch-theologisches Denken und anti-rabbinische Polemik in Matthäus 23, 1–12.* ANTZ 4. Berlin: Institut Kirche und Judentum, 1990. **Bowman, J.** "Phylacteries." *SE* 1 [= TU 73] (1959) 523–38. **Byrskog, S.** *Jesus the Only Teacher: Didactic Authority and Transmission in Ancient Israel, Ancient Judaism and the Matthean Community.* ConBNT 24. Stockholm: Almquist & Wiksell, 1994. **Derrett, J. D. M.** "Mt 23,8–10: A Midrash on Is 54,13 and Jer 31,33–34." *Bib* 62 (1981) 372–86. **Donaldson, J.** "The Title Rabbi in the Gospels." *JQR* 63 (1972–73) 287–91. **Fascher, E.** "Jesus der Lehrer." *TLZ* 79 (1954) 325–42. **Fox, G. G.** "The Matthean Misrepresentation of *tephillin.*" *JNES* 1 (1942) 373–77. **Fuller, R. C.** "Call None Your Father in Earth." *Scr* 5 (1952) 103–4. **Goma Civit, I.** "Fraternité et service pastoral (Mt. 23,1–12)." *AsSeign* 62 (1970) 21–32. **Hengel, M.** "Proseuche und Synagoge: Jüdische Gemeinde, Gotteshaus und Gottesdienst in der Diaspora und in Palästina." In *Tradition und Glaube: Das frühe Christentum in seiner Umwelt,* ed. G. Jeremias et al. Göttingen: Vandenhoeck & Ruprecht, 1971. 157–86. **Hoet, R.** *"Omnes autem vos fratres estis": Étude de concept ecclésiologique des "frères" selon Mt 23,8–12.* Analecta Gregoriana 232. Rome: Università Gregoriana Editrice, 1982. **Kohler, K.** "Abba, Father: Title of Spiritual Leader and Saint." *JQR* 13 (1900–1901) 567–80. **Limbeck, M.** "Die nichts bewegen wollen! Zum Gesetzesverständnis des Evangelisten Matthäus." *TQ* 168 (1988) 299–300. **Marquet, C.** "Ne vous faites pas appeler 'maître': Matthieu 23,8–12." *CHR* 30 (1983) 88–102. **Mason, S.** "Pharisaic Dominance before 70 CE and the Gospels' Hypocrisy Charge (Matt 23:2–3)." *HTR* 83 (1990) 363–81. **Michaels, J. R.** "Christian Prophecy and Matthew 23:8–12: A Test Exegesis." In *Society of Biblical Literature, 1976 Seminar Papers*. Missoula, MT: Scholars, 1976. 305–10. **Nestle, E.** "They Enlarge the Borders of Their Garments." *ExpTim* 20 (1908–1909) 188. **Newport, K. G. C.** "A Note on the 'Seat of Moses' (Matthew 23:2)." *AUSS* 28 (1990) 53–58. **Rahmani, L. Y.** "Stone Synagogue Chairs: Their Identification, Use and Significance." *IEJ* 40 (1990) 192–214. **Reilly, W. S.** "Titles in Mt 23,8–12." *CBQ* 1 (1939) 249–50. **Roth, C.** "The 'Chair of Moses' and Its Survivals." *PEQ* 81 (1949) 100–111. **Saggin, L.** "Magister vester unus est, Christus." *VD* 30 (1952) 205–13. **Shanks, H.** "Is the Title 'Rabbi' Anachronistic in the Gospels?" *JQR* 53 (1962–63) 337–45. **Spicq, C.** "Une allusion au Docteur de Justice in Matthieu, XXIII, 10?" *RB* 66 (1959) 387–96. **Sukenik, E. L.** *Ancient Synagogues in Palestine and Greece*. London: Oxford UP, 1934. **Tigay, J. H.** "On the Term Phylacteries (Matt 23:5)." *HTR* 72 (1979) 45–52. **Townsend, J. T.** "Matthew XXIII. 9." *JTS* 12 (1961) 56–59. **Viviano, B. T.** "Social World and Community Leadership: The Case of Matthew 23.1–12, 34." *JSNT* 39 (1990) 3–21. **Welch, A.** "Scribes and Pharisees in Moses' Seat." *ExpTim* 7 (1895–96) 522–26. **Winter, B. W.** "The Messiah as Tutor: The Meaning of καθηγητής in Matthew 23:10." *TynB* 42 (1991) 151–57. **Zimmermann, A. F.** *Die urchristlichen Lehrer*. WUNT 2.12. Tübingen: Mohr, 1984.

### Translation

[1] *Then Jesus spoke to the crowds and to his disciples,* [2] *saying: "The scribes and the Pharisees sit upon the seat of Moses.* [3] *Therefore do and keep* [a] *everything which they say to you,* [b] *but do not imitate* [c] *their deeds. For they say one thing and do another.* [d] [4] *And they tie up heavy [and difficult to bear]* [e] *burdens and place them upon the shoulders of others,* [f] *and they themselves* [g] *are not willing to move them even with their finger.* [5] *But they do all their deeds to be seen by others. For they make their phylacteries large, and they make their tassels* [h] *long.* [6] *And they love the seat of honor at banquets and the important seats in the synagogues* [7] *and the salutations of respect in the marketplaces and to be called 'Rabbi'* [i] *by others.* [j]

[8] *"You, however, are not to be called* [k] *'Rabbi.' For there is one who is your teacher,* [l,m] *but you all are brothers and sisters.* [n] [9] *And do not call anyone on earth your* [o] *'father.' For there is one who is your father—your heavenly* [p] *Father.* [10] *Nor are you to be called 'tutors,' because there is one* [q] *who is your tutor, the Christ.* [11] *But the one who is the greatest among you must be your servant.* [12] *And those* [r] *who exalt themselves* [s] *will be humbled, and those* [t] *who humble themselves* [u] *will be exalted."*

### Notes

[a] W *f*[13] TR lat sy[p,h] reverse the order of the verbs, changing the aorist to the present ποιεῖτε, "continue to do" (D *f*[1] also change the tense); sy[c] has ἀκούετε καὶ ποιεῖτε, "hear and do"; ℵ* (Γ) sy[s]? have simply ποιήσατε, "do"; Φ has simply τηρεῖτε, "keep." These changes were made either to bring about the same tense in both verbs or to avoid the problem of two verbs with the same meaning.

[b] Many MSS (W *f*[13] TR sy[p,h]) add τηρεῖν "to keep"; Γ adds ποιεῖν, "to do."

[c] κατὰ δὲ τὰ ἔργα αὐτῶν μὴ ποιεῖτε, lit. "do not do according to their deeds."

[d] λέγουσιν γὰρ καὶ οὐ ποιοῦσιν, lit. "for they say and do not do."

[e] καὶ δυσβάστακτα, "and difficult to bear," is lacking in L *f*[1] it sy[s,c,p] bo; after φορτία, "burdens," ℵ has simply μεγάλα βαρέα, "very heavy." The omission can have been caused by homoioteleuton, i.e., the skipping of the eye from the καί to the καί following the adjective. Favoring the text are B D W Θ *f*[13] TR lat sy[h] sa (mae). Because the word δυσβάστακτα may have been imported from the parallel in Luke 11:46, however, it is placed in brackets. Metzger appends his opinion that the words are an

interpolation from Luke 11:46 and should not be considered a part of the original text. If they were original, he asks, why are they omitted "from such a rich variety of witnesses"? *TCGNT*, 59–60.

[f] *ἀνθρώπων*, lit. "men."

[g] *αὐτοί*, "themselves," is omitted by many MSS (W Θ $f^{1,13}$ TR lat $sy^{h}$).

[h] Many MSS (L W $f^{13}$ TR it sy bo) add *τῶν ἱματίων αὐτῶν* (the last word is lacking in L), "of their garments."

[i] Many MSS (D W $f^{13}$ TR $sy^{s,c,h}$) repeat the word *ῥαββί*, "Rabbi," which is probably a scribal heightening. *TCGNT*, 60.

[j] *ἀνθρώπων*, lit. "men."

[k] Θ ($sy^{s,c}$) have the active imperative *μηδένα καλέσητε*, "call no one."

[l] *διδάσκαλος*, "teacher." $\aleph^{*,2}$ D L W Θ $f^{1,13}$ TR, however, have the synonym *καθηγητής* (cf. v 10).

[m] Many MSS (K Γ Δ TR $sy^{c,h**}$) insert *ὁ Χριστός*, "the Christ," probably through conformity with v 10.

[n] "And sisters" added to translation.

[o] D Θ lat $sy^{s,c,p}$ sa bo read *ὑμῖν*, "for you," possibly reflecting a "Semitic ethical dative." Cf. *TCGNT*, 60. The odd placement of the genitive *ὑμῶν* could account for scribes altering it to the dative.

[p] D W Δ Θ $f^{1}$ read *ἐν οὐρανοῖς*, while TR $sy^{h}$ read *ἐν τοῖς οὐρανοῖς*, both meaning "in the heavens."

[q] *εἷς*, "one," is omitted by Θ $f^{1,13}$ $sy^{s,c}$.

[r] *ὅστις*, lit. "whoever."

[s] *ἑαυτόν*, lit. "himself."

[t] *ὅστις*, lit. "whoever."

[u] *ἑαυτόν*, lit. "himself."

## *Form/Structure/Setting*

A. This pericope begins a rather lengthy and sharp denunciation of the scribes and Pharisees that takes up most of the chapter in preparation for the judgment announced in chap. 24. It begins, however, with an appreciation of the Pharisees and their desire to interpret the law. This appreciation is one in principle only; that is, it regards their task and intent, not their accomplishment. Thereafter the tone quickly turns to criticism of the pride of the Pharisees with a lesson concerning the humility meant to prevail among the disciples.

B. Only in three shorter sections within the pericope do Matthew's sources seem apparent. The logion (v 4) referring to the loading up of persons with heavy burdens and not moving the latter with a finger is apparently a Q saying, being found also in Luke 11:46 (where "woe" is pronounced upon *τοῖς νομικοῖς*, "the lawyers"). The form and wording are similar but not the same (common words: *φορτία* ["burdens"], *τοὺς ἀνθρώπους* ["men"], *δυσβάστακτα* ["difficult to bear"], *αὐτοί* ["themselves"], and *δακτύλων* ["fingers"]). Luke probably reflects Q more closely, whereas Matthew has worked the material into his larger pericope. The logion of v 12 also appears to be a Q saying, with only slightly different wording (cf. Luke 14:11 = Luke 18:14b). Finally, the references to *τὴν πρωτοκλισίαν ἐν τοῖς δείπνοις*, "the place of honor at banquets," *τὰς πρωτοκαθεδρίας ἐν ταῖς συναγωγαῖς*, "the chief seats in the synagogues," and *τοὺς ἀσπασμοὺς ἐν ταῖς ἀγοραῖς*, "the salutations in the marketplaces" (vv 6–7a), are found very nearly verbatim in Mark 12:38c–39 (where the clauses are, however, in reverse order) and in Luke 20:46 and 11:43 (where they are part of a "woe" saying). Mark 12:38b also contains a clause not included by Matthew: *τῶν θελόντων ἐν στολαῖς περιπατεῖν*, "the ones who want to walk about in long robes." The Markan logia are introduced with *καὶ ἐν τῇ διδαχῇ αὐτοῦ ἔλεγεν· βλέπετε ἀπὸ τῶν γραμματέων*, "and in his teaching he was saying: 'Beware of the scribes.'" Matthew's material, by contrast, addressed specifically to the crowds and Jesus' disciples, refers to the scribes and the Pharisees and begins with a positive statement about them. The logion in v 11 ("the greatest of you will be your servant") is very similar to Mark 10:43b ("whoever wants to be great among you will be your servant"), a saying found also in 20:26, where it is dependent on this Markan passage. Matthew's reflection of Markan material is the last until the Olivet Discourse, beginning in chap. 24. For the remainder of the pericope Matthew uses his own special source, as is the case for the remainder of the chapter, except for occasional possibilities of the use of Q material.

C. This first part of the extended discourse of Jesus divides into two major sections: the first a description of the Pharisees and the second a closely related exhortation to the disciples concerning humility. The following outline may be suggested: (1) the Pharisees, subdivided into (a) appreciation of the Pharisees as interpreters of Moses (vv 1–3a), (b) the failure of their deeds to match their words (v 3b–c), (c) the heavy burdens they impose (v 4), and (d) their love of the praise of others (vv 5–7); and (2) the disciples of Jesus, subdivided into (a) the need to avoid titles, (i) "rabbi" (v 8), (ii) "father" (v 9), and (iii) "teacher" (v 10), (b) greatness in service (v 11), and (c) eschatological reversal (v 12). Vv 8–12 can accordingly be thought of as a kind of small "community rule" (Haenchen, *ZTK* 48 [1951] 38–63). Having returned to an extended teaching discourse of Jesus, the evangelist provides again a large amount of parallel or symmetrical syntax. Pairs of parallel verbs occur in v 3 (λέγουσιν—ποιοῦσιν, "say"—"do") and in v 4 (δεσμεύουσιν—ἐπιτεθέασιν, "tie"—"put upon"), and v 5 contains parallel clauses: πλατύνουσιν τὰ φυλακτήρια αὐτῶν καὶ μεγαλύνουσιν τὰ κράσπεδα, "they make their phylacteries large, and they make their tassels long." The parallelism in the first three direct objects of the verb φιλοῦσιν, "they love," in vv 6–7 is striking; each is modified by a prepositional phrase beginning with ἐν: τὴν πρωτοκλισίαν ἐν τοῖς δείπνοις καὶ τὰς πρωτοκαθεδρίας ἐν ταῖς συναγωγαῖς καὶ τοὺς ἀσπασμοὺς ἐν ταῖς ἀγοραῖς, "the seat of honor at banquets and the important seats in the synagogues and the salutations in the marketplaces." The fourth object clause (καὶ καλεῖσθαι ὑπὸ τῶν ἀνθρώπων ῥαββί, "and to be called 'rabbi' by people") breaks the parallelism. The symmetrical syntax of vv 8–10 is striking: three imperative clauses (the first and third passive [κληθῆτε, "be called"], the second active [καλέσητε, "call"]) are each followed directly by words concerning "the one": in the first two instances, εἷς γάρ ἐστιν ὑμῶν, "for one is your" (vv 8, 9), in the third, ὅτι καθηγητὴς ὑμῶν ἐστιν εἷς, "because your tutor is one" (v 10). This basic structure is broken only by the parenthetical insertion in v 8c, πάντες δὲ ὑμεῖς ἀδελφοί ἐστε, "but all of you are brothers." The only other slight, but significant, variation is the conclusion of v 10 with its identification of the one tutor as ὁ Χριστός, "the Christ." Finally, note the exactly symmetrical parallelism of the two logia in v 12. The structural parallelism of parts of this pericope is impressive. Again it may point to the probability that the sayings of Jesus were deliberately transmitted so as to enable easy memorization, although the activity of the evangelist in this regard also should not be minimized.

*Comment*

**1–3a**  Matthew's τότε, "then," is again only a connective rather than a strict chronological note (cf. 4:1; the word occurs in Matthew ninety times, compared to six times in Mark and fifteen in Luke). As also in the Sermon on the Mount (chaps.

5–7), Jesus addresses τοῖς ὄχλοις καὶ τοῖς μαθηταῖς αὐτοῦ, "the crowds and his disciples" (cf. vv 8–12). The crowds will hear the nature of Jesus' indictment of the Pharisees; the disciples will in addition learn more of the righteousness required of them, that which exceeds the scribes' and Pharisees' righteousness (5:20), as well as something of the dangers that confront those who pursue righteousness. Down to the end of the chapter, no mention is made of the Pharisees being among the hearers, although they are addressed (at least rhetorically) in vv 13–34 and perhaps as part of the Jewish leadership. To begin with, Jesus makes a positive statement concerning the Pharisees that applauds them in principle for being those who occupy themselves with the important task of interpretation of the teaching of Moses. The statement up through v 3a could almost be put in quotation marks since it reflects the widely held view of the Pharisees. Jesus too shares this view, although he is soon to qualify it. The Pharisees, together with their professional Torah scholars, οἱ γραμματεῖς, "the scribes" (cf. the same combination in 5:20; 12:38; 15:1 and in the "woes" beginning in v 13), are said to "sit upon Moses' seat" (ἐπὶ τῆς Μωϋσέως καθέδρας ἐκάθισαν). This means that as the custodians of Moses' teaching they share in his authority and are accordingly to be respected. Although the term may be metaphorical here, there was in fact somewhat later a special chair of Moses in synagogues in which sat the one who expounded the Torah to the congregation (see Sukenik, 57–61; Newport). Because (or as it soon must be qualified, "insofar as") the Pharisees expound the Mosaic Torah, one is to follow their teaching. This is put absolutely and quite emphatically by the combination of πάντα and ὅσα, lit. "everything whatsoever," and the use of two nearly synonymous verbs, ποιήσατε καὶ τηρεῖτε, "do and keep." That their strong assertion is an approval in principle rather than fact, despite its emphasis, becomes clear from vv 13–33, and especially vv 16–22, where Jesus explicitly rejects what the Pharisees say (cf. v 4). This interpretation is more consonant with Matthew's concern to affirm Jesus' loyalty to the righteousness of Torah than is the conclusion that the statement is ironic or sarcastic (*pace* Carson). Furthermore, Jesus has on several occasions earlier in Matthew distanced himself markedly from the teaching of the Pharisees (cf. 9:10–11, 14; 12:1–2, 10–14; 15:1–20; 19:3–9) and at one point actually warned his disciples to "beware of the leaven [i.e., the teaching] of the Pharisees and Sadducees" (16:6, 11–12). On the historical question of the dominance of the Pharisees as the authoritative interpreters of the law before A.D. 70, see Mason.

**3b** The initial criticism of the Pharisees involves a discrepancy between their words and their deeds. Thus though one is to follow what they say, one is *not* necessarily to follow the example of their deeds: κατὰ δὲ τὰ ἔργα αὐτῶν μὴ ποιεῖτε, "do not do according to their works." They "say," i.e., speak concerning righteousness (presumably here, as in v 3a, correct statements concerning the righteousness of Torah), but they do not "do" or act in accordance with their own teaching (cf. Rom 2:21–24). Specific instances of this hypocrisy will be mentioned in the "woes" beginning in v 13, where repeatedly the scribes and Pharisees are addressed as "hypocrites" (cf. too esp. 15:6–7).

**4** This statement involves criticism of the teaching of the Pharisees for its burdensome character and of the insensitivity of the Pharisees in this regard. The reference to the tying up of φορτία βαρέα [καὶ δυσβάστακτα], "heavy [and difficult to bear] burdens," and placing them on people's shoulders (the burdensomeness of the law referred to in Acts 15:10, 28 refers to the commands of the written Torah itself, apart from the Pharisaic elaborations of those commands) points clearly to the Pharisees' distinctive oral Torah with its difficult and complicated casuistry (*pace* Gundry; cf. vv 16–18, 23, 25). The Pharisees, in a well-motivated but misled attempt to protect the obedience of the written Torah, had built up an elaborate fence around the Torah through the detailed stipulations of their special tradition (which in tragic irony had the effect of canceling out what it had been intended to explicate; cf. 15:3, 6). This they firmly imposed on others, without being willing to make adjustments to the burden, not even by so slight an exertion as the moving of a finger. Cf. 11:28 and *Comment* there.

**5** A major flaw among the Pharisees now emerges: their love of the praise and admiration of others. They perform their righteous deeds in order "to be seen by others" (πρὸς τὸ θεαθῆναι τοῖς ἀνθρώποις; see the criticism of this in 6:1, 5, 16). Examples supporting this conclusion are next provided. The Pharisees make the badges of their piety conspicuously large. τὰ φυλακτήρια αὐτῶν, "their phylacteries" (the word occurs in the NT only here), refers to the boxes, usually leather, that contained written passages of scripture and were strapped to their foreheads and arms in literal obedience to Exod 13:9 and Deut 6:8; 11:18. The κράσπεδα, "tassels" (Heb., צִיצִת, ṣîṣît), each with a cord of blue, were attached to the four corners of a garment, corresponding to the commandment of Num 15:37–39 and Deut 22:12, as a reminder to obey God's commandments (Jesus also wore such tassels; cf. 9:20; 14:36). The Pharisees called attention to their piety by the size of these items (πλατύνειν, "make large," occurs in the Gospels only here)—a symbolism ironically in keeping with the great burdens they imposed (vv 3–4).

**6–7** As further indications of the inordinate pride of the scribes and Pharisees, Jesus points out how "they love" (φιλοῦσιν) being shown deference and honor. Four items are mentioned in this connection. The first two have to do with seating at banquets and in the synagogue. τὴν πρωτοκλισίαν ἐν τοῖς δείπνοις, "the seat of honor at banquets," refers to being seated at the right hand of the host or master of the house (cf. Luke 14:7–8). τὰς πρωτοκαθεδρίας ἐν ταῖς συναγωγαῖς, "the places of honor in the synagogues," refers presumably to those seats at the front of the synagogue in full view of the congregation (cf. Jas 2:1–4). τοὺς ἀσπασμοὺς ἐν ταῖς ἀγοραῖς, "salutations in the marketplaces," are the respectful and deferential formalities that would have been offered to eminent religious authorities. One title of honor included in these words was that of "rabbi" (lit. "my great one," in the sense of "master"), a designation loved by the Pharisees (in Matthew, besides v 8, the word occurs again only in 26:25, 49, where Judas uses it to address Jesus; but cf. Mark 9:5; 11:21; John 1:49; 3:2; etc.). The term is synonymous with "teacher," as the following verse shows (cf. too John 1:38). As spoken by Jesus, the word used here and in v 8 probably does not mean "rabbi" in the later, technical sense of the word. In relation to that meaning of the word, we are here to understand "proto-rabbi." See Shanks for arguments against "rabbi" as an anachronism in the Gospels. The scribes and the Pharisees were motivated not so much by the claimed concern to obey God as by the ego-satisfying praise and honor of others.

**8** Jesus' disciples, by contrast (emphatic ὑμεῖς, "you"), should not allow themselves to be called "rabbi." This is all the more remarkable since the disciple of Jesus has in fact earlier been likened to a "scribe trained for the kingdom of heaven" (13:52). But the disciples have only one real "teacher" (διδάσκαλος), who is to be set apart from others as "rabbi" (for the equivalence of "rabbi" and "teacher," see John 1:38). Although the "one teacher" is not specified here, there can be no doubt that he is the same as the one tutor of v 10, i.e., the Christ. The point here is not to deny that the Christian community has teachers but rather to put up a barrier against the elevation of some above others and the pride that so naturally accompanies such differentiation. The stress thus falls on the egalitarian statement "all [πάντες] of you are brothers and sisters." All are equally dependent upon the single authoritative teacher of the community, Jesus (for the ramifications of this, see Byrskog). Behind this emphasis lies a polemic against the de facto authority of the Pharisees and scribes. Possible eschatological overtones, in the context of the announcement of the new covenant, are found in Jeremiah's declaration that no one will need teaching because they will all know the Lord directly (Jer 31:34).

**9** The disciples of Jesus should also avoid referring to anyone as "father" in an honorary or reverential sense (for an example of this use, see Acts 7:2; 22:1). The grammatical ambiguities of the Greek syntax (esp. ὑμῶν, "your") are to be decided upon in light of the preceding and following statements: i.e., "call no one your father." In the present context the word "father" is probably to be understood as connoting "teacher" (see Byrskog, 299–300) and does not constitute a reference to being descended from the patriarchs (*pace* Townsend, Michaels). Cf. the mishnaic tractate *Sayings of the Fathers* (ʾ*Abot*); Gal 1:14; Jos., *Ant.* 13.10.6 §297; 13.16.2 §408. Besides one's earthly father (for whom the title is not in question), only one other may be referred to as "Father," i.e., God himself, who, as here, is so often referred to in Matthew as our "heavenly Father" (for ὁ πατὴρ ὁ οὐράνιος, "heavenly Father," cf. 5:48; 6:14, 26, 32; 15:13; 18:35). Cf. Mal 2:10 (the sense of spiritual "father" in 1 Cor 4:14–15 is rather different from what is entailed here).

**10** A further title the disciples should avoid is that of καθηγητής, "tutor." This word occurs only here in the NT and not at all in the LXX. It does occur in other Greek sources (see Spicq), where it generally means "teacher" or "master." B. W. Winter's study of the terms in POxy 2190 (c. A.D. 70–90) points to the more specific meaning "tutor," in the sense of one who provides private instruction to a student outside the framework of a formal school. The argument is the same as in the two preceding instances: only one is worthy to be called "Teacher" or "Master," and now that one is at last explicitly and climactically identified as ὁ Χριστός, "the Christ (= Messiah)." The three occurrences of εἷς, "one," in vv 8–10 constitute an "implicit didactic christology" and at the same time may involve an allusion to the Shema, with the implication that "adherence to Jesus as teacher relates to the confession of the one and only God" (Byrskog, 300). The immediately underlying lesson, however, continues to be the humility of the disciple, as the final logia make clear.

**11** As in the important close parallel in 20:26–27, the future ἔσται, lit. "will be," is to be understood as an imperative, "must be." The one who would be "great" (μείζων) must become a "servant" (διάκονος). The final position of διάκονος, "servant," is emphatic in both passages.

**12** The reversal described in this saying happens not in this life but in connection with the enjoyment of eschatological rewards. Exaltation of oneself in the present will mean a humbling in the eschaton, while the humbling of oneself now will mean an exaltation in the future (cf. 18:4). Such a reversal is already anticipated in the OT (cf. Prov 29:23; Job 22:29; Ezek 17:24; 21:26) and is taken up in the NT, probably in dependence upon the teaching of Jesus (cf. Jas 4:10; 2 Cor 11:7; the pattern is seen even in Jesus' own mission as described in Phil 2:8–9). The very close parallels in Luke 14:11; 18:14, although slightly different in form, reflect the same symmetrical parallelism of Matthew's logion (note especially the same future passive forms in all three passages). The call of the disciple in the present is not to the pride of exalted status but to humility and servanthood. Only such demeanor can lead to eschatological exaltation (see further, Viviano).

### Explanation

Jesus respects the position of the scribes and Pharisees as interpreters of the law of Moses. Although he seems at first glance to give an unqualified approval to their teaching, it is clear in light of his criticism of their teaching elsewhere that his words are not to be taken in this sense. They are a way, instead, of emphasizing the importance of the law and must be understood with the strong qualification "insofar as their teachings are appropriate interpretations of Moses." Another way of putting this from the evangelist's perspective would be "insofar as their interpretation of the law overlaps with Jesus' interpretation," which may in actuality have been to no small extent. Yet for Matthew Jesus alone is the true interpreter of Moses, and he is therefore the one rabbi, teacher, and tutor. He, not the Pharisaic rabbis, gives authoritative interpretation of Torah. And the scribes and Pharisees come under harsh criticism for both their teaching and their deeds in the material that follows. Jesus faults them particularly for their desire to impress others and their love of prestige and position. Such dangers also threaten Christians, and Jesus thus warns his disciples. They are to avoid titles that would set them apart from, and above, others in the community of faith, not because the particular titles are reprehensible but because of the assumption of superiority and elitism that so often goes with them. The demeanor of the disciples is to be characterized above all by the virtues of service and humility. Christians of every era and every circumstance, especially those in leadership roles, must learn again that true greatness consists in service and that self-humbling now is the path to exaltation in the eschaton. Only by such a radical departure from the values and priorities of the world will Christians in authority be the disciples of the one Teacher and Lord.

# The Seven Woes against the Scribes and Pharisees (23:13–33)

### Bibliography

**Brandt, W.** "Jüdische Reinheitslehre und ihre Beschreibung in den Evangelien." *ZAW* 19 (1910) 1–62. **Derrett, J. D. M.** "Receptacles and Tombs (Mt 23,24–30)." *ZNW* 77 (1986) 255–66. ———.

"You Build the Tombs of the Prophets (Lk. 11,47–51, Mt. 23,29–31)." *SE* 4 [= TU 102)] (1968) 187–93. **Flowers, H. J.** "Matthew xxiii. 15." *ExpTim* 73 (1961–62) 67–69. **Hoad, J.** "On Matthew xxiii. 15: A Rejoinder." *ExpTim* 73 (1961–62) 211–12. **Jeremias, J.** *Heiligengräber in Jesu Umwelt (Mt. 23,29; Lk. 11,47).* Göttingen: Vandenhoeck & Ruprecht, 1958. **Kinniburgh, E.** "Hard Sayings III [Mt 23.33]." *Th* 66 (1963) 414. **Klein, G.** "Rein und unrein: Mt 23,25; Lc 11,37.42." *ZNW* 7 (1906) 252–54. **Kümmel, W. G.** "Die Weherufe über die Schriftgelehrten und Pharisäer: Matthäus 23,13–36." In *Antijudaismus im Neuen Testament?* ed. W. Eckert et al. Munich: Kaiser, 1967. 135–47. **Lachs, S. T.** "On Matthew 23:27–28." *HTR* 68 (1975) 385–88. **Ludin Janson, H.** "Existait-il à l'époque hellénistique des prédicateurs itinérants juifs?" *RHPR* 18 (1938) 242–54. **Maccoby, H.** "The Washing of Cups." *JNTS* 14 (1982) 3–15. **McKnight, S.** *A Light among the Gentiles: Jewish Missionary Activity in the Second Temple Period.* Minneapolis: Fortress, 1991. **Miller, R. J.** "The Inside Is (Not) the Outside: Q 11:39–41 and GThom 89." *Forum* 5 (1989) 92–105. **Minear, P. S.** "Yes or No: The Demand for Honesty in the Early Church." *NovT* 13 (1971) 1–13. **Neusner, J.** "'First Cleanse the Inside': The 'Halakhic' Background of a Controversy-Saying." *NTS* 22 (1976) 486–95. **Pernot, H.** "Matthieu XXIII, 29–36; Luc XI, 47–51." *RHPR* 13 (1933) 262–67. **Schwartz, D. R.** "Viewing the Holy Utensils (P. Ox. V,840)." *NTS* 32 (1986) 153–59.

### Translation

[13] *"But[a] woe to you, scribes and Pharisees, hypocrites, because you shut the kingdom of heaven to people. For you yourselves are not entering into it, nor do you permit those who would enter[b] it to do so.[c,d]*

[15] *"Woe to you, scribes and Pharisees, hypocrites, because you travel about on the sea and the dry land to make one proselyte, and when you succeed in doing so,[e] you make that person an offspring of Gehenna twice as bad as you are.*

[16] *"Woe to you, blind leaders, who say: 'If a person swears[f] by the temple, it is nothing; but whoever swears by the gold of the temple is bound by the oath.'[g]* [17] *Foolish and blind people! For what is greater, the gold or the temple that sanctified[h] the gold?* [18] *And you say, 'If a person swears[i] by the altar, it is nothing; but whoever swears by the gift that is on it is bound by the oath.'[j]* [19] *Blind[k] people! For what is greater, the gift or the altar that sanctifies the gift?* [20] *The one, therefore, who swears by the altar swears by it and everything upon it.* [21] *And whoever swears by the temple swears by it and by the One who dwells in it.* [22] *And the person who swears by heaven swears by the throne of God and by the One who sits upon it.*

[23] *"Woe to you, scribes and Pharisees, hypocrites, because you tithe mint and dill and cummin, and you have neglected the weightier matters of the law: justice, mercy, and faithfulness. [But][l] these things you ought to have done while not neglecting the others.* [24] *You are[m] blind guides, you who strain out the gnat but swallow the camel!*

[25] *"Woe to you, scribes and Pharisees, hypocrites, because you clean the outside of the cup and the dish, but inside they are filled with greediness and self-indulgence.[n]* [26] *Blind Pharisees! Clean the inside of the cup[o] first in order that its[p] outside may also be clean.*

[27] *"Woe to you, scribes and Pharisees, hypocrites, because you are like whitewashed tombs, which[q] on the outside appear beautiful but inside are filled with the bones of the dead and all sorts of impurity.* [28] *Thus too you yourselves on the outside appear righteous to people, but on the inside you are full of hypocrisy and iniquity.*

[29] *"Woe to you, scribes and Pharisees, hypocrites, because you build the tombs of the prophets and you beautify the monuments of the righteous* [30] *and you say: 'If we had lived in the days of our fathers, we would not have shared with them in killing the*

*prophets!'*[r] [31] *So that you bear witness against yourselves that you are the children*[s] *of those who murdered the prophets.* [32] *And you yourselves:*[t] *Bring to the full*[u] *the measure of your fathers!* [33] *Serpents, offspring of vipers! How will you escape from the judgment of Gehenna?"*

### Notes

[a] A number of MSS (אֶ* K W Γ Δ sy^{c.p.h} sa^{ms} bo^{pt}) omit δέ, "but."

[b] τοὺς εἰσερχομένους, lit. "those who are entering."

[c] The words "it to do so" are added to the translation for clarity.

[d] An additional verse is added here, as v 14, by *f*^{13} it vg^{cl} sy^{c} bo^{pt}; a majority of late MSS (W TR sy^{p.h} bo^{mss}) also add the verse but place it after v 12. In all these witnesses, the verse runs as follows: Οὐαὶ δὲ ὑμῖν, γραμματεῖς καὶ φαρισαῖοι ὑποκριταί, ὅτι κατεσθίετε τὰς οἰκίας τῶν χηρῶν καὶ προφάσει μακρὰ προσευχόμενοι· διὰ τοῦτο λήμψεσθε περισσότερον κρίμα, "Woe to you, scribes and Pharisees, hypocrites, because you devour the households of the widows, and for appearance's sake you pray at length. On account of this, you will receive greater judgment." These words, not found in the earliest MSS of Alexandrian, Western, or Caesarean traditions (אֶ B D L Z Θ *f*^1 vg sy^{s} sa mae bo pt), are apparently drawn from the parallel in Mark 12:40 (cf. Luke 20:47) and structured according to the Matthean pattern, including the introductory "woe." Its different position in the later MSS also testifies to its later insertion. *TCGNT*, 60.

[e] ὅταν γένηται, lit. "when it happens."

[f] ὃς ἂν ὀμόσῃ, lit. "whoever swears."

[g] "By the oath" added to translation.

[h] Most later MSS (C L W Θ *f*^{1,13} TR co) have the present participle ἁγιάζων, "sanctifies."

[i] ὃς ἂν ὀμόσῃ, lit. "whoever swears."

[j] "By the oath" added to translation.

[k] Many MSS (B C W *f*^{13} TR sy^{p.h} co) insert μωροὶ καί, "foolish and," before τυφλοί, "blind," probably in imitation of the words at the beginning of v 17. *TCGNT*, 61.

[l] δέ, "but," is lacking in אֶ D Γ Θ *f*^{1,13} lat sa^{ms} mae bo but present in B C K L W Δ sy sa^{mss}. This division of the witnesses causes the editors to put the word in brackets.

[m] "You are" added to translation.

[n] A few MSS (C K Γ sy^{p}) have ἀδικίας, "unrighteousness"; W (sy^{h}) has ἀκρασίας ἀδικίας, "unrighteous self-indulgence"; Σ lat sy^{s} co have ἀκαθαρσίας, "uncleanness"; and M has πλεονεξίας, "covetousness." The MS evidence favoring ἀκρασίας, "self-indulgence," is extremely strong by comparison.

[o] Many MSS (אֶ B C L W *f*^{13} TR lat sy^{p.h} co) add καὶ τῆς παροψίδος, "and the dish," perhaps influenced by the words in the preceding verse. Omitting the words are D Θ *f*^1 sy^{s}. Despite the relatively weak attestation of the shorter text, the editors favor it because of the instances supporting the singular αὐτοῦ, "its," in the following clause. See next *Note* and *TCGNT*, 61.

[p] Many MSS (אֶ B^2 C L W TR sy^{p.h}) have the plural αὐτῶν, "their," to agree with an immediately preceding reference to both the cup and the dish (X lat mae lack any pronoun). In favor of the singular αὐτοῦ, "its," are B* D Θ *f*^{1,13} sy^{s}. See preceding *Note*.

[q] D (mae) has ἔξωθεν ὁ τάφος φαίνεται ὡραῖος, ἔσωθεν δὲ γέμει, "on the outside the tomb appears beautiful, but inside it is filled"; the important cursive 33 has οἵτινες ἔξωθεν μὲν φαίνεσθε τοῖς ἀνθρώποις δίκαιοι, "you who on the outside appear righteous to people," thus anticipating the words of v 28.

[r] οὐκ ἂν ἤμεθα αὐτῶν κοινωνοὶ ἐν τῷ αἵματι τῶν προφητῶν, lit. "we would not have been sharers with them in the blood of the prophets." Many MSS (P^{77} אֶ C L W TR) reverse the unusual order of αὐτῶν κοινωνοί, "sharers with them." Θ omits αὐτῶν, "with them," altogether.

[s] υἱοί, lit. "sons."

[t] καὶ ὑμεῖς can also be taken with the preceding sentence, resulting in the added emphasis "even you."

[u] D reads ἐπληρώσατε, "you have fulfilled."

### Form/Structure/Setting

A. Seven woes against the scribes and the Pharisees make up the central section of chap. 23. For the first time in the chapter the Pharisees are addressed directly. The hypocrisy mentioned generally in v 3c ("they say, but they do not do") is now illustrated through specific examples. The first two woes (vv 13–15) are further-more related to the criticism of the scribes and Pharisees already articulated in v 4, while the fifth and sixth (vv 25–28) are related to vv 5–7. The final woe (vv 29–33) serves as a biting climax to the seven with its indictment of the scribes and Phari-sees as those who stand solidly in line with the murderers of the prophets. As their fathers did, so also will they persecute those sent to Israel by God. The very posi-tioning of this material at the end of the account of the ministry of Jesus, just prior to the eschatological discourse with its reference to the destruction of Jerusalem as the judgment of God (cf. the earlier position of the parallel material in Luke 11), also lends a climactic note to the entire chapter.

B. Matthew's seven woes are shaped by the evangelist to some extent on the model of, and utilizing elements of, traditional material available to him. In this pericope, the only parallel to Mark is in the textually doubtful v 14 (see above *Note* d), which appears to be a later insertion of the Markan material (Mark 12:40) prefaced by Matthew's woe formula. Matthew's pericope apparently depends on a combination of logia drawn from Q (cf. Luke 11:39–52, which contains six woe sayings, corre-sponding to Matthew's as follows: 1 = 4; [2 = 23:6–7]; 3 = 6; [4 = 23:4]; 5 = 7) and from Matthew's special source, all of which is then put into its present form by the evange-list and put in its parallel form by the repeated introductory woe formulae.

The first woe (v 13) accordingly finds a parallel in the woe saying of Luke 11:52. The latter, however, is addressed to τοῖς νομικοῖς, "the lawyers," rather than to the scribes and Pharisees (and none of the Lukan woe sayings employs ὑποκριταί, "hypocrites," as in Matthew). Luke also refers to the lawyers as taking away τὴν κλεῖδα τῆς γνώσεως, "the key of knowledge" (contrast Matthew's positive statement in vv 2–3a; Matthew uses the word κλείς, "key," only in connection with the authority given to Peter in 16:19). Although the wording is rather different, there can be no doubt that Matthew and Luke record the same logion: Matthew's κλείετε, "shut up," corresponds to Luke's κλεῖδα, "key"; both evangelists refer to a failure to enter in; and Luke's τοὺς εἰσερχομένους ἐκωλύσατε, "you prevent those who (would) enter in," is the equivalent of Matthew's οὐδὲ τοὺς εἰσερχομένους ἀφίετε εἰσελθεῖν, "nor do you permit to enter those who (would) enter in." Matthew appears to have reworked the logion of Q, which Luke probably presents more accurately. There are no Lukan parallels to the second and third woe sayings (vv 15–22). The fourth woe (vv 23–24), however, finds a parallel in Luke 11:42, which is addressed to the Pharisees. In the first part Luke agrees nearly verbatim except in the reference to the second and third items that were tithed: thus for Matthew's τὸ ἄνηθον, "dill," Luke has τὸ πήγανον, "rue," and for τὸ κύμινον, "cummin," Luke has πᾶν λάχανον, "every herb" (a Lukan modification of Q?). Accord-ing to Luke, what has been neglected (only Matthew refers to τὰ βαρύτερα τοῦ νόμου, "the weightier things of the law") are τὴν κρίσιν, "justice," as in Matthew, and τὴν ἀγάπην τοῦ θεοῦ, "the love of God," which takes the place of Matthew's second and third items, τὸ ἔλεος καὶ τὴν πίστιν, "mercy and faithfulness." Both evangelists agree almost exactly in the following sentence: ταῦτα δὲ ἔδει ποιῆσαι κἀκεῖνα μὴ ἀφιέναι (Luke: παρεῖναι), "these things you ought to have done without neglecting the others." Luke has no par-allel to v 24. Matthew's fifth woe (vv 25–26) finds parallel material in Luke 11:39–40, which, however, although addressed to the Pharisees, is not in the form of a woe say-ing. V 25 agrees closely with Luke 11:39, except for Matthew's τῆς παροψίδος for Luke's τοῦ πίνακος, both meaning "dish" (the former occurs only here in the NT; Matthew uses the latter only in 14:8, 11) and Matthew's ἀκρασίας, "self-indulgence" (in the Gos-pels only here), for Luke's πονηρίας, "evil." V 26, on the other hand, differs markedly from Luke 11:40–41. Matthew's φαρισαῖε τυφλέ, "blind Pharisee," corresponds to Luke's ἄφρονες, "fools." Matthew does not contain Luke's rhetorical question, "Did not the maker make both the outside and the inside?" Matthew's καθάρισον πρῶτον τὸ ἐντὸς τοῦ ποτηρίου, "cleanse first the inside of the cup," takes the place of Luke's πλὴν τὰ ἐνόντα δότε ἐλεημοσύνην, "but give the inner things for alms"; Matthew lacks Luke's καὶ ἰδοὺ πάντα καθαρὰ ὑμῖν ἐστιν, "and behold everything is clean for you" (which probably was in Q), concluding rather with ἵνα γένηται καὶ τὸ ἐκτὸς αὐτοῦ καθαρόν, "in order that the outside may also become clean." The sixth woe (vv 27–28) finds a partial parallel in the woe saying of Luke 11:44 (the address to the Pharisees is assumed from Luke 11:43), which, however, is parallel more in thought than in words: "For you are like graves [τὰ μνημεῖα; cf. Matthew's τάφοις, "tombs"] which are not seen, and men walk over them without knowing it." Matthew has probably rewritten the logion to make it accord more with his emphasis on hypocrisy, i.e., something seeming to be what it is not (cf. the application in v 28, lacking altogether in Luke). The seventh woe (vv 29–33) is paralleled in Luke 11:47 (the address "lawyers" is assumed from the preceding verse), where the opening words are almost exactly the same: ὅτι οἰκοδομεῖτε τὰ μνημεῖα [Matthew: τοὺς τάφους] τῶν προφητῶν, "because you build the monuments of the prophets." To this Matthew has added "and you adorn the monuments [τὰ μνημεῖα] of the righteous [δικαίων]." The thought that follows in both Matthew and Luke is the same, but Matthew has it in considerably expanded form by referring to a claim of the scribes and Pharisees that they would not have killed the prophets as did their fathers. Thus they bear witness against themselves that they are the sons of those who murdered the prophets (cf. Luke's simple "but your fathers killed them"). Luke concludes the saying with the comment that by building the tombs of the prophets they give implicit consent to the deeds of their fathers (Luke 11:48). Matthew, on the other hand, bitterly exhorts the scribes and Pharisees to "fill up the measure of your fathers," presumably referring to their opposition to Jesus and his disciples (cf. vv 34–36). This note is heightened by the caustic rhetorical question of v 33, which is again lacking in Luke.

In summary, it may be said that Matthew has used the Q tradition creatively, by bringing material together into seven parallel woe sayings, each of which is restated and sometimes expanded with Matthew's own material, so that together they enable Matthew to make the emphasis he desires at this climactic point in the Gospel.

C. The seven woes that make up the centerpiece of the denunciation of the scribes and Pharisees are constructed by Matthew for maximal impact. The fact that there are seven woes (cf. six woes in Luke 11:42–52) is itself significant symbolism, pointing to a fullness of corruption. Each of these begins with the identical formula, οὐαὶ ὑμῖν, γραμματεῖς καὶ φαρισαῖοι ὑποκριταί, ὅτι, "Woe to you, scribes and Pharisees, hypocrites, because . . . ," except for the third (v 16), which begins οὐαὶ ὑμῖν, ὁδηγοὶ τυφλοὶ οἱ λέγοντες, "woe to you, blind guides, who say . . ." (the variation is probably more than stylistic, being related to the content of the woe saying; see Comment). Several of the woe sayings include further vocative insertions: thus the third has two (v 17, μωροὶ καὶ τυφλοί, "fools and blind people," and v 19, τυφλοί, "blind people"), the fourth and fifth each have one (v 24, ὁδηγοὶ τυφλοί, "blind guides" [cf. v 16], and v 26, φαρισαῖε τυφλέ, "blind Pharisee"), and the seventh has one, the last words being epexegetical (v 33, ὄφεις, γεννήματα ἐχιδνῶν, "serpents, offspring of vipers"). The first six woes appear to be linked in pairs, with the seventh serving as a climax: the first and second (vv 13–15) concern the effect of the scribes and Pharisees on their disciples; the third and fourth (vv 16–24) concern their teaching; the fifth and sixth (vv 25–28) concern the problem of externalism; the seventh the rejection of those sent by God. The woes may be outlined as follows: (1) for shutting out others from the kingdom (v 13); (2) for bringing condemnation to proselytes (v 15); (3) for a casuistic approach to oaths (vv 16–22); (4) for letting minutiae eclipse what is important (vv 23–24); (5) for letting external cleanness hide the need for inner cleanness (vv 25–26); (6) for letting outward piety hide inner uncleanness (vv 27–28); and (7) for rejection of God's messengers (vv 29–33).

The content of the first two woe sayings, which are about the same length, exhibits little structural parallelism. By contrast, the third (vv 16–22) is much longer and is filled with structural parallelism. Its length and structural complexity, together with its distinctive formula, may argue for its independent formulation prior to being incorporated into the present collection. Two examples of casuistry in oath taking are given, the first concerning the temple and the gold of the temple and the second concerning the altar and the gift on the altar. In each instance the Pharisees' teaching is given (vv 16, 18, in exactly parallel syntax), and in each instance a rhetorical question is asked (vv 17, 19, again in exactly parallel syntax, the first introduced with μωροὶ καὶ τυφλοί, "fools and blind people," the second with simply τυφλοί, "blind people"). The implied answer in each case condemns the casuistic practice of the scribes and Pharisees. A three-fold concluding (οὖν, "therefore") statement (vv 20–22, again with each element in exactly parallel syntax) is then provided, which refers to altar and temple (in that order, and thus chiastically), followed by a third element concerning swearing ἐν τῷ οὐρανῷ, "by heaven," hitherto not mentioned in the woe saying but parallel to the immediately preceding references to the altar and the temple. Again this material (vv 16–22) looks very much as if it has been designed for transmission by memory. The fourth woe (vv 23–24) also reveals symmetrical parallelism in its syntax. Structurally, the three herbs tithed by the Pharisees are matched by the three "weightier matters of the law" that they neglect. There is parallelism in the infinitive clauses of v 23, ταῦτα . . . ποιῆσαι, "to have done these things," and κἀκεῖνα μὴ ἀφιέναι, "and not to have neglected those." Further parallelism is found in the participles and objects in the logion of v 24. The fifth woe (vv 25–26) consists of parallel syntax heightened by the contrast between ἔξωθεν, "outer," and ἔσωθεν, "inner." The double τοῦ ποτηρίου καὶ τῆς παροψίδος, "cup and dish," is paralleled by the double ἁρπαγῆς καὶ ἀκρασίας, "greediness and self-indulgence." The exhortation of v 26 places "clean" chiastically at the beginning and the end in relation to the inside and outside of the cup. The sixth woe (vv 27–28) contains two parallel contrasts (each employing μέν . . . δέ), again with respect to matters ἔξωθεν, "outwardly," and ἔσωθεν, "inwardly." V 28 thus essentially repeats the preceding two clauses of v 27 but moves from the analogy of the tombs to the more direct address of the second person. Thus δίκαιοι, "righteous," corresponds to ὡραῖοι, "beautiful," and ὑποκρίσεως καὶ ἀνομίας, "hypocrisy and iniquity," correspond to ὀστέων νεκρῶν καὶ πάσης ἀκαθαρσίας, "bones of the dead and all sorts of uncleanness." The final woe (vv 29–33) contains less syntactic parallelism, although it begins (v 29) with exactly parallel sentences, οἰκοδομεῖτε, "build," corresponding to κοσμεῖτε, "beautify," and τοὺς τάφους τῶν προφητῶν, "the tombs of the prophets," corresponding to τὰ μνημεῖα τῶν δικαίων, "the monuments of the righteous." The seven woes thus give clear and abundant evidence of Matthew's literary artistry. Taking up traditional elements, the evangelist has put them together to produce a powerful critique of the main opponents of Jesus in the Gospel.

D. Justin Martyr shows a knowledge of Matthew in his allusion to vv 27 and 24 in *Dial.* 112.4 (for v 27, cf. also the *Gos. Naass.* [= *Gospel of the Egyptians?* See E. Hennecke, *New Testament Apocrypha*, ed. W. Schneemelcher (Philadelphia: Westminster, 1963) 1:169–70; citing Hippolytus, *Refut. omn. haer.* 5.7.8–9]).

## Comment

**13** The woe saying is a painful statement of displeasure involving an implied judgment (see the helpful discussion of Garland, *The Intention of Matthew 23,* 64–90)—hence it serves as the opposite of the beatitude. Woe sayings are found elsewhere in Matthew (11:21; 18:7; 24:19; 26:24), but the seven woes of the present pericope form a distinctive set (all are identical with the present formula [cf. vv 15, 23, 25, 27, 29] except for v 16). Woe sayings are not uncommon in the OT, and a piling up of a succession of woe oracles is occasionally also found (cf. Isa 5:8–22 for a series of six; Hab 2:6–20 for five). See *Comment* on v 2 for the combination of γραμματεῖς καὶ φαρισαῖοι, "scribes and Pharisees." Here the woe sayings condemn the perspective and practice of the Pharisees and those Torah scholars who were responsible for the articulation of this viewpoint. ὑποκριταί, "hypocrites" (five further occurrences in this passage: vv 15, 23, 25, 27, 29), which elsewhere in Matthew is generally used in reference to the Pharisees (cf. 6:2, 5, 16; 7:5; 15:7 [explicitly]; 22:18 [explicitly]; 24:51), describes those who "play-act" or who want to appear to be something they are not (see *Comment* on 6:2). The issue, therefore, is deception of others rather than self-deception, as claimed by Via (see "Appendix: A Dialogue with Dan O. Via, Jr., on Hypocrisy in Matthew," in the second edition of Gundry's commentary [1994]). The Pharisees, as those who sit in Moses' seat (v 2), made claim to being the true interpreters of the righteousness of the Torah; in actuality, however, their teaching and practice were false and thus misled others. The statement that they "shut up the kingdom of heaven to people" (κλείετε τὴν βασιλείαν τῶν οὐρανῶν ἔμπροσθεν τῶν ἀνθρώπων), implies that their teaching of Torah should have been the key (cf. the cognate noun κλείς, "key," and its use in 16:19) that opened the door for others to enjoy the rule of God (for τὴν βασιλείαν τῶν οὐρανῶν, "the kingdom of heaven," see *Comment* on 3:2). The Pharisees and their scribes were not themselves (ὑμεῖς, "you," is emphatic) entering that rule, but worse than that, their false teaching did not permit those who followed them in the hope of entering the kingdom to do so. The failure of the Pharisees is a failure of responsibility. By implication—but it is *only* implication—the true interpreter of Torah is Jesus, whose teaching and work alone provide the possibility of entering the kingdom.

**15** The second woe, which begins with the identical opening formula, follows closely upon the concluding point of the first woe. Inasmuch as the misconceived teaching and practice of the Pharisees and their scribes actually prevent their disciples from arriving at their goal, the effect is disastrous: a proselyte is so misled that he becomes "twice as much a child of Gehenna" (υἱὸν γεέννης διπλότερον ὑμῶν), i.e., destined for divine judgment (cf. v 33). This statement (esp. "twice as much"), without denying its seriousness, is hyperbolic rhetoric that need not be taken literally. The extent of the Pharisees' dedication to making "a proselyte" (προσήλυτον; the word elsewhere in the NT always refers to gentile proselytes to Judaism; cf. Acts 2:11; 6:5; 13:43), is underlined by the reference to crossing sea and dry land to gain just ἕνα, "one."

> The question of the extent of the missionary activity of first-century Jews is a difficult one. Most scholars have concluded that there was a flourishing Jewish mission among the Gentiles (see esp. J. Jeremias, *Jesus' Promise to the Nations*, SBT 24 [London: SCM, 1958] 11–19). S. McKnight, however, has recently called attention to the tenuous nature of the evidence for this conclusion. It may well be the case, therefore, that the present verse has in mind not the conversion of pagan Gentiles to Judaism but the conversion of the God-fearing Gentiles (i.e., those already partial converts to Judaism) to full proselytes adhering in particular to the Pharisaic understanding of the righteousness of Torah (see McKnight, 106–8).

**16–19** The formula common to all the other woe sayings of this pericope is lacking here in the third woe. The unique formula οὐαὶ ὑμῖν, ὁδηγοὶ τυφλοὶ οἱ λέγοντες, "Woe to you, blind guides, who say," may reflect the prior, independent existence of this material (vv 16–22). But if the material with its opening formula already existed as it is when the evangelist took it up, there is no reason why he could not have altered the formula to agree with his own in the other six woes. It seems more likely, however, that Matthew deliberately varies the opening formula here in keeping with the content of what follows. Thus "blind guides" (the same expression has been used in describing the Pharisees in 15:14; it is used again in v 24 below) is particularly appropriate to describe those who teach in the casuistic manner of the examples that follow (cf. too the inserted vocatives in v 17, μωροὶ καὶ τυφλοί, "fools and blind people," and v 19, τυφλοί, "blind people"). In the two matters now mentioned, the Pharisees made distinctions between oaths taken ἐν τῷ ναῷ, "in [the name of] the temple," and ἐν τῷ χρυσῷ τοῦ ναοῦ, "by the gold of the temple," on the one hand, and ἐν τῷ θυσιαστηρίῳ, "by the altar," and ἐν τῷ δώρῳ τῷ ἐπάνω αὐτοῦ, "by the gift upon it" (this is also referred to in 5:23), on the other. In each case the former is regarded as not binding (οὐδέν ἐστιν, "it is nothing") while the latter is taken as binding (ὀφείλει, "he is obligated"). In each case, after the repeated address, "blind people" (the first also referring to "fools"), the point is made via a rhetorical question that the temple that makes the gold holy (ἁγιάσας) and the altar that makes the gift holy (ἁγιάζον; cf. Exod 29:37) are greater than that which they made holy. The point is not that the Pharisees simply had matters reversed but that an oath must in every case be regarded as binding (for a similar perspective, see *m. Ned.* 1:1). The supposed exceptions allowed by the Pharisees were deceiving and as such were disallowed by Jesus.

**20–21** This point is reaffirmed by these two statements. In swearing by the altar or temple, one swears by all that is associated with them, including above all the very presence of God. Thus the subtle distinctions of the Pharisees were indefensible. Jesus here argues minimally, and on the ground of the Pharisees themselves, for loyalty to all oaths (cf. 5:33). In his own view, however, oaths were altogether unnecessary: a yes or a no was good enough (see *Comment* on 5:34–37).

**22**   Oddly, a third summarizing statement on exactly the same pattern as those of vv 20–21 is added, although this particular oath has not been mentioned earlier (i.e., in vv 16–19). The principle is the same. Working backwards, we can conclude that the Pharisees said "if one swears by heaven or by the throne of God, it is nothing; but if one swears by the one who sits upon the throne, he is bound by the oath." Since in vv 20 and 21 ὀμνύει, "swears," is followed by ἐν αὐτῷ, which refers to the antecedent preceding the verb, so here ἐν τῷ θρόνῳ τοῦ θεοῦ, "by the throne of God," is probably equivalent to the preceding ἐν τῷ οὐρανῷ, "by heaven" (as it is in 5:34). To swear "by heaven" or "by the throne of God" is tantamount to swearing by the "One sitting upon the throne"—God himself. (It is difficult here to imagine the counterpart to vv 17 and 19, since nothing, not even heaven itself, could be greater than the One who sits upon the throne.) The conclusion is again clear: the implied distinctions are unjustified, and thus all oaths must be honored. Oath taking is always in effect an agreement in God's presence.

**23**   The fourth woe indicates the preoccupation of the Pharisees with minutiae and the resultant neglect of things that really mattered. The Pharisees took the principle of tithing one's crops, which is firmly fixed among the commandments of the OT (cf. Lev 27:30; Deut 14:22–23), to include even such herbs as τὸ ἡδύοσμον καὶ τὸ ἄνηθον καὶ τὸ κύμινον, "mint, dill, and cummin." This scrupulosity in tithing (cf. too Luke 11:42, which refers also to "rue" and πᾶν λάχανον, "every garden herb," and Luke 18:12) went beyond the requirement of the law, which, referring to "the seed of the land," "grain," and "the fruit of the trees," had in mind proper crops rather than garden herbs used for flavoring foods. (cf. *m. Šeb.* 9:1, which exempts certain herbs from tithing). The Pharisees were going the extra mile, to change the metaphor. Their fault, however, was that they had failed (ἀφήκατε, "you have neglected") to give heed to the more important things (τὰ βαρύτερα, lit. "the weightier things") of the law, enumerated here as τὴν κρίσιν καὶ τὸ ἔλεος καὶ τὴν πίστιν, "justice, mercy, and faithfulness." The call to these virtues is clear in the OT (for examples, cf. *justice:* Isa 1:17; Jer 22:3; *mercy:* Hos 6:6; Zech 7:9–10; and the combination of them in Mic 6:8; *faithfulness:* Hab 2:4). The context here favors translating τὴν πίστιν as "faithfulness" rather than "faith" (*pace* Gundry), despite the fact that Matthew does not otherwise use the word in this sense (but cf. the cognate adjective in 24:45). These three matters are at the heart of the OT, and their close affinity to the love commandment, the summary of the law (cf. 22:37–40), is thus readily apparent. These things (ταῦτα) especially, i.e., the more important matters of the law, they ought to have done, insists Jesus, adding κἀκεῖνα μὴ ἀφιέναι, "and not forsaking the others," i.e., the practice of tithing herbs already mentioned. Jesus accordingly sanctions the OT command to tithe, even the Pharisees' extension of it to include garden herbs. His reasoning appears to be: If the Pharisees wish to tithe even the smallest herbs, well and good—let them, as long as they give attention at the same time to the most important items of the law, items that bear directly on the welfare of others around them. Here Jesus strikingly resembles the OT prophets.

**24**   For ὁδηγοὶ τυφλοί, "blind guides," see v 16 (cf. 15:14). The point of the preceding is brought home by a humorous analogy that was perhaps already a proverbial saying (the underlying Aramaic probably contained a pun through similar-sounding words: קַלְמָא, *qalmā᾽* [or possibly even קַמְלָא, *qamlā᾽* ; cf. the inscription *Sefire* i.A.31 for this order of the consonants], for "gnat" and גַּמְלָא, *gamlā*, for "camel"; see M. Black, *Aramaic Approach*, 175–76). By dwelling on minutiae and neglecting the more important matters of the law, the Pharisees show themselves to be like those who carefully filter out τὸν κώνωπα, "the gnat," from their drink, in attempting to obey Lev 11:23, 41, only to swallow τὴν κάμηλον, "the camel." Since the law also designates the camel as unclean and hence disallows it as food (Lev 11:4), the point becomes perhaps even sharper. Concern for the small and relatively insignificant is accompanied by the ignoring of something enormous in size or importance. This appears to be precisely the Pharisees' problem, as the preceding verse has dramatically shown.

**25–26** The fifth woe, which begins with the same opening formula, turns the reader's attention to another weakness that characterized the Pharisees: their concern for outward cleanness at the expense of equal attention to inner cleanness. At first glance, the woe saying seems to be addressing the strict ritual cleanness practiced by the Pharisees in their use of various cups, vessels, and containers: καθαρίζετε τὸ ἔξωθεν τοῦ ποτηρίου καὶ τῆς παροψίδος, "you cleanse the outside of the cup and the plate" (cf. Mark 7:4). But when the inside (ἔσωθεν) is said to be "filled with greediness and self-indulgence" (γέμουσιν ἐξ ἁρπαγῆς καὶ ἀκρασίας) it becomes clear that the ritual cleanness (or perhaps only hygienic cleanness; thus Maccoby against Neusner) of objects is being used only as an analogy for moral cleanness. It is possible to appear righteous outwardly (cf. v 5) while in fact that appearance covers an inward uncleanness. Since the root cause of unrighteousness is internal (cf. 15:11, 19–20), it is useless to be overly concerned with external cleanness (for a somewhat similar critique of the Pharisees, see *As. Mos.* 7.7–10). The Pharisees should begin with what is important; internal purity must precede (πρῶτον, "first") external purity. Φαρισαῖε τυφλέ, "blind Pharisee," is addressed in the style of debate as to a hypothetical opponent (the phrase occurs only here in the NT; cf. vv 16, 17, 19, 24; 15:14; John 9:40).

**27–28** The sixth woe makes the same point using other imagery. This time, following the identical opening formula, the verb παρομοιάζετε, "you are like" (only here in the NT), makes the presence of an analogy clear from the start. Tombs were often "whitewashed" (κεκονιαμένοις; the only other NT occurrence of the word is in Acts 23:3, where it receives the same application), in order to make them conspicuous so that Jews might not inadvertently come into contact with them thereby rendering themselves unclean for seven days (Num 19:16; cf. Luke 11:44). This was done especially before Passover with its massive influx of pilgrims (see Str-B 1:936–37). The paradoxical result was that tombs γέμουσιν ὀστέων νεκρῶν καὶ πάσης ἀκαθαρσίας, "filled with bones of the dead and all sorts of uncleanness," were in this way actually ἔξωθεν, "outwardly," rendered ὡραῖοι, "beautiful." The latter word is used here, in sharp irony, precisely because it is so incongruous when applied to a place that hides the corruption of death. So, too, the Pharisees who "outwardly appear righteous to people" (ἔξωθεν μὲν φαίνεσθε τοῖς ἀνθρώποις δίκαιοι; cf. Luke 16:15; for a similar use of φαίνειν, see 6:5, 16, 18), were in truth ἔσωθεν, "inwardly," filled with ὑποκρίσεως καὶ ἀνομίας, "hypocrisy and iniquity" (the former noun occurs in Matthew only here; cf. Luke 12:1; for the latter noun, cf. 7:23; 13:41; 24:12). The fundamental flaw of the Pharisees, their hypocrisy, was in their concerted attempt to appear to be what they unfortunately were not. While they wanted to appear righteous, in fact they were unrighteous.

**29–30**  The final, seventh woe, after the usual formula, faults the Pharisees for constructing τοὺς τάφους τῶν προφητῶν, "the tombs of the prophets," and for beautifying τὰ μνημεῖα τῶν δικαίων, "the monuments of the righteous." The graves of such ancient worthies were often still known (cf. Acts 2:29), and they could be the object of such late attention (see esp. Jeremias). "Prophets" and "righteous persons" are linked several times in Matthew (cf. 10:41; 13:17). The Pharisees thereby give the impression that they honor these persons and regard themselves as champions of the principles they represented. Furthermore, they attempt explicitly to dissociate themselves from those responsible for killing the prophets: they would not have been κοινωνοὶ ἐν τῷ αἵματι τῶν προφητῶν, lit. "sharers in the blood of the prophets."

**31–32**  All of this, however, was again but a facade covering an endemic lack of receptivity to the messengers sent to Israel by God. It is an irony that the very claim that they would not have participated with their ("your") fathers (cf. τῶν πατέρων ἡμῶν, "our fathers," in v 30) in killing the prophets (cf. 5:12) does establish them as the υἱοί, "sons," of τῶν φονευσάντων, "those who murdered," the prophets. The implication is that the sons are, at least in the present instance, inescapably like their fathers. In making their disclaimer, they inadvertently also bear witness against themselves (ὥστε μαρτυρεῖτε ἑαυτοῖς, "so that you bear witness against yourselves"). For the sons, by their hostile rejection of Jesus and his disciples, are repeating what their fathers had done in rejecting the prophets. There is a certain bitter and ironic inevitability in this—hence the sharp exhortation πληρώσατε τὸ μέτρον τῶν πατέρων ὑμῶν, "Fill up the measure of your fathers." What the fathers began will be completed by their sons (cf. v 34; and the fulfillment in Acts 7:52; 1 Thess 2:15–16 [with ἀναπληρῶσαι αὐτῶν τὰς ἁμαρτίας, "filling up of their sins"]). And no rejection of God's messengers is more grievous than the Pharisees' rejection of God's supreme messenger, Jesus.

**33**  The rising crescendo of bitterness in the preceding lines reaches its climax in a rhetorical question that is at the same time a condemnation. The words are similar to those of John the Baptist in 3:7 (γεννήματα ἐχιδνῶν, "offspring of vipers," is found there verbatim [so too in 12:34], as well as the notion of fleeing [φεύγειν in both instances]; "coming wrath" in 3:7 is the equivalent of κρίσεως τῆς γεέννης, "judgment of Gehenna"). "Vipers" refers here to poisonous snakes. The condemnatory use of the virtual synonym ὄφεις, "serpents," occurs in Matthew only here. The application of this kind of language to the representatives of Israel is shocking in the highest degree. Those who turn against Jesus and his disciples will not escape the eschatological judgment. For "judgment" (κρίσις), see *Comment* on 5:21 (cf. 5:22; 10:15; 11:22, 24; 12:36, 41, 42). For "Gehenna" (γέεννα), see *Comment* on 5:22 (cf. v 15; 5:29–30; 10:28; 18:9).

### Explanation

This passage is certainly one of the most, if not *the* most, painful in the NT—and even worse, it is from the mouth of Jesus (*pace* Haenchen, *ZTK* 48 [1951] 38–63, who attributes the passage to the pre-70 Jewish-Christian church). At the same time, modern scholarship has become increasingly sensitive to the positive, admirable character of the Pharisees (see *Introduction* to chap. 23). This hardly means, however, that the content of this pericope must automatically be dismissed as unhistorical. If the Pharisees and Jesus differed on some fundamental issues, as they undoubtedly did (and especially on the central importance Jesus assigned himself in his proclamation of the kingdom, present and future), it is extremely unlikely that there was no hostility between them or that Jesus could not have criticized them very sharply on occasion. Indeed, it can be expected that it was just because they sat on Moses' seat and were themselves often so close to the truth that Jesus' criticism of them was as harsh as the Gospels record it. The clash between Jesus and the Pharisees was unavoidable, and thus a concrete historical context exists for woe sayings such as the ones in this pericope. At the same time, however, the following points should be noted: (1) it is hardly the case that all Pharisees were like those described here; (2) the present pericope, probably a special construction of the evangelist, gathers together in one place woe sayings spoken by Jesus at different times (cf. their scattered occurrence in Luke), thereby giving them a special impact; (3) the pericope lacks any word of grace, although the Pharisees were not excluded from Jesus' invitation (cf. Acts 15:15); and finally (4) very probably the intensity of the woe sayings to some extent reflects the growing hostility between the church and synagogue in Matthew's day, and thus the sayings may well have been sharpened in their bitter tone. There is today only one proper Christian use of the woe sayings of this pericope. It is found not primarily in the application of the passage to the historical Pharisees, and even less to modern Judaism as a religion, but in the application of the passage to members of the church. Hypocrisy is the real enemy of this pericope, not the scribes, the Pharisees, or the Jews. If, on the model of this pericope, a bitter woe is to be pronounced against anyone today, it must be directed *solely* against hypocrisy in the church (cf. 1 Peter 2:1).

# *Appendix to the Seventh Woe* *(23:34–36)*

## *Bibliography*

**Blank, S. H.** "The Death of Zechariah in Rabbinic Literature." *HUCA* 12–13 (1937–38) 327–46. **Boring, M. E.** "Christian Prophecy and Matthew 23:34–36: A Test Exegesis." In *Society of Biblical Literature, 1977 Seminar Papers.* Missoula, MT: Scholars, 1977. 117–26. **Chapman, J.** "Zacharias Slain between Temple and Altar: Mt 23.35." *JTS* 13 (1912) 398–410. **Christ, F.** "Das Weisheitswort." In *Jesus Sophia.* Zürich: Zwingli, 1970. 120–35. **Kennard, J. S.** "The Lament over Jerusalem: A Restudy of the Zacharias Passage." *ATR* 29 (1947) 173–79. **Légasse, S.** "L'oracle contre cette génération (Mt 23,34–36 par. Lc 11,49–51) et la polémique judéo-chrétinne dans la Source des Logia." In *Logia: Les paroles de Jésus.* FS J. Coppens, ed. J. Delobel. BETL 59. Leuven: Peeters, 1982. 237–56. **McNamara, M.** "Zechariah the Son of Barachiah: Mt. 23:35 and Tg. Lam. 2,20." In *The New Testament and Palestinian Targum to the Pentateuch.* Rome: Pontifical Biblical Institute, 1966. 160–63. **Miller, R. J.** "The Rejection of the Prophets in Q." *JBL* 107 (1988) 225–40. **Nestle, Eb.** "Between Temple and Altar." *ExpTim* 13 (1901–2) 562. **Pernot, H.** "Matthieu XXIII, 29–36; Luc XI, 47–51." *RHPR* 13 (1933) 262–67. **Ross, J. M.** "Which Zachariah?" *IBS* 9 (1987) 70–73. **Seitz, O. J. F.** "The Commission of Prophets and 'Apostles': A Reexamination of Matthew 23,34 with Luke 11,49." *SE* 4 [= TU 102] (1968) 236–40. **Steck, O. H.** *Israel und die gewaltsame Geschick der Propheten.* WMANT 23. Neukirchen: Neukirchener, 1967. **Winkle, R. E.** "The Jeremiah Model for Jesus in the Temple." *AUSS* 24 (1986) 155–72.

### Translation

[34] *"In keeping with this, look, I am sending prophets and wise men and scribes to you. Some* [a] *of them you will kill and crucify, and* [b] *others of them you will scourge in your synagogues and persecute from city to city,* [35] *so that all the innocent blood poured out upon the earth* [c] *shall be laid to your account,* [d] *even from the blood of Abel the righteous to the blood of Zechariah son of Barachiah,* [e] *whom you murdered between the temple and the altar.* [36] *Truly I tell you, all these things will happen in* [f] *this generation."*

### Notes

[a] Many MSS (C D L TR it vg^ww sy^h bo) begin this sentence with καί, "and," probably through the influence of the parallel in Luke 11:49.

[b] D a omit καί, "and."

[c] τῆς γῆς is possibly to be translated "the land" (i.e., Israel).

[d] ἔλθῃ ἐφ᾿ ὑμᾶς, lit. "will come upon you."

[e] א* omits υἱοῦ βαραχίου, "son of Barachiah," through homoioteleuton or, more probably, the influence of the parallel in Luke 11:51, together with its historical difficulty. See *Comment.*

[f] ἥξει ... ἐπί, lit. "will come upon."

### Form/Structure/Setting

A. The subject of the preceding woe (vv 29–33), the murdering of the prophets together with the likening of the sons to the fathers, leads to an appendix prophesying the persecution and killing of the contemporary generation of God's messengers, i.e., the disciples of Jesus. The Pharisees will in this way "fill up the measure" of their fathers (v 32). The final statement of the pericope indicates the relative imminence of this outbreak of hostility. Gnilka regards vv 32–39 as a unity reflecting the repeated threefold structure of invective (vv 34, 37), threat (vv 35, 38), and confirmation (vv 36, 39) on the prophetic model, for example, of 1 Kgs 1:3–4.

B. Matthew draws the pericope from Q (cf. Luke 11:49–51). In Luke, however, it is ἡ σοφία τοῦ θεοῦ, "the Wisdom of God," who speaks and sends the messengers (Luke 11:49). Matthew has probably altered Q at this point, introducing his favorite ἰδού, "look," and, more importantly, identifying Jesus with Wisdom and making him the speaker and sender: ἰδοὺ ἐγὼ ἀποστέλλω, "look, I am sending." Matthew is also probably responsible for the alteration of the material from Luke's (and Q's) third-person statement to the more direct address in the second person, "you" (thereby also making the material part of the preceding pericope). For those sent, Luke has "prophets and apostles [ἀποστόλους]," which seems to be an alteration of what is probably Matthew's closer following of Q: "prophets and wise men [σοφούς] and scribes [γραμματεῖς]"—this in keeping with Matthew's ability to refer to the followers of Jesus in Jewish vocabulary (for "scribes," cf. 13:52). Matthew probably expands Q by the insertion of "and crucify, and some of them you will scourge in your synagogues," which perhaps reflects the reality known to Matthew and his church (cf. 10:17). Matthew also inserts ἀπὸ πόλεως εἰς πόλιν, "from city to city," after the reference to persecution (cf. 10:23). Matthew's emphatic indictment ἔλθη ἐφ᾽ ὑμᾶς, "may come upon you" (v 35), is more primitive than Luke's technical ἐκζητηθῇ . . . ἀπὸ τῆς γενεᾶς ταύτης, "may be required from this generation" (Luke 11:50). On the other hand, it may be that Luke's τὸ αἷμα πάντων τῶν προφητῶν, "the blood of all the prophets," is more primitive, and thus reflects Q, than Matthew's πᾶν αἷμα δίκαιον, "all innocent blood." Matthew's lack of ἀπὸ καταβολῆς κόσμου, "from the foundation of the world" (Luke 11:50), is probably an abbreviation of Q. Matthew adds the descriptive genitives τοῦ δικαίου, "the righteous" (cf. the same word in v 29), following Abel, and υἱοῦ Βαραχίου, "son of Barachiah," after Zechariah, which may not have been in Q (cf. Luke 11:51). Matthew substitutes the emphatic ἐφονεύσατε, "you murdered" (cf. the same verb in v 31), for Luke's, and probably Q's, τοῦ ἀπολομένου, "who perished." Matthew's ναοῦ, "temple," replaces Luke's οἴκου, "house," and the order of temple and altar is reversed. Finally, in v 36 Matthew's characteristic ἀμήν, "truly," replaces ναί, "yes" (Luke 11:51), and ἥξει ταῦτα πάντα, "all these things will come," probably preserves Q, where Luke has ἐκζητηθήσεται, "will be required (of)." The agreement between Matthew and Luke is significant, yet Matthew has probably taken more freedom in adapting the Q material, while Luke follows Q rather more closely.

C. The pericope is a prophecy of things to come. Its form, especially that of the final sentence (v 36), is appropriate to prophecy. The following is an outline: (1) the sending of messengers (v 34a); (2) the maltreatment of the messengers (v 34b); (3) the guilt of the Pharisees (v 35); and (4) the imminence of persecution and judgment (v 36). The structure of the pericope reveals some symmetrical parallelism. V 34a has the threefold direct object of the verb "send." The remainder of the verse has four parallel future verbs; the first and third of these are prefaced with the words ἐξ αὐτῶν, "(some) of these." Also note a further parallelism in the ἀπό, "from," and ἕως, "until," phrases of v 35, as well as the appositional genitives modifying the names Abel and Zechariah. The final prophecy (v 36) is given emphasis by the formulaic ἀμὴν λέγω ὑμῖν, "Truly I tell you."

## Comment

**34** Διὰ τοῦτο, "on account of this," relates not just to the preceding verse but to the whole of the preceding woe saying and, indeed, to the entire pericope. It is probably to be understood in the sense of "accordingly" or "in keeping with this" rather than meaning strictly "for that reason" (*pace* Blomberg). The ἰδού, "look," as usual in Matthew introduces something particularly noteworthy. Matthew's ἐγώ, "I," is emphatic: it is Jesus who now sends his messengers as God had previously sent his. As in 11:19 Matthew thus identifies Jesus as the Wisdom of God (cf. Luke 11:49). The present tense is futuristic enough to include at least that generation (cf. v 36). Given the future tenses that follow, προφήτας καὶ σοφοὺς καὶ γραμματεῖς must refer to Christian "prophets and wise men and scribes" (the model of the sending of God's messengers and their rejection is, to be sure, the same as in the OT; cf. Jer 7:25–26; 25:4 among many passages). In view are those "sent" by Jesus to carry on his work, that is, his "apostles" and their associates, the leadership of the new community (although some bear the title "prophet" in that community [see 10:41; cf. 7:22], it is unclear whether the word here is meant in the technical sense [as in 1 Cor 12:28–29; Eph 4:11; 3:5; *Did.* 11.3] or in a more general sense as those who speak for God; cf. Seitz). (For the background of the persecution of the prophets and the fate of Israel under God's judgment, according to the deuteronomistic perspective of history, see Steck.) The prophets intended here, therefore, are those responsible for the community's instruction in the way of righteousness (this is probably also the sense of "wise men" and "scribes" [cf. 13:52]). This is fully congruent with the emphasis upon teaching in Matthew. Some of these leaders will be killed (for ἀποκτείνειν, "kill," in reference to the followers of Jesus, cf. 10:28; 24:9) or crucified (cf. the need for the disciple to take up his or her cross [σταυρός] in 10:38; 16:24, although literal crucifixion is the subject here). Since crucifixion was a Roman and not Jewish form of execution, the passage probably refers to Jewish instigation of Roman authorities against Christians, examples of which we have in Acts. It is unlikely (*pace* Garland, *The Intention of Matthew 23*, 177) that the crucifixion of Jesus is intended since it is those *sent* by Jesus who are crucified. The prophecy that the followers of Jesus would be scourged (μαστιγοῦν) in "their" synagogues has already been made in 10:17; again the evangelist distances himself and his community from the Jews by the pronoun "your" synagogues. The reference to being persecuted ἀπὸ πόλεως εἰς πόλιν, "from city to city," echoes the language of 10:23. Here, as in chap. 10, the mention of being scourged, crucified, and killed puts the disciples directly in the footsteps of Jesus (cf. the same verbs applied to Jesus in 16:21; 17:23 [cf. 21:39]; 20:19; 26:2). The three-stage pattern is complete: as the prophets were killed (vv 29–31), so too will Jesus (cf. 1 Thess 2:15) and those sent by him be killed.

**35** The Jewish leadership's treatment of these Christian messengers will confirm the extent to which, despite their disclaimer (v 30), they are one with their fathers in killing those sent by God. This is the sense of the purposive ὅπως, "so that." The Jewish religious leadership, represented by the scribes and Pharisees, will not only be guilty of the blood of Jesus and those whom he sends but will also be considered in principle guilty of the blood of the OT prophets murdered by their fathers. Because of their solidarity with their fathers' evil deeds, they become guilty of πᾶν αἷμα δίκαιον, "all innocent blood," from that of the first person murdered in the OT to the last. For the expression of blood coming "upon" someone, cf. 27:25; Acts 5:28; 18:6 (for its OT background, see 2 Sam 1:16; Jer 51:35). αἷμα δίκαιον is lit. "righteous blood" in the sense of "innocent blood" (cf. Joel 4:19; Jonah 1:14; Prov 6:17). The first murder recorded in the OT refers to the crying out of Abel's blood from the ground (i.e., innocent blood crying out for vengeance [Gen 4:8, 10]). For the description of Abel as δίκαιος, "righteous," cf. Heb 11:4; 1 John 3:12. The question of the identity of the Zechariah mentioned here is a difficult one (it was already discussed by the time of Origen, *Matt.* 23:35).

Although Matthew designates Zechariah as υἱοῦ Βαραχίου, "the son of Barachiah" (in an apparent addition to his source [Q], unless it was in Q and deleted by Luke [Luke 11:51]), there is no evidence that the Zechariah so designated, i.e., apparently one of the twelve minor prophets (Zech 1:1), died an unnatural death. Two questions arise: Who was the murdered Zechariah that was in Jesus' or Matthew's mind? How did this Zechariah come to be identified as "the son of Barachiah"? Among the more than thirty Zechariahs known to us from the OT, only three emerge as possible candidates: a son of the high priest Jehoiada, who was murdered in the court of the temple (2 Chr 24:20–22); the son of Jeberechiah (which becomes Barachiah in the LXX), one of Isaiah's two witnesses in Isa 8:1–2; and the son of Berechiah (Barachiah in the LXX) son of Iddo (Zech 1:1, 7). A fourth Zechariah, known to us only from Josephus (*J.W.* 4.5.4 §§334–43), the son of Bareis (or, according to other MSS of Josephus, Bariscaeus or Baruch), was a wealthy man murdered by the Zealots "in the midst of the temple" in about A.D. 69, just before the destruction of Jerusalem. We may omit the second and third of these because of the lack of any tradition of a violent death for either of them. The lack of this absolutely crucial element is far more important than the mere presence of the proper patronymic. Opting for the fourth would mean that the saying could not derive from Jesus but was the creation of the evangelist, assuming a post-70 date for the Gospel. This is by no means an impossibility. The passage then would involve a reference to the very first murder and to the most recent murder known to the evangelist (see esp. Kennard; Gnilka; Harrington). But this conclusion involves no less than three suppositions: that the evangelist knew of the story recounted in Josephus, that the Gospel was written after A.D. 70, and that the saying does not derive from Jesus. Far more likely is the conclusion held by the majority of commentators (see too esp. Chapman) that the Zechariah in view is that of 2 Chr 24. Although his murder took place in the ninth century, in the reign of Joash, it is the last recorded murder of a messenger of God in the historical books of the Hebrew Bible (although Uriah was murdered several centuries later [Jer 26:23]). Since 2 Chronicles is the last book of the Hebrew Bible (the last of the division known as the *kĕṯûḇîm*, the Writings), the statement "from the blood of Abel to the blood of Zechariah" means in effect from the beginning to the end of the Bible, thus including the first to the last of the righteous martyrs of the OT, as well as all between. To be sure, a question has been raised about whether the order of the canonical books was fixed as early as the time of the evangelist so that 2 Chronicles could have been thought of as the last book of the Bible (see Kennard; Ross). This point has been vigorously defended, however, by R. Beckwith (*The Old Testament Canon of the New Testament and Its Background in Early Judaism* [Grand Rapids: Eerdmans, 1985] 211–22; cf. Str-B 4.1:422–23). A further significant similarity exists between Abel and Zechariah the son of Jehoiada in that just as Abel's blood cries out from the ground (for vengeance) in Gen 4:10 so too the dying Zechariah cries out "May the Lord see and avenge" (2 Chr 24:22); in both instances "righteous blood" is shed (cf. v 35 of our passage). Furthermore, this Zechariah was a priest who was murdered "in the court of the house of the Lord" (2 Chr 24:21), and this corresponds with Matthew's "between the temple [ναοῦ] and the altar [θυσιαστηρίου]." We are still left with the question of Matthew's identification of Zechariah as the son of Barachiah. To suppose that this verse refers to yet another Zechariah, who was the son of Barachiah, who was also murdered in the temple, one altogether unknown to us but known to the evangelist (thus esp. Ross), is needlessly to grasp at a straw. Already in ancient tradition there was a tendency to conflate the Zechariah of 2 Chronicles and the canonical prophet, as we can see from the Tg. to Lam 2:20 (see McNamara, 160–63; Nestle; and Blank, who traces the death of Zechariah in the rabbinic literature). The best conclusion concerning our passage, then, is that probably sometime early in the transmission of this material, or perhaps by the evangelist himself, Zechariah was identified as the prophet (cf. the reference to prophets in the preceding verse), i.e., the son of Barachiah.

Since the blood poured out concerns the biblical history, possibly τῆς γῆς means "the land," but more likely that history of martyrdom is understood as prototypical of the shedding of innocent blood in all the earth (cf. Gen 4:10). The Pharisees' imminent persecution of the messengers sent by Jesus demonstrates that they are no different from their fathers. Thus they, as murderers of the righteous, may be said to stand with their fathers in what the latter did: referring to Zechariah, Jesus says ὃν ἐφονεύσατε, "whom you murdered." They with their fathers are guilty of "all innocent blood" of God's messengers.

**36** The ἀμὴν λέγω ὑμῖν, "truly I tell you," formula (see *Comment* on 5:18) lends gravity to the concluding sentence. ταῦτα πάντα, "all these things," refers to the persecutions prophesied in v 34 and τὴν γενεὰν ταύτην, "this generation," to the lifetime of those listening to Jesus' words (see *Comment* on 11:16). The statement is in this sense very similar to those of 12:45 and 24:34 (cf. 10:23). Now Jesus refers not to the religious leadership of Israel, as in the preceding, but to the populace as a whole. The passage serves as a triple warning: first, to the scribes and Pharisees, whose hostile actions against those sent by Jesus will inescapably bring them into judgment (cf. v 33); second, to the masses who have not accepted Jesus; but also, third, to the followers of Jesus, who must prepare themselves for the reality of imminent suffering in the name of their Lord.

### Explanation

The work of Jesus was to be carried on by his followers. But as he has informed them on more than one occasion (cf. 10:16–23, 28; 16:24–25; 21:22–23), they must expect to be treated no differently than he was to be. Their lot was not immediate triumph and the unalloyed blessing and glory of the kingdom here and now but the experience of hatred, persecution, and death for the sake of Jesus and the gospel. The members of Matthew's church must have known the reality of this suffering and have drawn comfort from knowing that Jesus had foretold it. The words of Jesus spoke not merely to the situation and needs of the first Christian generation but to them and to those who would follow them. The Jewish religious leadership, on the other hand, paid no heed to Jesus' words. Solidly aligned with those of previous generations, they filled to the full the measure of their fathers (v 32) and so inescapably brought themselves into the judgment that was to be theirs. Already in that generation they were to experience a foreshadowing of eschatological judgment in the destruction of Jerusalem and their temple (see 2 Chr 36:15–16 for the same rationale as in our passage). This pericope thus leads naturally to the eschatological discourse of chaps. 24–25. But before that, one final allusion will be made to the grace that was being offered them.

## *The Lament over Jerusalem    (23:37–39)*

### Bibliography

**Allison, D. C., Jr.** "Matt. 23:39 – Luke 13:35b as a Conditional Prophecy." *JSNT* 18 (1983) 75–84. **Christ, F.** "Das Jerusalemwort." In *Jesus Sophia*. ATANT 57. Zürich: Zwingli, 1970. 136–52.

**Kwaak, H. van der.** "Die Klage über Jerusalem (Matth. xxiii 37–39)." *NovT* 8 (1966) 156–70.
**Plath, M.** "Der neutestamentlichen Wehruf über Jerusalem." *TSK* 78 (1905) 455–60.

## Translation

[37] *"Jerusalem, Jerusalem, who kills the prophets and stones those who have been sent to her,*[a] *how often I have wanted to gather your children, in the same way as a bird gathers her*[b] *young under her wings, and you would not have it.*[c] [38] *Look, your house is left to you desolate.*[d] [39] *For I tell you, you will in no wise see me again from now until the time when you say:*
*Blessed is the One who comes in the name of the Lord.*[e] *"*

## Notes

[a] D lat sy$^s$ have σε, "you," probably through the influence of the direct second-person address in the material that follows.

[b] αὐτῆς, "her." Many MSS (א$^2$ C L Θ $f^{1,13}$ TR) have ἑαυτῆς, "her own," perhaps through the influence of the parallel in Luke 13:34; B* lacks a modifier here.

[c] καὶ οὐκ ἠθελήσατε, lit. "and you did not want (it)."

[d] A few MSS (B L sy$^s$ sa bo$^{pt}$) omit ἔρημος, "desolate," perhaps through the influence of the parallel in Luke 13:35 or because the word was thought redundant following ἀφίεται, "abandoned." It is possible, but less likely, that ἔρημος was added to produce agreement with Jer 22:5; the external evidence overwhelmingly supports the presence of the word. *TCGNT*, 61.

[e] D has θεοῦ, "God."

## Form/Structure/Setting

A. After the preceding intense and bitter criticism, this pericope begins with a burst of warm sunshine. If it does not cancel out the character of the earlier contents of chap. 23, it at least indicates that the religious leaders of Jerusalem, Jesus' opponents from almost the beginning, were not outside the scope of God's love and grace. In a most tender metaphor, Jesus indicates his repeated desire to receive them into his fold. They had not been prejudged; they had not been ruled out of God's saving purposes. But they had ruled themselves out by their rejection of Jesus and his message. The result was to be catastrophic. And thus Matthew immediately adjoins to this pericope the last of the five discourses (chaps. 24–25), that concerning eschatological judgment. Yet Matthew's last word in this chapter (v 39) is to be understood ultimately as a positive note of grace and thus hope.

B. This pericope is apparently drawn from Q, being found in nearly verbatim agreement in Luke 13:34–35. The differences with the Lukan parallel are only slight. The most significant difference is Matthew's ἔρημος, "desolate" (v 38), which is lacking in Luke 13:35 (where it may have been omitted as superfluous). Matthew's plural τὰ νοσσία αὐτῆς, "her young," is probably an alteration of Q (with the plural address of the earlier material of chap. 23 in mind), which may more accurately be reflected in Luke's τὴν ἑαυτῆς νοσσιάν, "her own brood." The remaining differences, apart from some variations in word order, are Matthew's second aorist infinitive ἐπισυναγαγεῖν (v 37) for Luke's first aorist ἐπισυνάξαι, "to gather together"; Matthew's insertion of ἐπισυνάγει, "gathers" (v 37, probably added for emphasis); and in v 39 Matthew's γάρ, "for," for Luke's δέ, "but," his insertion of ἀπ' ἄρτι, "from now," and his omission of the rough but textually suspect ἥξει ὅτε, "it will come when," of Luke 13:35. Again, for the most part, Luke rather than Matthew appears to follow Q more closely.

C. The lament is signaled by the opening repetition, "Jerusalem, Jerusalem." It is followed by two concluding remarks. The following outline may be suggested: (1) lament (v 37); (2) judgment (v 38); and (3) promise (v 39). The pericope reveals little structural distinctiveness. The only parallelism, apart from the analogy employing the two occurrences of ἐπισυνάγειν, "gather together," in v 37, is in the feminine participles ἀποκτείνουσα, "killing," and λιθοβολοῦσα, "stoning," also in v 37, each with a direct object, τοὺς προφήτας, "the prophets," and τοὺς ἀπεσταλμένους πρὸς αὐτήν, "those sent to her." The LXX quotation that closes the pericope and chapter, drawn from Ps 118:21, contains an element of hope.

## Comment

**37**   In the opening of the lament, the poignant repetition "Jerusalem, Jerusalem" is directed primarily to the inhabitants of Jerusalem (cf. Luke 19:41–44), represented especially by the religious leadership criticized earlier in the chapter. By extension the lament may point also to Jerusalem as representative of the Jewish nation. Only here does Matthew use the Hebraic form Ἰερουσαλήμ (cf. Heb. יְרוּשָׁלֵם, yĕrûšālēm); elsewhere in the Gospel he prefers the Hellenized form Ἰεροσόλυμα (e.g., 2:1; 3:5; 4:25; 5:35; 21:1). The personified Jerusalem is the subject of the two participial clauses that follow. The first, ἀποκτείνουσα τοὺς προφήτας, "killing the prophets," picks up the language of v 31 (cf. v 34; 5:12; Acts 7:52). The second, λιθοβολοῦσα τοὺς ἀπεσταλμένους πρὸς αὐτήν, "stoning those sent to her," is a motif found elsewhere in Matthew only in the parable of the wicked tenants (21:35). The reference to stoning has an appropriateness here, given that this was the method used in the killing of Zechariah, who is referred to in v 35 (it was also the way in which the first Christian martyr was killed, as the evangelist doubtless knew [Acts 7:59]). Jerusalem had become heir to a tragic tradition wherein God's messengers were persecuted and killed (cf. the ironical remark in Luke 13:33). This was true of the past, and it was to be true of the future. Yet Jesus had often longed to gather its people tenderly, indeed, as τέκνα, "children." The image of a mothering bird who gathers her young under her wings suggests such things as security, nurture, and well-being (cf. Ruth 2:12; Pss 17:8; 36:7; Isa 31:5 among many OT examples). It points to the experience of fulfillment and salvation. In the message of the dawning of the kingdom, this salvation had been offered repeatedly to the Jews. ποσάκις, "how often," may hint at an earlier Judean ministry not recorded in the Synoptics (cf. the early chapters of John), although a larger perspective may be intended. Despite the invitation to receive what Jesus was bringing, the Jews refused it: καὶ οὐκ ἠθελήσατε, "and you would not have it" (cf. 22:3; Luke 19:14; John 1:11; 5:40).

**38**   ἰδού, "look," here introduces an emphatic statement of judgment. ὁ οἶκος ὑμῶν, "your house," refers in the first instance to the temple (for "house" meaning the temple, cf. 1 Kgs 9:7–8; Isa 64:10–11; John 12:7) as the center of the people's religious faith but may also allude to the city (cf. Tob 14:4) and the nation, i.e., the people themselves. The statement is based on OT models (see esp. Jer 22:5 [cf. Jer 12:7], with its references to the house becoming a "desolation"; LXX uses the cognate noun ἐρήμωσιν). The passive verb ἀφίεται, "left (to you)," both connotes abandonment by God and alludes to the future destruction of the temple. Very similar language occurs in Ezekiel anticipating the destruction of the first temple (e.g., Ezek 8:6, 12; 9:3, 9; 11:23; cf. Bar 4:12). The destruction of Jerusalem and the temple becomes a major subject in the discourse that follows (cf. 24:2, 15; Acts 6:14).

**39** This is Jesus' last public appearance in the narrative. The discourse of chaps. 24–25 is given "privately" to the disciples, and chap. 26 leads quickly to the arrest of Jesus. A major point in the narrative has been reached. He thus solemnly and emphatically ("I tell you") informs his opponents that they will not see him again (cf. John 14:19) until his eschatological revelation as the glorious Son of Man (cf. 24:30). At that time there will be no alternative for them but to acknowledge him for who he is and to count him as the blessed one who comes in the name of the Lord (for ὁ ἐρχόμενος, "the coming one," cf. 3:11; 11:3; John 11:27; Heb 10:37). It is possible, if only remotely, that the statement describes a welcoming reception of Jesus in faith (for understanding the passage as a conditional promise of salvation, see Allison). Ps 118:26 is quoted here in verbatim agreement with the LXX. The same words were again cited exactly in 21:9 when Jesus was welcomed into Jerusalem as the messianic Son of David—this a foreshadowing of the eschatological appearance anticipated here. When Jesus returns in the parousia of the last days, even those who had rejected him will of necessity affirm him as "the coming one" (cf. Rev 1:4), the crucified, risen Messiah (cf. Phil 2:10–11), whether in gladness or remorse (cf. *1 Enoch* 62:5–6, 9–10).

### Explanation

The scribes and Pharisees had become the enemies of Jesus set upon destroying him; nevertheless, they too were invited to the new reality of the dawning kingdom. Despite Jesus' stern criticism of them, he has longed for them to receive him and his message so that he could bring them into the fold of those who enjoy his benefits. If they had only allowed him, he would have gathered them with the tenderness of a bird gathering her young—thus his lament over Jerusalem, its inhabitants, and especially its religious leadership. But as it is, only tragedy awaits the capital city. Judgment is soon to come upon the temple, and the Jews would not again see their Messiah until the coming of the eschaton. Again all turns upon the reaction to Jesus. Acceptance means salvation; rejection of him means inevitable judgment (cf. 10:32–33, 40; 12:41). It is possible to link the future acceptance of Christ implied in the words of Ps 118:26 to the eschatological salvation of Israel referred to by Paul in Rom 11:26, 31, but this probably goes well beyond what Matthew and his readers understood by this concluding statement.

# The Fifth Discourse:
# The Destruction of the Temple and
# the End of the World    (24:1–25:46)

*Bibliography*

**Agbanou, V. K.** *Le discours eschatologique de Matthieu 24–25: Tradition et rédaction.* EBib n.s. 2. Paris: Gabalda, 1983. **Barclay, W.** "Great Themes of the New Testament: VI. Matthew xxiv." *ExpTim* 70 (1958–59) 326–30; 71 (1959–60) 376–79. **Bauckham, R. J.** "The Delay of the Parousia." *TynB* 31 (1980) 3–33. **Beare, F. W.** "The Synoptic Apocalypse: Matthean Version." In *Understanding the Sacred Text.* FS M. S. Enslin, ed. J. Reumann. Valley Forge, PA: Judson, 1972. 115–33. **Beasley-Murray, G. R.** "The Eschatological Discourse of Jesus." *RevExp* 57 (1960) 153–66. ———. *Jesus and the Last Days: The Interpretation of the Olivet Discourse.* Peabody, MA: Hendrickson, 1993. **Beibitz, J. H.** "The End of the Age: Some Critical Notes on St. Matthew, Chap. xxiv." *ExpTim* 13 (1901–2) 443–50. **Blenkinsopp, J.** "The Hidden Messiah and His Entry into Jerusalem." *Scr* 13 (1961) 51–56, 81–87. **Brandon, S. G. F.** *The Fall of Jerusalem and the Christian Church.* London: SPCK, 1951. **Broer, I.** "Redaktionsgeschichtliche Aspekte von Mt. 24:1–28." *NovT* 35 (1993) 209–33. **Brown, S.** "The Matthean Apocalypse." *JSNT* 4 (1979) 2–27. **Burnett, F. W.** "Prolegomenon to Reading Matthew's Eschatological Discourse: Redundancy and the Education of the Reader in Matthew." *Semeia* 31 (1985) 91–109. ———. *The Testament of Jesus-Sophia: A Redaction-Critical Study of the Eschatological Discourse in Matthew.* Lanham, MD: University Press of America, 1981. **Cotter, A. E.** "The Eschatological Discourse." *CBQ* 1 (1939) 125–32, 204–13. **Dupont, J.** *Les trois apocalypses synoptiques: Marc 13; Matthieu 24–25; Luc 21.* LD 121. Paris: Cerf, 1985. **Feuillet, A.** "Le sens du mot Parousie dans l'Évangile de Matthieu: Comparaison entre Matth. xxiv et Jac. v. 1–11." In *The Background of the New Testament and Its Eschatology.* FS C. H. Dodd, ed. W. D. Davies and D. Daube. Cambridge: Cambridge UP, 1956. 261–80. ———. "La synthèse eschatologique de saint Matthieu (24–25)." *RB* 56 (1949) 340–64; 57 (1950) 62–91, 180–211. **Fuller, G. C.** "The Olivet Discourse: An Apocalyptic Timetable." *WTJ* 28 (1966) 157–63. **Gaston, L.** *No Stone on Another: Studies in the Significance of the Fall of Jerusalem in the Synoptic Gospels.* NovTSup 23. Leiden: Brill, 1970. **Grässer, E.** *Das Problem der Parusieverzögerung in den synoptischen Evangelien.* BZNW 22. 2nd ed. Berlin: Töpelmann, 1960. **Hagner, D. A.** "Apocalyptic Motifs in the Gospel of Matthew: Continuity and Discontinuity." *HBT* 7 (1985) 53–82. ———. "Imminence and Parousia in the Gospel of Matthew." In *Texts and Contexts.* FS L. Hartman, ed. T. Fornberg and D. Hellholm. Oslo/Boston: Scandinavian UP, 1995. 77–92. ———. "Matthew's Eschatology." In *To Tell the Mystery.* FS R. H. Gundry, ed. M. Silva and T. E. Schmidt. Sheffield: JSOT, 1994. 49–71. **Hahn, F.** "Die eschatologische Rede Matthäus 24 und 25." In *Studien zum Matthäusevangelium.* FS W. Pesch, ed. L. Schenke. Stuttgart: Katholisches Bibelwerk, 1988. 107–26. **Harnisch, W.** *Verhängnis und Verheissung der Geschichte.* FRLANT 97. Göttingen: Vandenhoeck & Ruprecht, 1969. **Harrington, D. J.** "Polemical Parables in Matthew 24–25." *USQR* 44 (1991) 287–98. **Hartman, L.** *Prophecy Interpreted: The Formation of Some Jewish Apocalyptic Texts and of the Eschatological Discourse Mark 13 Par.* ConBNT 1. Lund: Gleerup, 1966. **Kik, J. M.** *Matthew Twenty-Four.* 1948. Reprint, Philadelphia: Presbyterian and Reformed, 1961. **Knockaert, A.** "A Fresh Look at the Eschatological Discourse (Mt 24–25)." *LVit* 40 (1985) 167–79. **Knox, D. B.** "The Five Comings of Jesus, Matthew 24 and 25." *RTR* 34 (1975) 44–54. **Kümmel, W.**

**G.** *Promise and Fulfilment: The Eschatological Message of Jesus.* SBT 23. Naperville, IL: Allenson, 1957. **Lagrange, M.-J.** "L'Avènement du Fils de l'Homme." *RB* n.s. 3 (1906) 382–411, 561–74. **Lambrecht, J.** "The Parousia Discourse: Composition and Content in Mt. XXIV–XXV." In *L'Évangile selon Matthieu: Redaction et théologie,* ed. M. Didier. BETL 29. Paris: Gembloux, 1972. 309–42. **Loisy, A.** "L'apocalypse synoptique." *RB* 5 (1896) 173–98; 335–59. **Marguerat, D.** *Le jugement dans l'évangile de Matthieu.* Geneva: Labor et Fides, 1981. 479–561. **Martin, F.** "Le signe du fils de l'homme: Analyse de chapitres 24 et 25 de l'évangile de Matthieu." *LumVie* 160 (1982) 61–77. **Monsarrat, V.** "Matthieu 24–25." *FV* 5 (1977) 67–80. **Moore, A. L.** *The Parousia in the New Testament.* NovTSup 13. Leiden: Brill, 1966. **O'Flynn, J. S.** "The Eschatological Discourse." *ITQ* 18 (1951) 277–81. **Perrot, C.** "Essai sur le discours eschatologique (Mc XIII, 1–37; Mt XXIV, 1–36; Lc XXI, 5–36)." *RSR* 47 (1959) 481–514. **Pesch, R.** "Eschatologie und Ethik: Auslegung von Mt 24,1–36." *BibLeb* 11 (1970) 223–38. **Puig i Tàrrech, A.** "Temps i història en Mt 24–25." *Revista Catalana de Teologia* 6 (1981) 299–335. **Reicke, B.** "Synoptic Prophecies on the Destruction of Jerusalem." In *Studies in New Testament and Early Christian Literature,* ed. D. E. Aune. NovTSup 33. Leiden: Brill, 1972. 121–34. **Rigaux, B.** "La seconde venue du Messie." In *La venue du Messie: Messianisme et eschatologie.* RechBib 6. Bruges: Desclée de Brouwer, 1962. 177–216. **Roark, D. M.** "The Great Eschatological Discourse." *NovT* 7 (1964–65) 123–27. **Shaw, R. H.** "A Conjecture on the Signs of the End." *ATR* 47 (1965) 96–102. **Sibinga, J. S.** "The Structure of Apocalyptic Discourse: Matthew 24 and 25." *ST* 29 (1975) 71–79. **Spitta, F.** "Die grosse eschatologische Rede Jesu." *TSK* 82 (1909) 348–401. **Summers, R.** "Matthew 24–25: An Exposition." *RevExp* 59 (1962) 501–11. **Thompson, W. G.** "An Historical Perspective in the Gospel of Matthew." *JBL* 93 (1974) 243–62. **Turner, D. L.** "The Structure and Sequence of Matthew 24:1–41: Interaction with Evangelical Treatments." *GTJ* 10 (1989) 3–27. **Völter, D.** "Die eschatologische Rede Jesu und seine Weissagung von der Zerstörung Jerusalems." *STZ* 31 (1915) 180–202. **Vorster, W. S.** "A Reader-Response Approach to Matthew 24:3–28." *HTS* 47 (1991) 1099–1108. **Walter, N.** "Tempelzerstörung und synoptische Apokalypse." *ZNW* 57 (1966) 38–49. **Walvoord, J. F.** "Christ's Olivet Discourse on the Time of the End: Prophecies Fulfilled in the Present Age." *BSac* 128 (1971) 206–14. **Wenham, D.** *The Rediscovery of Jesus' Eschatological Discourse.* Gospel Perspectives 4. Sheffield: JSOT, 1984. **Wurzinger, A.** "Die eschatologischen Reden Jesu." In *Bibel und Zeitgemässer Glaube.* Klosterneuburger: Buch- und Kunstverlag, 1967. 37–67.

*Introduction*

The fifth and final discourse in the Gospel (chaps. 24–25), marked out by the customary concluding formula of 26:1, is devoted to the prophecy of future calamities, including especially the destruction of the temple and the holy city of Jerusalem, and to the prophecy of the coming of the Son of Man and the end of the present age. Because of the dramatic climax in the prophecy of the parousia and the central importance of the theme of the final judgment, the discourse is often called the "apocalyptic" discourse. These chapters are also known as "the Olivet discourse," indicating the location where the teaching was given as well as alluding to the apocalyptic associations of the Mount of Olives (Zech 14:4).

This description of the discourse as apocalyptic is of course appropriate. Much of the Gospel, indeed, has an apocalyptic tone, implicitly if not explicitly (see Hagner, *HBT* 7 [1985] 53–82). It should be remembered, however, that much of the discourse refers to phenomena of the interim period preceding the parousia—if only to indicate that the sufferings of the present are not themselves the end nor even necessarily the harbingers of the end. For all the similarities this discourse has to apocalyptic writings, there are at the same time some striking differences. Most important, the discourse does not attempt to provide a timetable for the end time. Information concerning the time of the parousia is conspicuously absent, denied even to Matthew's central figure, the Son of Man himself (24:36). Indeed, the thrust of the material is in quite another direction. The discourse does not intend to inflame the expectation of an imminent end, or even a predictable end. If anything, it cools such ideas. Tribulations that might have been thought to indicate an imminent end are described as "but the beginning of the birth pangs" (24:8). All that is assured in the discourse is the *fact* of the end. The time is deliberately left indeterminate, thus focusing on the need to be ready at any time. Consequently, the discourse retains its relevance in every Christian generation. It is addressed as much to the church as to the disciples. The one exception to this general indeterminacy is the significant time marker "immediately" ($\varepsilon\dot{v}\theta\dot{\varepsilon}\omega\varsigma$) of v 29, a redactional insertion of the evangelist, which along with the redaction of the disciples' question in v 3 clearly indicates that the evangelist shared the undoubtedly common view that the destruction of Jerusalem and the temple would mean the end of the age and the coming of the Son of Man.

As with the other discourses, the evangelist has constructed this discourse using traditions available to him. Clearly Mark 13 is the major source for chap. 24. There are, however, also sections apparently drawn from Q (e.g., the two parables with which chap. 24 ends [vv 37–44, 45–51] and the parable in 25:14–30). The discourse undoubtedly makes use of other material from oral tradition available to the evangelist (e.g., 25:31–46). As a construction of the evangelist using a variety of sources—sayings of Jesus spoken at different times in reference to different matters—it is easily conceivable that the discourse fails to separate this material clearly, thereby causing the problems of interpretation for which it is notorious. In particular, it is at least possible that material that originally referred to the fall of Jerusalem was applied to the end of the age and vice versa. As we have already noted, the evangelist could not separate the two. There is the further complicating factor that the horror of the fall of Jerusalem and the extraordinary suffering of that time apparently served as a type of the final judgment.

It is difficult to discern the structure of the discourse. Clearly we have basically two main types of material: exposition in 24:4–36 and parables of exhortation in the remainder of the discourse (24:37–25:46). The challenge is to identify the organization and chronological sequence, if any, of the material in 24:4–36. This is not possible apart from the interpretation of this section. In anticipation of the commentary that follows, however, we may suggest the following general divisions of the discourse: (1) 24:4–14: a time of suffering and of the proclamation of the gospel, referring in the first instance to the period before the destruction of Jerusalem but applicable also to the entire time period preceding the parousia; (2) 24:15–28: the fall of Jerusalem, not itself the end of the age, and the unmistakable character of the parousia, applicable also to the entire period preceding the parousia; (3) 24:29–36: the parousia of the Son of Man, inseparable from the fall of Jerusalem.

Beginning already in v 36, the predominant note of the parables that follow (through 25:13) is the unknowable time of the parousia. In the last two parables this motif recedes into the background, although not entirely, in favor of a more general hortatory emphasis on the importance of faithful discipleship.

This understanding of the discourse is based on the conviction that, in keeping with the question of v 3, the exposition section speaks both of the fall of Jerusalem and of the parousia of the Son of Man. Exactly here lies the main difficulty of interpreting this section of the discourse (24:4–36). Several possibilities lie open to the interpreter. A strictly futurist interpretation denies any reference here to events of the first century, including the fall of Jerusalem (e.g., Schlatter, Schniewind, Zahn, Gnilka, Agbanou, Dupont, Harrington). Dispensationalism also takes this view, asserting that everything in the passage lies yet in the future even for us (cf. Walvoord; for a refutation, see Carson, 494–95). Diametrically opposed is the preterist view, which regards the material up to v 35 as referring exclusively to the fall of Jerusalem (thus, e.g., Kik, Tasker, France, S. Brown, Garland). There are mediating views that find reference here both to the fall of Jerusalem and to the parousia of the Son of Man. As described in Turner's useful discussion, the "traditional preterist-futurist" view regards vv 4–14 as referring to the present age, vv 15–28 to the fall of Jerusalem, involving a double reference also to the end of the age, vv 29–31 to the parousia, and vv 32–41 to the certainty of the fulfillment of prophecy. With a variety of mutations (but with rejection by many of the idea of double reference), the preterist-futurist view is widely held (e.g., Barclay, Lambrecht, Gundry, Beasley-Murray, Carson, Blomberg; see esp. Appendix A to Wenham's discussion ["'This Generation Will Not Pass . . .'"; see *Bibliography* for 24:29–36]).

A familiar, basic tension in the discourse, apparent also from the outline just given, is the stress on the imminence of the parousia together with the stress on the unknowable time of the parousia. In particular, the arguments for the exclusively futurist and exclusively preterist explanations of the material center on the meaning of Matthew's redactional "immediately" ($\epsilon\upsilon\theta\epsilon\omega\varsigma$) in v 29, described by Grässer as "the puzzle of Matthew" (*Das Problem der Parusieverzögerung*, 218). For a hypothesis that explains this difficulty and our interpretation of the pertinent passages, see "Excursus: Imminence, Delay, and Matthew's $\epsilon\upsilon\theta\epsilon\omega\varsigma$" in the *Comment* on 24:29.

# The Prophecy of the Destruction of the Temple and the Disciples' Question (24:1–3)

## Bibliography

**Bockmuehl, M. N. A.** "Why Did Jesus Predict the Destruction of the Temple?" *Crux* 25 (1989) 11–18. **Dupont, J.** "Il n'en sera pas laissé pierre sur pierre." *Bib* 52 (1971) 301–20. **Fascher, E.** "Jerusalems Untergang in der urchristlichen und altkirchlichen Überlieferung." *TLZ* 89 (1964) 81–98. **Gaston L.** *No Stone on Another: Studies in the Significance of the Fall of Jerusalem in the Synoptic Gospels.* NovTSup 23. Leiden: Brill, 1970. **Meinertz, M.** "Die Tragweite der Weissagung Jesu von der Zerstörung des Tempels." *TGl* 35 (1943) 135–41. **Reicke, B.** "Synoptic Prophecies on the Destruction of Jerusalem." In *Studies in New Testament and Early Christian Literature,* ed. D. E. Aune. NovTSup 33. Leiden: Brill, 1972. 121–

34. **Schlosser, J.** "La parole de Jésus sur le fin du Temple." *NTS* 36 (1990) 398–414. **Vielhauer, P.** "Die Weissagungen von der Zerstörung und dem Wiederaufbau des Tempels." In *Oikodome: Aufsätze zum Neuen Testament,* ed. G. Klein. TBü 65. Munich: Kaiser, 1979. 2:59–66.

### Translation

[1] *And Jesus departed and was going away from* [a] *the temple, and his disciples came to him to show him the buildings of the temple.* [2] *But he answered and said to them: "You see all of these things, don't you?* [b] *Truly I tell you, not even a stone will be left here upon a stone; there is not one* [c] *that will not be broken down."*

[3] *While he was sitting on the Mount of Olives, the disciples came to him privately, saying: "Tell us, when will these things happen and what will be the sign of your coming and the* [d] *consummation of the age?"*

### Notes

[a] B has ἐκ, "out of," for ἀπό, "from," probably through the influence of the parallel in Mark 13:1.

[b] οὐ βλέπετε ταῦτα πάντα, begins with a negative that expects an affirmative answer.

[c] "There is not one" added for clarity.

[d] Many MSS (D W *f*[13] TR) insert the definite article τῆς, thereby suggesting a clear distinction between the coming of Jesus and the end of the age. (Even without the article, συντελείας, "consummation," must be translated as a definite noun in English.)

### Form/Structure/Setting

A. This brief pericope introduces the fifth and final discourse of Jesus, which is fittingly devoted to eschatology. The discourse is given in response to the disciples' direct question, which was in turn elicited by Jesus' remark that a time was coming when the temple would be destroyed. The disciples' association of the destruction of the temple with the end of the age becomes a key problem in the interpretation of the discourse that follows. The central importance of the theme of judgment in these chapters, especially as seen in the destruction of Jerusalem, receives emphasis by Matthew's omission of the Markan account of the widow's mite (Mark 12:41–44), thus connecting the discourse more closely with the woes of chap. 23.

B. Matthew's setting of the context of the discourse follows Mark closely (Mark 13:1–4; cf. Luke 21:5–7). He rewrites the opening sentence, avoiding the opening genitive absolute and the direct discourse of Mark 13:1 (which contains the address διδάσκαλε, "teacher"). In place of Mark's "one of the disciples," Matthew has "his disciples came [προσῆλθον]." To this Matthew adds the purposive infinitive clause ἐπιδεῖξαι αὐτῷ τὰς οἰκοδομὰς τοῦ ἱεροῦ, "to show him the buildings of the temple." In v 2 Matthew alters Mark's question by adding the negative οὐ and the adjective πάντα, "all," thereby bringing additional emphasis to the question: "You see all these things, don't you?" ταῦτα πάντα, "all these things," abbreviates Mark's ταύτας τὰς μεγάλας οἰκοδομάς, "these great buildings" (Mark 13:2). Matthew's insertion of ἀμὴν λέγω ὑμῖν, "truly I tell you," brings a note of authority as well as gravity to the following logion. The logion itself (v 2b) agrees verbatim with its form in Mark 13:2b except for Matthew's omission of the μή in the second double negative just before the final verb, which becomes the future passive καταλυθήσεται, "shall be destroyed," in place of Mark's subjunctive καταλυθῇ. Luke (21:6) agrees with Matthew in these two differences with Mark, perhaps as the result of the common influence of Q or oral tradition. In v 3 Matthew substitutes ἐπί for Mark's more unusual εἰς (both meaning "on") in the reference to Jesus sitting on the Mount of Olives. Matthew omits Mark's κατέναντι τοῦ ἱεροῦ, "opposite the temple," perhaps believing this information to be obvious or unnecessary. He furthermore substitutes his favorite προσῆλθον αὐτῷ οἱ μαθηταί, "his disciples came to him," in place of the names of the four disciples in Mark 13:3 (Luke also omits the four names [Luke 21:7]), again regarding this information as unnecessary. The first part of the question asked by the disciples agrees verbatim with Mark 13:4a, but for Mark's clause modifying σημεῖον, "sign," i.e., ὅταν μέλλῃ ταῦτα συντελεῖσθαι πάντα, "when all these things are about to be accomplished," Matthew writes τῆς σῆς παρουσίας καὶ συντελείας τοῦ αἰῶνος, "of your coming and consummation of the age." Matthew, probably with the content of the following discourse in mind, has thus brought more specificity to Mark's ταῦτα . . . πάντα, "all these things." (Luke's simple ὅταν μέλλῃ ταῦτα γίνεσθαι, "when these things are about to happen," clearly shifts the attention from eschatology to the destruction of Jerusalem.)

C. Serving as an introduction to the discourse itself, these verses present the fundamentally important question of the disciples about the future. Outline: (1) the observation of the temple buildings (v 1); (2) the judgment oracle (v 2); and (3) the disciples' question (v 3). Among structural features of this short segment of dialogue especially to be noted are the parallel genitive phrases that modify τὸ σημεῖον, "the sign," at the end of v 3, as well as the parallel questions concerning "when these things will be" and "what will be the sign" (v 3).

## Comment

**1–2** The departure of Jesus ἀπὸ τοῦ ἱεροῦ, "from the temple," is apparently not to be correlated with a previously specified visit; the last reference to Jesus entering the temple is in 21:23, and the intervening material presupposes the passage of considerable time. The disciples, apparently filled with wonder at the sight of τὰς οἰκοδομὰς τοῦ ἱεροῦ, "the buildings of the temple," wanted Jesus to share in their excitement, and they called his attention to the sight (ἐπιδεῖξαι αὐτῷ, "to show him"), probably looking back and down as they were part way up the Mount of Olives (cf. v 3) on the way back to Bethany (cf. 26:6). Herod's newly ornamented temple was famous for its gleaming beauty (see Jos., *J.W.* 6.4.8. §267: "the most marvelous edifice which we have ever seen or heard of, whether one considers its structure, its magnitude, the richness of its every detail"; cf. *Ant.* 15.11.3 §393; *b. B. Bat.* 4a). The disciples must have been astounded at the response of Jesus. A time was coming when these glorious structures would be leveled, when not a stone would be left upon a stone. This prophecy will later, in distorted form, be directed against Jesus by his opponents (cf. 26:61; 27:40). The disciples were not slow in recognizing the apocalyptic tone of the announcement, as their question in v 3 indicates. While they were familiar with Jeremiah's prophecies concerning the destruction of the first temple (cf. Jer 9:14; 9:11; Mic 3:12), which occurred in 586 B.C., the thought of the destruction of the second temple could, so they believed, only signal the time of final judgment, the end of the age. The statement that there will not be left λίθος ἐπὶ λίθον, "a stone upon a stone," a metaphor for total destruction (and one that reverses the building process [Hag 2:15]), is found again (besides in the synoptic parallels) in Luke 19:44, where it also refers to the destruction of Jerusalem (for the historical fulfillment, see Jos., *J.W.* 7.1.1 §§1–4). Jesus' statement receives added emphasis from the formulaic ἀμὴν λέγω ὑμῖν, "truly I tell you," which prefaces it.

**3** As Jesus sat down on the mountain to deliver the first Matthean discourse (cf. 5:1), so again he sits on a mountain, this time the Mount of Olives, while giving the fifth and last discourse. Thus Jesus delivers the eschatological discourse from the very place where the eschatological events were prophesied to begin (cf. Zech 14:4). The disciples, no doubt troubled by Jesus' prophecy, come to him privately for some privileged information (cf. the coming of the disciples κατ᾽ ἰδίαν, "privately," in 17:19). That the two parts of the question are asked in one breath indicates that the disciples could not dissociate the destruction of the temple from the end of the age. The misleading manner in which the questions are juxtaposed thus reflects the mindset of the disciples (including the evangelist, as may be determined by his redaction of Mark). The generalizing plural ταῦτα, "these things," apparently includes not only the leveling of the temple but events that had to accompany it, such as the fall of the city of Jerusalem. Remarkably, the first question, concerning "when" (πότε) these things were to occur, is not answered in the discourse. Although Jesus does not answer directly, however, v 34, insofar as it refers to the destruction of Jerusalem, would intimate that that event was to occur within that generation. The second question concerns τὸ σημεῖον, "the sign," that will point to the eschatological dénouement, indicating τῆς σῆς παρουσίας, "your coming," and συντελείας τοῦ αἰῶνος, "the consummation of the age." The conceptual unity of the parousia and the end of the age is indicated by the single Greek article governing both (Granville Sharp's Rule [see S. E. Porter, *Idioms of the Greek New Testament*, 2nd ed. (Sheffield: JSOT, 1994) 110–11]). The disciples thus were unable to separate the two events in their minds: the destruction of Jerusalem must entail the end of the age and the parousia of Jesus, inaugurating the eschaton. In the discourse Jesus will three times refer to ἡ παρουσία τοῦ υἱοῦ τοῦ ἀνθρώπου, "the coming of the Son of Man" (vv 27, 37, 39; the word "coming" does not occur in the other Gospels). "Parousia" now refers not to the visit or presence of an earthly king, as in the Hellenistic world, but is used technically to refer to the return of Jesus. The "consummation of the age" is not found in the remainder of the discourse (it is found, however, in 28:20, as well as in 13:39–40, 49; the only other occurrence in the NT is in Heb 9:26, where, however, the plural "ages" is used; cf. *T. Levi* 10; *2 Apoc. Bar.* 59:8; LXX Dan 11:35; 12:4, 13). Questions similar to those of the disciples are common in apocalyptic literature (cf. Dan 8:13; 12:6; 2 Esdr 4:33, 35; 6:7, 11–12; *2 Apoc. Bar.* 21:18–19). A similar concern is found in the rabbinic literature (*b. Sanh.* 98a; 99a; *Pesiq. R.* 1[46]).

### Explanation

As far as the apostles were concerned, the ominous words of Jesus concerning the destruction of the temple could point in only one direction: to the experiencing of the eschatological judgment. This was a subject to which Jesus had often alluded in his teaching ministry and therefore something they may well have expected him to indicate. They were accordingly eager to know how soon this might occur and what sign they might anticipate to indicate its approach. Their concern was not one of idle curiosity, for mere information's sake, but concern that they might be properly prepared for the time of judgment. From their perspective, the destruction of the temple must have meant the coming again of Jesus, not as he now was with them when his glory was veiled but as the clearly revealed Son of God for all to see. Jesus had now to instruct them more closely about these matters, about the future he had intimated in his dramatic oracle of judgment.

# *The Beginning of Birth Pangs    (24:4–8)*

## Bibliography

See *Bibliography* for *Introduction* to 24:1–25:46.

## Translation

> [4]*And Jesus answered and said to them: "Be careful lest anyone deceive you.* [5]*For many will come in my name, saying: 'I am the Messiah.' And they will deceive many.* [6]*And you will soon hear of wars and rumors of wars. See to it that you are not frightened. For these things* [a] *must happen, but the end is not yet.* [7]*For nation will rise up against nation and kingdom against kingdom, and there will be famines* [b] *and earthquakes in place after place.* [8]*But all these things are the beginning of birth pangs."*

## Notes

[a] "These things" added to translation for clarity ($\tau a \hat{v} \tau a$, "these things," is added to the text in lat sy*; cf. Luke 21:9). Many MSS (C W $f^{13}$ TR sy$^{p,h}$) add $\pi \acute{a} \nu \tau a$, "all (these things)," perhaps by the influence of v 8. The shortest reading, the simple $\delta \epsilon \hat{\iota} \gamma \grave{a} \rho \gamma \epsilon \nu \acute{\epsilon} \sigma \theta a \iota$, "for [they] must be" or "happen," is to be preferred. See *TCGNT*, 61.

[b] Many MSS (C $\Theta$ $f^{1,13}$ TR sy$^{p,h}$ mae) insert $\kappa a \grave{\iota} \lambda o \iota \mu o \acute{\iota}$, "and plagues," before $\kappa a \grave{\iota} \sigma \epsilon \iota \sigma \mu o \acute{\iota}$, "and earthquakes"; some other MSS (L W 33 lat) make $\lambda o \iota \mu o \acute{\iota}$, "plagues," the first of the three items. This insertion is a harmonization with the text of Luke 21:11 (followed most closely by the former group of MSS).

## Form/Structure/Setting

A. The eschatological discourse, given in response to the disciples' question, begins with the assertion that the world will yet experience much trouble before the coming of the final or eschatological judgment. The effect of this emphasis, although left implicit, is to make possible a separation of the destruction of the temple from the experiencing of the end of the age. In connection with the troubles to be experienced, messianic claimants will appear. But none of them is the Messiah; it is not yet the end of the age. This emphasis occurs repeatedly in this chapter as a kind of leitmotif (cf. vv 11, 23–36).

B. Matthew follows Mark closely, often verbatim, in this pericope. In v 4 he deletes Mark's ἤρξατο, "began" (Mark 13:5), and inserts the formulaic ἀποκριθείς, "answered" (which is commonly used with εἶπεν, "said," in Matthew). Matthew's inserted γάρ, "for," at the beginning of v 5 (cf. Luke 21:8) ties the sentences more closely together. Matthew's inserted ὁ Χριστός, "the Christ," completes the ἐγώ εἰμι, "I am," of Mark 13:6 (cf. Luke 21:8). In v 6 Matthew rewrites Mark by adding Mark's ὅταν δὲ ἀκούσητε, "whenever you hear," to μελλήσετε δὲ ἀκούειν, "you are about to hear," thus heightening the imminence of the expected troubles. In the same verse, Matthew inserts ὁρᾶτε, "see" (perhaps on the model of βλέπετε, "beware," in v 4), and γάρ, "for," after δεῖ, "it [they] must," and supplies the copula ἐστίν, "is," before τὸ τέλος, "the end." Matthew in v 7 smooths out Mark's syntax, and in v 8 adds πάντα, "all," to Mark's ταῦτα, "these (things)" (cf. the same phrase in v 2; 4:9; 6:23–24; 13:34, 51, 56; 19:20; and esp. 24:33–34).

C. Disastrous events were to occur in the future—events that would turn one's thoughts to eschatology. Yet the disciples were not to allow themselves to be deceived by these events. Outline: (1) warning not to be deceived (v 4); (2) the coming of false messiahs who will deceive many (v 5); (3) reports of war (v 6 a–b); (4) the delay of the end (v 6c); (5) future wars (v 7a); (6) future catastrophes (v 7b); and (7) the beginning of woes (v 8). The passage consists of a string of short sentences with not much syntactic parallelism. Some structural parallelism can be seen between βλέπετε and ὁρᾶτε, "see," in vv 4 and 6, both followed by μή with the prohibitive subjunctive. The two objects of ἀκούειν, "hear," in v 6 are parallel; v 7 furthermore has parallelism in the ἔθνος, "nation," and βασιλεία, "kingdom," clauses. λιμοί, "famines," and σεισμοί, "earthquakes," are put in parallel by Matthew. The ταῦτα πάντα, "all these things," of v 8 is recapitulative in force.

D. V 4b is quoted in *Did.* 6.1, but with the singular pronoun σε, "you," instead of the plural ὑμᾶς.

## Comment

**4–5** Jesus begins his answer to the disciples' questions by warning them not to be deceived by premature claims of the Messiah's presence, even when in conjunction with events that suggest the coming of the eschaton. The potential deception appears to be twofold: that the Messiah has come and that the eschatological judgment has begun. First, the attention is upon the πολλοί, "many," who will claim—presumably not at once, but over a period of time—ἐγώ εἰμι ὁ Χριστός, "I am the Christ [= Messiah]." The statement that such persons will come ἐπὶ τῷ ὀνόματί μου, "in my name," means either that they will come using the name of Jesus (see BAGD, 573a) or that they will come assuming the messianic office of Jesus (for ὀνόματι as "office," see BAGD, 573b), as is spelled out in the explicit claim that follows. The claim to be the Christ means here the claim to be the eschatological Messiah. (On the title, see *Comment* on 1:16.) Revolutionary leaders such as Judas the Galilean (Acts 5:37), Theudas (Acts 5:36), and the anonymous "Egyptian" (Acts 21:38), whose endeavors had clear eschatological overtones, might well qualify as the kind of pseudo-messiahs in view here, although not until Bar Kokhba in A.D. 135 do we have evidence of the claim of the title Messiah. For reference to such revolutionary leaders, see Josephus (e.g., *J.W.* 2.13.4 §259, 2.17.8–10 §§433–56; 6.5.2 §§285–87; *Ant.* 17.10.5–8 §§271–85). The prophecy that these messianic pretenders πολλοὺς πλανήσουσιν, "will lead many astray," is in view also in v 24, where ψευδόχριστοι, "pseudo-messiahs," are linked with ψευδοπροφῆται, "pseudo-prophets." For the latter, who "will deceive many," cf. v 11. The self-claims of false messiahs, or the claims of others on their behalf, stand in contrast with what will be the unmistakable evidence of the parousia of the Son of Man (v 27).

**6** The disciples will, in the not distant future, hear of πολέμους, "wars," and of ἀκοὰς πολέμων, "rumors of wars," i.e., of reports of wars more distant. The language is from the stock of apocalyptic literature (cf. *2 Apoc. Bar.* 48:30–41; 70:2–3; *Sib. Or.* 2:154–73). The horror and human suffering connected with war are bound to raise eschatological thoughts—and they have indeed throughout history—yet the disciples must realize that these terrible events (and those mentioned in v 7) do not in themselves signal the end (cf. vv 7–8). Accordingly, the disciples should not be unduly "disturbed" (θροεῖσθε) by these events. Behind δεῖ γὰρ γενέσθαι, "it is necessary for [these things] to happen," lies the Jewish concept of the absolute sovereignty of God in the affairs of this world (cf. the similar formula [δεῖ γενέσθαι] in Rev 1:1; 4:1; 22:6; Dan 2:28–29, 45 [Theod.] in reference to what "must" occur in the future). Despite what appears to point to the reality of eschatological judgment, οὔπω ἐστὶν τὸ τέλος, "the end is not yet." It is not yet the time of the proper eschatological work of the Messiah, and therefore the Messiah will not yet be present (cf. v 5). It is not yet the transition from "this age" (עוֹלָם הַזֶּה, ʿôlām hazzeh) to "that age," i.e., "the age to come" (עוֹלָם הַבָּא, ʿôlām habbāʾ). For the absolute use of τὸ τέλος, "the end," as it is used here, cf. vv 13–14; 10:22.

**7–8** The first half of v 7 refers again to wars but now using the more specific imagery of ἔθνος, "nation," and βασιλεία, "kingdom," rising up against their counterparts (cf. the language of 2 Chr 15:16; Isa 19:2). In addition to these events, not even λιμοὶ καὶ σεισμοί, "famines and earthquakes," in κατὰ τόπους, "various places," point to the end of the age. Much of the language of these verses again reflects standard apocalyptic imagery (for war, earthquakes, and famine, similarly linked, cf. *2 Apoc. Bar.* 70:8; 2 Esdr 9:3–4). All these terrifying events, and presumably others like them, are indeed but ἀρχὴ ὠδίνων, "the beginning of birth pangs." The imagery of "birth pangs" (*1 Enoch* 62:4; 2 Esdr 4:42; cf. *TDNT* 9:672–4) points to the commonly expected period of suffering (the "woes of the Messiah"; cf. *Mek. Exod.* 16:29; *b. Šabb.* 118a; *b. Sanh.* 96b–97a; cf. Str-B 4.2:977–86) that would immediately precede the birth of the messianic age (cf. the imagery of Isa 26:17; 66:7–8; Jer 22:23; Mic 4:9; and in the NT, 1 Thess 5:3). Only such an extended period of travail in birth could bring forth the "new birth" of the created order (cf. 19:28). The sufferings awaiting the disciples were but the beginning of that travail.

*Explanation*

Beginning in the OT and coming to its fullest expression in the apocalyptic literature of the intertestamental period, the experience of certain signs, preeminently of human suffering, was understood as pointing to the imminence of the turning of the ages. These sufferings were as closely linked with the dawning of a new reality as were the labor pains of a woman giving birth. The messianic woes would lead directly to the messianic age. Jesus accepts the basic correctness of the viewpoint but plays down the idea of imminence. Deep human suffering, terrifying in prospect, can be called but "the beginning" of the woes that will precede the coming of the Messiah and the end of the age. This suggests that this period of human suffering may be an extended one. The sufferings, then, cannot themselves be signs of the imminence of the end. It is clear indeed that the very things mentioned here have characterized the entire church age, the intervening period between the first coming of Jesus and his return. The signs point to and warn of the reality of future judgment, but not its time. Despite the emphasis of this passage, well-meaning but misled and misleading teachers have not resisted the temptation to interpret contemporary catastrophes as indicators of the imminence of the end. The apostle Paul had already to guard against this problem (2 Thess 2:2–3). "The godly are always prone to think that evils have reached their utmost limit" (Bengel). Things that may for the moment look out of control are nevertheless within God's purposes and providence. The time of the end is in God's hands alone.

# Persecution and Proclamation before the End (24:9–14)

### Bibliography

**Davison, J. E.** "*Anomia* and the Question of an Antinomian Polemic in Matthew." *JBL* 104 (1985) 617–35. **Dupont, J.** "La persécution comme situation missionaire (Marc 13, 9–11)." In *Die Kirche des Anfangs.* FS H. Schürmann, ed. R. Schnackenburg et al. Leipzig: St. Benno, 1977. 97–114. **Grassi, J. A.** "Matthew as a Second Testament Deuteronomy." *BTB* 19 (1989) 23–29. **Légasse, S.** "Le refroidissement de l'amour avant la fin (Mt 24,12)." *SNTU* 8 (1983) 91–102. **Lüthi, W.** "Missions as Promise and Commission." *Int* 8 (1954) 280–87. **Reicke, B.** "A Test of Synoptic Relationships: Matthew 10:17–23 and 24:9–14 with Parallels." In *New Synoptic Studies,* ed. W. R. Farmer. Macon, GA: Mercer UP, 1983. 209–29. **Taylor, J.** "'The Love of Many Will Grow Cold': Matt 24:9–13 and the Neronian Persecution." *RB* 96 (1989) 352–57. **Thompson, J. W.** "The Gentile Mission as an Eschatological Necessity." *ResQ* 14 (1971) 18–27. **Wenham, D.** "A Note on Matthew 24:10–12." *TynB* 31 (1980) 155–62.

### Translation

[9] *"Then they will hand you over to tribulation, and they will kill you, and you will be hated by all [a] the nations because of my name. [10] And then many will fall away, and they will betray one another, [b] and they will hate each other. [11] And many false prophets will arise, and they will deceive many. [12] And because of the proliferation of iniquity the love of many will grow cold. [13] But the one who endures to the end—this is the one who will be saved. [14] And this good news of the kingdom [c] will be preached throughout the whole world for a witness to all the nations, and then the end will come."*

## Notes

ᵃ πάντων, "all," is omitted by ℵ*, perhaps to soften the statement. Other MSS (C *f*¹ 1 [syᵃ] boᵐˢ) have only πάντων, "all," omitting τῶν ἐθνῶν, "the nations," through the influence of Mark 13:13 (cf. the same form of the saying in 10:22).

ᵇ ℵ omits the last clause, adding here εἰς θλῖψιν, "to tribulation," through the influence of v 9. Φ inserts εἰς θάνατον, "to death" (cf. v 9; Mark 13:12).

ᶜ A few MSS (1424 g¹ [l] Cyr) omit τῆς βασιλείας, "of the kingdom."

## Form/Structure/Setting

A. This section of the discourse indicates further suffering—specifically in the form of persecution—that must be endured before the end comes. Again allusion is made to false prophets who will mislead many, and now Jesus also warns of the increase of iniquity and the cooling of religious fervor. In the face of what must yet occur, only endurance to the end will bring salvation. V 14 introduces a new factor upon which the coming of the end is contingent—one that points to quite an extended time before the end. The gospel must be preached throughout the world before the end can come.

B. Matthew continues to follow Mark, here being somewhat dependent on Mark 13:9–13, a pericope already used by Matthew in nearly its entirety in 10:17–22. The dependence here is therefore not very great, although Matthew has not hesitated to use similar material a second time. Even in some of the new material introduced by Matthew (vv 10–12) Markan influence is to be seen. The first part of v 9 picks up the verb παραδώσουσιν, "they will betray," from Mark 13:9; Matthew's added εἰς θλῖψιν, "to tribulation," serves to summarize the Markan material. The second verb, ἀποκτενοῦσιν, "they will kill," may well reflect the synonym θανατώσουσιν at the end of Mark 13:12, especially since v 9b is clearly dependent on Mark 13:13, which Matthew follows verbatim except for the inserted τῶν ἐθνῶν, "the Gentiles," after πάντων, "all" (cf. v 14). V 10 seems to reflect Mark 13:12, with ἀλλήλους, "one another," corresponding to ἀδελφὸς ἀδελφόν, "brother [will betray] brother." Matthew's μισήσουσιν, "they will hate," is probably repeated from the preceding verse (cf. 10:22). Vv 11–12 are distinctive to Matthew (for ψευδοπροφῆται, "false prophets," leading many astray, cf. vv 5, 24). V 13 repeats Mark 13:13b verbatim, while v 14 (which was omitted in the use of Mark 13:9–13 in chap. 10) is borrowed from Mark 13:10 (Matthew adds τοῦτο, "this," before "gospel" and the further modifier τῆς βασιλείας, "of the kingdom" [cf. 4:23; 9:35], as well as the emphasizing words ἐν ὅλῃ τῇ οἰκουμένῃ εἰς μαρτύριον, "in all the world as a witness"). Mark's πρῶτον, "first," is replaced by Matthew's concluding clause καὶ τότε ἥξει τὸ τέλος, "and then the end will come."

C. If vv 4–8 describe what can be called "the beginning of birth pangs" of the full coming of the messianic age, the present verses describe more of those woes that will occur prior to the birth of the new age. But the passage ends on the announcement that the gospel must be preached universally. Only then will the end come. Outline: (1) the experience of persecution (vv 9–10); (2) the coming of false prophets (v 11); (3) the effect of increased iniquity (v 12); (4) salvation through endurance (v 13); and (5) the universal preaching of the gospel before the end (v 14). Note that structurally the passage consists of a series of short independent sentences linked mainly by καί, "and," probably reflecting the Semitic substratum of Jesus' words. Some parallelism of form is found in v 9a and v 10, where chiasm is also present (ἀλλήλους, "one another," plus verb, followed by verb plus ἀλλήλους). Also worth noting are the repeated παραδώσουσιν, "they will betray" (vv 9, 10), μισούμενοι, "hated," and μισήσουσιν, "they will hate (vv 9, 10). Indeed, v 10 is essentially a repetition of v 9. τέλος, "end," is also repeated in the pericope (vv 13, 14). "All the nations" are referred to in both v 9 and v 14 (inclusio).

D. The content of these verses is alluded to or cited frequently by the early church, which was often concerned with the danger of false prophets (see especially *Apocalypse of Peter* 1:2; *Did.* 16:3; Justin Martyr, *Dial.* 35.3; 82.1). *Did.* 16:3–5 follows the present pericope very closely, including most of its major elements. In addition to the passages mentioned, cf. *Barn.* 4:9.

E. The close similarity between this pericope and 10:17–22 suggests that the mission described in chap. 10 will extend even to the end of the age. Thus the tribulation described in chap. 10 is essentially the same as that described here (cf. esp. vv 9–10, 13 with 10:17, 22). And as the distress in chap. 10 occurs in connection with the proclamation of the kingdom (10:7), so too the references to anticipated sufferings in the present passage conclude with the note that the gospel of the kingdom must be preached throughout the world before the end comes. The frame of reference is fundamentally the same in the two passages, and only now (and in 28:19) does the reference to the Gentiles in 10:18 (where the mission had been explicitly limited to Israel; see 10:5–6) become clear. Persecution will be the lot of those who proclaim the gospel throughout the interim period before the coming of the Son of Man (cf. 10:23; 24:14, 30).

### Comment

**9–10** τότε is not to be taken in the sense of chronological sequence in either of its occurrences in these verses. Instead it points generally to the time of the messianic "birth pangs" mentioned in v 8, which are further described in the present pericope. The disciples must be prepared to face being handed over to tribulation (for παραδώσουσιν, "they will hand you over," which occurs twice in these verses, cf. 10:17, 19, 21; for θλῖψις, "tribulation," cf. vv 21, 29; 13:21) and even death (ἀποκτενοῦσιν ὑμᾶς, "they will kill you"; cf. 10:21, 28; John 16:2). The persecutors are presumably the ones who reject the message of the disciples. Those who proclaim the kingdom will furthermore be hated by the Gentiles because of the name of Jesus. The identical periphrastic construction ἔσεσθε μισούμενοι, "you will be hated" (cf. v 10), together with the following words in verbatim agreement (except for the lack of τῶν ἐθνῶν, "the Gentiles"), is found in 10:22a. Here τῶν ἐθνῶν, "the Gentiles," can be included since the gentile mission is announced with all clarity in v 14. The reference to the experience of persecution from "all the Gentiles" here stands in poignant relationship to the same phrase in v 14, for it is just "all the Gentiles" to whom the disciples are sent "for a witness." διὰ τὸ ὄνομά μου, "because of my name" (cf. 10:22), means because of the disciples' identification with Jesus. But there will also be disloyalty and treachery among those who are Jesus' disciples. σκανδαλισθήσονται πολλοί, "many will fall away" (cf. 13:21, 57; for the same verb form used similarly, see LXX Dan 11:41 [88 Sy]), undoubtedly because of the pressure of the persecution referred to in v 9. It will be a time of testing, but not all the disciples will survive it (cf. v 13). The repeated reciprocal ἀλλήλους, "one another," thus refers to betrayal (παραδώσουσιν, "they will betray"; cf. v 9) and hostility (μισήσουσιν, "they will hate"; cf. v 9) within the ranks of the followers of Jesus.

**11** In this extended time of woes before the end comes, πολλοὶ ψευδοπροφῆται, "many false prophets," will arise and πλανήσουσιν πολλούς, "they will lead many astray." The reference to "leading many astray" has already been made in v 5 (where the subject of the verb, however, is false messiahs; cf. v 4) and will again occur (without the "many") in v 24, where false messiahs and false prophets (who will do great signs and wonders) are mentioned together. In every instance it is clear that the end is not yet.

**12** The time of tribulation and persecution will bring with it the increase of ἀνομίαν, "iniquity," which will in turn be responsible for a failure in the fundamental Christian ethic of ἀγάπη, "love." The verb underlying "proliferation," lit. "be brought to the full" (πληθυνθῆναι), perhaps echoes the same verb in 23:32. The exact nature of the iniquity or "lawlessness" that will abound is not specified (see Davison), but for Matthew there is no more fundamental failure than this (cf. 7:15–27, esp. v 23; 13:41). For the expectation in the apocalyptic literature, cf. *1 Enoch* 91:7; 2 Esdr 5:2, 10; and Dan 12:4 (see Wenham). Also unclear is the exact sense in which the love practiced by "many" (τῶν πολλῶν) "will grow cold" (ψυγήσεται). The latter verb is also used figuratively in Josephus, *J.W.* 5.11.4 §472, referring to the cooling of hope. The failure of love refers more likely to love for others (hence, canceled by the treachery and hatred mentioned in the preceding verses) rather than a failure of love in relation to the truth (as in 2 Thess 2:10) or God (as in 2 Tim 3:4; cf. Rev 2:4), although these contexts too refer to the increase of iniquity. One must remember that love, for Matthew, is the summary of the law (cf. 22:36–40). Taylor's suggestion that the subject of these verses is specifically the Neronian persecution of Christians in Rome in A.D. 64, while not impossible, is not convincing.

**13** The logion of this verse is found verbatim in 10:22b (see *Comment* there). Again in a context of tribulation and persecution the promise of ultimate salvation is given to the one who endures εἰς τέλος, "to the end." Indirectly, the point is underlined that severe tribulation will be experienced before the coming of the end of the age.

**14** Another characteristic of the time that precedes the end is the universal proclamation of τοῦτο τὸ εὐαγγέλιον τῆς βασιλείας, "this gospel of the kingdom" (cf. 4:23; 9:35). This era is obviously to be sharply distinguished from the time of Jesus himself, when the mission of the twelve was explicitly restricted to Israel (10:5–6). This new time frame is inaugurated in the risen Jesus' commissioning of his disciples in 28:19 (cf. Luke 24:47; and the apocalyptic universalism of Rev 14:6). The verb κηρύσσειν, "proclaim," occurs regularly, as it does here, with εὐαγγέλιον, "gospel" (cf. 4:23; 9:35; 10:7; 26:13). Quite possibly Matthew's unique expression "*this gospel* of the kingdom" (so too in 26:13) is a deliberate paralleling of Jesus' teaching as recorded in his Gospel to Deuteronomy's reference to *this book* of the law, the Second Testament thus corresponding to the First Testament (thus Grassi). The universality of the proclamation is stressed by the words ἐν ὅλῃ τῇ οἰκουμένῃ, "in the whole world" (the last word occurs in Matthew only here). The proclamation involves the providing of a μαρτύριον, "witness" (cf. 8:4; 10:18), i.e., the recounting of the events that constitute the gospel or "kerygma." For πᾶσιν τοῖς ἔθνεσιν, "all the Gentiles," cf. v 9 and 28:19. The concluding statement καὶ τότε ἥξει τὸ τέλος, "and then the end will come," stands as the counterpart to the cautionary statement that "not yet is the end" in v 6 (cf. v 13; 10:22). The end of the present age, concerning which the disciples inquire in the question of v 3, cannot come immediately but must be preceded by a period of universal evangelization (see Thompson). The parousia must therefore be delayed.

### Explanation

The unavoidable time of tribulation and persecution that must come will have several effects: the commitment of many will grow cold; others will fall away and betray those with whom they formerly stood; and iniquity will abound. It will be a time that calls for great endurance from the faithful. At the same time, however, the period before the end will be marked by the proclamation of the good news that Jesus has been announcing in his ministry—the good news of the kingdom. But now that proclamation will go not just to the Jews but to "all the nations." This indeed appears to be the main reason for the delay of the parousia (cf. the similar logic of 2 Peter 3:9). This is not to say, however, that the coming of the end remains contingent on the evangelizing of every last tribe on the earth, as though it is in the power of the disciples to hasten or delay the coming of the end by their obedience or lack of obedience to the command to evangelize. In view, rather, is the widespread proclamation of the message of the kingdom without geographical or racial restriction. In this regard, for example, even though Paul had not reached the unevangelized territory of Spain (cf. Rom 15:20–24), he can speak of the spread of the gospel in the most comprehensive language (cf. Rom 10:18, where Ps 19:4 is quoted by analogy). Through the missionary work of the apostles, the gospel has "gone out to all the earth." This conclusion of course in no way weakens the continuing force of the missionary mandate throughout the interim period. But "the end" *could* already have come in the first century. The required conditions were all present. All the sufferings in vv 5–12 were experienced in the years prior to A.D. 70 and the fall of Jerusalem, and in varying degree they have been signs experienced by the church down to the present era. The signs of the end have been present to every Christian generation.

# Instructions to Flee from Jerusalem    (24:15–22)

### Bibliography

**Colunga, A.** "La abominación de la desolación." *CB* 17 (1960) 183–85. **Connell, F. J.** "An Exegetical Problem (on Mt. 24:21)." *AER* 113 (1945) 222–23. **Dodd, C. H.** "The Fall of Jerusalem and the 'Abomination of Desolation.'" *JRS* 37 (1947) 47–54. **Ford, D.** *The Abomination of Desolation in Biblical Eschatology.* Washington, DC: University Press of America, 1979. **Koester, C. R.** "The Origin and Significance of the Flight to Pella Tradition." *CBQ* 51 (1989) 90–106. **Lüdemann, G.** "The Successors of Earliest Jerusalem Christianity: An Analysis of the Pella Tradition." In *Opposition to Paul in Jewish Christianity*, tr. M. E. Boring. Minneapolis: Fortress, 1989. 200–213. **Rigaux, B.** *"ΒΔΕΛΥΓΜΑ ΤΗΣ ΕΡΗΜΩΣΕΩΣ* (Mc 13, 14; Mt. 24, 15)." *Bib* 40 (1959) 675–83. **Sowers, S.** "The Circumstances and Recollection of the Pella Flight." *TZ* 26 (1970) 305–20. **Stanton, G. N.** "'Pray That Your Flight May Not Be in Winter or on a Sabbath' (Matthew 24.20)." *JSNT* 37 (1989) 17–30 (reprinted in *A Gospel for a New People*, 192–206). **Thibaut, R.** "La grande tribulation." *NRT* 55 (1928) 373–76. **Wong, E. K.-C.** "The Matthean Understanding of the Sabbath: A Response to G. N. Stanton." *JSNT* 44 (1991) 3–18.

## Translation

[15] *"When therefore you see 'the abomination of desolation,' which was spoken of by the prophet Daniel, standing in the holy place* [a]—*let the reader understand*—[16]*then let those who are in Judea flee to* [b] *the mountains.* [17]*Let the one who is on the rooftop not come down to take the things* [c] *from his or her* [d] *house,* [18]*and let the one who is in the field not turn back to get his or her* [e] *garment.* [f] [19]*But woe to those women who are pregnant and those who are nursing in those days.*

[20] *"But pray that your flight may not be in winter or on a sabbath.* [21]*For then there will be great tribulation, of a kind that has not happened since the beginning of the world until the present, nor ever will be.* [22]*And if those days were not cut short, no human being* [g] *would be saved. But for the sake of the elect those days will be shortened."*

## Notes

[a] ἑστὸς ἐν τόπῳ ἁγίῳ, "standing in the holy place," is omitted in the minuscule MS 1010 and sy[s].

[b] Many MSS (ℵ K L W Z Γ *f*[13]) have ἐπί, lit. "upon," for εἰς, "to."

[c] D Θ *f*[1] latt have τι, "anything," instead of τά, "the (things)," probably by the influence of the parallel passage in Mark 13:15. ℵ* has τό, lit. "the (thing)."

[d] "or her" added in translation.

[e] "or her" added in translation.

[f] A few MSS (W Γ Δ f sy[h]) have the pl. τὰ ἱμάτια, "garments."

[g] πᾶσα σάρξ with the preceding οὐκ means lit. "no flesh."

## Form/Structure/Setting

A. Among the events to occur before the τέλος, "end," spoken of in v 14 is the "great tribulation" (v 21) spoken of in this pericope. As Luke makes very clear in the parallel passage (Luke 21:20), also dependent upon Mark 13, the present passage refers to the imminent destruction of Jerusalem, which was to take place in A.D. 70. This is marked very clearly by the opening reference in Matthew to "the abomination of desolation." This passage provides practical instructions concerning the flight from the city together with indications of the horrific suffering that is to be experienced. Indeed, so terrible will this tribulation be that it can be referred to in hyperbolic language befitting the eschatological judgment itself, of which in a way it becomes a prototype. V 22 most naturally belongs to the preceding verses (*pace* Carson) rather than with those that follow. Matthew's familiar marker τότε, "then," is the first word in v 23.

B. Matthew continues to be dependent upon Mark, following the order of the material in the Markan discourse (Mark 13:14–20). Matthew closely follows the Markan wording, making only the following significant alterations. In v 15, after the technical expression τὸ βδέλυγμα τῆς ἐρημώσεως, "the abomination of desolation" (Mark 13:14), Matthew adds τὸ ῥηθὲν διὰ Δανιὴλ τοῦ προφήτου, "that spoken of through the prophet Daniel," thereby pointing the reader to the OT background of the expression, using Matthew's favorite formula. In the same verse Matthew replaces Mark's masculine participle ἑστηκότα, "standing," with the neuter ἑστός, a grammatical improvement bringing about agreement with the neuter noun βδέλυγμα, "abomination." Matthew also replaces ὅπου οὐ δεῖ, "where it ought not to," with the specific identification ἐν τόπῳ ἁγίῳ, "in the holy place," i.e., in the temple (cf. Dan 11:31). In v 17 Matthew abbreviates Mark by omitting the redundant μηδὲ εἰσελθάτω, "nor let him go in" (Mark 13:15), and changes Mark's τι, "anything," to τά, "things." In v 20 Matthew supplies the missing subject ἡ φυγὴ ὑμῶν, "your flight," for the verb μὴ γένηται, "may not be" (Mark 13:18), and adds μηδὲ σαββάτῳ, "nor on a sabbath," as a matter of special concern for his Jewish readers. Matthew's syntax in v 21 improves the awkwardness of Mark's Greek (Mark 13:19) by making θλῖψις, "tribulation," the subject of the opening verb, substituting his favorite τότε, "then," for αἱ ἡμέραι ἐκεῖναι, "those days" (adding the expression twice in v 22), and omitting Mark's unnecessary τοιαύτη, "such a kind." Matthew also adds μεγάλη, "great," to modify θλῖψις, "tribulation." In the same verse Matthew alters Mark's κτίσεως, "creation," to κόσμου, "world," and omits Mark's redundant ἣν ἔκτισεν ὁ θεός, "which God created" (Mark 13:19). In v 22 Matthew replaces Mark's εἰ μὴ ἐκολόβωσεν κύριος τὰς ἡμέρας, "unless the Lord shortened the days" (Mark 13:20), with the Semitically more appropriate divine passive, εἰ μὴ ἐκολοβώθησαν αἱ ἡμέραι ἐκεῖναι, "unless those days were shortened." The phrase αἱ ἡμέραι ἐκεῖναι, "those days," also replaces Mark's τὰς ἡμέρας, "the days," at the end of the verse. Finally, Matthew omits Mark's redundant οὓς ἐξελέξατο, "whom he elected," following the noun ἐκλεκτούς, "elect."

C. These verses, referring to the destruction of Jerusalem, correspond specifically to the initial prophecy of v 2, and to the question, or at least part of the question, of v 3. The focus of the first part is on the flight from Jerusalem and Judea, and in the second part on the horror of the impending tribulation. Outline: (1) the exhortation to flee (vv 15–16); (2) the urgency of fleeing (vv 17–18); (3) the difficulty of the flight (vv 19–20); (4) the horror of the tribulation (v 21); and (5) the divine shortening of the tribulation (v 22). Very obvious structural parallelism can be seen between vv 17 and 18: the definite article ὁ functions as the pronoun subject in each sentence, both have negative imperative verbs, and in each instance the complementary infinitive clause begins with ἆραι, "to take." The added subject φυγή, "flight," picks up the root of the first main verb (φευγέτωσαν, "let them flee" [v 16]). The twofold αἱ ἡμέραι ἐκεῖναι, "those days," in v 22 picks up the same phrase in v 19. Parallelism may also be seen in v 22 between the opening εἰ μή, "unless," clause and the final clause with the same subject and same verb.

D. *Did.* 16.4, in referring to a coming time of trouble such as has never been seen before, appears to allude to v 20 of the present passage. Paul's reference in 2 Thess 2:3–4 to "the son of perdition" who takes his seat in the temple may also depend upon this material in oral form (v 15; see D. Wenham, *The Rediscovery of Jesus' Eschatological Discourse*).

E. The larger section of Matthew that begins here and runs through v 28 has been interpreted in a variety of ways. There appear to be several reasons for the difficulty of interpreting this material, the most important being the need to prepare for Matthew's "immediately after the tribulation of those days" in v 29, which, according to the majority of commentators, introduces the parousia. Therefore, it would seem that what is referred to in the verses preceding v 29 must concern an end-time tribulation that yet lies in the future just prior to the parousia. Furthermore, the reference here to a "great tribulation [θλῖψις μεγάλη], of a kind that has not happened since the beginning of the world until the present, nor ever will be" (v 21), sounds like an eschatological tribulation (cf. Rev 7:14: τῆς θλίψεως τῆς μεγάλης, "the great tribulation"), and thus many interpreters have been unable to resist identifying the "abomination of desolation" (v 15) with the eschatological Antichrist who "takes his seat in the temple of God, proclaiming himself to be God," referred to in 2 Thess 2:3–10 (cf. Rev 11:7; 12:9). The background for these images is found in certain apocalyptic passages of Daniel, e.g., 7:20–21, 24–25; 11:40–45; 12:1.

On the other hand, the statement of v 21 is a familiar topos that can indeed have been used to refer to the destruction of Jerusalem in A.D. 70 (see *Comment* there), and the meaning of the apocalyptic images of Daniel, 2 Thessalonians, and Revelation is debatable, to say the least. Many commentators therefore have concluded that vv 15–22 refer to the destruction of Jerusalem, although a good portion of them nevertheless feel constrained to separate vv 23–28 from vv 15–22 and to understand them as referring to events related to the end of time, again because of the influence of Matthew's "immediately" in reference to the parousia (v 29). There is nothing in the content of vv 23–28, however, that requires an eschatological understanding; indeed, these verses talk not about *the* Antichrist but about antichrists (v 24), and they repeat material already encountered in vv 4–5, ending moreover with a reference to this being *not* the time of the end (v 6; cf. vv 27–28). The view of this commentary is that vv 23–28 too refer most naturally to the time of the destruction of Jerusalem.

Feeling the force of the arguments for both interpretations, some commentators have opted here for a double reference, i.e., that the passage refers to both the destruction of Jerusalem and the eschatological tribulation (e.g., Hill; Bruner). It cannot be denied that these apocalyptic images by their nature can be used to refer to a number of interrelated pivotal events, as we already see in the application of the Danielic image of the abomination of desolation, which referred in the first instance to Antiochus Epiphanes in the second century B.C. and is now applied to another parallel event. Nevertheless, this does not justify seeing an actual double reference here—at least if we restrict ourselves to the evangelist's intention. We may perhaps see a further intimation of eschatological events and relate the images here to the apocalyptic material in 2 Thessalonians 2 and Revelation concerning the Antichrist, but exegesis requires us to limit ourselves to the intention of Matthew.

## Comment

**15** τὸ βδέλυγμα τῆς ἐρημώσεως, lit. "the abomination of the desolation," is language taken directly from the LXX of Daniel (exactly in Dan 12:11; without definite articles in 11:31; and with the plural τῶν ἐρημώσεων, "of the desolations," in 9:27), where it refers to an image set upon the altar of the temple in connection with the destruction of the city. It functions here, therefore, as a technical expression for an idolatrous "abomination" ( שִׁקּוּץ, *šiqqûṣ*, "detested," i.e., by God). The genitive construction is to be understood as meaning "the abomination that makes desolate," an allusion to the accompanying devastation of the sacrilege.

> The phrase "abomination of desolation" or "desolating abomination," already a technical term before the time of the evangelist, derives from the Hebrew שִׁקּוּץ שֹׁמֵם, *šiqqûṣ šōmēm* (cf. Dan 9:27). The expression in a slightly different form, as found in Dan 8:13, is הַפֶּשַׁע שֹׁמֵם, *happešaʿ sōmēm*, meaning "desolating rebellion" (cf. NRSV: "the transgression that makes desolate"). The phrase is apparently a pun on the name *Baʿal Šāmēm*, "Lord of Heaven," because of the similarity of the words "desolating" and "heaven." Baal is the "abomination" or "sacrilege" described in the other passages of Daniel (9:27; 11:31; 12:11) by the word *šiqqûṣ*, which has a numerical value of 490 and which is associated often with the word "desolating" in Jer 4; 7; 44; Ezek 5–7. See J. E. Goldingay, *Daniel*, WBC 30 (Dallas: Word, 1989) 212–13, 263.

The profanation of the temple referred to by Daniel took place in 168 B.C., accomplished by Antiochus Epiphanes as a part of his attempt to wipe out Judaism (the exact phrase βδέλυγμα ἐρημώσεως is used to refer to the image set upon the altar in the description of this event in 1 Macc 1:54; cf. too 2 Macc 8:17; for parallel instances concerning images, see Jos., *Ant.* 18.3.1 §§55–59; 18.8.2–9 §§261–309). Jesus adopts the same language to indicate that a similar desecration of the temple will occur. Matthew points specifically to the source of the expression in his added words τὸ ῥηθὲν διὰ Δανιὴλ τοῦ προφήτου, "which was spoken of by the prophet Daniel" (for this formula, see *Comment* on 1:22). Daniel, though included with the writings rather than the prophets in the Hebrew canon (in contrast to its position in the LXX), is referred to as a prophet in the sense of a vehicle of revelation (cf. 13:35). Although Matthew's ἐν τόπῳ ἁγίῳ, "in the holy place," i.e., in the temple (cf. 2 Macc 8:17; Acts 6:13; 21:28), clarifies Mark's "where it ought not (to be)," Matthew nevertheless retains Mark's ὁ ἀναγινώσκων νοείτω, "let the reader understand." The words as they stand in Matthew apparently refer to the understanding of an apocalyptic mystery (cf. Dan 8:15–17). The Danielic imagery was familiar to the readers. Now they were to know that what Daniel once referred to, fulfilled in the historical events of 167 B.C., was prophesied again by Jesus. This is thus privileged information about the future. Ironically, the understanding of "abomination of desolation" is much disputed.

> In Dan 9:27; 11:31; 12:11 the expression "abomination of desolation" (i.e., "that makes desolate") apparently refers to a specific historical event: the erection by Antiochus IV ("Epiphanes" = "[god] manifest") of an altar of Zeus upon the altar of Yahweh in the temple in 167 B.C. when Antiochus conquered Jerusalem. This is explicitly confirmed by the use of the same expression in 1 Macc 1:54 (cf. 1:59). So horrific was this event, however, that it became a convenient and elastic symbol for the great evils that were to engulf the people in the future, evils that could point to the struggles prior to the eschatological era itself. Thus, when in A.D. 40 the Roman emperor Caligula proposed setting up his own image in the temple, the Danielic language came immediately to mind. When Jesus prophesied the destruction of Jerusalem, he used the same symbolic language. So too in 2 Thess 2:4 Paul depends on the prophecy of Jesus, employing the same Danielic symbol, when he refers to the antichrist to come.

As we have already noted (*Form/Structure/Setting* §E), many interpreters have understood the desolating abomination in the present passage to refer to the eschatological antichrist of 2 Thess 2:4. Paul, like Matthew, thus associated the Danielic imagery with the end of the world. The fall of Jerusalem and the accompanying desecration of the temple could not help but bring with them the eschatological age. Matthew probably means by the words "let the reader understand" that the event referred to implies the end of the age brought about by the deed of a Roman (hence the importance of veiled language) invader—an event that vividly parallels the desecrating act of Antiochus. The words ὅταν οὖν ἴδητε, "when you see," correspond to the first part of the question of v 3, which in turn is directly prompted by the prophecy of v 2. Initially in view therefore is the destruction of Jerusalem and the concomitant setting up of the desolating abomination in the temple that occurred in A.D. 70. It is wrong to reject this conclusion by pressing the letter of the text (v 16) and insisting that only after the image was set up in the temple was the flight to take place (which would in fact have been too late). The meaning is more general, i.e., that the disciples should flee when events indicated that the desecration of the temple was inevitable.

Matthew writes about this before A.D. 70 in my opinion. The lack of exact, detailed correspondence with the actual events makes difficult the conclusion that Matthew's prophecy is a *vaticinium ex eventu* (see Reicke, "Synoptic Prophecies"). If Matthew means by the "abomination that desolates" something to be accomplished by the Romans in A.D. 70, that does not prevent the elastic symbol from also being applied to something lying in the future. But that possibility is not in the evangelist's mind.

**16**   That the destruction of Jerusalem (cf. Luke 21:20) is linked with the profanation of the temple becomes clear in this and the following verses. A time of terrible suffering was about to come. Those who are in Judea τότε, "at that time," are exhorted to flee εἰς τὰ ὄρη, "to the mountains." Perhaps in response to this remembered logion, much of the Christian community fled Judea for the mountains or foothills of the Transjordanian mountains (many settled eventually in Pella in the northern region; cf. Eusebius, *Historia Ecclesiastica* 3.5.3). The hills would provide safety as they did in the time of the Maccabean revolt (1 Macc 2:28). Although the identification of this flight with that referred to in the Pella tradition has been challenged (cf. Brandon, *The Fall of Jerusalem;* Lüdemann), it has also been defended by Sowers and C. R. Koester (the latter with reference only to the Lukan parallel [Luke 21:20–22]).

**17–18**   The severity of the impending distress is further underlined by the urgency of the need to depart (cf. Gen 19:17). The flight should be immediate, and thus there will be no time to retrieve possessions or clothing. The one on the housetop (the flat roof of the Palestinian house was a popular place to relax in the evening), as well as the one working in the field, must flee without delay (cf. Luke 17:31). Flight would also be easier without baggage.

**19–20**   Special circumstances—pregnancy, the necessity of nursing infants (cf. Luke 23:29), and possibly winter or the sabbath—will make the journey particularly difficult. Since the first two are not to be avoided, these women can only be pitied (οὐαί, "woe [to them]"). The other two, having to do with timing, may be avoidable, but the disciples are exhorted to pray that the necessary flight does not have to occur on the sabbath or in the winter, when flooding wadis and muddy hillsides could be dangerous (let alone a fording of the swollen Jordan) and bitter cold nights uncomfortable. While the point of the reference to the sabbath is hardly clear, probably what is meant is that an urgent flight on the sabbath would make any sabbath observance impossible (cf. Exod 16:29; Acts 1:12; and rabbinic elaboration limiting movement to "2000 cubits" in *m. ʿErub.* 4:3, 5:7). This apparently would still have been a serious matter for the Jewish-Christian membership of Matthew's church.

For a review of the possible ways of interpreting the sabbath reference, see Stanton's thorough discussion. Stanton's own proposal is that these verses refer not to any specific flight but generally to the need to flee from persecution, and in this case from the Jews (cf. 10:17, 23). The reference to the possible need to flee on the sabbath he then takes as something that would further antagonize the Jewish persecutors of Matthew's community. Stanton, however, too quickly rules out the traditional interpretation (taken above) by concluding that 12:1–14 must indicate that the sabbath was no longer an important issue for the Matthean community. But Matthew there omitted the logion of Mark 2:27 (a point made also in Wong's critique of Stanton's view), revealing his concern to tone down Mark's radicalism on the sabbath law. Every statement impinging upon the law in Matthew must be considered in the light of the conservative statement of 5:17–19. Nothing in the present context, furthermore, indicates that Jewish persecutors are in Matthew's purview. Rather, the context points to the imminent Roman invasion of Jerusalem. Although it is apparently true that already in the time of the Maccabees some Jews could bring themselves to fight on the sabbath, if necessary, rather than die (1 Macc 2:41; Jos., *Ant.* 12.6.2 §277), the view was hardly unanimous (cf. *Jub.* 50:12–13; 2 Macc 6:11; 15:1; and the qualification in Jos., *Ant.* 14.4.2 §63). If the Jews were not of a common mind on the subject in the time of the Jewish war (see M. Hengel, *The Zealots* [Edinburgh: T. & T. Clark, 1989] 287–90), it rings true to conclude with Wong that "at least some of the members of the Matthean community (probably some of the conservative Jewish Christians who still behave according to their tradition) would hesitate to flee on a Sabbath" (17). A flight on the sabbath could have divided members of the community with disastrous consequences. See too *Comment* on vv 15 and 16. France (following R. Banks) refers to the difficulties of gates being shut and provisions being unobtainable on the sabbath. The first might constitute a problem, but vv 17–18 prohibit the idea of acquiring provisions.

**21–22** The reason for the urgency of the flight is now finally stated. There will be a θλῖψις μεγάλη, "great tribulation." To emphasize the horror of the sufferings to be experienced, it is stated that no suffering, either before or after, will compare with the suffering of this tribulation. This is without question also the formulaic language of eschatological judgment (cf. Dan 12:1; Joel 2:2). In the present passage, we must conclude one of the following: the language (1) is used hyperbolically in reference to the fall of Jerusalem (there is no question concerning the horrible extent of the suffering; cf. Jos., *J.W.* 5.10.1 §§420–23; 5.11.3–4 §§460–72), (2) refers literally to the eschatological judgment of the end of the age, or (3) uses the destruction of Jerusalem as a type of foreshadowing of the last judgment, thereby applying to the former language strictly proper to the latter (see "Excursus: Imminence, Delay, and Matthew's εὐθέως" at 24:29). The appropriateness of such hyperbolic language in reference to the final six-month siege of Jerusalem in A.D. 70 is evident from the historical information provided by Josephus (*J.W.* 5.12.3 §§512–18). Well could it be said that worse suffering had never been seen nor would again be seen. See Beasley-Murray (*Jesus and the Last Days,* 419) for a defense of the language as formulaic and not literal (cf. passages cited by him: Exod 9:18; 10:14; 11:16; and esp. Dan 12:1; see too, Jos., *J.W.* Proem 4 §§9–12). The assertion of v 22 rests upon God's sovereign control of history, whereby he "curtails" (κολοβοῦν occurs in the NT only here and in Mark 13:20) the time of suffering. This statement again has the effect of underlining the gravity of the suffering. Had the time not been cut short, no one (this is the meaning of πᾶσα σάρξ, lit. "all flesh") would have survived (ἐσώθη, "saved" or "preserved," refers here to physical safety). The time of suffering will be shortened "for the sake of the elect" (cf. *2 Apoc. Bar.* 20:1–2; 83.1; 2 Tim 2:10). ἐκλεκτούς, "elect," is used elsewhere in Matthew only in vv 24, 31 and in 22:14. It must refer to those who have followed Jesus, i.e., Christians. But if the Christians have fled Jerusalem and the reference is to those in Jerusalem, it may include those who are elect in the sense of those who will yet come to faith in Jesus. The repeated expression αἱ ἡμέραι ἐκεῖναι, "those days," takes on the significance of a semi-technical phrase referring to a unique period of suffering (cf. vv 19, 29).

A problem sometimes mentioned concerning understanding vv 15–22 as referring to the fall of Jerusalem is the lack of exact correspondence between what is described here and what actually occurred. It is hardly likely, for example, that Titus erected a statue of himself on the site of the destroyed temple. As Beasley-Murray points out, "there is not a syllable which reflects knowledge of events which took place in the Jewish War, still less of the actual destruction of the city and temple" (*Jesus and the Last Days,* 407). This may provide confirmation that the passage reflects genuine prophecy of the events of A.D. 70 rather than having been written *ex eventu.*

### Explanation

The prophecy of the desolation of the temple pointed to a major turning point in the history of Israel. What had happened once by the hand of Antiochus a mere two hundred years earlier would happen again, this time, however, in conjunction with the destruction of the temple itself. Such a catastrophe could only be interpreted as an eschatological event, a repetition and final fulfillment of the prophecy of Daniel. It would cause a degree of suffering that was beyond words. Jesus accordingly instructs his disciples to flee from Jerusalem. Their survival is more important than any national loyalties that might motivate them to fight against the Romans. God indeed will not allow the suffering of that time to be prolonged so as to cause ultimate harm to his elect. Eschatological judgment is coming upon Jerusalem in advance of the final judgment of the eschaton. And beyond their immediate fulfillment the words of the prophecy also foreshadow a more distant and final fulfillment.

# *The Claims of Pseudo-Christs and False Prophets (24:23–28)*

### Bibliography

**Black, M.** "The Aramaic Dimension in Q with Notes on Luke 17.22 and Matthew 24.26 (Luke 17.23)." *JSNT* 40 (1990) 33–41. **Guenther, H. O.** "When 'Eagles' Draw Together."

*Forum* 5 (1989) 140–50. **Jonge, M. de.** "Jewish Expectations about the 'Messiah' according to the Fourth Gospel." *NTS* 19 (1972–73) 246–70.

### Translation

<sup></sup> ²³ *"Then if anyone says to you, 'Behold, the Christ is here!' or 'He is* ᵃ *there!' do not believe that person.*ᵇ ²⁴*For pseudo-christs and false prophets will arise, and they will perform great*ᶜ *signs and wonders, so that, if possible, they might deceive even the elect.* ²⁵*Take note, I have told you in advance.* ²⁶*If, therefore, they say to you, 'Look, he is in the wilderness!' do not bother to*ᵈ *go there.*ᵉ *Or if they say,*ᶠ *'Look, he is*ᵍ *in the inner rooms!' do not believe them.*ʰ ²⁷*For just as the lightning comes from the east and flashes to the west, thus will be the coming of the Son of Man.* ²⁸*Wherever*ⁱ *the corpse is, the vultures will be gathered together there."*

### Notes

ᵃ "He is" added.
ᵇ "That person" added.
ᶜ A few MSS (‭א‬ W* ff¹ r¹ boᵐˢ) lack μεγάλα, "great," probably by the influence of the parallel in Mark 13:22.
ᵈ "Bother to" added.
ᵉ "There" added.
ᶠ "Or if they say" added.
ᵍ "He is" added.
ʰ "Them" added.
ⁱ Many MSS (W *f*¹³ TR c ff² q syʰ mae) add γάρ, "for," thereby linking the proverb more closely with the preceding context.

### Form/Structure/Setting

A. The discourse continues with the motif with which it began in v 4, namely, the coming of messianic pretenders who will attempt to mislead the community of the faithful (cf. too v 11). The repetition of this theme here has the effect of emphasizing that the desecration of the temple just referred to does not entail the immediate dawning of the eschaton. This catastrophic event together with the destruction of Jerusalem, although a typological anticipation of the final judgment, is merely one event among many that must yet happen before the end of the age. Though their miraculous deeds and stupendous claims may be spectacular, the coming of pseudo-messiahs and false prophets must not be confused with the parousia of the Son of Man, which will happen in a sudden and dramatic way incapable of being missed.

B. For vv 23–25 Matthew follows Mark; v 26 is unique to Matthew; and vv 27–28 are probably drawn from Q (cf. Luke 17:24, 37b). Matthew's changes of the Markan text are minor: in v 24 he inserts μεγάλα, "great," after σημεῖα, "signs" (cf. Mark 13:22), thereby heightening the impact of the false messiahs and prophets; in the same verse Matthew inserts καί, "even," before τοὺς ἐκλεκτούς, "the elect," again for emphasis; Matthew (v 25) omits Mark's sentence ὑμεῖς δὲ βλέπετε, "but you beware" (Mark 13:23), probably regarding it as superfluous; and finally Matthew inserts ἰδού, "look," at the beginning of v 25 and omits Mark's πάντα, "everything" (Mark 13:23), the object of προείρηκα, "I have told you beforehand," probably regarding it as too comprehensive in the present context. In v 27 Matthew probably departs from Q in replacing ἀστράπτουσα ... λάμπει, "flashing ... shines" (Luke 17:24), with the less Semitic ἐξέρχεται ... καὶ φαίνεται, "comes ... and shines." So too Matthew probably alters ἐκ τῆς ὑπὸ τὸν οὐρανὸν εἰς τὴν ὑπ᾽ οὐρανόν, "from one part of the sky to another part of the sky" (Luke 17:24), to the smoother ἀπὸ ἀνατολῶν ... ἕως δυσμῶν, "from the east to the west" (v 27). In the same verse Matthew also has probably inserted ἡ παρουσία, "the parousia," perhaps using it in place of ἐν τῇ ἡμέρᾳ αὐτοῦ, "in his day," if this was in the Lukan text (Luke 17:24) and in Q. The only significant change in v 28 is the probable substitution of πτῶμα, "corpse," for σῶμα, "body" (Luke 17:37b), as more appropriate to the Matthean context.

C. The repeated warnings dominate the passage, giving the pericope the character of an admonitory exhortation. The supporting statements are designed to strengthen the main affirmation from the beginning of the discourse in v 4 that the end of the age is reached neither in the terrible sufferings to be experienced nor in the deceptive claims of wonder workers. As an outline, the following may be suggested: (1) exhortation not to believe false claims (v 23); (2) the impact of false messiahs and prophets (vv 24–25); (3) repetition of the exhortation (v 26); (4) the unmistakable character of the parousia of the Son of Man (v 27); and (5) an appended logion (v 28). The main structural feature of the pericope is the three prohibitory subjunctives of vv 23 and 26. These are parallel in the first two instances, with ἐάν clauses (though the second involves a plural ἐάν ... εἴπωσιν, "if they say" [v 26]). In the third instance the ἐάν clause is implied rather than stated. In all three instances an object clause is introduced by ἰδού, "look," though only the first has a subject, ὁ Χριστός, "the Christ," and only the second has a verb, ἐστίν, "he is," while the third has neither. The parallel between the first and third is heightened by the common verb μὴ πιστεύσητε, "do not believe." Each of the three prohibitions has a different location in view, the first ὧδε, "here" (twice), the second ἐν τῇ ἐρήμῳ, "in the wilderness" (as appropriate to the verb, μὴ ἐξέλθητε, "do not go out"), and the third ἐν τοῖς ταμείοις, "in the private rooms." V 24 contains three pairs of parallel elements worth noting: two subjects, two verbs, and two objects for the second of the verbs.

D. The sayings tradition here (cf. too vv 4–5, 11) probably serves in oral form as the source of Paul's statement, and even terminology to some extent, in 2 Thess 2:8–10 (see D. Wenham, *The Rediscovery of Jesus' Eschatological Discourse*). So too, the underlying tradition is probably reflected in *Did.* 16:4, and the Gospel itself in Justin Martyr, *Dial.* 35.3 (cf. 32.1–2).

## Comment

**23** The warning not to believe in messianic claimants resumes the main theme of the first part of the discourse, i.e., that despite great sufferings, including even the destruction of the temple and the destruction of Jerusalem, the end of the age remains in the future. The present statement repeats in slightly different form (third person, rather than first person) the warnings of vv 4–5 and 11 (see *Comment* on those verses). Here the claim is made in the third person on behalf of another: "Here is the Christ" (for a similar claim with regard to the kingdom, see Luke 17:21).

**24–25** While this is the only occurrence of ψευδόχριστος, "false messiah," in Matthew (the Markan parallel provides the only other NT occurrence; cf. the equivalent, ἀντίχριστος, "antichrist," in 1 John 2:18, 22; 4:3; 2 John 7), ψευδοπροφήτης, "false prophet," occurs also in v 11 and earlier in 7:15. There is no clear distinction between the words in this chapter: in each instance the verb πλανᾶν, "lead astray," is used (vv 5, 11, 24). So too in 1 John 4:1 false prophets are not distinguished from antichrists. In Rev 13:13 signs are performed by a second beast who leads astray the inhabitants of the earth. Perhaps the false prophets are to be understood as those who proclaim others as the Messiah (as for example the speakers in v 26). Both nouns are to be understood as the subjects of the verbs, i.e., ἐγερθήσονται, "will arise," and δώσουσιν, "will do" (διδόναι, lit. "give," can have this sense as well as ποιεῖν). One clear way in which these persons attempt to lead others astray is through the σημεῖα μεγάλα καὶ τέρατα, "great signs and wonders," they perform. The exact nature of these is not specified. τέρατα, "wonders," occurs in Matthew only here; σημεῖα, "signs," seldom has a positive meaning in Matthew and in the NT is modified by μεγάλα only in Luke 21:11; Acts 6:8; 8:13; Rev 12:1; 13:13; 15:1 (cf. Rev 19:20, where the false prophet does signs). The purpose of these mighty deeds is to lead astray the elect (ὥστε, "so that," and the infinitive here express purpose), if it were possible to do so. The implication of the εἰ δυνατόν, "if possible," is that the ἐκλεκτοί, "elect" or "chosen" (elsewhere in Matt 22:14; 24:22, 31), are in the care of their Father (cf. 10:29–31) and that it is therefore not within the power of these enemies to accomplish their purpose. The warnings in this passage against false prophets find an OT background in Deut 13:2–4. The disciples are not to be surprised by these developments: Jesus has foretold them (cf. John 13:19 where, however, a christological point is made of such foreknowledge).

**26** The warning of v 23 is now repeated in a twofold prohibition. The first claim, that the Messiah is ἐν τῇ ἐρήμῳ, "in the desert," results in the alteration of the negative formula from "do not believe" to μὴ ἐξέλθητε, "do not go out." That messianic deliverance would come from the desert was a widely shared expectation, which probably explains why John the Baptist began his ministry in the wilderness (cf. *Comment* on 3:1–12; see too 11:7; 1QS 8:12–14; Jos., *J.W.* 2.13.5 §261). The second claim, in abbreviated syntax, is that the Messiah is ἐν τοῖς ταμείοις, "in the private (or secret) rooms." This somewhat peculiar statement could have resulted from a misunderstanding of the underlying Aramaic, as Black speculates, which may have been bᵉʼidrayya, "in the Assemblies/Sanhedrin." More probably, however, the statement intends only a contrast with a fully public appearance in the desert (Matthew uses ταμεῖον in 6:6, referring to a private place of prayer; the only other NT occurrences of the word are in Luke 12:3, 24). Possibly underlying this warning is the notion that the Messiah would at first be only secretly present (cf. John 7:27; Str-B 1:86–87; see de Jonge). The disciples are not to believe (μὴ πιστεύσητε, "do not believe"; cf. v 23) such a claim in spite of whatever tribulation they may experience or whatever miraculous signs they may observe. As the evangelist next indicates, the return of the Son of Man will need no human heralds and will rest on no doubtful human claims.

**27** With the unmistakable clarity and suddenness of ἀστραπή, "lightning" (the only other occurrence in Matthew is in 28:3), flashing from one end of the sky to the other (cf. Luke 17:24; Zech 9:14; *2 Apoc. Bar.* 53:8–10), ἡ παρουσία τοῦ υἱοῦ τοῦ ἀνθρώπου, "the parousia of the Son of Man," will occur. Here finally is an answer to one of the questions asked by the disciples in v 3, namely, "What will be the sign of your parousia?" In addition to these two occurrences of the word παρουσία (lit. "coming" or "presence"), it occurs twice again in this chapter in precisely the same clause, οὕτως ἔσται ἡ παρουσία τοῦ υἱοῦ τοῦ ἀνθρώπου, "thus will be the coming of the Son of Man" (vv 37, 39), which thereby becomes a kind of refrain in response to the initial question. παρουσία, "parousia," which does not occur elsewhere in the Gospels, becomes an important word in the Pauline vocabulary (e.g., 1 Cor 15:23; 1 Thess 2:19; 3:13; and elsewhere) and also occurs in other NT writings (e.g., Jas 5:7–8:2; 2 Peter 3:4; 1 John 2:28). There is no special significance to Matthew's reference to east and west other than perhaps a smoothing out of Q (cf. Luke 17:24), although the language does connote comprehensiveness for Matthew (cf. 8:11). As there can be no doubt about the perception of lightning, there will be no doubt concerning the appearance of the Messiah, here referred to as the coming of the Son of Man.

**28** This proverb, rather more enigmatic than others in the Gospels, occurs also in Luke 17:37b, where it is spoken in response to the question "Where, Lord?" apparently concerning the location either of the one "taken" or the one "left." The imagery of flesh-eating birds is found elsewhere in the OT (Job 39:27–30; Hab 1:8) and NT (Rev 19:17–21). The most natural application of the imagery is to judgment, which may be the point of the proverb here. When the Son of Man comes, the judgment of the world will take place (cf. vv 30, 39, 51; 25:30, 46). On the other hand, since there is no reference to judgment in the immediate context, it may be that the proverb points primarily to the unmistakable character of the parousia. Thus, as surely as you know that where you see vultures gathered there is a carcass, so you will not be able to miss the coming of the Son of Man. This interpretation has the advantage of being fully consonant with the context of the immediately preceding verses. Whether οἱ ἀετοί refers to "eagles" or "vultures" does not matter (the two were often classed together), but a reference to the Romans does not make sense here, as it might have in the preceding pericope; nor does the carrion symbolize anything in particular. As tempting as it appears to many commentators, the proverb need not be allegorized.

*Explanation*

Jesus teaches his disciples not to be overeager in their acceptance of messianic claimants no matter what impressive miraculous deeds may accompany them and despite what may seem like an unwarranted delay in the appearance of the Messiah, aggravated by the ongoing experience of suffering. There is only one true answer to the church's agony and longing in the present interim period: the real coming of the Son of Man, whose advent will be as conspicuous as lightning in the sky. All those who offer easier alternatives in the present, who seem to offer a way out of sufferings and the promise of eschatological blessings before the eschaton, are pretenders: false prophets and false messiahs. The disciples are not to be taken in by their claims. There is in the church, of course, a degree of eschatology already realized through the ministry of the Holy Spirit. That experience of fulfillment, however, always stands in tension with the continuing fallenness of the world and our own unredeemed bodies. Every attempt to break that tension by greater claims of fulfillment, to force the kingdom by greater deeds of power or by messianic claims, must be regarded as false and dangerous. The parousia of the Son of Man brooks no rivals. It and it alone remains the hope of God's people. And by its very nature there is no way in which it can possibly be missed.

# *The Return of the Son of Man  (24:29–36)*

## *Bibliography*

**Burkitt, F. C.** "On *Immediately* in Mt 24.29." *JTS* 12 (1911) 460–61. **Dupont, J.** "La parable de figuier qui bourgeonne (Mc 13, 28–29 et par)." *RB* 75 (1968) 462–63. **Fascher, E.** "'Von dem Tage aber und von der Stunde weiss niemand . . .': Der Anstoss in Mark. 13, 32 (Matth. 24, 36): Eine exegetische Skizze zum Verhältnis von historisch-kritischer und christologischer Interpretation." In *Ruf und Antwort*. FS E. Fuchs. Leipzig: Koehler und Amelang, 1964. 475–83. **Glasson, T. F.** "The Ensign of the Son of Man ( Matt. xxiv. 30)." *JTS* 15 (1964) 299–300. **Grässer, E.** *Die Naherwartung Jesu*. SBS 61. Stuttgart: Katholisches Bibelwerk, 1973. **Higgins, A. J. B.** "The Sign of the Son of Man (Matt. xxiv. 30 )." *NTS* 9 (1962–63) 380–82. **Holman, C. L.** "The Idea of an Imminent Parousia in the Synoptic Gospels." *Studia Biblica et Theologica* 3 (1973) 15–31. **Joüon, P.** "Les forces des cieux seront ébranlées (Mt 24,29; Mc 13,25; Lc 21,26)." *RSR* 29 (1939) 114–15. **Kidder, S. J.** "'This Generation' in Matthew 24:34." *AUSS* 21 (1983) 203–9. **Kümmel, W. G.** "Die Naherwartung in der Verkündigung Jesu." In *Zeit und Geschichte*. FS R. Bultmann, ed. E. Dinkler. Tübingen: Mohr, 1964. 31–46. **Künzi, M.** *Das Naherwartungslogion Mk 9.1 par: Geschichte seiner Auslegung, mit einem Nachwort zur Auslegungsgeschichte von Markus 13.30 par.* Tübingen: Mohr, 1977. 213–24. **Lövestam, E.** "The ἡ γενεὰ αὕτη Eschatology in Mk 13, 30 parr." In *L'apocalypse johannique et l'apocalyptique dans le Nouveau Testament*, ed. J. Lambrecht. BETL 53. Gembloux: Duculot, 1980. 403–13. ———. *Jesus and 'this Generation.'* ConBNT 25. Stockholm: Almqvist & Wiksell, 1995. **Malvy, A.** "Cette géneration ne passera pas." *RSR* 14 (1924) 539–44. **Meinertz, M.** "'Dieses Geschlecht' im Neuen Testament." *BZ* 1 (1957) 283–89. **Merklein, H.** "Untergang und Neuschöpfung: Zur theologischen Bedeutung neutestamentlicher Texte vom 'Ende' der Welt." In *Biblische Randbemerkungen*. FS R. Schnackenburg, ed. H. Merklein und J. Lange. Würzburg: Echter, 1974. 349–60. **Oberlinner, L.** "Die Stellung der 'Terminworte' in der eschatologischen Verkündigung des Neuen Testaments." In *Gegenwart und kommendes Reich*. FS A. Vögtle, ed. P. Fiedler and D. Zeller. Stuttgart: Katholisches Bibelwerk, 1975. 51–66. **Schnackenburg, R.** "Kirche und Parusie." In *Gott in Welt*. FS K. Rahner, ed. J. B. Metz et al. Freiburg: Herder, 1964. 1:551–78. **Schütz, R.** "Das Feigengleichnis der Synoptikern." *ZNW* 10 (1909) 333–34. **Wenham, D.** "'This Generation Will Not Pass . . .': A Study of Jesus' Future Expectation in Mark 13." In *Christ the Lord*. FS D. Guthrie, ed. H. H. Rowdon. Leicester: InterVarsity, 1982. 127–50. **Winandy, J.** "Le logion de l'ignorance (*Mc*, xiii, 32; *Mt*, xxiv, 36)." *RB* 75 (1968) 63–79. **Zeller, D.** "Prophetisches Wissen um die Zukunft in synoptischen Jesusworten." *TP* 52 (1977) 258–71.

## *Translation*

[29] *"And immediately after the tribulation of those days, the sun will be made dark*

> *and the moon will not give its light*
> *and the stars will fall from the sky* [a]
> *and the powers of heaven*[b] *will be shaken.*

[30] *And then the sign of the Son of Man will appear in the sky,*[c] *and then*[d] *all the tribes of the earth will mourn, and they will see the Son of Man coming on the clouds of heaven with power and great glory.* [31] *And he will send his angels with a great trumpet call,*[e] *and they will gather together his chosen ones from the four winds, from one end of heaven to the other.*[f] [32] *Learn the meaning of the parable concerning the fig tree: Just when its branch becomes tender and it sprouts leaves, you know that summer is near.* [33] *Thus also you, when you see all these things, know that he*[g] *is near, at the doors.* [34] *Truly I tell you that this generation will by no means pass away before all these things*[h] *happen.* [35] *Heaven and earth will pass away, but my words will never pass away.*[i] [36] *But concerning that day and hour no one knows, neither the angels of heaven, nor the Son,*[j] *but the*[k] *Father alone.* "

## Notes

[a] τοῦ οὐρανοῦ, lit. "the heaven."

[b] τῶν οὐρανῶν, lit. "the heavens."

[c] Or, "in heaven." To οὐρανῷ many MSS add the definite article τῷ (W *f*[1,13] TR). D has the pl. οὐρανοῖς.

[d] A few MSS (ℵ* e mae) omit τότε, "then," which has already occurred at the beginning of the verse.

[e] σάλπιγγος μεγάλης, lit. "great trumpet"; many MSS (B *f*[13] TR sa) add φωνῆς, "sound (of)," or τῆς φωνῆς, "the sound (of)" (D lat), perhaps through the influence of Exod 19:16. See *TCGNT*, 61–62.

[f] D it add: "When the beginning of these things happens, look up and lift your heads because your redemption draws near," taken from the parallel in Luke 21:28, with which it agrees verbatim except for ἀναβλέψατε, "look up," for ἀνακύψατε, "stand up."

[g] Since the subject is included in the verb form, possibly "it."

[h] A few MSS (1424 aur b f ff[1] vg[mss]) omit ταῦτα, "these things," perhaps to soften the difficulty of the verse.

[i] ℵ* omits v 35 in its entirety, perhaps judging it alien to the context.

[j] Many MSS (ℵ[1] L W 0133 *f*[1] TR g[1] l vg sy co) omit οὐδὲ ὁ υἱός, "neither the Son," clearly for christological reasons. Including the phrase are ℵ[*2] B D Θ *f*[13] 28 it vg[mss]. Metzger notes that "the presence of μόνος ['only' or 'alone'] and the cast of the sentence as a whole" favor the originality of the phrase (*TCGNT*, 62).

[k] K W Γ f insert μου, "my."

## *Form/Structure/Setting*

A. After the extended discussion in vv 4–28 of the era preceding the coming of the Son of Man, with its full complement of trial and suffering leading the unknowledgeable to the hasty and mistaken conclusion that these events themselves marked the end, the discourse finally turns to the climactic event that *alone* signals the end of the age: the coming of the Son of Man on the clouds of heaven. This is described using apocalyptic imagery that emphasizes the gathering of the elect, while the concomitant judgment is left implicit (v 30). The pericope contains a striking juxtaposition of stress on imminence and reference to the indeterminacy of the time of the parousia of the Son of Man.

B. For this pericope Matthew continues to follow Mark very closely (here 13:24–32). Only in the first half of v 30 do we find a substantial departure from Mark, in material that is unique to Matthew, who probably has created the reference to "the sign of the Son of Man" to correspond to the question of v 3. The reference to the "tribes of the earth" mourning seems to be drawn from standard apocalyptic imagery. As for changes of the Markan text, the following should be noted. In v 29 Matthew adds (see Burkitt) the very problematic initial εὐθέως, "immediately," seemingly to tie this pericope more closely with what precedes. In v 30 Matthew conforms the language more closely to the language of Dan 7:13 by changing Mark's ἐν νεφέλαις, "in (the) clouds" (Mark 13:26), to ἐπὶ τῶν νεφελῶν τοῦ οὐρανοῦ, "on the clouds of heaven." In the same verse Matthew shifts πολλῆς, "much" or "great," to after δόξης, "glory," so that it also modifies the latter. In v 31 Matthew adds μετὰ σάλπιγγος μεγάλης, "with a great trumpet," again from standard apocalyptic vocabulary, and substitutes οὐρανῶν, "heavens," for Mark's γῆς, "earth" (Mark 13:27), thereby making the termini the ends of heaven rather than Mark's mixture of "the ends of the earth to the ends of heaven." Matthew's changes of the Markan text in the parable of the fig tree and the following logia are very minor. We may note only the addition in v 33 of πάντα, "all," to Mark's simple ταῦτα, "these things" (Mark 13:29; but cf. Mark 13:30); the omission of Mark's redundant γινόμενα, "happening," in the same clause; and finally the addition of the concluding μόνος, "only" (v 36), which adds force to the preceding negations. Formally, v 34 is strikingly similar to the syntax of 5:18.

C. This pericope finds more unity in content than of form, which consists of a quotation of OT material (v 29), a reference to the coming of the Son of Man (vv 30–31, with again allusion to the OT), a parable and its application (vv 32–33), a warning to the present generation (v 34), an independent logion (v 35), and finally a logion concerning knowledge of the time of the end (v 36). The following outline may be suggested: (1) the coming of the Son of Man (vv 29–30); (2) the gathering of the elect (v 31); (3) the lesson of the fig tree (vv 32–33); (4) fulfillment to the present generation (v 34); (5) the lasting character of Jesus' words (v 35); and (6) the time known only to the Father (v 36). Parallelism is found at two points in the pericope: in the four clauses of the OT material in v 29 (Matthew seems responsible for this parallelism, consisting of four subjects and four future verbs connected by καί) and in the parable and its application in vv 32 and 33, where syntactically the parallelism is nearly exact (ὅταν clauses; γινώσκετε; object clauses introduced by ὅτι). Also note the deliberately rhyming κόψονται, "they will mourn," and ὄψονται, "they will see," of v 30, probably reflecting the influence of oral tradition.

D. Vv 30–31 in pre-synoptic oral form are probably behind Paul's reference to the parousia of Christ in 1 Thess 4:16; even more extensive reflection of this same material is found in *Did.* 16:6–8; 10.5. A reference to the "changing" of sun, moon, and stars, probably dependent upon this material (v 29), occurs in *Barn.* 15:5, while *1 Clem.* 23:3–4 (and *2 Clem.* 11:2–3) may reflect the tradition underlying the fig-tree analogy (vv 32–33), used there in a discussion of the problem of the delay of the parousia.

### Comment

**29**   The meaning of τὴν θλῖψιν τῶν ἡμερῶν ἐκείνων, "the tribulation of those days," is much debated. Two major possibilities present themselves: (1) the words refer to the desecration of the temple and the destruction of Jerusalem prophesied in v 2 and probably referred to in vv 15–22 if not also vv 23–28 (see *Comment* for these two passages) or (2) a yet future experience of great suffering, an intensification of the suffering of the interim era, to be experienced just prior to the parousia, of which the judgment of Jerusalem is only a foreshadowing. The first interpretation would seem to have the clear advantage, given the context, were it not for the decidedly complicating presence of Matthew's added εὐθέως, "immediately."

### Excursus: Imminence, Delay, and Matthew's εὐθέως

Running through the the prophecies of eschatological or quasi-eschatological events in the Gospel of Matthew are strands of imminence and delay. One of the greatest challenges for the interpreter is to bring these diverse strands together, and that is also the particular challenge of the present discourse.

In regard to the length of time itself, several of the imminence sayings in Matthew fit the fall of Jerusalem particularly well. Thus the references to "this generation" not passing before some predicted event takes place (23:36; 24:34) and also the reference to "some standing here who will not taste death before . . ." (16:28) make especially good sense if they refer to the approximately forty years between the time of Jesus and the fall of Jerusalem. Possibly also 10:23 is to be understood in the same way.

References to the parousia and the accompanying final judgment, on the other hand, contain a consistent note of delay. We may point, for example, to 24:6, 8 but particularly to the parables of chaps. 24 and 25 (see esp. 24:48: "my master is delayed"; 25:5: "the bridegroom was delayed"; and 25:19: "after a long time"). In agreement with this motif of delay are such things as the choosing of the twelve (4:19), the building of the church (16:18–19; 18:18), the need to proclaim the gospel to the nations (24:14; 28:19), and Jesus' promise to be with his people to the end of the age (28:20). These verses presuppose an interim period of unspecified length between the death of Jesus and the parousia, although the evangelist may well have believed that the period of forty years satisfied the various requirements, including the preaching of the gospel to the nations (cf. Paul's view in Rom 10:18). He also may have regarded the interim as sufficiently long to account for the delay passages.

Two key facts provide the basis for understanding these complex data. The first of these is the statement of Jesus in 24:32 (= Mark 13:32) that "about that day and hour no one knows, neither the angels of heaven, nor the Son, but only the Father"—a statement that the early church can hardly have created. This overt statement concerning Jesus' own ignorance of the time of the parousia makes it virtually impossible that he ever himself spoke of the imminence of that event. The second key fact is that the disciples were unable to conceive of the fall of Jerusalem apart from the occurrence of the parousia and the end of the age (as the question of 24:3 indicates). In light of these two facts, the following conclusion becomes plausible. Although Jesus taught the imminent fall of Jerusalem, he did not teach the imminence of the parousia, leaving the latter to the undetermined future (cf. the sayings about the impossibility of knowing the time of the parousia and about the consequent need for being constantly ready: e.g., 24:42, 44, 50; 25:13). The disciples, however, upon hearing the prophecy of the destruction of the temple, thought immediately of the parousia and the end of the age. Knowing that Jesus had taught the imminence of the fall of the temple, they naturally assumed the imminence of the parousia. In their minds, the two were inseparable. Consequently, the imminence that was a part of the destruction of the temple prophecy now became attached to the parousia itself, and they began to speak of both as imminent.

We are now in a position to understand Matthew's redactional insertion of $\epsilon\dot{v}\theta\acute{\epsilon}\omega\varsigma$, "immediately," in v 29. He means that immediately (not simply "very soon after" as Bruner argues) after the destruction and desecration of the temple the parousia is to be expected. This, as we have argued, is only conceivable if the evangelist writes before and not after A.D. 70. To be sure, the material concerning the uncertainty of the time of the parousia noted above has not been integrated into the statement made by the evangelist here. No hypothesis, however, is able to dissolve completely the tensions that lie in the material of the discourse. In my opinion the evangelist uses material from Jesus that is not finally compatible with the association of the parousia with the fall of Jerusalem.

It need hardly be said that the words $\mu\epsilon\tau\grave{\alpha}\ \tau\grave{\eta}\nu\ \theta\lambda\hat{\iota}\psi\iota\nu\ \tau\hat{\omega}\nu\ \dot{\eta}\mu\epsilon\rho\hat{\omega}\nu\ \dot{\epsilon}\kappa\epsilon\acute{\iota}\nu\omega\nu$, "after the suffering of those days," governed by Matthew's "immediately," have been understood very differently. The futurist interpretation is the main rival to the view taken here. A priori convictions concerning a late, post A.D. 70 date together with the inserted "immediately" necessitate seeing the intended tribulation as a yet future one. Thus commonly vv 15–28 are taken, as we have seen, to refer to an eschatological tribulation and the coming of the Antichrist, as in 2 Thess 2:3–4 (as, e.g., McNeile, Grundmann, Hill, Schweizer, Gundry, Patte, and Harrington; cf. Burnett, Broer [who tries to soften Matthew's "immediately" to mean "still within this generation" (218)]). This conclusion means, however, that no answer is given in the discourse to the initial question concerning the fall of Jerusalem and that the discourse therefore has no relevance to the original readers of the Gospel. The setting up of the desolating abomination in the temple must also on this view either anticipate the rebuilding of the temple (referred to specifically in Matthew's redaction) or be taken metaphorically, and unnaturally, as referring to something such as the Holy Land or the community of God. It is furthermore hardly legitimate to read the passage in the light of 2 Thess 2:3–4, a passage that is based on the present material in oral form.

Other scholars, while allowing that vv 15–22 refer to the fall of Jerusalem, in order to accommodate the "immediately" of v 29 take vv 23–28 as referring to some other, later time just prior to the eschaton (cf. Morris; Blomberg; Carson: "the entire interadvent period of *thlipsis*"). It is clear, however, that the content of vv 23–28 corresponds closely to that of vv 4–14. These verses, which speak only vaguely of the danger of pseudo-messiahs and false prophets, effectively frame the only reference to a specific event in the whole of vv 4–28, namely, vv 15–22 with their reference to the desecration of the temple and the accompanying instructions about fleeing.

It is very difficult to believe that the words "immediately after the tribulation of those days" refer only to something general in the indeterminate future. Rather than something vague, the words seem to require a specific antecedent (note both the definite article $\tau\acute{\eta}\nu$ and the demonstrative pronoun $\dot{\epsilon}\kappa\epsilon\acute{\iota}\nu\omega\nu$). The only specific item in the preceding context that could correspond to "*the* suffering of *those* days" is the desecration of the temple referred to in v 15.

Finally, mention should be made of those who find a deliberate double reference in vv 15–28, both to the fall of Jerusalem and to the sufferings of the end time and the Antichrist (e.g., C. E. B. Cranfield, *The Gospel according to St Mark* [Cambridge: Cambridge UP, 1966] 402); Ford, *The Abomination of Desolation;* Agbanou, *Le discours eschatologique;* Meier; Bruner). While it is indeed true that from our perspective we may see a double reference in the material, it is extremely unlikely that the evangelist had any such thing in mind. The "immediately" of v 29, however, leaves no time for a secondary reference to something in the future that must precede the parousia. But just as Jesus and the evangelist had no trouble applying the symbolism of Daniel to the fall of Jerusalem yet to occur, so may we perceive the fall of Jerusalem as an anticipation of the final judgment. The desolating sacrilege of 24:15 and a time of indescribable suffering that is cut short only for the sake of the elect can easily suggest to us a time of future crisis that truly brings us to the brink of the eschaton. With Paul we can see the imagery as pointing ultimately to the Antichrist of the end of time (2 Thess 2:3–4). Matthew's "immediately," however, indicates that he thought of the end as imminent, as the concluding component of the destruction of Jerusalem. (For a fuller treatment of this subject, see Hagner, "Imminence and Parousia in the Gospel of Matthew.")

For solid refutation of the Dispensationalist understanding of this material, see Carson's and Bruner's perceptive remarks.

The lines used to describe the changes in the sun, moon and stars are drawn from the language of the LXX. Thus the reference to the sun being darkened and the moon not giving its light is taken from the apocalyptic material of Isa 13:10 (the only significant difference is Matthew's synonym φέγγος [cf. Joel 2:10 and 4:15] for φῶς, "light"). Although Isa 13:10 also mentions the stars not giving their light, Matthew next alludes to the LXX of Isa 34:4: "all the stars will fall [πεσεῖται] like leaves from a vine and as leaves fall from a fig tree [ἀπὸ συκῆς]" (with this last point, cf. the fig tree parable of vv 32–33). Only Matthew's ἀπὸ τοῦ οὐρανοῦ, "from the sky," added to complete the sense, is not verbally paralleled in these LXX passages. The fourth line, καὶ αἱ δυνάμεις τῶν οὐρανῶν σαλευθήσονται, "and the powers of heaven will be shaken," finds no direct parallel in the OT but is similar to the statement in Joel 2:10: "the heaven will be shaken" (σεισθήσεται); cf. Isa 34:4: "the heaven will be rolled up like a scroll" (cf. Isa 13:13; Hag 2:6; 2:21: "I will shake [σείω] the heavens"). Matthew's reference to αἱ δυνάμεις, "the powers," of heaven is probably not a reference to spiritual beings (as is probably the case in Rom 8:38; Eph 1:21; 1 Peter 3:22) but, in keeping with the first three lines, a further reference to the objects of the sky. As G. R. Beasley-Murray (*A Commentary on Mark Thirteen* [London: Macmillan, 1957] 87) points out, in some witnesses to the LXX text (B L) of Isa 34:4 the same Hebrew expression, כָּל־צְבָא, *kol-ṣĕbāʾ*, is alternately translated πᾶσαι αἱ δυνάμεις, "all the powers," and πάντα τὰ ἀστέρα, "all the stars." The coming of the Son of Man, in short, will be attended by unusual phenomena in the sky. Apocalyptic imagery of this sort became commonly used in depicting the coming of eschatological judgment (in addition to passages already cited, see Amos 8:9; Ezek 32:7–8; *1 Enoch* 80:2–8; 102:2; 2 Esdr 5:4–5; see Hagner, *NIDNTT* 3:730–37).

**30** When Matthew introduces the reference to the appearance of τὸ σημεῖον τοῦ υἱοῦ τοῦ ἀνθρώπου ἐν οὐρανῷ, "the sign of the Son of Man in heaven," with τότε, "then," and introduces the following reference to the actual coming of the Son of Man with another τότε, he makes it impossible to take the sign as either the phenomena in the sky of v 29 or as itself (as an appositional genitive) the coming of the Son of Man mentioned in the last half of the present verse (contra Gundry; Bruner). Matthew thus apparently regards the appearing of the sign of the Son of Man as something independent of both, but if so, it is very difficult to know what he had in mind. It is obviously some further spectacular event that will by its conspicuousness alert the world to what immediately follows, the parousia itself (cf. the question of v 3). Possibly the "sign" is the setting up of an "ensign," which is often mentioned (see, e.g., Isa 18:3; 49:22; Jer 4:21; 1QM 2:15–4:17) together with a trumpet call (thus Glasson, Schweizer, Hill). The early church eventually identified the sign as the cross (see *Apocalypse of Peter* 1; *Epistula Apostolorum* 16; so too Higgins), naturally identifying its symbol with the sign of the Son of Man, but its view like every other must remain speculative (for discussion see K. H. Rengstorf, *TDNT* 7:236–38).

Following the second τότε, "then," is the reference to the coming of the Son of Man, but this is preceded, probably for emphasis, by the reference to the mourning of "all the tribes of the earth" (πᾶσαι αἱ φυλαὶ τῆς γῆς), unique to Matthew. This language is virtually the same as that of Zech 12:10–14 (where both the same verb as in Matthew, κόψεται, "mourn," and the phrase πᾶσαι αἱ φυλαί, "all the tribes," as well as ἡ γῆ, here meant as "the land [of Israel]," occur—this in connection with looking on "me whom they have pierced" [LXX: "mocked"]). In keeping with Matthew's universal perspective, the tribes of the earth, which in the OT originally meant the tribes of Israel, are to be understood as all the nations of the earth (cf. 25:32). The same combination of Zech 12:10–14 and the Dan 7:13 reference to the coming of the Son of Man is found in Rev 1:7, which suggests that the combination depends upon early Christian tradition rather than upon a common source. The actual assertion concerning the parousia is made using the words from Dan 7:13, quoted again in the Gospel in 26:64 and alluded to earlier in 10:23. Carson is quite correct in denying any obstacle to understanding Dan 7:13–14 as a reference to the parousia, i.e., Christ's return to the earth. Here alone is mention made of μετὰ δυνάμεως καὶ δόξης πολλῆς, "with power and great glory," which is implied already in the words of Daniel, ἐπὶ τῶν νεφελῶν τοῦ οὐρανοῦ, "upon the clouds of heaven." The attempt of Tasker, S. Brown ("The Matthean Apocalypse"), France, and Garland to understand these words as referring not to the parousia but to the fall of Jerusalem in A.D. 70 is hardly convincing. It is apparently forced by Matthew's "immediately" but goes against the normal use of the language (see Wenham's critique). The parousia of the Son of Man has the marks of a theophany, here heightened by the eschatological and thus consummative character of this event. The mourning of humanity before the prospect of the imminent judgment that must accompany this event is readily comprehensible (cf. 16:27, where the glory of the return of the Son of Man is also connected with judgment; see too 2 Thess 1:7–8).

**31** A part of the end-time expectation of Israel was the gathering of the dispersed people of God from the four corners of the earth (see, e.g., Deut 30:4; Isa 60:4; Jer 32:37; Ezek 34:13; 36:24). Matthew's language (ἐκ τῶν τεσσάρων ἀνέμων ἀπ᾽ ἄκρων οὐρανῶν ἕως [τῶν] ἄκρων αὐτῶν, lit. "from the four winds, from the ends of heaven to its ends") is close to that of the LXX of Zech 2:10: ἐκ τῶν τεσσάρων ἀνέμων τοῦ οὐρανοῦ συνάξω ὑμᾶς, λέγει κύριος, "from the four winds of heaven I will gather you, says the Lord." The point of Matthew's (like Mark's) statement is the comprehensiveness or universality of the gathering of the saints. The involvement of the angels in this eschatological gathering of the people is referred to also in 13:41; 16:27; 25:31–32, where, however, in each case the gathering concerns the judgment of the wicked (a twofold gathering, for judgment and blessing, is found in 13:30, but the gathering of the righteous remains implicit in 13:41; cf. John 11:52). The gathering of the ἐκλεκτούς, "elect" (see too 22:14; 24:22, 24), refers here not simply to the gathering of Israel but to the gathering of Christian disciples, both Jews and Gentiles. The reference to the blowing of a great σάλπιγγος, "trumpet" (the word occurs in Matthew only here), in connection with the gathering of the righteous is found in Isa 27:13 (in the NT a reference to the eschatological trumpet occurs in conjunction with the descent of the Lord from heaven in 1 Thess 4:16; there as in 1 Cor 15:52 the trumpet is associated with the resurrection of the dead, which Matthew makes no mention of here). With the glorious coming of the Son of Man will be the gathering of the righteous and their subsequent vindication and reward (cf. 25:34).

**32–33** The point of the parable of the fig tree is a simple one. When a fig tree begins to sprout leaves, one knows that summer is near. In the same way, when certain events take place, one may know that the end is near. Yet the components of the analogy (v 33) are difficult to understand. Matthew's πάντα ταῦτα, "all these things" (cf. Mark's simple ταῦτα, "these things"), should probably be taken to include everything spoken of in vv 4–28, that is, all the signs prior to the parousia, including the fall of Jerusalem. The exegesis of this phrase cannot be separated from the understanding of the final clause of v 33, ἐγγύς ἐστιν ἐπὶ θύραις, "he [possibly: 'it'] is near, at the doors," which in turn may be governed by the understanding of v 34. With the immediately preceding context of this parable referring so unmistakably to the parousia of the Son of Man, the most natural understanding of "he (it) is near, at the doors" (for this expression, referring to the eschatological Judge, cf. Jas 5:9) is that it refers to the coming of the Son of Man. But just as the sprouting fig tree indicates that summer is near but not yet present, so the coming of the Son of Man is near but not yet present. The πάντα ταῦτα, "all these things," cannot include the parousia itself; they mean merely that all is in readiness. The coming of the Son of Man may occur at any time.

**34** The πάντα ταῦτα, "all these things," of this verse can include no more than the same phrase in the preceding verse and thus cannot include the coming of the Son of Man (so too Blomberg). The phrase refers not only to general marks of the interim period such as tribulation, distress, pseudo-messiahs, and false prophets but specifically, and dramatically, to the desecration of the temple and the destruction of Jerusalem (cf. vv 15–22). As in the other imminence sayings (cf. 16:28; 10:23; 23:36), all of which like the present logion are prefaced by the emphatic ἀμὴν λέγω ὑμῖν, "truly I tell you," formula, the main point is that the fall of Jerusalem was to be experienced by *that* generation (*pace* Kidder), those listening there and then to the teaching of Jesus (ἡ γενεὰ αὕτη, "this generation," is used consistently in the Gospel to refer to Jesus' contemporaries; cf. 11:16; 12:41–42, 45; 23:36). The attempt to explain ἡ γενεὰ αὕτη, "this generation," as the generation alive at the time of the parousia or more generally as the human race or people of God goes against the natural meaning of the phrase and makes the words irrelevant both to Jesus' listeners and to Matthew's readers. The fact that, as Lövestam has shown, the expression clearly alludes to a *sinful* generation, one ripe for judgment, fits the fall of Jerusalem (and not merely the end of the age, which is Lövestam's conclusion).

**35** This verse is parenthetical, perhaps having been initially suggested to the evangelist by the previous reference to the passing of "this generation." Heaven and earth, seemingly so permanent, are transitory and are destined to pass away in their present form with the dawning of the eschaton (cf. Isa 51:6; 2 Peter 3:7, 11–12). By contrast, the words of Jesus (οἱ δὲ λόγοι μου, "but my words") will endure forever. They are thereby made the equivalent of the word of God, which is the usual contrasting element in such statements (e.g., Isa 40:8). In the present context, the emphasis falls not on the teaching of Jesus generally (as, e.g., in 7:24, 26) but on the authority and reliability of his words concerning the future. Though all else of the present order will pass away, the words of Jesus will not fail.

**36** In very strong contrast to the emphasis in v 33 concerning what *can* be known—namely, the experienced signs of the interim up to the point of the nearness of the parousia of the Son of Man—the present verse clearly indicates the *impossibility* of knowing the time of the Son of Man's coming and the end of the age in advance of their actual occurrence (cf. the question of v 3 concerning πότε, "when," these events would occur). This stress on our ignorance of the actual time of the parousia continues through the next several pericopes (cf. vv 39, 42, 44, 50; 25:13). τῆς ἡμέρας ἐκείνης καὶ ὥρας, "of that day and hour," refers to *the* event, the climactic return of the Son of Man, which by this formula (for "day and hour," see v 50; 25:13; "day and hour" are split in vv 42, 44) is said to be beyond human determination altogether, and not just partially, e.g., so that, say, the month or year *could* be known (rightly Meinertz, Lövestam, Carson, Blomberg). What is so remarkable in the present verse is the statement that "neither the angels of heaven nor the Son [οὐδὲ ὁ υἱός]" know the time of the parousia. It is little wonder that many copyists (here, as in the Markan parallel) omitted this reference to the ignorance of the Son as seemingly incompatible with the Christology of the early church. The omniscience of the Son, however, is not a requirement of Matthew's very high Christology, and the ignorance of the Son on a matter such as this is compatible with the development of a kenosis doctrine (i.e., an "emptying" of divine prerogatives) such as Paul (Phil 2:6–8) and his predecessors had already developed—and with which Matthew, with his embracing of the full humanity of Jesus, would no doubt have been quite comfortable. The time of the coming of the Son of Man is in the keeping of "the Father alone" (ὁ πατὴρ μόνος; cf. Acts 1:7; for OT background, see the LXX of Zech 14:7: "there will be one day, and that day is known to the Lord [γνωστὴ τῷ κυρίῳ]"; cf. 2 *Apoc. Bar.* 21:8).

### Explanation

History will be full of suffering and evil, including the catastrophe of the fall of Jerusalem, that will seem to herald the eschaton and the coming of the promised one. But the coming of the Son of Man, when it occurs, will be so startling and conspicuous, so glorious and great, that it will need no proclaimers and no interpretation. In agreement with apocalyptic expectation of the first century, the nations will mourn the prospect of their judgment while the elect will be gathered together in joyful anticipation of entering into their inheritance. What must be differentiated, however, are the signs of the approach of the eschaton and the eschaton itself. The former can be known with all certainty; the time of the latter remains hidden. Consequently, every generation since the time of Jesus has been confronted with the reality of signs pointing to the end, and the Son of Man could have come to any of those generations, including the present generation. But the actual time of the parousia and the end of the age is known only to God. Uncertainty concerning the time is in a sense a non-issue; the *fact* of the future return of the Son of Man is what counts. The information that *is* available to us is intended not for its own sake, or to satisfy our curiosity about the future, or to enable us to relax until just before the event. Instead, what we can know, the signs that we *can* discern—everything that points to the apparent imminence of the end—all of this is meant, as the following pericopes will show, to motivate us to appropriate conduct in the present. NT teaching about eschatology finds its proper outcome in ethical living rather than in the speculations of so-called prophecy conferences.

# Uncertainty concerning the Time of the Return of the Son of Man (24:37–44)

### Bibliography

**Bauckham, R.** "Synoptic Parousia Parables and the Apocalypse." *NTS* 23 (1977) 165–69. **Falke, J.** "'Bei der Wiederkunft des Menschensohnes': Eine Meditation zu Mt 24,36–42." *BibLeb* 6 (1965) 208–12. **Geoltrain, P.** "Dans l'ignorance du jour, veillez." *AsSeign* 5 (1969) 17–29. **Gollinger, H.** "'Ihr wisst nicht, an welchem Tag euer Herr kommt': Auslegung von Mt 24,37–51." *BibLeb* 11 (1970) 238–47. **Lövestam, E.** "The Parable of the Thief at Night." In *Spiritual Wakefulness in the New Testament.* LUÅ n.s. 1.55.3. Lund: Gleerup, 1963. 95–107. **Strobel, A.** "Das Gleichnis vom nächtlichen Einbrecher (Mt 24,43f)." In *Untersuchungen zum eschatologischen Verzögerungsproblem.* Leiden: Brill, 1961. 207–15. **Walvoord, J. F.** "Is Posttribulational Rapture Revealed in Matt 24?" *GTJ* 6 (1985) 257–66.

### Translation

[37] *"For just as the days of Noah were, thus it will be* [a] *in the time of* [b] *the parousia of the Son of Man.* [38] *For as they were in [those]* [c] *days before the flood, eating and drinking, marrying and giving their children* [d] *in marriage, until the day Noah entered the ark—* [39] *and they did not know until the flood came and destroyed* [e] *all of them—thus will be [also]* [f] *the parousia of the Son of Man.* [40] *Then there will be two men in the field; one will be taken and one will be left.* [41] *Two women will be grinding at the mill; one will be taken and one will be left.* [g]

[42] *Watch, therefore, because you do not know on what day* [h] *your Lord is coming.* [43] *But know this: that if the master of the house had known in which night-watch the thief was coming, he would have watched and would not have permitted him to break into his house.* [44] *Because of this you yourselves must also be ready, because in an hour you do not expect, the Son of Man is coming."*

### Notes

[a] Many MSS, perhaps influenced by the καί in v 39b, add καί, "also" (D W Θ *f*[1,13] TR lat sy[h]).
[b] "In the time of" added for clarity.
[c] ἐκείναις, "those," is omitted by ℵ L W Θ *f*[1,13] TR lat mae bo, resulting in the reading "the days." Including ἐκείναις are B D it sa, and thus the word is retained by the *UBSGNT*, but in brackets.
[d] "Their children" added.
[e] ἦρεν, lit. "swept away."

ᶠ Some MSS omit καί, "also," here (B D it vgᵐˢˢ syˢ·ᵖ·ʰ co), perhaps by the influence of v 37 (see *Note* a). Including the καί are ℵ L W Θ *f*¹·¹³ TR syʰ. The *UBSGNT* indicates the difficulty of deciding the question by including the word in brackets.

ᵍ D *f*¹³ it vgˢ add "two will be in one bed; one will be taken and one will be left," which is taken nearly verbatim from the parallel in Luke 17:34.

ʰ Many MSS (K L Γ TR lat syˢ·ᵖ saᵐˢ boᵖᵗ) have ὥρα, "hour," instead of "day," perhaps by harmonization with v 44.

### Form/Structure/Setting

A. Departing from Mark, Matthew now adds three pericopes (vv 37–44; 45–51; 25:1–13) that serve to illustrate the truth of the centrally important logion of v 36. The motif throughout these passages is the uncertainty of the time of the parousia and the accompanying end of the age. As Blomberg astutely observes, in the first parable (vv 37–41) the return of Christ is completely unexpected, while in the second (vv 45–51) the return is sooner than expected and in the third (25:1–13) it is later than expected. Since the time of the coming of the Son of Man cannot be known, Christians are called to be in a state of continuous readiness. Thus the burden of the eschatological discourse becomes the motivation of the Christian's conduct. This ethical emphasis dominates to the end of the discourse.

B. Except for the logion of v 42, which is drawn from Mark 13:35, Matthew apparently draws on Q for this passage (cf. Luke 17:26–35; 12:39–40). For vv 37–39 the following redactional changes may be noted. For Q's "in the day(s) of" the coming or revelation of the Son of Man (Luke 17:26, 30) Matthew twice substitutes the technical expression παρουσία, "parousia" (vv 37, 39; already used in vv 3 and 27), of the Son of Man. Matthew's reference at the beginning of v 38 to "as they were in [those] days before the flood," which with the following present participles forms a periphrastic construction, may well be a Matthean addition to Q (rather than reflecting a Lukan deletion of the material), perhaps to emphasize the continuing action and thus the unexpected catastrophe of the flood, the mention of which reflects Matthew's special emphasis on the eschatological judgment. One further Matthean addition seems apparent, the parenthetical and awkward καὶ οὐκ ἔγνωσαν, "and they did not know," which repeats exactly the main point that Matthew wants to emphasize in these and the following verses. Matthew probably abbreviates Q by omitting the material in Luke 17:28–29 concerning the parallel instance of Lot as well as that in Luke 17:31–33, some of which he has already used (cf. 24:17–18, for which, however, he is dependent on Mark; cf. also 10:39). In vv 40–41 Matthew follows Q quite closely (cf. Luke 17:34–35), changing ἐπὶ κλίνης, "in bed," to ἐν τῷ ἀγρῷ, "in the field," and ἐπὶ τὸ αὐτό, "together," to ἐν τῷ μύλῳ, "at the mill," and abbreviating Q slightly but preserving the symmetrical parallelism. In v 42, which appears to be dependent on Mark 13:35, Matthew substitutes the nonspecific ποίᾳ ἡμέρᾳ, "what day," for Mark's πότε, "when," and ὑμῶν, "your," for τῆς οἰκίας, "of the house," as the modifier of κύριος, "Lord," since the latter makes no sense apart from the Markan context. Matthew omits the remainder of Mark's sentence, "in the evening, or at midnight, or at cockcrow, or at dawn," apparently regarding it as redundant after "what day," which for Matthew is the important issue. Vv 43 and 44 again follow Q fairly closely (in a different context in Luke; cf. Luke 12:39–40). The following alterations may be noted. In v 43 Matthew probably changes ὥρᾳ, "hour" (cf. Luke 12:39), to φυλακῇ, "watch" (given Luke 12:38, it is unlikely that Luke changed φυλακῇ to ὥρᾳ). In the same verse, Matthew inserts ἐγρηγόρησεν ἄν, "he would have watched," picking up the verb in the exhortation of v 42. Finally, at the beginning of v 44 Matthew adds διὰ τοῦτο, lit. "because of this," in order to emphasize the concluding application.

C. The basic components of the pericope are two analogies (vv 37–39, 43) and two exhortations (vv 42, 44), all related to the central point of the uncertainty of the time of the coming of the Son of Man. The following may be suggested as an outline: (1) the analogy with the days of Noah (vv 37–39); (2) the sudden separation (vv 40–41); (3) the key exhortation to "watch" (v 42); (4) the analogy of the thief (v 43); and (5) the concluding application (v 44). The first analogy consists of two parallel sentences that have exactly parallel main clauses, "thus will be the parousia of the Son of Man," and corresponding subordinate clauses (introduced by ὥσπερ/ὡς, "as"), the second providing much fuller information to make the analogy understandable. Matthew has broken up the structure somewhat by his insertion of the parenthetical καὶ οὐκ ἔγνωσαν, "and they did not know" (v 39), which is then awkwardly linked with the following ἕως, "until," clause (which goes with the periphrastic construction more naturally). Within the subordinate clause of the second sentence, the four parallel present participles should be noted. Vv 40 and 41 present nearly exact symmetry, broken only by the feminine participle ἀλήθουσαι, "grinding," for the verb ἔσονται, "will be."

D. Several motifs of this pericope are picked up in early Christian writings. Thus the coming of the Son "as a thief in the night" can be found in 1 Thess 5:2; 2 Peter 3:10; Rev 16:15; *Gos. Thom.* 21, 103. The exhortation to "watch" is found in 1 Thess 5:6; Rev 3:3; *Did.* 16:1; *Gos. Thom.* 21. The stress on the impossibility of knowing the time of the parousia is also found in Rev 3:3; *Did.* 16:1.

### Comment

**37–39** The parousia of the Son of Man is likened to the suddenness with which Noah's contemporaries were overwhelmed by the flood (see Gen 6:5–24). The judgment motif, though left implicit, is obviously also pertinent, for the coming of the Son of Man will mean judgment for the wicked. The term παρουσία, "parousia," found only in Matthew in the Gospels, first occurs in the disciples' question (v 3) and then in the clause οὕτως ἔσται ἡ παρουσία τοῦ υἱοῦ τοῦ ἀνθρώπου, "thus will be the coming of the Son of Man," which becomes like a refrain, occurring in v 27 and twice here (vv 37, 39). Noah is referred to in Matthew only here (for the flood as a warning to later generations, see 2 Peter 2:5; 3:6). The periphrastic construction (εἰμί + present participle) stresses the ongoing activity mentioned in the four participles (all with the euphony of the same endings): τρώγοντες καὶ πίνοντες, γαμοῦντες καὶ γαμίζοντες, "eating and drinking, marrying and giving in marriage." No special significance is to be read into these particular participles. They stand merely as indicators of the living of everyday, ordinary life. The people of Noah's day were oblivious to all else than their own pleasurable living. And they had no inkling of the judgment that was to come upon them until it was too late: "they did not know [οὐκ ἔγνωσαν (i.e., the imminent danger)] until the flood [κατακλυσμός] came and swept them away." The reference to Noah entering the ark in v 38 is very close to the language of the LXX of Gen 7:7. The parousia of the Son of Man will in a similar way come suddenly upon an unsuspecting generation that is carrying on its ordinary activities. This fact leads to the main exhortation of the passage in v 42.

**40–41** At the time of the coming of the Son of Man there will be a division of humanity; some will be taken, some left behind. This is put very vividly in the reference to two men working in a field and two women grinding at the mill (the repeated μία is feminine). They are going about their normal activities, unaware of what is about to befall them, when suddenly one of them is taken and the other is left. Presumably those who are "taken" are among the elect whom the angels of the Son of Man are to gather at his coming (v 31), while those who are left await the prospect of judgment. The application of these verses is made clear in the exhortation that follows (note the οὖν, "therefore," in the next verse).

**42** The main purpose of this section of the discourse, from the present pericope (i.e., v 37) down to 25:13, which is a repetition of the exhortation of this verse, is to impress upon the disciples and the church the importance of being ready for the parousia when it occurs. Because the time of the event must remain unknown (cf. vv 36, 44, 50; 25:13), the followers of Christ are to remain in a state of constant readiness. γρηγορεῖτε, "watch," connotes not simply looking for but being prepared for the coming of the Son of Man. Thus the watching involves an active dimension, namely, the faithful, righteous conduct of the disciples (cf. v 46) that becomes the focus of the end of the discourse (cf. 25:14–46). For this sense of spiritual vigilance, cf. the use of γρηγορεῖν in 1 Cor 16:13; 1 Thess 5:6; 1 Peter 5:8; Rev 3:2–3; 16:15 (see esp. Lövestam). Reference to uncertainty concerning the ἡμέρα, "day," is made also in vv 36, 50; 25:13. In the present passage the second element, the "hour," is mentioned in v 44. This is the only place in Matthew where the expression κύριος ὑμῶν, "your Lord," is used.

**43** The further, simple analogy is drawn with the reference to the householder who would have watched had he known the time when the thief was going to break into his house. But since Christians cannot know the time of the coming of the Son of Man, it is implied that they must continuously watch, i.e., be always prepared, for his coming. From this logion of Jesus is drawn the image of his return as a thief in the night, where the point of comparison is, of course, only the sudden unexpectedness of his coming (cf. 1 Thess 5:2; 2 Peter 3:10; Rev 3:3; 16:15). The language of the thief breaking in (same noun, κλέπτης, "thief," and verb, διορύσσειν, lit. "to dig through [a house wall of dried mud]") has been used earlier by Matthew in 6:19–20. The οἰκοδεσπότης, "master of a house," also provides a number of analogies in Matthew (cf. 10:25; 13:27, 52; 20:1, 11; 21:33). Matthew's noun φυλακῇ, "watch" (cf. 14:25), fits particularly well with the verb ἐγρηγόρησεν ἄν, "he would have watched."

**44** A concluding application is made here, introduced by διὰ τοῦτο, "therefore" or lit. "on account of this." Inasmuch as the situation of Christians is similar to that of the housemaster, who did not know the time in which the thief would come, they (the ὑμεῖς, "you," is emphatic) are to be ἕτοιμοι, "ready" (the word is used in the very same sense, but as a noun, in 25:10; the only other occurrences of the word in Matthew are in 22:4, 8). The reason for the necessity of this readiness is stipulated once again in the ὅτι, "because," clause, which reaffirms the point already made in vv 36 and 42: the time of the parousia of the Son of Man cannot be known in advance. He is coming ἧ οὐ δοκεῖτε ὥρᾳ, "in an hour you do not expect." This is the only reference of this kind to ὥρα, "hour," alone and not to "day" too, probably because of the context provided by the preceding verse, where it is in an hour of the night that the thief breaks in. The "day" has been mentioned in v 42. Being "ready" here, as in the exhortation to "watch" in v 42 (and 25:13), means to be living righteously.

### Explanation

Although the world will have seen and experienced much that hints at the proximity of the eschaton, and perhaps precisely because of the pervasiveness of and the consequent inurement to, such "signs," there will be no time to prepare for the parousia of the Son of Man. In fact, since the time of this event cannot be known in advance, it will catch many by surprise, and they will consequently not be "ready." The exhortation to the disciples and the church, however, is to maintain themselves in a state of constant readiness. That is, disciples should be acting as disciples are supposed to act. Spiritual wakefulness, as Lövestam points out, means the living of life "in communion with the Lord and in faithfulness to him" (106). They must not be embarrassed at the time of the parousia, whenever it may occur. And thus in Jesus' eschatological discourse, at the beginning of the stream of eschatology in the the NT, eschatology and ethics are brought together. The NT writers, to their credit, never allow this connection to be broken. Eschatology is never presented for the sake of mere information but always and consistently as the motivation for ethical living. Again, the fact of the parousia, not the time of the parousia, is what matters. The evangelist stresses the need to be prepared for that coming reality.

# The Faithful and Wicked Servants    (24:45–51)

### Bibliography

**Bauckham, R.** "Synoptic Parousia Parables and the Apocalypse." *NTS* 23 (1977) 165–69. **Betz, O.** "The Dichotomized Servant and the End of Judas Iscariot." *RevQ* 5 (1964) 43–58. **Dewey, A. J.** "A Prophetic Pronouncement: Q 12:42–46." *Forum* 5 (1989) 99–108. **DuBuit, F. M.** "Les paraboles de l'Attente et de la Miséricorde (Mt 24,43–44; 24,45–48; 25,14–30)." *Évangile: Cahiers bibliques* 49 (1968) 5–57. **Pesch, R.,** and **Kratz, R.** "Gleichnis vom guten und vom bösen Knecht." In *So liest Man synoptisch*. Frankfurt am Main: Knecht, 1978. 5:561–66. **Schwarz, G.** "τὴν τροφὴν ([τὸ] σιτομέτριον) ἐν καιρῷ? Mt 24,45/Lk 12,42." *BibNot* 59 (1991) 44. **Strobel, A.** "Das Gleichnis vom heimkehrenden Hausherrn und seinem Knecht (Mt 24,45–51)." In *Untersuchungen zum eschatologischen Verzögerungsproblem*. NovTSup 2. Leiden: Brill, 1961. 215–22. **Weiser, A.** "Das Gleichnis vom treuen und untreuen Knecht: Mt 24,45–51 par Lk 12,42–46,47f." In *Die Knechtsgleichnisse der synoptischen Evangelien*. SANT 29. Munich: Kösel, 1971. 178–225.

## Translation

45 "Who then are the faithful and wise servants[a] whom the[b] master appointed over his household servants[c] to give them their food at the right time? [46]Blessed are those servants whom their master comes and finds doing thus. [47]Truly I tell you that he will appoint them over all his possessions. [48]But if those[d] evil servants[e] should say in their heart, 'My master delays his return,'[f] [49]and begin to beat their fellow servants, and eat and drink with drunkards, [50]the master of those servants will come on a day which they do not expect and in an hour which they do not know, [51]and he will cut them to pieces and put their inheritance among the hypocrites, where there will be weeping and the grinding of teeth."

## Notes

a The sing. "servant" has been changed to the pl. (affecting also pronouns and related verbs) in order to avoid the masc. language.

b Many MSS (W Θ $f^{13}$ TR lat sy[h]) add αὐτοῦ, "his."

c ℵ q read οἰκίας, "house"; D $f^1$ TR e sy[s] read θεραπείας, "servant," probably by influence of the parallel in Luke 12:42. The word here, οἰκετείας, is "household," by metonymy, "household servants."

d ℵ* Γ Θ sy[s] sa mae omit ἐκεῖνος, "that," resulting in the reading "the (evil) servant."

e Sing. in the Gr. See Note a above.

f "His return" added for clarity. Thus too, many MSS (W $f^{[1]13}$ TR latt sy mae bo[mss]; and with slightly different word order, C D L Θ) add ὁ κύριός μου ἐλθεῖν, lit. "my master [delays] to come," to complete the sense of the clause. Cf. the ἔρχεσθαι, "to come," in the Lukan parallel (Luke 12:45).

## Form/Structure/Setting

A. This is the first of a succession of three passages that have to do with the requirement of appropriate conduct (= watchfulness) in the period prior to the coming of the Son of Man. The emphasis in this and the second parable (25:1–13) remains on the unknown and unknowable time of the coming of the Son of Man (cf. v 50; 25:13), whereas the great third apocalyptic passage focuses on the final judgment.

B. Matthew probably draws the pericope from Q (cf. Luke 12:42–46), preferring it to the omitted brief parable of Mark 13:34–36. The agreement between Matthew and Luke is quite close. The setting of the parable in Luke 12:41 and the introductory formula καὶ εἶπεν ὁ κύριος, "and the master said" (Luke 12:42), were probably not a part of Q. The following more significant differences between Matthew and Luke may be noted. In v 45 Matthew has δοῦλος, "slave," where Luke has οἰκονόμος, "steward" (Luke 12:42; but cf. δοῦλος in Luke 12:45). It is difficult to know here and in Matthew's οἰκετείας, "household servants" (Luke: θεραπείας, "servants"), and τὴν τροφήν, "food" (Luke: [τὸ] σιτομέτριον, lit. "measure of grain"), whether Matthew or Luke reflects what was actually in Q. In v 47, on the other hand, Matthew's ἀμήν, lit. "amen," is probably an alteration of Q's ἀληθῶς, "truly" (Luke 12:44), to the more usual formulaic expression. In v 48 Matthew probably alters Q in order to refer to a second servant (cf. the ἐκεῖνος in v 46) as the κακός, "bad (one)," as the somewhat clumsy retention of ἐκεῖνος, "that one," seems to betray (in contrast to Luke's single servant [Luke 12:45]).

Luke's ἔρχεσθαι, "to come" (Luke 12:45), is probably an addition to Q and there-fore is not found in Matthew. In v 49, Matthew's τοὺς συνδούλους αὐτοῦ, "his fellow servants," may well be a condensing of Luke's τοὺς παῖδας καὶ τὰς παιδίσκας, "the menservants and the maidservants" (Luke 12:45). In the same verse, Matthew's μετὰ τῶν μεθυόντων, "with the drunkards," is probably original to Q, with Luke's καὶ μεθύσκεσθαι, "and to become drunk" (Luke 12:45), being an al-teration of Q (cf. the tension concerning Jesus' association with the outcasts in Luke). Matthew's ὑποκριτῶν, "hypocrites," in v 51 is almost certainly an alteration of Q (Luke 12:46: ἀπίστων, "unfaithful") in the direction of his favorite vocabu-lary. And finally, the concluding clause, ἐκεῖ ἔσται ὁ κλαυθμὸς καὶ ὁ βρυγμὸς τῶν ὀδόντων, "where there will be weeping and the grinding of teeth," is an obviously Matthean addition to Q (cf. 8:12; 13:42, 50; 22:13; 25:30).

C. The opening question (v 45) concerning a hypothetical servant who is given certain responsibilities indicates the parabolic character of this pericope (cf. Luke 12:41: τὴν παραβολὴν ταύτην, "this parable"). Its point is to illustrate the impor-tance of faithful conduct during the era prior to the unknown time of the return of the Son of Man (cf. v 50). Its didactic character leads Dewey to conclude that it represents "a prophetic pronouncement of Wisdom" (103). A suggested outline: (1) the faithful servant (vv 45–47), further divided into (a) the question (v 45), (b) the identification (v 46), and (c) the reward (v 47); and (2) the wicked ser-vant (vv 48–51), further divided into (a) the identification (vv 48–49), (b) the unexpected return of the master (v 50), and (c) the punishment (v 51). As the outline shows, there is some general parallelism between the two halves of the pericope. Syntactical parallelism may be seen in the two sentences composing v 45 and the beatitude of v 46, both with the subject δοῦλος, "slave," and relative clauses beginning with ὅν, "whom." In vv 48–51a we encounter one of the most complex sentences in Matthew, with three parallel main verbs in the future tense, ἥξει, "he will come," διχοτομήσει, "he will cut," and θήσει, "he will put," as well as an extended ἐάν, "if," clause with four parallel verbs, εἴπῃ, "say," ἄρξηται, "be-gin," ἐσθίῃ, "eat," and πίνῃ, "drink." V 50 contains the striking parallel construction ἐν ἡμέρᾳ ᾗ οὐ προσδοκᾷ καὶ ἐν ὥρᾳ ᾗ οὐ γινώσκει, "in a day he does not expect and in an hour he does not know." V 51b contains a common Matthean formula. The passage (esp. v 49) is alluded to in the *Gospel according to the Hebrews* (Eusebius, *Theophania* [*PG* 24.685]).

## Comment

**45–47** The rhetorical question with which the passage begins concerns the identification of ὁ πιστὸς δοῦλος καὶ φρόνιμος, "the faithful and wise servant." Close to this is the "good [ἀγαθέ] and faithful servant" spoken of in 25:21, 23 (these verses contain the only other reference to πιστός, "faithful," in Matthew). φρόνιμος, "wise," is used elsewhere in Matthew to describe appropriate disciple-ship in 7:24; 10:16, and most conspicuously in the parable of the "wise virgins" (25:2, 4, 8, 9). The idea of delegated authority is not uncommon in the Bible (cf. Gen 39:4–5) and is also used by Matthew in 25:21, 23 in an illustration making a point similar to that of the present passage (cf. Mark 13:34). The giving of food in due season is common biblical imagery for provision of needs (cf. Pss 104:27

[LXX 103:27, where the language is close to Matthew's]; 145:15 [LXX 144:15]). V 46 characterizes as μακάριος, "blessed" (cf. esp. 5:3–11; the word is used also in 11:6; 13:16; 16:17), i.e., truly and deeply happy, that servant who is found faithfully doing what had been assigned to him or her (cf. Luke 12:38). The clause ἐλθὼν ὁ κύριος αὐτοῦ, "when his master comes," alludes, of course, to the coming of the Son of Man referred to in the preceding passage (cf. esp. v 42, ὁ κύριος there meaning "Lord" and echoed in the present passage, and v 44). The servant who is found faithfully fulfilling the master's commission is rewarded by being delegated greater responsibility, indeed over πᾶσιν, "all," the master's possessions (cf. 25:21, 23, where the good and faithful servant is granted authority ἐπὶ πολλῶν, "over much"). The ἀμὴν λέγω ὑμῖν, "truly I tell you," formula adds weight to the promised reward.

**48–49** Matthew's insertion of κακός, "bad," before δοῦλος ἐκεῖνος, "that servant," directs the reader to another contrasting servant rather than, as in Luke, the same servant who is thought of as entertaining an altogether different train of thought and engaging in a very different behavior (Luke 12:45). The "bad" servant (κακός is used to refer to persons elsewhere in Matthew only in 21:41) begins to act shamefully. Rather than providing for the needs of his fellow servants, the bad servant beats them (for other mistreatment of σύνδουλοι, "fellow servants," in Matthew, see 18:28–33) and begins to eat and drink with profligates (μεθυόντων, lit. "drunkards"). Cf. 1 Thess 5:7, where the "drunk" are contrasted with the sober and watchful (in a context stressing the sudden coming of the Lord). The reason for this shameful conduct is all important in the context. This servant says "in his or her heart" (for which, cf. LXX Deut 8:17; Isa 47:8), "My master delays" (for χρονίζειν, "to delay," see 25:5; on the problem of the delay, see 2 Peter 3:4). Since the master is delayed, the wicked servant takes advantage of his absence, violates the commands of his master, and acts irresponsibly. What the present passage says through a parable, Luke 21:34–36, ending the Lukan eschatological discourse, says in a straightforward admonitory exhortation.

**50** The reason one ought not to fall into such shameful conduct is that despite the present apparent delay of the coming of the master (i.e., the Son of Man), he will return, and that return will be ἐν ἡμέρᾳ ᾗ οὐ προσδοκᾷ καὶ ἐν ὥρᾳ ᾗ οὐ γινώσκει, "on a day which you do not expect and in an hour which you do not know." Matthew returns here to the central point of this section of the discourse: the unknown time of the parousia of the Son of Man (cf. vv 36, 39, 42, 44; 25:13). That the time remains unknown should have motivational power for ethical living in the present.

**51** The wicked servant faces a dreadful punishment: dismembering and a future place (for this meaning of μέρος, lit. "share," see BAGD, 506b) among the hypocrites in the eschatological judgment. διχοτομήσει, lit. "will cut in two," is found in the NT only here and in the Lukan parallel (it is used similarly in *3 Apoc. Bar.* 16:3 [tr. H. E. Gaylord, Jr., as "punish them with the sword and death" in *The Old Testament Pseudepigrapha,* ed. J. H. Charlesworth (Garden City, NY: Doubleday, 1983) 1:677]; cf. Heb 11:37; for other references cf. BAGD, 200b).

Quite possibly this verb is the result of a mistranslation of the underlying Aramaic. According to Jeremias' reconstruction, the original verb (פַּלֵּג, *pallēg*) meant to "distribute" (blows) as punishment (*Parables of Jesus,* 57, n. 31). More recently O. Betz has proposed קצץ (*qss*), "to cut," as the underlying verb. In view, then, would be the cutting off of the wicked servant from the people of God in eschatological judgment (cf. the parable at Qumran in 1QapGen 19:15–16). In Matthew, according to Betz, the verb shifts to the dramatic death (cf. Judas Iscariot, Ananias and Sapphira) that precedes eschatological torment.

For Matthew there is no worse group than the "hypocrites" (ὑποκριτῶν; cf. 6:2–18; 15:7; and esp. chap. 23), and the wicked servant of the parable was, if anything, a hypocrite. The Matthean formula ἐκεῖ ἔσται ὁ κλαυθμὸς καὶ ὁ βρυγμὸς τῶν ὀδόντων, "there will be weeping and grinding of teeth there," is found verbatim in 8:12; 13:42, 50; 22:13; 25:30.

### Explanation

A faithful and wise servant will by his or her ethical behavior be ready for the coming of the master, the Son of Man, at whatever time it may occur. The Lord may not come as soon as he is expected—he seems to be delayed. But that can be no reason to lessen one's commitment to obeying the teaching he has given. Only those who remain faithful in their living and obedient to their commission will be unembarrassed by his sudden coming. Again, the fact of that coming—not the time of it—is to be foremost in the minds of the disciples. The knowledge of *that* fact must govern the lives of the disciples in whatever time they find themselves.

# The Parable of the Wise and Foolish Virgins (25:1–13)

### Bibliography

**Argyle, A. W.** "Wedding Customs at the Time of Jesus." *ExpTim* 86 (1974–75) 214–15. **Batey, R. A.** *New Testament Nuptial Imagery.* Leiden: Brill, 1971. **Blinzler, J.** "Bereitschaft für das Kommen des Herrn." *BLit* 37 (1963–64) 89–100. **Bornkamm, G.** "Die Verzögerung der Parusie: Exegetische Bemerkungen zu zwei synoptischen Texten." In *Geschichte und Glaube I.* BEVT 48. (= *Gesammelte Aufsätze.* Vol. 3.) Munich: Kaiser, 1968. 1:46–55. **Burkitt, F. C.** "The Parable of the Ten Virgins: Mt 25.1–13." *JTS* 30 (1929) 267–70. **Deiss, L.** "La parabole des dix vierges (Mt 25, 1–13)." *AsSeign* 63 (1971) 20–32. **Derrett, J. D. M.** "La parabola delle vergini stolte." In *Studies in the New Testament.* Leiden: Brill, 1977. 1:128–42. **Donfried, K. P.** "The Allegory of the Ten Virgins (Matt. 25:1–13) as a Summary of Matthean Theology." *JBL* 93 (1974) 415–28. **Dupont, J.** "Le royaume des cieux est semblable à . . . ." *BeO* 6 (1964) 247–53. **Feuillet, A.** "Les épousailles messianiques et les références au Cantique des Cantiques dans les évangiles synoptiques." *RevThom* 84 (1984) 399–424. ———. "La parabole des vierges." *VSpir* 75 (1946) 667–77. **Ford, J. M.** "The Parable of the Foolish Scholars (Matt. xxv 1–13)." *NovT* 9 (1967) 107–23. **Goudge, H. L.** "The Parable of the Ten Virgins: Mt 25.1–13." *JTS* 30 (1929) 399–401. **Granqvist, H. M.** *Marriage Conditions in a*

*Palestinian Village.* 2 vols. Helsingfors: Centraltryckeriet, 1931, 1935. **Jeremias, J.** "Lampades in Matthew 25:1–13." In *Soli Deo Gloria.* FS W. C. Robinson, ed. J. M. Richards. Richmond, VA: John Knox, 1968. 83–87. **Kretzer, A.** "Das mt Basileiaverständnis in Ausblick auf Parusie und Gericht nach den eschatologischen Gleichnissen Mt 25." In *Die Herrschaft der Himmel und die Söhne des Reiches.* SBM 10. Würzburg: Echter, 1971. 187–224. **Lambrecht, J.** "The Wise and Foolish Virgins (Matthew 25:1–13)." In *Once More Astonished: The Parables of Jesus.* New York: Crossroad, 1981. 146–66. **Lövestam, E.** "The Parable of the Ten Virgins." In *Spiritual Wakefulness in the New Testament.* LUÅ n.s. 1.55.3. Lund: Gleerup, 1963. 108–22. **Maisch, I.** "Das Gleichnis von den klugen und törichten Jungfrauen: Auslegung von Mt 25,1–13." *BibLeb* 11 (1970) 247–59. **Meinertz, M.** "Die Tragweite des Gleichnisses von den zehn Jungfrauen." In *Synoptische Studien.* FS A. Wikenhauser. Munich: Kösel, 1954. 94–106. **Neuhäusler, E.** *Anspruch und Antwort Gottes.* Düsseldorf: Patmos, 1962. 226–34. **Puig i Tàrrech, A.** *La parabole des dix vierges (Mt 25, 1–13).* AnBib 102. Rome: Biblical Institute, 1984. **Rosaz, M.** "Passer sur l'autre rive." *CHR* 26 (1979) 323–32. **Schenk, W.** "Auferweckung der Toten oder Gericht nach den Werken: Tradition und Redaktion in Matthäus xxv 1–13." *NovT* 20 (1978) 278–99. **Schwarz, G.** "Zum Vokabular von Matthäus XXV. 1–12." *NTS* 27 (1981) 270–76. **Sherriff, J. M.** "Matthew 25:1–13: A Summary of Matthean Eschatology?" *Studia Biblica 1978,* II. *Papers on the Gospels,* ed. E. A. Livingstone. Sheffield: JSOT, 1980. 301–5. **Staats, R.** "Die törichten Jungfrauen von Matthäus 25 in gnostischer und antignostischer Literatur." In *Christentum und Gnosis.* Berlin: Töpelmann, 1969. 98–115. **Strobel, A.** "Das Gleichnis von den zehn Jungfraugen (Mt 25, 1–13)." In *Untersuchungen zum eschatologischen Verzögerungsproblem.* NovTSup 2. Leiden: Brill, 1961. 233–54. ———. "Zum Verständnis von Mt 25,1–13." *NovT* 2 (1958) 199–227. **Walvoord, J. F.** "Christ's Olivet Discourse on the End of the Age: The Parable of the Ten Virgins." *BibSac* 129 (1972) 99–105. **Weder, H.** "Die Parabel von den zehn Jungfrauen (Mt 25,1–13)." In *Die Gleichnisse Jesu als Metaphern.* FRLANT 120. Göttingen: Vandenhoeck & Ruprecht, 1978. 239–49. **Zumstein, J.** *La condition du croyant dans l'évangile selon Matthieu.* OBO 16. Göttingen: Vandenhoeck & Ruprecht, 1977. 271–81.

*Translation*

[1] *"Then the kingdom of heaven will be like the story of* [a] *the ten virgins who took their torches and went out to meet* [b] *the bridegroom.* [c] [2] *And five of them were foolish and five wise.* [3] *For the foolish ones, although they took their torches, did not take oil with them.* [d] [4] *But the wise ones took oil in flasks together with their torches.* [5] *And when the bridegroom delayed his coming,* [e] *they all became drowsy and fell asleep.* [6] *But in the middle of the night there was a cry: 'Look, the bridegroom! Come out* [f] *to meet* [g] *[him]!' *[7] *Then all those virgins arose, and they trimmed the wicks* [i] *of their torches.* [8] *And the foolish ones said to the wise: 'Give us some of your oil, because our torches are going out.'* [9] *But the wise answered, saying: 'There would by no means* [j] *be enough for both us and you. Go instead to the shops* [k] *and buy more* [l] *for yourselves.'* [10] *But when they had gone to buy more oil,* [m] *the bridegroom came, and the ones who were ready went in with him into the wedding banquet, and the door was shut.* [11] *And later the other virgins also came and said: 'Lord, lord, open the door* [n] *for us.'* [12] *But he answered and said: 'Truly I tell you, I do not know you.'* [13] *Watch, therefore, because you do not know the day or the hour.'* [o]

*Notes*

[a] "The story of" added to translation.

[b] ὑπάντησιν, "meeting." Many MSS (D L W Θ *f* [13] TR) have ἀπάντησιν (same meaning), perhaps through the influence of v 6.

ᶜ Some MSS (D Θ *f*¹ latt sy mae) add καὶ τῆς νύμφης, "and the bride," perhaps because copyists had in mind the bridegroom bringing the bride to his home for the wedding (see *TCGNT*, 62). See Burkitt for a defense of the longer reading.

ᵈ D and a few other witnesses add ἐν τοῖς ἀγγείοις αὐτῶν, "in their flasks," perhaps by the influence of v 4.

ᵉ "His coming" added to translation.

ᶠ A few MSS (Θ *f*¹) read ἐγείρεσθε, "rise up," probably a change prompted by the end of v 5.

ᵍ ἀπάντησιν, "meeting." Z Θ have the synonym ὑπάντησιν (cf. v 1); C has συνάντησιν αὐτῷ, "meeting with him."

ʰ Some important MSS (‭א‬ B Z) omit the pronoun αὐτοῦ, "him" (C has the dative αὐτῷ). Favoring the inclusion of αὐτοῦ are A D L W *f*¹,¹³ TR.

ⁱ ἐκόσμησαν, "they put in order." "The wicks of" added to translation.

ʲ The very strong οὐ μή, "by no means," is contained in B C D K W Δ *f*¹. Other MSS (‭א‬ A L Z [Θ] *f*¹³) have the simple and softer negative οὐκ, "not."

ᵏ τοὺς πωλοῦντας, lit. "the sellers."

ˡ "More" added to translation.

ᵐ "More oil" added to translation.

ⁿ "The door" added to translation.

ᵒ Many MSS (C³ *f*¹³ TR vgᵐˢˢ) add ἐν ᾗ ὁ υἱὸς τοῦ ἀνθρώπου ἔρχεται, "in which the Son of Man is coming," an obvious conforming of the text to 24:44. See *TCGNT*, 63.

## *Form/Structure/Setting*

A. In this second consecutive parable of the apocalyptic discourse (cf. τότε, "then") Matthew continues to address the importance of readiness for the coming of the Son of Man. The coming of the bridegroom and the wedding banquet have messianic associations (cf. 22:1–14), which make the parable particularly effective. This is the final pericope that stresses the need for constant preparedness, particularly because the time of the return of the Son of Man remains unknown and may involve a longer-than-expected delay.

B. Although there are stories in Mark and Luke centering on the necessity of "watching" (Mark 13:33–37; Luke 12:35–38) with motifs related to the present pericope (Mark: sleeping; Luke: burning torches and a wedding banquet) and a further passage in Luke 13:25–28 with other motifs common to our passage (shut door; the cry "Lord, open to us"; and the response οὐκ οἶδα ὑμᾶς, "I do not know you"), Matthew appears to be dependent on his own special source for the parable. For a full literary analysis, see A. Puig i Tàrrech.

C. The parable begins with a typical introductory formula and ends with an admonition that applies the parable to the readers (v 13). The following outline may be suggested: (1) the virgins' going out to meet the bridegroom (vv 1–5), with subdivisions (a) introduction (vv 1–2), (b) taking/not taking oil (vv 3–4), and (c) the bridegroom's delay (v 5); (2) the coming of the bridegroom (vv 6–7); (3) the difficulty of the foolish virgins (vv 8–9); (4) the entrance into the wedding banquet (v 10); (5) the return of the foolish virgins (vv 11–12); and (6) final admonition (v 13). The character of the passage is such that syntactic parallelism is limited to the contrasting statements in vv 2 and 3–4. *Did.* 16:1 probably alludes to this passage or its underlying tradition: "Be watchful [γρηγορεῖτε] for your life. Let not your lamps [οἱ λύχνοι] be quenched [μὴ σβεσθήτωσαν], and let not your loins be ungirded, but be ready [γίνεσθε ἕτοιμοι], for you do not know the hour [οὐ γὰρ οἴδατε τὴν ὥραν] in which your Lord comes."

D. While the main point of the parable has to do with the importance of pre-paredness, various specific elements carry obvious allegorical significance (see Lambrecht). Thus the bridegroom is Christ, his coming is the delayed parousia, the wise and foolish virgins are faithful and unfaithful disciples, and the final scene symbolizes the eschatological judgment. On the other hand, one almost certainly goes too far in concluding that torches symbolize good works and that this provides the "interpretive key" to the parable, as Donfried argues. J. M. Ford's hypothesis that the parable is directed against the hypocrisy of the Jewish teachers is possible only by an excessive allegorizing approach that regards the marriage feast as the symbol of the completion of Torah study with the torches as symbolic of Torah. On the issue of allegorical elements in the parables, see Hagner, *Matthew 1–13*, 364–65.

### Comment

**1–2** The introductory formula, ὁμοιωθήσεται ἡ βασιλεία τῶν οὐρανῶν, "the kingdom of heaven shall be like," is similar to that of 13:24; 18:23; 22:2 but employs the future tense because of its eschatological orientation (cf. 7:24, 26). The kingdom of heaven is likened not to the virgins but to the story of what happens to them: when the sudden arrival of the Son of Man occurs, some are ready and some are not. The παρθένοι, "virgins" (used elsewhere in Matthew only in 1:23), here understood in the general sense of unmarried maidens attending the bride, coming out in the night with their torches to meet the bridegroom probably reflects actual historical practice (*pace* Bornkamm; see Jeremias, *Parables of Jesus*, 171–174, who also refers to similar practices in modern Palestine; cf. Argyle, and the detailed discussion in Granqvist) rather than being a story with artificial details concocted for the purpose of teaching. All the same, it is difficult to know precisely where the bridesmaids were (i.e., at the home of the bride, or her family, or that of the bridegroom?). This point of information, however, is hardly crucial to the interpretation of the parable. The only other occurrence of νυμφίος, "bridegroom," in Matthew, outside of this passage, is in 9:15, which is important for its identification of Jesus as the "bridegroom" (cf. John 3:29). The careful reader cannot miss the allusion to Jesus here (cf. esp. the application in v 13). For ὑπάντησιν, "meeting," cf. 8:34, also in reference to Jesus. The mention in v 2 of the μωραί, "foolish" (elsewhere in Matthew: 5:22; 7:26; 23:17), virgins first indicates that they will become the focus of attention as the parable proceeds. For φρόνιμοι, "wise," in reference to disciples, see also 7:24 (opposite "foolish" in a judgment context and thus parallel to our passage); 10:16; 24:45.

**3–4** The wise virgins took extra oil (ἐν τοῖς ἀγγείοις, "in the flasks") for their λαμπάδας, "lamps" (i.e., torches [so Jeremias]; only here in the Synoptics; cf. John 18:3), having considered the eventuality of a delay of the bridegroom and in determination not to be caught unprepared. The foolish, on the other hand, again mentioned first, did not have the foresight to be prepared in the event of a delay of the bridegroom. The parable should not be allegorized to the extent that an equivalent to the oil is pursued (contra Garland, who follows Donfried in understanding the oil as referring to good works). The focus of the parable is the simple matter of preparedness versus unpreparedness and the tragic character of the latter.

**5** Although the idea of the bridegroom's delay is introduced as a particularly important element in the parable (cf. 24:48; 25:19; see Sherriff), it is far from unknown in rabbinic and current accounts of the Near Eastern wedding (see Jeremias, *Parables of Jesus,* 172, who suggests the delay resulted from negotiations concerning financial arrangements). When the bridegroom was delayed and as the hours of the night wore on, the virgins ἐνύσταξαν, "began to nod off" (in the Gospels only here), and πᾶσαι, "all," of them ἐκάθευδον, "fell asleep" (cf. 8:24; 9:24; 13:25; and esp. 26:40–46). The reference to sleep here and rising in v 7 are literal, not metaphors for death and resurrection (contra Schenk). No fault is attached to the wise for falling asleep (elsewhere "sleep" stands in obvious tension with "watching"; cf. 26:38–41; Mark 13:36; 1 Thess 5:6, but note v 10). Their preparedness lies in their having brought sufficient oil for their lamps. The delay of the bridegroom, like the delay of the master in 24:48, is directly linked to uncertainty concerning the time of the return of the Son of Man (cf. v 13; 24:48, 50; 25:19; see Bornkamm).

**6–7** μέσης δὲ νυκτός, "in the middle of the night," means that several hours have passed, apparently enough time for the oil in the lamps to have become rather low. Suddenly the κραυγή, "cry" (only here in Matthew), comes that the bridegroom has arrived and that the wedding attendants should come out to "meet" him (there is no discernible difference in meaning between ὑπάντησιν, "meeting," of v 1 and ἀπάντησιν here; for the latter, cf. Acts 28:15; 1 Thess 4:17). The virgins arise and "trim" (ἐκόσμησαν) their torches, i.e., clean and oil them so that they will burn brightly.

**8–9** The foolish virgins see that their oil is practically gone and that their torches σβέννυνται, "are going out" (elsewhere in Matthew only in 12:20), rather than burning brightly to hail the arrival of the bridegroom. Their torches apparently consisted of oil lamps tied atop poles. The image of the lamps of the wicked going out (where the same verb is used) is found in Prov 13:9 and Job 18:5 and may lie behind the imagery of the parable at this point. The wise virgins do not comply with the request of the foolish virgins to share their oil (i.e., from their reserve flasks) with them. They instead direct them to go and buy some more for themselves. Buying oil late in the night likely would not have been difficult in a little village in full celebration of a wedding. That they eventually succeeded in buying more oil is suggested by v 11. V 9 teaches not an example of Christian ethics (or violation thereof) but the importance of single-mindedness in being prepared with burning torches for the meeting of the bridegroom and the subsequent entry into the wedding banquet.

**10** At the coming of the bridegroom (i.e., the parousia of the Son of Man), it is αἱ ἕτοιμοι, "the ready" (for the word in this sense, see 24:44), who go in with him into the wedding (i.e., messianic) banquet. The γάμους, "wedding banquet," has been used with the same messianic associations in 22:1–14 (the same reality is described with different language in 8:11; see there for OT background). The symbolism of the shut door points to the time when it is too late to alter the division between the saved and the lost (cf. Isa 22:22; Luke 13:25; Rev 3:7; see Jeremias, *TDNT* 3:178). This point emerges clearly in the following two verses.

**11–12** The foolish virgins, now identified as αἱ λοιπαί, "the others" (in contrast to αἱ ἕτοιμοι, "the ready," in v 10), return, presumably with a new supply of oil, only to find a locked door. Their cry, κύριε, κύριε, "sir, sir," becomes in application the empty "Lord, Lord" of 7:21–22. After the coming of the Son of Man, it is too late for the knocking to which the door *will* open (cf. 7:7–8). Instead they hear the dreadful words ἀμὴν λέγω ὑμῖν, οὐκ οἶδα ὑμᾶς, "Truly I tell you, I do not know you" (cf. 7:23 and *Comment* above, together with the obviously related Luke 13:25). The foolish virgins, by being unprepared for the coming of the bridegroom with its unanticipated delay, are shut out from enjoying the wedding banquet, and no appeal can change that reality.

**13** The final exhortation, introduced with the strong οὖν, "therefore," indicates the main point to be drawn from the parable. One must γρηγορεῖτε, "watch." The point here is not the avoidance of literal sleep (creating an unnecessary tension with the preceding verses—the wise virgins *did* sleep) but spiritual wakefulness (see Lövestam), that is, keeping oneself in a state of constant readiness for the coming of the Son of Man (cf. 24:42–43). This vigilance is required because the time of the parousia, the day, the hour, cannot be known in advance (cf. 24:36, 42, 44, 50).

### Explanation

This parable makes yet once again, and in a most sobering way, the point that preparedness for the unexpected time of the coming of the Son of Man is of the utmost importance. That is, how one lives in the lengthening interim period between the first and second appearances of the Messiah must be consistent with one's claim to be a disciple. What matters is that one not be embarrassed by an "inopportune" coming of the Son of Man. The difference between the foolish and the wise is that the latter do all within their power to be ready for the parousia. They will join the Son of Man in the eschatological reward of the messianic banquet while the foolish will find themselves excluded and without recourse. The bottom line of the eschatological discourse is the importance of preparedness, which looms larger and larger toward the end of the discourse.

# The Parable about Fulfilling Responsibility
# (25:14–30)

### Bibliography

**Candlish, R.** "The Pounds and the Talents." *ExpTim* 23 (1911–12) 136–37. **Derrett, J. D. M.** "Law in the New Testament: The Parable of the Talents and Two Logia." *ZNW* 56 (1965) 184–95 (reprinted in *Law in the New Testament*. London: Longman and Todd, 1970. 17–31). **Didier, M.** "La parabole des talents (Mt 25,14–30)." *AsSeign* 93 (1965) 32–44. ———. "La parabole des talents et des mines." In *De Jésus aux Évangiles*. FS J. Coppens, ed. I. de la Potterie. BETL 25. Gembloux: Duculot, 1967. 248–71. **Dietzfelbinger, C.** "Das Gleichnis von den anvertrauten Geldern." *BTZ* 6 (1989) 222–33. **DuBuit, M.** "Les paraboles de l'Attente et de la Miséricorde (Mt 24,43–44; 24,45–48; 25,14–30)." *Évangile: Cahiers bibliques* 49 (1968) 5–57. **Dupont, J.** "La parabole des talents (Mt 25,14–30) ou des mines (Luc 19, 12–27)." *RTP* 49

(1969) 376–91. ———. "La parabole des talents (Mt 25, 14–30)." *AsSeign* 64 (1969) 18–28. **Ellul, J.** "La parabole des talents (du texte au sermon, 18)." *ETR* 48 (1973) 125–38. **Fiedler, P.** "Die übergegebenen Talente: Auslegung von Mt 25,14–30." *BibLeb* 11 (1970) 259–73. **Foerster, W.** "Das Gleichnis von den anvertrauten Pfunden." In *Verbum Dei manet in aeternum.* FS O. Schmitz, ed. W. Foerster. Witten: Luther, 1953. 37–56. **Ganne, P.** "La parabole des talents." *BVC* 45 (1962) 44–53. **Joüon, P.** "La parabole des mines (Lc 19,12–27) et la parabole des talents (Mt 25,14–30)." *RSR* 29 (1939) 489–93. **Kamlah, E.** "Kritik und Interpretation der Parabel von den anvertrauten Geldern: Mt. 25, 14ff.; Lk. 19, 12ff." *KD* 14 (1968) 28–38. **Lambrecht, J.** "The Talents and the Pounds (Matthew 25:14–30 and Luke 19:11–27)." In *Once More Astonished: The Parables of Jesus.* New York: Crossroad, 1983. 167–95. **Lindeskog, G.** "Logia Studien." *ST* 4 (1951) 129–89. **Lyss, D.** "Contre le salut par les oeuvres dans la prédication des talents." *ETR* 64 (1989) 331–40. **Manns, F.** "La parabole des talents: *Wirkungsgeschichte* et racines juives." *RevScRel* 65 (1991) 343–62. **Marcel, P.** "La parabole des talents (Matthieu 25:14–30)." *RRéf* 34 (1983) 49–54. **McCulloch, W.** "The Pounds and the Talents." *ExpTim* 23 (1911–12) 382–83. **McGaughy, L. C.** "The Fear of Yahweh and the Mission of Judaism: A Postexilic Maxim and Its Early Christian Expansion in the Parable of the Talents." *JBL* 94 (1975) 235–45. **Mutch, J.** "The Man with the One Talent." *ExpTim* 42 (1930–31) 332–34. **Naegele, J.** "Translation of *talanton* 'talent.'" *BT* 37 (1986) 441–43. **Neuhäusler, E.** "Mit welchem Massstab misst Gott die Menschen? Deutung zweier Jesussprüche." *BibLeb* 11 (1970) 104–13. **Pesch, R.,** and **Kratz, R.** "Gleichnis von den Talenten oder Minen." In *So liest Man synoptisch.* Frankfurt am Main: Knecht, 1978. 5:67–73. **Puig i Tàrrech, A.** "La parabole des talents (Mt 25,14–30) ou des mines (Lc 19,11–28)." *Revista Catalana Teologia* 10 (1985) 269–317. **Resenhöfft, R. W.** "Jesu Gleichnis von den Talenten, ergänzt durch die Lukas-Fassung." *NTS* 26 (1979–80) 318–31. **Ross, J. M.** "Talents." *ExpTim* 89 (1978) 307–9. **Spicq, C.** "Le chrétien doit porter du fruit." *VSpir* 84 (1951) 605–15. **Steinmetz, D. C.** "Matthew 25:14–30." *Int* 34 (1980) 172–76. **Weder, H.** "Die Parabel von den anvertrauten Geldern (Mt 25,14–30; Lk 19,11–27; HebEv fr 15)." In *Die Gleichnisse Jesu als Metaphern.* FRLANT 120. Göttingen: Vandenhoeck & Ruprecht, 1978. 193–210. **Weiser, A.** "Das Gleichnis von den anvertrauten Geldern: Mt 25,14–30 par Lk 19,12–27." In *Die Knechtsgleichnisse der synoptischen Evangelien.* Munich: Kösel, 1971. 226–72.

## Translation

14 "For the situation is ᵃ like when a man who was going on a journey called together his servants and gave over to them his money.ᵇ ¹⁵And to one he gave five talents, to another two, and to yet another one,ᶜ to each according to his own ability, and he went off on his journey.ᵈ Immediately ¹⁶the one who received the five talents went and worked with them, and he gained ᵉ another five.ᶠ ¹⁷Similarly, the one who had been entrusted ᵍ two gained ʰ another two. ¹⁸But the one who had received one went and dug a hole inⁱ the ground, and hid the money of his master. ¹⁹And after a long time the master of those servants came and settled accounts with them. ²⁰And the one who had received the five talents came forward and brought another five talents, saying: 'Master, you entrusted me with five talents. Look, I have earned another five talents.'ʲ ²¹His master said to him: 'Well done, good and faithful servant. Youᵏ were faithful over a little; I will put you in charge of much. Enter into the joy of your master.'²²[And]ˡ the one who had received ᵐ the two talents also came forward and said: 'Master, you entrusted me with two talents. Look, I have earned another two talents.'ⁿ ²³His master said to him: 'Well done, good and faithful servant. Youᵒ were faithful over a little; I will put you in charge of much. Enter into the joy of your master.' ²⁴But the one who had received the one talent also came forward and said: 'Master, I knew you ᵖ that you were a hard man, reaping where

*you did not sow and gathering where you did not scatter,* [25] *and being afraid, I went and hid your talent in the ground. Look, you have what is yours.'* [26] *And his master answered and said: 'Evil and lazy servant, did you know that I harvested where I did not sow and I gathered where I did not scatter?* [27] *You ought therefore to have put my money in the bank,*[q] *and when I came, I could have received what is mine with interest.* [28] *Take therefore the talent from him and give it to the one having the ten*[r] *talents.* [29] *For to all*[s] *who have, it shall be given and it shall be multiplied, but as for they*[t] *who do not have, even what they have*[u] *shall be taken from them.*[v] [30] *And cast the useless servant into the outer darkness. In that place there will be weeping and gnashing of teeth.'"*

## Notes

[a] "The situation is" added for clarity.

[b] τά ὑπάρχοντα αὐτοῦ, lit. "his possessions."

[c] "Yet another" added to translation.

[d] Many MSS (ℵ² A C D L W *f*¹³ TR aur l vg sy^{p.h}) insert the connective δέ, "but," after πορευθείς, "having gone," thereby indicating a full stop after εὐθέως, "immediately," so that it modifies the preceding ἀπεδήμησεν, thus "he immediately went away." Θ *f*¹ it sa mae have δέ after εὐθέως, indicating that it initiates a new sentence. The accepted text (without δέ altogether) is found in ℵ* B b g¹. Its ambiguity accounts for the various scribal insertions of δέ. See *TCGNT*, 63.

[e] ἐκέρδησεν, "gained" or "earned." Many MSS (ℵ* A^c W TR sy^h) have ἐποίησεν, "made."

[f] Many MSS (ℵ A C D W *f*¹,¹³ TR sy^h) add τάλαντα, "talents."

[g] "Who had been entrusted" added to translation.

[h] Many MSS (A C³ W Θ *f*¹,¹³ TR sy^h and D, but before the verb) add after ἐκέρδησεν, "he earned," the words καὶ αὐτός, "even he himself."

[i] "In" added for clarity. Many MSS (A [C²] D W Θ *f*¹,¹³ TR) alter the simple γῆν, "earth," to ἐν τῇ γῇ, "in the ground." Cf. v 25.

[j] Many MSS (A C W *f*¹,¹³ TR sy^{p.h}) read ἐκέρδησα ἐπ᾽ αὐτοῖς, "I have earned in addition to them."

[k] D lat co begin with ἐπεί, "since."

[l] The connective δέ, "and," is omitted by the important MSS ℵ* B as well as by sa.

[m] "Who had received" added to translation. Many MSS (ℵ D TR latt sa^{mss}) include λαβών, "having received," here.

[n] Many MSS (A C W *f*¹,¹³ TR sy^{p.h}) add ἐπ᾽ αὐτοῖς, "in addition to them." Cf. *Note* j above.

[o] D latt co begin with ἐπεί, "since." Cf. *Note* k above.

[p] D Θ lat sa mae omit a redundant σε, "you," of the Gr. text (not reflected in the translation above).

[q] τοῖς τραπεζίταις, lit. "to the bankers."

[r] D reads πέντε, "five."

[s] D W sy^p omit παντί, "everyone."

[t] The Gr. has a sing., which here and in the remainder of the verse is changed to a pl. to avoid masc. language.

[u] A few MSS (L Δ 33 lat sy^h mae) read δοκεῖ ἔχειν, "he seems to have" (cf. Luke 8:18).

[v] A few MSS (C³ H; after v 30 [Γ] *f*¹³) add ταῦτα λέγων ἐφώνει ὁ ἔχων ὦτα ἀκούειν ἀκουέτω, "saying these things, he cried: 'The one who has ears to hear, let that person hear.'"

## Form/Structure/Setting

A. This third successive parable, like the next and final pericope in the discourse, focuses on the responsibility of servants (disciples) to be about their master's work while he is "away." Here, although the parable alludes to a delay in the master's return (cf. v 19), hence relating this parable to the preceding parables, the attention of the reader is directed not to the surprise of his sudden return but more directly to the servants' conduct during the time he has been away. The parable sets the responsibility of the servants in terms of money ("talents"), but the symbolism points to something obviously more comprehensive.

B. It is difficult to know the source of Matthew's parable. A hint of the parable is given in Mark 13:34, to which the opening of our parable is similar. There are very significant parallels with Luke 19:11–27. Among these are the following: the going of a man (but in Luke a "noble") on a journey (but in Luke "to acquire a kingdom"); the calling together of his servants (but in Luke "ten," although only three report [Luke 19:16–21]); the entrusting to them of money (but in Luke a μνᾶ, "mina," a much smaller amount than a talent [one sixtieth of a talent]); the settling of accounts with the servants; the coming of three servants before the master, with the first two being rewarded for their industry (but the first earned ten times what he had been given and the second five times); the approbation of the first (but not the second) with the words εὖγε, ἀγαθὲ δοῦλε, "well done, good servant"; the granting of authority over more (but ten and five cities, respectively); the failure of the third to invest the money (but wrapped in a handkerchief); the statement of the third that he knew his master to be a stern man who "takes what you do not deposit" and "reaps what you do not sow"; the condemnation of that servant, addressed as πονηρὲ δοῦλε, "wicked servant"; the repetition of the servant's statement in the form of a question; the reference to depositing the money in the bank where it would have earned interest (but in the form of a second question); the command to take the mina (not talent) and give it to the one who had ten; and the logion about giving to everyone who has but taking away from the one who does not have. There is not a great amount of verbatim agreement, but, more importantly, there are a number of Lukan distinctives, perhaps drawn from a second parable, that give the Lukan passage a different cast from the one in Matthew (cf. esp. Luke 19:12, 14, 15a, 25, 27). Despite the strong similarities, therefore, it is by no means certain that Matthew's and Luke's source is Q. Unfortunately, one can only speculate about sources here, but it is difficult to explain either Matthew or Luke as a wholesale redaction of Q. It seems only plausible to argue that, unless Jesus spoke two similar parables, both passages go back originally to the same parable and that early in the process of transmission the parable assumed something like the two forms we encounter in Matthew and Luke and thus that there is no direct literary dependence upon Q here (see the discussions in Weiser, Lambrecht).

C. The parable lacks the typical introductory formula (its remnant is found in the initial ὥσπερ, lit. "just as," and near its end includes an inserted logion (v 29; cf. 13:12). It ends with the Matthean formula concerning "the outer darkness" (cf. 8:12; 22:13). The passage may be outlined as follows: (1) the entrusting of money to the servants (vv 14–15); (2) the work of the three servants (vv 16–18); (3) the settling of accounts (vv 19–27), subdivided into (a) the first servant (vv 20–21), (b) the second servant (vv 22–23), and (c) the third servant (vv 24–27); (4) giving to those who have (vv 28–29); and (5) the judgment of the wicked servant (v 30). By its nature the passage lends itself to syntactical parallelism. The similarity between the first two servants causes the verbatim repetition (except of course for the number referring to the talents) of larger blocks of material. Thus v 20b is repeated in v 22b, and the entirety of v 21 is repeated exactly in v 23. Syntactic parallelism may be noted in v 15 in the giving of the money to the three servants but even more conspicuously in vv 16–18 where the work of the three is described. Here all three sentences have a parallel subject clause, and the first and third sentences (vv 16, 18) have adverbial participles and compound predicate clauses. Similarly, the report of the three is initiated by three parallel sentence forms (vv 20, 22, 24, each with the adverbial participle προσελθών, "having come forward"). Note also the repeated reference to reaping/sowing and gathering/scattering in the statement of the third servant (v 24) and the question of his master (v 26). Syntactic parallelism is also apparent in the imperative clauses of v 28 and the future passive clauses of v 29. The explanation for all of this parallelism probably goes back to the formulation of the material in oral tradition and the facilitating of memorization of the words of Jesus.

D. Aspects of the pericope, or the underlying tradition, can be detected in the *Gospel of the Hebrews* (Eusebius, *Theophania* [*PG* 24.685]), which refers to three servants and specifically one who "hid the talent." In the *Gos. Thom.* 41 the logion of v 29 is reflected (but cf. 13:12). *2 Clem.* 8:5–6 refers to the one who is faithful in little being given much. Justin Martyr (*Dial.* 125.1–2) refers to the coming of the Lord and the time of settling of accounts in such a way as to reflect the present passage.

### Comment

**14–15**    The underlying theme of the parable is introduced at the outset: the absence of the master (the Son of Man) and the interim responsibility of the servants (disciples). The ἄνθρωπος, "man," is about to "take a journey" (ἀποδημῶν); cf. καὶ ἀπεδήμησεν, "and he departed on a journey," at the end of v 15. He calls his servants together to put them in charge of his money (τὰ ὑπάρχοντα αὐτοῦ, lit. "what belonged to him"). This is parallel to the commission in 24:45. Here, however, the responsibility is expressed in terms of money. It is difficult to know the value of the τάλαντον, "talent" (originally a measure of weight), but it was a very large amount of money, here probably silver coinage (cf. vv 18, 27): one talent equaled 6,000 denarii (one denarius was the equivalent of a day's wages for a common laborer). The talent was thus analogous to the modern "million" (so *EDNT* 3:332; cf. Naegele). Of course, the issue really at stake is not money but the stewardship of what has been given to individual disciples. Since this stewardship involves different "amounts" entrusted to the disciples (five, two, one talent[s]), the "talents" probably symbolize personal gifts and abilities rather than the gospel itself. This is supported by the phrase ἑκάστῳ κατὰ τὴν ἰδίαν δύναμιν, "to each according to his own ability" (perhaps picked up by Paul in Rom 12:3, 6–7). As at the present time for Matthew's readers, the master has "gone on a journey," and the stewardship of his servants is on trial.

**16–18**    The εὐθέως, "immediately," goes with the sentence that follows (cf. *Note* d) and indicates the proper urgency with which the first disciple goes about his business. The parable does not describe how the one who received the five talents ἠργάσατο ἐν αὐτοῖς, "worked with them," and doubled what had been given to him, but this is unimportant. It *is* important to the parable that he made good and effective use of what had initially been given him. The same is true of the second servant, who was also able to double the two talents that were entrusted to him. By contrast, the third servant, rather than using the money entrusted to him, took it and buried it (ὥρυξεν, "dug," elsewhere in Matthew only in 21:33) in the ground for safe-keeping (cf. 13:44 for treasure hidden in the ground). The word for "money" here, ἀργύριον, lit. "silver," shows that the talent was in the form of silver coinage. It is important to note the absence in v 18 of ἐκέρδησεν, "gained," in contrast to vv 16, 17. There is no gain here but mere preservation.

**19–23** μετὰ δὲ πολὺν χρόνον, "and after a long time," gives the servants sufficient time to work with the money but also reflects the delay of the parousia of the Son of Man, also the topic of 24:48; 25:5. Matthew's readers, if they received the Gospel in the late sixties, could only have taken comfort from the acknowledgment of the length of time. When ὁ κύριος, "the master," returns (the present tense in Greek is deliber-ate in Matthew), as with the return of the Son of Man, there is the unavoidable "settling of accounts" (συναίρει λόγον μετ᾽ αὐτῶν, lit. "he settles account with them"; cf. 18:23 where the same expression is used). This is obviously a figure for the eschatological judgment. Beginning in v 20, one by one the servants "come before" (προσελθών) the master (cf. vv 20, 22, 24). The words spoken by the first two agree verbatim (vv 20b, 22b) except for the number of talents gained. There is a report of the amount "entrusted" (παρέδωκας; for similar use of the verb, see v 14; cf. 11:27), and then of the amount "gained" (ἐκέρδησα; cf. 16:26; Jas 4:13). The entire response of the master (v 21) is repeated verbatim to the second servant (v 23), even including the introductory ἔφη αὐτῷ ὁ κύριος αὐτοῦ, "his master said to him." εὖ, lit. "well," is found in Matthew only here. Matthew refers to a "faithful [πιστέ] servant" who is also "wise" in 24:45; ἀγαθέ, "good," modifies servant only here in Matthew (cf. "good man" in 12:35). The accolade is followed by the statement "you were faithful over little, I will appoint you over much," which echoes the policy stated in 24:45–47 (cf. vv 28–29 and the articulation of a similar principle in Luke 16:10a). ὀλίγα, "little," here is ironic, given the large sums of money in question, but it also emphasizes the contrasting greatness of the divine generosity in eschatological blessing. Indeed, the parable of 24:45–51 makes very nearly the same point as the present parable. The μακάριος, "blessed," servant there (24:46) is the same as the "good and faithful" ser-vant here. The invitation to enter into τὴν χαρὰν τοῦ κυρίου σου, "the joy of your master," may refer to the happiness of a like prosperity. For Christian readers (both in the first century and in the present), however, the language cannot fail to connote the joy of eschatological blessing (cf. Heb 12:2), just as the judgment of the wicked servant (v 30) points to eschatological judgment.

**24–25** Unlike the first and second servants, the third servant does not begin with a reference to the amount with which he had been entrusted. He begins, rather, with an attempted justification of what he did with his one talent. He knew, he says, that his master was a σκληρός, "hard," man (the only use of the word in Matthew), reaping where he did not sow (the conjunction of reaping and sowing is found in 6:26) and gathering where he did not scatter (for συνάγειν in the sense of "harvesting," cf. 3:12; 6:26; 13:30; διασκορπίζειν, "sow," occurs in this sense only here in Matthew; but cf. 12:30). These two clauses seem to be equiva-lents, an example of synonymous parallelism (reap = gather; sow = scatter). The reader may surmise that by virtue of his position the master properly expected a profit from the labor of his servants. This understanding is confirmed when the servant's statement is turned against him in vv 26–27. Fear had motivated this servant, the fear of failure and losing the talent he had been given. And so he hid the talent in the ground (cf. 13:44). The result, announced by ἴδε, "look" (as in vv 20, 22), was that nothing had been gained (unlike the preceding two instances) except that the talent had been preserved and not lost: ἔχεις τὸ σόν, "you have what is yours." McGaughy speculates that in the parable as Jesus first taught it the answer of the third servant reflected popular bitterness concerning Yahweh's relation to his people, who had been entrusted with the traditions of the fathers. But this treats the parable too much as an allegory—one that moreover detracts from the main point of the parable as Matthew presents it.

**26–27**    Only here in Matthew is a "servant" described as πονηρέ, "wicked" (but elsewhere in Matthew the adjective can be applied to a man [13:35; cf. 7:11; 22:10] and, of course, frequently to a "generation"). The servant was wicked because of his bad stewardship, which the second adjective ὀκνηρέ, "lazy" (the only occurrence in Matthew), makes plain (cf. ἀχρεῖον, "useless," in v 30). The servant's culpability, rather than being lessened, is all the greater since he knew that his master expected a profit (cf. v 24). Therefore, he should have at least put the money in a bank where it could have earned some interest. The words τραπεζίταις, "bankers," and τόκῳ, "interest" (the latter is also found in the Lukan parallel), occur only here in the NT. There is no need to allegorize these or other details in the parable. Harrington's attempt to see the third servant as symbolic of Matthew's Jewish opponents, who failed to maintain an apocalyptic spirit, is not convincing. The parable's *three* servants are a problem for this view, but more significant is the fact that such an interpretation must impose a perspective upon the parable that detracts from its main and obvious point (Jeremias, *Parables of Jesus*, 60: "a *Parousia*-parable").

**28–29**    As the beginning of judgment (cf. v 30), the talent of the wicked and lazy servant is taken away from him and given to the good and faithful servant who had initially been given five but now had ten. This feature of the story gives rise to the articulation of the general principle in v 29, which captures both the positive and negative sides: positive, "to everyone who has, it shall be given and it shall abound" (cf. Prov. 9:9); negative, "from the one who does not have, even what he has will be taken away from him." The future passive verbs imply God as the acting subject. The logion (on which see Lindeskog) is the same as that of 13:12 (cf. Mark 4:25), and the wording of the two is very close (see *Comment* on 13:12). Faithfulness provides more blessing; unfaithfulness results in loss even of one's initial blessings. (For similar rabbinic ideas, cf. Str-B 1:660–61.)

**30**    A further word of judgment is spoken against the "wicked" and "lazy" servant (v 26), who is now referred to as ἀχρεῖον, "useless" (in the NT only here and in Luke 17:10), i.e., one who does not further the interests of the master. Two Matthean formulas come into play in the reference to the servant's condemnation: "cast into the outer darkness" (see 8:12; 22:13) and "there will be weeping and the grinding of teeth" (see 8:12; 13:42, 50; 22:13; 24:51). These are Matthew's favorite metaphors for the final lot of the wicked (see *Comment* on 8:12), and they stand in sharp contrast to the words of blessing spoken to the first two servants (vv 21, 23). For a refutation of the interpretation of the parable as teaching salvation by works, see D. Lyss. Lambrecht rightly characterizes the parable as stressing "gift" as well as involving "task."

## Explanation

Matthew, still building upon his assertion in 24:36 that the time of the coming of the Son of Man remains unknown, again addresses the importance of the disciples' conduct in the lengthy time that the Son of Man is "away." The imagery of the parable centers upon money. It is fitting, however, that the monetary unit referred to is the "talent," the Greek word that is the root of the common English word "talent," i.e., in the sense of "special aptitude" or "gift." Something like this (cf. the "spiritual gifts" of passages such as Rom 12:6–7; 1 Cor 7:7; 12:4–31) is probably in view here rather than literal money. Not everybody has been entrusted with the same "amount" (gift), but one must be faithful with what one has been given. Thus the two-talent person is given precisely the same accolade as the five-talent person (as would be the one-talent person, if only that talent had been used). The disciple who uses that with which he or she has been entrusted will receive the wonderful praise, "Well done, good and faithful servant," and will enter into the full joy of eschatological blessing. The disciple who, on the other hand, fails to make productive use of what has been given faces the terrifying prospect of ultimate loss. The faithful will be further blessed; the unfaithful will lose all. The point cannot be missed: before the Son of Man comes and until that time whenever it may be, disciples are called to faithful and steady service of the kingdom.

# The Last Judgment   (25:31–46)

## Bibliography

**Bligh, P. H.** "Eternal Fire, Eternal Punishment, Eternal Life (Mt 25,41–46)." *ExpTim* 83 (1971–72) 9–11. **Bonnard, P.** "Matthieu 25,31–46: Questions de lecture et d'interprétation." *FV* 76.5 (1977) 81–87. **Brändle, R.** "Zur Interpretation von Mt 25,31–46 im Matthäuskommentar des Origenes." *TZ* 36 (1980) 17–25. ———. *Matth. 25,31–46 im Werk des Johannes Chrysostomos.* BGBE 22. Tübingen: Mohr, 1979. **Brandenburger, E.** *Das Recht des Weltenrichters: Untersuchung zu Matthäus 25,31–46.*" SBS 99. Stuttgart: Katholisches Bibelwerk, 1980. **Brandt, W.** "Die geringsten Brüder." *JThSB* 8 (1937) 1–28. **Broer, I.** "Das Gericht des Menschensohnes über die Völker: Auslegung von Mt 25,31–46." *BibLeb* 11 (1970) 273–95. **Brown, S.** "Faith, the Poor and the Gentiles: A Tradition-Historical Reflection on Matthew 25:31–46." *TJT* 6 (1990) 171–81. ———. "The Matthean Apocalypse." *JSNT* 4 (1979) 2–27. **Burney, C. F.** "Mt 25.31–46 as a Hebrew Poem." *JTS* 14 (1913) 414–24. **Cadoux, A. T.** "The Parable of the Sheep and the Goats." *ExpTim* 41 (1929–30) 559–62. **Catchpole, D. R.** "The Poor on Earth and the Son of Man in Heaven: A Re-appraisal of Matthew XXV.31–46." *BJRL* 61 (1979) 355–97. **Christian, P.** *Jesus und seine geringsten Brüder: Mt 25,31–46 redaktionsgeschichtlich untersucht.* ETS 12. Leipzig: St. Benno, 1975. **Cope, O. L.** "Matthew xxv:31–46—'The Sheep and the Goats' Reinterpreted." *NovT* 11 (1969) 32–44. **Court, J. M.** "Right and Left: The Implications for Matthew 25.31–46." *NTS* 31 (1985) 223–33. **Cranfield, C. E. B.** "Diakonia: Mt 25,31–46." *LQHR* 30 (1961) 275–81. **Donahue, J. R.** "The 'Parable' of the Sheep and the Goats: A Challenge to Christians Ethics." *TS* 47 (1986) 3–31. **Duprez, A.** "Le jugement dernier (Mt 25)." *AsSeign* 65 (1973) 17–28. **Farahian,**

**E.** "Relire Matthieu 25,31–46." *Greg* 72 (1991) 437–57. **Feuillet, A.** "La caractère universel du jugement et la charité sans frontières en Mt 25,31–46." *NRT* 102 (1980) 179–96. **Forrest, R. G.** "Judgment." *ExpTim* 91 (1979) 48–49. **Friedrich, J.** *Gott im Bruder? Eine methodenkritische Untersuchung von Redaktion, Überlieferung und Traditionen in Mt 25,31–46.* Calwer theologische Monographien A.7. Stuttgart: Calwer, 1977. **Gay, G.** "The Judgment of the Gentiles in Matthew's Theology." In *Scripture, Tradition and Interpretation.* FS E. F. Harrison, ed. W. W. Gasque and W. S. LaSor. Grand Rapids: Eerdmans, 1978. 199–215. **Gewalt, D.** "Matthäus 25,31–46 im Erwartungshorizont heutiger Exegese." *LingBib* 25–26 (1973) 9–21. **Goppelt, L.** "Leben für die Barmherzigen." *Calwer Predigthilfen* 11 (1972) 221–28. **Grassi, J. A.** "'I Was Hungry and You Gave Me to Eat' (Matt. 25:35ff.): The Divine Identification Ethic in Matthew." *BTB* 11 (1981) 81–84. **Gray, S. W.** *The Least of My Brothers: Matthew 25:31–46: A History of Interpretation.* SBLDS 114. Atlanta: Scholars, 1989. **Gross, G.** "Die 'geringsten Brüder' Jesu in Mt 25,40 in Auseinandersetzung mit der neueren Exegese." *BibLeb* 5 (1964) 172–80. **Haufe, G.** "'Soviel ihr getan habt einem dieser meiner geringsten Brüder.'" In *Ruf und Antwort.* FS E. Fuchs. Leipzig: Koehler & Amelang, 1964. 484–93. **Herrmann, V.** "Anmerkungen zum Verständnis einiger Paralleltexts zu Mt 25,31ff aus der altägyptischen Religion." *BibNot* 59 (1991) 17–22. **Hülsbusch, W.** "Wenn der Menschensohn in seiner Herrlichkeit kommt: Predigtvorschlag für das Christkönigsfest nach Mt 25,31–46." *BibLeb* 13 (1972) 207–14. **Hutter, M.** "Mt 25:31–46 in der Deutung Manis." *NovT* 33 (1991) 276–82. **Ingelaere, J.-C.** "La 'parabole' du jugement dernier (Matthieu 25/31–46)." *RHPR* 50 (1970) 23–60. **Klein, L.** "Who Are the 'Least of the Brethren'?" *Dialog* 21 (1982) 139–42. **Knoch, O.** "Gott als Anwalt des Menschen: Die Bildrede vom Weltgericht: Mt 25/31–46." *BK* 24 (1969) 82–84. **Ladd, G. E.** "The Parable of the Sheep and the Goats in Recent Interpretation." In *New Dimensions in New Testament Study,* ed. R. N. Longenecker and M. C. Tenney. Grand Rapids: Eerdmans, 1974. 191–99. **Lambrecht, J.** "The Last Judgment (Matthew 25:31–46)." In *Once More Astonished: The Parables of Jesus.* New York: Crossroad, 1983. 196–235. **Lapoorta, J.** "'. . . whatever you did for one of the least of these . . . you did for me' (Matt. 25:31–46)." *Journal of Theology for Southern Africa* 68 (1989) 103–9. **Légasse, S.** "La parabole du jugement dernier (Mt., xxv, 36–46)." In *Jésus et l'enfant.* Paris: J. Gabalda, 1969. 85–100. **Maddox, R.** "Who Are the 'Sheep' and the 'Goats'? A Study of the Purpose and Meaning of Mt. 25,31–46." *AusBR* 13 (1965) 19–28. **Mánek, J.** "Mit wem identifiziert sich Jesus? Eine exegetische Rekonstruction ad Matt. 25:31–46." In *Christ and Spirit in the New Testament,* ed. B. Lindars and S. S. Smalley. Cambridge: Cambridge UP, 1973. 15–25. **Marguerat, D.** *Le jugement dans l'Évangile de Matthieu.* Geneva: Labor et Fides, 1981. **Martin, F.** "The Image of the Shepherd in the Gospel of St. Matthew." *ScEs* 27 (1975) 261–301. **Michaels, J. R.** "Apostolic Hardships and Righteous Gentiles: A Study of Matthew 25, 31–46." *JBL* 84 (1965) 27–37. **Mitton, C. L.** "Expository Problems: Present Justification and Final Judgment—A Discussion of the Parable of the Sheep and the Goats." *ExpTim* 68 (1956–57) 46–50. **Oudersluys, R. C.** "The Parable of the Sheep and the Goats (Matthew 25:31–46): Eschatology and Mission, Then and Now." *RefRev* 26 (1973) 151–61. **Pamment, M.** "Singleness and Matthew's Attitude to the Torah." *JSNT* 17 (1983) 73–86. **Pesch, W.** *Der Lohngedanke in der Lehre Jesu verglichen mit der religiösen Lohnlehre des Spätjudentums.* MTS 1. Munich: Zink, 1955. **Puzicha, M.** *Christus peregrinus: Die Fremdenaufnahme (Mt 25,35) als Werk der privaten Wohltätigkeit im Urteil der Alten Kirche.* Münsterische Beiträge zur Theologie 47. Münster: Aschendorff, 1980. **Rennes, J.** "À propos de Matthieu 25,31–46." *ETR* 44 (1969) 233–34. **Robinson, J. A. T.** "The 'Parable' of the Sheep and the Goats." *NTS* 2 (1955–56) 225–37. **Roy, M.** "Jugement et sanction: Matthieu 25,31–46; Luc 16,19–31." *CHR* 28 (1981) 440–49. **Sayer, J.** "'Ich hatte Durst, und ihr gabt mir zu trinken': Zum Ansatz einer Theologie der menschlichen Grundbedürfnisse nach Mt 25,31ff im Rahmen der Pastoral der Befreiung." *MTZ* 42 (1991) 151–67. **Schillebeeckx, E.** "A Glass of Water for a Fellow Human Being (Matt. 25,31–46)." In *God among Us.* London/New York: SCM/Crossroad, 1983. 59–62. **Steidle, B.** "Ich war krank und ihr habt mich besucht." *Erbe und Auftrag* 40 (1964) 443–58; 41 (1965) 36–52, 99–113, 189–206. **Turner, H. E. W.** "Expounding the Parables—The Parable of the Sheep and the Goats (Mt 25:31–46)." *ExpTim* 77 (1965–66) 243–46. **Via, D. O.** "Ethical Responsibility and Human Wholeness in Matthew 25:31–46." *HTR* 80 (1987) 79–100. **Wikenhauser, A.** "Die Liebeswerke im Gerichtsgemälde." *BZ* 20 (1932) 366–77. **Wilckens, U.** "Gottes geringste Brüder—zu Mt 25,31–46." In *Jesus und Paulus*. FS W. G. Kümmel, ed. E. E. Ellis and E. Grässer. Göttingen: Vandenhoeck & Ruprecht, 1975. 363–83. **Winandy, J.** "La scène du jugement dernier (Mt.25,31–46)." *SE* 18 (1966) 169–86. **Zumstein, J.** *La condition du croyant dans l'évangile selon Matthieu*. OBO 16. Göttingen: Vandenhoeck & Ruprecht, 1977.

## Translation

[31] *"When the Son of Man comes in his glory and all his angels* [a] *with him, then he will sit upon his glorious throne.* [32] *And all the nations will be gathered together before him, and he will separate them from one another, just as a shepherd separates the sheep from the goats.* [33] *And he will place the sheep at his right hand and the goats at his left.* [34] *Then the king will say to those at his right hand: 'Come, blessed ones of my Father, inherit the kingdom prepared for you from the foundation of the world.* [35] *For I was hungry and you gave me food* [b] *to eat; I was thirsty and you gave me something* [c] *to drink; I was a stranger and you received me as a guest;* [36] *naked and you clothed me; I was sick and you looked after me; I was in prison and you visited me.'* [37] *Then the righteous will respond to him, saying: 'Lord, when did we see you hungry and fed you, or thirsty and gave you a drink?* [38] *When did we see you a stranger and took you in as a guest, or naked and clothed you?* [39] *When did we see you sick or in prison and came to you?'* [40] *And the king will answer and say to them: 'Truly I tell you, insofar as you did these things* [d] *to one of the least of these my brothers* [e] *or sisters,* [f] *you did them* [g] *to me.'* [41] *Then he will say also to those on his left side: 'Depart from me, cursed ones, into the eternal fire which is prepared* [h] *for the devil and his angels.* [42] *For I was hungry and you gave me nothing to eat; I was thirsty and you gave me nothing to drink;* [43] *I was a stranger and you did not treat me as a guest; naked* [i] *and you did not clothe me; sick and in prison and you did not look after me.'* [44] *Then they themselves also will answer and say: 'Lord, when did we see you hungry, or thirsty, or a stranger, or naked, or sick, or in prison, and did not minister to you?'* [45] *Then he will answer and say to them: 'Truly I tell you, inasmuch as you did not do these things* [j] *to one of the least of these, you did not do them* [k] *to me.'* [46] *And these will go away to eternal punishment,* [l] *but the righteous to eternal life."*

## Notes

[a] Many MSS (A W *f*[13] TR sy[p.h] bo[pt]) read ἅγιοι, "saints," perhaps by the influence of the LXX of Zech 14:5. Supporting ἄγγελοι, "angels," are ℵ B D L Θ *f*[1] lat sa mae bo[pt]. Cf. Mark 8:38b; Luke 9:26b.

[b] "Food" added to translation, supplying a direct object.

[c] "Something" added to translation, supplying a direct object.

[d] "These things" added to translation, supplying a direct object.

[e] A few witnesses (B* 1424 ff[1] ff[2]) omit τῶν ἀδελφῶν μου, "my brothers," perhaps by the influence of v 45, where the phrase is not found.

[f] "Or sisters" added.

[g] "Them" added to translation, supplying a direct object.

[h] A few MSS (D *f*[1] it mae) read ὃ ἡτοίμασεν ὁ πατήρ μου, "which my Father prepared," instead of τὸ ἡτοιμασμένον, "which is prepared." This may be to parallel the τοῦ πατρός μου, "my Father," in v 34. On the other hand, if the former reading was the original, scribes may have been tempted to

soften the statement by the shorter one. The external evidence, however, strongly supports the shorter reading. See *TCGNT*, 63–64.

ⁱ p⁴⁵ h add ἤμην, "I was," on the model of v 35.

ʲ "These things" added to translation, supplying direct object.

ᵏ "Them" added to translation, supplying direct object.

ˡ One witness (it) reads *ignem*, "fire," by the influence of v 41.

## Form/Structure/Setting

A. The final section of the eschatological discourse ends fittingly in a great judgment scene. This pericope also ends the formal teaching of Jesus in the Gospel. The passage is again concerned with the return of the Son of Man (v 31) and the immediately subsequent judgment, with the blessing of the righteous and the punishment of the wicked. It is a time of accounting and a time of division. The passage concludes with no further exhortations or added logia; it is left to speak for itself. And the message concerning the importance of the disciples' conduct toward others can hardly have been made more poignantly.

B. The passage is unique to Matthew, being apparently drawn from the evangelist's special source. The only partial parallels are to its opening and close. Thus Mark 8:38b and Luke 9:26b both refer to the coming of the Son of Man in glory (Mark: of his Father; Luke: his and his Father's) with his holy angels. John 5:29, with its division between doers of good and of evil, is close to Matthew's concluding sentence but more in content than wording. Luke 13:27–28, "depart from me all workers of iniquity," is close to v 41. Two previous passages in Matthew anticipate parts of the present pericope. The content of the opening verses is stated concisely in 16:27, and in 7:23 one finds the command to "workers of iniquity" to "depart from me" (cf. v 41).

C. The pericope is artistically constructed and makes deliberate use of extensive repetition for effect and perhaps for ease in memorization. Unlike the preceding parables, however, this narrative is based not on a fictitious story but on the description of a very real, though future, event. Despite some clear parabolic elements, the passage with its future tense forms is more properly categorized as an apocalyptic revelation discourse (thus Friedrich; cf. Gnilka). The following outline reflects the parallel structure within the passage: (1) the glorious coming of the Son of Man (v 31); (2) the great separation (vv 32–33); (3) the reward of the righteous (vv 34–40), subdivided into (a) the reward (v 34), (b) its grounds (vv 35–36), (c) the protest (vv 37–39), and (d) the principle (v 40); (4) the judgment of the wicked (vv 41–45), subdivided into (a) the judgment (v 41), (b) its grounds (vv 42–43), (c) the protest (v 44), and (d) the principle (v 45); and (5) the final division (v 46). The most striking structural feature of the passage is the list of six needs, which occurs no less than four times (the fourth somewhat abbreviated), three times with corresponding lists of remedies (vv 35–36; 37–39; 42–43) and once with the summarizing remedy διηκονήσαμέν σοι, "we ministered to you." In all four lists the words and their order do not change: hungry, thirsty, stranger, naked, sick, in prison. The first repetition of the initial list, in the mouths of the righteous (vv 37–39), occurs as three questions, each pair being introduced by πότε σε εἴδομεν, "when did we see you?" The vocabulary of this list remains exactly the same except for ἐθρέψαμεν, "we nourished" (v 37), for "gave you to eat" (vv 35, 42). The second and third lists (vv 37–39; 42–43) agree in coalescing the fifth and sixth items so that only one remedy is given (ἤλθομεν, "we came," in v 39, which in the first list is the remedy to the sixth item, "in prison"; and ἐπεσκέψασθε, "look after," in v 43, which in the first list is the remedy to the fifth item, "sick"). The third list, addressed to the wicked, is, of course, further distinguished by the negatives before the remedies, "you did not." The fourth list (v 44) finally abbreviates drastically, simply listing the six items following the single πότε σε εἴδομεν, "when did we see you," and at the end offering the one comprehensive remedy διηκονήσαμέν σοι, "did we (not) minister to you?"

Several other parallels should be noted. The articulation of the principle in vv 40 and 45, both beginning with the ἀμὴν λέγω ὑμῖν, "truly I tell you," is verbatim, except for the two negatives in the second one and the omission in the second one of the phrase τῶν ἀδελφῶν μου, "my brothers." A further parallel construction occurs in vv 34 and 41, involving the description of the kingdom/the fire as ἡτοιμασμένην/ον, "prepared," and their respective modifiers, and in the same verses the oppositions in οἱ εὐλογημένοι, "the blessed," and [οἱ] κατηραμένοι, "[the] accursed" (cf. δεῦτε, "come"; πορεύεσθε, "depart"). Finally, note the parallel clauses in vv 33 and 46, involving the separation of the two groups.

D. Besides its influence upon other writings of the NT (see *Comment*), this passage is probably alluded to in 2 *Clem.* 6:7 ("eternal punishment"; cf. v 46); Justin Martyr, *Dial.* 76.5 ("depart into the outer darkness which the Father has prepared for Satan and his angels"; cf. v 41), and *Herm. Vis.* 3.9.2 ("look after one another and help one another . . . give to those who lack").

On the authenticity of the passage as going back to Jesus himself, see I. Broer (cf. J. A. T. Robinson; H. E. W. Turner). For a comparison of the passage with *1 Enoch* 62–63, see D. R. Catchpole.

## Comment

**31** For the last time in this discourse, the coming of the Son of Man takes center stage. Again the initial question of the disciples concerning the time of Jesus' parousia and the end of the age comes to mind (24:3). But here as in previous references to the coming of the Son of Man (cf. 24:27, 30, 37, 39, 44), the real issue is not the time but the significance of his coming and the consequent need to be prepared. For the coming of the Son of Man will mean judgment, as every pericope since 24:36 has emphasized. But the closest parallel to the present verse comes from 16:27, which also refers to the coming of the Son of Man but ἐν τῇ δόξῃ τοῦ πατρός, "in the glory of his Father," rather than ἐν τῇ δόξῃ αὐτοῦ, "in his glory," as here. That Matthew can alter this language so naturally is an indicator of his high Christology. The remainder of 16:27, "and then he will render to each according to his work," is, of course, the point of the present parable concerning the sheep and the goats. A second closely parallel verse is Matt 19:28, which speaks of the sitting of "the Son of Man on his glorious throne [ἐπὶ θρόνου δόξης αὐτοῦ]," giving rewards to his disciples. 24:30 has also referred to the coming of the Son of Man "on the clouds of heaven with power and great glory [μετὰ δυνάμεως καὶ δόξης πολλῆς]." So also 19:28 refers to the end of the age "when the

Son of Man is seated on the throne of his glory," in a context that refers to judgment. The accompanying angels have previously been mentioned in 13:41; 16:27; 24:31 (cf. 2 Thess 1:7; and for OT background, Zech 14:5 [see *Note* a] and LXX of Deut 32:43; 33:2). The background to this reference to the coming of the Son of Man is, as in the other references, primarily Dan 7:13–14. The language of this verse is also close to the following passages in *1 Enoch:* "the Son of Man sitting on the throne of his glory" (62:5; cf. 62:2–3); "he placed the Elect One on the throne of glory" (61:8). In both of these passages, the Son of Man brings about apocalyptic blessing for the righteous and judgment of the wicked (cf. 69:27–29; 1:9). Matthew again makes use of apocalyptic imagery for the coming of the Son of Man to his judgment throne (cf. 2 Thess 1:7–10; John 5:27). This event signals the great judgment scene that follows, in which Jesus as the Son of Man functions as judge—a role restricted to Yahweh in the OT.

**32–33** First, πάντα τὰ ἔθνη, "all the nations," are gathered before him. This comprehensiveness matches that of the commission to spread the gospel (cf. 24:14; 28:19). The gathering together (συναχθήσονται, "they will be gathered," a divine passive meaning "by God") described here probably refers to the same "gathering" of the righteous (cf. 3:12; 13:30) or of both righteous and wicked (cf. 13:47; 22:10) spoken of earlier in the Gospel. Probably included, therefore, are the gentile nations, Israel, and also the *corpus mixtum* of the Christian church— i.e., the reference is universal (thus too Cranfield, Catchpole, Via).

> The meaning of "all the nations" here is much disputed. In his encyclopedic survey of the interpretation of this pericope, S. W. Gray tabulates the following conclusions concerning the meaning of this phrase in descending order of popularity: (1) all human beings; (2) all Christians; (3) all non-Christians and non-Jews; (4) all non-Christians; and (5) all non-Jews (thus Allen; Brandenburger). Options 3, 4, and 5 understand the word τὰ ἔθνη as referring to the "heathen," in the sense of those who are not God's people (cf. Friedrich; Court; Garland; Lambrecht; Harrington, who points to the expectation of a particular judgment of the Gentiles in the apocalyptic literature), with conclusions varying depending on how the latter is understood. There are no clear markers in the text to indicate that any group is excluded (cf. 24:30), and, moreover, there are earlier indications in the Gospel that point to the future judgment of Christians (e.g., 7:21–23; 16:27). The second option is based in part on the difficulty of understanding the judgment of non-Christians by standards of which they are ignorant (see G. Gay). The basis for judgment, however, may not be deeds of mercy in general but only deeds that are indications of response to the message of the Gospel. The first option has the advantage of being consistent with the universality of the same phrase in 28:19, which includes both Gentiles and Jews (see *Comment* on that verse). The interpretation of "the nations" in the present passage is closely related to the interpretation of "the least of these my brothers" in v 40 (cf. v 45). See further *Comment* on that verse.

The great judgment scene portrayed here is alluded to elsewhere in the NT in such passages as Rom 14:10–12; 2 Cor 5:10; Rev 20:11–13 (cf. Acts 17:31). It involves a separation of the righteous and the wicked among the nations (ἀφορίσει, "he will separate," is also used in referring to the final judgment in 13:49; cf. 13:40–43). Despite the disagreement of the gender of αὐτούς, "them," the antecedent remains τὰ ἔθνη, "the nations" (rightly Gray, 353; cf. 28:19 for the same phenomenon). τὰ πρόβατα, "the sheep," is a common metaphor for the people of God, i.e., the righteous (e.g., 10:16; 26:31, citing Zech 13:7; cf. esp. John 10), although Matthew also uses the image of the lost or straying sheep (e.g., 9:36; 10:6; 15:24; Ezek 34:17, 20 call for a separation of sheep from sheep [i.e., the separation of males from females] but also of rams from goats). ἐρίφων, "goats," is used only here in Matthew and elsewhere in the NT only in Luke 15:29 (the slightly different, diminutive form ἐρίφιον in v 33, compared to ἔριφος in v 32, involves no change in meaning). ἐκ δεξιῶν αὐτοῦ, "at his right hand," refers generally to the place of honor (cf. 20:23; 22:44, citing Pss 110:1; 26:64; Acts 2:33–34; 5:31; 7:55–56; Rom 8:34). ἐξ εὐωνύμων, "at the left hand," however, need not indicate a position of disfavor (cf. esp. 20:21, 23). Some are sheep and some are goats; they are separated from each other into two groups as a setting for the bestowing of reward (and later judgment) together with the instruction that now follows.

**34** ὁ βασιλεύς, "the king," is the one described as sitting upon the throne in v 31, i.e., the Son of Man, and not another person. This is clear from the reference to those at "his right hand" (cf. v 33). The Son of Man is earlier identified as the Judge who hands out eschatological blessing or punishment in 16:27; 13:41–43 (cf. 2 Thess 1:7). Now again he is identified as Judge. The judgment seat of God (Rom 14:10–12) is no different from the judgment seat of Christ (2 Cor 5:10). The invitation δεῦτε, "come," vividly contrasts with the πορεύεσθε, "depart," of v 41, as do the other clusters of elements in the two verses. οἱ εὐλογημένοι, "the blessed" (contrast: [οἱ] κατηραμένοι, "[the] cursed"), is not elsewhere in Matthew or the NT an appellation used for the righteous (cf. specialized uses in 21:9; 23:39; Luke 1:42; Gal 3:9). They are uniquely the blessed τοῦ πατρός μου, "of my Father" (Matthean idiom; cf. 11:27; 20:23; 26:29, 53), reflecting thereby their special relationship to him. Now at last the righteous are to inherit the eschatological kingdom in all its fullness, the consummation of the fulfillment they had already begun to enjoy in their participation in the kingdom. In its other two occurrences in Matthew the verb κληρονομεῖν, "inherit," is also used in the future tense, once with respect to "the earth" (5:5) and once with respect to "eternal life" (19:29), other metaphors for the eschatological blessing now to be received (for the verb elsewhere in the NT, cf. esp. 1 Cor 6:9–10; 15:50; Gal 5:21). The βασιλείαν, "kingdom," to be inherited (for earlier references to this future kingdom, see, e.g., 5:19–20; 6:10; 7:21; 8:11; 18:3; 19:23; 20:21; 26:29) is said to have been ἡτοιμασμένην, "prepared" (for the same verb used in reference to eschatological blessing, see 20:23, with the addition "by my Father"; cf. 1 Cor 2:9), ἀπὸ καταβολῆς κόσμου, "from the foundation of the world" (for the same expression, see 13:35; cf. Luke 11:50; Heb 4:3; 9:26; Rev 13:8; 17:8), that is, from the beginning of time (cf. *m. ʾAbot* 5:6). In the blessing of the righteous, God's eternal purpose is being accomplished.

**35–36** There are six different situations of need, all in the aorist tense except for the ἤμην, "I was," in vv 35 and 36 (with regard to "a stranger" and "in prison"). The verb ἤμην, "I was," is also assumed for γυμνός, "naked," in v 36, following its use in v 35. The immediately startling fact (cf. vv 37–39) is that Jesus says he was in such situations of need, and the righteous in each instance met the need. The needs of hunger and thirst naturally go together, and one may have expected that the need of clothing would have been third rather than fourth, following the reference to being a stranger (for OT combination of the three, see Job 22:6–7; elsewhere in the OT hunger and nakedness are mentioned, with thirst probably assumed under hunger; cf. Isa 58:7; Ezek 18:7, 16; Tob 4:16; and Rom 12:20 citing Prov 25:21). The provision of food (drink) and clothing is regarded in the OT as the work of the righteous (of whom it is said they "shall surely live" in Ezek 18:9; for food see too Jas 2:15–17; for drink cf. Matt 10:42; Job 22:7). For the third item, hospitality to the stranger, see Job 31:32 (cf. in the NT, Heb 13:2; 1 Tim 5:10). Visiting the sick is mentioned in Sir 7:35 (together with the needy in Sir 7:32–34; cf. Jas 5:14; the verb ἐπισκέπτεσθαι, "look after," is used in Jas 1:27 but in connection with orphans and widows). On remembering those in prison, see Heb 13:3 (cf. *T. Jos.* 1.6). In the face of the needs mentioned, the righteous responded appropriately with deeds of mercy. The catalogue is, of course, only representative. It covers the most basic needs of life in order to represent the meeting of human need of every kind. The works themselves, however, serve as but "parabolic stageprops, as it were, used to convey the primary meaning of the parable" (Gray, 353).

**37–39** οἱ δίκαιοι, "the righteous" (a favorite word of Matthew's; cf. esp. v 46; 10:41; 13:43, 49), are understandably astonished at what Jesus has just said to them. They have taken it quite literally but remember no circumstance in which they ministered to Jesus in these ways—hence their threefold question, πότε σε εἴδομεν, "when did we see you?" at the beginning of vv 37, 38, 39. The substitution of ἐθρέψαμεν, "we fed" (τρέφειν is used elsewhere in Matthew only in 6:26), for ἐδώκατέ μοι φαγεῖν, "gave me to eat," is apparently only a matter of stylistic variation. A slight abridgment takes place in v 39, where the verb ἐπισκέπτεσθαι, "look after," used in v 36, is omitted. ἀσθενοῦντα, "sick," is instead combined with ἐν φυλακῇ, "in prison," and both are served by the single verb ἤλθομεν, "we came." A similar abbreviation takes place in v 43 where, however, the other verb, ἐπεσκέψασθε, "you looked after," becomes the predicate for both conditions of need.

**40** The confusion of the disciples at the statement of Jesus, disclosed in their questions, gives rise to the articulation of an astounding principle, central to the passage. Addressed with the formula ἀμὴν λέγω ὑμῖν, "truly I tell you," the mark of an especially weighty saying, the righteous are told that to the extent that they did these things ἑνὶ τούτων τῶν ἀδελφῶν μου τῶν ἐλαχίστων, "for one of the least of these my brothers," they had in effect done them for Jesus himself. Jesus thus identified himself fully with his disciples (cf. 1 Cor 8:12; 12:27; Acts 9:5).

There is much disagreement about the meaning of the phrase "the least of these my brothers." From Gray's survey of the options, we may list the following, in descending order of popularity: (1) everyone, i.e., particularly the needy among humankind; (2) all Christians; (3) Christian missionaries; and (4) Jewish Christians. The fourth option takes the word "brothers" too literally and therefore restricts it too narrowly to those Christians who are physically Jews. The distinction between options 2 and 3 is a small one, unless one insists in option 3 upon "missionary" in the technical sense of the term (thus Court, Gundry) as opposed to Christians generally—all of whom in some sense represent the Gospel (cf. 10:32). Nothing specific in the passage or context supports the speculation of Maddox that Christian leaders are intended. The real choice is between the first two options. The use of τῶν ἀδελφῶν μου, "my brothers," makes it almost certain that the statement refers not to human beings in general but rather to brothers and sisters of the Christian community. Elsewhere in the Gospel it is consistently the disciples whom Jesus calls "my brothers" (12:48–49; 28:10; see too 23:8; outside Matthew, see John 20:17; Rom 8:29; Heb 2:11–12). Although ἐλάχιστος, "least," is used elsewhere in Matthew to refer to persons only in 5:19, the true counterpart to the phrase "one of these least" is found in Matthew's distinctive οἱ μικροί, "the little ones" (of which ἐλάχιστος, "least," is the superlative), a phrase used by Matthew to refer to disciples generally (see 18:6, 10, 14, where the subject is also Christian treatment of Christians; see Winandy). A confirmation of the correctness of this conclusion is found in the use of the phrase in a sentence that makes much the same point as the present passage: "Whoever gives one of these little ones [ἕνα τῶν μικρῶν τούτων] a drink [ποτίσῃ, same verb as in the present passage] of cold water in the name of a disciple, truly I tell you, will in no wise lose his [her] reward" (10:42). This follows a statement about the identification of master and disciple that is very much in line with the thought of the present pericope: "The one who receives you receives me, and the one who receives me receives the one who sent me" (10:40). H. B. Green (206) not unjustly describes the present passage as "an extended dramatization" of 10:42 (see too Cope; Ingelaere). An intriguing OT antecedent is found in Prov 19:17: "Whoever is kind to the poor lends to the Lord and will be paid in full." See too the rabbinic parallel in *Midr. Tanhuma* on Deut 15:9: "My children, when you gave food to the poor I counted it as though you had given it to me" (see Jeremias, *Parables of Jesus*, 207).

The principle articulated here concerns in the first instance deeds of mercy done to disciples, brothers and sisters, and only by extrapolation to others (*pace* Grassi; Cranfield; Wilckens). Favoring this interpretation are Ladd, Michaels, Mánek, Cope, Oudersluys, Court, France, Catchpole, Via, Carson, Blomberg, Légasse, Lambrecht, and Donahue (whose discussion is particularly helpful). The hypothesis of J. Friedrich (cf. Catchpole) that, while this is the meaning of the text for the evangelist, Jesus' original words were universal in application is difficult to substantiate. Most astonishing in this pericope, however, is the intimate bond that identifies Jesus with his disciples. This identification cannot be explained on the basis of the *šaliah* model since then the righteous would know that the messengers represented the sender (thus rightly Catchpole; *pace* Michaels).

**41** The sequence of vv 34–40 is now repeated but in connection with the unrighteous. ἐξ εὐωνύμων, "on the left," picks up the phrase used of the goats in v 33. The command πορεύεσθε ἀπ᾽ ἐμοῦ, "depart from me" (contrast δεῦτε, "come" in v 34), is reminiscent of the judgment in 7:23 (citing Ps 6:8). κατηραμένοι, "cursed," is used of the unrighteous in the NT only here. Matthew frequently uses "fire" as a judgment metaphor (see *Comment* on 3:10); the phrase τὸ πῦρ τὸ αἰώνιον, "eternal fire," is used elsewhere in Matthew only in 18:8 (cf. πυρὶ ἀσβέστῳ, "with fire unquenchable," in 3:12). The judgment of the unrighteous condemns them to the place of eternal torment, the fire (cf. Rev 14:10; 19:20; 20:10, 14–15; 21:8) that has been "prepared" (cf. v 34) τῷ διαβόλῳ καὶ τοῖς ἀγγέλοις αὐτοῦ, "for the devil and his angels" (for "the devil" see *Comment* on 4:1; the notion of the devil's angels is found also in Rev 12:7, 9; 2 Cor 12:7).

**42–43** The same six items are mentioned as in vv 35–36 but now with the verbs of response consistently negated, "you did not." The fifth and sixth items are again joined under one verb (cf. v 39), this time, however, οὐκ ἐπεσκέψασθε, lit. "you did not look after." As consistently as the righteous are approved for their deeds of mercy, so now are the unrighteous faulted for their lack of charitable deeds toward Jesus.

**44** This provokes the same protest from the unrighteous as it did from the righteous. They still address Jesus as κύριε, "Lord" (as did the righteous in v 37), thereby reminding the readers of an earlier reference to those who addressed Jesus as "Lord, Lord" but who were nevertheless also turned away (7:21–23). In this case, however, rather than reflecting any form of discipleship, the address of Jesus as "Lord" is prompted by confrontation with the glorious Son of Man as Judge. Syntactically, Matthew now abridges by having one question (i.e., one πότε σε εἴδομεν, "when did we see you," rather than three as in vv 37–39), a list of the six situations of need separated by ἤ, "or," and a single, summarizing verb that covers all the needs, οὐ διηκονήσαμέν σοι, "and did not minister to you." These would-be disciples are equally puzzled by the claim of Jesus, in this case, that they had *not* done these deeds of charity to Jesus.

**45** Again the key principle is articulated (cf. v 40), this time, however, in the negative: not to have done deeds of kindness to others, again described as ἐνὶ τούτων τῶν ἐλαχίστων, "to one of the least of these," is to have failed to do them to Jesus. Here again under the figure "the least of these" are fellow disciples, the so-called "little ones" (cf. *Comment* on v 40). The omission of the phrase τῶν ἀδελφῶν μου, "my brothers," is a matter of abridgment and should not be taken to signal a change of meaning from the phrase in v 40.

**46** The last sentence of the parable refers to the final separation of the righteous and the wicked (cf. John 5:29; Dan 12:2). The wicked will go away εἰς κόλασιν αἰώνιον, "to eternal punishment" (cf. v 41; κόλασις is used elsewhere in the NT only in 1 John 4:18) while the righteous will receive ζωὴν αἰώνιον, "eternal life" (the phrase is used elsewhere in Matthew in 19:16, 29; see *Comment* on 19:16). The adjective αἰώνιον, "eternal," is used in both instances, pointing to the gravity of the issue at stake.

*Explanation*

The time of the great judgment wherein the righteous and the unrighteous are finally separated will arrive with the glorious coming of the Son of Man. All the nations of the world—that is, every individual of those nations—are to be judged on the basis of their treatment of disciples of Jesus. This perhaps surprising statement points at once to the unique relation between Jesus and those who follow him and to the supreme importance of the mission and message of the church to the world. To treat the disciple, the bringer and representative of the gospel, with deeds of kindness is in effect to have so treated Jesus. Conversely, to fail to meet the needs of the Christian missionary is to fail to meet the needs of Jesus. There is thus a most remarkable bond of solidarity between Jesus and his disciples. Although disciples are naturally also called to do good to all people (cf. 9:13; 12:7), deeds of kindness must begin with brothers and sisters of the faith, with the church (cf. Gal 6:10).

Although sometimes understood as confirming a salvation by works, this passage need not be understood as incompatible with the gospel of the kingdom as a divine gift. The apostle Paul, the champion of grace, can also stress the significance of good works (see esp. Gal 6:7–10; 2 Cor 5:10). Matthew does stress the importance of righteousness as good deeds, but as a part of a larger context in which God acts graciously for the salvation of his people (see Hagner, *Matthew 1–13*, lxi–lxiii and *Comment* on 5:20). The deeds of mercy in the present passage are symbolic of a deeper reality, and as Gray notes, "the main point of the parable is the acceptance or the rejection of the Christian faith" (353; cf. 359). For a balanced and helpful discussion of this problem, see esp. C. L. Mitton.

# The Story of Jesus' Death and Resurrection (26:1–28:20)

## Bibliography

**Alsup, J. E.** *The Post-Resurrection Appearance Stories of the Gospel Tradition.* Stuttgart: Calwer, 1975. **Bartsch, H.-W.** "Die Passions- und Ostergeschichten bei Matthäus." In *Entmythologisierende Auslegung.* TF 26. Hamburg: Reich, 1962. 80–92. **Benoit, P.** *The Passion and Resurrection of Jesus Christ.* New York: Herder and Herder, 1969. **Blinzler, J.** *Der Prozess Jesu.* 4th ed. Regensburg: Pustet, 1969. **Broer, I.** "Bemerkungen zur Redaktion der Passionsgeschichte durch Matthäus." In *Studien zum Matthäusevangelium.* FS W. Pesch, ed. L. Schenke. Stuttgart: Katholische Bibelwerk, 1988. 25–46. ———. *Die Urgemeinde und das Grab Jesu.* SANT 31. Munich: Kösel, 1972. **Brown, R. E.** *The Death of the Messiah.* 2 vols. New York: Doubleday, 1994. ———. "The Resurrection in Matthew (27:62–28:20)." *Worship* 64 (1990) 157–70. **Bruce, F. F.** "The Book of Zechariah and the Passion Narrative." *BJRL* 43 (1960–61) 336–53. ———. "The End of the First Gospel." *EvQ* 12 (1940) 203–14. **Buck, E.** "Anti-Judaic Sentiments in the Passion Narrative according to Matthew." In *Anti-Judaism in Early Christianity: Vol. 1. Paul and the Gospels*, ed. P. Richardson. Waterloo, Ontario: Wilfred Laurier University, 1986. 165–80. **Conzelmann, H.** "History and Theology in the Passion Narratives of the Synoptic Gospels." *Int* 24 (1970) 178–97. **Crossan, J. D.** *The Cross that Spoke: The Origins of the Passion Narrative.* San Francisco: Harper and Row, 1988. **Curtis, K. P. G.** "Three Points of Contact between Matthew and John in the Burial and Resurrection Narratives." *JTS* 23 (1972) 440–44. **Dahl, N. A.** "The Passion Narrative in Matthew." In *Jesus in the Memory of the Early Church.* Minneapolis: Augsburg, 1976. 37–51. ———. "Die Passionsgeschichte bei Matthäus." *NTS* 2 (1955–56) 17–32. **Descamps, A.** "Rédaction et christologie dans le récit matthéen de la Passion." In *L'Évangile selon Matthieu: Redaction et Théologie*, ed. M. Didier. BETL 29. Gembloux: Duculot, 1972. 359–415. **Dockx, S.** "Les étapes rédactionnelles du récit de la derniére céne chez les synoptiques." In *Chronologies néotestamentaires et vie de l'église primitive.* Leuven: Peeters, 1984. 207–32. **Finegan, J.** *Die Überlieferung der Leidens-und Auferstehungsgeschichte Jesu.* BZNW 15. Giessen: Töpelmann, 1934. **Fisher, K. M.** "Redaktionsgeschichtliche Bemerkungen zur Passionsgeschichte des Matthäus." In *Theologische Versuche*, ed. J. Rogge and G. Schille. Berlin: Evangelische, 1970. 2:109–28. **Fuller, R. H.** *The Formation of the Resurrection Narratives.* New York: Macmillan, 1971. **Garland, D. E.** *One Hundred Years of Study on the Passion Narratives.* NABPR Bibliographic Series 3. Macon, GA: Mercer UP, 1990. **Gerhardsson, B.** "Jésus livré et abandonné d'après la passion selon s. Matthieu." *RB* 76 (1969) 206–27. **Giblin, C. H.** "Structural and Thematic Correlation in the Matthean Burial-Resurrection Narrative (Matt. xxvii. 57–xxviii. 20)." *NTS* 21 (1974–75) 406–20. **Green, J. B.** *The Death of Jesus: Tradition and Interpretation in the Passion Narrative.* WUNT 33. Tübingen: Mohr, 1988. **Heil, J. P.** *The Death and Resurrection of Jesus: A Narrative-Critical Reading of Matthew 26–28.* Minneapolis: Fortress, 1991. ———. "The Narrative Structure of Matthew 27:55–28:20." *JBL* 110 (1991) 419–38. **Hendrickx, H.** *The Passion Narratives of the Synoptic Gospels.* 2nd ed. London: Chapman, 1984. **Hillmann, W.** *Aufbau und Deutung der synoptischen Leidensberichte.* Freiburg: Herder, 1941. **Horbury, W.** "The Passion Narratives and Historical Criticism." *Th* 75 (1972) 58–71. **Kratz, R.** *Auferweckung als Befreiung: Eine Studie zur Passions- und Auferstehungstheologie des Matthäus (besonders Mt 27,62–28,15).* SBS 65. Stuttgart: Katholisches Bibelwerk, 1973. **Kremer, J.** *Die Osterevangelien—Geschichten um Geschichte.* Stuttgart: Katholisches Bibelwerk, 1977. **Lambrecht, J.** "Het matteaanse lijdensverhaal." *Collationes* 30 (1984) 161–90. **LaVerdiere, E.** "The Passion Story as Prophecy." *Emmanuel* 93 (1987) 84–98. **Limbeck, M.,** ed. *Redaktion und Theologie des Passionsberichtes nach den*

*Synoptikern.* Wege der Forschung 481. Darmstadt: Wissenschaftliche Buchgesellschaft, 1981. **Lodge, J. G.** "Matthew's Passion-Resurrection Narrative." *Chicago Studies* 25 (1986) 3–20. **Lohse, E.** *History of the Suffering and Death of Jesus Christ.* Philadelphia: Fortress, 1967. **Martin, F.** "Mourir: Matthieu 26–28." *Sémiotique et Bible* 53 (1989) 18–47. ———— and **Panier, L.** "Dévoilement du péché et salut dans le récit de la passion selon Saint Matthieu." *LumVie* 36 (1987) 72–88. **Matera, F. J.** "The Passion according to Matthew: Part One. Jesus Unleashes the Passion, 26:1–75." *Clergy Review* 62 (1987) 93–97. ————. "The Passion according to Matthew: Part Two. Jesus Suffers the Passion, 27:1–66." *Priests & People* [London] 1 (1987) 13–17. **Meier, J. P.** "Commentary on the Passion, Death and Resurrection (Mt 26–28): The Turning Point of the Ages." In *The Vision of Matthew.* New York: Paulist, 1979. 179–219. **Moo, D. J.** *The Old Testament in the Passion Narratives.* Sheffield: Almond, 1983. **Overman, J. A.** "Heroes and Villains in Palestinian Lore: Matthew's Use of Traditional Polemic in the Passion Narrative." *Society of Biblical Literature Seminar Papers.* Atlanta: Scholars, 1990. 592–602. **Pesch, R.,** and **Kratz, R.** *So liest Man synoptisch: Anleitung und Kommentar zum Studien der synoptischen Evangelien.* VII. *Passionsgeschichte.* Part 2. Frankfurt am Main: Knecht, 1980. **Punnakottil, G.** "The Passion Narrative according to Matthew." *Biblebhashyam* 3 (1977) 20–47. **Rieckert, P. K.** "The Narrative Coherence in Matthew 26–28." *Neot* 16 (1982) 53–74. **Schelkle, K. H.** *Die Passion Jesu in der Verkündigung des Neuen Testaments.* Heidelberg: Kerle, 1949. **Senior, D.** "Matthew's Special Material in the Passion Story: Implications for the Evangelist's Redactional Technique and Theological Perspective." *ETL* 63 (1987) 272–94. ————. *The Passion Narrative according to Matthew: A Redactional Study.* BETL 39. Leuven: Leuven UP, 1975. ————. "The Passion Narrative in the Gospel of Matthew." In *L'Évangile selon Matthieu: Redaction et Théologie,* ed. M. Didier. BETL 29. Gembloux: Duculot, 1972. 343–57. ————. *The Passion of Jesus in the Gospel of Matthew.* Wilmington, DE: Glazier, 1985. **Smith, R.** "Celebrating Easter in the Matthean Mode." *CurTM* 11 (1984) 79–82. **Smyth, K.** "Matthew 28: Resurrection as Theophany." *ITQ* 42 (1975) 259–71. **Soards, M. L.** "Oral Tradition before, in, and outside the Canonical Passion Narratives." In *Jesus and the Oral Gospel Tradition,* ed. H. Wansbrough. JSNTSup 64. Sheffield: JSOT, 1991. 334–50. **Suggs, M. J.** "The Passion and Resurrection Narratives." In *Jesus and Man's Hope,* ed. D. G. Miller and D. Y. Hadidian. Pittsburgh: Pittsburgh Theological Seminary, 1971. 2:323–38. **Trilling, W.** "Die Passionsbericht nach Matthäus." *Am Tische des Wortes* 9 (1965) 33–44.

*Introduction*

In the story of the passion and resurrection of Jesus we come to the climax of the Gospel and by far the longest consecutive narrative in Matthew. Here the goal of Jesus' mission is realized. The death of Jesus on the cross is no surprise, nor does it indicate the failure of Jesus' mission. From the evangelist's point of view, it is the fulfillment of scripture (26:54, 56), the fixed will of God, and the deliberate choice of the obedient Son of God. This, indeed, is the unique *time* (*kairos*) of Jesus (26:18). Therefore, the tone of the narrative is not one of tragedy or defeat but one of accomplishment and victory even before we reach the triumph of the resurrection in chap. 28. There remains, to be sure, the deep mystery of the abandonment experienced by Jesus on the cross. Although we cannot penetrate that mystery, its meaning is surely to be related to the procuring of the forgiveness of sins through the redemptive death of the Son spoken of earlier in the narrative (1:21; 20:28; cf. 26:28). Jesus in this narrative accomplishes the purpose for which he came into this world.

The passion narrative is a literary masterpiece. It contains gripping drama that cannot but move the reader, yet there is nothing maudlin here. The crucifixion itself is not described but is referred to in the briefest way. Pervading the narrative is a deep sense of irony. Though sinful men do their best to thwart the mission of Jesus, they accomplish the very purpose for which he came and thus fulfill God's will. It is this that primarily accounts for the paradoxical tone of the narrative. But the plot is full of lesser ironies. One of the twelve betrays Jesus while the other disciples, who had profusely insisted upon their loyalty to Jesus, abandon their master in the moment of crisis. The hearings before members of the Sanhedrin and before Pilate are at best travesties of justice that condemn one who was truly innocent to his death. Yet it is the Roman prefect who knows Jesus' innocence (27:23–24; cf. Judas' regretful confession in 27:4). The mocking statements about Jesus' identity as Messiah, Son of God, coming Son of Man, and King of Israel—whether from Caiaphas, Pilate, or the unnamed mockers at the cross—are known from the earlier narratives of the Gospel to be true. The final and correct assessment of Jesus, which caps the crucifixion narrative, comes not from the Jews but from a most unlikely source, a Roman centurion and his soldiers, who conclude what the reader has been led to conclude throughout, namely, that "this was truly the Son of God" (27:54).

Matthew again follows his principal source, Mark, very closely, inserting only two new passages (27:3–10; 27:62–66 [cf. 28:11–15]). Form-critical scholars have established that a version of the passion narrative existed in connected form very early, long before the writing of the Gospels. The possibility of a pre-Markan passion narrative, perhaps used liturgically in the early church, is investigated by R. E. Brown (*Death of the Messiah*, 46–57; in the same work, M. L. Soards offers a review of scholarship on the question [1492–1524]).

In many respects the passion and resurrection narrative corresponds to the infancy narrative of the Gospel. The birth and death/resurrection of Jesus can be characterized as heavily laden with corresponding theological significance. Both are accompanied by unusual concentrations of extraordinary, sometimes supernatural, events. Both therefore raise the question of the historicity of the respective narratives. As with the birth/infancy narrative, we must avoid the bald alternative of *either* history *or* theological interpretation (see Hagner, *Matthew 1–13*, 2). Here, as there, the evangelist seems to be working creatively with the historical tradition to which he has access. The degree of that creativity is, of course, debatable. Again it seems most reasonable to resist the notion that Matthew's procedure can be regarded as wholesale creation. As throughout this commentary, the presupposition is that most, if not all, of the time Matthew's narrative has a historical core. However, as in the infancy narrative, Matthew at points in the passion narrative may well be utilizing and elaborating traditional materials whose literal historical basis may be questioned. Particularly problematic in the passion narrative are the events mentioned in 27:51–53 (see discussion in *Comment* below). Here it seems that Matthew makes use of a tradition that had a historical core, which was then elaborated (probably already before Matthew) to make a theological point. R. E. Brown's monumental commentary on the passion narratives of the four Gospels (*Death of the Messiah*) discusses the issue of historicity throughout and comes to sober, balanced, and relatively conservative conclusions. While I differ from Brown in my conclusions at a number of points,

I nevertheless highly recommend his informative and judicious treatment of the issues (see esp. his introductory discussion, 13–24).

The larger structure of the passion narrative in Matthew can be analyzed as follows:

I. Preliminaries
    A. The Plot to Kill Jesus (26:1–5)
    B. The Anointing of Jesus (26:6–13)
    C. Judas' Betrayal of Jesus (26:14–16)
    D. The Passover/Eucharist (26:17–30)
II. The Arrest of Jesus
    A. The Prediction of the Falling Away of the Disciples (26:31–35)
    B. Jesus' Struggle in Gethsemane (26:36–46)
    C. Jesus Apprehended (26:47–56)
III. The Trial before the Jewish Authorities
    A. Jesus before Caiaphas (26:57–68)
    B. Peter's Denial of Jesus (26:69–75)
IV. The Trial before Pilate
    A. Judas and the Blood Money (27:3–10)
    B. The Arraignment before Pilate (27:1–2, 11–14)
V. Jewish Complicity in the Crucifixion
    A. The Decision for Barabbas and against Jesus (27:15–23)
    B. Responsibility for the Death of Jesus (27:24–26)
VI. The Crucifixion of Jesus
    A. Mockery of Jesus by the Roman Soldiers (27:27–31)
    B. Jesus Crucified (27:32–37)
    C. Mockery of the Crucified One (27:38–44)
    D. The Death of Jesus (27:45–50)
VII. The Aftermath
    A. Spectacular Events (27:51–54)
    B. The Women at the Cross (27:55–56)
    C. The Burial of Jesus (27:57–61)
    D. The Posting of a Guard at the Tomb (27:62–66; cf. 28:11–15)

The last section of the passion narrative, the posting of a guard at the tomb, serves as a natural bridge to the resurrection narrative of chap. 28, which, of course, provides the real end to the story of the crucifixion. If the death of Jesus is the heart of the Gospel as a totality, that event is but a cul-de-sac apart from the reality of the resurrection of Jesus. The death of Jesus is thus rather like a climactic deceptive cadence at the end of a long fugue, a cadence that leads to a yet greater and more glorious final resolution.

The resurrection part of the story is given in remarkable brevity. Apart from the narrative concerning the Jewish authorities' attempt to cover up the truth (28:11–15), the evangelist provides only an account of the announcement of the resurrection to the women at the tomb (28:1–7) and two resurrection appearances, without elaboration, one to the women (28:8–10) and one to the eleven disciples (28:16–20). To be sure, the last passage provides a brilliant climax, not only to the narrative of Jesus' death and resurrection but to the whole of the Gospel. Here the risen, glorious Jesus sets the agenda for his disciples and promises his presence with them "to the end of the age."

It should not be surprising that we find in the passion and resurrection narrative—the climax of the story of the earthly Jesus—a recapitulation of earlier theological themes of the Gospel. For example, Matthew emphasizes the fulfillment theme and, through the eucharist, the theme of Jesus' death as the sacrifice that provides salvation, i.e., the forgiveness of sins. Paradoxically, however, Christology especially emerges in the passion narrative. This emphasis is apparent in a number of ways but preeminently in Jesus' answer to the high priest's question, which constitutes his most explicit self-confession in the Gospel and provides the promise of his triumphant return at the end of the age (26:63–64). We encounter Christology again at a climactic moment in the narrative in the response of the Roman centurion and soldiers to the events accompanying the crucifixion (27:54). It is no mere prophet, teacher, or healer who hangs upon the cross. This we finally see in all clarity in the appearance of the risen Christ in 28:16–20.

It is unfortunately true that Matthew intensifies Jewish guilt for the crucifixion of Jesus in his narrative. He does this by his redaction of Mark at points (as in 27:10) but more importantly by his inclusion of new material (e.g., 27:4; esp. 27:24–25; 27:62–64). R. E. Brown identifies this "haunting issue of responsibility" for the death of an innocent man as the main difference between the Matthean and Markan passion narratives (*Death of the Messiah*, 29). It is a mistake to conclude from Matthew's focus on the Jews, however, that he is to be regarded as anti-Semitic (see *Comment* on 27:25). Instead, Matthew's emphasis can largely be explained by the intense rivalry between Matthew's Christian community and the Jewish synagogue. It is the result of an intense intra-Jewish debate between Christian Jews and non-Christian Jews (see Hagner, *Matthew 1–13*, lxxi–lxxiii).

# *The Plot to Kill Jesus Gains Momentum*    *(26:1–5)*

### Bibliography

Fonck, L. "Cena Bethanica." *VD* 8 (1928) 65–75, 98–106. Segal, J. B. *The Hebrew Passover: From the Earliest Times to A.D. 70.* New York: Oxford UP, 1963. Wambacq, B. N. "Pesaḥ-Maṣṣôt." *Bib* 62 (1981) 499–518. Zerafa, P. "Passover and Unleavened Bread." *Ang* 41 (1964) 235–50.

### Translation

¹*And then*[a] *when Jesus had finished speaking*[b] *all these words, he said to his disciples:* ²*"Know*[c] *that after two days will be the Passover, and the Son of Man will be*[d] *handed over to be crucified."*

³*Then the chief priests*[e] *and the elders of the people*[f] *gathered together in the palace of the high priest, who was called Caiaphas,*[g] ⁴*and they took counsel together so that by deceit they might arrest Jesus and put him to death.*[h] ⁵*But they were saying, "Not during the feast, lest there be a riot among the people."*

## Notes

a καὶ ἐγένετο, lit. "and it came to pass," a Semitism (cf. LXX).

b "Speaking" added to translation.

c D omits οἴδατε, "know." The verb may also be construed (with the majority of translations) as an indicative, hence "you know." See *Comment*.

d παραδίδοται is present tense but here is obviously used as a future.

e Many MSS (TR it syᵖ·ʰ) add καὶ οἱ γραμματεῖς, "and the scribes" (cf. Mark 14:1). W adds καὶ οἱ Φαρισαῖοι, "and the Pharisees."

f B* omits τοῦ λαοῦ, "of the people."

g D it vgʷʷ sa mae read Καίφα, "Caipha."

h B* omits καὶ ἀποκτείνωσιν, "and put him to death," probably by homoioteleuton (with κρατήσωσιν).

### Form/Structure/Setting

A. This passage serves as a transition from the preceding major section of the Gospel, the fifth and final discourse of Jesus, to the climax of the story of Jesus, the passion and resurrection narrative. Matthew has juxtaposed Jesus' own statement concerning what is to befall him and the reference to the Jewish authorities contemplating how they might bring about his death. Thus the stage is set for the salvific death of Jesus, the accomplishment of God's purpose in sending Jesus to the world.

B. After the Matthean formula that marks the end of the discourse (v 1), Matthew resumes following Mark (Mark 14:1–2; cf. Luke 22:1–2) with these few changes. The notice about the Passover coming after two days is put into the mouth of Jesus but with the omission of καὶ τὰ ἄζυμα, "and the unleavened bread" (not needed for his Jewish readers). He further adds the note from Jesus that the Son of Man is to be handed over to be crucified (v 2b). In v 3 Matthew provides a setting for the gathering of the Jewish leaders in the reference to "the palace of the high priest Caiaphas" (cf. John 18:24). Matthew substitutes οἱ πρεσβύτεροι τοῦ λαοῦ, "the elders of the people" (unique to Matthew [cf. v 47; 21:23; 27:1] among the Gospels, except for Luke 22:66) for Mark's γραμματεῖς, perhaps as being a more inclusive term. Matthew substitutes συνεβουλεύσαντο, "they were taking counsel," for Mark's ἐζήτουν, "they were seeking," but otherwise follows Mark fairly closely.

C. These transitional verses set the direction of the conclusion of the Gospel. Jesus, after concluding his final teaching discourse, returns to the subject of his death, something that takes on a new degree of imminence with the mention of the counsel taken by the Jewish authorities. As an outline the following is offered: (1) a concluding formula (v 1); (2) Jesus' prophecy of his crucifixion (v 2); and (3) the meeting of the Jewish authorities (vv 3–5), further divided into (a) the plan to do away with Jesus (v 4) and (b) the fear of a popular revolt (v 5).

### Comment

1  Matthew ends the eschatological discourse, the last of the five, with the same formula he uses to end the others, καὶ ἐγένετο ὅτε ἐτέλεσεν ὁ Ἰησοῦς πάντας τοὺς λόγους τούτους, "and it came to pass that when Jesus finished all these words"

(cf. 7:28; 11:1; 13:53; 19:1). Here πάντας, "all," occurs for the first time, probably however referring only to the sayings in chaps. 24–25. On the other hand, very likely it includes a hint that this is formally the end of Jesus' teaching, the last of the great public discourses (cf. Deut 31:1 LXX, where almost the same formula is used of the formal end of Moses' teaching).

**2** Jesus now turns the minds of his disciples to the nearness of the Passover festival and the imminent death of the Son of Man. The note about the Passover is more than simply a note of the time. When it is connected, as here, with a reference to the death of Jesus, it gives the latter a sacrificial significance; implicitly Jesus is the paschal lamb (brought out clearly in vv 26–28; πάσχα, "Passover," is mentioned only in this chapter of Matthew; cf. vv 17–19; for explicit comparison of the Passover lamb and the death of Christ, see 1 Cor 5:7). οἴδατε may well be taken as an imperative, "know," rather than an indicative (thus Gnilka, following Lohmeyer), making the statement a solemn announcement rather than merely an acknowledgment of what the disciples already know. In fact, the disciples are here for the first time informed of the close connection between the Passover sacrifice and Jesus' death. The Passover feast probably fell on 15 Nisan in that year (a Saturday, or Sabbath day), beginning like all Jewish days at sundown of the previous day (so that the Passover meal would have normally been eaten on our Friday evening). Thus Jesus probably spoke these words to the disciples on Wednesday (or Tuesday night, which was regarded as the beginning of Wednesday). The prediction of the crucifixion recalls the earlier predictions in 16:21; 17:22–23; 20:18–19 (only the last, however, refers to crucifixion as the means of Jesus' death), where in contrast to the present passage the resurrection "on the third day" is consistently mentioned. The last two predictions also refer to "the Son of Man."

**3** Matthew's introductory τότε, "then," has the effect of making the plotting of the Jewish authorities the fulfillment of Jesus' prediction. οἱ ἀρχιερεῖς καὶ οἱ πρεσβύτεροι τοῦ λαοῦ, "the chief priests and the elders of the people" (see in 2:4 and 21:23, respectively), gather in the high priest's αὐλήν, "palace" (lit. "courtyard"; cf. 26:58, 69). Caiaphas was the ruling high priest (A.D. 18–36) and was the son-in-law of a previous high priest, Annas (shortened from Ananus), who is often mentioned with Caiaphas and who retained a strong influence as a kind of high priest emeritus (cf. Luke 3:2; John 18:13, 24; Acts 4:6). Jesus was ultimately brought before Caiaphas (v 57).

**4** The plotting to kill Jesus is not a new development (cf. 12:14; 22:15 [although the Pharisees are the agents in both instances], both with the cognate noun "counsel"; cf. later in the Gospel, 27:1, 7; and John 11:53). However, the recording of a meeting of powerful Jewish authorities at the beginning of the passion narrative gives it a new and ominous character. The plotting against Jesus is described as δόλῳ, "by deceit" (only occurrence in Matthew). Implied by this are both the innocence of Jesus and the unrighteousness of his opponents. The word is commonly used in the LXX to describe those who oppress the righteous (e.g., LXX Pss 9:28; 34:20; 51:2; 54:11; Prov 12:20; Jer 5:27).

**5** During the Passover Jerusalem would be jammed with many thousands of pilgrims, who would have their minds filled with nationalist fervor and longings. At that time the apprehension of a popular messianic figure could prove to be extremely dangerous. The one thing the authorities could not risk with the Romans, to whom they owed their privileged position, was a populist revolt (θόρυβος, "riot," is used elsewhere in Matthew only in 27:24; cf. Jos., *J.W.* 1.4.3 §88 for an example of such a riot). It would thus be better to wait until after the feast, or anyway so it seemed at the moment.

### Explanation

In this brief transition passage we are at a turning point, being set in motion toward the goal of the cross. The teaching and healing ministry of Jesus is essentially at an end, and we proceed now into the final and climactic stage of the Gospel narrative. Jesus calmly and confidently predicts what is to happen to him. This is indeed why he has come, and it is his primary work. There is a touch of irony in that directly after this prediction the Jewish authorities are recorded as busy in their deliberations concerning the need to be rid of this troublemaker. Thus unknowingly they industriously set about to accomplish the very purpose of God in Jesus. They cannot thwart God's plan; in their evil opposition to Jesus they become the very instruments of the fulfillment of that plan.

## The Anointing of Jesus    (26:6–13)

### Bibliography

**Beran, T. W.** "The Four Anointings." *ExpTim* 39 (1927–28) 137–39. **Daube, D.** "The Anointing at Bethany and Jesus' Burial." *ATR* 32 (1950) 186–99. **Derrett, J. D. M.** "The Anointing at Bethany and the Story of Zacchaeus." In *Law in the New Testament.* London: Longman and Todd, 1970, 1986. 266–85. ———. "The Anointing at Bethany." *SE* 2 [= TU 87] (1964) 174–82. **Feuillet, A.** "Les deux onctions fautes sur Jésus, et Marie-Madeleine." *RevThom* 75 (1975) 357–94. **Fiorenza, E. Schüssler.** *In Memory of Her: A Feminist Theological Reconstruction of Christian Origins.* New York: Crossroad, 1983. **Greenlee, J. H.** "'For Her Memorial': *Eis mnemosynon autes,* Mt 26.13, Mk 14.9." *ExpTim* 71 (1959–60) 245. **Holst, R.** "The Anointing of Jesus: Another Application of the Form-Critical Method." *JBL* 95 (1976) 435–46. **Jeremias, J.** "Mc 14.9." *ZNW* 44 (1952) 103–7. **Legault, A.** "An Application of the Form-Critique Method to the Anointings in Galilee (Lk 7,36–50) and Bethany (Mt 26,6–13; Mk 14,3–9; Jn 12,1–8)." *CBQ* 16 (1954) 131–45. **Pesch, R.** "Die Salbung Jesu in Bethanien (Mk 14.3–9)." In *Orientierung an Jesu.* FS J. Schmid, ed. P. Hoffmann et al. Freiburg: Herder, 1973. 267–85. **Riggans, W.** "Jesus and the Scriptures: Two Short Notes." *Themelios* 16 (1991) 15–16. **Schedl, C.** "Die Salbung Jesu in Betanien: Zur Kompositionskunst von Mk 14,3–9 und Mt 26,6–13." *BLit* 54 (1981) 151–62. **Storch, R.** "'Was soll diese Verschwendung?': Bemerkungen zur Auslegungsgeschichte von Mk 14,4f." In *Der Ruf Jesu und die Antwort der Gemeinde.* FS J. Jeremias, ed. E. Lohse et al. Göttingen: Vandenhoeck & Ruprecht, 1970. 247–58. **Thiemann, R. F.** "The Unnamed Woman at Bethany." *TToday* 44 (1987) 179–88.

### Translation

⁶*When Jesus was in Bethany in the house of Simon the leper,* ⁷*a woman came to him*

*who had an alabaster jar* [a] *of very expensive* [b] *ointment, and she poured it over his head as he was reclining at table.* [8]*But when the* [c] *disciples saw this,* [d] *they were indignant, saying: "What is the point of this waste?* [9]*For this* [e] *could have been sold for much and the money* [f] *given to the poor."* [10]*But Jesus knew their reasoning* [g] *and said to them: "Why are you causing trouble for the woman? For she has done a good work for me.* [11]*For you always have the poor among you, but you will not always have me.* [12]*For when she poured this ointment upon my body, she did it to prepare me for burial.* [13]*Truly I tell you, wherever this gospel is preached in the whole world, what she has done will also be told in memory of her."* [h]

### Notes

[a] "Jar" added in translation.

[b] βαρυτίμου, "very expensive." A number of important MSS (‍א A D L Θ sy^hmg) have the synonym πολυτίμου, probably through the influence of the parallel in John 12:3 (cf. Mark 14:3).

[c] Many MSS (A W f¹ TR sy sa^ms) insert αὐτοῦ, "his."

[d] "This" added, supplying direct object.

[e] Some MSS (K Γ f¹³) add τὸ μύρον, "ointment," through the influence of the parallel in Mark 14:5.

[f] "The money" added, supplying the implied subject.

[g] "Their reasoning" added, supplying direct object.

[h] In μνημόσυνον αὐτῆς the pronoun may also be taken as a subjective gen., resulting in the meaning "her memorial (to me)." See *Comment.*

### Form/Structure/Setting

A. In keeping with the transition to the passion narrative of the Gospel, the story of the anointing of Jesus—the preparation of his body for burial, as he interprets it—is told first (following the order in Mark but differing from its placement in Luke and John, if the latter are representations of the same story). It focuses indirectly, but poignantly, on the death of Jesus, with the plotting against Jesus immediately preceding and the betrayal of Jesus immediately following. The passage thus has an obvious christological orientation (Gnilka).

B. Matthew is dependent on Mark (14:3–9), whose wording he follows rather closely. Luke 7:36–50, on the other hand, is probably an independent story (so Legault, McNeile, Carson; *pace* Holst) with some cross-over influence from Mark, while John 12:1–8 is probably the same story as that of Matthew and Mark but with cross-over influence especially from the Lukan story (see Holst for the argument that all four narratives refer to the same incident). Among differences between Matthew and Mark, we note the following more significant ones. In v 7 Matthew has abbreviated Mark's description (14:3) of the ointment as νάρδου πιστικῆς πολυτελοῦς, "of very expensive nard" (the meaning of πιστικῆς is unclear), with the single word βαρυτίμου, "very expensive," perhaps regarding the detailed description of the ointment as unnecessary. Matthew in the same verse omits the reference to the woman breaking the alabaster jar, perhaps for the same reason. In v 8 Matthew specifies that it was οἱ μαθηταί, "the disciples," who were angry (for Mark's τινες, "some") and thereby stresses further the shortcomings of the disciples. In the same verse Matthew's omission of πρὸς ἑαυτούς, "to themselves" (Mark 14:4), makes the initial γνούς, "knowing," of v 10 rather difficult.

Matthew's typical abbreviation of Mark continues in v 8 with the omission of the unnecessary τοῦ μύρου γέγονεν, lit. "(this waste) of the ointment occurred" (Mark 14:4), and in v 9 of τὸ μύρον, "the ointment." For some reason Matthew replaces Mark's evaluation of the ointment at ἐπάνω δηναρίων τριακοσίων, "more than three hundred denarii," with the simple πολλοῦ, "much." Matthew omits Mark's next short sentence καὶ ἐνεβριμῶντο αὐτῇ, "and they scolded her" (Mark 14:5), as well as ἄφετε αὐτήν, "leave her alone" (Mark 14:6), thereby leaving the question of v 10, "why are you causing trouble for the woman?" with no apparent explanation. Matthew's εἰς ἐμέ for Mark's ἐν ἐμοί at the end of v 10 is an improvement. In v 11 Matthew omits Mark's sentence "and whenever you want, you are able to do good to them" (Mark 14:7), thereby sharpening the contrasting statement "but you do not always have me," immediately juxtaposing it with the preceding sentence. Shortly after that, Matthew omits the brief sentence "what she could she has done" (Mark 14:8), perhaps regarding it as unnecessary. Matthew's recasting of v 12 (cf. Mark 14:8) strengthens the statement. He adds τοῦτο, "this," after "gospel" for emphasis. Finally, ἐν ὅλῳ τῷ κόσμῳ, "in the whole world," is an improvement of Mark's εἰς ὅλον τὸν κόσμον, lit. "to the whole world." Matthew's redaction thus again reflects the usual abbreviation and stylistic improvement.

C. The pericope consists of narrative, explanation of the symbolism of the narrative, and a concluding logion. The following outline is suggested: (1) the woman's anointing of Jesus in Simon's house (vv 6–7); (2) the complaint of the disciples (vv 8–9); (3) Jesus' interpretation of the deed (vv 10–12); and (4) the memorial to the woman (v 13). The only striking structural feature is in the parallel statements of v 11: the contrast between having the poor always and not always having Jesus.

## Comment

**6** Βηθανίᾳ, "Bethany," was a village on the Mount of Olives nearly two miles east of Jerusalem. (Jesus had probably been staying in Bethany [cf. 21:17].) Simon "the leper" (τοῦ λεπροῦ) is not mentioned in the NT beyond the present reference and the Markan parallel. He would have been a leper who had been cured of his leprosy (by Jesus?); otherwise he would have been allowed no social intercourse.

**7** Strangely, the woman remains unnamed (perhaps just because she was a woman; see E. Schüssler Fiorenza) despite the emphasis at the end of the passage concerning the story being retold in memory of her (v 13; in John, where the last point is not made, the woman is identified as Mary, sister of Martha and Lazarus [John 12:3]). In a lavish gesture of devotion, the woman poured "an alabaster jar of very expensive perfumed ointment" (ἀλάβαστρον μύρου βαρυτίμου) over the head of Jesus. The alabaster flask accords with the costliness of its contents. αὐτοῦ ἀνακειμένου, "while he was reclining at table," refers to the usual posture at special meals. The anointing of the head, rather than the feet (usually anointed before the meal), was the normal custom with such an expensive ointment.

**8–9** The disciples, ever practical and oblivious to the deeper meanings of the act, protest indignantly (ἠγανάκτησαν, "they were indignant," used earlier in 20:24; 21:15) at what they could see only as a waste. Would it not have been better to sell (πιπράσκειν, "sell," is used elsewhere in Matthew in 13:46; 18:25) something so costly and distribute the money to the poor? The disciples must have been certain they were on the right track in their objection since the gospel entails "good news to the poor" (11:5) and they knew that Jesus had told a rich man to sell his possessions and give the money to the poor (19:21). In ordinary circumstances their objection might well have been apropos, but as Jesus goes on to explain, the present instance was an exceptional one.

**10** The word γνούς, "knowing," reflects Jesus' supernatural knowledge of the thinking of his disciples (cf. Mark's notice πρὸς ἑαυτούς, "to themselves" [Mark 14:4]; cf. the same participle for Jesus' special knowledge in 12:15; 16:8; 22:18). On the question "Why are you causing trouble for the woman?" see Mark's notice that the disciples "scolded her" (Mark 14:5). The idiom παρέχειν κόπους, "to cause trouble," is found also in Luke 11:7; 18:5; Gal 6:17. The ἔργον καλόν, lit. "good work," that the woman did is a special work of righteousness (a work of love rather than of almsgiving; cf. Jeremias, 103) because of the peculiar circumstance mentioned in v 12 (the expression occurs, but in the plural, in 5:16). The sense in which εἰς ἐμέ, "to me," is meant becomes clear in the next verse.

**11** The two parallel, but contrasting, statements of this verse are clear and indisputable. The poor are a reality in every society of every age (cf. Deut 15:11a). Jesus, on the other hand, will not always be physically with his disciples (cf. 9:15 and the several predictions of his death, including v 2 of the present chapter). The last statement becomes one of increasing prominence in the Gospel. One cannot miss what is implied: there will be opportunity in the future to minister to the needs of the poor; there will be no opportunity in the future to minister to Jesus. But even beyond this, the deed of kindness performed by the woman has a special significance.

**12** The woman had in effect anointed Jesus' body for burial. This was certainly not her intent. She was probably simply demonstrating her unlimited devotion to Jesus, perhaps in response to something Jesus had done for her or her family. Neither in the context, nor in the woman's intention, nor in Jesus' interpretation of her deed is there any suggestion of a royal, kingly anointing here. Only when Jesus interprets the act symbolically does the deed come to bear the significance of preparation for burial. In order to draw out the symbolism, ἐπὶ τοῦ σώματός μου, "upon my body," replaces the ἐπὶ τῆς κεφαλῆς αὐτοῦ, "upon his head," of v 7. τὸ μύρον τοῦτο, "this ointment," becomes emphatic. Such "ointment," being highly perfumed, was used in embalming (cf. the plural form of the word in Luke 23:56; other evidence in POxy 736.13; Artemidorus 1.5; Gen 50:2 LXX). The infinitive ἐνταφιάσαι, "to prepare for burial," is used in the NT only here and in John 19:40 (cf. the cognate noun in Mark 14:8; John 12:7). Matthew accordingly omits the Markan record of the women coming to the tomb to anoint the body (Mark 16:1).

**13** As an indirect reward for the woman's well-timed deed of love, Jesus solemnly affirms (ἀμὴν λέγω ὑμῖν, "truly I tell you") that this story will become a standard part of the gospel tradition and will come to be repeated everywhere the gospel is preached. The notion of τὸ εὐαγγέλιον τοῦτο, "this gospel," being "preached" (κηρυχθήσεται) in the whole world is found already in 24:14, where, however, the phrase is modified by "of the kingdom" (cf. 28:19). Only a forced exegesis could conclude that this preaching is not the church's proclamation of the gospel (wrongly supposing that Jesus could not have envisioned a worldwide mission) but an angelic proclamation of God's victory at the end of the age (thus

Jeremias, *Abba*, 115–20). Similarly, εἰς μνημόσυνον αὐτῆς, "in memory of her," may refer to the church's celebration of the wonderful deed performed by her rather than a divine remembering connected with eschatological reward (cf. *1 Enoch* 103:4; Sir 50:6), as Jeremias (*Abba*, 115–20) argues. On the other hand, perhaps the phrase involves a subjective genitive. Then the meaning would be that "what she has done will also be told as her memorial to me." This would be more in keeping with the fact that she is not named. (For this hypothesis, see Greenlee.) This unnamed woman broadens the category of disciples beyond the twelve (see Thiemann).

### Explanation

When a woman comes and lavishes her love and gratitude upon Jesus in the form of a costly ointment, with the thought of his imminent death uppermost in his mind he takes the anointing as a symbolic preparation of his body for burial. The central importance of the passion to the Gospel is such that it transforms the story. The fundamental question now is not the neediness of the poor. The disciples' concern for the poor is by no means incorrect. In this one instance, however, the timing was wrong. Jesus' statement "you always have the poor among you" (v 11) must not be taken to mean that as a consequence one need not worry about them or that all attempts to ameliorate the condition of the poor are ill-founded and futile. This cannot be made clearer than by citing the full text of Deut 15:11: "Since there will never cease to be some in need on the earth, I therefore command you, 'Open your hand to the poor and needy neighbor in your land.'" The ongoing presence of the poor does not provide an excuse to ignore them and their plight, but, quite the contrary, it provides the ongoing opportunity and stimulus to help them. But this one time responsibility to the poor may be legitimately set aside. All else assumes a subordinate place relative to the imminent death of Jesus. And the story of the woman who anointed his head is no longer one story among others but part of the story of the passion narrative itself.

# The Treachery of Judas   (26:14–16)

### Bibliography

**Bacon, B. W.** "What Did Judas Betray?" *HibJ* 19 (1920–21) 476–93. **Baumbach, G.** "Judas—Jünger und Verräter Jesu." *ZZ* 17 (1963) 91–98. **Cullmann, O.** "Die zwölfte Apostel." In *Vorträge und Aufsätze 1925 bis 1962*, ed. K. Fröhlich. Tübingen: Mohr, 1966. 214–22. **Enslin, M. S.** "How the Story Grew: Judas in Fact and Fiction." In *Festschrift to Honor F. Wilber Gingrich*, ed. E. H. Barth and E. E. Cocroft. Leiden: Brill, 1972. 123–41. **Gärtner, B.** *Iscariot.* Facet Books. Philadelphia: Fortress, 1971. **Klauck, H.-J.** *Judas—Ein Jünger des Herrn.* QD 111. Freiburg: Herder, 1987. **Levin-Goldschmidt, H.,** and **Limbeck, M.** *Heilvoller Verrat? Judas im Neuen Testament.* Stuttgart: Katholisches Bibelwerk, 1976. **Lüthi, K.** "Das Problem des Judas Iskariot—neu untersucht." *EvT* 16 (1956) 98–114. **Morin, J.-A.** "Les deux derniers des Douzes: Simon le Zélote et Judas Iskariôth." *RB* 80 (1973) 332–58. **Neirynck, F.** "ΑΠΟ

*TOTE HP≡ATO* and the Structure of Matthew." *ETL* 64 (1988) 21–59. **Plath, M.** "Warum hat die urchristliche Gemeinde auf die Überlieferung der Judaserzählungen Wert gelegt?" *ZNW* 17 (1916) 178–88. **Popkes, W.** *Christus Traditus: Eine Untersuchung zum Begriff der Dahingabe im Neuen Testament.* ATANT 49. Zürich: Zwingli, 1967. **Reiner, E.** "Thirty Pieces of Silver." *JAOS* 88 (1968) 186–90. **Roquefort, D.** "Judas: Une figure de la perversion." *ETR* 58 (1983) 501–13. **Stein-Schneider, H.** "A la recherche du Judas historique." *ETR* 60 (1985) 403–24. **Vogler, W.** *Judas Iskarioth: Untersuchung zu Tradition und Redaktion von Textes des Neuen Testaments und ausserkanonischer Schriften.* Theologische Arbeiten 42. Berlin: Evangelische Verlagsanstalt, 1983. **Wagner, H.,** ed. *Judas Iskariot: Menschliches oder heilsgeschichtliches Drama?* Frankfurt: Knecht, 1985. **Wrede, W.** "Judas Ischariot in der urchristlichen Überlieferung." In *Vorträge und Studien.* Tübingen: Mohr, 1907. 127–46.

### Translation

¹⁴ *Then one of the twelve, the one called Judas Iscariot,*[a] *came to the chief priests and* ¹⁵ *said:*[b] *"What will you give me so I will betray him to you?" And they set with*[c] *him the amount of*[d] *thirty silver coins.*[e] ¹⁶ *And from that time he began to seek an opportune time in order that he might betray him.*[f]

### Notes

[a] D Θ[c vid] lat read Σκαριώτης, "*Scariōtēs*," omitting the initial iota. See *Note* on 10:4.

[b] D adds αὐτοῖς, "to them."

[c] ἔστησαν, possibly "weighed out (to him)," which would indicate that he was paid immediately. The same verb occurs in the LXX of Zech 11:13.

[d] "The amount of" added for clarity.

[e] Some MSS (D *f*¹) read στατῆρας, "staters," specifying the kind of silver coins.

[f] Some MSS (D Θ it sa[ms] mae bo) add αὐτοῖς, "to them."

### Form/Structure/Setting

A. Following upon their meeting to devise a plan to do away with Jesus (vv 3–5), the chief priests are soon confronted with an ideal opportunity. No one less than an intimate of Jesus, one of the twelve, comes forward to betray his master into their hands. And now the story takes on a momentum that finds its end in the crucifixion of Jesus. If Jesus has been anointed for his burial in the preceding pericope, the inexorable process by which he comes to his death has its beginning here.

B. Matthew continues to follow Mark (here Mark 14:10–11; cf. Luke 22:3–6), in this case somewhat freely. Among Matthew's redactional changes, the following should be noted. At the start Matthew inserts τότε, "then," a favorite device, transposes εἷς τῶν δώδεκα, "one of the twelve," to the head of the sentence for emphasis, and alters Mark's Semitic Ἰσκαριώθ, "Iscariōth," to the Grecized Ἰσκαριώτης, "Iscariōtēs" (so too Luke 22:3). In v 15 Matthew alters Mark's narrative into direct discourse, inserting the phrase "what will you give me?" thereby adding pecuniary considerations to Judas' motive. In the same verse he omits Mark's ἀκούσαντες ἐχάρησαν, "and when they heard they were glad" (Mark 14:11), perhaps simply to abbreviate. Matthew also replaces Mark's ἐπηγγείλαντο, "they promised," with ἔστησαν, "they set," and specifies the amount agreed upon as τριάκοντα, "thirty," silver coins, in order to prepare the way for the use of Zech

11:13 later in the narrative (27:9). Finally, note Matthew's insertion of a characteristic ἀπὸ τότε, "from that time," at the beginning of v 16 and the use of the direct object εὐκαιρίαν, "opportune time" (so too Luke 22:6). We again note Matthew's tendency to abbreviate but also his ability to introduce new material for both stylistic and theological (or argumentative) reasons.

C. An outline of this short passage would do no more than enumerate the following items, proceeding verse by verse: Judas goes to the Jewish authorities (v 14), agrees upon a price for which to betray Jesus to their hands (v 15), and begins to look for an opportunity to betray him (v 16).

## Comment

**14** Matthew will not have the reader miss the irony that it was εἷς τῶν δώδεκα, "one of the twelve," which he moves to the beginning of his sentence, who actually betrayed Jesus (this is given even stronger emphasis in vv 20–25). The name Judas Iscariot has already been mentioned in the list of the twelve in chap. 10 (10:4). See the discussion there. For ἀρχιερεῖς, "chief priests," cf. vv 3, 47, 59.

**15** Matthew's casting of the passage seems to make Judas' motivation one of money since he asks what amount they are willing to pay. Possibly the verb here (see *Note* c) means "weighed out" in the sense of paid then and there, although it seems unlikely that the authorities would have paid in advance. All they needed was the agreement (cf. Mark 14:11). On the other hand, it may well be that Matthew inserts the question in order to prepare the way for the mention of the amount, i.e., the "thirty" (unique to Matthew) pieces of silver that will become important in the fulfillment of Zech 11:13 cited in 27:9 (cf. 27:3). Although the exact value of the silver pieces is not known, the amount was comparatively modest (coincidentally the price of a slave according to Exod 21:32; but perhaps a more insubstantial sum, even "paltry," if "thirty shekels" reflects an idiomatic Sumerian expression as Reiner argues). The modest amount and the lack of bargaining on Judas' part suggest that money was not his only or even his primary motive. Because of his treachery, Judas becomes known in the gospel tradition as "the betrayer" (cf. 10:4; 26:24–25, 46, 48; 27:3). Matthew (like Mark) makes no mention of "Satan" or "the devil" as a force acting upon Judas as do Luke (Luke 22:3) and John (John 13:2; cf. 6:70).

**16** The Lukan parallel makes clear the character of an εὐκαιρίαν, "good opportunity," namely one ἄτερ ὄχλου, "without a crowd" (Luke 22:6). This is in keeping with the earlier mentioned fear of a riot by the authorities (v 5). For them it would have been best "after the feast" (v 5) of Passover (and Unleavened Bread), but the opportunity that now presented itself was so ideal that it practically overruled all other considerations. Matthew's ἀπὸ τότε, "from that time," is characteristic, indicating a clear turning point in the narrative, though not so important as those of 4:17 and 16:21 (see Neirynck, 33–34).

## Explanation

It must be disconcerting to every disciple of Jesus that one of the twelve, that group so uniquely intimate with Jesus, became the betrayer of his master. It came as no surprise to Jesus, however, who knew the human heart so well. But it *was* a surprise to the disciples, who could not bring themselves to believe that one of their company would betray Jesus. We can only speculate regarding Judas' motives, though it seems unlikely that the motive was money alone. Perhaps he was disappointed in the direction of Jesus' ministry and wished to force his hand by having him arrested. Perhaps with the Zealots he shared the ardent expectation of a national-political kingdom that would end the Roman domination of Israel. It is unlikely, however, that Judas was offended at the anointing of Jesus because he understood it as an anointing of the King of the Jews (*pace* Bacon).

We must avoid, however, making Judas into a kind of unconscious hero of the faith for his role in initiating the process against Jesus that led to the redemptive event of the cross (contra Levin-Goldschmidt and Limbeck). Judas' betrayal was a sinister deed and is only spoken of in such terms by Jesus (see esp. 26:24). Because God can use that deed in accomplishing his will does not turn it into a commendable one, nor are we to think of Judas as a kind of saint (cf. the similar conclusion of Klauck).

# *Preparations for the Passover*     *(26:17–19)*

### Bibliography

**Arnott, A. G.** "'The first day of unleavened . . .': Mt 26.17, Mk 14.12, Lk 22.7." *BT* 35 (1984) 235–38. **Black, M.** "*ΕΦΦΑΘΑ* (Mk 7.34), [*TA*] *ΠΑΣΧΑ* (Mt 26.18W), [*TA*] *ΣΑΒΒΑΤΑ* (passim), [*TA*] *ΔΙΔΡΑΧΜΑ* (Mt 17.24 bis)." In *Mélanges bibliques.* FS B. Rigaux, ed. A. Descamps. Gembloux: Duculot, 1970. 57–62. **Chenderlin, F.** "Distributed Observance of the Passover: A Hypothesis." *Bib* 56 (1975) 369–93. ———. "Distributed Observance of the Passover: A Preliminary Test of the Hypothesis." *Bib* 57 (1976) 1–24. **Heawood, P. J.** "The Time of the Last Supper." *JQR* 42 (1951–52) 37–44. **Hoehner, H. W.** "The Day of Christ's Crucifixion." *BSac* 131 (1974) 241–64. **Jacob, R.** *Les péricopes de l'entrée à Jérusalem et de la préparation de la cène: Contribution à l'étude du problème synoptique.* Paris: Gabalda, 1973. **Jaubert, A.** *The Date of the Last Supper.* Staten Island, NY: Alba, 1965. **Strobel, A.** "Der Termin des Todes Jesu." *ZNW* 51 (1960) 69–101. **Zeitlin, S.** "The Time of the Passover Meal." *JQR* 42 (1951–52) 45–50.

### Translation

[17]*On the first day* [a] *of the festival of Unleavened Bread, the disciples came to Jesus and said: "Where do you want us to make preparation for you to eat the Passover meal?"* [18]*And he said: "Go into the city to the man and say to him: 'The teacher says:* [b] *"My time is near. At your place* [c] *I want to celebrate the Passover with my disciples."'"* [19]*And the disciples did as Jesus ordered them, and they made ready the Passover meal.*

### Notes

[a] "Day" added to translation.

## Form/Structure/Setting

A. This short passage serves as a prologue to the two following pericopes, which describe what took place at the Passover meal (i.e., vv 20–25, 26–30). Matthew's telling suggests that Jesus had taken steps to prepare for this important time rather than that a special divine providence was at work (as in Mark and Luke).

B. Matthew shows evidence of depending upon Mark (cf. Mark 14:12–17), but he has considerably abbreviated that material, taking up just the skeleton of the Markan passage. In v 17 only relatively insignificant omissions occur. Thus Matthew omits the unnecessary ἡμέρᾳ, "day," the somewhat difficult ὅτε τὸ πάσχα ἔθυον, "when they sacrificed the Passover lamb" (Matthew may have been bothered by the fact that the first day of the feast of Unleavened Bread was 15 Nisan while the lambs were sacrificed on 14 Nisan), and the redundant participle ἀπελθόντες, "having gone." But then Matthew omits altogether Mark's mysterious account of the sending of two disciples with the instructions that they would encounter a man carrying a jar of water whom they were to follow (Mark 14:13), that they were to go into the house and ask the master of the house where the guest room was (Mark 14:14), that he would show them a large upper room fully furnished where they were to prepare the Passover meal (Mark 14:15), and finally that they did this and found all just as Jesus had said (Mark 14:16). In contrast with this, Matthew preserves from Mark only that the disciples were to go into the city to a certain man and tell him that the teacher says he wants to eat the Passover there with his disciples. Matthew makes one significant insertion, ὁ καιρός μου ἐγγύς ἐστιν, "my time is near" (v 18). Matthew concludes by noting that the disciples obeyed Jesus and then in the last four words rejoins Mark verbatim: καὶ ἡτοίμασαν τὸ πάσχα, "and they prepared the Passover." It is perhaps surprising that Matthew here abbreviates Mark as much as he does. The reason is not that he has any objection to the material but more probably that he is pressed to conserve space; Mark's details are not necessary at this point. This is in keeping with Matthew's practice throughout the Gospel in his use of Mark.

C. The straightforward narrative consists of the disciples' question (v 17), Jesus' instructions (v 18), and the disciples' compliance with those instructions. Matthew seems to want to move quickly to the important events that follow.

D. Although it is not possible here to go into any detail regarding the problem of dating the Passover and the celebration of the meal by the disciples, the following brief remarks may be offered. The synoptic Gospels present the last supper as a Passover meal that took place at the normal time, i.e., on 15 Nisan, which began at sundown on Thursday. (The lambs were being sacrificed earlier that day, i.e., on 14 Nisan [cf. Mark 14:12].) The meal was eaten that night, and Jesus was arrested, given a mockery of a trial, and crucified on the same day, i.e., by Friday afternoon (on the problem of "the first day of Unleavened Bread," cf. *Comment* on v 17). In the Gospel of John, on the other hand, Jesus' death takes place at the time of the sacrificing of the Passover lambs, *before* the eating of the Passover meal (cf. John 18:28). On this reckoning, 15 Nisan began twenty-four hours later than in the Synoptics, i.e., on Friday at sundown. Commentators have appealed to the possibility of various calendrical reckonings (Jaubert [cf. Strobel]: solar calendar [e.g., Qumran, Synoptics] versus lunar calendar [e.g., Pharisees, John]; Hoehner: Galilean calendar [e.g., Pharisees, Synoptics] versus Judean calendar [e.g., Sadducees, John]); or "distributed observance" (Chenderlin); and, of course, a deliberate chronological shift for theological purposes (i.e., on John's part to line up the death of Jesus with the sacrifice of the lambs) has often been suggested. Any of these possibilities seems preferable to the Herculean attempt to harmonize the discordant chronologies (as, e.g., by Carson, 528–32).

*Comment*

**17** τῇ πρώτῃ τῶν ἀζύμων, "the first day of Unleavened Bread," was technically the first of the seven days of the festival; this first day occurred on 15 Nisan, the same day as the Passover celebration. Yet according to Matthew, following Mark, it is on this day that preparations are made for the Passover meal of the evening (reckoned as the next day, making it 16 Nisan, a day too late). For this reason some have attempted to understand τῇ πρώτῃ, "on the first," as a misunderstanding of the underlying Aramaic, which would have been קַמָּא, *qammāʾ*, or קַמֵּי, *qammê*, "before," rather than קַמָּאָה, *qammāʾāh*, "first" (thus Allen). The solution can only be guessed at, but the problem seems not to have bothered the evangelists. Perhaps the feast of Unleavened Bread could have been thought of as beginning a day before the Passover (cf. Exod 12:18, referring to the evening of 14 Nisan—thus eight days of Passover; cf. Jos., *J.W.* 5.3.1 §99; *Ant.* 2.15.1 §317 also refers to keeping the feast of Unleavened Bread for eight rather than seven days, thus including 14 Nisan [see Str-B 1:987–88]). Arnott's suggestion that the passage is referring to "unleavened things" goes against the natural meaning of the phrase τῶν ἀζύμων. The preparation would have included the obtaining of a suitable place, the sacrificing and preparation of the lamb, and the acquisition of other necessities such as herbs, wine, and bread (cf. Exod 12:1–20; and the Passover Haggadah). The feast of Unleavened Bread or Passover was one of the three major feasts involving pilgrimage to Jerusalem (see Deut 16:16). On this occasion the deliverance of Israel from the slavery of Egypt was commemorated. Lambs were slaughtered in remembrance of the sacrificial lambs of Exod 12:1–27. Now, however, a greater deliverance was to be accomplished by the unique sacrifice of God's Messiah (see vv 26–30).

**18** The disciples are instructed to go "into the city" (the Passover had to be celebrated in Jerusalem) πρὸς τὸν δεῖνα, "to the man," i.e., to someone known but not identified, with whom previous arrangements appear to have been made by Jesus. This man will apparently understand who "the teacher" is and recognize the signal ὁ καιρός μου ἐγγύς ἐστιν, "my time is near." The reference to this person as τὸν δεῖνα, "the man" or "so-and-so" (the only NT use of the word), i.e., someone who for some reason remains anonymous, together with the unusual message, retains in Matthew's account an unexplainable air of mystery when the Markan parts of the story have been removed (cf. the similar "mystery" in 21:2–3). Nevertheless, Matthew's version of the story is readily explainable as the result of Jesus' own prearrangement with the man, with precisely the need of a place to celebrate the Passover in mind (ποιῶ τὸ πάσχα, "I want to celebrate the Passover"; cf. LXX Exod 12:48; Num 9:2–5). The use of ὁ διδάσκαλος, "the teacher" (cf. 8:19; 9:11; 12:38; 17:24; 19:11; 22:16, 24, 36), seems to suggest that this particular man may not have been a follower of Jesus (in which case κύριος, "Lord," might have been expected in keeping with Matthew's usage). ὁ καιρός μου ἐγγύς ἐστιν, "my time is near," refers, of course, to the time of Jesus' death (cf. John 7:6, 8; but ὥρα μου, "my hour," is far more common in John), thereby connecting very closely the imminence of the death of Jesus with the Passover celebration. That the man knew the meaning of these words, however, remains unlikely. He need only know that Jesus required a place in which he and his disciples, i.e., the twelve, could celebrate the Passover together.

**19** The disciples did as Jesus "ordered them to do" (συνέταξεν; elsewhere in the NT only in 21:6 and 27:10), and they proceeded to prepare for the Passover meal. The setting is thus in place for the following pericopes.

### Explanation

Jesus was unquestionably aware of what important things he wanted to teach his disciples at the Passover meal. It is thus fully understandable that perhaps earlier in the week he had made inquiries concerning a suitable, i.e., private, location for this event. Already in the formula spoken to the man, "my time is near," the anticipated death of Jesus is associated with the eating of the Passover meal. This will be made quite explicit in vv 26–30. This Passover will be unlike any other Passover the disciples had experienced.

# Disclosure of the Betrayer  (26:20–25)

### Bibliography

**Bauer, J.** "Judas Schicksal und Selbstmord." *BLit* 20 (1952–53) 210–13. **Fensham, F. C.** "Judas' Hand in the Bowl and Qumran." *RQ* 5 (1965) 259–61. **Hein, K.** "Judas Iscariot: Key to the Last-Supper Narratives?" *NTS* 17 (1970–71) 227–32. **Hofbauer, J.** "Judas, der Verräter." *TPQ* 110 (1962) 36–42. **Leahy, D.** "The Meaning of Matt. xxvi,24." *Scr* 2 (1947) 82–84. **Preisker, H.** "Der Verrat des Judas und das Abendmahl." *ZNW* 41 (1942) 151–55. **Schwarz, G.** *Jesus und Judas.* BWANT 123. Stuttgart: Kohlhammer, 1988.

### Translation

[20]*And when evening came, he reclined at table with the twelve.*[a] [21]*And while they were eating, he said: "Truly I tell you that*[b] *one of you will betray me."* [22]*And becoming greatly distressed, they began to say to him,*[c] *one by one:*[d] *"I'm not the one, Lord, am I?"*[e] [23]*And he answered and said: "The one having dipped his hand with mine in the bowl, this one will betray me.* [24]*The Son of Man goes just as it has been written concerning him, but woe to that man through whom the Son of Man is betrayed. It would have been*

*better if that man had not been born."* [25] *And Judas, the one betraying him, answered and said: "I'm not the one, Rabbi, am I?"*[f] *Jesus* [g] *said to him: "You have said the truth."*[h]

### Notes

[a] Many MSS (‫ א‬A L W Δ Θ lat sy[h] sa[mss] mae bo) add μαθητῶν, "disciples" (cf. *Note* on 20:17). The evidence, however, slightly favors its omission. See *TCGNT*, 64.

[b] p[37] and p[45] omit ὅτι, "that."

[c] αὐτῷ, "to him," is omitted by p[37vid] p[45] D Θ *f*[13] latt sy[s] mae bo.

[d] εἷς ἕκαστος, lit. "each one." Some MSS (p[45] D Θ *f*[13] sy[s, p, hmg]) read εἷς ἐκ αὐτῶν, "one of them." p[64vid] omits εἷς ἕκαστος altogether.

[e] μήτι ἐγώ εἰμι, κύριε, lit. "it is not I, Lord?" expecting a negative answer.

[f] The question here has exactly the same form as in v 22 (see preceding *Note*).

[g] "Jesus" added to the translation for clarity. So, too, p[45] ‫ א‬it vg[mss] sy[p] add ὁ Ἰησοῦς, "Jesus."

[h] σὺ εἶπας, lit."you have said (it)."

### Form/Structure/Setting

A. In the intimate setting of their private, familial celebration of the Passover meal, Jesus makes the startling revelation that one of the twelve will be responsible for his betrayal. Since the betrayal leads to the death of Jesus, we again have the association of his death with the Passover. The connection becomes the central point of the pericope that follows the present one. The culpability of the betrayer is readily put together with the stress on the fulfillment of scripture (v 24).

B. Matthew continues to use Mark as his source for this passage (Mark 14:18–21; cf. Luke 22:21–23; and for a distinctive account, John 13:21–30). He follows Mark rather closely, especially in v 24, which is practically in verbatim agreement with Mark 14:21. Matthew makes a few typical omissions, mainly to abbreviate the Markan text. Thus in v 21 he omits Mark's ὁ Ἰησοῦς, "Jesus" (Mark 14:18), and the unnecessary short clause ὁ ἐσθίων μετ᾽ ἐμοῦ, "one who is eating with me" (a probable allusion to Ps 41:9); in v 23 he omits the awkward εἷς τῶν δώδεκα, "one of the twelve" (Mark 14:20); and at the beginning of v 24 he omits Mark's unnecessary ὅτι, "because" (Mark 14:21). Matthew makes two slight alterations: changing Mark's εἷς κατὰ εἷς, "one by one" (Mark 14:19), in v 22 and in v 24 adding the verb ἦν, "was," or here, "would have been." But Matthew also makes a few more substantial additions to his Markan source. Thus the whole of v 25 is an addition. Matthew further adds details of the setting in v 20, the poignant κύριε, "Lord," in v 22 (cf. Mark 14:19) and in v 23 the words τὴν χεῖρα, "the hand," as well as the emphatic οὗτός με παραδώσει, "this one will betray me," at the end of the verse (cf. Mark 14:20). Matthew thus again preserves and modifies his source.

C. The passage consists of straightforward historical narrative largely presented in the form of direct discourse. The following simple outline may be suggested: (1) the revelation that one of the twelve will betray Jesus (vv 20–21); (2) the distressed questioning of the disciples (v 22); (3) the partial answer (v 23); (4) the grievous sin of the betrayer (v 24); and (5) the full answer (v 25). A few structural features to be noted are: the identical questions of vv 22 and 25 but with the telltale difference in the latter of the address ραββί, "Rabbi"; the narrowing focus in the parallel utterances of vv 21 and 23, "one of you will betray me" and "this one will betray me"; and the twofold repetition and contrast of ὁ υἱὸς τοῦ ἀνθρώπου, "the Son of Man," and ὁ ἄνθρωπος ἐκεῖνος, "that man," in v 24. The tradition underlying the woe saying of v 24 is cited in *1 Clem.* 46.8, where it is combined with other material underlying 10:6. The saying "it were better for them not to have been born" is found in *Herm. Vis.* 4.2.6.

## Comment

**20–21** ὀψίας δὲ γενομένης, "when it was evening," reflects the custom that the Passover meal be eaten at night. This, according to our reckoning (see *Comment* on v 17), was Thursday night, the beginning of 15 Nisan. Jesus reclines with his disciples in order to partake of this special meal. While the first part of the meal was in progress (i.e., before the actual Passover ceremony, involving recitation of the Passover Haggadah), Jesus makes the shocking disclosure that one of them will betray him. The announcement is prefaced with the weighty formula ἀμὴν λέγω ὑμῖν, "truly I tell you." This would indeed turn out to be an unusual Passover meal!

**22** It is obvious that the disciples would be λυπούμενοι σφόδρα, "greatly distressed," by Jesus' words (the same expression occurs in 17:23 at the second announcement of the coming death of Jesus and in 18:31). One by one each disciple asks whether he is the betrayer. The initial word of the question, μήτι ἐγώ εἰμι, "It is not I?" produces the expectation of a negative answer (cf. NRSV: "Surely not I?"). The added κύριε, "Lord," points to true discipleship (though not necessarily; cf. 7:21), especially given the stark contrast with Judas' address of Jesus as ῥαββί, "Rabbi," when he asks the same question in v 25.

**23** Jesus' answer appears to take us no further than the original statement in v 21 that one of them would betray him. He adds only the point that the betrayer is presently eating with Jesus. The aorist participle, ἐμβάψας, "having dipped" (contrast Mark's present participle), together with μετ' ἐμοῦ, "with me," suggests only that the betrayer had already dipped his bread into the bowl at the same time that Jesus had (not just at that moment, *pace* Fensham). This is therefore not a clear indication of the betrayer's identity (contrast John 13:26). Judas' question in v 25 confirms this conclusion. The τρυβλίῳ, "bowl" (in the NT only here and in the Markan parallel), used often in the LXX, was an ordinary bowl containing a sauce or "dip" into which one dipped one's bread or other food (cf. John 13:26). Eating together—normally a sign of fellowship and human solidarity—here involves a violation of intimacy.

**24** The fate of Jesus is no accident of history, however, for ὁ μὲν υἱὸς τοῦ ἀνθρώπου ὑπάγει καθὼς γέγραπται περὶ αὐτοῦ, "the Son of Man goes as it is written concerning him." That is, the death of Jesus is the realization of God's plan and the fulfillment of scripture (cf. vv 54, 56; this emphasis is stronger in Luke; see esp. Luke 18:31; 24:25–27, 44–47). No reference is given here, but occasional OT quotations appear in the remainder of the passion narrative (cf. v 31; 27:9). The title "Son of Man" has been frequently linked with the earlier passion predictions (17:12, 22; 20:18, 28; 26:2, 45; cf. 12:40; 17:9; see "Excursus: Son of Man" at 8:20). The "woe" saying is very similar in form to the second one of 18:7 (which is linked with the καλόν ἐστιν, "better if," sayings [18:8–9]), where, however, the woe is pronounced upon the one "through whom the stumbling comes." The somber saying that "it were better had that man not been born" finds a parallel in the apocalyptic language of *1 Enoch* 38.2 and points unmistakably to the great seriousness of the offense. Judas' suicide (27:5) is quite in keeping with the woe pronounced upon him. See the *Comment* on 26:14–16.

**25** Finally, according to Matthew, Judas questions Jesus, perhaps just to see whether he really knew who the betrayer was. The reference to Judas as ὁ παραδιδοὺς αὐτόν, "the one betraying him" (present participle), perhaps points to the fact that the betrayal had already been initiated (cf. vv 14–16). His question follows precisely the same form that the other disciples had used, i.e., expecting a negative response (cf. v 22); yet he addresses Jesus as ῥαββί, "Rabbi," rather than as κύριε, "Lord." This is a particularly conspicuous difference since Matthew reserves the address κύριε for disciples or potential disciples while using other titles (e.g., "teacher") for address by those who resist or oppose Jesus (Judas uses "Rabbi" again in addressing Jesus in v 49; the word is used elsewhere in Matthew only in 23:7–8). Judas had not yet arrived at a proper estimation of Jesus. Jesus' response, σὺ εἶπας, lit. "you have said (it)," is obviously (as also in v 64 and similarly in 27:11) to be understood as an affirmation, albeit somewhat indirect. That is, yes, Judas *was* the betrayer as he himself well knew (for the syntax, see *Comment* on v 64). Although no reference is made to Judas' departure (cf. John 13:30), it is perhaps to be assumed here since Judas is next referred to as coming with the guards in vv 46–47.

### Explanation

At the beginning of their celebration of Passover together, Jesus makes it known that one of the twelve will betray him. The distress of the disciples leads to some inevitable soul searching even if their questions amount to defiant assertions of loyalty (cf. v 33). If the twelve, those who had known Jesus so intimately, who had accompanied him throughout his ministry, were prompted to ask the question of their loyalty to Jesus, how much more properly may Christians who have not had that privilege occasionally ask that question. The line between commitment and betrayal can be a thin one as the disciples themselves were to discover in the very near future. And although the sovereignty of God is always working itself out in the events of the Christian's life, this can never be made an excuse for failure—not in the case of Judas, nor in the case of the Christian. The Pharisees and the Qumran sect share with Christianity the sustained tension between God's sovereignty and human free will (and thus responsibility).

# Institution of the Eucharist   (26:26–30)

### Bibliography

**Aalen, S.** "Das Abendmahl als Opfermahl im Neuen Testament." *NovT* 6 (1963) 128–52. **Allen, W. C.** "The Last Supper Not a Passover Meal." *ExpTim* 20 (1908–9) 377. **Aulén, G.** *Eucharist and Sacrifice.* Tr. E. H. Wahlstrom. Philadelphia: Muhlenberg, 1958. **Bahr, G. J.**

"The Seder of Passover and the Eucharistic Words." *NovT* 12 (1970) 181–202. **Barth, M.** *Das Abendmahl: Passamahl, Bundesmahl und Messiasmahl.* Zürich: Evangelischer, 1945. **Beck, N. A.** "The Last Supper as an Efficacious Symbolic Act." *JBL* 89 (1970) 192–98. **Benoit, P.** "The Accounts of the Institution and What They Imply." In *The Eucharist in the New Testament,* ed. J. Delorme et al. Baltimore: Helicon, 1964. 71–101 **Bligh, J.** "Scriptural Inquiry: 'Do this in commemoration of me.'" *The Way* 5 (1965) 154–59. **Bokser, B. M.** "Was the Last Supper a Passover Seder?" *BR* 3.2 (1987) 24–33. **Braumann, G.** "Mit euch: Matth. 26.29." *TZ* 21 (1965) 161–69. **Burkitt, F. C.** "The Last Supper and the Paschal Meal." *JTS* 17 (1915–16) 291–97. **Carmichael, D. B.** "David Daube on the Eucharist and the Passover Seder." *JSNT* 42 (1991) 45–67. **Casey, M.** "The Original Aramaic Form of Jesus' Interpretation of the Cup." *JTS* 41 (1990) 1–12. **Cooke, B.** "Synoptic Presentation of the Eucharist as Covenant Sacrifice." *TS* 21 (1960) 1–44. **Cullmann, O.,** and **Leenhardt, F. J.** *Essays on the Lord's Supper.* London: Lutterworth, 1958. **Daly, R. J.** "The Eucharist and Redemption: The Last Supper and Jesus' Understanding of His Death." *BTB* 11 (1981) 21–27. **David, J.-E.** "Mt 26:28: Un faux problème." *Bib* 48 (1967) 291–92. **Delorme, J.** "The Last Supper and the Pasch in the New Testament." In *The Eucharist in the New Testament,* ed. J. Delorme et al. Baltimore: Helicon, 1964. 21–67. **Descamps, A.** "Les origines de l'Eucharistie." In *Jésus et l'Église: Études d'exégèse et de théologie.* BETL 77. Leuven: Leuven UP/Peeters, 1987. 455–96. **Dupont, J.** "'Ceci est mon corps,' 'Ceci est mon sang.'" *NTR* 80 (1958) 1025–41. **DuRoy, J.-B.** "Le dernier repas de Jésus." *BVC* 26 (1959) 44–52. **Edanad, A.** "Institution of the Eucharist according to the Synoptic Gospels." *Biblebhashyam* 4 (1978) 322–32. **Emerton, J. A.** "*TO AIMA MOY THΣ ΔΙΑΘΗΚΗΣ*: The Evidence of the Syriac Versions." *JTS* 13 (1962) 111–17. **Feld, H.** *Das Verständnis des Abendmahls.* Darmstadt: Wissenschaftliche Buchgesellschaft, 1976. **Feneberg, R.** *Christliche Passafeier und Abendmahl: Eine biblisch-hermeneutische Untersuchung der neutestamentlichen Einsetzungsberichte.* SANT 27. Munich: Kösel, 1971. **Fuller, R. H.** "The Double Origin of the Eucharist." *BR* 8 (1963) 60–72. **Galot, J.** "Eucharistie et Incarnation." *NRT* 105 (1983) 549–66. **Grail, A.** "Sacrement de la croix." *LumVie* 7 (1952) 11–27. **Gregg, D. W. A.** *Anamnesis in the Eucharist.* Nottingham: Grove, 1976. **Günther, J.** "Das Becherwort Jesu." *TGl* 45 (1955) 47–49. **Hahn, F.** "Die alttestamentliche Motive in der urchristlichen Abendmahlsüberlieferung." *EvT* 27 (1967) 337–74. ———. "Zum Stand der Erforschung des urchristlichen Herrenmahls." *EvT* 35 (1975) 553–63. **Higgins, A. J. B.** *The Lord's Supper in the New Testament.* SBT 6. London: SCM, 1956. ———. "The Origins of the Eucharist." *NTS* 1 (1954–55) 200–209. **Huser, T.** "Les récits de l'institution de la Cène: Dissemblances et traditions." *Hokhma* 21 (1982) 28–50. **Irwin, K. W.** "The Supper Text in the Gospel of Saint Matthew." *DunRev* 11 (1971) 170–84. **Jeremias, J.** *The Eucharistic Words of Jesus.* Philadelphia: Fortress, 1977. ———. "This is My Body. . . ." *ExpTim* 83 (1972) 196–203. **Käsemann, E.** "Das Abendmahl im Neuen Testament." In *Abendmahlsgemeinschaft?* ed. H. Asmussen et al. Munich: Kaiser, 1938. 60–93. **Kilpatrick, G. D.** "Eucharist as Sacrifice and Sacrament in the New Testament." In *Neues Testament und Kirche.* FS R. Schnackenburg, ed. J. Gnilka. Freiburg: Herder, 1974. 429–33. ———. "Living Issues in Biblical Scholarship: The Last Supper." *ExpTim* 64 (1952–53) 4–8. **Kollmann, B.** *Ursprung und Gestalten der frühchristlichen Mahlfeier.* GTA 43. Göttingen: Vandenhoeck & Ruprecht, 1990. **Kosmala, H.** "Das tut zu meinem Gedächtnis." *NovT* 4 (1960–61) 81–94. **Kuhn, K. G.** "Die Abendmahlswörte." *TLZ* 75 (1950) 399–408. **LaVerdiere, E.** "Do This in Remembrance of Me." *Emmanuel* 90 (1984) 365–69. **Leaney, A. R. C.** "What Was the Lord's Supper?" *Th* 70 (1967) 51–62. **Lebeau, P.** *Le vin nouveau du Royaume: Étude exégétique et patristique sur la parole eschatologique de Jésus à la Cène.* Museum Lessianum, Section biblique 5. Paris: Desclée de Brouwer, 1966. **Léon-Dufour, X.** "Prenez! Ceci est mon corps pour vous." *NRT* 104 (1982) 223–40. **Leroy, H.** *Zur Vergebung der Sünden: Die Botschaft der Evangelien.* SBS 73. Stuttgart: Katholisches Bibelwerk, 1974. **Lietzmann, H.** *Mass and Lord's Supper,* ed. R. D. Richardson. Tr. D. H. G. Reeve. Leiden: Brill, 1979. **Lohmeyer, E.** "Das Abendmahl in der Urgemeinde." *JBL* 56 (1937) 217–52. ———. "Vom urchristlichen Abendmahl." *TRu* n.s. 9 (1937) 168–227, 273–312; 10 (1938) 81–99. **Lyss, D.** "Mon corps, c'est ceci (Notule sur Mt 26, 26–28 et par.)." *ETR* 45 (1970) 389–90. **Marshall, I. H.** *Last Supper and Lord's Supper.* Grand Rapids: Eerdmans, 1981. **Mastin, B. A.** "Jesus Said Grace." *SJT* 24 (1971) 449–56. **Merklein, H.** "Erwägungen zur Überlieferung der neutestamentlichen Abendmahlstraditionen." *BZ* 21 (1977) 88–101, 235–44. **Meyer, B. F.** "The Expiation Motif in the Eucharistic Words: A Key to the History of Jesus?" *Greg* 69 (1988) 461–87. **Patsch, H.** *Abendmahl und historischer Jesus.* CTM 1. Stuttgart: Calwer, 1972. **Pesch, R.** *Das Abendmahl und Jesu Todesverständnis.* QD 80. Freiburg: Herder, 1978. ———. "The Last Supper and Jesus' Understanding of His Death." *Biblebhashyam* 3 (1977) 58–75. ———. *Wie Jesus das Abendmahl hielt: Der Grund der Eucharistie.* Freiburg: Herder, 1977. **Reumann, J.** *The Supper of the Lord: The New Testament, Ecumenical Dialogues, and Faith and Order on Eucharist.* Philadelphia: Fortress, 1984. **Saldarini, A. J.** *Jesus and Passover.* New York: Paulist, 1984. **Sanders, H. A.** "A Third Century Papyrus of Matthew and Acts." In *Quantulacumque.* FS K. Lake, ed. R. P. Casey et al. London: Christophers, 1937. 151–61. **Sandvik, B.** *Das Kommen des Herrn beim Abendmahl im Neuen Testament.* ATANT 58. Zürich: Zwingli, 1970. **Schelkle, K. H.** "Das Herrnmahl." In *Rechtfertigung.* FS E. Käsemann, ed. J. Friedrich, W. Pöhlmann, and P. Stuhlmacher. Tübingen/Göttingen: Mohr/Vandenhoeck & Ruprecht, 1976. 385–402. **Schürmann, H.** "Jesus' Words in the Light of His Actions at the Last Supper." In *The Breaking of Bread.* Concilium 40. New York: Paulist, 1969. 119–31. ———. "Das Mahl des Herrn." In *Ursprung und Gestalt: Erörterungen und Besinnungen zum Neuen Testament.* Düsseldorf: Patmos, 1970. 77–196. **Schweizer, E.** "Das Herrenmahl im Neuen Testament." *TLZ* 79 (1954) 577–92. ———. *The Lord's Supper according to the New Testament.* Facet Books. Philadelphia: Fortress, 1967. **Senn, F. C.** "The Lord's Supper, Not the Passover Seder." *Worship* 60 (1986) 362–68. **Stagg, F.** "The Lord's Supper in the New Testament." *RevExp* 66 (1969) 5–14. **Sykes, M. H.** "The Eucharist as 'Anamnesis.'" *ExpTim* 71 (1959–60) 115–18. **Temple, S.** "The Two Traditions of the Last Supper, Betrayal, and Arrest." *NTS* 7 (1960–61) 77–85. **Thyen, H.** *Studien zur Sündenvergebung im Neuen Testament und seinen alttestamentlichen und jüdischen Voraussetzungen.* FRLANT 96. Göttingen: Vandenhoeck & Ruprecht, 1970.

*Translation*

$^{26}$*And while they were eating, Jesus took a loaf of* [a] *bread, and when he had blessed God for it,* [b] *he broke it into pieces, and giving them* [c] *to his disciples, he said: "Take, eat; this is my body."* $^{27}$*And he took a cup,* [d] *and when he had given thanks, he gave it to them, saying: "All of you drink of it;* $^{28}$*for this is my blood of* [e] *the covenant,* [f] *which is poured out for all* [g] *for the forgiveness of sins.* $^{29}$*But I tell you, from now on I will not drink at all from this fruit of the vine until that day when I drink it with you new in the kingdom of my Father."* $^{30}$*And when they had sung a hymn, they went out to the Mount of Olives.*

*Notes*

[a] "A loaf of" added to translation.

[b] εὐλογήσας, "having blessed." Some MSS (A K W Γ Δ $f^{1,13}$ sy$^h$) have εὐχαριστήσας, "having given thanks," probably by the influence of the parallel in Luke 22:19; 1 Cor 11:24. But compare too the same verb in v 27.

[c] "Them" added, supplying the direct object.

[d] Some important witnesses (P$^{45}$ A C D K Γ $f^{13}$) include the definite article τό. The tendency of scribes would have been to add rather than delete the definite article. *TCGNT,* 64.

[e] Many MSS (A C W $f^{1,13}$ TR sy$^h$) insert the definite article τό before τῆς διαθήκης, producing an attributive adjectival phrase, "the blood of the covenant," which is much smoother than the accepted text. For that reason, it is probably not original.

ᶠ Many MSS (A C D W *f*¹·¹³ TR latt sy sa bo) insert καινῆς, "new," before "covenant," almost certainly from the parallel in Luke 22:20; 1 Cor 11:25. As Metzger points out, had the word been in the earliest MS, there is no reason it would have later been deleted. *TCGNT*, 64.

ᵍ περὶ πολλῶν, lit., "for many." See *Comment.*

## Form/Structure/Setting

A. We come now to a central component of the passion narrative. This pericope with its provision of a way for the followers of Jesus to commemorate the death of Jesus gives to the church what will become its central sacrament. The event recorded here not only anticipates the death of Jesus, but it also provides an interpretation of that event. Jesus takes basic elements of human sustenance, food and drink, and transforms the partaking of those elements into a symbolic portrayal of his redemptive death (cf. 1 Cor 11:26).

B. Matthew follows Mark very closely in this pericope (Mark 14:22–25; cf. Luke 22:15–20, which, however, is quite different [cf. 1 Cor 11:23–26]; cf. John 6:51–59, which also seems to bear some relationship to this material). There are only six substantive differences from the Markan text. Three additions are made: φάγετε, "eat," in v 26, a natural addition, but the present pericope is the only eucharist narrative with this imperative (cf. Mark 14:22); εἰς ἄφεσιν ἁμαρτιῶν, "for the forgiveness of sins," in v 28, implied in the preceding phrase, "poured out for many," but made explicit only in Matthew (cf. 1:21); and μεθ' ὑμῶν, "with you," in v 29, again unique to Matthew and recalling the reunion of Jesus with his disciples (cf. 24:31; 25:34). Matthew makes two significant alterations: he turns Mark's statement that all drank from the cup (Mark 14:23) into an imperative, πίετε ἐξ αὐτοῦ πάντες, "drink of it, all" (v 27), thus bringing about parallelism with the imperative "eat" (v 26) no doubt through liturgical influence; second, he changes Mark's reference to τῇ βασιλείᾳ τοῦ θεοῦ, "the kingdom of God," at the very end of the pericope (Mark 14:25) to τῇ βασιλείᾳ τοῦ πατρός μου, "the kingdom of my Father" (v 29; cf. a similar expression in 13:43). One omission may also be noted, that of Mark's ἀμήν, "truly" (Mark 14:25), in v 29, which thereby avoids the common formula (but it is difficult to know why). Other alterations of the Markan text are small and insignificant. In all, Matthew's relatively conservative preservation of his source attests to its importance to him.

C. The core of the passage consists of the "words of institution" as they later became called. The passage may be outlined as follows: (1) the eating of the bread (vv 26–27); (2) the drinking of the wine (vv 27–28); (3) the eschatological drinking of the wine (v 29); and (4) the departure (v 30). Structural parallelism can be seen in the reference to the bread and the cup. Thus in vv 26–27 we have λαβὼν ἄρτον/ποτήριον, "taking bread/cup," εὐλογήσας/εὐχαριστήσας, "blessing/giving thanks," followed by the parallel imperatives φάγετε, "eat," and πίετε, "drink," which are found only in Matthew among all the NT accounts (i.e., including Luke 22:15–20; 1 Cor 11:23–26). There are also the two parallel interpretive sentences of vv 26, 28: τοῦτό ἐστιν τὸ σῶμά μου, "this is my body," and τοῦτο γάρ ἐστιν τὸ αἷμά μου, "for this is my blood" (this parallelism is also in Mark), the latter being heavily modified with further interpretive material. Liturgical influence is probably to be detected in the form of the material as well as in choice of words. In addition to the parallel account of the institution of the eucharist in 1 Cor 11:23–26 (cf. allusion in 1 Cor 10:16), see too *Did.* 9.1–5 and Justin Martyr, *Apol.* 1.66.3.

D. The sense in which the bread and wine *are* the body and blood of Jesus in the Eucharist has been one of the notorious and divisive problems in the Christian church (for illuminating discussion of this along with other aspects, see Reumann; Cullmann and Leenhardt; Marshall). In the present note, only the following brief observations are possible. Jesus' use of the verb ἐστίν, "is" ("this is my body"; "this is my blood"), can hardly be meant literally when Jesus is physically present with them at the meal. The verb is to be taken seriously but as involving a deep and important symbolism. As the Passover meal involved rich symbolism, so Jesus instills a new dynamic symbolism into these elements. Christ *is* genuinely present in the elements, but without a change of these *into* his actual body and blood (as in transubstantiation). To eat of these elements is mysteriously to partake of Christ and his gifts, to enjoy the grace of the gospel (cf. John 6:56–57). Since the life of the Christian—the enjoyment of the gift of new life—depends so fundamentally upon the death of Jesus, the identification of the bread and wine of this supper as his body and blood is centrally significant. Yet although the eucharist points to the sacrifice of Jesus, it is not itself a sacrifice but a memorializing and contemporizing of the unique sacrifice accomplished by Jesus on the cross. Understandably, this commemoration of the sacrifice of Jesus for the forgiveness of sins becomes the central component of Christian worship. For helpful orientation, see Hahn, *EvT* 35 (1975) 553–63. On the issue of the historicity of the words of the institution, see Pesch, *Das Abendmahl.*

*Comment*

**26** Further on into the meal mentioned in the preceding verses, i.e., into the Passover celebration proper (cf. v 19), Jesus apparently interrupts the normal ceremony, takes the common (unleavened) bread and wine, and attaching new symbolic significance to them ("efficacious symbolic acts," thus Beck), invites his disciples to partake of them. Beginning with the bread (possibly the מַצָּה, *maṣṣāh*, "unleavened bread," reserved for the *afikoman* [אֲפִיקוֹמָן = ἐπικῶμον, "revelling"] or "after-meal dessert" of the Seder, which became symbolic of the coming of the Messiah; see Carmichael), which he consecrates or sets apart for its special use by prayer (εὐλογήσας, "having blessed [God]"; cf. 14:19 and *Comment* there), he breaks it into fragments that he then gives to the disciples (cf. Luke 24:30). The blessing of God and the breaking of the bread into fragments recalls the miraculous feeding of 14:9 and of 15:36. The words Jesus now speaks to them are astonishing in their import: λάβετε φάγετε, "take, eat," τοῦτό ἐστιν τὸ σῶμά μου, "this is my body" (cf. Luke 22:19; 1 Cor 11:2, both modified by a ὑπὲρ ὑμῶν, "for you," clause; cf. 1 Cor 10:16). Jesus identifies the bread with his body, the former a symbol of the latter (cf. *Form/Structure/Setting* §D above). As the various aspects of the Passover meal itself involved deep symbolism, so Jesus develops a new symbolism for the disciples' meal (cf. Schürmann, "Jesus' Words in the Light of His Actions at the Last Supper"). The bread symbolizes the body of Jesus, which is about to be given over to death on their behalf. The vicarious nature of this body (and its death) remains implicit here, but it becomes clear from the explanatory comments accompanying the reference to the blood in v 28. The background is that of the sacrifice of the Paschal lamb (cf. Exod 12:21, 27). On the supper as a Passover meal, see esp. Jeremias, *The Eucharistic Words of Jesus,* 15–88;

Higgins, *The Lord's Supper in the New Testament;* Marshall; Leaney; and Saldarini (to the contrary, Allen, Senn, Bokser).

**27–28**   It is uncertain at what point in relation to the traditional Passover meal Jesus introduced his new symbolism of the bread and wine and his atoning death (cf. Bahr). It is common, however, to relate the taking of the cup referred to here as the third cup, the so-called cup of blessing(cf. 1 Cor 10:16). This would have been preceded by the drinking of two earlier cups of wine (cf. Luke 22:17), in between which bitter herbs had been eaten, the Passover Haggadah recited, and the first part of the *Hallel* sung (i.e., Pss 113–18; see Str-B 4:41–76; *m. Pesah.* 10:1–7). "When he had given thanks" (εὐχαριστήσας; cf. 15:36, the only other occurrence of the word in Matthew), he gave the wine to them with the instruction πίετε ἐξ αὐτοῦ πάντες, "drink from it, all (of you)." The inclusive reference here to "all" probably has no significance beyond the importance of each disciple partaking of the wine (as of the bread, though not stipulated there). The symbolism of the bread and cup is only fulfilled in the participation of each individual disciple for whom Jesus' death was to be accomplished. In the parallel sentence to the saying of v 26 concerning the body of Jesus, τοῦτο γάρ ἐστιν τὸ αἷμά μου, "for this is my blood," we have the same type of symbolism at work: the wine symbolizes the blood of Jesus, and to drink that wine is symbolically to partake of the blood and its atoning effect. This is clear from the three interpretive phrases that follow. First, the blood is described as τῆς διαθήκης, "of the covenant." This phrase occurs in the OT (Exod 24:8; Zech 9:11; cf. Heb 9:20). The blood here is not the blood that was necessary to the first covenant (cf. Heb 9:18) but that which inaugurates the new covenant; thus although the word καινή, "new," does not occur here (although many MSS, but of inferior quality, include the word), it is to be presupposed (nor does it occur in Matthew's source, Mark 14:24; it is, however, found in Luke 22:20; 1 Cor 11:25). The phrase "blood of the covenant," without the adjective "new," referring to the blood of Christ, is found in Heb 10:29 (cf. 13:20; in the OT, Exod 24:8). The new covenant is that prophesied in Jer 31:31–34 (cf. Heb 8:6–13; 9:15–22). See David on the awkwardness of Matthew's Greek text here. Second, the blood is described as τὸ περὶ πολλῶν ἐκχυννόμενον, "which is poured out for many" (cf. Isa 53:12). The language "poured out" is itself an allusion to sacrifices of atonement in the temple ritual (e.g., Lev 4:7, 18, 25, 30, 34). Matthew's περί is not to be distinguished in meaning from Mark's ὑπέρ: i.e., it too means "on behalf of" (see BAGD, 644b). πολλῶν is probably used in the Semitic sense of "all" (as it is, e.g., in Rom 5:15, 19) and may point to the underlying Hebrew or Aramaic spoken at the meal. See *Comment* on 20:28 (where the analogous preposition ἀντί, "in place of," occurs). The pouring out of the blood of Jesus is to be taken not literally but metaphorically, referring to his death. Third, the blood (or more accurately, the pouring out of the blood) is described as being εἰς ἄφεσιν ἁμαρτιῶν, "for the forgiveness of sins" (see Leroy, 30–37). This notice links the death of Jesus both with that of the suffering servant of Isaiah (cf. Isa 53:12) and with the new covenant prophecy of Jeremiah (Jer 31:34). It is finally the real purpose of the coming of Jesus (cf. 1:21). As Jeremias points out, "Without Is 53 the Eucharistic words would remain incomprehensible" (*ExpTim* 83 [1972] 203; see *Eucharistic Words of Jesus,* 218–37, esp. 231). On the eucharist as sacrifice, see Kilpatrick. On the OT roots of the eucharist, see Hahn, *EvT* 27 (1967) 337–74.

**29** This somewhat difficult statement seems to function as an indication of the imminence of Jesus' death while pointing to the certainty of eschatological triumph. Jesus solemnly announces in a vow (cf. Num 30:2–17) that he will not drink wine after this occasion (contra Jeremias, who argues that Jesus abstained from food and drink at the meal; see Patsch's response), i.e., not again in this life. In the narrative he is arrested shortly after the conclusion of the Passover meal (cf. vv 47–56). When Jesus next drinks wine (τούτου τοῦ γενήματος τῆς ἀμπέλου, "this fruit of the vine," an alternate, Semitic way of referring to wine) with his disciples, it will be at the eschatological banquet (see *Comment* on 8:11; cf. 22:1–10). "The next meal of Jesus with his disciples will be the Messianic meal on a transformed earth" (Jeremias, *Eucharistic Words of Jesus*, 217). If his death is now a certainty, so is that joyous occasion when disciples and master will be reunited. At that time Jesus will drink the wine καινόν, "new," that is, the new wine in the new setting of eschatological fulfillment, and he will drink it μεθ' ὑμῶν, "with you," the Lord and Redeemer with his fully redeemed community of disciples. This will be the occasion of the experience of the consummated eschatological kingdom, here referred to as τῇ βασιλείᾳ τοῦ πατρός μου, "the kingdom of my Father" (cf. 13:43; 1 Cor 15:24).

**30** At the end of the Passover meal, the fourth and final cup was drunk and the conclusion of the *Hallel* (Pss 113–18, with various allusions to salvation) was sung (cf. *m. Pesaḥ*.10:7). It is very probably the singing of those prescribed Psalms that is referred to here (the only other reference to singing in the NT is in Acts 16:25; cf. 1 Cor 14:26; Eph 5:19; Col 3:16; Heb 2:12; Jas 5:13). Jesus and the disciples left Jerusalem to return to the Mount of Olives, presumably going directly to Gethsemane (v 36). A season of prayer would have been appropriate following the Passover celebration.

*Explanation*

Amidst the rich symbolism of the Passover meal, Jesus creates a new complex of symbols relating directly to his sacrificial death. It is not an accident of history but the working of divine sovereignty that Jesus was crucified at the Passover season. For Jesus was the new, eschatological Passover lamb (cf. 1 Cor 5:7), whose sacrificial death was the atonement for the sins of the world. The bread and wine, the commonest of elements, come in the institution of the Eucharist to bear sublime meaning as the expression of the very center of the Christian faith, the mystery of the death of God's own Son. For this reason the celebration of the Lord's Supper is at the center of Christian worship. The Eucharist becomes a Christian Passover. As A. J. B. Higgins puts it, "The Last Supper was the pattern of future celebrations of the Passover for the followers of Jesus" (*Lord's Supper in the New Testament*, 53). When the church repeats this sacramental meal, it looks simultaneously back to the redemptive death of its Lord, which is thereby commemorated, as well as forward to the future consummation of eschatology when Christians will be united with their Lord in the unalloyed enjoyment of the kingdom that is thereby celebrated (cf. 1 Cor 11:26). And for the present, the celebration of the sacrament brings a fresh experience of the grace of God through the forgiveness of sins, a renewed participation in salvation already enjoyed, and a renewed sense of the oneness of the members of the one body of

Christ (cf. 1 Cor 10:17). The disciples in the immediacy of the moment could not have begun to realize the significance of what Jesus was saying and doing. This they would first do after the resurrection. But by the time Matthew's readers read this account, the Eucharist had long since become a fixed component in their worship; hence they read the narrative with fuller understanding.

# The Prediction of the Falling Away of the Disciples and the Denial of Peter   (26:31–35)

## Bibliography

**Brown, R. E.** "The Passion according to Matthew." *Worship* 58 (1984) 98–107. **Evans, C. F.** "'I will go before you into Galilee.'" *JTS* n.s. 5 (1954) 3–18. **Kosmala, H.** "The Time of the Cock-Crow." *ASTI* 2 (1963) 118–20; 6 (1967–68) 132–34. **Kuntz, G.** "A Note on Matthew XXVI. 34 and XXVI. 75." *JTS* 50 (1949) 182–83. **Politi, J.** "'Not (Not I).'" *Literature and Theology* 6 (1992) 345–55. **Zeller, D.** "Prophetisches Wissen um die Zukunft in synoptischen Jesusworten." *TP* 52 (1977) 258–71.

## Translation

[31] *Then Jesus said [a] to them: "All of you will fall away during this night because of me. For it is written:*

*I will strike the shepherd*
*and the sheep of the flock will be scattered.*

[32] *But after I have been raised, I will go before you into Galilee."* [33] *But Peter, responding, said to him.[b] "If all fall away because of you,[c] I myself will never fall away."* [34] *Jesus said to him: "Truly I say to you that this night before the cock crows you will deny me three times."* [35] *Peter said [d] to him: "Even if I had to die with you, I would never deny you." All the disciples also spoke similarly.*

## Notes

[a] λέγει, historical present, lit. "says."
[b] P[37] sy[s] sa[ms] omit αὐτῷ, "to him."
[c] In P[53] ἐν σοί, "because of you," occurs after ἐγώ, "I," resulting in "If all fall away, I myself will never fall away because of you." Cf. ἐν ἐμοί, "on my account," in v 31.
[d] λέγει, historical present, lit. "says."

## Form/Structure/Setting

A. Only a short time before his arrest Jesus tells his disciples that they will be unable to remain loyal to him and that they will scatter like sheep. Not only will this happen, but Peter, who professes his loyalty most loudly, will deny Jesus three times before the coming dawn. These prophecies find their fulfillment before the end of the chapter (cf. vv 56, 69–75).

B. Again Matthew is dependent on Mark and follows his source very closely (Mark 14:26–31; cf. Luke 22:31–34; John 13:36–38). Matthew does not abbreviate as much as he customarily does, but the following more significant deletions may be noted. In v 34 Matthew omits σὺ σήμερον, "you today" (Mark 14:30), both words being redundant; ἢ δίς, "twice," being unnecessary after πρίν, "before"; and δίς, which would have introduced an unnecessary complication. Matthew also omits in v 35 Mark's descriptive adverb ἐκπερισσῶς, "with great emphasis" (Mark 14:31), although it is difficult to know why unless it is because in the next sentence all the disciples spoke ὁμοίως, "similarly." Meanwhile, however, Matthew makes an unusual number of additions of which the following should be noted. In v 31 Matthew adds the words ὑμεῖς, "you," and ἐν ἐμοὶ ἐν τῇ νυκτὶ ταύτῃ, lit., "in me in this night" (Mark 14:27), thereby supplying the specific identity of the subject (with emphasis), as well as the reason and the occasion referred to by the main verb (cf. v 34). In the quotation of Zech 13:7 in v 31, Matthew adds τῆς ποίμνης, "of the flock" (cf. Mark 14:27), bringing about closer agreement with the LXX (according to Alexandrinus) and relating the flock more closely to ποιμένα, "shepherd." In v 33 Matthew adds an unnecessary initial ἀποκριθείς, but in keeping with his style. In v 33 Matthew adds οὐδέποτε σκανδαλισθήσομαι, "I will never fall away" (cf. Mark 14:29), thereby repeating the verb and with the two verbs providing added emphasis. Finally, in v 35 Matthew adds οἱ μαθηταί, "the disciples" (cf. Mark 14:31), to emphasize the disciples' claim of loyalty. The several substitutions Matthew makes for Markan words are not particularly noteworthy.

C. The passage consists of prophecies of Jesus concerning the disciples and the responses of Peter. The following outline may be offered: (1) Jesus' prophecy concerning the falling away of the disciples (v 31); (2) the promise of going before them to Galilee (v 32); (3) Peter's assertion of loyalty (v 33); (4) Jesus' prophecy of Peter's denials (v 34); and (5) Peter's renewed assertion (v 35). Also note the OT citation in v 31 without fulfillment formula and the parenthetical character of v 32 with its prophecy that Jesus will go before the disciples to Galilee after he is raised. *Barn.* 5:12 seems to reflect a knowledge of Matthew in an allusion to this passage where Zech 13:7 is cited in a form similar to that of Matthew (i.e., τὰ πρόβατα τῆς ποίμνης, "the sheep of the flock").

### Comment

**31** The equivalent to σκανδαλισθήσεσθε ἐν ἐμοί, "you will fall away on my account," is found in 11:6; 13:57 (cf. John 6:61; 16:1). The verb can mean "to be offended by," "to cause to stumble," or "to be caused to stumble by" (for the construction, see BAGD, 752b). In the present context the meaning is a "falling away," an express disloyalty of the kind expressed in the verb used toward the end of the pericope, ἀπαρνεῖσθαι, "to deny" (vv 34–35). ἐν τῇ νυκτὶ ταύτῃ, "in this night" (cf. v 56), the disciples (πάντες ὑμεῖς, "all of you") would abandon their Lord in fear for their own lives. Even this sad turn of events had been foreseen in the scriptures. Zech 13:7 contains a reference both to the striking of the shepherd (in the sense of leader; cf. Ezek 34), which in the present context becomes an allusion to the death of Jesus, and to the scattering of the flock (the people), which in turn becomes readily understood as the flight of the disciples (the metaphor of shepherd and sheep is earlier used in 9:36). Matthew's διασκορπισθήσονται, "will be scattered," is drawn from Mark, which in turn follows the reading of the LXX according to A (cf. Heb. וּתְפוּצֶין, *ûṯĕpûṣeyn*, "and they will be scattered"). On the other hand, the form of the opening verb (πατάξω, "I will strike"), also taken from Mark, agrees with the Masoretic text against all the LXX witnesses. Since the quotation is introduced by Matthew with the formula γέγραπται, "it is written," it is easy to see the acting subject as God and not Peter (*pace* B. Lindars, *New Testament Apologetic*, 129). To say that God strikes the shepherd is to affirm that the death of Jesus is paradoxically the divine will (cf. esp. vv 24, 54). Important MSS of the LXX of Zech 13:7 (B ℵ*) refer to μικρούς, "little ones" (cf. Matt 10:42; 18:6, 10, 14), in parallel with πρόβατα, "sheep" (so too Heb. הַצֹּעֲרִים, *haṣṣōʿărîm*, "little ones"). Matthew puts the verb at the beginning of the clause to increase the parallel with the first clause and for emphasis. The shepherd will receive a mortal blow, and the sheep will flee even at the prospect of this calamity (cf. John 16:32; 10:15 for the shepherd who lays down his life for the sheep).

**32** This parenthetical statement provides the consoling thought that the smitten shepherd and the scattered sheep will be reunited. After his death, a theme that still dominates, Jesus is to "be raised" to new life (other occurrences of ἐγείρειν in reference to the future resurrection of Jesus are in 16:21; 17:9, 23; 20:19; cf. 27:63). And then like a shepherd leading his sheep, he will go before them into Galilee (cf. 28:7, 10; for the imagery of shepherd going ahead of the sheep, cf. John 10:4). Authoritative leadership may be alluded to here (see Evans). The meeting in Galilee after the death and the resurrection of Jesus is recorded in the last pericope of the Gospel (28:16–20; cf. 28:7).

**33** Peter, as is his habit in Matthew, plunges in to say what others are only thinking (cf. 14:28; 15:15; 16:16; 17:4; 18:21; 19:27). If others, indeed all (πάντες) others, should "fall away" (on σκανδαλίζειν, see *Comment* on v 31) because of what is to happen to Jesus (the construction assumes the prediction of v 31; cf. BDF §372[1c]), Peter says emphatically (ἐγώ, "I myself") that he will not. Indeed, not now, not ever (οὐδέποτε, "never"). This boast of Peter becomes even stronger in v 35.

**34** Jesus says to Peter, beginning with the weighty formula ἀμὴν λέγω σοι, "truly I tell you" (the last one in Matthew), that before the night is over he will have denied Jesus not once but three times. The ἐν ταύτῃ τῇ νυκτί, "in this night," echoes the same phrase (slightly different word order) in Jesus' initial statement in v 31. It is unlikely that the reference to the cock crowing in Matthew is to be understood as referring to a Roman division of the night watch (*pace* Kosmala). Rather than saying "before dawn," Jesus says πρὶν ἀλέκτορα φωνῆσαι, "before the cock crows," thereby preparing for what becomes a superb dramatic touch in the fulfillment recorded in vv 74–75. The thought of a threefold denial of Jesus must at this point have seemed unthinkable to Peter.

**35** Peter more vehemently than before insists that under no condition, not even under the threat of death, would he deny Jesus. That he regards the possibility of such a threat to be remote is indicated by the rare subjunctive verb δέῃ (lit. even if "it might be necessary"). Peter's perspective, so closely following the teaching of Jesus at the supper, serves as an instance of dramatic irony (thus Heil, *The Death and Resurrection of Jesus*, 41). This of course was precisely the circumstance in which he was soon to find himself. The verb for "deny" here (ἀπαρνεῖσθαι; in Matthew only in the present pericope, v 75, and 16:24) may possibly be more emphatic than, but not essentially different from, ἀρνεῖσθαι (cf. vv 70, 72), which is used in 10:33 in the statement "whoever denies me before others, I also will deny before my Father in heaven." Peter's denial of Jesus can thus be regarded as putting his own status before God in jeopardy. πάντες οἱ μαθηταί, "all the disciples," spoke ὁμοίως, "similarly," joining with Peter in their insistence that they would not deny Jesus, even in the face of death (v 56). But only the failure of Peter will be focused upon later in the chapter (vv 69–75).

*Explanation*

With the arrest of Jesus and the prospect of his death, his disciples—the ones closest to him—will scatter. Despite their protestations of loyalty, their courage will fail them and they will desert their Lord. The imminent failure of Peter, the first of the apostles, is focused upon, finding its corresponding fulfillment at the end of the chapter. The humanity of Peter and the disciples together with the very real frailty of every profession of commitment will be revealed. Despite the best of intentions, the disciples will not be able to be true to their deepest convictions (cf. v 56). They, like Peter, will have disappointed themselves as much as Jesus. But in the same breath Jesus gives notice that they will yet have a future with Jesus (v 32). All is not lost; the setback is only a temporary one though nonetheless serious for that. There is a way back from this failure. God's faithfulness to these vexed disciples remains unshakable just as his forgiveness and restoration are available to every follower of Jesus.

# *Jesus' Struggle in Gethsemane* (26:36–46)

*Bibliography*

**Aagaard, A. M.** "Doing God's Will: Matthew 26:36–46." *International Review of Mission* 77 (1988) 221–28. **Armbruster, C. J.** "The Messianic Significance of the Agony in the Garden." *Scr* 16 (1964) 111–19. **Barbour, R. S.** "Gethsemane in the Tradition of the Passion." *NTS* 16 (1969–70) 231–51. **Beck, B.** "Gethsemane in the Four Gospels." *EpR* 15 (1988) 57–65. **Birdsall, J. N.** "*Egrēgoreō.*" *JTS* n.s. 14 (1963) 390–91. **Blaising, C. A.** "Gethsemane: A Prayer of Faith." *JETS* 22 (1979) 333–43. **Boman, T.** "Der Gebetskampf Jesu." *NTS* 10 (1963–64) 261–73. **Braumann, G.** "Leidenskelch und Todestaufe." *ZNW* 56 (1965) 178–83. **Brongers, H. A.** "Der Zornesbecher." *OTS* 15 (1969) 177–92. **Cranfield, C. E. B.** "The Cup Metaphor in Mark 14:36 and Parallels." *ExpTim* 59 (1947–48) 137–38. **Daube, D.** "A Prayer Pattern in Judaism." *SE* 1 [= TU 73] (1959) 539–45. ———. "Two Incidents after the Lord's Supper." In *The New Testament and Rabbinic Judaism*. London: University of London, 1956. 330–35 (reprinted Peabody, MA: Hendrickson). **Dautzenburg, G.** "*Psyche* in Mk 14,34/Mt 26,38 und Jo 12,27." In *Sein Leben bewahren.* SANT 14. Munich: Kösel, 1966. 127–33. **Dibelius, M.** "Gethsemane." *CrQ* 12 (1935) 254–65. **Feldmeier, R.** *Die Krisis des Gottessohnes: Die Gethsemaneerzählung als Schlüssel der Markuspassion.* WUNT 2/21. Tübingen: Mohr, 1987.

**Feuillet, A.** *L'agonie de Gethsémani: Enquête exégétique et théologique suivie d'une étude de 'Mystère de Jésus' de Pascal.* Paris: Gabalda, 1977. **Héring, J.** "Simples remarques sur la prière à Gethsémané: Matthieu 26.36–46; Marc 14.32–42; Luc 22.40–46." *RHPR* 39 (1959) 97–102.
———. "Zwei exegetische Probleme in der Perikope von Jesus in Gethsemane (Markus XIV 32–42; Matthäus XXVI 36–46; Lukas XXII 40–46)." In *Neotestamentica et Patristica.* FS O. Cullmann, ed. W. C. van Unnik. NovTSup 6. Leiden: Brill, 1962. 64–69. **Holleran, J. W.** *The Synoptic Gethsemane.* Analecta Gregoriana 191. Rome: Gregorian University, 1973. **Johnson, S. L., Jr.** "The Agony of Christ." *BSac* 124 (1967) 303–13. **Kayalaparampil, T.** "Passion and Resurrection in the Gospel of Matthew." *Biblebhashyam* 16 (1990) 41–51. **Kenny, A.** "The Transfiguration and the Agony in the Garden." *CBQ* 19 (1957) 444–52. **Kuhn, K. G.** "Jesus in Gethsemane." *EvT* 12 (1952–53) 260–85. **Léon-Dufour, X.** "Jésus à Gethsémani: Essai de lecture synchronique." *ScEs* 31 (1979) 251–68. **Lescow, T.** "Jesus in Gethsemane." *EvT* 26 (1966) 141–59. **Lövestam, E.** *Spiritual Wakefulness in the New Testament.* Lund: Gleerup, 1963. **Mees, M.** "Die Bezeugung von Mt. 26, 20–40 auf Papyrus ($P^{63}$, $P^{64}$, $P^{65}$, $P^{66}$) und ihre Bedeutung." *Augustinianum* 11 (1971) 409–31. **Pelcé, F.** "Jésus à Gethsémani: Remarques comparatives sur les trois récits évangéliques." *FV* 65 (1966) 89–99. **Robinson, B. P.** "Gethsemane: The Synoptic and the Johannine Viewpoints." *CQR* 167 (1966) 4–11. **Roche, J.** "Que ta volonté soit faite." *VSpir* 93 (1955) 249–68. **Senior, D.** *The Passion Narrative according to Matthew: A Redactional Study.* BETL 39. Leuven: Leuven UP, 1975. ———. *The Passion of Jesus in the Gospel of Matthew.* Wilmington, DE: Michael Glazier, 1985. **Stanley, D. M.** "Matthew's Gethsemane (Mt 26:36–46)." In *Jesus in Gethsemane: The Early Church Reflects on the Sufferings of Jesus.* New York: Paulist, 1980. 155–87. **Starkie, W. J. M.** "Mt 26⁴⁵." *ExpTim* 31 (1919–20) 477. **Trémel, Y.-B.** "L'agonie de Christ." *LumVie* 68 (1964) 79–104.

### Translation

[36] Then Jesus came with them to the area called Gethsemane, and he said to the disciples:[a] "Sit here while I go there and pray." [37] And he took Peter and the two sons of Zebedee, and he began to be sorrowful and anxious. [38] Then he said to them: "My soul is very sad, even to death. Remain here and watch with me." [39] And when he had gone forward[b] a little, he fell upon his face in prayer,[c] saying: "My[d] Father, if it can be, let this cup pass from me. But not as I will, but as you do."[e] [40] And he came to the[f] disciples and found them sleeping, and he said to Peter: "Are you thus not strong enough to watch with me for one hour? [41] Watch and pray, in order that you may not enter into testing. On the one hand, the spirit is willing, but, on the other, the flesh is weak." [42] Again a second time he went and prayed, saying:[g] "My[h] Father, if this[i] cannot pass,[j] except that I drink it, let your will be done." [43] And when he came back, he again found them sleeping, for their eyes had become heavy. [44] And he left them;[k] again going some distance,[l] he prayed a third time,[m] saying again[n] the same prayer. [45] Then he came to the[o] disciples, and he said to them: "Sleep for the time that remains, and rest.[p] Look,[q] the hour has come near, and the Son of Man is betrayed into the hands of sinners. [46] Rise, let us go. Look, the one who betrays me has come near."

### Notes

[a] Θ $f^{13}$ have αὐτοῖς, "to them" (cf. Luke 22:40). A number of MSS (ℵ A C D W $f^1$ lat sy sa$^{ms}$ mae bo) add αὐτοῦ, "his," probably by the influence of the Markan parallel (Mark 14:32).

[b] Many MSS ($P^{53}$ ℵ A C D L W Θ $f^{1,13}$ TR sy$^h$) have προσελθών, "having gone to (there)." Supporting the text, προελθών, are $P^{37,45}$ B lat sy$^{s,p}$ co.

[c] προσευχόμενος καί, lit. "praying and."

<sup>d</sup> A few MSS (P<sup>53</sup>* L Δ *f* <sup>1</sup> vg<sup>ww</sup>) omit μου, "my," by the probable influence of the parallel in Mark 14:36; Luke 22:42.

<sup>e</sup> *f* <sup>13</sup> adds Luke 22:43–44, perhaps through the influence of the lectionary (see Nestle-Aland apparatus).

<sup>f</sup> D it vg<sup>cl</sup> sy<sup>s.p</sup> bo add αὐτοῦ, "his."

<sup>g</sup> λέγων, "saying," is omitted by B g<sup>1</sup>.

<sup>h</sup> P<sup>37</sup> and a few other witnesses omit μου, "my" (cf. v 39).

<sup>i</sup> Many MSS (Θ TR lat sy<sup>s.p</sup> mae bo and D *f* <sup>13</sup>, but in different word order) add τὸ ποτήριον, "cup," a natural addition because of the following verb, "drink."

<sup>j</sup> Many MSS (A C W *f* <sup>13</sup> TR sy<sup>h</sup>) add ἀπ' ἐμοῦ, "from me."

<sup>k</sup> Alternate punctuation puts καὶ ἀφεὶς αὐτούς, "and he left them," and even possibly πάλιν, "again," with the preceding sentence (v 43), thereby alleviating v 44 of some of its awkwardness. For an alternate translation of this clause, see *Comment*.

<sup>l</sup> "Some distance" added to translation in keeping with the participle ἀπελθών, "having gone."

<sup>m</sup> Some MSS (P<sup>37</sup> A D K *f* <sup>1</sup> it) omit ἐκ τρίτου, "a third time."

<sup>n</sup> πάλιν, "again," the last word of the Gr. sentence, may by different punctuation become the first word of the next sentence (v 45), thereby avoiding the awkwardness of two occurrences of the word in the same sentence (i.e., if the alternate punctuation mentioned above in *Note* k is not accepted). Many witnesses (A C D W *f* <sup>1,13</sup> TR lat sy<sup>p.h</sup> sa mae), on the other hand, omit this πάλιν altogether, in order to avoid the repetition of the word.

<sup>o</sup> D W Γ TR lat sy<sup>s.p</sup> bo insert αὐτοῦ, "his."

<sup>p</sup> The sentence may be intended as a question: "Are you still sleeping and taking your rest?" See *Comment* below.

<sup>q</sup> ἰδού, "look," is omitted by Θ *f* <sup>1</sup> mae, perhaps because of the occurrence of the word in v 46.

### Form/Structure/Setting

A. Just prior to his arrest, Jesus confronts his destiny in his agonizing prayer in the garden of Gethsemane. He knows well what lies ahead. This is the last pericope in which the earthly Jesus is together with his disciples. The inner core, Peter, James, and John, are unable to watch and pray in support of the trial of the soul through which Jesus passes. And thus again the disciples are portrayed as failures. At the crucial moment they are unable to pull themselves out of their sleepy stupor.

B. Matthew continues to follow Mark closely (Mark 14:32–42; cf. Luke 22:39–46, which, however, is quite different from Mark, and John 12:27–28, which is generally similar). Matthew makes the typical abbreviation of Mark.

The most substantial omissions are the following: in v 39 Matthew omits Mark's ἵνα εἰ δυνατόν ἐστιν παρέλθῃ ἀπ' αὐτοῦ ἡ ὥρα, "that if it is possible, the hour might pass from him" (Mark 14:35), although the first words εἰ δυνατόν ἐστιν, "if it is possible," are used in connection with the first petition in Matthew; also in v 39 Matthew omits Mark's first clause in the prayer, πάντα δυνατά σοι, "all things are possible for you" (Mark 14:36), perhaps as being irreconcilable with the prayer "if it is possible"; and in the same verse the evangelist omits Mark's Aramaic word ἀββά, "Father" (Mark 14:36, the only occurrence of the word in the Gospels); in v 40 he omits the first question to Peter in Mark, Σίμων, καθεύδεις; "Simon, are you sleeping?" (Mark 14:37), perhaps regarding it as unnecessary; in v 43 Matthew omits Mark's statement καὶ οὐκ ᾔδεισαν τί ἀποκριθῶσιν αὐτῷ, "and they did not know what to answer him" (Mark 14:40), perhaps as irrelevant to the narrative; and finally in v 45 Matthew omits Mark's somewhat puzzling ἀπέχει, "it is enough" (Mark 14:41).

On the other hand, however, Matthew makes a number of additions, among which the following may be noted: in v 36 Matthew adds μετ' αὐτῶν ὁ Ἰησοῦς, "Jesus with them" (cf. Mark 14:32), supplying a subject for the verb, introducing a new section, and preparing for Jesus' speaking with his disciples a little later in the verse; near the end of the same verse, Matthew adds ἀπελθὼν ἐκεῖ, "having gone there" (cf. Mark 14:32), indicating that the praying was done a little distance away. In v 38, as in v 40, Matthew adds μετ' ἐμοῦ, "with me," to the verb γρηγορεῖτε, "watch" (cf. Mark 14:34, 37). In v 39 Matthew adds μου, "my," after "Father" (cf. Mark 14:36). In v 40, Matthew adds πρὸς τοὺς μαθητάς, "to the disciples" (cf. Matthew 14:37), avoiding Mark's slightly abrupt syntax. In v 42 Matthew adds ἐκ δευτέρου, "a second time" (cf. Mark 14:39), thereby specifically enumerating all three instances that Jesus went to pray (cf. v 44; although Mark enumerates the times Jesus comes to the disciples [Mark 14:41]). In the same verse Matthew adds the content of the prayer, which varies a little from that in v 39 (contrast Mark 14:39: προσηύξατο τὸν αὐτὸν λόγον εἰπών, "he prayed, saying the same thing [lit. word]"). But in v 44 Matthew utilizes the Markan language just mentioned, adding it in the reference to the third prayer of Jesus. In v 45, Matthew again adds πρὸς τοὺς μαθητάς, "to the disciples" (cf. Mark 14:41), thereby bringing about parallelism with v 40. Finally, in the same verse, Matthew adds ἰδού, "look" (cf. Mark 14:41), one of his favorite markers of something particularly important.

Among Matthean substitutions, the following may be noted. In v 37 he substitutes τοὺς δύο υἱοὺς Ζεβεδαίου, "the two sons of Zebedee," for Mark's "James and John" (Mark 14:33); in the same verse, he substitutes λυπεῖσθαι, "to be sorrowful," for Mark's ἐκθαμβεῖσθαι, "to be distressed" (used four times in Mark but never in Matthew). In v 39 he substitutes πρόσωπον αὐτοῦ, "his face," for Mark's τῆς γῆς, "the ground" (Mark 14:35), a more suitable (Semitic) expression for prayer. In v 45 Matthew's favorite τότε, "then," replaces Mark's καί, "and" (Mark 14:41), and in the same verse, Matthew substitutes the more precise ἤγγικεν, "has come near," for ἦλθεν, "has come."

Thus, Matthew again follows his source closely while displaying a degree of freedom in his use of it.

C. The passage with its three references to Jesus praying and the disciples sleeping has clearly a dramatic character. It is structured around the instructions of Jesus to his disciples and his prayers. The passage ends with the dramatic utterance of Jesus that the time has come. The following is an outline of the pericope: (1) Jesus' and his disciples' entrance into the garden (v 36); (2) Jesus' and the inner circle of disciples' progression into the garden (vv 37–38); (3) Jesus' first prayer (vv 39–41), subdivided into (a) the prayer (v 39), (b) finding the disciples asleep (v 40), and (c) exhortation to the disciples (v 41); (4) Jesus' second prayer (vv 42–43), subdivided into (a) the prayer (v 42) and (b) finding the disciples asleep (v 43); (5) Jesus' third prayer (v 44); (6) the resignation (v 45a); and (7) the imminent betrayal (vv 45b–46). Certain structural features are easily seen. To begin with, there are the three times Jesus prayed (ἐκ δευτέρου, "a second time" [v 42], and ἐκ τρίτου, "a third time" [v 44]). Matthew, however, has not pressed for as much symmetry as he might have. Thus in the first instance (v 39) the aorist verb προσηύξατο, "he prayed," is not used, as it is in the second and third instances. The content of the prayer is given in the first two instances but not in the third (v 44), and both instances essentially agree in content (i.e., the affirmation of God's will; an if-clause pertaining to "that which is possible"; a reference to the "passing" of what is in view) yet hardly at all in form. Similarly, whereas there is an exhortation after the first prayer (v 41), this is not true of the others (in the second the sleepiness of the disciples is simply indicated [v 43], and the third ends in a note of resignation [v 45a]). Other minor structural parallelisms to be mentioned are the following: the correspondence of the command γρηγορεῖτε μετ' ἐμοῦ, "watch with me" (v 38), with the question using the same words in v 40; the πάτερ μου, "my Father," at the beginning of the two prayers (vv 39 and 42); the parallel οὐχ ὡς ἐγώ, "not as I," ἀλλ' ὡς σύ, "but as you," in the first prayer (v 39); the dual imperatives of v 41, γρηγορεῖτε καὶ προσεύχεσθε, "watch and pray"; the parallel structure of v 41b, τὸ μὲν πνεῦμα πρόθυμον, ἡ δὲ σὰρξ ἀσθενής, "the spirit (is) willing, but the flesh (is) weak"; the parallel imperatives in v 45, καθεύδετε, "sleep," and ἀναπαύεσθε, "rest"; and finally the repeated ἤγγικεν, "has come near" (the hour; the betrayer), in vv 45 and 46. Justin Martyr (*Dial.* 99.2; 103.8) quotes the Matthean version of the prayer that the cup, "if possible," might pass from Jesus (cf. v 39). The logion of v 41b is cited in Polycarp, *Phil.* 7:2. For comprehensive treatment of the pericope, see especially Feldmeier.

## Comment

**36**   Jesus and his disciples came to a χωρίον, a "place" or a "plot of land" (the only occurrence in Matthew), which was known as Γεθσημανί, "Gethsemane," the Greek transliteration of the Hebrew שְׁמָנֵי גַּת, *gat šĕmānê*, which means "oil press." More than a garden (cf. κῆπος, "garden," of John 18:1, 26), Gethsemane was probably an olive orchard. It was located across the Kidron valley on the lower slopes of the Mount of Olives. At a certain point Jesus instructs his disciples to sit down and to wait for him while he proceeds a little farther to pray (Matthew also records Jesus as praying in 14:23).

**37–38**   This is one of the special occasions in which only the inner core of disciples is allowed to participate (cf. earlier 17:1 [the transfiguration; for parallels with the present pericope, see Kenny]; Mark 5:37 [raising of a dead girl]). At this hour of trial, it is only natural that Jesus would want the emotional support of his closest friends (see Barbour for a discussion of Jesus' testing in the face of evil). The two sons of Zebedee are of course James and John (cf. 4:21; 10:2; Mark 14:33). The reason for Jesus' desire to pray is indicated in the infinitives λυπεῖσθαι and ἀδημονεῖν, namely, that he was "sorrowful" and "anxious." As the moment of his arrest approaches, Jesus is filled with dread. We are not told precisely the cause of this anguish. Perhaps Jesus faces the fear of death (thus Cullmann, *Immortality of the Soul or Resurrection of the Dead?* [London: Epworth, 1958] 21–22), but very probably what he faces here is the prospect of dying *as the bearer of sin* and thus as one who experiences the consequent wrath of God (cf. the pain of 27:46; see too esp. Heb 5:7; cf. Armbruster; R. E. Brown, *Death of the Messiah*, 234). Jesus' words in v 38, περίλυπός ἐστιν ἡ ψυχή μου, "my soul is very sorrowful" (cf. John 12:27: "troubled"), allude to similar language in the LXX of Pss 41:6, 12; 42:5 (where in all instances it occurs in the question "why are you sad, my soul?"). "Soul" here is to be understood in the sense of person. The expression of being sad ἕως θανάτου, "to death," that is, to the utmost limit or degree, is also biblical language (cf. LXX of Jonah 4:9; Sir 37:2, where in both instances it is linked with "sorrow"). Thus, using the language of the Bible, Jesus tells Peter, James, and John that his sorrow is so great that he is hardly able to bear it. The forgiveness of sins that he offers (cf. v 28) will be accomplished only at an incomprehensible personal cost that goes far beyond physical death. So, not as a brave martyr but in a state of extreme sorrow, he contemplates his death. He asks the three to remain there and charges them γρηγορεῖτε μετ᾽ ἐμοῦ, "watch with me." That is, they were to support Jesus by watching (present tense) not only "with" him, by assisting him with their conscious presence, but perhaps too with prayer (cf. v 41). Jesus does not want to face this time of anguish alone. The command to "watch" here and in vv 40 and 41 on the night of the Passover echoes the "night of vigil" referred to in Exod 12:42 (thus Gerhardsson).

**39** Jesus goes by himself μικρόν, "a little further," into the orchard, where he falls on his face before God in prayer (in the OT a common posture in special circumstances of worship, fear, or submission; in the NT, cf. 17:6; Rev 7:11; 11:16). In his prayer he addresses God with the intimate words πάτερ μου, "my Father" (very frequent in Matthew, but cf. esp. v 29; 11:25, 27; 25:34). τὸ ποτήριον τοῦτο, "this cup," is a metaphor for the suffering and death that he was soon to face (it is used as a metaphor for death also in 20:22–23; cf. John 18:11). For the related imagery of "the cup of God's wrath," also pertinent to the present context (see esp. Cranfield), cf. Rev 14:10; 16:19; and OT background in Isa 51:17, 22. Jesus then prays that εἰ δυνατόν ἐστιν, "if it is possible," he might not have to go the way of the cross. This conditioning of the prayer with "if it is possible" becomes more specific in the final clause of the prayer, πλὴν οὐχ ὡς ἐγὼ θέλω ἀλλ᾽ ὡς σύ, "but not as I will, but as you (will)" (cf. v 42). The governing reality then is not the will of Jesus, who would avoid what lies ahead, but the will of God, who is fixed in his intent to accomplish salvation for the world through the death of his Son (cf. John 6:38; 4:34). In actuality, if the will of the Father is done, it is *not* possible to avoid the cross (contra Blaising's insistence that the first-class condition necessitates a real possibility).

**40–41** When Jesus returns to the three disciples, he finds that they are sleeping and that he has received no support from them. They seem oblivious to what he is going through despite the indication of his anguish in v 38. καθεύδοντας, "sleeping," here and in v 43 is a culpable act (unlike in 25:5), especially after the command of v 38 (see Daube for the view that sleeping violated the fellowship of the Passover community [ḥăḇûrâ]), and becomes a metaphor in the NT for moral failure (cf. 1 Thess 5:6–7; Eph 5:14). Thus the rhetorical question to Peter conveys a rebuke (addressed to all the disciples as the plural form of the verb indicates), underlined by the reference to μίαν ὥραν, "one hour." γρηγορῆσαι μετ᾽ ἐμοῦ, "watch with me," corresponds exactly to the command of v 38 (see *Comment* there). For a second time the command to "watch" (γρηγορεῖτε) is given, but here it is linked with προσεύχεσθε, "pray." Now the focus is not upon watching μετ᾽ ἐμοῦ, "with me," but upon the need for vigilance in the future, threatening situation of the disciples. That is, they are to "watch and pray" (again plural verbs) so that *they* might not enter into testing. The lesson of Jesus' experience is thus applied to the disciples. Accordingly, the command to "watch" (γρηγορεῖν) becomes a standard feature in ethical catechism in the NT (in the sense of spiritual preparedness; cf. 1 Cor 16:13; Col 4:2; 1 Thess 5:6; 1 Peter 5:8; see Lövestam, *Spiritual Wakefulness in the New Testament*), as does the command to pray (cf. Eph 6:18; 1 Thess 5:17; 1 Peter 4:7). The reference to praying so as not to enter testing recalls the petition of the model prayer in reference to the great eschatological trial (6:13). (The experience of Jesus' own testing in the context of testing to be experienced by the disciples brings to mind Heb 2:18; 4:15). If Jesus' experience in Gethsemane underlines the truth that τὸ μὲν πνεῦμα πρόθυμον, ἡ δὲ σὰρξ ἀσθενής, "the spirit is willing, but the flesh is weak," how much more will this be the experience of the disciples in the struggles that await them. This logion points to the tension between the inner person, the center of volition, and the outer person, the bodily flesh with its more obvious inherent weakness (for the spirit-flesh distinction, see 1 Cor 7:34; 2 Cor 7:1; cf. Rom 8:4–17; Gal 5:17, where, however, flesh is contrasted with the Holy Spirit; for comparison with Qumran, see Kuhn).

**42–43** Matthew's addition of ἐκ δευτέρου, "a second time," is redundant after πάλιν, "again," but corresponds to ἐκ τρίτου, "a third time," in v 44. See above for structural similarities with the first prayer (v 39). Again Jesus begins his prayer with the words πάτερ μου, "my Father," asks that τοῦτο, "this (cup)," might pass, and conditions his prayer with the now negative εἰ οὐ δύναται, "if not possible"—reflecting a further stage of resignation—as well as the direct γενηθήτω τὸ θέλημά σου, "may your will be done" (cf. the petition in 6:10; Acts 21:14). The acceptance of God's will shows Jesus as one who is strong in his obedience, and thus Jesus is portrayed only positively in this pericope (see Dibelius). When Jesus returns from this time of prayer (v 43), he again finds the disciples καθεύδοντας, "sleeping" (as in v 40), but this time no actual rebuke is recorded, although one is clearly implicit (cf. Mark 14:40c). Only the comment that their eyes βεβαρημένοι, "were heavy," is added (the word is used similarly in Luke 9:32: "heavy with sleep"). The disciples continued to find it impossible to stay awake while Jesus was praying.

**44–45** Because the opening clause καὶ ἀφεὶς αὐτούς, usually translated "and having left them," is redundant (given the participle ἀπελθών, "having gone"), it may mean "having allowed them" (i.e., to sleep), a perfectly legitimate meaning of ἀφιέναι. This interpretation is consonant with the fact that Matthew in the preceding verse gives no report of Jesus saying anything to the disciples. It is also in agreement with the command of v 45 that they go on with their sleeping, unless this be taken as implying that only now after the third prayer is sleeping allowed. On the other hand, it is also possible that the participle means "having left" and that the redundant ἀπελθών, "having gone," is retained merely to strengthen the parallelism between this verse and v 42 where it also precedes προσηύξατο, "he prayed" (cf. προσελθών in v 39). Jesus prayed ἐκ τρίτου, "a third time" (cf. Mark 14:41; 2 Cor 12:8), πάλιν, "again," τὸν αὐτὸν λόγον, lit. "the same word" but in context "prayer." Possibly καθεύδετε [τὸ] λοιπὸν καὶ ἀναπαύεσθε is to be taken as a question (thus NRSV: "Are you still sleeping and taking your rest?") or an exclamation to the same point. The advantage of this interpretation is that it avoids the incongruity of the traditional rendering, "sleep for the remainder of the time and rest," with the initial words of v 46: "rise, let us go." On the other hand, from the NRSV translation one might expect ἔτι, "still," rather than [τὸ] λοιπόν, lit. "the remainder"; and the ἀναπαύεσθε, "rest," also seems to make less sense in a question than in an exhortation. If the words represent an exhortation, they may point simply to the reality of Jesus' final resignation to, and acceptance of, what lay ahead of him. The final sequence of events is about to begin, and now there is nothing the disciples can do. Thus they are invited to sleep and take their rest, although there is little time for such now.

ἰδοὺ ἤγγικεν ἡ ὥρα, "look, the hour has come near," signals the beginning of the passion (for ὥρα, "hour," as the hour of the passion of Jesus, see, e.g., John 2:4; 7:30; 12:27; 13:1; 17:1). ἐγγίζειν, "to draw near" or "to come," is used elsewhere in Matthew mainly in connection with the coming of the kingdom of heaven (3:2; 4:17; 10:7). The anticipated betrayal of the "Son of Man" (cf. in this chapter vv 2, 24; and earlier 17:12, 22; 20:18) now finds its fulfillment. Only here in Matthew is reference made to εἰς χεῖρας ἁμαρτωλῶν, "into the hands of sinners" (cf. 17:22: "into the hands of men"; the only other instance involving identification in the betrayal sayings refers to "the chief priests and scribes" [20:18]). While at times the "handing over" (= betrayal) of Jesus is expressed by a divine passive indicating God as the acting subject (e.g., 17:22; 20:18), here in light of the immediately following verses Judas is understood as the subject (cf. v 24).

**46** The words ἐγείρεσθε ἄγωμεν, "rise, let us go" (cf. the identical words in John 14:31), do not have flight in mind but rather going to meet the betrayer and those with him. Matthew's ἰδού, "look" (cf. v 45), yet again serves to call attention to a key event in the narrative. If the hour of the betrayal has come near (v 45), so too ἤγγικεν ὁ παραδιδούς με, "the one who betrays me is about to come" (cf. vv 15, 21, 23–25).

### Explanation

The thought of what he will have to undergo in the near future fills Jesus with dread and anguish. A real struggle within the soul of Jesus takes place in Gethsemane, and he craves the support of those who have been closest to him during his ministry. The mystery of the agony of God's unique Son cannot be fully penetrated. That it has to do with bearing the penalty of sin for the world to make salvation possible seems clear. What we do see in the narrative is Jesus pleading that if at all possible the cup of this suffering might pass from him without his having to drink of it, i.e., that he might even at this late moment bypass the agony of the cross. Yet here as elsewhere Jesus submits himself, however reluctantly, to the will of his Father. In all of this the disciples incidentally learn important lessons that may be summed up in Jesus' statement that while the spirit may be willing, the flesh is weak. Told to watch with Jesus, and no doubt eager to do so, they fail—being overcome with the combination of the Passover meal, the wine, and the lateness of the hour. No answer is given in the passage to the problem of the weakness of the flesh other than that it is a fact to be admitted and not to be underestimated. First this human failure, then the desertion of their master— the disciples are in for a bad time. They fail miserably at doing the will of their Lord. And yet despite it all, they remain disciples—disciples who have that status only through ongoing forgiveness. But Jesus knows their weakness and finally allows them the rest their frail humanity so craves. While the disciples in their sleepy stupor remain uncomprehending, for Jesus the immediate crisis is over and the final act about to begin. Now unwaveringly his face is set toward the cross and the fulfillment of his Father's will.

# *Jesus Taken into Custody    (26:47-56)*

*Bibliography*

**Black, M.** "The Arrest and Trial of Jesus and the Date of the Last Supper." In *New Testament Essays*. FS T. W. Manson, ed. A. J. B. Higgins. Manchester: Manchester UP, 1959. 19–33. **Crossan, R. D.** "Matthew 26:47–56—Jesus Arrested." In *Tradition as Openness to the Future*. FS W. W. Fisher, ed. F. O. Francis and R. P. Wallace. Lanham, MD: University Press of America, 1984. 175–90. **Daube, D.** "Three Notes Having to Do with Johanan Ben Zaccai: III. Slitting the High Priest's Ear." *JTS* n.s. 11 (1960) 59–62. **Deissmann, A.** "Friend, Wherefore Art Thou Come?" *ExpTim* 33 (1921–22) 491–93. **Dibelius, M.** "Jesus und der Judaskuss." In *Botschaft und Geschichte*. Tübingen: Mohr, 1953. 1:272–77. **Doeve, J. W.** "Die Gefangennahme Jesu in Gethsemane: Eine traditionsgeschichtliche Untersuchung." *SE* 1 [= TU 73] (1959) 458–80. **Eltester, W.** "'Freund, wozu du gekommen bist' (Mt. xxvi 50)." In *Neotestamentica et Patristica*. FS O. Cullmann, ed. W. C. van Unnik. NovTSup 6. Leiden: Brill, 1962. 70–91. **Harris, R.** "Deissmann on the Holy Grail." *ExpTim* 35 (1923–24) 523–24. **Harrison, E. F.** "The Son of God among the Sons of Men: XIII. Jesus and Judas." *BSac* 105 (1948) 170–81. **Klostermann, E.** "Zur Spiegelbergs Aufsatz 'Der Sinn von *eph ho parei* in Mt 26,50.'" *ZNW* 29 (1930) 311. **Kosmala, H.** "Matthew xxvi 52: A Quotation from the Targum." *NovT* 4 (1960–61) 3–5. **Krieger, N.** "Der Knecht des Hohenpriesters." *NovT* 2 (1957) 73–74. **Lee, G. M.** "Matthew xxvi.50: 'Ἑταῖρε ἐφ' ὃ πάρει.'" *ExpTim* 81 (1969–70) 55. **Limbeck, M.** "'Stecke dein Schwert in die Scheide . . . !' Die Jesusbewegung im Unterschied zu den Zeloten." *BK* 37 (1982) 98–104. **Owen, E. C. E.** "St Matthew xxvi.50." *JTS* 29 (1927–28) 384–86. **Peri, I.** "Der Weggefährte." *ZNW* 78 (1987) 127–31. **Rehkopf, F.** "Mt 26:50: *ETAIPE EΦ O ΠAPEI*." *ZNW* 52 (1961) 109–15. **Schneider, G.** "Die Verhaftung Jesu: Traditionsgeschichte von Mk 14.43–52." *ZNW* 63 (1972) 188–209. **Spiegelberg, W.** "Der Sinn von ἐφ' ὃ πάρει in Mt 26,50." *ZNW* 28 (1929) 341–43. **Suggit, J.** "Comrade Judas: Matthew 26:50." *Journal of Theology for Southern Africa* 63 (1988) 56–58. **Suhl, A.** "Die Funktion des Schwertstreichs bei der Gefangennahme Jesu: Beobachtungen zur Komposition und Theologie der synoptischen Evangelien (Mk 14,43–52; Mt 26,47–56; Lk 22,47–53)." In *The Four Gospels*. FS F. Neirynck, ed. F. Van Segbroeck et al. BETL 100. Leuven: Leuven UP, 1992. 1:295–323. **Wilson, J. P.** "Matthew 26,50: 'Friend, wherefore art thou come?'" *ExpTim* 41 (1929–30) 334.

*Translation*

[47]*And while he was yet speaking, look, Judas, one of the twelve, came and together with him a great crowd from the chief priests and elders of the people with swords and clubs.* [48]*And the one betraying him gave them a sign, saying: "The one I kiss—he is the one. Seize him."* [49]*And immediately when he had come to Jesus, he said:*[a] *"Hail, Rabbi"; and he kissed him.* [50]*But Jesus said to him:*[b] *"Friend, for this you come!"*[c] *Then they came, put their hands upon Jesus, and took him into custody.* [51]*And look, one of those with Jesus reached with his hand and drew his sword, and striking the servant of the high priest, he cut off his ear.* [52]*Then Jesus said to him: "Put your sword back in its place. For all who take the sword will by the sword perish.* [53]*Or do you think I am not able to call upon my Father, and he will send me*[d] *now*[e] *more than twelve legions of angels?* [54]*How therefore would the scriptures be fulfilled that thus it must be?"* [55]*At that point*[f] *Jesus said to the crowds: "Have you come out as for an insurrectionist to capture me with swords and clubs? I was sitting daily*[g] *in the temple teaching, and you did not*

*arrest me. ⁵⁶But this whole thing has happened in order that the writings of the prophets might be fulfilled." Then all the ʰ disciples abandoned him and fled.*

## Notes

ᵃ A few MSS (P³⁷ᵖ C [syˢ] saᵐˢ mae bo) add αὐτῷ, "to him."

ᵇ P³⁷ omits the words "Hail, Rabbi . . . to him," probably through homoioteleuton (αὐτῷ — αὐτῷ, "to him — to him" [the first of these is probably in P³⁷; see preceding *Note*]).

ᶜ ἐφ' ὃ πάρει, lit. "for which you come," may also be translated as a question: "Why have you come?" or as "Do what you are here to do." See *Comment*.

ᵈ אʹ* Θ f¹ (bo) insert ὧδε, "here."

ᵉ Many MSS (A C D W Θ f¹,¹³ TR it [syʰ mae]) place ἄρτι, "now," after δύναμαι, "I am able."

ᶠ ἐν ἐκείνῃ τῇ ὥρᾳ, lit. "in that hour."

ᵍ Many MSS ([A] C D W Θ f¹,¹³ TR latt syᵖ,ʰ mae) insert πρὸς ὑμᾶς, "with you," probably through the influence of the parallel in Mark 14:49.

ʰ A few MSS (B it syˢ sa) add αὐτοῦ, "his."

## Form/Structure/Setting

A. The preliminaries are over, and now the narrative moves into the sequence of events that culminates in the crucifixion of Jesus. The betrayer does his despicable deed; there is a brief attempt at resistance on the part of the disciples. But the central motif from the beginning of the final sequence, when Jesus is taken into custody by the Jewish authorities, is the fulfillment of the scriptures. From the arrest of Jesus the narrative moves immediately into his so-called trial and thence to his death. From this point on, the narrative takes on an inexorability that reflects a mysterious conjunction of human determination and divine superintendence.

B. Matthew again is closely dependent upon Mark (Mark 14:43–49; cf. Luke 22:47–53; John 18:2–12). The major differences from Mark are the addition of vv 52–54 (words of Jesus about the sword, angels, and the fulfillment of scripture), presumably from Matthew's special source, and the omission of Mark 14:50–52 (the enigmatic reference to the young man in the linen cloth). Beyond these we may note Matthew's omission in v 48 of Mark's καὶ ἀπάγετε ἀσφαλῶς, "and lead him away securely" (Mark 14:44), probably regarded as unnecessary, and in v 47 his omission of τῶν γραμματέων, "the scribes" (cf. Mark 14:43), probably to abbreviate. Three other omissions may be noted: in v 47 Mark's εὐθύς, "immediately" (Mark 14:43), redundant with the genitive absolute construction; in v 49 Mark's ἐλθών, "having come" (Mark 14:45), redundant given the following προσελθών, "having come to"; and in v 55 πρὸς ὑμᾶς, "with you" (Mark 14:49), probably to abbreviate. On the other hand, Matthew makes a number of additions to his Markan source. Most substantial, in addition to the one noted above, is in v 50, ὁ δὲ Ἰησοῦς εἶπεν αὐτῷ, ἑταῖρε, ἐφ' ὃ πάρει, "But Jesus said to him: 'Friend, for this you come'" (cf. Mark 14:45, where no words are spoken to Judas). This causes the addition of the following words, τότε προσελθόντες, "then having come," as well as ἐπὶ τὸν Ἰησοῦν, "upon Jesus" (cf. Mark 14:46). A few other additions are noteworthy. In v 47 Matthew adds πολύς, "great" (cf. the plural in v 55), in referring to the crowd (cf. Mark 14:43) and the modifier τοῦ λαοῦ, "of the people," to "the elders" (cf. 21:23, 26:3; 27:1). In v 49 he adds the greeting χαῖρε, "hail," as a dramatic touch (cf. Mark's simple "Rabbi" in Mark 14:45). In v 51 he inserts ἰδού, "look," in characteristic fashion (cf. Mark 14:47), and in the same verse he adds ἐκτείνας τὴν χεῖρα, "having reached (with) his hand," one of the few times in Matthew's redaction of Mark that he adds something not obviously useful or necessary. Note these few further additions: in v 55 Matthew adds ἐν ἐκείνῃ τῇ ὥρᾳ, "in that hour" (formulaic; cf. 8:13; 10:19; 18:1; cf. Mark 14:48); in the same verse he adds ἐκαθεζόμην, "I was sitting" (the usual posture for teaching); and at the beginning of v 56 he adds τοῦτο δὲ ὅλον γέγονεν, "this whole (thing) has happened," to complete Mark's sentence (Mark 14:49). Among Matthew's substitutions, we may note the more common σημεῖον, "sign," in v 48 for Mark's σύσσημον, "signal" (Mark 14:44, only here in the NT); τῷ Ἰησοῦ, "to Jesus," in v 49 for Mark's αὐτῷ, "to him" (Mark 14:45); and τοῖς ὄχλοις, "the crowds," in v 55 for αὐτοῖς, "them" (Mark 14:48). There is a degree of freedom in Matthew's use of Mark, yet in the main Matthew, as usual, follows his source closely.

C. The pericope consists of historical narrative but includes certain teaching elements (i.e., vv 52–54, 56). The following is a suggested outline: (1) the arrival of Judas and the guards (v 47); (2) the betrayal of Jesus (vv 48–49); (3) the arrest of Jesus (v 50); (4) a token of armed resistance (v 51); (5) Jesus' words to his disciple(s) (vv 52–54); (6) Jesus' words to the crowds (vv 55–56a); and (7) the flight of the disciples (v 56b). There is virtually no structural symmetry to speak of. Probably the most interesting feature is the reference to the fulfillment of scripture at the end both of the words to the disciple(s) (v 54) and of the words to the crowd (v 56a). The passage ends with the strongly negative note concerning the disciples' abandonment of Jesus.

### *Comment*

**47**    A further ἰδού, "look," calls attention to the arrival of Judas the betrayer, who is again deliberately mentioned as εἷς τῶν δώδεκα, "one of the twelve" (cf. vv 14, 21, 25). The ὄχλος πολύς, "large crowd," ἀπὸ τῶν ἀρχιερέων καὶ πρεσβυτέρων τοῦ λαοῦ, "from the chief priests and elders of the people" (linked also in 21:23; 26:3; 27:1), probably consisted of some of the temple guard, possibly expanded by some specially hired men, and perhaps even a contingent of Roman soldiers (cf. John 18:3, 12). Their number and their weapons, μετὰ μαχαιρῶν καὶ ξύλων, "with swords and clubs," seem to suggest that they intended to take into custody a serious criminal (cf. v 55). Perhaps they feared that the eleven would defend Jesus at any cost.

**48–49**    So that there would be no mistake in the darkness, Judas informs the guard that he will give them a sign by kissing Jesus, the customary practice of greeting between friends (see Dibelius) even down to the present in the Middle East (cf. Luke 7:45; Rom 16:16; 1 Cor 16:20; 2 Cor 13:12; 1 Thess 5:16; 1 Peter 5:14). This Judas does εὐθέως, "immediately," with the usual greeting χαῖρε, "hail" or "greetings" (cf. 28:9), the Greek probably reflecting an underlying, rather ironic, šālôm, "peace," and with the appellation ῥαββί, "Rabbi," again indicating that he has gone over to the opponents of Jesus (cf. v 25 and *Comment* there). The verb for "kiss" in v 49 is an intensive form (καταφιλεῖν) compared to the simple φιλεῖν in v 48.

**50**  Jesus' addressing of Judas as *ἐταῖρε*, "friend," should not be understood as involving a negative or sarcastic connotation, for the word can mean "comrade" or "companion" (in the NT used only in Matthew; cf. 11:16 [v.l.]; 20:13; 22:12; Socrates refers to his pupils using this word; cf. BAGD, 314b). Jesus' words *ἐφ᾽ ὅ πάρει* are extremely difficult to interpret. Literally they mean "for what you are come," which can be understood as a question (thus Deissmann), "Why do you (have you) come?" taking the relative as an interrogative. In this case, of course, the question would have to be rhetorical or ironical, since Jesus knows well why Judas has come. On the other hand, the words can be understood as a statement with an implied command, i.e., "what you have come to do, do it" (cf. NRSV: "do what you are here to do"; cf. John 13:27; cf. Owen). Yet Judas has already performed his act of betrayal in the kiss when Jesus speaks these words. It is the guard that acts next. Another possible understanding, however, is to take the words quite literally as a comment of resigned disappointment in Judas: "for *this* you come!" (cf. the irony of Luke 22:48). It reflects at once disappointment in Judas, a further stage of resignation to the will of God that will take him to his death, and a yielding to the final act of the story (cf. R. E. Brown, "Appendix III, C" [*Death of the Messiah*, 1385–88] and his conclusion that the phrase is a way of indicating Jesus' knowledge of what Judas is doing). (Cf. Wilson: "Companion, the thing you are here for!" Thus too Spiegelberg: "It is this for which you are here!"; cf. Rehkopf; Eltester.) The guards, having had their man pointed out to them, grab Jesus and take him into their custody (cf. John 18:12).

**51–52**  In a token of resistance on the part of the disciples, one of them (according to John 18:10–11, 26, it was Peter) takes his sword and slashes at *τὸν δοῦλον τοῦ ἀρχιερέως*, "the servant of the high priest" (the name Malchus is provided in John 18:10; Krieger suggests the servant was Judas!), slicing off his ear (only in the Lukan account does Jesus heal the severed ear [Luke 22:51], just as only in Luke do we learn that the disciples had with them two swords [Luke 22:38]). There can be little doubt that more serious harm was intended (*pace* Daube, who thinks of mutilation that would render one unfit for cultic service). Jesus, however, instructs his disciple to put the sword back in its scabbard and then utters the now-famous logion: *πάντες γὰρ οἱ λαβόντες μάχαιραν ἐν μαχαίρῃ ἀπολοῦνται*, "for all who take the sword will by the sword perish." This chiastically formed proverbial saying, which probably goes back to Gen 9:6 (where, however, it refers to capital punishment), describes the generally true principle that violence begets violence (cf. Rev 13:10, which takes up this logion). (Kosmala's argument that the logion comes from a Targum of Isa 50:11 is not more than a possibility.) This was no sensible way to proceed, even if it seemed like an appropriate indication of loyalty to Jesus. Furthermore, it opposed the teaching of Jesus already given in 5:39 (cf. 10:39).

**53–54**  If resistance were the right thing, Jesus had no need of swords or human assistance (cf. John 18:36, where Jesus denies any present claims that would justify violence). He makes the statement, in the form of a rhetorical question, that supernatural help is available to him at just a word to his Father. More than *δώδεκα λεγιῶνας ἀγγέλων*, "twelve legions of angels," is an enormous number (a legion of Roman troops amounted to about six thousand; thus here more than 72,000 angels!), but exactitude is no concern and the number twelve has obvious symbolic connotations. "Twelve" legions may be intended to correspond to the twelve tribes of Israel or to a full complement of twelve disciples. For the help of angels, cf. Ps 91:11–12 (cf. the use of this passage in Matt 4:6, where Jesus also does not avail himself of angelic assistance); for "innumerable angels," cf. Heb 12:22. Earlier in the Gospel the Son of Man sends angels (13:41; 24:31) and comes with his angels (16:27; 25:31). Belief in angels had increased dramatically in the period of the second temple. Here compare the militant angels who fight on the side of the sons of light in the Qumran writings (e.g., 1QM 7:6; 12:8). Again we see that Jesus' obedience to the will of the Father is not a matter of compulsion but of a free yielding to that will (cf. vv 39, 42). Even at this late moment all could be aborted, but then the scriptures would remain unfulfilled. It is implied in v 54 that if the scriptures are not fulfilled, the very faithfulness of God could be called into question. The scriptures state that οὕτως δεῖ γενέσθαι, "thus it must be" (δεῖ, "it must," reflecting divine necessity, is used in reference to the death of Jesus in 16:21; cf. related uses in 17:10; 24:6; the same construction, δεῖ γενέσθαι, is found in the LXX of Dan 2:28–29; 2:45 [Theod.]). God has ordained that things should be thus and since αἱ γραφαί, "the scriptures," reflect the will of God, they must be fulfilled. This same point is stressed again in v 56. Thus the emphasis on the fulfillment of scripture (on πληρωθῶσιν, "be fulfilled," see *Comment* on 1:22) is important in Matthew generally (cf. the "fulfillment quotations" and the discussion in Hagner, *Matthew 1–13*, liii–lvii) but also in connection with the death of Jesus specifically.

**55** Jesus turns at this point to speak to the mob (τοῖς ὄχλοις, lit. "to the crowds"). ἐν ἐκείνῃ τῇ ὥρᾳ, "in that hour," is formulaic and should be taken in the sense of "at that time" (see BAGD, 896b). Not far beneath the surface of Jesus' statement is a criticism of their cowardice. They could have arrested him when καθ᾽ ἡμέραν ἐν τῷ ἱερῷ ἐκαθεζόμην διδάσκων, "I was sitting daily in the temple teaching" (cf. 21:23; Luke 19:47; 21:37), but they were afraid of the people (cf. 14:5; 21:26, 46). Even in the middle of the night they have come with an oversized force of men armed μετὰ μαχαιρῶν καὶ ξύλων, "with swords and clubs" (cf. v 47), as though they were going to apprehend a violent revolutionary (λῃστήν can also mean "thief"; cf. 21:13; 27:38; but see BAGD, 473a). They are despicable opportunists.

**56** Yet Jesus returns to the outworking of God's superintending will in what is happening. τοῦτο ὅλον, "this whole," refers probably to the apprehension of Jesus, which is but the beginning of the passion. Jesus' path to the cross has been laid out in advance by the divine will. What happens does so not only in fulfillment of the plan devised by the chief priests and elders but, more importantly, in fulfillment of the scriptures (cf. v 54). The expression αἱ γραφαὶ τῶν προφητῶν, "the writings of the prophets," occurs only here in the NT (cf. Rom 16:26). It refers to the second division of the Hebrew Bible, the נְבִיאִים, nĕbîʾîm, "prophets," including especially such books as Isaiah (e.g., esp. chap. 53) and Zechariah (e.g., chaps. 12–13). On πληρωθῶσιν, "be fulfilled," also in v 54, see *Comment* on 1:22. The brief last sentence of the pericope records the abandonment of Jesus by the disciples. If the fulfillment of the scriptures meant that armed resistance was ruled out (v 52) and the only alternative was passive submission, the disciples would have nothing of it (πάντες, "all," of them is noteworthy). This brief note about their flight poignantly recalls the disciples' empty promise that if necessary they would die with Jesus (v 35) and simultaneously fulfills Jesus' prediction that they would fall away and be scattered (v 31; cf. John 16:32).

### Explanation

The betrayal with its "Judas kiss" and the arrest of Jesus are the shocking events with which the passion begins and which culminate in the crucifixion of Jesus. As implausible as it may look from a human perspective and especially from that of the fear-ridden disciples, God is in control of these events, and his will is mysteriously being done while evil men make their move against Jesus. The word concerning the fulfillment of scripture is addressed not only to the disciples but also to the mob. It cannot have meant much to them, and they probably took it as the raving of a deluded man. Even the disciples were unable to put much stock in Jesus' statements that these things were fixed in the divine will and that legions of angels could have been called upon had Jesus chosen the path of resistance. But what looks from a human point of view to be madness or tragedy is in this instance the mysterious working out of God's saving purposes.

It would be a mistake to take the saying that all who take the sword will die by the sword as a proof text for an absolute pacifism. The proverb, to be sure, discourages violence in general as an unproductive path. Peacefulness is surely a clear mark of those who belong to the kingdom of God (cf. 5:9). Violence only begets more violence. It may, however, at times be unavoidable (cf. Luke 22:36) and the lesser of two evils. In the present instance it was clearly out of place. Jesus had incalculable resources available to him if resistance had been an appropriate action. In this instance passive submission alone was consonant with the will of God.

# Jesus before Caiaphas and the Sanhedrin    (26:57–68)

### Bibliography

**Abrahams, I.** "The Tannaitic Tradition and the Trial Narratives." In *Studies in Pharisaism and the Gospels*. Cambridge: Cambridge UP, 1917–24. 2:129–37. **Bammel, E.** "Die Blutgerichtsbarkeit in der römischen Provinz Judäa vor dem ersten jüdischen Aufstand." *JJS* 25 (1974) 35–49. ———. "Kaiphas und der Prozess Jesu." *Neue Presse* (Coburg) (March 22, 1951). ———, ed. *The Trial of Jesus*. FS C. F. D. Moule. SBT 2.13. London: SCM, 1970. **Bartsch, H.-W.** "Wer verurteilte Jesu zum Tode?" *NovT* 7 (1964–65) 210–16. **Ben-Chorin, S.** "Wer hat Jesus zum Tode verurteilt?" *ZRGG* 37 (1985) 63–67. **Benoit, P.** "Jésus devant le Sanhédrin." *Ang* 20 (1943) 143–65. ———. "Les outrages à Jésus prophète (Mc 14,65 et par)." In *Neotestamentica et Patristica*. FS O. Cullmann, ed. W. C. van Unnik. NovTSup 6. Leiden: Brill, 1962. 92–110. **Betz, O.** "Probleme des Prozesses Jesu." *ANRW* 2.25.1 (1982) 565–647. ———. "The Temple Scroll and the Trial of Jesus." *SWJT* 30 (1988) 5–8. **Blinzler, J.** *Der Prozess Jesu*. Regensburg: Pustet, 1960. ———. "Das Synedrium von Jerusalem und die Strafprozessordnung der Mischna." *ZNW* 52 (1961) 54–65. ———. *The Trial of Jesus*.

2nd ed. Tr. J. & F. McHugh. Westminster, MD: Newman, 1959. ———. "The Trial of Jesus in the Light of History." *Judaism* 20 (1971) 49–55. **Bowker, J. W.** "The Offence and Trial of Jesus." In *Jesus and the Pharisees.* New York: Cambridge, 1973. 42–52. **Brandon, S. G. F.** "The Trial of Jesus." *Judaism* 20 (1971) 43–48. ———. *The Trial of Jesus of Nazareth.* New York: Stein and Day, 1968. **Broer, I.** "Der Prozess gegen Jesus nach Matthäus." In *Der Prozess gegen Jesus,* ed. K. Kertelge. QD 112. Freiburg: Herder, 1988. 84–110. **Büchsel, F.** "Die Blutgerichtsbarkeit des Synedrions." *ZNW* 30 (1931) 202–10. ———. "Noch einmal: Zur Blutgerichtsbarkeit des Synedrions." *ZNW* 33 (1934) 84–87. **Burkill, T. A.** "The Competence of the Sanhedrin." *VC* 10 (1956) 80–96. ———. "The Trial of Jesus." *VC* 12 (1958) 1–18. **Burnett, F. W.** "Characterization in Matthew: Reader Construction of the Disciple Peter." *McKendree Pastoral Review* (Lebanon, IL) 4 (1987) 13–43. **Catchpole, D. R.** "The Answer of Jesus to Caiaphas (Matt. xxvi. 64)." *NTS* 17 (1970–71) 213–26. ———. "The Problem of the Historicity of the Sanhedrin Trial." In *The Trial of Jesus.* FS C. F. D. Moule, ed. E. Bammel. SBT 2.13. London: SCM, 1970. 47–65. ———. *The Trial of Jesus: A Study in the Gospels and Jewish Historiography from 1770 to the Present Day.* SPB 18. Leiden: Brill, 1972. ———. "'You Have Heard His Blasphemy.'" *TynB* 16 (1965) 10–18. **Cohen, D.,** and **Paulus, C.** "Einige Bemerkungen zum Prozess Jesu bei den Synoptikern." *ZSSR* 102 (1985) 437–45. **Cohn, H.** "Reflections on the Trial of Jesus." *Judaism* 20 (1971) 10–23. ———. *The Trial and Death of Jesus.* New York: Harper and Row, 1971. **Danby, H.** "The Bearing of the Rabbinical Criminal Code on the Jewish Trial Narratives in the Gospels." *JTS* 21 (1919–20) 51–76. **Daube, D.** *The New Testament and Rabbinic Judaism.* London: Athlone, 1956. 23–26 (reprinted, Peabody, MA: Hendrickson). **Davies, A. T.** "The Jews and the Death of Jesus: Theological Reflections." *Int* 23 (1969) 207–17. **Dibelius, M.** "Das historische Problem der Leidensgeschichte." *ZNW* 30 (1931) 193–201. **Dodd, C. H.** "The Historical Problem of the Death of Jesus." In *More New Testament Studies.* Grand Rapids: Eerdmans, 1968. 84–101. **Dupont, J.** "'Assis à la droite de Dieu': L'interpretation du Ps. 110,1 dans le Nouveau Testament." In *Resurrexit: Acts du Symposium sur International la Résurrection de Jésus,* ed. E. Dhanis. Rome: Libreria Editrice Vaticana, 1974. 423–36. **Ebeling, H. J.** "Zur Frage nach der Kompetenz des Synhedrion." *ZNW* 35 (1936) 290–95. **Feuillet, A.** "Le triomphe du Fils de l'homme d'après la déclaration de Christ aux Sanhédrites (Mc. xiv, 62; Mt xxvi, 64; Lc, xxii, 69)." In *La venue du Messie,* ed. É. Massaux et al. RechBib 6. Bruges: Desclée de Brouwer, 1962. 149–71. **Flusser, D.** "At the Right Hand of Power." *Immanuel* 14 (1982) 42–46. ———. "Who Is It That Struck You?" *Immanuel* 20 (1986) 27–32. **France, R. T.** "Jésus devant Caïphe." *Hokhma* 15 (1980) 20–35. **Fricke, W.** *Standrechtlich gekreuzigt: Person und Prozess des Jesus aus Galiläa.* Frankfurt am Main: Mai, 1986. **Gerhardsson, B.** "Confession and Denial before Men: Observations on Matt. 26:57–27:2." *JSNT* 13 (1981) 46–66. ———. "Jésus livré et abandonné d'après la passion selon Saint Matthieu." *RB* 76 (1969) 206–27. **Gnilka, J.** "Der Prozess Jesu nach den Berichten des Markus und Matthäus mit einer Rekonstruktion des historischen Verlaufs." In *Der Prozess gegen Jesus,* ed. K. Kertelge. QD 112. Freiburg: Herder, 1988. 11–40. **Goldberg, A.** "Sitzend zur Rechten der Kraft." *BZ* 8 (1964) 284–93. **Gourgues, M.** "Marc 14:62 et Parallèles (Mt 26:64; Lc 22:69)." In *A la droite de Dieu: Résurrection de Jésus et actualisation du Psaume 110:1 dans le Nouveau Testament.* Paris: J. Gabalda, 1978. 143–61. **Grant, R. M.** "The Trial of Jesus in the Light of History." *Judaism* 20 (1971) 37–42. **Grappe, C.** "Mt 16,17–19 et le récit de la Passion." *RHPR* 72 (1992) 33–40. **Haufe, G.** "Der Prozess Jesu im Lichte der gegenwärtigen Forschung." *Die Zeichen der Zeit* 22 (1968) 93–101. **Hay, D. M.** *Glory at the Right Hand: Psalm 110 in Early Christianity.* SBLMS 18. Missoula, MT: Scholars, 1973. **Hill, D.** "Jesus before the Sanhedrin—On What Charge?" *IBS* 7 (1985) 174–86. **Holzmeister, U.** "Zur Frage der Blutgerichtsbarkeit des Synedriums." *Bib* 19 (1938) 43–59. **Horbury, W.** "The Trial of Jesus in Jewish Tradition." In *The Trial of Jesus.* FS C. F. D. Moule, ed. E. Bammel. SBT 2.13. London: SCM, 1970. 103–21. **Imbert, J.** "Le procès de Jésus." *Revue de l'Institut Catholique de Paris* 19 (1986) 53–66. **Jaubert, A.** "Les séances du sanhédrin et les récits de la Passion." *RHR* 166 (1964) 143–

169; 167 (1965) 1–33. **Jeremias, J.** "Zur Geschichtlichkeit des Verhörs Jesu vor dem Hohen Rat." *ZNW* 43 (1950–51) 145–50. **Jonge, M. de.** "The Use of HO CHRISTOS in the Passion Narratives." In *Jésus aux origines de la christologie,* ed. J. Dupont et al. BETL 40. Gembloux: Duculot, 1975. 169–92. **Juel, D.** *Messiah and Temple: The Trial of Jesus in the Gospel of Mark.* SBLDS 31. Missoula, MT: Scholars, 1977. **Kertelge, K.,** ed. *Der Prozess gegen Jesus: Historische Rückfrage und theologische Deutung.* QD 112. Freiburg: Herder, 1988. **Kilpatrick, G. D.** *The Trial of Jesus.* London: Oxford UP, 1953. **Koch, W.** *Zum Prozess Jesu: Mit Beiträgen von J. Blinzler, G. Klein, P. Winter.* Weiden Kr. Cologne: Der Löwe, 1967. **Kolping, A.** "'Standrechtlich gekreuzigt': Neuere Überlegungen zum Prozess Jesu." *TRev* 83 (1987) 265–76. **Lamarche, P.** "Le 'blasphème' de Jésus devant le sanhédrin." *RSR* 50 (1962) 74– 85. ———. "La déclaration de Jésus devant le sanhédrin." In *Christ vivant: Essai sur la christologie du Nouveau Testament.* LD 43. Paris: Cerf, 1966. 147–63. **Lapide, P.** *Wer war Schuld an Jesu Tod?* Gütersloh: Mohn, 1987. **Légasse, S.** "Jésus devant le Sanhédrin." *RTL* 5 (1974) 170–97. ———. *Le procès de Jésus: L'histoire.* LD 156. Paris: Cerf, 1994. **Lindeskog, G.** "Der Prozess Jesu im jüdisch-christlichen Religionsgespräch." In *Abraham unser Vater: Juden und Christen in Gespräch über die Bibel.* FS O. Michel, ed. O. Betz et al. Leiden: Brill, 1963. 325– 36. **Linton, O.** "The Trial of Jesus and the Interpretation of Psalm cx." *NTS* 7 (1960–61) 258–62. **Lövestam, E.** "Die Frage des Hohenpriesters (Mark 14,61, par. Matt. 26,63)." *SEÅ* 26 (1961) 93–107. **Lohse, E.** "Der Prozess Jesu Christi." In *Ecclesia und Res Publica.* FS K. L. Schmidt, ed. G. Kretschmar and B. Lohse. Göttingen: Vandenhoeck & Ruprecht, 1961. 24– 39. **Marcus, J.** "Mark 14:61: 'Are You the Messiah-Son-of-God?'" *NovT* 31 (1989) 125–41. **Matera, F. J.** "The Trial of Jesus: Problems and Proposals." *Int* 45 (1991) 5–16. **McRuer, J. C.** *The Trial of Jesus.* Toronto: Clark, Irwin, 1964. **Moule, C. F. D.** "The Gravamen against Jesus." In *Jesus, the Gospels, and the Church.* FS W. R. Farmer, ed. E. P. Sanders. Macon, GA: Mercer UP, 1987. 177–95. **Neirynck, F.** "Τίς ἐστιν ὁ παίσας σε: Mt 26,68/Lk 22,64 (diff. Mk 14,65)." *ETL* 63 (1987) 5–47. **O'Meara, T. F.** "The Trial of Jesus in an Age of Trials." *TToday* 28 (1972) 451–65. **O'Neill, J. C.** "The Charge of Blasphemy at Jesus' Trial before the Sanhedrin." In *The Trial of Jesus.* FS C. F. D. Moule, ed. E. Bammel. SBT 2.13. London: SCM, 1970. 72–77. **Paulus, C.** "Einige Bemerkungen zum Prozess Jesu bei den Synoptikern." *Zeitschrift der Savigny-Stiftung für Rechtsgeschichte* 102 (1985) 437–45. **Pawlikowski, J. T.** "The Trial and Death of Jesus: Reflections in Light of a New Understanding of Judaism." *Chicago Studies* 25 (1986) 79–94. **Pesch, R.** *Der Prozess Jesu geht weiter.* Freiburg: Herder, 1988. **Powell, M. A.** "The Plot to Kill Jesus from Three Different Perspectives: Point of View in Matthew." *Society of Biblical Literature Seminar Papers.* Atlanta: Scholars, 1990. 603–13. **Ramsay, W. M.** "The Denials of Peter." *ExpTim* 27 (1915–16) 360– 63; 28 (1916–17) 276–81. **Reichrath, H.** "Der Prozess Jesu." *Judaica* 20 (1964) 129–55. **Ritt, H.** "Wer war Schuld am Jesu Tod? Zeitgeschichte, Recht und theologische Deutung." *BZ* 31 (1987) 165–75. **Rivkin, E.** *What Crucified Jesus? The Political Execution of a Charismatic.* Nashville: Abingdon, 1984. **Rosenblatt, S.** "The Crucifixion of Jesus from the Standpoint of the Pharisaic Law." *JBL* 75 (1956) 315–21. **Sandmel, S.** "The Trial of Jesus: Reservations." *Judaism* 20 (1971) 69–74. **Schinzer, R.** "Die Bedeutung des Prozesses Jesu." *Neue Zeitschrift für systematische Theologie und Religionsphilosophie* 25 (1983) 138–54. **Schmidt, K. L.** "Der Todesprozess des Messias Jesus." *Judaica* 1 (1945) 1–40. **Schneider, G.** "Gab es eine vorsynoptische Szene 'Jesus vor dem Synedrium'?" *NovT* 12 (1970) 22–39. ———. "Jesus vor dem Synedrium." *BibLeb* 11 (1970) 1–15. **Schreiber, J.** "Das Schweigen Jesu." In *Theologie und Unterricht,* ed. K. Wegenast. Gütersloh: Mohn, 1969. 79–87. **Schubert, K.** "Die Juden und die Römer." *BLit* 36 (1962–63) 235–42. ———. "Das Verhör Jesu vor dem Hohen Rat." In *Bibel und zeitgemässer Glaube II,* ed. J. Sint. Klosterneuburg: Buch- und Kunstverlag, 1967. 97–130. **Schumann, H.** "Bemerkungen zum Prozess Jesu vor dem Synedrium." *Zeitschrift der Savigny-Stiftung für Rechtsgeschichte* 82 (1965) 315–20. **Scott, R. B. Y.** "Behold, He Cometh with Clouds." *NTS* 5 (1958–59) 127–32. **Sherwin-White, A. N.** "The Trial of Christ." In *History and Chronology in the New Testament.* Theological Collections 6. London:

SPCK, 1965. 97–116. **Sloyan, G. S.** "The History of the Tradition of the Trial in Matthew." In *Jesus on Trial.* Philadelphia: Fortress, 1973. 74–88. ———. "Recent Literature on the Trial Narratives of the Four Gospels." In *Critical History and Biblical Faith: New Testament Perspectives,* ed. T. J. Ryan. Villanova: College Theology Society, 1979. 136–76. **Sobosan, J. G.** "The Trial of Jesus." *JES* 10 (1973) 70–91. **Stewart, R. A.** "Judicial Procedure in New Testament Times." *EvQ* 47 (1975) 94–109. **Stonehouse, N. B.** "Who Crucified Jesus?" In *Paul before the Areopagus and Other New Testament Studies.* Grand Rapids: Eerdmans, 1957. 41–69. **Strobel, A.** *Die Stunde der Wahrheit: Untersuchungen zum Strafverfahren gegen Jesus.* WUNT 21. Tübingen: Mohr, 1980. **Theissen, G.** "Jesus' Temple Prophecy: Prophecy in the Tension between Town and Country." In *Social Reality and the Early Christians.* Tr. M. Kohl. Minneapolis: Fortress, 1992. 94–114. **Trilling, W.** "Der 'Prozess Jesu.'" In *Fragen zur Geschichtlichkeit Jesu.* Düsseldorf: Patmos, 1966. 130–41. **Unnik, W. C. van.** "Jesu Verhöhnung vor dem Synedrium." *ZNW* 29 (1930) 310–11 (reprinted in *Sparsa Collecta.* NovTSup 29. Leiden: Brill, 1980. 1:3–5). **Wilson, W. R.** *The Execution of Jesus: A Juridical and Historical Investigation.* New York: Scribners, 1970. **Winter, P.** *On the Trial of Jesus.* Berlin: de Gruyter, 1961. ———. "The Trial of Jesus and the Competence of the Sanhedrin." *NTS* 10 (1963–64) 494–99. **Wood, H. G.** "A Mythical Incident in the Trial of Jesus." *ExpTim* 28 (1916–17) 459–60. **Yamauchi, E. M.** "Historical Notes on the Trial and Crucifixion of Jesus Christ." *ChrTod* 15 (1970–71) 634–39. **Zeitlin, S.** "The Political and the Religious Synedrion." *JQR* 36 (1945) 109–40. ———. "Synedrion in Greek Literature, the Gospels and the Institution of the Sanhedrin." *JQR* 37 (1946) 189–98. ———. *Who Crucified Jesus?* New York: Harper and Row, 1942.

### Translation

[57]*And those who took Jesus into custody led him away to Caiaphas the high priest, where the scribes and elders had gathered together.* [58]*And Peter followed him from a distance as far as the courtyard of the high priest, and having entered it, he was sitting with the servants to see the outcome.*

[59]*Now the chief priests* [a] *and the whole Sanhedrin were seeking false testimony against Jesus so that they might have an excuse to* [b] *put him to death,* [60]*and they did not find any* [c] *evidence they could use* [d] *among the many false witnesses who came forward. But eventually two* [e] *came forward and* [61]*said: "This man said: 'I am able to destroy the temple of God and after three days to build it again.'"* [f] [62]*And the high priest rose and said to him: "Have you nothing to answer to what these men accuse you of?"* [63]*But Jesus was silent. And the high priest said* [g] *to him: "I adjure you by the living God that you tell us if you are the Messiah, the Son of God."* [h] [64]*Jesus said to him: "You have said the truth.* [i] *I furthermore tell you, in the future* [j] *you will see the Son of Man sitting at the right hand of the Power* [k] *and coming upon the clouds of heaven."* [65]*Then the high priest tore his garments, saying: "He has blasphemed!* [l] *Why do we still need witnesses? Look, you have now heard the* [m] *blasphemy.* [66]*What is your opinion?" And they* [n] *answered and said: "He is guilty and should die."* [o]

[67]*Then they spit in his face and struck him. And they slapped him,* [p] [68]*saying: "Prophesy to us, Messiah, who is it that has hit you?"*

### Notes

[a] Many MSS (A C W f[1] TR sy[p.h]) add καὶ οἱ πρεσβύτεροι, "and the elders" (cf. v 57).

[b] "Have an excuse to" added to translation to complete sense.

[c] Many MSS (A C[2] [D] W f[1],13 TR it sy[s],h) add καί, "and," after οὐχ εὗρον, "did not find," and repeat οὐχ εὗρον after ψευδομαρτύρων, "false witnesses," thereby making an extra, redundant sentence:

"They found none. And though many false witnesses came forward, they found none" (cf. KJV).

ᵈ "Evidence they could use" added to complete sense.

ᵉ Many MSS ([A] C D *f*¹³ TR latt syʰ) add ψευδομάρτυρες, "false witnesses."

ᶠ "It again" added to complete sense. A large number of MSS (א A C D L W TR lat) include the direct object αὐτόν, "it," either before or after οἰκοδομῆσαι, "to build." See *TCGNT*, 65.

ᵍ Many MSS (A C [D] W TR it sy) add ἀποκριθείς, "answered." See *TCGNT*, 65.

ʰ Some MSS (C* N W Δ vgᵐˢˢ syʰ saᵐˢˢ mae bo) add τοῦ ζῶντος, "the living" (cf. the use of the phrase earlier in the verse as well as in 16:16).

ⁱ σὺ εἶπας, lit. "you have said (it)."

ʲ ἀπ' ἄρτι, lit. "from now." See *Comment*.

ᵏ τῆς δυνάμεως, lit. "the Power," is a deliberate circumlocution for God (as, e.g., in "kingdom of heaven"). It could well be translated "God" here (cf. NEB, TEV, NIV), but it is better to retain the original. See *Comment* on vv 65–66.

ˡ א* syᵖ begin the high priest's statement with ἰδέ, "look." Many MSS have the recitative ὅτι (introducing a quotation) before the high priest's statement (A C*ᵛⁱᵈ W *f*¹,¹³ TR).

ᵐ Many MSS (A C W Θ *f*¹,¹³ TR it) add αὐτοῦ, "his."

ⁿ D it syˢ have ἀπεκρίθησαν πάντες καί, "they all answered and."

ᵒ ἔνοχος θανάτου ἐστίν, lit. "he is guilty of death."

ᵖ "Him" added as implied object. A few MSS (D G Φ *f*¹) make the object explicit by adding αὐτόν, "him."

### Form/Structure/Setting

A. The first stage of Jesus' trial is reached in this pericope, the trial before the Jewish authorities. This "trial" is obviously of an exceptional character with necessary departures from usual procedure because of the extraordinary circumstances. But at least a show of justice is made. On the grounds of his self-identification, a high christological point in the Gospel (v 64), Jesus is accused of blasphemy and given the death sentence; finally he is mocked and ridiculed before being handed over to the Romans.

B. Matthew again follows Mark closely for this pericope (Mark 14:53–65; cf. Luke 22:54–71; John 18:13–24). There are no lengthy omissions or additions. Among the omissions, the following are the most substantial: in v 58 Mark's "and he was warming himself at the fire" (Mark 14:54), as an unnecessary detail; in v 67 Mark's "and to blindfold him" (Mark 14:65), though presupposing this in v 68. Other more minor omissions are: in v 57 πάντες οἱ ἀρχιερεῖς, "all the chief priests" (cf. Mark 14:53), the evangelist perhaps being satisfied with the reference to the high priest; and in v 63 Mark's τοῦ εὐλογητοῦ, "the blessed" (cf. Mark 14:61), since it is unnecessary in the high priest's question. Several minor agreements with Luke against Mark (e.g., in vv 58, 63, 68) are most probably the result of the overlapping influence of oral tradition (see Neirynck on vv 67–68). It should also be noted that, for whatever reason, in vv 60–63 (cf. Mark 14:56–61) there are numerous omissions and vv 63–67 (cf. Mark 14:63–65) contain numerous additions.

In vv 60–63 many of the omissions involve obvious abbreviation. The following are noteworthy. In vv 60, 61 (cf. Mark 14:56, 59) Matthew omits the two references to the testimony of the false witnesses being in disagreement (Matthew regards the testimony as correct and valid; note his use of δύο, "two," in v 60). Matthew in fact omits Mark's reference to his accusers as ἐψευδομαρτύρουν κατ' αὐτοῦ, "bearing false witness against him" (v 60; cf. Mark 14:57), and his added ὕστερον, "finally" (v 60), distinguishes the two witnesses from the false witnesses just previously mentioned. In v 61 Matthew omits

Mark's reference to the temple as τοῦτον τὸν χειροποίητον, "this, made with hands," and the one to be built after three days as ἄλλον ἀχειροποίητον, "another, not made with hands" (cf. Mark 14:58), thereby preparing the way for the words about the temple to refer secondarily to the body of Jesus and its resurrection. The omissions in these verses involve various kinds of abbreviation, e.g., in v 63 Mark's καὶ οὐκ ἀπεκρίνατο οὐδέν, "and he answered nothing" (Mark 14:61), which is redundant following the statement that "Jesus was silent." Among additions to Mark the following should be mentioned: in v 57 the subject, οἱ κρατήσαντες, "those arresting him" (Mark 14:53), is provided and the high priest's name, Καϊάφαν, "Caiaphas," is given. At the end of v 58 Matthew adds ἰδεῖν τὸ τέλος, "to see the end," specifying the reason for Peter remaining in the vicinity. In v 59 he notes that the authorities were seeking ψευδομαρτυρίαν, "false testimony," against Jesus (cf. Mark 14:55). In v 61 he adds δύναμαι, "I am able" (cf. Mark 14:58), in the accusation against Jesus (see *Comment*).

Finally, we note the additions in vv 63–67. In v 63 Matthew prefaces the high priest's question with ἐξορκίζω σε κατὰ τοῦ θεοῦ τοῦ ζῶντος ἵνα ἡμῖν εἴπῃς, "I adjure you by the living God that you tell us" (cf. Mark 14:61), adding a certain gravity to the important question that follows. In the same verse Matthew introduces the allusion to Dan 7 with the emphatic πλὴν λέγω ὑμῖν, "but I tell you," as well as the somewhat difficult words ἀπ' ἄρτι, lit. "from now," just at the beginning of the allusion. In v 65 he adds the verb ἐβλασφήμησεν, "he has blasphemed," emphasizing the high priest's assessment, and the words ἴδε νῦν, "look, now," for emphasis (cf. Mark 14:63). In v 67 he adds εἰς τὸ πρόσωπον αὐτοῦ, "into his face," and ἡμῖν, χριστέ, τίς ἐστιν ὁ παίσας σε, "(prophesy) to us, Messiah, who is it that has hit you?" (the last four words are found in Luke 22:64 and constitute a minor agreement against Mark, probably to be explained through the influence of oral tradition; cf. Mark 14:65). Matthew also, as he often does, introduces τότε at the beginning of vv 65, 67, thereby bringing more sense of chronological succession to the narrative. Among the more significant substitutions, the following are to be noted: in v 60 δύο, "two," for Mark's τινες, "some" (Mark 14:57), in keeping with Matthew's interest in "two or three witnesses" (cf. 18:16); in v 63 τοῦ θεοῦ, "of God," for τοῦ εὐλογητοῦ, "the Blessed One," one of the more surprising changes by Matthew, who otherwise prefers circumlocution in referring to God; in v 64 the indirect admission σὺ εἶπας, "you have said," for Mark's bolder ἐγώ εἰμι, "I am," again perhaps surprising given Matthew's Christology (see *Comment*). In v 65 Matthew substitutes the more comprehensive and less specific τὰ ἱμάτια, "the garments," for τοὺς χιτῶνας, lit. "tunics" (Mark 14:63). In v 66 he substitutes δοκεῖ, "does it seem," for φαίνεται, "does it appear" (Mark 14:64). And last, in v 67 he has οἱ δὲ ἐράπισαν, "and they slapped (him)," avoiding Mark's introduction of a new subject in οἱ ὑπηρέται ῥαπίσμασιν αὐτὸν ἔλαβον, "the servants took him with slaps" (Mark 14:65). Despite the many changes noted (for a variety of reasons), in general Matthew still follows Mark quite closely.

C. The genre of historical narrative continues, with a focus on the evidence given against Jesus and the subsequent exchanges. Outline: (1) Jesus' being taken to the high priest (and being followed by Peter) (vv 57–58); (2) the authorities' seeking of evidence against Jesus (vv 59–61), further divided into (a) failure (v 60a) and (b) the evidence of two witnesses (vv 60b–61); (3) the high priest's key question (vv 62–63); (4) Jesus' answer (v 64); (5) the charge of blasphemy (v 65); (6) preliminary death sentence (v 66); and (7) the mocking of Jesus (vv 67–68). There are few noteworthy structural features. Parallel infinitives may be observed in the charge against Jesus in v 61, and also striking are the three parallel verbs of v 67. Of central significance in the passage is the citation of Dan 7:13 in v 64.

D. It has been observed by many scholars that the trial of Jesus here portrayed fails at many points to correspond to the procedures laid down in the Mishna,

*Sanh.* 4–7. (For full discussion of the problem, see R. E. Brown, *Death of the Messiah,* 328–97.) The trial is full of anomalies: held at night, on the eve of a holy day, minimal attendance of members of the council, irregular location, without proper conditions pertaining to a capital case, no witnesses for the accused, and so forth. Although all this cannot be denied, it is a mistake to conclude that the present account is unhistorical (for a defense of its historicity, see Sherwin-White). A key question, one that is virtually impossible to answer, is the extent to which the legal procedures laid down in the Mishna at the beginning of the third century were in effect at the time of Jesus (see Danby; to the contrary, Abrahams, who argues that the Mishna preserves authentic traditions regarding the first century). Apart from this difficult question, many commentators simply forget that this was a quite extraordinary event in which, from the perspective of the Jewish authorities, it was expedient, if not necessary, to bend the rules. Two key factors must be kept in mind. First, just as Judas' initial approach was unexpected, so the opportunity to apprehend Jesus in the privacy of the night presented itself unexpectedly, and they had to act quickly if they were to act at all. Second, the Jewish authorities were extremely eager to be rid of Jesus *immediately*—before the climax of the holy feast of Passover—and thus no doubt they found this opportunity impossible to resist. It is not difficult, therefore, to imagine a night meeting of the authorities, probably without the full membership of the council (despite Matthew's τὸ συνέδριον ὅλον, "the whole Sanhedrin" [v 59]; cf. his omission of Mark's πάντες οἱ ἀρχιερεῖς, "all the chief priests," in v 57), and an abbreviated quasi-legal process. Perhaps the present pericope really portrays a preliminary interrogation, prior to turning Jesus over to the Romans, rather than a trial (R. E. Brown, *Death of the Messiah,* leans toward this conclusion). Although an attempt was made at having a trial of sorts (cf. vv 59–62), by Mishnaic standards the trial was a sham. But under the very special circumstances, it could not have been otherwise. The Gospel of John which, relying on independent tradition, has no account of a formal trial before the Jewish authorities, mentions only what must be taken as an informal, semi-private hearing, first before Annas, the father-in-law of Caiaphas (John 18:13), and then before Caiaphas himself (18:24). Luke has a formal trial before the Sanhedrin as in Matthew—not at night, however, but "when day came" (cf. Matthew 27:1). There is no need to harmonize these discrepancies. The Synoptics agree that there was at least the semblance of a trial before the Jewish authorities; John provides his counterpart in the hearings before Annas and Caiaphas (on Jewish judicial procedure, see Stewart). It was the Romans, however, who would try Jesus and eventually execute him.

## Comment

**57** It is clear from this verse that the mob sent to apprehend Jesus had been sent by the Jewish authorities under the direction of the high priest. It is to his house that they return with their prisoner. On Caiaphas, see *Comment* on v 3. οἱ γραμματεῖς, "the scribes," are no doubt mentioned here (and not in v 3 or v 47) because of the importance Torah scholars would have in legal matters such as might emerge in a "trial" (see *Form/Structure/Setting* §D). On πρεσβύτεροι, "elders," see *Comment* on 16:21.

**58**    Peter, who had fled the scene of Jesus' apprehension along with the other disciples (cf. v 56), apparently did not go far but subsequently followed the mob ἀπὸ μακρόθεν, "from a distance," to the palace of the high priest. He went ἕως τῆς αὐλῆς, "as far as the courtyard," which in v 3 refers to the palace itself but here to the courtyard of the palace (cf. v 69; see too John's explanation of how Peter's entry into the courtyard was made possible [John 18:15–16]), and sat there with τῶν ὑπηρετῶν, "the servants" (perhaps "guards"; cf. John 7:32, 45–46; 18:3), waiting ἰδεῖν τὸ τέλος, "to see the outcome." This parenthetical sentence has the purpose of preparing the reader for the account of Peter's denial of Jesus in vv 69–75.

**59**    The Jewish authorities had perhaps begun to gather witnesses and formulate a case against Jesus immediately after Judas' offer to betray Jesus into their hands. However, they were not prepared for the suddenness with which the "trial" came upon them, and so they were still interviewing witnesses and trying to build their case against him. Their goal was not justice but the end of Jesus. Thus they were seeking ψευδομαρτυρίαν, "false testimony" (elsewhere in Matthew only in 15:19; cf. 19:18; Ps 27:12), a charge to use against Jesus ὅπως αὐτὸν θανατώσωσιν, "so that they might put him to death" (as had been the idea much earlier; cf. 12:14; 26:4).

οἱ ἀρχιερεῖς, "the chief priests," play a very important role in the passion narrative (cf. vv 4, 14, 47). τὸ συνέδριον ὅλον, "the whole Sanhedrin," need not be taken literally but as referring to the whole of the members then present, unless it anticipates the apparently fuller meeting of the Sanhedrin in the morning (as in 27:1, where the parallel [Mk 15:1] refers to "the whole Sanhedrin"; cf. Luke 22:66). Gnilka suggests the possibility of a subcommittee charged with such matters.

**60–61**    They were at first frustrated in their attempt to find something they could use from among "the many false witnesses who came forward" (πολλῶν προσελθόντων ψευδομαρτύρων). Then two men were found (δύο, "two"; for the importance of two witnesses, see 18:16; cf. John 8:17; Deut 17:6). Matthew avoids calling them "false witnesses," apparently regarding their evidence as true and not wanting to deny that Jesus had said what is reported by the witnesses. The logion, "I am able to destroy [καταλῦσαι] the temple of God [τὸν ναὸν τοῦ θεοῦ] and after three days to build it [οἰκοδομῆσαι]," is not found as an utterance of Jesus in Matthew or the other Synoptics (a form of it is found in John 2:19; cf. Mark 14:58; Acts 6:14). It is, however, on the lips of passersby in 27:40, and thus Matthew assumes its authenticity. Matthew has referred to the destruction of the temple using the same verb, καταλύειν, "destroy," in 24:2, but there it is not Jesus who does the destroying (for the unfounded charge that Jesus would destroy the temple, see Acts 6:14). Perhaps Matthew's δύναμαι, "I am able," is regarded as more truthful than Mark's "I will destroy" (Mark 14:58). Matthew also alludes to the resurrection of Jesus after three days (cf. in the mouth of the opponents, 27:63; cf. 12:40 and the Western text of Mark 13:2, which however probably depends on Mark 14:58) or, more regularly, on the third day (16:21; 17:23; 20:19). Nowhere, however, is there a reference to Jesus building the temple again in three days (for apocalyptic expectation of a rebuilding of the temple, see 1 Enoch 90.29; 91.13; Tob 14:4; Gnilka also cites the Targum of Isa 53:5, which refers to the Messiah building a new temple). The accusation thus mixes together two quite separate matters, the destruction of the temple and the resurrection of Jesus.

The explanation for this may well be found in the combination of the two motifs seen in the Gospel of John (2:19–21) where, however, the temple is explicitly interpreted as referring to τοῦ ναοῦ τοῦ σώματος αὐτοῦ, "the temple of his body," and where there is also evidence that the metaphorical reference confused the Jews. The only difference with the present logion is that there is no reference to Jesus as the one who destroys the body. No doubt the complexity of the tradition is caused by this double meaning of "temple" and Jesus' prediction of the destruction of the temple and of his own death and resurrection after three days.

**62–63a** Matthew says nothing about how grievous this charge may have been regarded, but the fact that this testimony was allowed after much else had been refused suggests that the prosecutors believed it would be useful. To speak of destroying the temple or even of the temple being destroyed would definitely have been regarded as an extremely serious, indeed a treasonous, offense, one deserving of capital punishment (cf. Acts 6:13–14). Matthew's δύναμαι, "I am able" (v 61), however, has the effect of shifting attention to the authority or power claimed in such a statement. And it was in the personal claims of Jesus that the Jewish authorities thought their best hope of doing away with Jesus lay (thus the high priest's question of v 63b). The high priest asks Jesus whether he has any response to the accusations made against him, no doubt hoping he would expose himself to further peril by what he said. Jesus, however, "kept silent" (ἐσιώπα). In his trial before the Jewish authorities, as before Pilate (27:14), Jesus makes no attempt to defend himself. The silence of Jesus is an important motif in the passion narrative and perhaps alludes retrospectively to Isa 53:7 (for another strand of the motif of silence, see Pss 38:14; 39:9; cf. Gerhardsson, *RB* 76 [1969] 206–27). It was probably understood by Caiaphas as consent to the truthfulness of the charge brought against him. Jesus submits to the faulty reasoning of his accusers and opponents in order to accomplish the will of God and so to fulfill the scriptures (cf. vv 54, 56). His silence was a sovereign silence.

**63b–64** The high priest's next question is made even weightier in Matthew than it is in Mark by the addition of the solemn words ἐξορκίζω σε κατὰ τοῦ θεοῦ τοῦ ζῶντος, "I adjure you by the living God." He charges Jesus under an oath to God (ἐξορκίζω, "I adjure," is used only here in the NT; ὁρκίζω, "I adjure," is found in Mark 5:7) to answer his question truthfully. The modifier τοῦ ζῶντος, "the living," in reference to God is found also in 16:16 (see *Comment*). The question is whether Jesus considers himself to be ὁ χριστὸς ὁ υἱὸς τοῦ θεοῦ, "the Messiah, the Son of God." There is no need to suppose by this language that the high priest meant exactly what the early church meant by this phrase in its Christology. That the Messiah would be the Son of God, even uniquely so (though of course metaphysically distinct from God), was quite probably the high priest's own understanding (for the view of the Son of God in Palestinian Judaism, see Hengel, *Son of God*, esp. 41–56). For "Son of God," see 14:33 (and *Comment* there); 16:16 (Messiah as Son of God); 27:40, 43, 54 (cf. John 11:27; 20:31). Jesus offers an answer to the direct question of the high priest, and it is an answer of the greatest significance. Nowhere does Jesus reveal himself more than here. In Matthew's account of Jesus' response, given in the historical present tense for vividness, the words σὺ εἶπας, "you have said," rather than being strictly evasive (or negative), amount to an affirmative answer (see esp. Catchpole; cf. v 25; 27:11 [to Pilate]; 27:43), but in a much less direct and emphatic way than Mark's ἐγώ εἰμι, "I am"

(Mark 14:62). In this alteration of Mark, Matthew probably intends to allow for qualification and to preserve the consistency of the indirectness of Jesus' messianic claims, especially vis-à-vis his opponents, throughout his narrative. Matthew, whose Christology is generally more explicit than Mark's, would not in principle have objected to Mark's ἐγώ εἰμι (cf. 14:27 and *Comment* there). Jesus' affirmation of being the Messiah, the Son of God (the background for the two combined titles may have been Ps 2; see Lövestam), may not yet in itself have been sufficient grounds for the high priest to regard him as blaspheming. But when Jesus adds to his answer the quoted material from Dan 7:13 and the allusion to Ps 110:2, identifying himself as *that* triumphant figure—and thus more than the Messiah as a merely human agent—as the one who is "given dominion and glory and kingship" whom all will serve and whose kingdom will see no end (Dan 7:13–14), the one who sits at the right hand of God (Ps 110:1), the high priest reacts to what he regards as horrifying blasphemy (cf. v 65). In the face of such a startling claim (Moule, 194), his reaction is understandable. πλήν, rather than being adversative in force, involves clarification of the meaning of Messiah (i.e., not one with present political aspirations), hence "furthermore" (see Catchpole, *NTS* 17 [1970–71] 213–26). λέγω ὑμῖν, "I tell you," though not the full formula (it lacks ἀμήν, "truly"; see *Comment* on 5:18), functions to give the following statement the character of a pronouncement.

Matthew's ἀπ᾽ ἄρτι is difficult. If taken in its ordinary sense, i.e., "from now on," it is not easy to understand how it can be applied to what they (Jesus addresses those present: ὑμῖν, "you," plural) "will see."

> To begin with, we are probably meant to take the expression in a general sense, meaning in the *near* future rather than from that actual moment (cf. the use of the phrase in 23:39 where they did continue to see Jesus for a while). It can hardly be stretched, however, to mean the distant future (as the NIV seems to take it). It is thus very possible to take it as referring to the events attending the crucifixion and the resurrection and its aftermath, that is, in and through the amazing events that will soon follow in their experience (R. E. Brown: "in the storyline the Sanhedrists could have seen dramatic signs of Jesus' vindication by God" [*Death of the Messiah*, 504]; a kind of "mental seeing of the Son of Man sitting on God's right hand" [Gundry, 545]). The Jews will see, presumably at the parousia and/or the final judgment (cf. Rev 1:7), the Son of Man sitting at God's right hand; this, however, is something that will begin with the imminent resurrection of Jesus (cf. 28:18). A further possibility, however, is that the phrase is to be taken as referring not to the imminent seeing but to the imminent *sitting* of the Son of Man at God's right hand, which will take place in the immediate future in the resurrection of Jesus (thus Zahn, who criticizes an inept translation). This is the sense of Luke's parallel ἀπὸ τοῦ νῦν, "from the present," in the easier statement of Luke 22:69: "From the present the Son of Man will be sitting at the right hand of the power of God"). As a third possibility, but less probably, ἀπ᾽ ἄρτι could be taken as a single word with the quite rare meaning "certainly" (cf. BAGD, 81a; BDF §12[3]); thus: "Assuredly you will see the Son of Man. . . ." This avoids the problem of ἀπ᾽ ἄρτι being placed before ὄψεσθε, "you will see," but if this is what the evangelist meant, he could have chosen much more obvious words or phrases.

Two key passages are combined here. The reference to "the Son of Man . . . coming on the clouds of heaven" is drawn almost verbatim from Dan 7:13 (the same material has been quoted in 24:30 and is also alluded to in 11:3; 16:27;

25:31; cf. 23:39; on this phrase, see Scott). The ready reference to the Son of Man (i.e., Jesus) in speaking about the Son of God shows simply that both titles could be used of the Messiah. The reference to "sitting at the right hand of the Power" is an allusion to Ps 110:1, cited earlier in 22:44 (cf. Mark 16:19; Acts 7:55–56.; *1 Enoch* 69:27 [according to B and C]), where it is also used to elucidate the meaning of "Messiah," "the Son of David." See *Comment* on 22:44. "The Power" (from Heb. גְּבוּרָה, *gĕbûrāh;* see Goldberg) is, of course, a way to refer to God without using the word "God" (the Hebrew text of Ps 110:1 refers to the right hand of Yahweh [LXX: κύριος, "LORD"]). This circumlocution becomes a very important consideration in the question of the culpability of Jesus in his reply to the high priest (cf. vv 65–66). Jesus in self-confession thus not only admits that he is the Messiah but goes on to elucidate his understanding of the Messiah in terms of the one like the Son of Man of Dan 7:13 and the Lord addressed in Ps 110:1 (cf. 22:41–46), this despite everything about the present moment that seems incompatible with such a statement. If not precisely claiming deity (cf. John 5:18; 10:33), Jesus was at least ranking himself with God in a unique status (cf. Lamarche, "La déclaration"). Thus Powell's analysis proves correct when he writes that "Matthew's passion narrative must be read and interpreted in light of Matthew's christology and, particularly, in light of Matthew's concept of Jesus as the Son of God" (612).

**65–66** The high priest finds Jesus' words intolerable. They seem not only so obviously untruthful but also so outrageously self-aggrandizing—indeed, sacrilegious—that he reacts in horror and tears his garments. This symbolic action is mentioned in the OT in connection with mourning (cf. Lev 10:6; 21:10; 2 Kgs 19:1), in the Mishna in connection with the pronouncing of the divine name (*m. Sanh.* 7:5), and in Acts 14:14 in connection with Paul and Barnabas being accorded divine honors.

The high priest's statement ἐβλασφήμησεν, "he has blasphemed," and the following statement, "Look, now you have heard the blasphemy [τὴν βλασφημίαν]" have raised the question whether Jesus' response and statement would *technically* have constituted blasphemy. According to the Mishna, "'The blasphemer' is not culpable unless he pronounces the Name itself" (*Sanh.* 7:5; cf. in the OT Lev 24:10–23). In Matthew's narrative (following Mark), however, Jesus avoids using even the word "God" (let alone pronouncing the divine name [i.e., Yahweh]), instead making use of the circumlocution τῆς δυνάμεως, "the Power" (v 64). This seems to be a deliberate attempt to show that Jesus was *not* guilty of blasphemy, at least technically, and that the cause of the high priest's reaction lay elsewhere, i.e., in the personal claims of Jesus (cf. 9:3 in connection with forgiving sins, which is characterized as blasphemy). In fact, however, blasphemy was used in a wider sense to refer to any insult of God, for example, by an arrogation to oneself of prerogatives that belong to him alone (rightly R. E. Brown, *Death of the Messiah*, 523). In that sense Jesus could well have been understood as being guilty of blasphemy (cf. v 64; see Linton; Lövestam; Dodd, 99). It was not the claim of Jesus to be the Messiah in itself that was considered grounds to do away with him; it was his personal delineation of that messiahship that did so (cf. John 19:7). "If the judges sought for a plea on which to condemn Jesus, his confession of the Messiahship would surely have sufficed, even if, in the most technical sense, it was not blasphemy" (Montefiore, *Synoptic Gospels,* 1:352). From this moment the high priest's case is made (cf. Luke 22:71), and Jesus' fate is sealed.

No further witnesses are necessary; what they might have offered has become redundant. The verdict of those present is ἔνοχος θανάτου ἐστίν, "he deserves to die." This verdict is hardly based on any consideration of the evidence even if the unwarranted charge of blasphemy naturally brought with it the suggestion of the death penalty (Lev 24:16); it simply carries out the predetermined purpose of the Jewish authorities to do away with Jesus (cf. v 4). The verdict of capital punishment taken here was perhaps an informal one, later formalized by the meeting of a larger number of Sanhedrin members at the early morning meeting mentioned in 27:1 (see *Comment*). The Jews themselves did not have the authority to carry out the death sentence (see Jeremias), so Jesus would have to be sent to the Roman authorities.

**67–68** The mistreatment and mocking of Jesus reflect the hateful animosity of the Jewish leaders toward him. Spitting upon and striking a person (cf. the parallel 27:30 for the same deeds from the Romans) involve insult and pain. The early church soon found this treatment of Jesus to be the fulfillment of scripture (e.g., esp. the servant of Isa 50:6; 53:3, 5; cf. too Mic 5:1). The mocking includes the blindfolding of Jesus (assumed but not mentioned by Matthew; cf. Mark 14:65) and the request for him to "prophesy" (προφήτευσον), i.e., tell supernaturally, who was striking him. The address "Messiah" or "Christ," which perhaps alludes to the confession in the trial, is, of course, used mockingly. The Messiah *would* be able to identify his mockers. But not for a minute did they suppose he could be what he claimed. He was for them at that moment a charlatan who deserved no respect.

### Explanation

It is clear that the Jewish authorities were biased against Jesus from the start and that it is hardly meaningful to call this hearing a "trial." They were fixed in their purpose to have Jesus put to death, so they sought no justice here and contrived only the facade of propriety. They needed merely the thinnest case against him, only enough to trigger a self-incriminating (from their perspective) response. They got more than they expected from Jesus: not only his admission that he was the Messiah but the unbelievable statement, his self-confession, that he would sit at God's right hand and that they would eventually see him in his glorious parousia, coming with divine glory. From their point of view, he suffered from a severe case of megalomania. He had gone too far in associating himself with God—which no doubt also accounted for his irresponsible behavior with regard to the law and the Pharisaic tradition. The impudent man and his movement had to be stopped. And thus in their zeal to be rid of Jesus, they unknowingly set in motion events that would forever and unshakably establish that movement. For the death of Jesus— the fate they deemed he deserved—is what fundamentally establishes the church. The one they now mock in their mistaken confidence is the one before whom they will some day stand as their judge. The Jewish people as a whole, of course, bear no responsibility for the death of Jesus. Still, there is no need to rewrite history to exculpate the Jews from their responsibility in the death of Jesus. As Stonehouse rightly notes: "There is a far deeper guarantee in Christianity of the rights of the Jew than any revision of one's estimate of the actual course of the events connected with the death of Jesus could provide" (69). Christians who want to assign responsibility for the death of Jesus should think of their own sin. And when they think of the Jews, they should think of their Lord and the source of their salvation.

# Peter's Denial of Jesus    (26:69–75)

*Bibliography*

**Boomershine, T. E.** "Peter's Denial as Polemic or Confession: The Implications of Media Criticism for Biblical Hermeneutics." *Semeia* 39 (1987) 47–68. **Derrett, J. D. M.** "The Reason for the Cock-Crowings." *NTS* 29 (1983) 142–44. **Ernst, J.** "Noch einmal: Die Verleugnung Jesu durch Petrus (Mk 14,54.66–72)." In *Petrus und Papst,* ed. A. Brandenburg and H. J. Urban. Münster: Aschendorff, 1977. 43–62. **Gardiner, W. D.** "The Denial of St. Peter." *ExpTim* 26 (1914–15) 424–26. **Gerhardsson, B.** "Confession and Denial before Men: Observations on Matt. 26:57–27:2." *JSNT* 13 (1981) 46–66. **Gewalt, D.** "Die Verleugnung des Petrus." *LingBib* 43 (1978) 113–44. **Goguel, M.** "Did Peter Deny His Lord?" *HTR* 25 (1932) 1–27. **Guyot, G. H.** "Peter Denies His Lord." *CBQ* 4 (1942) 111–18. **Klein, G.** "Die Verleugnung des Petrus: Eine traditionsgeschichtliche Untersuchung." *ZTK* 58 (1961) 285–328. **Kosmala, H.** "The Time of the Cock-Crow." *ASTI* 2 (1963) 118–20; 6 (1967–68) 132–34. **Kosnetter, J.** "Zur Geschichtlichkeit der Verleugnung Petri." In *Dienst an der Lehre.* FS F. König. Wiener Beiträge zur Theologie 10. Vienna: Herder, 1965. 127–43. **Lampe, G. W. H.** "St. Peter's Denial." *BJRL* 55 (1972–73) 346–68. **Lattey, C.** "A Note on Cockcrow." *Scr* 6 (1953) 53–55. **LaVerdiere, E. A.** "Peter Broke Down and Began to Cry." *Emmanuel* 92 (1986) 70–73. **Linnemann, E.** "Die Verleugnung des Petrus." *ZTK* 63 (1966) 1–32. **Masson, E.** "Le reniement de Pierre." *RHPR* 37 (1957) 24–35. **Mayo, C. H.** "St. Peter's Token of the Cock Crow." *JTS* 22 (1921) 367–70. **McEleney, N. J.** "Peter's Denials–How Many? To Whom?" *CBQ* 52 (1990) 467–72. **Merkel, H.** "Peter's Curse." In *The Trial of Jesus.* FS C. F. D. Moule, ed. E. Bammel. SBT 2.13. London: SCM, 1970. 66–71. **Murray, G.** "Saint Peter's Denials." *DR* 103 (1985) 296–98. **Pesch, R.** "Die Verleugnung des Petrus: Eine Studie zu Mk 14,54.66–72 (und Mk 14,26–31)." In *Neues Testament und Kirche.* FS R. Schnackenburg, ed. J. Gnilka. Freiburg: Herder, 1974. 42–62. **Ramsay, W. M.** "The Denials of Peter." *ExpTim* 27 (1915–16) 410–13, 471–72, 540–42; 28 (1916–17) 276–81. **Riesenfeld, H.** "The Meaning of the Verb ἀρνεῖσθαι." FS A. Fridrichsen. ConNT 11. Lund: Gleerup, 1947. 207–19. **Rothenaicher, F.** "Zu Mk. 14,70 und Mt. 26,73." *BZ* 23 (1935–36) 192–93. **Schwank, B.** "Petrus verleugnet Jesus." *SeinSend* 29 (1964) 51–65. **Smith, P. V.** "St. Peter's Threefold Denial of Our Lord." *Th* 17 (1928) 341–48. **Taylor, D. B.** "Jesus–of Nazareth?" *ExpTim* 92 (1981) 336–37. **Walter, N.** "Die Verleugnung des Petrus." *Theologische Versuche* 8 (1977) 45–61. **Wenham, J. W.** "How Many Cock-Crowings? The Problem of Harmonistic Text-Variants." *NTS* 25 (1978–79) 523–25. **Zuntz, G.** "A Note on Matthew XXVI. 34 and XXVI. 75." *JTS* 50 (1949) 182–83.

*Translation*

⁶⁹*Now Peter was sitting outside in the courtyard. And one servant girl came up to him and said: "You too were with Jesus the Galilean."*ᵃ ⁷⁰*But he denied it before them*ᵇ *all, saying: "I don't know*ᶜ *what you are talking about."*ᵈ ⁷¹*And another servant girl*ᵉ *saw him when he came out to the entrance and said to those who were there: "This*ᶠ *man*

*was with Jesus the Nazorean.*"[72]*And again he denied with an oath:*[g] *"I do not know the man."*[73]*And after a little while those who had been standing there came and said to Peter: "Truly you too*[h] *are one of them, for*[i] *your speech also betrays you."*[j] [74]*Then he began to curse and to swear: "I do not know the man!" And immediately the cock crowed.*[75]*And Peter remembered the word which Jesus had spoken:*[k] *"Before the cock crows you will deny me three times." And he went out and cried bitterly.*

### Notes

[a] C sy[p] have Ναζωραίου, "Nazorean," perhaps by the influence the parallel in Mark 14:67 (cf. v 71).

[b] "Them" added in translation. Some MSS (A C* W Γ Δ *f*[1]) include αὐτῶν, "them." On the other hand, K has only αὐτῶν, lacking πάντων, "all."

[c] D (Δ) *f*[1] it sy[s] add οὐδὲ ἐπίσταμαι, "nor do I understand," almost certainly from the parallel in Mark 14:68.

[d] τί λέγεις, lit. "what you are saying."

[e] ἄλλη, lit. "another," but since the word is feminine, "servant girl" is understood. D it vg[cl] make it explicit by adding the word παιδίσκη.

[f] Many MSS (A C L W Θ *f*[1,13] TR latt sy[p,h] bo) add καί, "also," perhaps by the influence of the Lukan parallel (Luke 22:59). See *TCGNT*, 65.

[g] D it mae add λέγων, "saying."

[h] D Θ *f*[1] sy[s] sa[mss] omit καὶ σύ, "also you," probably because of the parallel in Mark 14:70.

[i] C* Σ sy[h**] add Γαλιλαῖος εἶ καί, "You are a Galilean and," by the influence of the parallel in Mark 14:70.

[j] δῆλόν σε ποιεῖ, lit. "makes you plain." D it sy[s] have ὁμοιάζει, "is similar (to Jesus')."

[k] Many MSS (A C W Θ *f*[1,13] TR sy sa[ms] mae bo) add αὐτῷ, "to him."

### Form/Structure/Setting

A. In turning to this story about Peter (thereby interrupting the narrative of what befell Jesus), this pericope concludes the motif of the abandonment of Jesus by his disciples and provides the account of the fulfillment of Jesus' specific prediction concerning Peter's threefold denial of Jesus (vv 33–35). The poignancy of Peter's disloyalty to Jesus is deepened by the placement of this narrative between the account of Jesus before Caiaphas and the Jewish authorities and that of his appearance before Pilate. It is perhaps unexcelled in the Synoptics for its dramatic effect. The contrast of Peter's denial with Jesus' own confession (v 64) is deliberate. For the parallels between the passages (e.g., the three stages in each [see §C below]), see Gerhardsson, *JSNT* 13 (1981) 46–66.

B. Matthew follows Mark, as is his custom, but somewhat more freely in the present narrative than usual (Mark 14:66–72; cf. Luke 22:56–62; John 18:15–18, 25–27). The following are the more significant alterations. In v 69 Matthew omits Mark's note (Mark 14:66–67) that the servant girl was "one of the high priest's," the repeated reference to her looking at Peter, and that Peter was θερμαινόμενον, "warming himself." This reflects Matthew's practice of abbreviating by removing details he regards as unnecessary (he had earlier deleted Mark's reference to the fire (v 58; cf. Mark 14:54). In the same verse he replaces Mark's Ναζαρηνοῦ, "Nazarene," with Γαλιλαίου, "Galilean" (but he uses Ναζωραίου in v 71 and avoids Mark's Γαλιλαῖος in v 73). In v 70 he adds that Peter made his denial ἔμπροσθεν πάντων, "before everyone" (cf. Mark 14:68), in order to emphasize Peter's failure. On the other hand, in the same verse Matthew omits Mark's οὔτε ἐπίσταμαι, "nor do I understand," and Mark's σύ, "you" (emphatic subject), in order to abbreviate. In v 71 Matthew further omits καὶ ἀλέκτωρ ἐφώνησεν, "and the cock crowed" (which, however, is textually doubtful), since he has previously reduced the number of cock crowings from two to one in Jesus' foretelling of Peter's denials (v 34; cf. Mark 14:30; cf. Wenham). In the same verse he replaces Mark's προαύλιον, "forecourt" (Mark 14:18), with the more common πυλῶνα, "gate." Also in v 71 he turns Mark's same ἡ παιδίσκη, "servant girl" (cf. πάλιν, "again" [Mark 14:69]), into ἄλλη, "another," servant girl (cf. Luke's ἕτερος, "another," man [Luke 22:58]), this in keeping with his penchant for having two (or three) witnesses (cf. McEleney). Matthew further omits ἰδοῦσα αὐτὸν ἤρξατο πάλιν, "seeing him began again" (Mark 14:69), replaces παρεστῶσιν, "standing," with ἐκεῖ, "there," and omits the recitative ὅτι, "that"—all to abbreviate. He replaces ἐξ αὐτῶν ἐστιν, "is of them," with ἦν μετὰ Ἰησοῦ τοῦ Ναζωραίου, "was with Jesus the Nazorean," perhaps for emphasis upon Peter's denial of Jesus. In v 72 he supplies emphatic words to Mark's simple notice that "again he denied" by adding μετὰ ὅρκου ὅτι οὐκ οἶδα τὸν ἄνθρωπον, "with an oath: I do not know the man" (cf. Mark 14:70). In v 73 Matthew adds καὶ σύ, "also you" (cf. Mark 14:70), for emphasis, and in the same verse he substitutes the explanatory ἡ λαλιά σου δῆλόν σε ποιεῖ, "your speech betrays you," for Mark's Γαλιλαῖος εἶ, "you are a Galilean" (Mark 14:70). In v 74 he inserts his favorite initial τότε, "then," and omits Mark's τοῦτον ὃν λέγετε, "this one of whom you speak" (Mark 14:71), probably for the sake of abbreviation. In the same verse Matthew omits ἐκ δευτέρου, "a second time" (Mark 14:72), and in v 75 he omits δίς, "twice," in keeping with a single crowing of the cock. Finally, also in the same verse, Matthew substitutes ἐξελθὼν ἔξω, "having gone outside," for Mark's difficult ἐπιβαλών, "broke down" (?), and adds the touching adverb πικρῶς, "bitterly."

C. The pericope consists of the three charges and three escalating denials, which provide its basic structure, together with a brief account of Peter's response. It may be outlined as follows: (1) the first charge and denial (vv 69–70); (2) the second charge and denial (vv 71–72); (3) the third charge and denial (vv 73–74a); and (4) the crowing of the cock and Peter's recollection of Jesus' words (vv 74b–75). Although Matthew avoids strict parallelism in his account of the charges and denials, some correspondences are noteworthy. The charges are made by μία παιδίσκη, "one servant girl," and ἄλλη, "another (servant girl)" but in the third instance by οἱ ἑστῶτες, "the bystanders." While the first and third charges are addressed in the second person, καὶ σύ, "you also," the second charge is put in the third person, οὗτος, "this one." The first two charges accuse Peter of being μετὰ Ἰησοῦ, "with Jesus" (in the first modified by "the Galilean," in the second by "the Nazorean"), while the third charge accuses Peter of being ἐξ αὐτῶν, lit. "of them," and is intensified by the addition of ἀληθῶς, "truly." To the third charge, unlike the first two, is added the grounds of the charge. Whereas the verb ἠρνήσατο, "he denied," is used in the first two denials, in the second μετὰ ὅρκου, "with an oath," is added, and in the third the climactic ἤρξατο καταθεματίζειν καὶ ὀμνύειν, "he began to curse and to swear," is used. Matthew, who supplies words of Peter in each denial, uses οὐκ οἶδα, "I do not know," in all three instances but in the first has τί λέγεις, "what you are saying," as the object and in the second and third the identical and more specific τὸν ἄνθρωπον, "the man," thereby making the second and third denials identical (vv 72, 74). Thus the pericope is artistically constructed with an excellent sense of progression and dramatic climax, even to the last word, πικρῶς, "bitterly."

### Comment

**69–70** V 69a connects with and continues the narrative begun in v 58, where Peter was left sitting in the courtyard. The servant girls of vv 69, 71 had perhaps been among the crowds who had seen Jesus teaching and recognized Peter as having been with him (καὶ σύ, "you too," is emphatic). Jesus is referred to as τοῦ Γαλιλαίου, "the Galilean," only here in the NT, except for Luke 23:6 (cf. Matt 21:11). The charge involved the implicit threat that Peter too might be apprehended and suffer the same fate as that of Jesus (which ironically was what Peter had said he was prepared to do; cf. v 35). Peter, in the grip of fear (*pace* Gardiner, who argues for stubborn self-will), ἔμπροσθεν πάντων, "before all," i.e., all who overheard the woman's comment, denies that what she says is true: "I don't know what you are talking about." Peter thus denies even knowing about the matter, let alone being personally associated with Jesus. And ironically he makes his denials at the same time that Jesus boldly confesses his identity in response to the high priest's question. Here (and in v 72) the word ἀρνεῖσθαι, "deny," recalls both Jesus' prediction (v 34) and the warning of 10:33 (on the meaning of the word, see Riesenfeld). It anticipates the problem of persecution and apostasy in the later church (see Lampe).

**71–72** Peter, apparently sensing imminent personal threat and wishing to avoid any further questioning, begins to leave the courtyard (ἐξελθόντα εἰς τὸν πυλῶνα, "having gone into the entrance") only to be encountered by another servant girl who, recognizing him, makes the same charge, which is now, however, addressed to those standing there: οὗτος ἦν μετὰ Ἰησοῦ τοῦ Ναζωραίου, "this one was with Jesus the Nazorean." Reference to Jesus as "the Nazorean" (on Ναζωραῖος, see *Comment* on 2:23) is fairly common in the NT (2:23; Luke 18:37; John 18:5, 7; 19:19; Acts 2:22; 3:6; 4:10; 6:14; 22:8; 26:9; the alternate form Ναζαρηνός, "Nazarene," is preferred by Mark [Mark 1:24; 10:47; 14:67; 16:6]). Since Nazareth was a city in Galilee, the appellation is only a further specification of the latter. Peter's denial (note: πάλιν, "again") is now made μετὰ ὅρκου, "with an oath," i.e., with all the more strength (on the force of an oath, cf. 14:7, 9 and the teaching of Jesus in 5:33, here violated), and with the statement οὐκ οἶδα τὸν ἄνθρωπον, "I do not know the man." The reader cannot miss the deliberately impersonal "the man" (cf. v 74 for the same sentence verbatim). The Son of Man has become to the first of the disciples an anonymous "the man."

**73–74a** μετὰ μικρόν, "after a little while," a third charge comes, this time from others standing there, now men (as the masculine participle indicates) and thus more seriously threatening than the accusations of the women servants. Having heard him speak, they recognized his distinctive Galilean accent. "Truly [ἀληθῶς]," they claim, "you too [again emphatic] are one of them [ἐξ αὐτῶν]," i.e., one of the disciples of Jesus, most of whom were Galileans. The present tense εἶ, "are," is deliberate and all the more threatening to Peter. As evidence for their claim, they add "your speech [λαλιά] betrays you," lit. "makes you obvious." This is not the only time the Galilean Peter would become conspicuous in Judea (cf. Acts 4:13, where, however, the nuance is a little different). Peter's self-defensive reaction is vehement: he begins to curse and to swear. καταθεματίζειν, "to curse," and ὀμνύειν, "to swear," are difficult to distinguish in meaning: both may involve appeal to a deity's wrath to come upon oneself if the statement being made is not true. On the other hand, the first verb may possibly assume Jesus as its direct object, i.e., that Peter cursed or reviled Jesus (thus Merkel; Gerhardsson, *JSNT* 13 [1981] 46–66). The response οὐκ οἶδα τὸν ἄνθρωπον, "I do not know the man," is exactly the same as his second response (v 72). Gerhardsson puts it graphically: "In order to save his skin he howls with the wolfpack" (*JSNT* 13 [1981] 55).

**74b–75** The dramatic effect of the short sentence καὶ εὐθέως ἀλέκτωρ ἐφώνησεν, "and immediately the cock crowed," is especially powerful. The narrative repeats the prediction of Jesus (originally reported in v 34) and records Peter's reaction to hearing the cock crow and remembering the words of Jesus. The story ends with the brief, but especially poignant, ἔκλαυσεν πικρῶς, "he wept bitterly." Peter "does not rend his garments but he 'rends his heart'" (Gerhardsson, *JSNT* 13 [1981] 62). The reference to the "cock crowing" here does not refer to the marking of the Roman watch (12:00–3:00 A.M.) by that name (*pace* Mayo, Kosmala; see R. E. Brown, *Death of the Messiah*, 606) and is not used as a time indicator (nor does it have to do with evil spirits, *pace* Derrett). It points rather to the fulfillment of Jesus' prophecy in v 34 and at the same time, as a dramatic touch, serves to heighten Peter's shameful failure.

### Explanation

Peter's guilt is not greater than that of the other disciples who abandoned Jesus and who thus in effect also denied him. It is, of course, far more conspicuous because of the present passage. Peter is singled out, however, not merely because of his boastful claim that he would never deny Jesus even if it meant death (all the disciples spoke similarly according to v 35) but more particularly because of his central importance in Matthew. Peter, even when he was first designated "the rock," had been unable to face the prospect of a suffering Messiah (16:21–23), nor, we may be sure, did he relish the words then spoken by Jesus about the need for his disciples to take up their cross and to be willing to lose their lives for his sake (16:24–25). Now he had faced precisely that challenge and had failed miserably. We cannot be surprised at the bitterness of his soul at that moment. The fact that Peter, the prime apostle, the "rock" upon which Jesus promised to build his church, could exhibit this human weakness and failure should provide both a warning (cf. esp. 10:33) and encouragement to disciples of Jesus who read the Gospel of Matthew. Obviously it can never be appropriate for disciples to become overconfident in their own strength. The problem of human weakness must always be realistically faced, especially in cases when it is magnified by fear. (These insights are confirmed by Gewalt from a literary-critical point of view.) But if failure occurs, there is also the prospect of forgiveness and restoration (presupposed in Matthew [cf. the reference to "the eleven" in 28:16], where however Peter's name does not occur again; cf. Mark 16:7; Luke 24:12; John 20:2–7; 21:15–23). The Gospel of Matthew, for all its emphasis on the rigors of discipleship, is not overly optimistic about human performance. But neither is it lacking in emphasis upon forgiveness (e.g., 1:21; 9:2, 5–6; 12:31–32; 26:28).

# *Jesus Is Handed over to Pilate	(27:1–2)*

### Bibliography

**Kerr, I.** "Who Has Authority?" *ExpTim* 94 (1983) 146–47. **McGing, B. C.** "Pontius Pilate and the Sources." *CBQ* 53 (1991) 416–38.

### Translation

[1]*And when morning had come, all the chief priests and the elders of the people took* [a] *counsel together against Jesus with the resulting verdict that* [b] *he should be put to death.* [2]*And having bound him, they led him away and handed him* [c] *over to Pilate* [d] *the governor.*

### Notes

[a] ἔλαβον, " took." D vg^mss mae bo have ἐποίησαν, "made" (a consultation), by the influence of the parallel in Mark 15:1.

[b] "With the resulting verdict that" translates the simple ὥστε, lit. "so that."

[c] "Him" added, supplying direct object. Many MSS (A [C³] W Θ *f*^1,13 TR) insert the αὐτόν, "him."

[d] Many MSS (A C W Θ *f*^1,13 TR latt sy^h) insert Ποντίῳ, "Pontius," before "Pilate." Since there is no reason for its deletion, it was probably added to supply the full name. See *TCGNT,* 65.

### Form/Structure/Setting

A. Having established that Jesus should be put to death, the Jewish authorities proceed to the next stage of the process by turning him over to the Romans. The action introduced here is continued in vv 11–37 after the parenthetical account of the end of Judas (vv 3–10).

B. Matthew continues to be dependent on Mark, again following his source quite closely (cf. Mark 15:1; cf. Luke 23:1; John 18:28). Matthew recasts the beginning of v 1 with a genitive absolute, πρωΐας γενομένης, "when it was morning," and omits Mark's εὐθύς, "immediately," as unnecessary. He replaces Mark's ποιήσαντες, lit. "having made," with ἔλαβον, "took" (used consistently with συμβούλιον, "counsel," in Matthew; cf. 12:14; 22:15; 27:7; 28:12). Matthew inserts πάντες, "all," before οἱ ἀρχιερεῖς, "the chief priests," meaning again "all who were there"; he identifies the πρεσβύτεροι, "the elders," as τοῦ λαοῦ, "of the people" (as often elsewhere, e.g., 21:23; 26:3, 47, though never so in Mark); and he omits Mark's καὶ γραμματέων καὶ ὅλον τὸ συνέδριον, "and scribes and the whole Sanhedrin," perhaps regarding the latter as tautologous or as an overstatement though there seems to be no reason for the omission of the scribes, except abbreviation, since they are earlier mentioned as involved in the proceedings (cf. 26:57; 27:41). Matthew adds the reason for the gathering in the words κατὰ τοῦ Ἰησοῦ ὥστε θανατῶσαι αὐτόν, "against Jesus so that they might put him to death." In v 2 he replaces τὸν Ἰησοῦν, "Jesus," with the pronoun αὐτόν, "him," no doubt because he has used the name Jesus in the addition just mentioned. Matthew also adds τῷ ἡγεμόνι, "the governor," after the first reference to Pilate's name, providing a note of specific identification.

## Comment

**1–2** πρωΐας δὲ γενομένης, "and when it was morning," refers probably to first daylight. The phrase συμβούλιον ἔλαβον, "took counsel," occurs also in 12:14; 22:15; 27:7; 28:12 (the last two employing the participle λαβόντες, "having taken"). The last two instances, as here, may refer to formal meetings. In the present case we probably have a *de facto* second meeting of the Jewish authorities that same morning (cf. Luke 22:66)—still not legal by Mishnaic standards but perhaps somewhat more formal than in 26:57–68 and probably with more members of the Sanhedrin in attendance. Perhaps too the decision taken (as συμβούλιον ἔλαβον, "took counsel," may be understood) may be regarded as more formally official than the opinion expressed in 26:66. Alternatively, this meeting may be considered the final stage of the meeting described in 26:57–68 (thus R. E. Brown, *Death of the Messiah*, 632). Taking the decision are πάντες οἱ ἀρχιερεῖς καὶ οἱ πρεσβύτεροι τοῦ λαοῦ, "all the chief priests and the elders of the people," which appears to be a favorite Matthean shorthand for the Jewish authorities (cf. 21:23; 26:3, 47). The decision is κατὰ τοῦ Ἰησοῦ, "against Jesus," and involves the death penalty, ὥστε θανατῶσαι αὐτόν, "so that they should put him to death." Since the execution of the death penalty was probably not allowed to them (cf. John 18:31b), they bind Jesus as a criminal and hand him over (for the verb παραδιδόναι, see *Comment* on 17:22) to the Romans and specifically to Pilate, τῷ ἡγεμόνι, "the governor." Pilate was *praefectus* ("prefect," a position somewhat later designated "procurator"), the fifth over Judea, from A.D. 26/27 to 36. His *nomen* (representing the tribe), "Pontius," is given in Luke 3:1; Acts 4:27; 1 Tim 6:13. On Pilate, cf. Josephus *Ant.* 18.2.2 §35; 18.3.1–2 §§55–62; 18.4.1–2 §§85–89; *J.W.* 2.9.2–4 §§169–77; and Philo, *De legatione ad Gaium* 299–305. Pilate, who would normally have been resident in Caesarea Maritima, was conveniently in Jerusalem to provide some control during the Passover feast. For particularly useful studies of Pilate the man, see McGing; R. E. Brown, "Appendix IV: Overall View of Judas Iscariot," in *Death of the Messiah*, 1394–1418.

## Explanation

The fate of Jesus is decided by the Jewish authorities, although it is the Romans who must finally carry out the sentence against Jesus. This is not the last mention of Jewish complicity in the death of Jesus in Matthew, however, which comes to a kind of climax later in the chapter (vv 20–25). It is a motif the evangelist does not shy away from, despite his own Jewish background. It is also a motif that has had tragic and un-Christian consequences in the hatred and persecution of the Jewish people as a whole. See further the *Explanation* for 27:15–26.

# *Judas and the Blood Money  (27:3–10)*

## Bibliography

**Benoit, P.** "The Death of Judas." In *Jesus and the Gospel.* New York: Herder, 1973. 1:189–207. **Bernard, J. H.** "The Death of Judas: Mt 27.3–10." *Exp,* 6th series, 9 (1904) 422–30.

**Betz, O.** "The Dichotomized Servant and the End of Judas Iscariot." *RevQ* 5 (1964) 43–58. **Bruce, F. F.** "The Book of Zechariah and the Passion Narrative." *BJRL* 43 (1960–61) 336–53. **Colella, P.** "Trenta denari." *RivB* 21 (1973) 325–27. **Conard, A.** "The Fate of Judas: Matthew 27:3–10." *TJT* 7 (1991) 158–68. **Desautels, L.** "La mort de Judas (*Mt* 27,3–10; *Ac* 1,15–26)." *ScEs* 38 (1986) 221–39. **Escande, J.** "Judas et Pilate prisonniers d'une même structure (Mt 27,1–26)." *FV* 78 (1979) 92–100. **Findlay, J. A.** "The First Gospel and the Book of Testimonies." In *Amicitiae Corolla,* ed. H. G. Wood. London: University of London, 1933. 57–71. **Haugg, D.** *Judas Iskarioth in den neutestamentlichen Berichten.* Freiburg: Herder, 1930. **Herber, J.** "La mort de Judas." *RHR* 129 (1945) 47–56. **Jervell, J.** "The Field of Jesus' Blood: Mt. 27, 3–10." *NorTT* 69 (1968) 59–73. **Klauck, H.-J.** *Judas—ein Jünger des Herrn.* QD 111. Freiburg: Herder, 1987. **Lake, K.** "The Death of Judas." In *The Beginnings of Christianity: Part 1: The Acts of the Apostles,* ed. F. J. Foakes Jackson and K. Lake. New York: Macmillan, 1933. 5:22–30. **Manns, F.** "Un midrash chrétien: Le récit de la mort de Judas." *RevSR* 54 (1980) 197–203. **Menken, M. J. J.** "The References to Jeremiah in the Gospel according to Matthew (Mt 2,17; 16,14; 27,9)." *ETL* 60 (1984) 5–24. **Moeser, A. G.** "The Death of Judas." *BiTod* 30 (1992) 145–51. **Moo, D. J.** "Tradition and Old Testament in Matt 27:3–10." In *Gospel Perspectives,* ed. R. T. France and D. Wenham. Sheffield: JSOT, 1980. 3:157–75. **Munro, J. I.** "The Death of Judas (Matt. xxvii.3–8; Acts i.18–19)." *ExpTim* 24 (1912–13) 235–36. **Quesnel, M.** "Les citations de Jérémie dans l'évangle selon saint Matthieu." *EstBib* 47 (1989) 513–27. **Reiner, E.** "Thirty Pieces of Silver." In *Essays in Memory of E. A. Speiser,* ed. W. W. Hallo. *JAOS* 88 (1968) 186–90. **Roquefort, D.** "Judas: Une figure de la perversion." *ETR* 58 (1983) 501–13. **Schwarz, W.** "Die Doppelbedeutung des Judastodes." *BLit* 57 (1984) 227–33. **Senior, D.** "A Case Study in Matthean Creativity: Matthew 27: 3–10." *BR* 19 (1974) 23–26. ———. "The Fate of the Betrayer: A Redactional Study of Matthew XXVII,3–10." *ETL* 48 (1972) 372–426. **Sparks, H. F. D.** "St. Matthew's References to Jeremiah." *JTS* n.s. 1 (1950) 155–56. **Stein-Schneider, H.** "A la recherche du Judas historique: Une enquête exégètique à la lumière des textes de l'Ancien Testament et des Logia." *ETR* 60 (1985) 403–29. **Strecker, G.** "Die Judasperikope (Mt. 27,3–10)." In *Der Weg der Gerechtigkeit.* Göttingen: Vandenhoeck & Ruprecht, 1962. 76–82. **Sutcliffe. E. F.** "Matthew 27:9." *JTS* n.s. 3 (1952) 227–28. **Tilborg, S. van.** "Matthew 27:3–10: An Intertextual Reading." In *Intertextuality in Biblical Writings.* FS B. van Iersel, ed. S. Draisma. Kampen: Kok, 1989. 159–74. **Unnik, W. C. van.** "The Death of Judas in Saint Matthew's Gospel." In *Gospel Studies.* FS S. E. Johnson, ed. M. H. Shepherd and E. C. Hobbs. ATR Supplement Series 3. Evanston, IL: Anglican Theological Review, 1974. 44–57. **Upton, J. A.** "The Potter's Field and the Death of Judas." *Concordia Journal* 8 (1982) 213–19. **Vogler, W.** *Judas Iskarioth.* Theologische Arbeiten 42. Berlin: Evangelische, 1983.

### Translation

[3] *Then when Judas, the one who betrayed* [a] *him, saw that Jesus* [b] *was condemned to death,* [c] *he regretted what he had done and returned the thirty pieces of silver to the chief priests and elders,* [4] *saying: "I have sinned in having betrayed innocent* [d] *blood." But they said: "What difference is that to us? That's your problem."* [e] [5] *And when he had thrown the silver pieces* [f] *into the temple,* [g] *he departed. And he went and hanged himself.* [6] *And the chief priests, having taken up the silver pieces, said: "It is not permitted to put them into the treasury, since they are blood money."* [7] *And when they had counseled together, they bought the "potter's field" with the silver pieces* [h] *as a burial place for aliens.* [8] *Therefore that field was called the "field of blood" up to the present.* [9] *Then the word* [i] *was fulfilled which was spoken by the prophet Jeremiah,* [j] *which says: "And they took the thirty pieces of silver, the price of the precious One* [k] *upon whom a price had been set by the children* [l] *of Israel,* [10] *and they* [m] *gave the silver pieces* [n] *for the field of the potter, just as the Lord commanded me."*

## Notes

<sup></sup> ᵃ παραδιδούς, lit. "betraying." Many MSS (‭א‬ A C W Θ *f*¹·¹³ TR) have the aorist participle παραδούς, lit. "having betrayed."

ᵇ "Jesus" added for clarity, specifying the subject of the passive verb.

ᶜ "To death" added to translation for clarity.

ᵈ Some MSS (B¹ L Θ latt syˢ saᵐˢˢ mae bo) have δίκαιον, "righteous," perhaps by the influence of 23:35. See *TCGNT*, 66.

ᵉ τί πρὸς ἡμᾶς; σὺ ὄψῃ, lit. "What [is that] to us? You see [to it]."

ᶠ ‭א‬ adds τριάκοντα, "thirty," probably by the influence of v 3.

ᵍ εἰς τὸν ναόν (‭א‬ B L Θ *f*¹³). Many MSS (A C W *f*¹ TR) have ἐν τῷ ναῷ, "in the temple," which suggests that Judas was *in* the temple complex rather than outside. Throwing the silver pieces from the outside, as suggested by εἰς τὸν ναόν, implies "strong emotion and physical exertion." *TCGNT*, 66.

ʰ ἐξ αὐτῶν, lit. "from them."

ⁱ "Word" added for clarity.

ʲ A few MSS correct Ἰερεμίου, "Jeremiah," to Ζαχαρίου, "Zechariah" (22 syʰᵐᵍ armᵐˢˢ), and some simply omit the name altogether (Φ 33 itᵃ·ᵇ vgᵐˢ syˢ·ᵖ·ᵖᵃˡ boᵐˢ). Two MSS (21 itˡ) have "Isaiah." See *TCGNT*, 66–67.

ᵏ τοῦ τετιμημένου, lit. "the one having been priced." However, this can also be translated "the valued One" or "the precious One" (so NJB; NRSV margin). See *Comment*.

ˡ ἀπὸ υἱῶν Ἰσραήλ, "by the sons of Israel."

ᵐ Some MSS (‭א‬ B²ᵛⁱᵈ W sy) have ἔδωκα, "I gave," perhaps through the influence of Zech 11:13 (cf. μοι, "to me," at the end of the sentence). A*ᵛⁱᵈ has ἔδωκεν, "he gave." See *TCGNT*, 67.

ⁿ αὐτά, lit. "them."

## Form/Structure/Setting

A. Matthew at this point inserts the story of Judas' remorse and suicide together with the account of the purchase of the potter's field with his thirty pieces of silver. Matthew, the only Gospel with this story, has probably included it because of the correspondence between certain elements of historical tradition concerning the end of Judas and material in Zechariah, which leads him to the last of his special formula quotations stressing fulfillment. Thus, although this story interrupts the narrative of the condemnation of Jesus, it has the desirable effect of further indicating God's sovereign control over the events having to do with the betrayal and death of Jesus (cf. 26:54, 56).

B. In the present pericope, Matthew departs from his Markan source, used throughout the passion narrative. The evangelist is probably working creatively with traditional materials at his disposal. The only other NT account of the fate of Judas is found in Acts 1:15–20, which, however, differs from the present narrative in important respects (see Benoit). Nevertheless, there is an important connection between the two passages in the common reference to the "field of blood" (Acts 1:19). Another relatively early account of Judas' death is found in the obviously elaborated and fictional narrative in Papias, Fragment 3 (preserved by Apollinarus of Laodicea [for the Greek text, see Lake, 23, and for ET, see R. E. Brown, *Death of the Messiah*, 1408–9]).

C. Matthew's main goal in the pericope is obviously the fulfillment quotation with which it ends. The pericope is shaped with this in mind from the start, i.e., in the reference to Judas' return of the thirty pieces of silver (v 3) but also clearly in the deliberation of the chief priests and their purchase of the field (vv 6–8). This is another example of haggadic midrash (Gnilka: haggada; Benoit:

"midrashic interpretation" [206]) based on the quoted matter of the OT similar to that encountered also in the infancy narrative and in the temptation narrative of 4:1–11. This fact, however, does not necessarily exclude the reality and use of historical traditions here. The following outline may be suggested: (1) Judas' change of mind and return of the money (vv 3–4); (2) the suicide of Judas (v 5); (3) the purchase of the potter's field (vv 6–8); and (4) the consequent fulfillment of scripture (vv 9–10). The most notable structural feature is the correspondence between the narrative section and the quotation in the reference to τὰ τριάκοντα ἀργύρια, "the thirty pieces of silver" (vv 3, 9), and to τὸν ἀγρὸν τοῦ κεραμέως, "the field of the potter" (vv 7, 10).

*Comment*

**3** When Judas, ὁ παραδιδοὺς αὐτόν, "the one betraying him" (he is described similarly in 26:25, 48), saw that Jesus had been "condemned" (κατεκρίθη; the same verb is used in the prophecy of 20:18), he "changed his mind" about what he had done. It is impossible to know how Judas may have been affected psychologically by his act of betrayal. However, a high degree of remorse, if not technically repentance (μετανοεῖν would have been used in that case, with more positive connotations), is implied in the participle μεταμεληθείς, "regretted" (used also in 21:29, 32), and is confirmed by his statement in v 4 as well as by his deed in v 5b. The money he had obtained, τὰ τριάκοντα ἀργύρια, "the thirty pieces of silver" (cf. 26:15), now became reprehensible to him, and he attempted to return it to "the chief priests and elders" (see v 1).

**4–5** Judas is painfully aware of the injustice he has committed against Jesus. He thus declares that he "has sinned" (ἥμαρτον) in his betraying of αἷμα ἀθῷον, "innocent blood," a common expression in the OT. A specific injunction against doing just what Judas did is found in Deut 27:25: "Cursed be anyone who takes a bribe to shed innocent blood [LXX: αἵματος ἀθῴου]." Since it is obviously as wrong to give such a bribe as to take one, the Jewish authorities are themselves also guilty. This fact they ignore, however, in their response, τί πρὸς ἡμᾶς, lit. "what [is that] to us?" The process has gone too far to be reversed, and the Jewish authorities have no interest in regaining the money they had paid, let alone absolving Judas of his crime. σὺ ὄψῃ, lit. "you see [to it]" (the future tense is here, as in v 24, imperatival [BDF §362]), essentially turns the problem back upon Judas. (V 24 uses the same expression when Pilate refuses to find Jesus guilty; in the same verse Pilate declares himself ἀθῷος, "innocent," of τοῦ αἵματος, "the blood," of Jesus.) No doubt loathing himself as well as the Jewish authorities, Judas throws the coins εἰς τὸν ναόν, "into the temple," i.e., into the temple area (cf. Zech 11:13), perhaps through a gate or over the wall into the area restricted to the priests (an allusion to the practice referred to in *m. ʿArak.* 9:4 seems unlikely, *pace* Gnilka). The short notice of Judas's end is given in three words: καὶ ἀπελθὼν ἀπήγξατο, "and he went away and hanged himself" (ἀπάγχεσθαι is used only here in the NT; cf. 2 Sam 17:23 [but deliberate allusion to Ahithophel seems unlikely; with Gnilka; Moo, *The Old Testament in the Gospel Passion Narratives*, 190; *pace* R. E. Brown, *Death of the Messiah*, 643, 656]; Tob 3:10). Acts 1:18 attributes Judas's death to a cause other than suicide, reflecting God's judgment (for an early attempt to harmonize the disparate accounts, see Papias, Fragment 3 [see *Form/Structure/Setting* §B]). From a Greco-Roman perspective, suicide was the only honorable deed for one who betrayed his teacher (thus Moeser; but it is unclear how much Judas the Jew would have been influenced by this perspective).

**6** Because the money was "blood money" (τιμὴ αἵματος, lit. "the price of blood," i.e., "of a bloody deed"), it was contaminated and abhorrent to God (cf. Deut 23:18). Therefore, it could not be deposited εἰς τὸν κορβανᾶν, "in the (temple) treasury" (from Aramaic קָרְבָּנָא, *qorbānāʾ*; cf. Jos., *J.W.* 2.9.4 §175 and the word κορβᾶν, "Korban" or "gift," in Mark 7:11), the place from which it presumably had come. This much the chief priests would admit, though they are quite oblivious to their own complicity. On the importance of the notion of "blood money" (contrast "innocent blood") to the formation of the pericope and its place in the passion narrative, cf. Senior, *ETL* 48 (1972) 372–46.

**7–8** The chief priests then agree (the language is the same as in v 1: they "took counsel," or "decided") to use the money for something practical (and religiously correct) and buy with it a piece of land, identified by Matthew as τὸν ἀγρὸν τοῦ κεραμέως, "the field of the potter" (cf. the Hebrew of Zech 11:13), εἰς ταφὴν τοῖς ξένοις, "for a burial place for aliens" (i.e., for non-Jews, who were not allowed to be buried in the same cemetery with Jews). For this reason (διό, "wherefore"), i.e., because the field was purchased with "blood money" (v 6), it became known as ὁ ἀγρὸς αἵματος, "the field of blood," as it continued to be known down to the evangelist's own day (probably south-southwest of Jerusalem, across the valley of Hinnom). Acts 1:19 knows too of this "field [but χωρίον rather than ἀγρός] of blood," referring to it also using the transliterated Aramaic equivalent Ἁκελδαμάχ, "Hakeldamach" (= הֲקֵל דְּמָא, *hăqēl děmāʾ*). The story in Acts, however, connects the naming of the field to the manner of Judas' death in that field rather than to the kind of money used to buy it.

**9–10** Matthew's last fulfillment quotation (see Hagner, *Matthew 1–13*, liii–lvii) is fraught with difficulties. To begin with, the quotation is attributed to Ἰερεμίου τοῦ προφήτου, "Jeremiah the prophet," although it is taken mainly from Zech 11:13, where the shepherd doomed to slaughter (Zech 11:7) is valued at and paid "thirty shekels of silver" and instructed to throw the money to "the potter" (יוֹצֵר, *yôṣēr*, LXX: χωνευτήριον, "foundry," i.e., "to the moulder" or "smelter"; Syriac Peshitta has "treasury" [thus NSRV]). Almost certainly it is the reference to "the potter" in Zechariah that brought to mind the book of Jeremiah, where the potter assumes such a large role, causing the evangelist to cite it here (cf. Jer 18:1–12; 19:1–15) or causing the early church to relate and perhaps conflate the two passages. A rather less likely connection is with the reference to the buying of the field with seventeen shekels of silver in Jer 32:6–9. (Nowhere in Jeremiah are the potter and the field brought together, however.) The quotation as Matthew gives it is somewhat closer to the Hebrew than to the LXX.

The opening words, to be sure, are essentially Septuagintal: καὶ ἔλαβον τὰ τριάκοντα ἀργύρια (LXX: τοὺς τριάκοντα ἀργυροῦς), "and I [or 'they'] took the thirty silver coins." Matthew's next words, τὴν τιμὴν τοῦ τετιμημένου ὃν ἐτιμήσαντο, "the price of the one having been priced [or 'the precious One'], whom they priced," however, are closer to the Hebrew (אֶדֶר הַיְקָר אֲשֶׁר יָקַרְתִּי, *ʾeder hayqār ʾăšer yāqartî*, "the magnificence of the price with which I was priced") than to the LXX. The awkward redundancy of Matthew's

Greek is alleviated if one translates τοῦ τετιμημένου as "the precious One" (so NJB, NRSV margin). Something that is "priced" can from another perspective be understood as "valued as precious," and this may well be how Matthew's Christian readers understood the participle (McNeile). This difference in nuance may also be related to different vocalizations of הַיְקָר, i.e., הַיְקָר, hayqār, "the price"; הַיָּקָר, hayāqār, "the honored one" (Moo, "Tradition," 158). Matthew's ἀπὸ υἱῶν Ἰσραήλ, "by the sons of Israel," is not found in the Hebrew OT or in the LXX and is simply Matthew's expansion of "by them," with the action of the Jewish authorities in mind (the ἀπό probably reflects the Heb. מִן, min, in a partitive sense, i.e., "some of the sons of Israel"; cf. Stendahl, School of St. Matthew, 126). The words of v 10, καὶ ἔδωκαν αὐτὰ εἰς τὸν ἀγρὸν τοῦ κεραμέως, "and they gave them for the field of the potter," similarly find no actual counterpart in the OT (though, as indicated above, Jeremiah has references both to the potter and to the buying of a field). The final clause, καθὰ συνέταξέν μοι κύριος, "just as the Lord commanded me," a clause that is frequently found in the LXX without the μοι, "me," probably uses formulaic language to reflect the opening of Zech 11:13, καὶ εἶπεν κύριος πρός με, "and the Lord said to me"—which probably is also the explanation of the discordant μοι, "me" (the preceding verbs in the quotation are all plural, including the ambiguous ἔλαβον, "they took," which in the LXX is first person singular; i.e., it is the prophet who takes the money). It is remarkable that the very line in Zech 11:13 that suggested the Jeremiah passage, "and threw them [the thirty pieces of silver] to the potter [or into the treasury] in the house of the Lord," is not included in Matthew's quoted material (though earlier Matthew states that Judas took the silver pieces and threw them into the temple [v 5]). But he may have avoided this line because of the shift in subjects that would then have been necessary. Matthew's comment that the chief priests decided that the money could not go into κορβανᾶν, "the treasury" (v 6), suggests that he may have known of the variant rendering אוֹצָר, ʾôṣār, "treasury," for יוֹצֵר, yôṣer, "potter," in Zech 11:13 (Bruce, BJRL 43 [1960–61] 349–50; cf. Benoit).

If we attempt to reconstruct how Matthew came to this fulfillment quotation, we may conclude the following. Matthew had from Mark that Judas was paid ἀργύριον, "money" (Mark 14:10). Matthew may have had a separate tradition about the amount of "thirty," but perhaps it is more likely that he imports this detail from the Zechariah quotation in anticipation of using it later in connection with the "potter's field" (cf. its presence already in 26:15). Because Zech 9–14 was particularly important for the early church as a resource of prophecies fulfilled by Jesus (cf. in Matthew Zech 9:9 in 21:5; Zech 13:7 in 26:31; see esp. Bruce, BJRL 43 [1960–61] 336–53; Moo, The Old Testament in the Gospel Passion Narratives, 173–224) and in particular because Zech 11 speaks of a shepherd "doomed to slaughter," taken obviously by Matthew to refer to Jesus (cf. 26:31), Matthew finds the correspondence between Zech 11:13 and the story of Judas taking silver coins for betraying Jesus a compelling one. Matthew also probably had an element from historical tradition about a "field of blood" associated with Judas' reward money (cf. Acts 1:18), which he may also have known as "the potter's field." Thus Matthew finds a further correspondence in the twofold statement of Zech 11:13 that the pieces of silver were thrown "to the potter"—why else, according to Matthew, than to buy the field in question (v 7)? The combination of these motifs may thus be responsible for the association with Jeremiah.

The textual basis for the attribution of the quotation to Jeremiah is particularly strong (the reading "Zechariah" in 22 sy^hmg arm^mss is obviously a "correction") though there is no real quoted material from Jeremiah. If this attribution is not simply a blunder (thus Stendahl, *School of St. Matthew*, 123), how is it to be explained? Scholars have suggested the following possibilities, listed here in what is in my opinion an ascending order of probability: (1) the quotation is derived from an apocryphal book of Jeremiah (Origen; Jerome; Lohmeyer; Strecker, *Weg*); (2) the passage in question is in fact Jer 19:1–13 (E. W. Hengstenberg, *Christology of the Old Testament and a Commentary on the Messianic Predictions*, reprint [Grand Rapids: Kregel, 1956] 4:40–45; Gundry; Senior; Moo, "Traditions," who admits it is "the least obvious reference" [161]; Carson); (3) "Jeremiah" means "the prophets" collectively since in some canonical lists the book of Jeremiah stands at the head of the prophets (Str-B 1:1030; Sparks; Sutcliffe); (4) the Zechariah and Jeremiah passages in question were already associated by the early church and perhaps—although the hypothesis does not depend on this—conflated in a collection of *testimonia* under Jeremiah's name, which Matthew made use of (Findlay; Bruce, *BJRL* 43 [1960–61] 341). The first solution is of necessity pure speculation; the second depends on similarities too general in nature; and the third is based on insufficient evidence. On the importance of Jeremiah's understanding of a rejected Messiah for Matthew, cf. Menken and Sparks. Matthew's use of the quotation, as in several other of his fulfillment quotations, depends on the correspondences noted above, which are regarded not as coincidental but as divinely intended, so that the former foreshadow the latter and the latter are said to be the fulfillment of the former. Matthew is unconcerned about a number of details that do not correspond, e.g., that in Zechariah the prophet takes the money while in Matthew the evil chief priests take the money; that in Matthew the priests do not put the money into the temple treasury while in Zechariah the money is cast into "the house of the Lord." Instead, because of the important role played by Zech 9–14 in the polemic of the early church, Matthew all the more confidently bases his argument on the quotation of Zech 11:12–13 (for the generative function of the text in explaining the pericope, see R. E. Brown, *Death of the Messiah*, 657–60). What Judas and the Jewish authorities did had already been anticipated by the prophets. The narrative in effect identifies Jesus as the good shepherd-prophet of Zechariah and at the same time contrasts him with the chief priests, the evil sheep-owners (thus van Tilborg). —

### Explanation

Judas becomes aware too late of the full horror of his betrayal of Jesus. What lay behind his change of heart is difficult to say. He can hardly have expected a different decision than that reached by the Jewish authorities, namely, that Jesus should be condemned to death. Had he perhaps with national-political loyalties hoped he could force Jesus to act powerfully against his enemies and exert his messianic power (prematurely), as the devil had tempted him in the wilderness (4:1–11) and as he would be tempted upon the cross (27:40)? Or did it simply dawn upon Judas that he had been responsible for the great injustice of the condemnation of a truly righteous and good man? At the same time, the narrative has an unmistakable inevitability about it. We can pity Judas, but we cannot make a hero out of him, nor alas even a believer. As the Son of Man fulfills the prophecies, so too do Judas and the Jewish priests, as they act freely out of their own unfortunate motives, unwittingly acting as instruments for the accomplishment of God's purposes and the fulfillment of scripture. In no sense are we allowed to take Judas or the Jewish authorities as representing Jews or Judaism in general, let alone "the essence of Jewishness." In such thinking lies the evil root of anti-Semitism.

## *Jesus Arraigned before Pilate    (27:11–14)*

### Bibliography

**Allen, J. E.** "Why Pilate?" In *The Trial of Jesus.* FS C. F. D. Moule, ed. E. Bammel. SBT 2.13. London: SCM, 1970. 78–83. **Bammel, E.** "The Trial before Pilate." In *Jesus and the Politics of His Day,* ed. E. Bammel and C. F. D. Moule. Cambridge: Cambridge UP, 1984. 403–12. **Becq, J.** "Ponce Pilate et la mort de Jésus." *BTS* 57 (1963) 2–7. **Benoit, P.** "Praetorium, Lithostroton and Gabbatha." In *Jesus and the Gospel.* New York: Herder, 1973. 167–88. **Blinzler, J.** "Der Entscheid des Pilatus: Exekutionsbefehl oder Todesurteile?" *MTZ* 5 (1954) 171–84. **Brandon, S. G. F.** *Jesus and the Zealots.* New York: Scribners, 1967. **Cantinat, J.** "Jésus devant Pilate." *VSpir* 86 (1952) 227–47. **Chilton, C. W.** "The Roman Law of Treason under the Early Principate." *JRS* 45 (1955) 73–81. **Cullmann, O.** *Jesus and the Revolutionaries.* Tr. G. Putnam. New York: Harper & Row, 1970. **Erhardt, A.** "Was Pilate a Christian?" *CQR* 137 (1944) 157–67. **Escande, J.** "Judas et Pilate prisonniers d'une même structure (Mt 27, 1–26)." *FV* 78 (1979) 92–100. **Garnsey, P.** "The Criminal Jurisdiction of Governors." *JRS* 58 (1968) 51–59. **Harrison, E. F.** "Jesus and Pilate." *BSac* 105 (1948) 307–19. **Hengel, M.** *Was Jesus a Revolutionist?* Philadelphia: Fortress, 1971. **Horvath, T.** "Why Was Jesus Brought to Pilate?" *NovT* 11 (1969) 174–84. **Irmscher, J.** "σὺ λέγεις (Mark xv.2—Matt. xxvii.11—Luke xxiii.3)." *Studii Clasice* 2 (1960) 151–58. **Kastner, K.** *Jesus vor Pilatus: Ein Beitrag zur Leidensgeschichte des Herrn.* NTAbh 4.2–3. Münster: Aschendorff, 1912. **Lémonon, J.-P.** *Pilate et le gouvernement de la Judée: Textes et Monuments.* EBib. Paris: Gabalda, 1981. **Liberty, S.** "The Importance of Pontius Pilate in Creed and Gospel." *JTS* 45 (1944) 38–56. **Maier, P. L.** "Sejanus, Pilate, and the Date of the Crucifixion." *CH* 37 (1968) 3–13. **Marin, L.** "Jesus before Pilate: A Structural Analysis Essay." In *The New Testament and Structuralism,* ed. A. M. Johnson, Jr. Pittsburgh Theological Monograph 2. Pittsburgh: Pickwick, 1976. 97–144. **Matera, F.** "Mt 27.11–54." *Int* 38 (1984) 55–59. **Quinn, J. F.** "The Pilate Sequence in the Gospel of Matthew." *DunRev* 10 (1970) 154–77. **Riesner, R.** "Das Prätorium des Pilatus." *BK* 41 (1986) 34–37. **Robbins, V. K.** "The Crucifixion and the Speech of Jesus." *Forum* 4 (1988) 33–46. **Rogers, R. S.** "Treason in the Early Empire." *JRS* 49 (1959) 90–94. **Sherwin-White, A. N.** *Roman Society and Roman Law in the New Testament.* Oxford: Clarendon, 1963. **Staats, R. K.** "Pontius Pilatus im Bekenntnis der frühen Kirche." *ZTK* 84 (1987) 493–513. **Vincent, L. H.** "Le Lithostrotos évangélique." *RB* 59 (1952) 513–30. **Wansbrough, H.** "Suffered under Pontius Pilate." *Scr* 18 (1966) 84–93. **Winter, P.** "The Trial of Jesus as a Rebel against Rome." *The Jewish Quarterly* 16 (1968) 31–37.

See also *Bibliography* for 26:57–68.

## Translation

[11]Now Jesus stood before the governor, and the governor[a] asked him, saying: "Are you the king of the Jews?" And Jesus said:[b] "You speak the truth."[c] [12]And when he was accused by the chief priests and the elders, he answered nothing. [13]Then Pilate said to him: "Do you not hear how many things they bear witness against you?" [14]And he did not answer him, not even to a single charge, so that the governor was very amazed.

## Notes

[a] W Θ sy[s] omit ὁ ἡγεμών, "the governor," perhaps because of the immediately preceding occurrence of the word.

[b] Many MSS (A B W Θ f[1,13] TR lat sy mae) include αὐτῷ, "to him."

[c] σὺ λέγεις, lit. "you say." See Comment.

## Form/Structure/Setting

A. Following an interruption with the story of Judas, the narrative regarding Jesus' progress toward his crucifixion continues with his arraignment (an interrogation rather than a formal trial; see Bammel) before the Roman governor Pilate. The Roman arraignment is quite similar to that before the Jewish authorities (26:59–66). While Jesus admits to being the "king of the Jews," i.e., their Messiah, he makes no attempt to answer the accusations brought against him. Pilate is amazed at Jesus' demeanor and, unlike the Jewish authorities, ultimately refuses to find him guilty (cf. v 24).

B. Matthew resumes his dependence upon Mark in this short pericope (Mark 15:2–5; cf. Luke 23:2–5; John 18:29–38). The following more significant changes should be noted. Because of the previous interlude concerning Judas and the potter's field, Matthew adds the opening sentence to set the context: ὁ δὲ Ἰησοῦς ἐστάθη ἔμπροσθεν τοῦ ἡγεμόνος, "and Jesus stood before the governor." Also in v 11, Matthew substitutes ὁ ἡγεμών, "the governor," for ὁ Πιλᾶτος, "Pilate" (Mark 15:2), taking the word from his opening sentence. In the same verse Matthew omits Mark's unnecessary ἀποκριθεὶς αὐτῷ, "answering him." In v 12 Matthew omits πολλά, "many things" (Mark 15:3), referring to the accusations against Jesus, focusing instead on Jesus' silence by the addition of οὐδὲν ἀπεκρίνατο, "he answered nothing." In the same place Matthew adds καὶ πρεσβυτέρων, "and elders," in keeping with his usual dual reference to "chief priests and elders" (cf. 26:3, 47, 57; 27:1, 3, 20). In v 13 Matthew abbreviates by omitting Mark's question (Mark 15:4), "Do you not answer anything?" (probably because of his addition of the statement in v 12 that Jesus answered nothing); Matthew then turns Mark's statement concerning their accusations of Jesus into a question. In v 14 Matthew intensifies Mark by his replacement of οὐδέν, "nothing" (Mark 15:5), with πρὸς οὐδὲ ἓν ῥῆμα, "to not even one charge," and by the addition of λίαν, "greatly," to θαυμάζειν, "was amazed." He also replaces τὸν Πιλᾶτον, "Pilate," with τὸν ἡγεμόνα, "the governor" ("Pilate" was used by Matthew in v 13).

C. Structurally, the passage consists of the basic pattern of question and answer typical of an arraignment. It may be outlined as follows: (1) Pilate's question (v 11a–c); (2) Jesus' answer (v 11d); (3) Jesus' silence before his accusers (v 12); (4) Pilate's second question (v 13); and (5) Jesus' continued silence (v 14). The parallels with the narrative of Jesus before Caiaphas and the Jewish authorities are impressive: Jesus is brought before the key authority figure (v 11; cf. 26:57); he is asked a question concerning his understanding of himself (v 11: "King of the Jews"; cf. 26:63: "the Christ, the Son of God"); Jesus responds affirmatively though indirectly (v 11: σὺ λέγεις, "you say [so]"; 26:64: σὺ εἶπας, "you have said [so]"); both inquisitors ask Jesus for a response to the accusations (v 13; cf. 26:62); and in both cases Jesus is silent (vv 12, 14; cf. 26:63).

*Comment*

**11**  Jesus is now brought before the Roman governor Pilate, resuming the narrative from v 2 (see there concerning Pilate; for rich background material to the Roman trial, see R. E. Brown, *Death of the Messiah*, 676–722). For the location of this "trial," the *praetorium* in Herod's "lower" palace, see Riesner. Pilate's question, σὺ εἶ ὁ βασιλεὺς τῶν Ἰουδαίων, "are you the king of the Jews," amounts to the same question put by the high priest in 26:63 concerning whether Jesus is ὁ χριστὸς ὁ υἱὸς τοῦ θεοῦ, "the Messiah, the Son of God," but expressed now in more political language, reflecting no doubt the manner in which the charge was expressed to Pilate by the Jewish authorities (cf. John 18:34). Though the division is hardly absolute, a religious question was thus in effect turned into a political one, for the Romans would only be concerned about the latter. The Jews, however, would have said "King of Israel" (cf. v 42). The issue that concerns Pilate is whether Jesus was an insurrectionist who constituted a political threat to the Roman rule of Judea. Jesus' answer, σὺ λέγεις, "you say (so)," is an affirmation (see Catchpole, *NTS* 17 [1970–71] 213–26, on the similar response in 26:64) though indirect (all four Gospels have the same response by Jesus to Pilate's question; cf. 1 Tim 6:13, which probably refers to this event). Jesus thus admits to being "King of the Jews" but implies by the form of his answer that his kingship is not the sort that Pilate might suppose (cf. John 18:36–37). Jesus answers Pilate just as he did Caiaphas (26:64; cf. 26:25) although without any added qualifying words. Words such as Jesus had spoken to Caiaphas would be meaningless to the Roman prefect. Despite Jesus' answer, Pilate seems instinctively to know that Jesus is not really a threat to the political and social stability he was charged to preserve (cf. the Johannine explanation in John 18:36 and Jesus' recognition of Pilate's authority in John 19:11). He finds no reason to be worried about a Jewish "king" of this kind and perceives the issue to be nothing more than Jewish quibbling (cf. v 24). Although some have tried to construe Jesus as a political revolutionary (esp. Brandon), it is clear that such an understanding of Jesus is incorrect (see Cullmann; Hengel).

**12–13**  Jesus would not defend himself against the charges of τῶν ἀρχιερέων καὶ πρεσβυτέρων, "the chief priests and elders" (cf. 26:3, 27:1). Although Matthew does not specify the charges here, they were presumably of the order of those mentioned in 26:61 (the only other occurrence of κατηγορεῖν, "accuse," in Matthew is in 12:10 in connection with the violation of the sabbath; cf. Luke 23:10). Jesus was, in brief, a dangerous revolutionary bent on disturbing the status quo. This was the accusation of the Jewish authorities against Jesus, although it is unlikely (*pace* Horvath) that they had any idea that Jesus could or might overthrow Roman authority then and there. Matthew's readers almost certainly related the silence of Jesus before his accusers (cf. v 14) throughout the passion narrative, both here and before the Sanhedrin (26:62), to the servant of Isa 53:7, who like a lamb led to slaughter did not open his mouth. It is not the silence of defeat or confusion but of a triumphant resolution. Pilate's question about Jesus' silence reflects his surprise at Jesus' passive resignation (cf. 26:62, where the same verb, καταμαρτυροῦσιν, "they bear witness against," is used). Jesus appears to be no threat to him.

**14** Matthew sharpens the report of Jesus' silence in noting that Jesus responded πρὸς οὐδὲ ἕν ῥῆμα, "to not even one charge." ῥῆμα, lit. "word," in the present context can be taken to mean "matter" or "charge," especially when governed by πρός, "to." The result of Jesus' persistent silence was the great amazement of Pilate (for the silence of Jesus in the passion narrative, see *Comment* on 26:63). What kind of man is it, he must have wondered, who refuses to defend himself? The exceptionally unusual nature of this case is further brought to Pilate's attention in v 19.

### Explanation

The process whereby Jesus is "tried" continues toward its inexorable conclusion. Jesus now courageously faces the Roman interrogator who has the power of life or death (cf. John 19:10) in the settlement of the case. He quietly gives assent to the question whether he is the Jewish king but does not flinch in the face of his accusers' charges. He keeps silent now, just as he did before the Jewish authorities. The dignity of that silence impresses even Pilate, who could not, however, have known that he was participating in a divine drama of such historical consequences that his own name would thereby be immortalized. Jesus' commitment to the cross—the will of his Father—is firmly fixed. Nothing, no one, can turn Jesus away from that goal.

# The Decision for Barabbas and against Jesus (27:15–23)

### Bibliography

**Aus, R. D.** "The Release of Barabbas (Mark 15:6–15 par.; John 18:39–40), and Judaic Traditions in the Book of Esther." In *Barabbas and Esther and Other Studies*. Atlanta: Scholars, 1992. 1–27. **Bajsić, A.** "Pilatus, Jesus und Barabbas." *Bib* 48 (1967) 7–28. **Chavel, C. B.** "The Releasing of a Prisoner on the Eve of Passover in Ancient Jerusalem." *JBL* 60 (1941) 273–78. **Couchoud, P. L.,** and **Stahl, R.** "Jesus Barabbas." *HibJ* 25 (1926–27) 26–42. **Davies, S. L.** "Who is called Bar Abbas?" *NTS* 27 (1981) 260–62. **Derrett, J. D. M.** "Haggadah and the Account of the Passion: 'Have nothing to do with that just man!' (Matt. 27, 19)." In *Studies in the New Testament*. Leiden: Brill, 1982. 3:184–92. **Dunkerley, R.** "Was Barabbas Also Called

Jesus?" *ExpTim* 74 (1962–63) 126–27. **Fascher, E.** "Das Weib des Pilatus." *TLZ* 72 (1947) 201–4. ———. *Das Weib des Pilatus (Matthäus 27,19): Die Auferweckung der Heiligen (Matthäus 27,51–53)*. Hallische Monographien 20. Halle: Niemeyer, 1951. **Ford, J. M.** "'Crucify him, crucify him' and the Temple Scroll." *ExpTim* 87 (1976) 275–78. **Gillman, F. M.** "The Wife of Pilate (Matthew 27:19)." *LS* 17 (1992) 152–65. **Husband, R. W.** "The Pardoning of Prisoners by Pilate." *AJT* 21 (1917) 110–16. **Langdon, S.** "The Release of a Prisoner at the Passion." *ExpTim* 29 (1917–18) 328–30. **Maccoby, H. Z.** "Jesus and Barabbas." *NTS* 16 (1969–70) 55–60. **Merkel, J.** "Die Begnadigung am Passahfeste." *ZNW* 6 (1905) 292–316. **Merritt, R. L.** "Jesus Barabbas and the Paschal Pardon." *JBL* 104 (1985) 57–68. **Nevius, R. C.** "A Reply to Dr. Dunkerley." *ExpTim* 74 (1962–63) 255. **Oepke, A.** "Noch einmal das Weib des Pilatus: Fragment einer Dämonologie." *TLZ* 73 (1948) 743–46. **Ott, E.** "Wer war die Frau des Pilatus? Eine Geschichte für Heute." *GL* 59 (1986) 104–6. **Rigg, H. A., Jr.** "Barabbas." *JBL* 64 (1945) 417–56. **Trilling, W.** "Der Prozess vor Pilatus: 27,15–26." In *Das wahre Israel*. Munich: Kösel, 1964. 66–74. **Twomey, J. J.** "Barabbas Was a Robber." *Scr* 8 (1956) 115–19.

## Translation

¹⁵*And at the time of the feast, the governor was accustomed to release one prisoner to the crowd whom they wanted.* ¹⁶*And they had then a notorious prisoner named [Jesus]*ᵃ *Barabbas.*ᵇ ¹⁷*When they had gathered together, therefore, Pilate said to them: "Whom do you want me to release to you, [Jesus]*ᶜ *Barabbas or Jesus, the one called 'Messiah'?"* ¹⁸*For he knew that they had handed him over because of envy.*

¹⁹*And while he was sitting on his judgment throne, his wife sent a message*ᵈ *to him, saying: "Do not have anything to do with that righteous man.*ᵉ *For I have suffered many things today in a dream on his account."*

²⁰*Now the chief priests and the elders persuaded the crowds that they should ask for Barabbas and that they should destroy Jesus.* ²¹*But the governor answered them and said: "Which of the two men do you want me to release to you?" And they said: "Barabbas."* ²²*Pilate said to them: "What therefore shall I do*ᶠ *with Jesus, the one called 'Messiah'?" They all said:*ᵍ *"Let him be crucified."* ²³*But he*ʰ *said:*ⁱ *"Why? What bad thing has he done?" But they cried out all the more loudly, saying: "Let him be crucified!"*

## Notes

ᵃ The vast majority of MSS (א A B D L W *f*¹³ TR latt sy^{p.h} co) do not include Ἰησοῦν, "Jesus," while only a few include it (Θ *f*¹ 700* sy^s). It is, however, quite possible that the name, not an uncommon one (Josephus refers to more than half a dozen individuals named Jesus; cf. Col 4:11), was originally present and later suppressed out of reverence for the name "Jesus" (for which reason Origen in his commentary argued against the reading). Harmonization with Mark 15:6, where only the name Barabbas appears, may also have been a fact in its omission from Matthew. It is difficult, on the other hand, to know why it would have been introduced into later MSS. A marginal comment in S (tenth century) and twenty or so minuscule MSS notes that "many ancient copies" of Matthew referred here to Barabbas as also having the name Jesus. Because of the few witnesses, however, that contain the name here, it is placed in brackets by the *UBSGNT* committee. Cf. v 17. See *TCGNT*, 67–68. Against accepting the reading, see Dunkerley.

ᵇ Φ (sy^s mae) add ὃς διὰ φόνον καὶ στάσιν ἦν βεβλημένος εἰς φυλακήν, "who because of murder and insurrection had been thrown into prison," probably an importation of similar information from Mark 15:7.

c Many witnesses again (cf. v 16) omit Ἰησοῦν, "Jesus" (‏א‎ A D L W *f*¹³ TR latt syᵖ·ʰ co), while only a few include it (Θ *f*¹ 700* syˢ). See discussion above in *Note a*. In those MSS that include Ἰησοῦν, the definite article, τόν, appears between Ἰησοῦν and Βαραββᾶν. The reading of B, τὸν Βαραββᾶν, also suggests an earlier MS containing Ἰησοῦν τὸν Βαραββᾶν. A further reason for the omission of "Jesus" in this verse, in addition to reverence for that name, may be that the dative ΥΜΙΝ caused the omission of I̅N̅ (haplography), the standard abbreviation for Ἰησοῦν. See *TCGNT*, 67–68.

d "A message" added, supplying direct object.

e μηδὲν σοὶ καὶ τῷ δικαίῳ ἐκείνῳ, an idiom, lit. "nothing to you and to that righteous man." See *Comment*.

f D it have ποιήσωμεν, "shall we do."

g Many MSS (L Γ TR) add αὐτῷ, "to him."

h Many MSS (A D L W *f*¹ TR lat syʰ·ᵖ mae bo) insert ὁ ἡγεμών, "the governor."

i Some MSS (D L *f*¹ lat syᵖ mae bo) add αὐτοῖς, "to them."

## *Form/Structure/Setting*

A. The narrative turns now to the strange way in which Pilate's diffidence enables the crowd to bring about the decision to have Jesus crucified. The choice is between Barabbas and Jesus. The crowd is instigated by the chief priests and elders to bring about their own evil intent, and at the end of the pericope the repeated fateful cry is heard: "Let him be crucified."

B. Matthew continues to be dependent upon Mark in this pericope (Mark 15:6–14; cf. Luke 23:17–23; John 18:39–40). Matthew makes one major omission of Markan material and one major addition to it. In v 16 Matthew omits Mark's description of Barabbas as one associated with insurrectionists who had committed murder (Mark 15:7), being content simply to describe him as δέσμιον ἐπίσημον, "a notorious prisoner." This is probably because of Matthew's penchant for abbreviating Mark by ruling out material not regarded as essential. On the other hand, Matthew adds v 19, which refers to the message from Pilate's wife, perhaps from a piece of tradition known to him. A further omission may be noted in Matthew's abbreviation of Mark by substituting the simple genitive absolute συνηγμένων αὐτῶν, "when they gathered together" (v 17), for Mark's καὶ ἀναβὰς ὁ ὄχλος ἤρξατο αἰτεῖσθαι καθὼς ἐποίει αὐτοῖς, "and the crowd went up and began to ask just as he (usually) did for them" (Mark 15:8). Another significant alteration of Mark involves the adding of a question (v 21) to Mark's two questions, making Pilate ask a total of three questions (cf. Luke 23:22: τρίτον, "a third time"). Matthew phrases the first question (v 17) unlike Mark (Mark 15:9) in terms of an either/or, "Barabbas or Jesus?" Matthew's added second question (v 21) receives the answer οἱ δὲ εἶπαν· τὸν Βαραββᾶν, "and they said: 'Barabbas.'" In Matthew's first and third questions, he replaces Mark's τὸν βασιλέα τῶν Ἰουδαίων, "the king of the Jews" (Mark 15:9, 12), with Ἰησοῦν τὸν λεγόμενον Χριστόν, "Jesus, the one called Messiah" (vv 17, 22), thus emphasizing less the political and more the religious dimension of Jesus' identity as the anointed one of Israel. An important Matthean addition occurs in the words τὸν δὲ Ἰησοῦν ἀπολέσωσιν, "but they should destroy Jesus" (v 20; cf. Mark 15:11), which has the effect of heightening Jewish responsibility for the death of Jesus.

Among alterations of less importance, the following may be noted. At the beginning of the pericope Matthew inserts εἰώθει ὁ ἡγεμών, "the governor was accustomed" (v 15; cf. Mark 15:6), thereby immediately setting the scene for what follows. In the same verse he replaces Mark's αὐτοῖς, "to them," with the more specific τῷ ὄχλῳ, "to the crowd." In v 20 Matthew inserts καὶ οἱ πρεσβύτεροι, "and the elders" (cf. Mark 15:11), in keeping with his usual practice (cf. vv 12, 41). In v 21 Matthew substitutes ὁ ἡγεμών, "the governor," for Mark's ὁ Πιλᾶτος, "Pilate" (Mark 15:12), and in v 23 he omits ὁ Πιλᾶτος (Mark 15:14) but inserts it in v 22 (cf. Mark 15:12). Finally one may note Matthew's λέγουσιν πάντες, "all said," for Mark's οἱ δὲ πάλιν ἔκραξαν, "and they again cried out" (Mark 15:13), a substitution that again emphasizes the culpability of the Jews.

C. The passage takes its basic structure from the three questions of Pilate, which in turn depend on the custom of the release of a prisoner. The following is an outline of the passage: (1) the custom of releasing a prisoner (vv 15–16); (2) the first question (vv 17–18); (3) the parenthetical message from Pilate's wife (v 19); (4) the persuasion of the crowds (v 20); (5) the second question (v 21); and (6) the third question (v 22a), which leads finally to (7) the call for Jesus' crucifixion (vv 22b–23). There is little syntactic parallelism, again owing to the narrative character of the material. The Barabbas-Jesus alternative in Pilate's first question (v 17) becomes a strong contrast in v 20, where the crowds are persuaded to "ask for" Barabbas but to "destroy" Jesus, and in its implementation, where the crowds ask for "Barabbas" (v 21) and demand Jesus' crucifixion (vv 22b–23), the latter involving the repeated σταυρωθήτω, "Let him be crucified" (vv 22–23). In both instances where Pilate refers to Jesus, he is characterized as τὸν λεγόμενον Χριστόν, "the one called Messiah" (vv 17, 22). A striking contrast can be seen in the reference to Barabbas as a "notorious prisoner" (v 16) and to Jesus as "that righteous man" (v 19).

*Comment*

**15–16** Although the custom of the Romans' releasing a prisoner κατὰ δὲ ἑορτήν, "at the time of the feast" (i.e., here Passover; cf. John 18:39), later called the *privilegium paschale*, is not known outside the Gospels, there is no need to doubt its historicity (*pace* R. E. Brown, *Death of the Messiah*, 814–20, who, however, accepts the historicity of the release of Barabbas for reasons left unexplained). Pertinent Jewish evidence is perhaps to be seen indirectly in *m. Pesaḥ.* 8:6 (see Blinzler, *Prozess;* Chavel; Merritt). Husband argues that the practice was Pilate's own invention. There is no obvious reason why the evangelists would invent such an idea, and it fits with a pragmatic opportunism directed toward gaining a few points with the people (note: ὃν ἤθελον, "whom they wanted"), which the Roman governor of Judea might well engage in and in which indeed Pilate seems happy to do in the present passage. The subject of εἶχον, "they had," is the Roman authorities. As it happened, there was another Jesus (a common name in the first century; cf. *Note* a) in Roman custody, a certain Jesus Barabbas, who is described by Matthew only as ἐπίσημον, "notorious" (but possibly, according to context, "famous"). In Mark we read that he was associated with insurrection (see Twomey) and murder (Mark 15:7; more explicitly, Luke 23:19; John 18:40 describes him only as λῃστής, "a bandit"). Nothing beyond this is known of the man. His name is a patronymic, בַּר אַבָּא, *bar ʾabbāʾ*, lit. "son of Abba" (Jerome in his commentary on this verse notes that in Latin the name was rendered *filius magistri eorum*, i.e., "son of their teacher" [בַּר רַבָּן, *bar rabbān*]). The argument of Rigg, and later Maccoby and S. L. Davies, that Jesus Barabbas was actually no person but only another name for Jesus himself, depends more on imagination than evidence.

**17–18** Those who "gathered together" (συνηγμένων αὐτῶν) were the crowds assumed now to have congregated outside Pilate's Jerusalem headquarters, perhaps for the very purpose of receiving the customary gift of a released prisoner. Whether the governor commonly gave the crowd only two possibilities, as in the present case, cannot be known. On this occasion, in any event, they were given a choice between two men named Jesus (assuming the questionable text; see *Notes* a and c): one Barabbas and the other τὸν λεγόμενον Χριστόν, "the one called Messiah [i.e., Christ]" (as also in v 22; cf. 1:16). The participle λεγόμενον, "called," is used to reflect unbelief in such a claim, both on the part of the accusers and of Pilate. Yet the use of Χριστόν, "Messiah," at the same time paradoxically points to Jesus' true identity (16:16–17; cf. John 19:21). The additional statement ᾔδει γὰρ ὅτι διὰ φθόνον παρέδωκαν αὐτόν, "for he knew that it was on account of envy that they had handed him over," probably explains why Pilate was willing to release Jesus to them. Pilate had established to his own satisfaction that Jesus had been brought to him not because he was a genuine threat or really the promised Jewish Messiah but because of the Jewish leaders' envy of his influence among the people (or perhaps their "zeal," a closely related concept; cf. ζῆλος, BAGD, 337b). Pilate was therefore willing, indeed even perhaps inclined, to release Jesus.

**19** τοῦ βήματος, "the judgment seat," was the official tribunal from which legal judgments were made, located in the open air (cf. Acts 18:12, 16–17; 25:17). Pilate's wife, whom the tradition names Procla (*Acts of Pilate*, appendix), perhaps knew that her husband was presiding over the trial of Jesus and sent him an urgent message—so urgent that he was to be interrupted—about a dream she had had. Dreams were taken with great seriousness by the Romans, as were omens of various kinds. Early in the morning (σήμερον, "today") she "suffered many things" (πολλὰ ἔπαθον) in "a dream" or what might better be called a nightmare. There is no reason to conclude that she was a convert to Judaism. The reader is meant to understand supernatural agency here (κατ' ὄναρ, "in a dream," is elsewhere used in Matthew only for divine revelation; cf. 1:20; 2:12, 13, 19, 22). It is from the dream that she knows to refer to Jesus as τῷ δικαίῳ ἐκείνῳ, "that righteous man" (cf. the similar use of δίκαιος in Luke 23:47; Acts 3:14; 7:52), and that her husband should not become involved in condemning him (this may well account for Pilate's action in v 24). The idiom μηδὲν σοὶ καὶ τῷ δικαίῳ ἐκείνῳ, lit. "nothing to you and to that righteous man," is quite similar to that in 8:29 (see *Comment* there; cf. Mark 1:24; John 2:4). In the present context it means "have nothing to do with that righteous man." The dream serves as a divine vindication of Jesus. (See Gillman for further discussion.)

**20** The Jewish authorities, again described in Matthew's favorite phrase οἱ ἀρχιερεῖς καὶ πρεσβύτεροι, "the chief priests and elders" (especially in the passion narratives: 26:3, 47; 27:1, 3, 12), now press on to the achievement of their goal: the death of Jesus. It is therefore imperative for them to persuade the people to make the right choice. Although the arguments they used are not given, it is not difficult to imagine that Jesus was characterized as a charlatan and blasphemer, one who was misleading the people. It was clear that Jesus of Nazareth was not the promised Messiah; in no way could one so obviously helpless in the hands of the Romans be significant for the hope of Israel. Perhaps, on the other hand, Barabbas was set forth as a patriotic freedom fighter (ironically something the Jewish authorities were in reality against). However that may be, they were apparently so successful in their arguments that they persuaded the crowd not only to ask for the release of Barabbas but also to demand the death of Jesus. τὸν δὲ Ἰησοῦν ἀπολέσωσιν, lit. "they might destroy [i.e., 'kill'] Jesus," has as its subject the Jewish crowd and again stresses Jewish responsibility for the death of Jesus (cf. v 25 and *Comment* there). What is actually meant here, of course, is that they might have Jesus put to death, i.e., by means of the Romans.

**21–22** These two verses correspond to and carry out the two-part resolution of the preceding verse, i.e., the request for the release of Barabbas and the death of Jesus. Pilate first asks which of the two men they want released, which is followed by the blunt answer of the crowd: "Barabbas" (cf. the choice given in v 17). Then (v 22) Pilate asks what he should do with the other Jesus, τὸν λεγόμενον Χριστόν, "the one called Messiah [i.e., Christ]" (cf. v 17 and *Comment* there). The answer of the crowd to this question of Pilate is equally incisive: σταυρωθήτω, "let him be crucified" (a frenzied cry repeated again in v 23). Thus not only do they demand the death of Jesus, but they specify a most horrible form of death, that of crucifixion (used frequently by the Romans esp. in conquered realms but never administered to a Roman citizen). This means of death furthermore could bring with it a divine curse (Deut 21:23). From the Temple Scroll of Qumran, it now appears that crucifixion was not merely a Roman form of punishment but also a Jewish one (see Ford).

**23** Pilate asks a final question that itself and by the lack of an easy answer to it points indirectly to the innocence of Jesus (thus confirming the truth of the reference to Jesus as a "righteous man" by Pilate's wife [v 19]): "What bad [or 'evil'] thing [κακόν] has he done?" The issue is not whether he had done anything worthy of death but merely whether he had done anything of which he could justly be criticized or perhaps punished with a lighter sentence. The crowd at this point, however, is not strong on reasons. Their corporate response is simply to shout (ἔκραζον, "they cried out") their demand louder: "Let him be crucified" (cf. v 22). Pilate, clearly aware of this man's innocence (cf. v 24; Acts 3:13; 13:28), can react only with amazement.

## *Explanation*

Although Pilate may have been unhappy about the decision against Jesus, he was more than ready to take an opportunity to please the crowd, even at the expense of Jesus' life. He knew from his interrogation of him that Jesus had violated no Roman law. It was rather a matter of the internal religious squabbles among the Jews. He knew furthermore from his wife's urgent communication to him that Jesus was a righteous man. To his question "What wrong has this man done?" he receives no answer—because none could be given. Thus although Pilate will symbolically wash his hands and declare that he is innocent of the wrong of putting Jesus to death (v 24), yet in yielding to the demands of the crowd he, together with the Jews, can hardly escape being accounted guilty. It is shockingly clear from this passage that it is a righteous man who goes to his death and that therefore his death is the greatest of injustices. Deeper and more powerful forces are at work than the surface narrative can disclose.

# The Question of Guilt in the Crucifixion of Jesus (27:24–26)

## Bibliography

**Baum, G.** "The Gospel of Saint Matthew: Matthew 27,25." In *Is the New Testament Anti-Semitic?* Glen Rock, NJ: Paulist Press, 1965. 100–108. **Bowman, J.** "The Significance of Mt. 27:25." *Milla wa-Milla* 14 (1974) 26–31. **Cargal, T. B.** "'His Blood Be upon Us and upon Our Children': A Matthean Double Entendre?" *NTS* 37 (1991) 101–12. **Cope, O. L.** "The Matthean Crucifixion Narrative." In *Matthew: A Scribe Trained for the Kingdom of Heaven.* Washington, DC: Catholic Biblical Association of America, 1976. 102–10. **Fitzmyer, J. A.** "Anti-Semitism and the Cry of 'All the People' (Mt. 27:25)." *TS* 26 (1965) 667–71. **Frankemölle, H.** "27,25: *pas ho laos.*" In *Jahwebund und Kirche Christi.* NTAbh 10. Münster: Aschendorff, 1974. 204–11. **Haacker, K.** "'Sein Blut über uns': Erwägungen zu Matthäus 27,25." *Kirche und Israel* 1 (1986) 47–50. **Heil, J. P.** "The Blood of Jesus in Matthew: A Narrative-Critical Perspective." *PRS* 18 (1991) 117–24. **Joüon, P.** "Notes philologiques sur les Évangiles—Matthieu 27.25." *RSR* 18 (1928) 349–50. **Kampling, R.** *Das Blut Christi und die Juden: Mt 27,25 bei den lateinischsprachigen christlichen Autoren bis zu Leo dem Grossen.* NTAb 16. Münster: Aschendorff, 1984. **Koch, K.** "Der Spruch 'Sein Blut bleibe auf seinem Haupt' und die israelitische Auffasung vom vergossenen Blut." *VT* 12 (1962) 396–416. **Kosmala, H.** "His Blood on Us and Our Children (The Background of Matt. 27, 24–25)." *ASTI* 7 (1968–69) 94–126. **Lovsky, F.** "Comment comprendre 'Son sang sur nous et nos enfants.'" *ETR* 62 (1987) 343–62. **Matera, F. J.** "'His blood be on us and on our children.'" *BiTod* 27 (1989) 345–50. **Mora, V.** *Le refus d'Israël: Matthieu 27,25.* LD 124. Paris: Cerf, 1986. **Overstreet, L.** "Roman Law and the Trial of Christ." *BSac* 135 (1978) 323–32. **Pfisterer, R.** "'Sein Blut komme über uns. . . .'" In *Christen und Juden,* ed. W.-D. Marsch and K. Thieme. Mainz: Grünewald, 1961. 19–37. **Reventlow, H. G.** "'Sein Blut komme über sein Haupt.'" *VT* 10 (1960) 311–27. **Sanders, W.** "Das Blut Jesu und die Juden: Gedanken zu Matt. 27,25." *Una Sancta* 27 (1972) 168–71. **Schelkle, K. H.** "Die 'Selbstverfluchung' Israels nach Matthäus 27,23–25." In *Antijudäismus im Neuen Testament?* ed. W. P. Eckert et al. Munich: Kaiser, 1967. 148–56. **Smith, R. H.** "Matthew 27:25: The Hardest Verse in Matthew's Gospel." *CurTM* 17 (1990) 421–28. **Sullivan, D.** "New Insights into Matthew 27:24–25." *NB* 73 (1992) 453–57.

## Translation

²⁴*And when Pilate saw that he was getting nowhere* [a] *but that instead the clamor increased,* [b] *he took water and washed his hands before the crowd, saying: "I am innocent of this* [c] *man's blood. It is your responsibility."* [d] ²⁵*And the whole people answered and said: "His blood be upon us and upon our children!"* ²⁶*Then he released Barabbas to them, but when he had Jesus scourged, he handed him over* [e] *to be crucified.* [f]

## Notes

ᵃ οὐδὲν ὠφελεῖ, lit. "he is accomplishing nothing."

ᵇ θόρυβος γίνεται, lit. "there is a clamor."

ᶜ Many MSS (אּ L W *f*¹˒¹³ TR lat syᵖ˒ʰ saᵐˢˢ mae bo) have τοῦ δικαίου τούτου, "this righteous man" (so too A Δ but with slightly different word order), "an accretion intended to accentuate Pilate's protestation of Jesus' innocence" (*TCGNT*, 68). Cf. the similar variant in v 4.

ᵈ ὑμεῖς ὄψεσθε, lit. "you will see (to it)."

ᵉ Some MSS (אּ¹ D L N Θ *f*¹ lat syˢ) add αὐτοῖς, "to them."

ᶠ D Θ it have σταυρώσωσιν αὐτόν, "that they might crucify him."

## Form/Structure/Setting

A. Just prior to the handing over of Jesus to the Roman soldiers, Matthew includes an account of Pilate's declaration of his innocence in what is about to happen to Jesus. With that declaration, Matthew emphasizes the willing acceptance by the Jews of responsibility for the execution of Jesus. This pericope is in keeping with Matthew's intention of highlighting Jewish culpability for the crucifixion.

B. Only for v 26, with its mention of the release of Barabbas and the handing over of Jesus, is Matthew dependent on Mark (Mark 15:15; cf. Luke 23:24–25; John 19:16a). There Matthew omits Mark's ὁ δὲ Πιλᾶτος βουλόμενος τῷ ὄχλῳ τὸ ἱκανὸν ποιῆσαι, "but Pilate wishing to satisfy the crowd" (something already implicit in the narrative), but otherwise follows Mark's wording closely. Vv 24–25 are unique to Matthew among the Gospels, probably being drawn from historical tradition available to him.

C. The pericope has at its heart the two contrasting statements of vv 24 and 25, both pertaining to the "blood" of Jesus, i.e., the taking of his life. The following is a simple outline: (1) Pilate declares his innocence (v 24); (2) the people accept the responsibility (v 25); and (3) Jesus is handed over to be crucified (v 26). V 26 includes the contrast of previous verses (vv 17, 20) in its reference to the release of Barabbas and the giving of Jesus over to the soldiers for crucifixion. The reference to Pilate washing his hands is found also in *Gos. Pet.* 1, which, however, is probably dependent on Matthew.

## Comment

**24** Pilate quickly becomes aware that it is useless to try to reason with the crowd. Their minds were firmly made up concerning the death of Jesus (cf. v 20). He "was gaining nothing" (οὐδὲν ὠφελεῖ; the verb is used earlier in 15:5; 16:26). Worse than that, the crowd seemed volatile (for the expression θόρυβος γίνεται, which could be translated "a riot was beginning" [so NRSV], cf. 26:5). Although it is not so indicated by Matthew, Pilate must at that point have determined that he would have to yield to the request of the people for the execution of Jesus. But to dissociate himself from their resolve (perhaps with his wife's counsel in mind [v 19] since he personally was probably not much concerned with the matter), he performed before them the symbolic action of washing his hands—a public sign of his innocence in this matter. Since there is Hellenistic as well as Jewish background for this practice, it is not necessary to conclude that this statement is not historical (*pace* R. E. Brown, *Death of the Messiah*, 833). For OT background, cf. Pss 26:6; 73:13; and esp. Deut 21:6–8; for Hellenistic background, see Herodotus 1.35; Virgil, *Aeneid* 2.719: Sophocles, *Ajax* 654. The crowd could not have missed the significance of the sign since it was accompanied by the words ἀθῷός εἰμι ἀπὸ τοῦ αἵματος τούτου, "I am innocent of the blood of this one" (for "blood" in this sense, cf. v 4; 2 Sam 3:28; Sus 46). This is virtually an admission that Jesus has done nothing deserving of death. The reader of the Gospel knows that Pilate was correct. ὑμεῖς ὄψεσθε, lit. "you will see (to it)" (imperatival future as in v 4), means in this context the transferring of the responsibility for Jesus' death to the Jews, thus "it is your responsibility" (cf. the Jewish authorities' similar remark to Judas in v 4). Pilate's public display of "innocence" cannot, however, veil his own complicity, even if reluctant and passive, in the death of Jesus (cf. v 26).

**25** If Pilate is not willing to take responsibility for the death of Jesus, the inflamed crowds will! There may be no more fateful verse for the history of Jewish-Christian relations in the entire Bible than this one (see *Explanation* below). The crowd now seems obsessed with but one thought: the death of Jesus. Can they be wrong in following the prompting of their religious and spiritual leaders? And thus, now referred to deliberately as πᾶς ὁ λαός, "all the people" (= Israel; *pace* Kosmala), they readily take upon themselves the responsibility for the death of this man. The idea of blood being "upon someone" (or more often "upon their head") is found in both the OT (e.g., 2 Sam 1:16; Jer 26:15; cf. 51:35; see discussion of the expression in Reventlow) and the NT (Acts 5:28; 18:6). The implication of τὰ τέκνα ἡμῶν, "our children," depends on the well-established familial solidarity of the OT (going back to such passages as Josh 7:24; 2 Kgs 24:3–4; Lam 5:7; cf. the proverb "The parents have eaten sour grapes, and the children's teeth are set on edge" in Jer 31:29; Ezek 18:2, against which both prophets argue). A proper understanding of this text, however, must begin with the realization that those demanding Jesus' death are primarily the Jewish leaders or at most the particular crowds whipped up by them. It is certainly only the Jews of that generation—and indeed, only *some* of them—who were responsible for the death of Jesus, not the Jews of later centuries. And that generation (and their children if they must be included despite Jer 31:30; Ezek 18:19–32) could from Matthew's perspective easily have been regarded as suffering God's judgment in the fall of Jerusalem when it occurred. This verse was not intended to encourage Christians to bring vengeance upon the Jews. The Lord says "vengeance is mine" (Deut 32:35; Rom 12:19; Heb 10:30), and Christians taught by Jesus will love their "enemies" (5:11, 44; Rom 12:19–21). The verse points painfully to the theological reality and historical tragedy of the failure of the Jews to welcome their Messiah (see Mora; Fitzmyer) and to understand the church as the fulfillment of Israel's hope (cf. 21:43). Nevertheless, Jesus has forgiven those responsible for his death (cf. Luke 23:34; the "ignorance" motif is picked up in Acts 3:14–17; 1 Cor 2:8), and God continues to love the Jews and will yet remember his covenant loyalty to them (cf. 23:39; but more clearly, Rom 11:26–32). The blood of which the first-century Jews are guilty will yet be the source of their forgiveness (cf. Acts 2:39: "to you and your children"). The blood of Christ means not condemnation but salvation (Schelkle). That is the long view (see W. Sanders), however, and one can hardly read from Matthew's text the idea that the blood is upon the Jews in a redemptive sense (*pace* R. H. Smith and Cargal, who argues for an intentional double entendre).

**26** In keeping with his initial offer (v 17) and the subsequent decision (vv 20–23), Pilate releases Barabbas to the people and accedes to their request to have Jesus crucified. He then "handed over" Jesus to the Roman soldiers (cf. v 27). This is the last occurrence of παραδιδόναι, "hand over," which occurs so frequently in these chapters that Gnilka (2:459–60) refers to it as a *cantus firmus* of the passion narrative. In handing over an innocent man to death, however, he does not violate Roman law because Jesus was not a Roman citizen (see Overstreet). φραγελλώσας, "having scourged," refers to flogging with a lash having sharp bits for tearing the flesh (cf. Jesus' prophecy in 20:19 where, however, the verb is μαστιγοῦν). This was commonly administered to a person before crucifixion (cf. Jos., *J.W.* 2.14.9 §306; 5.11.1 §449), perhaps to hasten death on the cross. The charge for which Jesus was to be crucified remains unspecified (but cf. v 11; v 37, with its political overtones; and see John 19:12).

### Explanation

In this pericope the inference can be drawn that Pilate is innocent and the Jews alone are guilty of the death of Jesus. We have seen, however, that Pilate must also be regarded as guilty though in a somewhat different way. At the same time, there can be no mistaking the fact that Matthew portrays the Jews in an exceptionally bad light. The words recorded in v 25, "his blood be upon us and upon our children," to some extent also reflect the hostility between Matthew's church and the synagogue that characterized the last half of the first century. That hostility, I have argued (see Hagner, *Matthew 1–13*, lxxi–lxxiii), was between Jews, those who had accepted Jesus as their Messiah and those who had not. That there would be especially strong feelings in the first generation of disagreement is understandable. This particular verse, sad to say, has been used to justify "Christian" persecution of the Jews down through the centuries. Regarding Jesus as the incarnation of God, Christians of subsequent generations found it easy to think of Jews as guilty of deicide. It is as shocking as it is true that anti-Semitism accordingly became a Christian virtue, indeed, a Christian duty. After all, had not the Jews all but wished revenge upon themselves in the words they spoke to Pilate? We may only hope and pray in this post-Holocaust era that Christians no longer need to be told how unthinkable such a conclusion is and what a tragic abuse of v 25 it is to use this statement in support of anti-Semitism. The salvation enjoyed by gentile Christians is in reality the gift of the Jewish people by whom it has come, as the Fourth Evangelist puts it (John 4:22), and with that Matthew would have no reason to disagree (cf. 1:1). It is right therefore for Christians to honor the Jews, for the light that has dawned in Christ is also meant to be glory to God's people Israel (Luke 2:32; and again Matthew would not disagree). As for the responsibility for the death of Jesus, theologically there is only one possible answer: it is sin, the universal malady of all human beings, that drives Jesus to the cross. The crucifixion is in this sense a piece of the autobiography of every man and woman ever to walk this earth. It is "I" who am guilty of crucifying Jesus.

# The Mocking of Jesus by the Roman Soldiers (27:27–31)

## Bibliography

**Bonner, C.** "The Crown of Thorns." *HTR* 46 (1953) 47–48. **Delbrueck, R.** "Antiquarisches zu den Verspottungen Jesu." *ZNW* 41 (1942) 124–45. **Ha-Reubéni, E.** "Recherches sur les plantes de l'Évangile: L'éine de la couronne de Jésus." *RB* 42 (1933) 230–34. **Kastner, K.** "Christi Dornenkrönung und Verspottung durch die römische Soldateska." *BZ* 6 (1908) 378–92. ———. "Nochmals die Verspottung Christi." *BZ* 9 (1911) 56. **Lübeck, K.** *Die Dornenkrönung Christi.* Regensburg: Pustet, 1906. **Schlier, H.** "Der Dornengekrönte." *SeinSend* 29 (1964) 148–60.

## Translation

[27] *Then when the governor's soldiers had taken Jesus into the praetorium, the whole cohort gathered together around him.* [28] *And they took his clothes off*[a] *and put*[b] *a scarlet robe around him.* [29] *And they wove together a crown of thorns and placed it upon his head and a staff in his right hand. And they fell on their knees before him and mocked*[c] *him, saying: "Hail, King of the Jews!"* [30] *And having spit upon him, they took the staff and began to beat him upon his head.* [31] *And when they had mocked him, they took off the robe and put on his own garments, and they led him away to be crucified.*

## Notes

[a] Some MSS (ℵ² B D it syˢ) have ἐνδύσαντες, "they clothed him," probably a correction, given the nudity presupposed in the flogging referred to in v 26 (cf. the sequence unclothed-clothed in v 31). Cf. Mark 15:17. *TCGNT*, 68. A few witnesses (064 33 syʰᵐᵍ saᵐˢ mae boᵐˢ) add τὰ ἱμάτια αὐτοῦ, "his clothes," which is also added to this translation as the object of the verb.

[b] D it (syˢ) insert ἱμάτιον πορφυροῦν καί, "a purple garment and," no doubt by the influence of the parallel in Mark 15:17; John 19:2.

[c] Many MSS (A W Θ *f*¹,¹³ TR) have the imperfect tense ἐνέπαιζον, "they were mocking," instead of the aorist tense, perhaps to harmonize with the imperfect ἔτυπτον, "they were beating" or "began to beat," of v 30. *TCGNT*, 68.

## Form/Structure/Setting

A. Just prior to the crucifixion itself occurs a further mocking scene parallel to that which took place after Jesus had been accused of blasphemy by the Jewish authorities (cf. details of 26:67–68). The Roman soldiers had, of course, less appreciation of the nature and meaning of Jesus' offense. Yet the irony remains here as in the early scene that the one being mocked truly is the king and Messiah of the Jews. Jesus' prophecy in 20:19 is specifically fulfilled in this pericope (and in v 26).

B. For the most part Matthew follows Mark closely, although the material is rearranged with some freedom (Mark 15:16–20; cf. John 19:2–3). Thus in v 29 Matthew substitutes γονυπετήσαντες ἔμπροσθεν αὐτοῦ, "fell on their knees before him," for Mark's redundant τιθέντες τὰ γόνατα προσεκύνουν αὐτῷ, "kneeling down they paid homage to him" (Mark 15:19), and transposes it to before the mocking words "Hail, King of the Jews." In v 30 he reverses the order of the reference to the beating upon Jesus' head and spitting upon him in Mark 15:18 although the language remains similar. Other changes to be noted are the following. In v 27 Matthew inserts a favorite initial τότε, "then," and identifies the soldiers by the addition of τοῦ ἡγέμονος, "of the governor" (cf. Mark 15:16). In the same verse he substitutes συνήγαγον, "gathered together," for Mark's συγκαλοῦσιν, "called together." In v 28 Matthew inserts καὶ ἐκδύσαντες αὐτόν, "and they stripped him," prior to the reference to the robe that was put upon him, thereby replacing Mark's redundant ἐνδιδύσκουσιν αὐτόν, "they clothed him" (Mark 15:17). In the same place he substitutes χλαμύδα κοκκίνην, "red cloak," for Mark's πορφύραν, "purple (garment)." So too in v 31 Matthew substitutes χλαμύδα, "cloak," for πορφύραν, "purple" (Mark 15:20). Although Roman soldiers also were described as wearing "purple" cloaks (as in Mark), Matthew appears to think that "red" is more accurate. In v 29 Matthew adds the following information, curiously lacking but presupposed in Mark (cf. Mark 15:17, 19): ἐπέθηκαν ἐπὶ τῆς κεφαλῆς αὐτοῦ καὶ κάλαμον ἐν τῇ δεξιᾷ αὐτοῦ, "they placed it on his head and a staff in his right hand" (with the first half, cf. verbatim John 19:2). Finally, Matthew substitutes the more appropriate ἐνέπαιξαν, "mocked," for Mark's ἀσπάζεσθαι, "saluted" (Mark 15:18). Other very minor differences in wording need not be noted here.

C. The pericope is in the form of dramatic narrative consisting of a series of relatively short sentences linked with the repeated καί, "and." It may be outlined as follows: (1) Jesus before the Roman soldiers (v 27); (2) mockery of Jesus as the Jewish king (vv 28–29), divided further into (a) royal garment (v 28), (b) crown and scepter (v 29a), and (c) adulation (v 29b); (3) further physical abuse (v 30); and (4) Jesus' being led off to be crucified (v 31). The structural element that stands out and is central to the pericope is the mocking adulation: "Hail, King of the Jews" (v 29). In allusions to the present pericope, both the *Gos. Pet.* 6:8 (ἔθηκεν ἐπὶ τῆς κεφαλῆς αὐτοῦ, "they placed it upon his head") and *Barn.* 7:9 (τὸν κόκκινον, "the scarlet [garment]") show evidence of the knowledge of Matthew or at least of the underlying tradition.

### Comment

**27** The Roman soldiers who are now charged with the task of crucifying Jesus first bring him εἰς τὸ πραιτώριον, "into the praetorium," to make sport of him. The praetorium was the governor's official residence, probably the old palace of Herod the Great in the western part of the city but possibly the fortress Antonia just northwest of the temple (see BAGD, 697b for lit.). The statement that ὅλην τὴν σπεῖραν, "the whole cohort," gathered together around Jesus is probably hyperbolic. Technically a "cohort" consisted of 600 soldiers, although the number varied. It was, however, apparently a fairly large number of rough men who mocked Jesus with their crass humor.

**28–29** The soldiers had probably crucified many, but this man, because of the charges against him, would be the source of some extra fun. There is little reason to suspect the historicity of this scene, which has the ring of plausibility (for parallels, cf. Philo, *In Flaccum* 36–39; Dio Cassius, *Hist.* 15.20–21). They decided to dress Jesus like a king, and so they provided him with a robe, a crown, and a scepter. They took off his clothes (he had apparently been dressed again after his flogging [v 26]) and put on him one of the red cloaks (χλαμύδα κοκκίνην) that the Roman soldiers wore. This was his royal robe. For his crown they wove together branches with thorns and placed it on his head (perhaps decorative rather than torturous; see Bonner). And for a scepter, the other symbol of his rule, they placed in his right hand a κάλαμον, lit. "reed" but in the context (cf. v 30) more probably a wooden "staff" (cf. BAGD, 398b). Then they made obeisance to him as to a ruler, mockingly; i.e., they "fell down before him on their knees" (γονυπετήσαντες ἔμπροσθεν αὐτοῦ; the verb is used again in Matthew only in 17:14). The statement that ἐνέπαιξαν αὐτῷ, "they mocked him" (cf. vv 31, 41), is the fulfillment of Jesus' prophecy in 20:19 (cf. Ps 22:8). In their cry of mocking adulation, χαῖρε, βασιλεῦ τῶν Ἰουδαίων, "Hail, King of the Jews," the Roman soldiers, like Caiaphas (26:63) and Pilate (27:11), unwittingly speak the truth. For the greeting χαῖρε, "hail," see Judas' greeting of Jesus in Gethsemane (26:49).

**30–31** ἐμπτύσαντες εἰς αὐτόν, "when they had spat on him," recalls the same action of the Jews in 26:67–68 as does the soldiers' hitting Jesus in the head. The κάλαμον must be a wooden "staff" rather than a "reed" (cf. v 29) to make sense here. The acts perpetrated against Jesus mentioned here would have brought to the early church's remembrance a passage in the third servant song of Isaiah, viz. Isa 50:6: "I gave my back to those who struck me, and my cheeks to those who pulled out the beard; I did not hide my face from insult and spitting." When they were finished with their cruel play (for ἐνέπαιξαν αὐτῷ, "they mocked him," cf. v 29), the soldiers took off the cloak, clothed Jesus with his own garments (an exception to normal practice, probably for the sake of the sensitivities of the Jewish crowds in the city for the Feast of Passover), and they led him off to be crucified.

### Explanation

The Roman soldiers in their mocking cruelty provide Jesus with royal robe, crown, and scepter—the symbols of a kingly authority that are rightly his. These immature soldiers could not know that one day they would again kneel before and confess as exalted Lord (Phil 2:10–11) the very one whom they now sarcastically hailed as the "King of the Jews." Meanwhile, Jesus submits to their mockery without resistance, meekly and mildly, determined to fulfill the will of his Father. His experience of humanity in all of its fallenness must have brought a deeper realization of the meaning of his mission on the cross.

# The Crucifixion   (27:32–37)

### Bibliography

**Bammel, E.** "Crucifixion as a Punishment in Palestine." In *The Trial of Jesus.* FS C. F. D. Moule, ed. E. Bammel. SBT 2.13. London: SCM, 1970. 162–65. ———. "The *titulus.*" In

*Jesus and the Politics of His Day,* ed. E. Bammel and C. F. D. Moule. Cambridge: Cambridge UP, 1984. 353–64. **Bishop, E. F. F.** "Simon and Lucius: Where Did They Come From?" *ExpTim* 51 (1939–40) 148–53. **Brandenburger, E.** *"Stauros,* Kreuzigung Jesu und Kreuzestheologie." *WD* 10 (1969) 17–43. **Buhlmann, W.** "Die Kreuzigung Jesu." *HL* 9 (1981) 3–12. **Cantinat, J.** "Le crucifiement de Jésus." *VSpir* 84 (1951) 142–53. **Charlesworth, J. H.** "Jesus and Jehohanan: An Archaeological Note on Crucifixion." *ExpTim* 84 (1972–73) 147–50. **Fitzmyer, J. A.** "Crucifixion in Ancient Palestine, Qumran Literature, and the New Testament." *CBQ* 40 (1978) 493–513. **Fuller, R. C.** "The Drink Offered to Christ at Calvary." *Scr* 2 (1947) 114–15. **Gese, H.** "Psalm 22 und das Neue Testament." *ZTK* 65 (1968) 1–22. **Hengel, M.** *Crucifixion in the Ancient World and the Folly of the Message of the Cross.* Philadelphia: Fortress, 1977. **Hewitt, J. W.** "The Use of Nails in the Crucifixion." *HTR* 25 (1932) 29–46. **Jeremias, J.** *Golgotha.* Leipzig: Pfeiffer, 1926. **Kuhn, H.-W.** "Die Kreuzesstraf während der frühen Kaiserzeit: Ihre Wirklichkeit und Wertung in der Umwelt des Urchristentums." *ANRW* 2.25.1 (1982) 648–793. **Lee, G. M.** "The Inscription on the Cross." *PEQ* 100 (1968) 144. **O'Rahilly, A.** "The Title on the Cross." *Irish Ecclesiastical Record* 65 (1945) 289–97. **Osborne, G. R.** "Redactional Trajectories in the Crucifixion Narrative." *EvQ* 51 (1979) 80–96. **Parrot, A.** *Golgotha and the Church of the Holy Sepulchre.* Tr. E. Hudson. London: SCM, 1957. **Reumann, J. H.** "Psalm 22 at the Cross." *Int* 28 (1974) 39–58. **Riesner, R.** "Golgotha und die Archäologie." *BK* 40 (1985) 21–26. **Schneider, G.** "Die theologische Sicht des Todes Jesu in den Kreuzigungsberichten der Evangelien." *TPQ* 126 (1978) 14–22. **Taylor, V.** "The Narrative of the Crucifixion." *NTS* 8 (1961–62) 333–34. **Tzaferis, V.** "Crucifixion: The Archaeological Evidence." *BARev* 11 (1985) 44–53. **Unnik, W. C. van.** "Der Fluch der Gekreuzigten." In *Theologia Crucis—Signum Crucis.* FS E. Dinkler, ed. C. Andresen and G. Klein. Tübingen: Mohr, 1979. 483–99. **Vogt, J.** "Crucifixion etiam pro nobis: Historische Anmerkungen zum Kreuzestod." *Internationale kirchliche Zeitschrift* 2 (1973) 186–91. **Wansbrough, H.** "The Crucifixion of Jesus." *Clergy Review* 56 (1971) 251–61. **Willcock, J.** "'When he had tasted' (Matt. xxvii.34)." *ExpTim* 32 (1920–21) 426. **Yadin, Y.** "Epigraphy and Crucifixion." *IEJ* 23 (1973) 19–22. **Zias, J.,** and **Charlesworth, J. H.** "Crucifixion: Archaeology, Jesus, and the Dead Sea Scrolls." In *Jesus and the Dead Sea Scrolls,* ed. J. H. Charlesworth. New York: Doubleday, 1992. 273–89. **Zias, J.,** and **Sekeles, E.** "The Crucified Man from Giv'at ha-Mivtar: A Reappraisal." *IEJ* (1985) 22–27.

## Translation

[32]*And as they came out, they found a man from Cyrene* [a] *named Simon. They forced this man to carry his cross.*

[33]*And when they came to a place called Golgotha, that is, called* [b] *the "Place of the Skull,"* [34]*they gave him wine* [c] *mixed with gall to drink. And when he tasted it, he did not want to drink it.* [d] [35]*And when they crucified him, they divided his garments, casting lots for them,* [e] [36]*and they sat down and were watching him there.* [37]*And they placed above his head his crime in writing:* [f] *THIS IS JESUS THE KING OF THE JEWS.*

## Notes

[a] D it vg^mss insert εἰς ἀπάντησιν αὐτοῦ, "to meet him," to be taken with the initial participle ἐξερχόμενοι, "coming out" (for the construction, cf. 25:6). MS 33 has ἐρχόμενον ἀπ' ἀγροῦ, "coming from a field," by the influence of the parallel Mark 15:21.

[b] א¹ D Γ Θ lat sa bo lack λεγόμενος, "called," perhaps because of its occurrence six words earlier.

[c] Many MSS (A W TR sy^{p.h} mae bo^{mss}) read ὄξος, "vinegar," perhaps through the influence of Ps 69:21 (a psalm that in other respects was widely regarded as anticipating the crucifixion narrative).

[d] "It" added in translation, supplying the direct object.

<sup>e</sup> "For them" added to translation to complete the sense (892* sy* co? supply ἐπ' αὐτά, "for them"; cf. Mark 15:24). Δ Θ *f*<sup>1,13</sup> it vg<sup>cl</sup> sy<sup>h</sup> mae insert ἵνα πληρωθῇ τὸ ῥηθὲν διὰ [ὑπό, *f*<sup>1,13</sup>] τοῦ προφήτου· διεμερίσαντο [-σαν, Θ] τὰ ἱμάτιά μου ἑαυτοῖς, καὶ ἐπὶ τὸν ἱματισμόν μου ἔβαλον κλῆρον, "in order that the word spoken through [by] the prophet might be fulfilled: 'They divided my garments for them-selves, and for my clothing they cast lots,'" almost certainly through the influence of John 19:24, with a Matthean introductory formula added (the quotation is from Ps 22:18). A slight possibility exists that this material was omitted through homoioteleuton (κλῆρον, end of v 35—κλῆρον, end of inserted quotation), yet the MS evidence is overwhelmingly against its inclusion. *TCGNT,* 69.

<sup>f</sup> τὴν αἰτία αὐτοῦ γεγραμμένην, lit. "the charge against him written."

## Form/Structure/Setting

A. After two trials and two mockings, the climax, or the first of several climaxes, of the narrative is reached in the crucifixion itself. Especially noteworthy is the restraint of the text. No sensationalism or emotionalism hinders the account. The horrible deed of the crucifixion is itself mentioned only by means of a subordi-nate participle, almost as if in passing. Matthew allows himself two more pericopes (vv 38–44; 45–50) before he records the death of Jesus.

B. In this pericope Matthew continues his practice of following Mark closely (Mark 15:21–26; cf. Luke 22:33–34; John 19:17b–19). Matthew makes only two substantial omissions of Markan material. First, Matthew in v 32 omits Mark's fur-ther information about Simon the Cyrenian, ἐρχόμενον ἀπ' ἀγροῦ, τὸν πατέρα Ἀλεξάνδρου καὶ Ῥούφου, "coming from a field, the father of Alexander and Rufus" (Mark 15:21), probably regarding it as superfluous, although the first part might have been thought to involve something improper on the day of the feast. Sec-ond, in v 36 Matthew omits Mark's ἐπ' αὐτὰ τίς τί ἄρῃ, "for them, who would take what" (Mark 15:24), perhaps regarding this as obvious, and the immediately fol-lowing sentence, ἦν δὲ ὥρα τρίτη καὶ ἐσταύρωσαν αὐτόν, "and it was the third hour, and they crucified him" (Mark 15:25), perhaps because the crucifixion has been mentioned as already having taken place in the participle σταυρώσαντες, "having crucified," at the beginning of v 35. On the other hand, Matthew makes the following additions. In v 34 he adds πιεῖν, "to drink," which is understood in Mark 15:23, and καὶ γευσάμενος, "and when he had tasted (it)," thus providing a reason for his refusal to drink. The whole of v 36 is also added: καὶ καθήμενοι ἐτήρουν αὐτὸν ἐκεῖ, "and sitting down, they were watching him there," which takes the place of the omitted Mark 15:25 and prepares for subsequent references to the soldiers. In v 37 Matthew adds καὶ ἐπέθηκαν ἐπάνω τῆς κεφαλῆς αὐτοῦ, "and they placed above his head," indicating the exact place of the sign, and to the words that were written on the sign Matthew adds οὗτός ἐστιν Ἰησοῦς, "this is Jesus," making more of a declarative statement. A few other alterations to be noted are: Matthew's general recasting of the opening sentence (v 32; cf. Mark 15:21) together with the use of εὖρον, "they found," and the omission of Mark's παράγοντά τινα, "a certain passerby"; in v 33 the substitution of ἐλθόντες, "having come," for φέρουσιν αὐτόν, "they bring him," and λεγόμενος, "called," for μεθερμηνευόμενον, "being interpreted"; in v 34 the substitution of μετὰ χολῆς μεμιγμένον, "mixed with gall," for ἐσμυρνισμένον, "mixed with myrrh" (Mark 15:23), in order to bring about agreement with Ps 69:22; and finally in v 35 the use of the subordinate participle σταυρώσαντες, "having crucified," for Mark's finite verb σταυροῦσιν, "they crucified," thereby avoiding the direct statement.

C. Structurally, it is remarkable that the two central events of the pericope, the arrival at Golgotha and the crucifixion itself, are stated not in main clauses but in subordinate participial clauses. In each instance, the emphasis of the main clause involves the fulfillment of OT anticipation, i.e., in the giving of wine and gall to Jesus (Ps 69:21) and in the dividing of his garments by the casting of lots (Ps 22:18). The superscription, "This is Jesus the King of the Jews," has a climactic effect in its irony. The following outline may be suggested: (1) Simon's conscription to bear the cross (v 32); (2) Jesus' declining the drink at Golgotha (vv 33–34); (3) the guards' dividing of his garments (vv 35–36); and (4) the superscription on the cross (v 37). Both *Gos. Pet.* 15 and *Barn.* 7:3, 5 allude to Matthew in their mention of χολή, "gall," given to Jesus to drink (found only in Matthew's account).

### Comment

**32**  ἐξερχόμενοι, "as they came out," refers either to coming out of the praetorium or coming out of the city, i.e., outside the city wall (cf. Mark 15:21, where Simon is described as "coming in from the field," and *Comment* on v 33). The man named Simon (a very common first-century Jewish name) was a Jew originally from Cyrene in North Africa. He may have been either a settler in Jerusalem (where there was a synagogue attended by Cyrenians; cf. Acts 6:9) or a pilgrim there for the festival of Passover. This man, encountered by accident, ἠγγάρευσαν, "they forced," to carry the heavy wooden cross, perhaps only the crossbeam rather than the entire cross, which Jesus was apparently unable to carry after the scourging he had received. The verb ἀγγαρεύειν has the semi-technical meaning "to press into service" (cf. 5:41), which the Roman soldiers apparently could require of any person they encountered. A tradition later arose that this Simon (= Simeon called Niger in Acts 13:1?) eventually became a Christian (cf. the mention in Mark 15:21 of his two sons with the common names Alexander and Rufus, the latter of which *may* be referred to in Rom. 16:13; cf. *Acts of Peter and Andrew* 1, 4).

**33–34**  The name Γολγοθᾶ, "Golgotha," is the transliteration (but with two unexpected omicrons for vowels as well as a missing lambda) of the Aramaic word for "skull," גֻּלְגָּלְתָּא, *gulgultā'*. A Greek translation of the word as a place name is given in the Greek Κρανίου Τόπος, "Place of the Skull" (Latin for "skull" is *calvaria*, from which "Calvary" is derived). It refers obviously to a place where executions were carried out, perhaps a skull-shaped knoll, although its exact location just outside the city wall has long been debated. It is much more probable, however, that it was located where the present Church of the Holy Sepulcher is located (see Riesner) than in the area where the so-called Garden (Gordon's) Tomb is located. Although inside the city wall (the so-called third wall) since the time of Herod Agrippa I, the former location was outside the wall at the time of the crucifixion. Crucifixion was performed alongside main thoroughfares so that many might be terrified by the warning (note the passersby in v 39). When they arrived at the site, Jesus was offered a drink of οἶνον μετὰ χολῆς μεμιγμένον, "wine mixed with gall." χολή, "gall," refers to something bitter tasting and can on occasion mean something poisonous. Probably this particular word was chosen because of an intended allusion to the first line of the LXX of Ps 68:22 (MT 69:21;

the word is translated "poison" by NRSV even though bread, not wine, is in view). The evangelist is thereby able to bring about agreement with both lines of Ps 69:21, the second line finding its fulfillment in the wine of v 48. The wine here is therefore perhaps to be distinguished from the drugged wine, the wine mixed with myrrh (Mark 15:23), generally offered to a person before crucifixion in order to deaden the senses and lessen the pain. The offering of this wine involves cruelty and mockery consistent with the context of the Ps 69 reference (see R. E. Brown, *Death of the Messiah*, 942–44; Moo, *Old Testament in the Gospel Passion Narratives*, 249–52). When Jesus tasted the wine and discovered that it was bitter, he refused to drink it.

**35–36** Matthew refuses to dwell on the details of the crucifixion. Even his mention of the crucifixion itself is made only by means of an introductory, subordinate participle, $\sigma\tau\alpha\upsilon\rho\acute{\omega}\sigma\alpha\nu\tau\epsilon\varsigma$ $\delta\grave{\epsilon}$ $\alpha\mathring{\upsilon}\tau\acute{o}\nu$, "and when they had crucified him." (For information on crucifixion, see Bammel; Hengel; Fitzmyer; Kuhn; R. E. Brown, *Death of the Messiah*, 945–52; on the pre-70 skeletal remains of a crucified man found in a private tomb at Giv'at ha-Mivtar northeast of Jerusalem, see Charlesworth; Zias and Charlesworth; Tzaferis; Yadin.) The attention is focused not on Jesus' sufferings on the cross, which, however, cannot be far from the readers' minds, but upon the activity of the soldiers at the foot of the cross who unknowingly fulfill what the scriptures anticipated. Although Matthew does not use a fulfillment formula, there can be no question but that in keeping with his practice elsewhere he could have. The use of the language of the LXX (21:19) of Ps 22:18 is deliberate: $\delta\iota\epsilon\mu\epsilon\rho\acute{\iota}\sigma\alpha\nu\tau o$ $\tau\grave{\alpha}$ $\acute{\iota}\mu\acute{\alpha}\tau\iota\alpha$ $\alpha\mathring{\upsilon}\tau o\hat{\upsilon}$, "they divided his garments," is verbatim from the LXX, except for the LXX's first person $\mu o\upsilon$, "my [garments]"; $\beta\acute{\alpha}\lambda\lambda o\nu\tau\epsilon\varsigma$ [LXX: $\acute{\epsilon}\beta\alpha\lambda o\nu$, "they cast"] $\kappa\lambda\hat{\eta}\rho o\nu$, "casting lots," is also nearly verbatim from the LXX (cf. John 19:23–25, which elaborates the tradition and provides a fulfillment formula quotation of the LXX's Ps 21:19 verbatim). This is the first of a series of allusions to Ps 22 in Matthew's passion narrative (cf. vv 39, 42–43, 46). On the importance of Ps 22 to the passion narrative, see Reumann; Gese. Matthew's unusual addition: $\kappa\alpha\grave{\iota}$ $\kappa\alpha\theta\acute{\eta}\mu\epsilon\nu o\iota$ $\acute{\epsilon}\tau\acute{\eta}\rho o\upsilon\nu$ $\alpha\mathring{\upsilon}\tau\grave{o}\nu$ $\acute{\epsilon}\kappa\epsilon\hat{\iota}$, "and sitting down, they were watching him there," suggests more than just the fulfillment of duty (lest his disciples remove him from the cross before he died), implying already something unusual about this victim, and may prepare the way for the confession of v 54.

**37** It was apparently the custom in some instances to include on a placard nailed to the cross the crime for which a person had been executed, perhaps because of its inhibitory impact upon others. $\acute{\epsilon}\pi\acute{\alpha}\nu\omega$ $\tau\hat{\eta}\varsigma$ $\kappa\epsilon\phi\alpha\lambda\hat{\eta}\varsigma$ $\alpha\mathring{\upsilon}\tau o\hat{\upsilon}$, "above his head," indicates incidentally that Jesus was crucified on the traditional, rather than a T-shaped, cross. $\tau\grave{\eta}\nu$ $\alpha\grave{\iota}\tau\acute{\iota}\alpha\nu$ $\alpha\mathring{\upsilon}\tau o\hat{\upsilon}$, "the charge against him," uses a technical legal expression for the ground of the conviction (cf. the use of the word in John 18:38b; 19:4; Acts 13:28; 28:18). The charge itself, written in the superscription, $o\mathring{\upsilon}\tau\acute{o}\varsigma$ $\acute{\epsilon}\sigma\tau\iota\nu$ $\acute{I}\eta\sigma o\hat{\upsilon}\varsigma$ $\acute{o}$ $\beta\alpha\sigma\iota\lambda\epsilon\grave{\upsilon}\varsigma$ $\tau\hat{\omega}\nu$ $\acute{I}o\upsilon\delta\alpha\acute{\iota}\omega\nu$, "This is Jesus the King of the Jews," reflects the question of Pilate and Jesus' affirmative answer in v 11, and thus from the Roman perspective the crime was a political one, probably perceived as treason or insurrection (all four Gospels agree at least in the words "king of the Jews"). To the Jews, on the other hand, the title had a distinctly religious ring, for it pointed to the Messiah as Son of David (cf. the question of

Caiaphas in 26:63 and Jesus' affirmative answer; the protest of the chief priests to the superscription recorded in John 19:21 is particularly revealing in this respect). At the end of the crucifixion pericope the superscription stands as a declaration of the crime for which Jesus is executed and, paradoxically, as a statement of the truth: this Jesus is the king of the Jews.

### Explanation

Matthew records this momentous event in a remarkably matter-of-fact way. His focus is on how even incidental occurrences connected with the crucifixion are the fulfillment of scripture and thus the will of God. Without intending to do so, the soldiers fulfilled a higher plan and purpose. And the indictment they wrote in mockery, "This is Jesus the King of the Jews," ironically, could not have been truer. Mysteriously it is the Jewish Messiah, the Lord of all, who has been crucified like a common criminal and who hangs upon the cross in helpless agony. A divine drama is being enacted before the very eyes of the Roman soldiers, a drama of which they remain totally oblivious. A turning point in the ages has been reached, the accomplishment of the salvation of the world, while the soldiers like blind fools vie for the garments of the man they have crucified. What they perceive as but the death of another criminal is in reality the accomplishment of a sacrifice that will atone for the sins of the world (cf. 1:21; 20:28; 26:28)—including theirs!—and thus remedy the fundamental malaise that has troubled all humanity of every era. It is a wondrous narrative filled with paradoxes when read by Christian eyes.

# Mocking of the Crucified One (27:38–44)

### Bibliography

**Aytoun, R. A.** "'Himself He cannot save' (Ps. xxii 29 and Mark xv 31)." *JTS* 21 (1919–20) 245–48. **Daube, D.** "The Veil of the Temple." In *The New Testament and Rabbinic Judaism.* London: Athlone, 1956. 23–26. **Donaldson, T. L.** "The Mockers and the Son of God (Matthew 27.37–44): Two Characters in Matthew's Story of Jesus." *JSNT* 41 (1991) 3–18.

### Translation

[38] *Then they crucified two thieves with him, one on his right hand* [a] *and one on his left.* [39] *Those passing by were blaspheming him, shaking their heads* [40] *and saying: "You, the one who would destroy the temple and in three days rebuild it,* [b] *save yourself, if you are the Son of God, [and]* [c] *come down from the cross."* [41] *In a similar way the chief priests with the scribes and elders* [d] *were also mocking him and saying:* [42] *"He saved others, but he is unable to save himself.* [e] *He is the king of Israel;* [f] *let him now come down from the cross and we will believe* [g] *in him.* [43] *'He* [h] *trusted in God; let him now deliver*

*him,*[i] *if he delights in him.' For he said: 'I am the Son of God.'"* [44]*And the thieves who had been crucified with him chided him in the same manner also.*

## Notes

[a] The relatively late Latin MS c (Colbertinus, 12th–13th cent.) identifies the two thieves by name: on his right, *nomine Zoatham*, and on his left, *nomine Camma.* Other Old Latin MSS provide different names at Luke 23:32, as does *Acts of Pilate* 9.4.

[b] ὁ καταλύων τὸν ναὸν καὶ ἐν τρισὶν ἡμέραις οἰκοδομῶν, lit. "the (one) destroying the temple and in three days building (it)."

[c] Many MSS (ℵ² B L W Θ *f*[1,13] TR lat sy[h] co?) omit καί, "and." Those including it are ℵ* A D it sy[(s).p]. It may have been accidentally omitted because of the κατ- beginning the next word, or it may have been inserted by someone who took the preceding clause, "if you are the Son of God," as modifying the preceding words, "save yourself." Because of this difficulty, the word is kept but in brackets. *TCGNT*, 69.

[d] D W it sy[s] read Φαρισαίων, "Pharisees." Many MSS (TR sy[p,h] bo[pt]) add Φαρισαίων to πρεσβυτέρων, "elders." Γ has neither word, probably by the influence of the parallel in Mark 15:31.

[e] ἑαυτὸν οὐ δύναται σῶσαι can also be understood as a question: "Is he unable to save himself?"

[f] Many MSS (A W Θ *f*[1,13] TR lat sy mae bo) insert εἰ, "if," at the beginning of the sentence. But ℵ B D L 33 do not have the word. Metzger suggests that it may have been added by copyists who missed the irony (*TCGNT*, 70).

[g] Some MSS (ℵ L W Γ Δ Θ *f*[13] 33) have πιστεύσωμεν, "(that) we might believe in him," probably by the influence of the parallel in Mark 15:32.

[h] D Θ *f*[1] it co insert εἰ, "if," probably to imply that he did not trust in God, ignoring the allusion to Ps 22:8.

[i] "Him" added to translation, supplying the direct object. Many MSS (A[*vid] D W Θ *f*[1,13] TR lat) do include αὐτόν, "him." Although the pronoun, which is unnecessary in the Gr., could have been deleted by an Alexandrian editor, the *UBSGNT* committee thought it more likely that it was added through the influence of the LXX passage (LXX Ps 21:9). *TCGNT*, 70.

## Form/Structure/Setting

A. The taunting of Jesus on the cross is the last human indignity he must face. In this pericope the motif of sarcastic unbelief continues. Perhaps the taunts and challenges also presented Jesus with his last hour of testing. A line of continuity runs from the testing of Jesus in the wilderness (4:1–11) through the rebuke of Peter (16:22–23) and the experience in Gethsemane (26:36–56) to the present narrative. Jesus could at any moment have refused to go on the path God had predetermined for him. He could have come down from the cross and thus at the last instant avoided his fate. Still, ironically, his opponents have no idea who he really is and that he *could* have come down from the cross.

B. Matthew follows his Markan source very closely in the present pericope (Mark 15:27–32; cf. Luke 23:35–39). Apart from very minor changes and differences in word order, the following is a complete list of departures from Mark. In v 38 Matthew replaces Mark's καί, "and" (Mark 15:27), with his own favored τότε, "then." In v 40 Matthew omits Mark's emotive οὐά, "aha" (Mark 15:29), at the beginning of the words of those passing by. In the same verse he inserts εἰ υἱὸς εἶ τοῦ θεοῦ, "if you are the Son of God," thereby sharpening both the mockery and the irony. In v 41 Matthew omits Mark's πρὸς ἀλλήλους, "to one another" (Mark 15:31), regarding it as unnecessary, and in the same verse he inserts καὶ πρεσβυτέρων, "and elders," a group he has referred to quite consistently in the passion narrative, providing here complete representation of the Sanhedrin. In v

42 Matthew omits ὁ Χριστός, "the Messiah" (Mark 15:32), perhaps wanting to refer only to the title included on the *titulus* above Jesus' head (v 37), and supplies the verb ἐστίν, "is," understood by Mark. The OT quotation of v 43 is unique to Matthew. And finally, in v 44 Matthew inserts τὸ δ' αὐτὸ καὶ οἱ λῃσταί, "and the same also the thieves" (cf. Mark 15:32), thus resuming the subject of v 38 and making it easier for the reader to realize the identity of these last mockers.

C. Again this pericope consists of historical narrative. Now, however, the focus falls upon the mocking words that are spoken either to or concerning the crucified Jesus. The following serves as an outline: (1) two thieves crucified with Jesus (v 38); (2) the mockery of those passing by (vv 39–40); (3) the mockery of the Jewish authorities (vv 41–43); and (4) the mockery of the thieves (v 44). Clearly we encounter a deliberate pattern of three mockeries. In the case of the thieves' mockery, it is only noted that they said τὸ αὐτό, "the same thing." In the case of those passing by and the Jewish authorities, however, the content of the mockery is spelled out. Note the similarity between what is said by both groups (cf. ὁμοίως, "similarly" [v 41]). Again a basic threefold pattern becomes clear: (1) "save yourself"/"unable to save himself" (vv 40, 41), (2) "son of God"/"king of Israel" (vv 40, 42), and (3) "come down from the cross" (vv 40, 42). The mockery of the Jewish authorities is extended by the quotation of Ps 22:8 and the concluding and climactic statement "For he said: 'I am the Son of God'" (v 43; cf. "if you are the Son of God" in v 40). Justin Martyr reflects a knowledge of Matthew in his allusion to the Psalm quotation of v 43 in *Dial.* 101.3 and *Apol.* 1.38.6–8.

## Comment

**38**   The mention of the two "thieves" or "bandits" (λῃσταί, perhaps "insurrectionists"; used elsewhere in Matthew in v 44; 21:13; 26:55) crucified (the vividness of Mark's historical present tense is retained here by Matthew) with Jesus prepares the way for the reference to their joining in with the mockery of Jesus in v 44. It recalls Jesus' statement about the Jewish authorities coming to arrest him as though he were a "thief" (26:55), and the early church undoubtedly thought of the words of Isa 53:12, "he was numbered with the transgressors," when they described Jesus with a thief on either side of him. The incongruity of this righteous man crucified between two nefarious criminals is striking.

**39–40**   When it is said that those passing by ἐβλασφήμουν αὐτόν, lit. "they were blaspheming him," what is meant is probably not blasphemy in the technical sense but that they were "reviling" or "deriding" (so NSRV) him. They were κινοῦντες τὰς κεφαλὰς αὐτῶν, "shaking their heads," in disapproving scorn, a further allusion to Ps 22 (LXX 21:8), the next verse of which will be quoted in v 43 (cf. Ps 109:25; Lam 2:15; Jer 18:16). Their reference to Jesus as ὁ καταλύων τὸν ναὸν καὶ ἐν τρισὶν ἡμέραις οἰκοδομῶν, "the one destroying the temple and in three days building it," is precisely the charge brought against Jesus in 26:61 (see *Comment* there). The truth of the metaphor will be realized in the death and resurrection of Jesus. The passersby, assumed to be Jews, may have picked up knowledge of the charge against Jesus (partly evident from the *titulus*) as well as the claim about being the Son of God from conversations with others watching the spectacle. To those passersby Jesus was no more than a charlatan. εἰ υἱὸς εἶ τοῦ θεοῦ, "if you are the Son of God," echoes verbatim the repeated clause in the temptation narrative (cf. 4:3, 6) as well as the question of the high priest (26:63), and it anticipates the statement at the end of v 43. If Jesus is the Son of God and capable of miracles, he must surely be able to save himself and to come down from the cross. Implicit in the words σῶσον σεαυτόν, "save yourself," and the words κατάβηθι ἀπὸ τοῦ σταυροῦ, "come down from the cross," is, of course, the belief that such things are impossible (cf. the οὐ δύναται, "he is not able," of v 42). And behind that lies the assumption that something so unspeakable could never happen to one who was truly the Messiah, the Son of God (cf. 16:22).

**41–42** The Jewish authorities, now identified by Matthew as including οἱ ἀρχιερεῖς . . . μετὰ τῶν γραμματέων καὶ πρεσβυτέρων, "the chief priests . . . with the scribes and elders," mock Jesus ὁμοίως, "in a similar way." While the chief priests and elders figure prominently in the passion narrative, the scribes or "scripture scholars" are mentioned only here and in 26:57. It is not necessary to conclude that these men were at the crucifixion scene; their mocking may well have been behind closed doors where they were no doubt congratulating themselves on their success in being rid of Jesus for good. The verb ἐμπαίζοντες, "mocking," is used earlier in the passion narrative in vv 29, 31 (cf. 20:19). The words ἄλλους ἔσωσεν, "he saved others," in the mouth of the Jewish authorities must be an allusion to the healing ministry of Jesus (cf. 9:21–22 for σώζειν in this sense). Matthew's readers, however, would not have missed the irony that it was in not saving himself that he *was* saving others (cf. σώζειν as used in 1:21). The unbelief underlying ἑαυτὸν οὐ δύναται σῶσαι, "himself he is not able to save," must also underlie the following words βασιλεὺς Ἰσραήλ ἐστιν, "he is the king of Israel" (for the title, cf. Zeph 3:15), which were written on the *titulus* (v 37) with the Jewish substitute of "Israel" for "the Jews." These words are to be understood sarcastically. As in v 40, so here too the issue raised in the trial before Caiaphas is again raised. As with those who passed by (cf. v 40), so here too the challenge is "let him come down from the cross." Let him do that one miracle καὶ πιστεύσομεν ἐπ᾽ αὐτόν, "and we will believe in him" (note the Pauline formula; e.g., Rom 4:24; 9:33; 10:11). The claim is hardly a true one. So set were they against him that had he come down from the cross they might well have charged him with sorcery (which, indeed, was their explanation of his miracles; cf. 10:25; 12:24). Indeed, when confronted with an even greater miracle in the resurrection, they demonstrated how deep and immovable their unbelief was (cf. 28:11–15; Luke 16:31). For Jesus, to have come down from the cross would have been to bypass the will of God, a temptation he had already faced and overcome in Gethsemane (26:39, 42, 44). At the same time, it would have contradicted Jesus' own repeated exhortation to his disciples to take up their cross and face death squarely (e.g., 10:38–39; 16:24–26). The point is not that Jesus *could* not come down from the cross but that he *would* not because he had freely chosen to follow his Father's will (Gerhardsson). Jesus becomes "the enthroned Son" because he remains "the obedient Son of Israel" (thus Donaldson).

**43** Without introductory formula, perhaps because the verse is quoted misleadingly, words very close to Ps 22:8 (LXX Ps 21:9) are appealed to by the Jewish leaders: πέποιθεν [LXX: ἤλπισεν] ἐπὶ τὸν θεόν [LXX: κύριον] · ῥυσάσθω [LXX adds: αὐτόν] νῦν εἰ [LXX: ὅτι] θέλει αὐτόν, "he has trusted [LXX: hoped] in God [LXX:

the Lord], let him deliver [LXX adds: him] now if [LXX: because] he wants him."
If the Christians can appeal to Ps 22 as prefiguring the suffering of Christ (cf. the
centrally important quotation of Ps 22:1 in v 46), then the opponents of Christ can
now quote the same psalm. From their perspective the words seemed to have a
degree of plausibility, regardless of the fact to which they seem oblivious, that in
the psalm they are also spoken mockingly by the taunters of the righteous one who
suffers. It is generally true from the perspective of the scriptures that they who
trust in God may have confidence that God will deliver them (cf. the close connections of Wis 2:18–20 with the present verse). For the moment, however, and by the
clear will of God, in this unique situation there is no deliverance. If, however, one
looks forward to the resurrection, one may say that God did indeed deliver him in
a greater deliverance—from death (cf. Heb 5:7 for just this perspective)—and that
thus the objection of the mockers amounts to nothing. It is perhaps the last words
of the quotation, "if he wants him," or more suggestively (from the Hebrew), "if he
delights in him," that prompts the final words εἶπεν γὰρ ὅτι θεοῦ εἰμι υἱός, "for he
said: 'I am the Son of God!'" (The word "if" reflects a possible translation of the
Hebrew כִּי, kî.) It is pre-eminently the Son of God, the one in whom God delights
(cf. 3:17; 17:5), whom he will preserve (this is the point of the tempter's argument
in 4:5–6). It was before these same Jewish leaders that Jesus in response to Caiaphas'
question admitted to being the Son of God (26:63; in the present chapter, see vv
40, 54; cf. 14:33; 16:16 for the disciples' confession; see *Comment* on 16:16).

**44** As a final indignity in this extended mockery scene, even the thieves who
had been crucified on either side of Jesus joined in the derision (ὀνειδίζειν, lit.
"reproach," occurs elsewhere in Matthew in 5:11; 11:20). Among the four evangelists only Luke expands on the incongruity of the thieves' participation in the
mocking (Luke 23:39–41, where indeed only one thief is said to deride Jesus).

### Explanation

Throughout this pericope, as in the preceding pericopes, the underlying paradox cannot be missed. What these mockers scornfully ridicule, what they regard
as impossible, what they look upon as the wild claim of a charlatan is paradoxically the truth. The words with which they so confidently taunt Jesus, "Son of
God," "king of Israel," are fully true, as the original readers of Matthew knew
well. The key piece of information unknown to the mockers is that Jesus under-
goes in his humiliation and crucifixion nothing other than the intended will of
God. Their notion of the Son of God, the messianic king of Israel, as a triumphant, self-assertive, and powerful figure was mistaken—or at least partially so
since he will ultimately appear as such in his future parousia. They cannot guess
that they are speaking the truth about Jesus. In their blind opposition to the truth,
they but accomplish the will of God.

# The Death of Jesus (27:45–50)

*Bibliography*

**Baker, N. B.** "The Cry of Dereliction." *ExpTim* 70 (1958–59) 54–55. **Bligh, J.** "Christ's Death Cry." *HeyJ* 1 (1960) 142–46. **Blight, W.** "The Cry of Dereliction." *ExpTim* 68 (1956–57) 285. **Blinzler, J.** "Ist Jesus am Kreuz gestorben?" *Glaube und Leben* 10 (1954) 562–76. **Boman, T.** "Das letzte Wort Jesu." *ST* 17 (1963) 103–19. **Brower, K.** "Elijah in the Markan Passion Narrative." *JSNT* 18 (1983) 85–101. **Buckler, F. W.** "Eli, Eli, Lama Sabachthani?" *AJSL* 55 (1938) 378–91. **Cohn-Sherbok, D.** "Jesus' Cry on the Cross: An Alternative View." *ExpTim* 93 (1982) 215–17. **Danker, F. W.** "The Demonic Secret in Mark: A Reexamination of the Cry of Dereliction (15, 34)." *ZNW* 61 (1970) 48–69. **Deissler, A.** "'Mein Gott, warum hast du mich verlassen . . . !' (Ps 22, 2): Das Reden zu Gott und von Gott in den Psalmen—am Beispiel von Psalm 22." In *"Ich will euer Gott werden": Beispiele biblischen Redens von Gott*, ed. H. Merklein and E. Zenger. SBS 100. Stuttgart: Katholisches Bibelwerk, 1981. 97–121. **Delamare, J.** "Les sept paroles de Christ en croix." *VSpir* 88 (1953) 254–71. **Duquoc, C.** "L'abandonné." In *Christologie: Essai dogmatique*. Paris: Cerf, 1972. 39–51. **Edwards, W. D., Gabel, W. J.,** and **Hosmer, F. E.** "On the Physical Death of Jesus Christ." *Journal of the American Medical Association* 255 (1986) 1455–63. **Eichrodt, O.** "'Mein Gott' in Alten Testament." *ZAW* 61 (1945–46) 3–16. **Floris, É.** "L'abandon de Jésus et la mort de Dieu." *ETR* 42 (1967) 277–98. **Gnilka, J.** "Mein Gott, mein Gott, warum hast du mich verlassen? (Mk 15,34 Par.)." *BZ* 3 (1959) 294–97. **Guichard, D.** "La reprise du Psaume 22 dans le récit de la mort de Jésus." *FV* 87 (1988) 59–65. **Guillaume, A.** "Mt. XXVII,46 in Light of the Dead Sea Scroll of Isaiah." *PEQ* 83 (1951) 78–81. **Hasenzahl, W.** *Die Gottverlassenheit des Christus nach dem Kreuzeswort bei Matthäus und Markus und das christologische Verständnis des griechisches Psalters: Eine exegetische Studie.* BFCT 39. Gütersloh: Bertelsman, 1938. **Holzmeister, U.** "Die Finsternis beim Tode Jesu." *Bib* 22 (1941) 404–11. **Johnson, S. L., Jr.** "The Death of Christ (Mt. 27:45–46)." *BSac* 125 (1968) 10–19. **Johnston, J.** "The Words from the Cross—IV. The Cry of Desolation." *ExpTim* 41 (1929–30) 281–83. **Kenneally, W. J.** "Eli, Eli, Lamma Sabacthani? (Mt. 27:46)." *CBQ* 8 (1946) 124–34. **Killermann, S.** "Die Finsternis beim Tode Jesu." *TGl* 23 (1941) 165–66. **Lacan, M.-F.** "Mon Dieu, mon Dieu, pourquoi? (Mt 27,46)." *LumVie* 66 (1964) 33–53. **Lange, H. D.** "The Relationship between Psalm 22 and the Passion Narrative." *CTM* 48 (1972) 610–21. **Lange, J.** "Zur Ausgestaltung der Szene vom Sterben Jesu in den synoptischen Evangelien." In *Biblische Randbemerkungen.* FS R. Schnackenburg, ed. H. Merklein and J. Lange. Freiburg: Echter, 1974. 40–55. **Léon-Dufour, X.** "Le dernier cri de Jésus." *Études* 348 (1978) 666–82. **Lofthouse, W. F.** "The Cry of Dereliction." *ExpTim* 53 (1941–42) 188–92. **Michaels, J. R.** "The Centurion's Confession and the Spear Thrust." *CBQ* 29 (1967) 102–9. **Nestle, Eb.** "Die Sonnenfinsternis bei Jesu Tod." *ZNW* 3 (1902) 246–47. **Pennells, S.** "The Spear Thrust (Mt. 27,49b, *v.l.*/Jn. 19,34)." *JSNT* 19 (1983) 99–115. **Ramsay, W. M.** "The Denials of Peter." *ExpTim* 27 (1915–16) 296–301; 28 (1916–17) 276–81. **Read, D. H. C.** "The Cry of Dereliction." *ExpTim* 68 (1956–57) 260–62. **Rehm, M.** "Eli, Eli, lamma sabacthani?" *BZ* n.s. 2 (1958) 275–78. **Reumann, J. H.** "Psalm 22 at the Cross: Lament and Thanksgiving for Jesus Christ." *Int* 28 (1974) 39–58. **Rossé, G.** *The Cry of Jesus on the Cross: A Biblical and Theological Study.* Tr. S. W. Arndt. New York: Paulist, 1987. **Sagne, J.-C.** "The Cry of Jesus on the Cross." *Concil* 169 (1983) 52–58. **Schützeichel, H.** "Der Todesschrei Jesu: Bemerkungen zu einer Theologie des Kreuzes." *TTZ* 83 (1974) 1–16. **Sidersky, D.** "La parole suprême de Jésus." *RHR* 103 (1931) 151–56. **Smith, F.** "The Strangest 'Word' of Jesus." *ExpTim* 44 (1932–33) 259–61. **Tilliette, X.** "Der Kreuzesschrei." *EvT* 43 (1983) 3–15. **Trudinger, L. P.** "'Eli, Eli, Lama Sabachthani?' A Cry of Dereliction or Victory?" *JETS* 17 (1974) 235–38. **Wilkinson, J.** "The Physical Cause of the Death of Christ." *ExpTim* 83 (1971–72) 104–7. **Willcock, J.** "When He Had Tasted." *ExpTim* 32 (1920–21) 426. **Wilson, W. E.,** and **Smallbone, J. A.** "Our Lord's Cry on the Cross." *ExpTim* 31 (1919–20) 519–20. **Worden, T.** "My God, my God, why hast thou forsaken me?" *Scr* 6 (1953) 6–16. **Zimmermann, F.** "The Last Words of Jesus." *JBL* 66 (1947) 465–66. **Zugibe, F. T.** "Two Questions about Crucifixion: Does the Victim Die of Asphyxiation? Would Nails in the Hands Hold the Weight of the Body?" *BibRev* 5 (1989) 34–43.

## Translation

⁴⁵*And from the sixth hour darkness came upon the whole land*ᵃ *lasting until the ninth hour.* ⁴⁶*And about the ninth hour Jesus cried out with a loud voice, saying:* "Ēli, Ēli,ᵇ lemaᶜ sabachthani?"ᵈ *That is, "My God, my God, why have you forsaken me?"* ⁴⁷*And when some of those standing there heard the voice,*ᵉ *they said: "This man is calling for Elijah."* ⁴⁸*And immediately one of them*ᶠ *ran and took a sponge and filled it*ᵍ *with sour wine, and putting it on a stick, he gave it*ᵍ *to him to drink.* ⁴⁹*And the others were saying: "Wait, let us see if Elijah comes to save him."*ʰ ⁵⁰*But Jesus cried out again with a loud voice and stopped breathing.*ⁱ

## Notes

ᵃ Or possibly "earth." See *Comment.*

ᵇ ηλι ηλι (representing the Heb. אֵלִי אֵלִי, ʾēlî, ʾēlî, "my God, my God") is the reading of most MSS (A D [L] W Θ *f*¹·¹³ TR). The important MSS ℵ B 33 co have ελωι ελωι (representing the Aram. אֱלָהּ אֱלָהּ, ʾĕlāhî, ʾĕlāhî, "my God, my God"), but probably by conformity to the parallel in Mark 15:34. *TCGNT*, 70. On the other hand, the reading ηλι ηλι could be secondary, caused by the influence of the reference to Ἠλίαν, "Elijah," in v 47.

ᶜ ℵ B 33 700 have λεμα (representing the Aram. לְמָא, lĕmaʾ, "why?"). The Aram. is also reflected in the variant spellings λιμα (A K U Γ Δ Π) and λειμα (E F G H M S V). λαμα, on the other hand, is the equivalent of the Heb. לָמָּה, lāmmāh, "why?" (D Θ).

ᵈ Almost all MSS have σαβαχθανι (representing the Aram. שְׁבַקְתַּנִי, šĕḇaqtanî, "you have forsaken me") or a spelling variant thereof, σαβαχθανει (ℵ A Δ), σαβακτανει (B). Only D*, the single MS with all three words in their Heb. form, has the equivalent of the Heb. ζαφθανει (representing the Heb. עֲזַבְתַּנִי, ʿăzaḇtanî, "you have forsaken me"). See *TCGNT*, 70.

ᵉ "The voice" added for clarity.

ᶠ ℵ omits ἐξ αὐτῶν, "of them." Cf. Mark 15:36.

ᵍ "It" added for clarity.

ʰ Some important MSS (ℵ B C L Γ vgᵐˢˢ mae) add ἄλλος δὲ λαβὼν λόγχην ἔνυξεν αὐτοῦ τὴν πλευράν, καὶ ἐξῆλθεν ὕδωρ καὶ αἷμα, "and another man took a spear and pierced his side, and water and blood came out," which is, however, probably an insertion from John 19:34. "It is probable that the Johannine passage was written by some reader in the margin of Matthew from memory . . . and a later copyist awkwardly introduced it into the text" (Metzger, *TCGNT*, 71). See Pennells for an improbable speculation that the reading was original but later covered up by the church because it did not fit its theology of death by crucifixion.

ⁱ ἀφῆκεν τὸ πνεῦμα may also be translated "gave up the spirit."

## Form/Structure/Setting

A. The death of Jesus is not only the climax of the passion narrative but also the climax of Jesus' earthly work. The Gospels are books of "good news" primarily because of what is accomplished through the death of Jesus. Here we come to *the* gospel. At the heart of the story is Jesus' death in fulfillment of God's will and for the salvation of the world. But the death of God's Son involves impenetrable mystery. It is attended by a supernatural darkness and followed by remarkable events. Matthew's account of the death itself is nevertheless simple, sober, and restrained in character.

B. Matthew continues to follow Mark very closely (Mark 15:33–37; cf. Luke 23:44–46; John 19:28–30). There are no major differences, but the following alterations should nevertheless be noted. In v 45 Matthew begins with ἀπό, "from," replacing Mark's γενομένης, "being" (Mark 15:33), and in v 46 περί, "about," plus the accusative replaces Mark's simple dative implying "at" (Mark 15:34). In the same verse Matthew alters Mark's Aramaic ελωι ελωι, *elōi elōi*, to the Hebrew ηλι ηλι, *ēli ēli*, despite the fact that the remaining words are in Aramaic (see *Notes* b–d above). This was probably done to produce a closer phonetic similarity with Ἡλίαν, "Elijah," of v 47 and so to produce a more plausible narrative. Also in the same place Matthew omits Mark's unnecessary μεθερμηνευόμενον, "being interpreted," and alters Mark's repeated ὁ θεός, "God," to the more proper repeated vocative θεέ, "God." In the quotation, furthermore, he alters Mark's εἰς τί, "why," to the synonymous ἱνατί in keeping with the LXX. In v 47 Matthew substitutes a recitative ὅτι (equivalent to quotation marks) for Mark's ἴδε, "look" (Mark 15:35), and adds οὗτος, "this man," giving the sentence more balance by providing a subject. In v 48 Matthew adds a favorite word, εὐθέως, "immediately," and writes εἷς ἐξ αὐτῶν, "one of them," for Mark's simple τις, "a certain one," and λάβων, "having taken" (cf. Mark 15:36). V 49 begins with Matthew's added οἱ δὲ λοιποί ἔλεγον, "and the others were saying," for Mark's λέγων, "saying," which has as its subject the man who gave Jesus the drink (Mark 15:36). In the same verse he replaces Mark's καθελεῖν, "take down" (Mark 15:36), with σώσων, lit. "saving" (i.e., "to save"). In v 50 Matthew adds πάλιν, "again" (cf. v 46), substitutes the more usual κράξας, "crying out," for Mark's ἀφείς, "letting go," and finally, substitutes ἀφῆκεν τὸ πνεῦμα, lit. "gave up the spirit" or "stopped breathing," for Mark's ἐξέπνευσεν, "breathed his last" (Mark 15:37).

C. The genre of historical narrative continues in this pericope. Of central importance is the cry of despair from the crucified Jesus (v 46) in words drawn from Ps 22:1, given both in transliterated Hebrew/Aramaic and then in Greek translation. This is the first cry with a φωνῇ μεγάλῃ, "loud voice"; the second cry without words, described with the same phrase (cf. πάλιν, "again"), occurs as Jesus actually expires in v 50. The following simple outline may be suggested: (1) the darkness (v 45); (2) the cry of despair (v 46); (3) the misunderstanding (vv 47–49), including the parenthetic reference to giving Jesus a drink; and (4) the last breath of Jesus (v 50). The form of the words of Jesus quoted on the cross found in Justin Martyr, *Dial.* 99.1, may reflect a knowledge of Matthew (cf. ἱνατί, "why").

## Comment

**45** A preternatural darkness (not to rule out the possible instrumentality of natural causes; see discussion in Holzmeister) descended ἐπὶ πᾶσαν τὴν γῆν, "upon all the land." This phrase probably means "the land of Judea" (cf. *Gos. Pet.* 5.15) rather than "the earth," although the evangelist may mean the whole "earth," which is the way he generally uses the word γῆ (cf. for example 5:13, 18; 6:10, 19; 11:25; 12:42; 24:35; 28:18; but in reference to a more limited "land," cf. 2:6, 20, 21; 4:15; 10:15, all with modifiers; see too 9:26, 31). The idea of the sun going down at midday is an apocalyptic image for a time of great sorrow and mourning employed in Amos 8:9 (cf. Jer 15:9). Darkness is, of course, also a common metaphor for judgment that will come on "the Day of the Lord" (cf. such passages as Joel 2:2, 31; Zeph 1:15). The hours are reckoned here according to the Roman system with ἕκτης ὥρας, "the sixth hour," meaning "noon" and ὥρας ἐνάτης, "the ninth hour," meaning "three o'clock in the afternoon," the darkness lasting for a three-hour period.

**46** As this period drew to a close, Jesus cried out loudly with the heart-rending words that begin Ps 22: "*Eli, Eli, lama sabachthani?*" As the passion narrative began with Jesus' prayer in Gethsemane (26:39), now it comes to a close with Jesus' prayer as he experiences drinking the cup he had earlier prayed would pass. In Matthew's version of these words, "*Eli*" represents the Hebrew, "My God," while the following words are Aramaic for "Why have you forsaken me?" (see *Notes* b–d above). It appears that Jesus, rather than quoting the words in Hebrew, quoted them in their Aramaic equivalent (using the language he normally spoke) and that Matthew altered the word for "God" (the Aramaic ελωι in his Markan source) to ηλι (Hebrew, "my God"), perhaps with an eye on the confusion with the name of Elijah in v 47. (The Targum of Ps 22, however, also retains the Hebrew form *Eli;* see Str-B 1:1042.) The form of the words is one thing. The meaning of the words in the mouth of Jesus, the Son of God, is something about which the reader and the exegete can only wonder. It may fairly be said that it was whatever occurred here—this breach with his Father (although the prayer avoids this intimate term, using simply "God")—and not the excruciating pain or ignominious death of crucifixion that Jesus dreaded above all else. Jesus clearly feels abandoned (and *is* abandoned by God; contra Baker; on the seriousness of the abandonment, see esp. Rossé; cf. Read; Moo, *Old Testament in the Gospel Passion Narratives,* 274–75) and articulates his feeling with words from Ps 22:1. No doubt his heart took courage from the words of scripture, for Ps 22 is not only a psalm of lament but simultaneously also a psalm of trust (thus rightly Gerhardsson; Reumann). The abandoned one, who still prays to his God, can also say of his ancestors: "To you they cried, and were saved; in you they trusted and were not put to shame" (Ps 22:5; cf. 22:24). In no way, however, does this lessen the reality of present abandonment (*pace* Senior, *Passion of Jesus;* see R. E. Brown's discussion, *Death of the Messiah,* 1044–51), and it is going too far to take Jesus' cry as a cry of victory (*pace* Trudinger). For the importance of Ps 22 in the passion narrative, see *Comment* on v 35 (see too Deissler, who describes Ps 22 as paradigmatic for all prayer). The evangelists (i.e., Mark and Matthew) avoid interpretive comment on the words of Jesus, and although other writers of the NT, whose task *is* interpretation, never refer to the words, it is not difficult to see the direct relevance of passages such as Rom 3:25; 2 Cor 5:21; Col 1:20; Heb 5:7–10; 7:27; 9:11–14. Jesus as the sin-bearing sacrifice (cf. 1:21; 20:28; 26:28) must endure the temporary abandonment of his Father, i.e., separation from God. Horrible as this would be for any creature of God, when it concerns one who is uniquely the Son of God (cf. 1:23; 3:17; 11:27; 14:33; 16:16; 26:63–64), not to use later trinitarian language (28:19), it is impossible to assess what this may have meant to Jesus. This is one of the most impenetrable mysteries of the entire Gospel narrative.

**47–49** When "some of those standing there" (τινὲς δὲ τῶν ἐκεῖ ἑστηκότων, implying Jews rather than Roman soldiers) heard Jesus crying out ηλι ηλι, *Ēli Ēli*, they thought he was calling upon Elijah. This would have been an easy mistake to make, according to Matthew's text, because of the similarity between אֵלִי, *'ēlî*, and אֵלִיָּה, *'ēliyah* (although according to Guillaume the latter can also be an alternative form for "my God" in Hebrew), which is nicely reflected in the similarity between the Greek transliteration ηλι and the name Elijah in Greek, Ἠλία, *Ēlia*. There was furthermore the plausibility of such an appeal to Elijah who might be thought to be available as a deliverer of those in need; earlier in the Gospel Elijah's coming has eschatological overtones (see 11:14; 16:14; 17:3–12, esp. v 11; see too Brower). There is little need, however, to argue that the bystanders had clearly worked-out views on the subject! They thought they heard Elijah's name and so thought that Jesus was crying out to be delivered (cf. v 49; Str-B 4:769–71). Perhaps struck by his piteous cry, it is parenthetically inserted, one of the bystanders "ran immediately" (εὐθέως δραμών) to get him something to drink. ὄξους, "sour wine," was a favorite cheap beverage (cf. Ruth 2:14 and the "wine vinegar" of Num 6:3) that "relieved thirst more effectively than water" (BAGD, 574a). The only way it could be given to Jesus as he hung on the cross was by means of a soaked sponge put on the end of a stick. This wine, unlike that of v 34, Jesus drank (cf. John 19:30). This apparently incidental account is probably regarded as important by the evangelist because of the allusion it provided to Ps 69, where according to v 21b (LXX Ps 68:22) "for my thirst they gave me vinegar [LXX: ὄξος as in Matthew] to drink" (see too *Comment* on v 34; cf. John 19:28 for specific stress on fulfillment in this connection). That οἱ δὲ λοιποί, "and the others," were probably Jews is suggested by their half-serious expectation that Elijah might come to deliver (σώσων, lit. "saving") him as ἄφες ἴδωμεν, "wait, let us see," suggests. Their comment may imply that some of them at least regarded Jesus as a righteous man who did not deserve this fate. Here the coming of Elijah is almost certainly thought of as related to the deliverance of a righteous man in his hour of need and not as the eschatological precursor of the Messiah (as for example in 11:14).

**50** The death of Jesus, a climactic point in the narrative, is described very simply: a last φωνῇ μεγάλῃ, "loud cry," of agony (cf. the same phrase in v 46) and then the end. Nothing in the text suggests that this cry is any different from the first cry—for example, a cry of triumph (*pace* Senior, *Passion of Jesus*)—and there is no need to identify the cry as the logion of Luke 23:46 (*pace* Bligh). Because of the ambiguous meaning of πνεῦμα, which can mean "breath" or "spirit," it is difficult to know how to understand the words ἀφῆκεν τὸ πνεῦμα, which can be taken as "gave up his breath," i.e., "breathed his last" (NRSV, REB) or "gave up his spirit" (cf. NJB). Matthew's expression seems halfway between Mark's ἐξέπνευσεν, "he expired" (so too Luke 23:46), and John's παρέδωκεν τὸ πνεῦμα, "he gave over (up) the spirit" (John 19:30). It is clear that his death is meant and that at the least the expression means that he stopped breathing. The word πνεῦμα can mean "breath" (cf. the cognate verb ἐκπνεῖν in Matthew's source, Mark 15:37). It is unlikely that Matthew means by this expression that Jesus sovereignly chose the moment of his death as a number of commentators allege (see Wilkinson, who concludes that Jesus did not die of any physical cause!). Whether included in this idea is the related notion of the departure of "the spirit," i.e., his spiritual being from the physical body, is uncertain although perhaps not likely. Danker's argument that the parallel in Mark 15:37 describes the expulsion of a demon is without basis. It is also most unlikely that the phrase refers to the Holy Spirit (*pace* Schniewind). On the physical cause of Jesus' death, see the debate between Edwards et al. (asphyxiation) and Zugibe (shock).

*Explanation*

Christians universally regard the death of Jesus as salvific in nature. It is one of the central mysteries of the Christian faith. In the death of Jesus, he, the Righteous One, bears for sinners the righteous wrath of God against sin. Matthew's church, like the church throughout the ages, would have regularly celebrated that death and its consequences in their eucharistic services—not that they or any others in the history of the church have been able to fathom what happened in the cross (cf. esp. 1 Cor 1:18, 23–25, 30). Jesus did not call for Elijah to deliver him; his heart was set to accomplish the will of the Father. Yet in obedience to that very will, he must for the time being undergo the Father's rejection. Thus in agony of soul as much as of body Jesus cries out the biting words, "My God, my God, why have you forsaken me?" Perhaps it is best simply to let the words stand as they are—stark in their impenetrability to us mortals.

# Spectacular Events Following the Death of Jesus   (27:51–54)

*Bibliography*

**Aguirre, R.** "Cross and Kingdom in Matthew's Theology." *TD* 29 (1981) 149–53. **Blinzler, J.** "Zur Erklärung von Mt 27,51b–53: Totenauferstehung am Karfreitag?" *TGl* 35 (1943) 91–93. **Essame, W. G.** "Matthew xxvii.51–54 and John v.25–29." *ExpTim* 76 (1964–65) 103. **Fascher, E.** *Das Weib des Pilatus (Matthäus 27,19): Die Auferweckung der Heiligen (Matthäus 27,51–53).* Hallische Monographien 20. Halle: Niemeyer, 1951. **Fuller, R. C.** "The Bodies of the Saints, Matt 27, 52–53." *Scr* 3 (1948) 86–88. **Grassi, J. A.** "Ezekiel 37,1–14 and the New Testament." *NTS* 11 (1964–65) 162–64. **Hill, D.** "Matthew 27:51–53 in the Theology of the Evangelist." *IBS* 7 (1985) 76–87. **Hutton, D. D.** "The Resurrection of the Holy Ones (Mt 27:51b–53): A Study of the Theology of the Matthean Passion Narrative." Diss., Harvard Divinity School, 1970. **Jonge, M. de.** "Matthew 27:51 in Early Christian Exegesis." *HTR* 79 (1986) 67–79. **Kratz, R.** *Auferweckung als Befreiung: Eine Studie zur Passions- und Auferstehungstheologie des Matthäus.* SBS 65. Stuttgart: Katholisches Bibelwerk, 1973. **Lange, J.** "Zur Ausgestaltung der Szene vom Sterben Jesu in den synoptischen Evangelien." In

*Biblische Randbemerkungen.* FS R. Schnackenburg, ed. H. Merklein and J. Lange. Würzburg: Echter, 1974. 40–55. **Lindeskog, G.** "The Veil of the Temple." In *In honorem A. Fridrichsen sexagenarii.* Edenda curavit Seminarium Neotestamenticum Upsaliense. ConNT 11. Lund: Gleerup, 1947. 132–37. **Maisch, I.** "Die österliche Dimension des Todes Jesu: Zur Osterverkündigung in Mt 27,51–54." In *Auferstehung Jesus—Auferstehung der Christen: Deutungen des Osterglaubens.* FS A. Vögtle, ed. I. Broer. QD 105. Freiburg: Herder, 1986. 96–123. **Monasterio, R. A.** *Exegesis de Mateo 27:51b–53: Para una teologia de la muerte de Jesús en el Evangelio de Mateo.* Biblica Victoriensa 4. Vitoria, Spain: Eset, 1980. **Nestle, Eb.** "Matt 27,51 und Parallelen." *ZNW* 3 (1902) 167–69. **Pelletier, A.** "La tradition synoptique du 'voile déchire' à la lumière des réalités archéologiques." *RSR* 46 (1958) 161–80. **Pobee, J.** "The Cry of the Centurion—A Cry of Defeat." In *The Trial of Jesus.* FS C. F. D. Moule, ed. E. Bammel. SBT 2.13. London: SCM, 1970. 91–102. **Riebl, M.** *Auferstehung Jesu in der Stunde seines Todes? Zur Botschaft von Mt 27,51b–53.* SBS 8. Stuttgart: Katholisches Bibelwerk, 1978. ———. "Jesu Tod und Auferstehung—Hoffnung für unser Sterben." *BibLit* 57 (1984) 208–13. **Schneider, C.** "Der Hauptmann am Kreuz." *ZNW* 33 (1934) 1–17. **Senior, D.** "The Death of God's Son and the Beginning of the New Age (Matthew 27:51–54)." In *The Language of the Cross,* ed. A. Lacomara. Chicago: Franciscan Herald Press, 1977. 29–51. ———. "The Death of Jesus and the Birth of the New World: Matthew's Theology of History in the Passion Narrative." *CurTM* 19 (1992) 416–23. ———. "The Death of Jesus and the Resurrection of the Holy Ones (Mt 27:51–53)." *CBQ* 38 (1976) 312–29. **Simpson, J.** "Matthew xxvii.51–53." *ExpTim* 14 (1902–3) 527–28. **Verseput, D.** "The Role and Meaning of the 'Son of God' Title in Matthew's Gospel." *NTS* 33 (1987) 532–56. **Wenham, D.** "The Resurrection Narratives in Matthew's Gospel." *TynB* 24 (1973) 21–54. **Wenham, J. W.** "When Were the Saints Raised? A Note on the Punctuation of Matthew xxvii.51–3." *JTS* 32 (1981) 150–52. **Williams, W. H.** "The Veil Was Rent." *RevExp* 48 (1951) 275–85. **Winklhofer, A.** "*Corpora Sanctorum.*" *TQ* 133 (1953) 30–67, 210–17. **Witherup, R. D.** "The Death of Jesus and the Raising of the Saints: Matthew 27:51–54 in Context." In *Society of Biblical Literature Seminar Papers 1987.* 574–85. **Zeller, H.** "*Corpora Sanctorum:* Eine Studie zu Mt 27,52–53." *ZKT* 71 (1949) 385–465.

## Translation

[51]*And look, the curtain of the temple was torn in two from the top to the bottom.*[a] *And the ground was made to quake, and the rocks were split open.* [52]*And the tombs were opened, and many bodies of saints who had died* [b] *were raised.* [53]*And when they had come out of the tombs after his resurrection, they entered into the holy city and were seen by many.*

[54]*Now the centurion and those watching Jesus with him, when they saw the earthquake and the things that happened, were terribly afraid and said: "Truly this was the Son of God."*[c]

## Notes

[a] The word order of the preceding eight words (six in Gr. text) varies considerably among the MSS, but no change of meaning is caused thereby. D latt? add the word μέρη, "parts," after δύο, "two."

[b] τῶν κεκοιμημένων, lit. "having fallen asleep."

[c] θεοῦ υἱός may also be translated "a son of God." See *Comment.*

## Form/Structure/Setting

A. More supernatural events take place after the death of Jesus, that is, in addition to the darkness while Jesus was on the cross. For any Christian reader, these events are filled with obvious theological significance, although Matthew does not elaborate upon this. The events themselves are apocalyptic in character and point to the decisive importance of the death of Jesus not only for that generation but for all of subsequent history. There is an air both of judgment and of eschatology in this material. In light of the strange events, the only conclusion to be drawn is that of the centurion and his soldiers: "Truly this man was the Son of God." This is the climactic statement of the passion narrative. What remains is the account of Jesus' burial and resurrection.

B. While the insertion of vv 52–53 is without parallel in the other Gospels, coming either from tradition or from Matthew himself, vv 51, 54 are derived from Mark (Mark 15:38–39; cf. Luke 23:45, 47). In v 51 Matthew follows Mark verbatim except for slight variation in word order and the insertion of his favorite ἰδού, "look" (Mark 15:38). V 54, on the other hand, is quite different from Mark 15:39. Matthew omits Mark's ὁ παρεστηκὼς ἐξ ἐναντίας αὐτοῦ, "who was standing opposite him," as unnecessary. Matthew inserts new material corresponding to earlier elements in his narrative. Thus καὶ οἱ μετ' αὐτοῦ τηροῦντες τὸν Ἰησοῦν, "and those with him watching Jesus," corresponds to v 36, and τὸν σεισμὸν καὶ τὰ γενόμενα, "the earthquake and the things that happened," corresponds to at least some of the events of vv 51–52. Matthew also adds the note that the "centurion" (he substitutes the more usual ἑκατόνταρχος for Mark's Latin κεντυρίων) and his soldiers ἐφοβήθησαν σφόδρα, "were terribly afraid." Matthew furthermore has the centurion *and* his soldiers (hence a plurality of witnesses) make the statement about Jesus as "the Son of God" (v 54), attributing it not, as in Mark, to the manner of Jesus' death (ὅτι οὕτως ἐξέπνευσεν, "that thus he died" [Mark 15:39]) but to the spectacular events referred to in vv 51b–52 (τὸν σεισμὸν καὶ τὰ γενόμενα, "the earthquake and the things that happened"). By altering the word order of the statement, putting θεοῦ υἱός, lit. "of God the Son" (emphatic word order), immediately after ἀληθῶς, "truly," and putting οὗτος, "this," at the end of the sentence, Matthew has heightened the impact of the statement in comparison with its form in Mark 15:39. A final alteration, the omission of Mark's ὁ ἄνθρωπος, "man," is consonant with the stronger form of the Matthean statement.

C. The passage contains obviously symbolic and apocalyptic motifs yet continues in the genre of historical narrative. The astonishment of the Roman soldiers finds expression in the climactic utterance with which the pericope and indeed the passion narrative itself ends. The following outline may be suggested: (1) the rending of the curtain (v 51a); (2) the earthquake (vv 51b–53), subdivided into (a) the opening of the tombs (v 52a), (b) the rising of the saints (vv 52b), and (c) their appearance in Jerusalem (v 53); and (3) the response of the Roman soldiers (v 54). Structurally, the five successive aorist passive verbs ("divine" passives in which God is understood to be the acting subject) in vv 51–52 should be noted.

### Comment

**51a** τὸ καταπέτασμα τοῦ ναοῦ, "the curtain of the temple," refers most probably to the "second" (cf. Heb 9:3) or innermost curtain (cf. Heb 6:19) that separated the Holy of Holies from the rest of the temple (the word καταπέτασμα most often refers to the inner curtain; see Exod 26:31–35) rather than the "outer" curtain that covered the entrance to the temple structure itself. The splitting of the curtain ἀπ' ἄνωθεν ἕως κάτω, "from top to bottom," together with the passive verb ἐσχίσθη, "was split," implying divine action, points to the event as an act of God (possibly, as Daube suggests, this is comparable to the rending of one's garments because of great sorrow as the high priest does in 26:65). A remarkable symbolism is involved, which none of the evangelists stops to explain. Clearly, however, the tearing of the veil is a type of apocalyptic sign pointing, on the one hand, to the wrath and judgment of God against the Jewish authorities (cf. *T. Levi* 10:3) and, on the other, to the end of the temple, where God is no longer present. It seems also probable, however (*pace* R. E. Brown, *Death of the Messiah*, 1108–9), that Matthew's church perceived another symbolism in the torn curtain, namely, that by his sacrificial death, Jesus obviates the sacrifices and priesthood, making available to all people a new, bold, unrestricted access into God's very presence. The negative symbolism of the torn veil cannot but entail inescapable positive connotations. The evangelist can leave this unexplained because it was so familiar to the early church. The curtains of the temple, like the various temple courts, restricted access to the presence of God. The Holy of Holies was entered only once a year, on the Day of Atonement, by the high priest alone to make atonement for the sins of the people (cf. Heb 9:7). With the atoning death of Jesus, toward which the sacrificial cultus pointed, this system has come to an end. From that time on, every believer, Jew and Gentile, has immediate and unrestricted access to God and to the forgiveness of sins accomplished through the death of Jesus on the cross. Witherup rightly calls the event "a salvation-historical indicator" (580). The author of Hebrews makes the point succinctly, alluding to the curtain now divided in two (for a common tradition underlying the Gospels and Hebrews here, see Lindeskog), when he writes that "we have confidence to enter the sanctuary by the blood of Jesus, by the new and living way that he opened for us through the curtain (that is, through his flesh)" (Heb 10:19–20). The death of Jesus establishes the priesthood of all believers.

**51b–53** According to Matthew alone among the evangelists there was an earthquake (as again in 28:2) following the death of Jesus (perhaps to be related to the splitting of the curtain). The earth was shaken and rocks ἐσχίσθησαν, "were split open" (the same verb as in the tearing of the curtain; cf. Nah 1:56; Zech 14:4). Earthquakes are particularly important apocalyptic portents for Matthew (see 24:7; 28:2; for OT background, cf. Isa 24:19; 29:6; Jer 10:10; Amos 8:8; and many other texts). Through the violent tremors, some rock tombs in the area ἀνεῴχθησαν, "were opened." For the raising of the dead "in their tombs," see the LXX of Isa 26:19. See especially, however, Ezek 37:13, which is possibly the basis for the present passage. Without explanation, Matthew notes the resurrection of πολλὰ σώματα τῶν κεκοιμημένων ἁγίων, "many bodies of the saints who had fallen asleep" (for κοιμᾶσθαι, "fall asleep," as a metaphor for death, see *Comment* on 9:24; cf. Acts 7:10; 1 Cor 15:6, 18, 20; *1 Enoch* 91:10; 2 Esdr 7:32). The "saints" or "holy ones" here must be the righteous Jews (the δίκαιοι, "righteous") of the time before Jesus, perhaps the patriarchs, prophets, or martyrs, although Matthew's readers will be thinking of the eventual resurrection of Christians. It is highly unlikely (*pace* McNeile) that we are meant to relate this resurrection to the descent of Christ into Hades (despite 12:40, which was later related to 1 Peter

3:18–20; 4:6) since the saints seem to be raised at the moment of the death of Jesus. Salvation (resurrection) is thus brought into the closest causal connection with the death of Jesus. The death of Jesus breaks the power of death itself. Matthew adds that these resurrected saints entered into Jerusalem (τὴν ἁγίαν πόλιν, "the holy city"; for this expression, see 4:5) and ἐνεφανίσθησαν πολλοῖς, "were seen by many." The text gives not the slightest indication that the heavenly Jerusalem is in view here (*pace* Benoit). Nor does it give any indication that the saints arise to "testify against" Israel (*pace* Witherup). It is difficult to know whether the phrase μετὰ τὴν ἔγερσιν αὐτοῦ, "after his resurrection" (v 53), is to be taken with the preceding participial clause, i.e., that they came out of the tombs after the resurrection of Jesus (thus R. C. Fuller; J. W. Wenham), or with the following verb, i.e., that after the resurrection of Jesus they entered into the city (Schlatter; Zahn). On balance the latter seems more likely since v 52 seems to say that the saints ἠγέρθησαν, "were raised," in connection with the opening of the tombs and since the phrase in question is closer to the following verb (it could have preceded the participle ἐξελθόντες, "having come out," had Matthew wanted to make it clear that their resurrection occurred only after Jesus' resurrection). But if the phrase "after his resurrection" points forward to the verb, then the difficult question remains concerning the whereabouts of these resurrected saints during the three days before Jesus is himself raised from the dead. (Gundry goes so far as to say that Matthew means that the saints [all the OT saints!] were raised to life at the death of Jesus but stayed in the tombs until after Jesus' resurrection!) This particular difficulty is avoided if the earthquake referred to here actually occurred in connection with the opening of the tomb after Jesus' resurrection and is thus the same earthquake as that referred to in 28:2 (thus McNeile) but placed here to relate the resurrection directly to the death of Jesus. Matthew seems clearly, however, to have two separate earthquakes in mind. The suggestion that the singular pronoun αὐτοῦ, "his," was substituted for the plural αὐτῶν, "their," thus not after "his" (Jesus') but "their" resurrection, is purely speculative.

This is a difficult and much discussed passage. A straightforward historical reading of these verses must face difficulties beyond those already mentioned. For example, there is the question of the nature of the bodies of the resurrected saints. Do these saints have what may be called new-order resurrection bodies, i.e., permanent bodies not subject to decay, or are they resuscitated bodies (like that of Lazarus) that later died again? (Could they have new-order resurrection bodies before Jesus, "the first-fruits of the dead" [1 Cor 15:20], did?) Related to this is the further question about what happened to these saints after they made their appearance in Jerusalem. (Were they raptured to heaven and, if so, when? Did they remain on the earth and, if so, where?) Furthermore, why is such a spectacular event "seen by many"—surely of great apologetic significance—referred to only here in the NT and not at all outside the NT? A further question concerns the basis on which this number of saints and these particular saints, and no others, were raised from the dead (was it arbitrary or do unknown criteria come into play?).

A surprising number of commentators sidestep the historical question altogether. Those who do raise it can be found to use terms such as "puzzling," "strange," "mysterious." Stalwart commentators known for their conservatism are given to hesitance here: A. B. Bruce: "We seem here to be in the region of Christian legend" (*The Expositor's Greek Testament*, ed. W. R. Nicoll [Grand Rapids: Eerdmans, 1897] 332); A. Plummer: "a tradition with a legendary element in it" (402); W. Grundmann: "mythic-legendary" (562). Even those disposed to accept the historicity of the passage can indicate a degree of discomfort: R. T. France: "its character as 'sober history' (*i.e.* what a cine-camera might have recorded) can only be, in the absence of corroborative evidence, a matter of faith, not of objective demonstration. It was, in any case, a unique occurrence and is not to be judged by the canons of 'normal' experience" (401); L. Morris: "Since there are no other records of these appearances, it appears to be impossible to say anything about them. But Matthew is surely giving expression to his conviction that Jesus is Lord over both the living and the dead" (725); C. Blomberg: "All kinds of historical questions remain unanswered about both events [the tearing of the temple curtain and the raising of the saints], but their significance clearly lies in the theology Matthew wishes to convey" (421).

The question of the historicity of the event described in the present passage remains problematic. We should not, of course, rule out a priori that Matthew may be recording historical events in these verses. If God raised Jesus from the dead, he surely can have raised a number of saints prior to the time of the general resurrection. The question here, however, is one of historical plausibility. It is not in principle that difficult for one whose view of reality permits it (i.e., who has a biblical view of reality) to believe in the historicity of this event. The problem is that the event makes little historical sense, whereas what *does* make sense is the theological point that is being made. The various difficulties mentioned above together with the obvious symbolic-apocalyptic character of the language (e.g., darkness, earthquake, opening of tombs, resurrection) raise the strong possibility that Matthew in these verses is making a theological point rather than simply relating history. This hardly means that the evangelist, or those before him with whom the tradition may have originated, is necessarily inventing all the exceptional events in his narrative (*pace* R. E. Brown, *Death of the Messiah*, 1137–40). More likely, here as in the birth narratives a historical core of events, such as the darkness and the earthquake, has given rise to a degree of elaboration in the passing on of the tradition. This elaboration extends the original events and in so doing draws out the theological significance of the death of Jesus. Theology and a historical core of events are by no means mutually exclusive. See Lange, who concludes: "We must learn the alphabet of the language in which the evangelists—and the Spirit which they promote—have tried to make the 'kernel of the matter' accessible to us" (54–55).

I side, therefore, with such recent commentators as Gundry, Senior (*Passion of Jesus*), Gnilka, Bruner, Harrington, D. R. A. Hare (*Matthew*, Interpretation [Louisville: Westminster/John Knox, 1993]), and R. E. Brown (*Death of the Messiah*) in concluding that the rising of the saints from the tombs in this passage is a piece of theology set forth as history. Sabourin is probably correct when he writes: "Matthew took for historical facts popular reports of what would have taken place at the time of Jesus. He used these stories to convey his own theological message" (919; so too R. E. Brown, *Death of the Messiah*, 1138). It is obvious that by the inclusion of this material Matthew wanted to draw out the theological significance of the death (and resurrection) of Jesus. That significance is found in the establishing of the basis of the future resurrection of the saints. We may thus regard the passage as a piece of realized and historicized apocalyptic depending on OT motifs found in such passages as Isa 26:19; Dan 12:2; and especially Ezek 37:12–14 (though Monasterio, Riebl, Gnilka, and others probably speculate too much in concluding Matthew's dependence on a Jewish apocalyptic text oriented to Ezek 37; contrast Maisch who opts for Matthean composition). Ezek 37:12–14 is apposite: "Therefore prophesy, and say to them, Thus says the Lord GOD: I am going to open your graves, and bring you up from your graves, O my people. . . . And you shall know that I am the LORD, when I open your graves, and bring you out of your graves, O my people. I will put my spirit within you, and you shall live. . . ." For the importance of Ezek 37:1–14 in the synagogue at Passover time, see Grassi (cf. Hill, *IBS* 7 [1985] 76–87).

R. E. Brown (*Death of the Messiah*) is probably correct when he concludes that Matthew wants to communicate that the death and resurrection of Jesus mark "the beginning of the last times" (so too Maisch; Senior, *CBQ* 38 [1976] 312–29; Hill, *IBS* 7 [1985] 76–87; *pace* Witherup, who, however, correctly sees that a salvation-historical turning point has been reached in Matthew's narrative). Already in the events accompanying the death of Jesus Matthew finds the anticipation of the good news of the conquering of death itself and hence of the reality of resurrection for the people of God. The death of Jesus as well as the resurrection of Jesus is gospel, for that death is life-giving (Senior, *CBQ* 38 [1976] 312–29).

If there was an earthquake that opened up some tombs (a not uncommon experience in Palestine), it is very possible that the opened tombs suggested the resurrection of the dead to the original witnesses. Matthew recorded the tradition, believing that it foreshadowed the reality of the eventual resurrection of saints, which in turn corresponded to and depended upon the resurrection of Jesus. It may well be that the clue in Matthew's redactional work in this regard is found in the awkward, telltale insertion μετὰ τὴν ἔγερσιν αὐτοῦ, "after his resurrection," which is not only syntactically difficult, as we have noted, but which also betrays the anachronistic character of these unusual verses (cf. 1 Cor 15:20–23; Col 1:18; Rev 1:5). Matthew wants to connect the open tombs with the resurrection of dead saints yet must reckon with the theological fact that Jesus must be the first to rise.

**54** The Roman ἑκατόνταρχος, "centurion," and his soldiers, together watching Jesus, ἐφοβήθησαν σφόδρα, "became terribly afraid" (the words are used earlier in 17:6), having experienced τὸν σεισμὸν καὶ τὰ γενόμενα, "the earthquake and the things that happened." How much is to be included in the last phrase is somewhat uncertain. They would have seen the darkness (v 45), felt the earthquake (v 51), and perhaps seen nearby tombs split open (v 52). They would not, however, have seen the rending of the temple curtain (v 51) and probably did not see resurrected bodies coming out of the tombs since Matthew would hardly have omitted pointing this out specifically. What they did see, however, was enough to terrify them. The emphatic (see *Form/Structure/Setting* §B) conclusion they drew, ἀληθῶς θεοῦ υἱὸς ἦν οὗτος, "truly this was the Son of God," is nearly identical to that drawn earlier by the disciples in 14:33 (cf. 16:16). Although technically the translation "a son of God" is possible since no definite article is present, the technical expression already carries a definiteness by its previous use in the Gospel (see too the lack of the definite article in 4:3, 6; 27:40, 43). This is the assessment of Jesus at the climax of his earthly work, and it is virtually impossible that Matthew means us to understand the confession to be that he was merely *a* son of God (on the title here, see Verseput, 547–49). It is, of course, also the conclusion of the evangelist as well as his readers. From the centurion's perspective, on the other hand, Jesus was probably perceived as possessing divine power, and thus the centurion's confession amounts to an admission of both Jesus' innocence and Roman guilt (thus Pobee). There is both irony and tragedy in the fact that the statement is made by Roman soldiers (cf. 8:10–11) and not the Jews to whom Jesus had come—just as in 2:2, 11 it is Gentiles who acknowledge the truth and not the Jews, anticipating the salvation-historical shift that will be articulated in 28:19. The soldiers in their fear mouth words whose real significance they could hardly have known. What they had seen was enough to make them receptive to Jesus' claim (which they would have heard from the Jewish authorities [see 27:43]), and ultimately their confession does not differ greatly from that of Matthew's church. On the other hand, the very claim made here was largely responsible for the Jewish rejection of Jesus (cf. 26:63; 27:40, 43).

### Explanation

Through the death of Jesus, a turning point of the eons has been reached. When Jesus dies, a number of spectacular things take place. Two in particular are laden with symbolic significance. The rending of the temple curtain in two symbolizes and, indeed, foreshadows the end of the sacrificial cultus of the temple, although it would continue another forty years—until the temple was destroyed in A.D. 70 (cf. 23:38). Now that the supreme sacrifice for sin has been offered, to which indeed the temple cultus pointed, the latter has become superfluous. The way to the presence of God is now through the sacrifice of his Son, which provides free and ready access to God's very presence. Second, the earthquake and the opened tombs symbolize the reality of the future resurrection of the saints and the direct dependence of this event upon the death and resurrection of Jesus. Since Jesus has died and been raised, the resurrection of those who believe in him is assured. If a group of saints was literally raised and walked about Jerusalem, they become yet further evidence of the reality of the coming resurrection of all the saints. If this did not literally happen, a symbolic anticipation of what literally *will* happen is nevertheless supplied with the purpose of increasing confidence in the resurrection that awaits Christians, should they fall asleep before Jesus returns. The cross and the spectacular events that immediately followed point together to the reality of Jesus as the Son of God. It was the Son of God who died so miserably, as a criminal and as one cursed by God. Little wonder that this death was attended by spectacular signs. Judgment and salvation are bound up in this wondrous event.

# The Women at the Cross    (27:55–56)

### Bibliography

**Gerhardsson, B.** "Mark and the Female Witnesses." In *DUMU-E₂-DUB-BA-A*. FS Å. W. Sjöberg, ed. H. Behrens et al. Philadelphia: University of Pennsylvania, 1989. 217–26. **Heil, J. P.** "The Narrative Structure of Matthew 27:55–28:20." *JBL* 110 (1991) 419–38. **Hengel, M.** "Maria Magdalene und die Frauen als Zeugen." In *Abraham unser Vater.* FS O. Michel, ed. O. Betz et al. Leiden: Brill, 1963. 243–56

### Translation

⁵⁵ *And there were many women there watching from a distance, who had followed Jesus from Galilee, serving him,* ⁵⁶ *among whom were Mary* ᵃ *Magdelene and Mary* ᵃ *the mother of James and Joseph,* ᵇ *and the mother of the sons of Zebedee.*

### Notes

ᵃ Μαρία, "Mary." In both places C (L) Δ Θ (f¹) sa⁽ᵐˢˢ⁾ have Μαριάμ, "Miriam," more closely reflecting the Heb. מִרְיָם, *miryām*.

ᵇ A great number of MSS (A B C Dᶜ f¹,¹³ TR sy⁽ᵖ⁾ʰ saᵐˢˢ) have Ἰωσή, "Jose" (itself a shortened form of "Joseph"), perhaps to bring about more conformity with the parallel in Mark 15:40, which has the alternate (Grecized) form of the same name, Ἰωσῆτος, "Jose." After "Mary Magdelene and Mary the mother of James," ℵ* has καὶ ἡ Μαρία ἡ Ἰωσὴφ καὶ ἡ Μαριάμ τῶν υἱῶν Ζεβεδαίου, "and Mary the (mother of) Joseph and Mary the (mother of) the sons of Zebedee," thus producing a total of four women, all with the name "Mary."

### Form/Structure/Setting

A. The note about the Galilean women at the cross is an important one in the Gospel tradition (it occurs in all four Gospels, although only John has a story attached to the note [John 19:25–27]). The presence of the women here and at the tomb provides a kind of continuity of the community of disciples from the time that the twelve themselves flee until the women report the resurrection of Jesus to them (they indeed are not active again in the story until 28:16). These verses belong naturally with the preceding narrative, and thus Heil's proposal concerning structure, which finds 27:55–28:20 a single unit, remains unconvincing (see discussion in R. E. Brown, *Death of the Messiah*, 1300–1301).

B. Matthew depends upon Mark 15:40–41 for these verses (cf. Luke 23:49; John 19:25–27). Matthew reorders the Markan material somewhat and abbreviates a little but otherwise follows Mark very closely. The only alterations that need to be noted are Matthew's substitution of ἐκεῖ, "there," for Mark's καί, "also," in v 55 (cf. Mark 15:40); his omission of τοῦ μικροῦ, "the small" (or "less"), after the name "James" in v 56 (cf. Mark 15:40); and in the same verse his substitution of ἡ μήτηρ τῶν υἱῶν Ζεβεδαίου, "the mother of the sons of Zebedee," for Mark's Σαλώμη, "Salome" (Mark 15:40), where Matthew apparently wishes to identify this "Salome" or to substitute a better-known woman (cf. 20:20). Matthew's abbreviation is found mainly in his omission of Mark 15:41b, "and there were many other women who had come up with him to Jerusalem," which is reflected only in his insertion of πολλαί, "many," in v 55 (cf. Mark 15:40).

### Comment

**55** Jesus had been grateful earlier for the support women had given to his Galilean ministry (cf. Luke 8:2–3 where διηκόνουν, "ministering," is also used; cf. διακονοῦσαι, "serving," in the present passage). These women, many of whom had been delivered from various maladies by him, continued to look after him right up to the end. Furthermore, it is the two Marys who were at the burial

(27:61), who went to the tomb (28:1; cf. Mark 16:1, where they go to "anoint" the body of Jesus), and who first encountered the risen Jesus (28:9). The women watched ἀπὸ μακρόθεν, "from a distance," which was the only thing they could do at this point. They had "followed" (ἠκολούθησαν) Jesus both literally and in discipleship, but now all seemed to have come to an end. They have no more hope than do the men.

**56** Three of these women are singled out, two by the name of Mary: Mary Magdalene (i.e., of Magdala on the Sea of Galilee), who is always named first (cf. Hengel), and Mary the mother of James and Joseph, neither of whom has been mentioned earlier by Matthew (the only mention of Mary Magdalene in the Gospels outside the passion and resurrection narratives is in Luke 8:2, where it is recorded that she had been exorcized of seven demons; nothing is known of the second Mary, who was perhaps the wife of Clopas, the sister of Mary the mother of Jesus [cf. John 19:25], but who is not referred to outside the passion and resurrection narratives). The two Marys are mentioned by Matthew again in v 61 and in 28:1–10. Nothing is known of the two sons, James and Joseph, unless the former (described as τοῦ μικροῦ, "the less" or "the small," in Mark 15:40) is to be identified with James the son of Alphaeus, one of the twelve, although this is perhaps unlikely. The third woman is the mother of the "sons of Zebedee," who are, of course, James and John of the twelve. She has appeared earlier in the narrative (20:20), where, however, she also remains nameless. If the parallel in Mark 15:41 refers to the same person, her name was Salome (she too is sometimes taken to be the "Mary the wife of Clopas" in John 19:25).

*Explanation*

At the very end it is the women, and not the disciples, who are there at the cross. They thus reflect a greater loyalty to their master. As they had faithfully supported him during his ministry, so now it is they who remain with him, even if at a distance, to the bitter end. They therefore deserve this special note of recognition as witnesses of his crucifixion and death. And it is they who will soon convey the message concerning the resurrection of Jesus to the disciples, for it is to the women that he first appeared.

# The Burial of Jesus (27:57–61)

*Bibliography*

**Bahat, D.** "Does the Holy Sepulchre Church Mark the Burial of Jesus?" *BARev* 12.2 (1986) 26–45. **Bakhuizen van der Brink, J. N.** "Eine Paradosis zu der Leidensgeschichte." *ZNW* 26 (1927) 213–19. **Barkay, G.** "The Garden Tomb: Was Jesus Buried Here?" *BARev* 12.3 (1986) 40–57. **Barrick, W. B.** "The Rich Man from Arimathea (Matt 27:57–60) and 1QIsaᵃ." *JBL* 96 (1977) 235–39. **Blinzler, J.** "Die Grablegung Jesu in historischer Sicht." In *Resurrexit: Actes du* *symposium international sur la résurrection de Jésus,* ed. É. Dhanis. Vatican: Libreria Editrice Vaticana, 1974. 56–107. ———. "Zur Auslegung der Evangelienberichte über Jesu Begräbnis." *MTZ* 3 (1952) 403–14. **Bornhäuser, K.** "Die Kreuzesabnahme und das Begräbnis Jesu." *NKZ* 42 (1931) 38–56. **Braun, F.-M.** "La sépulture de Jésus." *RB* 45 (1936) 34–52, 184–200, 346–63. **Briend, J.** "La sépulture d'un crucifié." *BTS* 133 (1971) 6–10. **Broer, I.** *Die Urgemeinde und das Grab Jesu: Eine Analyse der Grablegungsgeschichte im Neuen Testament.* SANT 31. Munich: Kösel, 1972. **Cousin, H.** "Sépulture criminelle et sépulture prophétique." *RB* 81 (1974) 373–93. **Curtis, K. P. G.** "Three Points of Contact between Matthew and John in the Burial and Resurrection Narratives." *JTS* 23 (1972) 440–44. **Dobschütz, E. von.** "Joseph von Arimathäa." *ZKG* 23 (1902) 1–17. **Gaechter, P.** "Zum Begräbnis Jesu." *ZTK* 75 (1953) 220–25. **Giblin, C. H.** "Structural and Thematic Correlation in the Matthean Burial-Resurrection Narrative (Matt. xxvii. 57–xxviii. 20)." *NTS* 21 (1974–75) 406–20. **Holtzmann, O.** "Das Begräbnis Jesu." *ZNW* 30 (1931) 311–13. **Jackson, C.** "Joseph of Arimathea." *JR* 16 (1936) 332–40. **Jeremias, J.** *Heiligengräber in Jesu Umwelt.* Göttingen: Vandenhoeck & Ruprecht, 1958. **Joüon, P.** "Matthieu 27,59: σινδών καθαρά, 'un drap d'un blanc pur.'" *RSR* 24 (1934) 93–95. **Kennard, J. S., Jr.** "The Burial of Jesus." *JBL* 74 (1955) 227–38. **Lai, P. H.** "Production du sens par la foi: Autorités religieuses contestées, fondées: Analyse structurale de Matthieu 27,57–28,20." *RSR* 61 (1973) 65–96. **Mercurio, R.** "A Baptismal Motif in the Gospel Narratives of the Burial." *CBQ* 21 (1959) 39–54. **Michel, O.** "Jüdische Bestattung und urchristliche Ostergeschichte." *Judaica* 16 (1960) 1–5. **O'Rahilly, A.** "The Burial of Christ." *Irish Ecclesiastical Review* 58 (1941) 302–16, 493–503; 59 (1942) 150–71. **Price, R. M.** "Jesus' Burial in a Garden: The Strange Growth of the Tradition." *Religious Traditions* 12 (1989) 17–30. **Riesner, R.** "Golgota und die Archaeologie." *BK* 40 (1985) 21–26. **Scholz, G.** "'Joseph of Arimathea' und 'Barabbas.'" *LingBib* 57 (1985) 81–94. **Schottroff, L.** "Maria Magdalena und die Frauen am Grabe Jesu." *EvT* 42 (1982) 3–25. **Schreiber, J.** "Die Bestattung Jesu: Redaktionsgeschichtliche Beobachtungen zu Mk 15,42–47 par." *ZNW* 72 (1981) 142–77. **Senior, D.** "Matthew's Account of the Burial of Jesus (Mt 27,57–61)." In *The Four Gospels 1992.* FS F. Neirynck, ed. F. Segbroeck et al. BETL 100. Leuven: Leuven UP, 1992. 1433–48. **Smith, R. H.** "The Tomb of Jesus." *BA* 30 (1967) 74–90. **Turiot, C.** "Sémiotique et lisibilité du texte évangélique." *RSR* 73 (1985) 161–75. **Vincent, L.-H.** "Garden Tomb: Histoire d'un mythe." *RB* 34 (1925) 401–31. **Whitaker, D.** "What Happened to the Body of Jesus?" *ExpTim* 81 (1969–70) 307–11.

## Translation

⁵⁷*Now when it was evening, a rich man from Arimathea by the name of Joseph came, who himself also had become a disciple of Jesus.* ⁵⁸*This man, having come to Pilate, asked for the body of Jesus. Then Pilate commanded it*ᵃ *to be given over to him.*ᵇ ⁵⁹*And Joseph took the body, wrapped it in a clean linen cloth,* ⁶⁰*and placed it in his new tomb, which he had cut in the rock. And when he had rolled in place a large stone to serve as*ᶜ *the door of the tomb, he departed.* ⁶¹*And Mary*ᵈ *Magdelene and the other Mary were there sitting opposite the tomb.*

## Notes

ᵃ "It" added to translation. Many MSS (A C D W Θ Σ *f*¹³ TR lat syᵖ·ʰ) have τὸ σῶμα, "the body," thus supplying the direct object. Σ syʰᵐᵍ add τοῦ Ἰησοῦ, "of Jesus."

ᵇ "To him" added to translation for clarity. A few MSS (237 sa mae) add αὐτῷ, "to him."

ᶜ "To serve as" added to the translation for clarity.

ᵈ Although many MSS (A D W *f*¹³ TR sa bo) have Μαρία, "Mary," the better MSS (א B C L Δ Θ *f*¹ mae boᵐˢ) have Μαριάμ, "Mariam" or "Miriam," a more Hebraic spelling of the name.

## *Form/Structure/Setting*

A. After the account of the death of Jesus and the parenthetical note concerning the women watching from a distance, this pericope concerning the burial of Jesus follows naturally. The body of Jesus is taken and buried by an influential man who was a disciple of Jesus. The location of the tomb in which the body of Jesus was placed is thus directly known to a disciple of Jesus. And a further guarantee of the location of the tomb is the note that the two Marys were also there opposite the tomb. (For an argument that 27:57–28:20 forms a single connected burial-resurrection narrative in a chiastic structure with 28:1–10 at the center, see Giblin; and for a critique, see Senior).

B. Matthew again follows Mark fairly closely but with some changes (Mark 15:42–47; cf. Luke 23:50–56; John 19:38–42). Matthew's pericope is only half as long as Mark's. The biggest departure from the Markan text involves the omission of Mark 15:44–45a concerning Pilate's inquiry about whether Jesus was in fact dead (omitted also by Luke). Matthew apparently felt no need to defend the death of Jesus against a theory that Jesus may only have appeared to be dead and later revived in the coolness of the tomb. Matthew's concern was to answer the claim that Jesus' body had been stolen (cf. vv 62–66; 28:11–15).

Other Matthean omissions to be noted are: in v 57 Mark's ἤδη, "already," and ἐπεὶ ἦν παρασκευὴ ὅ ἐστιν προσάββατον, "since it was the day of preparation, which is just before the sabbath" (cf. Mark 15:42), a somewhat awkward chronological note with which Matthew has no disagreement but which he apparently regards as unnecessary or perhaps confusing. Further alterations include the following. In v 57 Matthew refers to Joseph as ἄνθρωπος πλούσιος, "a rich man," in place of Mark's εὐσχήμων βουλευτής, "a prominent member of the council" (Mark 15:43), perhaps not wanting to associate Joseph with the enemies of Jesus (cf. Luke's necessary addition in Luke 22:51 that Joseph had not been part of the decision against Jesus). Also in v 57 he replaces Mark's ἦν προσδεχόμενος τὴν βασιλείαν τοῦ θεοῦ, "he was waiting expectantly for the kingdom of God" (Mark 15:43), with the more explicit ἐμαθητεύθη τῷ Ἰησοῦ, lit. "he had become a disciple of Jesus." In the same place Matthew omits Mark's τολμήσας, "dared," in reference to going to Pilate to make his request. In v 58 Matthew abbreviates Mark's ἐδωρήσατο τὸ πτῶμα τῷ Ἰωσήφ, "he gave the corpse to Joseph" (Mark 15:45), with ἐκέλευσεν ἀποδοθῆναι, "he commanded (it) to be given over." Matthew recasts v 59, with the resultant omission of ἀγοράσας, "bought," by the use of the synonym ἐνετύλιξεν, "he wrapped" (so too Luke 23:53; cf. John 20:7), for Mark's ἐνείλησεν, and the addition of καθαρᾷ, "clean" (cf. Mark 15:46). In v 60 Matthew adds τῷ καινῷ αὐτοῦ, "his new," to modify μνημείῳ, "tomb" (cf. Luke 23:53; John 19:42); μέγαν, "large," to modify λίθον, "stone," thereby emphasizing the security of the tomb (cf. Mark 16:4); and ἀπῆλθεν, "he departed," to round out the narrative (cf. Mark 15:46). In v 61 Matthew describes the second Mary as simply ἡ ἄλλη, "the other," in place of Mark's peculiar ἡ Ἰωσῆτος, "the mother of Joses" (cf. Mark 15:40, 47), and he replaces Mark's ἐθεώρουν ποῦ τέθειται, "they were watching where it [the body] was laid," with καθήμεναι ἀπέναντι τοῦ τάφου, "were sitting opposite the tomb."

C. The pericope is again in the genre of historical narrative, telling the story of how the body of Jesus came to be buried. A new character is introduced in the person of Joseph of Arimathea. The final verse of the passage (v 61) is not really part of the story itself but is added in preparation for 28:1. The passage may be simply outlined as follows: (1) Joseph asks Pilate for the body of Jesus (vv 57–58); (2) Joseph buries Jesus (vv 59–60); and (3) the women appear as witnesses (v 61).

*Comment*

**57–58** ὀψίας δὲ γενομένης, "and as evening came," i.e., Friday but before the beginning of the sabbath, the dead body of Jesus still hung on the cross. A man named Joseph, who was from Arimathea (a city in Judea [= Ramathaim?] mentioned only at this point in the four Gospels), whom Matthew describes only with the word πλούσιος, "rich," along with the indication that he ἐμαθητεύθη τῷ Ἰησοῦ, "had become a disciple of Jesus" (for the verb, cf. 13:52; 28:19), decided to bury Jesus in a tomb he had recently prepared (cf. Isa 53:9, which is possibly in Matthew's mind). According to the Markan and Lukan parallels, he was a member of the council of the Sanhedrin (Mark 15:42; Luke 23:50) and would thus have been well apprised of Jesus' fate, concerning which, as a disciple of Jesus (though "a secret one," according to John 19:38), he would have had special interest. Because of the way in which Mark describes Joseph, R. E. Brown (*Death of the Messiah*) concludes that he became a disciple of Jesus only *after* the resurrection. Matthew uses the word "rich" to indicate the kind of power and influence Joseph had to make his request of Pilate and to have it granted. It would have been not at all unusual for a disciple to bury his master, and it is doubtful that Joseph would have had to justify his request beyond that. In addition, from the Jewish perspective it was a requirement that the body of an executed criminal not be allowed to remain hanging "on a tree" through the night (Deut 21:22–23), especially at the onset of the sabbath, and this is more probably the reason Joseph gave for his request. In any event Pilate seems to have readily acceded to this small request of an influential man. It would not hurt him to accede to Jewish sensitivities on this point, and, furthermore, he saw no political threat from the followers of Jesus. (According to *Gos. Pet.* 3–5, 23–24, the disposition of the body of Jesus was the prerogative of Herod and the Jews, whom Pilate [described as a "friend" of Joseph's!] had to ask before the body could be granted to Joseph! But there is nothing historical here.)

**59–60** Unless the press of time did not permit it (as Mark 16:1 seems to imply), the body of Jesus would have been anointed with spices as it was wrapped in the linen cloth (cf. John 19:39–40). ἐντύλιξεν αὐτὸ [ἐν] σινδόνι καθαρᾷ, "he wrapped it in a clean linen cloth," employs the special terminology used in referring to contemporary burial practice. καθαρᾷ, "clean," could also be understood in the sense of "white" when applied to burial clothes (thus Joüon). So too it was the custom to bury in tombs carved out of rock, at least where this could be afforded, and to roll a huge stone in front of the opening to seal the tomb. The vocabulary μνημείῳ ὃ ἐλατόμησεν ἐν τῇ πέτρᾳ, "tomb which he cut out of the rock," is found in the LXX of Isa 22:16. A tomb cut out of rock would have been particularly expensive. This tomb into which Joseph placed the body of Jesus was τῷ καινῷ αὐτοῦ μνημείῳ, "his new tomb," one that he had recently prepared (cf. John 19:41; Curtis finds Johannine dependence on Matthew), perhaps for a close relative who was elderly or near death. A new tomb would obviously have contained no other body, thereby obviating the possibility of a later confusion of bodies. That Joseph put Jesus into the tomb is a tribute to his deep attachment to Jesus (cf. 1 Kgs 13:29–30). The λίθον μέγαν, "large stone" (cf. Mark 16:4), being round, was designed to be rolled into place along a kind of track (cf. 28:2; Mark 16:4; John 12:38–39). Having fulfilled his sad task, Joseph ἀπῆλθεν, "departed," and with this the pericope ends, except for the following added note about the women. Jesus, crucified as a criminal and from the Jewish point of view cursed by God, is nevertheless given an honorable burial. Indeed, he is buried in the tomb of a rich man (cf. Isa 53:9; see Barrick).

**61** Some of the women who had been watching Jesus on the cross presumably followed to see what became of the body when it was taken down (on the importance of the women in the passion narrative, see Schottroff). Perhaps they themselves hoped to give Jesus a better burial than would ordinarily be given someone who had been crucified, namely, the depositing of the body in a common grave used for criminals. ἡ ἄλλα Μαρία, "the other Mary," is almost certainly the Mary identified as "the mother of James and Joseph" in v 56 who there, as here, is also mentioned with Mary Magdalene (cf. too 28:1). The two Galilean Marys sat ἀπέναντι τοῦ τάφου, "across from the tomb," where they would have been able to watch Joseph put the body in the tomb and seal it with the huge stone. This note functions to certify correct knowledge concerning the specific tomb into which Jesus had been placed. Thus the empty tomb these same two women (i.e., the two witnesses; cf. 18:16) encounter in 28:1, 6 could not have been the wrong tomb. The word used for "tomb" here and in the following verses (τάφος) is a synonym for μνημεῖον (see the parallel use of the two words in 23:29). For a defense of the conclusion that the site of the original tomb lies beneath the present Church of the Holy Sepulchre, see R. E. Brown, *Death of the Messiah*, 1279–83; Bahat; cf. Barkay.

## Explanation

Jesus is spared the final ignominy of having his body buried with those of criminals in a common grave. A wealthy disciple of Jesus, Joseph of Arimathea, in an act of devotion to his Lord requests the body from Pilate in order that he might bury it in his nearby private tomb, newly hewn out of rock. It is this disciple's action that prevents Jesus' body from remaining on the cross (the Roman practice) and from being given a dishonorable burial in the anonymity of a common grave. It is noted by the evangelists that the two Marys sat opposite the tomb in which Jesus was buried, apparently watching Joseph as he placed the body in the tomb. In all of this the providence of God is at work preparing for the scene, shortly to follow, of the women meeting the angel at the empty tomb. Joseph of Arimathea, otherwise unknown to us, by his act of love provides the venue for the first experience of the news of the resurrection of Jesus—the revolutionary event that makes possible the faith we call Christianity. In the kerygma of the early church it is not only the death of Jesus that is important but also his burial (see 1 Cor 15:3–4; Acts 13:29). The burial is further confirmation of the reality of Jesus' death; together they provide the necessary prelude to the resurrection itself. As with the death and resurrection, the burial of Jesus is applied spiritually to the life of the Christian in the Pauline letters (Rom 6:4; Col 2:12).

# The Posting of the Guard at the Tomb    (27:62–66)

## Bibliography

**Broer, I.** "Mt 27,62–66." In *Die Urgemeinde und das Grab Jesu.* Munich: Kösel, 1972. 69–78. **Craig, W. L.** "The Guard at the Tomb." *NTS* 30 (1984) 273–81. **Lee, G. M.** "The Guard at the Tomb." *Th* 72 (1969) 169–75. **McArthur, H. K.** "On the Third Day." *NTS* 18 (1971) 81–86. **Metzger, B. M.** "The Nazareth Inscription Once Again." In *Jesus und Paulus.* FS W. G. Kümmel, ed. E. E. Ellis and E. Grässer. Göttingen: Vandenhoeck & Ruprecht, 1975. 221–38 (reprinted in *New Testament Studies.* Leiden: Brill, 1980. 75–92). **Ritt, H.** "Die Frauen und die Osterbotschaft: Synopse der Grabesgeschichten (Mk 16,1–8; Mt 27,62–28,15; Lk 24,1–12; Joh 20,1–18)." In *Die Frau im Urchristentum,* ed. G. Dautzenberg, H. Merklein, and D. Müller. QD 95. Freiburg: Herder, 1983. 117–33. **Samain, P.** "L'accusation de magie contre le Christ dans les Évangiles." *ETL* 15 (1938) 456–64. **Smyth, K.** "The Guard at the Tomb." *HeyJ* 2 (1961) 157–59. **Walker, N.** "'After three days' (Matt 27:63)." *NovT* 4 (1960) 261–62. **Wenham, D.** "The Resurrection Narratives in Matthew's Gospel." *TynB* 24 (1973) 21–54. **Zulueta, F. de.** "Violation of Sepulture in Palestine at the Beginning of the Christian Era." *JRS* 22 (1932) 184–97.

See also *Bibliography* on 28:11–15.

## Translation

[62] *And on the next day, which was the day* [a] *after the preparation, the high priests and the Pharisees gathered together before Pilate,* [63] *saying: "Your Excellency, we remember that, when he was alive, that deceiver said: 'After three days I will rise.'* [64] *Give orders, therefore, that the tomb be made secure until the third day, lest his* [b] *disciples come and steal him* [c] *and say to the people: 'He has been raised from the dead,' and the last deception will be worse than the first."* [65] *Pilate* [d] *said to them: "Take* [e] *a guard.* [f] *Go, make it as secure as you know how to."* [66] *And they went and made the tomb secure, having sealed the stone, and leaving* [g] *the guard.* [h]

## Notes

[a] "The day" added to complete sense.

[b] א B arm geo[pt] omit αὐτοῦ, "his." The remaining οἱ μαθηταί, lit. "the disciples," may, however, also be translated "his disciples."

[c] Some MSS (C³ L S Γ sy[s,p]) include νυκτός, "by night," either before or after "steal him." This is probably an addition prompted by 28:13. *TCGNT*, 71.

[d] Some MSS (א A C D W Δ f¹ sy[h]** bo[pt]) add the connective δέ, "but" or "and."

e ἔχετε, lit. "you have." See *Comment.*

f D* it mae bo have φυλακάς, the proper Gr. word for "guard" rather than the equivalent Latin loanword κουστωδίαν.

g μετά, lit. "with."

h D* it mae bo^pt again have τῶν φυλακῶν for τῆς κουστωδίας. See above, *Note* f.

### Form/Structure/Setting

A. Just prior to the resurrection account itself, Matthew inserts this pericope concerning the measures taken by the Jewish authorities to assure that the body of Jesus could not be stolen. This pericope is obviously related very closely to 28:11–15 where the Jewish authorities concoct the story of the disciples stealing Jesus' body. Indeed, R. E. Brown may be correct in concluding that originally these verses were part of one connected narrative into which Matthew inserted the pericope concerning the women at the tomb (28:1–10; *Death of the Messiah,* 1301–5). The key to Matthew's purpose in both pericopes is the final sentence of 28:15: "and this story has spread among the Jews until this day." Matthew intends to show how groundless any such claim is. Matthew's Jewish readership provided the motivation for the inclusion of this material. They would have been familiar with this explanation of the empty tomb.

B. The passage is unique to Matthew. The material may depend on a source used by Matthew, or it may be the result of the evangelist's reconstruction based on his knowledge of the presence of a guard at the tomb. The parallel material in *Gos. Pet.* 28–34 (where Pilate sends a centurion named Petronius and some soldiers to guard the tomb) is probably an elaboration of the Matthean account rather than an independent witness to the same tradition (thus Gnilka; but for the latter view [in addition to dependence on Matthew], cf. R. E. Brown, *Death of the Messiah,* 1307).

C. Apart from the introductory and concluding verses, the pericope consists of dialogue between the Jewish authorities and Pilate. The following outline may be suggested: (1) the Jewish authorities come to Pilate (v 62); (2) they recall Jesus' prophecy of his resurrection (v 63); (3) they ask for a tomb guard (v 64); (4) Pilate grants them a guard (v 65); and (5) the tomb is secured (v 66). The polemical tone of v 64 finds its explanation in the reality of the subsequent resurrection and the concocted story of the Jews in 28:11–15.

D. The question concerning the historical reliability of this narrative (and that of 28:11–15) is difficult. In a balanced discussion R. E. Brown finally decides against its historicity because of the difficulty of reconciling Matthew's story with that of the other evangelists (*Death of the Messiah,* 1310–13). The latter, indeed, know nothing of the story (they did not have to contend with the Jewish explanation of the empty tomb). Apart from that fact, if there was a Roman guard at the tomb, how would the women have hoped to gain access to it to accomplish their purpose of anointing the body of Jesus (Mark 16:1; Luke 24:1)? One may respond that perhaps they had no knowledge of the guard, or if they did, they still had some slim hope of persuading them to gain entrance for their special purpose. Matthew, to be sure, alters Mark by having the women witness the rolling back of the stone (28:2), thereby adding assurance to the unbroken security of the tomb. The women *see* the tomb opened. But this liberty is not different from what we have seen in the evangelist's use of his sources and need not undermine the historicity of the core here. (For support of the historicity of this pericope, see Wenham, 47–51, and Craig, who, however, argues for a Jewish rather than a Roman guard; and for arguments against the historicity, see Broer, 60–78.)

*Comment*

**62**  τῇ δὲ ἐπαύριον, "and on the next day," is the day after the crucifixion, identified further as the day μετὰ τὴν παρασκευήν, "after the preparation" (cf. Mark 15:42), for the sabbath, i.e., more directly, the sabbath or Saturday. Although the gathering together of οἱ ἀρχιερεῖς καὶ οἱ φαρισαῖοι, "the chief priests and the Pharisees" (a somewhat unusual coupling made earlier in 21:45), need not be thought of as a formally constituted gathering of the Sanhedrin authorities, it would nevertheless have been extraordinary for this to have occurred on the sabbath. It need hardly be thought impossible, however, given the extraordinary circumstances and the fact that the concern of these Jewish authorities was an urgent one. Matthew, however, makes no point of the violation of the sabbath.

**63**  The address of Pilate as κύριος means "Sir" or "Your Excellency" rather than "Lord," although it is not impossible that the error of the Jewish authorities in not accepting Jesus as their κύριος, "Lord," is hinted at. This is the only place in the Gospels where Jesus is called πλάνος, "deceiver" (cf. the cognate verb used in reference to Jesus in John 7:12, 47; cf. the same point but different language in Luke 23:14). For the prophecy μετὰ τρεῖς ἡμέρας ἐγείρομαι, "after three days I will rise," spoken as a sign to the scribes and Pharisees, cf. 12:40 (see too 26:61; 27:40, both in reference to rebuilding the temple in "three days"). The typical Matthean formula, however, is τῇ τρίτῃ ἡμέρᾳ, "on the third day" (cf. 16:21; 17:23; 20:19), in each instance spoken to the disciples (see Walker, who argues that "after three days" is to be reckoned from the rejection of Jesus at the Sanhedrin trial). It is a mistake to suppose that the Jewish authorities had a very clear conception of what Jesus had predicted. Matthew's formulation of their words reflects later, more specific knowledge.

**64**  The Pharisees believed in the future resurrection of the dead; to the extent that the chief priests were of Sadducean persuasion, they denied the possibility of resurrection altogether (cf. Acts 23:6–10). But none of these Jews believed that Jesus would really rise from the dead, nor, of course, when he had risen did they believe the report (hence the concocted story referred to in 28:11–15). They wanted Pilate "to put the tomb under guard" (ἀσφαλισθῆναι τὸν τάφον) not to prevent the resurrection but to keep the disciples from stealing the body, as is clearly stated here. The phrase ἕως τῆς τρίτης ἡμέρας, "until the third day," reckoned from the time of the request (i.e., Saturday), would provide one day's extra protection (cf. μετὰ τρεῖς ἡμέρας, "after three days" [v 63]). The reference to the disciples stealing the body reflects the very story the Jewish authorities themselves later find it necessary to invent (cf. 28:13). The imagined statement ἠγέρθη ἀπὸ τῶν νεκρῶν, "he has been raised from the dead," becomes ironically the central element of the church's kerygma (e.g., Acts 2:24; 3:15; 10:40; 13:30). And the fear expressed in the words καὶ ἔσται ἡ ἐσχάτη πλάνη χείρων τῆς πρώτης, "and the last deception will be worse than the first" (for the same idiom, cf. 12:45;

2 Peter 2:20), proves ironically true in the sense that the proclamation of the resurrection of Jesus brought forth a more positive response to Jesus than his actual ministry, limited in space and time, could ever have produced. It seems clear that the material of this and the preceding verse has been formulated with a degree of hindsight on the evangelist's part.

**65–66** Pilate's response: ἔχετε κουστωδίαν is problematic since it can be taken literally to mean "you have a guard (already)" or "take a guard," i.e., "there, you have a guard" (for which, see BAGD, 333b). It is more probably a guard of Roman soldiers (κουστωδίαν is appropriately a Latin loanword) as can be seen from the fact that they were answerable to Pilate (cf. 28:11, 14; 28:12 uses στρατιῶται, "soldiers," a word that usually means Roman soldiers [as in 27:27]; see esp. Smyth, who provides parallel examples of the use of ἔχετε as an imperative). Pilate, of course, has little genuine interest in the matter, but ever intent on building good relations with the Jewish authorities, he gives them authority to secure the tomb with the provided guard. They are given directions to secure the tomb as well as they know how to do it (ὡς οἴδατε, "as you know"). They depart to the tomb where they post the guard and seal the tomb. The tomb had, of course, already been closed by the great stone that Joseph of Arimathea had rolled into place after having placed Jesus' body in it (v 60). Although it is not impossible that σφραγίσαντες τὸν λίθον μετὰ τῆς κουστωδίας is meant metaphorically, i.e., "sealing the stone with the presence of a guard" (cf. BAGD, 510a), it is perhaps more likely that the stone was actually sealed shut with official seals that if broken would attest the opening of the tomb (cf. the practice referred to in Dan 6:17). The security of tombs was important enough to have become the subject of a Roman imperial edict between 50 B.C. and A.D. 50 (see Metzger). Since this strategy was not formulated until "the next day" (v 62), the tomb in fact remained unguarded over Friday night. As R. E. Brown (*Death of the Messiah*, 1309, n. 53) rightly points out, however, the guard would hardly have sealed the tomb without first checking to see if the body was there. If Matthew created this story *ex nihilo*, however, it is more likely that he would have had the guard posted immediately after the interment (rightly, Carson).

### Explanation

It is remarkable that Jesus' opponents remember the prediction of Jesus' resurrection. If they knew that Jesus had said he would rise from the dead, they certainly did not believe it. Whatever they knew or had heard rumor of, it was enough to motivate them to take the precaution of guarding the tomb lest the disciples deceive the people by stealing the body and making the claim that he had risen from the dead. There is a twofold miscalculation here. First, the Jewish authorities underestimate Jesus by failing to realize God's purpose in and through him. That Jesus could rise from the dead they wrongly rule out a priori. And when they have no explanation for what happened to the body of Jesus, ironically they invent the very lie they attempted to protect against (28:13). Second, they overestimate the disciples, who were not thinking of Jesus' words about rising from the dead and whose psychological condition hardly made it possible for them to perpetrate such a hoax as the Jewish authorities feared. The incongruous, ironical result is that the opponents took Jesus' words about rising from the dead more seriously than did the disciples. A vague fear in this case was a greater motivation than the hope of the disciples. Calling attention to the irony in the passage, Gnilka aptly concludes: "The laughter of God roars through the pericope" (2:489). Such must be said also of the pericope that completes this one (28:11–15).

# The Resurrection Narrative (28:1-20)

## Bibliography

**Alsup, J. E.** *The Post-Resurrection Appearance Stories of the Gospel Tradition: A History-of-Tradition Analysis with Text-Synopsis.* CTM 5. Stuttgart: Calwer, 1975. **Brown, R. E.** "The Resurrection in Matthew (27:62-28:20)." *Worship* 64 (1990) 157-70. ———. *A Risen Christ in Eastertide: Essays on the Gospel Narratives of the Resurrection.* Collegeville, MN: Liturgical, 1991. **Bruce, F. F.** "The End of the First Gospel." *EvQ* 12 (1940) 203-14. **Fuller, D. P.** *Easter Faith and History.* Grand Rapids: Eerdmans, 1965. **Fuller, R. H.** *The Formation of the Resurrection Narratives.* New York: Macmillan, 1971. **Gardner-Smith, P.** *The Narratives of the Resurrection: A Critical Study.* London: Methuen, 1926. **Grass, H.** *Ostergeschehen und Osterberichte.* 3rd ed. Göttingen: Vandenhoeck & Ruprecht, 1964. **Gutbrod, K.** *Die Auferstehung Jesu im Neuen Testament.* Stuttgart: Calwer, 1969. **Heil, J. P.** *The Death and Resurrection of Jesus: A Narrative-Critical Reading of Matthew 26-28.* Minneapolis: Fortress, 1991. **Hendrickx, H.** *The Resurrection Narratives of the Synoptic Gospels.* Rev. ed. London: Chapman, 1984. **Kremer, J.** *Die Osterbotschaft der vier Evangelien: Versuch einer Auslegung der Berichte über das leere Grab und die Erscheinungen des Auferstandenen.* Stuttgart: Katholisches Bibelwerk, 1968. **Reeves, K. H.** *The Resurrection Narrative in Matthew: A Literary-Critical Examination.* Lewiston, New York: Mellen, 1993. **Smith, R. H.** "Celebrating Easter in the Matthean Mode." *CurTM* 11 (1984) 79-82. ———. *Easter Gospels: The Resurrection of Jesus according to the Four Gospels.* Minneapolis: Augsburg, 1983. **Smyth, K.** "Matthew 28: Resurrection as Theophany." *ITQ* 42 (1975) 259-71.

# The Announcement of the Resurrection to the Women at the Tomb (28:1-7)

## Bibliography

**Aarde, A. G. van.** "' Ἠγέρθη ἀπὸ τῶν νεκρῶν' (Mt 28:7): A Textual Evidence on the Separation of Judaism and Christianity." *Neot* 23 (1989) 219-33 (reprinted in *God-with-Us: The Dominant Perspective in Matthew's Story.* Hervormde Teologiese Studies Supplementum 5. Pretoria: Nederduitsch Hervormde Kerk, 1994. 248-60). **Albertz, M.** "Zur Formgeschichte der Auferstehungsberichte." *ZNW* 21 (1922) 259-69. **Bickermann, E.** "Das leere Grab." *ZNW* 23 (1924) 281-92. **Bode, E. L.** *The First Easter Morning: The Gospel Accounts of the Women's Visit to the Tomb of Jesus.* AnBib 45. Rome: Biblical Institute, 1970. ———. "A Liturgical *Sitz im Leben* for the Gospel Tradition of the Women's Easter Visit to the Tomb of Jesus?" *CBQ* 32 (1970) 237-42. **Broer, I.** "Zur heutigen Diskussion der Grabesgeschichte." *BibLeb* 10 (1969) 40-52. **Campenhausen, H. von.** "The Events of the Easter and the Empty Tomb." In *Tradition and Life in the Church.* Philadelphia: Fortress, 1968. 42-89. **Craig, W. L.** "The Empty Tomb of Jesus." In *Gospel Perspectives*, ed. R. T. France and D. Wenham. Sheffield: JSOT, 1981. 2:173-200. **Dockx, S.** "Étapes rédactionelles du récit des apparitions aux saintes femmes." In *Chronologies néotestamentaires et vie de l'Église primitive.* Leuven: Peeters, 1984. 233-53. **Driver, G. R.** "Two Problems in the New Testament." *JTS* 16 (1965)

327–37. **Gerhardsson, B.** "Mark and the Female Witnesses." In *DUMU-E₂-DUB-BA-A.* FS Å. W. Sjöberg, ed. H. Behrens et al. Philadelphia: University of Pennsylvania, 1989. 217–26. **Goulder, M. D.** "Mark xvi. 1–8 and Parallels." *NTS* 24 (1977–78) 235–40. **Hengel, M.** "Maria Magdalena und die Frauen als Zeugen." In *Abraham unser Vater.* FS O. Michel, ed. O. Betz et al. Leiden: Brill, 1963. 243–56. **Hodges, Z. C.** "The Women and the Empty Tomb." *BSac* 123 (1966) 301–9. **Jenkins, A. K.** "Young Man or Angel." *ExpTim* 94 (1983) 237–40. **Krücke, A.** "Der Engel am Grabe Christi." *ZNW* 33 (1934) 313–17. **LaVerdiere, E.** "The Resurrection according to Matthew." *Emmanuel* 93 (1987) 126–35. **Léon-Dufour, X.** "The Easter Message according to Matthew." In *The Resurrection and the Message of Easter.* Tr. R. N. Wilson. New York: Holt, Rinehart and Winston, 1971. 139–49. **Longstaff, T. R. W.** "The Women at the Tomb: Matthew 28:1 Reexamined." *NTS* 27 (1981) 277–82. **Margoliouth, D. S.** "The Visit to the Tomb." *ExpTim* 38 (1927) 278–80. **Marin, L.** "Les femmes au tombeau." In *Études sémiologiques.* Paris: Klincksieck, 1971. **Martini, C. M.** "Les signes de la résurrection (Mt 28,1–10)." *AsSeign* 21 (1969) 48–57. **McKenzie, R. A.** "As the First Day of the Week Dawned: Mt 28.1–20." In *The First Day of the Week.* New York: Paulist, 1985. 22–39. **Minear, P.** "Matthew 28.1–10." *Int* 38 (1984) 59–63. **Nauck, W.** "Die Bedeutung des leeren Grabes für den Glauben an den Auferstandenen." *ZNW* 47 (1956) 243–67. **Neirynck, F.** "Les femmes au tombeau: Étude de la rédaction Matthéenne (Matt. xxviii:1–10)." *NTS* 15 (1968–69) 168–90. ———. "John and the Synoptics: The Empty Tomb Stories." *NTS* 30 (1984) 161–87. **O'Collins, G.,** and **Kendall, D.** "Mary Magdalene as Major Witness to Jesus' Resurrection." *TS* 48 (1987) 631–46. **Oppermann, R.** "Eine Beobachtung in Bezug auf das Problem des Markusschlusses." *BibNot* 40 (1987) 24–29. **Rigaux, B.** "Mt 28,1–8." In *Dieu l'a ressuscité: Exégèse et théologie biblique.* Gembloux: Duculot, 1973. 200–204. **Ritt, H.** "Die Frauen und die Osterbotschaft Synopse der Grabesgeschichten (Mk 16,1–8; Mt 27,62–28,15; Lk 24,1–12; Joh 20,1–18)." In *Die Frau im Urchristentum,* ed. G. Dautzenberg et al. QD 95. Freiburg: Herder, 1983. 117–33. **Stein, R. H.** "Was the Tomb Really Empty?" *JETS* 20 (1977) 23–29. **Trilling, W.** "Die Auferstehung Jesu: Anfang der neuen Weltzeit (Mt 28,1–8)." In *Christusverkündigung in den synoptischen Evangelien: Beispiele gattungsgemässer Auslegung.* Biblische Handbibliothek 4. Munich: Kösel, 1969. 212–43. ———. "Das leere Grab bei Matthäus (Mt 28,1–7)." In *Vielfalt und Einheit im Neuen Testament.* Einsiedeln: Benziger, 1968. 112–24. **Walker, D. A.** "Resurrection, Empty Tomb and Easter Faith." *ExpTim* 101 (1990) 172–75. **Walter, N.** "Eine vormatthäische Schilderung der Auferstehung Jesu." *NTS* 19 (1972–73) 415–29. **Webster, C. A.** "St. Matthew 28,1.3." *ExpTim* 42 (1930–31) 381–82. **Whitaker, D.** "What Happened to the Body of Jesus?" *ExpTim* 81 (1969–70) 307–11. **Wilckens U.** "Die Perikope vom leere Grabe Jesu in der nachmarkinischen Traditionsgeschichte." In *Festschrift für Friedrich Smend zum 70. Geburtstag.* Berlin: Merseburger, 1963. 30–41.

### Translation

¹*And after the sabbath at dawn on the first day of the week, Mary* [a] *Magdalene and the other Mary came to look at the tomb.* ²*And look, there was a great earthquake! For an angel of the Lord, having come down from heaven and having approached the place,* [b] *rolled the stone away* [c] *and was sitting upon it.* ³*And his appearance was like lightning, and his clothing was white as snow.* ⁴*And through fear of him those keeping guard were shaken, and they became like dead men.* ⁵*But the angel answered and said to the women: "Do not you too become afraid. For I know that you look for Jesus the crucified one.* ⁶*He is not here, for he has been raised, just as he said he would be.* [d] *Come, see the place where he* [e] *was lying.* ⁷*And go quickly and say to his disciples that he has been raised from the dead!* [f] *And look, he is going before you into Galilee. There you will see him. Look, I have told it* [g] *to you!"*

## Notes

ᵃ Μαριάμ, lit. "Mariam" or "Miriam," a more Hebraic rendering of the name. Many MSS (A B D W *f*¹·¹³ TR sa bo) have Μαρία, "Mary." See *Note* a on 27:56.

ᵇ "The place" added to supply direct object.

ᶜ Some MSS (C K W Δ syᵖ) add ἀπὸ τῆς θύρας, "from the door." Other MSS (A L Γ Θ *f*¹·¹³ syʰ mae bo) include that addition plus τοῦ μνημείου, "of the tomb."

ᵈ "He would be" added to the translation to complete the sense of the sentence.

ᵉ Many MSS (A C D L W *f*¹·¹³ TR lat sy[ᵖ]ʰ) insert ὁ κύριος, "the Lord," 1424 inserts τὸ σῶμα τοῦ κυρίου, "the body of the Lord," and Φ inserts ὁ Ἰησοῦς, "Jesus," all of which supply a subject for ἔκειτο, "was lying."

ᶠ D lat syˢ arm omit ἀπὸ τῶν νεκρῶν, "from the dead," perhaps influenced by the simple ἠγέρθη, "he was raised," of v 6. See *TCGNT*, 71–72.

ᵍ "It" added to supply direct object.

## Form/Structure/Setting

A. The resurrection narrative begins with the empty tomb account. This pericope gains forcefulness by following immediately upon the story concerning the precautions taken by the Jewish authorities to guard against any intrusion into the tomb. The narrative presupposes the resurrection of Jesus rather than giving an account of how or when it happened. It is fundamentally an announcement of the fact of the resurrection without an actual resurrection appearance. The startling announcement is made with appropriately spectacular accompaniments: an earthquake, an open tomb, the appearance of an angel, and the revelation of instructions for the disciples.

B. Matthew remains dependent upon Mark for this pericope, although he does not follow very closely (Mark 16:1–7; cf. Luke 24:1–8; John 20:1). Is it possible that for vv 9–10 and even vv 16–20 Matthew is dependent upon the original, now lost, ending of Mark (thus Gundry)? See esp. Neirynck (*NTS* 15 [1968–69] 168–90) for Matthew's redaction of Mark. Matthew omits Mark 16:1 with its reference to the three women coming to embalm the body of Jesus, instead referring in v 1 to the two Marys, who come only to look at the tomb (cf. the anointing in 26:6–13). Matthew also omits Mark 16:3–4, where the women wonder how they will gain access to the inside of the tomb only to discover that the stone had been rolled back, replacing this with the account of a σεισμὸς μέγας, "great earthquake," and the descent of an ἄγγελος κυρίου, "angel of the Lord," who rolls back the stone and sits upon it (v 2, corresponding to Mark's νεανίσκον, "young man," sitting inside the tomb ἐν τοῖς δεξιοῖς, "on the right side"). In this way Matthew tightens up the sequence of events so as not to have an open tomb without witnesses before the arrival of the women. In Matthew the women do not enter the tomb as they do in Mark (Mark 10:5). While both evangelists talk of the white raiment of the angel/man, Matthew adds ἦν δὲ ἡ εἰδέα αὐτοῦ ὡς ἀστραπή, "and his appearance was like lightning" (cf. Luke 24:4). Mark's reference to the alarm of the women (ἐξεθαμβήθησαν, "they were alarmed") becomes in Matthew a reference to the fear of the guards who ἐγενήθησαν ὡς νεκροί, "became like dead men" (v 4; cf. Mark 16:5). The message from the angel/man remains essentially the same. Matthew, however, adds in v 5 the emphatic ὑμεῖς, "you" (in contrast to the guards), and οἶδα ὅτι, "I know that" (supernatural knowledge may be expected in an angel from heaven), and in v 6 καθὼς εἶπεν, "even as he said," pointing to the resurrection predictions (cf. Mark 16:6). Only at this point is there an invitation to enter the tomb in Matthew's added δεῦτε, "come." Also in v 6 ὅπου ἔκειτο, "where he lay," replaces Mark's ὅπου ἔθηκαν αὐτόν, "where they laid him" (cf. Mark 16:6). In v 7 Matthew adds ταχύ, "quickly," and supplies the specific message of the resurrection ὅτι ἠγέρθη ἀπὸ τῶν νεκρῶν, "that he has been raised from the dead," to the message that "he goes before you to Galilee" (cf. Mark 16:7), thereby emphasizing the message about the resurrection of Jesus. Given the prominence of Peter in Matthew, it is very surprising that Matthew omits καὶ τῷ Πέτρῳ, "and to Peter," but the evangelist apparently did not think it important to single out Peter at this point (cf. Mark 16:7). Peter's forgiveness is taken for granted (he is among the eleven in 28:16). Finally note Matthew's alteration of Mark's καθὼς εἶπεν ὑμῖν, "just as he said to you," to ἰδοὺ εἶπον ὑμῖν, "behold, I have told you," perhaps because of the insertion of καθὼς εἶπεν, "just as he said," in the preceding verse but more probably because of Matthew's addition in v 10 (v 7; cf. Mark 16:7).

C. The pericope consists essentially of the coming of the angel and the message of the angel; thus the first half consists of narrative, the second of speech. As an outline the following may be suggested: (1) the women's arrival at the tomb (v 1); (2) the earthquake and the appearance of the angel (vv 2–3); (3) the fear of the guards (v 4); and of central importance (4) the message of the angel (vv 5–7), subdivided into (a) exhortation not to fear (v 5), (b) statement that Jesus is risen (v 6), and (c) command to go and tell the disciples (v 7). Note the structural device of the five parallel imperatives spoken by the angelic messenger: do not fear, come, see, go (an imperatival participle), and tell.

D. The problem of reconciling the resurrection narratives in the four Gospels is notorious. There is, however, no need to harmonize the details of these discrete accounts. We do well to allow each Gospel to present its own account with its own distinctives. As L. Morris points out, "Each of the Evangelists tells the story as best he knows without trying to harmonize it with what somebody else says" (733). It is enough (with Morris) to stress that all the Gospels have in common an empty tomb, the announcement of the resurrection of Jesus to the women, and the appearance of the risen Jesus to the disciples. On the historicity of the empty tomb, see Stein, Nauck, and especially Craig.

*Comment*

1 Although ὀψέ literally means "evening," ὀψὲ δὲ σαββάτων here means "and after the sabbath" (for ὀψέ as "an improper preposition" with the genitive, see BAGD, 601b; BDF §164[4]) as the following phrase, τῇ ἐπιφωσκούσῃ εἰς μίαν σαββάτων, "at the dawning on the first (day) of the seven (i.e., week)," indicates (cf. 1 Cor 16:2). The time indicated is thus early Sunday morning (with Goulder; *pace* Gundry, who argues for Saturday evening). Here, indeed, we find the impetus for Christian worship on the first day of the week (thus Bode, *CBQ* 32 [1970] 237–42). ἡ ἄλλη Μαρία, "the other Mary," is presumably Mary the mother of James and Joseph, referred to in 27:56 together with Mary Magdalene. The latter is of key importance as a witness to the resurrection, being mentioned first in every

resurrection narrative in the Gospels (see O'Collins and Kendall). No mention is made of the third woman, the mother of the sons of Zebedee, also mentioned in 27:56 (thus no equivalent to Mark's third woman, Σαλώμη, "Salome," is given here, in contrast to 27:56). According to Matthew, they come only θεωρῆσαι τὸν τάφον, "to see the tomb," perhaps to pray or to mourn (cf. their presence near the tomb during Jesus' interment [27:61]). Less probable is Longstaff's argument that their visit reflects a Jewish custom of visiting the tomb of a loved one until the third day to insure against premature burial (cf. *Sem.* 8.1 from the third century).

**2–3** Matthew again calls attention to the unusual with his ἰδού, "look!" Only Matthew refers to an earthquake here, σεισμὸς μέγας, "a great earthquake," which is conceivably the same as that referred to in 27:51, 54 but possibly also meant as a fresh one (an aftershock of the first?). The mention of an earthquake here involves apocalyptic symbolism as elsewhere in Matthew but need not for that reason alone be regarded as not actually happening (cf. 24:7; 27:54; 8:24; Matthew uses σεισμός, "earthquake," four times compared to one reference in Mark and in Luke [both = Matt 24:7]). The earthquake in this instance is related to (note γάρ, "for") the descent ἐξ οὐρανοῦ, "from heaven," of ἄγγελος κυρίου, "an angel of the Lord" (the first reappearance of the phrase since the infancy narrative; cf. 1:20, 24; 2:13, 19), a reference that also stresses the apocalyptic character of the event. The angel ἀπεκύλισεν τὸν λίθον, "rolled away the stone" (cf. the reference to λίθον μέγαν, "very large stone," in 27:60), and was triumphantly "sitting above it" (ἐκάθητο [imperfect] ἐπάνω αὐτοῦ). The εἰδέα (= ἰδέα), "appearance," though possibly "face" (in the NT only here), of the angel is described as being ὡς ἀστραπή, "like lightning," i.e., having a startling brilliance (cf. Dan 10:6; Matt 13:43). For dazzling "white" (λευκόν) garments, cf. 17:2 ("white as light"); Acts 1:10; Rev 3:5; 4:4; etc. (for "white as snow," cf. Dan 7:9).

**4** If the earthquake did not frighten the guards enough, the appearance of an angel with such a glistening visage, sitting moreover upon the large tombstone that had been rolled away, frightened them to death. ἀπὸ δὲ τοῦ φόβου αὐτοῦ, "and for fear of him," they trembled (ἐσείσθησων, lit. "were shaken," now not by an earthquake but by their anxiety) and ἐγενήθησαν ὡς νεκροί, "they became like dead men" (for the same expression as a sign of fear, cf. Rev 1:17). Perhaps it is meant that they fainted from the shock. The irony is not to be missed: the ones assigned to guard the dead themselves appear dead while the dead one has been made alive.

**5** The angel first directs his attention to calming the women's fears: μὴ φοβεῖσθε ὑμεῖς, "Do not you too become afraid" (emphatic ὑμεῖς, "you," i.e., as did the guards). It is not uncommon for such heavenly messengers similarly to exhort those whom they approach not to fear (e.g., Luke 1:13, 30; 2:10; pertaining to Jesus, cf. v 10 in the present pericope; 14:27; 17:7; Rev 1:17). With the tomb now open, the women can be correctly described as "seeking" (ζητεῖτε) Jesus who, having accomplished his goal—hence as the risen one—can now also remarkably be described as τὸν ἐσταυρωμένον, "the crucified one" (the perfect participle reflecting his ongoing status as such; the same form is used in describing the heart of the kerygma in 1 Cor 1:23; 2:2; cf. Gal 3:1). But the crucified one is not in the tomb where the women expect him to be, indeed, where they had seen him buried two days earlier (27:61).

**6** The women are told οὐκ ἔστιν ὧδε, "he is not here." The angel has not opened the tomb so that Jesus may come out. No one, indeed, saw Jesus come out of the tomb. All the women have thus far are the brief words of the angel. The reason he is not there is made very plain in the triumphant words ἠγέρθη γάρ, "for he has been raised," a divine passive with God as the acting subject (cf. v 7). This declaration rules out all alternative explanations of the empty tomb. *It* alone explains the empty tomb. The words καθὼς εἶπεν, "just as he said," refer to his predictions of his resurrection in 16:21; 17:23; 20:19 (cf. 12:40; 26:61; 27:40, 63). The women are invited into the tomb to see where Jesus "lay" (ἔκειτο) as proof that the body was not there. Yet faith in the resurrection does not result from the empty tomb itself (Nauck). The women will yet see the risen Jesus for themselves.

**7** It is the faithful and devoted women who are to go ταχύ, "quickly," to bear the good tidings of Jesus' resurrection τοῖς μαθηταῖς αὐτοῦ, "to his disciples." Matthew uses repetition to emphasize their clearly defined message, ὅτι ἠγέρθη ἀπὸ τῶν νεκρῶν, "that he has been raised from the dead" (cf. the same verb in v 6), which would become the cornerstone of the kerygma of the apostles and the early church (see, e.g., Acts 3:15; 4:10; 13:30; Rom 10:9; 1 Cor 15:12; in all these references except the last, the passive verb of the Synoptics now receives its understood subject: God raised Jesus from the dead). The words beginning καὶ ἰδού, "and look," are also probably meant to be part of the message to the disciples but are probably equally addressed to the women. The statement προάγει ὑμᾶς εἰς τὴν Γαλιλαίαν, "he goes before you to Galilee," recalls words of Jesus himself recorded in 26:32; it is repeated by the risen Jesus in v 10 and finds it fulfillment in v 16. The resurrection of Jesus, however, is to be more than a report for the disciples. In Galilee (ἐκεῖ, "there") αὐτὸν ὄψεσθε, "you will see him," a promise repeated to the women by the risen Jesus in v 10. The added words ἰδοὺ εἶπον ὑμῖν, "look, I have told you," function to call attention once again to the angelic, and thus heavenly, source for this revelation, thereby emphasizing the authority of the words.

### Explanation

The event of the resurrection is not described by the evangelists. The first evidence of the resurrection of Jesus consists only of the report, spectacular as it is in Matthew's account, of an angelic being accompanied by the hard evidence of the empty tomb. Yet the empty tomb remains circumstantial evidence that only begins to awaken faith; the real proof of the resurrection is the encounter with the risen Jesus in vv 8–10. In the context of the proclaimed resurrection of Jesus, the description of the guards as "like dead men" takes on an almost comical aspect. But the focus of the narrative is on the proclamation that Jesus has been raised from the dead—the key element of the message preached by the earliest Christian church and the hallmark of authentic Christian proclamation down to the present. It is striking—indeed, in the contemporary Jewish context, simply astonishing—that the women became the first custodians of this message and thus in effect became the first proclaimers of the key element of the kerygma. The absent disciples must at first rely on the testimony of women. All this supports the historical reality of this pericope. No invented story in that culture would have given the women such prominence and entrusted the first proclamation of the resurrection, and indeed the initial witness of it (vv 8–10), to such questionable witnesses (see Origen, *contra Celsum* 2.55; note the absence of reference to the women in the list of witnesses to the resurrection in 1 Cor 15:5–8). We may note finally that if the tomb in which Jesus was buried had not been empty, it would have been impossible for the church to proclaim the resurrection of Jesus in its kerygma.

# The Appearance of the Risen Jesus to the Women (28:8–10)

## Bibliography

**Allen, D.** "Resurrection Appearances as Evidence." *TToday* 30 (1973) 3–11. **Alsup, J. E.** "Resurrection and Historicity." *ASB* 103 (1988) 5–18. **Anderson, H.** "The Easter Witness of the Evangelists." In *The New Testament in Historical and Contemporary Perspective.* FS G. H. C. MacGregor, ed. H. Anderson and W. Barclay. Oxford: Blackwell, 1965. 35–56. **Barta, K. A.** "Resurrection Narratives: Thresholds of Faith." *BiTod* 27 (1989) 160–65. **Bartsch, H.-W.** "Der Ursprung des Osterglaubens." *SNTU* 13 (1988) 81–100. **Broer, I.** "'Seid stets bereit, jedem Rede und Antwort zu stehen, der nach der Hoffnung fragt, die euch erfüllt' (1 Petr 3,15): Das leere Grab und die Erscheinungen Jesu im Lichte der historischen Kritik." In *"Der Herr ist warhaft auferstanden" (Lk 24,34): Biblische und systematische Beiträge zur Entstehung des Osterglaubens,* ed. I. Broer and J. Werbick. SBS 134. Stuttgart: Katholisches Bibelwerk, 1988. 29–61. **Craig, W. L.** *Assessing the New Testament Evidence for the Historicity of the Resurrection of Jesus.* Lewiston, NY: Mellen, 1989. ———. "The Bodily Resurrection of Jesus." In *Gospel Perspectives,* ed. R. T. France and D. Wenham. Sheffield: JSOT, 1980. 1:47–74. **Cranfield, C. E. B.** "The Resurrection of Jesus." *ExpTim* 101 (1990) 167–72. **Dodd, C. H.** "The Appearances of the Risen Christ: An Essay in Form-Criticism of the Gospels." In *Studies in the Gospels.* FS R. H. Lightfoot, ed. D. E. Nineham. Oxford: Blackwell, 1955. 9–35. **Drane, J.** "Some Ideas of Resurrection in the New Testament Period." *TynB* 24 (1973) 99–110. **Galvin, J. P.** "The Origin of Faith in the Resurrection of Jesus: Two Recent Perspectives." *TS* 49 (1988) 25–44. **Goppelt, L.** "Die Auferstehung im der Kritik, ihr Sinn und ihre Glaubwürdigkeit." In *Grundlagen des Glaubens,* ed. P. Rieger and J. Strauss. Munich: Kösel, 1970. 55–74. **Hengel, M.** "Ist der Osterglauben noch zu retten?" *TQ* 153 (1973) 252–69. **Hübner, H.** "Kreuz und Auferstehung im Neuen Testament." *TRu* 54 (1989) 262–306; 57 (1992) 58–82. **Kendall, D.,** and **O'Collins, G.** "The Uniqueness of the Resurrection Appearances." *CBQ* 54 (1992) 287–307. **Koch, G.** "Um den Realitätscharacter der Ostererscheinungen." *TRev* 73 (1977) 441–50. **Ladd, G. E.** *I Believe in the Resurrection of Jesus.* Grand Rapids: Eerdmans, 1975. **Moule, C. F. D.,** ed. *The Significance of the Message of the Resurrection for Faith in Jesus Christ.* SBT 2.8. Naperville, IL: Allenson, 1968. **Orr, J.** *The Resurrection of Jesus.* London: Hodder and Stoughton, 1908. **Osborne, G. R.** *The Resurrection Narratives: A Redactional Study.* Grand Rapids: Baker, 1984. **Perkins, P.** *Resurrection: New Testament Witness and Contemporary Reflection.* Garden City, NY: Doubleday, 1984. **Robinson, W. C.** "The Bodily Resurrection of Christ." *TZ* 13 (1957) 81–101. **Schweizer, E.** "Resurrection—Fact or Illusion?" *HBT* 1 (1979) 137–59. **Trompf, G. W.** "The First Resurrection Appearance and the Ending of Mark's Gospel." *NTS* 18 (1972) 308–30. **Westcott, B. F.** *The Gospel of the Resurrection: Thoughts on Its Relation to Reason and History.* London: Macmillan, 1906. **Wilckens, U.** *Resurrection: Biblical Testimony to the Resurrection: An Historical Examination and Explanation.* Atlanta: John Knox, 1978.

## Translation

⁸*And they departed from the tomb quickly, and with fear and great joy they ran to announce the news* ª *to his disciples.* ⁹*And look,*ᵇ *Jesus met them! And he said: "Greetings." And they came to him and grasped his feet and worshiped him.* ¹⁰*Then Jesus said to them: "Do not be afraid. Go, proclaim the news* ᶜ *to my brethren* ᵈ *so that they may go to Galilee, and there they* ᵉ *will see me."*

## Notes

ª "The news" added, supplying direct object.

ᵇ Many MSS (A C L *f*¹ TR syʰ) add ὡς δὲ ἐπορεύοντο ἀπαγγεῖλαι τοῖς μαθηταῖς αὐτοῦ, "but as they were going to announce (the news) to his disciples," before καὶ ἰδού, "and look." The words could have dropped out through homoioteleuton (αὐτοῦ—αὐτοῦ), but, given the MSS lacking the words (𝕏 B D W Θ *f*¹³ lat syᵖ co), they could also be "a natural expression derived from the sense of the preceding verse" (*TCGNT*, 72).

ᶜ "The news" added, supplying direct object; cf. *Note* a.

ᵈ 𝕏* omits μου, "my," resulting in τοῖς ἀδελφοῖς, "the brethren." A few MSS (e.g., 157 Cyrᵖᵗ) have μαθηταῖς μου, "my disciples." It is not difficult to see christological commitments as the cause of these changes.

ᵉ D e h have ὄψεσθε, "you will see," probably by the influence of v 7.

## Form/Structure/Setting

A. As the women go on their way to fulfill the angel's commission to announce the thrilling news of Jesus' resurrection, they are met by the risen Jesus himself. To the women's surprise, their message becomes reality, and they fall down before him in worship. What Jesus says to them in v 10 repeats various elements of the angel's initial instructions in vv 5–7. This pericope, like the preceding one, thus prepares the way for the climactic final verses of the Gospel (vv 16–20).

B. Only for the first part of v 8 does Matthew reflect dependence on Mark, and even here Matthew shows considerable freedom in using his source (Mark 16:8; cf. Luke 24:9; John 20:2). In v 8 Matthew's ταχύ, "quickly," takes the place of Mark's ἔφυγον, "they fled." Matthew's μετὰ φόβου καὶ χαρᾶς μεγάλης, "with fear and great joy," represents Mark's τρόμος καὶ ἔκστασις, "trembling and astonishment" (cf. Mark's final ἐφοβοῦντο γάρ, "for they were afraid"). Matthew omits Mark's statement καὶ οὐδενὶ οὐδὲν εἶπαν, "and they told nothing to anyone," as unnecessary and probably out of place. The remaining words of v 8, ἔδραμον ἀπαγγεῖλαι τοῖς μαθηταῖς αὐτοῦ, "they ran to proclaim (the news) to his disciples," are the logical fulfillment of the commission they had been given in v 7 (cf. Luke 24:9). Matthew's account of the risen Jesus meeting the women in v 9 is paralleled only in John 20:14 (to Mary Magdalene alone; so too the later Mark 16:9), which also parallels Matthew's reference to holding onto Jesus' feet. V 10, as already mentioned, is but the repetition of material from vv 5–7 (partly paralleled by Mark 16:6–7). See the following section.

C. The core of the pericope is found in v 9 with the encountering of the risen Jesus by the women. The passage consists of narrative except for the instructions provided in v 10. It may be outlined as follows: (1) the women depart (v 8); (2) they meet and worship the risen Jesus (v 9); and (3) Jesus gives them his message to his disciples (v 10). The five components of the message in v 10 are all paralleled in vv 5, 7: (1) fear not, (2) go, (3) proclaim the news, (4) they should go to Galilee (in v 7: "he goes before you into Galilee"), and (5) they will see Jesus there.

D. The bodily resurrection of Jesus is the *sine qua non* of the Christian faith (thus forcefully Paul in 1 Cor 15:14). This is the decisive miracle of the narrative that makes the Gospel coherent and compelling. Without the reality of this miracle we would be left with puzzle upon puzzle. In a very important sense too this miracle provides a test case for whether we have a view of reality that is compatible with the NT proclamation. That view of reality must at least be open to the possibility of supernatural events happening in time and space. If, as with the virgin birth (cf. Hagner, *Matthew 1–13,* 16), we are in a realm where the historian *qua* historian is incapacitated, that does not reduce us to depending upon a blind faith. R. E. Brown's statement concerning the story of the angel rolling back the stone from Jesus' tomb (v 2) is also especially apropos in reference to the resurrection itself:

> I do not deem it methodologically sound to let such a priori rejection of the supernatural determine historicity, and indeed that principle would rule out the discussion of any resurrection narrative. In my judgment the possibility or plausibility of this story must be discussed on the same basis as that of any other Gospel story. (*Death of the Messiah,* 310)

None of the alternative explanations of the resurrection of Jesus—whether a stolen body, a Jesus who only "swooned," or a mistaken tomb—is adequate to explain the total range of phenomena that must be explained. Although outside the range of the historian, the best explanation *historically*—i.e., that provides a comprehensive account of what happened—is the reality of the resurrection of Jesus. See further Ladd, Schweizer, Cranfield.

### Comment

**8** The reference to the women leaving the tomb ταχύ, "quickly," corresponds to the angel's command ταχὺ πορευθεῖσαι, "go quickly" (v 7). Although the women had not overcome their fear (μετὰ φόβου, "with fear"), despite the exhortation of the angel not to fear (v 5), they were simultaneously filled with χαρᾶς μεγάλης, "a great joy" (the phrase occurs elsewhere in Matthew only in 2:10). There was no doubt in their hearts about the truthfulness of what they had been told about Jesus being raised from the dead, and they ran to tell the news τοῖς μαθηταῖς αὐτοῦ, "to his disciples" (cf. v 10). ἀπαγγεῖλαι, "announce" or "proclaim (the news)," used also in vv 10, 11, occurs earlier in Matthew in 2:8; 8:33; 11:4; 14:12.

**9** A climactic point in the Gospel occurs here in the appearance of the risen Jesus to the two women. Matthew's characteristic ἰδού, "look," catches the reader's attention. The women had heard the words that he had been raised from the dead. Now they encountered the risen Jesus. The reality of the resurrection was confirmed by sight (cf. John 20:29). The extraordinary meeting is described in very ordinary words: "Jesus met them." ὑπήντησεν, "met," is the regular verb for meeting (it occurs earlier in Matthew in 8:28). No description of the risen Jesus is provided here or in the remainder of the Gospel. The first word spoken by Jesus, χαίρετε, "Greetings," is the ordinary everyday greeting used in that culture (cf. 26:49). The women apparently recognized Jesus immediately. In that culture the grasping of feet (note the fact that Jesus was tangible) was to make an obeisance, usually to a ruler or king, expressing submission and homage. When combined, as in the present context, with the verb προσεκύνησαν, worship is clearly entailed (the latter verb also signifies "worship" in v 17, as in 4:9–10; 14:33). The only way the women can react to their cumulative experience is to fall at Jesus' feet in worship. See Drane for a survey of various views of resurrection in antiquity and discussion of the uniqueness of Jesus' resurrection.

**10** As the angel did in v 5, Jesus tells the women not to be afraid (on μὴ φοβεῖσθε, "do not be afraid," see *Comment* on v 5). They are then instructed to do as the angel had told them, i.e., to "go" (ὑπάγετε) and "announce" (ἀπαγγείλατε) the news (cf. v 8), τοῖς ἀδελφοῖς μου, "to my brothers." This comes as rather a surprise since one expects "my disciples" as in vv 7, 8, yet Matthew has in several previous passages recorded words of Jesus in which the disciples are called his "brothers" (cf. 12:48–50; 25:40; see too esp. the parallel to the present passage in John 20:17). The point here may well be that the risen Lord continues to refer to his disciples as his brothers (and sisters) now even after they have abandoned him. The disciples are thus forgiven for their failure in the hour of crisis. There is no indication that "brothers" here is to be understood as referring to the larger group of Galilean disciples of Jesus who were in Jerusalem, let alone to other Jerusalem appearances of the risen Jesus (*pace* Carson). Apart from the present pericope Matthew records only the Galilean appearance to the disciples (vv 16–20). Jesus repeats the angel's instruction that the disciples are to go to Galilee (cf. vv 7, 16) and that κἀκεῖ με ὄψονται, "there they will see me" (cf. vv 7, 17). The way is prepared now for the climactic meeting of Jesus and his disciples in Galilee.

*Explanation*

The crowning events of the resurrection narrative are the appearances of the risen Jesus first to the women and then to his disciples, i.e., the eleven. The empty tomb, for all of its impressiveness and importance, is not sufficient evidence in itself for the resurrection of Jesus. What alone can be decisive is reliable eyewitness testimony that Jesus had been raised from the dead. The women, the two Marys, are not only given the first responsibility to convey the message that Jesus had risen from the dead but are also given the privilege of being the first to see the risen Jesus himself. When they encounter him, they respond with unalloyed worship (contrast v 17). They worship him not so much because he had come back to life but because his resurrection vindicates all that he had said and done during his ministry. And now it must have become exceedingly clear that this was not a special man among fellow humans but the unique manifestation of God's grace and wisdom, who now reflected the new order of life that would be the portion of all his followers in the consummation of the eschatological age.

# The Jewish Authorities Concoct a Story  (28:11–15)

### Bibliography

**Metzger, B. M.** "The Nazareth Inscription Once Again." In *Jesus und Paulus.* FS W. G. Kümmel, ed. E. Ellis and E. Grässer. Göttingen: Vandenhoeck & Ruprecht, 1975. 221–38. **Michaelis, W.** *Die Erscheinungen des Auferstandenen.* Basel: Heinrich Majer, 1944. **Pesch, R.** "Eine alttestamentliche Ausführungsformel in Matthäus-Evangelium." *BZ* 10 (1966) 220–45; 11 (1967) 79–95.

See also *Bibliography* on 27:62–66.

### Translation

[11]*And while the women* [a] *were on their way, look, some of the guard came into the city and recounted to the chief priests everything that had happened.* [12]*And when the latter* [b] *had gathered together with the elders and considered the matter, they gave quite a large amount of money to the soldiers,* [13]*saying: "Say, 'His disciples came by night and stole him while we were sleeping.'* [14]*And if this should come to the governor's attention, we ourselves will conciliate [him],* [c] *and we will keep you blameless."* [15]*And they took the money and did as they were instructed. And this story has spread widely among the Jews until the present [day].* [d]

### Notes

[a] *αὐτῶν* in a genitive absolute construction, lit. "they."
[b] "The latter" added to make the subject of the participle clear.
[c] A few important MSS (ℵ B Θ 33e) omit the direct object *αὐτόν*, "him."
[d] Gr.: *μέχρι τῆς σήμερον [ἡμέρας]*, lit. "until the today [day]." *ἡμέρας*, "day," here is omitted by many MSS (ℵ A W *f*[1,13] TR) but is present in B D L Θ lat. Because of this difficult division among the MSS, the word is put in brackets. No difference in meaning is at stake.

### Form/Structure/Setting

A. The reality of the resurrection of Jesus has been established in the preceding pericopes, and the one thing the Jewish authorities feared—an empty tomb—is now something they must explain to counteract the claims of the Christians. The pericope is the sequel to the closely related pericope of 27:62–66 and may originally have composed with it one single, connected narrative (thus R. E.

Brown, *Death of the Messiah*, 1301–5). The concluding sentence, the last mention of the Jews in the Gospel, provides a sad commentary on widespread Jewish unbelief in the evangelist's day. The "sign of Jonah" (12:38–40) cannot overcome their fixed opinion of Jesus, and they will lie to preserve that opinion.

B. This pericope, like its counterpart in 27:62–66, is unique to Matthew and is either composed by the evangelist or dependent on a now unknown source. The related tradition in *Gos. Pet.* 45–49 is very probably dependent itself on Matthew as must also be said of the parallel in Justin Martyr, *Dial.* 108.2.

C. Again this pericope is a mixture of narrative and direct discourse. It focuses on the story made up in v 13, which the guards are to spread, and on the final comment made by the evangelist in v 15b. The following outline may be suggested: (1) the report of the guards (v 11); (2) the bribing of the guards (v 12); (3) the concocted story (v 13); (4) the protection from Pilate (v 14); (5) the compliance of the guards (v 15a); and (6) the evangelist's summarizing comment (v 15b).

### Comment

**11** Some of the Roman κουστωδίας, "guard" (as in 27:65–66), quickly (πορευομένων δὲ αὐτῶν, "while they [the women] were going") make a report to the chief priests who had put them in charge of the tomb and thus to whom they were responsible (cf. 27:62). εἰς τὴν πόλιν, "into the city," indicates that the tomb, like the place of crucifixion, was located outside the city walls. The description of this report as containing ἅπαντα τὰ γενόμενα, "everything that had happened," raises the question of how much they had in fact witnessed before they lapsed into unconsciousness, if that is what v 4 implies. They perhaps remembered at least the earthquake, the rolled-back stone, and the brilliant visage of the angel. It could have been enough to cause the Jewish authorities to rethink their estimate of Jesus had not their minds been irreversibly made up. Thus their guilt is intensified.

**12** For the last time in the Gospel the chief priests "took counsel together" (συμβούλιόν λαβόντες) with the elders. These two groups are frequently mentioned together in Matthew as representative of the Jewish authorities, especially in the passion narrative (cf. 16:21; 21:23; 26:3, 47; 27:1, 3, 12, 20). The best course of action, they decide, is to bribe τοῖς στρατιώταις, "the soldiers," to keep them from telling the truth. They thus give the soldiers ἀργύρια ἱκανά, lit. "enough money," i.e., a relatively large amount of money. The statement is reminiscent of, and serves as an inclusio to, the gathering of the same authorities at the beginning of the passion narrative (cf. 26:3–4) and the offering of ἀργύρια, "silver [money]" (as here and in v 15), to Judas in return for his betrayal of Jesus (26:15).

**13** With the money comes instructions about the story they are to tell. There is a certain irony in that the very thing they had hoped to prevent by posting a guard—the stealing of the body (cf. 27:64)—becomes the story they concoct to explain the empty tomb. The guards are to say that οἱ μαθηταὶ αὐτοῦ νυκτὸς ἐλθόντες ἔκλεψαν αὐτόν, "his disciples came by night and stole him," and that this happened ἡμῶν κοιμωμένων, "while we were sleeping." There is a comical aspect to these final two words since it simultaneously shows them to be irresponsible (some soldiers of the guard were supposed to have been awake through the night; the penalty for failure could amount to capital punishment) and raises the awkward question of how they knew what happened if they were sleeping, not to mention the fact that they would have had to be sleeping extremely soundly if they were not able to hear the large stone being rolled away from the door of the tomb.

**14** The τοῦτο, "this," of which Pilate the governor, their supreme commanding officer (cf. 27:65), might possibly become cognizant is presumably the story of the body being stolen (thus pointing to the ineffective performance of their duty) rather than the matter of the bribery itself, which would have remained a well-kept secret between them. Should this happen, they say, ἡμεῖς πείσομεν [αὐτόν], "we ourselves will conciliate [him]" (for πείθειν in this sense, see BAGD, 639b), and ὑμᾶς ἀμερίμνους ποιήσομεν, "you we will hold blameless." How this would be accomplished is not specified, but at a minimum the Jewish authorities would certainly offer no complaint concerning the guards' performance—precisely what they *would* have done, no doubt, if the body *had* been stolen. Had the guard been a group from the Jewish temple guard, they would hardly have had to worry about Pilate.

**15** It must have been with a degree of bewildered delight that the soldiers walked away with the large amount of money in their pockets when they had no doubt expected to be censured and perhaps sent back to Pilate with a complaint for not having succeeded in their mission. They were happy to do ὡς ἐδιδάχθησαν, "as they had been instructed" (the only use of διδάσκειν in Matthew for something other than religious teaching). The story concocted by the Jewish authorities (ὁ λόγος οὗτος, "this word [i.e., story]") διεφημίσθη, "was spread widely" (used elsewhere in Matthew only in 9:31 where it refers to the news about Jesus' power to heal), as the explanation of the empty tomb and the disappearance of Jesus' body—"a type of antigospel" (R. E. Brown, *Death of the Messiah*, 1298). The story was particularly effective παρὰ Ἰουδαίοις, "among Jews," as an explanation of the Christian claim concerning the resurrection and empty tomb. The word Ἰουδαῖοι occurs elsewhere in Matthew only in the phrase "king of the Jews" applied to Jesus (cf. 2:2; 27:11, 29, 37). Here for the first time the word is given a negative connotation, referring to those who do not accept the evidence for the resurrection of Jesus—not that this is the only reference to the unbelief of the Jews. The unreceptiveness of the Jews to Jesus' ministry and claims has been a frequent motif in the Gospel, beginning as early as 9:3, 34. At the time the evangelist writes (μέχρι τῆς σήμερον [ἡμέρας], "until the present [day]"), the story that the body had been stolen by Jesus' disciples continued to be widely disseminated among the Jewish people (several decades later it is reflected in Justin Martyr, *Dial.* 108.2). This statement provides no indication of the date of the Gospel but is fully compatible with a pre-70 date.

## Explanation

The bribed guards knew well that the story about the body being stolen by Jesus' disciples was untrue. We are not told what the Jewish authorities thought about the original report of the guards. But they too knew that their concocted story was mere fabrication. They appear to be desperate men determined at any cost to bring the whole matter of Jesus and his movement to an end. Their propaganda campaign, however, had only limited success. To some it seemed indeed a convenient way around a disconcerting piece of evidence. A little thought shows, however, that the disciples were in no frame of mind to steal the body of Jesus. Nor would they later have been prepared to die as martyrs for what they knew to be a lie. The only way to comprehend the dramatic change in the disciples is the actual resurrection of Jesus. And for this, the determinative argument is not the empty tomb—which is after all only circumstantial evidence—but the personal confrontation of the disciples with the risen Jesus. If the Jewish authorities had not invented the story of the stolen body, others would have. Down to the present time there are some, Jews and non-Jews, who believe this explanation of the empty tomb. So easily would they think to cancel out the Christian gospel! But the hypothesis of the stolen body leaves one with a number of other difficulties that must either be ignored or explained in such ways as to reveal a foolish a priori bias against the possibility of the supernatural in history. It is this view that is untenable, not the Christian view.

# The Appearance of Jesus to the Eleven in Galilee and the Great Commission    (28:16–20)

## Bibliography

**Aarde, A. G. van.** "Ἠγέρθη ἀπὸ τῶν νεκρῶν (Mt 28:7): A Textual Evidence on the Separation of Judaism and Christianity." *Neot* 23 (1989) 219–33. **Abramowski, L.** "Die Entstehung der dreigliedrigen Taufformel–ein Versuch: Mit einem Exkurs: Jesus der Naziräer." *ZTK* 81 (1984) 417–46. **Barth, K.** "An Exegetical Study of Matthew 28:16–20." In *The Theology of the Christian Mission*, ed. G. H. Anderson. New York: McGraw Hill, 1961. 55–71. **Bartnicki, R.** "Der Bereich der Tätigkeit der Jünger nach Mt 10,5b–6." *BZ* 31 (1987) 250–56. **Basset, J.-J.** "Dernières paroles du ressuscité et mission de l'Église aujourd'hui." *RTP* 114 (1982) 349–67. **Baumbach, G.** "Die Mission im Matthäus-Evangelium." *TLZ* 92 (1967) 889–94. **Benoit, P.** "Mission Universelle." In *Passion et résurrection de Seigneur.* Paris: Editions du Cerf, 1966. 355–87. ———. *The Passion and Resurrection of Jesus Christ.* Tr. B. Weatherhead. New York: Herder and Herder, 1969. **Bornkamm, G.** "The Risen Lord and the Earthly Jesus: Mt 28, 16–20." In *The Future of Our Religious Past.* FS R. Bultmann, ed. J. M. Robinson. Tr. C. E. Carlston and R. P. Scharlemann. New York: Harper and Row, 1971. 203–29. **Brooks, O. S., Sr.** "Matthew xxviii 16–20 and the Design of the First Gospel." *JSNT* 10 (1981) 2–18. **Brown, S.** "The Matthean Community and the Gentile Mission." *NovT* 22 (1980) 193–221. **Bruce, F. F.** "The End of the First Gospel." *EvQ* 12 (1940) 203–14. **Chavasse, C.** "Not the Mountain Appointed: Studies in Texts: Matthew 28:16." *Th* 74 (1971) 478. **Conybeare, F. C.** "The Eusebian Form of the Text in Matthew 28, 19." *ZNW* 2 (1901) 275–88. **Davies, W. D., and Allison, D. C.** "Matt. 28:16–20: Texts behind the Text." *RHPR* 72 (1992) 89–98. **Eager, B.** "The Lord Is with You." *Scr* 12 (1960) 48–54. **Ellis, I. P.** "But Some Doubted." *NTS* 14 (1967–68) 574–80. **Flusser, D.** "The Conclusion of Matthew in a New Jewish Christian Source." *ASTI* 5 (1967) 110–20. **Friedrich, G.** "Die formale Struktur von Mt 28, 18–20." *ZTK* 80 (1983) 137–83. **Giblin, C. H.** "A Note on Doubt and Reassurance in Mt 28:16–20." *CBQ* 37 (1975) 68–75. **Grayston, K.** "The Translation of Matthew 28:17." *JSNT* 21 (1984)

105–9. **Green, H. B.** "The Command to Baptize and Other Matthean Interpolations." *SE* 4 [= TU 102] (1968) 60–63. **Hahn, F.** *Mission in the New Testament.* SBT 47. Tr. F. Clarke. Naperville, IL: Allenson, 1965. ———. "Der Sendungsauftrag des Auferstandenen." In *Fides pro mundi vita.* FS H.-W. Gensichen, ed. T. Sundermeier, H.-J. Becken, and B. H. Willeke. Gütersloh: Mohn, 1980. 28–43. **Hare, D. R. A.,** and **Harrington, D. J.** "Make Disciples of All the Gentiles (Matthew 28:19)." *CBQ* 37 (1975) 359–69. **Hartman, L.** "'Into the Name of Jesus': A Suggestion Concerning the Earliest Meaning of the Phrase." *NTS* 20 (1974) 432–40. **Hendrickx, H.** *The Resurrection Narratives of the Synoptic Gospels.* Rev. ed. London: Chapman, 1984. **Hiebert, D. E.** "An Expository Study of Matthew 28:16–20." *BSac* 149 (1992) 338–54. **Hill, D.** "The Conclusion of Matthew's Gospel: Some Literary Critical Observations." *IBS* 8 (1986) 54–63. **Horst, P. W. van der.** "Once More: The Translation of *hoi de* in Matthew 28.17." *JSNT* 27 (1986) 27–30. **Howard, G.** "A Note on the Short Ending of Matthew." *HTR* 81 (1988) 117–20. **Howe, E. M.** "'But Some Doubted' (Matt. 28:17): A Re-Appraisal of Factors Influencing the Easter Faith of the Early Christian Community." *JETS* 18 (1975) 173–80. **Hre Kio, S.** "Understanding and Translating 'Nations' in Mt 29.19." *BT* 41 (1990) 230–38. **Hubbard, B. J.** *The Matthean Redaction of a Primitive Apostolic Commissioning: An Exegesis of Matthew 28:16–20.* SBLDS 19. Missoula, MT: Scholars, 1974. **Jeremias, J.** *Jesus' Promise to the Nations.* SBT 24. Tr. S. H. Hooke. Naperville, IL: Allenson, 1958. **Kertelge, K.** "Der sogenannte Taufbefehl Jesu." In *Zeichen des Glaubens: Studien zu Taufe und Firmung.* FS B. Fischer, ed. H. Auf der Maur and B. Kleinheyer. Zürich: Benziger, 1972. 29–40. **Kingsbury, J. D.** "The Composition and Christology of Matt 28:16–20." *JBL* 93 (1974) 573–84. **Kosmala, H.** "The Conclusion of Matthew." *ASTI* 4 (1965) 132–47. **Kvalbein, H.** "'Go therefore and make disciples': The Concept of Discipleship in the New Testament." *Themelios* 13 (1988) 48–53. **Kwik, J.** "Some Doubted." *ExpTim* 77 (1965–66) 181. **LaGrand, J.** "The Earliest Christian Mission to 'All Nations' in the Light of Matthew's Gospel." Diss., University of Basel, 1989. **Lange, J.** *Das Erscheinen des Auferstandenen im Evangelium nach Mattäus: Eine traditions- und redaktionsgeschichtliche Untersuchung zu Mt 28, 16–20.* Würzburg: Echter, 1973. **Legrand, L.** "The Missionary Command of the Risen Lord Mt 28:16–20." *Indian Theological Studies* 24 (1987) 5–28. **Léon-Dufour, X.** "The Origin of the Narratives of Christ's Appearances." In *The Resurrection and the Message of Easter.* New York: Holt, Rinehart and Winston, 1971. 94–104. ———. "Présence du Seigneur ressuscité." In *À cause de l'Évangile.* FS J. Dupont. LD 123. Paris: Cerf, 1985. 71–72. **Lindblom, J.** *Jesu Missions- och Dopbefallning: Matth. 28, 18–20.* Stockholm: Svenska Kirkans Diakonistyrelses Bokförlag, 1919. **Lohmeyer, E.** "'Mir ist gegeben alle Gewalt!' Eine Exegese von Mt 28, 16–20." In *In Memoriam Ernst Lohmeyer,* ed. W. Schmauch. Stuttgart: Evangelisches, 1951. 22–49. **Luck, U.** "Herrenwort und Geschichte in Matth. 28, 16–20." *EvT* 27 (1967) 494–508. **Malina, B. J.** "The Literary Structure and Form of Matt. xxviii, 16–20." *NTS* 17 (1970–71) 87–103. **Manus, C.** "'King-Christology': The Result of a Critical Study of Matt 28:16–20 as an Example of Contextual Exegesis in Africa." *Scr* 39 (1991) 25–42. **Mather, P. B.** "Christian Prophecy and Matthew 28:16–20: A Test Exegesis." In *Society of Biblical Literature Seminar Papers* (1977) 103–15. **McKay, K. L.** "The Use of *hoi de* in Matthew 28.17: A Response to K. Grayston." *JSNT* 24 (1985) 71–72. **Meier, J. P.** "Nations or Gentiles in Matthew 28:18?" *CBQ* 39 (1977) 94–102. ———. "Two Disputed Questions in Matt 28:16–20." *JBL* 96 (1977) 407–24. **Meye, R. P.** "The Christological Conclusion of Matthew's Gospel." *Foundations* 11 (1968) 9–26. **Michel, O.** "The Conclusion of Matthew's Gospel: A Contribution to the History of the Easter Message." In *The Interpretation of Matthew,* ed. G. N. Stanton. Philadelphia: Fortress, 1983. 30–41. **Morris, W. D.** "Matthew xxviii.17: καὶ ἰδόντες αὐτὸν προσεκύνησαν αὐτῷ οἱ δὲ ἐδίστασαν." *ExpTim* 47 (1935–36) 142. **Neirynck, F.** "Excursus: οἱ δέ in Mt 28, 17." *ETL* 63 (1987) 33–36. **Nielen, J. M.** "Zur Grundlegung einer neutestamentlichen Ekklesiologie." In *Aus Theologie und Philosophie.* FS F. Tillmann, ed. T. Steinbüchel and T. Müncker. Düsseldorf: Patmos, 1950. 370–97. **O'Brien, P. T.** "The Great Commission of Matthew 28:18–20—A Missionary Mandate or Not?" *Evangelical Re-*

*view of Theology* 2 (1978) 254–67. **Osborne, G. R.** "Redaction Criticism and the Great Commission: A Case Study toward a Biblical Understanding of Inerrancy." *JETS* 19 (1976) 73–85. **Parker, H. M.** "The Great Commission." *Int* 2 (1948) 74–75. **Parkhurst Jr., L. G.** "Matthew 28¹⁶⁻²⁰ Reconsidered." *ExpTim* 90 (1979) 179–80. **Perkins, P.** "Christology and Mission: Matthew 28:16–20." *Listening* [Romeoville, IL] 24 (1989) 302–9. **Quesnell, Q.** "I am with you always." *The Way* 3 (1963) 105–14. **Rigaux, B.** "Mt 28,16–20." In *Dieu l'a ressuscité: Exégèse et théologie biblique.* Gembloux: Duculot, 1973. 254–58. **Rogers, C.** "The Great Commission." *BSac* 130 (1973) 258–67. **Russ, R.** "Kirche des Matthäus–Kirche heute: Entwurf einer Predigt zu Mt 28,18–20." *BK* 26 (1971) 68–71. **Sawatzky, H.** "But Some Doubted." *ExpTim* 90 (1979) 178–79. **Scaer, D. P.** "The Relation of Matthew 28:16–20 to the Rest of the Gospel." *CTQ* 55 (1991) 245–66. **Schaberg, J.** *The Father, the Son and the Holy Spirit: The Triadic Phrase in Matthew 28:19b.* SBLDS 61. Chico, CA: Scholars, 1981. **Schelbert, G.** "'Mir ist alle Gewalt gegeben' (Matth 28,18): Auferstehung und Aussendung den Erhöhten nach Matthäus." *BK* 20 (1965) 37–59. **Schieber, H.** "The Conclusion of Matthew's Gospel." *TD* 27 (1979) 155–58. ———. "Konzentrik im Matthäusschluss: Ein form- und gattungskritischer Versuch zu Mt 28,16–20." *Kairos* 19 (1977) 286–307. **Strecker, G.** "Die Grundlegung (Mt 28, 16–20)." In *Der Weg der Gerechtigkeit.* Göttingen: Vandenhoeck & Ruprecht, 1962. 208–14. **Strobel, A.** "Der Berg der Offenbarung (Mt 28, 16; Apg 1, 12): Erwägungen zu einem urchristlichen Erwartungstopos." In *Verborum Veritas.* FS G. Stählin, ed. O. Böcher and K. Haacker. Wuppertal: Brockhaus, 1970. 133–46. **Tassin, C.** "La mission selon Matthieu: Deux contextes pour lire Mt 28,16–20." *Spiritus* [Paris] 29 (1988) 366–85. **Thomas, J.** "'Allez donc . . .': Matthieu 28,17–20." *CHR* 108 (1980) 446–57. **Trilling, W.** "Der Inhalt des Manifests 28, 18–20." In *Das wahre Israel.* Munich: Kösel, 1964. 21–51. ———. "Das Kirchenverständnis nach Matthäus (Mt 28, 18–20)." In *Vielfalt und Einheit im Neuen Testament.* Einsiedeln: Benziger, 1968. 125–39. ———. "Les traits essentiels de l'Église de Christ (Mt 28,18–20)." *AsSeign* 53 (1964) 20–33. **Vögtle, A.** "Das christologische und ekklesiologische Anliegen von Mt 28, 18–20." *SE* 2 [= TU 87] (1964) 266–94 (reprinted in *Das Evangelium und die Evangelien.* Dusseldorf: Patmos, 1971. 253–72). ———. *Was Ostern bedeutet: Meditation zu Matthäus 28, 16–20.* Freiburg: Herder, 1983. **Walsh, B. J.,** and **Keesmaat, S. C.** "Reflections on the Ascension." *Th* 95 (1992) 193–200. **Watson, P. S.** "The Blessed Trinity." *ExpTim* 90 (1979) 242–43. **Zumstein, J.** "Matthieu 28: 16–20." *RTP* 22 (1972) 14–33.

### Translation

¹⁶*Now the eleven disciples went into Galilee to the mountain to which Jesus had ordered them.* ¹⁷*And when they saw him, they worshiped him,*[a] *but they*[b] *doubted.* ¹⁸*And Jesus came and spoke to them, saying: "All authority in heaven and upon [the]*[c] *earth has been given to me.*[d] ¹⁹*Go, therefore,*[e] *and make disciples of all the nations. Baptize them in the name of the Father and of the Son and of the Holy Spirit,* ²⁰*and teach them to keep everything—as much as I have commanded you. And, look, I am with you all the days until the consummation of the age!"*[f]

### Notes

[a] "Him" added, supplying the direct object. Many MSS (A W Θ *f*¹,¹³ TR) add the dat. pronoun αὐτῷ, "him." Γ 28 700* 1241 add the accusative pronoun αὐτόν, "him." The text (without pronoun) is supported by א B D 33 lat, judged by the *UBSGNT* committee to be superior. *TCGNT*, 72.

[b] οἱ, the pl. of the definite article, may also be translated "some." See *Comment.*

[c] The definite article τῆς is omitted by many MSS (א A W Θ *f*¹,¹³ TR). Favoring its inclusion are **B** D 892.

ᵈ Θ syᵖ add καθὼς ἀπέστειλέν με ὁ πατήρ, κἀγὼ ἀποστελῶ ὑμᾶς, "just as the Father sent me, I also will send you," an apposite importation from John 20:21.

ᵉ οὖν, "therefore." D it have νῦν, "now." Many MSS (‍‍א A *f*¹³ TR boᵖᵗ) omit οὖν. Favoring οὖν are B W Δ Θ *f*¹ lat sy sa mae boᵖᵗ.

ᶠ Many MSS (Aᶜ Θ *f*¹³ TR it vgᵐˢˢ sy boᵖᵗ) add ἀμήν, "amen," probably "reflecting the liturgical usage of the text" (*TCGNT*, 72). No reason exists for the deliberate omission of the word if it had been part of the original text.

## *Form/Structure/Setting*

A. The resurrection narrative comes to its climax, as does the entire Gospel, in this its final majestic pericope. The women have seen the empty tomb and have met the resurrected Jesus. It is assumed in the present passage that they relayed Jesus' message to the disciples, for now the latter are found in Galilee. Here, as promised, the risen Jesus appears to them. And here they receive their commission in the famous words that have become the hallmark of the Gospel of Matthew. For these words, perhaps more than any others, distill the outlook and various emphases of the Gospel (see Vögtle, *SE* 2 [1964] 266–94). O. Michel goes so far as to say, in italics, that "Matt. 28:18–20 is the key to the understanding of the whole book" (35; cf. P. F. Ellis, *Matthew: His Mind and His Message*, 22–25). Here we find especially Christology and discipleship but also ecclesiology (see Trilling, "Das Kirchenverständnis") and righteousness—emphases familiar from the earlier parts of the Gospel (see Lange's thorough study). These final five verses not only conclude the passion-resurrection narrative of chaps. 26–28 but also serve as the conclusion to the entire Gospel. According to Brooks this pericope is basic to the narrative framework of the entire Gospel since it stresses authority and teaching—emphases found in every section of the Gospel.

B. The passage as it stands is unique to Matthew. That traditional elements underlie at least some of the material seems indicated by a few parallels that do exist, especially in Luke, John, and the longer ending of Mark. Thus Luke 24:47 refers to the necessity that κηρυχθῆναι ἐπὶ τῷ ὀνόματι αὐτοῦ μετάνοιαν εἰς ἄφεσιν ἁμαρτιῶν εἰς πάντα τὰ ἔθνη, "repentance for the forgiveness of sins be proclaimed in his name to all the nations" (cf. v 19). Parallel to Matthew's reference to the disciples' doubting (v 17) is Luke's account of the risen Jesus asking διὰ τί διαλογισμοὶ ἀναβαίνουσιν ἐν τῇ καρδίᾳ ὑμῶν, "Why do doubts arise in your heart?" (Luke 24:38), and the reference to the disciples ἔτι δὲ ἀπιστούντων αὐτῶν, "and they yet disbelieving" (Luke 24:41). With Matthew's reference to the disciples' worshiping the risen Jesus, cf. καὶ αὐτοὶ προσκυνήσαντες αὐτόν, "and they were worshiping him" (Luke 24:52). And with Matthew's reference to the authority of Jesus and his ongoing presence with them, cf. καὶ [ἰδοὺ] ἐγὼ ἀποστέλλω τὴν ἐπαγγελίαν τοῦ πατρός μου ἐφ᾽ ὑμᾶς, "and [behold] I send the promise of my Father upon you," and ἐνδύσησθε ἐξ ὕψους δύναμιν, "you will be clothed with power from on high" (Luke 24:49). There is also some similarity with the Gospel of John, which preserves tradition independent of the Synoptics. Thus Matthew's commission is similar to John's εἰρήνη ὑμῖν· καθὼς ἀπέσταλκέν με ὁ πατήρ, κἀγὼ πέμπω ὑμᾶς, "peace be with you; as the Father sent me, so I send you" (John 20:21; cf. 20:23: "if you forgive the sins of any they are forgiven"). With Matthew's emphasis on keeping Jesus' commandments, cf. ἐάν τις ἀγαπᾷ με τὸν λόγον μου τηρήσει, "if anyone loves me that person will keep my word," and with the promise of Jesus' presence, cf. καὶ πρὸς αὐτὸν ἐλευσόμεθα καὶ μονὴν παρ᾽ αὐτῷ ποιησόμεθα, "and we [i.e., Jesus and the Father] will come to him and make our abode with him" (John 14:23). The parallel with Mark 16:14–18, verses not found in the earliest MSS, almost certainly reflects dependence on Matthew and therefore cannot be used as independent confirmation of Matthew's material. (Thus Mark 16:14 mentions the ἕνδεκα, "eleven," and refers to Jesus rebuking the disciples for their unbelief; Mark 16:15 records the commission πορευθέντες εἰς τὸν κόσμον ἅπαντα κηρύξατε τὸ εὐαγγέλιον πάσῃ τῇ κτίσει, "Go into the whole world and preach the gospel to every creature"; Mark 16:16 refers to baptizing converts, βαπτισθείς, "having been baptized"; and Mark 16:17 has the phrase ἐν τῷ ὀνόματί μου, "in my name," where, however, it refers to demon exorcism.) The parallel in *Did.* 7.1, where the commission to baptize using the triadic formula is presented, also probably depends on Matthew. And the same must be said of *Herm. Sim.* 5.7.3; 6.4, where reference is made to the authority Jesus received from the Father.

C. The pericope of course finds its raison d'être not only in the appearance of Jesus to the disciples but especially in the words of Jesus with which the Gospel concludes. The following is a suggested outline: (1) the disciples return to Galilee (v 16); (2) they see the risen Jesus (v 17); and (3) Jesus commissions them (vv 18–19), subdivided into (a) the statement of the authority of Jesus (v 18b), (b) the command to make disciples of the nations (19a), baptize them (19b), and teach them (v 20a); and (c) the promise of Jesus' presence (v 20b). Thus Jesus declares his authority, commissions his disciples, and assures them of his presence in the future. In the narrative material (vv 16–17) there is little to comment on structurally except for the opposition προσεκύνησαν, "they worshiped," and ἐδίστασαν, "they doubted," in v 17. In the commission section, several structural features may be pointed out. After the initial statement concerning Jesus' authority, which has the parallelism ἐν οὐρανῷ καὶ ἐπὶ [τῆς] γῆς, "in heaven and on [the] earth" (v 18b), the commission proper consists syntactically of the main verb μαθητεύσατε, "make disciples," with three parallel subordinate participles: πορευθέντες, "going," βαπτίζοντες, "baptizing," and διδάσκοντες, "teaching" (vv 19–20a). The participles when linked with the imperative verb themselves take on imperatival force and function as imperatives. Under the second of these participles is the parallel triadic formula εἰς τὸ ὄνομα τοῦ πατρὸς καὶ τοῦ υἱοῦ καὶ τοῦ ἁγίου πνεύματος, "in the name of the Father, and of the Son, and of the Holy Spirit" (v 19b). The final sentence (v 20b), with the forceful introductory ἰδού, "look," the ἐγὼ μεθ᾽ ὑμῶν εἰμι, "I am with you," and the final phrase ἕως τῆς συντελείας τοῦ αἰῶνος, "until the consummation of the age," functions as a grand concluding cadence to the pericope and the entire Gospel. The commission proper (vv 19–20a) is thus preceded by the assertion of Jesus' authority (v 18) and followed by the promise of Jesus' presence (v 20b). Indeed, it is possible to see, with Schieber, a concentric structure: A, authority (v 18b); B, making disciples (v 19a); C, the central element, baptizing (v 19b); B', teaching (v 20a); and A', presence (v 20b). Also note the occurrence of the word "all" no less than four times, pointing again to the scope of the passage (v 18 [authority], v 19 [nations], and twice in v 20 [ Jesus' commands; days]).

D. Several attempts have been made to classify this pericope in terms of genre. A common explanation is that 28:18–20 is an "enthronement hymn" with an eye on parallel texts in Dan 7:13–14; Phil 2:9–11 (Michel, 36; Jeremias, 38–39; Hahn, *Mission*, 66–67). B. J. Hubbard provides a brief survey of scholarship, including other theories (e.g., cult legend [Bultmann, *History of the Synoptic Tradition*, 306], word of revelation, theophany, farewell speech, priestly blessing, covenant renewal [Frankemölle, *Jahwebund*, 53–67; cf. K. Baltzer, *Das Bundesformular*, WMANT 4 (Neukirchen: Neukirchener, 1964)], official decree [e.g., 2 Chr 36:23; thus Malina; cf. Lange]). Hubbard himself looks to the commissioning narratives (concerning patriarchs and prophets) of the Hebrew Bible for a parallel form to the present pericope. The fullest pattern contains the elements of introduction, confrontation, reaction, commission, protest, reassurance, and conclusion. Of these the present pericope lacks protest and conclusion (which records obedience). Clearly our passage resembles both enthronement (presentation, proclamation, acclamation) and commissioning narratives. Yet it fits no specific literary genre *exactly* (see Meier, *JBL* 96 [1977] 407–24; O'Brien; Friedrich; Schieber, *Kairos* 19 [1977] 286–307; and Hill, *IBS* 8 [1968] 54–63). Although the present pericope has some relationship to Dan 7, the contents are not extensive enough to warrant Schaberg's characterization of it as a midrash on that passage. The text is sui generis in the same way that the event is sui generis.

E. The question of the authenticity of the words of Jesus in vv 18–20 is rather easier than for earlier passages of the Gospel, assuming one accepts the reality of the risen Jesus. For it is that glorious figure who speaks here and who may readily be thought of as capable of such words. The limitations of the earthly Jesus have been left behind. Here from the mouth of Jesus is the vindication of the legitimacy of the gentile mission (*pace* Hill). At the same time, it is very clear that the words are recast in Matthew's style and vocabulary (see Kingsbury, *JBL* 93 [1974] 573–84). This fact, however, does not amount to a demonstration that Matthew composed the passage ex nihilo (*pace* S. Brown, Lange, Kingsbury). He may simply have worked over and re-presented a tradition available to him (thus Gnilka, 505; Meier, *JBL* 96 [1977] 407–24; cf. Osborne). Davies and Allison (*RHPR* 72 [1992] 89–98) argue for an original commissioning logion from Jesus reinterpreted by means of Dan 7:13–14 and finally glossed with Moses-Joshua traditions (Deut 31:14–15, 23; Joshua 1:1–9). For a denial of the influence of Dan 7, however, see Vögtle (*SE* 2 [1964] 266–94).

## Comment

**16** For the first time the disciples are referred to using the poignant term οἱ ἕνδεκα, "the eleven," rather than οἱ δώδεκα, "the twelve" (cf. 10:1–2, 5; 11:1; 20:17; 26:14, 20, 47). For "the eleven" in this sense, i.e., the twelve minus Judas, cf. Mark 16:14; Luke 24:9, 33; Acts 1:26. Note, however, that "the eleven" *includes* Peter. The eleven disciples travel up to Galilee as they had been commanded to do both by Jesus and by the angel at the tomb (cf. vv 7, 10; and Jesus' statement in 26:32). The consummation of the story will thus take place where the ministry began: in "Galilee of the Gentiles" the light dawns that overcomes the shadow of death (4:15–16) and makes possible the mission to the Gentiles (v 19). No reference has been made earlier in Matthew to a specific mountain in Galilee where the disciples were to meet Jesus (τὸ ὄρος οὗ ἐτάξατο αὐτοῖς ὁ Ἰησοῦς, "the mountain to which Jesus had summoned them"), and here it may simply reflect Matthew's concern to set this revelatory expression of Jesus at an appropriately holy mountain, as elsewhere in the Gospels, i.e., a place of revelation. Traditionally the mountain has been identified with Tabor, the mount of the transfiguration. (On this, the seventh of Matthew's mountains [including 14:23], see Donaldson, *Jesus on the Mountain,* 170–90; Strobel argues for an actual, rather than symbolic, place.)

**17** When the disciples saw Jesus they, like the women earlier (v 9), προσεκύνησαν, "worshiped," him. This would seem to indicate not only that they recognized Jesus but that they thus believed that he had risen from the dead. The reader is accordingly unprepared for the last three words of the verse: οἱ δὲ ἐδίστασαν, "but they doubted." Two major problems here must be addressed. First, to what exactly does the definite article οἱ refer? Second, what is the nuance of ἐδίστασαν, "they doubted?"

Grammatical considerations alone cannot answer the first question. Even without the corresponding οἱ μέν to go with οἱ δέ (i.e., "some, on the one hand, . . . but others"), the latter words can have a partitive sense meaning "some of the eleven." On the other hand, οἱ δέ can simply be taken as a pronoun meaning "they," i.e., all of the eleven (for evidence of both possiblities, see BAGD, 549b–550a). An examination of the οἱ δέ construction in Matthew seems mainly to support the latter usage (see 2:5; 4:20, 22; 14:17, 33; 15:34; 16:7, 14; 20:5, 31; 21:25; 22:19; 26:15; 26:67; 27:4, 21, 23; 28:15). Granted that some of these occurrences may be ambiguous, none of them demands a division. All of them could be, and several must be, taken as inclusive (if "some" is occasionally meant, they represent the whole group) rather than partitive (26:67, listed by BAGD as partitive, is hardly necessarily so). Grayston has this right, McKay notwithstanding. Van der Horst's overstated case to the contrary (οἱ δέ "*must* be part of the disciples" [29]) is based solely upon Hellenistic usage and ignores Matthean usage. Furthermore, if the evangelist had wanted to say "some," he had available to him the unmistakable τινές or τινὲς αὐτῶν to make his point. For strong support for taking οἱ δέ as referring to all the eleven, see Giblin; Neirynck; Reeves; Kwik; and Hahn, "Der Sendungsauftrag" (among the commentators, cf. Grundmann, Bonnard, Viviano, Bruner, Garland). In fact, however, the decision about the sense of the construction in 28:17 is usually influenced by the problem posed by the idea of all eleven "doubting." And thus a considerable number of commentators continue to opt for translating οἱ δέ with "some," i.e., some of the eleven worshiped, some doubted (e.g., Hill; Gundry; Fenton; Hubbard, *The Matthean Redaction;* France; Gnilka; Harrington; Blomberg). Some indeed cannot tolerate the idea of *any* of the eleven doubting and thus argue, with no actual evidence, that οἱ δέ means "some" *others* who were on the mountain and not the eleven (Allen; McNeile; Plummer; Lohmeyer; Klostermann; and more recently, Carson; L. Morris [if tentatively]; Hiebert, *BSac* 149 [1992] 338–54).

At the root of the problem for those who have trouble accepting that all eleven disciples were involved is the meaning of the word ἐδίστασαν, usually translated "they doubted." The question is whether doubt, in the sense of unbelief, is compatible with the worship referred to in the first clause. Some would avoid the problem by understanding ἐδίστασαν as a pluperfect, i.e., they "had doubted" but no longer did (thus Jerome, Lagrange). This view is disallowed, however, by the clearly aorist verb of the first clause. Others argue for a weakened sense of προσεκύνησαν, taking it not as worship but as a posture from which to beseech Jesus for mercy (Grayston). Another way of dealing with the difficulty is by specifying the object of the doubt. For Grayston the doubt concerns whether Jesus will forgive them for their recent disloyalty. Others assert that the doubt concerned the identity of Jesus (thus Hendricksen; Filson; Walvoord, *Matthew: Thy Kingdom Come* [Chicago: Moody, 1974]). Some suggest that they were uncertain about the propriety of worshiping Jesus (Parkhurst, Harrington; cf. Lange). In both cases one may ask why then the disciples worshiped Jesus. As to the latter, clearly the worship of Jesus is no problem for the evangelist, and he would hardly make it one for the disciples (Blomberg suggests the reverse problem, i.e., "confusion about how to behave in the presence of a supernaturally manifested, exalted, and holy being" [430]). As a final example of the lengths to which some have been driven to solve this puzzle, note W. D. Morris' emendation of the text to οἱ δὲ διέστησαν, i.e., "but they stood apart," i.e., not approaching the risen Jesus.

The key to a proper understanding of the statement is the definition of the verb διστάζειν. To begin with, it must be stressed that the verb does not refer to unbelief, nor even perplexity. As I. P. Ellis has pointed out, the evangelist had available ἀπιστεῖν for "disbelieve" and ἀπορεῖν for "be perplexed." The word occurs in the NT only here and in 14:31. In the latter passage, Peter walks on the water until he sees the wind and becomes afraid. Then Jesus addresses him as ὀλιγόπιστε, "O little faith," and asks εἰς τί ἐδίστασας, "Why did you doubt?" The doubt here amounts to hesitation, indecision (Ellis documents this meaning of the word in Plato and Aristotle), and perhaps uncertainty. In Peter's case the doubt indicates a divided mind brought about by a lack of an adequate measure of faith, not a lack of faith altogether. This appears to be somewhat, but not altogether, different from the reference to διαλογισμοί, "doubts," that were arising in the hearts of the disciples as they confronted the risen Jesus according to Luke 24:38. To be noted, incidentally, is the fact that a few lines later Luke can refer to a combination of ἀπιστούντων, "disbelieving," and χαρᾶς, "joy," in the minds of (all, not some) of the disciples (Luke 24:41).

It is natural to believe that the eleven disciples would have been in a state of hesitation and indecision. Too much had happened too fast for them to be able to assimilate it. They did not doubt that it was Jesus whom they saw and whom they gladly worshiped. If their faith was too small in measure, that was because they were in a state of uncertainty about what the recent events meant and what might happen next. They found themselves in "a situation of cognitive dissonance *par excellence*" (Walsh and Keesmaat, 195). It is precisely this state of mind that is addressed in the words that Jesus speaks to the disciples in the following verses (vv 18–20; see Giblin, who refers to "reassurance"). Jesus' words will accomplish what the sight of the risen Jesus alone could not. Two things remain intriguing, however: first, that Matthew bothers at all to insert the reference to their doubting, and second, that Matthew records no resolution of their uncertain state of mind (cf. Leon-Dufour, "Origin"). It seems clear that Matthew wanted members of his community to apply the truth to themselves. This can be put in a variety of ways. Garland writes: "Matthew understands that the fluctuation between worship and indecision is every disciple's struggle. What is needed is confidence that Jesus is Lord of all and present with them at all times" (266). Other writers have appropriately made room for doubt alongside faith in the believer (see Grundmann, Bruner, Reeves, Walsh and Keesmaat, and Viviano, who concludes that the passage refers to "a common psychological experience which gives hope to moderns" [674]). To such people, who are far from being perfect, Jesus gives the commission to make disciples of the nations (Bruner, Stendahl)—a commission, as we have already noted, that is framed with a comforting statement and promise.

**18** Jesus now "comes to them" (προσελθών), a comforting approach that takes the initiative to reestablish an intimate relationship with them, and speaks the wonderful concluding words of the Gospel. He does not rebuke them for their disloyalty or their doubt. He begins with a vitally important prelude to the formal commissioning of the disciples, namely, the assertion of his authority: ἐδόθη μοι πᾶσα ἐξουσία ἐν οὐρανῷ καὶ ἐπὶ [τῆς] γῆς, "all authority has been given to me in heaven and upon [the] earth." The passive verb assumes God as the acting subject: God has given Jesus this comprehensive sovereignty over the whole of the created order. Already during his ministry he had made statements about his authority. In 9:6 (cf. 9:8) he referred to the ἐξουσίαν, "authority," given to the Son of Man ἐπὶ τῆς γῆς, "upon the earth," in this case to forgive sins (cf. Dan 7:14 with respect to the Son of Man). In 11:27 he made the astonishing claim that πάντα μοι παρεδόθη ὑπὸ τοῦ πατρός μου, "all things have been given to me by my Father" (see *Comment* on this verse and Lange's discussion, 25–96; cf. John 3:35). From the risen Jesus, however, such a claim has all the more convincing power (cf. the exalted passage concerning the authority specifically of the risen Jesus in Eph 1:20–23). The resurrection serves as a vindication of the words and deeds of Jesus during his ministry. Now the resurrected (not resuscitated!) Jesus who appears before the disciples is one who partakes of a new order of existence and who here anticipates his glorious exaltation (enthronement; cf. 2 Sam 7:13) at God's right hand (cf. Luke 24:51; Acts 1:9; Phil 2:9–11) and indeed the parousia itself. As on the mount of the transfiguration (17:1–8), the veil is taken away— but now permanently—so that the glorious identity of Jesus becomes plain (cf. 26:64). It is accordingly the one who has "all authority in heaven and on earth," i.e., the sovereign authority of God, who now sends out his disciples on the mission to evangelize the world. This is to provide them in turn with authority and supply them with confidence as they go. The authority of the risen one is not categorically new but now depends upon a new basis—the arrival at a new stage of salvation history. Dan 7:13–14 provides important background material to vv 18–20, referring to one like a Son of Man who receives "dominion and glory and kingship," an everlasting dominion, "that all peoples, nations and languages should serve him" (for the Dan 7 background to this pericope, see Schaberg's discussion, 111–221).

**19** This connection between the authority of Jesus and the fulfilling of the tasks now assigned to the disciples and those who come after them in Matthew's and every church is made plain in the connective οὖν, "therefore." Jesus' authority (v 18) and his presence (v 20) will empower his disciples to fulfill the commission he now gives them. The commission itself is given by means of one main imperative verb, μαθητεύσατε, "make disciples," together with three syntactically subordinate participles that take on an imperatival force (thus rightly Friedrich, 154) because of the main verb. The first of these, πορευθέντες, precedes the main verb. The disciples are to "go" and "make disciples." Since the main verb has for its object πάντα τὰ ἔθνη, "all the nations," it is implied that the disciples are to go into all the world. The universal authority of Jesus is the basis of the universal mission of the church. The verb μαθητεύσατε, "make disciples," is characteristically Matthean (cf. 13:52; 27:57; the only other NT occurrence is in Acts 14:21 where it is linked with εὐαγγελισάμενοι, "having evangelized"). The word "disciple" means above all "learner" or "pupil." The emphasis in the commission thus falls not on the initial proclamation of the gospel but more on the arduous task of nurturing into the experience of discipleship, an emphasis that is strengthened and explained by the instruction "teaching them to keep all that I have commanded" in v 20a. To be made a disciple in Matthew means above all to follow after righteousness as articulated in the teaching of Jesus (see Kvalbein, *Themelios* 13 [1988] 48–53).

Now, after the death and resurrection of Jesus, for the first time the limitation of the gospel to Israel (cf. 10:5; 15:24) is removed. The direct commission is given to take the message of Jesus to πάντα τὰ ἔθνη, "all the nations" (a development anticipated in 24:14; 26:13), a task acknowledged and fulfilled by the early church (cf. Mark 16:15; Acts 1:8; Col. 1:23). Now we finally arrive at the full inclusion of the Gentiles (on this, see Hre Kio) in the history of salvation (cf. Dan 7:14), something hinted at in the Gospel from the very beginning and throughout (cf. the allusion to Abraham in 1:1 but also the magi in 2:1–12, the centurion in 8:5–13, and the Canaanite woman's daughter in 15:21–28). The problem of the slowness of the early church to engage in the evangelization of the Gentiles is no necessary obstacle to the historicity of these words of commission. In all probability the earliest church believed that Israel was to be won first before the "time of the Gentiles" would begin (Gerhardsson). The commission as it stands in Matthew does not exclude the Jews, nor (*pace* Hare and Harrington; see esp. Meier, *CBQ* 39 [1977] 94–104), of course, did the early church understand its task in such a way as to exclude further evangelization of the Jews (cf. Rom 1:16; 10:18; 1 Cor 9:20). Probably already in 24:9; 25:32 the Jews are included under the rubric τὰ ἔθνη, "the nations." It *is* shocking now to find Israel thus subordinated and absorbed into the comprehensive reference to the nations. In the now completed salvific work of the Messiah, Israel has accomplished her special role in salvation history. She now too is to enjoy the fruit of that accomplishment as *primus inter pares* (cf. Rom 1:16). The reference to "all nations" here, of course, cannot be understood as the collective conversion of national groups (in which case αὐτά, the neuter plural pronoun, would be expected rather than αὐτούς, "them" [masculine], as in our text).

The disciples are further told to "baptize" (βαπτίζοντες; the second of the participles functioning as supplementary imperatives) new disciples. The command to baptize comes as somewhat of a surprise since baptism is referred to earlier only in chap. 3 (and 21:25) where only John's baptism is described (among the Gospels only in John 3:22; 4:1–2 do we read of Jesus' or his disciples' baptizing others). Matthew tells us nothing concerning his view of Christian baptism. Only Matthew records this command of Jesus, but the practice of the early church suggests its historicity (cf. Acts 2:38, 41; 8:12, 38; 9:18; etc.). The threefold name (at most only an incipient trinitarianism) in which the baptism was to be performed, on the other hand, seems clearly to be a liturgical expansion of the evangelist consonant with the practice of his day (thus Hubbard; cf. *Did.* 7.1). There is a good possibility that in its original form, as witnessed by the ante-Nicene

Eusebian form, the text read "make disciples *in my name*" (see Conybeare). This shorter reading preserves the symmetrical rhythm of the passage, whereas the triadic formula fits awkwardly into the structure as one might expect if it were an interpolation (see H. B. Green; cf. Howard; Hill [*IBS* 8 (1986) 54–63], on the other hand, argues for a concentric design with the triadic formula at its center). It is Kosmala, however, who has argued most effectively for the shorter reading, pointing to the central importance of the "name of Jesus" in early Christian preaching, the early practice of baptism in the name of Jesus, and the singular "in his name" with reference to the hope of the Gentiles in Isa 42:4b, quoted by Matthew in 12:18–21. As Carson rightly notes of our passage: "There is no evidence we have Jesus' *ipsissima verba* here" (598). The narrative of Acts notes the use of the name only of "Jesus Christ" in baptism (Acts 2:38; 8:16 10:48; 19:5; cf. Rom 6:3; Gal 3:27) or simply "the Lord Jesus" (τοῦ κυρίου Ἰησοῦ; Acts 8:16; 19:5). Baptism εἰς, lit. "into," the "name" (the singular ὄνομα, "name," points to the unity of the three) of the Father, the Son, and the Holy Spirit reflects the Hebrew/Aramaic expression לְשֵׁם, *lĕšēm*, which has a cultic sense and means "fundamentally determined by" (Hartman). In contrast to John's baptism, this baptism brings a person into an existence that is fundamentally determined by, i.e., ruled by, Father, Son, and Holy Spirit (cf. εἰς τὸ ἐμὸν ὄνομα, "in my name," in 18:20). Schaberg's theory that the triadic formula goes back to the triad in Dan 7 (Ancient of Days, one like a son of man, and angels) remains an improbable speculation.

**20** The final element of the commission is found in διδάσκοντες, "teach" (the third participle functioning as an imperative). They are thus told to do what Jesus himself did (Jesus is referred to as teaching in 4:23; 5:2; 7:29; 9:35; 11:1; 13:34; 21:23; 26:55). This command recalls the explicit teaching of 5:19. The exalted Jesus stands in continuity with the historical Jesus (thus Luck). The object of the participle is the clause τηρεῖν πάντα ὅσα ἐνετειλάμην ὑμῖν, lit. "to keep everything whatsoever I have commanded you." This is obviously a concern that has often been close to the heart of the evangelist earlier in the Gospel, especially in the first discourse of Jesus, the Sermon on the Mount, namely, *obedience* to the teaching of Jesus (cf. esp. 5:17–20; 7:21–27). "Righteousness" for Matthew finds its final and authoritative definition in the teaching of Jesus, who is the *one* teacher (23:8, 10). And indeed, the Gospel of Matthew provided the church with an excellent handbook containing that teaching. And it is thus the particular responsibility of the church to hand on that teaching and to see to it that new disciples make it their way of life (cf. the similar Johannine emphasis [John 14:23]). The commission of the disciples is followed by a promise that must have cheered the hearts of those to whom so much responsibility was being given. Matthew calls attention to its special character with his ἰδού, "look." The promise is that ἐγὼ μεθ' ὑμῶν εἰμι, "I am with you," words that recall the promise of 18:20 as well as echo especially the identification of Jesus as Emmanuel, "God with us" (1:23; cf. Hag 1:13 where the words are found verbatim in slightly different order; in fact, the promise echoes numerous OT passages that promise the presence of Yahweh with his people, e.g., Gen 28:15; Exod 3:12; Josh 1:5, 9; Isa 41:10). Where Yahweh was formerly with his people, Jesus is now with his people, the church. Jesus, though not physically present among them, will not have abandoned them. He will be in their midst, though unseen, and will empower them to fulfill the commission he has given them. Those who receive the messengers of the good news will receive Jesus himself (10:40). And the promise of Jesus' continuing presence with them is not restricted to any special circumstances (but includes persecution as well as ministry), nor is it made simply for the immediate future. He will be with them πάσας τὰς ἡμέρας ἕως τῆς συντελείας τοῦ αἰῶνος, "all the days until the consummation of the age." The last phrase, "the consummation of the age," is also found in 13:39–40, 49; 24:3 and for Matthew (contrast Heb 9:26) refers to end of the present age through the parousia of the Son of Man and the experience of the final judgment of the wicked and reward of the righteous. Jesus promises his disciples that he will be with them until the end of time as presently known. The promise thus applies not only to the future of the disciples themselves but to their successors and their successors' successors in the church. The evangelist here not only writes history but provides a promise having relevance to his own contemporaries and indeed to the disciples composing the church down to the end of the eon.

## Explanation

The risen Jesus is central to the existence and proclamation of the church. There would be no gospel if there had been no resurrection. The resurrection, however, is not simply a datum of history, words about a past event. The resurrection has enormous consequence for present Christian existence (which, however, it is left to certain NT epistles to expound). It is the risen Jesus, to whom all authority in heaven and earth has been given, who here commissions his disciples and in effect the church of every period of history. They are to go everywhere with the message of good news in the name and authority of Jesus. Theirs is indeed an awesome responsibility: to go, make disciples of all nations, baptize, and teach. If left to their own devices and strength, the task would be overwhelming. Yet they are not left alone in this assignment. The risen, enthroned Jesus promises to be with them in their fulfillment of it, not intermittently but always. Evidence of the truth of that promise is readily available in the narrative of the book of Acts as well as in the history of the church (cf. 16:18), which has seen a network of believers around the world in every land, of every race, come into existence from what began just after the death of Jesus with but a handful of doubting, confused, and powerless disciples. The statements that frame the commission on either side concerning the authority and the presence of Jesus alone allow the church to continue in the world. Only the ongoing reality of these facts can continue to equip the church for its mission—a mission that will continue until the consummation of the age. The great commission and its frame with which Matthew ends remain, like the whole Gospel itself, one of the priceless treasures of the Christian church, providing comfort, strength, and hope until the final dawning of the eschaton. "And this good news of the kingdom will be proclaimed throughout the world, as a testimony to all nations; and then the end will come" (24:14).

# Index of Modern Authors

# Index of Principal Topics

# Index of Biblical and Other Ancient Sources

## The Old Testament

# The New Testament

## Old Testament Apocrypha

# Jewish Pseudepigrapha

# Rabbinic Writings

# Apostolic Fathers

# Other Early Christian Writings

# Other Ancient and Classical Texts

# Papyri and Inscriptions